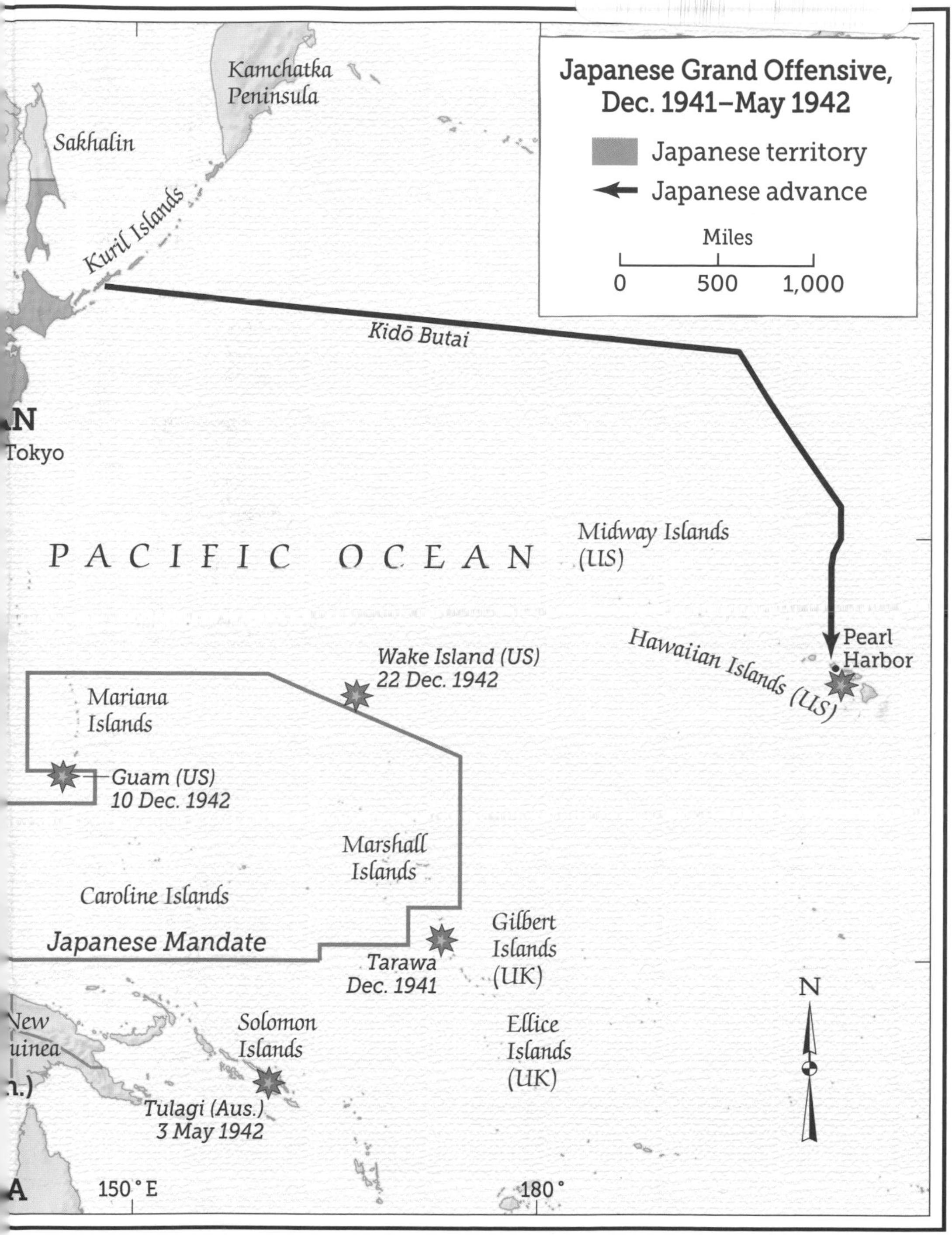

Kamchatka
Peninsula

Sakhalin

Kuril Islands

Japanese Grand Offensive, Dec. 1941–May 1942

▨ Japanese territory

← Japanese advance

Miles

0   500   1,000

Kidō Butai

N

Tokyo

PACIFIC   OCEAN

Midway Islands
(US)

Hawaiian Islands (US)

Pearl
Harbor

Wake Island (US)
22 Dec. 1942

Mariana
Islands

Guam (US)
10 Dec. 1942

Marshall
Islands

Caroline Islands

Japanese Mandate

Tarawa
Dec. 1941

Gilbert
Islands
(UK)

N

New
Guinea

Solomon
Islands

Ellice
Islands
(UK)

h.)

Tulagi (Aus.)
3 May 1942

150°E

180°

A

TOWER OF
SKULLS

ALSO BY RICHARD B. FRANK

MacArthur: A Biography

Downfall: The End of the Imperial Japanese Empire

Guadalcanal: The Definitive Account of the Landmark Battle

TOWER OF SKULLS

A HISTORY OF

THE ASIA-PACIFIC WAR

JULY 1937–MAY 1942

RICHARD B. FRANK

W. W. NORTON & COMPANY

Independent Publishers Since 1923

For information about permission to reproduce selections from this book, write to
Permissions, W. W. Norton & Company, Inc., 500 Fifth Avenue, New York, NY 10110

For information about special discounts for bulk purchases, please contact
W. W. Norton Special Sales at specialsales@wwnorton.com or 800-233-4830

Manufacturing by LSC Communications, Harrisonburg
Book design by Chris Welch
Production manager: Lauren Abbate

Library of Congress Cataloging-in-Publication Data

Names: Frank, Richard B., author.
Title: Tower of skulls : a history of the Asia-Pacific war / Richard B. Frank.
Other titles: History of the Asia-Pacific war
Description: First edition. | New York : W. W. Norton & Company, [2020–] |
Includes bibliographical references and index. | Contents: volume 1. July 1937–May 1942—
Identifiers: LCCN 2019033200 | ISBN 9781324002109 (v. 1 ; hardcover) |
ISBN 9781324002116 (v. 1 ; epub)
Subjects: LCSH: World War, 1939–1945—Campaigns—Pacific Area. |
World War, 1939–1945—Casualties—Pacific Area.
Classification: LCC D767 .F73 2020 | DDC 940.54/25—dc23
LC record available at https://lccn.loc.gov/2019033200

W. W. Norton & Company, Inc., 500 Fifth Avenue, New York, N.Y. 10110
www.wwnorton.com

W. W. Norton & Company Ltd., 15 Carlisle Street, London W1D 3BS

1 2 3 4 5 6 7 8 9 0

To Samuel Eliot Morison, for the inspiration to love and study history.

You are building your conception of an Asia which
would be raised on a tower of skulls.

BENGALI POET RABINDRANATH TAGORE IN A LETTER TO THE
JAPANESE POET AND NATIONALIST YONEJIRO NOGUCHI, 1938

I believe that the fundamental proposition that we must
recognize is that the hostilities in Europe, in Africa,
and in Asia are all parts of a single world conflict.

PRESIDENT FRANKLIN D. ROOSEVELT, JANUARY 1941

CONTENTS

TOWER OF SKULLS

:

The Marco Polo Bridge

Eight miles southwest of Beijing the old Lugouqiao Bridge girds the Yongding River. Eleven arches suspend an elegant roadway stretching nearly three hundred yards. Since the bridge was first constructed in the twelfth-century reign of the Jin dynasty, countless footfalls and wheel scrapes have smoothed the stone surface. The balustrades flanking the roadway rest on 250 marble posts and mount over 400 carved white ornamental lion statues. Diminutive lion sculptures—no two alike—adorn the larger ones.

When Marco Polo gazed upon the span during his thirteenth-century travels, he pronounced it without peer in Europe. By July 1937 the bridge was known outside China as the Marco Polo Bridge, a name accentuating foreign ascendancy and Chinese decline. That same month saw the Lugouqiao Bridge set the scene as the curtain rose on a calamitous drama that would engulf first China and then the world over the next eight years. That drama would be best known as "The Marco Polo Bridge Incident."

CHINA IN 1937 was deeply divided, and its sovereignty was in peril. With the collapse of the Qing dynasty in 1911, thousands of years of Chinese dynastic rule came to a convulsive end. The country fragmented into zones governed by competing regional leaders, often branded as "warlords." That term accentuates the military measure of these competing leaders, but all rivals for political ascendancy ultimately rely upon arms to maintain or expand their power. These regional leaders differed not just in military terms, but also in a wide spectrum of economic and political environments in which they operated. The Kuomintang (KMT) or Nationalist Party formed the leading faction. Its founder was Dr. Sun Yat-sen (Sun Zhongshan), the most revered figure to emerge from the dense (and often lethal) Chinese political thickets of the first three decades of the twentieth century. Sun's forte proved to be his visionary pronouncements, most famously his Three Principles (*San min zhu yi*) carrying the tang of contemporary Western intellectual currents of nationalism, democracy, and socialism ("people's livelihood"). But Sun believed that democracy must be cautiously grafted onto China after a period of benign authoritarianism that he called "tutelage."

Sun created the Nationalist Party in 1919. One of his followers was a soldier whose steadfast loyalty won Sun's confidence and affection. In repayment Sun bestowed on his Cantonese protégé the name by which he is best known in the West: Chiang Kai-shek.

Before he died of cancer in March 1925, Sun adopted for himself the title of "Generalissimo." He formed an alliance with the Soviet Union (telling Vladimir Lenin that Chiang was "his most trusted deputy") and organized the Nationalists along Marxist-Leninist lines. Upon Sun's death, Jingwei Wang, a handsome, intelligent, charismatic, long-standing Nationalist leader, appeared—not least to his own satisfaction—as Sun's obvious successor. Chiang lacked any lofty post within the inner party hierarchy, which dismissed his qualifications. But ordinary Nationalist members eyed Chiang as a forceful military leader and an independent, incorruptible, and faithful disciple of Sun. Chiang also carried credentials as the Nationalist figure most knowledgeable about the Soviet Union, now the party's principal backer. The succession struggle played out with violence and subterfuge over some time, but to the surprise of all but a few observers, Chiang became the new "Generalissimo" of the Nationalists. After this defeat, Jingwei Wang did not leave the world stage but would go on to make his name perhaps the most iniquitous in twentieth-century Chinese history.

As historian Gregor Benton phrased it, the Nationalists were "an aggregation of relatively autonomous cliques and powerful personalities rather than a political party in the modern sense." The ideological outlook of at least six distinct cliques and even more major personalities formed a kaleidoscope whose political philosophy spanned from left to far right. Lacking an established power base within the Nationalist Party, Chiang held sway by skillfully balancing one faction against another. His limited sources of personal loyalty derived from ties to his native Zhejiang province and a network of graduates of the Whampoa Military Academy he once headed. He never purified the Nationalists' incoherent ideological components, perhaps realizing it was infeasible or even that the multiple viewpoints were useful for his purposes, and he fell back on the techniques of nepotism, favoritism, suppression, and ultimately terror to further his control.

In 1926, against the counsel of Chinese and Soviet advisers and the expectations of nearly all Western observers, Chiang gathered his National Revolutionary Army (NRA) and launched the "Northern Expedition" to realize Sun's dream of unifying the nation. Despite being outnumbered about ten to one by regional military forces, and with only about 20 percent of Chiang's 100,000-man army reliably loyal to him, by the end of the year the Nationalists had expanded from their original base in Guangdong province to control six more provinces with a combined population of 170 million, roughly one-third of China's total. Chiang displayed boldness in maneuvers that kept his enemies off balance and deft political agility in forming alliances with regional leaders.

Nevertheless, by the time of the "Marco Polo Bridge Incident" in July 1937, Chiang had not expanded his domain and still effectively controlled only a fraction of the country. Outside of his seven provinces in South Central China, numerous other regional leaders held effective sway. Of these, one of the least in territorial control and military power was China's Communists under their relentless, visionary, and ruthless leader Mao Zedong.

Presciently, Chiang sensed China's Communists represented a serious—perhaps mortal—challenge. The Japanese, he once remarked, were a disease of the skin while the Communists were a disease of the heart. Chiang had struck murderously against the Communist presence within the Nationalists in 1927. Then he ordered successive "anti-bandit" campaigns against the main Communist enclave in the Jiangxi/Fujian border region in Southeast China. The first four of these campaigns commanded by Chiang's subordinates failed, some spectacularly. Chiang took personal command of the fifth in 1934, combining military and political programs. This forced the Communists out of their base area onto what became Mao's "Long March," a 6,000-mile journey during which Mao emerged as the top leader. Of the approximately 86,000 men (and a few women) in the ranks at the beginning of the trek, only about 5,000 to perhaps 9,000 survived. Besides colossal casualties, the march ended in northern Shaanxi province, just south of the Great Wall in northwestern China, a remote, desperately poor region. By 1937 the Communist territory contained only 1.45 million people, about 0.3 percent of China's population. The Red Army mustered roughly 30,000 ill-armed men, who formed about 1.5 percent of all Chinese under arms. It seemed utterly unimaginable that some twelve chaotic years later Mao would unify mainland China once more under his rule.

CHINA'S MILITARY and diplomatic weakness produced one of the most grating manifestations of its degraded sovereignty: the presence of foreign troops on its soil, not just the customary embassy guards but thousands of foreign soldiers and marines in major cities like Shanghai, Hong Kong, Tianjin,

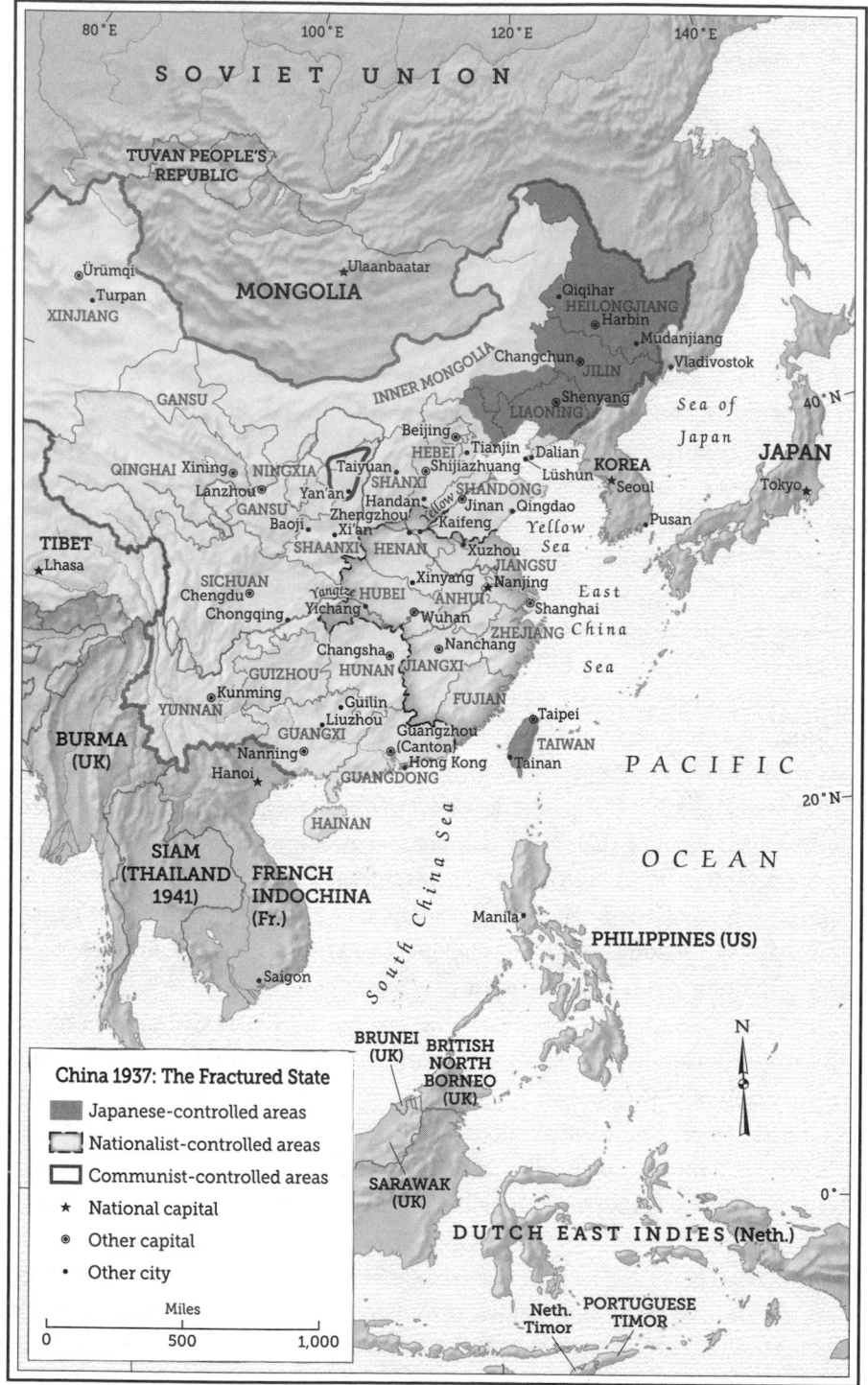

China 1937: The Fractured State

- ▨ Japanese-controlled areas
- ▨ Nationalist-controlled areas
- □ Communist-controlled areas
- ★ National capital
- ◎ Other capital
- • Other city

Miles

0   500   1,000

and most prominently Beijing. The presence of foreign soldiers in Beijing stemmed from the 1901 event known in the West as the "Boxer Rebellion." The term "Boxer" reflected the title (more accurately rendered as "Boxers United in Righteousness") of an early Chinese nationalist confederation of poor, young, male peasants known for their martial rites. They viewed Christian missionaries and their Chinese converts as a prime cause of China's decline. During their revolt, they singled out for killing both missionaries and those Chinese suspected rightly or wrongly to be Christians. Gaining the support of Qing Dowager Empress Cixi, the Boxers laid siege to the foreign diplomatic compounds of Beijing before a 20,000-man international relief force intervened. The settlement of this episode included an explicit provision to permit foreign troops to be stationed in Beijing to protect the foreign legations in perpetuity.

Of all the foreign garrisons in Beijing, by far the largest was Japanese. Thus, on the moonless night of 7 July 1937, the 8th Company of Maj. Kiyonao Ikki's 3rd Battalion, 1st Independent Infantry Regiment marched from its compound in a suburb of Beijing for a night maneuver with live ammunition in a desolate area about 0.6 miles from the Marco Polo Bridge. Ikki answered to his regimental commander, Col. Renya Mutaguchi, a preening firebrand in an army replete with hotspurs. Mutaguchi's unit formed part of Japan's 5,600-man "China Garrison Army." The "Boxer" settlement not only sanctioned the presence of this "army" but also a warrant to conduct field exercises without prior notice to Chinese officials. What animated frequent Japanese exercises proximate to the Marco Polo Bridge was not the structure itself, but the nearby railway bridge linking strategically vital lines to the northwest, south, and southeast via the junction town of Wanping. Of late, the Japanese, out of courtesy, routinely informed local Chinese commanders of such maneuvers. But this night they tendered no forewarning.

As the Japanese company commenced the first part of the exercise at 2230 hours (10:30 p.m.), roughly a dozen small arms rounds went whizzing past them. It was the seventh day of the seventh month of the seventh year of the decade. "In Chinese philosophy," notes historian S. C. M. Paine, "the number seven is associated with fire, bitterness, burning, war, blood, and the color red." Although who fired these shots remains unresolved, the most likely source was a soldier of the Chinese Twenty-Ninth Route Army—quite understandably on hair-trigger alert after years of repeated Japanese encroachments on China's sovereignty. The Japanese returned fire, and then roll call was conducted. Private Kikujiro Shimura from Tokyo initially failed to answer—though he showed up soon after (popular history has enshrined the possibility that Shimura had gone off to relieve himself). The report of the "missing" soldier reached higher commands, but not word of his return. Ikki mustered the main body of his battalion for a search. Near dawn, more shots were fired at the milling Japanese soldiers. Although Mutaguchi initially endorsed Ikki's proposal to negotiate, not fight, Mutaguchi ordered Ikki to respond to the renewed firing with an attack and rejected Ikki's protest that they should avoid escalating the episode into an international incident. Notwithstanding the prompt mutual apologies by Japanese and Chinese liaison officers over the incident, Mutaguchi declared his refusal to back down with artillery fire.

More volleys by Chinese troops on 8 July triggered a small but violent skirmish ending—all too typically—in a Chinese rout. To Imperial Army Chief of Staff Prince Kotohito Kan'in in Tokyo, events around the bridge appeared as merely yet another of the numerous small-scale eruptions between Japanese and Chinese stretching back for decades. He ordered the "China Garrison Army" "to avoid further use of force so as to prevent extension of the conflict."

But the "extension" Prince Kan'in feared came.

The Marco Polo Bridge incident proved fateful for three key Japanese participants. Private Shimura, who had failed to answer the roll call, died in battle in Burma in 1943. With him expired the explanation for his failure to answer that night. His regimental commander, Mutaguchi, was later elevated to Burma Army command during 1944. He cited his oppressive sense of responsibility for igniting the war as part of the rationale for flinging his men into a disastrous invasion of India, which ended in the most humiliating defeat in the history of the Imperial Army. His one-time deputy, Ikki, had by then fallen leading his unit into virtual annihilation on the island of Guadalcanal in 1942—the turning point of the Pacific War. The presence of Mutaguchi in India and Ikki at Guadalcanal marked the farthest poles of Japan's conquests—a march to disaster and a turning point in human history that began on the Marco Polo Bridge.

Indeed, it is the Marco Polo Bridge Incident that immediately initiated a train of events ending with the dissolution of the Asian empires of Britain, the Netherlands, Japan, and France in favor of at least nineteen sovereign nations; the division of Korea; the Communist takeover of China and continuing conflict over the status of Taiwan; and the American military hegemony over Japan and the East Pacific that persists to this day.

The incident secured only transient international attention in the newspapers of the time, and the regional war it triggered has for too long been seen as subsidiary to the US-Japan collision and the concurrent conflict in Europe.

However, it is now clear from a twenty-first-century perspective that the tumult in Asia and across the Pacific transformed those regions the way the First World War upended Europe. The role of the war in the rise of Asian nations in the new century demands a fundamental reappraisal of World War II. Such is the goal of *Tower of Skulls* and the trilogy of which it is the first volume.

TOWER OF SKULLS takes the story of the Asia-Pacific War from the shots fired that July night near the Marco Polo (Lugouqiao) Bridge to the surrender of Filipino and American forces on Corregidor on 6 May 1942. At that moment, the Empire of Japan arguably reached its apogee—though its descent would begin immediately.

The Second World War is often cited as the greatest event in human history. This claim is based both on the unmatched global span of the conflict and the unparalleled loss of life, now placed at 60 million deaths or more. There is a massive literature on the war. What then distinguishes this work from this enormous library? It is the first work in English—or any language—that takes as its fundamental perspective on World War II the whole canvas of Asia and the Pacific Region. The prior literature concerns only portions of this part of the war, and those taking the widest view treat this war as one involving Japan and the United States, with all other aspects as peripheral, if mentioned at all. Thus, this trilogy aims to create a new standard narrative of one-half of the greatest event in human history.

Besides seeking this critical, wide, and novel perspective, this work strives to accord a fair balance to all nations and peoples. "Peoples" is a very important category, for when the war began, the expanse of the globe from India, around what is now Indonesia and up past the Pacific coast of Japan, with about one-half the total population of the world, contained just four nation-states with some claim to sovereignty: Mongolia, Thailand, China, and Japan. The rest of the peoples of this region lived under some form of colonialism. Now there are at least nineteen major nations in this region with just under one-half the world's total population. The Asia-Pacific War is fundamental to this transformation, though the specific paths of many of these nations is complex in relationship to the war. Ultimately the trilogy argues that its contemporary relevance is immense because the world of the twenty-first century is fundamentally the product of the Asia-Pacific War.

Another intention of the narrative is to keep constantly in mind the relationship between military and political events in Europe and what transpired in the Asia-Pacific region. This is an aspect in which a great deal of the existing literature is, in my view, too often cursory. In this volume, this relationship becomes a vastly important theme in the second half of 1941 when the German assault on the Soviet Union emerges as the critical factor in the relations between the United States and Japan.

The chronology of political and military events serves as the skeleton, but the narrative paints a portrait of far more than domestic and international politics or battlefields on land, in the air, or at sea. The flavor of individual experience, broader social history, and economics all figure importantly. The foremost intent is to restore to Western literature on the war a framework in which events on the Asian continent rise to at least an equal position with the clash unfolding across the Pacific between Japan and the United States. And if events on the Asian continent are to be given equal treatment, then above all the extraordinary story of China takes primacy.

The war launched China into a calamitous four-decade upheaval in which it soared to a triumph of great power status, bringing the astonishing rise of China's Communists from near impotence to dominance. The number of dead heaped around these milestones is measured in the tens of millions. This volume attempts to restore the notion of a "Heroic China" carrying on in the face of Japanese aggression, with horrific levels of death and destruction and with very sparse international support. That achievement marked a decisive shift from a century or more of China's inability to sustain hostilities with any industrialized power that trampled its sovereignty. The possibility that China could hold out in a conflict with Japan for more than weeks, or at most months, was wholly discounted throughout the world in 1937.

A deeper discussion of the issues raised by occupation, collaboration, and the contests between the Nationalist coalition, the Communists, and the Japanese is deferred from volume one to subsequent volumes. This first volume, however, already reflects a huge upsurge in the specialist literature on China, fueled by the release of documentary evidence from both sides of the Taiwan Straits. That literature remains very little read or understood in the United States. For those steeped in the almost unrelieved negative vision of Chiang Kai-shek's China created by Gen. Joseph Stilwell and his acolytes, this story, based on a much richer archival base, will serve as a corrective.

CHAPTER 1

⠿

"China Cannot Be Lost"*

NORTH CHINA TO SHANGHAI

Backing into War

The immediate reactions of two influential officers in Tokyo to the Marco Polo (Lugouqiao) Bridge clash illuminates the schism within the Imperial Japanese Army. On the Army General Staff, a key officer in the Operations Division, Col. Akira Mutô, asserted "something wonderful has happened" (*yukai na*). On the other hand, a China specialist in the War Ministry, Col. Kenjirô Shibayama, sensed, "something troubling has occurred" (*yakkai na*).

Mutô's eager feeling of opportunity reflected the predominant attitude within the Imperial Army and mirrored a society-wide view of China. A modernized Meiji era Japan had achieved its first external military victory with the trouncing of China on land and sea in the First Sino-Japanese War of 1891–1895. Expecting to encounter an opulent and refined civilization—the fount of so much Japanese culture—Japanese soldiers returned from the continent full of derisive accounts of squalor and debasement. After 1911 the Chinese Empire splintered into armed fiefdoms that more and more represented to the Japanese a decadent civilization but not a country. Said one Japanese writer: "[China] is . . . dead, only its corpse is wriggling."

Chinese weakness had long roused the predatory impulses of other nations. During the nineteenth century, Western powers relentlessly violated Chinese sovereignty, demanding "extraterritoriality" rights (i.e., exemption

---

* "China Cannot Be Lost": a Chinese patriotic slogan. Diana Lary, *The Chinese People at War: Human Suffering and Social Transformation, 1937–1945* (Cambridge: Cambridge University Press, 2010), 38.

of their citizens from Chinese law) and carving off enclaves, most famously Hong Kong. Japan belatedly entered this game, seeking to reduce China to a Japanese vassal state with the "Twenty-One Demands" of 1915 until international pressure forced it to backpedal after China joined the war against the Central Powers.

After World War I, the power of those in Japan advocating Western style society and more participatory government waxed, but those favoring an ultra-nationalistic, military-dominated political and social orientation remained potent, especially in the economically distressed countryside. The Great Depression particularly savaged rural Japan, as the price of rice toppled down and the bottom dropped out of the silk industry. Farmers were impoverished; some sold their daughters into prostitution. The situation was aggravated by the erection of trade barriers. These events resonated both within the officer corps of the Imperial Army, by now comprised about 80 percent from commoners, and the enlisted ranks, heavily drawn from rural areas. Collectively the economic troubles served to discredit Western-oriented market and democratic policies.

However, it was war with Russia, not China, that appeared inevitable to many Japanese soldiers. By the early 1930s the burgeoning Soviet economy threatened to produce an overwhelming military arsenal—and at the same time offered an example of the apparent superiority of centralized state direction over market forces. This blended with the ideological threat Communism posed to what most Japanese saw as their uniquely virtuous society. A prospective Soviet clash underscored the vital importance of safeguarding the Japanese rear in China and mobilizing Chinese resources for Japan's war machine. Surging Chinese nationalism in the 1920s and early 1930s disquieted Imperial Army officers, who worried that China might either undergo Communist revolution, or at any rate ally itself with the Soviet Union against Japan, a prospect that Sun Yat-sen's and later Chiang Kai-shek's warm relationship with the USSR underscored.* Crushing Chiang and his regime increasingly appeared the remedy for this danger. Even officers who questioned this radical step believed strongly that Japan must ruthlessly answer any "insult" from the Chinese.

---

* The Mandarin rendering of Chiang's name is usually Jiang Jieshi. Because during the period addressed in this work the most common (Cantonese) rendering of his name was Chiang Kai-shek (particularly on official documents and accounts outside China), and because that name for decades has been by far the most familiar to those outside China, for purposes of clarity Chiang Kai-shek will be used.

Against this backdrop, the thinking of one of the more colorful figures of the period, Kanji Ishiwara, is instructive. In fact, it reveals "the immediate ideological genesis" of the Asia-Pacific War. In 1931 Ishiwara was an obscure lieutenant colonel stationed in a frontier outpost in southern Manchuria (obtained by Japan by the treaty ending the Russo-Japanese War of 1904–1905) as a member of Japan's Kwantung Army. Ishiwara reached Manchuria fresh from duty as a war college instructor, where he mesmerized officers with presentations blending historical and military analysis with apocalyptic religious prophesy taken from Nichiren Buddhism. This uniformed sooth-sayer foretold a "clash of civilizations" culminating in a "final war" that would pit Japan, the synthesis of all that was best of the East, against the United States, the champion of the degenerate West. This confrontation would be an Armageddon decided by globe-circling aircraft capable of annihilating great cities in a day. It would be a war in which every living person would be a com-batant. It would be a war for which Japan must prepare first by seizing the resources of Manchuria and then establishing a national security state.

Ishiwara was no idle theorist. On the night of 18 September 1931, a faction of Kwantung Army officers he helped lead detonated a small bomb near a line of the Japanese South Manchuria Railroad. Using the pretext that the culprits were anti-Japanese Chinese, the conspirators unleashed the Kwantung Army into a coordinated assault that within three days thrashed Chinese units and seized all of Jilin province. The government of Japanese prime minister Reijiro Wakatsuki protested the Kwantung Army actions and initially demanded the "incident" be curtailed. But Wakatsuki's courage soon wilted. While Ishiwara and his compatriots marched the Kwantung Army into the other two Man-churian provinces, chauvinistic reports in Japan's media roused public enthu-siasm for the action.

The Wakatsuki government resigned in December 1931. The succeeding cabinet of Tsuyoshi Inukai proved equally incapable of bridling the Kwantung Army. By February 1932 the Kwantung Army occupied all three Manchurian provinces. The next month, the Kwantung Army proclaimed that these ter-ritories now formed the independent state of Manchukuo under the regency of Henry Pu Yi, the last Qing emperor.

The seizure of Manchuria proved to be far more than some obscure epi-sode highlighting undisciplined, hot-headed, middle-grade officers in the Imperial Army. Its immediate effect included a lethal blow in Japan to the halting steps toward democracy based on popularly elected political parties. Premier Inukai was assassinated on 15 May 1932 for his lack of support for the seizure of Manchuria. (One bizarre aspect of Inukai's murder was that the rebels schemed to also assassinate the American actor Charlie Chaplin, who happened to be in Tokyo. At his trial, one rebel testified that he believed killing Chaplin would trigger a war between Japan and the United States, which the rebels sought.) No prime minister would come from a popularly elected political party after Inukai's death. Instead, the emperor appointed a prime minister (henceforward usually an army or navy officer) who formed a so-called "national unity" cabinet.

The seizure of Manchuria figures fundamentally in Japan's history for the next decade and a half. Between 1933 and 1943, Japan would directly invest more capital in Manchukuo than Britain devoted to India in two hundred years of imperial rule. This transformed Manchuria into the most industrialized part of Asia outside Japan. It provided Japan with a host of valuable minerals, including coal and iron in particular. Without the resources of Manchuria, Japan could not have mounted a war with the United States. But Japan also embarked on a massive colonization project in Manchuria, aimed particularly at providing an outlet for the poorest stratum of the nation's burgeoning population. Hundreds of thousands of impoverished Japanese farmers sought and found a better life in Manchuria. Manchurian development helped Japan extract itself expeditiously from the worldwide Great Depression. For a huge swath of the population, the role of the Imperial Army in bringing these benefits to all levels of society formed an important bond with the nation's soldiers. Conversely, the loss of Manchuria struck a heavy blow at China, depriving the nation of a large fraction of its industry and forests.

Against this background of eroding civilian control in Tokyo, the designs of the Imperial Army on North China continued unabated. To this end the Imperial Army combined overt military intimidation with covert subversive activities of its special service (military intelligence) organs (*tokumu kikan*) to expel Nationalist authority effectively from Rehe, Chahar, and Hebei provinces. This secured Japanese dominance of Chinese territory down to the Great Wall by 1937. The Manchurian Incident foreshadows the Asian-Pacific War and must loom large in our understanding of the Japanese Empire at the outset of the Second World War. Certain structural defects of the Meiji constitution of 1889 placed the military beyond civilian control. Eventually, factions within the armed forces manufactured conflicts in an atmosphere of irresolution and confusion. Terrorism added another critical element. The assassination of Prime Minister Inukai in 1932 was the second killing of a Japanese premier within two years (Prime Minister Osachi Hamaguchi had been assassinated in 1930 for signing a naval limitation treaty). They are only two names on a lengthy roll of political terror victims.

Military adventurism would later figure in sweeping explanations of the tragedy of the next fifteen years. The postwar trials of top Japanese officials (commonly styled "The Tokyo War Crimes Trials") first codified this interpretation by declaring that a "common conspiracy" by a "select group of militarists" steered Japan through this period. Subsequently, a Marxist view emerged that the root cause of these events stemmed from basic defects in Japan's post-Meiji capitalist society, so that the "conspirators" included the emperor and the established order. This point of view also preserves the belief that the Japanese people were "victims" themselves of a conspiracy. But an understanding of Ishiwara reveals that Japanese uniformed and civilian officials as well as a large swath of the population fundamentally shared a conviction between 1931 and 1945 that they were the chosen and beneficent agents of destiny.

In Ishiwara's worldview, the seizure of Manchuria only served as the means to a greater and noble end: Pan-Asianism. This very amorphous concept at its most benign and elementary level merely celebrated a common arc of civilization from India to Japan that elevated Eastern spiritualism over Western materialism. A more pragmatic model of Pan-Asianism ventured into the secular realm and advocated an alliance of free and equal Asian nation-states. But Ishiwara subscribed to a third variant in which "Pan-Asianism" served as the rationale that legitimized Japan's armed crusade to liberate Asia from Western domination and exalted Japan as an exemplar of how to modernize and yet maintain ancient Asian spiritual values. Conservatives in Japan glorified this vision of Japan as the "liberator." But "liberation" proved not to be the term of choice for many Asians who experienced Japanese occupation in subsequent years—worse in the vast majority of cases than their encounters with Western colonialism.

Ishiwara's swashbuckling background as coconspirator of the Manchurian Incident won him the prestigious post of chief of the operations division of the Army General Staff in 1937. Moreover, with a figurehead imperial prince as the chief of staff and with a vice chief of staff and chief intelligence officer virtually incapacitated by illness or drink, Ishiwara bore far weightier responsibility for policy formulation than was customary in his new position.

But Ishiwara's reaction to the Marco Polo Bridge Incident was far more ambivalent than one might expect. While he deemed Japan's seizure of Manchuria as essential for the ultimate good of all Asians, by 1937 Ishiwara urged that Japan abandon its divide-and-rule policy in North China for a new policy of "benevolence" (jinai). In his mind, benevolent rule would transform China from a rebellious colony to a zealous servant of Japan's preparations to confront the Soviets. Just as importantly, Ishiwara foresaw that quelling China would require at least fifteen divisions for at least six months, mobilization at home, and an expenditure of 5.5 billion yen. This titanic entanglement— Ishiwara presciently warned it would be "an endless bog" to Japan, as Spain had proved to Napoleon—would be folly.

But Ishiwara and his few allies in Tokyo were outnumbered by hardliners. A majority of officers below the rank of lieutenant colonel in the Army Ministry and Army General Staff clamored for settling the matter of the Marco Polo Bridge with gunpowder, not paper. The emperor's brother, Prince Nobuhito Takamatsu, scribbled in his diary: "The mood in the army today is that we're really going to smash China so that it will be ten years before they can stand up again." The chief of the General Staff, Prince Kan'in, and the war minister, Gen. Gen Sugiyama, assured the emperor that fighting in China would end in two or three months. As one officer declared, Japan must exploit the episode to annex Hopei province (which stretched far south of Beijing) to "eradicate once and for all roots of future difficulties." Likewise, overseas senior leaders in China, Korea, and the Kwantung Army agitated for a comprehensive thrashing of the Chinese. Yet another source of bellicosity multiplied the odds against restraint. Hot-headed officers selectively fed pieces of information to a press edited to expurgate news of a potential accord and incite the public to strident demands for "decisive measures" against the "barbaric Chinese."

Between 9 July and 27 July, Tokyo oscillated repeatedly between actions to terminate or to expand the incident. At one point, Ishiwara proposed that Prime Minister Fumimaro Konoe fly to Nanjing and negotiate directly with Chiang. At another point, Konoe dispatched to Nanjing two peace negotiators. Imperial Army code breakers, however, learned of Konoe's maneuver via Chinese diplomatic messages, and the Imperial Army arrested the two negotiators. Each time Japanese policy makers started to wind down hostilities, they reversed themselves. The most significant factor in this wavering proved to be a series of reports from the military attaché's office in Nanjing warning that the Nationalist government was mobilizing and deploying massive troop concentrations to North China that threatened to overwhelm the China Garrison Army and imperil about 12,000 Japanese civilians in the area. These reports even bent Ishiwara to support deployment of troops from the Korean and Kwantung Armies as well as three divisions from the Japanese homeland to China at a crucial point on 11 July. That evening a public announcement named the affair "The North China Incident." Putting a title on the episode would prove far easier than controlling it.

The "North China Incident" first appeared to follow a long pattern of Chinese futility in the face of Japanese ferocity. The war began with Imperial Army forces numbering 90,000 men in the Kwantung Army who occupied positions all the way down to the Great Wall. Supplementing them were allied Chinese forces about 57,000 strong. About 5,600 Japanese soldiers of the China Garrison Army held positions in an arc along the rail lines from Tianjin to Beijing and Beijing to Shanhaiguan. They faced about 75,000 Chinese of the Twenty-Ninth Route Army. The Japanese rushed to the Beijing area two brigades and a division by 18 July. On 26 July Tokyo authorized 210,000 men for duty in North China, but even before they all arrived the Japanese subdued Beijing on 28 July and secured their supply line to the capital through the key port of Tianjin two days later.

On 29 July at Tongzhou, near Beijing, the Chinese seemed to confirm the worst fears of Japanese officials. After witnessing the Japanese execute about five hundred Nationalist soldiers who refused to surrender their arms, a body of Chinese puppet troops mutinied and joined the Nationalist survivors to annihilate a small Japanese military detachment and then set about slaughtering with great brutality two hundred civilians. The victims numbered

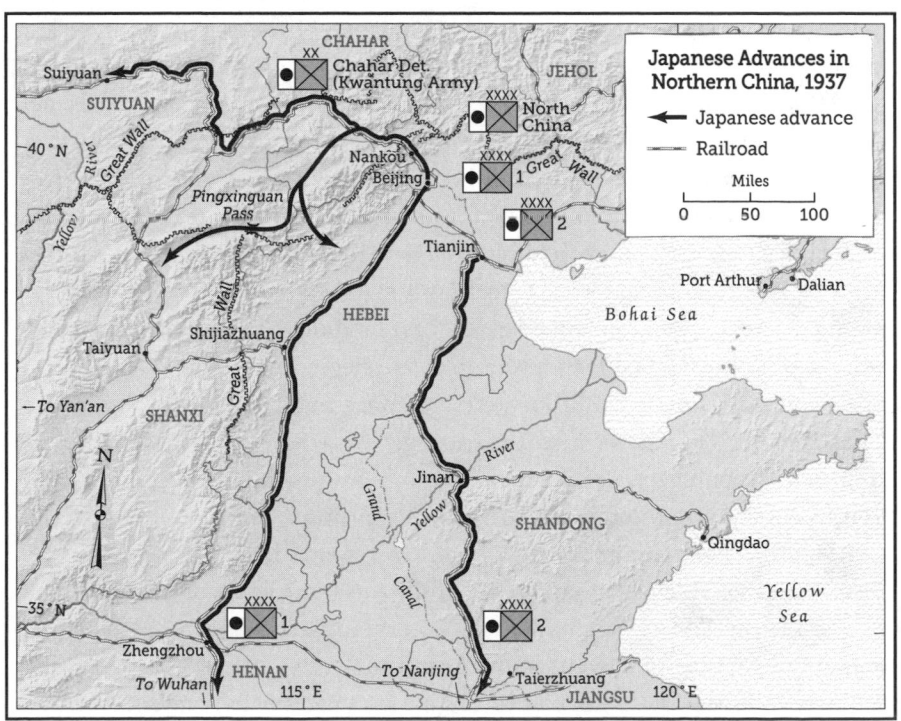

many women (frequently raped before death), children, and infants. The dead divided about equally between Japanese and Koreans. News of this incident inflamed public opinion in Japan.

To direct the now massively reinforced China Garrison Army, on 31 August Imperial Headquarters appointed Gen. Hisaichi Terauchi commander of the new North China Area Army of eight divisions. Tokyo declined to declare a formal state of war because Japanese leaders expected Terauchi to crush Chinese forces in North China and enforce a swift political settlement. Terauchi split his command, sending one part south about eighty-eight miles along the Beijing-Hankou railway toward Baoding, while the other part advanced to the east along the Tianjin-Pukou rail line a similar distance. Terauchi intended for the two armies to encircle and annihilate the main Chinese forces. His maneuver reflected the shackles that railroad-dominated logistics imposed on the Imperial Army throughout the war, limiting operations to regions within 150 to 180 miles from a rail head.

According to American correspondent Theodore White, the Chinese defenders from regional armies comprised ill-equipped and poorly supplied "ragamuffin hordes" that "broke like a wall of dust" before the Japanese. A German Army observer reported that "most forces simply have never offered resistance." The Central Army units Chiang sent to the north had casualty lists attesting to their fighting, but the collapse of the regional forces left them with no option but retreat. Terauchi explained his flagrant disregard for a stop line dictated in Tokyo with the comment that "the officers and men shouldn't return without filling their canteens with water from the Yellow River as a souvenir." Later defying further restrictions, Terauchi even propelled units south of the Yellow River. Terauchi's conduct foretold another enduring pattern: Japanese field commanders habitually disobeyed strictures promulgated in Tokyo. When Terauchi was satisfied, he halted the campaign by his 90,000-strong command at the cost of about 1,500 killed and 4,000 wounded. But he settled for souvenirs, not strategic achievement.

Concurrent with Terauchi's march, the Kwantung Army looked to conquer Chahar province to safeguard the strategic western flank of Manchukuo. Imperial Headquarters concurred and on 14 August authorized an expeditionary headquarters commanded by the Kwantung Army's chief of staff, Lt. Gen. Hideki Tôjô, who in four years would be Japan's fateful prime minister. Three brigades (including Japan's sole fully mechanized force) and later one division fell under Tôjô's command. Two other divisions extended Japanese operations that terminated with the Kwantung Army mastery over Chahar, Suiyuan, and the northern half of Shanxi provinces. The Imperial Army's exasperating experience with the mechanical defects and the logistical impositions of the mechanized brigade was noted, but rather than digest these lessons as challenges to overcome to maintain parity with future sophisticated foes, the Imperial Army disbanded the unit.

These excursions produced an episode with a dramatically inverse relationship between its scale and its repercussions on Chinese morale and the foreign perception of Chinese Communist forces. The Japanese sent a regimental-size task force to parry the threat posed by Chinese forces near Pingxingguan Pass. While Chiang's Central Army units battled the Japanese regiment in front, the Chinese Communist 115th Division with about 6,000 effectives under twenty-nine-year-old Lin Biao set up an ambush to the rear. Lin Biao nearly annihilated two supply columns of seventy horse-drawn and eighty motor vehicles respectively. Approximately two hundred of the three hundred trapped Japanese died. But in the widely disseminated Communist version of the event, which greatly bolstered national morale and burnished the reputation of Communist forces, a Japanese "brigade" or in some versions even a "division" had been "nearly annihilated," with the losses variously reported over the years into the thousands. The conflicting evidence confirms the small-scale tactical victory involving near-annihilation of the supply columns. Far from marking a material contribution by Chinese Communist forces to the conflict, this small action represented the only significant conventional engagement by Chinese Communist forces prior to 1940.

The "North China Incident" Becomes the "China Incident"

As Ishiwara emerged as a farsighted figure working to swerve Japan away from the precipice, Generalissimo Chiang Kai-shek steered China full tilt into a struggle that would prove ultimately fatal to Imperial Japan. It also eventually proved fatal to his regime, so that when he died in 1974 at age 87, Chiang seemed, in the words of China scholar Jonathan D. Spence, "a failure, a piece of Chinese flotsam left awkwardly adrift in the wake of Mao Zedong's revolutionary victories." But by the twenty-first century, Spence observed: "Now it is not so easy to be sure." The resurrection of Chiang's reputation in the People's Republic of China forms the latest gyration of Chiang's widely varying image since the 1920s.

Chiang was born in 1887 to a salt merchant and his villager wife, in South

Central China near the treaty port of Ningbo in Zhejiang province. When Chiang was just fourteen, his mother arranged a marriage with a nineteen-year-old illiterate bride, Fumei Mao. The belated consummation of that union produced a son in April 1910, Ching-kuo. (Chiang divorced Mao after twenty years of increasingly estranged relations.) From very early in his life, Chiang relentlessly pursued two goals: reunification of China, and the extirpation of foreign domination. Japan's victory over Russia in 1904–1905 likely inspired Chiang to embark on a military career. But in that time, military and political careers were not easily divorced.

Chiang found his mentor in Dr. Sun Yat-sen. Though their relationship was close, Sun chided Chiang for his "fiery temper, and your hatred of mediocrity [that] often leads you to quarrels and renders cooperation difficult." A long-serving reporter for the *New York Times* glossed Chiang's image as a rising leader with a slender, quick-moving body, and "magnificent flashing eyes." The British journalist Freda Utley depicted those eyes (in perhaps what now would be seen as an "Orientalist" tone) as "large, very dark and bright, extremely intelligent, completely unrevealing of his personality. They are the eyes of a man whose human feelings have been completely subordinated to his conception of his destiny."

Chiang's own misadventures in business and his avid readings tilted him decidedly to the left in matters of economics, but his vision was not fenced by economics. He developed a "neo-Confucian" outlook described by his able biographer Jay Taylor as encompassing "[an] emphasis on character development, self-discipline, and the conscious cultivation of the self, along with a sense of duty, courage, honor and activism rather than passive contemplation." This "neo-Confucian" viewpoint formed the basis for a political order reflecting a harmonious, orderly society. His focus on inculcating a set of individual virtues rather than some sweeping socioeconomic schema proved a fundamental defect in Chiang's vision.

As a soldier, Chiang had a unique background. He became first head of the Whampoa Military Academy—where Chinese military practice underwent a renaissance and he forged a lifelong bond with the Communist political commissar, Zhou Enlai. He studied at Japanese military academies (where Chiang learned to speak and read Japanese fairly well and assured he would become the first Chinese future national leader to have traveled outside the country). He served with Bolshevik officers in the field, and from the 1920s to the 1940s he fought Chinese Communist forces in guerrilla and regular combat. In the 1930s, he worked closely with a cadre of German military advisers and in the next decade with future American generals such as Joseph

Stilwell and Claire Chennault. Despite exposure to a veritable encyclopedia of twentieth-century military thought, Chiang never distilled any signature approach to war. Rather, he remained a pragmatic military leader addressing each challenge on its own merits.

After Sun's death in 1925, Chiang vaulted to leadership of the Nationalists. Then he led his National Revolutionary Army to triumph between 1926 and 1927, greatly expanding Nationalist control of China. In April 1927, Chiang launched a reign of terror against his erstwhile Communist allies. This came shortly after Stalin confided to party workers in Moscow that "when the [Nationalist] Right is of no more use, Chiang Kai-shek will be squeezed out like a lemon and flung away." While Chiang did not know of Stalin's remarks, convincing evidence had reached him of the Chinese Communists' plots to take over the Nationalists and depose him. Meanwhile, the Communists had unleashed lethal class warfare in the countryside. In response, Chiang loyalists killed between three and four thousand Communists and approximately 30,000 others.

In December 1927, Chiang married Mayling Soong, a Christian, English-speaking, American college graduate, youngest daughter of an American-educated wealthy Chinese, Charles Jones Soong. Later an American diplomat described her as "intelligent, liberally minded, self-assertive, magnetic, reasonably good looking, intense, somewhat impulsive, determined and devoted to her husband and China." She carved out a powerful leadership niche, and as *Time* magazine would note: "No woman in the West holds so great a position as Madame Chiang Kai-shek holds in China." The Soong family formed its own galaxy within China's elite. Brother T. V. Soong exerted great power as a Nationalist financier and diplomat. Oldest sister Ailing Soong married Xiangxsi Kong (H. H. Kung), the "financial architect" of Chiang's government. Middle sister Qingling Soong was the widow of Sun Yat-sen.

In 1928 Chiang seized Nanjing and made it his capital. This triumph left costs. It furthered a culture of violence within Chinese politics, accentuated military fragmentation, and inflamed bitter personal rivalries that hobbled momentum toward Chinese political and military unity.

The "Nanjing Decade" that followed Chiang's consolidation of power commenced in economic chaos and strife. Natural disaster and then the worldwide depression pummeled China. Chiang jousted with internal rivals among the Nationalists and took to the field again to suppress regional uprisings in 1930–1931. When Japan seized Manchuria in 1931, Chiang bitterly recognized that China lacked the military capacity to challenge the aggression. While at one time most historians found scant merit in the "Nanjing Decade," since the 1980s a substantial body of work now credits Chiang with major accomplishments politically and economically, many of which anticipated modernization that would continue after the Communist triumph in 1949.

The centerpiece of Chiang's vision was a small but modern elite force of professional military units, foreign-trained and -equipped. This army would serve directly as a rallying point to revive Chinese nationalism. Just as important, Chiang employed it for the ambitious goal of reversing negative Chinese cultural attitudes toward military service, a change essential to create the armed forces the nation needed to reestablish its full sovereignty. But a refurbished army formed only one component of a comprehensive reform revolution aimed at reshaping China. The other components included an honest and efficient political structure, an economy that could produce modern implements (particularly those for war-making), and a revamped social system that featured healthy, disciplined, educated citizens and modern communications. As historian Hans van de Ven summarized it, the whole tapestry of policies heeled to an "aesthetic of vigorous nationalist modernity."

But Chiang and his party manifested other facets that leached away at efforts to expand their popular support. The Nationalists used both legal and extralegal methods to stifle, undermine, or in some cases assassinate critics. Another chronic problem was corruption. Chiang was personally honest and eschewed ostentation. He openly spoke out against corruption among the Nationalists and military and even executed a few officers for this crime. But he failed to take decisive measures, because the issue of corruption, along with the issue of land reform, touched Nationalist party members and his military supporters. Corruption was especially flagrant at the local level, where Nationalist officials abused tax powers to extort abusive sums from farmers.

By "Double Ten Day" (10 October) in 1936 (the anniversary date of the rebellion that overthrew the Qing dynasty), Chiang was seen as an indispensable and "far-seeing leader who so long as the nation had been torn by internal struggles, had wisely avoided confrontation with the Japanese." A habitually critical publication conceded that "The people's confidence [in Chiang] seems as though revived from the dead." A balanced view of Chiang at this stage would acknowledge some palpable progress in rousing China from a protracted nightmare of political chaos. That said, while urban areas generally enjoyed economic strides and farmers savored rich harvests in 1935 and 1936, the vast majority of Chinese remained deeply scarred by abject poverty. Because Chiang held effective sway over only roughly one-third of the population, the penetration of his reforms into the nation remained shallow and urban.

As early as November 1931, Chiang defined his approach to confronting Japan as "first unity, then resistance." His domestic critics taunted him that this really meant craven appeasement of Japan so that Chiang could focus grotesquely on his real target: China's Communists. Foreign critics and later historians replicated these accusations as indisputable facts. To this array of Chiang detractors, only the December 1936 Xi'an Incident explains Chiang's will to war in 1937.

The architect of the Xi'an Incident was Xueliang Zhang ("The Young Marshal"). In 1928 the Japanese had assassinated his father Zuolin Zhang ("The Old Marshal"), the regional leader of Manchuria. Xueliang Zhang succeeded his father, but in 1931 the Japanese ousted him and his army from Manchuria. Thereafter, Zhang and his restless soldiers agitated for a redemptive war with Japan. They were by no means alone. The vociferous advocates of such a course included many students and intellectuals. Zhang believed the essential prerequisite to confronting Japan was the formation of a national unity government bringing together Chiang's Nationalists with other factions, particularly the Chinese Communists.

Zhang—an "opium-addled playboy" who counted a daughter of Benito Mussolini among his mistresses—was unaware that Stalin had ordered a shift to a "United Front" policy whereby Communist parties allied against real or alleged fascists worldwide. This led to secret negotiations between Chiang and the CCP resulting in a nascent agreement (not finalized until September 1937) calling for the CCP forces to come under Chiang's military command and abandon the most radical revolutionary policies, like land confiscation, while Chiang abandoned his demands for the abolition of the Chinese Communist Party and of a separate Red Army. Oblivious to all this, Zhang staged his own conspiracy. He asked Chiang to come to Xi'an on the pretext that Chiang's appearance would mollify Zhang's soldiers who were demanding hostilities with Japan. Once there, Zhang seized Chiang and offered him the choice of death or war with Japan—staged in concert with the Communists. News of Chiang's capture on 12 December 1936 delighted the Communist leader Mao Zedong and his chief subordinates. They wanted Chiang killed, but mindful of their subordinate status, Mao requested instructions from Moscow. Stalin found Chiang's imprisonment a source of serious alarm. A Chinese contact explained that without Chiang "China would be without a leader to fight the Japanese and this would not benefit the Soviet Union." A galvanizing bit of news from Europe seemed to confirm this threat. Chiang's longtime rival for Nationalist leadership, Jingwei Wang, had met with Hitler to discuss the prospect of China enlisting in the anti-Communist Axis in return for expanded German aid to China.

Chiang refused to formally agree to anything while a captive and appeared fully prepared to accept a martyr's death rather than submission. When word of Chiang's abduction spread throughout China, it triggered what an American diplomat described as an "extraordinarily widespread" outpouring of popular support on his behalf. Zhang, realizing his misjudgment, received Mao's trusted deputy Zhou Enlai, who warned Zhang not to harm Chiang. Chiang and Zhou finalized the agreement that had been in tentative form prior to Xi'an, whereby the Communists acceded to accept orders from Chiang in a national unity coalition, but Chiang relented on his demand that the Communists abolish their own independent army. When Chiang returned to Nanjing a free man, enormous throngs packed the streets to shower a rapturous, firecracker-accented welcome upon him. Edgar Snow declared that the generalissimo returned from Xi'an with a national standing "higher than that of any leader in modern Chinese history." "Chiang had left for Xi'an a popular leader," explained his biographer Jay Taylor, "but returned a national hero." Without Stalin's intervention Chiang likely would have been killed. Among the frightening alternative paths history might then have taken are Wang Jingwei's ascendency in the Nationalist Party, possible agreement with Japan to defeat the Chinese Communists, and the freeing up of Japan to attack the Soviets in 1941.

Chiang's decision for war in 1937 stemmed from many factors linked with the Xi'an Incident, perhaps more for its temporal proximity than its weight. Upon his return from Xi'an, Chiang commanded armies of 2,029,000 troops of highly variegated capability and loyalty. His personal forces included an elite cadre of 300,000 German-trained and 80,000 German-armed men. Chiang received the news that the head of his German advisory mission, Gen. Alexander von Falkenhausen (with whom Chiang conversed in their common language: Japanese), had reversed his cautious assessment that Chiang's units needed two more years of training before challenging the Japanese, and now pronounced them ready to drive "the Japanese over the [Great] Wall." This misplaced optimism by Chiang and his German adviser about the capability of his troops exerted a strong influence over Chiang's decisions in July 1937.

A second stratum of the Chinese armies, numbering roughly 600,000, included various regional commands loyal to Chiang in the past that generally conformed to his directives. These troops were better armed and trained than the rest. The third category encompassed regional armies mustering roughly a million men who were neither loyal nor obedient to Chiang. Among these were about 50,000 Red Army troops, of which just 29,650 possessed weapons. Finally, there were the perhaps 200,000 to 250,000 strong "armies" in Northeastern China and Manchuria. These elements had been defeated and displaced by the Japanese and generally disintegrated very early in the war, with some becoming Japanese puppet troops or reverting to bandit ways.

Another factor bolstered Chiang's sense that it was the hour to confront Japan. Contrary to the view of his detractors that was embedded in many accounts for decades, Chiang had long recognized that a true revival of China's sovereignty inevitably meant war with Japan. In March 1934, Chiang told a group of senior political leaders that "fewer than 1,100 days remained" before war with Japan, an estimate off by only forty-three days. Presciently, he also foretold that the conflict would last ten years, that foreign powers would eventually intervene, and that a world war would erupt.

Chiang quietly had opened the throttle for war preparations a half decade before the Marco Polo Bridge Incident. As early as 1932, Chiang created a secret National Defense Planning Council to analyze how confronting foreign aggression would affect an array of material, financial, and social issues. Chiang recruited a contingent of German military advisers to apply their expertise to fashioning China's modern forces. He arranged to trade Chinese raw materials, especially tungsten, for German arms. The first National Defense Plan of 1932 underwent a series of revisions over the next several years. By 1936 Sichuan province emerged as the general base area, and material preparations commenced. The proposals from both Chinese and German sources included adjustments of rail and road nets to support new fortification lines, plans to divide China into five "War Zones," mobilization of basic and military industry, and the establishment of military depots. In addition to stockpiling small arms ammunition, Chiang also had gathered food for men, forage for horses, medical facilities, and fuel supplies. Antiaircraft protection for Nanjing and Wuhan also received attention.

While these factors played a significant role in Chiang's considerations, probably the single most important impetus for Chiang to fight in 1937 was elemental: survival as China's preeminent leader. "If we allow one more inch of our territory to be lost, we shall be guilty of an unpardonable crime against our race," publicly declared Chiang. Chiang implied it would be an "unpardonable crime" if he failed to fight, and he would forfeit his claim to national leadership. Despite his sound belief as a soldier that uniting the country must precede embarking on the colossal task of taking on Japan, he recognized as a statesman that he could no longer demand forbearance from those Chinese whose good graces he must retain. Privately he weighed the strategic calculus: if the Japanese used the pretext of the incident to seize Beijing, they would be positioned in the middle of China, able to strike fatal blows at Chiang and the Nationalists. No wonder in his diary he termed this "the turning point for existence or obliteration."

As for how such a war would be waged, debate centered on two options. One contemplated permitting Japan to seize coastal areas and drive inland where the Chinese would make their stand and outlast the Japanese. On the contrary, General von Falkenhausen argued that China must immediately meet a Japanese attack, for the Chinese people would not abide the enormous sacrifices of the withdrawal strategy if they did not see serious sacrifices by the Nationalists. While von Falkenhausen won on basic strategy, he also cautioned that there was scarce hope for international intervention on China's behalf.

Both strategies would be employed; both involved huge risks for Chiang. Severe depletion of his armies would imperil his position both against Japan and domestically. He could also anticipate huge popular dissatisfaction from the massive loss of territory and population in the withdrawal strategy. Further, there was no small danger that however the war was fought, it might open the door to the triumph of the Communists. These thoughts—and the urging of many leaders and intellectuals not to embark upon war (one warned that in a war between Japan and Chiang's Nationalist government "at best both sides lose")—may have produced Chiang's caution upon the first news of the Marco Polo Bridge Incident. In his diary he asked: "Is this an isolated episode or the overture to further Japanese incursions into China?" Chiang's first orders to the local Twenty-Ninth Route Army commander in Beijing hedged: negotiate but do not yield "one iota of sovereignty." At the same time, he ordered all senior military and civilian officials to institute martial law and a general mobilization. He further dispatched three of his best German-trained divisions toward North China. When he learned on 12 July that three Japanese divisions had arrived at Tianjin, Chiang informed the Twenty-Ninth Route Army commander, "I am now determined to declare war on Japan."

When Japanese troops attacked near Beijing on 27 July, Chiang scrawled in his diary, "War is inevitable. We must fight. . . . I must not do anything to cause people to be ashamed of me." After a national conference at Lushan failed to sanction Chiang's proposed declaration of war, on 2 August Chiang officially declared his resolve to fight the Japanese in a telegram to provincial civil and military leaders. He invited them to Nanjing to discuss strategy. In a momentous act, most key provincial authorities put aside their rivalries and suspicions in favor of the national interest and participated in the 7 August meeting of the National Defense Council. Chiang deprecated the likelihood of intervention by the United States or Britain; China would have to protect itself. "Do we fight, or shall we be destroyed?" The participants agreed to obey Chiang without hesitation. "The conference," said railroad minister Jia'ao Zhang, "united the entire nation—unseen for centuries."

The Battle for Shanghai

China would fight, but where? The selection of Shanghai as the principal front reflected a combination of political and military factors. Shanghai housed the massive Anglo-American International Settlement and the French Concession, enclaves carved out by foreign nations that operated outside of Chinese sovereignty. These enclaves contained Western diplomats, businessmen, and journalists who would provide witnesses and hopefully advocates on China's behalf. As Chiang appealed to the League of Nations to condemn Japanese aggression, he also may have entertained a hope that events in Shanghai would mirror an earlier incident in 1932, when Japan had aborted a bombardment of Shanghai after a League of Nations–imposed cease-fire. But subsequent events left little chance the League would take any meaningful action. Europe and America remained riveted upon economic tribulations and the menace of Hitler. Chiang's key adviser, the Australian W. H. Donald, predicted it would be years before the West intervened.

Even if Western intervention was far-fetched, there were other compelling reasons to fight in Shanghai. The relatively level terrain in North China maximized Imperial Army advantages in mobility, equipment, and the military craft, and conversely accentuated Chinese weakness in all these categories. By contrast, Shanghai's naturally congested urban labyrinth diminished many Japanese advantages and magnified the utility of Chinese strength in raw numbers and small arms. Further, although Chiang stood as the titular top political leader and the commander in chief of China's armed forces, forces loyal to him actually comprised perhaps one-quarter of the total, making it risky to empower the northern regional commanders to provide critical leadership, as events soon confirmed.

Beyond these two considerations rested a pair of additional calculations. Japanese advances in North China threatened to cut the resupply route from the Soviet Union through Shanxi province. This constituted Chiang's only major outside source of material support. As Chiang anticipated, the Shang-

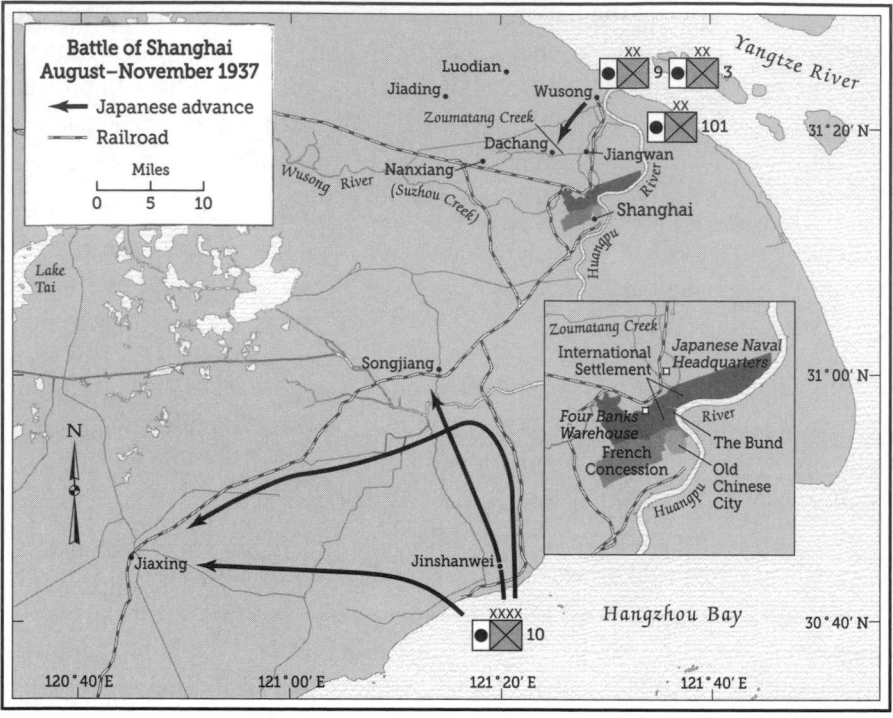

hai front acted as a magnet drawing Japanese troops from North China, thus safeguarding the Soviet supply line. A major Shanghai battlefront also threatened to tie up so much of the Imperial Army that Japan's Manchurian client state would become vulnerable to Soviet depredations. Unlike the remote prospects of intervention by the Western powers or the League of Nations, the Soviet threat might impose a real inhibition on Japan's appetite for Chinese territory. Chiang also perceived that a fight for Shanghai would psychologically mobilize China's masses behind the war in a way that war in the more remote North would not.

News of Japanese warships concentrating at Shanghai prompted Chiang to order two of his best units, the 87th and 88th Divisions, to assume defensive positions in the city. At the same time, however, he reined in his local commander, Zhizhong Zhang, from launching a preemptive attack without Chiang's express authority. "The Chinese [troops] wear olive drab uniforms," the *New York Times* advised its readers, and are "well armed, cheerful and confident." An estimated 50,000 Chinese civilians, sensing the ominous portents, began fleeing Shanghai's northern suburbs for the International Settlement.

In the words of eminent Japanese historian Ikuhiko Hata, the rapidity and completeness of Japanese conquests in North China by the end of July made it appear "as though a full-scale war could be averted." This brief illusion later produced an argument that the Imperial Navy was responsible for what Japan began to call the "China Incident" by insisting on expanding the fighting to Shanghai and Nanjing. But Hata dismissed this "simple explanation," for when China unexpectedly continued resistance, Shanghai and Nanjing loomed as the obvious next targets, coupling military accessibility with likely political impact to force China to yield. Tensions in Shanghai were already running high when on 9 August Chinese troops killed two Japanese sailors who ventured near a Chinese airbase. The Japanese immediately demanded that Chinese armed forces abandon Shanghai. On 10 August, the Japanese cabinet approved the recommendation of naval leaders that Japan should attack in Shanghai twenty days after army forces mobilized. Just two days later, the Army Ministry ordered 300,000 troops to Shanghai.

On 13 August, Chiang was still rebuffing his local commander's request to attack, but events on the ground careened out of control. After skirmishes between Chinese and Japanese troops erupted, Japanese warships bombarded the Chinese quarter of Shanghai. The Chinese attempted to retaliate by an air strike the next day. The Chinese bombs horribly missed their intended Japanese ship targets and instead landed in Chinese territory, killing, by one count, 1,142 civilians. The Imperial Japanese Navy answered Chinese air raids on 14 August, escalating hostilities in raids aimed at Chinese air bases. The Japanese planes flew history's first transoceanic flights to their targets from bases on Taiwan, a carrier, and even the city of Omura in Japan, a feat that amazed the world.

In the face of Chinese aerial attacks on Japanese ships, the Imperial Navy jettisoned their usual skeptical stance toward enterprises of the Imperial Army and advocated land campaigns from Shanghai to Nanjing. In the meantime, the navy itself rushed men to Shanghai to bring its forces to 4,000, but they were outnumbered at least ten to one. On 17 August, Imperial General Headquarters created the Shanghai Expeditionary Army. The emperor himself directed the commander, Lt. Gen. Iwane Matsui, to protect Shanghai's Japanese nationals. Short and slender, with hands and shoulders that shook as though afflicted with palsy, Matsui nonetheless spoke sharply and incisively. His outstanding feature, noted a journalist, was "his large, long ears, resembling those found upon Japanese and Chinese temple idols and supposed to denote men of great wisdom and intelligence." When the increasingly perturbed emperor demanded a strategy to halt the fighting, his chiefs of staff advocated sharp escalation: a pulverizing bombing campaign to shatter Chinese will coupled with occupation of vital points in North China, capped by a blockade of China's coast.

The main Chinese offensive to oust the Japanese from Shanghai began on 17 August. It demonstrates in microcosm the enduring patterns in the long struggle to follow. Conscious that they needed to strike swiftly before the Japanese reinforced, the Chinese launched an assault to crush the Japanese Shanghai enclave. But the best tactical approaches would have pressed through parts of the International Settlement and French Concession. Avoiding offense to international opinion, the Chinese thrust along paths heading into prepared Japanese defenses, namely the headquarters of the Japanese naval troops guarding the Japanese settlement. This massive building was a fortress bristling with machine guns nestled in concrete or sandbagged emplacements and protected by barbed wire entanglements. Covering fire from Japanese warships in the river bolstered the Japanese defenders. Though the Chinese showed an important grasp of the war's political dimensions, their military approach pitted flesh against bullets and shells. By late August, the bullets and shells had won. Moreover, the Chinese commanders proved unable to mass forces and coordinate action to make their numerical advantages decisive. "Every building was bullet-marked and the haze of gunpowder hung over the town," reported a visiting Japanese literary figure, Fusao Hayashi, describing the atmosphere of deadlock. Under the blazing August sun, combat flared mostly at night, leaving the sunlit hours in "eerie silence" broken only by swarms of blue flies.

On 20 August, Chiang issued a "General War Directive for the National Army." It provided for five "War Zones" and fitted the Shanghai battle into an overall strategy of a war of attrition. Historian Hans van de Ven later identified this as "the point of no return" for China. On 21 August, the Imperial Army submitted plans to mobilize three more divisions. Meanwhile, the Imperial Navy's shore forces were barely hanging on when the 3rd Division landed on 22 August with the mission of striking west from the International Settlement to clear Chinese opposition. At the same time, the 11th Division went ashore about twenty miles north of Shanghai and struck out southwest for Luodian, a key communications hub for the entire region.

The Combatants

The entry of Japan and China into a huge battle at Shanghai provides an opportunity to compare the real combat capabilities of each contestant. In the air and at sea, Japanese forces possessed not just a superiority, but marked supremacy, both in terms of modern aircraft and ships in overwhelming multitude, but also generally in individual war machines and the men who manned them. On the ground, the Imperial Army enjoyed marked superiority at all levels in firepower from automatic weapons to artillery. A comparison of the average Japanese regular army division and one of Chiang's elite Central Army divisions conveys some sense of the disparity.

Nominal Japanese and Chinese Divisions

	JAPANESE	CHINESE
Personnel	24,400/28,200*	10,923
Rifles	9,586	3,821
Light Machine Guns	292	274
Heavy Machine Guns	96	54
Grenade Launchers	304	243
Mountain/Field Guns	48	16
Mortars	56	30

* Japanese divisions usually had two different authorized strengths at this time.

This table reflects a well-equipped, regular Japanese division with four infantry regiments. But only about twenty "reformed," German-trained and -equipped Chinese divisions of Chiang's Central Army possessed the scale of men and arms listed above. The other two hundred or so Chinese "divisions" fell far short of this complement of men and equipment, particularly weapons heavier than a rifle, making the disparity in combat power far greater than this table indicates. Indeed, the figures for artillery apply only to about a dozen Chinese divisions in 1937. Further, the enormous diversity of their foreign and domestic manufacturers compounded the general shortage of Chinese weapons. Moreover, Chinese signal equipment was sparse and often unreliable. Messengers or telegrams might take days to arrive. As to mobility and logistics, a Japanese division also normally fielded 6,000 to 7,000 horses and two to three hundred motor vehicles. There were just 3,000 military vehicles in all of China, and Chinese divisions lacked all but small numbers of horses.

At the start of the war, the Japanese accorded the most respect to Chiang's Central Army units, including the Whampoa cadets, referring to them as the "core central forces." The Japanese also respected the Guangxi Army, the Northwestern Army, and Northeastern Army, and some Uyghur Army units.

By contrast, the Japanese held in low esteem the Guangdong Army, Shanxi Army, and provincial forces such as the Yunnan and Sichuan Armies.

One subjective expression of the immense gaps between the combat power of Japanese and Chinese units of comparable size appears in the general rule adopted by experienced Japanese commanders that a single Japanese regiment was a match for a full division of Chiang's Central Army. A single Japanese battalion could grapple on even terms with a division from regional forces. Frank Dorn, an American military observer, calculated that the average Japanese division possessed three to twelve times as much combat power as its ostensible Chinese equivalent.

A huge reason for this acknowledged gap in capabilities between Japanese and Chinese units rested in the officer corps. Japan's modernization program included the establishment of a comprehensive tier of officer training schools from the tactical to higher command and staff functions. The Chinese failed to suit their military educational system to their needs. Even when Chinese units possessed competent leaders, they all too often lacked a complement of staff officers to address the voluminous details of modern combat. The result was that Chinese units typically possessed muscle, but even if they enjoyed a talented brain, they lacked a nervous system to coordinate the movement of their muscles within their unit, much less with adjacent units.

BOTH THE JAPANESE IITH AND 3RD Divisions confronted a maze of natural and manmade obstacles. The 11th Division advanced north of Shanghai through well-tilled lands, lightly veined with crude roads and composed of dry rice paddies framed by steep five-foot-high embankments. A jumble of creeks and canals crosshatched the land. This terrain dispersed Japanese formations into inhabited locations ranging from individual farms to small towns, both affording natural redoubts with husky, reinforced brick walls. An old China hand, *New York Times* journalist Hallett Abend, underlined how the Chinese also exploited "large and small conical grave mounds with which the countryside surrounding Shanghai is dotted. These grass covered mounds provide good camouflage for prepared positions and the ground in front of them and between them is heavily mined."

Meanwhile, the 3rd Division struggled in the bewildering labyrinth of Shanghai beyond the International Settlement. A Catholic missionary described this urban battleground as

a maze of tiny streets, few of which run for as much as 100 yards before turning a right angle, many where two [rickshaws] have to go carefully in passing each other and all paved unevenly with sharp stones. The houses lean into each other, filling solidly all the space between the streets; in general the rooms of each house centre on a tiny square courtyard, whose top light, two stories up, is all the lighting the lower rooms get.

Factories, warehouses, businesses, and municipal structures of solid brick formed an archipelago of natural fortresses within the dense disordered sea of residences. The constricted avenues of movement, the severely curbed vision, and the tiny fields of fire caused troops to stumble into ambush sites where they could be laced with sniper, machine-gun, or mortar fire.

One foreign observer described another element of Chinese resistance that would soon drive Japanese soldiers into countless ruthless reprisals and pre-emptive executions:

> The anti-Japanese feeling of the Chinese people is now at such a pitch that almost every Chinese in this area is a potential sniper if only he could procure a revolver or a rifle, and Shanghai is facing the prospect of a long period of ruthless killings, imprisonments, inquisitions, sudden counterstrokes and savage retaliation.

Considering the difficulties, the 3rd and 11th Divisions progressed remarkably, but at an appalling cost. The Imperial Army mobilized ten reserve battalions to replace casualties. Fatalities occurred not only because of Chinese weapons but also because Japanese divisions arrived without heavy artillery or tank units due to the erroneous staff assessments that the ground was too soft to bear their weight. Neglect of minimal combat support requirements found Japanese infantrymen shoved into combat without their logistical or medical units. Japanese industry could not meet the abrupt surge in demand for artillery ammunition.

A casualty of a different sort was Ishiwara in Tokyo. When the navy demanded troops for Shanghai, Ishiwara countered with a proposal to evacuate Japanese nationals as much cheaper than full-scale war. During August and September his advocacy of a swift negotiated settlement provoked heated shouting matches in the halls of the General Staff. By mid-September, Prince Kinmochi Saionji, the last of the elder statesmen from the Meiji era, advised Premier Konoe that Ishiwara's influence was so low "he is like a candle in the wind ready to be snuffed out at any moment." The actual snuffing followed at the end of the month. But in a typically convoluted maneuver, the new vice chief of staff Gen. Hayao Tada (a moderate like Ishiwara) packaged Ishiwara's replacement (by another moderate) with a purge of some of Ishiwara's most vociferous foes on the General Staff. Tada and other acolytes of Ishiwara's strategic sense continued to work to curtail the war.

Ishiwara's resistance, the erratic record of decisions in Tokyo in 1937, as well as the appointment of Tada, are facts that challenge the beguiling interpretation styled "The Fifteen Years War," which argues that Japan followed a seamless path from Manchuria in 1931 to the USS *Missouri* in 1945. "The Fifteen Years War" appears on the surface as a logical narrative of these events, and some Japanese leaders did press policies that link all these events. But the fact that Ishiwara—of all personalities, given his role in 1931—vigorously sought to steer Japan away from further entanglement in China, and the staggering, stumbling steps Tokyo took into full-scale war, raise the more compelling alternative interpretation: contingency rather than inevitability produced the Sino-Japanese War of 1937–1945.

Even as the tide began to turn unmistakably against the Chinese defenders in Shanghai, Chiang believed a demonstration of sacrifice would rally the whole nation. He pushed into Shanghai as many as 750,000 men (to face a final Japanese commitment of 250,000). This number would assure that Shanghai was the largest urban battle in World War II prior to Stalingrad. Chiang also sought to secure a League of Nations censure of Japan for aggression. That effort resulted in a conference set to convene in Brussels, Belgium, on 30 October, involving the signatories to the Nine-Power Treaty signed in Washington in 1922, which had guaranteed China's right to self-determination and affirmed the American "Open Door Policy" of equal access to trade. In a Nanjing speech on 9 October, Chiang cautioned his countrymen not to expect any near-term Western aid: "international sympathy, though the source of great encouragement, should not be permitted to awaken false and ill-grounded hopes." They must not expect others to fight China's battles but must brace themselves for "ever increasing hardships and afflictions and be prepared to face situations and experiences ten times more difficult and harrowing than those faced today." But as to more distant horizons, Chiang wrote on 15 October, "By the time the war has lasted six months, next March at the latest, Japan will be facing either internal turmoil or external threat. We will hold out." He himself moved to Suzhou 62 miles from Shanghai to take direct command of the battle.

The International Settlement formed a peculiar facet of the Battle of Shanghai. At first, little appeared to change. As before the war, down its wide and ordered streets, often flanked by fine brick buildings, swirled an array of humanity in a pageant of Eastern and Western dress, speaking every imaginable language. Treaties provided authority for its existence, but contingents of Western soldiers, sailors, and marines enforced its actual immunity from battle, though not from stray bullets, shells, and bombs. The scene was like a row of opera boxes fronting a stage of carnage. By October, however, the fighting no longer seemed remote. Heavy guns sounded every half hour against an almost continuous melody of machine-gun bursts. The only other sound was the doleful chiming on the quarter hours from the darkened customs house on the famous Bund. The Sunday church chimes often were overpowered by the sounds of artillery. Bitter smoke from the struggle wafted through the air of the deserted streets. Almost all buildings were shuttered and sandbagged. The few cinemas open showed only comedies, with Walt Disney the patrons' favored fare. "The city shrinks apprehensively on hearing loaded bombers droning high overhead," recorded one reporter. He went on to write that "Dreary cabarets catering to soldiers and sailors with plain dancing partners cannot develop even alcoholic gayety."

With an eye to the Brussels meeting and a growing fear of Soviet entry into the war by November, Tokyo committed three more divisions to Shanghai to end the fighting during October. One of these, the 101st, originally earmarked for garrison duty, was filled with overage reservists in their thirties, many with wives and families. On 29 September, Matsui threw four divisions into a concerted assault. Two days later his soldiers hit the Chinese main line of resistance in western Shanghai along a feature named Wusong Creek. Far from being a minor watercourse, it was about one hundred to three hundred feet wide and too deep to ford. The far shore housed Chinese fortifications. Forfeiting his artillery advantage, Matsui resorted to massing infantry along narrow sectors—about 60,000 men along a front of only about six to eight miles—to overpower the defenders in brute frontal assaults.

The Chinese resisted fiercely, often skillfully, and with undeniable heroism. For the first time, they managed to pummel the Japanese with concentrated artillery fire. They mounted repeated but poorly coordinated counterattacks to negate Japanese advances. House-to-house fighting, where a dwelling changed hands several times, was common. The Chinese fought in the rubble of pulverized positions and refused to surrender, even when surrounded—though in reality neither side customarily took prisoners. In overrun positions, Japanese soldiers found dead Chinese, some with disturbingly childlike features. Others still clutched weapons, as though, said some Japanese, their ghosts had returned to continue resistance. The Chinese sought to avoid combat except at such close ranges—often just a few yards—so that the Japanese could not bring their artillery into play. One Japanese diplomatic observer wrote in his diary about this struggle that Japan had "viewed [China] as a dog, [it] now emerges as a wolf." Still, a persistent fundamental defect remained the Chinese failure to create true multitiered defenses in depth.

When the reserve 101st Division plunged into the maelstrom on 7 October, they found themselves, like their regular army comrades, transported back to the trench warfare of World War I. Their zigzagging trench network facing Wusong Creek tendered a partial shield from Chinese fire. The soldiers dug angled approach trenches to the creek itself. Nerving themselves in these rain-soaked jump-off points, they manhandled assault boats into the creek under fire, guided by volunteer swimmers. At the far shore, the survivors attempted to scale the six-foot-high barbed-wire-crowned embankment with bamboo ladders. The thin bands who cleared all these challenges then as often as not found themselves in diabolically prepared killing zones for Chinese machine guns and mortars. Even once the Japanese penetrated the Wusong Creek line, they faced a further belt of similar defenses along a series of creeks anchored by Zoumatang Creek. After only four days the 101st Division reported 3,000 casualties. The bloodletting among these reservists sent a shock wave through Japan. Matsui shifted the 101st to a lesser role. The main burden of the attack devolved back to the regular 3rd and 9th Divisions.

As days turned into weeks and weeks into months, the Japanese experienced acute embarrassment over their inability to smash the Chinese armies around Shanghai. A few foreign military observers took the wrong lesson from the Chinese defense; the battle, they concluded, demonstrated that Japan presented no threat to any first-class power. The *New York Times* dryly recorded a novel rationale offered by an official Japanese spokesman for the stalemate: "In explanation of the slowness of their progress around Shanghai, the Japanese complained that the Chinese, ignorant of tactics, did not know when to retreat."

On 25 October, the Japanese 9th Division completed, at the cost of 9,556 casualties, the last lap of the 2.5-mile advance in twenty days from Wusong to Zoumatang Creeks, aided by newly arrived heavy artillery and the unrelenting pummeling of the Chinese by Japanese airmen. In the shroud of darkness that night, exhausted Japanese soldiers trudged across bamboo bridges over the barrier. After being rebuffed three times, one battalion finally breached the Chinese main defenses by daybreak. The 3rd Division followed and expanded the foothold the next day. The Chinese defenders, exhausted and likewise having suffered ghastly losses, finally began to retreat.

The collapse of Chinese resistance in Shanghai led to much celebration in Japan. Processions of flag-waving schoolchildren drawn from the Tokyo region marched past the Imperial Palace by day on 27 October. That night some 20,000 lantern-bearing youths paraded.

Total Japanese casualties officially numbered 40,372 (9,115 killed and 31,257 wounded), but these figures fail to convey the severe losses sustained by the four most heavily engaged divisions. The Ninth Division suffered an astonishing 94 percent casualty rate, based on its original strength. Only the infusion of replacements, mostly reservists, kept these formations going. But in the end, quite often a rifle company comprised just twenty men commanded by a corporal. Even the exemplary Japanese élan was shaken. The government abruptly stopped releasing complete casualty lists. Tokyo policemen fended off demonstrators before the home of a regimental commander whose unit sustained severe losses. The widow of another regimental commander who fell in Shanghai committed suicide to escape the venom aimed at her husband.

The Chinese toll was more terrible still. An official report on 5 November set Chinese casualties at 187,200 killed and wounded, about four-and-one-half times Japan's losses. Later historians set the number as high as 250,000, or six times Japanese losses. Not only did these raw numbers include a majority of Chiang's best German-trained and -equipped troops, whose losses degraded the immediate Chinese resistance capacity; they included a large swath—estimated as high as 70 percent—of the approximately 30,000 academy-trained Chinese officers. The loss of these trained officers deprived the Chinese armies of the key leaders needed to create and direct future combat-effective units.

A year later, Chiang admitted he committed a grave error by failing to withdraw his troops from Shanghai before the collapse. "We were totally defeated. It was my fault." But without downplaying the horrific casualties or the detriment to immediate Chinese prospects, it must be said that the Battle of Shanghai nonetheless provided tremendous benefits for China. Despite sometimes severe discord among China's various generals and armies (even including some plotting against Chiang), a genuine coalition formed that would largely endure over the whole war—something that had not existed for about a century. Further, decades of political and social agitation had failed to rouse the Chinese masses to unite to withstand Japanese incursions. While many Chinese in the vast countryside remained ignorant of the war, news of the ferocity of Japanese soldiers against combatant and civilian alike kindled in key sections of the population a conflagration of patriotic fury that "for the first time . . . transcended regionalism, localism and familism." These Chinese saw the struggle as not just some new iteration of the ancient human impulse for territorial aggrandizement, but as a stark race war—short of the genocidal descent in Europe—in which the Japanese regarded them as a lower order of being. The struggle would be known as *"Kangri Zhanzheng"*: The War of Resistance Against Japan.

The month-after-month struggle for Shanghai demonstrated that effective and sustained resistance was feasible, rousing impassioned spirits dormant after a century of humiliations. Official news and word of mouth carried across China the saga of the valiant street-by-street, house-by-house defense of Shanghai. A near-hourly series of dispatches by the Chinese and foreign press created an epic symbolic narrative of the defense of the Four Banks Warehouse across Suzhou Creek from the International Settlement by "The Lost Battalion" of "Eight Hundred Heroes." This unit (the 1st Battalion, 524th Regiment, 88th Division) only numbered somewhat over four hundred men. It fought a spectacularly dramatic battle from 26 to 31 October before the eyes of foreign and cheering Chinese witnesses in the International Settlement. After suffering about a hundred fatalities, the survivors were interned in the International Settlement.

Memorable national slogans—some originating at the top but all reflecting actual mass sentiment—swept across the land. "China Cannot Be Lost" emerged as perhaps the most common, painted on countless walls and buildings. The war birthed an entirely new Chinese social phenomenon: mass singing. A famous soldier's tune of the period contained the key lyrics, "Never to come back until our hills and rivers are returned to us!" An almost daily outpouring of new Chinese songs and the free use of traditional Chinese and borrowed Western melodies followed. These were songs to recruit or inspire soldiers, laments of parting and homesickness, songs of fury, and songs of freedom.

One song that became famous during this period would later be the national anthem: "The March of the Volunteers." This one song would come to symbolize much of China's twentieth-century history. The melody was written in 1934 by the composer Nie Er with words by the playwright Tian Han to protest Japan's aggression in Manchuria. Er had died in a swimming accident while visiting Japan in 1935, so he would never know the unlikely fate of his creation. After the Communist triumph in 1949, the song (with different lyrics) was made the official national anthem of the People's Republic of China, which it remains. Er's collaborator, Tian Han, survived the war, but died in a Maoist prison camp during the Cultural Revolution. His service to the Chinese people in their greatest hour of need failed to save him from the charge of being a "poisonous weed."

CHAPTER 2

"The Bombs and the Bullets and the Bayonets of the Japanese Are Ruthless"*

NANJING

Hangzhou Bay

To complete the crushing of Chinese forces near Shanghai, Tokyo created the potent new Tenth Army with four divisions under Lt. Gen. Heisuke Yanagawa. From the outset, Yanagawa set his sights not on annihilating Shanghai's defenders but on the glory of seizing Nanjing, the Nationalist capital. As early as 20 August the Chinese detected Japanese reconnaissance probes of Hangzhou Bay south of Shanghai. But they wrongly surmised that Japanese intentions extended only to a one-division secondary effort. (Later Chiang admitted in his diary that the neglect of Hangzhou Bay defenses constituted "our biggest strategic mistake" in the struggle for Shanghai.) On 5 November, the Japanese Tenth Army overpowered the Chinese 63rd Division by landing two divisions covered by naval gunfire. The Japanese then trounced Chinese Central Army reinforcements. The Chinese fronts both at Suzhou Creek and Hangzhou Bay collapsed. The chaos of disorganized units, trailing in their wake huge quantities of discarded weapons

---

* "The bombs and the bullets and the bayonets of the Japanese are ruthless": Madame Chiang Kai-shek to Mrs. A. L. Luce, 2 May 1938, Papers of Harry L. Hopkins, Sherwood Collection, Book 3: Background of Lend Lease—Book 4, Russia Attacked, Box 305, Folder Book 3: China Pre-Pearl Harbor 4, FDRL. Luce was a college classmate of Madame Chiang.

and ammunition, devastated the high morale that had fueled the ferocious Chinese resistance at Shanghai. Wounded were abandoned; some officers deserted. Chinese commanders could neither persuade nor compel their men to rally at the prepared defensive works between Shanghai and Nanjing.

Once Shanghai fell, some Imperial Army officers preached rest for the troops. But others insisted that the army must surge onward along the 170 miles to Nanjing. On 7 November, Tokyo created the provisional Central China Field Army under Lt. Gen. Iwane Matsui, who concurrently commanded his own Shanghai Expeditionary Army as well as Yanagawa's Tenth Army. Matsui's mission remained the destruction of Chinese forces around Shanghai. The next day, the Japanese split their forces. The Shanghai Expeditionary Army headed west along the Shanghai-Nanjing railway. Yanagawa's Tenth Army surged west along the southern bank of Lake Tai. By 15 November, Yanagawa discarded any restraint. He agitated for a vigorous offensive against the Chinese remnants and encirclement of Nanjing. With Nanjing surrounded, Yanagawa would avoid costly frontal assaults and instead unleash Japanese aircraft to bludgeon any defenders into submission with mustard gas and incendiaries. But the chief of staff of the Imperial Army, Imperial Prince Kan'in, ordered Yanagawa's superior, Matsui, that "the use of gas and tear gas shall await further directives." The Japanese generals now aimed for a comprehensive, war-ending victory. Japan then could dictate a settlement that would validate not only their local gains, but all the encroachments in North China obtained over the past several months.

As Japanese columns converged on Nanjing on 13 November, Chiang Kai-shek displaced the government to Chungking and his military headquarters to Wuhan to gird for a protracted War of Resistance. On 17 November, Chiang confided in his diary: "Should we defend Nanjing or abandon it? It is hard to decide." Most senior commanders and General von Falkenhausen opposed defending Nanjing to the last man. Some voices rose for symbolic resistance or guerrilla warfare. Minister of Foreign Affairs Shijie Wang counseled against embarking on "a sacrifice which is unnecessary, meaningless and without strategic benefit" for the Republic.

Both internal advocates for terminating the conflict and international factors buffeted Chiang. As early as September, Chiang heard domestic critics favoring appeasement. With the loss of Shanghai, the minister of justice, Ju Zheng, executed an about-face from prosecuting appeasers to becoming a champion for negotiations. An exasperated Chiang tartly pointed out the folly of certain "men of letters" who now urged "appeasement after military

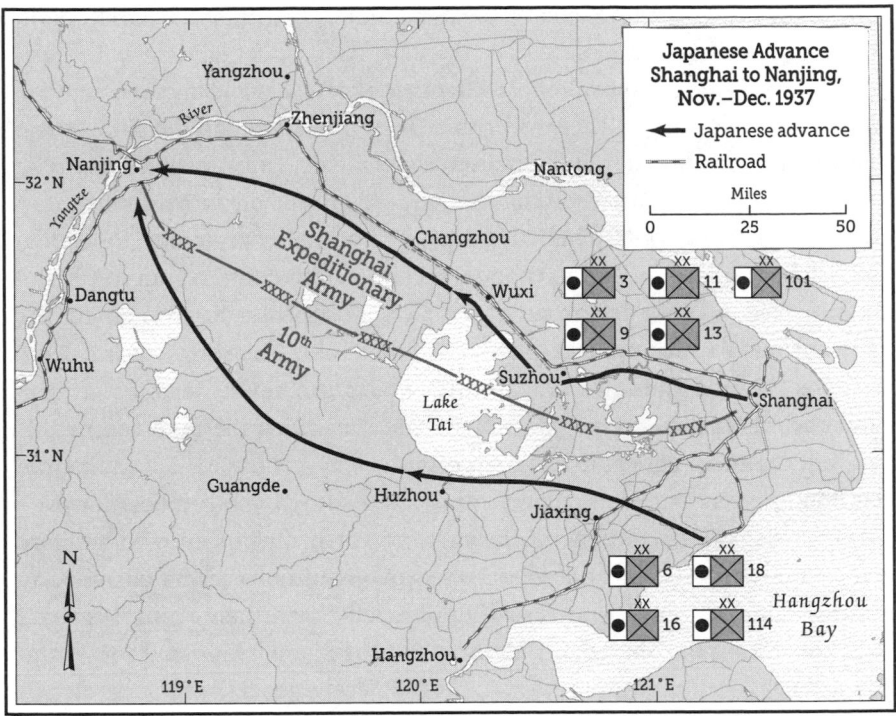

defeat." More ominously, Chiang was beset by even some ranking officers, who formerly sounded the tocsin for war but now had "lost their guts."

Chiang continued efforts to meld domestic politics and military strategy with endeavors to ply international support. China's realistic hopes of foreign intervention rested precariously with the Soviet Union. The Soviets signed a nonaggression treaty with China on 21 August and became beleaguered China's only significant munitions supplier. These concrete measures prompted Chiang on 1 September to predict ultimate Soviet intervention. On 11 November, Marshal K. Ye. Voroshilov outfitted a Chinese military delegation departing from Moscow with a message for Chiang that the Soviets would not stand idly by if the situation became critical. Chiang acknowledged this message in a cable to Stalin on 30 November and added: "China has made its last and largest efforts for national survival. We have to retreat from Nanjing. We are looking forward to the powerful support from our ally the Soviet Union. We sincerely hope that you will send troops." Two factors pushed Chiang's fateful order to defend Nanjing "to the death": the need (for both domestic and international reasons) to display his unyielding will, backed by the Chinese people, for protracted resistance to Japan, and anticipation that the stand might induce Soviet intervention.

Chiang also juggled two other diplomatic efforts, one old and one new. He had vested "great hope" that the Brussels meeting, based on the Nine-Power Treaty, might rally material international support for China or at least impose sanctions on Japan. But when the conferees adjourned on 24 November, they left behind bland words abstractly affirming international support for China, but eschewing any call for sanctions, much less direct intervention. Chiang then turned to a new demarche via the German ambassador to Japan, Oskar Trautmann. As historian Ikuhiko Hata observed, the secret peace negotiations between China and Japan through Trautmann, as Japanese armies approached Nanjing, were "the only instance in which the high commands of both countries agreed to a certain extent on the conditions for ending the conflict. . . . This was the last opportunity for ending the hostilities."

True statecraft required the Japanese to hitch diplomacy with military restraint. Astute Japanese leaders urged magnanimous terms designed to salvage Chinese "face" while avoiding protracted war; their counsels gained traction during the Shanghai stalemate. But the Shanghai breakthrough and then the prospective capture of Nanjing—an event generally not expected in Tokyo before 1938—incited hardline officers as well as their civilian allies to demand ever more onerous terms. Some even entertained visions of replacing Chiang with a pro-Japanese government. By 6 December, Chiang agreed to negotiations along the more generous lines Japan originally proposed, but he also insisted on preserving Chinese territorial integrity and instituting a cease-fire before the negotiations. Under the heady illusion that a decisive victory at Nanjing beckoned, Japanese leaders deferred their response until January 1938. That response would emerge as a disastrous monument to Japanese strategic folly.

Chiang's senior subordinates remonstrated with him over his original plan to take personal command of the defense of Nanjing and President Sun Yat-sen's adjacent mausoleum. On 19 November, Chiang instead entrusted Nanjing to the general who volunteered for the job: Shengzhi Tang. According to historian Jonathan Spence, "Tang's distinguishing feature was the abiding faith he held in his Buddhist spiritual adviser," who urged Tang to take charge of Nanjing's defenses. Chiang confessed Tang's dim prospects in his diary on 27 November: "It is hard to defend Nanjing, but we must do it." In fact, geography shaped Nanjing into a natural trap for its defenders. The Yangtze flowed north and then curved east, creating a loop around the city to the southwest, west, north, and northeast. The Chinese defenders awaiting the Japanese approach from the east and southeast thus had their backs to the river. The only withdrawal route from the city across the river was via the "back door" called Xiaguan Gate. But there was no bridge, so soldiers would need watercraft to cross the Yangtze. A *New York Times* reporter who interviewed Tang came away with the conviction that the Chinese fully recognized the likelihood of the entrapment of their forces but aimed to make the Japanese pay a stiff price for the capital "in a final heroic gesture so dear to the Chinese heart."

Although Chiang failed in his endeavors to secure foreign intervention, his government nonetheless displayed greater agility at coordinating military and diplomatic strategy than did his Japanese adversaries. In the opening clashes, the Japanese field forces in China intermingled restraint and overreaching, while senior officers in Tokyo fumbled for some consistent policy, stumbling into a piecemeal commitment of forces. As they steered the nation into a quagmire, Japan's uniformed leaders denied information and meaningful consultation to the civilian government under Prime Minister Konoe. The armed forces instituted an Imperial General Headquarters for the first time since the Russo-Japanese War, a mark of the gravity of the conflict. But they denied Konoe a seat at the headquarters, and only met his threat of resignation with the grudging establishment of a (Cabinet) Liaison Conference that served as the sole conduit for civilian governmental input into war strategy.

Imperial General Headquarters formally came into existence on 20 November, but Japan's uniformed leaders only met with top civilians in a Liaison Conference five days later. That same day, 25 November, word that commanders in China contemplated an attack on Nanjing triggered an uproar and an order for Matsui to rein in the Tenth Army. But the intelligence reaching Matsui the next day pictured Chinese losses as half the eighty-three divisions committed to the area and characterized the morale of the remainder as devastated by hunger and lack of ammunition. This persuaded Matsui that capturing Nanjing would inflict a mortal stroke on Chinese resistance.

In an abrupt about-face, on 1 December, Tokyo not only authorized Matsui to seize Nanjing but also elevated him from command of the provisional Central China Area Army to commander, China Expeditionary Army. Leadership of the Shanghai Expeditionary Army devolved from Matsui to Prince Asaka Yasuhiko, the emperor's uncle by marriage. Matsui initially ordered maneuvers bypassing Nanjing, but the disintegration of Chinese defenses prompted him on 5 December to direct the capture of the capital city.

That same day, a message from Stalin dispelled the hopes Chiang nurtured of immediate intervention. The Soviet leader declared that his nation would only send troops if sanctioned by a majority of the other nations of the

Nine-Power Treaty and endorsed by the Supreme Soviet, set to convene in six to eight weeks. Stalin also astutely pointed out that if his troops interposed in China, the Western powers, more fearful at that point of Bolsheviks than Hitler's Nazis, might toss their sympathies to Japan. Chiang's diary shows he now clearly understood that no Soviet intervention was in prospect. Nonetheless, the next day he gave false encouragement in a dispatch to his generals: "We must defend Nanjing. In one month, the international situation may change dramatically. China may avoid disaster."

Both logistics and tactics regulated the Japanese march to Nanjing. One junior officer in the Tenth Army advancing astride the Yangtze River likened the march to a training exercise, but without sustenance. The army supply system forwarded only essential combat and medical supplies. Only plunder from the Chinese population provided food for Matsui's soldiers. A progression of smoke pillars visually charted the approach of Japanese spearheads as soldiers engaged in a frenzy of arson, torching residences or other dwellings to deny the Chinese ambush sites. Japanese officers only partly quelled this practice by pointing out the buildings might afford shelter in the coming winter. Most soldiers essentially did as they liked, and they liked pillage, rape, and slaughter. Behind the advancing columns lay a thick wake of murdered prisoners and violated women. The open terrain, the antithesis of Shanghai, emancipated the Imperial Army to wield its vast superiority in maneuver and unleash its equally great advantages in air and artillery bombardment. The Japanese sent increasing numbers of bombers to Nanjing to herald their imminent arrival.

Nanjing and Its Defenders

Nanjing once had served as China's capital during the Ming dynasty (1368–1644 CE). An approximately twenty-one-mile-long wall with thirteen gates enclosed the inner metropolis. This rampart, facing outward over a moat, thrust up fifty feet high and was forty feet wide at the top. The devilishly intricate gates funneled invaders into courtyards where they could be assailed from all sides. Barbed-wire entanglements, pillboxes, and other prepared works amended these superannuated defenses with modern enhancements. Nanjing became the rebel capital during the great Taiping Revolt. That upheaval's bloody ending transpired at Nanjing in 1864. Central government troops recaptured the city and then not only dispatched the rebels, but also massacred many of the inhabitants. Little more than scorched stone structures still stood in the aftermath. Chiang had moved the national capital from Beijing to Nanjing because there he held the strongest military and political control. To project the modernity and majesty of his reign, Chiang remodeled the center of Nanjing with the ornamental grandeur of broad boulevards, fine squares, imposing government buildings, and plenty of open space thriving with lakes, ponds, and thickets. From the east on Purple Mountain, Sun Yat-sen's tomb overlooked the city, casting an aura of political legitimacy over it and magnifying the impact of the physical symbolism Chiang sought to instill.

As the Imperial Army approached, a handful of European and American stalwarts who remained in Nanjing mobilized under the title International Committee to create the Nanjing Safety Zone to provide a 1.5-square-mile sanctuary for civilians. Although Americans, mostly missionaries, comprised the majority of the twenty-two-member committee, the chairman was a white-haired, fifty-five-year-old German, John Rabe, later famous as "the Good Man of Nanjing." Besides possessing a strong and winning personality, being fluent in English, and having a more British than German penchant for irony and humor, Rabe's elevation also stemmed from his seniority among Western residents due to his long service with a subsidiary of Siemens. Rabe's membership in the Nazi Party also outfitted him with entrées to the Japanese that no American or Briton could match. Rabe anticipated direct help from Hitler, writing in his diary: "The Führer won't leave me in the lurch." Rabe's hope for Hitler's help was in vain, but Rabe proved "fearless and untiring."

While Chinese soldiers braced to defend Nanjing, Chinese civilian officials fled, devolving the city government on the International Committee, making Rabe "something very like an acting mayor." The committee labored frantically to secure sanction from both sides for a safety zone for civilians encompassing approximately one-eighth of the city. Not all Chinese favorably viewed the committee's efforts. A Chinese colonel barked at Rabe: "Every inch of soil that the Japanese conquer should be fertilized with our blood. Nanking must be defended to the last man. If you had not established your safety zone, people now fleeing into the Zone could have helped our soldiers."

The committee also mounted frenetic efforts to stock the zone with food and services for Chinese refugees. Despite the committee's pledges to bar Chinese soldiers and weapons from the safety zone, thousands of terrified Chinese soldiers, both in units and as individual deserters, sought sanctuary in the safety zone to evade imprisonment—or (more likely) death. "We assured them that if they gave up their equipment their lives would be spared by the Japanese," wrote one American of the International Committee. "But it

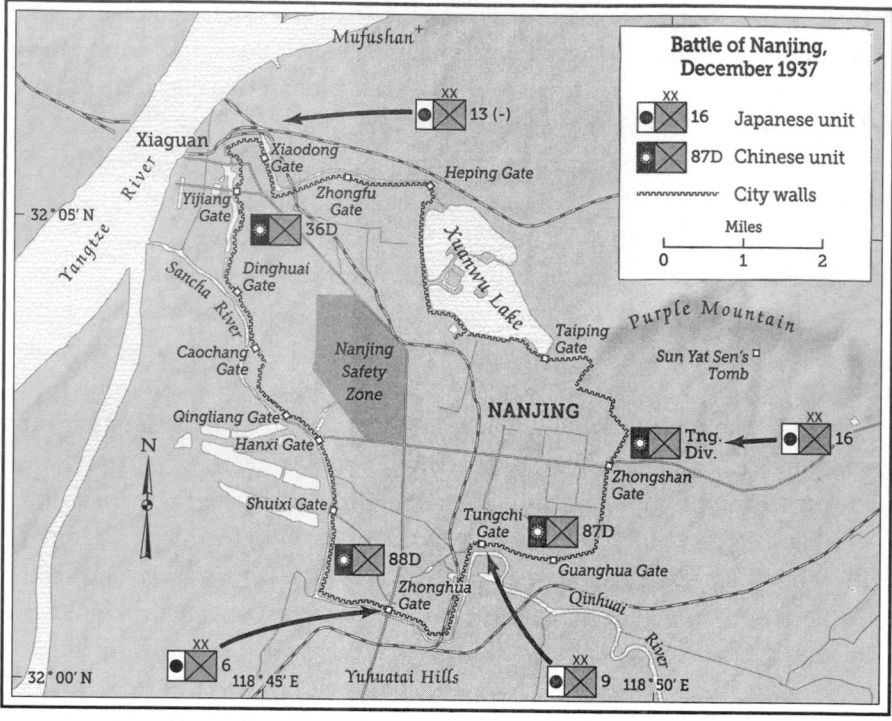

was a vain promise. All would have preferred to die fighting than to be taken out and shot or sabered or used for bayonet practice, as they all were later on."

The formal order of battle of the Chinese forces mustered to defend Nanjing featured five elite, German-trained National Army Divisions as well as the "Training Brigade" (a "super elite" unit with the strength of a division). Added to these were eight provincial divisions. Severe losses among six of these eight provincial divisions at Shanghai diminished their combat power to very low levels. For example, only 1,000 to 2,000 men remained in the ranks of the 103rd Division. Chiang summoned five divisions and two brigades of Sichuan troops to bolster Nanjing defenses, but this force bolted away when confronted with the Japanese—validating the low reputation of Sichuan's soldiers for battle worthiness.

Figures for the Chinese defenders have varied widely at between 20,000 and 150,000, but subsequent events make the actual numbers very important. The best estimate, based on a thorough analysis of the archival material from Chinese, Japanese, and other sources, is that the defending garrison in the proximate Nanjing vicinity numbered from 73,800 to 81,500. This total includes about 32,000 auxiliaries. The eyes of another German resident, Horst

Baerensprung, caught the spectacularly varied quality of Nanjing's defenders. The best units contained tough-looking fighters shouldering modern rifles with grenades stuck in belts, trailed by mules packing machine guns and small cannon, well protected under canvas. But against the drooping temperatures even these men wore only thin summer uniforms with a blanket or piece of canvas slung in a roll over their shoulder and just straw sandals. Every unit trailed a wake of auxiliaries (or, as Baerensprung bluntly put it, "coolies") toting loads on bamboo poles, with perhaps several hefting a huge kettle that served as the unit's field kitchen. These auxiliaries—sometimes early teenage boys or younger—lacked arms or training and frequently had been coerced into service.

Taking these auxiliaries into account would nominally yield 49,000 "fighting troops." But this would be deceptive as well, for this number incorporated approximately 30,400 raw recruits, most without any military training. Rabe observed throngs of such cannonfodder, dressed in ragged civilian clothes with a bundle for a pack and a rusty rifle in hand. Rabe noted "entire columns . . . without any footwear. They all march by in total silence, an endless mute procession of weary figures." The effective defense of Nanjing thus fell on fewer than 20,000 trained combatants.

East of Nanjing, the Chinese hastily set up two thinly manned outer tiers of defenses. One comprised an arc set out twenty to thirty miles from the city; a second was five to ten miles out. The first fell on 8 December, the second two days later. The Japanese 16th Division knifed down to the city outskirts from the northeast while the 9th and 3rd Divisions pried at the easterly gates. From the south came the 6th and 114th Divisions. The Chinese fought, sometimes ferociously, and even mounted counterattacks; casualties piled up on both sides. As the Japanese closed in on Nanjing, the Chinese employed "scorched earth" tactics and burned with abandon public buildings as well as outlying villages and residential areas in Nanjing.

When the Chinese rejected Matsui's demand for surrender by noon, 10 December, the Japanese surged against the walls that night, following a heavy artillery preparation. On 11 December, the Imperial Army's 6th Division penetrated the city from the southwest and the 9th Division entered from the east. But on 12 December, the Chinese continued their "fierce resistance" until that afternoon, when artillery fire in the 6th Division sector crumbled the southwest protective walls. Japanese soldiers ignited houses to create a smokescreen and spanned the moat in sampans to scale the remaining heights with bamboo ladders. Japanese engineers, using their bodies as supports, bridged the moat by late afternoon. When Rabe gazed out at about 1830 hours, 12 December, artillery fire coupled to lightning and thunder seemed to set the Purple Mountain aflame. He remembered an old Chinese adage: "When Purple Mountain burns, Nanjing is lost."

"The Rape of Nanjing"*

Although Chiang delegated command of Nanjing's defense to Tang, the generalissimo stationed himself in Nanjing as the Japanese approached, underscoring the capital's importance. He only flew out on 8 December. At that point, the dire prospects for a successful defense or even a heroic sacrificial fight were clear, but Chiang did not order the city abandoned. After Tang declared he would lead a fight to the death, at 0700 on 13 December, with the city reeling under artillery fire and Japanese troops lodged inside the walls, he abruptly ordered the city abandoned. Tang immediately and shamefully obeyed his own order, crossing the Yangtze by boat and leaving the Chinese forces leaderless and with no direction or plan for an orderly withdrawal. This triggered indescribable confusion, followed by an epidemic of hysterical panic as the defenders learned of their abandonment by Tang and that the Japanese had closed a trap around the city. While some units continued stiff resistance, others lost discipline and dissolved into fearful bands of terrified men. The Central Army 36th Division opened fire on Chinese soldiers attempting to flee the city. The worst stampede rushed toward Xiaguan Gate. There, converging throngs congealed into human waves bashing into the narrow opening, crushing hundreds or thousands whose bodies stacked up like barricades. For days, dogs would gnaw at the bodies heaped five feet tall. Other soldiers tied their clothes together to form makeshift scaling lines to surmount Nanjing's famous walls. Once beyond the walls, soldiers leaped onto junks or makeshift rafts, usually capsizing them before they could cross the river. Thousands drowned.

Matsui originally ordered his two subordinate armies to select two or three infantry battalions and military police units to enter the city. But as fighting flared in the eastern and northwestern areas, Yanagawa commanded his

---

* According to Suping Lu, the American missionary George A. Fitch first coined the phrase "Rape of Nanking" in a 6 January 1938 letter. The phrase first appeared in print in the 16 March 1938 edition of the English language *South China Morning Post*, published in Hong Kong. *They Were in Nanjing: The Nanjing Massacre Witnessed by American and British Nationals* (Hong Kong: Hong Kong University Press, 2004), 32, 97–98.

Tenth Army to crush resistance. This sent about 70,000 men surging into the city, free to use artillery, arson, or any means necessary to quell all resistance. Street fighting erupted, bringing orders from the chief of staff, 114th Division, in the southeast sector of the city, to burn two-story buildings to eliminate resistance. Orders were again given to beware of Chinese "stragglers," as historians Satoshi Hattori and Edward Drea put it, "meaning everyone from prisoners of war to suspicious-looking civilians."

The Japanese showered the city with leaflets promising civilians good treatment. Indeed, as one European correspondent noted, "At first sight of the Japanese, a sense of relief seemed to pass through the Chinese civilian population, and they came out ready to accept the Japanese if they would have behaved humanely." F. Tillman Durdin, the *New York Times* correspondent who provided some of the most searing eyewitness testimony about the Japanese occupation of Nanjing, reported scattered cheers echoed from some crowds as the Japanese marched in. Here and there, Japanese flags fluttered from the homes of rich and poor in a vain display of servility intended to buy exemption from whatever exactions the conquerors sought.

Durdin acknowledged that some Japanese units exercised restraint and that "certain Japanese officers tempered power with generosity and compassion." A Westerner working on the International Committee confirmed, "We have had some very pleasant Japanese who have treated us with courtesy and respect. . . . Occasionally, have I seen a Japanese soldier helping some Chinese, or picking . up a Chinese baby to play with it." But "soldiers with a conscience are few and far between," recorded an American witness. "The Japanese might have gained a wide measure of support and confidence from the Nanking Chinese," Durdin informed his readers. "Instead they drove deeper into the Chinese soul a hatred of Japan and set back to a distant future prospects for gaining the Chinese cooperation for which they profess to be fighting China."

During the first twenty-four hours of occupation, Japanese soldiers primarily focused their energies on their most primal needs: food and shelter. The starving soldiery sifted the city for edible items. Then in exhaustion many tossed Chinese out of their homes simply to acquire a bed covered by a roof. But from 14 December, the Japanese occupation descended into a demoniacal frenzy of looting of businesses and private dwellings. As Rabe recorded the scenes in his diary:

> The Japanese march through the city in groups of ten to twenty soldiers and loot the shops. If I had not seen it with my own eyes I would not have believed it. They smash open windows and doors and take whatever they

like. Allegedly because they are short of rations . . . some Japanese soldiers dragged their booty away in crates, others requisitioned [rickshaws]
to transport their stolen goods to safety.

Ruifang Cheng, an administrator at Ginling College, a major refugee camp
within the Safety Zone, kept the only known contemporary Chinese diary
during this period. Cheng wryly termed the looting the Japanese version of
the "Open Door Policy." Nor did the Japanese confine their requisitions to
the Chinese populace. "Every foreign house is a sight to behold, untouched
until the Japanese army arrived; nothing untouched since. Every lock has
been broken, every trunk ransacked. Their search for money and valuables
had led them to the flues and inside pianos." The Japanese carted off massive amounts of goods and personal effects, leaving the street in front of each
ransacked dwelling carpeted in cast-out items. After spreading depredations
from end to end of the main commercial thoroughfares, Japanese soldiers
torched most stores and devastated many homes, however humble, to "cover
up evidence of very thorough looting." Day and night, all around the city
flames consumed ever-increasing proportions of the building stock and saturated the air with acrid smoke. It would be 17 January before the fires halted.

But the Japanese occupation of Nanjing would not be remembered for vast
material destruction via looting and arson; it would go down in history as
"The Rape of Nanking" for its carnival of violation and its festival of killing. Throughout history, the soldiers of triumphant armies have commonly
viewed women of the vanquished population as spoils. In December 1937 the
Imperial Army transformed Nanjing into a modern symbol of this barbarism at its worst. "Rape! Rape! Rape! We estimate at least 1,000 cases a night
and many by day. In case of resistance or anything that seems like disapproval there is a bayonet or a bullet," wrote one American witness at the end
of the first week of the Japanese occupation of Nanjing. For weeks after the
fall of Nanjing, Japanese soldiers roamed the streets and alleys calling for
"hwa guniang" (young girls), some as young as twelve. Nor were women of
fifty or sixty spared. And when they could not find young girls, the soldiers
sometimes took teenage boys.

The best documentation of mass rape rests in the diaries and letters of
Western witnesses. Minnie Vautrin, acting president of Ginling College,
managed a refugee camp in the Safety Zone originally intended to hold 2,700
women and children, which at its peak held 10,000. This location was about
as secure as any in the Safety Zone, yet her diary describes repeatedly how she
personally warded off Japanese soldiers bent on rape, sometimes interrupt-

ing a rape in progress. Other entries in her diary record the contemporaneous accounts given to her by Chinese victims. Vautrin's diary entries parallel
those of Cheng, her deputy, as well as Rabe and at least two American members of the International Committee.

On 17 December, one American wrote that "one poor woman was raped
thirty-seven times. Another had her five-month-old infant deliberately smoth-
ered by the brute to stop its crying while he raped her. Resistance means the
bayonet." Rabe confided in his dairy this same date, "If husbands or brothers intervene, they are shot." Another December 1937 American diary entry
described "a woman six months pregnant, who resisted, had 16 knife wounds
in her face and body, one piercing the abdomen. She lost her baby, but her
life will be spared." Eleven days after the Japanese occupied the city, Vautrin
wrote of the agonized choice facing younger married Chinese women:

> Many young women are faced with a terrible dilemma—to stay with
> their husbands and be raped by soldiers when their husbands are turned
> out of house at point of bayonet; [or] to come to Ginling, and leave their
> husbands—the latter then runs risk of being carried off and killed.

A Japanese-sponsored newspaper in its 21 January 1938 edition featured an
article titled "Japanese Troops Gently Soothe the Refugees. The harmonious Atmosphere of Nanjing City Develops Enjoyably." Although the intensity
of the serial assault on Chinese women had attenuated by this date, as late
as 5 February 1938 women from other disbanded refugee camps sought refuge at Ginling from the sexual predations of the occupying army. At the postwar Tokyo War Crimes trial, the number of rapes in Nanjing was estimated
as at least 20,000. The lowest estimates are 4,000 to 5,000.

But Chinese women were not all simply passive victims. Cheng docu-
mented the extraordinary heroism of two Chinese women. As the Japanese
prepared to haul some male captives away for summary execution, an aging
Chinese woman

> came out to identify [as relatives,] three men she did not know at all.
> She just wanted to save them. Another young lady came out to identify
> [one man] as her brother. Then, she went inside to change clothes and
> came out again to identify more men as her relatives.

The Chinese driver for the American embassy exclaimed to Vautrin, "The
only thing that had saved the Chinese people from utter destruction was the

fact that there were a handful of foreigners in Nanking." Vautrin's courageous and tireless work on behalf of her charges won her the name among the Chinese of "The Goddess of Mercy." In February, when, in the words of Cheng, the "very capable and courageous" John Rabe reluctantly obeyed orders to leave Nanjing, he emerged from a farewell tea Vautrin sponsored at Ginling College to find a crowd of 3,000 women who "all knelt and began to weep and implore" him to stay.

But even the record of pillage and rape in Nanjing is overshadowed by sheer slaughter. The Chinese dead can be divided between combatants and non-combatants. In Shanghai, where both sides took few prisoners, Chinese soldiers had learned all too well what to expect. They instinctively resorted to the accepted norm during China's intramural wars—swift doffing of uniforms to blend in to the recesses of the city. Durdin witnessed "the wholesale undressing of an army that was almost comic." Some Chinese soldiers stripped off uniforms as they marched; others ran into alleys. Chinese policemen ventured about in their underwear looking for civilian garb. The streets became instant junkyards of the Chinese Army's cast-aside physical possessions, scattered in an artless collage: trucks, buses, staff cars, wagons, uniforms, firearms, swords, grenades, knapsacks, helmets, and overcoats. A last-moment torching of some public buildings set off stores of munitions whose detonations provided a frenetic sound track to the rout, joined by the screams of horses caught in the blazes. Wounded men hobbled around, dragging themselves through alleyways; many eventually lay down to die in the streets.

The Japanese branded these former combatants now in civilian guise as "plainclothes soldiers." Officers and men in the Imperial Army believed with justification that many of these "plainclothes soldiers" were likely to return to the Chinese ranks, and not a few of them might snipe at the Japanese as they mingled with noncombatants. The internationally codified law of war entitled the Japanese to execute summarily "plainclothes soldiers" caught in the act of sniping, but immediate apprehension of such assailants was rare. The applicable warfare law proscribed summary execution of suspected soldiers caught in civilian clothes unless and until a military tribunal pronounced them to be spies or guerrillas. But most if not all Japanese units just presumed that any nonuniformed male of military age was a "plainclothes soldier." The Japanese deemed the presence of knapsack or rifle butt marks on the shoulders or even the mere presence of calloused hands (common to any manual laborer) as damning evidence of a "plainclothes soldier." Translating these dim or nondescript inferences into death warrants, the Japanese dispensed with even cursory judicial process and usually proceeded straight to summary execution.

As Durdin gazed out from his Shanghai-bound ship, he witnessed the execution of two hundred Chinese men, "lined against a wall and then shot." After that, "a number of Japanese, armed with pistols, trod nonchalantly around the crumpled bodies, pumping bullets into any that were still kicking." The Japanese soldiers invited their naval counterparts to join an audience with "a large group of military spectators [who] apparently greatly enjoyed the spectacle." Durdin personally observed at least three mass executions, characterized by standing groups of a dozen Chinese males by a dugout, then shooting them and tossing the bodies into the dugout. A Reuters correspondent watched as about 1,000 Chinese in a field were led away in small groups. They were "forced to kneel and . . . then shot in the back of the head. We had observed some 100 such executions, when the Japanese officer in charge noticed us and ordered us to leave at once." A few survivors found their way to Western doctors, where the grisly evidence of severe burns about the head and shoulders testified to the practice of dousing bodies of executed Chinese males with gasoline and then igniting it to dispose of the dead. Vautrin's diary recorded another practice. She found a pond with "scores of black charred bodies and among them two empty kerosene or gasoline cans. The hands of the men were wired behind them."

These contemporary eyewitness accounts establish the existence but not the scope of mass executions. The best evidence emerges from Japanese official reports and private diaries. For example, the 9th Division's report blandly acknowledged that in "mopping up" in Nanjing, it alone annihilated (*senmetsu*) some 7,000 "stragglers." The 16th Division's commander, Lt. Gen. Kesago Nakajima, confided to his diary on 13 December that army policy was "Accept no prisoners!" He noted how the division contemplated using a "huge ditch" to dispose of a batch of 7,000 to 8,000 prisoners, until "someone suggested this plan: Divide them up into groups of 100 to 200, and then lure them to some suitable spot for finishing off."

On this same date, 13 December, an entry in the diary of the 13th Brigade commander, Maj. Gen. Toichi Sasaki, recounted that his unit alone had accounted for over 20,000 Chinese. This toll included about 10,000 "abandoned bodies" (apparently referring to those killed in battle), with another 10,000 killed by Japanese fire while trying to escape across the Yangtze or executed after capture. The battle report of the 1st Battalion, 66th Regiment records that it received an order from 13th Brigade headquarters at 1400 on 13 December to "kill all POWs," coupled with the advice that the prisoners should be "[tied] up in groups less than twenty" and shot "one by one." The report went on to explain how the battalion parceled its 1,657 prisoners among three companies. Each company escorted small groups of captives to its own killing ground. There the prisoners, "resigned to their fate, stuck out their heads before our swords and stood tall before our bayonets with no sign of fear. Some of them, however, wailed and pleaded for mercy, especially when unit commanders came to make their rounds."

But the worst single known episode of prisoner executions involved Maj. Gen. Ryuhei Ogisu's 13th Division at Mufushan, on the Yangtze banks north of Nanjing's city walls. That division's 65th Regiment comprised second- and third-tier reservists in their thirties to early forties, not the typical regulars in their twenties. A contemporary Japanese newspaper account (and at least one personal diary) reported that 14,777 Chinese troops of the 18th [sic] and 88th Divisions and the Cadet Training unit surrendered to this regiment on 14 December. There is good evidence that the regiment's ultimate prisoner total crossed 17,000 the next day and that the final number may have approached 20,000. One diarist of an artillery unit recorded how 7,000 prisoners were shot to death on 16 December. Those who survived the gunfire were finished off with bayonets and swords ("the prisoner's agonized cries of death were indescribably horrific"). He ended his entry: "Having witnessed a scene never to be forgotten in our lives, we returned at about [2130]." Another soldier's diary reports that after the machine gunning, they closed in on the survivors with bayonets and swords:

> I figured that I'd never get another chance like this, so I stabbed thirty of the damned Chinks. Climbing atop the mountain of corpses, I felt like a real devil-slayer, stabbing again and again, with all my might. "Ugh, ugh," the Chinks groaned. There were old folks as well as kids, but we killed them lock, stock, and barrel. I also borrowed a buddy's sword and tried to decapitate some. I've never experienced anything so unusual.

On the 17th and continuing to the morning of the 18th, another 10,000 to 13,000 were marched into a barbed-wire enclosed semicircle, with the open end on the Yangtze, and machine gunned. A diary entry described this as "a totally inconceivable, unimaginable sight." The regiment attempted to burn most of the bodies, but dumped some into the Yangtze.

One conscientious attempt to extract a full accounting from just these Japanese sources wrestled with the facts: (1) only about one-third of the Japanese units at Nanjing recorded evidence on this issue, (2) the entries often were vague about precise death counts, (3) a widespread tendency existed (by no means unique to the Japanese) to overestimate enemy fatalities, and (4) undoubtedly such entries included indisputable Chinese combatants killed in battle who could not be categorized as "massacre victims." Even allowing for all these factors, this historian produced an estimated death count from these sources of 109,475. Of these, he reckoned that at least 29,240 were "clearly illegal, unjustifiable killings." Less rigorous criteria produced a figure of 46,215 "estimated illegal, unjustifiable killings" (or "massacre victims") and still another definition a toll of 63,260 "arguably illegal, unjustifiable killings."

Civilian victim figures—and indeed whether or not victim status applies only to civilians and not to any Chinese soldiers, no matter if they were helpless POWs—provoke bitter dispute that is relevant to Sino-Japanese relations to this day. The contested facts commence with temporal and geographical definitions of the event. Those arguing for minimal figures contend that the time span only includes the period from 13 December, when the close assault began, to 17 December, when General Matsui conducted his victory parade in Nanjing. They also confine the relevant area to the walled city of Nanjing. At the other extreme are those who count the entire Yangtze Valley between Shanghai and Nanking and set the beginning of the event as August 1937 and the end in February 1938, when some normalcy returned to Nanjing, or even March 1938 when a collaboration government took charge.

Japanese historians who deny or minimize the event choose the smallest perimeters in time and geography to argue that there was no "massacre" or that the "victim" total was as low as a few dozens to a few thousands. But others as early as the 1950s began referring to "massive butchery" (*daigyakusatsu*), with a death toll in the 200,000 to 300,000 range. Chiang was on record during the war as setting a total of "over 200,000." At the postwar Tokyo War Crimes trials, the number of dead was described as "over 200,000" in or around the city in six or seven weeks. A subsidiary war crimes trial in Nanjing pegged the number at "over 300,000." Subsequently Chinese historians and others have urged a broader framework and advance numbers reaching from 300,000 to 400,000.

Logically, fixing the number of Chinese civilians in Nanjing when the occupation began would appear as the starting point for calculating death totals. But neither Chinese nor Japanese sources provide such figures. Only Western accounts provide contemporary evidence on the count of the civilian inhabitants when Japanese troops arrived. These indicate the vast majority of the one million residents of Nanjing vacated the city as the Japanese approached, spurred on by rumors of what Japanese occupation entailed. Minnie Vautrin's invaluable diary reports that an exodus began "weeks and weeks" prior to 13 December. First the wealthy vacated by truck, car, and boat, heading west, many to Hankou. The middle class followed and then the poor. "For days and days," Vautrin wrote, "you could see [rickshaws] going past loaded with boxes and rolls of bedding and people. All who could possibly do so got out of the city, the poor going into the country, especially taking the sons and daughters of the family, leaving the old to take care of their homes." By 7 December, Rabe wrote in his diary that "only the very poor are still here." Western sources indicate that the overwhelming portion (the most frequently cited figure is 200,000) of the remaining civilian population fled into the International Safety Zone. A Japanese registration effort starting on 24 December counted between 150,000 and 160,000 residents in the International Safety Zone, but excluded all children under ten and "old women" above the age of sixty. Adjusting demographically for these two omitted categories yields projected numbers between 226,000 and 235,000.

Some historians press for much higher Nanjing population figures in December 1937. The most well-known advocate of larger figures was the late Iris Chang, whose book, *The Rape of Nanking*, became an international best seller. Chang set the population as the Japanese arrived at 600,000 to "perhaps" 700,000. Relying on the work of a Chinese scholar, she reported about a half-million of the original approximately one million residents remained. To this she added 90,000 military personnel and "tens of thousands" of refugees from the countryside fleeing the Japanese. Chang's figures are at odds with the Western estimates at the time and require a considerable vault into speculation on how many refugees from other areas packed into Nanjing. While there is no number that can now be certified as accurate, the more credible evidence points to lower, not higher numbers.

The next possible source of evidence on deaths comprises burial records. Contemporary evidence verifies the work of the Red Swastika Society (RSS), a private charitable organization.* Records of that organization tender credible figures of about 40,000 to 43,000 burials. Some of this total included actual combatants, so it does not equal "massacre victims," and these figures would not include disposals of remains by the Japanese. At the time of postwar judicial proceedings, reports appeared of 112,267 burials by an organization known as the Chongshantang (CST). Scrutiny of the contemporary evidence on the very existence of this organization and the internal credibility

---

* Chinese Buddhist iconography had long incorporated the swastika. The Red Swastika Society (Hongwanzihui) was formed to imitate the Red Cross but used the swastika to remove the Christian connotations. It had no relationship to Hitler's National Socialists.

of its purported figures revealed profound problems that make its numbers highly dubious.* Those pressing for higher numbers properly point out that the Japanese reported dumping remains into the Yangtze or cremating them. Thus, burials would not equal deaths. While many bodies may have been tossed into the Yangtze, skeptics point out that the crews of Chinese, Japanese, or Western shippers in the Yangtze recorded no contemporary observations of a surge of corpses adrift that such dispositions presumably would have created. Likewise, cremations running into the many tens of thousands are hard to credit in the absence of the infrastructure later used by the Germans in death camps.

After a lengthy, well-informed, and tightly reasoned survey of the evidence, historian Bob Tadashi Wakabayashi concluded that the most reasonable parameters for the "Rape of Nanjing" are the Nanking Special Administrative District, comprising the walled city and the six surrounding counties, and a time front from early December 1937 to March 1938. Given this definition, Wakabayashi found that scholarly legitimacy could be accorded to death totals from 40,000 to 200,000 for victims of unlawful killing, both civilians and captured combatants—a vast range reflecting the manifest inadequacies of fully reliable evidence. Wakabayashi also noted that the accomplished Japanese military historian Hata Ikuhiko (sometimes unfairly described as a "denier") found a 300,000 number as credible for all the Chinese belligerents and civilians killed in the five-month-long Shanghai and Nanjing campaigns.

After reviewing the contentious literature on this topic, this writer concurs with Wakabayashi's ultimate judgment that the most credible figures for unlawful deaths in the span between December 1937 and March 1938 in and immediately around Nanjing and the six adjacent counties mostly likely fall in the range of over 100,000 but less than 200,000. Of these, approximately 50,000 were noncombatants and over 50,000 were combatants killed illegally. The figure excludes battle deaths of Chinese soldiers.

Turning to the causes of the human catastrophe in Nanjing, Chinese leaders cannot be wholly absolved of blame, although they are not remotely as

---

* There are four major challenges to the CST reports: (1) its existence is not confirmed by the 1937–1938 records, (2) the CST reports purport that its work crews buried 104,718 corpses in only twenty-three days in April–May 1938, or 4,553 per day, with a work crew of forty-five (which works out to an incredible 101 burials per man per day), (3) the location of 59,318 corpses cannot be correct, given the credible information about locations of civilians and Chinese defenders, and (4) postwar sources maintained that the CST conducted burials only in the eastern part of Nanjing whereas the RSS worked in the western part, at a minimum indicating double counting of the work of RSS and CST.

culpable as their Japanese counterparts. The "scorched earth" policy that aimed to deny the Japanese shelter and sustenance also served inadvertently to swell the ranks of refugees and ultimately victims in Nanjing. Even granting the importance for domestic and international reasons not to abandon the capital, making the final stand within the natural trap formed by the city walls and Yangtze River represented folly, compounded by Tang's precipitous and disgraceful abandonment of his men. Among the efforts to maintain order and discipline occurred instances of Chinese troops deliberately killing other Chinese combatants who had panicked or straggled. However, it is unlikely that an organized capitulation of the Chinese defenders might have diminished their subsequent slaughter. Lacking food for their own men, the Japanese had none to spare for a mass of prisoners and no military police to handle captives or control their own troops. They also could expect that if they simply turned the Chinese prisoners loose, many would return to face them as combatants in the future. The Imperial Army created this quandary, making it extremely hard to imagine that Japanese officers would not have resorted to mass executions even with an organized surrender. But there is at least a fair prospect that an organized surrender might have diminished to some degree civilian losses.

It is a mistake to separate analysis of Nanjing from that of the larger pattern of the Japanese war in China—though it would be equally wrong to assume that Nanjing reflects the pattern of Japanese occupation in *all* places and at *all* times. The rampage in the Chinese capital encompasses a host of factors applicable far beyond the boundaries of the weeks after the city fell. At the outset of the conflict, Tokyo planted the first seeds of events in Nanjing. In earlier conflicts, the pursuit of equal international status animated Japan's adoption of Western rules of warfare that dictated humane treatment of prisoners of war. The emperor of Japan had promulgated Imperial edicts declaring war against China in 1894, Russia in 1904, and Germany in 1914; each expressly commanded Japanese soldiers and sailors to abide by international law. But there would be no Imperial edict declaring a state of war with China and enjoining Japan's warriors to adhere to international law. Instead, on 5 August, the Army Ministry sent notice to the China commands that "It is inappropriate to act strictly in accordance with various stipulations in treaties and Practices Governing Land Warfare and other laws of War." In October, Matsui publicly warned that "[to] those who bear arms against Japan the Japanese army will show no mercy"—a statement clearly implying Japan recognized no legal bar to summary execution of Chinese soldiers.

The Japanese government would maintain for the entire conflict that events in China were an "incident," not a war. Using the term "incident" instead of "war" stemmed in part from the fact that under the US Neutrality Acts of the 1930s, formal recognition of Japan and China as belligerents would compel the United States to deny both access to certain raw materials. Japan particularly could not do without oil imports from America. But behind such technical considerations lurked a fundamental Japanese notion that China was not then a sovereign nation but a loose amalgamation of decadent satrapies. Further, Tokyo, or at least the senior Japanese commanders in China, sent Japanese troops marching from Shanghai to Nanjing with virtually no food supplies. This forced these men to plunder Chinese dwellings and farms for basic subsistence. That constituted an infallible prescription for abuse. It also provided an excuse for not taking prisoners at all and then for executing prisoners taken.

Yet another important contributor to this tragedy and many others to come was the Imperial Army's socialization of officers and men through habitual discipline by physical violence. Not only did noncommissioned officers beat common soldiers, but so did officers strike junior officers and enlisted men. Not surprisingly, this instilled in enlisted men the outlook that they were in turn entitled to physically abuse those with still lower status, like civilians and prisoners. Further, by the 1930s the Japanese armed forces inculcated the belief that there was unbearable shame in surrender. Anyone who would offer to surrender was contemptible. Finally, physical violence against women was rampant in Japanese society.

Tokyo's lifting of legal norms, the encouragement of physical violence against inferiors (and women), and the sense of unbearable shame in surrender provided the backdrop to Nanjing and a host of other episodes. But in Nanjing this backdrop acted in synergy with two other immediate factors: combat-induced emotional fever and *gekokujo*. Some Japanese divisions, though by no means all, entering Nanjing had sustained severe losses in Shanghai. For example, the 9th Division amended its casualty roll with the names of another 460 killed and 1,156 wounded. This brought its cumulative casualties since entering combat in August to 14,026, or 106 percent of its original strength. Searing memories of fallen comrades undoubtedly set loose the desire for revenge. Combat-heightened emotions also exacerbated the contempt for any soldier who surrendered—whether Chinese or Japanese—which made it easy for some to discard the cloak of pan-Asianism. In fact, to many Japanese steeped in the notion that Japan's noble cause was to redress the wrongs of imperialism against all Asians, Chinese resistance was particularly infuriating. And finally, some Japanese regarded the Chinese as abjectly inferior beings. A Japanese journalist, Shigehara Matsumoto, then working for Domei News Agency in Shanghai, quoted a Kwantung Army staff officer, Ryukichi Tanaka, as saying, "To be perfectly frank, the ways you (Matsumoto) and I look at the Chinese are fundamentally different. You seem to think of them as human, but I see them as pigs."

Having been left by their superiors without legal injunction to treat prisoners humanely and without a means to deal with masses of captives, and fearful that freed Chinese prisoners would take up arms again, Japanese officers and men began slaughtering any Chinese of military age in uniform or not. Once this process began largely spontaneously or at least without explicit coordinated command from the most senior levels, the phenomena of *gekokujo*, literally "the top deferring to the bottom," then propelled the process. *Gekokujo* in practice meant senior officers abdicated command and control to their subordinates. It is revealing in this regard that the post-hostilities war crimes trials dismissed charges based on commission against the top Japanese officer, Matsui, and instead convicted him of a crime of omission—that he knew of the violations of the laws of warfare by his soldiers but failed to control them.

Such is the persistence of the controversy that at least some advocates deem the failure to support a figure of 300,000 or more "massacre victims" as tantamount to denying any slaughter took place at all. Not only is this attitude logically defective, it also manages to distract focus from a reality that is appalling. "The Nanjing Massacre" has taken on an imposing gravitas; it is now undeniable (based not least on contemporary Japanese records) that something horrifying took place in the city. Or as historian Frank Gibney simply phrased it: "The important thing about the Massacre is that it occurred. All responsible writers on the subject, Japanese and foreign, agree that tens of thousands of innocent people were killed."

⋮

CHAPTER 3

"Water as a Substitute for Soldiers"

TAIERZHUANG SPRING; WUHAN SUMMER

"Ruthless Cruelty"

Quite apart from any moral issues, Japan committed two egregious strategic blunders between 13 December 1937 and 16 January 1938 that flung away perhaps the one golden opportunity to halt the slide into a quagmire. First, the loss of Nanjing not only failed to bludgeon the Chinese into submission, but also its harrowing aftermath would affect Japan's relations with China for decades. Even more than Japanese arms, "the domineering attitude of her soldiers . . . instill[ed] a hatred of all thing Japanese into all classes from the illiterate coolie upwards.'" Then followed the disastrous demolition of the Trautmann Mediation.

On 11 January, Emperor Hirohito presided in his full dress army uniform over the first Imperial Conference in twenty-five years. This ritualized convocation of government figures consecrated a course already fixed by Prime Minister Konoe's cabinet. Konoe "rethought" policy toward Chiang after Nanjing's capture. He jettisoned somewhat conciliatory terms supported by the Imperial Navy that had been conceived during the Shanghai stalemate. Instead, Konoe's government assembled demands aimed for Chinese thralldom as the price of peace: (1) China's de jure recognition of Manchukuo, (2) tracts of North and Central China and Inner Mongolia would become "demilitarized zones" (but occupied by Japanese troops), (3) China's abandonment of Soviet ties and complete cooperation in fighting Communism, (4) the indefinite stationing of Japanese troops in China, and (5) China's payment of war reparations to Japan. The Imperial Conference met to sanction not only this portfolio, but also a capstone proviso that if Chiang spurned these conditions Japan would cease to treat him as the legitimate ruler of China and seek a regime more pliant than that of the Nationalists.

The Army Ministry and many junior officers advocated these stern terms. But Ishiwara's faction on the Imperial Army General Staff remained profoundly alarmed at the already prodigious effusion of treasure and thoroughly appalled by the specter of a protracted war against the "wrong" enemy. They predicted that Chiang would reject the terms and that the only recourse of an "unrecognized" Chiang would be to prosecute the war. Even Chief of Staff Prince Kan'in uttered "a mild reservation" about the wisdom of this policy, but halted short of forthright opposition. Hopes of some officers that Hirohito might intervene to rein in the hardliners were dashed when Kinmochi Saionji (who earlier called for Ishiwara's ouster) steered the emperor to accept the government's decision without even making inquiries. When Chiang refused to kowtow to the terms, on 16 January Konoe publicly announced that the Japanese government no longer recognized Chiang's Nationalists as the legitimate government of China.

Far from being driven by "militarists," Konoe chose to align himself with the most unyielding factions within the armed services. Grossly misreading the situation, Konoe thought the Chinese must see Japan's ultimate purposes as nobly serving their common goal of an Asia freed from Western imperialism. He and other Japanese leaders could not comprehend that many Chinese now viewed Japan as another imperialist intruder. Likewise, the emperor's principal adviser, Lord Keeper of the Privy Seal Marquis Koichi Kido, backed harsh terms and anticipated Chiang's replacement by a more tractable regime. Konoe would confess retrospectively that "no large amount of intelligence is necessary" to realize this posture was "a serious mistake."

At the time of Konoe's nonrecognition proclamation, foreign observers almost unanimously shared Japan's expectations that China must yield and a thoroughly discredited Chiang must fall. On New Year's Day, 1938, a *New York Times* headline advised its readers, "Defeatist Tone of Official Chinese Statements Believed to Be Propaganda for Surrender." Some foreigners viewed this as good for China, perceiving Japan as the avatar of modernity against superstition and backwardness.

But American naval officers equipped President Franklin D. Roosevelt with an accurate portrait of the situation and advised him to brace for continued conflict. A December 1937 letter from Admiral Harry Yarnell, commander in chief, Asiatic Fleet, explained:

One phase of this war which I had not expected of the Japanese is their ruthless cruelty towards the Chinese. Killing of noncombatants is an ordinary occurrence and the Chinese populace is so terrified that up to the present that they refuse to return to their homes in any of the occupied territory. The number of dead in this war . . . will run into the many millions before it is over. . . . There is today throughout China a universal and deep seated hatred of the Japanese which is not going to be eliminated for a long time.

A missive from Yarnell's chief of staff, Captain Riley F. McConnell, confirmed that "no government in China could today make peace and remain in power." McConnell added, "There is no personality today in China who can take the place of the generalissimo."

Chiang convened a meeting of the senior military leadership at Wuhan in January 1938. There he argued that despite the loss of Shanghai and Nanjing, thwarting Japanese plans for a swift victory constituted a Chinese strategic triumph. Then Chiang resoundingly communicated his resolve and that of the leadership to fight on. On 24 January 1938, General Fuju Han was executed, transfiguring him into an iniquitous symbol: the highest ranking Chinese officer in modern history to pay with his life for treachery, malfeasance, and cowardice. Since 1930, Han had been the governor of Shandong province, the nation's most populous. With the outbreak of full-scale war in July 1937, Han not only failed to rally to the national cause, he also schemed for a separate bargain with the Japanese. The Japanese repaid Han's parlays with bombers and then a massive ground onslaught; he abandoned his capital of Jinan with his 80,000-strong army. Then on 5 January, Han deserted his army, taking with him his personal possessions and much of the provincial treasury. After his apprehension, a tribunal of senior officers swiftly condemned him to death. He defiantly cried out as he was led away, "I take responsibility for losing Shandong. But who takes responsibility for losing Nanjing?"

The execution of Han illuminated much about China's leadership at this point. The perception of Chiang as China's supreme leader commanding rigid obedience grossly parts company from reality. In military affairs Chiang served only as the "presiding coordinator of a loose federation of forces." This status stemmed from both the fragmented political structure of China and hence its armies, and from the diverse origins of the elite uniformed leadership. Modernizing China commenced the schooling of officers at military academies. Sun Yat-sen detailed Chiang to open the Whampoa Academy in

1923. "The aim," noted historian Hans van de Ven, "was to nurture a new type of officer: literate, honest, disciplined, militarily competent, drawn from across the country, dedicated to the revolution." Before the outbreak of war, the Whampoa Academy admitted seventeen classes that prepared graduates for junior officer slots, and it embraced a rising reputation as the premier training ground for aspiring officers.

The clique of Whampoa graduates formed a key nucleus for Chiang's power. But Whampoa graduates lacked seniority and experience for the very top commands. Below Chiang, not one of the next six ranking commanders was a Whampoa graduate; four were graduates of the Baoding Military Academy. In 1937, Baoding accounted for 35 percent of army commanders and 20 percent of division commanders, while the figures for Whampoa were 10 and 11 percent, respectively.

The differences between Baoding and Whampoa combined professional as well as generational divides. "At Whampoa political education and party discipline along Leninist lines were stressed," explained historian Stephen MacKinnon, "whereas at Baoding the training was professionally focused (along German and Japanese models), non-political, and Confucian in the sense that personal loyalty was stressed." Baoding emphasized service to the nation and competence, whereas Whampoa imprinted its graduates with loyalties first to the Nationalists and Chiang, a goal that detracted from inculcation of sheer competence.

For these top officers, the execution of Fuju Han reverberated both symbolically and practically. It dramatized recognition that the Japanese design of conquest loomed as a threat to the central government unequaled since the Manchus in the early seventeenth century. This could only be countered by patriotically putting aside personal histories of distrust and enmity for the sake of the common cause. There could be no tolerance whatever for any officer's failure to resist, much less for collaboration with the invaders. But the bonding of these officers before the Japanese peril remained rooted in their shared training and an intense camaraderie of experiences, not in unquestioning fealty to Chiang.

The commanders Chiang assembled at Wuhan in January 1938 pledged absolute commitment to defend Xuzhou as a key point in the strategy of in-depth defense of the Yangtze Valley—"perhaps," pronounced MacKinnon, "the most important [Chinese decision] of the war." To implement this strategy, the Chinese generals divided command, reflecting an underlying reality. The combination of losses to Chiang's most loyal troops (including China's best, those German-trained and -equipped), the nonparticipation of the Communists, and the dispersion of Chinese units in the North left the main strength of Chinese resistance in the regional armies from the Southwest and Northwest. This lineup included the armies of Zongren Li and Chongxi Bai (Guangxi province, called "China's Sparta"), Yun Long (Yunnan), Sen Yang (Sichuan), Fakui Zhang and Xue Yue (Guangdong), and Xishan Yan (Shanxi-Suiyuan) area.

Accordingly, command organization mirrored both geography and sources of military power. The area north of the Yangtze (Anhui, Henan, and part of Hubei provinces) became the Fifth War Zone under Gen. Zongren Li (described by one historian as "'aggressive, ambitious, intelligent, nationalistic, puritanical, efficient, honest, daring, and innovative"). His command numbered about fifty divisions mustering 450,000 men. These comprised mostly his regional armies (about 80,000 strong) as well as some of Chiang's forces. The area south of the Yangtze became the Ninth War Zone under Gen. Cheng Chen, a Chiang loyalist with undoubted ability. This territory included Hunan, Jiangxi, and the other part of Hubei provinces as well as the Wuhan tri-city area. Chen directed seventy-eight divisions with about 700,000 men. These comprised a medley of provincial units (including displaced units of doubtful loyalty), a collection of Chiang's forces, and even a smattering of just-hatched guerrilla units of the Communist New Fourth Army. While the numerical strength of the Chinese armies remained impressive, losses among the best-trained and -equipped Chinese units in the 1937 campaigns served to widen the gap with Japan's forces in equipment, firepower, mobility, and air support.

The defeat and retreats of 1937 made it obligatory to convince the Chinese people that continuing the war, already marked by horrific sacrifices, was necessary. Chiang also needed to persuade the people that he and his government could provide leadership on through to ultimate victory. Between 29 March and 1 April, the Nationalists convened an extraordinary party congress in Wuhan. Chiang's oration linked the War of Resistance to national redemption. The congress adopted the Organic Law of War for Resistance and National Reconstruction. The law pronounced that the war "requires all people of the country to join together in our common cause and shoulder these tasks together." The war's purpose must be to realize "the Three People's Principles and the Testament of Sun Yat-sen." Among the law's injunctions was a call to subordinate all former divisions to the cause, to arm the population, and to initiate a broad guerrilla war. The law stated the war would be fought under the leadership of the Nationalists and Chiang. The law also attempted to redefine the Chinese polity. No longer was the critical dividing line between various

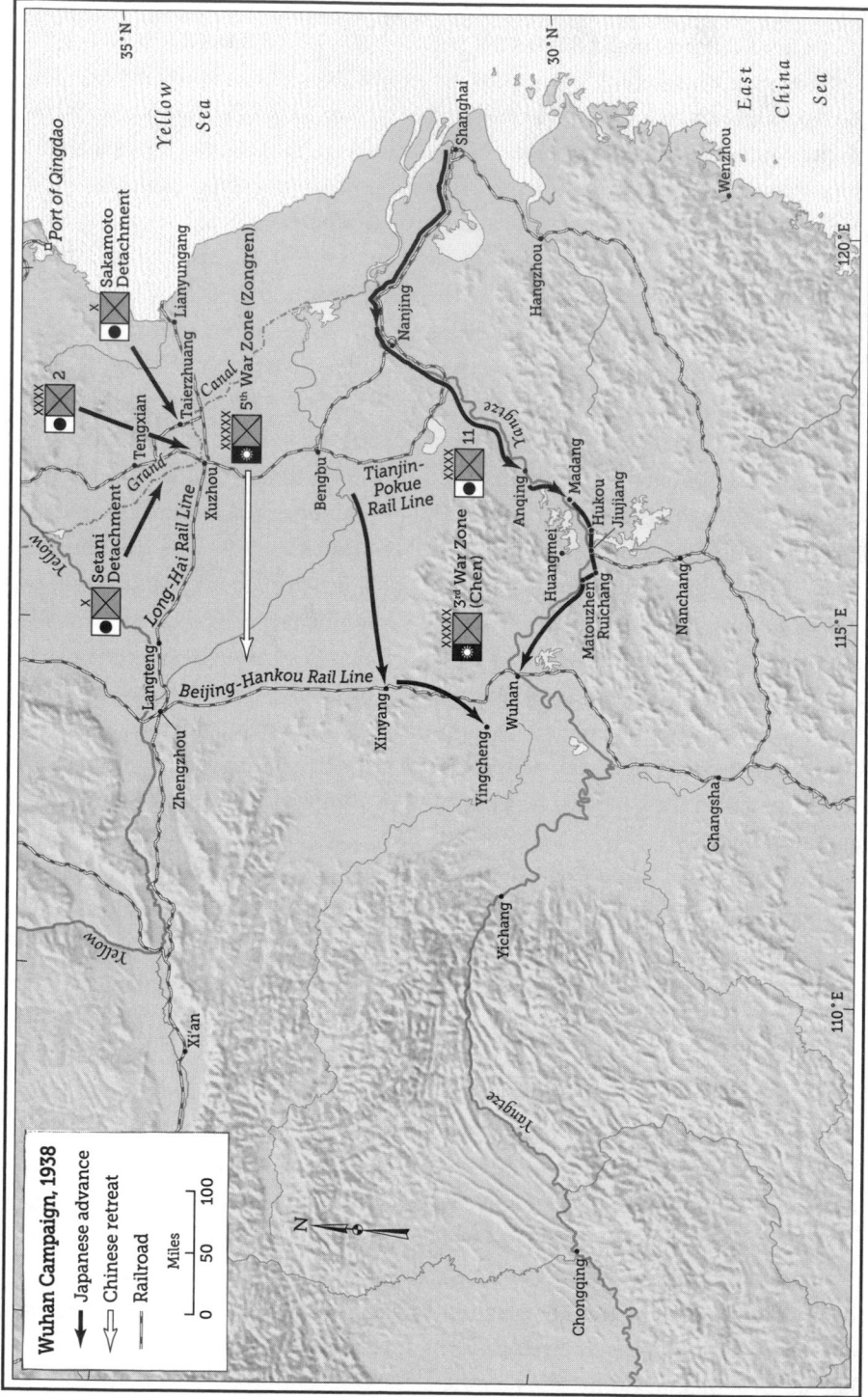

Wuhan Campaign, 1938

Japanese advance
Chinese retreat
Railroad

Miles
0   50   100

political factions; it was "between those committed to fighting for the idea of China as a culture, race, and nation, and 'Hanjian'" (national traitors).

For Japan, the end of 1937 found sixteen divisions and some 600,000 men of the Imperial Army in China. This virtually equaled the entire peacetime army. Moreover, the 1937 campaigns exhausted units in Central China. Casualties vastly exceeded expectations, and Japan's industrial mobilization lagged far behind the output needed to sustain intense operations. Imperial General Headquarters directed a lull in offensive operations to permit the refitting of the divisions in China, the raising of ten additional divisions in the Japanese homeland, and the expansion of the industrial infrastructure. Campaigning might resume in the summer, but thoughts also turned to creating a collaborationist regime. The emperor officially sanctioned this policy at a 16 February 1938 Imperial Conference.

The actual implementation and ultimate fate of this grand design affords yet another case study in the want of rudimentary discipline among Japan's soldiers. The Soviet Union loomed as the ultimate enemy to the General Staff. These officers tailored the doubling of the Imperial Army's strength to thirty-four divisions to segregate regular army soldiers for duty in Manchukuo or as a reserve in case of war with the Soviet Union. Perforce, the army assigned most first- and second-line reservists, often married men with children and civilian jobs, to units in China. The result, noted historian Edward Drea, was that

> as of August 1, 1938, just over 11 percent of Japanese soldiers in the China Expeditionary Army were regulars, 22.6 percent were from the first reserve (aged 24–28), 45.2 percent from the second reserve (aged 29–34), and 20.9 percent from the conscript reserve, the last consisting of untrained or semi-trained personnel used as replacements mainly in transport and logistical units.

Uncurbed by Tokyo's directive to halt further advances, Japanese commanders in North China remained fixed on destroying the Chinese field forces. Repeated Japanese success in maneuver emboldened commanders to divide their own units into widely separated flanking columns, even when heavily outnumbered. This predilection produced disaster.

In mid-February elements of the Japanese Second Army pressed south from Tianjin toward the key Xuzhou railroad junction. They were snagged at Tengxian, a railway stop roughly seventy-five miles north of Xuzhou. Bolstered by tanks, heavy artillery, and air cover, in mid-March the numerically superior Japanese finally overwhelmed the Chinese defenders from Sichuan, who were largely unbloodied and weakly armed (some toted rifles dating from the Qing dynasty).

Another Japanese column landed at the port of Qingdao in mid-February and tramped southwest cross-country toward Xuzhou. Large Chinese forces confronted this body in a three-week battle at Linyi, approximately thirty miles northeast of Xuzhou. One Chinese commander, Zizhong Zhang, in disgrace since surrendering Beijing without a fight, became a national and international hero overnight based on his unyielding resistance at Linyi.

Still greater opportunity presented itself to Zhang and other Chinese commanders in mid-March. After a pause, the focus of the fighting shifted to the small town of Taierzhuang, roughly thirteen miles northeast of Xuzhou. The Japanese Setani Detachment (the Japanese customarily named units after the senior commander) of the 10th Division, advancing on Taierzhuang from the northwest, encountered massed Chinese defenders. A second Japanese column, the Sakamoto Detachment of the 5th Division, embarked on a flanking movement from the northeast. In desperate need of a success after the loss of Nanjing, Chiang demanded a victory and issued an order threatening Zongren Li, his chief of staff Chongxi Bai, and Enbo Tang (commander of Chiang's Central Army forces under Li) with "punishment" if they lost—a threat representing no rhetorical flourish given Han's fate.

For once the Chinese skillfully massed Enbo Tang's crack Central Army units against one and then the other Japanese column in engagements between 22 March and 7 April—often at night and hand-to-hand. Although the Chinese sustained approximately 20,000 casualties and claimed an equal number of Japanese, actual Japanese losses numbered about 8,000. Whether the Japanese pulled back because of defeat at Chinese hands, shortage of ammunition, or by mistake when the Setani Detachment withdrew in the erroneous belief that the Sakamoto Detachment was withdrawing, the fact remained that it marked the first major Japanese retreat in the war. The battered and exhausted Chinese units mustered no attempt to pursue the Japanese as they retreated from the charred remains of Taierzhuang. Nine Chinese generals died in the battle, but just one hailed from the immediate area. This single fact illuminated a much larger dynamic of tremendous importance: breaking a nearly century-old pattern, Chinese soldiers rose to fight not just for their native places but for the nation of China.

Taierzhuang ignited exuberant victory celebrations across China. It proved an enormous fillip to Chinese morale and yielded tremendous political benefits on two levels. Domestically, it validated the endorsement of continuing the war at simultaneous national and Nationalist conferences. Moreover, the February–April battles reversed international opinion: the war might be headed to stalemate, but it was not tumbling to a Chinese collapse.

On 7 April, the same day the first phase of the Battle of Taierzhuang ended in a Chinese victory, Imperial Headquarters issued a new directive. Seven divisions and supporting elements totaling about 200,000 men would stage an envelopment of Xuzhou from north and south. The immense strategic value of Xuzhou stemmed from the railway net, which visually resembled an "H—". The east-west Long-Hai railway represented the bar of the "H" with Xuzhou on the right (east) and Zhengzhou on the left (west). The bar pointing roughly east from the "H" represented the extension of the Long-Hai railway from Xuzhou to the port of Lianyungang. The vertical line on the right (east) represented the Tianjin-Pukou line and the vertical line on the left (west) the Beijing-Hankou line. In Japanese hands, the combination of the port of Lianyungang and the railway system would enormously simplify their logistics in central China. Xuzhou would become a secure springboard for full-throated advance west along the Long-Hai line to where it intersected at Zhengzhou with the other great north-south rail line from Beijing to Hankou. From Zhengzhou it was only 373 miles south to Wuhan, a path unimpeded by significant natural obstacles. Besides seizing Xuzhou, the Japanese also aimed to create a pocket trapping up to fifty Chinese divisions.

As one of the strongest pieces of evidence rebutting the canard that Chiang had failed to prepare for war, Xuzhou stands out as the long-anticipated key interior battleground against the Japanese. This area not only formed the focus of much discussion at Chinese military academies but also the site of staff exercise trips to examine the terrain. But shrewd forethought on where to fight was not matched by equally astute dispositions. The defenders of Xuzhou, outnumbering the Japanese overall by a factor of perhaps six to one in the entire Central Yangtze Valley, adhered to German thinking in organization with the two great field armies (the Fifth and Ninth War Zones). But the Chinese commanders adopted Soviet concepts of positional warfare, stacking their units along lines of communication, like rail lines. This worked well for logistics, but it left little or lightly defended areas, providing ready gaps for Japanese maneuver. At this juncture, the Chinese had not fully mobilized guerrilla units to supplement the regulars and harass the Japanese. The terrible losses at Shanghai and Nanjing revived the propensity of Chinese commanders to avoid decisive engagements for fear of irretrievable losses of scarce men, equipment, and supplies, vital to survival of regional commanders.

Buttressed by much superior ground and air firepower, the Japanese clamped a ring of eight divisions around Xuzhou's defenders by mid-May. Japanese officers claimed that they were about to achieve a historic feat surpassing the ancient classic annihilation battles of Cannae or its World War I equivalent at Tannenberg. But all too typically, Japanese commanders pushed their men into marches that stretched and then snapped logistical support. Starved Japanese soldiers, some desperately short of ammunition, could not seal a ring around the defenders. After securing Chiang's concurrence, Gen. Zongren Li ordered a breakout of his surviving troops. Marching by night and hiding by day, and aided by a providential cloak of fog and a sandstorm, about 200,000 to 300,000 of Li's men managed to elude the Japanese noose. The Japanese stomped into Xuzhou on 19 May, taking about 30,000 Chinese prisoners. Two days later, Li reported that his retreat was complete. The fighting devastated the region around Xuzhou. Of Xuzhou's original population of 20,000, by the end of the fighting the inhabitants numbered just seven: six women and an eighty-five-year-old male.

Li combined the steel core of a soldier with a cultivated personality at ease with poetry. Although he received a hero's welcome at Wuhan, Li was hospitalized. An old war wound provided the official reason; the more likely reason was depression over his losses. Bai replaced Li as commander of the Fifth War Zone.

Valiant and skilled Chinese resistance at Taierzhuang revived Chinese spirits, but the loss of Xuzhou sent them down again. The Chinese, however, had entangled and embarrassed the Japanese, who were compelled to rush reinforcements from Manchuria and Nanjing. These unexpected drains on Japanese resources delayed planned campaigns up the Yangtze from Nanjing as well as west and north from Taiyuan. The protracted battle for Xuzhou forced a reshuffling of troop allocations and a shakeup of commands. It compelled the Japanese to treat Central China as their premier concern, to the detriment of their earlier commitment to the Soviet threat.

Yellow River Floods and Zhangguofeng

With the failure to annihilate the main Chinese armies at Xuzhou, Imperial General Headquarters discarded the chimera of a single "decisive battle" in China in favor of staking out the dominance of vital strategic centers. Tokyo selected Wuhan as the key target for the new strategy. Wuhan served Nationalist China as the civilian government center and military hub for the armies guarding the Central Yangtze Region. Moreover, Wuhan figured symbolically as a rallying point for Chinese resistance in 1938. In late May, the Japanese cabinet approved a plan to seize Wuhan and to attack Guangzhou (Canton) simultaneously. They would then establish "a new government opposed to war, opposed to Chiang Kai-shek, and opposed to communism." They expected that the vast territory the Chinese had already lost, followed by the loss of Wuhan and Guangzhou, would end the war and give them control of China.

Chiang met the renewed Japanese drive on Wuhan with a colossal and desperate measure. From Xuzhou, Japanese troops marched west along the Long-Hai rail line. By 6 June they threatened to cross the Yellow River and attack at Zhengzhou on the Beijing-Hankou rail line. From Zhengzhou, their route south to Wuhan would be logistically secure and bereft of natural obstacles. Chiang flew to Zhengzhou at the end of May and made one of his most fateful decisions of the war.

The Chinese refer to the Yellow River as simply "The River." Its middle reaches and its tributary, the Wei, gave birth to Chinese civilization. Massive dykes with rock and rubble core and earthen embankments contain the river in its middle and lower reaches, where the riverbed often flows above the adjacent land. Epic catastrophic floods on the Yellow River, usually caused by a combination of natural forces and government negligence, punctuate Chinese history and evoked a second name for the river: "China's Sorrow." Maintaining the dykes formed a virtually sacred task of all Chinese central governments. Under the traditional "mandate of heaven" theory that undergirded imperial rule, a flood signified the loss of mandate. The dyke system profoundly molded the very core of historic Chinese political arrangements, for the obligation to maintain dykes to preserve the mandate led to "an obsession with control, and an authoritarian system of government which ensured that control."

With the defeat of Li's Fifth War Zone at Xuzhou, total defeat by Japan loomed terrifyingly before senior Chinese leaders. No battle-worthy Chinese force remained to impede the Japanese thrust along the Long-Hai rail line to Zhengzhou. At a minimum, the Chinese desperately needed time for Li's forces to reassemble and to at least permit the central government to displace to the west, with its administrative infrastructure and much of its surviving munitions industry now ensconced in Wuhan. Chinese leaders also feared the prospect of more Nanjings, large and small. In this fraught atmosphere, Qian Cheng, commander of the First War Zone encompassing the middle reaches of the Yellow River, and Cheng Chen, minister of war, proposed to Chiang breaching the dykes to cut the Long-Hai rail line. None of Chiang's principal subordinates uttered any objection and Chiang made the final decision himself to use "water as a substitute for soldiers" (yi shui dai bing).

The moment chosen for breaching the dykes fell in early summer, the sole time of year when the river flowed high and fast. At other seasons, low and sluggish waters would have precluded a huge flood. But this moment also fell at the most critical time of the year for farmers, as they were least apt to flee with their crops verging on harvest. A breach was opened in Henan province on 9 June roughly thirty miles from the Japanese vanguard. Manual labor initiated the rupture; the river did the rest. About three-quarters of the main current surged out from its normal northeast course to the southwest, sluicing across a flat plain.

The flood cut the Long-Hai railroad just south of the breach. Heeding no human design, the torrents inundated enormous stretches of productive agricultural land in Henan, Anhui, and Jiangsu provinces before dividing into three watery talons that punched to the sea. The unbounded deluge inflicted a calamity of almost unimaginable proportions. In 1948 the Chinese government reconstructed figures for the dead and their proportion to the population in the forty counties affected. These imply that individuals near the original breach gained some forewarning and priceless opportunity to seek safety. The waters typically took those further distant unawares, with no time for flight on the plains graded perfectly level by several millennia of repeated flooding. Of those who did not drown immediately, thousands died of hunger or disease in the weeks that followed.

The flood also inflicted a titanic environmental disaster. The people were dead or expelled—likewise the livestock. Houses, roads, bridges, and other public structures were demolished. Often only the angular lines formed by the tops of the walls of county towns protruded above the surface of the flooded expanse. The inundation not only destroyed the standing crops, it also erased centuries of irrigation canal networks and coated the earth with silt that ruined the soil for cultivation. Much of the region west of Xuzhou became void of living presence.

Later figures for fatalities and refugees widely differ, although there is no dispute they were stupendous. Official Nationalist government figures assembled in 1948 looked as follows:

Casualties of the Yellow River Flood, June 1938

PROVINCE	HENAN	ANHUI	JIANGSU	TOTALS
Deaths	325,589	407,514	160,200	893,303
Refugees	1,172,639	2,536,315	202,400	3,911,354

As horrifying as these numbers are, the actual figures may have been still higher. Although initially the Communist government employed lesser numbers, it reverted to the Nationalists' approximate 1948 figures in the 1970s to 1990s. An official history in 1994 set the dead at 900,000 and the destitute and homeless at nearly 10 million. More recent academic work from archival materials included a 1995 Taiwan study that fixed the deaths at 400,000–500,000, the number of refugees at three million, and the number of people affected at five million. A subsequent study put the number of dead and homeless at 500,000 each.

The Nationalist government at first tried to blame the breach falsely on Japanese bombs. The Japanese vigorously denounced this claim and countercharged that the incident had killed 300,000 peasants and demonstrated the "ruthless contempt for human life" of Chiang's government. The Communists, largely mute at first, adopted the same theme—that the incident confirmed the inhumanity of the Nationalist government. But the evidence favors the conclusion that it was not sheer callousness, but confusion and panic at the highest echelons that drove Chiang's decision. Chiang never mentioned the event in his diary, nor did he express remorse. Those caught in the path of the flood tended to blame both sides. During the rest of the war and into the civil war that followed, swaths of the flooded area became stalwart base areas for Communist guerrillas.

What effect did this immense sacrifice purchase? The Japanese reoriented their main approach for their own reasons toward Wuhan from what had shaped up as a north-to-south thrust from Zhengzhou to an east-to-west advance up both banks of the Yangtze. There, however, the Chinese Ninth War Zone mounted protracted resistance. A second thrust southwest across country from Xuzhou faced much more difficult terrain. The delayed advance proved to have very important strategic effects, to which we will return. But the price of using the Yellow River for the first time in Chinese history against an invader would be to raise a profound question about the mandate of the Nationalist government.

As there was virtually no media coverage of this horror at the time, it has rested in obscurity ever since. The final telling word on the Yellow River flood of 1938 is provided by the Western historian who has done the most to preserve the memory outside China, Diana Lary:

> We are left to make an almost impossible leap in imagination to understand the suffering on such a vast scale, and to grasp the horror of it.

The written accounts do not help us. Most of them simply list figures, with very little descriptive detail, no names of the victims, no personal stories, to underline the magnitude of the suffering. It is inconceivable that this would be the treatment of so vast a tragedy . . . in the history of the Second World War in Europe.

Part of the reason it proved difficult to measure the effects of the Yellow River floods on Japanese actions is that, shortly after the catastrophe, Tokyo's attention was forcefully directed to the north. Between the Japanese seizure of Manchuria in 1931 and 1938, the Soviets nearly tripled troop deployments along this frontier from about eight to twenty-four divisions and 450,000 men. Aircraft strength surged tenfold from 200 to about 2,000. This far outpaced Japanese efforts to maintain parity. By 1938 the Kwantung Army mustered only about 200,000 men, including eight divisions and roughly 230 aircraft. The vague borderlines generated numerous minor clashes, but in 1937, the Soviets appeared to back down swiftly from a more sizable episode. The Japanese interpreted Soviet accommodation as signaling weakness, reflecting the effects of the bloody Stalinist purges ravaging the Red Army's senior ranks.

Nonetheless, Hirohito rebuffed proposals from the army to launch an attack to expel Soviet troops who had occupied disputed high ground around Zhangguofeng (Changkuofeng in many Western accounts; Lake Khasan in Soviet accounts) along the Korean border in July 1938. To foreclose repetition of the unilateral action by Imperial Army units in Korea in 1931, Hirohito forbade moving troops without his express approval. In flagrant disregard for the imperial order, the local Japanese commander launched an unauthorized attack on the night of 30–31 July. The army then obtained Hirohito's retroactive sanction by falsely informing him that the attack merely retaliated for Soviet assaults. The Soviets countered massively with three divisions supported by air and artillery against the approximately 7,000 Japanese defenders. By the time of a cease-fire on 11 August, Japanese casualties hit 1,400 Japanese (500 dead), and official Soviet casualties were 850 (the real number may have approached 6,000).

Japanese officers distilled from the episode dangerously false conclusions. They interpreted the obvious effort of the Soviets to confine the encounter to a patch of disputed land as evidence of Soviet predisposition to back down when powerfully confronted. Further, Imperial Army officers believed the tactical aspects of the battle validated their appraisal that the Soviet commanders were clumsy and that the superior élan and grit of the Japanese soldier could overcome marked Soviet numerical superiority in manpower and weaponry.

Wuhan Summer

Hard Chinese fighting around Xuzhou, the Yellow River floods, and the clash around Zhangguofeng purchased a summer respite in Wuhan that became a singular moment in twentieth-century Chinese history: a preview of a China with political and artistic freedom as well as new directions in public policy. Moreover, Wuhan also exerted a powerful international effect. Foreign reporters and military attachés transmitted to the world compelling messages about the suffering and heroism of the Chinese and linked China to global events.

Wuhan comprises the tri-cities of Hankou, Wuchang, and Hanyang along the Yangtze—here flowing "coppery brown, turbid with the red soil of the west washed down in its wild course through mountainous [Sichuan]." The prewar economy particularly revolved around the great inland port of Hankou, where oceangoing vessels could dock and offload commodities or processed goods for distribution. The war shut the water route to Hankou, abruptly capping off the economy's wellspring, but in its place came a massive upsurge in capital, labor, and managerial investments in war industries.

As prodigious columns of refugees sought safety across China, Wuhan's population doubled within a few months. Moreover, the swollen census included nearly all notable members of China's intellectual elite— philosophers, dramatists, novelists, editors, and writers— displaced from the coastal cities that had nurtured the vanguard of modernization. Likewise, Wuhan became a Mecca for fleeing university faculty and students from all over China. A sense of miraculous deliverance united these heterogeneous refugees. "Uniting to make a last stand became a moral necessity and, psychologically, a way of facing survivor guilt," noted MacKinnon, the Western bard of the "Wuhan Summer."

Heretofore, the modest numbers of Chinese publications free of censorship had existed only at a distance from the central government, ironically in regions run by certain regional leaders and amid Western gashes in Chinese sovereignty, like Shanghai. But now, under the benign reign of Baoding military commanders, Wuhan witnessed an immense geyser of unfettered and widely diverse political and artistic expression. The political culture produced "more diversity of public opinion in Wuhan than in any Chinese capital before or since."

An explosion of print outlets characterized the openness of Wuhan. In the first quarter of 1938, the number of daily papers jumped from three to fourteen, and journals soared from thirty to over two hundred. Censorship evaporated and not one editor was assassinated or arrested. Commentary covered the entire spectrum from Communist to far right. For at least this brief interval, the Nationalists and CCP forged a genuine United Front. Communist leaders Zhou Enlai and Wang Ming roused rapt crowds with orations linking the struggle against fascism in Spain centered at Madrid with the defense of Wuhan. Part of the reason for the Nationalist-CCP truce, however, derived from the fact that as in Spain, the Communists were obsessed more with left-wing enemies (particularly "Trotskyites") than right-wing adversaries.

Heretofore "serious" novels and theater reflected a deadening obsession with the family and the personal tribulations of rarified upper-class Chinese life. Now, in a cultural earthquake paralleling the political upheaval, artistic expression abandoned the narrow conversation among elites for a concerted movement into the popular culture to mobilize the urban and rural masses to defend Wuhan and support the War of Resistance.

Of 108 institutions of higher learning in the areas occupied by Japan, no fewer than 94 shut their doors or relocated, many up to five times. Between 1935 and 1937, only about 46,758 students (about a tiny 0.01 percent of the population) attended college-level institutions. The number of students at the secondary level totaled a mere 546,212, or about 0.12 percent. (These figures also illustrate a severe constraint on the ability of the Chinese to muster qualified officers for the armed forces in both combat and technical roles.) Over 100,000 of this cohort of secondary and higher level scholars passed through Wuhan in the summer of 1938. By virtue of their family backgrounds—from businessmen, government officials, and educators—they overwhelmingly shared elite origins, but now in Wuhan for the first time students from all across China were tossed together.

Despite these overall relatively minuscule numbers, in the twentieth century and continuing to the twenty-first century, Chinese students have obtained and retained a reputation as the conscience of the nation. They also stand out for their potent sense of theatrics and the deft use of symbolism in rallies, as part of their penchant for blurring boundaries between political and artistic expression. Ubiquitous wall posters and wall newspapers formed the hallmark of the student presence. In these early years they jettisoned their earlier penchant for demonstrations against Chinese authorities for fervent support of the war effort.

Beyond atmospherics in public discourse and the arts of freedom, the summer also birthed at least baby steps toward pluralism. In March, the Nationalist government created the People's Political Council. Of its two hundred members, half could not be associated with the Nationalists. Third parties, though small, barked vigorous criticism of the Nationalists and Communists.

For millennia, national and province-level authorities had confined their public service activities to flood control via large works and grain reserve storage for famine relief. Localities and private benefactors performed all other social services in China. Instead of triggering despair and disintegration, the dire prospects of Japanese occupation and the appearance of masses of refugees spawned in Wuhan an unprecedented sense of community. It manifested itself particularly in the creation of public services for women and children. An especially potent symbol proved to be the creation of state-run orphanages, a program vigorously advocated by the formidable female lawyer Shi Liang and in the newspapers, and then approved by Chiang in May. This evolved into a national program that by war's end cared for hundreds of thousands of orphans. The images of orphans being nurtured under the approving eye of high officials (Madame Chiang Kai-shek took a leading role) also served China well in building international support. A stellar collection of Chinese medical luminaries, propelled by the war into Wuhan, created new models of state-run medical services that served as prototypes for both the PRC and Taiwan. The relief efforts in Wuhan at least equaled the far better-highlighted efforts in the international quarters of Shanghai. These measures set important precedents for creating a new milieu of community, bridging a huge gap between the nation and province, and between the family and clan.

The Wuhan summer played a huge role in shaping the international image of China and the significance of its struggles with Japan. Initially, the clash seemed, in the words of poet W. H. Auden, "off stage a war, thuds like the slamming of a distant door." But when the fighting failed to flicker out after a few months, China's travails seemed to mesh into a sequence of ominous events: Japan's seizure of Manchuria (1931–1932), the Italian conquest of Ethiopia (1935–1936), the Spanish Civil War (1936–1939), Hitler's remilitarization of the Rhineland (March 1936), Germany's annexation of Austria (March 1938), and a building tension over Czechoslovakia that would produce the Munich Agreement in September 1938. From Western perspectives, malevolent forces stalked the world, and there seemed no clear barrier assembling to halt their depredations.

A major metamorphosis of the Western intermediaries between China and their peoples enhanced China's prospects quite independently of any Chinese effort. An old guard of diplomats, journalists, and soldiers conspicuously huddled in isolated compounds remained tethered to traditional views. They found merit in Japanese claims of representing a modernizing force revitalizing a decayed and dysfunctional China. Some British diplomats, for example, looking warily at Germany's ascent and Soviet fanfares about international revolution, thought it prudent to avoid Asian entanglements or even to maneuver for an eventual alliance with Japan.

But change was afoot with the infusion of a fresh wave of journalists and soldiers. The war's movement away from Beijing and Shanghai left behind the established cadre of journalists. In their place came reporters like Edgar Snow, Agnes Smedley, Freda Utley, Tilman Durdin, and Jack Belden. Their relative youth and energy primed them to forgo comforts and seek out stories at the front, at rallies, or at bars. Seeing China "being invaded and brutalized," as Durdin recalled, swiftly tilted their sympathies to the Chinese. The arrival of other journalists like Robert Capa (still building his legendary career as photographer), and literary figures like W. H. Auden and Christopher Isherwood, helped to harness the Chinese struggle with "anti-Fascism" elsewhere, notably the contemporary perception of Spain. With the arguable exception of Utley, this cadre of reporters and intellectuals skewed largely left. Smedley, in fact, having acted as a secret agent of Imperial Germany to further Indian independence during World War I, spent the last three decades of her life as a covert Communist agent. Whatever his instinctive leanings, rough hewn Belden (who spoke "like a Brooklyn taxi diver," noted another journalist) stands apart for his foresight on where the Chinese Communists would take the country if they gained control.

Among the soldiers, the most significant development in 1938 was the displacement of Chiang's German military advisers by a Red Army mission. Japanese pressure prompted Hitler to overrule his Sinophile Army General Staff and recall Chiang's German advisers. Among several Germans who chose to remain privately was Walther Stennes, a former intelligence officer who claimed to have been the former Berlin Brown Shirt leader who led a failed putsch against Hitler in 1931. He charmed his way into Madame Chiang's trust to become the head of Chiang's bodyguard, but he also was a Soviet agent. Following the signing of a Sino-Soviet nonaggression pact on 21 August 1937, a body of Red Army officers arrived to replace the Germans.

A shift in primary military suppliers paralleled the transition of advisers. For the first sixteen months of the war, China obtained 60 percent of its arms from Germany. The Sino-Soviet nonaggression pact contained secret clauses promising arms worth 100 million Chinese dollars. Subsequently, Soviet loans in 1938 and 1939, totaling $223 million, financed more arms in exchange for Chinese tea, tungsten, and wool. With the weapons would come not only high-level advisers, but artillerists and an initial tranche of 450 Soviet pilots and aviation personnel. During August 1938, many citizens of Wuhan remained outside to watch Soviet and Chinese pilots in Soviet and American aircraft contest the Japanese air raids.*

A standout military observer in Wuhan was the well-connected Dutchman Henri de Fremery, who enjoyed easy access to Chiang's chief of staff, Yingqin He. But a contingent of American military observers in Wuhan exerted the most important influence. These individuals included Evans F. Carlson of the US Marine Corps and Joseph Stilwell, David Barrett, and Frank Dorn from the US Army. They traveled widely and mined the work of journalists and diplomats to assemble their reports.

Perhaps the most interesting facet of the very effective Chinese propaganda campaign was that its talented leader, Hollington Tong, with Chiang's explicit concurrence, chose to empower foreign journalists to roam unhindered and report uncensored, confident that the stories they would tell would feature China's heroism in the face of Japanese barbarism. This approach worked effectively to win over Western correspondents to China's cause, and in 1938 few stories appeared highlighting government mismanagement or corruption or the divisions between the Nationalists and the Communists.

To facilitate efforts, however, in March 1938, the Chinese government opened the Chinese News Service office in New York City. While a Chinese headed the enterprise, his staff comprised American reporters and missionaries. The Chinese News Service highlighted stories of Japanese atrocities

---

* During the war, the Soviets provided 1,250 aircraft of all types, including 348 bombers and about 663 fighters. In addition, the Soviets provided 82 tanks, 2,118 vehicles, 1,140 artillery pieces, 9,720 machine guns, and 50,000 rifles. About 3,000 Soviet officers served as advisers, including such later luminaries as Georgiy Zhukov and Vasiliy Chuikov. About 2,000 Soviet pilots served in China. Van de Ven, *War and Nationalism*, 199; Paine, *The Wars of Asia*, 144–45. The most authoritative English language account of Soviet fighter pilots in China is Mikhail Maslov, *Osprey Aircraft of the Aces*, 95, *Polikarpov I-15, I-16 and I-153 Aces* (Oxford: Osprey Publishing, 2010), chap. two, "Swallows Over China." Maslov says Soviet pilots claimed eighty-one Japanese planes. About one hundred Soviet pilots died in battle and a "similar number" in accidents.

and China's resistance. From this seed would grow what would later be styled "The China Lobby."

At this stage of the war both the Nationalists and Communists sought to conceal their differences to outsiders. Tong permitted open contact with Communists and publication of their newspaper. Bluntly pro-Communist journalists like Agnes Smedley and Logan ("Red Baron") Roots herded colleagues into interviews and contacts, notably with the charismatic Zhou Enlai, who in the long run would powerfully influence foreign journalists.

Edgar Snow published *Red Star over China* in 1937, arguably one of the most significant books by an American journalist in the twentieth century. For decades, Snow's multiple naive misrepresentations of the Chinese Communist Party and especially Mao Zedong and "The Long March" would beguile both huge Western and (in translation) Chinese audiences. But the influential *Foreign Affairs* magazine also carried Snow's much read hagiography of Chiang in 1938, titled "China's Fighting Generalissimo." At the popular level, the powerful Time-Life publication empire was headed by the son of Presbyterian missionaries to China, Henry Luce. Luce's support for China, and particularly Chiang, proved fervent and enduring. In January 1938 *Time* magazine chose Generalissimo and Madame Chiang as the Man and Wife of the Year (1937).

Attacking and Defending Wuhan

In a key step to implement the Japanese strategic blueprint to end the war by capturing Wuhan and Guangzhou (Canton), in July 1938 the Imperial Army organized the new Eleventh Army in the Central China Expeditionary Army, under Gen. Yasuji Okamura, a well-reputed China expert. The army consisted of the 6th, 9th, 27th, 101st, and 106th Divisions and the Namita Detachment (a portion of the Taiwan Composite Brigade). For the rest of the war in China, the Eleventh Army (about double the strength of a normal Japanese "army") would remain the largest formation tasked with shattering Nationalist resistance.

Counting the Eleventh Army, the Japanese fielded fourteen divisions and 300,000 to 400,000 men south of the Great Wall. Nine of these divisions pitched into the Wuhan campaign in the summer under overall command of Gen. Shunroku Hata. A potent column built around the Eleventh Army and naval units advanced from Nanjing westward up the Yangtze. A much smaller column from the North China Area Army would approach Wuhan over rugged terrain from the northeast.

Convinced that Wuhan could be held, Chiang massed at least 800,000 men to defend the tri-cities and the Central Yangtze Valley. Theater commander Cheng Chen and his subordinates, rather than Chiang, devised the basic defense scheme. The Fifth War Zone confronted the Japanese prong approaching from the northeast, and the Ninth War Zone met the thrust up the Yangtze. The Chinese aimed to exploit harsh terrain to the north and fortifications along the Yangtze approaches to the south.

Geography parceled out handicaps and advantages to each side, while weather and disease stood impartial. The Japanese tramping from Xuzhou toward Wuhan from the northeast faced the fine-grained terrain of a succession of narrow valleys between small mountain ranges, littered with numerous river crossings and conspicuously lacking roads. While the Yangtze offered the defenders several natural blocking positions, it was also at high water, enabling the Japanese Third Fleet with 120 vessels to bolster the ground advance with heavy naval gunfire. At the same time, supplies could be floated much more efficiently upstream than hauled overland—and largely immune to Chinese guerrilla attacks to boot. Summer tormented both sides with sweltering temperatures as high as 104 Fahrenheit. The blazing sun and the high humidity exhausted marching soldiers and accelerated the epidemic-level spread of diseases such as malaria, cholera, and dysentery.

Japanese air support (three hundred aircraft covering the Yangtze advance alone) remained much more formidable than its largely nonexistent Chinese counterpart. But the Japanese also wielded a more sinister trump card: poison gas. Under the code name "special smoke," they deployed this terror weapon to make up for the dulled edge of their units to subdue generally stiff Chinese resistance.

The Japanese secured two coups in their initial push up the Yangtze. Anqing, about one hundred miles directly west of Nanjing (and more than double that distance on the Yangtze), fell with humiliating swiftness to an amphibious hook. Next at Madang, the Japanese eschewed a frontal attack on major Chinese fortifications in favor of encirclement by 24 June. They doused the Chinese with poison gas and Madang fell on 29 June. Chiang ordered the execution of one divisional commander and the court-martial of other officers at Madang, but took no action against their more culpable superior, a Whampoa graduate, who ignored warnings of Japanese intentions.

Thereafter, the Chinese displayed more effectiveness. They only lost Hukou after five hard days of battle. But at the next major river port city of Jiujiang, just one hundred miles downstream from Wuhan), Yue Xue, a Baoding Academy product, mishandled his command and then abruptly retreated, leaving the civilian population to fall into Japanese hands. Those hands produced a miniature of the Nanjing massacre—they may also have used poison gas to take Jiujiang. In any event, an outbreak of cholera then halted the conquerors. At Ruichang, a commercial center about ten miles distant from the Yangtze on the road leading to the Wuhan-Canton rail line, the Chinese locked the attackers into a costly seesaw struggle that lasted for a month.

The Chinese commanders, already famed for the defense of Xuzhou, turned in a much better record in the Fifth War Zone to the north. Their stout defensive efforts retarded the Japanese advance to 9 September. This proved a preview of even stiffer resistance at Matouzhen. There Gen. Yue Xue and his Cantonese command atoned for their earlier failure at Jiujiang with obdurate resistance and even a counterattack that knocked the Japanese back and forced the local Japanese commander to summon emergency reinforcements. The struggle here did not let up until Wuhan itself fell in October.

The Chinese made a last stand before Wuhan at a sophisticated river fortress at Tianjiazhen. Only a batch of poison gas on the fortress permitted the Japanese finally to break into the abandoned, charred ruins of the city. Thereafter, Chinese resistance south of the Yangtze ceased. While the principal struggles occurred east and northeast of Wuhan, the Japanese unleashed the Second Army of four divisions, rerouted by the Yellow River floods, on a circuitous route following rail lines first west from Xuzhou to Xinyang to sever the Beijing-Hankou rail line, and then south along the rail line to approach Wuhan from the north. Tough battles along the approaches to Xinyang kept that city in Chinese hands until 30 September. Gen. Zongnan Hu was supposed to keep Xinyang in Chinese hands while General Li's much-worn Fifth War Zone divisions withdrew to the mountains to the west. But to Li's rage, Hu abandoned Xinyang without a fight.

The loss of Xinyang bestowed the Japanese access to the rail line approach to Wuhan from the north, just as Hata's command completed its last strides along the Yangtze to close in on Wuhan from the south. Heeding the painfully acquired lessons of Shanghai and Nanjing, Chiang authorized a timely withdrawal from Wuhan. The governmental and military command apparatus evacuated up the Yangtze to Chongqing, deep in Sichuan province. From July and gathering momentum into October, a Herculean mobilization disassembled the tri-cities industries, particularly key munitions plants for portage upriver. Wuhan fell on 25 October. The Japanese staged a triumphal entry ceremony on 3 November, but commanders enforced strict discipline, and there was no repetition of the "unlawful acts" in Nanjing.

By the numbers, the ten-month campaign to defend the Yangtze valley in 1938 cost the lives of approximately a million Chinese civilians. Extremely rudimentary Chinese medical services (where any existed at all) and rampant disease combined with combat to bring death and injury to a half-million Chinese soldiers. The main Japanese force, the Eleventh Army, sustained 4,567 killed (including 172 officers) and 17,380 wounded (including 526 officers). The army reported Chinese losses as 143,493 abandoned corpses and 9,581 POWs.

The loss of Wuhan marked only one of a season of three Chinese reverses, one self-inflicted. With many of the best Guangdong (Cantonese) forces shouldering the defense of Wuhan, to Chiang's shock and chagrin the Japanese landed the Twenty-First Army in their home region and captured Guangzhou (Canton) on 21 October. Typical of the uneven performance of Chinese command, the retreat from Wuhan appeared to leave the strategic city of Changsha, one hundred miles to the south, bereft of defenses. In 1938 Changsha was a wealthy provincial town with a rich cultural tradition. It sat at a major trade crossroads and featured important rice markets as well as one of South China's historic centers of learning. Not only generations of mandarins and intellectuals, but young Mao Zedong studied there. Moreover, the Hunanese bore fame as antiforeign and political radicals. During the war, Changsha would emerge as the Chinese Leningrad, apotheosized as the essence of heroism and resistance.

False intelligence sounded an alarm that the Japanese would swoop down on Changsha from the east. Chiang had just given a rousing speech in Changsha, proposing the city be torched if in danger of capture, following the example of the Russians burning Moscow in 1812 to deny it to Napoleon. In one of his worst mistakes of the war, Chiang flung aside the forceful objections of Cheng Chen and ordered the city burned. Starting on 12 November 1938, flames consumed this capital of Hunan province for three days. When the smoke cleared, a huge rice store was gone, along with about two-thirds of all structures. The dead numbered about 10,000, including masses of wounded soldiers who could not move. The appalling extent of civilian suffering and the failure of the Japanese to approach propelled Chiang to shift responsibility. Three mid-level police officials paid with their lives while Chiang shielded the provincial governor, his trusted lieutenant Zhizhong Zhang, from accountability.

Changsha graphically illustrated the Chinese scorched earth policy that wrote innumerable tragic chapters in the War of Resistance. Precedents for the policy, usually a desperate tactic of the weaker combatant, existed in China's own history, but prewar Chinese strategists took bearings from more modern examples. Implemented as early as the Battle of Shanghai, it became formal policy during the struggle for Wuhan, after which Chiang declared Japanese advances must only find "scorched earth and empty cities." It directly denied the Japanese profits from their successes while harboring an implied message to the Chinese people that China ultimately would triumph. Retreating Chinese forces routinely burned or demolished roads, railroads, bridges, water vessels, factories, and food stores, as well as civilian dwellings, stores, and public services. Seldom were the Nationalists able to provide any succor for their own countrymen suffering loss or mortal peril due to this policy. Historian Hans van de Ven astutely noted the policy had a "somewhat paradoxical effect, on the one hand strengthening the national will to resist Japan come what may, but also undermining the legitimacy of the Nationalists."

The Japanese sought to follow up military success with political maneuvers. On 3 November Konoe sought to swaddle Japan's exertions in China in noble robes—touting them as an enterprise devoted to Pan-Asian uplift under the rubric of a "New Order in East Asia" based on "cooperation of Japan, Manchuria and China." European colonial powers and the United States interpreted this as a rejection of the international legal and economic status quo, a posture that increased their willingness to assist Chiang. At the same time, Tokyo aspired to find a Chinese interlocutor who could deliver two blessings: a replacement for Chiang and his implacable opposition to Japan's goals, and a legitimate authority to sanction a peace accord. By 20 November, Chiang's long-time rival, Jingwei Wang, stepped forward to play the role scripted for him by the Japanese as the head of Japan's puppet government in China.

Wang carried brilliantly burnished credentials as an authentic Chinese patriotic hero. During the 1911 Revolution, he attempted to assassinate a Manchu prince and later became one of Sun Yat-sen's closest followers. The remarkably handsome Wang possessed abundant charm and intelligence. In individual meetings he appeared unassuming, but before a crowd he metamorphosed into a rousing orator—"like a crazed lion" marveled a Japanese journalist. A reviewer of a volume of Wang's poetry, translated into English in 1938, observed: "In this poet I discover a fervent reformer, yet fond of long conversations with a friend, fond of wine, a lover, a husband, and one who delights in little children and in that perpetual innocence of sea, sky and land." But the reviewer missed another fateful Wang trait: a proclivity for taking reckless gambles. He regarded himself as the obviously best-fitted heir to Sun and bitterly resented his displacement by Chiang.

From mid-1938, Wang conducted a tortuous courtship with the Japanese. He initially and correctly affirmed that only if the Japanese would grant him real independence and power would he be able to undermine support for the War of Resistance and deliver Japan from its entanglement. He accepted a promise from lower level Japanese negotiators to withdraw Japanese troops from all regions south of the Great Wall, save where Communists held out, to abandon extraterritoriality, and to return leased territories. Wang in turn promised to recognize Japan's occupation of Manchuria, grant Japan preferential rights in Chinese resource development, and cooperate economically and in opposition to communism. But Konoe effectively reneged on the vital promise of troop withdrawals. This was hopelessly shortsighted and left Wang irreparably compromised. When Wang revealed his decision, he thereafter sealed his reputation as a "traitor for a thousand generations" to the Chinese masses. Only a tiny handful of Chinese political figures followed Wang. More significantly, despite Japanese endeavors to turn Chinese military leaders, particularly those who had trained in Japan, not one of any note switched sides.

Wuhan—A Pivot Point of the War

The stock-taking on both sides after the fall of Wuhan marked a fundamental pivot point in the Sino-Japanese conflict. The year commenced for China with the vile aftertaste of defeat at Shanghai, and humiliation at Nanjing followed closely by an outbreak of the initial stages of what threatened to be a fatal epidemic of panic and demoralization. With few exceptions, foreign observers predicted a rapid end to the hostilities and the swift fall of Chiang. The saga over the following ten months witnessed yet more Chinese defeat, stupendous human and material loss, serious territorial loss, the epic Yellow River floods, the fall of Wuhan, the disastrous burning of Changsha, and creation of a rival puppet government under Wang. Logically, this litany must seem inexorably to portend the collapse of Chinese resistance.

But on the contrary, 1938 produced an inverse effect on the attitudes of the combatants. Besides defeat and loss, there had been victory, or at least perceived victory, at Taierzhuang and a stubborn defense of the Yangtze Valley. These glimmers on the military horizon, plus the resolution to carry on the war coursing through much of the Chinese population, endowed Chinese military leaders with a grim but real confidence that they could prevail ultimately in a protracted war. Notwithstanding that many provincial troops fought far from home and faced a far more lavishly equipped foe, relatively few deserted. But the year also increased losses among irreplaceable academy-trained officers and expended munitions at an unsustainable rate based on China's resources alone. Chiang's best Central Army units emerged generally weaker rather than stronger after Wuhan.

As became a feature of the war, senior Chinese military leaders assembled for a conference at Nanyue, 25–28 November 1938. With his leadership on the agenda, Chiang delivered what one historian called a "bravura" performance. He insisted that the war to date had progressed according to plan: luring the Japanese into the interior where they could be bogged down, dispersed, and eventually defeated. He evoked parallels to the Taiping Rebellion, where initial disaster was followed by victory that saved Chinese civilization. He was unsparing in a list of "twelve points of shame" of Chinese units. These included items like failing to bury the dead, letting wounded become beggars, and failing to feed soldiers so they pillaged from civilians. For the future, he set out an elaborate and thoughtful program of reforms and operations, highlighting the need to develop guerilla warfare.

In sixteen months of war, Chiang had made many errors, some—like his breaching of the Yellow River dykes and the burning of Changsha—of appalling magnitude. But whatever their reservations about his operational and tactical acumen, his subordinates recognized that he had emerged as the luminous beacon of resistance—and his personal courage was beyond dispute. In the face of deadly peril from Japanese aircraft, Chiang flew into Xuzhou, Zhengzhou, Madang, Xinyang, and Changsha just before battles to affirm his leadership. He flew out of Wuhan on 24 October, only hours before the Japanese marched in. Parallels would be Winston Churchill flying into Dunkirk or Singapore or Franklin Roosevelt into Guadalcanal or Bastogne. No other top political and military figure in World War II would match this scroll of personal feats of courage.

Conversely, ten months of fighting for Wuhan demolished the optimism gamboling among Tokyo elites at the New Year. After Wuhan, Imperial Headquarters somberly concluded that ending the war solely by military means was beyond Japan's grasp—a conclusion Prime Minister Konoe shared. Only now the Japanese belatedly recognized that their operational military supremacy could not avail them in the absence of a coherent grand political strategy. Only now they seriously addressed this folly by fabricating a rival but subservient Chinese government to undermine Chiang Kai-shek's regime. Military operations shifted to emphasis on bringing "peace and order" to the huge swaths of China now under nominal Japanese control. In Northern and Eastern China, the Japanese garrisons effectively controlled only cities and towns and kept open the roads and rail lines between them. Most of this landscape, however, remained a limbo area. The Chinese governments, both Nationalist coalition and Communist, claimed parts. Elsewhere bandits, puppet forces, and guerrilla units contended for dominance. Guerrillas, for example, operated in the hills just outside Beijing. In the long term, Tokyo aspired to reduce by half the 800,000 men now bogged down in China.

The paradox of Wuhan mystified Japanese officers at the time and Japanese historians since. The exhausted Japanese awakened to the horrifying reality that at enormous cost they had only procured a quagmire, not a victory. While the Chinese eventually lost Wuhan at a stupendous toll, they gained political strength and permanently shifted international opinion in their favor and against Japan. The Chinese achievement created expectations within the country about outside aid that never materialized. Wuhan also induced outside impressions of robust Chinese political unity and military effectiveness, but these impressions would sour in future years.

⁞

CHAPTER 4

"The Greatest Migration of People in All History"*

REFUGEE FLIGHT AND AMERICAN POLICY

Terror and the Masses

In the opening weeks of the war, the Japanese overran much of Northern China. In areas where they encountered little or no resistance, Japanese "conduct was excellent," observed British writer William H. Chamberlain. Moreover, those Chinese who fled their country's northern tier often expected just a brief absence. One poet, vividly reflecting the delusion shared by some intellectuals that once China resolved to fight, the Japanese would be swiftly overcome, declaimed: "Is war so dreadful? Not at all our four hundred million people are eagerly looking forward to its arrival. We welcome it because this is the time when we can liberate ourselves." But before many weeks had passed, it was not the Chinese bidding welcome to war, but war bidding welcome to a vast swath of Chinese.

Certainly, a multitude of massive upheavals littered China's long history. The late stages of the Qing dynasty included the Taiping (1850–1864), Nian (1851–1868), and Boxer (1898–1901) Rebellions as well as foreign interventions (like the 1839–1842 and 1856–1860 Opium Wars). More domestic convulsions roiled China after the Qing fall in 1911, including the regional or "warlord" struggles. These sowed devastation over the country and uprooted populations. Decades of war inured the Chinese masses to riptides of danger

---

* Lu Liu, "A Whole Nation Walking: The 'Great Retreat' in the War of Resistance, 1937–45," PhD diss., University of California–San Diego, 2002, 34–35, Proquest Information and Learning Company [hereafter Liu, "A Whole Nation Walking"].

to life and property, but that history also taught that however locally severe the slash marks, they never left more than scattered narrow scars over the sprawling expanse of the nation. During both the Taiping Rebellion (which produced as many as 30 million deaths) and again in the revolution of 1911, Qing armies torched Hankou, yet left the adjacent twin city of Wuchang unscathed. "By the twentieth century, urban populations in particular had learned to view war as an unwelcome guest or temporary pestilence that had to be waited out."

Regional soldiers instilled deep fears in the Chinese populace. Many regional leaders employed low or absent recruiting standards (they sometimes welcomed bandits and outlaws with predictable results), administered loose discipline at best, and provided erratic pay, leaving soldiers to seek other means of compensation. Not surprisingly, a regional army's presence featured looting. This paled, however, compared to the routine practice of murder, rape, and arson. Even such rote generic terms only faintly evoke the vivid horrors they perpetrated in beheading, dismemberment, disemboweling, eye gouging, flaying alive, and a bulging catalogue of grotesque mutilations. Chinese folklore of the period recorded the peoples' "cries [that] shook the earth" with a central mantra: "Burn, kill, rape, and rob; there was nothing they did not do."

But none of this history provided an adequate tutorial for the Japanese rampage that quantitatively rivaled and qualitatively outstripped the torments lashed upon the Chinese people from internal convulsion or Western imperialistic incursions since the mid-ninetieth century. Japanese soldiers possessed the mobility to range widely and rapidly by foot, animal, or motor, as well as firepower far beyond any prior entry in the millennia of Chinese chronicles. Perhaps most malevolent of all were Japanese aircraft, an utterly novel form of warfare for most Chinese. Between 15 August and 13 October 1937 alone, Japanese planes wreaked destruction on fifty-eight Chinese cities across nine provinces. A Chinese journalist recorded that many of his countrymen feared Japanese planes as though they were "ghosts and spirits."

The nearby sights and sounds of fighting animated Chinese civilians to take foot. But rumors that proved all too accurate of massive killing by Japanese troops galloped across the face of China—nominally on the pretext that males of military age were likely soldiers attempting to melt back into the population—and the dreadful fates of females, particularly young girls. These rumors persuaded most Chinese that the Japanese deliberately employed terror to break their will to resist. "After the Nanjing Massacre . . . many civilians were convinced," wrote historian Diana Lary, "that they too would be killed simply because they were Chinese, and that Japan was engaged in a race war against China." At one time, the Chinese had referred to Westerners encroaching on their land as "ocean devils," but now they referred to the Japanese as "devils," and their "tone was quite different, stark terror rather than bemusement." A famous Chinese newspaper of the era, *Dagong bao* (*L'Impartial*), declared this "the first war of the entire nation in Chinese history. In comparison, all those preceding were merely partial wars."

The most visible symbol of the havoc inflicted by Japan was the tidal wave of fleeing by terrorized individuals—many animated in what is now called "survivor flight" by direct experience. A Catholic priest described just one example of this near Xuzhou:

> On the road to the southwest, a long ribbon of ox carts stretches without interruption. This is the whole population of the North in flight. The women and children are on the carts, in the middle of bundles, baskets, sacks, chicks, goats, etc. Many are in tears, the children are crying. The men beat the oxen. [It is] impossible to stop, only to go on. In the middle of all this are incredible numbers of soldiers. To go faster, they pass through the wheat. One would say that there is no air. All is gloom. One only breathes the dust.

As correspondents Theodore White and Annalee Jacoby declared, this spectacle was "one of the greatest mass migrations in human history" and produced "a sight unmatched since the days of nomad hordes." The Chinese writer Lin Yutang flat out pronounced it "the greatest migration of people in all of history." But historian Stephen MacKinnon acknowledged "the anti-Japanese war did not produce a Chinese Tolstoy" to record this saga. Moreover, the war spawned political events that ironically suppressed the collection of data, the normal accretion of individual memories, and the production of formal written histories of this aspect—among many—of the war.

A girdle of twenty-one of China's thirty provinces, arching from Manchuria to the border of Indochina and far inland along the major waterways, fell in whole or in part under Japanese domination. The unrelenting march of Japanese soldiers and the visitations of its aviators uprooted many Chinese more than once. Refugee estimates range from an early and obviously incomplete and inaccurate figure of three million to a postwar figure of 95 million persons.* The most systematic calculations by the Nationalists in 1946 yielded figures of about 60 million in the initial two years of the struggle, with a grand total for the whole period of about 95 million, though these numbers enfold those enduring multiple moves. A judicious estimate by Dr. Lu Liu that the refugee total numbered about 45 million is probably very conservative but navigates these complexities as well as can be achieved. While China's prewar population numbered about 450 million, this stupendous surge spurted out from the perhaps 266 million or so Chinese within the territories overrun by Japan. By comparison, between 8 and 10 million French people of a population over 40 million fled the German attack in May–June 1940. In the Soviet Union, estimates of refugees during the German onslaught range from 7.5 to 25 million from a population of about 200 million.

The titanic forced migration of the first years of the war curled up in a trio of enormous waves. Between July and August 1937, the first crest billowed from the north generally to the south as the Japanese seized Beijing and regions east and south. The city of Jinan afforded a horrendous barometer of this phase. Its population doubled from 300,000 to more than 600,000 nearly overnight. But occupation by the Japanese put to flight all but about 100,000 of its inhabitants. The second wave constituted teeming urban populations from the East Central Coast, scrambling inland generally up the Yangtze valley. The total number of Chinese in this migration may have numbered about 16 million. Shanghai, for example, contributed approximately 600,000 panic-stricken civilians. Over half set out west while approximately 250,000 crammed into Shanghai's safety zones in the International Settlements. The third wave commenced in December 1937 and crashed through January 1938. The Nanjing massacre energized dense masses of survivors trekking toward Wuhan and Guangdong. A further wave from the north overlapped the hordes fleeing from the horrors in the Yangtze valley. When Guangdong fell in late 1938, Hong Kong and Macau suddenly absorbed about a million refugees.

Data on the composition of this vast exodus are sparse and contradictory.

---

* The common meaning of the word *refugee* is one who flees his home or country to seek refuge elsewhere in time of war, persecution, natural disaster, etc. Under modern international law, however, "refugee" has acquired legal baggage confining its application to those who leave the country of their nationality. A Chinese word for individuals fleeing within their own country is *"nanmin"* meaning "victim of catastrophe." The word *refugee* will be used here in its common English meaning and as an approximation of *nanmin*.

The swollen Wuhan population in 1938 appeared to mirror a fair cross section of China between rich and poor, urban and rural. A specific survey prepared in 1939 of refugees from Hunan disclosed a rough gender balance, with about one in three a child under age sixteen. But the survey also confirmed a stark dearth of persons over age sixty. One Nationalist official estimated that "cultural and educational workers accounted for 55 percent [of all refugees], government functionaries and employees of social institutions accounted for 21 percent, businessmen ten percent, and industrial workers six percent, while peasants only accounted for two percent." This estimate underscores the fact that the Japanese had seized the great intellectual centers of China, so that a disproportionate fraction of the refugees included "most of the important names in Chinese literary, art, drama, and university worlds." Likewise, most of the major national press fled the Japanese. Not surprisingly, these cadres of intellectuals not only complained loudly of their fate, but also reeled off many enduring accounts of their travails.

Besides the government functionaries, another category strongly represented was small businessmen and artisans. The self-employed benefited from a superior capacity to displace their work from one location to another and often possessed the financial resources to sustain distant movement. These heavily represented categories featured skills, talent, or financial mobility and backgrounds that explain why most refugees flowing into the interior settled into urban settings. Conversely, the underrepresentation of peasant farmers among the refugees, or at least those who fled over great distances, reflected their lack of financial resources and their tethers to the land necessary for simple survival, which precluded more than temporary absence.

The effects of this refugee flight and other depredations wreaked by the Japanese profoundly transformed Chinese society. At the opening of the war, 75–90 percent of Chinese resided in the countryside, where life quietly pulsed within the tight confines of centuries of calcified customs. Rural China remained not in the thrall of distant rulers or the gravitational tugs of modernity but of diverse religious beliefs. Peasants issued regular prayers to ancestors reverently remembered for guidance and temporal help and turned to fortune tellers before acquiring property or arranging marriages. They tilled the soil by hand and hauled their produce to market on their backs. They lived with their animals—without electricity, indoor plumbing, or safe water. They celebrated no weekly day of rest, for they measured the year not in weeks or months but by festivals, like the lunar New Year. Journeys commenced on auspicious days (like any date with a three in it). Their world revolved around extended families, the ideal being four generations under one roof, and the families in turn meshed with clans, a grouping which might connect land-lords to the poorest tenants. Deference extended to elders and to the gentry elite, though the basis for the elite's status now rested less on education than economic power. Only a small entering wedge of change affected the rigid subordinate status of women, who faced arranged marriage and polygamy as a norm. Clothes remained homespun cotton garments dyed blue (though the wealthy distinguished themselves with long gowns and jackets).

In the last decades of the nineteenth and first decades of the twentieth century, cracks emerged in this cocoon of ancient cultural, economic, and political systems swaddling China, though no one knew what would emerge when this cocoon finally shattered. Yet to most Chinese, these political changes touched their daily lives about as much as the cycle of the stars in the firmament. The fissures that would remake China emerged first in the treaty ports, eastern cities, and missionary schools (which provided coeducation). It was from these that modernity entered, bringing revolutionary changes in industry, transportation, and communications accompanied by stimulating and seductive Western ideas in science, medicine, literature, education, music, and popular culture.

Rising to the top of Chinese society by the 1930s was a thin crust of a Western-oriented, and in many cases, Western-educated urban elite. They wore Western clothes or Japanese style military jackets, men and women cut their hair short, and cigarette smoking became a major fad. They included intellectuals, engineers, and businessmen, and they clustered particularly in Beijing and Shanghai. They despised China's backwardness and subservience to foreign powers. They were painfully aware that, unlike the Manchu invaders who had barred intermarriage but adopted the culture, many if not all Westerners not only looked different but held Chinese culture in contempt. Ironically, they exploited the freedom of expression in foreign enclaves like Shanghai to publish criticism that they could never print in the heartland. As one historian acknowledged: "The early 1930's was the most open period that Mainland China has ever experienced, with the kind of freedom now seen only in Hong Kong and Taiwan." This vanguard class nurtured much anger and directed it particularly at Chiang and the Nationalists. The war would unmask a lingering ambivalence about ancient China even among this modernizing urban vanguard. Many city dwellers, even those several generations removed from country living, when taking flight would head for a rural ancestral home that most had never seen.

After the first weeks, and particularly after the fall of Shanghai, most refugees understood that their flight would be hard and not temporary. But even those prepared for "endless and incessant bitterness," as one man predicted, remained woefully unready for the physical and psychological distances they would ultimately traverse. Money, talent, and hard-earned social éclat might spur flight, but many Chinese believed the random pattern of survival reflected "fate (yuanfen), the mysterious force that many Chinese believed guided their lives." To become a refugee was like a blind leap onto a steep slide of unpredictable vector and length. The descent ruptured ties to family and geography; it ruthlessly stripped away wealth, privilege, and property; it dissolved marriages and "spawned desperate romance." Social and class lineages became unrecognizably mashed as merchants, soldiers, scholars, peasants, artisans, workers, and students joined, as one said, in a "fellowship of war and misfortune and hope."

Exhaustion and soon starvation became the most constant companions. One constant was that "at times of crisis, the family was the core default unit." This in turn led to soul-wrecking horrors described by journalist Freda Utley:

> Many [families] had been on the march for weeks, some for months. Families which had set out with five or six children had reached Hankou with only one or two. Small girl children were scarce; when the mother and father have no more strength to carry the little children, and when the smaller children were too exhausted to move another step, some have to be left on the road to die. . . . With what agony of mind must some children be abandoned so that the rest can be saved! Who can even imagine the infinite number of small individual tragedies amongst the millions who have been driven from their homes by the Japanese.

As nearly unimaginable as the abandonment of children during flight, there was a further horror in the experience of millions. Even in urban settings, Chinese still tried to adhere to an ideal of three or four generations living under one roof. Before setting out in flight, families faced the agonizing decision of whether elderly members should even attempt the movement. The figures collected on refugees indicate the answer was usually no—or that the elderly, as well as children, often were abandoned along the way.

Historian Stephen MacKinnon vividly described the long-term effects of this tumult:

> China's population was being forcefully redistributed and remixed. . . .
> Chinese who spoke different dialects and differed in class, educational, and regional backgrounds were being thrown together in new places and

new ways. . . . Thus the war was a great leveler, achieving more lasting change in the way of social, cultural, and linguistic integration between the urban and the rural than Mao Zedong's forced migration or *xiafang* campaigns of the 1950s and 1960s.

Despite the abrupt discontinuity with history that the mass flight evinced, and the countless severe-to-catastrophic individual traumas it produced, "[it] did not become a chaotic rout but rather unrolled with a great deal of dignity and endurance, as if ordinary Chinese people were trying to tell Japan that they could be defeated but not destroyed."

The Nationalist Response

The challenges presented by this mass refugee movement proved important to both the immediate and ultimate fortunes of the Nationalist government and for the long-term arc of China's modern nation-building. The first response of the Nationalist government to the refugee issue occurred in early September 1937. Nanjing established the Emergency Refugee Relief Commission (*feichang shiqi nanmin jiuji weiyuanhui*). Initially the organization played the traditional role of providing overall supervision, while local organizations provided actual services. One of these local organizations was an international committee in Shanghai under French Catholic priest Pere Jacquinot. But a consortium of local Chinese benefactors from the Chinese local elite (to include gangsters) set up the Union of All-Shanghai Voluntary Agencies, which soon operated sixty relief stations servicing a half-million persons. Notwithstanding these efforts, the breakdown of sanitation and sustenance throughout the city produced at least 100,000 civilian deaths by the end of the year.

The shortcomings disclosed in the Shanghai relief experience provoked pointed criticism by both the media and local elites that the state must play a direct relief role. This proved critical to the evolution of the wartime welfare policies of the Nationalist government. The displacement of the government to Wuhan enforced a hiatus in central government action, but still louder demands for action marked this pause, and they were boosted by the direct example in the streets of Wuhan. On 23 April 1938, the Nationalist government created the Development and Relief Commission (*Zhenji weiyuanhui* [DRC]), which superseded prior government organizations. The DRC would have been historically significant simply by interjecting the state directly into the provision of relief. But its mandate went far beyond that. In an address to DRC officials, H. H. Kung, president of the Executive Yuan, stated: "The government is duty bound to do all the work related to [the refugees'] alleviation and relief. There is no shirking this responsibility." To this end, the DRC "developed a gigantic new welfare complex to provide refugees with medical care, housing, transportation, logistical support, job placement, development projects, small loans, child care centers and nursery schools, education in state-supported schools, and hostels for overseas Chinese returnees."

Bypassing customary civil administrative structures, the DRC created a transit system based on emerging battle zones in Northern and Eastern China. The DRC established eight relief zones and delineated specific routes for civilian evacuation, provided relief stations along the routes, and assigned refugees a certain destination. In the peak of refugee flight during 1938–1941, at least 26 million refugees received help from some institution, with about 70 percent relying on the DRC. By early 1941, the DRC claimed it supported more than nine million persons.

Between 1937 and 1940, the heretofore historically crucial role of native-place associations as providers of direct relief entered what proved to be a permanent decline—a development working in parallel with a profound change in the identification of the average Chinese. At the beginning of the war, many residents of small cities and rural hamlets impressed contemporary intellectuals with their lack of national consciousness. "Who did a better job in the battle, Chinese or Japanese?" This sort of detached observation characterized multitudes of nonurban Chinese as well as many refugees. But the mission assigned by the Nationalist government to the DRC included linking the practical provision of aid to a larger narrative and bolstering national strength. The refugees were imbued gradually with the notion that they were not simply the victims of a calamity, but warriors in a conflict for national salvation.

The spread of a national rather than a regional identity among the refugees and the expansion of state responsibility over civil society would ultimately prove to be very mixed blessings for the Nationalists. As the refugees recognized their new status as warriors serving the nation, they also draped around themselves the mantle of moral superiority attained by their undoubted sacrifice. They demanded the government banish the term *refugees* for the title *people of righteousness* (*yi min*) and redesignate the DRC relief facilities as "stations for righteous people." This change of self-perception presaged increased demands that the Nationalist government ultimately could not meet fully.

Moreover, it was part of another sensibility that the war spread through the nation: geographically defined patriotism. Lin Wenbang, a clerk on the

Beijing-Hankou railroad, evacuated with the Nationalist army to the interior. Noting, however, that many who originally accompanied him had returned, he wrote to the publication, "The Resistance," as follows:

> In a time of national resistance against the Japanese, to sacrifice all that we have is our duty as citizens. We should embrace all the hardships and fight together with our compatriots. . . . If you only think of personal safety now and thus betray [the country] to serve the Japanese, how will you face your nationalist compatriots in the future when we win the war? At that time, not only will you be despised and cursed by your fellow countrymen, but your descendants also [will] be disgraced generation after generation.

The massive flight of tens of millions of Chinese before the Japanese advances is a fundamental turning point in modern Chinese history. For the state, it led to unprecedented levels of centralized power and a new direct commitment to the provision of relief measures. For the society, it proved a potent impetus to creating a national rather than a local or regional identity. For the individual, it inflicted severe damage to the ancient primary identity with a multigenerational family and clan and commenced a profound psychological slide toward atomization that would permit the herding of the population for a quarter century after 1949 into social and economic experiments, some of which proved stupendously destructive.

By late 1938, much of the world knew that flight and mass death formed defining characteristics of Japan's war in China. A Japanese poet and nationalist, Yonejiro Noguchi, wrote to the Bengali poet Rabindranath Tagore to defend his nation's actions. Tagore, a polymath and the first non-Westerner to win the Nobel Prize in literature in 1913, denounced Noguchi's justifications for Japan's path in one searing sentence: "You are building your conception of an Asia which would be raised on a tower of skulls."

A Turning Point in America's China Policy

Concomitant with the fraught changes in Chinese society in the first two years of war, a fundamental change in China's role in the Far East transpired. President Herbert Hoover viewed the 1931 seizure of Manchuria as not just morally reprehensible, but as a blunt assault on the entire post–World War I global peace structure. Hoover's concern focused on two treaties: the

Nine-Power Treaty (part of the 1922 Washington agreements), which promised China's independence and provided equal-trade opportunities for foreign nations in China (codifying internationally the American "Open Door Policy"), and the Kellogg-Briand Pact (1928) that purported to outlaw war. Both, but particularly the latter, rested on the concept that "world opinion" constituted the enforcing mechanism—not military threats or countermeasures. The Japanese annexation of Manchuria thus struck at the heart of the reigning American conceit that it could rely on cool tangible paper and heated intangible moral umbrage to prevent or reverse armed aggression.

Hoover sought earnestly for some measure to validate the credibility of the treaty structure. He immediately ruled out force (his military subordinates told him a war with Japan would take four years) as well as economic sanctions that would only light a fuse that would detonate a war. Chinese resistance to Japan's aggression largely evaporated, vitiating both moral and pragmatic arguments about defending Chinese sovereignty. All of these considerations ultimately yielded a "Non-recognition Doctrine"—the United States would refuse to recognize the changes in Manchuria wreaked by force. When Roosevelt became president in 1933, he gratefully accepted the "Non-recognition Doctrine" inheritance from Hoover.

Roosevelt, like Hoover, faced severe curbs on his options. On the one hand, some Americans argued that the United States should simply abandon any interests in the Far East. In 1936 the US investment in China amounted to $298.8 million, just 8.6 percent of total foreign investment in China. Since overtaking Great Britain in 1931, Japan stood first ($1,394 million or 40 percent) and Great Britain second ($1,220.8 million or 35 percent). Those opposing American involvement in the Sino-Japanese War ridiculed the paltry US investment ("slightly more than we paid for chewing gum [in 1936]" remarked one). Only roughly 3 percent of American overseas trade was with China. Japan ("far and away our best customer in the Far East," explained the anti-interventionist New York Daily News) accounted for four to five times that total. The 1934 Tydings-McDuffie Act, promising the Philippines independence after a ten-year transition (with US naval base rights for two further years), stood as another landmark of aversion to Asian involvement. It would extract the United States from its morally ambiguous adventure in colonialism, remove a potential flash point for war, and halt a drain on the US treasury.

As full-scale war in China erupted in 1937, the Roosevelt administration initially maintained its posture of expounding principles but taking no meaningful action to implement them. Meanwhile, American public opinion swiftly tilted overwhelmingly toward China. An August 1937 Gallup poll showed 55 percent of Americans volunteered sympathy to neither side, 43 percent to China, and 2 percent to Japan. But by February 1940, fully 76 percent of Americans sympathized with China, 22 percent professed indifference and a still minuscule 2 percent favored Japan.

From a historical—not to mention a racial—context, this marked American affinity for China appears inexplicable. The American national census of 1940 disclosed a population of 132,164,569. Of this total, just 77,504 (0.05 percent) were persons of Chinese descent and 126,947 were persons of Japanese descent (0.08 percent). No person of Chinese descent occupied any commanding political, economic, or cultural position. A lengthy and bitter history of anti-Chinese discrimination from the nineteenth century culminated in the Chinese Exclusion Act of 1882 and a legal ban on Asian immigration in 1924. But what has been called the American romance with China also stretches back to at least the colonial period, with exotic Chinese themes common in interior decoration. Indeed, sophisticated American art collectors exhibited a marked preference for Chinese art over its pre-Columbian, African, Indian, Southeast Asian, or Islamic rivals.

Tangible factors shaping American opinion included exposure to graphic images in the newsreels most Americans saw on average about twice a week when they attended the movies. Up until Pearl Harbor, the visual library available to Americans contained vastly more searing images of Japanese depredations in China than those of Germany in Europe. Another multidimensional factor was religion. The prospect of mass conversion of Chinese to Christianity—and a corollary belief that the Chinese particularly aspired to be like Americans—enthralled a vast number of devoted Americans and energized a potent missionary movement. Madame Chiang was a Methodist and Chiang was widely depicted as a model convert. Henry Luce's publications, *Time* and *Life*, featured the American religious connection to China and particularly China's leader and his wife. (Later assertions that Chiang's Christian leanings were purely for show are belied by his diaries). Yet another factor shaping American opinion was communications by missionaries in China back to congregations in the United States. Although its scope and impact are hard to document, this channel existed and exerted the power of its very personal accounts.

Even among the staunch opponents of overseas intervention, the stories and images from China prompted revulsion. Former president Herbert Hoover in November 1938 denounced Japan's war in China for being as horrible "as that of Genghis Khan." The *Chicago Tribune* newspaper classified

Japan's actions in China as on par with those of Hitler's persecutions or Stalin's murder of millions. But moral outrage generated less impetus for Roosevelt's reaction than the niche China filled in a much broader global pattern: Italy and Germany on an aggressive march. In a 5 October 1937 address thereafter called the "quarantine speech," Roosevelt declared:

> It would seem to be unfortunately true that the epidemic of world lawlessness is spreading. When an epidemic of physical disease starts to spread the community approves and joins in a quarantine of the patients in order to protect the health of the community against the spread of the disease.

Roosevelt left a typically muddled record as to what exactly he meant by a "quarantine." He fruitlessly solicited some form of a joint naval blockade from the British, but London, riveted on Hitler, dismissed a potentially explosive move in the Far East. The president likewise assessed sanctions, but rejected this by September, when he lamented to Secretary of the Interior Harold Ickes that, as to Spain or China, "what has happened in those countries has happened" and he planned no active measures.

The "quarantine" speech sparked a public uproar that swiftly forced Roosevelt to backpedal. The term *isolationist* became the damning label slapped on those Americans who opposed what they regarded as Roosevelt's march to war. They rejected the "isolationist" appellation for what they deemed a more accurate identification as "anti-interventionists" or "noninterventionists." In the apt phrase of historian Justus Doenecke, there were "many mansions of anti-interventionism," for it canvassed a diverse set of viewpoints spanning the full ideological spectrum. On the extreme right were a few tens of thousands of individuals who joined outfits like the Silver Shirts or the German-American Bund, openly supporting Hitler and Germany. On the extreme left, the Communist Party USA, marching in lockstep to Moscow's orders, would first advocate action against Germany, then after the August 1939 Soviet-German Pact stridently oppose Roosevelt's efforts to support China and the Western Allies, only to turn literally overnight in June 1941 with Hitler's attack on the Soviet Union to shrieks for every manner of action against Germany.

But far right and left organizations formed no more than a fraction of Americans opposing US participation in overseas hostilities. By the numbers, the Midwest and members of the Republican Party formed the main strongholds for these views. But they were by no means confined by geography, political affiliation, employment, or class. Representative Hamilton Fish, from the congressional district of Roosevelt's personal residence in Hyde Park, New York, figured prominently, as did Senator Burton K. Wheeler, a Democrat from Montana. The most prominent labor leader in the country, John L. Lewis of the United Mine Workers, lent his mesmerizing voice in opposition, but so did various business leaders.

The fundamental starting point for understanding "anti-interventionism" is to acknowledge it as a core component of traditional American foreign policy for a century and a half. Socioeconomic factors provided the bedrock foundation for this tradition. An overwhelmingly agrarian, small-community America formed for most Americans a basic perspective that recognized few vital links to a wider world. Moreover, two vast oceans flanking the continent and the technology of transportation and communications conferred decades of insulation from overseas events.

This traditional foreign policy featured two major prongs that enjoyed almost universal popular and political support: nonintervention in Europe and unilateralism. Excepting the expeditionary force in 1917–1918, for 150 years no American troops had fought in Europe. After extinguishing its alliance with France following the American Revolution, the country abjured what Thomas Jefferson called "entangling alliances." But far from viewing "unilateral" as a synonym for unconstrained or even reckless, "isolationists" believed that "unilateral" action served to preserve American sovereignty and, critically, was consonant with the American concept of democracy, because such actions would be subject to direct review by the American people rather than outsourcing American policy to foreign bodies or peoples.

But the term *isolationist* grotesquely distorted this viewpoint by implying that those sharing this traditional perspective wished to seal off the United States hermetically from relations with the rest of the world. Some "anti-interventionists" had no intention of snipping off international credit relations or trade. Others were keenly attentive to foreign affairs. What perhaps surprises most novices to these events is the fact that prior to 1940 the majority of the best-recognized spokesmen for the so-called "isolationists"—such as Senators William Borah, Hiram Johnson, George Norris, and Gerald Nye—were "progressives" and irregular Roosevelt allies on domestic issues.

During the 1940 election, the America First Committee emerged as the foremost anti-interventionist grouping. When it disbanded on 11 December 1941, it fielded 450 units with total membership of approximately a quarter-million. While "progressives" like Norris, Wheeler, and Nye continued to speak out prominently, America First particularly featured staunch conservatives, like the famous aviator Charles A. Lindbergh (who only joined in April 1941). This evolution accounts for the fact that "isolationism" became mistakenly linked almost solely to conservatives and Roosevelt's opponents on domestic issues, when the fact is that the "anti-interventionists" were a far more ideologically diverse grouping.

The domestic and foreign policy visions of "progressives" among the "anti-interventionists" shared several features. Perhaps above all, they feared bigness and concentrated power. They found virtue in individualism, rural and small-town denizens, workers over employers, debtors over creditors, small but not large businesses, democracy over monarchy or authoritarian governments, legislative over executive or judicial branches, and equality over special privilege of any sort. Their lineage clearly fitted classical Jeffersonians, not Hamiltonians. Their bêtes noires included the big cities, Wall Street, the East, and Europe—with England cast as Lucifer incarnate. A minority of "anti-interventionists," as exemplified by Senator Hiram Johnson of California, shared with Roosevelt a dark and long-standing suspicion of Japan and were prepared to exempt Asia or Latin America from their general opposition to intervention.

As a historic tide in America, "isolationism" crested just as dramatic strides in naval and air power provided aggressive foreign powers with the ability to vault the natural moats provided by the Atlantic and Pacific Oceans. The mid-1930s atmosphere of disillusionment with the outcome of World War I and the apparent discrediting of capitalism by the Great Depression led to articles and books weaving these two threads together in the charge that "merchants of death" allegedly deceived the nation into entry into World War I. "Progressive" Senator Gerald Nye of North Dakota chaired a sensational set of hearings that probed into the role in American participation in World War I of munitions makers and financiers as well as US military and civilian officials. In the words of a fellow senator, the hearings were "probably the most effective medium for channeling American public opinion into isolationism during this period."

Turmoil in Europe proved a catalyst for specific legislation in the Neutrality Acts. While the 1935 and 1936 editions were temporary, in 1937 Congress adapted a "permanent" neutrality law applicable to international conflicts and civil wars, designed to prohibit the type of events alleged to have pulled America into World War I. This legislation imposed a mandatory arms embargo on foreign wars, a ban on loans and credits to belligerents, and a ban on travel by Americans on belligerent ships. The new law further proscribed the arming of American merchant ships trading with belligerents and the use of American ships to carry arms to belligerents. It did allow the president discretion to permit sale of nonembargoed goods to belligerents on a "cash and carry basis." This meant the title to the items had to be transferred to non-American hands, and then the items had to be transported to the belligerents in non-American ships.

While broad public opposition to entanglement in the Sino-Japanese war, spearheaded by "anti-interventionists," presented a huge impediment to more active US policy, Roosevelt manufactured another himself. Interpreting his huge electoral victory in 1936 as a virtually unlimited mandate, he attempted a "court packing" plan to empower him to appoint more justices to change fundamentally the ideological composition of the Supreme Court and halt its nullifications of his domestic agenda. A large majority of Americans, including many customary allies, found this proposal a terrifying strike at one of the most fundamental tenets of the constitution, the separation of powers. Roosevelt suffered a humiliating rebuke when the Democrat-controlled Congress rejected the plan. Then the economy plunged downward, reversing gains since 1933, an event viewed as linked to Roosevelt's policies. Finally, Roosevelt permitted his frustrations to override his normally acute political judgment in an extremely ill-conceived effort to purge certain conservative Democratic senators by endorsing their primary challengers. Roosevelt's favorites lost nearly across the board. Thus, within the span of a year after his triumphant reelection, the president almost singlehandedly squandered his vast political capital on domestic matters and even undercut his leadership on foreign affairs.

This background set the parameters for Roosevelt's initial reactions to the Sino-Japanese War. At the Brussels Nine-Power Conference in November 1937, Roosevelt wished to validate the sanctity of treaties but would not back that goal with coercion in any form on the basis that neither Congress nor the people would accept such action. The next month an event confirmed that Roosevelt's acute sense of public opinion had revived. The USS *Panay*, a gunboat designed for China river patrols, was about twenty-eight miles up the Yangtze River from Nanjing on the morning of 12 December 1937. Besides the mission of evacuating Americans from Nanjing, *Panay* was also engaged in protecting US property in the form of three Standard Oil river tankers. Although the ship was clearly marked with two large American flags painted on canvas awnings, Japanese naval aircraft led by Lt. Shigeharu Murata (who would lead Japanese torpedo bombers in the Pearl Harbor raid exactly four

years less five days later) attacked and sank it with two bomb hits. Two crewmen and one civilian died; forty-three crew and five civilians were wounded.*

The Japanese government declared the attack a completely inadvertent
mistake and offered a formal apology and $2,214,007 in reparations for the
Panay and for the oil tankers sunk or damaged with it. (To quell the crisis,
at Roosevelt's request, Universal Pictures edited its dramatic newsreel footage of the attack to eliminate sequences showing Japanese aircraft passing so
close to the *Panay* that the pilots' faces were visible, potent evidence that the
mistaken identity claim was not true.) An Imperial Army officer in the vicinity, Col. Kingoro Hashimoto, a founder of one of the right-wing secret societ-
ies in Japan, ordered firing on the *Panay* as it was sinking as well as on British
vessels whose identities he knew. There were repercussions for the Japanese
naval officers, though not severe, but none against Hashimoto.

Reports of the incident, complete with dramatic newsreel footage of part of
the attack and of the *Panay* sinking, prompted a reaction in the United States
that illustrates the frigid temperature of public opinion toward foreign hostilities, even in the face of a clear act of war. Pending at that time before the
House of Representatives was the Ludlow Amendment to the Constitution. It
would require that if a declaration of war passed the Congress, it would then
be submitted to the American people for a referendum to make it effective, in
the absence of a direct attack on the nation. The amendment had been bottled
up in a congressional committee. News of the *Panay* Incident energized its
supporters to force a record vote on a measure to bring it to the floor of the
House for debate. This procedural action was narrowly voted down (209 to
188) on 10 January 1938.

The vote on the Ludlow Amendment represented a watershed unrecognized at that time. For four years, the "anti-interventionists" had dictated
successfully a legislative agenda of neutrality measures designed to keep
the United States out of war. The defeat of the Ludlow Amendment, however, marked a momentum swing. From here on out, Roosevelt and his allies

---

* The Standard Vacuum Oil Company river tankers were the *Mei Ping*, *Mei Hsia*, and *Mei
An*, each about 1,000 tons displacement. Irvine H. Anderson Jr. highlights one customarily
neglected fact about this episode. The trio carried about eight hundred Chinese employees
of Standard Vacuum Oil and their families. Besides *Panay*, Japanese aircraft sank all three of
these riverboats as well as two of four other small company-owned craft. Presumably losses
were high among these passengers, but apart from the Caucasian master of *Mei An*, they go
unmentioned in the records. *The Standard-Vacuum Oil Company and United States East Asian
Policy, 1933–1941* (Princeton: Princeton University Press, 1975), 107–8.

would fight many hard battles against the "anti-interventionists." But henceforth, Roosevelt would be acting and the "anti-interventionists" reacting.

And at the end of 1937 and into 1938, China gifted to Roosevelt a strikingly new foundation for US policy. Up to the fall of 1937, US policymakers viewed China solely as a potential prize, not as a participant in the Far Eastern strategic competition. As the Battle for Shanghai entered September and then continued into October, American diplomats and military and naval attachés shed their accustomed images of the ineffectiveness of Chinese arms and the inevitability of Chinese concessions. The key figure was US Marine Capt. Evans Carlson. He combined perhaps the greatest emotional commitment to China of any American observer with direct access to Roosevelt. As a junior officer, Carlson established a personal bond with Roosevelt as commander of the Marine detachment at Roosevelt's Warm Springs, Georgia, home. That assignment also secured for him the friendship of Roosevelt's son James and particularly his personal secretary Marguerite "Missy" LeHand. "To have her favor was the best possible channel to [Roosevelt's] attention," wrote John Gunther. Carlson's letters, ostensibly addressed to LeHand, routinely became Roosevelt reading material, and Roosevelt even read some of Carlson's letters to his cabinet. Carlson wrote to the president from China that the Chinese soldiers were doing "remarkably well," while declaring the new unity of China "unbelievable." (Neither of these views was a fiction at that time.) The crusty American head military attaché, Col. Joseph W. Stilwell, proved a greater skeptic, but by November even he admitted that "nothing less than a miracle" could make true his early prognostication that China would quickly fold.

These weeks also produced a momentous change in the attitude of Stanley Hornbeck, a key State Department official in Far Eastern affairs. Heretofore, the absence of Chinese resistance had prompted Hornbeck to counsel American distance from China's abuse at Japanese hands. But now, with evidence of Chinese resolve, Hornbeck swung toward the role he would play over the next four years as a vigorous and persistent advocate of stalwart support for China.

Defeat in Shanghai and the loss of Nanjing administered a "serious blow to Chinese morale and American hopes." These twin strokes drove Chiang from his main power and financial bases just as news leaked out of the attempted Trautmann mediation. "Things look very black again" reported the American military attaché office. The American ambassador to China, Nelson T. Johnson, cabled gloom to Washington: Japan would conquer China and soon. Johnson's second secretary opined: "China is helpless and China as an independent nation is finished."

Then in March and April 1938 American optimism rebounded. The protracted defense of Xuzhou was followed by outright victory at Taierzhuang. Carlson particularly trumpeted Taierzhuang as evidence not only that China would continue to fight, but that it might prevail. Even Stilwell admitted that "it is possible for China to win." Though Taierzhuang represented the sole reasonably clear Chinese victory in 1938, while the long Wuhan campaign ended in Chinese defeat, newfound American confidence in China remained unshaken. The resilience of American optimism might seem oddly disconnected from the facts of individual engagements, and no doubt mirrors American bias toward China. But it does not seem fallacious when considered against the Imperial Headquarters admission at the end of 1938 that Japan could not force a conclusion to the war by military means. The implications of the radically new American perspective of China as a player in Far Eastern geopolitics, not merely a victimized bystander, would swell to huge significance by the fall of 1941. But in the short term, an effort spearheaded by Secretary of the Treasury Henry Morgenthau produced the first important tangible American support for China: a $25 million loan for arms purchases.

CHAPTER 5

:

"A Despicable Urge to Live!"

1939: A YEAR OF ATTRITION

New Year, New War

Accounts of the Sino-Japanese conflict after 1938 speak often of stalemate. This framework is valid if measured by the modest changes in territories occupied by Japan after 1938 (excepting 1944) and the fact that Japanese energies veered from pursuit of military decision toward consolidation and a political program to undermine the Nationalists. But the dying by no means halted or sharply declined, particularly during 1939–1940. Nationalist figures, while imperfect, still disclose a crowded roll of battles, with casualties averaging 50,000 per month, only 10,000 fewer than during the span from the Battle of Shanghai to the fall of Wuhan.

The first notable event on the 1939 calendar was the resignation of Prime Minister Konoe, triggered by the obdurate refusal of the military to provide him with information or policy input on the China War. The emperor issued an Imperial Order for Konoe's choice, Kiichiro Hiranuma, the chairman of the Privy Council, to form a new government. Proclaiming his goal as "national unity," the new prime minister, once counted among the most radical right-wing nationalists, proved cautious and moderate.

For the long term, Chiang recognized that defeating the "dwarf pirates" depended as much on his diplomatic skill as on his battlefield prowess. China could not defeat Japan alone. It must acquire allies and the obvious candidates were those nations plainly athwart Japan's Asian ambitions: the Soviet Union, the United Kingdom, and the United States. Mao's thinking ran broadly along the same lines. "China's strength alone," he remarked, "will not be sufficient to defeat [the Japanese], and we shall also have to rely on the support of inter-national forces." But Mao presumably thought the outside help would come from only the Soviet Union or perhaps other Marxist revolutionary forces—maybe even including a revolt in Japan.

Meanwhile, the Nationalists looked to establish a solid base for a war of endurance. The densely populated and agriculturally self-sufficient Sichuan province, with no feasible rail or river approaches for the Japanese, became the foundation of resistance. But a chain of now ten "War Zones" radiated out from this base, forming barriers confronting the Japanese along the entire perimeter of Japanese-occupied territory. These "War Zones" forced the Jap-anese to disperse their forces. They interdicted rail lines connecting Japa-nese occupied territories. They also protected Chinese supply lines from the Soviet Union in the North (where the Nationalists shifted a concentration of forces) and from Burma and Indochina in the South. Further, the Chi-nese now turned in earnest to creating guerrilla areas to harass the Japanese, maintain political sway over populations under Japanese occupation, and keep the entire nation engaged in war. Finally, to refurbish their armies for a protracted conflict, the Nationalists instituted a program of reducing field forces by one-third, coupled to an intensified retraining program.

Chiang and his Nationalists met the challenge of devising a sound mili-tary strategy for waging protracted war with Japan. Dealing with the severe economic perils birthed by the struggle proved far more intractable. Unlike its Western and Japanese rivals, the Qing Dynasty never mastered the task of extracting massive tax revenues. The Qing relied on two major sources of income: the land tax and customs duties. By the late nineteenth century the land tax was mired in hopeless inefficiency and pervasive corruption. By the twentieth century customs duties provided the major conduit of wealth for the national government. Due to gross mismanagement, however, creditors forced the Qing dynasty to place administration of this bountiful stream into British hands to service foreign loans and the regime's debts. Supplementing the flow from customs duties was a hodgepodge of taxes on agricultural prod-ucts and consumer items as well as internal transit duties.

The financial situation of the Nationalist government improved dramati-cally after T. V. Soong (Song Ziwen) took charge of finances. He established the Central Bank of China and imposed monetary reform, and, most impor-tantly, his skilled negotiations extracted autonomy on tariffs from foreign governments in 1928 in exchange for abolition of the land tax. The National-ist government fiscal year ending on 30 June 1937, just a week prior to the Marco Polo Bridge Incident, reflected total revenues of 739 million yuan

(Chinese dollars) or about 222 million US dollars. The government obtained barely under 50 percent of its total revenue from customs duties, one-quarter from the salt tax, and one-fifth from the "consolidated tax."[*] The remainder, approximately 5 percent, flowed from a combination of taxes on tobacco and wine, stamps, income, and mining. But the Nationalist budget still reflected a 37 percent deficit of expenditure over revenue.

The war inflicted an "economic catastrophe" on the Nationalist regime. The Japanese occupied most of the economically productive regions of China and particularly its great ports. Consequently, tax receipts from customs duties by one calculation plummeted by 85 percent. Of the other two major revenue sources in the 1930s, the salt tax receipts withered by 65 percent while the "consolidated tax" fell by 90 percent. This would leave the government with only 20 to 25 percent of its prewar income. The Nationalists faced just two dire choices: radically cut expenditures (an impossibility if the war was to continue), or print money (and unleash the demon of inflation). A Nationalist yuan plummeted in value from thirty cents per dollar in 1937 to four cents in 1941. The attempt to control expenditures by capping salaries of government workers and soldiers slashed the economic status of precisely those people the regime most depended upon for support.

The war also ravaged the foundations of the nation's internal economy. Battle (including Chinese "scorched-earth tactics") and bombing so disrupted rail- and water-borne transportation that long distance internal trade virtually ceased. In the swiftly occupied areas, the war inflicted less direct damage to transportation, but the occupiers cut merchants off from customary interior markets and imposed discriminatory preferences for Japanese and Korean businesses. The resulting seesaw effect on prices, particularly in the Yangtze Valley, spread havoc both there and in many other areas. Prices collapsed in areas vastly oversupplied with fish or rice, while prices pitched into a steep upward climb in areas of deficit.

Another scourge unleashed by war was looting that vastly exceeded any experience from the "warlord" era. An observer in Suzhou, an exceptionally wealthy city, wrote in 1937:

> Between November 21st and December [11th] we went into [Suzhou] nearly every day. We saw that every bank and shop, every residence had

---

[*] The items in the "consolidated tax" were: rolled tobacco, cotton yarn, flour, matches, cement, and cured tobacco.

been forced open. Japanese soldiers were passing in and out of them like ants loaded down with bales of silk, eiderdown quilts, shop goods and household effects of every description.

Looting as well as battle stripped vast numbers of Chinese families of "records, books, letters and mementoes." The loss of these irreplaceable objects, the tangible symbols of revered lineage stretching back, in many cases, numberless generations, inflicted on countless Chinese not just present pain but the ceaseless agony of parting from the treasured past.

The Chinese "Dunkirk"

One of the Chinese epics of the war took place off the battlefield: the evacuation of Chinese industry into the interior. China's modest industrial development proliferated overwhelmingly along the coast and in a few great river cities. The 1932 Battle of Shanghai served notice to Chiang and the Nationalists that a sustained conflict with Japan demanded a plan to transport China's existing industrial infrastructure to the interior coupled to a program to locate new industries in strategic depth. Two major existing arsenals displaced inland during 1932–1933, but then the program halted to maintain production to nourish Chiang's campaigns against the Communists.

Through the middle 1930s new construction projects, particularly featuring vital metals (like tungsten, steel, and copper), coal, oil, electrical manufacturing, and machines, appeared only in Central China—not near the coast. Directing this development program, unprecedented in China's history, was the National Resources Committee (*ziyuan weiyuanhui*) (NRC). The head of this body was Dr. Wenhao Weng, China's first PhD in geology. American journalists described him as "a tiny man, a scholarly doodler. He had a deep cleft in his forehead that made him oddly attractive, and his smile was unfailing." In later war years he remained one of few officials never accused of corruption.

Deeply impressed with Weng's pioneering reports on China's natural resources, Chiang attempted to entice Weng into the Nationalist state bureaucracy. But Weng, like most other academics in the first decades of the twentieth century, maintained his independence from a bureaucracy that had fallen from a pinnacle of power and prestige in the late imperial era due to corrupted standards within the recruiting system and the stigma of associations with unpopular government. "For the sake of the anti-communist cause," however,

Weng signed on as head of the NRC in 1932 and eventually would rise to be minister of economic affairs. His reputation for probity brought in a galaxy of other talented individuals. In the 1930s the NRC comprehensively audited China's physical and human resources for their war utility. The effort especially focused on Western China, where military strategists were planning to fight a protracted war against Japan. The NRC forms a milestone in the history of modern China. It validated the concepts of enlisting outside technical expertise and central planning for at least the military-industrial sector, and it proved a means of advancing state control over society.

The outbreak of war in July 1937, however, aborted the NRC's master plan for military construction in Central China. Chiang turned to Weng to direct the evacuation of existing industrial infrastructure. Weng tackled the immediate issue of extricating Shanghai's trove of industries (1,279 private factories alone)—indeed, purchasing time for Weng's program provided one reinforcing reason for Chiang to conduct a major battle there. Arsenals stood out as the obvious priority for evacuation. Jiyong Liu, the former dean of an engineering college, spearheaded the effort. The heroic sacrifices of industrial workers awed him, an attitude likewise emphasized in China's media. Amidst Japanese bombs, Liu reported that the workers "seeing their colleagues die, they simply move the corpse aside and keep working with tears in their eyes. Cold machines are painted with warm blood." Before Shanghai's fall, 146 factories with 14,600 tons of machinery and 2,500 technicians migrated inland, mostly to Wuhan. At least sixty other factories migrated from North, East, and South China to the interior.

Liu also praised those industrialists trying to move their establishments as "zealous for the common weal and steadfastly pursuing righteousness." But later criticism stressed the fact that the 146 factories represented only about 11 percent of Shanghai's total. Ire rained upon those industrialists who failed to act for lack of patriotism (or just plain selfishness). "The large majority of industrialists . . . preferred the amenities of Hong Kong or of the International Settlement in Shanghai to the rigors and uncertainties of the interior," noted historian Lloyd Eastman acidly. But the major reasons why more factories were not evacuated were that many fell outside the NRC's priority list of essential military industries, lack of transportation resources, and lack of government funds to sustain the evacuation. Liu cogently argued that those unable to evacuate even for valid reasons could still have destroyed their enterprise rather than let it slip into Japanese hands.

A second major phase of industrial evacuation transpired with the loss of Wuhan. From January 1938, the NRC prepared for a mass retreat of industries from Wuhan. Infected with the patriotic fevers of Wuhan, industrialists proved markedly more receptive to evacuation than their counterparts in Shanghai. No fewer than 170 migrant industries and 150 local Wuhan factories departed from Wuhan. But the great obstacle to evacuation was transportation. With military operations monopolizing 95 percent of river steamer capacity, about 170 factories moved by water or rail southwest or northwest. The 138 factories, totaling 130,000 tons of equipment, and 10,000 workers that displaced up the Yangtze became a symbol of resolute resistance hailed as "China's Dunkirk Retreat."

The greatest hero of this effort was Zuofu Lu, the entrepreneur who created Minsheng, a Yangtze transportation company. With his savvy and salesmanship, his company and an armada of 850 wooden junks, like the "splinter fleet" of Dunkirk, would haul nearly 200,000 tons of materials (including sixteen arsenals) and 1.5 million persons out of Wuhan before the last stage of the retreat. Although, as at Dunkirk, the larger steam-powered vessels rescued the most men, the Chinese, like the English, were enthralled by the role of the small craft. National pride swelled over the image of knots of tow-rope pullers "walking on rocks hundreds of feet above the river line" as the junks were dragged over shoals and through whirlpools. "We were embracing chilly winds, sweating all over our bodies, blood boiling, breathing out hot air," recalled one, "our backs higher than our heads." Those industrialists, technical experts, and workers who moved into the interior were hailed as patriots. This formed part of a critical element of the state's new definition of pure patriotism: true Chinese identified themselves by where they arrayed themselves geographically. Those who remained in Japanese-occupied territory invited the label of "traitors."

Hainan, Nanchang, and Changsha

Mutual exhaustion after the 1938 fighting induced a four-month lull, broken by the Japanese capture of Hainan Island, just off the coast of Guangdong province. This oval-shaped island measures about 160 miles east to west and about 130 miles north to south. With all regular Chinese troops redeployed to other regions, the Japanese landing in February 1939 quickly dispersed local militia units. The Japanese installed air bases and commenced attacks to interdict supplies flowing north from French Indochina.

The next series of battles commenced in the spring of 1939 for the strategic southern Yangtze Valley railway cities of Nanchang and Changsha. Nanchang, the capital of Jiangxi province, provided a hub for transshipment of supplies to war zones in Central and Southern China. The Chinese amassed about 230,000 men, including guerrillas to protect the city along the natural defense line of the Xiu River, north of the city. Overall command rested with Yue Xue, with tactical orchestration by Zhuoying Luo. Gen. Yasuji Okamura thrust his men across the river on 20 March 1939. The Japanese not only fully employed their firepower advantage in artillery (the campaign opened with the largest artillery barrage of the whole war) and air strikes, but also poison gas. The Japanese only entered Nanchang on 27 March, expelling hundreds of thousands of refugees in their path.

The Chinese defenders refused to collapse and yielded ground only grudgingly. Their commanders applied the lessons of 1938 and mounted a strong counterattack in April from the southwest. By 26 April, at the cost of heavy casualties, the Chinese restored their grasp on the Nanchang airfield. The Japanese summoned reinforcements and pummeled the Chinese with air strikes and poison gas. Chiang issued an order on 1 May: "Capture Nanchang! If this goal is not accomplished, all commanders above the rank of brigadier will be punished." The reinvigorated onslaught verged upon triumph when on 8 May Japanese fire killed one Chinese division commander and wounded the other. This broke Chinese morale; Chiang bitterly authorized a retreat. Nanchang remained in the control of the Japanese for the rest of the war, but they would not venture farther south until 1944. Japanese killed in action numbered about 500, and the wounded almost 1,700. The Chinese losses were reported as nearly 24,000 killed and about 8,600 POWs.

The Chinese obtained a second opportunity to display their new level of operational and tactical skill when the Japanese thrust south toward Changsha in early August 1939. Changsha was now one of the most strategic locales in China. It formed the terminus of the vital rail line along which most military supplies reaching the Nationalists flowed from Hong Kong. Changsha also served as the key to Hunan province, a rice- and raw-material treasure chest whose loss threatened to inflict a serious, perhaps mortal, blow on Chinese resistance. The Japanese further intended to seize Changsha to deliver a huge political bonus by having it coincide with the formal inauguration of a puppet government under Jingwei Wang.

Gen. Cheng Chen, with 365,000 men of the Ninth War Zone, faced General Okamura with 120,000 men. In April 1939 Chiang had instructed Changsha defenders to evade a frontal clash, permit the Japanese to approach

Changsha, and then unleash a mighty counterattack. Chen's subordinate, Yue Xue elaborated on this scheme. He erected three defense lines north of Changsha and divided his forces into what he designated as a field army, a garrison force, an assault force, and a reserve. The garrison force would delay the Japanese through three defense lines north of Changsha and lure them into prepared ambush sites. The field army would wage guerrilla attacks on the Japanese rear to disrupt their transport and communications routes and prey upon rear-area logistical facilities. The assault force harassed the Japanese flanks. They also "slipped into the battlefield in civilian clothes" to "set ambushes, kill commanding officers at various levels, destroy communications, and create chaos." Reserve forces guarded strategic areas and reinforced counterattacks by the assault forces. Prior to the Japanese advance, the Chinese stripped the countryside to deny supplies and moved the population into the hills.

As the Japanese columns approached Changsha, Chen unleashed a timely counterattack from all sides that cut Japanese supply lines. The three most forward Japanese divisions wheeled about and desperately cut their muddy way back to their start point. For once, it was the emperor's soldiers who endured galling artillery fire from a handful of Chinese pieces. Typically, Japanese and Chinese versions of the battle shared sparse common ground. The Japanese explained that the thrust had only been a spoiling attack, never intended to occupy Changsha permanently. They reported their losses at just about 850 killed and 2,700 wounded while claiming they killed nearly 44,000 Chinese and captured almost 4,000. Foreign military observers estimated Chinese losses much lower, at 20,000, while pegging Japanese losses probably much too high at 30,000. The indisputable fact was that Changsha remained in Chinese hands, a vital buttress to Chinese morale in a dark passage.

Following upon Changsha was a battle on a much smaller scale that packed significant political and military implications. The town of Shiqi (Shekki), famous as the birthplace of Sun Yat-sen, rests along the Pearl River delta, with Guangdong (Canton) to the north and Portuguese Macau to the south. After a series of abortive Imperial Navy thrusts beginning in June, Imperial Army troops captured Shiqi on 8 October. But after a mere two days of occupation, the Japanese withdrew. The protracted struggle for Shiqi, followed by its loss and then abandonment, symbolized obdurate Chinese resistance and the inability of the Japanese to pacify the countryside in regions they ostensibly occupied.

The Disputed Manchurian Frontier

In between the two main battles in China at Nanchang and Changsha during the first three seasons of 1939 came an Asian event of profound importance in the whole global struggle. As if this were not enough to command detailed attention, this clash between Japan and the Soviet Union affords a matchless insight into the thirty-year evolution of the mind and soul of the Imperial Army that would endure for the whole Asia-Pacific War.

Manchuria sticks north into the Soviet Union and its client Mongolian People's Republic (Outer Mongolia) like a stout thumb, creating a nearly 3,000-mile border vaguely defined in treaties written in Chinese and Russian and often obscured by forests, mountains, and featureless deserts. From the outset, the Japanese occupation ignited flare-ups—by Japanese numbers totaling 1,600 to the year 1945 (by Soviet math 1,850)—progressing from verbal altercations on to trespasses, abductions, airspace violations, sniping, and full-scale lethal gunfire exchanges. Of the succession of border incidents, two stand out before 1939. The first involved a relatively low-level confrontation along the Amur River in northern Manchuria during June–July 1937. The episode convinced Japanese officers that Stalin's purges had seriously weakened the Red Army.

A second already mentioned incident in July and August 1938—the Battle of Lake Khasan (Soviet title) or Battle of Changkuofeng (Japanese title)—proved even more significant. A telling feature of this episode was that the local commander, Gen. Kamezo Suetaka, had defied Tokyo authorities, including the emperor. Rather than disciplinary action and disgrace, Suetaka's insubordination won the admiration and support of senior officers in Tokyo. But from Changkuofeng the Imperial Army extracted two "lessons." It extolled the first night attack by a Japanese rifle battalion against the Red Army as vindication for a tactical doctrine that emphasized nocturnal infantry movement to launch a close assault climaxed by hand-to-hand fighting and relying ultimately on morale to carry the day. Further, the Imperial Army imbibed the "lesson" that its resolute riflemen could hold despite being deluged by Soviet artillery and assailed by three times their numbers. Stalin provided an endorsement of Japanese perceptions of success: he had the Soviet commander, Vasily Blyukher, tortured to death.

Changkuofeng roused the emperor to a sensational dressing down of the army chief of staff. The army's defiance of officials in Tokyo, including the emperor's prerogatives, was "outrageous in the extreme," declared Hirohito. But this tirade did not curb the army from deceiving the emperor that the Kwantung Army had acted only in self-defense.

The apparent vindication of Imperial Army doctrine at Changkuofeng proved a matter of tremendous moment not only to proximate events, but to the whole path the Imperial Army followed to 1945. Imperial Japan adopted a formal strategic plan in 1907 identifying Russia, the United States, and China as its main potential foes. But the services divided sharply on the rank order of these prospective enemies. The Imperial Army placed priority on Russia while the Imperial Navy focused on the United States. Both services neglected China. The fundamentals of the plan were reaffirmed in 1918, 1923, and 1936, save for the addition of Great Britain as a potential foe in 1936.

One Japanese officer explained that the "supreme command exhausted its wits in thinking out countermeasures" to burgeoning Soviet might fueled by Stalin's forced draft industrialization by the early 1930s. Imperial Army reaction to the Soviet menace splintered. Some officers sought solace in rank racism. As one Japanese analyst typically declared in 1938, "as long as the essence of the Russian people does not change" the Soviet armed forces would be "uncontrolled, in a state of confusion, and corrupt in morale." More reflective officers bowed to the reality of Japan's smaller population and economy. They saw the army's salvation in the development of an integrated strategic, operational, and tactical doctrine that would permit the Imperial Army to triumph despite its numerical and material inferiority.

The dialectical exchange between the spiritual- and material-minded camps within the Imperial Army resulted ultimately in a doctrine of a quick, decisive war (*sokusen sokketsu*). This doctrine aimed to offset factors that could be enumerated, such as men and machines, with what the Japanese viewed as their unique racial superiority in extraordinary courage and audacity that was best exploited by relentlessly seizing the initiative with bold, dispersed maneuvers under the mask of terrain or darkness to avoid ruinous casualties. These maneuvers aimed to surprise Soviet units from the flank or rear and then deliver the coup de grace with a sudden charge to hand-to-hand combat.

Japanese soldiers were inculcated with absolute conviction in ultimate victory and their individual superiority, particularly in bayonet and hand-to-hand fighting. They were imbued with the mystique "that night attacks exploited the unique Japanese characteristics of bravery, tenacity, shrewdness and audacity." The Imperial Army trained as no other for nocturnal combat under the motto that "the night is worth a million reinforcements."

The new tactics required junior officers with exceptional capabilities, noted historian Edward Drea, "but it required high-quality, well-trained junior officers who were concerned about their troops' welfare and who matured by continual service with their regiments." The grinding war in China, however, seriously diluted officer quality. Losses not only depleted rosters of junior officers, but also the rapid promotion of company officers to field grade left the rifle companies with fewer experienced leaders.

In 1933 the Imperial Army published a forty-nine-page booklet titled *How to Fight the Soviets*. This work declared that the Soviet people, and consequently their army, were docile, submissive, and blindly obedient servants. Red Army soldiers were dully stolid, captives of orders, and tenacious in set defense but wanting for imagination or initiative. When subjected to the unexpected, like a flank attack or encirclement, they fell to despair, depression, and panic. In sum, the manual pinpointed the essence of the Red Army in racial characteristics, not in weapons, doctrine, tactics, or strategy. (This indoctrination prompted Japanese soldiers to jibe that the Soviet soldiers manifested "a despicable urge to live!") Up to 1939, battlefield experience seemed to validate the new tactics. Outnumbered Japanese units routinely defeated, if not routed, Chinese soldiery. The Imperial Army chose to classify the less decisive results at Changkuofeng as a victory.

Nomonhan (Khalkhin Gol): Incident and Escalation

In 1939 a Manchurian border clash escalated into a battle that rightly deserves ranking among the most important of World War II. On 4 May about a fifty-strong band of Soviet-allied Outer Mongolian horsemen meandered into one of the innumerable disputed Manchurian border sectors. In this area, the Japanese maintained that the Halha River (Soviet name: Khalkhin Gol) marked the border. The Soviets insisted that a pair of straight lines meeting east of the river near the nondescript village of Nomonhan delineated the border. The escalating clash ended on 28–29 May when the Soviets virtually annihilated a 220-man Japanese contingent under Lt. Col. Yaozo Azuma.

Where Azuma met his fate rested in the middle of what would be the main battlefield, in a rectangle of desert about twenty miles north to south and thirty miles east to west. The fine but firmly packed sandy soil arranged itself in wavy dunes forming indistinguishable undulations that provided no obstacle to mechanized movement and scant concealment. As one Japanese officer explained, "When you hear the word 'heights,' you imagine a mountain or at least a hill. But here it meant something like a raised pancake, with a diameter of about [two miles]." During the combat peak, Japanese soldiers found their way at night by stench: guiding themselves by the smell of the putrefying corpses of men and horses.

The inclination of the Kwantung Army to overlook Azuma's disaster ended when the Soviets thrust more troops into the disputed ground. The Kwantung Army then detailed the 23rd Division to settle the matter, a unit a mere six months old. The commander, Lt. Gen. Michitaro Komatsubara, was intelligent but theoretical. He and his staff lacked combat experience, and junior officers were unseasoned. Among Japanese divisions, it wielded the oldest artillery pieces and the fewest machine guns. The senior ordnance officer provided his verdict on the division's equipment as it marched off to battle: he killed himself.

The Yasuoka Detachment (named for its commander Lt. Gen. Masaomi Yasuoka) significantly reinforced the 23rd Division. It comprised two tank battalions, a motorized infantry regiment, and a truck regiment from the 7th Division. Total committed forces now included 73 tanks, 400 trucks (only about one-fourth of the logistical need), 112 antitank guns, 24 antiaircraft guns, 180 planes, and 13 infantry battalions.

Displaying an "amoral and devious attitude" according to Imperial Headquarters, the Kwantung Army concealed its intent to initiate the offensive with a preemptive air attack on 27 June deep beyond the border into Soviet-dominated Outer Mongolia. A Soviet general paid with his life for the serious damage the preemptive attack inflicted on Soviet air strength.

Nor did the cavalier attitude about international boundaries restrain the Kwantung Army's operational plans for the ground assault. Key advisers from Kwantung Army headquarters to Komatsubara were Maj. Masanobu Tsuji and Lt. Col. Takushiro Hattori, officers who would play a huge subsequent role in Japan's fortunes far out of order with their rank. The plan for the initial attack was a double envelopment on a basically southern axis. The right wing (or western) prong comprised the 23rd Division's main force. It would cross the Halha River (thus violating even the border claimed by Japan) and press south parallel to the west bank of the river toward the Kawamata Bridge. The left wing (or eastern) prong was the Yasuoka Detachment, which would thrust down the east bank of the Halha River to the bridge.

The 23rd Division launched its attack on 1 July, crossing the Halha River. Inept Soviet armor handling permitted the Japanese to decimate Soviet vehicle inventories, with its limited number of antitank guns supplemented by Japanese infantry in "human bullet" assaults (nikuhaku kogeki) using incendiary bottles and explosive charges. But after the Japanese infantry assaults

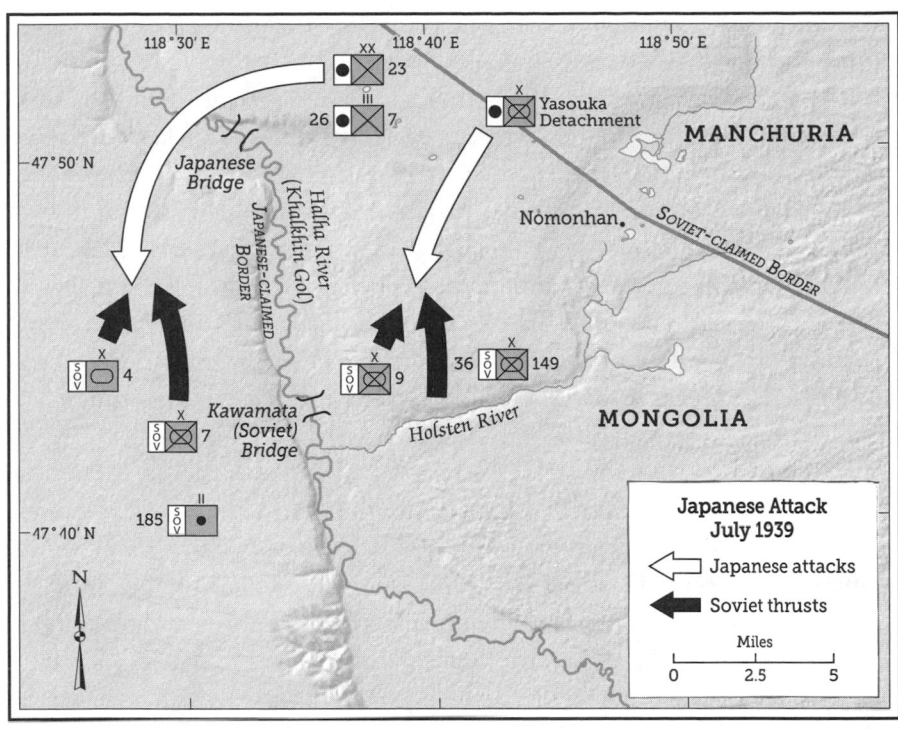

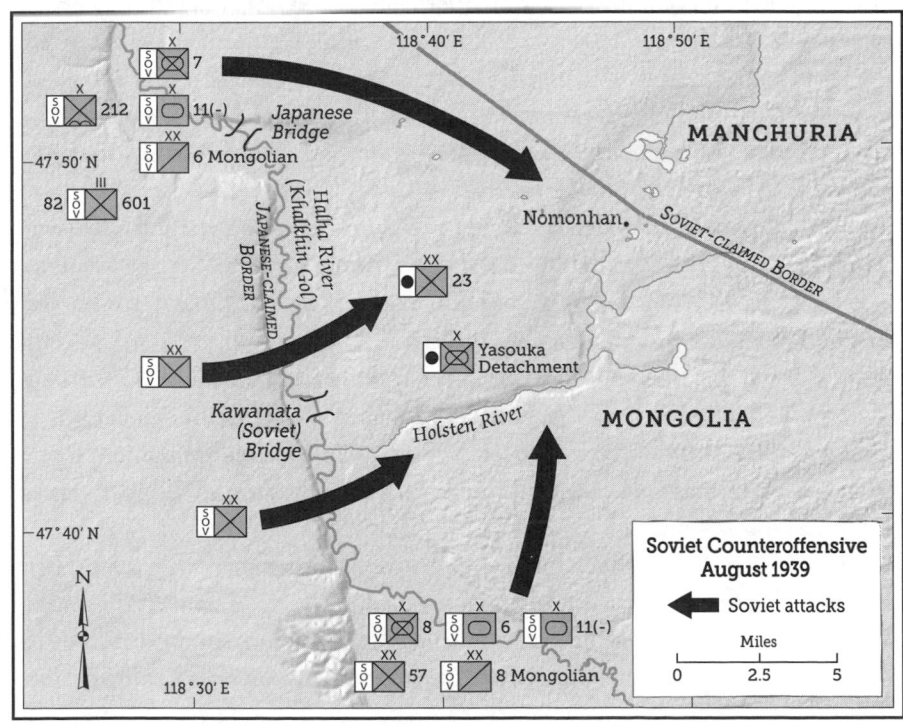

stalled, two tank battalions of the Yasuoka Detachment attempted a break-through, only to be shattered by Soviet fire.

Next, the Kwantung Army sought to neutralize overpowering Soviet batteries with a detachment from Japan of thirty-five pieces of (by Japanese standards) heavy field artillery. These artillery units were the most prestigious in the Imperial Army; one of the batteries was commanded by an Imperial prince who was the emperor's prospective son-in-law. Outgunned and out-ranged, Japanese gunners found each shot they fired drew several, if not scores, in return. The marked Soviet firepower made it suicidal for Japanese infantry to remain in advanced positions visible to enemy artillery observers or tanks. The Japanese offensive ended in bloody exhaustion on 26 July.

The Soviet Counteroffensive

Japanese intercepts of Soviet communications from late July into August alerted Imperial Army officers of an impending Soviet counterattack. But the Japanese gained no clear picture of the scale or schedule of the Soviet stroke, partly due to sophisticated Soviet deceptions. Imperial Army staff officers also strongly believed that multidivision operations could not be mounted beyond a 120-to-150-mile radius from a major supply hub. Nomonhan sat about 150 miles from the nearest Japanese logistical node, whereas 450 miles separated the Soviets from their supply hubs in the USSR and Ondorhann. Accordingly, Japanese staff officers assured themselves that the Soviets could support at most two rifle divisions at the front.

With Moscow's approval, the Red Army moved massive reinforcements to Nomonhan, now designated the First Army under General Georgiy Zhukov. This was accomplished with a fleet of 9,200 supply and tanker trucks—far beyond Japanese imagination. By the evening of 19 August, Zhukov completed his deployments. Soviet forces numbered over 57,000, more than double the Japanese rosters, and were even more disparate in combat power and mobility. Zhukov planned to execute a classic double envelopment using mechanized forces on a basically eastern axis to sweep around the open flanks of the 23rd Division.

The Soviets began their massive offensive on 20 August with a thunder-clap of air attacks ("a veritable circus overhead," snapped one Japanese officer). Stupendous artillery barrages followed the aerial onslaught. Up to three incoming rounds every second reverberated, to one Japanese soldier, "like the gongs of hell." When the barrages finally lifted, the Soviet infantry and armored units advanced, in some areas behind flame-throwing tanks spurting red darts of fire "spitting like the tongues of snakes," noted one Japanese colonel. Both Soviet wings rolled forward, with only the northern arm experiencing a serious check. Once the overall encirclement was completed, the battle followed a consistent pattern. The Soviets methodically isolated and then nearly exterminated Japanese units platoon by platoon, company by company, and battalion by battalion.

An eyewitness account of the battle's final minutes for the 71st Infantry Regiment exemplifies the fate of trapped Japanese units. Lt. Col. Munehara Higashi assembled his pitiful band of only seventeen men and announced the end was at hand. They burned the sacred regimental colors. Then, in a scene the unit historians noted "would move demons to tears," the seventeen men gave three lusty cheers for the emperor. Higashi leaped up erect, brandishing his sword, and shouted, "I am Lieutenant Colonel Higashi, 49 years old!" He ran forward in a pathetic but valorous charge with his handful of upright, able-bodied men. Following them was a wiggling trail of crawling wounded desperately seeking with their last strength to join the final sortie.

An attempted Japanese counterattack on 24 August was smashed. When the hopeless situation of the 23rd Division finally became indisputable, the Kwantung Army ordered division commander Komatsubara out. He barely managed to extract four hundred men with him. Like other survivors, they carried haunting memories of the wounded begging to be taken along. Often when the wounded were abandoned, they were handed grenades to commit suicide.

It was not just local calculations that prompted the Soviets to halt precisely along the boundary they claimed. The height of the fighting in Nomonhan coincided with a diplomatic thunderbolt: the German-Soviet Nonaggression Pact signed on 24 August 1939. (According to the German interpreter, Stalin boasted to German Foreign Minister Joachim von Ribbentrop that the Red Army had slaughtered 20,000 Japanese at Nomonhan. "That is the only language these Asiatics understand. After all, I am an Asiatic too, so I ought to understand.") The detonation of this news toppled the Hiranuma cabinet on 28 August. For almost a month, no one would accept the portfolio of foreign minister in the tumbled diplomatic world for the palpably feeble new government under Gen. Nobuyuki Abe. The outbreak of war in Europe on 1 September jolted Abe's government again. Abe could manage but a minimal announcement that Japan would not participate but would seek to end the China Incident.

Although Hitler had asked Stalin to join the German invasion of Poland from the outset, Stalin demurred. But the unexpectedly swift German advances in Poland stirred Stalin to launch his own forces far sooner than he had anticipated across the chunk of Poland promised him in the August pact. Under these circumstances, eliminating any prospect of a two-front war mobilized Moscow to agree to cease Nomonhan hostilities on 16 September. It was no mere coincidence that the day after halting hostilities in the Far East, Soviet armies rolled into Poland.

Japanese losses reflected a severe trouncing. The Kwantung Army provided figures of 75,736 men committed (in the whole region) and losses totaling 17,716 (8,629 killed, 9,087 wounded). Proportionally, this soared above the prior Japanese benchmark for severe casualties at Mukden in the Russo-Japanese War. The 23rd Division reported it mustered 15,975 men at Nomonhan. Of these 11,958, or 79 percent, became casualties: 4,976 dead, 5,321 wounded, 349 missing, and 1,312 sick. Red Army sources initially provided a figure of 9,284 killed and wounded for Soviet-Mongolian losses. Decades later casualties were admitted as actually having reached 25,655 (9,703 killed and 15,952 wounded). These numbers reversed the impression that the Soviets had inflicted disproportionate losses on their adversaries. Even the original lower numbers served to start Zhukov's reputation among Soviet soldiers for heavy casualties. The Japanese fared better in the sky. The Soviets deployed about 600 aircraft during the campaign; the Japanese fewer than half that total. Approximately 207 Soviet aircraft were lost with Japanese losses about half that figure.

The Red Army at first rejected Japanese requests to recover their dead within the Soviet lines, but the Soviet atheists oddly relented to the spurious argument of a clever Japanese staff officer who claimed falsely that Buddhism strictly mandated the Japanese attend to their own slain comrades. Historian Alvin Coox noted that body recovery teams found numerous tableaus, "bordering on the supernatural . . . depicting self-sacrifice and devotion to comrades, flags and units."

The cease-fire agreement provided for an exchange of prisoners. The Japanese promptly returned eighty-seven men. The Soviets presented about two hundred Japanese—those who permitted themselves to be handed over. Perhaps as many as one thousand Japanese captured at Nomonhan refused repatriation. They rightly feared the consequences and the unutterable disgrace. One of the returned prisoners was Acting Corp. Chosaku Negishi of the 1st Heavy Artillery Regiment. As his unit faced annihilation, his senior remaining officer gave the order for the survivors to commit suicide and proceeded to kill himself. Lacking even last bullets, Negishi dutifully lined up opposite another soldier and they simultaneously ran each other through the throat with bayonets. Miraculously, his comrade's thrust missed any vital point and Negishi revived in a Soviet hospital. Repatriation brought Negishi a court-martial where he was found "guilty" of the "crime" of becoming a prisoner of war. But unlike in the cases of other repatriated men, the physical evidence supporting Negishi's account was so clear-cut and moving that his sentence was only three days of confinement.

The Imperial Army typically subjected other returned enlisted prisoners of war to far harsher penalties. After punishment, they were not returned to their units. Instead, they were reassigned to other units—no two together—outside the Japanese homeland. For repatriated officers, including at least one pilot captured unconscious, the Imperial Army provided only one option: suicide. A particularly egregious fate overtook Lt. Col. Eiichi Ioki. His inspirational leadership of the tenacious defense of a key hill hung up the northern wing of the Soviet pincers and disrupted Zhukov's timetable. In other armies, his feat would be the stuff of heroic legend. But when his last capacity for defense evaporated, Ioki pulled his pitiful survivors off at the last extremity without orders. Withdrawal without orders disgraced Ioki, no matter what the circumstances, and he was forced to commit suicide.

These specific stories reflect the culmination of a gradual but dramatic shift in institutional and societal attitudes about surrender. During the Tokugawa Era (1603–1868), the warrior class adhered to a cultural norm of suicide to atone for error or defeat. The frequent beheading of prisoners incentivized those outside the warrior class to follow suit, but surrender to promote reconciliation in frequent regional wars or by agreement was also accepted. In the early Meiji Era, the national government welcomed surrender by rank and file rebels and junior officers. Officers discouraged any thought of surrender during the Sino-Japanese War (1894–1895) with dire warnings of cruel death at Chinese hands. By the eve of the Russo-Japanese War (1904–1905), the Imperial Army inculcated the unwritten norm that death was preferable to the shame of surrender and its connotation of cowardice. Most returned prisoners of war faced a gauntlet of derision, jeers, and insults that no apology or explanation served to deflect. "Along with ideas of racial superiority, national uniqueness, and *seishin* [fighting spirit]," noted Edward Drea, "the myth of death before dishonor slowly permeated postwar society, incubating until the army would use it again."

During the 1932 Battle of Shanghai, gravely wounded Maj. Noburo Kugo was taken prisoner. After the Chinese returned him, pitiless peer pressure for atonement and his own depression steered him to suicide. No fewer than

five movies and one play extolled Kugo's "example" and solidified the concept of death before surrender as a norm no less rigid for being informal.
Another incident raised three enlisted men to parallel peaks of moral stature.
They charged a Chinese fortification with an improvised explosive device in a
bamboo mat. The device prematurely blew up, killing all three. In the sensa-
tionalized retelling of the incident, the soldiers were extolled into "war gods"
who had deliberately made themselves human bombs. Thus, by a lengthy
evolution, what had started as a mythologized ideal of death before surrender
of ambiguous historical origins had morphed into an unwritten but rigidly
enforced norm—soon to be formally inscribed in 1941 regulations.

Without disclosing many particulars, the Imperial Army did release
a public announcement admitting defeat and a shocking figure of 18,000
casualties—a number not far from the exact truth. There followed a purge, of
sorts. The list of relieved general officers began with the deputy chief of the
General Staff, ran down through the Kwantung Army commander and many
of his staff, and finally to the Sixth Army commander and Komatsubara of
the 23rd Division (although the last two were handled discreetly). As events
would prove, the new commander of the Kwantung Army, Lt. Gen. Yoshijiro
Umezu, a favorite of the emperor, finally stamped out in his new command
the insubordinate schemes and actions that had marked the past decade.
Umezu's forceful assertion of authority came just in time to halt fantastic
plans to reverse the verdict on the battlefield with a revenge campaign in
1939 followed by the possibility of full-scale war with the Soviets in 1940. But
justice definitely faltered. The two field grade officers who exhorted for the
most disastrously aggressive policy did not merely survive, they flourished.
Lt. Col. Hattori served as Tôjô's private secretary and chief of the prestigious
operations section of the Army General Staff. Maj. Tsuji went on to play an
important and controversial role in a whole series of important actions in the
Pacific and Southeast Asia. Thus, far from teaching the perils of defiance of
Tokyo and the virtues of prudence, Nomonhan exemplified the army's willingness to blame strategic and doctrinal errors on subordinates and to reward
recklessness.

On the Soviet side, Zhukov would go on to become a legendary figure in
the titanic clash with Germany. But in the treacherous world of the Stalinist
state, one of Zhukov's most able subordinates, Gen. G. M. Shtern, would be
mysteriously removed from his command a week before the German invasion
and executed in October 1941.

Nomonhan shocked the Imperial Army to its core. The image or conceit of
the "Invincible Kwantung Army" suffered irreparable damage. The doctrine

created to offset Soviet numbers and material superiority by quick, relentless, offensive action by sparsely equipped foot soldiers had been tested and failed against a doctrine emphasizing combined arms and protracted warfare. But Japanese strategists could not see a clear path to a new doctrinal solution. Japan simply lacked the economic resources to support more than a light infantry force structure, very modestly supplemented with mechanized assets. Drea aptly captured the Imperial Army's quandary in 1939:

> To alter drastically [Imperial Army] tactical doctrine was, in effect, to pull the props from under Japanese spirit—the intangibles of battle—to deny the martial values themselves. Perhaps it could have been done, and the end result would have been an army with a glittering array of weaponry, but no soul.

Two Treaties

Two moves on the international diplomatic scene coincided with Nomonhan. In mid-1939, the Roosevelt administration could no longer ignore the powerful tides of indignant American public opinion over Japanese bombing in China. In June 1939, Secretary of State Cordell Hull publicly urged American firms to cease shipping Japan aircraft or aerial armaments. But this so-called "moral embargo" failed to stay Senator Key Pittman from introducing a resolution authorizing the president to embargo trade with any party to the Nine-Power Treaty threatening the life or legal rights of any American citizens. Pittman's unmistakable target was Japan. His embargo would ratchet American pressure from mere words to dangerous deeds.

Roosevelt and Hull contrived a deft counter to what they regarded as the excessive provocation of Pittman's resolution, which simultaneously bowed to public opinion and (they hoped) might sober the increasingly strident Japanese. On 26 July, Roosevelt issued notice of intention to abrogate the 1911 Treaty of Commerce and Navigation with Japan. Public acclaim greeted the move. Indeed, a stalwart in the anti-interventionist camp, Senator Borah, bestowed his approval. Chiang thanked the American ambassador for the step and the timing.

The Soviet-German Nonaggression Pact of 24 August 1939 far overshadowed the jolt of the American move. The immediate role of Nomonhan in producing the pact is clear. But the long-term consequences of the pact confounded Stalin. Up to this point, he had displayed a far sounder grip on the intricacies of Asian diplomacy than his Western counterparts. He pushed the "United Front" strategy on his Chinese minions to halt the civil war and mobilize the Chinese to bog down the Japanese. By entangling the Japanese in a regional war quagmire, he aimed to keep them from joining Germany in a potentially lethal two-front attack on the Soviet Union. Nomonhan at one level seemed to further this strategy. The drubbing of the Imperial Army shocked the Japanese and provided another powerful deterrent to renewing hostilities with the Soviets, even in conjunction with Germany. But what Stalin did not foresee was that he had unleashed Hitler to overrun Western Europe the next year. Hitler came very close to eliminating all his adversaries in the West, which would have freed up his armies for a massive drive on the Soviet Union. Further, the pact also severely affected the flow of Soviet aid to China, particularly aircraft. Since the Soviet Union stood as China's only major source of munitions, this left China's continued resistance in peril. As events would later demonstrate, a collapse of Chinese resistance represented a potential global catastrophe to the anti-Axis cause.

This geopolitical earthquake collapsed the hapless Hiranuma government. Hirohito appointed General Nobuyuki Abe as the new prime minister on 30 August and admonished him to "cooperate" with Britain and the United States. Abe in turn anointed the retired Admiral Kichisaburō Nomura, a confirmed friend of America, as his foreign minister.

Up to the moment word of the pact reached Tokyo, Imperial Army officers fended off recommendations for negotiations over Nomonhan on the basis that Japan's bleak situation in the field made its hand too weak. But with their western front secure, the Soviets could now transfer still more forces to the Far East. Consequently, the new Abe government promptly negotiated a settlement. But on the very day Abe's government took office, 1 September 1939, Germany attacked Poland. Declarations of war by Poland's allies, Britain and France, followed on 3 September. Completely befuddled by the radical changes in the geostrategic order, the Abe government resigned on 14 January 1940.

Nanning and the Chinese Winter Offensive of 1939

As fall approached in 1939, Chiang faced a host of challenges. In September he admitted to American diplomats that he feared the British might attempt to revive their treaty with Japan after the Nazi-Soviet Pact. This had serious implications for vital supply routes to China through Hong Kong and ultimately Burma. At the same time, Jingwei Wang's collaborationist regime generated energy for Chinese seeking accommodation with Japan. A major northern regional commander, Xishan Yan, reached an understanding with the Japanese in November 1939. In return for arms and Japanese withdrawal from some areas in Shanxi, he switched the target of his military efforts from the Japanese to the Chinese Communists.

Chiang answered these challenges with a massive nationwide offensive employing as many as eighty divisions. Its goal was to prove both domestically and internationally that the Nationalists could sustain active hostilities with Japan. The plan called for major offensives by the Second and Fifth War Zones to cut major rail lines while the Third War Zone attempted to interdict traffic on the Yangtze. There would be subsidiary operations by the First, Fourth, Eighth, and Ninth War Zones. Simultaneously with these endeavors, guerrillas in the Shandong-Jiangsu and Hebei-Chahar regions would strike.

At the Second Nanyue Military Conference in October 1939, Chiang attempted to rouse enthusiasm for the forthcoming offensive. He acknowledged that the Soviet-German Pact now precluded hopes for an alliance of Britain, France, and the Soviets against Japan. But he affirmed that the quality of Japanese troops in China had declined (it had) and that heroic defense of Changsha now made Japanese troops "afraid" (it had not). He also insisted that a world war remained inevitable and would lead to triumph in the War of Resistance (it would).

On 15 November, the Japanese struck first. They launched an offensive in Guangxi province to sever the road and rail routes for supplies reaching Chiang's forces from French Indochina. The Japanese aspired not only to deliver a heavy military blow to Chiang but also to create a schism between southern regional political leaders and Chiang. The Japanese deployed the two divisions supported by strong air and naval forces. By 24 November, the Japanese seized Nanning, the hub of a logistical artery where the railroad from Hanoi linked to a road. But the net effect of the thrust was not to throttle the supply route from Hanoi, but to bend it to the west.

The great Nationalist Winter Offensive of 1939 began on 12 December and continued for nearly forty days to about 20 January 1940, on almost all fronts in North, Central, and South China. Ironically, both sides gauged the outcome on a narrow scale from unsatisfactory to disastrous. Chiang graded Chinese performance as bad, and particularly singled out the ineffectual efforts of the Third War Zone to interdict the Yangtze. The operation again revealed the chronic Chinese inability to coordinate effectively various arms and even operations of adjacent units. Most offensive operations ceased after a few days. Chiang's postmortem as usual featured harsh denunciations of several commanders who retreated at the approach of the Japanese or who had tendered a resignation rather than lead their troops into battle. He also condemned the pernicious effects on morale of widespread smuggling and gambling.

One relative bright spot appeared as the Japanese simultaneously attempted to drive northeast from Nanning deeper into Guangxi province. Chiang committed elite forces as both armies wrestled for the key Kunlan Pass, which provided an avenue to reach deeper into Guangxi and even threaten further advances into Yunnan, where sat Kunming, a key logistical hub from both Burma and Indochina and the site of important air bases. Both sides sustained serious losses; the Chinese killed the senior Japanese commander at the pass, Maj. Gen. Masao Nakamura. In fighting that dragged well into 1940, the Japanese rebuffed Chinese attempts to retake Nanning but remained hemmed in around its vicinity.

While the Chinese found much that was wanting in their efforts, the Japanese regarded the offensive as something they survived rather than defeated. Chinese coordination at the tactical or operational level was often lackluster, but the offensive revealed Chinese strategic coordination across most of China that startled the Japanese. This precluded the usual Japanese counter of shifting units from quiet areas to confront Chinese thrusts. The Japanese Eleventh Army, the Imperial Army's premier combat command in China, submitted a particularly telling report. The army claimed to have slain 51,000 Chinese and captured 987 prisoners of war. But the army's own casualties totaled 2,141 killed (including 109 officers) and 6,126 wounded (including 225 officers). Only the much more protracted Battle of Wuhan had produced greater losses.

The view from Tokyo in the aftermath of the Winter Offensive was grim. It reinforced the conclusion manifest after the fall of Wuhan that China had become a sinkhole consuming the resources needed for preparations for the expected showdown with the Soviets. The defeat at Nomonhan added urgency to the need for modernization, and German triumphs in Europe beckoned to open other opportunities for useful employment of Japan's arms. Tokyo realized that it must scale back the commitment in China to prepare for the Soviets or other eventualities. The Army Ministry drafted schemes to reduce strength in China from 850,000 men to 700,000 by the end of 1939 and 500,000 by the end of 1940. Some officers even proposed withdrawals to limit Japanese control to northern China to facilitate the troop drawdown. The major Japanese command in China, now titled the China Expedition-

ary Army, strenuously objected to force reductions and indeed asked for reinforcement. The upshot was a May 1940 compromise that awarded the China
Expeditionary Army two more maneuver divisions in exchange for an overall
reduction of 100,000 men by the end of the year.

On New Year's Day, 1940, Chiang faced a future full of uncertainties. To
the amazement of the world, he had fought Imperial Japan to a standstill after
two-and-a-half years. But he had lost his original base area together with vast
tracts of China. He also had lost his principal sources of revenue. He had
expended priceless amounts of human capital in his armed forces as well as
munitions China could not itself replace. He remained convinced, however,
that his grand strategic vision of world war would come true and that the
acquisition of allies would enable the defeat of Japan. What he did not know
was that he faced two of the hardest and darkest years of the war and that during this span the hold of his regime would begin to erode in alarming ways.

⋮

CHAPTER 6

"Japan's Prince of Self-Destruction"

THE CALAMITOUS YEAR OF 1940

Yichang by Land

The anti-Axis cause, not least Nationalist China, staggered through 1940 in a cavalcade of disasters. It began as two events from 1939 penetrated the new year. The inconclusive Nationalist Winter Offensive in China trickled out and the Japanese consolidated their new holdings in the far south of China. Similarly, the Soviet attack on Finland in November 1939, known as the Winter War, continued to March 1940. Grossly outnumbered Finnish soldiers inflicted humiliating defeats on Red Army columns, but ultimately Soviet numbers and firepower prevailed.

In the spring, the Japanese struck another devastating blow by seizing Yichang. Through decrypted Chinese military messages, the Japanese anticipated a Chinese summer offensive toward Wuhan in 1940 by the Fifth and Ninth War Zones. To forestall this, on 1 May the Imperial Army unleashed a major offensive: the Zaoyang-Yichang Campaign up the Yangtze toward Chongqing. Three divisions of the Japanese Eleventh Army (now under Lt. Gen. Waichiro Sonobe) sought to encircle and destroy the Chinese Thirty-First Army Group under Gen. Enbo Tang. Tang prepared to execute the successful Changsha counterpunch choreography, but the Japanese dashed around him. When the Chinese Thirty-Third Army group under Gen. Zizhong Zhang marched to support Tang, two Japanese divisions pivoted to confront Zhang. Tang roughly cuffed one Japanese division, but the Japanese swiftly rallied, massed their forces, and pitched back Tang and Zhang's forces numbering about 300,000 men. Japanese machine-gun fire cut down Zhang (a graduate of the Japanese Military Academy and hero of the Battle of Taierzhuang), who personally refused to retreat. The Japanese bestowed a respectful burial on Zhang, the most senior Chinese commander to die in battle during the war.

Strained logistics leashed Japanese pursuit of the withdrawing Chinese forces, but the issue of occupying Yichang revived a festering discord among Japanese commanders. Some 110 miles up the Yangtze from Hankou, Yichang abuts the eastern edge of Sichuan province where the Yangtze spills from gorges down onto a plain. It afforded a vital link between Chongqing and the Fifth and Ninth War Zones. The Imperial Navy coveted Yichang as a forward air base for bombing Chongqing. Imperial Army opponents of garrisoning Yichang argued it would exacerbate the army's overextension in China. Typical of Imperial Army conduct in China, the occupation proponents won out, and in June the Imperial Army began an occupation of Yichang that endured for most of the rest of the war. The stunning German success in Western Europe provided a potent spur to the decision to occupy Yichang. Japanese officers touted the idea that German triumphs coupled with the loss of Yichang might finally convince Chiang to punctuate ongoing secret negotiations with an agreement to end the war. It did not.

The Eleventh Army toted up campaign losses of 1,403 killed (including 106 officers) and 4,639 wounded (including 203 officers). By Japanese tally, Chinese casualties numbered 63,127 killed and 4,797 captured. Later called a "devastating blow" to Chiang's coalition, the loss of Yichang seriously impaired communications thereafter from Chongqing to the war zones across China. The concurrent loss of north Hebei also cost Chiang a source of food and recruits. But the Japanese did not achieve their overarching objective of ending the war, and yet again overextended their forces. The campaign weakened Chiang but at the price of diluting Japanese control of the countryside. Only the Communists pocketed a full profit from Yichang.

Chongqing by Air

Japanese bombing in China and particularly what the Chinese call the "Great Bombing of Chongqing" remain little noted in the West. The backdrop to this savaging commenced in 1915, when a Japanese naval lieutenant, Chikuhei Nakajima, drafted the first writing advocating bombing the civilian population to crush a nation's resistance. In World War I, Germany launched a succession of attacks on England, first with airships and later with bombers. These raids killed 1,413 (including 296 military personnel or 20 percent) and wounded 3,407 (including 521 military personnel or 15 percent). The raids exerted a hugely disproportionate psychological impact. The first daylight bombings of London in 1917 incited vigilante mob aggression against persons or places with "German" names. Heretofore known as the House of Saxe-Coburg and Gotha (German bombers were called "Gothas," after their manufacturer), the British Royal family hastily rechristened itself as the House of Windsor.

In the years between 1919 and 1937, Europeans continued a practice begun in 1913 of employing aircraft for colonial "policing" actions. The cumulative number of "policing" deaths perhaps ran into the thousands, but almost always occurred in small individual episodes. Meanwhile, two contestants disputed the use of air weapons against (white) cities. Some idealists attempted to erect a taboo against such bombing by legal provisions and moral suasion. Their antagonists were air-power theorists, most notably the Italian Giulio Douhet, who held civilian masses in terrorized thrall with prophesies of a future European conflict characterized by huge sky fleets pulverizing great metropolises with bombs or perhaps poison gas.

But Japan first breached the embryonic legal injunctions and moral taboos about bombing cities. In 1932 Japanese air ordnance accounted for probably a majority of the 2,000 to 6,000 Chinese civilians killed in the Battle of Shanghai. This was, noted historian Mark Peattie, "the most destructive aerial attack on an urban center until the [German] Condor Legion's assault on Guernica five years later." Art and maybe race, not fact, elevated Guernica to supremacy as a timeless international symbol of civilian bombing. Although depicted as a holocaust that purportedly left 1,654 dead civilians and 889 wounded, the raid killed "only" about 300. Artist Pablo Picasso's *Guernica* enshrined that Basque city as the premier world martyr to "terror bombing," completely overshadowing far more massive slaughter in Shanghai. City raids in Spain remained sporadic, so China acquired the lamentable distinction of becoming "the first country to be subjected to systematic bombing of civilian targets."

Japan entered its war with China in 1937 with a respectable modern air arm, though numerically it trailed both Europe and the United States. The Japanese Imperial Army aircraft inventory stood at about 1,000, while the Imperial Navy counted approximately 800 aircraft on hand. Japan passed an important milestone in 1937 by transitioning from dependence on foreign designs to reliance on a domestic industry, now featuring several models of world-class aircraft, notably the Imperial Navy's Mitsubishi A5M Type 96 monoplane fighter and the Mitsubishi G3M Type 96 land-based bomber, and the Imperial Army's Kawasaki Ki-10 speedy biplane fighter.* These aircraft formed only a small minority of frontline strength in July 1937. China by contrast lagged far behind in total air strength at about 300 and remained wholly dependent on a potpourri of foreign design and manufacture, save for a minuscule licensed-production output. China's roster of approximately 700 trained flyers faced about 10,000 Japanese counterparts.

With the outbreak of hostilities, the Japanese divided air responsibilities between the two services. The Imperial Army covered North China, scene of little air combat, while the Imperial Navy took responsibility for Central and Southern China. The Imperial Army fettered its airmen largely to ground support roles, but the Imperial Navy aimed to establish immediate air superiority with preemptive surprise attacks on Chinese aviation installations. The cost of air control over Shanghai proved high. The skilled Imperial Navy airmen prided themselves particularly on the sleek new twin-engine Mitsubishi G3M Type 96 ("Nell") land-based bomber. The first forty-two-strong unit of Type 96s lost nearly half its inventory in the early phase of operations in a psychologically jolting manner. Chinese fighters readily set alight G3Ms. Then before the horrified eyes of fellow aviators, the flames drove the crews of the stricken aircraft into the front cabin. In one crew, the plane captain was

---

* The complex Japanese aircraft designation systems proved confusing during and after the war. Several forms of nomenclature applied to Imperial Navy aircraft, but just two are important. The first system ("short form") comprised a letter, number, letter (e.g., A5M). The first letter identified mission (A = carrier fighter, B = carrier bomber, G = land-based bomber, etc.). This was followed by a numeral indicating the numerical sequence of that model for the mission (5 = fifth carrier fighter). The second letter designated the manufacturer (the most important were A = Aichi, K = Kawanishi, M = Mitsubishi, N = Nakajima). The second major system was the type number from the year of service introduction under the Japanese calendar. By the Japanese calendar, 1936 was Year 2596, from which "96" was taken as the year of introduction. The year 1940 was Year 2600, hence the famous designation of the Mitsubishi A6M Carrier Fighter as the Type "0" or "Zero." Imperial Army aircraft bore a Kitai (airframe) number (e.g., Ki-27), a type number/mission designator based on the Japanese calendar (Army Type 97 fighter had a 1937 year of introduction), and sometimes a name. The Imperial Navy resisted the use of names before capitulating to this system in 1943. To unify and simplify the identification of Japanese aircraft, the United States adopted a system by 1943 of providing male (fighters) and female (bombers) names for Japanese aircraft. Hence, the A6M "Zero" became officially the "Zeke" (although the Zero alone of Japanese aircraft continued to be widely known by that designation), while the "Nell" stood for the G3M and "Betty" for the G4M. This system has become so entrenched in decades of literature about the Pacific War that it will be used here for purposes of clarity.

observed placing his arms around his comrades just as the flames enveloped them and the aircraft plunged earthward in a fiery plume. By the end of 1938, the Imperial Navy counted 158 aircraft lost (51 carrier fighters, 27 carrier dive bombers, 21 carrier attack bombers, and 18 land-based medium bombers).

The Chinese airmen, mostly ill- or modestly trained, soon found themselves severely handicapped as the quality of their mounts declined precipitously in comparison to the new types the Japanese rapidly introduced. The Chinese Air Force achieved a few notable early successes but at very high cost. Operational strength plummeted from 145 aircraft to just 31 by mid-November 1937. The Soviet Union stepped in to provide China with aircraft and volunteer airmen. On 21 November 1937, Soviet fighter pilots first engaged the Japanese over Nanjing. Proportionate to Chinese efforts, the Soviet pilots accomplished more. Nevertheless, the Japanese still came out on the winning side of most air battles—though these remained very small compared to later battles in China and those in the last four years of the European phase of the war. Even with more competitive Soviet equipment like the Polikarpov I-15 and I-16 fighters and the Tupolev SB bombers, Chinese airmen continued to suffer heavy losses and at times were compelled effectively to suspend operations.

Facing the specter of a stalemate, on 2 December 1938 Imperial Headquarters issued directives that gave top priority to attacks against "strategic and political" targets in Central China. Japanese flyers concentrated efforts on northern supply routes from the Soviet Union and southern routes from Indochina and Burma. While dozens of Chinese cities and towns suffered the lash of Japanese air assault, by far the most bombed location was Chongqing. That city, originally of about 339,200, served as an important economic center of Sichuan province, a vast triangle larger in population and area than Britain or France at that time. A Chinese saying boasted that whatever grows anywhere in China sprouts better in Sichuan, but Sichuan cultivated virtually no industry. From 1937, Chongqing donned the mantle of wartime capital. Its population swelled officially to 702,387 by 1941, including the national government, military high command, many evacuated students, teachers, and workers and, not least, massive hordes of refugees.

Chongqing became arguably the preeminent crossroads of China. "All the dialects of China mixed together in [Chongqing] in a weird, happy cacophony of snarls, burrs, drawls, and staccatos," observed journalists Theodore White and Annalee Jacoby. "A foreigner who asked directions in halting Mandarin dialect was likely to be answered by a Cantonese who spoke Mandarin even worse." Business signs like "Nanking Hat Shop" and "Shanghai Garage" memorialized the prior haunts of refugee entrepreneurs. There were restaurants to salute each regional palate.

The inhabitants of Chongqing entered a hard bargain: they traded comfort for security from Japan's ground legions. The nearly impregnable city perched on cliffs at the juncture of the Jialing and Yangtze Rivers, well up from the great rocky gorges that pinched the mighty Yangtze. Chongqing was a city parsimonious with roads along the peninsula formed by the paired rivers, but lavish with steep flights of stairs that hung like spider webs across cliff faces. Wood and bamboo dwellings balanced on long piles clasped the precipitous hillsides in a dense lattice.

In winter, rain and mist bearing a moist chill shrouded Chongqing and covered streets and stairs with muddy slime that daubed bedrooms and grand council chambers with ugly smears. But the endless cloud cover and fog provided the city effective air defense. Known in China as one of "three furnaces of the Yangtze Valley" (along with Wuhan and Nanjing), in summer Chongqing tormented the population with torrid heat of over 100 degrees Fahrenheit by day and no lower than 80 degrees Fahrenheit by night, enervating humidity, and a dusty crust to supplant winter's mud. Besides sultry temperatures, the long summer from May to October brought clear skies and Japanese bombs.

The first major Japanese raid of 1939 struck Chongqing on 3–4 May. Both high-explosive and incendiary bombs pelted the commercial and residential areas of the Old City, igniting horrifying conflagrations. A British journalist described how "Hundreds tried to escape [the fires] by climbing the old city wall but were caught by the pursing flames, and, as if by magic, shriveled into cinders." The estimated casualties were 4,400 killed and 3,100 injured. This raid shocked and terrorized the population, leaving the streets barren for a week. But in an early glimpse of a worldwide phenomenon, the shock and terror did not instill a chronic paralysis, but receded swiftly like an acute fever, leaving only a nagging anxiety.

The disaster infused energy into the city's active and passive defenses. Even without radar, the Chinese ingeniously created an extraordinarily effective air-raid warning system. A network of thousands of observation posts linked by radio and telephone lines to Chongqing issued immediate alarms when Japanese aircraft lofted from their Wuhan bases and then tracked their approach. In addition to sirens, the municipal officials installed towering gallows-like poles on hill peaks and surrounding mountain rims. Accompanying the first burst of sirens, each pole dangled a mammoth paper red lantern to signal—day or night—that enemy planes were potentially an hour away. Two red lanterns announced the planes were closing. When the lanterns dropped, the sirens shrieked a three-minute staccato wail signaling imminent attack. The civil defense command squandered no time with nocturnal dimouts or brownouts when Japanese planes droned within fifty miles; they simply pulled a central switch that instantly doused power all over the city. Anyone imprudent enough to permit light to escape from a flashlight, cigarette, or other source was apt to draw a warning bullet from a patrolling policeman.

The population adapted swiftly, organizing life around air raids. Any day, especially in the summer, threatening clear skies vetoed inclinations for roaming far from home, a location that increasingly coincided with the workplace. The air raid alarms triggered a scene compared to the mighty, merciless Yangtze itself in full spat: "people were rushing in every direction, small carts piled with luggage, rickshaws weighted down with six or seven packing cases, even bicycles were loaded with family property." Yet this surface tumult belied the fact that "there is haste but no confusion. It is like an exciting play which has been performed so often it has lost meaning for the actors."

Apart from those who believed they could reach the countryside, the common destination was a shelter. The air raid shelter program drew from Chiang's personal exhortations and guidance, and much exhausting chiseling by rhythmically chanting, mallet-wielding workers into Chongqing's solid sandstone to excavate a multitude of caves and tunnels. By 1941 the program provided spaces for 370,000 persons and by the next year 428,000. Shelters flourished in endless varieties: caves, dugouts, or simple trenches with wood-and-dirt overhead cover to "elaborate privately run shelters charging admission fees and offering such amenities as chairs and tables, electric lamps and refrigerators, bathrooms, and reading material for those who could afford to pass the time in leisure." Indeed, the enterprising bombing entrepreneurs managed 930 of approximately 1,400 shelters in 1941. But by law, no one could be refused admission to even these privately staffed shelters after the final warning siren, so at the last moment crowds might rush in. Two additional civil defense programs comprised mass evacuation of about 300,000 persons to the surrounding countryside and the ruthless clearing of a grid of firebreaks to contain conflagrations. Much-amended city building codes demanded use of stone and brick rather than wood and bamboo in new structures.

Entering a cave or tunnel shelter, even those housing government offices, customarily meant dipping under lines of wet clothes and stepping around gurgling infants and small children at play as the facilities took on the function of residences. Writer Han Suyin described a typical shelter experience:

> We sit in the stifling damp, drenched with sweat, fanning, stirring up the foul air to no purpose. In the dim cave light faces are white, glistening with sweat. Babies lie in stupor in their mothers' arms, dead still as though anaesthetized. Listless, the older children sit hunched on the benches, drugged with exhaustion.

Bomb-ruptured water lines rendered bathing bodies or clothes so arduous that the inhabitants moved in a haze of goatlike stench. The periodic night raid left the population sleep-deprived. Dirt-stained, aging clothes, and eyes framed with dark circles, provided surrogate badges of honor for officials and common citizens alike. The city's mayor Hongkun Li, a portly, American-educated intellectual, set an inspiring example by fearlessly dashing about Chongqing during raids to exhort firefighting and rescue teams. These fire and rescue teams achieved a high state of effectiveness, quenching fires swiftly with hoses or slowly with bucket brigades when Japanese bombs ruptured the water mains. They extracted the hurt and dead, filled craters in roads with rubble, and finessed Japanese efforts to wipe out electrical power. (One macabre new industry involved "corpse carriers." Paid by authorities with rice, they transported remains on boats out of the city to the "new coffin mountain.") Endless bombing, destruction, and death instilled a degree of callousness. On one street, crews might be extracting corpses from wreckage while the next street over, well-dressed crowds sauntered to see a movie, eyes uplifted to large signs depicting Hollywood stars. Like other national leaders, Chiang was much concerned about the morale of the capital city's population. He was quick to extol Chongqing's demonstrated resilience as a model for the nation.*

A typical Japanese raid in 1939 featured eighteen to thirty-six aircraft. In 1940, that average ranged from fifty to ninety as the Imperial Navy launched "Operation 101." This was not only Japan's first truly strategic bombing cam-

---

* Japanese bombing prompted a pronounced long-term social effect on China. Because it made moving far from home a hazard, it instilled the practice of maintaining close proximity between living and working locations. This led to the adoption after 1949 of "work units" clustering living and work places, a system not dismantled until the 1990s. Mitter, *Forgotten Ally*, 13.

paign but the first in history in which the attacker explicitly admitted the purpose of forcing a national surrender by terrorizing civilians. About 120 Imperial Navy G3Ms, later joined by Imperial Army bombers, gathered around Wuhan to strike by day and night at Chongqing and relatively near airfields. The Japanese divided Chongqing into five sectors and set about systematically blasting and burning each. To a Japanese aviator, the "honey-combed ruins [of Chongqing] looked like the excavated remains of a very ancient civilization." Japanese planes unleashed strings of bombs "bursting and throwing up myriads of freakish cloud formations, movie slow motion wise, like so many brown roses bursting to bloom." Japanese bomb loads notched gaps across the city, leaving lines of roofless, partial walls with fire-scorched, empty windows or just-mounded, formless debris from what had been houses or buildings.

Chongqing sat some 497 miles from Japanese bases at Wuhan, far beyond fighter escort range of just about 373 miles. It translated into an exhausting seven-hour round trip for Japanese raiders, who faced Chinese and Soviet air and ground defenses. Antiaircraft fire nurtured Chinese morale but claimed few raiders. Even modest aerial challenges ended abruptly in August 1940 when the famous Mitsubishi A6M "Type 0" (ever after commonly called "Zeros") fighters debuted. The specification for the design reflected combat experience in China, especially a demand for unprecedented range, as well as requirements for speed, firepower, and maneuverability so intimidating that one aircraft company immediately dropped out of competition. Chinese interceptors at first simply evaded combat with the formidable new Japanese fighter, but on 13 September, thirty-four Chinese fighters soared up to defend Chongqing. Thirteen A6Ms pounced, shooting down an equal number of defending aircraft and damaging eleven more. Ten Chinese pilots were killed and eight injured. Only four of the A6Ms sustained light damage. There would be a parallel one-sided massacre in March 1941. In the face of over-whelming Japanese qualitative and quantitative superiority, the Chinese Air Force was reduced to the aerial equivalent of guerrilla warfare.

During 1940, Japanese ledgers recorded 3,715 sorties in 182 raids (all but 14 by day) during which some 2,000 tons of bombs showered down in Chong-qing's vicinity.* This campaign cost the Japanese nine planes lost and one hundred damaged. Vast damage to Chongqing, however, failed to achieve its strategic goal of forcing China to bow. But motion and still pictures, as well as

---

*   A sortie with respect to military aviation means one flight by one plane.

print accounts, of the bombing heaped international abuse upon Japan. These terrifying images from Asia merged with startling news from Europe.

German Triumph; American Reaction

As Ambassador Joseph Grew observed, when the Treaty of Commerce and Navigation expired on 26 January 1940, the prospect of American sanctions dangled over Japan like a "sword of Damocles." It soon developed that the Japanese reaction turned infinitely less on American trade than on German triumph.

On 9 April 1940, Hitler flung his legions into Denmark. The Danish government ordered a cease-fire by 0600 that morning, ending resistance from the nation's 17,000-strong armed forces. That same day, the German Navy and Luftwaffe pierced through the supposedly impenetrable shield of the British Royal Navy to land forces at multiple locations in Norway. The Royal Navy counterattacked with mixed results, and a combined Polish exile, French, and British army fought the Germans until a June evacuation. Losses numbered about 6,800 total Allied casualties and about 5,500 Germans. The Germans dazzled with their audacity and the superior skill of their air and ground forces—though heavy German naval losses loomed large by the summer. The Norwegian government and King Haakon VII chose to go into exile in Britain.

Then, on 10 May, German columns of tanks and mechanized elements thrust through the Ardennes forest in France and Belgium. In the spring of 1940, Allied forces in Western Europe included four million soldiers in 151 divisions. Germany committed around three million soldiers in 141 divisions and three brigades. The German artillery park numbered 7,378 pieces versus about 14,000 Allied. A paltry 2,439 German battle tanks faced 4,204 Allied peers. In the air, the Allies readied 4,469 fighters and bombers at the front or rear areas compared to Germany's 3,578 combat aircraft.

Luxembourg, the Netherlands, and Belgium all surrendered by 28 May. France had held out for four years in the prior war, but its government surrendered in just 44 days on 22 June. German losses in all these campaigns totaled 163,213 (including 29,640 killed). Suddenly Germany looked unbeatable in the air and on the ground. It now stood astride the whole of Western Europe; it had shattered the world's strategic balance. To many Japanese leaders, particularly in the Imperial Army, the stunning displays of German battlefield virtuosity seemed to guarantee German victory against any adversary, no matter the numerical odds. The perception that German triumph was a near certainty fatefully colored Japanese statecraft for the next two years or more.

Dispatches from Europe convulsed the heretofore complacent American public and Congress. For the first time in the nation's history, Congress authorized a peacetime draft, but stipulated that draftees could not serve outside the Western Hemisphere, except for US possessions. Even more startling was the mobilization of the nation's finances. In January 1940, Roosevelt asked for $1.181 billion for national defense—and Congress looked to pare this figure downward. After Germany's sweep, the final set of appropriations and authorizations for current and future spending soared to $17.692 billion.

For Japan, the most important aspect of this funding upsurge involved ships. Congressman Carl Vinson explained to his colleagues that the United States could shortly be left to face five million tons of hostile war vessels with only a fleet of 1.9 million tons. By 11 July, Congress passed two acts creating what was known as the "Two Ocean Navy." The combined building program mirrored navy projections that to act offensively in one ocean and defensively in the other, the United States needed a building program of 32 battleships, 15 carriers, 87 cruisers, 373 destroyers, and 185 submarines.

The "Two Ocean Navy" legislation punctured the delusions of a vast number of Imperial Navy officers. Despite recognition of superior US industrial power, many Imperial Navy officers drew the false conclusion that Japan could abandon treaty-building limitations without penalty because the Americans lacked the will, or perhaps the funds (due to the Depression), to maintain a full treaty strength fleet. Faced now with the prospect of a colossal American building program, Imperial Navy staff officers did their sums. The ratio of Japan's warships to US warships would plunge to 50 percent by 1943 and dip to 30 percent or less by 1944—and by that time, the United States would hold a ten-to-one advantage in aircraft production. The numbers demonstrated that the most favorable ratio between Japan and the United States would be 76 percent. It would occur at the end of 1941.

When France surrendered, Britain's prospects looked dire. Roosevelt commented to Postmaster General James A. Farley that Britain's chances of survival were "about one in three." European defeats reverberated in Asia as the British announced closure of the Burma Road to China. Roosevelt juggled an array of issues presented by these events—all complicated by his reelection campaign and his public pledge to keep the country out of war. Deterring Japan remained a priority. Therefore, he reaffirmed the decision made in April 1940 to move the US fleet to Pearl Harbor—a decision made before Hitler totally reordered the world power balance.

Roosevelt, however, remained focused on avoiding active hostilities with Japan. This figured directly in how he handled the authority that the July National Defense Act granted him to control critical exports to streamline procurement of vital raw materials for defense preparations. Roosevelt designated Lt. Col. (soon Brig. Gen.) Russell L. Maxwell of the US Army as export control administrator. But Roosevelt also installed two key limits on Maxwell's writ. First, although Maxwell could prescribe guidelines and procedures, the State Department's Division of Controls alone could issue the necessary export licenses. Further, Maxwell received confidential instructions to defer to Hull on all matters with foreign policy implications. This effectively gave cautious Hull and the State Department a double veto over proposals to halt exports.

Secretary of the Treasury Morgenthau promptly validated Roosevelt's concern about the repercussions of export controls. On 19 July Morgenthau presented the president with a four-point plan he said "might give us peace in three to six months": a total embargo of all American oil shipments; Britain to be sustained by oil from Venezuela and Colombia; Anglo-Dutch destruction of Netherlands East Indies Oil facilities; and British bombing of German synthetic oil plants.

Initially Roosevelt professed tremendous interest in Morgenthau's scheme, which did not involve the United States firing a shot. But he dropped his support after Under Secretary of State Sumner Welles warned that the likely Japanese reaction would be to seize the Netherlands East Indies and its oil. Then Welles and Roosevelt became aware of massive new Japanese orders for aviation grade gasoline and lubricating oil from American suppliers. The upshot was that the president rejected a total oil embargo but imposed restrictions on aviation-grade petroleum products. This could be and was justified as a measure to support US national defense, not as a punitive action against Japan. American producers promptly protested that the original published expansive definition of the grades of petroleum products subject to export controls would ensnarl nearly the whole oil market. The revised version, however, so narrowed the controlled categories that Japan could purchase unrestricted quantities of lower grade gasoline with octane ratings still usable for aviation purposes. The American qualitative petroleum limitations effectively were moot because from July 1940 to December 1941, it was Japan's inability to provide tankers or other means to haul away American petroleum that effectively curbed its purchases.

On 18 June, Churchill pleaded for the transfer of some overaged US destroyers to Britain for convoy protection against German U-Boats as a "matter of life and death." Two issues pointed to a denial of Churchill's request. The first was the looming prospect that a likely British capitulation might shift custody of the transferred destroyers into German hands. It was not Churchill's inspirational orations that allayed this fear, but his deeds. After the surrender of Britain's former French ally in June, Churchill greatly feared that the French fleet might fall into German hands. This would pose a dire threat to Britain's continued control of the oceans and hence its very existence. On 3 July at Mers-el-Kébir (near Oran in Africa), the French commander rejected a set of options the British offered to assure his ships could not fall into German grasp. With Churchill's authorization, a British squadron then attacked the French ships, sinking or disabling most and killing large numbers of French sailors. Roosevelt's key adviser, Harry Hopkins, later confided to Churchill that this event persuaded Roosevelt that—contrary to the reports he was receiving from American Ambassador Joseph P. Kennedy in London—Britain would fight on with resolution. Further, as July and then early August passed, Britain remained very much in the war.

The second issue was whether Roosevelt could legally transfer the vessels without congressional approval—and review by a Congress with many anti-interventionists threatened a major political storm and maybe even rejection of the deal. But the Roosevelt administration finessed this obstacle by linking the destroyer transfer to an exchange for base rights on multiple British possessions in the Western Hemisphere. The manifest value of the bases to American defense secured public approval and left noninterventionists objecting more to Roosevelt's alleged "dictatorial" means (Roosevelt used an executive order bypassing congressional authorization) rather than the substance of the deal. The noninterventionists objected to one other development that Churchill deemed a virtue: the deal "brought the United States definitely near to us and to the war."

German Triumph; Japanese Reaction

The German sweep of Western Europe suddenly unveiled a dazzling array of prospects for Japan among the Dutch, French, and British colonial holdings in the Far East. One Japanese leader termed this a "golden opportunity that comes once in a thousand years." Among Imperial Army officers, and a swath of lower level Imperial Navy officers, sentiment for a formal German alliance—burgeoning since 1938—ignited to a white-hot fervor. Yet voices of caution remained. Emperor Hirohito disfavored any German alliance not solely directed against the Soviets. Some senior Imperial Navy officers feared a German alliance might force an unready Japan into a war with the Anglo-American powers, and that Britain and the United States would counter a Japanese pact with Hitler with expanded aid to China, thus prolonging that quagmire.

Adm. Mitsumasa Yonai, the man appointed prime minister after the Abe cabinet fell in January 1940, adamantly opposed a German alliance. The Imperial Army ordered the war minister to resign, thus under Japanese law toppling Yonai's cabinet. On 17 July, Hirohito ordered Prince Fumimaro Konoe to form a new government. Konoe enjoyed the active support of his friend, the new privy seal, Kōichi Kido, as well as the trust of Hirohito.

"Modern Japanese history," wrote historian Marius B. Jensen, "has not known a more enigmatic man" than Konoe. Born in October 1891, Konoe descended from a noble family second only to the imperial family itself. Given this exalted lineage, Konoe, alone of Hirohito's ministers and advisers, displayed a relaxed familiarity in conversational sessions with the emperor—even sitting with his legs casually crossed, to the consternation of court watchers.

But exalted birth afforded no shield from successive tragic blows. A fever claimed his mother only eight days after his birth; his father married his mother's sister. Years later an embittered Fumimaro learned that the woman he always believed to be his mother was his stepmother. This instilled in him the corrosive idea that "the world is filled with lies." At age twelve, Konoe's father, a prominent political figure (and stalwart friend of China) died. His stepmother remained aloof, and loneliness obtained a life-long grip on him.

During his school years, Konoe avidly plunged into philosophy and consumed a library of leftist literature, including Marx. Konoe also inherited special privilege as the son of his father's friend Prince Kinmochi Saionji, one of the great Meiji Era "Wise Men." Saionji took the twenty-seven-year-old Konoe to the Versailles Peace Conference in 1919, an event Konoe denounced in an essay as an "Anglo-American Peace." Konoe asserted that the world was divided into "haves" and "have-nots." The Western powers rigged the international system to protect the status quo favoring them as "haves." For the rest of his life, Konoe basically approached foreign affairs with this outlook.

Creditors carted away many family heirlooms (which seared him with a suspicion of the rich), but they could not divest Konoe of his title as prince, which gained him a place in the House of Peers, the upper chamber of Japan's parliament, at age sixteen. He donned the mantle as the great hope of Japan's fretful aristocrats in politics. During the 1920s and 1930s he ascended political rungs, not without missteps that made his judgment suspect to Saionji, and he acquired a reputation for his free-wheeling personal life despite being married. His handsome face, tall frame, nonchalance, and youth contrasted starkly with a blur of drab senior political figures and adorned him with "an enchanting aura of elegance." Despite his pedigree and acknowledged intellectual power, he never projected arrogance. Rather, he won plaudits for his easy intimacy and courtesy to others. When he first became prime minister, he engendered wildly inflated public confidence that he was the savior Japan desperately needed to lead itself out of its problems and perils.

For Konoe, a veneer of casual aristocratic gentility and worldly sophistication overlay a core of suspicion of other humans and of a world order maliciously canted by the West against "have-not" nations like Japan. Konoe possessed the breeding and knowledge to stand easily with any actor within Japan's political filament, but he soon found the limited powers of the prime minister's role made it difficult or impossible to control others. He acquired a well-merited reputation for indecision and far too late recognized how he blundered step-by-step toward catastrophe.

Two Konoe cabinet appointments proved fateful. For foreign minister, he turned to Yosuke Matsuoka, a self-confident, even flamboyant figure and a favorite of the army. Born into an impoverished family, Matsuoka was shuttled to the United States to find his way with relatives from age thirteen to twenty-two. He thrived in the Pacific Northwest, then a raw frontier suffused with a pioneering spirit he extolled all his life. He gained a law degree from the University of Oregon and acquired fluency in English, but thanks to the heritage of his principal teacher, English emerged out of Matsuoka's Japanese mouth with a Scottish burr.

Matsuoka, with a protracted foreign youth and college degree, cut an exotic figure among insular Japanese elites. The day before he assumed his post, Matsuoka lectured American reporters: "The era of democracy is finished and the democratic system bankrupt." But there is no truth to the charge that Matsuoka nursed implacable hostility to the United States, engendered by racial discrimination. In fact, he often recounted to his children his positive experiences in the United States and urged them to think large and nurture big ambitions like Americans. The real source of Matsuoka's denigration of the United States in public during his tenure stemmed from his travel through the country in 1934, during the nadir of the Great Depression. The shocking scenes he witnessed convinced him that Americans had lost the qualities that he had so admired in his youth.

Matsuoka calculated that his background precluded him from becoming premier at that time, but he saw his appointment as an entrée into political power to implement his grand strategy. Konoe lacked a firm grasp of foreign affairs and sought Matsuoka to fill that void. Konoe also (mistakenly) thought Matsuoka might help him control the army. They reached a mutually satisfactory agreement: Matsuoka obtained a free rein in foreign policy so Konoe could concentrate on restructuring the country.

The second key Konoe appointment was fifty-five-year-old Gen. Hideki Tôjô as war minister. Tôjô's father Hidenori was a humble member of the samurai class dispossessed of its rights and income during the Meiji Restoration. Hidenori rose to the rank of lieutenant general in the Imperial Army by dint of sheer merit. His eldest son Hideki followed the new conventional path to high rank. Hideki graduated tenth of 363 in the 1905 (Seventeenth) Class in the military academy. In contrast to his charming, energetic, college-educated wife, Katsu Ito, Hideki offset his glitter-free personality with a ceaseless nervous energy propelling him to endless work. "If only you apply yourself," he once remarked, "you will be able to accomplish whatever you set out to do." He early exhibited genuine talent as a superbly efficient administrator.

Tôjô graduated with honors from the War College in 1915 (Twenty-Seventh Class). The Imperial Army shipped him to Europe, as it did a large majority of its most promising officers—but the army detailed few officers to study the United Kingdom or the United States, thus creating a profound institutional gap in its understanding of the Anglo-Americans. En route back to Japan in 1922, Tôjô traversed the United States, but what impression this made on him, if any, is unknown.

When the February 1936 army mutiny broke out in Tokyo, Tôjô (now a major general) was then military police commander in the Kwantung Army. He quashed any support for the mutineers. This reflected his highly legalistic worldview: Japan's armed services answered to the emperor, and absolute obedience to the imperial will represented the path of true duty. Any action without imperial sanction constituted an unthinkable act of rebellion that must be punished severely. This mindset may not have guaranteed his eventual rise to the premiership, but it certainly elevated his standing compared to that of other officers when the army's indiscipline loomed as a serious challenge to the emperor and the government. Thus, in mid-1940, the combination of Tôjô's emphasis on discipline in the army and his ability to work across factional lines elevated him to the front rank of candidate war ministers.

In addition to Matsuoka and Tôjô, Konoe appointed Adm. Zengo Yoshida as navy minister. On 19 July, Konoe assembled at his private residence these three central figures in the incoming cabinet, in what newspapers styled the "Four Pillars Conference." Matsuoka presented a draft program for the incoming administration. Konoe would oversee the foremost priority: the establishment of a comprehensive war economy. This was regarded as an essential prerequisite to resolution of the China Incident and would position Japan to cope with the radically changed international situation.

Matsuoka's agenda for foreign affairs included strengthening relations with the Axis powers, securing a nonaggression pact with the Soviets, and taking "appropriate measures" to incorporate former European colonies into the New Order in East Asia while avoiding "unnecessary conflicts" with the United States. The China Incident would be ended via a combination of military strokes to cut Chiang's supply lines and support for Jingwei Wang's rival government. Chongqing would then accept a peace acceding to Japanese dominance. This program was copied almost wholly from an Imperial Army policy paper, endorsed by the navy, thus guaranteeing the support of the armed forces.

The Tripartite Pact

The first public photograph of the new Konoe government's central figures showed Yoshida and Tôjô in dull uniforms and Konoe in somber traditional attire. But Matsuoka instantly signaled an image as a man of action by donning a striking white flax jacket. He followed this up with the "Matsuoka Cyclone": a wholesale shake-up of the Foreign Ministry. Having thus raised expectations of major accomplishments, Matsuoka did not disappoint.

Matsuoka conceived a multistep diplomatic strategy to authenticate Japan's status as a great power and its dominance over at least East Asia—a strategy that ultimately played a crucial role in wreaking national disaster. He first addressed a German alliance to cement his claim to dazzling leadership. Germany's stunning triumphs and the expected subjugation of Great Britain to Luftwaffe attacks mesmerized all strata of Japanese society with vistas of a heretofore unimaginable extension of Japan's writ. Current best sellers in Japan included Hitler's *Mein Kampf* and Paul Joseph Goebbels's *diary*, while Sawada Ken's *Life of Hitler* garnered acclaim "as a work worthy to be read alongside Plutarch."

Matsuoka harbored no special sympathy for Nazi Germany, and especially not its anti-Semitism. But he believed an alliance with Germany would restrain the United States and permit Japan to negotiate on an "equal footing." Japan would seek alignment with the United States or alternatively the Soviets to obtain bargaining leverage against the other. Further, Matsuoka eyed the forthcoming US presidential election. He believed preventing a Pacific War required denying Roosevelt a third term and that somehow a quick alliance would encourage German-Americans to vote against the incumbent.

Britain's refusal to buckle and the "destroyers for bases" deal sobered up Hitler from the intoxication of his unexpectedly huge victories. He dispatched to Tokyo envoy Heinrich Stahmer to pursue an alliance. Before Stahmer arrived, a major shift transpired among the elite leadership. The Imperial Navy stood as the fundamental obstacle to the alliance. Several important senior officers, including former prime minister Yonai, Adm. Isoroku Yamamoto (former navy vice minister and now commander in chief, combined fleet), and current navy minister Yoshida, vehemently objected to any pact automatically dragooning Japan into a war with the United States—a war they believed Japan could not win. Yoshida, however, toiled under severe pressure from the army and public opinion, as well as middle-rank officers of his own service, not to "miss the bus" in coupling Japan to the new European warrior colossus. Yoshida's health, not his reasoning, broke down. The psychological pressure overwhelmed him. He was hospitalized on 3 September and resigned the next day. Adm. Koshirō Oikawa replaced him on 5 September. Oikawa's dubious career highlights were evading difficult problems and bowing to others' opinions.

For nearly three weeks after Stahmer reached the Japanese capital on 7 September, negotiations hinged on whether Japan would submit to treaty language firmly committing it to enter any war between Germany and the United States due to an American "attack." The treaty, signed on 27 September in Berlin, was officially in English—a choice that appears like a diplomatic smirk at its intended main target. Article 3 formed the heart of the pact. Under it Germany, Italy, and Japan "undertake to assist one another with all political, economic and military means when one of the three Contracting Parties is attacked by a power at present not involved in the European War or in the Sino-Japanese Conflict." Thus, on its face, the pact bound Japan into the rigid commitment to a war with the United States that was stoutly resisted by the Imperial Navy.

But at the same time Matsuoka and Germany's Ambassador Eugen Ott exchanged letters providing a secret protocol reflecting a stratagem devised by the Imperial Navy to assuage the anxieties of many of its leaders. The key covert provision stated: "the question of whether an attack within the meaning of Article 3 of the pact has taken place must be determined through joint consultation by the three consulting parties." In other words, the secret protocol effectively gutted Japan's automatic commitment to join the war upon an "attack" and reserved Japan's right to decide independently whether to enter the war. But Ott and Stahmer nullified the Japanese stratagem with one of their own: they never forwarded the letters to Berlin. The secret protocol thus remained hidden from the world, including Berlin and Rome—and was nonbinding. Ott and Stahmer acted strictly on their own authority, without sanction or even subsequent review by Berlin.

It is difficult to overstate how crucially the Tripartite Pact figured in the outcome of the war. Japanese leaders, foremost Matsuoka, viewed the Tripartite Treaty as a vehicle to acquire vital allies. They failed to recognize it served even more to acquire vehement enemies. "From the British and American point of view," noted historian S. C. M. Paine, "the alliance with Germany transformed Japan from a regional irritant into a key player in the worldwide threat to overturn the global order." And the calculations that injected Japan into the highest strategic calculus for the global war likewise promoted China's role to the same level. Chiang immediately grasped how disastrous the pact would prove for Japan. In his diary he acclaimed Konoe as "Japan's prince of self-destruction."

While basking in public acclaim for the Tripartite Treaty, Matsuoka candidly confided to an aide, "The Army is the playwright [of the pact] and I am a mere actor."[*] Further, the success reinforced Matsuoka's instinct toward a "Lone Ranger" style of diplomacy. This cut him off from extracting solutions and alternatives from the Foreign Ministry in the future; the army was only too ready to fill the void. Finally, he created a mirage that he was a miracle worker. Whatever current benefit accrued to Matsuoka from this image, in the not distant future it threatened to make any faltering in his program seem far more disillusioning.

Simultaneously with negotiating the Tripartite Pact, Matsuoka wrestled with another diplomatic issue, where he was by no means an actor following the Imperial Army's script. The fall of France exposed its Indochina colonies.

---

[*] Matsuoka's statement appears to place the onus for the Tripartite Pact on the Imperial Army and himself. But an important faction within Japan's Foreign Ministry, the so-called "reformists" including figures like Mamoru Shigemitsu and Toshio Shiratori, envisioned an overthrow of the capitalist, liberal order worldwide and thus saw Nazi Germany as a desirable partner in that enterprise. Likewise, there was a pro-German faction within the Imperial Navy enthusiastic about the pact. This background illustrates how distorted the postwar narrative was that placed the blame for Japan's path to defeat almost solely on Imperial Army officers. Takeda Tomoki, "The Path to the Tripartite Alliance of Japan, Germany and Italy," in Kiyotada Tsutsui, ed., *Fifteen Lectures on Showa Japan: Road to Pacific War in Recent Historiography* (Tokyo: Japan Publishing Industry for Culture, 2016).

As early as 17 June, the local French governor announced the suspension of all arms traffic to China. The Imperial Army, however, leaped to eliminate permanently a supply route believed to be providing Chiang's Nationalists with nearly half their munitions. Further, the Imperial Army looked to secure permission to move troops through Indochina to attack into Southern China and to obtain air bases for operations against the Nationalists.

On 18 June, a meeting between representatives of the Army General Staff and the Army Ministry produced a fiery clash over the means to these ends. The chief of the Operations Division of the Army General Staff, Maj. Gen. Kyōji Tominaga, urged a prompt invasion of French Indochina. Army Ministry officials condemned Tominaga's bellicosity as "against the spirit of the samurai" and urged diplomacy. The upshot was the dispatch of Maj. Gen. Issaku Nishihara to negotiate with the French in Indochina.

Initially, Matsuoka appeared as tough-minded as the most rabid army officers in his approach to the French. Despite the implicit menace of a Japanese invasion, the French played their weak hand with skill. In the end, Matsuoka emphasized diplomacy over force, and the French bowed to terms satisfactory to Matsuoka and Tōjō. This should have ended the matter—but it did not.

In a vastly complex series of events featuring orders, counter-orders, a forged order, and flagrant refusal to obey lawful orders, Tominaga and like-minded officers in the Army General Staff in Tokyo as well as officers of the Twenty-Second Army and the 5th Division in China, launched Japanese troops in an armed onslaught across the Indochina border in the opening minutes of 23 September 1940. Even after it became clear that this attack violated the diplomatic agreement sanctioned by the Japanese government, and even after lawful orders from Imperial Headquarters reached the South China Army demanding a halt to any combat, various officers ignored orders and sought to turn the forceful occupation of part of Indochina into a fait accompli. This included a combat landing of Japanese troops, who advanced into Haiphong without opposition, and then the accidental bombing of that city, killing a number of Vietnamese.

Tōjō vowed to take stern measures to restore obviously shattered discipline. Tominaga (who forged a purported order from Imperial Headquarters) and certain other Army General Staff officers were dismissed from their posts and transferred to lesser duties. The commanders of the South China Army and Twenty-Second Army were placed in reserve status, but no retribution fell upon their culpable staff officers. Yet within a year, Tōjō himself would restore to influential posts most of these same officers. (Tominaga, for example, became chief of the Army Ministry's Personnel Bureau, later vice minister and a trusted Tôjô adviser!). The fierce contempt from the now dominant radical officers ended Nishihara's career over his obedience to legitimate directives from Tokyo. Some middle-grade officers in the Imperial Navy implicated in the unsanctioned use of force in Indochina remained in their posts and would play a key role in maneuvering the navy into support for the decision for war in 1941. One Japanese historian affirmed that Tôjô's actions "did result in a decline in the tendency for junior officers to assert their views over those of their superiors and strengthened the position of the Army Ministry and leaders of the General Staff." But the fact remains that it would have been unthinkable in the American or British Army (or probably the German or Red Army) for any senior officer to have forged a purported order from supreme headquarters and to have held subsequently any responsible post.

Then Matsuoka made a terrible error with fateful consequences. The army had by no means resolved to advance from Northern into Southern French Indochina. At a liaison conference on 12 December 1940, Matsuoka appeared to give his tacit approval to a plan to move into Southern Indochina. As biographer David Lu observed:

> The military could take it to mean that diplomatically the occupation of Southern French Indochina would not pose any more serious problems than the ones encountered at the time of the occupation of the northern part. What the utterance did was to encourage the military to look again at the prospect seriously. This was especially regrettable in that when the army and navy finally decided to move to Southern Indochina in the summer of 1941, Matsuoka was the lone and articulate dissenter against that course of action. By then his credibility had already been tarnished.

Breaking "Purple"

In one of those moments when history turns mischievous and bonds two highly disparate but vital events, the Tripartite Pact coincided with one of the great feats of code breaking in history. Japanese diplomatic messages sent on what the Japanese called the "A Type" cipher machine in late 1938 forewarned of a change to a new "B Type" cipher machine. American code breakers also read the messages, for they had solved the "A Type" cipher machine, which they had dubbed "Red." On 20 February 1939, Japanese diplomats at eleven key embassies shifted over to use of the "B Type" machine. In the history of American code breaking, the "B Type" machine would ever afterward be immortalized by its code name: "Purple."

Initial analysis demonstrated the markedly higher frequency of six of the twenty-six Roman letters. This appeared to parallel the same characteristic of the "Red" machine, where the six letters emerged as vowels (A, E, I, O, U, and Y). Further study, however, indicated the new machine was no mere modification of "Red." The earlier machine encrypted the "6s" by means of a "commutator" (a wheel with forty-seven connector points) geared to another, or break wheel, that advanced the "commutator" one, two, or three steps at a time. The new machine, however, ran on a consistent cycle through twenty-five alphabets. Each alphabet scrambled the letters differently, but the sequence of the scrambled alphabets, one after another, remained constant. An "indicator" controlled where the operators of the machine set the correct starting point for a message among these alphabets. Using tested techniques, just under two months later the code breakers could ferret out the "6s" (vowels) in any lengthy message. They deduced that although there were 25 starting points (one for each scrambled alphabet), the Japanese employed "only" 120 "indicators" to mark these starting points at the beginning of one of these alphabets in the series, so there were four to five "indicators" for each alphabet starting point.

When the "6s" popped out from decipherment, they formed skeletons of words or phrases in the plain text. Astute deductions based on the vowels and the context could then fill in the blank spaces. For example:

Cipher: B H A X E F Q C E V Q O O X H E C F D L N H Q R V Q P P L C
    E R P
"6s": _ _ E _ A _ A _ E _ E _ O _ E _ _ _ E _ _ _ E _ U E _ _ _ _ _ A _
Plain: T H E J A P A N E S E G O V E R N M E N T R E Q U E S T S T H
    A T

An underlying plain text in English greatly facilitated the work of the code breakers. This was both because virtually all the code breakers understood no Japanese and because the few translators could spare little time for this work. The code breakers gained a tremendous boost to their work when inspired guesses of probable phrases from the "6s" prompted linkage of the cryptographic text with a document sent or received by Japanese diplomats in English. If the job of the code breakers increased tremendously when the plain text was in Japanese, on 1 May 1939, the Japanese zoomed the difficulty to staggering complexity by adapting a "species" of the "Phillips Code." The

"Phillips Code" referred to a method of shortening the length of commercial telegrams and thus reducing their costs. As applied here, it comprised a lengthy series of arbitrary letters and abbreviations standing for numbers, punctuation marks, words, syllables, and sometimes phrases. It produced this sort of plain text at the beginning of a message:

Cipher: FGPXP IXUDB DGECZ LBLNU ZQOQH YNMRQ ARJOP
"Plain": XFCGJ WFOVD DNOBB FYXFO CFYLC CFMSG TSJVR

The actual meaning of this plain text was: "Number 15 (part 1 of 2 parts) Secret, to be kept within the Department paragraph, On March 16th the American Ambassador, Grew," etc.

Eventually, the code breakers painstakingly unmasked the plain texts for parts of fifteen fairly lengthy messages. But exhaustive study of these messages delivered a shock. There was "complete and absolute absence of any causal repetitions within any single message, no matter how long, or between two messages with different indicators the same day." Even when repetitions of three or four cipher letters occurred, they never represented the same plain text. "In fact," noted the head of the US Army code-breaking unit William Friedman, "statistical calculation gave the astonishing result that the number of repetitions actually present in these cryptograms was less than the number to be expected had the letters comprising them been drawn at random out of a hat." Thus, the Americans realized the machine had been designed ingeniously and purposely to suppress all plain text repetition.

The code breakers slowly grasped that they could not identify basic cyclically repeating cipher sequences like those produced by such familiar hardware as rotating commutators, rotors, and the like found in the known Hebern and Enigma type machines. This then forced them to redirect a final attack at locating several messages on the same day in the same indicator, or else to convert several messages in the same indicator on different days to the same base. This method nominally required twenty to twenty-five messages in the same indicator on the same day, but no more than two messages in the same indicator on the same day were available. That meant they had to convert several messages in the same indicator on different days to the same base.

Through a process too complex even for Friedman to describe in his final report, the code breakers managed to secure a set of merely six messages, all in one indicator that they reduced to the same base. Only two of these messages were complete or near complete; just fragments of the other four were known. From this minuscule sample of six messages, the code breakers finally discerned brief and scattered intervals of repeated sequences on 20 September 1940, at about 1400—nineteen months to the day from its introduction.

As one of the staff working on these select messages, Miss Genevieve Grotjan conducted yet another tedious examination of worksheets on the messages. She finally located in multiple locations correlations between plain text and cipher text equivalents. With her manner radiating a sense of excitement, she summoned the team leader, Frank Rowlett, and two other cryptanalysts, Robert Ferner and Albert Small. She directed their attention successively to four areas she had circled on the worksheets. Rowlett and the others instantly grasped the monumental significance of this first small hole through the previously impervious wall of secrecy of "Purple." With his arms upraised and clasped like a victorious prize fighter, Small began a jig around her desk and exclaimed "Whoopee!" The normally sedate Ferner shouted "Hurrah, Hurrah" as he clapped his hands. Even Rowlett began jumping up and down and letting loose with cries of "That's it! That's it! Gene has found what we've been looking for!" In classic understatement, Friedman noted, "There was much excitement at this first glimmer of light upon a subject that had for so many months been shrouded in complete darkness and regarded occasionally with some discouragement." It was a sublime moment that demanded that the normally rigid traces of bureaucratic dignity be released in exuberant celebration. So the code breakers—with Friedman's approval—kicked up their collective heels by an order of Coca-Colas all around.

Even with these initial clues of some cyclic or symmetric sequences, the underlying basic cryptographic laws that would explain the shifts from one sequence to another at first defied solution. But the reenergized team accelerated its tempo with much night work, so that only one week later they could hand in two translations of fresh messages representing the very first solution of the "Purple" machine. The date was 27 September: by remarkable coincidence, the date the Tripartite Pact was signed.

With one indicator identified, the next phase involved not only the solution of the remaining 119 indicators, but also the transformation of the theoretical principles of construction and operation of the machine, derived from pure logic, into construction of an equivalent machine. The machine consisted of thirteen rotary, six-level, twenty-five-point switches of the type called "stepping switches" employed in automatic telephony. One of the thirteen switches controlled the encipherment of the "6s" and advanced through the same twenty-five-point cycle over and over again, as often as was required to complete the message. As to the "20s," these were enciphered by three banks of four switches each, with each bank having 500 cross connections, making a total of 1,500 subcircuits available for enciphering any given letter.

Postwar congressional hearings on the Pearl Harbor attack would publicize this critical breakthrough. In 1974 the revelation that the Allies had triumphed against German codes, particularly those generated by the Enigma Machine, spawned a vast celebratory library. This raises the intriguing question as to which, if either, of these feats is more impressive. From a purely technical standpoint, "Purple" and first Enigma three-rotor machines were roughly on par. The later four-rotor Enigma machine was more challenging than "Purple." The British enjoyed two enormous head starts in their efforts. First, a commercial, open market version of the Enigma machine provided fundamental insight into the structure and operation of the machine. Second, important work by Polish code breakers handed over to the British facilitated the attack. By contrast, breaking "Purple" represented the brute application of pure logic to recover the cryptographic laws governing the system, and then Friedman's team turned that theoretical knowledge into a duplicate of a machine they had never seen. Breaking "Purple" *and* creating an analog is arguably the more stunning achievement.

The 1940 American Presidential Election

The Tripartite Pact also overlapped with the 1940 American presidential election. The East Coast Republican establishment contrived to nominate Wendell L. Willkie, an attractive and articulate Wall Street lawyer turned utilities executive. They outmaneuvered the party's more conservative midwestern core constituency, whose members were not pleased with a nominee who had been a Democrat most of his life and who had voted for Roosevelt in 1932. Moreover, Willkie had pledged all-out support for Britain, thus potentially neutralizing the war and peace issue.

Roosevelt coyly held out the prospect that he would not seek an unprecedented third term, but his paladins found it easy to secure his nomination from the delegates in Chicago. Over the opposition of many party faithful, Roosevelt insisted on the very liberal Henry Wallace as his vice-presidential running mate. Since Wallace had been a Republican in 1932, this created the curious spectacle of both parties placing at the top of the ticket nominees who recently had been with the opposite party.

What followed bids for first place as the most vicious presidential campaign in American history; its angry tides continued to roil up to the time of Pearl Harbor. Besides apoplexy over the New Deal, the Republicans returned again and again to the charge that Roosevelt's real ambition was to overthrow democracy and install a dictatorship in America. A second theme was that Roosevelt intended to take America into the war against the wishes of a clear majority of Americans and would use any tactic to that end. Up until the last weeks of the campaign, Roosevelt cagily ignored his challenger, carrying on as though too consumed with his executive duties, particularly overseeing the massive defense buildup authorized since mid-year.

Willkie started instinctively on the high road, but facing daunting polling numbers favoring Roosevelt by as much as 60 percent, and frustrated by Roosevelt's refusal to engage him, shifted to ever more savage attacks. Willkie tried to establish a real material difference between them over war and peace and domestically over democracy. Willkie called the destroyers-for-bases deal with Britain "the most dictatorial and arbitrary act of any President in the history of the United States." With the polls apparently indicating a tightening race, Roosevelt was compelled to declare publicly, "I have said this before, and but shall say it again and again and again: Your boys are not going to be sent into any foreign war."

But in answering charges of warmongering, Roosevelt and the Democrats more than matched their adversaries in venom. Not content to call the Republican position unwise or perilous to American freedom and independence, the Democrats denounced their adversaries as flat-out traitors. In his acceptance speech for the party nomination, Roosevelt characterized his opponents as "appeaser fifth-columnists." (The term "Fifth Columnist," from the Spanish Civil War, was one species of "traitor.")[*] This theme did not begin or end with the 1940 campaign; ominously, it reflected deeply held beliefs. By the fall of 1941, Secretary of the Interior Ickes delivered a public speech declaring opponents of Roosevelt's policies to be those "who consciously or unconsciously are playing the traitor's part." Not only did this invite later retribution in kind, the fact is that Roosevelt and many of his senior subordinates genuinely believed that much of the Axis triumph was due to "Fifth Column" activity. They further believed anti-interventionists were directed and funded by

---

[*] During the Spanish Civil War, a Nationalist general commented at one point that they were advancing on Madrid with four military columns and that there was a fifth column of sympathizers in Madrid itself. The phrase caught on and for years thereafter, the term "Fifth Columnist" meant a traitor, covert or open, working from within to secure the victory of the enemy.

the Axis powers. The administration launched multiple investigations by Federal agencies to confirm these beliefs, including wire-tapping by the Federal Bureau of Investigation and the Treasury Department. Although these failed to confirm the existence of Axis control of domestic critics, the belief endured and would have grave consequences for some Americans after Pearl Harbor. On 4 November, the American people reelected Roosevelt by a wide margin of 27 million to 22 million votes.

China's Communists

"In 1937 . . . the [Chinese Communist Party, or CCP] was still a tiny, battered rump of survivors, far from the centers of Chinese life," wrote historian Diana Lary. She emphasized further that there was no inexorable connection that links the often ragtag radical movements, including the Communists, in the 1920s and the ultimate triumph of Mao Zedong's armies in 1949. The outbreak of war in 1937 found the Communists so marginalized compared to Chiang and the Nationalists that Stalin experienced no qualms in supporting the latter over the former based on who really could contain Japan. Mao himself would famously respond to a penitent Japanese prime minister Kakuei Tanaka in 1972 that were it not for Japan's aggression, he would never have succeeded. The ultimate triumph of Mao and the CCP was not, however, simply a matter of default. It also derived from Mao's and Stalin's usually astute choices about political and military strategy.

Vladimir Lenin sent two operatives as the initiating spark for the formation of the CCP in 1920. The party—then numbering fifty-three members—convened its first congress at Shanghai in July 1921. Mao Zedong was among the twelve delegates, a group dominated by teachers, journalists, and intellectuals. There were no workers or peasants.

Mao Zedong was born on 26 December 1893, in the village of Shaoshan, in the province of Hunan, South China. He was the third born, but first surviving son to Mao Yichang. Typical of peasants in rural China, the elder Mao consulted a Daoist fortune teller who recommended the name Mao Zedong ("Benefactor of the East"). Mao Yichang himself grew up in abject poverty. He served as a soldier for a time and used his army pay to redeem family-tilled land. Then by dint of shrewdness and ceaseless work, he raised himself into the respectable orbit of a relatively rich peasant who rented out some of his own lands.

In later life, Mao Zedong depicted a contentious relationship with an ill-tempered and even cruel father —though not as cruel as the father of one of Mao's great generals, Zhu De. (Zhu's desperately poor father drowned with his own hand five of his children in a pond.) Whatever their differences, Mao's father faithfully subsidized the son through a protracted and erratic academic voyage that eventually led to the son's fateful landfall with Marxism. From an early age Mao exhibited the stubbornness consistent with the Chinese stereotype of the Hunanese: "hot like their food." His kind and generous mother Wen Qimei (literally "Seventh Sister Wen" because girls were only entitled to numbers, not separate names), whom Mao loved deeply, served as a peacemaker between the rebellious offspring and his father. In about 1907, Mao Zedong's parents picked out a wife for him four years his senior. Mao Zedong insisted the marriage was never consummated and he abandoned her. (She died young of dysentery shrouded by a rumor that Mao's father had taken her as a concubine.)

With his actual life experiences opening only a minute peephole vision of the world, Mao Zedong avidly turned to books. His voracious reading accented a Chinese history replete with ruthless emperors and rebellions, which stamped his mind for life and ignited his fevered ambition. Mao particularly admired Emperor Liu Bang, the first to rise from a commoner, who overthrew one despot only to become another and to kill all his faithful lieutenants as potential rivals. Another favorite was Qin Shi Huangdi, whose infamous cruelties included an episode in which he buried alive 460 Confucian scholars. But even Mao's relatively modest early education vaulted him into the top 2.5 percent of the population and instilled a lofty sense of superior station that made performing menial tasks like hauling his own water beneath him.

Writing stood preeminent among subjects in Chinese schools, and Mao's highest marks came there—he also was agile with poetry. "[Mao] wrote quickly," one contemporary recalled, "as if sparks were flying from his writing brush." From age twenty and into his forties, Mao was tall and lanky, with an impressive presence. His handsome face featured dark, sad eyes, and a broad and high forehead framed on three sides by dense black hair gradually receding at the top. Prominent cheeks flanked a long, curved ridge of nose, below which was what American radical Agnes Smedley dared call a feminine mouth. He pulled himself up a ladder of institutions to Beijing University by 1918. By now Mao, who combined "the air of both a peasant and an old-style scholar," eagerly partook of the intellectual brew that freely mingled traditional Chinese thought with classical liberalism, socialism, anarchism, and even vegetarianism. He started as just an assistant librarian, with a monthly income about half that of the average rickshaw puller in Beijing. But he made his mark with his scribing and married his first wife, Yang Kaihui ("Dawn" or "Little Dawn"), the daughter of one of his favorite teachers.

A university professor first proselytized Bolshevism to China's intellectual class. In November 1920, Mao became a convert. In the words of insightful biographers Alexander Pantsov and Steven Levine, it was not "the romance of universal equality" that drew Mao to Communism, but "the apologia for violence, the triumph of will, and the celebration of power." For the next fifteen years, the fortunes of the CCP and of Mao would wax and wane markedly. Funding constituted Moscow's ultimate means of control, for without Soviet money the CCP would scarcely have risen above an ineffectual collection of radical thinkers. Representatives dispatched by the Communist International (Comintern) headquarters in Moscow formed the direct control mechanism. Mao's own status fluctuated, gaining and losing top party posts. His judgment also erred at times, but less so than the typical breed of Chinese intellectual who ran the party on the fumes of theories they absorbed in Moscow classrooms. Mao and similar leaders walked a narrow line between ostensible fealty to Comintern dictates, and efforts to displace Moscow-anointed superiors and take the party in radically deviant directions.

Ultimately Mao's three critical contributions extracted the CCP from impotence. First, he recognized that the CCP must have its own army, using the later famous aphorism that "political power is obtained from the barrel of the gun." Second, he (with help from Zhu De) incubated tactics for the Red Army. These tactics were integral to what later became globally known as the strategy of People's War. With his trademark facility for pithy summary, he described this in a 1929 letter to party leaders as: "The enemy advances, we retreat; the enemy camps, we harass; the enemy tires, we attack; the enemy retreats, we pursue."

Third (but by no means the least important), Mao eventually won the argument that the CCP must emphasize the peasant masses. This spectacularly diverged from classic "scientific" Marxist theory of the inexorable tramp of history from feudalism to bourgeois democracy to a proletarian-led revolutionary finale. Like (or worse than) Russia, however, China contained a tiny proletariat compared to the peasantry. Unlike Shanghai-based intellectuals, Mao personally investigated conditions in the countryside and parlayed his research into a reputation as the party's leading authority on the peasantry. Events demonstrated all too tragically that Mao's later policies would inflict catastrophes on China's peasants. The font of these disasters proved to be the complexity of China's countryside, which belied the crude portrait of a binary class structure of a few rich landlords grasping virtually all the land and a sea of landless peasants.

"One characteristic feature of village life in China," explained Pantsov and Levine, "was the division of society not into gentry and peasantry, as in the West, but into two deeply antagonistic parts: those who had land, including not only the rich but all who could feed themselves, and those without land, the rural lumpen proletariat." The chasm between even poor farmers who rented their land and this lumpen proletariat was "a hundred times greater than that between rich and poor peasants." The lumpen proletariat who lacked the means to feed themselves turned to crime and violence, driving even landless tenant farmers to identify their interests with those of the landlords.

The stark clan divisions among the villages inserted yet more complexity. In the average village or collection of villages, everyone was related, closely or distantly, as exemplified by the same surname that all carried. Incomes might vary widely, but blood relationships outweighed class consciousness. The sense of a blood-based community was buttressed by the fact that rents were often advantageous rather than grossly exploitative, and also by shared membership in the local militias that provided desperately needed security for life and property from rural bandits and especially from other clans.

Traditional yawning chasms between rich and poor clans marked another pervasive schism in China, especially Southern China. The poor clans normally comprised those that had migrated often centuries earlier, commonly from North to South China. The southerners labeled them *Hakka*, the sound of the word in the northern dialect for *kejia* (guest). The *Hakka* (numbering about 30 million in South China) typically had not integrated culturally or socially and normally only rented the less fertile lands, often on exploitative terms. (*Hakka* women did not bind their feet because they had to work steep upland fields.) The original local clans, called *bendi* ("core inhabitants") harbored both contempt and fear of the *Hakka*. For *bendi*, land redistribution where there was already a gross shortage of fertile land threatened to leave the majority with even less land to sustain themselves. For their part, the *Hakka* and rural lumpen proletariat hankered not for land redistribution but for the power to humiliate or even to annihilate the *bendi*.

Terror had coursed through dynastic Chinese history for millennia, but in the Republican Era it shifted from sporadic to systematic toward the end of the 1920s. From at least 1926, the CCP (notably including Mao, who in early 1927 called for a reign of terror in the countryside) made terror an official policy and nurtured armed peasant associations who commenced murdering those they called "local bullies and evil gentry." Their opponents struck back in kind, but these outbursts were uncoordinated. Chiang secured indisputable evidence in January 1927 that Mikhail Borodin, the Comintern representative, had attempted to replace him with Zongren Li. On 6 April 1927, Chiang obtained documentary evidence confirming Moscow's close control of the CCP.

Chiang decided to strike a decisive blow against the Communists just as his Northern Expedition achieved his goals. On 12 April, his supporters, accompanied by Green Gang gangster contingents, launched a "White Terror" campaign commencing in Shanghai. Over the next several months the campaign killed 3,000 to 4,000 Communists and as many as 30,000 others. This formalized the beginning of a twenty-two-year civil war. Thereafter, Chiang launched four "Anti-Bandit" Campaigns designed to eradicate Communist strongholds in the countryside, especially that of Mao in Jiangxi. These failed, both due to Mao's clever tactics and the fact that Chiang's efforts were dispersed to deal with both rebellious regional leaders and the Japanese.

In December 1930, the Futian Incident, sometimes known as the A-B *tuan* (AB Corps) Incident, unfolded amid the "Anti-Bandit" campaigns with an Intra–Communist Party bloodbath. Some local Communist Party members challenged what they viewed as the extreme radicalism of Mao's rural policies. Mao turned terror inward on the party itself. A frenzied purge took place, using the torture of party members and sometimes their wives to secure "confessions" implicating other party members. The final toll numbered in the tens of thousands. It is of historical note that Mao unleashed large-scale terror on fellow party members well prior to such episodes by Hitler or Stalin.

In 1933, Chiang took personal command of the Fifth "Anti-Bandit" Campaign. This time Chiang installed a tight blockade and combined it with effective political warfare. On Moscow's order, in October 1934 Mao embarked on "The Long March." In January 1935, Mao was elected to senior military and political posts. He and his faction gained an ascendancy they would never lose thenceforth. In October 1935, Mao and his vastly diminished column reached Northern Shaanxi Province, just south of the Great Wall. This event became the "glorious foundation myth" of the CCP, but behind the legend were the basic points that it was a disaster in terms of losses and, in fact, where the march ended was dictated by happenstance, not by plan, as customarily presented.

From the outbreak of the war in July 1937, Mao conceded Chiang's genuine opposition to Japan, but neither of them saw the United Front as more than a temporary passage to be followed by renewed struggle. Chiang recognized separate Red Army forces, titled the Eighth Route Army, originally three divisions with 30,000 men. Their base was the Special Border Region of the Chinese Republic; it included about 1.45 million persons (roughly 0.3 percent of China's population) in eighteen counties in Shaanxi, Gansu, and Ningxia provinces in Northwest China. A little later Chiang bestowed recognition on a separate 12,000-man command in Central China, designated the New Fourth Army.

Mao severely faulted Chiang's willingness to engage in conventional battle with the Japanese. Yet some Communist leaders argued for committing Red Army units to such combat. Moscow itself directed maintenance of the United Front and maximum effort against the Japanese. Mao objected that not only were the very weak Red Army units completely unsuited to such warfare, but also that this would lead to loss of party control of its armed forces and thus facilitate what Mao saw as Chiang's ultimate aim for the decimation of armed Communist units followed by the occupation of Communist base areas by Chiang's forces. Mao entertained an even more paranoid view, peaking in 1940, that Chiang would surrender to the Japanese and then combine with them to eradicate the Communists. Throughout, Mao dictated absolute priority to guerrilla operations or "sparrow war" as he called it. Communist guerrillas confined Japanese control to urban areas and their linking lines of communication over large expanses of northern and northwestern China. At the same time, Mao shrewdly seized the opportunity the war presented to rapidly extend Communist political control from its extremely low starting point.

Mao's strategy proved very economical in casualties but left by far the main burden of fighting the Japanese to Chiang's coalition. Indeed, Mao insisted that no more than one-third of the main Red Army forces be sent to fight the Japanese and 25 percent be maintained in reserve to defend against Nationalist attack. In January 1940, Stalin read a secret report from Zhou Enlai summarizing the war through the first two years. According to Zhou, during this period Chinese armed forces overall sustained a million men killed and wounded. But of this total, he stated, Communist military units lost just 31,000 killed and wounded—less than 3 percent of the total.

During Mao's reign, the entrenched version of the CCP's rise during the war was that his lieutenants faithfully followed Mao's brilliant concepts of People's War, emphasizing the mobilization of the rural masses through class warfare. But historians within and outside the PRC now present a far more nuanced accounting that emphasizes the highly diverse paths local CCP organizations followed. Among these varied stories, that of the New Fourth Army stands apart. The New Fourth Army sprouted from unconnected guerrilla bands left behind after the "Long March." From 1937, they penetrated from their mountain refuges down into largely level, densely populated East Central China, astride the Yangtze River. The profile of the New Fourth Army, compared to Mao's main force, the Eighth Route Army, disclosed more workers, intellectuals, women, the offspring of gentry, returned overseas Chinese, and younger cadres. Its sophisticated cadres reflected their birth and education in China's entrepôt for modernity in economics and culture. By contrast, their northern counterparts grew up in and now proselytized in the far more backward northwestern region. Unlike the Eighth Route Army, the New Fourth Army stressed "Machiavelli, not Marx" according to their most devoted Western chronicler, Gregor Benton. It appealed to United Front unity rather than class struggle cleavages. The New Fourth Army flexibly calibrated its allure from province to province and county to county, wooing and sometimes betraying the full spectrum of Chinese classes, clans, and associations.

The northwestern haunts of the Eighth Route Army differed radically from the east central regions contested by the New Fourth Army. Topographically, the forests and mountains in the north provided the prerequisites for guerrilla bases, an environment lacking in the level, open eastern central region. The Nationalists had never achieved a firm grip in the north, exercising what sway they could predominantly through alliances with local power brokers. Under the Japanese onslaught, these preexisting governmental structures collapsed. The Japanese forces held cities and key lines of communications but left a vacuum in the countryside into which the Communists flowed easily. Here blunt appeals to class warfare resonated through a countryside impoverished even by the low standards of northern China. By contrast, East Central China formed a major locus of prewar Nationalist power and loomed as a critical region in a postwar struggle for supremacy between the Nationalists and CCP. Even after the Japanese swept over the area, the Nationalists retained both a major political and a military presence. Moreover, in the wake of Japanese legions, not only the Nationalists and the New Fourth Army squabbled, but also Japanese puppet forces, bandit gangs, and autonomous contingents devoid of ideological affiliation.

In April 1940, Mao ordered the commanders of the Eighth Route and New Fourth Armies to press for expansion of activities wherever they could and "not to be bound by the Kuomintang's restrictions." By about that time, the New Fourth Army counted some 90,000 men and the Eighth Route Army roughly four times that number. The extension of Communist control beyond originally sanctioned territories resulted in an agreement in Chongqing between Chiang and Zhou Enlai—who consistently appeared to work cooperatively to preserve the United Front—for the Eighth Route and New Fourth Armies to confine their operations to north of the Yellow River. Zhou agreed, probably because he recognized that Chiang was sanctioning Communist control in a vast swath of North China, including Beijing and Tianjin, which would also provide a direct link between Mao and the Soviet border. Mao, however, rejected the proposal, for he sought opportunities to expand his control to territories south of both the Yellow and Yangtze Rivers.

In August and September 1940, the Eighth Route Army launched the "Hundred Regiments Campaign." Eventually involving 104 "regiments," it constituted the sole major Communist conventional campaign of the war. While officially targeting North China railroad lines to cut down Japan's supplies of vital high-quality coking coal, the enterprise also aimed to restore recent losses in base areas and to stifle criticism of the CCP's paltry military effort. The initial surge procured some profit, but massed Japanese reinforcements—augmented with poison gas—crushed the offensive. Superior Japanese firepower emphatically trumped superior Chinese numbers—a senior Chinese Communist general confessed that even outnumbered seven to one, the Japanese prevailed. Communist losses totaled about 22,000 killed and wounded and reached about 100,000, counting desertions, out of an original force of about 570,000. Japanese losses were about 3,000 to 4,000.

This military retaliation paled compared to Japan's doctrine of the "Three Alls" ("kill all, burn all, destroy all"), a near-extermination campaign against civilians. Japanese soldiers surged over rural locations in the plains suspected of harboring Communists, torching dwellings and crops, demolishing dikes and wells, and slaughtering livestock and men, women, and children regardless of age. The population within this Communist-dominated area plummeted at least temporarily from 44 million to 25 million. Never again would Mao mount any conventional or massed guerrilla campaign during the war.

In the middle of the "Hundred Regiments" Campaign, the Communist New Fourth Army crushed the Nationalist Eighty-Ninth Army in October 1940. This followed several other full-scale battles between Nationalists and Communists and highlighted the New Fourth Army's unauthorized intrusions into Jiangsu and Shandong provinces north of the Yangtze River. At Chiang's urging, the Military Council, the top military command authority under the United Front, promulgated formal orders ultimately commanding the New Fourth Army to be north of the Yangtze by 31 December 1940, heading to a final position north of the Yellow River.

Gen. Ying Xiang, the commander of the New Fourth Army, led a division south rather than north on 4 January 1941. Nationalist forces surrounded and killed or captured about 10,000 men of the New Fourth Army. Xiang escaped but was murdered by a bounty hunter in March 1941. Much controversy over who is to blame surrounds this event. Some charged Chiang as deliberately plotting the attack; some alleged Mao manipulated Xiang to produce an episode to discredit Chiang and the Nationalists; others placed all the blame on Xiang.

A People's Republic of China historian, Kuisong Yang, gained unique access to Communist files. He asserts that the Nationalists and Communists were in regular communication. The Nationalists prepared and stocked two exit routes for Xiang to the north, but Xiang's plunge south surprised Mao, Chongqing, and the Nationalist local commanders. Mao did not connive Xiang's movements, and Chiang did not order the attack. But Yang concluded that the deep suspicions emanating from a decade of civil war made some such clash inevitable.

The Communists leveraged defeat in the field into a huge propaganda victory. Blame for the incident both within and outside China cascaded upon Chiang. The governments of Britain and the United States expressed disapproval, but like the Soviets, did not halt aid to Chiang. The oft-ventured assertion that the incident signaled the death of the United Front exaggerates the level of cooperation before and the level of overt hostilities thereafter. From 1941 to 1945, the Communists and Chiang fired far more volleys of recriminations and abuse than bullets at each other.

Within China, however, the "incident" exerted two profound effects. First, it effectively checked Chiang's efforts to confine the expansion of Communist influence into ever greater reaches of the country. This would have enormous consequences in the 1945–1949 Civil War. Second, the New Fourth Army's rival political strategy—emphasizing unity as well as features of pluralism and accommodation—was aborted and replaced by Mao's generally cruder class warfare banner, though tactically Mao would sometimes only deploy the slogans of class warfare, but not actually implement them, by concrete measures like land confiscation or even rent and interest reduction. For nearly three decades after his triumph in the Civil War, Mao would implement much purer class warfare policies that would have lethal and horrific consequences for tens of millions of Chinese. The possibility that the New Fourth Army's political program might have provided a much different course for Communist China under the rival leadership of Xiang makes the New Fourth Army Incident far more than an obscure chapter in the war.

Thus, historian Hans van de Ven observed that, as the calendar turned to 1941, "The Nationalists were on their knees"—but so too was the whole anti-Axis cause.

:

CHAPTER 7

"One Hundred Evils and Not a Single Good"

PARLEYS AND FOLLIES JANUARY TO JUNE 1941

The "Matsuoka Troupe"

Mere "diplomatic triumph" like the Tripartite Pact could not satiate Matsuoka's ego; he craved celebrity status as a "star on the diplomatic stage." Thus, upon departing Tokyo on 12 March 1941 for a fateful European hegira, Matsuoka mischievously christened his entourage the "Matsuoka troupe"—evoking the image of a circus act. The inaugural run of the "troupe" featured performances in Berlin and Rome affirming Tripartite Pact solidarity and a deal-making interlude in Moscow. Following this adventure, he envisioned state visits to Hawaii to consecrate a sphere of influence agreement with the United States that would divide the Pacific, and then to Chongqing, where he would settle the China War.

Ensconced in his coach on the Trans-Siberian Express, Matsuoka shocked his subordinates by vocally reflecting on Japan's Soviet relations. Attributing past conflicts to the malign manipulations of the United States and the United Kingdom, he declared his devotion to opening a new chapter of close and cordial relations. At first his companions thought Matsuoka stunningly oblivious to the undoubted Soviet bugging of their compartments. But it gradually dawned on his young acolytes that Matsuoka had commenced wooing the Kremlin via the eavesdropping.

At a brief halt in Moscow en route to Berlin, Matsuoka talked to American ambassador Lawrence Steinhardt, denying Japanese designs on Singapore and tendering his wish to see FDR mediate the Sino-Japanese conflict. In Berlin, German officials urged a Japanese attack on Singapore, and Hitler volunteered the inducement that "if Japan gets into a conflict with the United States, Germany on her part will take the necessary steps at once." Matsuoka adroitly protested his lack of authority to discuss military matters, but he detected an ominous sharp deterioration in German-Soviet relations. Excited by Japan's opportunities in a German-Soviet conflict, Japanese ambassador Ōshima Hiroshi urged Matsuoka to avoid even parchment shackles on Japan's hands with the Soviets.

While the "Matsuoka troupe" cavorted across Europe, Germany again flaunted its military prowess. In the aftermath of the French capitulation and wary of Soviet ambitions, Romania tossed its lot in with the Axis. Hitler shifted ground and air units into Romania to protect the massive oil fields, essential to the German war effort. This unilateral infringement on an Italian sphere of interest enraged Mussolini. He decided to retaliate by seizing Greece without prior notice to Berlin. "If anyone makes any difficulties about beating the Greeks," declared Mussolini, "I shall resign from being an Italian." He hurled his army from Albania into Greece on 28 October 1940. The Greeks amazed the world by flinging back the Italians in November and defeating another Italian attack in March 1941. In the New Year, the British sought to enlist the Greeks, Yugoslavia, and Turkey to resist Germany. This grand design failed, but Churchill pledged to aid Greece.

Hitler was furious. Mussolini's rogue endeavor served the British a pretext for establishing air bases in Greece, threatening not only Italy but also the Romanian oil fields. As German units massed in Bulgaria, Berlin tried to recruit Yugoslavia to the Axis cause. On 25 March 1941, the Yugoslav government buckled to German pressure. Two days later an anti-Nazi coup d'état installed a new government that not only rejected German demands, but also signed a nonaggression pact with the Soviets on 5 April. The coup infuriated Hitler, who unleashed an attack on Yugoslavia on 6 April. The onslaught commenced with a massive punitive bombing of Belgrade that killed 17,000. The Italians, Bulgarians, and Hungarians marched with the Germans. Yugoslavia fell in just eleven days.

Dusty German columns marched or motored through Yugoslavia into Greece. An Australian–New Zealand corps drawn from the Western Desert fought alongside the Greek Army. Despite a few local reverses, the Germans hustled Allied forces out of Greece by May. The British Royal Navy evacuated most of the Commonwealth contingent despite German air supremacy. Hitler's rapid defeat of hard-fighting Greek and Commonwealth forces in terrain highly favorable to defense further burnished the reputation of German arms.

Still more awesome was the German conquest of Crete in May. In the world's first massed airborne assault, German paratroopers, despite horrifying casualties, bested numerically superior Commonwealth defenders. The Royal Navy suffered dreadful losses in yet another evacuation. For the first time the British people contemplated defeat; one British soldier wrote: "The infallibility of the Germans is an idea that is rapidly gaining ground."

Matsuoka arrived in Moscow as Germany pummeled Yugoslavia and Greece. He exclaimed: "I can now have my treaty," correctly recognizing Stalin's enormously bolstered interest in stabilizing his eastern flank as the Germans closed in from the west. Both uniformed and civilian Japanese leaders had been weaned on virulent anti-Russian and later anti-Soviet ideology. The Russian/Soviet colossus stood astride avenues of Japanese interest or outright advance on the Asian continent. But a broad section of Imperial Army leadership now regarded ending the China War as the primary task. If diplomacy could maneuver the Soviets into an agreement that would cut off the supply line from the Soviet Union to China, it would strike a deadly practical and potent symbolic blow against the ability and resolve of Chiang to continue the war. Reinforcing this first tier of thinking came a second. German triumph in Europe in June 1940 opened Japan's vistas for a southern advance. Securing Japan's northern frontiers formed a prerequisite to such a thrust, thus further increasing the importance of a Soviet settlement.

By 13 April, Matsuoka had his treaty. The Soviets declined to sign a nonaggression pact as Matsuoka hoped, but did agree to a five-year neutrality pact— thus implicitly securing Japan's northern flank to free it for a strike south. The terms of the pact were simple and direct. Each party promised to respect "the territorial integrity and inviolability of the other contracting party," and they vouched effectively that Japan would stay neutral in a Soviet-German war and the Soviets would stay neutral in a US-Japan war. Much to Chinese anger, the Soviets also recognized Manchukuo.

Following a vodka-and-champagne-soaked revel, Stalin and Foreign Minister Molotov escorted an inebriated Matsuoka to his departing train. But if Stalin sought to affirm his satisfaction with his new agreement with Japan with this most unusual gesture, he also took the occasion to display misgivings about the durability of his bond with Hitler. Grabbing the German ambassador by the shoulders, Stalin exclaimed: "We must remain friends and you must now do everything to that end." The Soviet-Japanese Neutrality Pact delivered a severe jolt to Chiang's government, although the Soviets provided reassurances that their relationship would not change. The United States responded on 25 April with a $50 million loan.

The American loan to China was the lesser of two major American initiatives during this period. US neutrality laws forced the British (and other Axis opponents) to pay with cash for munitions purchased in the United States. On 8 December 1940, Churchill wrote to Roosevelt an extraordinarily candid letter explaining that Britain would soon run out of funds to pay for vital war supplies. The president's first public response came on 29 December 1940. In one of his most important "Fireside Chats" by radio to the American public, Roosevelt pledged his commitment to keeping the country out of war, but emphasized that to achieve that the nation must become the "Great Arsenal of Democracy." This led directly to the Lend-Lease Program designed to "lend" the output of the "arsenal" to the nations holding the line against the Axis powers without requiring payment first. The noninterventionists mounted a powerful campaign against the concept, but Roosevelt coined a brilliantly simple analogy that the act was like lending your neighbor a fire hose so he could fight a fire in his house. The law passed the legislative branch on 11 March 1941, by votes of 317 to 71 in the House and 60 to 31 in the Senate. These strong majorities reflected a public disposition to accept the bill on the terms presented by Roosevelt: it would avoid US entry into the war by arming opponents of the Axis.

China Endures

If the end of 1940 found Chiang's coalition on its knees, the first half of 1941 remained a trial—particularly on the psychological front—but with both some immediate success and heartening glimmers of improved fortunes toward the end of this period. Militarily, the period began with two major Japanese offensives geared to destroy a pair of the largest war zones now tenuously connected to Chongqing. The Japanese first placed their sights on the Fifth War Zone in the Battle of Southern Henan (South Central China) from 25 January to 10 February. About 150,000 Japanese troops marched north from Wuhan astride the Hankou-Beijing railroad. The Chinese again barely contested the Japanese advance at first. As the Japanese became extended and exhausted their supplies, the Chinese fell on their rear. The end of the campaign found the Japanese back to their jump-off positions, less their casualties, which may have exceeded those of the Chinese.

The Japanese then wheeled to attack the Ninth War Zone. The prize was the city of Shanggao, which donated its name to the battle. From this locale, the Ninth War Zone threatened Japanese holdings along Yangtze. In Japanese hands, it would open a route to attack the still more important city of Changsha from the west. The battle unfolded like reruns of excerpts from prior clashes. The Japanese sought to converge on Shanggao in three columns. The Nationalists employed their now-proven tactics of only harassing the Japanese at first before falling on their rear, cutting off one column, encircling a second, and forestalling any linkup in Shanggao. The result was a Chinese victory, less well known than Taierzhuang but "at least as impressive" in the judgment of historian Hans van de Ven. The Japanese then scored a triumph in the Zhongtiao Mountains of Southern Shanxi. From this position the Nationalist First War Zone threatened the Japanese presence in North China and impeded communications between the Communist stronghold in Yan'an and other Communist areas. But the Japanese ejected the Nationalist forces from the mountains, partly offsetting defeat at Shanggao.

The companion to this mostly good news on the military front was a political event of great moment. Roosevelt dispatched his economic aide, Canadian-born Lauchlin Currie, to China on an inspection trip in February 1941. Currie's report emphasized the need for increased aid to China, and he became a mainstay of this effort, notably in the Lend-Lease Program. Not surprisingly for a covert Soviet agent, Currie's report displayed muted affinity for the Chinese Communists and catalogued the discontent with Chiang's government at numerous levels, from the prospective of "liberal and progressive" elements. But Currie's portrait of Chiang personally was balanced. Currie emphasized Chiang as a "true Chinese patriot" bent on unifying China, not merely a tool of "property interests." Currie highlighted the need to provide China aircraft and airmen; this would soon bear fruit. After Currie returned, the president sent his son, James, conspicuously wearing his uniform as a Marine Corps officer, to Hong Kong and Chongqing. The visit's obvious symbolism also worked to the aid of those advocating a stronger garrison in Hong Kong.

State Department officials endorsed a major theme of Currie's report: the increasingly disastrous state of Chongqing finances. By Currie's March 1941 figures, even with tax reforms boosting central government revenues in 1941, receipts still would barely equal one-third of estimated annual expenditure. As an American financial adviser noted in May, the government covered the deficit by printing money. That, plus the actual shortage of goods, created an inflation estimated at 700 percent from 1937 to the end of 1940. By the end of 1941, the American ambassador calculated Chinese government expenditures were "nearer" 10 billion Chinese dollars while revenues from all sources totaled only about 10 percent of that figure. The ambassador further estimated that the amount of Chinese currency in circulation had leaped from 2.5 billion in 1937 to about 14 billion in 1941. In Currie's accurate view, inflation exerted even more dire social and political effects that exceeded its severe purely economic aspects.

US-Japanese Negotiations Commence

Matsuoka parted Moscow in a stupor but arrived in Tokyo sober enough to deliver a report to the emperor shaded to his hopes rather than his fears: "the outlook for German-Soviet relations was 60 percent for the conclusion of an agreement and 40 percent for war." But the cables awaiting him recounting US-Japanese negotiations enraged him. The story of US-Japanese diplomatic relations in the year before the outbreak of the Pacific War is an exceedingly complex, multitiered tale. On both sides, a host of institutions and actors clashed while other nations pulled and tugged on decisions in Washington and Tokyo. The center of these events is the figure appointed as Japan's Washington ambassador on 8 November 1940, retired admiral Kichisaburō Nomura. All these institutions, actors, and forces intersected in Nomura's earnest, self-appointed crusade to stave off war.

In 1898 Nomura received a pair of binoculars from Emperor Meiji's own hands to award his standing as the number-two man in his naval academy class. Over the next decades, his superiors groomed Nomura for high rank with a series of choice billets both naval and diplomatic. Nomura forged enduring friendships with important American naval officers, who warmed to his frank and outspoken personality. In 1922, as a young rear admiral, he supervised the education of Crown Prince Hirohito. Besides picking up German and (halting) English, Nomura grasped the value to Japan of the Washington Treaty; he understood that the nexus between industrial capacity and ultimate sea power far overshadowed current fleet lists. Nomura believed that Japan must never get into a war with the American economic titan. Moreover, he stood out as one of the few senior Japanese who comprehended the ideological factor in American foreign policy. He warned his government that "The majority of Americans, above all the president, see the present world war as a struggle between 'democratic' and 'totalitarian' camps . . . and will aid Britain, the stronghold of the democracies, to the hilt." American secretary of state Hull described Nomura as "tall, robust, in fine health, with an open face." Still tall and robust-looking, Nomura, sixty-four years old, had heavy jowl lines formed like parentheses around his nose and mouth.

By 1940 Nomura discerned that the only remaining bulwark against a war between Japan and the United States would be a resolute stand by the navy's top leadership acknowledging that Japan could not prevail. But Nomura also knew the Imperial Navy was no monolith. Indeed, its middle and lower echelons teemed with officers devoted to the Tripartite Pact and a southward advance strategy as a necessary step toward what they regarded as an "inevitable" war with the United States. Navy Minister Oikawa and Vice Minister Teijirō Toyoda courted him to become Japan's ambassador to the United States—professing their opposition to war with the United States, thus enhancing Nomura's hope that the navy might still arrest Japan from a final leap into the abyss. And the naval hierarchy tendered a tangible symbol of their commitment: rather than funnel his views as ambassador solely via the Foreign Ministry, Nomura would enjoy a secret direct line of communication to the elite naval leadership in Tokyo through Japan's naval attaché in Washington, Capt. Ichiro Yokoyama.

Nomura specifically sought and received assurance from Konoe, Oikawa, and Fushimi that the Tripartite Pact did not automatically commit Japan to war against the United States and Britain. Still, Nomura received warnings that his mission might prove futile. Commander in chief of the Combined Fleet, Adm. Isoroku Yamamoto, expressed doubts that any prospect remained of a diplomatic settlement between the two nations. Former prime minister Yonai went further, warning Nomura that the naval leadership "won't hesitate to pull the ladder out from under you once they've got you to climb up it."

Nomura's ostensible boss, Matsuoka, regarded the admiral as "an awfully nice guy, but not a bright one." The foreign minister intended to use Nomura's appointment as a mere nod toward a friendly atmosphere to pave the way for Matsuoka's own dazzling turn, when he would personally negotiate a settlement with the United States to Japan's advantage. Matsuoka disclosed his real vision of Nomura's insignificant role by dispatching him with no real instructions or negotiating tools.

At the Washington embassy, Nomura found Captain Yokoyama of like mind. Yokoyama had warned Tokyo that an attack on British colonial holdings in Southeast Asia would yield "one hundred evils and not a single good." But Europe, not Asia, drew Washington's attention as Nomura arrived. A British military mission reached Washington in January to conduct secret talks—pointedly, the Americans treated these as explorations of purely technical military questions and refused to permit State Department or Foreign Office participation. The British sought active American participation in the war against Germany and American measures to deter Japan. The Americans bristled at least inwardly at what they perceived as their guests' ill-founded façade of superiority, as British military performance to date had left the hosts decidedly unimpressed. Their combined labors produced the American-British-Canadian Agreement (ABC-1). The Americans pledged to give priority to the defeat of Germany in the event of war. They also promised to supply munitions to the United Kingdom, to protect trans-Atlantic convoys bearing those munitions, and ultimately to gird for a joint invasion of Europe. The parties divided on deterring Japan. The Americans acknowledged the need for deterrence but rebuffed the British plea for stationing US warships at Singapore—an act that would abrade American anticolonial ideals. In a letter advising his fleet commanders of the future foretold by the conference, Admiral Harold Stark, chief of naval operations, declared: "The question as to our entry into the war now seems to be *when* and not *whether*."

As the ABC-1 talks flourished, on 14 February—Valentine's Day—Nomura presented his credentials to Roosevelt. A "marked spirit of cordiality and personal friendliness" suffused their encounter. They reminisced fondly on their prior relationship during World War I, when Nomura was Japan's naval attaché and Roosevelt the assistant secretary of the navy. Drawing from this well of goodwill, Roosevelt declared he would call Nomura admiral rather than ambassador to evince the easy candor on which the president sought to moor their relationship. Nomura's detailed account of the interview to both Matsuoka and navy leaders stressed Roosevelt's warning about stiffening American public opinion toward Japan and the dangers of a southward advance.

A diverse cast of characters on both sides of the Pacific rushed into the vacuum created by Matsuoka's lack of instructions to Nomura. Under their pseudonym of the "John Doe Associates," they became a timeless lesson in the pitfalls of private diplomacy. The key figures of the "John Doe Associates" were Father James M. Drought, vicar general of the Roman Catholic Foreign Mission Society of America at Maryknoll in New York, and his superior Bishop James E. Walsh, the superior general of the Maryknoll Order (which specialized in missions to Asia). In November 1940, Drought and Walsh hawked in Tokyo a memorandum tailored to delight the Japanese with a prescription for a Japanese "Far Eastern Monroe Doctrine" and for steps leading to a high-level conference that would seal an agreement between Japan and the United States as the twin pillars of a Pacific community.

Drought and Walsh acted on behalf of a group in the United States led by Frank C. Walker and Lewis L. Strauss. Walker, a prominent Catholic layman and a key political figure in the Roosevelt administration, served as the postmaster general of the United States. Strauss was the private secretary to former president Herbert Hoover. The thread linking these four Americans was Irish Catholicism. Drought and Walsh approached a Japanese banker, Tadao

Ikawa, thought to have links with Prime Minister Konoe and Col. Hideo Iwakuro, the chief of the Military Affairs Section of the powerful Army Ministry's Military Affairs Bureau. Iwakuro had at best a tenuous connection with Konoe. Far from being—as Ambassador Grew mistakenly believed—"one of the most important leaders of the young officers' group" and a confidant of War Minister Tôjô, Iwakuro was viewed by Tôjô and others as a pompous, disruptive force in the ministry. Matsuoka unwisely chose to meet privately with the two clergymen in December 1940. The pair parlayed the faux legitimacy of this interview into a meeting with Roosevelt in January 1941.

The memorandum Drought and Walsh presented to Roosevelt differed radically from the one they peddled in Tokyo. This document fantastically purported to represent the views of "conservative" Japanese seeking "cooperation with the United States," who were preparing to turn on—or even declare war on—Germany. The memorandum proposed a Pacific spheres-of-influence agreement between Japan and the United States. Correctly believing the State Department would treat their concepts as anathema, the group proposed to bypass that institution and consummate their design in a summit meeting of Roosevelt and Konoe.

Of fundamental importance in explaining the extremely convoluted path of the "John Doe Associates" is that Drought foisted on his Japanese and American contacts the appearance of his inside access to both President Roosevelt and Prime Minister Konoe. Added to this, Colonel Iwakuro reached Washington in February 1941 and beguiled Walker with his supposed credentials to "negotiate concrete terms for a settlement of all Far Eastern issues." Walker duly relayed this claim to Roosevelt. Drought and Iwakuro soon ensnared the novice Nomura into their machinations.

The ultimate results of this eventually unsuccessful and obscure diplomatic drama are far more significant than its byzantine course between March and June, but some key highlights of that path stand out. First, Nomura's dispatches to the senior naval leadership emphasized the "indivisibility" of Britain and the United States and warned that a Japanese attack on Singapore or the Netherlands East Indies would guarantee US entry into hostilities. In such a war the United States would subdue Japan by campaigns of strangulation and attrition. Therefore, Japan must urgently plan a settlement with the United States—not a war.

Second, the "Draft Understanding" formed the centerpiece of the effort. This document, however, underwent dizzying multiple revisions by both sides wherein the specific terms reflected alternatively Japanese then diametrically opposed American views. The confusion peaked when at one point a

Japanese version of the "Draft Understanding" was relayed to Japanese officials as an *American proposal*, while Secretary of State Hull urged his Japanese interlocutors to present the same draft formally to the United States as a *Japanese proposal*.

Third, in April Hull sought to steer the negotiations away from the specifics of the "Draft Understanding" into a preliminary agreement on "Four Principles." These were (1) respect for the territorial integrity and sovereignty of all nations, (2) noninterference in the internal affairs of other nations, (3) equality of economic opportunity for all nations, and (4) no change in the status quo in the Pacific except by peaceful means.

Nomura then committed what his biographer Peter Mauch characterized accurately as "a blunder of monumental proportions." Nomura probably rationalized that if Japan ended its war in China and announced its peaceful intentions in Southeast Asia, it would substantially satisfy Hull's quartet of principles. On the other hand, if he forwarded Hull's "principles" to his government, the talks might become fruitlessly mired in abstractions. Nomura cabled Tokyo a current and Japan-favorable version of the "Draft Understanding" as an *American proposal*, but not Hull's "principles." By this decision Nomura inverted Hull's intent: Tokyo concluded that the United States was so eager to avoid a Pacific clash that it would "yield on some important issues."

It was at this point that Matsuoka, having just returned from his European swing, obtained his first perusal of the "Draft Understanding." The fact that Nomura never forwarded the original English text of the document raised his suspicions. But Matsuoka's fury stemmed fundamentally from the affront to his policy and his psyche. At its core, the version of the "Draft Understanding" Matsuoka examined traded Japan's abandonment of the Tripartite Pact for an end to the China War and Chinese recognition of Manchukuo. But negating the deterrent effect of the Tripartite Pact on the United States, the "Draft Understanding" would derail the whole train of Matsuoka's grand strategic design, culminating in a triumphant turn in Washington. With Navy Minister Oikawa vetting the proposal as finally a way out of the China War, and former Prime Minister Hiranuma raising the specter of popular upheaval if Japan hesitated to accept it, however, Matsuoka first deployed a delaying tactic: Was it acceptable to Germany?

Matsuoka's initial mild counter masked how the "Draft Understanding" fundamentally unhinged him. He thereafter pummeled with uncontrolled fury his government colleagues and his Foreign Ministry subordinates (especially Nomura). Only a flare-up of tuberculosis (that would eventually kill him in 1946) enforced some lulls in his self-destructive behavior. His words and conduct raised serious doubts about his mental stability in Tokyo and Washington.

During 7–11 May, an obviously embarrassed Nomura appeared for interviews with Hull where he delivered in part—for he refused to recite the more inflammatory "oral statements"—Matsuoka's oral and written bombs designed to blow up the "Draft Understanding." Nomura appealed to the naval leadership to save the "Draft Understanding." Their dismaying response on 8 May conspicuously lacked their prior endorsement of the "Draft Understanding." Instead, the fresh cable scoffed at the prospect of the United States embarking on war with Germany and asserted that, if confronted with a firm Japanese stand, the United States would bow to Japanese terms. That same day, 8 May, in a Liaison Conference, Oikawa asserted that soon Germany would crush England and this would produce a "major change" in US policy. Only now did Nomura finally relay Hull's "Four Principles," but he failed to convey just how central they were to Hull's view of the negotiations.

Matsuoka's comprehensive counterproposal on 11 May effectively demanded a complete American capitulation: abandon opposition to Hitler or face Japan's entry into the war as Germany's ally, and force Chiang to submit to the same one-sided settlement of the China Incident that Japan had forced on Jingwei Wang. Matsuoka completed this thorough evisceration of the prior substance of the "Draft Understanding" by even striking the pledge that Japan would not use force in moving southward.

Nomura duly reported this revised text to Hull and met with him nine times between 12 May and 7 June. What Nomura failed to do, in gross violation of his duties, was to report back to Tokyo written and oral American reservations at these sessions. On learning of the American statements through Ambassador Grew in Tokyo, Matsuoka fired off a scathing rebuke to Nomura. Meanwhile, Matsuoka, sublimely confident in his own negotiating prowess, pursued a direct meeting with Roosevelt. Grew seconded the request, not in expectation that it would produce a settlement, but so that Matsuoka "might learn at firsthand of the determination of the United States that the Axis must be defeated."

Trans-Pacific intrigues thwarted Matsuoka's aspiration for what he hoped would be a crowning achievement. In Tokyo, a spokesman for anonymous cabinet members (almost certainly including Matsuoka's implacable enemy Hiranuma) sought to convince Grew that Konoe would not allow Matsuoka to go to Washington even if invited. Meanwhile, purely for selfish reasons to retain his pivotal position, Drought in the United States poisoned American officials about the proposed visit.

"Magic" code breaking delivered to Hull not only the oral and written submissions Nomura made (or did not make) but also disclosed the contentious relationship of Nomura and officials in Tokyo, particularly Matsuoka. With apparent hope that Nomura's views might prevail, Hull developed an "unofficial" American response to Matsuoka's 11 May revised "Draft Understanding." When delivered to the Japanese on 31 May, it essentially confirmed the impasse between the two nations as it laid out nearly the reciprocal of Matsuoka's "revisions." Iwakuro transmitted it to his army superiors in Tokyo, who shared it with their navy counterparts. The obviously diametrically opposite provisions on the Tripartite Pact, China, and the southern advance convinced them that there was no common ground for agreement.

What abruptly extinguished the last embers of the "John Doe Associates" was Hitler's shattering attack on the Soviet Union. But the episode expired only after inflicting a trio of evils. First, it wasted perhaps the best if uncertain opportunity for Nomura to make progress on his arrival in an adjustment of US-Japanese relations. Second, it played a spoiler role in preventing a meeting between Roosevelt and Matsuoka, which offered some prospect for at least far better comprehension in Tokyo of American resolve. Third, while Matsuoka properly ferreted out the lack of authenticity in the "Draft Understanding," he failed to carve out the one great gem it could have placed in his hands: support within some quarters of the Imperial Army for a withdrawal from China. This was particularly tragic, because Matsuoka himself, whatever his other failings, was one of the few Japanese leaders who read correctly and with sympathy Chinese nationalism and who believed the war in China was a colossal mistake that must be rectified. Matsuoka also had an ally on this policy in Tôjô, who believed the China War was causing severe damage to the discipline and character of the army. If Matsuoka had carried in his pocket this extremely valuable trading point to a meeting with Roosevelt, perhaps history might have taken a better course for Japan. But any settlement at this point (or later in 1941) essentially required that the Imperial Army acquiesce in a withdrawal from China. It is by no means clear this would have occurred. This was a prospect that was anathema to senior Imperial Army officers in China, as well as to those of like mind in the middle echelons of the army, all of whom remained steadfast in support for Wang's regime and who believed that any settlement in China must adhere to the one-sided conditions imposed on Wang.

CHAPTER 8

⁝

"Leaping off the Veranda"

JUNE TO OCTOBER 1941

Hitler Turns East

US Ambassador to Japan Joseph Grew exemplified the increasing professionalism of the US diplomatic corps at the outset of World War II. Grew rose in a changing milieu mixing imperfect meritocracy and an "aristocratic ethos." Born of a prominent Boston business family, he married into wealth. When President Herbert Hoover appointed Grew to be ambassador to Japan in 1932, it marked the first time a career diplomat assumed that role with a first-class power. His wife, Alice de Vermandois Perry (a distant relative of commodore Matthew Perry who, in the American view, "opened" Japan in the 1850s), enormously aided her husband, for she knew Japanese and the subtleties of Japanese customs. Historian David Mayers characterized Grew's personality as "optimis[tic], averse to flamboyance, [and] unfailingly polite." The one great fault in Grew's perspective was that he viewed Japan through a lens created by his circle of Japanese friends and associates, who represented the conservative but internationalist elite now rapidly declining in influence.

Grew had known Franklin Roosevelt when they were boys together at the elite Groton School. Grew thus exercised the privilege of addressing letters to the president: "Dear Frank." In December 1940, Grew asked for Roosevelt's views on "Japan and all her works." Roosevelt replied: "I believe that the fundamental proposition that we must recognize is that the hostilities in Europe, in Africa, and in Asia are all parts of a single world conflict." This statement captures the essence of Roosevelt's profound insight that all the components of the war were linked. FDR's ability to see the connections between China's role, Soviet survival, and the ultimate triumph of the anti-Axis cause form the surest guide to his statecraft in 1941.

As early as 31 July 1940, in the updraft of exhilaration over the conquest of Western Europe, Hitler divulged his intention to turn and crush the Soviet Union. The formal directive for what became Operation Barbarossa was promulgated on 18 December 1940. In Moscow, Soviet intelligence snared a profusion of clues of an impending German onslaught, not least a copy of Hitler's December 1940 directive.

Washington and London also warned Stalin. On 20 March, the US government forwarded a copy of Hitler's December 1940 decree for a Soviet attack. On 3 April, Churchill risked disclosing to Stalin critical breakthroughs in British attacks on German codes with intelligence verifying Hitler's intentions. Britain subsequently shared still more telling revelations. Stalin neither raised the alert status nor the dispositions of forces on the Soviet western border, but he did react to these warnings by ordering the mobilization and positioning of deep reserves that played a key role in stalling the German drives from July onward.

At 0315, 22 June 1941, surprise German air attacks on Soviet airfields heralded the opening of Operation Barbarossa, history's greatest land onslaught. Along a colossal front from the Baltic to the Black Sea, Hitler unleashed some three million men organized in an Army of Norway and a Finnish Army in the far north and then, in order, Army Groups North, Center, and South, incorporating at least 152 German, 14 Finnish, and 14 Romanian divisions. Equipment inventories numbered about 3,350 tanks, 7,200 guns, and 2,770 aircraft. The strategic objectives were: Leningrad (Army Group North), Moscow (Army Group Center), and Kiev (Army Group South).

Soviet defenders reeled back in the north and center but proved staunch initially in the south. The breakdown of command and control left Moscow groping for information—at times telephoning local commissars to find out if the Germans had reached their location. Stalin later confided to Churchill, "I prefer fear to convictions, because convictions change." To this end, Stalin had slaughtered many of the Red Army's officers in murderous purges in the 1930s. Now this terror inculcated paralyzing timidity in most survivors. Save for isolated instances, however, ill training, mechanical failure, and lack of fuel squandered the Soviet advantages of numerically and in some cases technically superior tank inventories. Berlin furnished the world what appeared to be the indisputable indicator of the situation: communiqués identified one Soviet city after another falling from west to east. On 23 June, Secretary of War Stimson delivered to Roosevelt the grim but unanimous prediction of the US Army, including Chief of Staff Marshall, that Germany will be "thoroughly occupied with beating Russia for a minimum of one month and a possible maximum of three months." The Soviet military situation was characterized as "grave" at a 30 June London War Cabinet meeting. Expecting Hitler to wheel back west after crushing the Soviets, Churchill ordered counterinvasion preparations brought to a "concert pitch" by 1 September.

Although Stimson had already served Roosevelt well since the summer of 1940, from this point forward his role would become increasingly vital in the war to come. Henry L. Stimson personified the best of upper crust America. A hawk-like face suggested a formidable intellect and personal force. He completed the educational trifecta of Philips Andover, Yale, and Harvard Law School and lived life on a big scale with vigorous outdoor activities and worldwide travel. During World War I he served as an artillery officer, and thereafter preferred the title "Colonel," though he had been both a secretary of war and of state. Stimson's rigid probity in both public and private spheres knew no superior. He prided himself on avoiding vulgar racism, but displayed little overt sympathy for the aspirations of Blacks or Filipinos. He could be archaic socially: even old and dear friends were no longer admitted into his home if they were divorced. He inspired matchless loyalty and veneration from his subordinates because, as one explained, they knew he "would never manipulate them, or betray them, or do anything for his own advantage." Though unflappable in the face of adversity, he often confided to his invaluable diary his disenchantment with Roosevelt's disordered governing methods.

Meanwhile, Barbarossa reality differed radically from the communiqués and public war maps. At the cost of horrendously disproportionate losses—sometimes ranging up to ten dead Soviet soldiers for every German—the men and equipment of Hitler's frontline units were being ground down. Strategic errors by Stalin, like the huge encirclement of Soviet armies near Kiev and before Moscow, sometimes grossly magnified Soviet losses. Moreover, sober preinvasion analysis of German logistics demonstrated that German forces must deal a mortal blow to the Soviets within a few hundred miles of the border, or German defeat loomed. But German generals, not just Hitler, replaced such rational analysis with the notion that unshakable "will," not material factors, would somehow produce triumph.

Stalin immediately grasped the importance of China to prevent the Japanese from opening a potentially fatal second front in the Far East. Moscow ordered the Chinese Communists, whose base areas lay proximate to Japanese-Soviet borders, to provide intelligence on Japanese intentions and for the 200,000–300,000-man Eighth Route Army to stage diversionary attacks. Mao balked. He reported the Eighth Route Army possessed only about twenty rounds of ammunition per rifle and was massively deficient in machine guns and artillery. Conventional battle would destroy the Red Army with the subsequent loss of Communist base areas. Consequently, Mao prioritized his long-term interests in building up forces as he had done since 1937, not answering desperate Soviet needs.

Operation Barbarossa marked a milestone in the global war's moral dimensions. When Hitler invaded Poland in September 1939, his regime by that date had murdered perhaps 10,000 persons. By that same date, Stalin's regime alone had killed at least eight million people, overwhelmingly in domestic convulsions like collectivization, the terror famine, and the purges. Japan's march since the Marco Polo Bridge Incident had produced approximately four million Chinese deaths. By 22 June 1941, Hitler, via war and terror, had killed around 600,000 human beings. Stalin's regime added to its prior toll a minimum of about 200,000 Finns, Poles, and people of the Baltic States. The dead in China due to Japanese aggression now approached 7.5 million. Thus, retrospective assumptions that Hitler's butchery soared above all others—or that European slaughters generally far overshadowed those in Asia—do not match the facts as they stood from 1939 to mid-1941.

Up to this point in the war, Churchill, Roosevelt, and their peoples understood Hitler employed terror, but its extent remained veiled and its vast upward leap in June 1941 unimaginable. Behind the German columns advanced SS "Einsatzgruppen," followed by "Order Police" battalions, as well as three SS military brigades. Initially "Einsatzgruppen" incited "self-cleansing" by local anti-Semitic groups to murder Jews and Communists. The "Einsatzgruppen" were tasked to kill Communist Party officials, partisans, and saboteurs, and "Jews in party and state positions." The killing began against Jewish males, but by August moved to include women and children. A great many local peoples, often those seared by Stalin's murderous policies, eagerly assisted the German program. The German Army tendered extensive though not universal assistance for this program, mostly administrative and logistical rather than direct killing. Bullets were the primary means of execution. By the end of 1942, an estimated 1.35 million persons in the bounds of the Soviet empire had been executed by gunshot.

But Hitler's slaughter program also included cleansing the east of "Slavs" to create living space for his envisioned racially pure utopia. Under the "Hunger Plan," clearing the east involved starving to death tens of millions. The Germans first applied the "Hunger Plan" to Soviet prisoners of war. Of the

3.5 million captured in the first months of the war, over two million perished from deliberate starvation.

These numbers underscore the moral calculus of the war in two important dimensions. First, Hitler only began to rival Stalin and Imperial Japan in mass murder in the second half of 1941. Second, Britain and the United States lacked any rational strategic alternative to an effective alliance with the Soviet Union, but they did not want for choice as to how the alliance would be portrayed to their publics. Rather than couching the relationship as an arm's length exercise grounded on shared interests ("my enemy's enemy is my friend"), London and Washington extolled the alliance as a union based on shared values. When Churchill, one of the most prominent anti-Communist figures in the world, was pressed by Foreign Minister Anthony Eden to portray the relationship as strictly a limited, military-only alliance, the prime minister vehemently and emotionally declared it must be presented foremost as founded on Hitler's slaughter of Russian peasants. Roosevelt chose to rouse the American public by depicting the war as a stark contrast between Axis totalitarianism and Anglo-American freedom, "regardless of Soviet realities."

In Britain, George Orwell found the Ministry of Information's published "guidelines" to steer coverage of "Soviet realities" such an egregious affront to truth that he wrote his classic work *Animal Farm*—only to have it suppressed during the war. American diplomat George Kennan recoiled at depicting the Soviet alliance as based on shared values: "To welcome Russia as an associate in the defense of democracy would invite misunderstanding of our own position and would lend to the German war effort a gratuitous and sorely needed aura of morality." During the war, Western public debate legitimately included criticism of European colonialism and Chiang's undemocratic and repressive regime. But the simultaneous and systematic misrepresentation of Stalin's regime by Britain and the United States attenuates the moral force of such criticism at the time—not to mention retrospectively.

Barbarossa did not surprise Japan's uniformed leaders. A 5 June message from Ambassador Ōshima in Berlin relayed confidences directly from Hitler and Ribbentrop that Germany would soon attack the Soviet Union. Hitler and his foreign minister predicted victory in two or three months, to be followed by an autumn invasion of Great Britain. With curiously mixed symbolism, Foreign Minister Matsuoka learned of Hitler's onslaught while entertaining Jingwei Wang at a kabuki theater at 1600 hours on 22 June. Within ninety minutes, Matsuoka faced the emperor to urge that Japan strike north against the Soviets. Matsuoka's advocacy paralleled the initial opportunism of the

Army General Staff, but deep rifts within that service and across the entire leadership emerged swiftly.

It is now that the multiple structural dysfunctions in the Japanese government and severe factionalism among Japan's leadership most starkly surfaced in the slide to an expanded war. The deepest roots of structural dysfunction rested in the 1889 Meiji constitution, which, as one historian phrased it, created "a curious sort of pluralism in which many participated and no one was ultimately accountable." That document installed a civilian government merging two divergent models: the then-new German Empire for the government and ostensibly Britain for the monarchy. The constitution divided power within the government structure, but it certified the emperor as divine, the paramount figure in Japan. The drafters of the constitution exempted the emperor from democratic accountability, but they also safeguarded his aura of infallibility by insulating him from active participation in governing. The constitution thus spawned a fundamental ambiguity about the emperor's role: Did he rule or merely preside? The Meiji constitution conferred the "right of autonomous command" (*Tosuiken Dokuritsu*) on the chiefs of staff of the army and navy. This meant they answered not to the government, but directly to the emperor. With the armed services thus outside the authority of the government and the emperor's actual control ambiguous, this left the nation's arms bearers potentially without a master. Some indirect checks existed. The cabinet could persuade the army and navy ministers to steer the armed forces down an agreed path, and the Diet (the Japanese parliament) held ultimate power over appropriations.

An ad hoc solution to this structural vacuum in the Meiji Era appeared as the *genro*: a body of elder statesmen exercising coordination of both the government and the military and thus domestic and foreign policy. Accordingly, control of the military rested upon personalities working harmoniously outside the legal structure of Japan's government. (The reality was hardly placid as the *genro* exhibited frequent internal discord.) Kinmochi Saionji, the last of the original *genro*, died in November 1940. No formal mechanism existed to replace the *genro*. To some extent the *jushin*, comprised of former prime ministers, assumed the function of the *genro* following Saionji's passing. The *jushin* likewise lacked authority under the constitution and moreover lacked the *genro*'s stature, further diluting its informal power.

Yet more structural problems plagued Japan's government. Lacking recognition within the constitution itself, the cabinet's legal authority derived from the 1889 Regulations for Governing the Cabinet. The title translated in

English as "prime minister" in Japanese was *Shuhan* (literally "Head Position [in a group]"). The Japanese prime minister did not exercise the level of control over the government or even the cabinet customarily awarded that role in other nations. Critically, the prime minister did not select the army or navy ministers; that power resided in the services themselves. Further, the resignation of an army or navy minister automatically toppled the government, thus bestowing a military veto over civilian authority.

Yet another Japanese policymaking participant exerted power outside the constitution: the elite bureaucracy. Its power rested in its functions: drafting legislation, controlling information reaching cabinet members, and implementing laws. Some of its most senior members would even become cabinet members. Supposedly a neutral body of "officials of the emperor," in practice the bureaucracy became politicized.

Adding a final level of complexity to policymaking was the Imperial Household Ministry. While on the surface it existed only to manage domestic arrangements for the Imperial Family, it exerted both powerful indirect and direct effects on Japan's path. The Imperial Household Ministry fundamentally shaped Hirohito's outlook with its careful management of his education in Japan's history and institutions and the history of the rest of the world. It also formed a web or "court group," tied through wealth to both traditional and new elites, and through the military, which channeled information to the emperor. Perhaps most importantly, Marquis Kōichi Kido, a hereditary aristocrat and the lord keeper of the privy seal within the Imperial Household Ministry, became Hirohito's most trusted adviser. He also exercised a vital role in selecting prime ministers.

From at least the Manchurian Incident in 1931, factionalism among uniformed and civilian elites enormously increased the dangerous diffusion of control and accountability embedded in the government's structural defects. After the war, the civilians (including the emperor and his supporters) as well as naval officers concocted an account that fanatics in the Imperial Army had hijacked the nation into a war with the West over their objections. In fact, profound responsibility tarred all these elites. Factionalism began with the divergent outlooks of the armed services. As noted earlier, the gaze of the Imperial Army looked north toward the Asian continent, where stood a Russian and later Soviet colossus. The Imperial Army neglected the Anglo-American powers and thus possessed little understanding of them. The Imperial Navy looked outward and indeed around the globe. Its gaze naturally fell upon the Royal and United States Navies as measuring sticks of power and justifications for resources. Since at least 1905, this basic divide left Japan with no coherent national defense policy, as each service prepared only for war with its own envisioned opponent.

But factionalism extended deep within both the Imperial Army and Navy. By the 1930s the Imperial Army fault lines produced what were called the "Imperial Way" (*Kōdō*) and the "Control" (*Tōsei*) factions. At one level, the essence of the "Imperial Way" faction appeared as an obsession with spiritual values and hence morale over material factors. Its leaders railed against corrosive Western concepts like capitalism or communism; they extolled a mystical bond between the army and the throne. The "Imperial Way" sought to revive its selectively edited concept of the traditional Japanese warrior ethos *bushidō* as physically manifested by the 1934 order for company grade officers to remove their French army–style swords for the classic Japanese versions. "Imperial Way" generals insisted on maintaining the army's maximum possible active duty strength even at the expense of modernization. This policy stemmed from their strategic outlook: Japan's mortal enemy was Russia and then later the Soviet Union and its Communist ideology. Only a large active duty army would permit quick victory in the opening battles against the Soviets. The corollary to this outlook was that "Imperial Way" officers opposed any dispersion of effort toward large-scale entanglement with China or any southward advance.

The "Control" Faction looked not at the past, but the future. From World War I its adherents gleaned the conclusion that future conflicts demanded a planned national economy that could support a modernized military and gird it for a protracted war. Its leaders would trade reduced active duty manpower strength for new weapons, particularly aircraft and vehicles. "Control" officers certainly acknowledged the Soviet threat but did not rule out a southward advance, as a matter of first principles.

A group of radical "Imperial Way" junior officers staged a mutiny in February 1936. They struck across Tokyo and targeted selected officials for assassination. Shocked at the murder of some of his ministers, Hirohito intervened decisively to quash the rebellion. The incident shifted leadership of the army toward the "Control" Faction. In the view of Konoe, the ascendency of "Control" over "Imperial Way" officers in 1936 figured importantly in 1941, as it removed a major barrier to Japan's turn south.

From at least the Washington Treaty system of 1922, the Imperial Navy likewise fractured internally. A "Treaty Faction" believed the pacts served Japan by effectively making it supreme in the Western Pacific via the halt of a building race and the denial of Britain and the United States of advanced naval bases necessary for projection of naval power into the waters adjacent to Japan and the Asian continent. The "Fleet Faction" was obsessed with the numerically inferior fleet the treaties awarded Japan. The "5–5–3" ratio of capital ships for Britain, the United States, and Japan respectively meant that Japan possessed only 60 percent of the naval power of either of its two main rivals. The Fleet Faction worshipped certain arcane calculations that Japan's chances to prevail in a war against either rival depended upon whether its navy had at least 70 percent of the strength of its adversary.

By 1941 the "Fleet Faction" ideology infected most middle echelon officers in the Imperial Navy. They pressed for policies they recognized would likely lead to war with not only the Netherlands and Great Britain, but also the United States. Their vocabulary featured incantations that this path was mandated for Japan's "self-existence" and "self-defense" against Japan's "encirclement" by the "ABCD" (American, British, Chinese, and Dutch) powers. More cautious senior officers, however, presented the service's policy to army counterparts as "war preparations without war determination." Army officers suspected that the Imperial Navy was merely feigning the intention to go to war to sustain its claim to a preponderance of national arms resources.

The middle echelon "Fleet Faction" officers in the Imperial Navy and their equally rabid counterparts in the Imperial Army exemplified yet further distinctive and dysfunctional phenomena of Japan's leadership. Their sobriquet was *bakuryo*, literally "officers behind the curtains." Their functions in coordinating policy between the senior staff and ministries and devising plans gave them enormous power behind the scenes. Their baneful draftsmanship channeled discussion along increasingly aggressive paths, and they formed a constituency that superiors sought to pacify by projecting a single-minded warrior toughness instead of their proper role as prudent stewards of the nation's destiny.

Added to all these other elements of dysfunction was a deep-rooted culture of insubordination and outright rebellion integral to Japanese military life from the 1860s. It has already appeared in these pages repeatedly in the disregard by Japanese commanders in China for orders from Tokyo and the extraordinary defiance that produced the attack on French Indochina in 1940. Four elements created this situation. First, the structural defect in the Meiji state that ostensibly was founded on supremacy of the emperor, but left others, not the emperor, to formulate and execute actual policy. This, noted historian Danny Orbach, created "inexhaustible . . . ideological ammunition for dissenters" who could always tout that they represented the "true will" of the emperor, not the "betrayal" of that will by legal authorities. Second, the Meiji state's core ideology espoused relentless expansion of the empire, but third, there was no defined stopping point for this expansion. The legal hierarchy thus found it difficult or impossible to sanction the "patriots" who took unauthorized action to expand the empire, and these "patriots" could generally count upon their unilateral actions to be retroactively accepted. Fourth, rebels against the existing order created the Meiji state. For over seven decades thereafter, the government extolled their rebellion, but failed to stipulate that other than that one unique historical moment, rebellion was a high crime. Exacerbating all of this were the complex interpersonal networks that linked officers high and low horizontally who could and did negate official vertical hierarchies.

The jolt of the German attack on the Soviets interacted with the structural dysfunction of the Japanese government, severe factionalism, and the culture of insubordination and rebellion to send Japan careening down a disastrous path. Key Imperial Navy officers forged a rapid consensus to block Imperial Army schemes to attack the Soviet Union. The navy counter-prescribed a southern advance to seize the raw materials, especially the oil of the Netherlands East Indies, which Japan desperately needed. Some of the navy's middle echelon officers, convinced of the "inevitability" of a war with the United States, produced a paper in June dismissing Nomura's talks as hopeless and demanding that the navy formally commit to a southern advance—even if it meant war with the United States. While the commitment to a southern advance extended elsewhere in the naval hierarchy, another faction of officers still regarded it as premature to commit formally to war with the United States. But army officers remained skeptical when Navy Chief of Staff Nagano declared that Japan must embark on the southern advance and take on any country that opposed it. (It bears heavy emphasis that Nagano's announcement was *before the US trade embargo addressed below.*) The soldiers suspected that the newfound fervor of Nagano and other navy officers for hostilities with the United States reflected merely a tactic to ward off shifts in budgetary allocations.

Intense and protracted conferences among Japanese leaders later in June found Imperial Army General Staff officers and Foreign Minister Matsuoka prepared to pitch into the German-Soviet struggle. (Matsuoka memorably pronounced: "Great men will change their minds. Previously I advocated going south, but now I favor the north.") The navy minister remained opposed to joining the attack on the Soviet Union. He commented at one meeting that, "The Navy is confident about a war against the United States and Britain, but not confident about a war against the United States, Britain, and the Soviet

Union." The cautious Army Ministry representatives advocated a wait-and-see policy. At the Liaison Conferences on 27 and 30 June, War Minister Tôjô tellingly observed that deciding whether to strike north or south would be easy "if it weren't for the China Incident." Ultimately these exchanges produced an uneasy consensus for a "ripe persimmon" policy of the Army Ministry: Japan would jump in to take advantage of decisive German success against the Soviets (like waiting for a ripe persimmon to drop naturally from a tree). But until the "persimmon" fell, Japan would stay its hand in the North.[*]

Further exchanges between army and navy officers with input from the Foreign Ministry eventually produced a critical document entitled "Outline of National Policies in View of the Changing Situation," presented before the emperor at an Imperial Conference on 2 July. The paper defined the nation's fundamental policy as establishment of the "Greater East Asia Co-prosperity Sphere" and proposed the following toward that end:

> Our Empire will continue its efforts to effect a settlement of the China Incident, and will seek to establish a solid basis for the security and preservation of the nation. This will involve taking steps to advance south, and, depending on changes in the situation, will involve a settlement of the Northern Question as well.

The "outline" called for actions "to force the capitulation of the Chiang regime." It endorsed taking measures approved in prior policy papers with respect to French Indochina and Thailand "for the purpose of strengthening our advance into the southern regions." It declared that "our Empire will not be deterred by the possibility of being involved in a war with Great Britain and the United States." Though necessary preparations would commence, Japan would enter the German-Soviet war only if events developed "to the advantage of our Empire." Meanwhile, the nation would strive "to the utmost . . . to prevent the entry of the United States into the European War." But if the United States entered the European war, Japan would act in accordance with the Tripartite Pact, but would "decide independently as to the time and method of resorting to force."

This was the first time a supreme-level Japanese policy document expressly

---

[*]   Notwithstanding the deadly serious consequences of these discussions, one bit of no doubt unintended black humor appeared. In the midst of one of many protracted and contentious meetings, Prince Yasuhiko Asaka commented: "Aren't we being too careful, compared with the way Germany does things?" Ike, *Japan's Decision for War*, 75.

contemplated war with Britain and the United States. Moreover, several illu-minating points emerged during the discussions before the emperor. Army Chief of Staff Sugiyama asserted that the advance into Southern Indochina aimed to cut off British and American aid to the Chinese Nationalists. But the Navy Chief of Staff Nagano affirmed that the advance into Southern Indochina and Thailand represented a "first step" to enhance "our ability to move southward." Creating another ominous precedent, this marked the first time a top navy leader expressed willingness to make war with the Anglo-American powers.

A critical error in the thinking of top Japanese Army and Navy leaders (except Navy Chief of Staff Nagano), as well as Konoe, was the delusion that the United States would not react vigorously to an advance into Southern Indochina. This delusion rested on the belief, first, that the United States would abide the advance due to its preoccupation with events in Europe and, second, that since the advance ostensibly resulted from a diplomatic agree-ment with the Vichy authorities, it was not an aggressive military occupation. Ironically, because of his pivotal role in steering Japan into a perilous situa-tion, Matsuoka, after initially endorsing the move south, did an about-face and predicted it would bring "disaster."

Read literally, the 2 July Imperial Conference policy paper did not expressly authorize attacks either north toward the Soviets nor south toward Malaya or the Netherlands East Indies. It represents an example of the Japanese sys-tem of *Ryoron-heiki*, defined as the recording in a formal document of two opposing opinions as they stand, without any mutual accommodation. The paper ruled out an immediate war with the Soviet Union and sanctioned pri-ority for preparations for a southward advance. But while all of this seemed to bow to the navy's strategy of a southern advance, as well as to the army ministry's "wait-and-see" attitude toward the German-Soviet war, the paper stopped just short of authorizing specific advances beyond Thailand and French Indochina.

Yet focusing on this text without context is disingenuous. At no point between 1937 and 1941 did Japanese leaders formally adopt a paper authoriz-ing a specific timetable of aggression by the multiple successive steps Japan opportunistically followed ever deeper into China and then across the Asian continent and the Pacific. The ambiguous compromise acceptable to all the participants in the Tokyo policy contests in July 1941 may only have autho-rized the next small steps, but they also crafted a menu (and momentum) for further vast aggression from which Japan's leaders could order "depending on changes in the situation." Despite the attempt to link further advances into French Indochina with the struggle against Chiang, Southern Indochina in fact played no role in the China Incident; but, as Admiral Nagano confirmed, it formed an essential springboard for conquering Malaya and the Netherlands East Indies.

Just after the 2 July Imperial Conference, the conflict over the "Strike North" or "Strike South" strategy merged with the parlous state of Japanese-US relations to incite a cabinet change. On 21 June, Hull formally tendered to Nomura the American counterproposal to Matsuoka's radically revised "Draft Understanding" of 11 May that represented American capitulation on all important points. In an accompanying oral statement, Hull denounced those Japanese leaders—singling out a statement by Matsuoka—committed to supporting Nazi Germany. Hull pronounced it "illusory" to believe the United States could reach an agreement with such men.

When the Japanese government took up Hull's 21 June note at the Liaison Conferences on 10 and 12 July, Matsuoka proposed breaking off US negotiations. Both army and navy leaders, however, deemed it imprudent to flatly rebuff Hull's proposals while Japan negotiated the occupation of Southern Indochina with French officials. The armed forces leadership naively convinced itself that it was Matsuoka, not very fundamental policy divergences, that precluded a settlement with the United States. Moreover, Matsuoka had progressively alienated his cabinet colleagues with his abrasive behavior and his disturbing actions. Crowning these considerations was Matsuoka's obvious ambition to displace Konoe. Consequently, Konoe ejected Matsuoka by forcing the whole cabinet to resign en masse and then on 17 July reappointing everyone except Matsuoka. Vice Admiral Teijirō Toyoda picked up the Foreign Ministry portfolio.

Thrust and Response

On 1 July, FDR wrote to Secretary of the Interior Harold Ickes that the Japanese were "engaged in a real drag down and knockout fight" as they tried "to decide which way they are going to jump-attack Russia, attack the South Seas (thus throwing their lot definitely with Germany), or whether they will sit on the fence and be more friendly with us." "Magic" diplomatic intercepts disclosed the substance of the 2 July Imperial Conference, but the translation only appeared on 8 August. The "Magic" version, however, rendered the new policy as a formal commitment to a southward advance, rather than categorizing the southward advance as just an option, albeit one gathering extremely perilous momentum.

"Magic" disclosed on 21 July that Vichy capitulated to a 12 July Japanese ultimatum demanding that Vichy submit to the Japanese occupation of Southern Indochina. The preemptive American response was twofold. On 21 July, Acting Secretary of State Welles delivered a warning to Japan's Washington embassy that such a move might extinguish the talks with Nomura. Three days later Roosevelt—displaying his very best side—devised an exceedingly imaginative and bold stroke. Roosevelt's overarching goal remained the defeat of Hitler. Supporting Britain and now the Soviet Union furthered that purpose while a war with Japan did not. Roosevelt now unveiled in Nomura's presence the most conciliatory American diplomatic initiative of 1941: an international agreement to neutralize Indochina. This step offered a trio of benefits: defusing a serious escalation of tensions between the two nations; securing key raw materials for the United States, like tin and rubber; and providing an adroit way for the Japanese to commence decoupling themselves from Germany. Roosevelt deftly edited from the proposal any linkage to the intractable issue of the Sino-Japanese conflict.

Roosevelt's plan to arrest the downward spiral toward war energized Ambassador Grew. He met with Foreign Minister Toyoda on 27 July to champion the initiative, but Toyoda claimed Nomura had not reported it. (The "Magic" intercept of Nomura's report of his meeting with Roosevelt demonstrated that the ambassador had indeed described Roosevelt's scheme, but failed to highlight it. It is also possible that pro-Axis elements in the Foreign Ministry culled the reference from the version of the wire shown Toyoda.) Japanese troops landed in Southern Indochina on 28 July. The formal Japanese response to Roosevelt's neutralization proposal (now amended to include Thailand) only appeared on 6 August. Japan stated it would withdraw troops from Indochina upon conclusion of the China Incident—thus merging once again two issues Roosevelt had carefully sundered. The Japanese note offered a promise of no advance beyond French Indochina if the United States abandoned military measures in the Southwest Pacific and restored trade. The note reiterated the demand for the United States to help negotiate a settlement between Japan and China.

The next American responses to the new Japanese Indochina thrust proved fateful. China remained at the center of Far Eastern calculations. China's resistance since 1940, pinning down huge Japanese forces, protected European colonial holdings and thus indirectly aided Britain's ability to prosecute its war against Germany. Now the inability of the Imperial Army to mass its might to strike north to join the German onslaught into the Soviet Union steeply multiplied China's strategic value. On 23 July, Roosevelt authorized a military mission to China under Brig. Gen. John Magruder to coordinate delivery of Lend-Lease supplies.

Yet to date, as one British observer commented, Roosevelt only had been "willing to give Chiang Kai-shek just enough, but no more than enough, aid to continue the war and counteract the defeatists in [Chongqing]." As of July 1941, the administration had authorized 821,000 tons of supplies for the British and just 16,000 for China. Reports from China deprecated Chiang's actual military effort against the Japanese, highlighted the lack of a true United Front between Chiang's coalition and the Communists, and warned of serious issues of inflation, corruption, and waning morale. These took their toll on American enthusiasm for Chiang, but logistics towered as the foremost impediment to supporting China. Between the occupation of ports and the naval blockade along China's Pacific rim, and the seizure of Northern Indochina, Japan effectively isolated China from outside supply, save three routes. The least noted but "primary source of war material from aboard" after 1937 was Hong Kong. About 60,000 tons per month reached China via Hong Kong during the first sixteen months of the war; even after Guangzhou (Canton) fell, Hong Kong still forwarded inland along road and rail lines as well as coastal shipping about 3,000 tons per month until December 1941.

The second major route from August 1937 to June 1941 wound down from the Soviet Union through Northwest China. Unlike the British in Hong Kong, the Soviets supplied finished weapons (notably aircraft and artillery), but on average only about 2,000 to 3,000 tons per month—much of which arrived on the backs of 50,000 camels! But the Soviets tapered down support after the August 1939 Soviet-German Pact and ended it after the German invasion.

The third major China supply pathway was the Burma Road. Only completed in December 1938, the British closed it from July to October 1940 to placate the Japanese during Britain's hour of greatest strategic peril. The "road" commenced at the port of Rangoon and continued by rail line to Lashio in northeast Burma, from whence trucks hauled the supplies 710 miles east to Kunming, China. The poorly surfaced road—rarely more than crushed rock—featured dangerous hairpin turns, steep grades, and eroded shoulders. Trucks with jerking transmissions negotiated fourteen passes with an elevation of more than 7,000 feet. Worse than the road's serious physical impairments was the administration by sixteen different Chinese agencies. A June 1941 British report estimated that only 7,000 tons per month left Lashio and just 3,000 arrived in Kunming. The report allocated about 30 percent of the tonnage for fuel for the trip and about 25 percent for commercial goods, and allowed another 15 percent for smuggling. An American report estimated that 14,000 tons would have to leave Lashio to get 5,000 to Kunming—and Kunming was still hundreds of miles from the front.[*]

Air power provided the one notable if modest escalation of American support for China in July 1941. The continual pummeling by Japanese airmen turned Chinese thoughts naturally from mere defense to retaliation. Chiang asked for five hundred American planes. He began to receive some, but only obsolete models. But Chiang's importuning led, after a complex and halting series of negotiations through 1940, to a session of the administration's "mature brains" (Stimson's phrase), who rejected various fanciful schemes, including one to provide China B-17s flown by American pilots to bomb Japanese cities. Instead, Washington authorized Claire Chennault, a former Army Air Corps pilot now acting as an aviation adviser to Chiang, to recruit reserve and regular officers who "left" the US armed forces for an American Volunteer Group (AVG), later famed as the "Flying Tigers." The British agreed to spare from their orders one hundred Curtiss P-40 fighters in exchange for a promise of double that number of more advanced models. Ultimately, Chennault enlisted a total of ninety-nine pilots, who sailed 8 July for China from San Francisco.

Roosevelt's other major move involved the Philippines. On 26 July, Roosevelt ordered the nascent army of the Republic of the Philippines into US service and recalled Lt. Gen. Douglas MacArthur to active duty. MacArthur assumed command of the US Army Forces in the Far East (USAFFE), which incorporated the American and Philippine air and ground forces in the Philippines.

Coincident with the alarming development in Southern Indochina, in the last ten days of July Washington received glimmers of potentially vital

---

[*]   A curious fourth way existed for supplies to find their way into the hands of those resisting Japan. The Japanese sought to pay for their naval blockade by increasing exports to China, so that they ran a very favorable trade balance. This made it appear that the Chinese effectively paid for the blockade. The reality, however was that the porous routes of connection between occupied and Free China meant Japanese goods could end up in the hands of Free Chinese. A historian who studied this problem noted: "Unwittingly, the Japanese naval blockade, which was supposed to prevent goods from being transported to the enemy, established economic conditions that produced exactly the reverse. Ironically, legitimate trade conveyed large amounts of militarily useful goods to the enemy and so contributed to the enemy war effort." Ken-ichi Arakawa, "Japanese Naval Blockade of China in the Second Sino-Japanese War, 1937–41," in Bruce A. Elleman and S. C. M. Paine, *Naval Blockades and Seapower, Strategies and Counter-Strategies* (London and New York: Routledge, 2006), 114–15.

news from Europe. As July began, the situation in the Soviet Union appeared extremely grim. Stimson wrote in his diary that "the terrible German Moloch seems to be pushing on and killing or capturing uncounted hosts of Russians who have done nothing worse than trying to defend their own country." But in the last ten days of July both Soviet and German daily communiqués concurred that Soviet resistance remained strong and that the German advance had been halted—or at least had paused. A combination of extremely dogged, though horrendously costly, Soviet fighting, the progressive thinning of German ranks, the huge loss of vehicles from both combat and mechanical failure, and debilitating German logistical failings, stabilized the front for several weeks. In fact, early August marked a turning point. Germany had failed to crush Soviet armies near the borders, the essential prerequisite for victory in 1941. This turning point was not recognized in Washington or London; what was clear was that for the first time in the war a major German land onslaught appeared to falter and Soviet collapse no longer seemed foreordained. Prospective Soviet survival enormously bolstered the importance of China in keeping the Japanese from attacking the Soviet rear.

Roosevelt unveiled what proved his most controversial response to Japan's occupation of Southern French Indochina at a cabinet meeting on 24 July. He would freeze all Japanese financial assets in the United States (as he already had German and Italian funds), a move made effective on 26 July. In addition to the existing requirement that the Japanese obtain an export license from the US agency charged with control of items related to national defense, Roosevelt now stipulated that the Japanese also secure a license to unfreeze funds to pay for each licensed export shipment. The British and Dutch followed the American lead. On 1 August 1941, the United States revoked the outstanding Japanese licenses for huge quantities of oil. This order halted all pending oil shipments and left future shipments up in the air.*

---

* The fund-freezing order also followed the dashing of an illusion about Japan's financial situation. From 1937 to the end of 1940, some US officials entertained a fond hope: that Japan would exhaust its dollar holdings for foreign exchange. An inability to pay for vital imports, especially US oil, would compel Japan to cease its aggression without the United States firing a shot. But at the end of 1940, American investigators discovered that the Japanese had fraudulently concealed a massive war chest of dollars in their US bank branches. The investigators estimated these dollars could finance Japan's war activities into 1944. Realizing the Americans had uncovered their scheme, the Japanese migrated dollars as rapidly as possible, most to South American destinations. Edward S. Miller, *Bankrupting the Enemy: The U.S. Financial Siege of Japan Before Pearl Harbor* (Annapolis, MD: Naval Institute Press, 2007), 73–74, 106–7, 168–69 [hereafter Miller, *Bankrupting the Enemy*].

A significant historical controversy festers around arguments that subordinate officials subverted Roosevelt's original intent to create a flexible instrument of economic pressure to deter, not provoke, Japan. On 18 July, for example, Roosevelt lectured his cabinet officers on how cutting off all oil shipments might propel Japan into war. The hawkish Ickes complained that Roosevelt "was still unwilling to draw the noose tight. He thought it might be better to slip the noose around Japan's neck and give it a jerk now and then." Some historians maintain that subordinate officials—with Dean Acheson, the assistant secretary of state for economic affairs, as the prime culprit—converted a policy designed to control trade with Japan into an effective total embargo of oil exports to Japan. (One historian described him as an individual "uniting a pungent personality with a mind so keen his opponents scurried from its sweep.") Acheson is depicted as using his perch on the interagency Foreign Funds Control Committee to freeze completely Japanese funds. Without funds, there could be no oil exports.

But historian Waldo Heinrichs discovered compelling evidence that the idea of effectively halting *all* oil exports by refusing to release funds *initially* came from top authority. On 29 July, Sumner Welles (then effectively the secretary of state, as Hull was ill) told Acheson that "for the next week or so the happiest solution" would be "to take no action on Japanese applications" to unfreeze funds. Given Welles's position, his close relationship with Roosevelt, and the momentous importance of this decision, it is almost inconceivable that Welles acted without instructions from the president himself. As the Japanese pondered when American oil might start flowing again, another signal event occurred.

On 9 August, Franklin D. Roosevelt and Winston Churchill met for the first time as national leaders at a secret rendezvous at Placentia Bay, Newfoundland, a stunning setting that Roosevelt described as "high mountains, deep water, & fjord like arms of the sea." Roosevelt waited aboard the anchored heavy cruiser *Augusta*, its light peacetime paint and polished fittings reflecting its nation's ostensible neutrality. Precisely at the appointed hour of 0900, Churchill peered down from the regal bridge of the battleship *Prince of Wales* as it glided into the bay, swathed in dapples of multihued war paint and parting curtains of fog that abruptly yielded to a sparkling deep blue sky.

Sunday, 10 August, the conferees attended a joint Divine Services on the *Prince of Wales*. Churchill personally stage-managed the scene: on the quarterdeck beneath the awesome barrels of the battleship's great guns, sailors of both navies surrounded an altar draped with the flags of both nations in blatant symbolism of Churchill's ardent hopes. The prime minister picked the hymns ("O God Our Help in Ages Past" and "Onward Christian Soldiers," while Roosevelt added the emotionally powerful "Eternal Father Strong to Save") for an event he wanted "fully choral and fully photographic." One of Churchill's secretaries remarked, "You would have had to be pretty hard boiled not to be moved by it all." The motion and still images of this session still strike a chord for the fact that soon many of the battleship's company would perish.

While Roosevelt and Churchill met, their diplomatic and military staffs also conferred. The British delegation pursued the great prize: American entry into European hostilities. They had to settle for American pledges to take up some additional burdens in the Atlantic. Roosevelt consented to Churchill's Far East measures: discourage Japanese encroachment on Thailand, insist on withdrawal of Japanese troops from Southern Indochina, and present Tokyo with "a very severe warning" that Churchill argued was "in the highest degree important."

The meeting became best known for "The Atlantic Charter" that set forth "certain common principles" both nations supported and on which they based "hopes for a better future for the world." In summary, these were: "no aggrandizement, territorial or other"; "no territorial changes that do not accord with the freely expressed wishes of the peoples concerned"; the right of all people to choose their own form of government and the restoration of self-government to those peoples forcefully deprived of that right; the establishment of free trade and access to raw materials for all nations ("with due respect for their existing obligations"); establishment of the fullest possible international collaboration to improve "labor standards, economic advancement and social security"; "after final destruction of the Nazi Tyranny," the establishment of a safe peace; freedom of the seas; and, finally, the abandonment of the use of force and the establishment of an international government body. With this charter Roosevelt secured a key goal: certifying "the political basis for waging and winning the war."

The *Prince of Wales*'s passengers also included Roosevelt's key adviser, Harry Hopkins, fresh from a presidentially commissioned mission that included a fateful Moscow visit. There, Stalin personally divulged to Hopkins battlefront details never confided previously to a foreigner. Stalin affirmed: "Give us anti-aircraft guns, and the aluminum, and we can fight for three or four years." The fact that aluminum could only be used to make planes well in the future powerfully implied Stalin's confidence that his country would withstand the current onslaught and fight on. Hopkins came away uneasy with the palpable aura of terror suffusing Stalin's reign, but convinced that the Soviets were not about to collapse and would form a formidable and enduring ally against Germany. But Hopkins delivered a second strategic insight. Soviet Foreign Minister Vyacheslav Molotov pointedly raised to Hopkins the threat posed by Japan. Molotov asked for an American warning to Japan that if Japan struck in Siberia the United States "would come to the assistance of the Soviet Union." While Hopkins could make no such commitment, this exchange accentuated the nexus between Soviet survival and the prevention of Japan's striking north.

When Roosevelt returned to Washington, the hiatus in oil shipments to Japan became permanent. One view holds that by now Roosevelt dared not provoke incandescent national outrage by retreating from the now fervently supported embargo, coupled to concern that such appeasement might further embolden hardliners in Japan. But placing the sequence of events in the context of vital shifts in the geostrategic balance, the evidence better aligns with the interpretation that Roosevelt simply reexamined the concept of elastic trade sanctions after obtaining new evidence of the huge implications of Soviet survival. Saving the Soviets translated into forestalling a Japanese attack that might undermine, perhaps catastrophically, Soviet resistance. Two vital constraints tethered Japanese capabilities: Chinese resistance bogging down a huge part of the Imperial Army, and utter Japanese dependence on imported US oil—oil that "might encourage or permit" a potential fatal Japanese blow against the Soviet Union. Thus, it is not surprising that after returning from his meeting with Churchill and receiving Hopkins's report, Roosevelt acquiesced to an indefinite extension of the effective oil embargo.

There is a further moral dimension to the oil embargo. Japan imported about 90 percent of its petroleum needs, of which 75 to 80 percent came from the United States. Inevitably that meant that American oil largely powered the Japanese war machine that by now was ultimately responsible for approximately 7.5 million dead Chinese. Had Hitler's war machine run to this extent on American oil, continuing the supply would have unleashed clamorous historical condemnation. Previously, Roosevelt based his refusal to permit an oil cutoff on a fear that this would prompt Japan to seize oil in the Netherlands East Indies, an act the American public would not view as justification for a US declaration of war. Although strategic considerations undergirded the embargo now, they also thus harbored a profound moral dimension.

Upon return to England, Churchill faced a crestfallen cabinet that had hoped the meeting would mark the entry of the United States into the war with Germany. According to Churchill, Roosevelt said "he would wage war, but not declare it." Putting the best face on events, Churchill took pains to convince members of his government that he had established a close personal bond with FDR. "I am sure I have established warm and deep personal relations with our great friend," he wrote Deputy Prime Minister Clement Attlee.

Whether Churchill accurately conveyed Roosevelt's words or not, the president's actions demonstrated he still hoped to confine the US role to providing aid to allies to defeat the Axis, while not entering formal hostilities. In keeping with this course, he inflicted further discouragement in British quarters when he muffled his promised stern warning to Japan. New circumstances, not faintheartedness, animated Roosevelt's restrained tone. To their shock, the Japanese gradually realized that the Americans were translating the financial freeze into an effective embargo of trade, especially oil. No one was more stunned than Konoe. After compiling a long record of drift and misjudgment, Konoe very belatedly grasped the extreme gravity of the situation. On 8 August, Nomura unveiled Konoe's emergency maneuver to Hull: Konoe proposed a meeting with Roosevelt to resolve face-to-face the critical issues between the two nations.

From the American standpoint, the proposal's intrinsic problem stemmed from Konoe's lack of credentials as a peacemaker. In 1937–1938, he led Japan into an ever-widening war in China, disastrously declared that Japan would not recognize Chiang's government, sanctioned Jingwei Wang's puppet government, and proclaimed Japan's goal of a "New Order in Asia" that appeared to leave little if any space for the interests of other nations. Then in 1940 he oversaw the advance into Northern Indochina, followed by a formal pact with Germany and Italy. The immediate cause of the current crisis was the latest piece of Konoe statecraft: the advance into Southern Indochina, which posed a threat to British, US, and Dutch positions. And Konoe exacerbated the current crisis with incredibly maladroit diplomacy: rebuffing the neutralization proposal *before* asking for the summit meeting.

A second great shadow beclouded Konoe's overture: Would the forces that had propelled Japanese aggression for years now grant benediction over any halt, not to mention a reverse course? To Ambassador Grew, Konoe argued that he was the only Japanese political figure with the courage and clout to head off the slide to war. Foreign ministry emissaries in Tokyo and Washington echoed this, and they maintained that Konoe had support from top leaders of the army and navy as well as from the imperial court, including the emperor. But they also spoke of dangerous pro-Axis forces dedicated to preventing a settlement, of the peril of assassination (specifically targeting Konoe, who escaped an actual assassination plot in September, as did the foreign minister), of a possible coup attempt, and of their fear that if Konoe failed he would be replaced by a military dictatorship. These arguments could hardly fail to reinforce rather than reduce American doubts about the durability of any agreement with Konoe. Yet another severe blow to Konoe's credibility was inflicted by a fateful coincidence. His proposal appeared the same day (8 August) that the "Magic" translation of the report of the 2 July Imperial Conference reached American leaders. Japanese blandishments, however, gained support from one American quarter. Ambassador Grew cabled Washington to urge "with all the force at [his] command" that the Japanese proposal not be turned aside without "very prayerful consideration." He warned of "appalling consequences" if the leaders' meeting failed.

But consequences—appalling or not—of a Konoe-Roosevelt meeting were very much on American minds in Washington. At a meeting with Nomura on 17 August, Roosevelt delivered a very tepid version of the "warning" sought by the British but then expressed interest in meeting Konoe. The president imposed, however, a critical precondition: the Japanese government must present a "clearer statement" of its "attitude and plans." As Hull elaborated to Nomura, the United States believed the conference should consummate the "ratification of essential points" of agreement reached prior to the meeting. The American interrogatories about terms seemed to be little-disguised tests to see if Konoe really sought a settlement despite his prior record.

And as Roosevelt and Churchill met, the Imperial Army General Staff calculated that a "Strike North" hinged on Soviet withdrawal of half their estimated thirty divisions and two-thirds of their 2,800 aircraft from the Far East. Under the guise of "special maneuvers," the Imperial Army mounted a stupendous logistical effort to shift 500,000 men, plus their associated horses and equipment, to reinforce the twelve divisions currently in Manchuria. By December 740,000 Japanese troops stood watch in Manchuria and Korea. But weather would preclude operations in Siberia after mid-October. Thus, the cabinet must authorize an attack by 10 August, so that it could begin by mid-September.

While the Army General Staff advocated the "Strike North," the Army Ministry exerted caution; indeed, it throttled down the flow of reinforcements to Manchuria, lest the Kwantung Army unilaterally plunge the nation into war with the Soviets. By 9 August, however, Soviet survival through 1941 appeared likely, and the failure of the Soviets to withdraw massive forces from the Far East convinced even the Army General Staff to look to a 1942 date for "Strike North." But there was another reason there could be no "Strike North" in 1941: the oil embargo rendered operations against the Soviets "extremely difficult," and "securing enough oil suppressed the argument for the northern advance."

The Japanese were not alone in experiencing painful curbs on their military capabilities. When the US Congress authorized the first peacetime draft in the nation's history in 1940, the law only required service for one year. By the summer of 1941 Roosevelt faced the prospect that his newly strengthened army might abruptly wither back to a mere constabulary guard. With just 51 percent of popular opinion favoring extension of draftee service, Roosevelt sent a powerful message personally demanding such legislation. With twenty-one senators abstaining, just forty-five "ayes" passed the measure, but it only authorized eighteen months of service, not the duration of the emergency that FDR had requested. The measure squeaked by the House of Representatives on 12 August by just a single vote, 203–202. It seemed an extremely powerful signal of the nation's profound reluctance to go to war.

In Tokyo, Japanese leaders scrambled to deal with the oil embargo and to design a "clearer statement" of Japan's "attitudes and plans." The upshot was a paper titled "The Essentials for Carrying Out the Empire's Policies." This declared that Japan would embark on the southern operations, and, "if necessary," open hostilities with the United States, Great Britain, and the Netherlands. But the Empire would concurrently press diplomatic measures to "endeavor to attain our objectives." If there was "no prospect" of a diplomatic settlement the first ten days of October, "we will immediately decide to commence hostilities against the United States, Great Britain, and the Netherlands."

The paper then defined Japan's "minimum demands" to be attained by diplomacy. The United States and Great Britain must "neither interfere with nor obstruct the settlement of the China Incident by our empire" on the basis of the submissive terms Japan imposed on Wang. They would close the Burma Road "and cease to assist the Chiang Kai-shek regime militarily, politically, and economically." Japan pledged "in principle" to withdraw troops from China following a settlement, and it was also prepared to affirm there would be no restriction on US and British economic activities in China on an equitable basis. The Anglo-Americans must restore commercial relations and "supply those goods from their territories in the Southwest Pacific that our Empire urgently needs to sustain itself."

Then the paper defined Japan's maximum concessions as: (1) a promise "not to advance militarily from the bases in French Indochina to neighboring areas other than China," (2) preparation to withdraw forces from French Indochina after a "just peace" is established in the Far East, and (3) a guarantee of Philippine neutrality. In sum, this framework demanded that the United States, Britain, and the Netherlands capitulate to Japan by immediate concrete actions on virtually all key issues while Japanese "concessions" floated nebulously in the realm of future actions.

On 5 September, Konoe stood before Kido and the emperor. Why did "The Essentials" award precedence to war over diplomacy, asked the emperor? Konoe lamely protested that the draft really emphasized diplomacy. When Sugiyama and Nagano presented themselves, the emperor, observed historian Eri Hotta, "displayed the incisiveness he was capable of when utterly compelled—which did not happen often." How long would war last with the United States?, he demanded. Sugiyama volunteered only three months. The emperor rejoined that Sugiyama had told him the China Incident would end in about one month, and now four years later it still raged. Sugiyama haltingly replied that China proved to have a vast hinterland. A clearly riled emperor retorted: "If the hinterland of China is vast isn't the Pacific Ocean even more immense?" Then the emperor demanded, "Can you guarantee our victory?" As Sugiyama's evasive answer failed to satisfy the emperor, Nagano then interjected with a simple analogy. He likened the situation to that where a doctor says that an operation offers a 70 percent chance of survival for a dying person. Would not the decision be for the operation? According to Konoe's account, the emperor pressed again: "I take it that the supreme command will place emphasis on diplomacy. Is that correct?" Both chiefs of staff answered affirmatively, and Nagano added that the three-part draft resolution did not favor war and merely provided for the circumstance when war was unavoidable. When Konoe asked if the emperor wanted to change the agenda for the Imperial Conference, the apparently mollified emperor replied, "There is no need to change anything."

For two hours on the morning of 6 September, the Imperial Conference reviewed "The Essentials." Since a Pacific War must emphasize the naval dimension, the most important assessment spilled from the lips of the chief of the Naval General Staff. Nagano confessed that the Americans would likely embark on a protracted war and that the current moment favored Japan, but by the end of 1942 the situation would be problematic. If Japan struck immediately to seize territory and resources, it could establish "an impregnable position" and create "the basis for a prolonged war." Thereafter, "the situation then depended on the tangible and intangible elements of national power" and "on developments in the world situation."

A document accompanying the basic policy paper expressly identified the China Incident as the "central problem" challenging Japan's manifest destiny of leading a New Order in Asia—thus fixing China as the fundamental issue between Japan and the United States, even after the embargo. This paper painted prospects for Germany in highly optimistic colors: destruction of the main Soviet armies by the end of 1941, followed by an invasion of Britain in the summer of 1942.

Primed by Kido, Privy Council President Yoshimichi Hara posed the emperor's critique: why the draft prioritized war over diplomacy. Navy Minister Oikawa asserted that the paper made war and diplomacy equal—thus contradicting Konoe's claim the day before of priority for diplomacy. Then by the staid standards of imperial conferences, this one climaxed in high drama. The emperor read a famous *tanka* poem from Emperor Meiji: "Across the four seas all are brothers. In such a world why do the waves rage, the winds roar?" He added, "I always read this composition with humility, endeavoring to be instructed in the late emperor's peace-loving spirit." Sugiyama and Nagano were stunned and abruptly professed to concur with the priority for diplomacy over war. Upon returning to his office from the conference, Tôjô exclaimed: "His Majesty's wish is for peace, I tell you!" And to a member of the Military Affairs Bureau Maj. Gen. Akira Muto blurted out: "War is absolutely out of the question! Listen up now. His Majesty told us to reach a diplomatic settlement on this, no matter what it takes."

However accurate may be these reports of the initial reaction to the emperor's intervention by Sugiyama, Nagano, Tôjô, Mutô, or other figures, it produced no meaningful change. None of these figures—nor Konoe and Toyoda—ever fundamentally revisited the terms set in "The Essentials." And although "The Essentials" again did not lock Japan irrevocably into war, it further accelerated the momentum toward war created by the July Imperial Conference. Perhaps worst of all, "The Essentials" now installed a dangerously narrow negotiating straitjacket and locked it within a specific deadline for diplomacy. And the increasingly bellicose language erected ever loftier psychological barriers within the army and navy to the sort of compromise essential to forestall hostilities.

Konoe's indecisive character over the weeks following the 6 September

Imperial Conference makes difficult any firm conclusion as to his expectations and goals (army leaders likened pinning down Konoe to "trying to nail jelly to a wall"). To meet Roosevelt's request for terms, Konoe transmitted less than comprehensive versions of the proposals sanctioned at the Imperial Conference. They included the deal breaker that the United States effectively withdraw all support for China and endorse a one-sided settlement of the "China Incident" favoring Japan.

As one Japanese historian emphasized, however, Konoe "was obsessed with holding the summit itself rather than its content." Konoe and his intermediaries tried to convey that before Roosevelt he would jettison these provisos for something mutually acceptable that would halt the now quick-step march to war. Ambassador Grew seconded the proposition that only at an actual meeting with Roosevelt, not before, could Konoe "offer assurances which, because of their far reaching character, will not fail to satisfy the United States." Grew warned that if no meeting transpired, Konoe's cabinet was likely to be replaced by a military dictatorship. The ambassador concluded ominously that "Japanese psychology . . . cannot be measured, nor can Japanese actions be predicted by any Western measuring rod."

At a 25 September Liaison Conference, Nagano and Sugiyama proposed a deadline of 15 October for diplomacy. An Imperial Army observer recorded that this proposal staggered Konoe. The next day, Konoe announced to Kido his intent to resign, but the Privy Seal admonished Konoe that because he had contrived the 6 September Imperial Conference, as prime minister he could not now just walk away.

Yet, in the first fortnight of October, a glimmer appeared in Tokyo that a settlement might be reached. At a joint service staff conference, the chief of the Navy Operations Division, Adm. Shigeru Fukudome, admitted that by the third year of a war with the United States, Japan would lack the merchant shipping to sustain its industrial base. Even Tôjô and Sugiyama recognized this meant Japan's defeat in a war with the United States. At a meeting with Navy Minister Oikawa, Tôjô acknowledged that he could not bear to give up in China after loss of "200,000 souls," but the army minister was prepared even to abandon his staunch insistence on stationing troops in China if the navy had no confidence in the outcome of a Pacific War certain to produce still higher death tolls. Thus, the fateful burden fell on Oikawa: if he clearly expressed the view that the navy lacked conviction for success in a war with the United States, Japan might halt its plummet to war. For several days Oikawa hid his opinion behind a smokescreen of ambiguity. Then at a 12 October meeting with Konoe, Toyoda, and Tôjô, Oikawa refused to state that the navy had no confidence in the outcome of war. Instead, he pronounced that the decision for war was a political decision and hence up to Konoe.

Determining whether the summit proposal represented a lost opportunity to avoid war requires an answer to two questions: Was a Konoe-Roosevelt agreement possible, and then, could Konoe secure the agreement's enforcement? The crucial issues loomed: Japanese troop withdrawal from Southern Indochina to restore the flow of oil; Japanese troop withdrawal from China; and Japan's obligations under the Tripartite Pact. The most revealing evidence is the summit negotiating position draft that Konoe actively helped write. It conspicuously lacked reference to withdrawal of Japanese troops from Indochina, essential to renewing oil shipments. (And when Nomura and Roosevelt mooted this trade later, it went nowhere in Tokyo. This leaves little reason to believe it could have been agreed upon and enforced during Konoe's tenure.) Konoe's draft only allowed that Japan agreed as "a general principle" to withdraw from China, and it would only conduct an independent review of obligations under the Tripartite Pact. Perhaps even more telling is the fact that Konoe did not even present the "general principle" of troop withdrawal from China at the 6 September Imperial Conference. Instead, he allowed a Foreign Ministry proposal to be adopted that only promised withdrawal from China after the Sino-Japanese War was settled.

Quite fundamentally, by the second half of 1941 no common ground existed on China. All of the Japanese proposals in 1941 included a formula assuring Japan's clear-cut victory over China. American leaders adamantly declined to support any settlement leaving a defeated China—and thus freeing Japan to strike north or south. Even if Konoe agreed to end the China Incident with an independent China exercising sovereignty over nearly all its 1937 territory, there is virtually no chance that the key Imperial Army and Navy leaders would have openly supported him. Tôjô, by now shaping up as the most committed figure among the senior leadership pressing to unleash war, exclaimed that the only acceptable US response to Japanese terms was "yes" or "no."

Yet the extremely dim prospects for agreement on China stemmed not from blindness to the measures necessary to avoid a disastrous war, but from a want of moral courage pervasive among Japan's leaders in 1941. From August to mid-October, key army and navy leaders left ample evidence of their sound individual grasp of the situation—starkly at odds with

their customary strident façades in council. On 27 August 1941, a delegation from the Total War Research Institute presented the cabinet with their
rigorous analysis concluding that Japan must necessarily lose a war with the
United States. The attentive Tôjô "grew noticeably pale, as though his worst
fears had been confirmed," as the presentation paralleled reports Tôjô had
perused from the War Ministry and the intelligence section of the Army
General Staff. He attempted to rebut the conclusion by arguing it omitted
intangibles like unpredictability. Two days later, the War Guidance Office of
the Army General Staff journal predicted Konoe would cave to US demands,
but deemed this better than war. Meanwhile, the officer designated to
accompany Konoe to the summit from the Military Affairs Bureau of the
War Ministry forecast that the emperor would overrule all army objections
to any agreement Konoe might reach with Roosevelt. Then on 29 September, the chief of the Military Affairs Bureau of the Army Ministry informed
his staff that even withdrawal of troops from China was preferable to war
with the United States.

But the most damning evidence of the private doubts masked by a bristling
surface attitude emerged from the top Imperial Navy leadership. On 29 September, Combined Fleet commander Yamamoto wrote Chief of Staff Nagano
that a "war with so little chance of success should not be fought." At a private
meeting with Konoe on 1 October, Navy Minister Oikawa stated that if Konoe
would "swallow all the U.S. demands" to normalize relations and head off
war, "the Navy will back you up fully, and the army should follow." According
to Navy Vice Minister Sawamoto, Oikawa then met Nagano, who also pledged
to support Konoe to avoid war.

Yet at a Liaison Conference on 4 October, Nagano blustered that "It is no
longer time for discussion. We should [set a timetable for war] right away!"
Then at a naval leadership conclave on 6 October, a consensus emerged for
avoiding war, even if it meant a graduated troop withdrawal from China. But
Nagano refused to confront the army over this course. The next day Tôjô
sought to pin down Oikawa on the navy's confidence in victory. "That, I am
afraid, I do not have . . . ," replied Oikawa, "if war continues for a few years,
we do not know what the outcome will be. . . . What I have said should not go
beyond this room." Far from castigating Oikawa for his admission of moral
cowardice, Tôjô declared in measured tones that if the navy lacked confidence,
then the path the government was embarked upon must be reversed. Nonetheless, the very next day, when Konoe importuned the war minister to accept
American terms, particularly withdrawal from China, Tôjô replied with per-

haps the most memorable remark of his life: "Occasionally, one must conjure up enough courage, close one's eyes and leap off the veranda of [the] Kiyomizu [Temple]."* And these are only some of the examples of the gloomy inner judgments of senior leaders contradicting their bellicose postures in decision-making forums.

There was yet a further serious obstacle to Japanese acceptance of any agreement satisfactory to the United States: the Japanese public. As Nomura explained, the Japanese government must be able to "present to the Japanese people some reward for [their] sacrifice[s in China] or some alternative attractive gain." Another historian has pointed out that, thanks to the government's educational indoctrination and manipulation of the press, the public was "more jingoistic than Japan's top leaders from 1931 to 1941."

The Tôjô Cabinet

Konoe resigned on 16 October. He recognized that his policy of protracted if not limitless negotiations faced adamant opposition from the army. Faced with the prospect of leading Japan into war with the West, his brittle character shattered and he sought to escape responsibility. Coincident with, though not a proximate cause of, Konoe's resignation appeared devastating news of betrayal by an aide.

Richard Sorge had stalked Tokyo since 1933 as a dashing German expatriate whose friends included the German ambassador Eugen Ott (Sorge's mistresses may have included Ott's wife). Sorge appeared to be a freelance journalist; he was really a Soviet spy. His espionage network included Hotsumi Ozaki, a trusted member of Konoe's inner circle and likewise a secret Communist. Sorge's warnings of Operation Barbarossa were among the

---

* The Buddhist Kiyomizu Temple (literally "Pure Water Temple"), perched high on a hill east of Kyoto, is famous for its veranda (or stage) built entirely without nails about forty-three feet off the ground, offering a spectacular view of Kyoto and the nearby countryside. The expression "leaping off the veranda of the Kiyomizu" is usually depicted as a rough equivalent of the English phrase "taking a wild leap." Prior to the banning of the practice, however, pilgrims would dive off the veranda on the superstitious belief that if you survived the fall, your wish would be granted. The 85 percent survival rate of the jumpers indicates a nuance in Tôjô's comment, implying a gamble under very favorable odds that a literal translation conceals.   https://www.google.com/culturalinstitute/entity/%2Fm%2Fo2yn3g?projectId=world -wonders (last viewed 27 November 2013).

many received in Moscow. But thanks to Ozaki and other sources, including Ott, Sorge notified Moscow that Japan would not attack in 1941. Pursuit of an unrelated case stunned Tokyo police when it unraveled evidence that Ozaki was a Soviet spy. Police arrested Ozaki on 15 October and Sorge on the 17th —Konoe's resignation fell exactly between those dates. (Sorge and Ozaki were executed in November 1944.)[*]

Both Konoe and Tôjô favored Prince Naruhiko Higashikuni, an army officer and a blood relative of Hirohito, the new prime minister. Konoe advanced Higashikuni as a war opponent. Tôjô envisioned a dual role for the prince: a unifying symbol for the armed forces and nation if Japan took on the West, but also, conversely, as the singular figure, if backed by the emperor, who could contain the national convulsion sure to detonate if Japan yielded to American demands. But Kido and the other elder statesmen aborted this proposal both because Higashikuni lacked political experience and more importantly because he would bind the war directly to the imperial family; defeat would thus threaten Hirohito's grip on the throne.

With Prince Higashikuni out of the picture, Konoe recommended Tôjô to Kido out of both the fear that Tôjô alone might be able to control the army, and the hope that Tôjô might reverse the decisions of the September Imperial Conference based on the navy's lack of confidence in a war. In an unprecedented intervention, Kido steered a meeting of the elder statesmen to anoint Tôjô as

---

[*]   Some accounts give primacy to Sorge's reports, which Stalin read, as the trigger for the shift of Soviet forces from the Far East, which played a vital role in halting and then throwing back the German drive on Moscow. This, however, may overstate Sorge's importance. David Glantz, a highly respected authority on the Soviet-German war, argues that even without the reports of Sorge or other intelligence that the Japanese would not attack in 1941, Stalin would still have moved massive forces from the Far East to defend Moscow. Glantz notes that Stalin in 1941 faced a dilemma as to whether to take risks with or even abandon large areas in the Far East to the Japanese to assure the strategically critical defense of Moscow. This was the same challenge Soviet leaders confronted in 1921–1922 during the Russian Civil War and Allied intervention. Those Soviet leaders chose to move Far Eastern forces westward and thus concede to the Japanese (temporarily as it turned out) a large tract of the Soviet Far East. Therefore, Glantz maintains that Stalin probably would have made the same decision. Further, Glantz notes that the Soviets raised new formations in the Far East, albeit not well trained or equipped. These additional formations sustained or even increased the Soviet Far Eastern order of battle through 1941, thus easing Stalin's ability to shift forces to the west.

Jonathan Haslam maintains that the key evidence prompting Stalin's shift of forces from the Far East to the West came from Soviet code breaking of Japanese communications. He further argues that Moscow did not trust Sorge and that, if the Japanese had not executed Sorge, the Soviets would have. *Near and Distant Neighbors: A New History of Soviet Intelligence* (New York: Farrar, Straus and Giroux, 2015), 118, 126–28.

the new prime minister. The news left Tôjô "absolutely . . . dumbfounded" in his own words. Tôjô would simultaneously hold the portfolios of war minister and home minister. Other key members of the cabinet formed on 17 October included Shigenori Tōgō as foreign minister, and Shigetarō Shimada as navy minister (a "simpleton" according to Isoroku Yamamoto).

Curiously, Foreign Minister Tōgō, like Matsuoka, stood out like an exotic creature among Japan's typically staid leadership. Historian Eri Hotta described him as a "sixty-year-old dandy with copious graying hair." His background overshadowed even his striking physical appearance. He descended from a Korean family of potters, renowned for their ceramic arts, dragged forcibly to Japan during the sixteenth century. They had preserved their Korean heritage over hundreds of years. His father achieved great economic success and bought the family name Tōgō when his son, then named Shigenori Park, was five. Shigenori married a German woman but rejected Nazism. On the other hand, he had no affinity toward the Anglo-Americans. His Korean lineage made him suspect to some Japanese, so Tōgō radiated an ostentatious Japanese patriotism; yet he stood out for clear thinking when it was in short supply in Tokyo.

Kido relayed the emperor's desire that the new cabinet reexamine the whole question of relations with the United States by "wiping the slate clean," i.e., without regard to the 6 September Imperial Conference. But Kido seriously compromised what might have been another singular opportunity to halt the march to war. First, he conveyed this instruction only to the government, not to the independent supreme command. Second, the command to "wipe the slate clean" was not accompanied by a command that at whatever sacrifice, the nation must avoid war with the United States.

In this hour of crisis, Japan desperately needed an outstanding statesman, but in Tôjô it secured only an outstanding clerk. Tôjô seemed to grasp that if the navy lacked confidence in victory, then Japan must reverse its whole trajectory of statecraft since July. Now, as prime minister, he fell back on his forte as superefficient administrator and dutifully officiated at the façade of the "wipe the slate clean review." But he could not rise above his background as an army officer and his rigid personality; nor could he prioritize his role as prime minister over his simultaneous appointments as war minister and home minister. Process, not substance, obsessed him, so he compounded Kido's error by failing to proselytize actively to avoid war with the West, even at grievous cost. And since Tôjô empowered essentially the same cast of characters that devised the old policy to conduct the "review," the outcome was foreordained.

A marathon series of liaison conferences convened to reconsider the 6 September resolution on all but one day from 23 to 30 October. They were marked by the appearance of the exploration of key issues, like the nation's capability for war, including its economic stamina, the strategic situation in Europe and Asia, and not only US-Japan relations, but also the viability of the alliance with Germany. The armed forces representatives from the vice ministers and the vice chiefs of staff on down formed a chorus clamoring for an immediate decision for war. Foreign Minister Tōgō and Finance Minister Okinori Kaya tried their best to subject a lot of very shallow analysis to rigorous scrutiny.

The superficial or even fraudulent character of the review is exemplified by the crucial issue of the capacity of Japan's merchant fleet to endure losses and still transport critical war-fighting materials from resource areas to the Japanese homeland. One initial Imperial Navy internal projection pointed to catastrophic losses. But other staff officers manufactured counterfeit figures for the liaison conferences showing losses averaging 700,000 tons per year for the first three years of the war. (This gave a total loss of 2.1 million tons over that span—the actual loss proved to be almost 7.3 million tons.)

During this interval, the Imperial Army General Staff furnished arguably the signature moment of 1941 Japanese strategic thinking: "It is first and foremost necessary, at this point, to make up our minds [for war]. Then and only then can we calibrate our national capabilities and direct the nation to prepare for war." In other words, decide to go to war first, and only afterward look at the nation's war capabilities. During all of 1941, neither the Imperial Army nor the Imperial Navy ever conducted an objective comparison of Japanese and American capabilities. Some army officers professed that since naval aspects must dominate the war, that task belonged to the Imperial Navy. In fact, a May 1940 Imperial Navy map exercise had exceeded any earlier or later examination of Japan's prospects in a Pacific War. The exercise highlighted with alarming clarity the chasm between Japanese and US economic potential and Japan's utter inability to prevail in a protracted conflict. Then Navy Minister Zengo Yoshida summarized a key finding that since Japan could not control the sea routes to southern resource areas, "Would it not be pointless to occupy the [Netherlands] East Indies?"

The Liaison Conference met on 1 November 1941, in a fateful seventeen-hour marathon rent by "great tension and angry exchanges between participants." Navy Minister Shimada had just switched from war opponent to proponent. But now Shimada hijacked this utmost consequential moment into yet another iteration of endless resource allocation quarrels. He presented the conference with effectively a ransom note: give the navy more materials, especially steel, and I will vote for war. Shimada's stance perplexed Tōjō and others: Was it a ploy to stave off war with outrageous demands, or the navy's self-serving exploitation of the crisis? After exhausting hours of debate, they acceded to Shimada's demand. And as unimaginably reckless as Shimada's extortion appears, it was worse: he ostensibly traded his ballot on his country's fate for what proved only the chimera of extra steel production.

Having settled the wrangle with Shimada, the assembly turned to the trio of options on the agenda. Option one looked to purchase peace via concessions to the United States that required great Japanese hardships. It gained no serious traction. The Army General Staff urged option two: an immediate decision for war with political and military strategies aligned to that end. But the army ministry, the navy, and the foreign ministry all rallied to option three: a decision for war, but with war preparations and diplomacy marching side by side in a manner that permitted diplomacy to succeed.

Then the conference turned to the manifestly decisive question: Could Japan prevail in a Pacific War? Speaking "with great emphasis" according to the conference record, Nagano declared, " 'Now! The time for war will not come later!' " (Yet when pressed about Japan's prospects at sea in three years, Nagano only rated Japan's chances as 50–50.) The other participants counted Shimada's silence as concurrence with Nagano. Chief of the Planning Board Suzuki, the supposed careful accountant of Japan's capacity for war, convicted himself of moral cowardice: he radiated worry but seconded Nagano's assertion: better war now than later. (The skeptics, Foreign Minister Tōgō, and Finance Minister Kaya, before, during, and after this meeting probed for more objective examination of Japan's prospects. They made no headway because the army and the navy declared relevant data secret!) Tōjō contributed to the routing of facts by exhorting, "At the time of the Russo-Japanese War, we took our stand with no prospect of victory. . . . Yet we won."

The participants next turned to the practical elements of option three. Foreign Minister Tōgō denounced as "outrageous" the diplomacy deadlines of 13 and 20 November proposed by the Imperial Army and Imperial Navy respectively. The soaring tempers in these exchanges triggered a twenty-minute recess. Fearful that Tōgō might resign and collapse the cabinet, which could result in a less hawkish new government, the armed forces retreated to a deadline of midnight, 30 November, five days before the then-projected start of hostilities.

Tōgō then introduced the previously vetted Japanese formula for a settlement known thereafter as Proposal A. It addressed four key issues:

(1) Japanese troops in China: Japan would confine occupation to designated

areas of North China, Mongolia, and Hainan Island for "as long as is neces-sary" after peace was concluded between Japan and China. Withdrawal of other forces would commence "the minute" peace was signed under a sepa-rate Japanese-Chinese accord and would be concluded within two years. An annotation to this provision defined "as long as necessary" as "roughly 25 years." (Tôjô remarked that 25 years was "a way of saying close to eternity.")

(2) Indochina: Japan would declare its commitment to the territorial sov-ereignty of French Indochina and pledged to withdraw its troops stationed there "upon the settlement of the China Incident or upon the establishment of a just peace in the Far East."

(3) Nondiscrimination in trade: "The Japanese government acknowledges the principle of nondiscrimination will be applied to the entire Pacific region and China as well, insofar as that principle is applied throughout the world."

(4) Tripartite Pact: Japan would not unduly broaden its definition of the right of self-defense and would "act on its own discretion" in interpreting and observing the pact.

To the consternation of army and navy officers, Tōgō also unveiled for the first time an alternative, known thereafter as Proposal B. Of its four key pro-visos, the first two survived scrutiny, but the army's vociferous objections resulted in the redrafting of point three and adding point four in a manner designed to assure American rejection:

(1) Japan and the United States would mutually pledge not to make "any advances by military force into Southeast Asia and the South Pacific region, other than French Indochina."

(2) Both governments would cooperate "to guarantee the procurement of necessary resources from the Dutch East Indies."

(3) Both governments would work "to restore trade relations to what they were prior to the freezing of assets, and the United States will promise to sup-ply Japan with the petroleum it needs."

(4) "The United States government shall not engage in such actions as may hinder efforts toward peace by Japan and China." On its face these words seemed innocuous, but Japan's diplomats had made clear earlier and later that by this Japan meant the United States would halt all military, financial, and political support for China once talks commenced.

In sum, the revised drafts of Japanese diplomatic demands still insisted upon a China defeated (Proposal A) or a China abandoned (Proposal B)—with defeat inevitably to follow.

In the customary ritual, on 5 November, an Imperial Conference convened to bestow the emperor's sanction on the determinations reached in the liaison conference. Tōgō delivered a gloomy recitation, concluding that "there is no prospect of the negotiations coming to a successful conclusion quickly if things continue as they have in the past." Neither of the chiefs of staff, Nagano or Sugiyama, spoke of or was interrogated about Japan's prospects in a protracted war. At the end, the conference sanctioned Proposals A and B and the deadline for negotiations. This was not a slate "wiped clean," but one etched with a negotiating posture and a deadline tilted far more to produce not agreement but war.

CHAPTER 9

"Our Anxiety Is About China"

NOVEMBER 1941: TIME RUNS OUT

Diplomacy in a Global Context

On 5 November, Army Chief of Staff Marshall and Chief of Naval Operations Stark advised President Roosevelt that the United States must avoid a Pacific War and that aid to China, while desirable, must remain subordinated to British and Soviet needs. Shortly afterward Marshall presented the president an upbeat forecast that by March 1942 American forces in the Philippines, including air reinforcements and mobilized Philippine units, coupled to British Far East naval deployments, would erect a powerful deterrent to Japanese designs. Marshall urged "clever diplomacy" to purchase vital time with concessions like easing the oil embargo.*

---

* A message from Japan's Washington embassy to Tokyo decrypted on 6 November 1941 contained startling domestic American political news. Hidenari Terasaki, the embassy's first secretary and secret intelligence chief, had been in contact with American "C. K. Armstrong," who worked for a group secretly funded by Japan to promote friendly relations between Japan and the United States. "Armstrong" confided information about Tyler Kent, formerly a code clerk in the US London embassy in 1940. In that capacity, Kent illicitly saved copies of more than 250 secret wires between President Roosevelt and Prime Minister Churchill. At British request, the Roosevelt administration waived Kent's diplomatic immunity. The British then located Kent's cache of documents and secretly tried and imprisoned him. This prevented him from returning to the United States during the 1940 presidential campaign, where a public trial would inevitably reveal the secret communications that might have proved a serious embarrassment to Roosevelt's stance that he was laboring to keep the United States out of the war. "Armstrong" claimed that "[Charles] Lindbergh and [Robert] McCormick, owner of the *Chicago Tribune*, want to use these documents in impeaching

Roosevelt began November doubting whether even "clever diplomacy" could buy sufficient time. After visiting Roosevelt just as November began, Canadian Prime Minister William L. Mackenzie King confided to a reporter that the president regarded war with Japan as "almost certain" within "30 days." On 9 November, at a meeting with Harry Balfour, the British undersecretary of state for air, Roosevelt warned that his policy of "stalling and holding off" Japan could either lead to a hiatus in the Far East for months, or it "may blow up in the very near future." "Magic" provided the main source of Roosevelt's fears of an imminent "blowup." It not only delivered Japan's Proposals A and B to American eyes, it also divulged Foreign Minister Tōgō's exhortation to Nomura that they represented a "last effort." A settlement was "absolutely necessary" by 25 November.

From August to the first half of November, mixed signals emerged from the all-important Soviet front. German advances resumed in August, and then on 6 September Hitler directed his generals to make Moscow the primary objective. Secretary Stimson's diary recorded oscillating assessments of Soviet prospects in September, though he acknowledged the Soviets had "a mighty good army and they are making a terrific fight." News in early October looked "very bad," but Stimson recorded a glowing report from American officers who "likened [Soviet] spirit to those of crusaders." On 28 October, the American embassy (now decamped from Moscow to Kuybyshev) cabled that the Soviets did not expect to hold Moscow. But by 13 November, the embassy revised its position: Moscow's fall no longer appeared inevitable. Since the waning days of October, both Soviet and German communiqués described the German drive on Moscow as stalled. The German official communiqué of 10 November claimed that so far, German forces had captured 3,632,000 Soviet prisoners of war (a figure by itself several multiples of total US armed forces), a trenchant reminder of the stupendous scale of the struggle. On 16 November, a major article in the *New York Times* assured readers that "Winter and Russians Rob Hitler of Victory." This optimism proved premature.

---

the President." SDRJ No. 16,337, Washington (Nomura) to Tokyo, Nov 6, 1941; translated 11/8/41 in SDRJ series, Box 19, RG 457, National Archives and Records Center. Whether Roosevelt or other administration officials saw this message is not certain, but it would have reinforced already well-developed administration fears about "Fifth Column" activity in the United States. For the Tyler Kent affair (save the "Magic" intercept), see Peter Rand, *Conspiracy of One: Tyler Kent's Secret Plot Against FDR, Churchill, and the Allied War Effort* (Guilford, CT: Lyons Press, 2013), especially 55–56, 63, 77–78, 82–83, 89–91, 105–6, 109–14, 163–66, 176–78, 180.

While the Soviet front ranked first in importance, other global developments also shaped Washington's calculations. The Chinese faced a huge test. In April 1941, the very aggressive Gen. Korechika Anami, commander of the Eleventh Army, urged the seizure of the strategically important city of Changsha (the nexus of the South China rail network) to destroy the 300,000-man Chinese forces in Hunan province, and thus to deny the Chinese the granary and the source of manpower to sustain resistance. He maintained this campaign would end the China War. Only after the decision to defer a campaign against the Soviets until spring 1942 did Tokyo unleash Anami on the premise that his blow might either convince Britain and the United States to abandon China as a worthless ally or even to knock China out of the war.

The Chinese destroyed the road and rail net along the northern approaches to Changsha to impede Japanese logistics and force them to advance by foot and horse. Anami fielded six divisions and four independent brigades totaling 120,000 men. Supporting them were twenty naval vessels and two hundred motorized boats to exploit the waterway routes to Changsha, while one hundred Japanese aircraft commanded the skies. Facing this host under the competent Gen. Yue Xue was the Ninth War Zone, which comprised twenty-five Chinese divisions in ten armies formed into the Thirty-First and Thirty-Third Army Groups.

At first all went well for the Japanese. An attack on 16 September caught the Chinese by surprise. Japanese columns thrust south, taking care to place forces to guard open flanks. On 27 September, the Japanese reached Changsha. But this success proved very brief. With the Japanese fully strung out, commencing on 24 September three Chinese armies sprang out of the hills marking the long Japanese left (eastern) flank. The threat to cut off his leading columns forced Anami to abandon Changsha after only four days. The Japanese battled backward, enduring for once massed Chinese artillery fire. By 8 October the Japanese, with many vacancies in their ranks, were back to their starting point.

Soviet advisers, particularly Lt. Gen. Vasiliy Chuikov (the 1942 hero at Stalingrad), contributed importantly to the overall planning of the defense, but Chinese officers directed the actual counterattack. At the urging of Soviet advisers that the Changsha action provided an opportunity to counterattack to retake the key city of Yichang, the Chinese struck on 26 September. With an exceedingly rare equality or even superiority in artillery, the Chinese penetrated the city walls on 8 October. Their morale high, the Chinese fought furiously, but Japanese ground reinforcements (including two divisions rushed back from Anami's command), air strikes, and then the major use of poison gas finally threw back the Chinese attack.

The Chinese victory in the major battle at Changsha thwarted Japanese aims to undermine China's value to its allies and perhaps finally knock it out of the war. Instead, the Japanese underscored China's continued serious resistance. And China's main value rested in large-scale conventional battle, not scattered guerrilla warfare. Failure at Changsha forms a powerful back story to Japan's terms in Proposals A and B to defeat China with diplomacy when arms had failed.

The premier component of the Anglo-American struggle against Hitler remained the Battle of the Atlantic. October saw ship losses in a decline and heading to a monthly low for 1941. But British naval resources remained stretched taut, and day by day almost all the latest additions to the US fleet reported for duty in the Atlantic. In mid-October a U-Boat damaged the destroyer *Kearny*, producing the first American military fatalities (eleven) of the undeclared war. Then on 31 October, another submarine sank the destroyer *Reuben James* and killed 115 sailors. Admiral Stark declared: "Whether the country knows it or not, we are at war." US public opinion polls taken after these two incidents on 5 November, however, underscored public disagreement with Stark. While 11 percent of the respondents declined to offer an opinion, the surveys found 63 percent were still opposed to declaring war on Germany compared to just 26 percent in favor.

The first half of November produced further momentum in the confrontation with Japan and then reversed Western optimism about the Soviet situation. Marshall ordered Philippine reinforcements "expedited in every way" on 8 November. Churchill contributed a British deterrent on 10 November when he publicly revealed the dispatch of a "powerful naval force of heavy ships" to the Indian and Pacific Oceans (this was the task force built around battleship *Prince of Wales* and battle cruiser *Repulse*). He added that if the United States became embroiled in war with Japan, a British declaration of war would follow "within the hour." On 14 November, Roosevelt ordered the last major Marine detachments from China to the Philippines. But then the short-lived complacency about Soviet survival through 1941 toppled. Plummeting temperatures solidified the ground. Across this frozen landscape from 15 November German panzer thrusts stamped ominous enveloping arms north and south of Moscow. Thus, the backdrop for US-Japanese diplomacy in November included firm Chinese resistance, hopes that permanent deterrence of Japan from striking south might soon be at hand, and first confidence and then rising fears about Soviet survival.

Tokyo and Washington

No American labored harder than Ambassador Joseph Grew in Tokyo to prevent war in the fall of 1941. But Grew maintained close links to only the lesser voices among Japan's decision elites. Hence, his messages, commencing in late October and building in intensity during November, argued that: (1) Tôjô's cabinet, incentivized by the emperor, genuinely sought a settlement, (2) total Japanese troop withdrawal from China could not be reasonably expected, (3) these were now final negotiations with time crucial, and (4) failure of negotiations likely meant war. Grew warned on 3 November that "Japanese sanity cannot be measured by American standards of logic," and that Japan might well "rush headlong into a suicidal struggle with the United States." On 17 November, he wired Washington that tight Japanese security measures negated any prospect for his embassy to provide advance warning of a Japanese move that might "exploit every possible tactical advantage like surprise."

No Japanese labored harder than Kichisaburō Nomura in Washington to prevent war in the fall of 1941. After a period in limbo between the Konoe and the Tôjô cabinets, Tōgō finally enlightened Nomura on 4 November of Proposals A and B. Tōgō also dispatched Saburō Kurusu as a special envoy to assist Nomura. Tōgō did not trust Nomura and particularly admonished Kurusu that they must strictly follow Tokyo's bidding. Tōgō outfitted Kurusu with two more versions of Proposal B. The most conciliatory variant essentially called for a return to the status quo of early July: withdrawal of Japanese troops to Northern Indochina in exchange for resumption of trade.

Fifty-five when he arrived in Washington, Kurusu was both younger and much shorter than Nomura. The new representative was trim, with neatly combed-back, thick, dark hair only beginning to gray, wide-set eyebrows, intelligent eyes behind silver wired glasses, and a well-kept mustache. His well-tailored suits and careful manners signaled his "polished personality." Moreover, he had an American wife and spoke excellent English—thus eliminating the risk of misunderstanding always at play in Nomura's encounters with US officials.

Nomura delivered to Hull on 7 November a formal version of Proposal A. It provided that Japanese soldiers would remain in "specified areas" of North China, Inner Mongolia, and Hainan Island "for a certain required duration after restoration of peaceful relations between Japan and China."

All other forces in China would commence withdrawal "as soon as a general peace is restored between Japan and China, and the withdrawal will proceed according to separate arrangements between Japan and China and will be completed within two years with the firm establishment of peace and order." Japan guaranteed the territorial integrity of French Indochina and the withdrawal of troops "as soon as the China Affair is settled or an equitable peace is established in East Asia." Finally, Japan would apply the principle of nondiscrimination in trade in East Asia, provided the principle is "applied uniformly to the rest of the entire world as well." Three days later, Tōgō personally informed Grew that Proposal A represented Japan's "maximum possible concessions." If Japan was compelled to abandon the "fruits" of its four years of war, Tōgō declared that "she must inevitably collapse." He added that US economic sanctions "menac[ed] the national existence to a greater degree than the direct use of force" and might prompt Japan to act in self-defense.

Thanks to intercepts, Hull already knew the substance of Proposal A, and he also knew that behind it waited Proposal B. As noted, Proposal A defined a China defeated and unable to play a material role in the ongoing war. With China's collapse, Japan would gain freedom of action against the British, the Dutch, and the Soviets. As Tōgō expected, Proposal A gained no favor in Washington.

From early November onward, Roosevelt intervened personally in the diplomatic volleys with Japan. On 6 November, no doubt spurred by the plea of his military advisers for time, he sketched for Stimson the concept of presenting the new Japanese envoy Kurusu with a six-month "truce" of no further moves of troops or armaments. During that time China and Japan would attempt a settlement. Stimson objected that it would halt the American buildup in the Philippines and that the Chinese would likely feel abandoned.

On 10 November 1941, Nomura met with FDR and Hull. The admiral, echoing Tōgō's communication to Grew the same day, stated that while a complete Japanese troop withdrawal from China may be "desirable," it is "impracticable under present circumstances." Mindful of the need to buy time, Roosevelt raised for the first time to Tokyo through Nomura the possibility of a temporary agreement, a modus vivendi. Nomura reported that Roosevelt's initiative was

> a so-called modus vivendi [and] was necessary in order for the people to live and stated that this term might be translated as "method of living"

or the like. While it is not at all clear what this means, we must follow
up and ascertain beforehand whether it means a provisional agreement.

Roosevelt's comments, rather than Hull's interminable abstract lectures and
aversion to grappling with a settlement's substance, signaled that the United
States might accept an interim agreement that would break the momentum
to war. Roosevelt's intervention underscored a further point. As the president viewed him, Hull's value to the administration stemmed from his high
standing with Congress based on his service as a member of the House
of Representatives and as a senator, where he displayed keen attention to
international relations. In the words of one historian, Roosevelt personally
viewed Hull "as a cross between a Tennessee rube and a Wilsonian funda-
mentalist" and preferred to be his own secretary of state. It did not help that
Roosevelt did not have high regard for the State Department professionals
as a whole. But Roosevelt's intrusion into the substance of the negotiations
with the modus vivendi signaled his focused attention on the increasingly
fraught situation.

   A 14 November wire to Tokyo contained Nomura's astute depiction of the
core of US policy. He emphasized that Washington aimed to prevent a Japanese thrust not just south but also north. To that end, the Americans would
employ "every economic weapon they possess," a comment that included the
oil embargo as part of the deterrent package. Further, the Americans were
making every military and every other type of preparation as well as "conspir-
ing" with other nations to prevent Japan from striking north or south. Finally,
he underscored that "for the sake of peace in the Pacific, the United States will
not favor us at the sacrifice of China."

   On 17 November, Nomura presented the newly arrived Kurusu to Hull
and Roosevelt. During their conversation, Kurusu attempted to persuade his
hosts of Tôjô's commitment to peace, and he defended Japan's intention not to
withdraw all its troops from China. Kurusu further stressed the importance
of time. To protests of peaceful intent by Japanese envoys, Hull's typically
acerbic rejoinder was that Japan's new order in Asia was aimed "to dominate
entirely, politically, economically, socially and otherwise by military force all
the Pacific area." With Hull having played the "Bad Cop" to the hilt, Roosevelt
intervened as the "Good Cop." The president commented: "The United States
is not trying to intervene or mediate in the problems between Japan and
China. I don't know whether there is such a word in the parlance of diplomats
or not, but the United States' only intention is to become an 'introducer.'" No

doubt Roosevelt offered these comments to nudge along the possibility of an interim agreement. But Tokyo may have interpreted his remarks as veering close to the Japanese position that the United States would bring China to the negotiation table with Japan and then abandon it.

On this same day, 17 November, and probably after this session, Roosevelt elaborated on his thoughts on a modus vivendi. He mooted to Hull a six-month bargain, swapping an American relaxation of trade restrictions ("some oil and rice now—more later") for a Japanese pledge not to march additional troops north or south and not to enter a war between Germany and the United States under the Tripartite Alliance.

Nomura informed Hull on 18 November of the "very pressing" situation in Japan and the urgent need "to arrest a further deterioration in the relations between the two countries." The two Japanese diplomats recognized that the original version of Proposal B could not secure American blessing. Nomura tried to explain to Tokyo that settlement of the key issue, the Sino-Japanese conflict, "would have to wait until the end of the world." Accordingly, the Japanese envoys carved out of Tōgō's additional variants of Proposal B a return to the status quo ante of July: Japan would withdraw troops from Southern Indochina in exchange for the unfreezing of assets and the resumption of trade.

From the American standpoint the 18 November initiative by Nomura and Kurusu constituted a hand outstretched to grasp Roosevelt's concept of a modus vivendi. But when Nomura and Kurusu cabled word of their initiative to Tokyo, Tōgō erupted. His Washington envoys not only skipped over the American official silence so far on Proposal A, but also without authorization plucked a single term from the most yielding version of Proposal B. Tōgō shot back a sharp rebuke and ordered them to retract their offer and present the original (and most rigid) version of Proposal B. Tōgō further instructed his envoys: "Please bear in mind that paragraph 4 [the one requiring the United States "not (to) engage in such actions as may hinder efforts toward peace by Japan and China"] means the cessation of all help to Chiang Kai-shek by the United States." Nomura and Kurusu duly submitted the original Proposal B on Thanksgiving Day, 20 November. It included the proviso: "The government of the United States undertakes to refrain from such measures and actions as will be prejudicial to the endeavors for the restoration of general peace between Japan and China." While Hull stated he wished to study the proposal before any further comments, he demonstrated he clearly grasped the demand for US abandonment of China when he pointedly asked the Japanese representatives what they thought the reaction would be if the administration proposed to "discontinue aid to Great Britain." Nomura emphasized to Tokyo that Hull found the abandonment of China an impossible term.[*]

While Proposal B extended more of a partial bridge toward the United States than Proposal A, B still retained the wholly unacceptable requirement that the United States effectively abandon all forms of support for Chiang during Chinese-Japanese talks. Still, the Japanese offer required an American response. Notwithstanding his accustomed inflexible stance before the Japanese, Hull requested alternative terms for a settlement from his staff. Harry Dexter White of Treasury also entered the picture with a sweeping proposal geared not just to the current crisis but to the friction points between the United States and Japan going back to the start of the century.[†] For the two days after Thanksgiving, Hull and his staff sifted all the proposals, including Proposal B, and devised a modus vivendi and a comprehensive agreement.

The modus echoed the Nomura-Kurusu concept: a three-month moratorium that would return to the status quo of early July with Japanese troops pulling back "forthwith" to Northern Indochina, where the total garrison

---

[*]   Secretary of the Interior Harold Ickes characteristically advanced the most radical bit of policy advice Roosevelt received in November 1941. On the 21st, Ickes urged Roosevelt to have the Pacific Fleet launch a preemptive attack on the Japanese fleet in its home waters to free up forces for use in Europe! This recommendation fell into deserved obscurity, but it does reflect the emphasis on European matters prevalent in the administration. Stetson Conn, Rose E. Engelman, and Byron Fairchild, *United States Army in World War II, Guarding the United States and Its Outposts* (Washington, DC: Center of Military History, 1989), 176.

[†]   In 1995, a retired KGB agent, Vladimir Pavlov, claimed that he met in 1941 with Harry Dexter White, a senior official in the Treasury Department who often exerted important influence on Secretary Morgenthau. Pavlov asserted that he inveigled White to steer American policy on a path to provoke Japan into driving south against the United States rather than north against the Soviet Union, thus securing the Soviet Union's Far Eastern flank as it faced the German onslaught. "The Time Has Come to Talk About Operation 'Snow,'" *Novosti razvedki i kontrrazvedki* (News of Intelligence and Counterintelligence), Moscow, 1995. ["Snow" was a play on White's name and the popular Walt Disney animated movie, *Snow White*.] White was a Soviet agent, though a nervous one who at times refused Soviet instructions. As John Earl Hayes and Harvey Klehr point out, Pavlov's article was an effort to burnish the image of Soviet intelligence agencies. Further, they found Pavlov's account "purposely misleading" over any specifics, and accordingly they found it unconvincing. *Venona: Decoding Soviet Espionage in America* (New Haven, CT: Yale Nota Bene Book, 1999), 412n58. Edward S. Miller buttresses this conclusion with a description of the chronology of White's actions in relationship to his reported encounter with Pavlov and the actions of other administration officials. *Bankrupting the Enemy*, 272n42. In fact, White's memorandum for a general settlement can be read as advancing two goals shared in Washington and Moscow: to keep China an active belligerent, and to prevent a Pacific War to avoid diverting American resources away from the war with Germany.

was not to exceed 25,000. In exchange, the United States would adjust trade restrictions to permit export of nonmilitary commodities including food and cotton and, subject to monthly adjustments, lower-grade petroleum in quantities gauged to civilian consumption. The Japanese would pledge no further cross-border military incursions, but no restrictions would curb further American-British-Dutch reinforcements or existing Japanese deployments beyond Indochina's borders. The proposal omitted any reference to the irreconcilable issue of Japan's adherence to the Tripartite Pact.

The draft modus approached the vital issue of peace in China obliquely. The United States offered to bring the two together for talks in the Philippines. The United States would "not look with disfavor" if an armistice accompanied the talk, thus raising the possibility that in such an event the United States might suspend aid to China during the talks. Critically, however, the draft did not incorporate China-Japan talks as a condition for the modus. In sum, the draft modus purchased time by extending a modest outreach on peace in China and partly opening the oil spigot, but it remained ambiguous at best on the key Japanese demand for the effective US abandonment of China.

The comprehensive proposal set down the steep costs to Japan for restoration of trade and an overall settlement. Japanese troops must vacate China and Indochina. Tokyo must recognize Chiang as the only legitimate government of China and negotiate the status of Manchuria with him. Japan as well as the Western powers would surrender extraterritorial rights and concessions in China. Japan would make the Tripartite Pact a dead letter, and all the parties to the settlement would sign a nonaggression pact and pledge the neutrality of Indochina.

Hull presented both proposals to British, Chinese, Dutch, and Australian representatives on 22 November. Although the British tentatively approved Hull's proposals, the Chinese ambassador Shi Hu immediately pointed out that getting the Japanese out of Southern Indochina was a positive step, but forced Hull to admit that the modus would not curb any Japanese action in China. Hu added that China would be "very reluctant" to agree to any relaxation of the embargo.

London exercised an advantage over Washington during these days. Not only were the British reading Japanese diplomatic messages, they were also reading Chongqing's messages to its ambassadors. Further, London was decrypting some German Eastern Front messages, presenting more timely indications of how the German drive on Moscow and elsewhere on the Eastern Front was being halted. In a memorandum to Foreign Minister Eden on 23 November, Churchill allowed that a partial relaxation of pressure on Japan might be acceptable, but only if it did not encompass the abandonment or suspension of aid to China or make it possible for Japan to attack the Soviet Union.

The 25 November formal comments from the Foreign Office in London declared the Japanese proposal "clearly unacceptable," but London recommended that it be regarded as the beginning of bargaining. If so, the United States would take the helm, but the British outlined very stiff terms. Japan must first withdraw all forces from Indochina and promise to suspend advances not just in China, but also in Southeast Asia, the Southern Pacific, and the Soviet Union. Only then, and with progress toward a general settlement, could the embargo be somewhat relaxed—but not on oil. But Chongqing broadcast its volcanic reaction via Owen Lattimore, Chiang's American adviser, as well as Shi Hu and T. V. Soong in Washington. Lattimore noted he had never seen the generalissimo so "really agitated before." Chiang's objection to the number of Japanese troops permitted to remain in Indochina was merely a terse overture to his main theme that "leaving Japan entrenched in China" would cause the Chinese people to feel "completely sacrificed" by the United States. American omission of China's plight constituted appeasement of Japan "at the expense of China." It would demolish American prestige in China the way British prestige was shredded by the closure of the Burma Road.

Roosevelt forwarded a copy of the proposed modus to Churchill. The president deemed it fair, but he was "not hopeful" of Tokyo's acceptance. He added, "we must all be prepared for real trouble, possibly soon." Churchill responded during the night of 25–26 November. Like Roosevelt, he too saw how China fitted into the global strategic picture and what their "joint dangers" were:

> Of course it is for you to handle this business and we certainly do not want an additional war. There is only one point that disquiets us. What about Chiang Kai-shek? Is he not having a very thin diet. Our anxiety is about China. If they collapse our joint dangers would enormously increase.

While the United States prepared new draft proposals and received reviews from its allies, "Magic" provided several devastating pieces of information. Between 22 and 24 November, intercepts disclosed to Hull first on the 22nd that the Japanese deadline for an agreement had been extended to 29 November, and "after that things are automatically going to happen." But two days later, "Magic" revealed that the actual deadline was 28 November, Japanese time. Then adding to the Allied reservations on Hull's drafts of proposals,

"Magic" demonstrated that Tokyo insisted that China be "made to express her friendly intentions toward Japan." An armistice would follow, leading to negotiations, but Japan would settle for no less than the cessation of all American support for China during peace talks. On 24 November, Tōgō emphasized that merely a return to the status quo of July (Japanese withdrawal of troops from Southern Indochina, and US restoration of trade) was not acceptable. The United States must cease aid to Chiang and restore petroleum shipments.

With the very ominous Japanese negotiation deadline now clear, and with rapidly vanishing prospects for even an interim settlement, on 25 November Roosevelt discussed the situation with Stimson, Secretary of the Navy Frank Knox, Marshall, and Stark. According to Stimson, Roosevelt thought that

> we were likely to be attacked perhaps next Monday [December 1], for the Japanese are notorious for making an attack without warning, and the question was what we should do. The question was how we should maneuver them into the position of firing the first shot without allowing too much danger to ourselves.

Later, some accounts would edit Stimson's words down to the phrase about "how [the United States] should maneuver them into the position of firing the first shot without allowing too much danger to ourselves." It would then be asserted that this phrase evidenced a master plan to provoke Japan into war. But Stimson's comment simply reflects that the domestic US political situation barred the United States from initiating war and thus dictated that the United States had to absorb the first blow (hopefully without too much damage). The quote may also highlight another facet of the situation. American leaders entertained deep concerns that the Japanese might launch attacks on British and Dutch colonial holdings but leave American interests, including the Philippines, untouched. Assuring that Japan unmistakably was the aggressor in that event would be vital to securing US public support for entering the war.

When Stimson returned to his office he read a very disturbing report. Japanese war plans looked to strike at the Philippines, Thailand, Malaya, and Burma as well as other locales immediately upon the outbreak of war, about 8 December (Tokyo time). Starting from at least 20 November for warships and still earlier for transports bearing troops, equipment, and supplies, massive numbers of Japanese ships sortied from Japanese waters or ports like Shanghai on the Chinese coast. These included one aircraft carrier, two battleships, eleven heavy and ten light cruisers, at least fifty-five destroyers,

fourteen submarines, and several score of lesser combatants like minelayers, patrol boats, escorts, and submarine chasers. The numbers of transports
lifting expeditionary forces likewise numbered well over one hundred. The
elements intended for an attack on Thailand, Malaya, and Burma gathered at
Hainan Island. Those for the Philippines mostly assembled in the Pescado-
res and Formosa. The great majority of this huge and unmistakable stream
of ships passed through the heavily traveled waters near the China coast.
According to Stimson's diary, the G-2 reported that five divisions had come
down from Shantung and Shansi to Shanghai, and there they had embarked
on an estimated thirty to fifty ships. This convoy had now been sighted south
of Formosa. Stimson immediately informed Hull by telephone and sent copies of the message to the president.

The 26th of November was a crucial day. In an early telephone conversation, Hull informed Stimson that, due to Chinese objections to the modus,
he was inclined to "kick the whole thing over" and inform the Japanese he
had nothing further to offer. Only minutes later, Stimson asked the president
on the phone whether he had received the report sent over the night before
"about the Japanese having started a new expedition from Shanghai down
towards Indo-China." According to Stimson, Roosevelt

> fairly blew up—jumped up into the air, so to speak, and said he hadn't
> seen it and that that changed the whole situation because it was evidence
> of bad faith on the part of the Japanese that while they were negotiat-
> ing for an entire truce—and entire withdrawal—they should be sending
> this expedition down there to Indo-China.

Hull met with Nomura and Kurusu later that day. Hull had abandoned both
the draft modus and the comprehensive settlement and instead presented
them with what afterward was called the "Hull Note." The "Note" compiled a
list of the most stringent American positions over the year, starting with reaf-
firmation of "Hull's Four Principles." The major other provisions included (1)
a Pacific nonaggression pact among the governments of the British Empire,
China, Japan, the Netherlands, the Soviet Union, Thailand, and the United
States, (2) Japanese withdrawal of "all military, naval, air and police forces"
from China and Indochina, (3) Japanese recognition of only Chiang Kai-shek
as the legitimate ruler of China, (4) the United States and Japan to give up
extraterritorial rights in China, including international settlements and concessions under the Boxer Protocol, and seek to have the British and other
governments do likewise, and (5) a provision that would basically void any Japa-

nese obligations under the Tripartite Pact. The Japanese envoys were stunned. Kurusu declared that Japan's government would "throw up its hands" at Hull's proposal. He even suggested it should not be forwarded to Tokyo.

As Kurusu expected, the "Hull Note" shocked Tokyo. Tōgō "was struck by despair." In the words of one historian, he believed "the note rejected willfully and categorically all the efforts of the two countries." Tôjô's government and some later historians called the "Hull Note" an ultimatum. But the note was marked "Strictly Confidential, Tentative and Without Commitment"; it also lacked a deadline for acceptance, contained no threat that failure to adopt the proposal would lead to war, and effectively sought the continuation of negotiations, albeit with notice of a modified US stance. The absence of any deadline or threat of war and the note's call to continue negotiations made the note legally insufficient as an ultimatum, regardless of any attempt to label it otherwise.

For the Japanese militarists, however, the note was "nothing short of a miracle." One interpretation of the situation is that at this point profitable negotiations ended. In fact, they ended with the "Magic" disclosures of 18–24 November. In rapid succession, the core substance of Japan's stance was revealed as an absolute negotiation deadline of 28 November (Tokyo time); summary rejection of Nomura and Kurusu's attempt at a modus on 18 November; and Tōgō's affirmation that US abandonment of China formed a minimal condition for any settlement—not to mention resumption of oil shipments.[*] On 27 November, Hull informed Stimson that he had "washed my hands of [the negotiations] and it is now in the hands of you and Knox the Army and the Navy."

But in a meeting with Nomura and Kurusu, Roosevelt declared that he had not given up hope of a peaceful settlement "although the situation is serious and that fact should be recognized." During an exchange with Kurusu, the

---

[*] As if enough obstacles to a settlement did not exist, Japanese militarists had experienced anxieties that perhaps the United States might agree to Proposal B. Accordingly, they sought to add a further humiliating condition designed to make Americans choke at the last moment by demanding that acceptance of Proposal B also required submission to Japanese demands for massive amounts of petroleum. Hence, Tōgō sent a message on 26 November informing Nomura and Kurusu that, assuming the United States agreed to Proposal B, then it was "essential" that Washington also promise to deliver to Japan 4 million tons of petroleum per year (roughly 333,000 tons per month) of types as per the situation prior to the freezing order. The Dutch were to pledge 1 million tons per year. No. 169 Tokyo to Washington, No. 833, November 26, 1941 (translated November 26, 1941), The "Magic" Background to Pearl Harbor, appendix 4, A92.

president again brought up the concept of "introducing" Japan and China for talks. Both Roosevelt and Hull stated in various forms that an agreement could be reached if Japan's leadership chose to follow the path of peace, but that recent statements and acts emanating from Japan suggested this was not the case.

The following day, 28 November, Stimson presented Roosevelt with a G-2 estimate of Japanese intentions with regard to their large troop and shipping concentrations. G-2's list of potential Japanese options included reinforcing Indochina or making strikes at the Philippines, Thailand, Singapore, or the Netherlands East Indies. But Roosevelt immediately singled out yet another Japanese option: a landing on the Kra Isthmus and then a march to Rangoon to cut the Burma Road at its very origins. It marked another signal that the president remained highly alert to the fate of China. When Roosevelt mooted the idea of sending a telegram directly to the emperor, Stimson snorted that "One does not warn an emperor." During this day, "Magic" produced a translation of Tōgō's message of the same date commending Nomura and Kurusu for their "superhuman efforts" in the negotiations. Tōgō concluded that since Tokyo could not accept the US proposal, "the negotiations will be de facto ruptured. This is inevitable. However, I do not wish you to give the impression that the negotiations are broken off."

When clocks struck midnight, 28 November in Tokyo, the time for successful negotiations expired. The enormous literature scrutinizing these events often attempts to identify some step missed that might have prevented war. There certainly is fault to be found. The multiple meanings and subtle nuances of some Japanese words and phrases in general and the propensity for Japanese diplomats to flaunt their erudition with obscure classical references presented a formidable translation problem. Not surprisingly, some "Magic" translations erred. But did these errors critically undermine American belief in the sincerity and honesty of Japan's representations toward a settlement? This argument elevates mood and subjective factors over the real issue of terms mirroring irreconcilable strategic objectives that left no space for compromise.

The performance of Secretary of State Cordell Hull likewise often garners low marks. His sermonizing sessions with Nomura and Kurusu are painful to read and no doubt were excruciating to endure. But beneath Hull's outward predilection for intoning abstract principles rested clear-eyed perception of some implacable realities. Like his equally chastised main adviser, Stanley Hornbeck, Hull recognized correctly that Japanese aggression not only stemmed from a cabal of militarists, but represented a policy endorsed widely by much of the civilian leadership and the public. Hull thought that only a long-term process of humiliating this leadership by defeat, particularly in China, could restore Japan to the liberal political and economic order of the 1920s, which Hull extolled as the sound basis for international relations. Given this outlook, it is no wonder he remained skeptical of any interim settlement. Hornbeck and others, like Dean Acheson, were steered by the conviction that Japanese leaders knew they could not win a war with the United States, and hence the United States believed that if it just held rigidly to its terms, the Japanese ultimately would back down. Thus, those who entertained such convictions by no means supported the embargo because they felt it would provoke Japan into war. Quite the contrary, they could not believe, as Grew grasped, that given a choice between disastrous war and humiliation, the Japanese would choose war.

Whatever Nomura's failings, he did correctly inform his superiors that the United States would not abandon China and sought to prevent Japan's thrust north or south. In the end, Nomura and Kurusu devised an interim solution compatible with the concepts Roosevelt endorsed—which Tokyo promptly renounced. Konoe, a figure of manifest inadequacy for his role, at least comprehended that Japanese occupation of vast Chinese territories since 1937 was the decisive divide. In the last days of his final cabinet, Konoe desperately attempted to secure Tôjô's sanction for a ploy to ostensibly agree to troop withdrawal on paper, but to nullify the agreement in practice. Tôjô refused even to consider this feint to avoid war.

This brings us to the key point. Even if "Magic" had perfectly translated all Japanese messages and all the American policymakers had possessed great perspicacity and reposed trust in the sincerity of Japanese proposals, the path to any settlement satisfactory to the United States and enjoying any prospect of Japanese acceptance remained blocked. Quite fundamentally, the irreducible American and Japanese strategic objectives in the fall of 1941 could not be reconciled. For the United States, the defeat of Germany constituted the preeminent strategic goal. This meant keeping the United Kingdom and the Soviet Union in the war—which meant at least concentrated US support for these combatants, if not direct US intervention. But other considerations clashed with this top priority. On the one hand, a settlement with Japan promised to avoid diverting any effort by the Soviets, the United Kingdom, or the United States away from Germany. But keeping the Soviet Union in the war at all and sustaining Great Britain also awarded vast value to sustaining China as an active combatant—and China clearly demonstrated its worth in this capacity. A Chinese collapse would free Japan to deliver perhaps a fatal blow to the Soviets. A Chinese collapse would also unshackle Japan to strike south against the British and the Dutch. This might not have the same immediate effect as an attack on the Soviets, but it certainly would reduce the ability of Britain to deal with Germany and perhaps also bring the United States into a full-scale war in Asia that would detract from or even prevent action against Germany.

For Japan, the transcendent strategic goal in 1941 was ending the China War. The attempt to yet again achieve this by arms failed around Changsha in September and October. When Japan reverted to diplomacy, it adopted Proposal A, which defined a defeated China, and Proposal B, which defined an abandoned China—with the collapse of its resistance to follow. Proposals A and B sought no less than US submission to Japan's overarching strategic goal. If the "Hull Note" deserves the label of "ultimatum," then the same applies to the most fundamental tenets of Proposals A and B. Tōgō recognized the unbridgeable gap between American and Japanese strategic objectives and originally drafted Proposal B to omit the China issue. But the other elite leadership at the 1 November Liaison Conference insisted on adding to Proposal B the demand for US abandonment of China. When Nomura and Kurusu, on their own initiative, presented a modus that evaded the China issue, and which would have placed at least a temporary settlement within reach, Tōgō summarily rejected this and ordered them to present the original version of Proposal B, stressing that the US abandonment of China was an indispensable term for any settlement. It appears far less likely that Tōgō's command represented a change in his views than that it reflected his resignation to the fact that the rest of the leadership would accept no less.

Arguments that condemn the US stance, on the basis that China was not a vital interest warranting the risk of war, ignore that by the second half of 1941 China not only served as a critical ally for the United States, the United Kingdom, and the Netherlands in the Asian-Pacific region, but also that it figured functionally as an indispensable ally of the Soviet Union. Churchill captured the point on 25 November: "Our anxiety is about China. If they collapse our joint dangers would enormously increase." From his memorandum to Eden on 23 November, we know the "joint dangers" the British prime minister emphasized, entailed not only Japanese strikes against the British, the Dutch, and the Americans *but also* concerned the role of China in preventing Japan from striking perhaps a mortal blow to the Soviet Union. The ill-founded deprecation of China's contributions, beginning in the late war period and continuing for decades postwar, distorted understanding of its vital role in 1941, especially after Germany's attack on the Soviet Union.

Understanding the core of Japanese terms also is vital for assigning responsibility. Some historiography depicts Japanese actions as simply reactions to provocative American measures. This inverts reality. From at least 1937, American economic measures culminating in the effective oil embargo all followed and responded to Japan's march of conquest through China and then on into Indochina. This pattern consistently was one of US reaction, not provocation. The occupation of Northern Indochina possessed a clear relationship to the war in China. The occupation of Southern Indochina did not, but it did menace British, Dutch, and American interests. Japan not only rejected Roosevelt's Indochina neutralization proposal, but also did so while Konoe was seeking a summit meeting. This action, as well as what we know of Konoe's actual portfolio of proposals, indicates that expectations that the meeting could have averted war—which make the huge assumption that Konoe could have made concessions that would have been acceptable to Japan's militarists—are misplaced.

In the final months leading up to Pearl Harbor, all of Japan's elites, whether in uniform or not, had contributed to pushing the nation to war. Moreover, the civilian and military leadership had roused the public to support their bellicose path. A great many of Japan's senior soldiers and sailors understood only too well that a war with the United States could end in catastrophe. These top officers shared deeply ingrained cultural sensibilities as warriors of the elite *yamato* race. They also viewed any retreat on China as a betrayal of their countrymen who had given their lives since 1937. Their failing was not fanatical blindness to their situation, but ultimately a lack of the moral courage that their stewardship of the nation required.

:::

CHAPTER 10

"This Dispatch Is to Be Considered a War Warning"

TARGETING PEARL HARBOR

Dogma Enshrined, Dogma Overturned

The Japanese attack on Pearl Harbor towers as one of the most consequential moments of World War II and twentieth-century history. It has birthed a vast library, including a large annex dedicated to various conspiracy theories asserting that US officials, including President Roosevelt, or UK officials, including Prime Minister Churchill, had advance warning of the attack. But the successful Japanese attack resulted from no conspiracy. It did stem from surprise and deception. But those words serve only as terse surface headings beneath which rest complex depths. The Japanese achieved surprise at three distinct levels in at least four ways. Similarly, Japanese deception rested upon both concealment of actual whereabouts of the Japanese carrier task force and simultaneous provision of false but persuasive evidence of where it was not.

Surprise formed a matrix of strategic, operational, and tactical levels, but strategic surprise stands foremost. Imperial Navy officers constructed their strategic outlook from two sources, the first provided ironically by an American naval officer, Alfred Thayer Mahan. According to one Japanese officer, Mahan's *The Influence of Sea Power on History, 1660–1783*, taught "certain immutable principles": (1) battleships constituted the decisive ship type, (2) battleships must be gathered in one battle fleet that must seek to destroy the enemy battle fleet in a decisive battle, and (3) victory or defeat in the decisive battle would decide the nation's fate. The second of these served as the core dogma in the Imperial Navy *Kantai Kessen* ("Great All Out Battle"). But Japanese sailors also extracted equal if not greater inspiration from their own naval theorists and from their service's seminal experience: the battle-line victory at Tsushima in 1905 that secured a victor's peace in the Russo-Japanese War.

The Washington treaties of 1922 fundamentally altered the balance between the world's major navies. Besides snuffing out a budding post–World War I naval arms race, the agreements declared a ten-year "holiday" on battleship construction. They instituted limits on the size and armament of battleships, aircraft carriers, and cruisers, and restricted the permissible fleet tonnage in these categories in the ratio of 5:5:3 among Great Britain, the United States, and Japan, respectively. They also restricted US and British base development to guarantee Japan supremacy in the Western Pacific. The 1930 London Naval Treaty extended the battleship construction "holiday" for five years and adjusted ratios on cruisers and other craft in ways that favored Japan, but not to the degree demanded by some Japanese naval officers. One critical barometer of Japan's domestic political situation is that anger at the Washington agreements and the London Treaty produced the assassination of the responsible prime ministers, Takashi Hara and Osachi Hamaguchi.

In response to the numerical inferiority in battleships to the United States, the Imperial Navy devised an overture to the climactic *Kantai Kessen*, titled *yogeki sakusen* ("interceptive operations"). Japan would commence hostilities by seizing the American bases in Guam and the Philippine Islands and then await the inevitable US counterattack. Japanese submarines and air units would both track and deplete the US fleet as it trundled its way across the Central Pacific past islands mandated by the League of Nations to Japan after World War I. Then, at a location in the Western Pacific chosen by the Imperial Navy, the enemy fleet would be pummeled with severe further attrition in massed night torpedo attacks, and the following day the main batteries of Japan's battleships would crush the enfeebled remnants of the US fleet.

Intensive interwar study of a possible war with Japan (and revelations from intercepted communications during Japanese naval maneuvers) disclosed to American naval officers that the Japanese would wait in the Western Pacific for the US fleet to approach. American professionals deemed this the "correct" Japanese stance. Thus, the critical first step in understanding the stunning strategic surprise of the Pearl Harbor attack is that it totally inverted the "accepted" pattern of a Pacific war codified on both sides of the ocean. Instead of waiting in the Western Pacific, a major component of the Japanese fleet would strike in the Central Pacific.

The indispensable figure in the Pearl Harbor attack was Isoroku Yamamoto, the commander of the Combined Fleet from 1939. Yamamoto "possesses more brains than any other Japanese in High Command," emphasized the US Pacific Fleet intelligence officer in 1941, Lt. Cdr. Edwin Layton. Historian Sadao Asada aptly remarked that what set Yamamoto wholly apart from his peers was "his pronounced individuality [which] was so rare among Japanese navy men that one former officer remarked that he was almost 'the product of mutation.'"

Yamamoto recognized one damning fact about *Kantai Kessen*: it failed in repeated war games to produce a complete Japanese victory. Amazingly, the Imperial Navy never tested the comprehensive *Kantai Kessen* in an actual sea exercise. Two factors steered Yamamoto's quest for an alternative to the *Kantai Kessen*. He was a keen exponent of naval aviation. He also came equipped with a gambler's soul—he even jested about leaving the navy for that passion.

Yamamoto displayed the first glimmer of the idea of a Pearl Harbor raid in around March or April 1940. That September, Yamamoto prophetically warned Prime Minister Konoe: "If I am told to fight regardless of the consequences, I shall run wild for the first six months or a year, but I have utterly no confidence for the second and third year." In November 1940, the Royal Navy staged a stunningly successful night torpedo plane attack on the Italian fleet in Taranto Harbor, sinking or disabling three battleships. Since Yamamoto had already mooted the idea, it is probably too much to claim that Taranto did more than reinforce the idea of a carrier raid on Pearl Harbor. But Yamamoto did order a secret study of the concept in the fall. In a January 1941 letter to Navy Minister Kōshiro Oikawa, Yamamoto declared that from "the very first day" the Combined Fleet must "fiercely attack and destroy the U.S. main fleet . . . so that the morale of the U.S. Navy and her people" would "sink to the extent that it could not be recovered."

Historians have bestowed both extravagant praise and savage criticism on Yamamoto's Pearl Harbor attack strategy. While Yamamoto's exact thinking remains in dispute, the evidence supports the deduction that he reasoned from three fundamental principles. First, Japan possessed no chance of victory in a long war. Second, *Kantai Kessen* would not achieve victory in a short war. Third, Japan lacked the means to attack the United States itself and impose a peace by arms. Therefore, Yamamoto identified only one conceivable strategic option: undermine American will to prosecute the conflict at the outset.

But Yamamoto left an ambiguous record on his appraisal of the vulnerability of American morale. When he spoke to Konoe in the summer of 1941, he probably gave his most measured view:

> There are those who say that if we give a terrible blow to the enemy at the outset of the war, warships cannot be replenished quickly, so Americans will raise their hands and surrender. But such a view totally ignores Americans' national wealth, industrial might, national character, etc.

There stood one other feature in this matrix of thinking: the US Pacific Fleet represented the only element of Allied power that could plausibly bar Japan from securing the vital southern resource areas. Although Yamamoto spoke firmly on the superiority of naval aviation over battleships, he identified destruction of at least four American battleships as the key objective of the Pearl Harbor raid. This number presumably represented the reduction in the total number of available American battleships (not just those in the Pacific) through May 1942 that would deter any interference with the Southern Operations.

But Yamamoto thought far beyond simplistic conventional calculations. He perceived battleships not as dominant weapons, but as foremost symbols. Yamamoto hoped the destruction of the most majestic emblems of American power would hammer a shattering blow to American morale. Close behind this stunning blow, a barrage of staggering punches would propel the American populace and government to a negotiated peace. In sum, Yamamoto's strategy sought to exploit the small window of favorable balance of forces to attack the only American vulnerability accessible to Japan and end the war before America's overwhelming material superiority could dictate an inevitable outcome.

The foremost ground for challenging Yamamoto's overarching strategy concerns its focus on American will as the center of gravity for Japan. In 1941 the American people remained deeply ambivalent about war. It is by no means clear that Congress would have declared war if Japan left American territory untouched. But leaving the US astride the vital sea routes to the resource areas that it could readily throttle if it entered the war later, harbored huge perils that must have seemed to outweigh its attractions. If Japan did not strike in the fall of 1941, it would shortly lose any prospect of success in a sea war. The most generous interpretation of Yamamoto's vision is not that he thought it afforded a high chance of complete victory for Japan, but that it afforded the only slim chance of success—and perhaps the only way to salvage the Imperial Navy's honor.

The next level of surprise was the operational level, which is where tactics are meshed into strategic goals. Surprise here fell at two distinct levels. The first of these concerned the movement of the task force centered on six fleet (large) carriers to Hawaii. Imperial Navy ship design philosophy incorporated modest fuel capacity requirements because it expected a main fight in the Western Pacific. Only the carriers *Kaga*, *Shōkaku*, and *Zuikaku* possessed a fuel load great enough to permit a strike on Pearl Harbor and return. The carriers *Akagi*, *Sōryū*, and *Hiryū* lacked that capability as did most of the task force escorting vessels. The improvised solution was to load extra fuel on the carriers, except *Shōkaku* and *Zuikaku*, and two cruisers and to attach to the task force seven oilers that conducted what was for the Imperial Navy the highly novel exercise of underway refueling. Before the attack, the Imperial Navy had never exhibited the capability of projecting a major part of itself so far across the Pacific.

A revolutionary step in naval warfare constituted the second part of operational surprise. Prior to 1941, navies generally kept their carriers dispersed, not massed, because they were "eggshells armed with hammers," to apply Churchill's evocative phrase originally intended for battle cruisers. Because of treaty limitations on size, carriers generally traded off defensive protection for aircraft capacity. They also housed vast loads of dangerous aviation gasoline and aircraft munitions. War experience highlighted the serious vulnerabilities in all the carriers built before the war. In December 1941 the United States had seven and the Japanese six fleet carriers in service; each navy lost four within a year.

The exponential increase in the striking power of carrier aircraft in the 1930s markedly elevated their offensive value. But before radar, only eyes could detect approaching aircraft. Exercises repeatedly demonstrated that carriers could be found and then damaged or sunk. Consequently, prior to 1941, the US and Japanese Navies reasoned that dispersion represented the best defense for carriers, so that no one wave of attackers could knock out the fleet's entire carrier force.

Based on lessons in China about the value of massed formations of attack planes escorted by fighters, in mid-1940 Rear Adm. Jisaburō Ozawa urged Yamamoto to place the navy's air units under a single "air fleet" command. In December 1940, Yamamoto authorized the formation of two air fleets. The first, designated the Eleventh Air Fleet, comprised all the land-based naval aviation. The second, consisting of carriers, was organized on 1 April 1941 and named the First Air Fleet (also commonly referred to as the *Kido Butai* or Striking Force). By the fall of 1941, it comprised Carrier Division 1 (*Akagi* and

Kaga), Carrier Division 2 (*Sōryū* and *Hiryū*), and Carrier Division 5 (*Shōkaku* and *Zuikaku*).* Conceived originally as a weapon to destroy US carriers in a preemptive strike, the First Air Fleet found a new target in Pearl Harbor.

It is nearly impossible to overstate the Japanese revolution in the massing of six fleet carriers in one tactical formation. It is also nearly impossible to overstate the Japanese folly of massing six fleet carriers in one tactical formation. American naval officers who discounted the prospect of a massed carrier formation understood that only a parallel leap in defensive capabilities would keep the benefits of the leap in offensive capability viable. The grouping of fleet carriers in one formation permitted the Japanese triumph at Pearl Harbor in December 1941; it also led in a straight line to the Japanese catastrophe at Midway in June 1942. In that battle American carrier planes found and simultaneously inflicted fatal damage on three of four Japanese fleet carriers operating in a single formation (and the fourth later that day); Japanese carrier planes found and severely damaged only one American carrier (later sunk by a submarine) of three operating in dispersed formations.

Having taken a revolutionary step in creating the First Air Fleet, the Imperial Navy gave in to its fetish for seniority and protocol by appointing as its commander fifty-five-year-old Vice Adm. Chuichi Nagumo. He had what historian Gordon Prange described as a bald "cannonball of a head" and a face that could readily shift from smiles to frowns. He habitually thrust out his husky chest and cocked his hat at a jaunty angle. He was generous, kind, and a hearty friend with a soul flashing signs of nobility. He looked and acted the picture of a Japanese sea dog, but that was the problem because all his experience was with surface ships.

To provide technical expertise, Nagumo's chief of staff was Rear Adm. Ryunosuke Kusaka. A gifted officer with an aviation background, he was not himself a pilot. But below Nagumo and Kusaka were two individuals central to resolving the daunting practical problems in effective operations of a massed carrier formation. The first was Cdr. Minoru Genda, who in decades of postwar writing bore the sobriquet "genius" like a title of nobil-

---

* Two Japanese terms manifest here—and frequently later—present translation issues. The term *Kido Butai* is defined by historians Jon Parshall and Mike Wenger as "a Japanese term (literally, 'mobile force') that referred to any naval force that contained an aircraft carrier, and was capable of independent operation. In terms of the Hawaiian Operation, the term was a euphemism for 'Carrier Striking Force.'" The Japanese designation for units of paired carriers was *kōkū sentai*, usually rendered as "Air Flotilla." The Japanese used the same term for land-based units, and it has been the custom in Western writing to style carrier units "carrier divisions" following US Navy practice for the purposes of clarity.

ity. He looked the part of a lean aristocrat, with level dense eyebrows, precise straight line strokes for nose and chin, and eyes that gleamed with intensity and intellectual acuity. In February 1941 he was charged with putting flesh on Yamamoto's skeleton concept. Genda emphasized that secrecy and surprise constituted the two indispensable prerequisites for success. He also devised a target priority list subversive of Yamamoto's grand design: he identified the vital targets as American carriers and land-based aircraft, not battleships.

The second key figure was Lt. Cdr. Mitsuo Fuchida, a "clever, fiery, fearless and outspoken" aviator. From his appointment in August, Fuchida and senior carrier flyers worked out in less than four months the intricate details of how the sextet of carriers would organize massive strike groups, rapidly launch them, assemble them under one commander, conduct a coordinated attack, reform, and return to the carriers. There was no means by which American intelligence could glean exactly what the Japanese were developing in this abbreviated time frame.

The six carriers in combination packed 416 aircraft: 144 Nakajima B5N "Kate" carrier attack planes, 133 Aichi D3A "Val" dive bombers, and 139 Mitsubishi A6M "Zero" fighter aircraft. Because there were quality issues in all six of the carrier air groups, only the long-established units in Carrier Divisions 1 and 2 could be entrusted with the most demanding attack roles. The most potent ship killers in the First Air Fleet were the three-seat "Kate" carrier attack planes. Of these, Carrier Divisions 1 and 2 deployed 90. The "Kates" could be rigged alternatively to deliver torpedoes or bombs.

The employment of these "Kates" brings us to the last level of surprise: the tactical. Ordinary aerial torpedoes dipped one hundred feet or more below the surface on the initial drop. This precluded their use in the shallow water of Pearl Harbor, only thirty to forty-five feet deep. The Americans also customarily berthed battleships two abreast, rendering the inboard ship invulnerable to torpedoes, and they might deploy antitorpedo nets to protect the outboard ships. If the Japanese failed to solve the technical problem of shallow water torpedo dropping, or the Americans deployed antitorpedo nets, the Japanese would lose their most potent antiship weapon.

Technicians ingeniously surmounted this challenge by attaching sets of wooden fins to the torpedoes. The fins caused the torpedoes to enter the water at a much shallower angle that kept their initial dive within acceptable parameters. On impact, the fins then snapped off, leaving the torpedo free to run normally. The validation of this technological innovation came after persistent failure, only during 11–13 November 1941, less than a month before the attack. A batch of the modified torpedoes reached the carriers just two days before they sailed.* Thus, till nearly the eve of the task force sortie, it appeared that half of the most important attack aircraft would be impotent.

While "Val" dive bombers could achieve great accuracy, the Japanese lacked a bomb for the "Val" that would penetrate the thick armored decks of a battleship and reach vital areas. The "Kate" level bombers could carry a heavy bomb, but practice demonstrated that to achieve reasonable accuracy they had to fly at an altitude of about 9,800 feet. This was too low to permit available armor-piercing bombs to gain enough velocity to penetrate battleship protective decks. Japanese airmen solved this dilemma by converting regular 410 mm (16.1-inch) armor-piercing shells into special bombs. Intense practice also perfected the technique of a five plane "V" formation with four planes dropping simultaneously on the lead aircraft manned by the most skilled pilot and bomb aimer. The two-seat "Vals" carried 551-pound semi-armor-piercing or general-purpose bombs. The armor-piercing weapons could be employed effectively against carriers and cruisers but could cause no more than superficial damage to heavily armored battleships. The general-purpose bombs were suitable for attacks on lesser warships or precision land targets, like hangars, dispersed aircraft, etc.

Like the multiple layers of surprise, the Japanese also employed two levels of deception. The first was by maintaining complete radio silence during their stealthy approach across the little-traveled Northern Pacific. But the Japanese actively and passively provided plausible evidence of where the carriers were not. The Japanese left behind certain radio personnel from their carriers to conduct dummy traffic. (To other skilled listeners, each radio operator has a distinctive "fist" or keying style as revealing as a fingerprint. By leaving behind normal carrier radio operators, the Japanese cleverly created the impression that the carriers remained in home waters.) Other home-based aviation units mimicked carrier plane radio traffic. These ruses worked very well and were duly reported as evidence that the carriers remained close to Japan on 27 November. Three days later, false traffic generated by the Japanese deception program created the mirage that carrier *Akagi* waited in home waters. Further, the massing of forces for the Southern Operations provided a passive but very plausible explanation that Japanese carriers remained in

---

* A factory in Nagasaki produced the modified torpedoes. It was directly below where the atomic bomb would detonate on 9 August 1945.

home waters, prepared to counter any American effort to thwart the Southern Operations.

The Imperial Navy looked to enhance the attack's effectiveness with the other new weapon of sea power: the submarine. Japan possessed only forty-eight submarines with trans-Pacific range on 7 December 1941. No fewer than thirty participated in the Pearl Harbor operation. Three screened ahead of the Striking Force. Twenty submarines manned patrol lines to sink or damage US warships in Hawaiian waters. One submarine scouted the Fijis and Samoa while a second investigated the Aleutian Islands. Five specially modified submarines ported midget submarines to the waters just off Pearl Harbor. There they would release their brood and then mount a close blockade in hopes of catching American ships fleeing the harbor.

The use of submarines raised the hackles of the aviators, who feared, presciently, that detection of a submarine might ruin the element of surprise vital to the success of the attack. Vastly enhancing the peril was Yamamoto's authorization for the midget submarines to penetrate the harbor citadel itself before the air attack. Although originally the midget submarines were to lie in wait of units attempting to exit the harbor or to attack the night of the air attack, the crews' pleas won authorization to attack simultaneously with the aviators. This scheme both exponentially raised the danger of triggering an alarm and turned the midget submarines into almost certain suicide craft.

Still another monumental issue emerged in planning. Yamamoto's staff recommended exploiting the surprise Pearl Harbor attack (*kōgeki*) with an immediate invasion (*kōryaku*) of Hawaii. This proposal sparked vehement objection from the Naval General Staff. In the end, Yamamoto ruled out the immediate invasion. Final approval from Chief of the Naval General Staff Nagano for the Pearl Harbor attack only came on 19 October. Nagano maintained his strong opposition, but he yielded to Yamamoto's threat to resign with his staff if his strategy were not accepted.

The Striking Force secretly assembled in lonely Hitokappu Bay in the Kuril Islands, north of Hokkaidō. Its final composition was six carriers, two battleships, two heavy cruisers, one light cruiser, nine destroyers, seven oilers, and three submarines. The fleet sailed at 0600, 26 November, Japanese time, as snow swirled across the half-lighted, lead-colored waters. Each ship was just a gray smudge, even to its nearby consorts. Nagumo's mighty host followed a concealed course across the North Pacific, well away from shipping lanes and in often heavy weather. The fleet maintained absolute radio silence but monitored radioed intelligence updates from Tokyo. Strict orders required the fleet to abandon the mission if a diplomatic settlement was secured.

But even if Yamamoto's gamble on the Pearl Harbor attack produced at least tactical success, his further decisions cast profound doubts about his judgment. If refueling should prove impossible, Yamamoto authorized the attack to go forward with just *Shōkaku*, *Zuikaku*, and *Kaga*. This effectively meant the total arsenal for damaging his primary targets would be twelve torpedoes and fifteen armor-piercing bombs on *Kaga*, for the other two carriers lacked any of these weapons. Yamamoto ordered the task force to execute the attack even in the face of alerted defenses if it were detected within the last twenty-four hours of the approach—a circumstance war games showed could produce limited results for heavy loss. Then there was the romantic but extraordinarily risky sanction for the midget submarines to trade the permanent loss of half or more of his fleet carriers for four battleships, either sunk or out of action for only six months. This provides the full measure of how much Yamamoto ultimately was gambling that the breaking of American will was worth costs unthinkable to any other Imperial Navy officer.

At Pearl Harbor

In April 1940, Roosevelt ordered the Pacific Fleet to shift its base from the West Coast to Pearl Harbor, at first indefinitely and then permanently. The Pacific Fleet Commander, Adm. James O. Richardson, "strongly and repeatedly disagreed with FDR" regarding the move. Richardson maintained that a West Coast–based fleet could far better prepare itself for projecting American sea power into the Western Pacific, and this would be understood in Tokyo.[*] The abrupt separation from family, friends, and the amenities of California also blighted crew morale. As Capt. Raymond G. O'Connor recalled: "Complaining, allegedly the sole right accorded servicemen reached a crescendo, and the usual excesses of a sailor's liberty attained awesome proportions."

But Richardson's abrupt dismissal did not arise from his objections about the Pearl Harbor base—which Richardson admitted never related to the dan-

---

[*]   Daniel C. Fuguea provides powerful support for Richardson in his study of the employment of the old battleships of the Pacific Fleet in the year after Pearl Harbor. The surviving battleships, and reinforcements of like vessels from the Atlantic Fleet, were organized as Task Force One. Fuguea demonstrates that they attained both superior material condition as well as a much higher state of training on the West Coast than they had attained at Pearl Harbor (from August 1942), or when four advanced to the South Pacific (November 1942). "Task Force One: The Wasted Assets of the United States Pacific Battleship Fleet, 1942," *Journal of Military History* 61 (October 1997): 715.

ger of a Japanese attack. Rather, Richardson triggered a rupture in October 1940 when he commented to Roosevelt that "senior officers of the Navy" lacked "trust and confidence in the civilian leadership of this country" for "the successful prosecution of a war in the Pacific." Richardson probably intended to relay the view he shared with other senior officers that certain administration civilians, particularly the State Department's Stanley Hornbeck, had foisted the unsound base shift on the president. But Richardson later realized his comments had shocked FDR—who may have heard the remark as an aspersion of his competence as commander in chief.

Three months after this meeting, Roosevelt tapped the very junior Adm. Husband E. Kimmel, a fifty-eight-year-old, trim but powerfully built, blue-eyed native of Kentucky, to replace Richardson. Historian Gordon Prange, who knew the admiral, believed Kimmel lacked "the spark of creative imagination" and was "an easier man to admire than to love."

The command change produced a fateful scene. A staff officer read to Kimmel and Richardson an appraisal by Adm. Thomas C. Hart, commander in chief, Asiatic Fleet, an uncannily prescient word portrait of Yamamoto in truncated cablegram shorthand:

> Energetic. Highly able. Bold in contrast to most [Imperial Navy officers] who are inclined to be cautious. Decisive. . . . Highly thought of by rank and file of [Japanese] Navy. Personally likes Americans. . . . Very air minded.

Only three days after Kimmel gripped the helm of the Pacific Fleet, his new army counterpart, Maj. Gen. Walter C. Short, reached Hawaii. During the interwar period, the commanders of the army's Hawaii garrison comprised an exceptional group of talented officers recognized as skilled strategists. Short's professional forte, however, was training. Marshall issued piercingly clear instructions to Short: "the fullest protection for the Fleet is *the* rather than *a* major consideration." By 7 December, Short's Hawaiian Department numbered about 43,177 men, by far the largest command outside the continental United States, a fact reflected by Short's elevation to the grade of lieutenant general. Marshall apparently picked Short with an eye to raising the proficiency of the enlarged garrison, not warding off an attack. Short, moreover, was a micromanager who could not delegate and was overwhelmed by the details of his huge command.

Kimmel and Short established excellent personal relations, but even the most cordial association could not surmount a fundamental flaw. Their superiors made Kimmel and Short functional equals—as was the historical precedent in American armed services. Therefore, cooperation, not subordination, controlled their relations. (There was a local agreement allowing for unity of command in Hawaii, but it was never implemented prior to the attack.) Exacerbating the division of responsibility was that Rear Adm. Claude C. Bloch, commander of the Fourteenth Naval District, not Kimmel, via his local administrative command, held sway over base facilities and their defense in Hawaii. According to one observant staff officer, "Admiral Bloch . . . looked down his nose at Admiral Kimmel." Bloch's only glimmer of brilliance proved his adroit maneuvers out from his rightful heavy burden of culpability.

Richardson and then Kimmel adhered to a predictable schedule of fleet operations driven by legal restrictions on the use of congressionally appropriated funds dictating enforced economy on tug hires and harbor dredging by contractors essential for base operation and development. But logistics also sharply constrained Kimmel's options. When Kimmel took over, he reorganized the fleet into three task forces. Fuel shortages, and particularly the scarcity of oilers that could perform underway replenishment for ships at sea, defeated his original plan to keep two constantly at sea.

Richardson had dismissed the use of antitorpedo nets to protect ships in Pearl Harbor on the basis that air-dropped torpedoes would not function in its shallow waters. With the British attack on Taranto in mind, Stark wrote Kimmel directly in February 1941 to assure him that technical examination confirmed that the "minimum depth of water of seventy-five feet may be assumed necessary to successfully drop torpedoes from planes." This was about twice the depth of Pearl Harbor. Then on 13 June, Stark warned that both the United States and the British had developed aerial torpedoes that could function in Pearl Harbor. What the United States and the British could do, the Japanese might do. But Kimmel still rejected antitorpedo nets.

Yet Kimmel was by no means indifferent to the danger of a Japanese attack on his base. At his direction, Rear Adm. Patrick Bellinger and Maj. Gen. Frederick L. Martin, the commanders of noncarrier aviation in Hawaii, collaborated on a study of a Japanese attack. The prescient Martin-Bellinger Report of 31 March 1941 emphasized that "the most likely and dangerous form of attack on Oahu would be an air attack . . . [from] one or more carriers." They went on that "a dawn air attack" could be delivered with a "high probability" of "complete surprise." The report further foresaw that the presence of any single submarine might "indicate the presence of a considerable undiscovered surface force composed of fast ships accompanied by a carrier."

The study then stated that the countermeasure to foil "the most likely and dangerous form of attack" was "daily [air] patrols as far as possible to seaward through 360 degrees to reduce the probabilities of surface or air surprise." The report went on to lament that available personnel and planes could only mount such patrols for "a very short period" and thus would not be effective unless other intelligence pointed to a "rather narrow" time frame of need. What was true in March remained true in December. By that date, Bellinger's command on Oahu numbered just sixty-six Catalina PBYs (PBY was a US Navy designation for long-range patrol [bomber] aircraft). Of the sixty-one operational PBYs on Oahu, a mere seven were in the air on antisubmarine patrol or on training exercises on the morning of 7 December.

Whether Hawaii could have mounted an adequate patrol plane search of the distant approaches to Pearl Harbor, or whether it lacked the necessary resources for such measures, constitutes a complex issue. The first question is the sector to be searched. Defenders of Kimmel and Short maintain they required far more PBYs (possibly supplemented by B-17s) than Washington supplied to sustain for more than about four or five days a 360-degree search network cited in the Martin-Bellinger report. The counter to this is that a narrow sector to the north constituted by far the most likely threat. For the Japanese, it combined the virtues of meshing the best concealed approach route from Japan through the little-traveled North Pacific, with favorable prevailing winds for carrier aircraft launching. Search planes available to the Hawaiian commanders could have covered such a narrowed sector.

Two other factors figure in any alternative search plane scenario. War experience on the vagaries of search plane success demonstrated that there was no guarantee that a search focused on the north would certainly have detected the Japanese carriers. But mooting the entire issue of search plane assets or broad or narrow search sectors are the facts that Kimmel was so focused on saving his search planes for a critical scouting role in his own ambitious offensive plans, and that he totally discounted the prospect of a carrier raid. Thus, it is hard to imagine that he would have authorized a comprehensive or even a lesser search, even if his search plane resources were substantially greater.

Whatever the patrol plane situation may have been, Washington did provide Short and Kimmel with the sinews for an effective air-warning system—radars and an air information center to direct fighter interception. By 7 December, the army fielded six operational radar sets on Oahu, each with a nominal detection range of 75 to 125 miles. A rudimentary control center had also been set up and tested in September. Further, the navy donated to Short the services of Lt. Cdr. William E. Taylor, an officer well versed in both British and American experience in radar-equipped air-warning systems. Taylor's postwar testimony blamed Short for lack of "impetus" to set up a fully functional system. But the navy failed to provide liaison watch officers equipped with knowledge of deployment of navy aircraft. Without such staffing, the air information center lacked the essential ability to identify incoming enemy aircraft detected by radar or other means.

The army displayed more confidence than actual capability in its antiaircraft guns. There were only 86 of 100 planned 3-inch antiaircraft guns. Worse still, there were just 20 of 144 of the 37 mm automatic cannon and 109 of 516 planned .50 caliber weapons, with virtually no ammunition for the former and little for the later.

The army air garrison of Hawaii totaled 234 aircraft. Fighters numbered 152, but included 14 obsolete P-26s dating from the early 1930s. The balance consisted of 39 P-36As and 99 P-40Bs and Cs. The latter two modern types, with experienced pilots (of which the Hawaiian air force possessed many) and appropriate tactics, could have fought the A6Ms and could have wreaked havoc on "Vals" and "Kates." On the morning of 7 December, 94 of these fighters were operational: 64 P-40s, 20 P-36s, and 10 P-26s. Twenty-five modern bombers also stood ready, including 12 B-17Ds, one B-24A, and 12 A-20As. The bomber inventory additionally featured 38 obsolete types: 33 B-18s, three B-12As, and two A-12As. There were another 24 aircraft of miscellaneous types and marginal use. Nonetheless, Washington communicated its assessment of priorities by posting to the Philippines larger numbers of the most formidable bombers (35 B-17s) and fighters (including 24 P-40Bs and 67 of the latest P-40Es, none of which was sent to Hawaii). Further, Washington dispatched another 200 P-40s to the Soviet Union to bolster defense against Hitler and help deter Japan.

The sea services contribution was numerically greater at 301, but skewed to patrol (69), battleship and cruiser float observation planes (92), and utility and transport models (54) rather than fighter or attack types (86). The combat types included 24 fighters, 60 scout bombers, and two torpedo planes. These raw numbers were further reduced by the fact that there were 52 replacement aircraft in storage status (nine fighters, six scout bombers, one torpedo plane, 33 observation planes, and three utility aircraft). Deducting aircraft in major overhaul or minor repair status left operational on the morning of 7 December just 202 navy planes: 61 PBYs, 10 fighters, 41 scout bombers, 53 float observation planes, and 37 utility types. The upshot of all these figures is the usually overlooked but startling fact that despite a raw complement of 535 aircraft, the American garrison mustered just 160 effective combat-type aircraft on 7 December to meet 350 attackers.

The priority to support Britain against Germany and deter Japan in the Western Pacific affected Kimmel and Short in more ways than in allocations of PBYs. In April and May 1941, Roosevelt and his principal lieutenants, Stimson, Knox, Hull, and Morgenthau, debated a fundamental reassignment of American naval power from the Pacific to the Atlantic. Although Stimson advocated virtually a total shift as a means of securing the Western Atlantic and buttressing battered England, concerns for strategic deterrence and of diplomatic leverage over Japan produced a compromise, but one that still cost Kimmel about one-quarter of his strength.

As the following table indicates, dozens of decisions in Washington on the distribution of American naval resources ultimately resulted by 7 December in a division of the fleet into two approximately equal halves.

Naval Force Strength and Dispositions
7 December 1941

	IMPERIAL NAVY	UNITED STATES NAVY			
		US TOTAL	ASIATIC FLEET	PACIFIC FLEET	ATLANTIC FLEET
Carriers	9+1*	7+1*	0	3	4 + 1*
Battleships	10	17	0	9	8
Heavy Cruisers	18	18	1	12	5
Light Cruisers	17	19	2	9	8
Destroyers					
Old	33	70	13	21	36
New	69	97	0	45	52
Total	102	167	13	66	88
Submarines					
Old	31	55	6	6	43
New	32	49	23	21	5
Total	63	104	29	27	48

* Small escort carriers

"War Warnings"

In April 1941, Washington sent an advisory to senior naval commanders, noting the Axis powers' propensity to commence action on weekends and holidays and ordering commanders to "take such steps on such days to see that proper watches and precautions are in effect." This message set standards for clarity, simplicity, and emphasis. Washington dispatched a series of such messages in November 1941 collectively known as "War Warnings" after the most famous of the number. The November series prompted a high alert by Gen. Frank Andrews in the Panama Canal Zone. Why it did not in Hawaii remains a major issue.*

The War Department issued an alert upon the imposition of stiffer American economic sanctions in July 1941, prompting Short to place his command on full war footing, a stronger measure than he would take in November and December 1941. On 16 October, Stark advised his fleet commanders of the cabinet changes in Japan and commented that these created a "strong possibility" of hostilities between Japan and Russia but only "a possibility" of hostilities between Japan and the United States and United Kingdom. Stark further dulled the edge of the 16 October message with a personal letter to Kimmel the very next day, explaining, "Personally I do not believe the Japs are going to sail into us and the message I sent you merely stated the 'possibility' [of hostilities]." The parallel War Department message to Short in mid-

---

* On 19 November, the Japanese Foreign Ministry cabled to various diplomatic stations what became known as the "Winds Code." Tokyo to Washington, No. 2353 & 2354, November 19, 1941 (2353 translated November 28, 1941; 2354 translated November 26), *The "Magic" Background to Pearl Harbor*, Appendix 4, A81. The message set up a plain language "code" to be broadcast on regular Japanese weather reports in case normal communications with diplomatic stations were impaired. The code message would alert the distant stations that Japanese diplomatic relations with three countries were "in danger." "East Wind Rain" was the "code" message indicating peril for Japan–United States relations. Postwar US congressional hearings and later writings devoted enormous attention to whether or not an authentic "East Wind Rain" message was intercepted prior to the attack. For a meticulous and exhaustive examination of this convoluted controversy, and several additional plain language "codes" set up by the Japanese Foreign Ministry, see Robert J. Hanyok and David P. Mowry, *United States Cryptologic History, Series 4: World War II, Volume 10, West Wind Clear: Crytology and the Winds Message Controversy—A Documentary History* (Center for Cryptologic History, National Security Agency, 2008), http://www.nsa.gov/about/_files/cryptologic_heritage/publications/wwii/west_wind_clear.pdf (accessed 4 March 2014). They show, among many other matters, that no such message was sent in time to have served any purpose prior to the attack.

October 1941 likewise conveyed reassurance that although "tension between United States and Japan remains strained . . . no abrupt change in Japanese foreign policy appears imminent."

Stark painted a much more ominous situation in a message to his Pacific commanders on 24 November:

> Chances of favorable outcome of negotiations with Japan [are] very doubtful. This situation . . . indicate[s] in our opinion that the possibility of a surprise aggressive move in any direction including an attack on the Philippines and Guam is a possibility.

The input of key advisers and intelligence officers modulated the concerns of Stark and Marshall until near the end of November. Rear Adm. Richmond Kelly Turner headed the War Plans office under Stark. He possessed brains, an imperious presence, and absolute conviction in his opinions. Until well into November, Turner insisted the Japanese would strike north, not south. Turner also misinformed Stark that Kimmel and Short possessed their own "Purple Machine" and thus were independently reading key diplomatic intercepts.

Marshall was ill-served by Brig. Gen. Sherman Miles's G-2 (General Staff, Intelligence Division). On 28 November, G-2 declared Japan was "completely extended militarily and economically" and thus "was momentarily unable to concentrate anywhere a military Striking Force sufficient to assure victory." On 5 December, G-2 affirmed that Germany would "remain the only power capable of launching large scale strategic offensives." Stimson and Roosevelt recognized Miles's inadequacy, but only relieved him after the Pearl Harbor attack.

The day after the "Hull Note," 27 November, Stimson managed the dispatch of a War Department message to Pacific commands:

> Negotiations with Japan appear to be terminated to all practical purposes with only the barest possibilities that the Japanese Government might come back and offer to continue. Japanese future action unpredictable but hostile action possible at any moment. If hostilities cannot, repeat cannot, be avoided, the United States desires that Japan commit the first overt act. This policy should not, repeat not, be construed as restricting you to a course of action that might jeopardize your defense. Prior to hostile Japanese action, you are directed to take such reconnaissance and other measures as you deem necessary but these measures

should be carried out so as not, repeat not, to alarm the civil population or disclose intent. Report measures taken.

While a specific reference to the danger of sabotage was stricken from the draft version of this message, an alert about "subversive activities" appeared in a separate G-2 message on 28 November. Army Air Force Chief Henry Arnold sent a parallel dispatch through Short to the local air commander Martin that again underscored the threat from sabotage. In yet another example of faulty coordination, a 28 November Navy Department message ordered heightened alert against sabotage to Naval Districts 1–15 (except the 14th in Hawaii!), the Washington, DC Navy Yard, and Guam.

Short responded tersely on the 28th that his command was "alerted to prevent sabotage." Short's comprehensive response to the warnings reached Washington on 1 December. Short stated he had instituted Alert No. 1, as defined in the new standing Operating Procedure of 5 November 1941. This alert level contemplated increased danger from sabotage and subversion, but not any external threat. Short did order operation of the air warning system each morning from 0400 to 0700. But he also directed that his aircraft be parked close together to permit easier guarding against sabotage. The mobile antiaircraft batteries previously deployed were stored in hangars and ammunition for the fixed guns securely locked. Air crews had stood ready for weeks to respond immediately to a warning; now they were released to a much lower alert level. Short's orders totally disconnected the ability to detect external air danger and the capacity to meet it.

Short later pointedly contrasted the language of Marshall's message to his predecessor commander on 27 June 1940 with the phrases of the 27 November message. The June dispatch trilled urgency: "Immediately alert complete defensive organization to deal with possible trans-Pacific raid, to greatest extent possible without creating public hysteria or provoking undue curiosity of newspapers or alien agents." In contrast to this, the 27 November message and its two follow-up communications conveyed no express warning of an external attack at Hawaii but emphasized internal threats. Further, the 27 November message contained few "do's" with numerous cautionary "don'ts." How, for example, could Short fail to violate the taboo against "alarm[ing] the civilian population" if he elevated the Hawaiian Department to a state of full, hyperalertness? And as Short reasonably pointed out, he was also adjured "that no international incident must take place in Hawaii that would provoke the Japanese or give them an excuse [to declare war]."

Short's reports indicating a vigil against sabotage alone passed in Washington under the eyes of Col. Charles W. Bundy and Brig. Gen. Leonard T. Gerow in the War Plans Division and up to Marshall. None of them attempted to fault Short for his exclusive focus on internal dangers. Bundy and Gerow clearly saw and initialed Short's reply, and Marshall later testified that he presumed he saw it. "That was my opportunity to intervene," Marshall would tell congressional investigators later, "and I did not do it." Though Marshall shouldered his responsibility, the actual failure rested on Bundy and Gerow whose duties included understanding fully what "Alert No. 1" in the Hawaiian Department signified. Gerow manfully admitted his culpability at a congressional investigation; Bundy was killed in a plane crash during a fact-finding mission to Pearl Harbor in December 1941.

On the same day, the War Department issued a warning, 27 November, the Navy Department radioed to Pacific naval commands:

> This dispatch is to be considered a war warning. Negotiations with Japan looking forward toward stabilization of conditions in the Pacific have ceased and an aggressive move by Japan is expected within the next few days. The number and equipment of Jap[anese] troops and the organization of naval task forces indicates an amphibious expedition against either the Philippines or Kra Peninsula or possibly Borneo. Execute an appropriate defensive deployment preparatory to carrying out the tasks assigned in [the current war plan].

Officers in Washington were keenly aware that the phrase "war warning" was unprecedented in any prior message. On its face this language seemed to instruct Kimmel to go to a state just short of active hostilities, but the multiple implications between the succeeding lines diluted this impact. Most glaring was the fact that Stark specified as Japanese targets only the Philippines, Malaya (Kra Peninsula), and Borneo. He conspicuously omitted Hawaii. Kimmel's one decisive reaction to this message is instructive. He deemed a submarine attack as the likely Japanese threat to Hawaii. Kimmel not only ordered an alert against this danger, but also authorized the depth charging of any submarine found around the Oahu operating areas. This would have included international waters, and such action could have been taken as an act of war.

Washington assigned priority on air assets to the Philippines and consequently emphasized the provision of still more airpower, particularly heavy bombers, there. To protect key bases along the bomber ferry route to the Philippines, Washington proposed that Short redistribute one squadron of twenty-five P-40s (his best fighters) to Midway and a second squadron of twenty-five P-40s to Wake Island as well as troops to both outposts. These proposals left discretion on whether and how to execute them to the Hawaiian commanders. The senior Hawaiian commanders discussed these proposals on 27 November (just before the two "War Warning" messages were received). When an army aviator protested that this would compromise the primary mission of protecting Oahu, Kimmel responded: "Do you think we are in danger of an attack?" When the army officer pointed out the Japanese capability to attack, Kimmel turned to Capt. Charles E. McMorris, the Fleet War Plans Officer, and queried: "What do you think about the prospects of a Japanese air attack." McMorris shot back: "None, absolutely none." The proposal to strip Short of half his most modern interceptors demonstrated that like McMorris, Washington scoffed at the prospect of an attack on Hawaii.

Kimmel worked out an alternate plan with unanticipated consequences. He decided to substitute squadrons of Marine Corps aircraft for the army planes: a squadron of fighters to Wake and dive bombers to Midway. The Marine aircraft, unlike army aircraft, could be recovered later and redeployed by carriers. The mission of taking the first Marine squadron to Wake went to Vice Adm. William F. Halsey Jr. and his carrier *Enterprise* task force. When *Enterprise* sailed on 28 November, Halsey put his command on full war alert. A task force built around carrier *Lexington* sailed on 5 December with a squadron of Marine dive bombers for Midway. Thus, local decisions on the execution of the proposed redeployment of air units to Wake and Midway, not direct Washington orders, would ultimately result in the fact that Pearl Harbor held no carriers on the morning of 7 December. The third Pacific Fleet carrier, *Saratoga*, was undergoing scheduled maintenance on the West Coast.

The Pearl Harbor Intelligence Battle

On 27 January 1941, Ambassador Joseph Grew had written to Washington from Tokyo:

> My Peruvian Colleague told a member of my staff that he had heard from many sources including a Japanese source that the Japanese military forces planned, in the event of trouble with the United States, to attempt a surprise mass attack on Pearl Harbor using all of their military facilities.

This seemed sensational when revealed in postwar hearings, but no basis for the story beyond rumor ever emerged. The account duly reached the navy against the background of frequent flirtations with the notion by both the Imperial and US Navies and (broadly) fiction writers about a Pearl Harbor attack in the interwar period. When a paraphrase of the message was forwarded to the Pacific Fleet, it was conveyed with a caution that naval intelligence placed little credence in the story.

As early as the summer of 1940, the foreign ministry staff of the Japanese Honolulu consulate began forwarding detailed information on American military and naval activities in Hawaii, but in March 1941, a trained intelligence agent arrived. A medically retired Imperial Navy lieutenant and naval academy graduate, Takeo Yoshikawa proved a fountain of indispensable information to Tokyo. Yoshikawa's postwar accounts proved credible in asserting he avoided contact generally with individuals of Japanese ancestry in Hawaii. But they do confirm that the head of the consulate and the code clerk, as well as a cab driver (who frequently conveyed Yoshikawa to convenient overlooks of American military facilities) and the owner of a restaurant with an overview of Pearl Harbor, all clearly understood Yoshikawa's actual intentions. Short of declaring the entire island of Oahu a restricted military zone, a measure the American government refused to take as a potential "provocation" of Japan, there was no way to prevent Yoshikawa from observing Pearl Harbor and other installations from easily accessible public viewing locations. Among the most vital data Yoshikawa telegraphed to Tokyo were the operating routines making it predictable that the fleet would be in Pearl Harbor on Sunday. American counterintelligence officers in Hawaii never detected Yoshikawa.

Meanwhile, back in Washington in August 1941 the British alerted J. Edgar Hoover of the Federal Bureau of Investigation about "Tricycle," the code name of Dusko Popov, a German agent sent to set up an espionage ring in the United States. The Germans outfitted "Tricycle" with a three-page priority list of targets, about one-third comprised of detailed inquiries about Hawaii. "Tricycle" was a British double agent. He met Hoover, who also scrutinized the priority list. A careful reading of Popov's specific targets for investigation in Hawaii discloses almost an entire emphasis on targets for sabotage, not an air raid focused on ships in harbor and planes dispersed about airfields. Further, the Japanese never disclosed their plan to stage a carrier plane attack on Hawaii, so German orders to Popov were never connected to the actual attack. Notions that Hoover missed a stunning tip-off to the raid are without merit.

If "Tricycle" was a false alarm, one priceless tidbit of information concerning Yoshikawa did fall into American hands. A 24 September 1941 message from Tokyo routed to the Japanese consulate in Honolulu outfitted Yoshikawa with an imaginary grid over Pearl Harbor and commanded him to com-mence reporting the precise position of ships in the harbor. This would go down in history as the "Bomb Plot Message." Many other intercepted mes-sages betrayed Japanese interest in the enumeration of American ships in multiple locations in the Pacific, consistent with the gathering of strategic intelligence—but Tokyo asked for exact ship locations at no other port. As the defenders of Admiral Kimmel and General Short later cogently argued, information at this level of detail pointed to tactical intentions to stage some manner of attack or perhaps sabotage.

Senior Washington army and navy intelligence officers and Admiral Stark saw the "Bomb Plot" message. Amazingly, only one army intelligence officer sensed that the dispatch emitted an attack alert signal. None of the naval offi-cers, including Stark, picked up on the unique character of the message or its significance. No one informed Kimmel or Short of the message.

Proximate to the "Bomb Plot Message," Washington squandered another opportunity that might have foreclosed or impeded the Pearl Harbor attack. A congressional proposal arose for investigations of Japanese subversive activi-ties, including those involving "Japanese consular officials in Hawaii." Sec-retary of State Hull blocked the proposed investigations, arguing that they might derail diplomatic negotiations. It is not clear that if the investigations had gone forward, they might have disrupted espionage in Hawaii and if so, whether this could have prevented the attack. It is possible though far from certain, however, that if espionage had been snuffed out from the consulate in Honolulu, the attack might have been aborted for lack of reliable information on the Pacific Fleet's whereabouts.

The failure to forward the "Bomb Plot Message" to Hawaii connects to another issue. By December 1941, American code breakers had produced a total of eight "Purple Machines." Of these, Washington retained four that clattered away incessantly decoding Japanese diplomatic traffic. One machine was sent to the Asiatic Fleet both because of its exposed position and its excel-lent intercept opportunities. London received two machines. When the eighth machine became available, it too went to the British. The upshot was that nei-ther the army nor navy commands in Hawaii possessed a "Purple Machine."

The lack of a "Purple Machine" in Hawaii made Kimmel and Short wholly dependent on Washington to forward all relevant diplomatic intercepts. Kim-mel trusted in Stark's solemn promises to keep him fully informed. Stark dutifully not only sent Kimmel a stream of official messages, but he also wrote long personal letters attempting to keep the Pacific Fleet commander informed of thinking in Washington.

While Kimmel lacked direct access to "Purple," he still enjoyed ready access to an array of radio intelligence on Japanese forces. Radio intelligence encompasses the art and science of deriving information from the external and internal characteristics of a radio communications system. The simplest form of radio intelligence is direction finding (DF): locating the direction in which a transmitter lies by means of very specialized receiving equipment. The specific geographic position of a radio transmitter may be determined under favorable conditions by triangulation from two or more monitoring sites. The next level of radio intelligence is traffic analysis. This involves gathering information by deducing the identities of the senders and addresses of radio messages (usually concealed in alphanumeric address groups termed "call signs") and the patterns formed by the frequency, priority, and location of radio transmissions. Both direction finding and traffic analysis work from only the external characteristics of radio communications, that is, without any understanding of the contents of messages usually concealed by codes or ciphers.

Direction findings and traffic analysis dominated American and Allied radio intelligence on the Imperial Navy prior to Pearl Harbor, yet the most attention has focused on code breaking. In fact, Allied and particularly American cryptographic attacks on Japanese naval codes and ciphers form a vital subject, not only for the period leading up to the Pearl Harbor attack but also throughout the remainder of the war. Because of the centrality of its role from now until the end of the war, an understanding of the main Imperial Navy operational code and cipher system is essential.

By far the most important Japanese naval code is known to history by the designation assigned by US Navy code breakers: JN-25. The actual Japanese designation was Code Book D. The term *code book* distinguishes the Japanese naval system that employed a book code and a book cipher system from the Japanese "Purple" diplomatic system that used a cipher machine (like the German "Enigma" machine).* Thus, no relationship existed between the two

* "A code consists of thousands of words, phrases, letters or syllables with the codewords or codenumbers (or more generally code groups) that replace these [plain text] elements," according to the magisterial work by David Kahn. "In ciphers, on the other hand, the basic unit is the letter, sometimes the letter pair (digraph or bigram), very rarely larger groups of letters (polygrams). . . . There is no sharp theoretical dividing line between codes and ciphers; the latter shade into the former as they grow larger . . . a more penetrating and useful distinction is that code operates on linguistic entities, dividing its raw material into meaningful elements like words and syllables, whereas cipher does not—cipher will split the *t*

systems and success against the diplomatic ciphers affords no evidence what-
soever as to the ability to break into naval codes and ciphers.

The initial JN-25 code book comprised lists of 33,333 five-digit numbers
ranging from 00003 to 99999, each divisible by three as a simple check
of "garbles" (erroneously sent or copied digits). The code book linked each
five-digit number with a meaning such as a ship name, word, phrase, letter,
numeral, etc. The Japanese left an approximately 3,000 five-digit numbers
blank either as a security feature or to allow for future expansion. They also
assigned multiple code groups for frequently used words, phrases, and so on.
The key point about the code book is that intelligence information could be
extracted only by comprehending *the meaning of sufficient five-digit code numbers in a message.*

By this point in history it was well understood that competent code breakers could "read" such a code if they acquired a sufficient volume of traffic in
the code and information that permitted them to deduce the meaning of a
quantity of the five-digit numbers. Therefore, the Imperial Navy masked the
actual five-digit code numbers with a cipher. The cipher for JN-25 consisted
of a book of additive tables. The tables comprised randomly selected five-digit
numbers. The additive book contained pages, each with a 10 by 10 square of
random five-digit numbers. A code clerk selected a page and a starting position in the additive book. From that point, he followed the sequence of random numbers to the end of the code text. He "added" each random number to
the original code value using "false" or modulo arithmetic (i.e., no carrying or
borrowing, thus "9" plus "4" gave "3"). For example:

Original code group:	91113
Additive random number:	52139
Final message text transmitted:	43242

Communications procedures designated a specific point in each message
to tell the recipient the starting page and position in the additive book. This
five-digit number was termed the indicator group or key. It was transmitted
twice in each message to prevent garbles. The Japanese disguised the indicator group or key with a separate list of random numbers using the same "addi-

---

from the *h* in *the*." *The Code Breakers* (New York: Macmillan Publishing, 1967), xiv–xv. As a
practical example, suppose the code group for "aircraft" is 33333. This code group is then enciphered by adding it to a randomly selected five-digit group 55555. The resulting enciphered
text transmitted is 88888.

tion" practice. They concealed the "key" not only by separate cipher, but also by a formula for scrambling the digits. This resulting random number was called the key additive.

In addition to the code groups housing the actual text of the message, each message contained a header or text preamble. This header or text preamble incorporated essential communications system information like the call signs of the sender and addresses, precedence, a message number, transmission date/time, and a total of five-digit groups. This basic structure essentially remained in use throughout the war, but the Japanese progressively introduced numerous complications.

JN-25 first entered use on 1 June 1939. By American nomenclature, the code book was "JN-25A" and the first additive table was Book 1. The additive book contained 300 pages, each with a 10 by 10 grid of random five-digit numbers for a total of 30,000 additives. The key additives totaled 999, chosen by date to mask the indicator group. Further, to avoid the vulnerability of stereotypical headings or endings to messages, standing orders directed the code clerks to start the enciphering somewhere in the middle of the body of the message, continue to the end, and only then go back to encipher the first part of the message, like cutting a deck of cards. Each message contained a "begin message here" group to show where the actual message text commenced. Moreover, each unit was assigned an initial start point in the additive book and instructed to work through the book from that point with no repetition until the complete book had been used.

As an American report observed about success against JN-25: "no system's security [is] greater than the care of those who [use] it." From the outset the seemingly insuperable difficulty of the system rendered some Imperial Navy code clerks complacent, and they ignored instructions (much like their German counterparts). They started messages at the actual beginning and did not work through the additive book in the directed order, instead repeating the same pages (usually the early pages of the additive book). These violations eased additive recoveries and introduced vulnerabilities in recovering plain text from stereotypical beginnings and endings of messages.

The "JN-25A" version remained in use until 1 December 1940, when it was replaced by the "B" version of JN-25. During the interval between 1 June 1939 and 1 October 1940, a total of four additive books were used. Additive Book 5 entered service on 1 October 1940 and remained in use until 1 February 1941. Thus, it overlapped the change of code books from the "JN-25A" to the "JN-25B" version. Additive Book 5 contained 500 pages, each of 100 numbers, for a total of 50,000 additives.

JN-25B would remain in effect until 27 May 1942 (Japanese time). Its refinements included an upper case or "Auxiliary Table," which permitted two meanings to be assigned to a code group. This feature applied to the first two-thirds of the code book, thus raising the total number of code group values to around 55,000. (Practically speaking, this meant that prior to a code group for which the second meaning was intended, there would be an "Auxiliary Table indicator" alerting the recipient that the group carried the second meaning. This might apply to several sequential code groups.) The "B" version also discarded the so-called "hatted" pattern of ordering code groups so that the meanings of the text concealed by the five-digit numbers progressed sequentially through the Japanese syllabary from low to high numbers. The "B" version thus required two books, one for encoding and one for decoding, making what is called a two-part code. Moreover, it introduced three special tables for encoding positions, geographical designators, and date/time groups. In practice, these special tables were reserved for particularly critical instances of those subjects.

This account of how the Imperial Navy deployed JN-25 to May 1942 illuminates the basic tasks before the communications intelligence activities. Like all naval communications in that period, the messages were transmitted in Morse code by hand tapping on an electrical keying device by skilled radio operators at speeds of forty words per minute or greater. They had to be intercepted by highly trained radio intercept operators who recognized the distinctive Japanese traffic and could copy it down on specially modified typewriters ("code mills") at full speed. (Japanese Morse code was in *kana* symbols with seventy-five different characters, plus suffixes denoting *hanigori* [a harsh sound] and *nigori* [a soft sound]). The copied messages were forwarded to the code-breaking centers in Washington, the Philippines, and Hawaii. (In 1941 there was no dedicated secure radio or cable communications link between all the code-breaking centers, and most copied messages were forwarded by mail or messenger taking days or weeks.) At these centers, the message texts were attacked to extract the additive tables so that the underlying code groups could be studied. Only then could the process begin of determining the meaning of individual code groups. Extracting usable intelligence required the accumulation of enough code group values to reveal useful information.

In November 1940, just before the change to "JN-25B," code breakers had extracted the meaning of about 1,300 five-digit groups from the "A" code version and entertained aspirations of being able to "read" code traffic by year's end. The introduction of "JN-25B" dashed those hopes. The reality is that while the tempo of additive group recoveries increased greatly in 1941, the number of recovered code values through December 1941 remained far less than needed to "read" messages. A report by the main American code-breaking unit in Washington reflects about 3,800 values (of 55,000, or about 7 percent) that were recovered by 1 December 1941. The laborious business of recovering actual meaning or values, however, spawned numerous instances of erroneous assignments of meaning that required later correction, and so the process was not a steady cadence of breakthroughs. Another report drafted in Washington asserts that one or a few very short, highly stereotyped "movement reports" (messages verifying the departures and arrivals of a vessel) could be discerned by the small code-breaking unit in the Philippines in JN-25 traffic. The report of the Philippine unit makes no such claim.[*] In any event, no message could be "read" that shed material light on Japanese plans or intentions prior to the Pearl Harbor attack.

The attack on JN-25 required specialists trained in the arcane arts of copying Japanese navy messages, dedicated and secure communications between intercept operators and code-breaking organizations; those skilled at breaking codes; and competent translators. But like so much else of American defense resources, personnel with these abilities were in extremely short supply. On Pearl Harbor day, 7 December 1941, just 331 US Army personnel worked on all aspects of communications intelligence. On VJ Day (15 August 1945) that roster numbered 10,371, an increase by a factor of 31. Parallel figures for the US Navy were 738 on 7 December and 9,157 in July 1945, an increase by 12 times. Because of the massive investment in labor-saving machinery during the war (ten times more for the navy alone by December 1943), the actual capability of the workforce at the end of the war was far greater than the simple manpower figures would indicate.

---

[*] Two subsequent reports are very illuminating on the issue of accurate code group recoveries. A Washington report as of 8 January 1942 (after a significant upgrade in resources devoted to the attack on JN-25B) noted that by then some 5,366 code values were believed recovered, but of these only "roughly 3,000" were deemed verified. RG 38, CNSG Library Box 116 5750/201 CNSG-OP-20-GY-P History (2 of 2), "File # 62, War diary File on History and Function of OP-20-G Officers from Dec 42–Oct 45," National Archives and Records Administration [hereafter NARA]. A summary by the Corregidor unit dated 10 March 1942 after still more time and resources were devoted to attacking JN-25B lists a total of 10,247 code group recoveries, but only 3,522 were confirmed and another 70 were good. Another 2,185 were deemed questionable, 3,531 very questionable, and 939 without classification. RG 38, CNSG Library, Box 119, File 5750/221, "Summary of C.I. Activity," NARA.

Decisions to spread the few bodies into multiple endeavors tremendously exacerbated the limited capabilities due to personnel shortages. For example, the US Navy's Washington office (Station Negat) contained a unit designated GY-1 working on Japanese codes. It mustered just ten individuals in the first quarter of 1941 and abandoned work on JN-25 for part of 1941 to concentrate on German codes, only to return in August. It only grew to a total of 22 personnel by the fourth quarter, but two years later mustered nearly 30 times as many personnel (656).

Two factors most strongly influenced this dispersion of effort. First was the priority of daily "Purple" intercept production for both army and navy Washington communications intelligence operations. Ironically, breaking "Purple" produced not only valuable intelligence but also profound distortion of the overall communications intelligence effort. As policymakers became addicted to a daily take of "Purple," the army soon found its resources inadequate, particularly as to translation capacity. Beginning in February 1941, the services split this duty with the navy, handling "Purple" traffic on odd-numbered days with the army taking care of it on even-numbered days. By Pearl Harbor day, fully 50 percent of the navy's translation capability in Washington worked only "Purple." According to the army's original translator, John Hurt, that service had just two translators who could produce rapid and accurate translations; both worked "Purple."

The concentration on "Purple" exerted multiple ripple effects. Knowledge that "Purple" transmitted the highest grade of Japanese diplomatic traffic spawned the presumption that it also carried the most valuable intelligence. Consequently, lesser systems were worked only as scarce resources permitted. One of these neglected lower grade systems was that used by the Honolulu consulate that turned out to carry revealing espionage information highly suggestive of attack preparations in messages finally translated after the attack.[*]

The second factor dispersing the decryption effort was the administra-

---

[*] The lesser cryptographic systems included those designated J-19, PA-K2, and LA. Effort also was directed at plain text traffic and standard broadcasts. Although the lesser cryptographic systems were more easily broken than "Purple," concentration on "Purple" meant as a practical matter that, for example, about two-thirds of the "Purple" traffic was decrypted and translated from 1 November to 7 December 1941, but only about 16 percent of J-19 traffic. PHA, Part 37, 1081-83. Further, translation of decrypted J-19 messages frequently occurred days later than for "Purple." "Friedman notes of meeting with Captain Safford," page 11, Folder 4217, "Pearl Harbor Investigation and Miscellaneous Material," RG 457, Entry 9032, Box 1360, NARA.

tion's "Germany First" strategy. A large contingent of the navy's communications intelligence effort in Washington aimed at German and to a much lesser degree Italian naval traffic. Efforts were even divided between the two Pacific sub units, Station Cast in the Philippines and Station Hypo in Hawaii. Station Cast enjoyed superior intercept ability due to proximity to Japan. It worked on JN-25, but likewise with only a very small complement of personnel. A "Purple Machine" had been shipped to the Philippines so that General MacArthur and Admiral Hart had access to diplomatic intercepts, but at the cost of diverting effort from JN-25. Washington tasked Station Hypo with working on the "AD" or in shorthand "the Admiral's Code." This system was believed to harbor top level operational intelligence and hence enormous value. The effort proved fruitless, however, primarily because not enough "AD" traffic was intercepted to permit an effective attack.

Besides the American enterprises, the Dutch and the British also worked on Japanese codes. The Dutch had a small intercept and code-breaking element stationed in the Netherlands East Indies known as *Kamer* (Room) 14. The Dutch achieved considerable progress in solving Japanese manual diplomatic systems, but little headway with machine ciphers such as "Purple" or Japanese military or naval cryptographic systems. In a restricted exchange program between the Dutch and the British, the latter sent diplomatic intercepts to Bandung, while the Dutch shared copies of all their intercepts, including Japanese military and naval messages. The Dutch, on occasion, did pass some translations of intercepted Japanese diplomatic messages to the American military attaché office in the East Indies. The British Far East Combined Bureau (FECB) in Singapore, supported modestly by a small contingent at the Government Code and Cipher School at Bletchley Park (which famously broke the German "Enigma" system), worked on Japanese codes. The FECB and Station Cast in the Philippines began exchanging recoveries of additives and code groups to mutual profit in February 1941. But like the Americans, neither the Dutch nor the British could obtain useful intelligence from JN-25 prior to Pearl Harbor.

In summary, by far the best and most credible evidence on American and Allied code breaking against JN-25 prior to Pearl Harbor demonstrates what can be hailed as cryptographic success but lamented as intelligence failure. Cryptographically, the system was "solved" in the sense that it was identified as a combined book code and cipher system employing five-digit code numbers concealed by additives. During 1940 to 1941, progressively greater success emerged in stripping away additive groups. But recovery of the meaning of code groups remained minuscule. Some rough sense of the status of code group recovery can be gleaned by imagining that on a page of text in this work, roughly thirty, typically nonconsecutive "words" (code groups) could be made out—and not all those "words" were correct. Thus, no meaningful intelligence could be extracted about Japanese military or naval plans and intentions from code breaking.

Intelligence in Hawaii

The intelligence reaching Kimmel in Hawaii comprised both open and secret sources. The accounts appearing in local newspapers certainly conveyed a crisis atmosphere. On 30 November, for example, the *Honolulu Advertiser* headlined: "Japanese May Strike Over Weekend." Secret intelligence sources included dispatches from staff offices in Washington, Allied naval attaché cables, reports from British intelligence sources in the Far East, and some State Department reports. Reports of Japanese merchant ships uniformly steaming homeward between August and November 1941 provided perhaps the earliest indicator of Japanese preparations for hostilities. State Department and naval attaché reports reflected open observations of Japanese troop movements pointing to the mounting of an amphibious operation to the south of Japan. Between 1 November and 6 December, however, the daily summary from the Fourteenth Naval District radio intelligence unit (Station Hypo) delivered to Kimmel his most valuable information. These summaries reflected the radio intelligence gathered from traffic analysis and direction finding without input from decryption of Japanese messages.

The radio intelligence summaries demonstrated unmistakably a very large Japanese task force headed south of ships supported by land-based aircraft linked to troop convoys. In the days before 7 December, the Japanese cleverly kept down total radio traffic, but that traffic contained an unusual number of high precedence messages. In this same span, Japanese intelligence organizations in Tokyo prolifically spewed out messages, as did the Navy Ministry and the Naval General Staff. None of these signs pointed to Pearl Harbor.

With respect to Japanese aircraft carriers, one division (two carriers) appeared to be linked to the huge task force headed south. On 3 November, a call sign recovery for the first time gave the title "First Air Fleet." This was, in fact, the massive carrier force assembling for the Pearl Harbor attack. Kimmel's intelligence officers, however, thought the command represented both sea- and land-based air, thus missing an important clue. Later when the title "Eleventh Air Fleet" (the command over the Imperial Navy's land-based aircraft) emerged, they confessed uncertainty over its composition. Up through 17 November, traffic appeared (correctly) to locate most carriers in Japanese ports. By 24 November, Kimmel's intelligence summary lamented that there was "no definite indication of location" of the carriers. The Hawaii unit surmised that the long-standing association with carriers of some destroyers located in the Marshall Islands on 30 November pointed to the presence also of carriers. This deduction was rejected by the closer intercept unit in the Philippines. That unit, in fact, projected on 27 November that "all large carrier forces," including ten carriers, were part of a task force being assembled for operations in Southeast Asia.

The Imperial Navy had changed all radio call signs of units on 1 November. When it again changed all call signs on 1 December, the shift after just one month was totally unprecedented. Further, the Japanese altered procedures to make call sign recoveries more difficult and thus seriously impede traffic analysis. On 2 December, Kimmel's radio intelligence summary confessed an "almost complete blank of information on the carriers today." While about two hundred call signs had already been recovered, not one was linked to a carrier. This resulted in a scene recalled later by Fleet Intelligence Officer Lt. Cdr. Edwin Layton.

"You mean to say," Kimmel asked, "that you are the intelligence officer of the Pacific Fleet and you don't know where the [Japanese] carriers are?"

[Layton] "No, sir, I don't."

[Kimmel] "For all you know, they could be coming around Diamond Head [by Honolulu], and you wouldn't know it."

[Layton] "Yes, sir, but I hope they'd have been sighted by now."

From 4 to 6 December, the summary noted but did not emphasize an extremely ominous sign: the commanders of the Second and Third Fleets, who had been extremely talkative since 1 November, suddenly fell silent—a clear signal of an impending operation.

Looking over these reports, three pieces of information stand out. The first was the 1 December unprecedented change of Imperial Navy call signs after only one month. On 2 December, Kimmel's intelligence officer advised him that the whereabouts of Japan's most potent aircraft carriers were unknown because of a lack of verified radio traffic for fifteen to twenty-five days. Then on 3 December, Kimmel learned that Tokyo ordered Japanese embassies (including Washington) to destroy code material, another indicator of incipient hostilities. Kimmel failed to share any of this information with Short.

In the decades that followed Pearl Harbor, conspiracy theories thrived and centered on the idea that there was some missed signal or tip-off to the attack—or that Washington or London detected the signal but concealed it from the commanders in Hawaii (or London concealed its findings from Roosevelt) for purposes of getting the United States into the war via the "back door." These theories share some fundamental defects. First, all diplomatic code breaking revealed at best was an *oral* promise from Hitler (or on his behalf) that if Japan got into war with the United States, then Germany would follow. Given Hitler's overall record with written much less oral commitments, and his stunning betrayal of Japan in the Nazi-Soviet Pact of August 1939, it would require an energetic leap of faith to base strategic calculations on the premise that a German declaration of war would follow assuredly after a Japanese attack—or that an American public would mindlessly demand a declaration of war against Japan *and* Germany. The possibility that Germany would not declare war and that the United States would find itself solely enmeshed in war with Japan was perhaps among the worst nightmares of officials in Washington and London.

Second, when the mechanics of the handling of radio intelligence are understood, it is clear that many people would have to have participated in such a conspiracy and then maintained perfect secrecy. Further, the suppression or alteration of records to conceal such nefarious activity would have to extend not only back from 7 December, but also forward well into 1942. Third, if code-breaking success permitted foreknowledge of the Pearl Harbor attack, where is evidence of such capability concerning Japan's other opening moves and during the campaigns that followed the attack? Fourth, and particularly telling, such arguments presume that any hint via code breaking, direction finding, or interception of alleged radio signals in the North Pacific would have tipped off the extraordinary and unprecedented nature and scale of the actual attack. Fifth and finally, the US Pacific Fleet was the vital bulwark for the defense of the British Asian Empire. The idea that Winston Churchill's government would remain silent if aware of danger to the Pacific Fleet is thus preposterous.

What conspiracy theories have accomplished is to divert attention from the key explanations of this historical turning point. The first of these aspects is that the Japanese success arose from the multiple layers of surprise and deception. American and Allied intelligence failed to sift out Yamamoto's audacious inversion of the mutually shared presumption of how a Pacific conflict would be conducted strategically. There was no precedent for, nor intelligence clue that unmasked, the development of the new Japanese operational capabilities for moving a major task force to Hawaii or the massing of six fleet carriers. Further, there was no solid evidence of a Japanese breakthrough at the tactical level in capabilities of their air-launched torpedoes or bombs. And a well-thought-out and executed deception plan crowned these schemes. That deception plan included rigorous radio silence by the First Air Fleet coupled to a plausible pattern of false information locating the carriers in home waters, notably via fictitious carrier radio traffic purporting to originate from carriers and their "aircraft" on training flights. Although not explicitly part of the deception plan, the massing of the huge task forces for attacks on Malaya and the Philippines further provided a highly plausible explanation that the carriers, like most of Japan's battleships, were held in home waters as a distant cover for the southern offensives against intervention by the US Pacific Fleet.

Conspiracy mania also has served to obscure the division of responsibility between Hawaii and Washington for the disaster. After the attack, Washington worked assiduously to heap virtually all the blame on Kimmel and Short in Hawaii. This was grossly unjust, but these officers were not blameless. Their failure to set up an effective air information center alone prevents their exoneration. They also were responsible for material failures to share information, like Kimmel's failure to inform Short that the whereabouts of Japan's carriers were unknown and Short's failure to explain to Kimmel that his alert was only against sabotage or subversion. Short's decisions to *decrease* his level of alertness to external threats after the "War Warning" and to decouple the ability of his command to react to a radar warning of an air attack remain indefensible. Kimmel likewise bears responsibility for failing to verify the actual defenses available to protect the fleet in port. They share responsibility for failing to invoke the plans for unity of command and joint operations carefully prepared earlier that year.

But Washington garners its own damning list of faults. The first was moving the fleet from the West Coast, where it was immune to carrier attack, to Pearl Harbor where it was exposed. This was done for the sake of deterrence and not to bait a Japanese attack, but it was executed over the objections of the fleet commander who was relieved for his protests. Second, leaders in Washington issued "War Warnings" alerting Pacific commanders of a strategic threat, but the warnings conspicuously diverted attention away from Hawaii when identifying likely Japanese targets for attack. Third, when Short duly notified Washington that he interpreted his "War Warnings" as only a stimulus to guard against sabotage or subversion, none of his superiors objected that his response was inadequate.

The Last Week of Pacific Peace

1 December 1941 proved to be an extremely important day in the Japanese and American capitals. In Tokyo, an Imperial Conference convened. Foreign Minister Tōgō blamed the breakdown of negotiations entirely on American intransigence, culminating in the "Hull Note," which he characterized as an "unreasonable proposal, which completely disregarded the negotiations that had gone on for a year." Tōgō denounced the refusal of the United States to "stop giving aid to Chiang" and described this as an obstruction of "the establishment of peace" between Japan and China. This event was purely ritual. Policy had been set on 5 November. If the United States did not meet either Proposal A or Proposal B, Japan would commit to war by 1 December. As the United States refused to accept either proposal, only one course remained.

Had these men not shackled themselves to a rigid deadline for a war decision, within a week or perhaps two of this date, the defeat of German armies in the Soviet Union might have caused them to radically alter their stance. Insofar as Japanese leaders entertained some concept of how the war they intended to start would end satisfactorily for Japan, their thoughts rested most heavily on Germany knocking out the Soviets and then hopefully Great Britain. Manifest German failure in the Soviet Union might have prompted Japan's leaders to pull back from the precipice, no matter how bitter the alternative.

In Washington this same day, 1 December, "Magic" disclosed Tokyo's orders for destruction of code machines and various codes at offices in London, Hong Kong, Singapore, and Manila. Even more significant, translation on 1 December of a 29 November message from Ambassador Ōshima in Berlin revealed Foreign Minister Ribbentrop's affirmation that "should Japan become engaged in a war against the United States, Germany, of course, would join the war immediately." A 30 November message from Tokyo to Berlin was also translated this day that contained urgent instructions for Ōshima to interview Hitler and Ribbentrop and explain "very secretly" that a war between Japan and the Anglo-Saxon nations "may come quicker than anyone realizes."

In the afternoon of 1 December Roosevelt summoned the British Ambassador Lord Halifax. After months of silence in response to British requests for an explicit pledge of support if Japan attacked in the Far East, Roosevelt announced that if the Japanese moved into Thailand, he would support the British counteraction, including a thrust into Thai territory in the Kra Isthmus (Operation Matador).[*] The president then commented—with a casualness that belied the import of his words—that if the Japanese attacked British or Dutch holdings directly, "we should obviously all be together." On 3 December Roosevelt clarified his informal language and affirmed to Halifax that "support" meant armed support. On 4 December, Roosevelt expanded his commitment to back Operation Matador, even if the Japanese only attacked northern Thailand.

On 2 December, Roosevelt personally directed the Asiatic Fleet to charter three small vessels to form a "Defensive Information Patrol." To meet minimum requirements to establish them as US warships, they must be commanded by a US naval officer and mount "a small gun and 1 machine gun." Crews would be a minimum number of US Naval personnel supplemented by Filipinos. Their mission was "to observe and report by radio Japanese movements in the West China Sea and Gulf of Siam." The purpose of this "Defensive Information Patrol" may have been, as the title indicated, an ad hoc measure to secure information on the large Japanese troop movements under way by ship. Another possibility is that Roosevelt sought to goad the Japanese to sink a US warship to form a casus belli even if Japan otherwise avoided US territory. This latter purpose would seem to contradict the idea that Roosevelt knew for certain that Japan was about to strike Pearl Harbor or some other US location that would provide a far more compelling rationale for war. In any event, the "Defensive Information Patrol" never reached its station before the war began.

On 4 December, Robert McCormick's *Chicago Tribune* newspaper bleated in a huge banner headline: *FDR'S SECRET WAR PLANS REVEALED!* The same article appeared in the capital in the *Washington Times-Herald*, published by McCormick's cousin Cissy Patterson. The exposé described a leaked copy of a top secret administration plan (styled "The Victory Program") for mobilization of 10 million men and then a dispatch of a 5 million man European expeditionary force by July 1943. The plan's official origin stemmed from an order issued by Roosevelt in July 1941 for a blueprint for "overall pro-

---

[*]   The strategically important Kra Isthmus is the slender southern extension of Thailand connecting it to Malaya to the south and providing access to a similar narrow extension of Burma on the west.

duction requirements required to defeat our potential enemies." The real origin was that Stimson and other officials had finally compelled the president to install some order in the shockingly chaotic efforts to mobilize—primarily due to Roosevelt's refusal to set up structure, priorities, and comprehensive goals. The *Tribune* story spun the study as a war plan, whereas it looked to America's needs as either a belligerent or a nonbelligerent.

When shocked and furious senior administration officials gathered, Stimson demanded the rooting out of "this infernal disloyalty which we now have working in America First and in these McCormick family papers." The cabinet bruited a trial of McCormick and others under the Espionage Act, which carried a possible death penalty. Had not the episode been entirely overtaken by the Japanese attack on Pearl Harbor three days later, it would have rivaled or exceeded the significance of the Pentagon Papers case of 1971.

A sorely needed ray of hope in Washington as the month began came from the Libyan Desert. There the British Commonwealth Army had launched an offensive on 18 November against German Gen. Erwin Rommel and his Italian-German army. It was only at the end of the month, however, that the Commonwealth forces finally gained the upper hand, and the first days of December brought progressively more upbeat reports. By contrast, the situation on the Soviet Front remained perilous from the last days of November into the first days of December. Some positive news twinkled out from the otherwise sober picture on 25 November, when Soviet forces on the extreme southern end of the gigantic front launched an offensive that ejected the Germans from Rostov. But this was overshadowed by Soviet acknowledgment of the critical situation before Moscow. On 4 and 5 December, news began to appear of Soviet counterattacks easing the situation. Secretary of the Interior Ickes recorded the acute anxiety in Washington: "The Germans are making a supreme effort to capture Moscow at whatever cost for the moral effect, not only on their own people, but on the allies, including the United States. There can hardly be any doubt that if Moscow should fall the effect would be highly unfavorable."

On 4 December (Japanese time) Nagumo's Striking Force pivoted bows from the easterly heading, maintained since 26 November, to a southeasterly course. After an anxious final refueling evolution, the task force aimed prows for a point over seven hundred miles northeast of Oahu—an approach that would have evaded American search planes flying only due north. On 6 December (Hawaii time), Nagumo's ships veered to a southwesterly course for the final dash to the launch point.

On 6 December in Washington, word came that British reconnaissance aircraft flying from Malaya had sighted the previous day three large Japanese troop convoys in the Gulf of Siam before contact was lost due to weather. This latest ominous news provided a backdrop for two final actions by Roosevelt. He personally drafted a message to Emperor Hirohito pointing to reports of a large buildup of Japanese forces in Southern Indochina which threatened peoples in the Philippines as well as British and Dutch possessions. Roosevelt pleaded that there was no American intention to attack Southern Indochina and that similar guarantees could be obtained from the British, Dutch, Thai, and Chinese governments. He asked the emperor to agree to withdraw Japanese forces from Indochina and to preserve the peace. Imperial Army officers delayed the telegram so that the emperor only saw it after Japanese bombs fell on Pearl Harbor.

Roosevelt may have hoped for but did not expect a reply from the emperor. Accordingly, he also ordered the State Department to draft a far more difficult communication. It would strive to present a convincing case to a skeptical public and many members of Congress that the United States should enter the war in the Far East even if Japan confined its overt hostilities only to British or Dutch possessions or Thailand and avoided acts of war against American territory.

During 6 December, the Japanese Foreign Ministry telegraphed the first thirteen parts of a fourteen-part message as a formal reply to the "Hull Note." At about 2130, Lieutenant Lester R. Schultz, an assistant naval aide, entered the president's study bearing the copy of the intercept. He found Roosevelt and Hopkins in conversation. He handed the message to the president. The opening phrases explained Japan's view of events since 1937, placing China as the fundamental issue:

> It is the immutable policy of the Japanese government to insure the stability of East Asia and to promote world peace and thereby to enable all nations to find each its proper place in the world. Ever since the China affair broke out owing to the failure on the part of China to comprehend Japan's true intentions, the Japanese government has striven for the restoration of peace. . . . However, both the United States and Great Britain have resorted to every possible measure to assist the Chungking regime so as to obstruct the general peace between Japan and China.

The note declared that while the Japanese government had manifested "the spirit of conciliation" in negotiations since April, the United States and Great Britain had "willfully misrepresent[ed]" Japan's deployment of forces in accordance with an agreement with the French for the "joint defense" of Indochina as a threat and instituted freezing measures and the military encirclement of Japan that "endangers the very existence of our Empire." The note presented Japan's 20 November proposal as fair and conciliatory. It acknowledged that its terms included the requirement that the United States "undertakes not to resort to measures and actions prejudicial to the endeavors for the restoration of general peace between Japan and China" once negotiations began between Japan and China, i.e., the abandonment of China by the United States once negotiations began. Not only had the United States rejected the proposal but it had made known its intent "to continue its aid to Chiang Kai-shek." The last section of the note charged that the United States and Great Britain had conspired to defeat Japan's aim "to adjust Japanese–American relations and to preserve and promote peace."

To Schultz's recollection, after digesting the document the president stated "this means war" or words to that effect—a fair surmise that the fourteenth part would contain a declaration of war. Roosevelt and Hopkins then exchanged views on where the Japanese might strike. Schultz could recall mention only of Indochina, but he also extracted a sense that the outbreak of hostilities was still some time off—which left Schultz so surprised the next day. Hopkins observed that the Japanese would strike when their forces were in the optimal position and lamented that since war was inevitable, it was unfortunate that the United States could not strike first and prevent surprise. Roosevelt nodded but said, "No, we can't do that. We are a democracy and peaceful people." Then raising his voice, Roosevelt said, "But we have a good record." Before Schultz left, Roosevelt tried to contact Admiral Stark. On learning his senior naval officer was at the National Theater watching a play, Roosevelt decided not to have Stark summoned because this might cause public alarm.

Couriers on similar missions delivered the "Magic" decrypt of the thirteen-part message to other officials that night. Neither the president nor any of his senior officials sought to issue further warnings or to consult about any other measure. The reason is simple: like Lieutenant Schultz, no American official suspected that Tokyo would combine the delivery of the complete note the following day, 7 December 1941, with the opening of hostilities.

CHAPTER 11

"Air Raid, Pearl Harbor, This Is No Drill"

DAY OF INFAMY

Vanguard and Alarms

Five midget submarines—the world's first successful models of this type—constituted the vanguard of the attack. Each two-man craft weighed 46 tons, measured 78.5 feet long, and pointed two 18-inch-diameter torpedoes from its bow. Five specially modified submarines, *I-16*, *I-18*, *I-20*, *I-22*, and *I-24*, transported them piggyback to the waters near the entrance to Pearl Harbor. Beginning at about midnight, 7 December, the mother subs commenced releasing their brood in bubble geysers for their harbor penetration mission. Only American ineptitude prevented this appallingly bad idea from wreaking catastrophe on the attackers.

At 0342, minesweeper *Condor*, performing the numbing sentry function south of the antisubmarine nets protecting the harbor entrance, sighted a periscope. *Condor*'s alarm brought to the scene World War I–era duty destroyer *Ward*. Decommissioned in 1921 after just three years' service, *Ward* returned to the fleet in February 1941, manned largely by reservists from Minnesota. It acquired its incumbent captain, Lt. William W. Outerbridge, on 5 December. After a briefing that afternoon on his mission, Outerbridge took *Ward*—his first command—to sea the next day. Thus, when history called, Outerbridge had logged less than forty-eight hours as a skipper and less than twenty-four hours at sea as a ship captain. When *Ward*'s sonar detected nothing, its officers adduced this as another in a series of false alarms over the past months. They issued no report. When *Condor* and its consort *Crossbill* headed back into the harbor, no one closed the protective nets behind them that were designed to keep out torpedoes that would also have halted the midget submarines.

In these last hours of peace, alarming omens alternated between Hawaii and Washington. As the midget submarines cast off from their mother ships, American intercept stations pulled from the ether Foreign Minister Tōgō's wire with the fourteenth and last part of the final Japanese note. It concluded: "The Japanese government regrets to have to notify hereby the American government that in view of the attitude of the American government it cannot but consider that it is impossible to reach an agreement through further negotiations."

By about 0940 (9:40 a.m.) in Washington (0410 in Hawaii), the code breakers set before Roosevelt the fourteenth part. While the president feared the night before that the first thirteen parts formed a bill of indictment for a declaration of war, the final part announced just a breakoff of negotiations. Naval intelligence officers and Stark mulled what the new decode signified but could not agree on further action. Nor did the State Department react. The absence of Washington's alarm when the entire fourteen-part message became available is both understandable and important. The note's alternately strident and wounded tone ended in a whimper, without severing diplomatic relations, much less making a declaration of war.

At the War Department, just before 0900, Col. Rufus S. Bratton began to reread the complete fourteen-part message to tease out any new implications. As he did so he was handed the latest decrypt. In it Tōgō commanded Ambassador Nomura: "Will the Ambassador please submit to the United States government (if possible to the Secretary of State) our reply to the United States at 1:00 p.m. [1300] on the 7th your time."

The new communication—ever after known as "the 1 o'clock message"— electrified Bratton. It not only activated the fourteen-part message; the order to deliver the message at a specified time on a Sunday, not a normal workday for diplomats, was unprecedented. Bratton vaulted into action to assure that Pacific commands were alerted that Japan might strike at that time—but as Bratton later testified, he never suspected that Pearl Harbor might be a target because he believed the fleet was at sea. Bratton was by no means alone in believing the Pacific Fleet had gone to sea. In the paired ironies of this day, Tokyo possessed a better grasp of the deployment of the Pacific Fleet than many senior officers in Washington—while Washington knew the contents and status of Japan's diplomatic note better than Tokyo's Washington representatives.

Bratton needed the approval of his superiors to dispatch an alert message to the Pacific, but he found that intelligence chief Brig. Gen. Sherman Miles,

Brig. Gen. Leonard T. Gerow (chief of the War Plans Division), and Marshall were not at their offices. Bratton learned Marshall had gone horseback riding. It was 1030 hours when Bratton hailed Marshall by phone. The chief of staff announced he would come to the office to see the message.

While Bratton tracked down Marshall, Stimson and Knox sat down with Hull to look over the fourteen-part message. As Stimson recorded in his diary, Hull was "very certain that the Japs are planning some deviltry and we are all wondering when the blow will strike."

When Lt. Cdr. Alwin Kramer returned to his office after delivering the fourteenth part of the message to the White House and Navy Department, he found waiting "the 1 o'clock message." Kramer performed a routine exercise of converting this hour in Washington into time on the West Coast, Honolulu, Manila, and Tokyo. This demonstrated it would be 0730 in Hawaii. But Kramer was more impressed with the fact that it would be several hours before dawn off Malaya, the "normal time" for an amphibious landing.

Kramer handed a copy of "the 1 o'clock message" to Cdr. Arthur McCollum outside Stark's office. Both Kramer and McCollum emphasized the relationship of the Washington time to the time in Hawaii and the Far East. But both Kramer and McCollum, in next briefing Knox, placed far more emphasis on the time off Malaya than in Hawaii.

The Japanese embassy presented a stark contrast to the formidable American efficiency in preparing decoded copies of these messages for circulation. Ironically, Foreign Minister Tōgō, not Japan's militarists, instinctively thought to commence war without prior notification, but Prime Minister Tôjô and the emperor directed otherwise. On 3 December, Tōgō's staff crafted a draft note explicitly announcing the end of negotiations and a declaration of war. The Imperial Navy vehemently objected that this might compromise surprise. Some officers even advocated delivery of the note twenty-four hours after the attack! The navy relented on delivery the same day of the strike when Tōgō's redraft note ended benignly with notice only of the end of negotiations. The exact timing of the notification was set by the vice chief of the naval general staff, Rear Adm. Seiichi Itō. Originally he proposed 1230 (12:30 p.m.), 7 December, Washington time, which was 0700 in Hawaii. But on the 5th, Itō demanded the time be moved back to 1300 (1:00 p.m.), which was 0730 in Hawaii. Ito explained that practical experience in fleet exercises indicated the attack would probably come twenty minutes late. He therefore calculated the new time would give a fifty-minute advance notice—early enough to constitute prior notice but not so early as to give the Americans adequate time to prepare.

Early on 6 December, Washington time, Tōgō notified his Washington

embassy that he was forwarding in parts a memorandum in English respond-
ing to the "Hull Note" of 26 November. "You will refine the wording," Tōgō
directed, "and complete all other advance preparations beforehand, so as to be
able to deliver it to the United States whenever so directed" by a separate telegram. The first thirteen parts clattered off cable lines in Washington starting
from noon 6 December and the fourteenth part by 0900, 7 December, Washington time. This left little margin to prepare a clean copy to deliver. Tōgō
further expressly forbade the embassy from employing any regular (American) clerical personnel for security reasons. The only senior staff member
with even rudimentary typing skills (on Japanese language typewriters) was
First Secretary Katzuso Okumura. His task was still more challenging since
the message had to be typed on an English language typewriter. But neither
Okumura nor anyone else of the senior staff lingered at the embassy during
the night of 6–7 December. Many had left for a going-away party for one of
the secretaries—held at a Chinese restaurant. Few gastronomic exercises in
diplomatic history have generated such controversy.

Thanks primarily to the missing staff, there were delays in decoding the
messages. Okamura only commenced his fumbling onslaught on the English
typewriter after he arrived in the morning. About 1100 hours, just as Okamura embarked on retyping a clean, corrected copy of the memorandum, a
new dispatch ordered delivery of the memorandum at 1:00 p.m. [1300], Washington time. A hurried phone call arranged an appointment at that hour with
Hull as Okumura pecked furiously to prepare the memorandum for delivery.
No one in the embassy was privy to the real reason for the 1:00 p.m. delivery time. Indeed, Nomura had convinced himself that a war was certain, but
that it would follow a three-step scenario: Japan would advance in Thailand;
the United States would respond by deploying forces to the Netherlands East
Indies; and then Japan, desperate for oil, would attack that location, starting
hostilities. Accordingly, Nomura believed that the note would at worst only provide notice of the advance into Thailand, meaning that belated delivery would
be of little consequence. Okumura only completed typing at 1:50 p.m. [1350].
Consequently, it would only be at 2:00 p.m. [1400] that Nomura and Kurusu
arrived with the note to see Hull—just as Hull received news of the attack.

From these contretemps some Japanese historians fabricated a controversy
by arguing the blame for the "surprise attack" that fueled American fury
rested on Washington embassy staff, particularly Okumura, not Japan's military. The reality is that even had the memorandum been delivered precisely as
ordered, it could not have attenuated American rage. The memorandum itself
was not an explicit declaration of war. Even if it had been interpreted as such,

there was no practical way, with 1941 communications, that the 1:00 p.m. delivery (between eighteen and twenty-five minutes before the first shot in Hawaii) would have permitted timely notice to Hawaii that could have materially reduced the surprise or the casualties.

At 0550 Hawaiian time, just twenty minutes after Okumura read "the 1 o'clock message" in Washington, Nagumo's task force wheeled to port onto a course north of due east and raised speed to twenty-four knots. Ironically, although steam propulsion had unshackled ships from the dominion of wind for the first time in several millennia, aircraft carriers had regressed to dependency on breezes to permit the safe launching and recovery of planes. Now the sextet of Japanese carriers slammed into an endless succession of rising waves propelled by blasts of air which, coupled to ship speed, reached hurricane ferocity. Oscillating bows dipped, canted port or starboard, and then pitched high, hurling aft white, frothy spray peeled off the wave crests. These conditions would have terminated flight operations in peacetime exercises. But there could be no halting now: the massive cavalcade of Japan's opening operations was synchronized around this assault on Pearl Harbor.

The Striking Force mingled the latest technology—the esthetically pleasing as well as the utilitarian ugly— with ancient tradition. *Hiryū, Sōryū, Shōkaku,* and *Zuikaku* represented the low-slung, streamlined look of advanced carrier design. By contrast, atop the original capital ships hulls of *Akagi* and *Kaga,* flight decks and their supporting structure reared up in ugly jumbled tiers of angular or rounded supports, a maze of catwalks, enormous downward curved funnels, and a disordered mix of boats, cranes, grills, guns, and radio towers. The six wood-planked flight decks teemed with sleek, state-of-the-art monoplanes. Mitsubishi A6M2 Type Zero and Aichi D3A1 Type 99 (Allied code name "Val") dive bombers featured titillating, air-show style livery of overall pale hemp shade with black cowlings. The Nakajima B5N2 Type 97 (Allied code name "Kate") torpedo and level bombers mostly eschewed such gaudy schemes for a warlike cloak of solid or mottled dark green upper surfaces. Yet juxtaposed to the lethal modernity of their mounts, each flight crew member wore warm bulky flight togs that resembled brown animal hides reminiscent of prehistoric warriors. Each forehead displayed a white *hachimaki* bandana inscribed with the word *Hisshō* ("Certain Victory"), linking each man and machine to Japan's samurai tradition.

At 0605, the first wave, led by Cdr. Mitsuo Fuchida, began launching. It numbered 183 of 189 planned planes: 40 "Kates" carrying torpedoes, 49 "Kates" with 16.1-inch naval shells converted to armor-piercing bombs, and 51

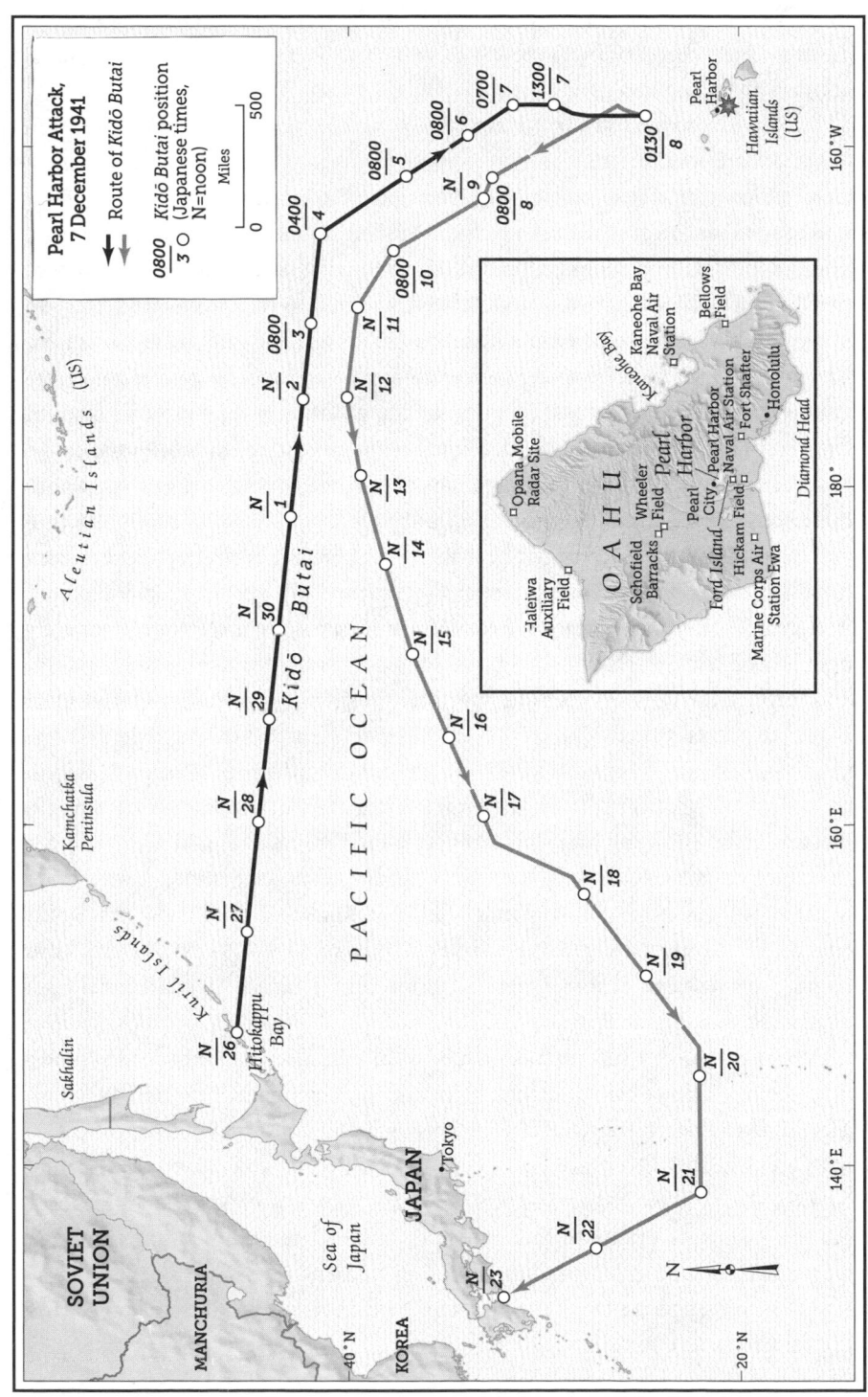

"Vals," each with a 250 kg (551 pound) bomb and 43 Zeros. One "Kate" with an armor-piercing bomb, three "Vals," and two Zeros, for assorted reasons, aborted the mission.

In Washington, Miles, the army's chief intelligence officer, joined Bratton at the War Department. The fourteen-part message and "the 1 o'clock message" convinced Miles that "war was very likely" and that "something is going to happen coincident with the 1 o'clock Washington time."

Marshall arrived at his office about 1125, just after Nagumo's carriers pointed their bows into the wind the first time. When Miles and Bratton entered, they observed Marshall methodically reading the entire fourteen-part message. Both Miles and Bratton attempted to direct his attention immediately to "the 1 o'clock message," but Marshall impassively finished reading the text of the Japanese diplomatic note before taking up the additional cable. Marshall later testified he immediately recognized "the 1 o'clock message" had "some very definite significance," but he asked Miles and Bratton to provide their opinion. Both urged that the message meant the Japanese meant to strike some American installation at or shortly after 1 o'clock. They all thought of American outposts in the Pacific, but no one thought immediately or solely of Pearl Harbor.

Marshall took out a sheet of paper and personally wrote a longhand message. He paused to call Stark at the Navy Department. Stark had been discussing the same messages with a staff officer, but initially he counseled Marshall against sending a warning on the premise that they had already sent enough. But about five minutes later, Stark called back. He had changed his mind and now offered the use of navy communications, which he stated "were quite rapid when the occasion demanded it." But Marshall demurred that army communications could get the message "through very quickly." Stark gave in on the condition that the message should instruct army commanders to notify "Navy opposites."

Marshall handed his draft dispatch to Bratton and ordered him to convey it to the message center to dispatch "at once by the fastest safe means." Both Marshall and Stark had available telephones and could have called Short or Kimmel directly. But Stark had been warned by his communications chief that the "scrambler" telephone was not truly secure, and Marshall later testified that securing phone connections was a time-consuming process and that he would have called Manila first and then Panama.

At the message center, Bratton deciphered Marshall's handwriting for the signal personnel. It read:

The Japanese are presenting at one p.m. Eastern Standard Time today
what amounts to an ultimatum also they are under orders to destroy
their Code machine immediately. Just what significance the hour set
may have we do not know but be on alert accordingly. Inform naval
authorities of this communication. Marshall.

When Bratton left the message center to return to Marshall's office he glanced
at his watch. It was 1158. Off Hawaii, it was 0628.

The exhausts of 183 planes of the first wave inscribed paired white moving dots against the half-lit dome of the sky. They merged into compact formations behind lead planes showing yellow lights. At the fore beckoned one
orange light marking Fuchida's command plane. The orange light turned
toward Pearl Harbor shortly before Bratton peered at his watch.

When Bratton reentered Marshall's office, the chief of staff told him to
return to the message center and find out how long it would take to get the dispatch out. A senior signal officer estimated thirty to forty minutes for Bratton,
but this did not include time to decipher the text and deliver it to the recipient.
The first message went out at 1200, but to the Caribbean Defense Command
(which included Panama). Then over the next twelve minutes, the dispatch
went to the West Coast and Manila. But intense static blanketed the connection to Honolulu. The signal officer considered turning to the navy, but instead
opted to send it via the commercial Western Union cable to San Francisco and
then on by RCA (Radio Corporation of America) cable to Honolulu. The message left at 1247 (12:17 p.m. in Washington), which was 0647 in Hawaii.

At 0630, just seventeen minutes before Western Union transmitted Marshall's warning, as the stores ship *Antares* approached the Pearl Harbor
entrance, its alert lookouts spotted a small submarine conning tower. *Antares*
summoned watchdog *Ward*. On that ship, the phone rang, waking skipper
Outerbridge in his sea cabin. The officer of the deck barked, "Captain, come on
the bridge." Outerbridge responded with a short but tart lecture to the young
reserve lieutenant about the impropriety of issuing an order, not a request, to
his commanding officer. The junior officer stalwartly replied: "Captain, come
on the bridge." This rocketed Outerbridge to his post. A bare seven minutes
from the *Antares* signal, one of just two shots aimed by *Ward*'s gunners perfo-
rated the base of the conning tower of the midget submarine where it joined
the hull. (Some sixty years later, divers located the hulk of a midget submarine in this vicinity with a hole drilled through its conning tower in exactly
that spot.) *Ward* broadcast a startling report: "We Have Attacked, Fired Upon

and Dropped Depth Charges on a Submarine Operating in the Defensive Sea Area." Elderly *Ward*, its reservist crew and its neophyte skipper, thus concluded the only near flawless American performance of the day.

As naval communicators processed the alert from *Ward*, Nagumo's carriers again nosed into the east wind and rough waves at 0705 and immediately commenced launching the second wave—fifteen minutes earlier than scheduled. This comprised 167 of 171 planned planes—35 Zeros, 54 "Kate" high-level bombers, and 78 "Val" dive bombers. Since surprise would have been long since lost, no aircraft carried torpedoes on this strike.

About 0720, just fifteen minutes after the second wave began launching, *Ward*'s message and that of a PBY which joined the fracas were relayed through the headquarters of the Commandant, Fourteenth Naval District, to Admiral Kimmel's duty officer. Initially, the recent spate of false alarms prompted skepticism, but the news propelled Kimmel from his quarters toward his office. It also motivated orders at 0751 for destroyer *Monaghan* to join *Ward*. No one, however, deemed it appropriate to order the vessels in the harbor to go to General Quarters.

Navy authorities did not deign to notify their army counterparts of *Ward*'s escapades, but the army had forfeited any grounds to complain about a communications failure. Three of the army's six radar sets on Oahu in operation from 0400 to 0700 detected and reported at about 0645 tracks of two float reconnaissance planes from Japanese cruisers *Chikuma* and *Tone* scouting ahead of the first wave of attackers. But a navy officer dismissed this news on the basis that they must be navy planes. Meanwhile, at the best and northernmost radar site at Opana, two very junior enlisted men, Joseph L. Lockhart and George E. Elliot, were about to shut off their set on schedule when at 0702 they saw by far the most sizable return echo they had ever observed. The American radio waves etching a startling, broad, vertical spike on the Opana oscilloscope rebounded from some of the 183 aircraft of the first wave of the Japanese attackers. The perplexed pair reported about 0715 to the Information Center at Fort Shafter a major flight of aircraft to the north, now about eighty-eight miles distant.

Only two men manned the center. The switchboard operator relayed the call to his superior, Lt. Kermit Tyler. But Tyler was not the regular controller and was merely present for training. As Tyler listened to the report, he recalled that a flight of B-17s was due in from the West Coast that morning. The bearing seemed approximately correct for the flight (the two tracks were in fact close). During their conversation, Tyler failed to explain that the flight comprised only about a dozen aircraft and the privates failed to volunteer that the echo signified at least fifty aircraft. Even after Tyler dismissed the report as the expected B-17s at about 0720, the Opana crew tracked the flight until it was about twenty miles distant at 0739.

The Japanese thus had volunteered three potential tactical warnings of the coming onslaught. Even had an effective Air Information Center been operating, it is probably dubious that radar contact around 0645 with the two float reconnaissance planes would have prompted a dramatic reaction. The detection of the massive first wave about forty minutes before the first bombs fell, however, should have triggered a full alarm by at least twenty minutes before the attack. Since it only required about eight to ten minutes to get battleships to general quarters with all watertight enclosures secured at sea, and less time for smaller vessels, even doubling that time for the less prepared situation that morning in Pearl Harbor, the attack still should have found the ship defenders alert and ready. Army antiaircraft batteries probably would still have been mobilizing, as likely would have been the defending fighters. *Ward*'s message describing its encounter with a submarine about five minutes after the report of a massive radar contact at a minimum should have reinforced the urgency of the reaction, though alternatively it could have started a full alert through the naval command chain. While Washington committed many sins against Kimmel and Short, the failure of their commands to exploit these tactical warning remains their most damning failure.

Airmen and Airfields

As the Japanese air armada approached, Pearl Harbor held ninety-six ships of the United States Pacific Fleet. These included eight of the fleet's nine battleships (*Colorado* was under overhaul at Puget Sound, Washington). At least fifteen of the vessels were undergoing repairs that diminished or eliminated the effectiveness of their armament. By no means did Pearl Harbor contain the entire Pacific Fleet. Not present were another forty-two ships, including all three aircraft carriers. The *Enterprise* task force ran into heavy weather on the 5th ("It looks like the North Atlantic instead of the Blue Pacific," noted one diarist). This unexpected development not only forced the task force to slow, but impeded essential destroyer refueling operations. Consequently, *Enterprise* and its consorts were about two hundred miles west of Pearl Harbor as dawn broke. *Lexington* on a similar delivery mission to Midway Island maneuvered still farther away with its eight escorts. The third carrier, *Saratoga*, was on the West Coast.

Cumulus clouds, mostly clustered over the mountains, streaked about 40 percent of the habitual crystalline blue skies over Oahu. Visibility at Pearl Harbor was good, with a ten-knot wind from the north. The only major vessel underway was destroyer *Helm*, leisurely shifting its berth. As the clock swept up toward 0800, all over the harbor crisply uniformed details prepared for the rituals of morning colors to be followed by religious services. On the battleships, bandsmen clustered near the stern while color parties stood by with the folded national banners, ready to snap them smartly to hoists. The time of the attack on the harbor was fixed by the fact that it coincided with the preparatory signal for these ceremonies at 0755. At that moment officers and men all around the harbor heard a discordant choir of powerful aircraft engines. A glance upward located many aircraft. Some, like glimmering crosses, arranged themselves in neat formations—others appeared to be diving.

The maneuvers witnessed by the uncomprehending Americans actually signified the collapse of the intricate Japanese attack plan. The commander of the first wave, Cdr. Fuchida, chose from a menu of two scenarios. He would fire one red flare if surprise were gained, unleashing the torpedo planes to attack first. If surprise were lost, he would fire two red flares, prompting the level and dive bombers to initiate the attack so as to distract attention from the more vulnerable torpedo planes. Fuchida's resort to visual signals underscored a serious Japanese technological shortcoming. Imperial Naval aircraft radios were wretchedly bulky, maliciously awkward to operate, and fitfully reliable. Consequently, Japanese formation leaders were stripped of any command and control technique more sophisticated than clumsy visual signals and still more crude "follow me" leadership techniques.

Seeing no evidence of American preparations, Fuchida duly fired off one red flare signaling surprise. But when he feared one group of planes failed to see the signal, he blasted off a second red flare. Although substantial time separated the two flares, which should have transmitted Fuchida's actual intentions, nonetheless the dive and level bomber leaders immediately launched their charges into the attack. Fuchida's radioman tapped out in *Wabun* (Japanese Morse code) "Tora, Tora, Tora," the code word for a successful surprise attack. Listeners not only on Nagumo's flagship *Akagi* heard the tapping, but so did eager ears on Yamamoto's distant flagship *Nagato*.

The mischance over the flare signals irrevocably disorganized the Japanese first wave and could have had very serious consequences if it had been confronted by even modest American readiness. The attack descended into what historian Alan Zimm condemned as "the same level of organization as the Kentucky Derby after the horses are turned loose." The startled Americans experienced the attack as a tumultuous, simultaneous onslaught from every direction and altitude. What scant framework may be imposed over the subsequent minutes stems from the fact that the Japanese units detailed to attack American air facilities needed less distance to fly and hence commenced delivering their ordnance first.

While the Japanese attack aimed foremost to disable the Pacific Fleet, Nagumo's airmen assigned over half the strike groups (183 of 350 aircraft) to the equally vital task of knocking out American airpower to preclude a counterattack. Probably about 0748, relays of Zeros and "Kates" administered to the US Navy's principal seaplane base in Hawaii at Kaneohe on Oahu's east coast the most annihilating onslaught of the day in terms of material damage. Of 33 PBYs, 26 were total losses and seven not air-worthy due to damage.

The US Army Air Force maintained two major and two minor (dispersal) bases on Oahu. The first major base, Wheeler Field, northwest of Pearl Harbor, housed 140 fighters. Starting at about 0751, roughly six minutes before the first torpedo hit, Japanese bullets and bombs set scores of American fighters blazing in puddles of flaming fuel and melting aluminum. The perverse fortune favoring the defenders was that massive smoky fires kindled amid the modern aircraft on the eastern end of the field masked obsolete aircraft on the western end.

The second major base, Hickam Field, just south of the Pearl Harbor naval base, hosted most bombers and a major repair installation. Here "Vals," Zeros, and "Kates" strafed and bombed in series, destroying many aircraft, hangars, repair shops, the base chapel, the guard house, and a mess hall. For good measure, the Japanese destroyed the base fire engine and the water main, thus precluding effective efforts to control flames.

Ewa (pronounced "Evva") Field, west of Pearl Harbor, served Marine Air Group (MAG)-21. Zeros pounced to destroy or render unserviceable all but two of forty-seven planes. Marines blazed away with rifles, pistols, and machine guns, downing one attacker.

Despite all this devastation and ill-preparedness, the defending fighter force managed to get off a combined total of sixteen sorties (two pilots managed two sorties each) with both P-40s and P-36s. Six pilots drove frantically amid strafing from Wheeler to the dispersal field at Haleiwa in the northern part of the island, overlooked by the Japanese. All told, four American pilots were killed, but they did succeed in shooting down at least eight Japanese planes, with Lt. George Welch gaining half these successes.

Besides the aircraft present at dawn on 7 December, three other groups of planes reached the island during or after the attack. At 0615 carrier *Enterprise* launched 18 Douglas SBD dive bombers. These planes flew into the middle of the attack. Six SBDs were shot down (five by the Japanese, one by army gunners); eight more Americans died. In the evening, jittery gunners shot down four of six *Enterprise* Wildcat fighters trying to land on Ford Island. Three pilots perished.

Twelve B-17s also flew into war. (In a great stroke of luck for the Japanese, the approach of this flight toward the Opana radar tracked along the same general bearing of the first wave.) None carried ammunition because they loaded extra gasoline for the 2,000-mile flight from California. Considering their situation, the crews did very well. They largely evaded the attackers and found refuge at various fields around the island. Only one Fortress was destroyed after landing at Hickam, and a second was cannibalized for spare parts.

"Air Raid, Pearl Harbor, This Is No Drill"

While other Japanese flyers commenced pummeling American air installations, eighty-nine "Kates" lagged behind by several minutes as they traced longer approach routes to the primary targets: the battleships of the Pacific Fleet. The deadliest punch of forty "Kates" toting torpedoes divided into two units. Twenty-four aircraft from *Akagi* and *Kaga* circled west as they lunged down to make runs at "Battleship Row" along the southern side of Ford Island in the center of Pearl Harbor. Sixteen "Kates" from *Hiryū* and *Sōryū* circled east before banking and descending to make runs on the berths normally occupied by carriers on the north side of Ford Island.

The demanding very low (about 60 feet) and very slow (about 140–150 knots) flight profile for a successful torpedo drop in Pearl Harbor taxed each pilot's skill to the maximum. After being buffeted by updrafts over land and buildings, every plane had to dip down abruptly over the water for a mere fifteen-second run. Each pilot stuck his head out of the cockpit to gauge his distance above the harbor in comparison to his wingspan. He could neither watch his airspeed and altitude instruments nor keep a steady eye on his target. These demands left scant opportunity to assess the success of earlier planes and resulted in overconcentration at the two most obvious targets: the battleships *Oklahoma* and *West Virginia*. Meanwhile, the forty-nine "Kate" horizontal bombers swept westward and shuffled into a sequence of five-plane "V" formations to attack American battleships.

Before the torpedo planes released their deadly cargoes, nine *Shōkaku* "Vals" heralded the attack with bombs that erupted on the seaplane slips on Ford Island. Amazingly, the first bomb at 0755 entirely missed Ford Island,

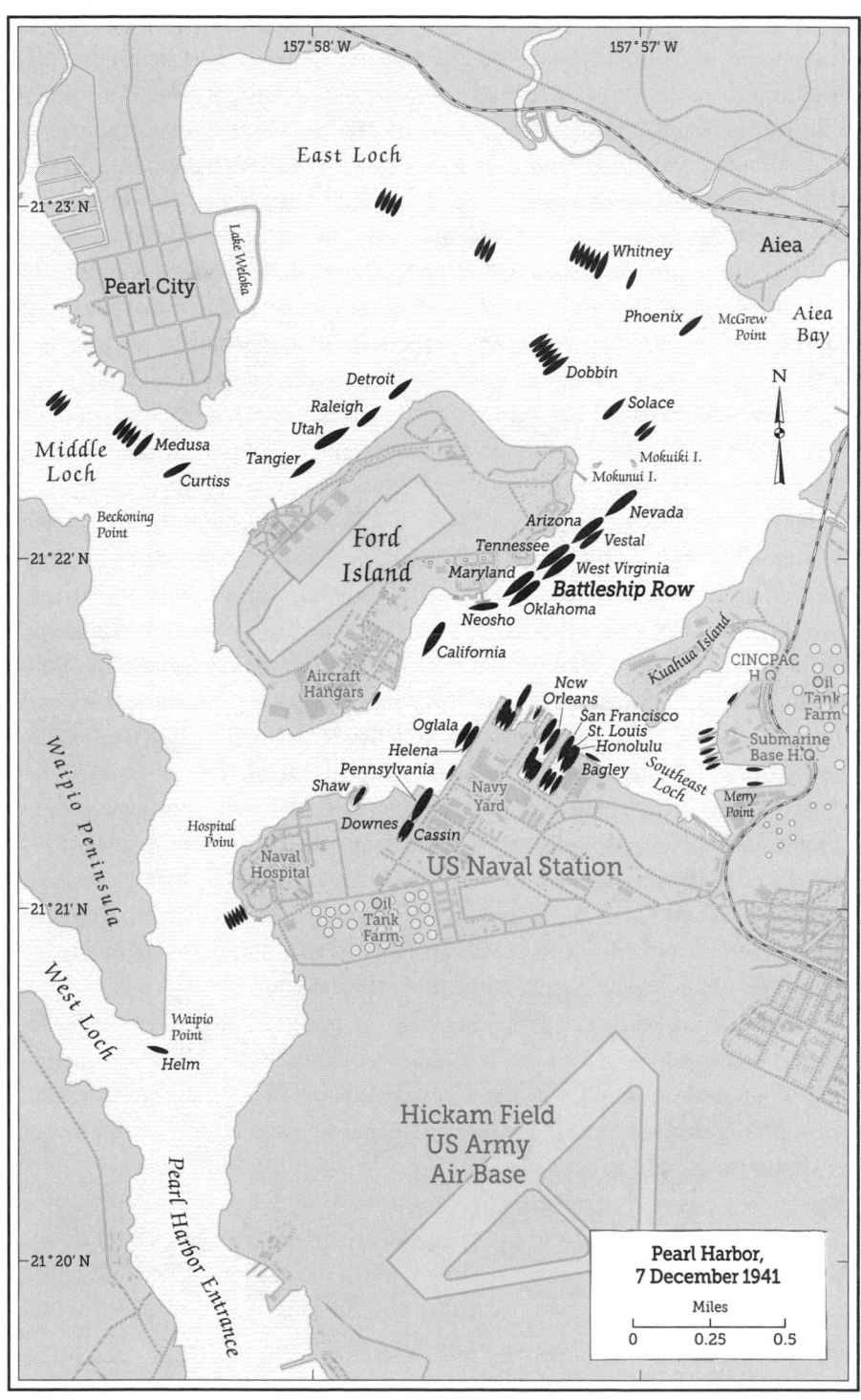

157° 58' W   157° 57' W

East Loch

21° 23' N

Lake Weloha

Pearl City

Whitney   Aiea

Phoenix   McGrew   Aiea
               Point   Bay

Detroit   Dobbin

Raleigh   Solace

Utah   Mokuiki I.
Tangier   Mokunui I.

Middle   Medusa
Loch
        Curtiss

Beckoning   Arizona   Nevada
Point
21° 22' N   Ford   Tennessee   Vestal
                 Island   Maryland   West Virginia
                                    Battleship Row
                          Neosho   Oklahoma
                                           Kuahua Island
                     California   CINCPAC
                                                       H.Q.   Oil
                     Aircraft   Tank
                     Hangars   Farm
                                    New   Submarine
                                    Orleans   Base H.Q.
                          Oglala   San Francisco
                                   St. Louis
                          Helena   Honolulu   Southeast
                       Pennsylvania   Bagley   Loch
Waipio Peninsula Shaw   Merry
                          Downes   Navy   Point
              Hospital   Yard
              Point   Cassin
                     Naval
                     Hospital   **US Naval Station**

21° 21' N
                  Oil
                  Tank
                  Farm

West Loch

              Waipio
              Point
               Helm

                     Hickam Field
                     US Army
                     Air Base

Pearl Harbor Entrance

21° 20' N

**Pearl Harbor,
7 December 1941**

Miles

0   0.25   0.5

but subsequent bombs blasted a hangar and ignited fires. All over the area, Americans who initially assessed the swooping planes as friendly aircraft conducting exercises, suddenly grasped the abrupt end of peace. Within a minute, Cdr. Logan Ramsey on Ford Island ordered a radio message that electrified the navy and the nation: "AIR RAID, PEARL HARBOR, THIS IS NO DRILL." The Japanese airmen either destroyed or damaged every one of the twenty-six PBYs present on Ford Island as well as two utility aircraft.

Just behind the spearhead "Vals" charged sixteen *Hiryū* and *Sōryū* "Kates" at low level led by *Hiryū*'s Lt. Hirata Matsumara. Arranged in a row from east to west were old light cruisers *Detroit* and *Raleigh*, target ship *Utah*, and seaplane tender *Tangier*. Sun glare baffled Matsumara's attempts at target identification, and six of his eight planes became separated in a turn. Meanwhile the eight *Sōryū* planes continued on toward their designated targets along Ford Island's northern moorings.

Four *Sōryū* "Kates" aimed at *Utah*, a former battleship commissioned in August 1911, but since 1932 rebuilt without main armament as a radio-controlled gunnery practice target. Just barely one minute into the attack, two torpedoes speared *Utah* on its port side, causing catastrophic flooding. It pitched over to port in an unstoppable roll until it was capsized. Capt. Robert B. Simons of *Raleigh* could see the heavy six-by-twelve-inch timbers laid over *Utah*'s guns to protect them from practice bombs rolling down onto "the unfortunate members of her crew as they came up the hatches." Chief Water Tender Peter Tomich, one of the first great heroes of this day, stayed to secure *Utah*'s boilers from explosion to save his shipmates at the certain cost of his life. Later in the day, a party cut a hole in its overturned hull and extracted Fireman Second Class John B. Vaessen. Having just been freed from his tomb, Vaessen took one deep breath and then climbed back inside in a futile search for other survivors. Sixty-four men perished on *Utah*.

A torpedo hit *Raleigh* at 0755, knocking out power. It heeled over radically to port and hung poised to capsize. Except for gun crews, all hands turned to jettison topside weights by hand power. Just before 0900 a bomb knifed through the ship—missing one man by inches and slicing within ten feet of tanks housing 3,500 gallons of aviation gasoline—to explode outside the ship. *Raleigh* warned of its extremely precarious stability when it suddenly rolled from eleven degrees to port to eight degrees to starboard. Desperate measures kept it upright, and more amazing still, none of its crew was killed and only a few sustained injury. Luck smiled on *Detroit* and *Tangier*. One torpedo missed *Detroit* astern by about ten yards while *Tangier* was untouched.

The leader of *Sōryū*'s "Kates" recognized the ships looming before him on the north side of Ford Island as lesser prey, so he banked around the south side of Ford Island and then aimed at the berth that normally secured the fleet flagship, but which was now occupied by light cruiser *Helena*, with the aged minelayer *Oglala* tied to its outboard starboard side. The confusing silhouette of the two ships convinced the attacker they were a battleship. The torpedo ran under *Oglala* to rip a hole in *Helena* at 0757. The blast, however, pried apart seams in *Oglala's* weary hull structure. Flooding could not be checked and it lost power. (A mount captain on *Helena* asked the bridge watch on *Oglala* to clear out as he intended to fire *through Oglala* at Japanese planes. They complied.) About two hours after the hit, *Oglala* capsized.

The frightening predicament of a group of *Helena* sailors in its forward boiler room illustrates the distinctive feature of modern naval warfare: a majority of crewmen sealed in an interior compartment enjoyed no direct sensory perception of the combat around them. The torpedo struck just aft of the forward boiler room. Light and power instantly failed, pitching the men in this compartment below the water line into absolute darkness accompanied by the sounds of inrushing water through a ruptured bulkhead. As if this were not terrifying enough, a raucous horn blared a frantic warning that they were in imminent danger of being scalded to death by superheated steam from the boilers. Nonetheless, intelligent discipline (and courage) kept these men in the compartment methodically seeking to remedy the situation until they were evacuated when water reached chest depth.

"Battleship Row"

In the absence of their foremost target—the American carriers—the Japanese aviators switched to their secondary goal: sink or disable the American battleships in "Battleship Row" on the south side of Ford Island. This was the primary objective of twenty-four "Kate" torpedo bombers under Lieutenant Commander Murata from *Akagi* and *Kaga* and forty-nine "Kate" level bombers under Fuchida from *Akagi*, *Kaga*, *Hiryū*, and *Sōryū*. The long column of *Akagi* and *Kaga* "Kates" grew disordered; Murata himself became detached from the following planes and the *Hiryū* and *Sōryū* interlopers bashed through the larger formation, exacerbating the disorder. By Japanese timepieces, the torpedo plane runs began at 0758 and took about ten minutes. The Japanese claimed that twenty-nine aircraft scored twenty-three torpedo hits along "Battleship Row." They certainly scored no fewer than fifteen at the cost of five of their number.

California, the flagship of Vice Adm. William S. Pye, commander, Battle Force, Pacific Fleet, was at the head of the moored column. For purposes of a planned inspection to check for fuel leaks, access to ten voids on the port side was open, compromising *California*'s watertight integrity.* Within the first five minutes after the attack began, two torpedoes struck *California* almost simultaneously, one forward and one aft. The hits stilled the ship's power plant. Unorthodox countermeasures orchestrated by Ens. Edgar Fain arrested *California* from capsizing. A bomb struck the ship at about 0900 and exploded below the bridge structure on the second deck; another near-miss bomb off the port bow aggravated the flooding challenge. As if these hazards were not enough, flaming oil floating on the harbor surface surged down and threatened to envelop the ship. Altogether, the punishment inflicted by the Japanese killed ninety-eight *California* sailors and wounded forty-eight. It took three days for the flooding finally to run its course and sink *California* to the harbor floor.

Fleet oiler *Neosho* was moored between *California* and the next pair of American battleships, *Oklahoma* and *Maryland*. In a lucky stroke, *Neosho* had finished discharging the last of its extremely volatile cargo of aviation gasoline into tanks on Ford Island at 0750, about five minutes before the attack began. If *Neosho* had been hit while still burdened with this cargo, the effects might have been catastrophic for one or more battleships. To get out of what its log described as the "focal point" of the attack and to clear a path for *Maryland*, it got under way at 0842 and headed over to a berth near the submarine base.

Oklahoma had commenced the same sort of inner bottom inspection as *California* the prior day, thus likewise compromising its watertight integrity— but no ship of its size could have survived the horrific devastation of at least five torpedo hits on its exposed port side within the first few minutes of the attack. *Oklahoma*'s 32,000-ton hull first rocked from side to side from the repeated blast of Japanese explosives and then began to twist to port. Water surged into its compartments through gashes bored by torpedo warheads knocking out power to the pumps. As the decks dipped into the harbor, water

---

* Like other late World War I–era American battleships, *California*'s protective system against underwater damage comprised a "sandwich" arrangement of four separate longitudinal bulkheads running from nearly bow to stern from the outer hull plates inboard. These in turn were divided by athwart ship bulkheads into a series of compartments. By filling some of these compartments with fuel and leaving others empty, the system would dissipate the effects of an explosion and control flooding. But in this case, the plates over the access holes into some of these compartments were off, thus permitting the flow of water.

began to smash down from overhead via hatches, portholes, access trunks, shafts, and ventilators.

As he struggled to his battle station in the aftermost main battery turret, Seaman Steven B. Young recalled, "I saw the faces of my shipmates, frightened, anxious, unbelieving." Their ears heard "the roar of the water invading the ship [that] drowned out the cries of the sailors as it engulfed them." In the two forward main battery turrets a sailor and an officer respectively sacrificed their lives holding flashlights that illuminated the only escape hatch for their shipmates, but in Young's turret, the officer in charge left his post without ordering his men out.

To counter the ever-increasing list, sailors gripped everything in sight to remain upright. But gear and equipment secured for ordinary purposes burst restraints and careened down, knocking countless crewmen into the liquid abyss from which there was no return. In the final moments of this horror, objects as huge as the 14-inch shells (each weighing about 1,500 pounds) slipped their holdfasts to crush screaming men. Within at most ten minutes of the first hit, *Oklahoma* canted over sharply to port and kept right on going until its masts dug into the harbor bottom, leaving only *Oklahoma*'s starboard bilge and a single forlorn propeller thrust skyward above the water like an askew cross over the graves of 415 men.

In the midst of the continuing attack, officers and men from *Oklahoma* and the repair ship *Argonne* began frantic rescue work. Tapping established the location of men trapped in air pockets, and cutting equipment was deployed to slice into the overturned hull. In this manner, thirty-two men, including Steven Young, were plucked from certain death.

On battleship *Maryland*, moored inboard of *Oklahoma*, Seaman Leslie V. Short was writing letters and Christmas cards by the forward machine-gun group when he glanced up and saw attacking planes. He leaped into action, loading and then firing a .50 caliber machine gun, and brought down one of the torpedo plane attackers. *Maryland*'s position masked it from Japanese torpedoes, but not bombs. At about 0909, one bomb hit forward, killing four men and wounding fourteen while fragments from another three bombs punctured *Maryland*'s stem.

Next astern of *Oklahoma* and *Maryland* were *West Virginia* and (inboard) *Tennessee*. Two bombs from "Kates" struck *Tennessee*. One exploded on a gun barrel from the forward main battery turret II while the second penetrated the roof armor of after turret III. Both detonations were of low order. Together they killed only four *Tennessee* sailors and wounded twenty-three, but a fragment gutted *West Virginia*'s Capt. Mervyn S. Bennion. *West Virginia*'s sunken hull pinned it to its moorings, but *Tennessee* kept its screws turning over with revolutions for ten knots to help push away blazing oil.

Mixed fortunes marked *West Virginia*'s fate. The first bomb explosion occurred along the sight line from *West Virginia* toward *California* and was mistaken for an explosion on the latter. The order rang out "Away Fire and Rescue Party." This alarm started crewmen boiling up from lower decks to topside, saving many lives. Within the initial minutes of the attack, the first pair of seven torpedoes slammed into *West Virginia*, transmitting heavy shocks through its 33,000-ton hull. *West Virginia* tilted over to port with alarming speed.

Courage, discipline, and above all ingenuity saved *West Virginia* from sharing *Oklahoma*'s fate. Lt. Cdr. John D. Harper, the damage control officer, scrambled down to his post in Central Station—deep below the waterline in a ship with an already fearful list. As Harper rallied the effort to save the ship, men covered with water and oil from rapidly filling compartments forward began to enter Central Station through the starboard (uphill) door. Meanwhile, other desperate shipmates seeking salvation pounded on the port (downhill) sealed access door. Harper urged these men to try to go around to starboard, but ordered that door remain closed. None of these men survived. Water soon gushed into Central Station and Harper ordered everyone out, save himself and one coolheaded enlisted communicator. This pair only left when the water was nearly six feet deep.

Without coordinated direction to save the ship, *West Virginia*'s prospects looked bleak. But Lt. Claude V. Ricketts took matters into his own hands. In one of the most inspiring stories of a day that produced many, Ricketts (who seemed to be everywhere at once) instigated an unorthodox counterflooding campaign, enlisting valorous shipmates to clamber along listing decks and open valves to fill starboard side voids to counterbalance the port list. These efforts prevented capsizing.

Fire added to the perils of flood. Blazing oil from *Arizona* and flames from a bomb hit set *West Virginia* alight along a large part of its length. Crewmen mounted sedulous efforts to check the flames. On the bridge, Captain Bennion lay dying of severe abdominal wounds. To the very end, he thought only of his ship and his men. When raging fires surrounded the bridge, Bennion urged the officers and men maintaining a devoted vigil over their fallen leader, including Ricketts and Mess Attendant Doris Miller (the first African American hero of the war), to save themselves. They refused to leave their gallant captain, who expired before the senior surviving officer gave the order to abandon ship.

Arizona was next astern of *Tennessee* and *West Virginia* with the repair ship *Vestal* moored outboard on its port side. Two five-plane flights of "Kates" scored four direct hits and two near misses. (One of the near misses off the port bow gave rise to the mistaken belief that *Arizona* was torpedoed.) Ens. Guy S. Flanagan Jr. recorded the effect of one nearby bomb hit below decks: a "whish with a gust of hot air and sparks flew" followed by "very nauseating gas and smoke."

Cdr. Erick V. Hakansson, a navy doctor aboard hospital ship *Solace*, dashed out on its stern with a movie camera in hand. He focused the camera on the starboard side of *Arizona*, roughly six hundred yards away. Hakansson triggered his camera and captured a sequence that would become the most horrifying image of the attack. It commenced about one-half second after a bomb hit around *Arizona*'s two forward main battery turrets. An intense fire flared up, engulfing the ship as far aft as the mainmast. Just short of seven seconds later, a stupendous explosion erupted. A pulsing fireball jetted skyward with a halo of smoke that instantly transformed from black to white, a certain sign that the explosion represented the detonation of *Arizona*'s forward magazines. The mainmast pitched forward, not because of direct damage, but because the forward half of the ship was shattered.

These few inches of celluloid became the iconic image of the Pearl Harbor attack, replayed times beyond counting in future decades. But there is a twist. The film was first printed reversed (i.e., as though it was taken from *Arizona*'s port side), so the picture imprinted in millions of minds is a mirror image of what Hakansson witnessed. There was a hideous element to the moment the film could not transmit. "I was conscious of a sweetish, sickening smell to the flame," stated one of *Arizona*'s survivors, stopping short of admitting that this was the odor of seared flesh.

The catastrophic structural devastation of the forward part of the ship obliterated evidence of the exact cause. The most likely explanation for its loss is that one of the 16.1-inch shells converted to a bomb dropped by a *Hiryū* "Kate" sliced through *Arizona*'s armored deck to touch off its magazines.[*]

---

[*] A second theory on the cause of the loss of *Arizona* starts from the fact that between its two forward main battery turrets below the armored deck was a compartment with 1,075 pounds of black powder used only for its ceremonial saluting guns in peacetime. Unlike the "smokeless" powder propellant for *Arizona*'s fourteen-inch guns, which is hard to ignite for safety considerations, black powder is notoriously volatile. In this rival theory, a *Hiryū* bomb ignited a fire that reached down through an unsecured hatch directly over the black powder magazine. The detonation of the black powder magazine ignited the smokeless powder magazines, causing the catastrophic explosion. This second theory reflected the unwillingness of officials involved in the *Arizona*'s design to admit that a Japanese bomb defeated its armored deck, though that is far more likely than not.

The human devastation was also catastrophic. Deaths on *Arizona* totaled 1,177 of a complement of 1,514, or 77.7 percent. These included one or both of thirty-five of thirty-six sets of brothers and one father and son. The blast killed Capt. Franklin Van Valkenburgh, the ship's commander, and Rear Adm. Isaac C. Kidd, the commander of Battleship Division One. Of Kidd, all that was found was his Naval Academy ring fused to the conning tower. There were just 337 survivors, including those ashore at the time of the attack. Two bombs aimed at *Arizona* instead hit repair ship *Vestal*, and *Arizona*'s thunderous destruction ignited fires. *Vestal* got under way and beached herself to prevent sinking.

Nevada's position as the last ship in "Battleship Row" spared it the attention of most Japanese aircraft in the initial attack. It did sustain a torpedo hit on the port bow, but it got under way at 0840 after Chief Boatswain Mate Edwin J. Hill cast off its lines and swam back to the ship. The sight of *Nevada*—wreathed in smoke, its superstructure spurting flashes of flame as its antiaircraft guns blazed—standing out past its moored or sinking sisters, lifted the spirits of all hands who saw it.

Nevada's gallant sally coincided with the arrival of the second wave attack. When the seventy-eight "Vals" of this wave arrived over Pearl Harbor, they were greeted by what the aircrew described as the most ferocious antiaircraft barrage they had ever seen. That fire shot down no fewer than fourteen "Vals" and damaged a like number so badly that they had to be jettisoned on return (a 36 percent overall loss rate). Further, low clouds and massive globs of drifting smoke from damaged ships and blazing airfields not only blanketed many vessels from view or prompted misidentification of targets, but also arranged a curtain midway between the pushover point and the target, often negating standard dive attacks.

Twenty-three *Kaga* "Vals" assailed *Nevada*, hoping to sink it and block the channel. Five bombs churned *Nevada*'s once smart forecastle into contorted wood and ruptured metal and killed the gallant Hill, while hits around its superstructure burnt out the bridge area. *Nevada* did not come to ultimate grief from Japanese hits but from a combination of the poor material condition of an old ship, a circulation system of flawed design, and a huge damage-control mistake when an order to flood the forward magazines was incorrectly understood to include flooding the after magazines. This combination compelled its beaching to prevent sinking.

To the south of "Battleship Row," across a channel, lay the Pearl Harbor Navy Yard packed with ships undergoing updating and repairs. Pacific

Fleet flagship battleship *Pennsylvania* rested in dry dock; just ahead of it sat destroyer *Downes* with destroyer *Cassin* to port. Around 0900, "Vals" attacked this trio. Three bombs hit *Downes*. Soon after the last man left, a torpedo tube mount blew up with a "terrific explosion." *Cassin* rolled to starboard into *Downes*. Another bomb exploded in a secondary battery casemate on *Pennsylvania*. In an ill-considered attempt to combat the flames on the destroyers, the dock was flooded but the oil-fueled conflagration just rose with the water level. Dive bombers hit destroyer *Shaw* in a floating dry dock nearby with three bombs. Its forward magazines erupted in a spectacular explosion that sank the ship and the floating dry dock and became one of the famous images of the attack.

Elsewhere in the Navy Yard were three cruisers, seven destroyer types, and two auxiliary vessels. These ships plus destroyer *Bagley*, four submarines in the submarine base, and five more auxiliary vessels to the south and east were perched directly athwart the approach path of the main Japanese "Battleship Row" torpedo plane attack. Their fire, mainly by machine guns and small arms, with some assistance from the battleships, knocked down five of the last seven attacking torpedo planes. This record strongly suggests that had all these vessels been at General Quarters at the onset of the attack, they might have exacted terrific execution among the "Kates" and sharply reduced the number of battleship torpedo hits. Cruiser *New Orleans* contributed to American folklore as its Chaplain, Howell M. Forgy, coached crewmen to "praise the Lord and pass the ammunition," a phrase later set to music in a popular song.

In an arc from northeast to northwest of Ford Island were moored seven nests of destroyer types with two tenders, as well as four other singly moored ships. Destroyer *Monaghan* got under way and headed down the channel north of Ford Island. *Monaghan* noted seaplane tender *Curtiss* hoisting signal flags to warn of a submarine. *Curtiss* and two other vessels provided an exclamation point to this warning with gunfire at the midget submarine, which retaliated with a torpedo that missed *Monaghan*. In a tricky bit of seamanship, *Monaghan* rang up flank speed to ram the submarine. *Monaghan* gave a slight tremor as it passed over the submarine. Alert crewmen released two depth charges set for a depth of only thirty feet that blasted the submarine partly to the surface—to the frantic cheers of *Curtiss* sailors. *Monaghan*'s lunge caused it to embrace momentarily a derrick barge, but it promptly disentangled itself and headed out to sea.

At 0905 antiaircraft fire from *Curtiss* crippled a "Val" pulling out of a dive on Ford Island. The plane turned to plunge down and crashed into *Curtiss*, igniting a serious fire. Seven minutes later, one of four bombs aimed at *Curtiss* exploded in the hangar. Its crew subdued the fires, but it suffered sixty-nine dead or missing and thirty-three wounded.

The destroyers and their tenders attracted relatively little Japanese attention. Most of these smaller vessels concentrated on getting under way, a task much easier for them than for larger types. Destroyer *Aylwin* stood out under command of the senior officers aboard—a quartet of ensigns. Likewise, another ensign took command of *Blue* and cleared it past the harbor entrance at twenty-five knots.

The Accounting

The Japanese attack achieved tremendous tactical success. They sank four battleships (*California, Oklahoma, West Virginia,* and *Arizona*), seriously damaged one (*Nevada*), and inflicted minor damage on three (*Maryland, Tennessee,* and *Pennsylvania*). Two cruisers were seriously damaged (*Raleigh* and *Helena*), and three destroyers (*Shaw, Cassin,* and *Downes*) and an elderly minelayer (*Oglala*) were sunk.

The exact number of American aircraft losses that day remains unsettled. While aircraft totally destroyed can be fixed with accuracy, there remain lingering problems with the number of aircraft damaged but ultimately scrapped. Given these challenges, a reasonable total is eighty-seven navy (thirteen fighters, twenty-one dive bombers, forty-six patrol and reconnaissance planes, two transports, and five others) and seventy-seven army (four B-17s, twelve B-18s, two A-20s, thirty-two P-40s, twenty P-36s, four P-26s, and three others). To this total of 164 planes on Oahu should be added ten *Enterprise* planes, making a grand total of 174.

American casualties on 7 December 1941 were:

	KILLED, MISSING, AND DIED OF WOUNDS	WOUNDED
Navy	2,008	710
Marine Corps	109	69
Army	218	364
Civilians	68	35
Total	2,403	1,178

This was the highest single-day fatality total for American forces in the entire war.* On the other hand, because all the ships sunk were in harbor, a far higher proportion of crewmen survived than would have been the case on the open sea. Those well-trained sailors provided the backbone of the fleet that won key battles in 1942 and stiffened crews in later campaigns.

As best could be calculated, the Pacific Fleet fired 6,143 shells and 272,556 rounds of smaller caliber fire at the attackers. Destroyer *Dale* reported that once outside harbor it observed a large number of splashes which represented 5-inch antiaircraft shells whose fuses were improperly cut and did not function. At a hospital, one reporter saw the body of a "little girl in a red sweater, barefoot, still clutch[ing] a piece of jump-rope in her hand." This small child, like the great majority of the civilian casualties, was likely killed by such errant missiles.

In achieving these results, the Japanese lost twenty-nine planes (with fifty-five aircrew killed) and five midget submarines with nine crewmen killed. One marker of American response was that the first wave lost only nine planes (5 percent) while the second wave lost twenty (12 percent). Indeed, the heavy losses among the last of the torpedo planes to attack "Battleship Row" and among the second wave powerfully suggest that with a twenty- to-forty-minute tactical warning for the defenders, the effectiveness of the Japanese attack would have been attenuated and the cost steep. About fifteen returning planes were so damaged that they were jettisoned, and two were ditched.

One peculiar aspect of the official Japanese depiction of the attack was that the crews of the five lost midget submarines became the objects of cult status, not the aviators who did all the damage. An instantly famous portrait with the faces of the nine dead midget submarine crewmen over a picture of Pearl Harbor became a decoration in many homes. An awkward fact was that the face of one of the ten crewmen was absent. Ens. Kazuo Sakamaki became the first Japanese serviceman taken prisoner by the United States.

---

* The only other day that American losses potentially could have exceeded this toll was 6 June 1944 at the Normandy landings. Joseph Balkowski, an outstanding American scholar of this day, advised the author that it never proved possible to total American losses definitively. A great many men were carried as "missing," and it would require scrutiny of literally thousands of "morning report" entries of small units over about a three-month span to settle the final status of all of the "missing." Nevertheless, based on his in-depth work in the records, even allowing generously for potential fatalities among the "missing," it seems very likely that the final toll of D-Day would have fallen short by several hundred of the death count at Pearl Harbor. Emails Balkowski to author, 4 and 6 May 2016.

From a rigorous tactical standpoint, the attack had some conspicuous shortfalls. The overwhelming majority of the damage to ships was inflicted in the first ten to twelve minutes of the attack—all the battleships lost were hit in this span, though the story of *Nevada* required further twists. Thereafter, the accuracy of Japanese bombing fell off markedly, especially among the second wave "Vals," due to vigorous antiaircraft fire and massive smoke and cloud target obscuration. Thanks in large part to Short's orders to group his planes closely, the Japanese achieved an extraordinary degree of success against American aircraft, though mostly in the first wave. While Japanese aerial torpedoes worked brilliantly, both the converted 16.1-inch shells used as armor-piercing bombs and the 551-pound bombs fitted to the "Vals" displayed a damningly high rate of failure and low order detonation.

Little remarked upon for years was the overall failure of the large submarine force deployed to support the attack. The only notable achievements occurred over a month after the attack: *I-6* damaged carrier *Saratoga* on 11 January 1942 with a torpedo that kept the carrier out of action until June, and *I-172* sank the oiler *Neches* on 23 January, which aborted a planned US carrier raid on Wake Island. The Japanese submarine force managed to sink only seven merchant vessels in the vicinity of Hawaii and two on the American West Coast. On 10 December, carrier planes from *Enterprise* sank *I-70* with its crew of 93. The returning Japanese skippers faced accusations of cowardice.

Starting from a few days after the attack and later enshrined in Samuel Eliot Morison's influential postwar history, American naval officers asserted that the attack might have inflicted even more long-term damage had the Japanese launched a third attack wave directed at the vulnerable fuel tanks and ship repair installations. They argued that loss of fuel stores and repair capacity would have set back the American position in the Pacific much longer than the damage to ships and loss of aircraft. The so-called "third strike thesis" achieved status as a fixture in Pearl Harbor accounts. But it is a myth.

The first set of issues concerning the "third strike" involves practical realities. Nagumo's orders allowed for the possibility of a "third strike," but dictated target priorities that did not include oil tanks or repair installations. No formal contingency plan existed for such a strike. The extremely narrow fuel margins in the Striking Force, especially for destroyers, meant the "third strike" had to be launched on 7 December or not at all. Otherwise, the Striking Force could not renew its attack until it had expended four or more days in refueling, by which time the defenses would be strengthened and alert.

The exact number of aircraft the Striking Force could have launched on a "third strike" on 7 December remains unsettled because Japanese records lack clarity on the damaged aircraft that could have been readied for another sortie that day. A reasonable estimate by historian H. P. Willmott is that 235 aircraft from the first two waves would have been available (111 "Kates," 68 "Vals," 56 Zeros). This is 77 percent of the "Kates" but only 53 percent of the "Vals." The "Val" dive bombers represented the key element of a third attack, as only they could be expected to hit precision targets like machine shops. Moreover, the Japanese certainly would have retained half or more of the remaining "Kates" and "Vals" to search for and possibly attack the missing American carriers.

But the available daylight makes these other calculations moot. Each strike consumed about four hours from launch to recovery. At best, it would require between two and three hours to formulate and issue a plan for a "third strike" as well as concurrently to repair, refuel, and rearm aircraft. At the very best, this means no launch of a third strike before 1415 with a more likely time of about 1500. This translates into recovery between 1815 and 1900. But sunset on 7 December 1941 occurred at 1712, and the last trace of the horizon disappeared at the end of nautical twilight at 1805. Thus, the "third strike" would have had to land in darkness. This factor alone would render the whole concept infeasible.

The Inquisitional Innings

One metric of the shock of Pearl Harbor is that it triggered no fewer than ten investigations spread over fifty-four years (1941–1995). Secretary of the Navy Frank Knox initiated this parade with a 9–14 December 1941 inspection trip. He reported that Admiral Kimmel and General Short

> admitted that they did not expect [the air attack] and had taken no adequate measures to meet one if it came. Both Kimmel and Short evidently regarded an air attack as extremely unlikely. . . . Both felt that if any surprise attack was attempted it would be in the Far East.

His critique prompted President Roosevelt to relieve Kimmel and Short, effective 17 December, and to appoint Supreme Court Associate Justice Owen J. Roberts to head a panel with two army and two navy flag officers. Roosevelt's charter dictated only two choices to them: did the disaster stem from dereliction of duty or errors of judgment. The panel immediately compromised its independence by meeting informally and deferentially with Stimson and

Knox and others in Washington, despite the manifest issue of what role these parties played in the matter. As Roberts later acknowledged, with these figures they confined their examination to the narrow issue of whether Washington issued "war warnings" to Hawaii. In Hawaii, after assuring Kimmel and Short that they were not targets, the panel donned inquisitional robes and trampled on elemental principles of due process. The White House publicly released the panel's grossly skewed report in late January 1942. It found Kimmel and Short guilty of the extremely onerous charge of "dereliction of duty" and placed virtually all blame on their shoulders.

During the war, the navy and the army each commissioned three investigations. These inquiries spread the blame far beyond—and above—Short and Kimmel. The public learned of none of these, however, so the Roberts Commission report remained the definitive official statement. In a display of patriotic self-abnegation, Kimmel and Short deferred their right to demand a court-martial since the proceedings were certain to get into matters like radio intelligence that had to remain secret. With the end of the war, the Congress, though controlled by Democrats, bowed to tremendous public pressure to probe the disaster. A bipartisan Joint Congressional Committee conducted a stunningly open investigation between 15 November 1945 and 23 May 1946. Among the key findings of the committee was that Kimmel and Short made "errors of judgment" but were not guilty of "dereliction of duty."

In 1995 an effort by the families to permit the posthumous restoration of the highest held ranks of Kimmel and Short, as was done for other senior officers relieved of their commands, prompted yet another review. This review became known as the Dorn Report, after Assistant Secretary of Defense Edwin Dorn, who oversaw the effort. In important aspects this inquiry easily surpassed what had gone before in terms of a clear-eyed look at many facets of Pearl Harbor, particularly failures in Washington. The Dorn Report did find that, notwithstanding a far more widespread sharing of errors, restoration of rank for Kimmel and Short was not an appropriate remedy.

Washington, DC, 7–8 December 1941

"Navy is Superior to Any, Says Knox," announced the front-page headline of the 7 December 1941 edition of the *New York Times*, quoting from the secretary of the navy's just released annual report. Elsewhere, a *Times* correspondent in Tokyo described how "a great majority of the [Japanese] still instinctively refuse to believe" a war with the United States was possible. While their economy appeared to be booming, each day a "white brigade" of wounded soldiers in hospital garb exercised in Hibiya Park next to the Imperial Palace, a mournful reminder of the unending war in China.

The front-page headline that same morning in the *Washington Post* exclaimed: "Roosevelt Appeals Direct to Emperor As Japan Masses More Men, Proclaims Crisis Is At Hand." The *Post* demoted Knox's report to page 20, but plucked from it the quote: "The American people may feel fully confident in their Navy." A *Post* columnist pronounced: "At the moment this is written we are extremely close to war with Japan." In contrast to this anecdotal impression of Japanese public opinion in the *Times*, a Gallup poll that closed on 6 December 1941 asked a representative sample of Americans: "Do you think the U.S. will go to war with Japan in the near future?" Fifty-two percent of the respondents said yes, 27 percent said no, and 21 percent declined to answer.

After weeks of beguilingly mild and sunny weather that seemed to refute the approach of winter, the "near future" of 7 December in Washington broke wintry and windy with temperatures straining to ascend from 32 to 43 degrees Fahrenheit. The downtown streets at midday remained "unusually bare" of traffic, with "the usual lines in front of the big motion picture houses . . . shriveled to scant dozens of youths and maidens and their elders," with the breeze whipping overcoats and skirts in swirls.

After sessions that morning with his physician and the Chinese ambassador Dr. Shi Hu, President Roosevelt ate lunch in the Oval Office with Harry Hopkins. Their conversation rambled over "things far removed from war" when the phone rang at 1340 (1:40 p.m.)—twenty-five minutes or less after the first bomb fell in Hawaii. It was Knox, who announced word of an attack on Pearl Harbor. An incredulous Hopkins thought "there must be some mistake . . . surely Japan would not attack in Honolulu." Roosevelt, however, immediately credited the report as true, for it was "just the kind of unexpected thing the Japanese would do and that at the very time they were discussing peace in the Pacific they were plotting to overthrow it."

Nomura and Kurusu arrived at the State Department at 1405 (2:05 p.m.). Under Roosevelt's instructions not to reveal knowledge of the attack, Hull received them at 1420 (2:20 p.m.). The secretary did not ask them to sit. Nomura apologized for their tardiness. He explained his government had ordered him to deliver the message at 1:00 p.m.—why, his government had not explained—but decoding the cable caused the delay. Although Hull already knew the contents of the memorandum, he proceeded to adjust his black-ribboned pince-nez and read it as though for the first time. Then he looked to the Japanese representatives and, according to his aide, said:

> In all my 50 years of public service I have never seen a document that was more crowded with infamous falsehoods and distortions—infamous falsehoods and distortion on a scale so huge that I never imagined until today that any Government on this planet was capable of uttering them.

Alistair Cooke, then a rising reporter for the British Broadcasting Corporation, knew Hull well and demurred with this official version as a "pale, formal paraphrase of the Secretary's words." Cooke earnestly lamented the loss of Hull's actual "abusive idiom, deriving half from animal biology, half from the Bible, of which the Tennessee mountaineers need never be ashamed." Hull waved the Japanese representatives out—calling them, as Cooke suspected, "scoundrels and piss-ants"—with no chance to respond.

After 1500 (3:00 p.m.), Hull, Marshall, and other officials gathered in Roosevelt's office. Updates reached them by phone from Stark, whose voice betrayed his "shocked disbelief." Roosevelt's personal secretary, Grace Tully, took the calls and transcribed the messages in shorthand before typing them to hand to the president. "With each new message," Tully recalled, Roosevelt "shook his head grimly and tightened the expression of his mouth."

A graying sun was already sliding down over the Lincoln Memorial when the White House announced the news at 1422 (2:22 p.m.). From there the shattering word flashed to the country's ordinary citizens, initially on home and car radios. A great many Americans, including large numbers who thought themselves "well informed," struggled mentally to locate Pearl Harbor. "A crowd arose as though from the streets in front of the White House as the word got around that Japan had begun shooting in the Pacific," reported the *Washington Post*. "The crowd included men, women and children" but "mostly men with angry faces" who stood shoulder-to-shoulder "studying the high, lighted windows in the White House Executive Offices as though for some sign of what was to come now." People pulled themselves up on the wrought iron fences. Autos went by at "snail's pace with heads thrust from windows." Throngs assembled first on Pennsylvania Avenue, but later a bigger crowd packed into the small street between the White House and the Treasury building. Some held children aloft. There was "a lot of quiet evenly spoken, emphatic and bitter cussing."

Some 27,102 fans assembled to watch the Washington Redskins play football against the Philadelphia Eagles before the news arrived. When word reached the press box, the stadium managers decided not to make a general announcement. Eight minutes into the game, the public address system announcer began calling out by name officers of the armed forces, civilian officials, and eventually reporters and editors, directing each to report to his office. One by one, a contingent of photographers peeled off to other locations like the White House and the Japanese Embassy until only one cameraman remained to cover the final score: Redskins 20, Eagles 14. The next day the sportswriters of the *Washington Post* would use an insouciant sub-headline in coverage of the game: "Japan Kicks Off."

Another crowd, eventually numbering around a thousand, lapped around the white stucco structure housing the Japanese embassy. By 1630 (4:30 p.m.) dense auto traffic drifted by the building. These witnesses could see Japanese officials stacking 145 containers on the embassy grounds and then systematically burning the contents. The crowd remained silent and "the only sound was the whirring of news cameras recording the scene." The *New York Times* advised its readers of information confirming that Ambassadors Nomura and Kurusu were "astounded" by the news. Through the embassy windows they could occasionally be seen sitting "glumly" or glancing out at the crowd.

In Pittsburgh, Pennsylvania, approximately 2,500 people packed into Soldiers and Sailors Memorial Hall to hear America First Committee speakers. Just before Senator Gerald Nye, the featured orator, went on, a journalist informed him of the White House report of an attack on Pearl Harbor. Recalling the early and misleading reports about the *Greer* incident, Nye remained skeptical. But when he finally began his talk about 1700 (5:00 p.m.), another note advised him that Japan had announced it was at war with the United States and Britain. Nye informed the audience of the report and quickly closed what proved to be the very last public meeting of the America First Committee.

"The White House press room already had that air of tobacco-choked energy that is the Washington odor of panic," explained Cooke. "Everybody was smoking, walking nervously around to see how they should adjust to their first world-shaking crisis," as Steve Early, the president's press secretary, disclosed that the president would meet with the cabinet at 2030 (8:30 p.m.) and with congressional leaders a half hour later. By the appointed hour, policemen and soldiers, some nervously clutching submachine guns and rifles, teemed on the White House grounds and around other key government buildings.

Senator W. Lee O'Daniel of Texas contributed inadvertent humor to the otherwise somber proceedings. O'Daniel, better known for his affinity for hillbilly bands and biscuits, appeared uninvited at the White House to try to "learn a few things" and "to make sure Texas is represented at this conference." But the imposing senior senator from Texas, the formidable Tom Connally, chairman of the Foreign Relations Committee, provided the Lone Star State with ample representation. "Professing a desire for peace and under the pretext that she coveted amiable relations with us," intoned Connally to reporters with his customary rhetorical flourish, "Japan stealthily concealed under her robes a dagger of assassination and villainy."

At 2030 (8:30 p.m.), the cabinet formed in a seated semicircle in front of the president's desk in the second-floor Red Room study. Steve Early sat by FDR and handled dispatches that arrived every few minutes. The president "opened by telling us that this was the most serious meeting of the Cabinet that had taken place since 1861," recorded Stimson in his diary, "and then he proceeded to enumerate the blows which had fallen upon us in Hawaii." While "the president was his usual calm self," admitted Attorney General Francis Biddle, "most of us were deeply shocked at the terrific loss." Claude Wickard, the secretary of agriculture, noted that Knox "had lost his air of bravado."

Roosevelt then read his draft message for Congress. Hull protested that "the most important war in 500 years deserved more than a short statement" and asked for an extended recital of the events leading up to the attack. Stimson urged the president to charge that Germany "inspired and planned this whole affair," and to demand a declaration of war against Germany. But Roosevelt disagreed with both his lieutenants and stuck to his terse draft.

When congressional leaders entered, Roosevelt provided a very detailed account of the reports he had received. These described three, possibly four, battleships sunk, two others badly damaged. He added that "casualties, I am sorry to say, were extremely heavy." He studiously fended off questions that invited him to suggest the losses were not heavily one-sided. Stimson observed the tremendous effect of this recital. The congressional leaders "sat in dead silence." The one who found words was Senator Connally, who exploded with thoughts very much abounding in that room and across the nation: "I am amazed at the attack by Japan, but I am still more astounded at what happened to our Navy. They were all asleep. Where were our patrols?" The president had no answer. Primed by radio intelligence but concealing the source, Roosevelt also pointedly advised them: "We have reason to believe that the Germans have told the Japanese that if Japan declares war, they will too." He concluded by cautioning that defeating Japan would not be quick but would require a protracted campaign of "starvation" and "exhaustion."

During the eventful afternoon and evening, the president worked on his message to Congress. The opening line originally read, "Yesterday, December 7, 1941, a date which will live in world history. . . ." With his own hand, he scratched out the last two words and replaced them with one that would make the phrase immortal. Very late that night, Roosevelt shared a dinner of beer and sandwiches with journalist Edward R. Murrow. With a thump of his fist on the table, Roosevelt poured out the humiliation he regarded as most galling of all: "Our planes were destroyed on the ground, by God, on the ground!"

8 December 1941 brought a distinctive sign of the abrupt change in the capital city atmosphere. For generations, active duty officers had worn civilian clothes to work in Washington as one symbol of American abhorrence of large standing military or naval institutions. This morning officers pulled out their uniforms—most stored in camphor acquired from the Japanese colony of Formosa (Taiwan)—and donned them before reporting to work. It was a traditional ritual proclaiming the nation was at war.

The daybreak headline in the *Washington Post* exclaimed: "Japan Declares War Against U.S.; Hawaii Attacked Without Warning With Heavy Loss; Philippines Are Bombed." The featured picture caption read: "Japanese Emissaries Set Fire to Papers in Embassy Gardens." Across the nation, other newspaper headlines on 8 December seethed with outrage. "Strike With All Might," demanded the *Chicago Tribune*, heretofore a bulwark of nonintervention. The *Los Angeles Times* termed the attack the "act of a mad dog." *New York Times* military analyst Hanson Baldwin highlighted a truly fundamental point: the Japanese attack had "merged the Chinese War and European War into a war of the world." The editors of Baldwin's paper classified the Japanese attack as "sublime insanity." But they swiftly added that Japan was the "lesser danger" and "the real battle of our times will not be fought in the Far East. It will be fought on the English Channel." With the defeat of Hitler "the situation in the Far East will take care of itself."

News accounts from Hawaii tilted more to fiction than fact. The attack was said to have included 50 to 150 Japanese planes from a "carrier anchored off Barber's Point." The battleship *Oklahoma*, named in broadcasts from Tokyo and Berlin, was reputedly "set afire by torpedo planes" when it was actually sitting capsized in the mud. Some "witnesses" reported Japanese paratroopers dropped on the island, while others told of gun flashes from a US fleet that had intercepted Japanese carriers. On the West Coast, the FBI and soldiers had rounded up some Japanese citizens and quarantined Japanese fishermen at Terminal Island in Los Angeles harbor. In San Francisco, the Golden Gate Bridge was blacked out, but the nearby San Francisco–Oakland Bridge remained ablaze with light. Amazingly, papers published the first list of service fatalities with fourteen names. Even in disaster, however, commercial instincts remained alert. An ad in the *Times* screamed: "For the Japanese Plan of Attack see pages 468–78 in *That Day Alone* by Pierre Van Paassen, The Dial Press, $3.75 call Murray Hill 5-2776."

Just before noon the big black limousine bearing Roosevelt debouched from the east gate of the White House in a sputter of gravel and merged into the middle of a protective convoy of vehicles. The president rested in the vehicle's deep cushions dressed in a high silk hat and swathed in the long folds of a huge naval boat cloak. Secret Service men in soft hats stood on each running board, while the presidential car was flanked on each side by open-topped escort autos with three Secret Service agents on the running boards on each side with .38 caliber revolvers. Four more agents were clustered inside each escort car, everyone clutching sawed-off riot guns. All eyed the crowds intently. Policemen three hundred–strong formed deep ranks around the capital; Secret Service agents stood on vantage points or roamed the crowds. Marines with fixed bayonets barred entries, turning away idlers and even the wives and children of congressmen who lacked the foresight to realize that on this day a mere verbal vouching as to their identity would not be accepted. It took Senator Connally's personal word to get the bayonets pulled back from in front of the Asian face of the Chinese ambassador, Dr. Shi Hu.

Inside the Capitol building, Roosevelt waited in the Speaker's room. Secretary of Agriculture Wickard thought the president "looked as serious as I have ever seen him, yet he showed no signs of nervousness." On the floor of the House chamber, congressmen in their best suits formed conversational knots, while elsewhere on the floor a dozen or more children squirmed in their fathers' laps and only intermittently obeyed shushes for a dignified quiet. At five minutes past noon, with a mighty thud of his largest gavel, House Speaker Sam Rayburn summoned the scene to order. Through the doorway at the central aisle entered the Senate, led by Vice President Henry Wallace, towing at a slow pace on his strong arm the aged and withered Senator Carter Glass of Virginia. When the senators filled their places, eight glaring spotlights illuminated the podium for the cameras. The Supreme Court and then the cabinet trod the aisle to their reserved sections.

Rayburn lifted his other, smaller gavel, and called out the traditional cry "The President of the United States!" The whole chamber and the galleries sprang to their feet. "For an instant," noted reporter James Reston, "there was silence and then suddenly there was an ever increasing round of applause which terminated suddenly as Speaker Rayburn rapped with his gavel." An ovation recommenced that lasted over a minute. It was the greatest of Roosevelt's eight years as president. The audience first saw James Roosevelt, the president's son, in the midnight blue tunic and sky blue trousers of his dress Marine Corps uniform. He walked at a funereal pace next to the president, "a bulky man in mourning clothes with a weary face." With one hand locked on his son's arm and his "other hand feeling every inch of the long sloping rail," the president ascended the ramp to the dais, his massive shoulders and great head lurching from side to side. By fate, not plan, Roosevelt's entry foretold the country's story: a body mending from a crippling blow, but already rising by an undaunted spirit.

Time magazine reported that in the nimbus of blazing white light and to the atonal accompaniment of grinding movie cameras, "Mr. Roosevelt gripped the reading clerk's stand, flipped open his black, loose-leaf schoolboy's notebook. He took a long, steady look at the Congress and the battery of floodlights, and began to read." The famously patrician voice declared: "Yesterday, December 7, 1941—a date which will live in infamy—the United States was suddenly and deliberately attacked by naval and air forces of the Empire of Japan." The Japanese onslaught had severely damaged American naval and military forces and "very many American lives have been lost." Roosevelt then rhythmically recited a litany of further Japanese onslaughts against American and British posts in the Pacific. He continued "that always will our whole nation remember the character of the onslaught against us." At this comment "the room roared with a cry of vengeance." Roosevelt pledged that the war would be pursued to "absolute victory," a perhaps important signal that he already contemplated what he later enunciated as the policy of "unconditional surrender." And he concluded: "I ask that the Congress declare that since the unprovoked and dastardly attack by Japan on Sunday, December 7, 1941, a state of war has existed between the United States and the Japanese Empire." Reston noted that only at the very end did Roosevelt acknowledge the response of the crowd with a smile and wave of his hand.

Action followed swiftly. The Senate unanimously adopted a Declaration of War at 1300 (1:00 p.m.); the vote was 82–0. There was one vacancy as well as 13 absences from travel delays. The House followed at 1310 (1:10 p.m.), but by a vote of 388–1, with 46 absences due to travel delays. White-haired, sixty-one-year-old Miss Jeanette Rankin, Republican of Montana, an unshakable pacifist, cast the sole "nay." She had voted against the declaration of war in 1917. Now she vainly sought recognition by Speaker Rayburn, raising her hand and crying out "Mr. Speaker." Rayburn ignored her while a voice from another congressman shouted "Sit Down, Sister!" After the roll call, a pack of reporters pursued her out of the chamber. She sought refuge in a telephone booth like a "cornered rabbit" until rescued by Capitol police. Exactly one hour after the House voted, the president signed the joint resolution at 1410 (2:10 p.m.). Roosevelt cabled Churchill immediately: "Today all of us are in the same boat with you and the people of the Empire and it is a ship which will not and cannot be sunk."

In summarizing these events, *Time* magazine wrote: "But the war came as a great relief, like a reverse earthquake, that in one terrible jerk shook everything disjointed, distorted, askew back into place. Japanese bombs had finally brought national unity to the U.S." Yet by no means were all the noninterventionists convinced that there had not been an alternative to war. In a private letter the same day as Roosevelt's address, former president Herbert Hoover wrote: "You and I know this continuous putting pins in rattlesnakes finally got the country bitten. We also know that if Japan had been allowed to go without these trade restrictions and provocations, she would have collapsed from internal economic reasons alone within a couple of years." Those sharing Hoover's doubts, however, stowed them out of the public eye.

Whatever the attack had achieved at the operational and tactical level, it looms now as a strategic catastrophe—for Japan. Rather than a divided and disheartened public, the attack fused virtually the entire American nation together into a ferocious resolve to crush the Empire of Japan. Further, Japanese statecraft now arrayed against the nation the world's most populous country, the world's greatest empire, and the world's most advanced industrial power.

The underlying cause of all of this measureless folly was China—a nation that defied a century of its recent history to mount four and one-half years of sustained resistance. For this, China paid an enormous price: to this point probably more total deaths than any of the anti-Axis powers, and proportionally more of its wealthiest, most modern, and most industrialized regions than even the Soviet Union. While Great Britain is justly celebrated for its heroic vigil "alone" as the last major power standing against Nazi Germany from June 1940 to June 1941, the British still received more material help from their empire and the United States than China obtained for her isolated stance against Japan yearly from at least 1939 to 1941.

⋮

CHAPTER 12

"Issue in Doubt"

DECEMBER 1941: DISASTERS AND DECISIONS

Japan's Great Offensive Begins

In Japan on 8 December, a typical headline announcing the war read "Great, Death Defying Air Attack on Pearl Harbor, Hawaii." Ubiquitous posters appeared, "Slaughter them! The English and Americans are our enemies! Advance like a hundred million balls of fire!" The Emperor's Rescript placed responsibility for the war on Great Britain and the United States, who had "disturbed the peace" in Asia by supporting China and had "inordinate ambition to dominate the Orient." Premier Tôjô warned of a long war, but the government swiftly mobilized the public in support so that "doubts, fears and concerns remained largely unvoiced," though many countenances reflected such thoughts. Even intellectuals previously wary of Japan's path commonly were swept away with patriotic fever. Novelist Sei Itō found exhilaration in the news of American ship losses. In his diary he wrote that "Our destiny is such that we cannot realize our qualifications as first class people unless we have fought with the top ranking white men."

In the immediate aftermath of the Pearl Harbor attack what had been two regional wars (if effectively one since late July 1941) now merged into one global struggle. News of the blow made Hitler ecstatic. He hastened to validate his prior promises to Japan and, with appropriate ceremony, declared war on the United States on 11 December. His actions reflected two delusions: that the Imperial Navy was superior to the US Navy, and that it was myth, not fact, that the entry of the United States into World War I proved critical to Germany's defeat. Hitler's action freed the Roosevelt administration from facing a very divisive national debate on whether the United States would make war in Europe as well as Asia.

The Pearl Harbor strike aimed to free Japan to conduct the Southern Operations with the foremost strategic goal of securing oil supplies in Borneo and the Netherlands East Indies. Initially the Imperial Navy conceived the advance toward the oil-producing areas as a "clockwise" or eastern sweep basically from the Philippines. The Imperial Army advocated a "counterclockwise" or western sweep toward the same objectives basically down through Malaya. In a conspicuous manifestation of the inability of the two services to compromise, the Japanese did both.

The forces earmarked for the Southern Operations comprised as a core 11 of the Imperial Army's 51 divisions and 70 of a total of 151 air squadrons with around 300,000 men, counting both combat and support elements.[*] About two million tons of shipping—just under one-third of all Japanese shipping—supported the southern offensive. Plans called for these forces to be transported and guarded by the Imperial Navy at enormous distances from Japan. The size, oceanic reach, and astonishing tempo of these operations were without historical precedent. In addition to these main thrusts, Japan added several subsidiary operations designed to deal with Hong Kong and to secure key Pacific locations: Guam and Wake Islands, as well as Rabaul on New Britain in the South Pacific. Chronologically, all these subsidiary operations (save Rabaul) transpired at the very outset of the stunning Japanese thrust, and they produced the one sharp, though temporary setback—and the one arguably significant defeat in the opening six months of the war.

Guam and Wake

The United States acquired Guam in the southern Mariana Islands during the Spanish-American War (1898). The rugged, jungle-thatched island totaled 228 square miles and had some 20,000 inhabitants known as Chamorros. Although its geographic position offered advantages as an air and submarine base, Japanese-held islands snuggled close by. The US Congress refused to fund a serious defense of Guam, so by December 1941, US Navy Captain George J. McMillin commanded a garrison of a mere 670 personnel.

Japanese aircraft hit Guam on 8 December. They returned the next day while a massive invasion force closed the island with the "South Seas Detach-

---

[*]   Besides the 11 divisions assigned to the Southern Operations, the Imperial Army deployed 15 divisions in Manchuria and Korea to counter the Soviets and 24 divisions in China.

ment" of 5,500 men (Maj. Gen. Tomitarō Horii), covered by powerful naval forces. Although the Americans and Chamorros mounted a spirited resistance at the island's capital, Agana, McMillin feared that ultimately hopeless resistance might provoke severe Japanese retribution against his Chamorro wards. He surrendered Guam on 10 December. The Japanese treated decently the captured military personnel, but their treatment became far less benign when they were evacuated to Japan.

WAKE, A VOLCANIC ATOLL, proved a very different story. From a distance it mesmerizes the eye as "a horseshoe of bright turquoise, framed in flashing white, stand[ing] out against the indigo blue of encircling ocean." Wake comprises a reef girding three islands totaling a mere 2.5 square miles arranged like "a broken, mold-covered wishbone." The two arms of Wake Island proper stretch to the northwest, ending in narrow channels across which sit Peale Island to the north and Wilkes Island to the south.

Location accorded Wake strategic value—2,004 nautical miles almost due west from Honolulu, triple the distance from any Japanese harbor. The airplane abruptly terminated Wake's languid obscurity. Pan American Airlines began a clipper seaplane passenger service in 1935 to the Far East, enlisting Wake as way station. American armed forces, however, identified two roles for Wake. Army flyers coveted an airfield stepping-stone for moving heavy bombers to the Philippines. In 1941 Admiral Kimmel drafted plans not only to use Wake to support operations against the Marshall Islands, but also to turn Wake into bait to draw out a portion of the Imperial Navy for extinction.

Kimmel energized a massive base expansion project. Some 1,146 civilian contractors aged from their twenties to seventy-two soon radically increased Wake's value. Meanwhile, Kimmel fabricated a garrison, with the main element a detachment of the Marine 1st Defense Battalion. Under Maj. James P. S. Devereux, this detachment's artillery numbered six 5-inch coast defense guns, a dozen 3-inch antiaircraft guns, and four dozen machine guns for ground and antiaircraft defense. Cdr. Winfield S. Cunningham arrived as the island commander only on 28 November. By the outbreak of hostilities, there were 524 American military personnel on Wake and 1,218 civilians. Last-minute bolstering included patrols by fleet submarines *Tambor* and *Triton* off Wake, and on 4 December, Admiral Halsey's *Enterprise* delivered twelve Grumman F4F-3 Wildcat fighter planes of Marine Fighter Squadron VMF-211.

Word of the Pearl Harbor attack reached Wake in time to sound the alarm and send up a dawn patrol of four Wildcats. Summoned to sound the "Call

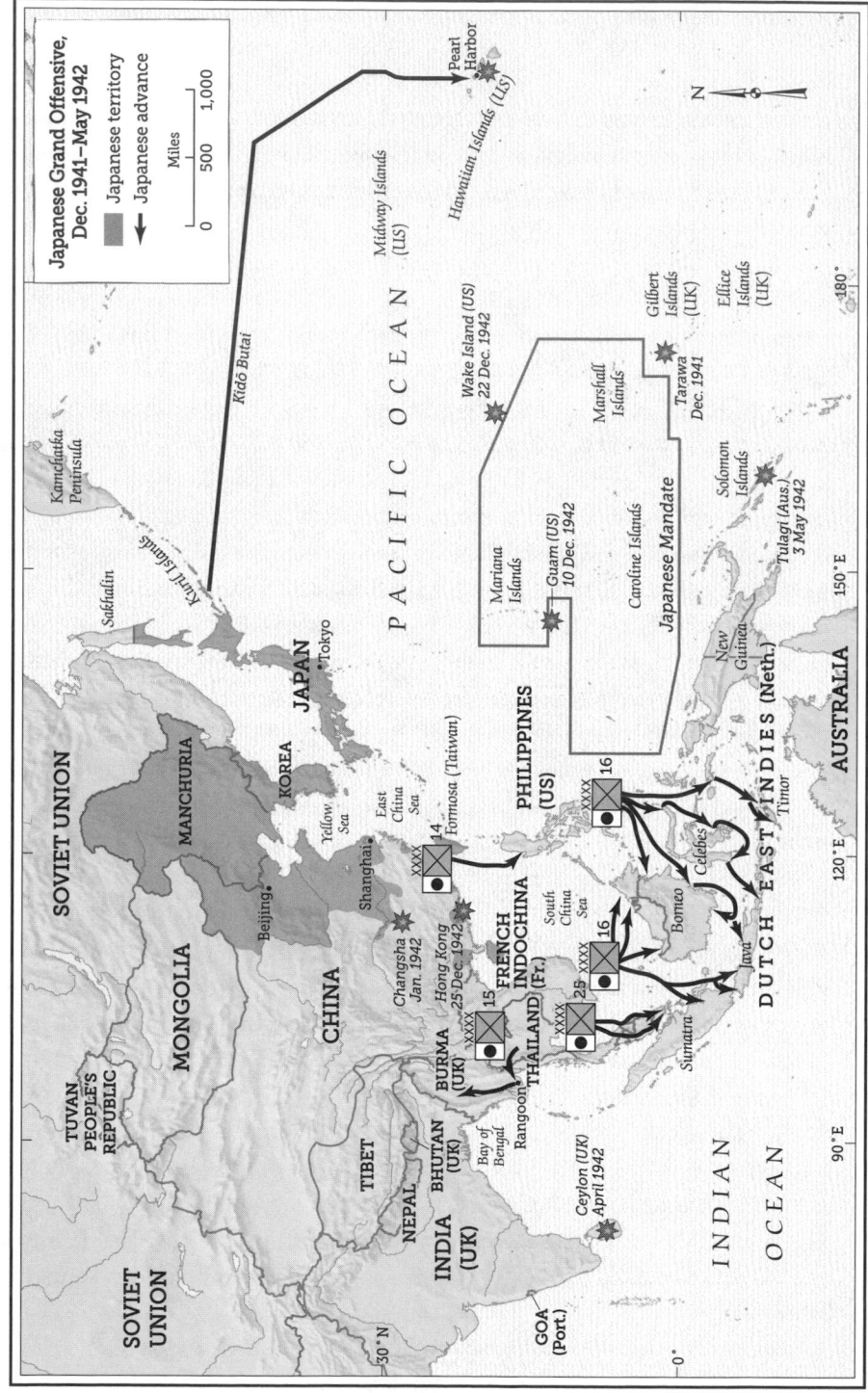

Japanese Grand Offensive,
Dec. 1941–May 1942

Japanese territory
Japanese advance

Miles
0　　500　　1,000

to Arms," bugler Alvin J. Waronker stumbled through a "demented medley" of inappropriate calls in a quest for the correct one. Waronker's misadventure illustrates that Wake's Marine defenders comprised an average assortment of the Corps, not supermen; but in the days ahead they demonstrated the remarkable quality of the "average" Leatherneck.

At 1150, thirty-six G3M2 twin-engine "Nell" bombers of the Marshall Islands–based Chitose Air Group hit Wake. Wake lacked radar, and low squalls veiled the attackers from observers ashore and aloft. The crashing surf muffled aural warning. The Japanese airmen inflicted massive damage to aviation facilities and personnel and left just three Wildcats operational after the Japanese run (one later repaired).

Two more days of Japanese air strikes followed. About 186 contractors volunteered and contributed valuable assistance in defending the garrison. Many American servicemen, however, developed acute animosity that more of the contractors failed to step forward. The contractors, however, having heard of Japanese conduct in China, rationally feared savage retribution if they participated in combat as civilians.

Before dawn on 11 December, Rear Adm. Sadamichi Kajioka's Wake Island attack force closed in on the island. Kajioka flew his flag in the light cruiser *Yubari*. His other major warships—all well aged—included light cruisers *Tatsuta* and *Tenryu*, and six destroyers. The assault force numbered 450 men carried in two very old destroyers converted to small transports, *Patrol Boats 32* and *33*, as well as a pair of relatively modern medium transport ships.

The intelligence reaching Kajioka credited the garrison with 1,000 fighting men and 600 laborers—reversing their proportions. As light broke over Wake, Kajioka's *Yubari* steamed smartly up toward the southeastern tip of the atoll, swung to port, and commenced bombarding the south shore with its six 5.5-inch guns. Its two light cruiser consorts added the fire of their combined eight weapons of the same caliber. The absence of any return fire seemed to confirm the effective handiwork of Japanese airmen.

Devereux sternly ordered the Marine defenders, crouching by their weapons, to wait until he gave an explicit order to engage. A man of aristocratic background and tastes in a slender, balding figure only five-foot-five inches tall, the Marine major seemed wildly miscast to direct a desperate defense. Indeed, up to this moment, his men largely detested him; one described him as a rigid, small-minded, by-the-book martinet. Devereux rightly reasoned, however, that he must draw the Japanese into very close range to make the fire of his old and limited coastal batteries effective.

Goggle-eyed Marines unleashed a torrent of indignant demands for permission to fire, but Devereux stubbornly rebuffed them. Finally, about 0615, Devereux barked "Fire." The Marine five-inch batteries bellowed rapid salvoes. *Yubari* fled unscathed but a Marine shell detonated a magazine in charging destroyer *Hayate* ("Squall"); it disappeared with all but one of 168 hands. Four Wildcats then swooped down and one of their bombs started a fatal fire on destroyer *Kisaragi* ("February"). It blew up in "a ball of flame" and sank with all 157 souls. The Japanese withdrew.

News of the repulsed attack transmitted a tremendous tonic to American morale and made instant national heroes of Devereux and his Marines.[*] From 9 December Admiral Kimmel looked to succor Wake—and perhaps retrieve his reputation. For decades a common view, as expressed by one historian, was that "Kimmel's plan for relieving Wake was sound, but the execution was attended by many misfortunes." The sorrowful reality was that the "many misfortunes" in execution (and probably a narrow escape from disaster) arose because of an unsound basic plan.

Kimmel's aggressive scheme looked to both relieve Wake and possibly inflict defeat on a portion of the Imperial Navy. Task Force 14, built around carrier *Saratoga*, mounted the main effort. It would add armed strength to Wake, evacuate contractors, and deliver a Marine fighter squadron. Although *Saratoga* embarked Rear Adm. Aubrey W. Fitch, an aviator, Kimmel assigned leadership of Task Force 14 to an officer he highly regarded—Rear Adm. Frank Jack Fletcher, who commanded the task force cruisers and was senior. Kimmel also deployed carrier task forces built around *Lexington* and *Enterprise*, but scattered them beyond any meaningful mutual support range.

If dispersion was Kimmel's main mistake, delay ran a close second. The clock ticked away while the seaplane tender *Tangier* (delegated to haul reinforcements and supplies) loaded and *Saratoga* consumed extra days getting to Pearl. With no better choice, Kimmel outfitted Fletcher with the slow oiler *Neches*, which limited the advance to about twelve knots. Fletcher discovered

---

[*] Newspapers not only trumpeted stories of the Marine success on 11 December, but also purported that the garrison sent a defiant radio message: "Send us more Japs." Only years later did the facts emerge. One of two ensigns charged with encoding messages from Cunningham followed procedure and attached at the beginning and end of each message "padding." This was supposed to be nonsense words or phrases designed to defeat code breaking by eliminating stereotypical headings and conclusions of messages. On one message the ensign used the phrase "send us more Japs" as padding in the belief that no right-minded person would think that was part of an actual message. Alas, the ensign was innocent of the ways of publicists and journalists. Urwin, *Facing Fearful Odds*, 358; Cressman, *The Magnificent Fight*, 162.

Dueling Visions for China

Generalissimo Chiang Kai-shek, leader of the Nationalist Party, June 1938. New evidence provides a far more nuanced understanding of his achievements and failures.

Mao Zedong speaking in 1938. He led the Chinese Communist Party from extraordinarily low ebb in 1937 to control of unified China by 1949—an outcome utterly beyond belief in 1937.

Critical Battles, 1937

The USS *Augusta* in Shanghai, flagship of Adm. Harry Yarnell (inset), commander of the Asiatic Fleet. He predicts Japan's aggression will kill millions of Chinese, but the Chinese will not quit.

Some of Chiang Kai-shek's German-equipped and -trained troops, China's best, but only a small fraction of the Chinese soldiers facing the formidable Imperial Army.

Japanese troops triumph in Nanjing, 1937, an event now seared in Chinese memory.

Chinese Retreat; Japanese Bombing; American Reaction

Driven from their base area by 1939, the Nationalists established a wartime capital in Chongqing, far up the Yangtze River, its steep hills covered in a lattice of dwellings.

Intense Japanese bombing struck scores of Chinese cities (here Shanghai, 1937).

These are two classic images among many depicting Japanese bombing in China. They gave the American people a far larger visual library of Japanese barbarity than anything available relating to German crimes prior to 1945.

Agonies of the Chinese People

"The Greatest Migration in Human History": here a handful of the at least 45 million Chinese refugees the war produced. This and other trials of war forged a much more potent national identity across vast swaths of China.

The greatest single tragedy of the Asia-Pacific War: the breaching of the Yellow River dykes in June 1938 in a desperate measure to stave off China's defeat. At least 500,000 perished in an episode virtually unknown outside of China.

A Global War

LEFT: President Franklin D. Roosevelt grasped fully that the wars in Europe and Asia were closely connected. His statecraft throughout World War II profoundly reflected that principle. RIGHT: After Hitler's attack on the Soviet Union in June 1941 (shown here), Washington and London viewed China's role as crucial for preventing Japan from joining Hitler in what was feared would be a fatal blow to Soviet resistance.

In August 1941, aboard the British battleship *Prince of Wales*, President Roosevelt and Prime Minister Winston Churchill (seated) agreed on their joint war aims in the "Atlantic Charter."

Japan's Desperate Plunge

Despite images like this, designed to depict Emperor Hirohito as all powerful, in reality he sat atop a decision-making structure designed to insulate him from participation in active policymaking. That structure also proved incredibly dysfunctional as it steered Japan into ever wider war.

When Japan desperately needed a statesman as prime minister in October 1941, the role fell upon a superb clerk: Gen. Hideki Tôjô.

Ill-Fated Diplomacy

American ambassador Joseph Grew worked tirelessly to stave off war from his post in Tokyo.

Ambassador Kichisaburō Nomura and Special Envoy Saburō Kurusu sought shrewdly but vainly to forestall Japan's war with the United States. American code breaking revealed that Japan's terms for a diplomatic agreement required that the US agree to China's defeat, or abandonment with defeat to follow.

"Air Raid, Pearl Harbor, This Is No Drill"

The opening minutes of Pearl Harbor attack, looking southeast over Ford Island at "Battleship Row." A torpedo is exploding against the battleship *Oklahoma*.

Almost half of all Americans who died at Pearl Harbor perished on the USS *Arizona*.

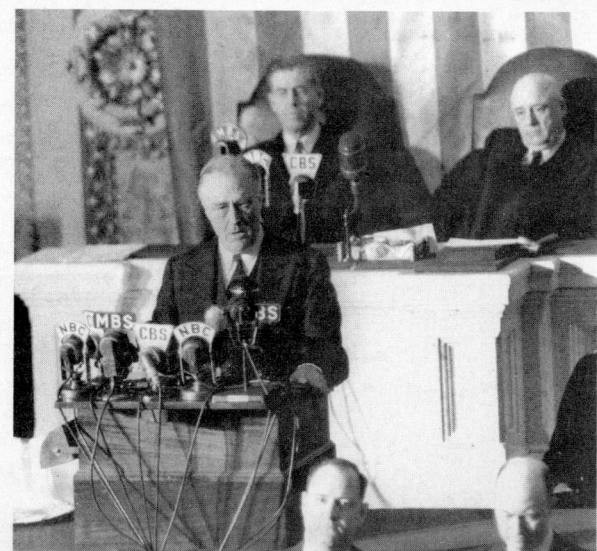

President Roosevelt delivers his 8 December 1941 "Day of Infamy" speech before Congress. The Pearl Harbor attack fundamentally altered the US relationship to the rest of the globe. The deepest underlying cause of the Japanese attack was US refusal to abandon China to Japanese aggression.

Allied Disaster in the South China Sea

New battleship
Prince of Wales
in Singapore,
2 December.

Handled brilliantly by
her captain, the aged
battlecruiser *Repulse*
resisted Japanese air
attacks better than her
new consort until finally
overcome.

A dramatic photograph
of the last minutes of
the *Prince of Wales*.
Her loss marked the
first time aircraft sank
a fully maneuvering
capital ship.

Key Aerial Adversaries

LEFT: The sleek but vulnerable Mitsubishi G3M (Allied code name "Nell") bomber was the principal instrument of Japanese bombing in China from 1937 to 1941. RIGHT: American-made Brewster Buffalo fighter aircraft in Singapore. Its degraded performance in the tropics contributed heavily to British and Dutch loss of air control.

LEFT: The Mitsubishi A6M ("Zero") fighter aircraft loomed as the most feared adversary of Allied pilots commencing with its combat debut in 1940. It was also the first fighter aircraft with strategic range. This aircraft was the first captured when its pilot became lost on a ferry flight and set down on the China coast on 26 November 1941. It is in the process of being restored to flight status. RIGHT: A kinetic image from a film of a Nakajima B5N (Allied code name "Kate") torpedo and level bomber. These potent aircraft inflicted the most damage at Pearl Harbor.

Singapore: Greatest Japanese Military Triumph

LEFT: Lt. Gen. Archibald E. Percival: As a staff officer he had few superiors; as a commander he had few inferiors. RIGHT: Gen. Tomoyuki Yamashita, commander of the Twenty-Fifth Army, conqueror of Singapore. A general possessed of tremendous daring and vision.

LEFT: This striking image of an Australian antitank gun crew and some of the Japanese tanks they destroyed illustrates the close-quarter fighting of the Malayan campaign, where Japanese tanks spearheaded Japan's victory. RIGHT: The British surrender delegation at Singapore. The Japanese officer in the darker uniform, right center, Col. Ichiji Sugita, also would be part of the Japanese surrender delegation on the USS *Missouri* in September 1945.

Defense of the Philippines

Filipino and American forces would hold out in the Philippines far longer than Allied forces elsewhere in Asia and the Pacific after Pearl Harbor. This made General Douglas MacArthur a huge hero and masked his serious misjudgments and command errors. He is seen here in his only visit to Bataan, in January 1942.

The twenty-nine submarines in the Asiatic Fleet formed the most potent potential Philippine defense capability. The ineffectiveness of this contingent, with a few exceptions like *Swordfish* (SS-182), shown here, constituted the single most abysmal failure in the defense of the Philippines.

The "Flying Tigers"

A perpetual outsider in the Army Air Corps, Claire Chennault proved himself a master air tactician in China. He became an international hero, but his fitness for higher-level command remained untested.

Despite their Curtiss P-40s' lackluster performance, Chennault's astute tactics made the "Flying Tigers" justly famous. Their success also highlighted the woeful performance of the American Far Eastern Air Force in the Philippines.

Fate of the Netherlands East Indies

A Japanese official history acknowledged that it was "no exaggeration" to say Japan embarked on its southward advance between December 1941 and May 1942 primarily to capture these oil refineries at Palembang, Sumatra.

LEFT: Capt. Hector "Hec" M. L. Waller, commanded his ship, HMAS *Perth*, faithfully followed by the USS *Houston* in the desperate Battle of Bantam Bay. Allied naval defeats sealed the fate of the Netherlands East Indies. RIGHT: The USS *Houston* (CA-30), one of President Roosevelt's favorite ships, fought valiantly before being sunk in Bantam Bay.

Burma

Lt. Gen. Joseph W. Stilwell (inset) leading his "walkout" from Burma. This made him famous in America, but his failure to come out of Burma with any substantial body of Chinese troops poisoned his relations with Chiang Kai-shek.

Gen. William Slim displayed exemplary leadership in the retreat from Burma. He obtained lessons on fighting the Japanese from Chinese officers, which he applied to gain his great victories in 1944–1945.

Glimmers of Allied Hope

LEFT: Gen. Douglas MacArthur, after his arrival in Australia, confers with Prime Minister John Curtin. Both leaders tugged Allied strategy in directions resisted in Washington and London. RIGHT: Adm. Chester W. Nimitz (left) took command of the Pacific Fleet and soon found his tenure imperiled. Vice Adm. William F. Halsey Jr. (with Nimitz later in the war, when Halsey was a full admiral) gained fame and Nimitz's enduring gratitude for his aggressive actions.

Raids in early 1942 by American aircraft carriers like *Enterprise* (CV-6 shown here) were relative pinpricks but prepared them for the great carrier battles to come.

The Doolittle Raid of 18 April 1942 on Japan, sent American morale soaring, but provoked tragic consequences in China.

that peacetime projections miserably underestimated the fuel demands of his destroyers, and weather and lack of practice at underway fueling in heavy weather further hobbled the advance.

Vice Adm. William S. Pye replaced Kimmel on 17 December as temporary steward of the Pacific Fleet, pending arrival on Christmas Day of the new commander, Adm. Chester W. Nimitz. Pye carried a reputation as a formidable strategist and a tactician never bested in war games. But caretaker Pye faced brutal reality, not a war game.

Fletcher's orders required him to arrive off Wake by 2130, 23 December (local time) and get *Tangier* to Wake on 24 December, and recommended that he refuel his task force before the final run in at a distance beyond the range of Japanese search planes from the Marshalls. Despite the slow speed of the task force, Fletcher was on schedule when he commenced fueling 515 miles from Wake on 22 December (Wake time) for the final approach. Sea conditions inflicted yet more refueling delays so that by 0800, 23 December *Saratoga* remained 425 miles from Wake.

Stung by the initial landing repulse, the Japanese did not remain idle. Marshall Island–based Japanese aviators in bombers and flying boats raided day and night between 11 and 20 December. At dusk on 17 December, about twenty-five miles southwest of Wake, the Japanese submarine *RO-62* accidentally rammed and sank *RO-66*. There were just three survivors of the sixty-six-man crew of *RO-66*.

For the second effort to capture Wake, Admiral Kajioka's invasion force remained substantially the same, with two destroyers filling in for the two lost ones. *Patrol Boats 32* and *33*, transport *Kinryu Maru*, and destroyers *Mutsuki* and *Oite* lifted a first wave assault force of about nine hundred sailors. Kajioka also readied a second wave of 1,100 sailors from ships' crews. Tremendously boosting the firepower of Kajioka's command was Rear Adm. Arimoto Goto's Cruiser Division 6, a quartet of 8-inch gunned heavy cruisers (*Aoba*, *Kinugasa*, *Furutaka*, and *Kako*). But still more potent was a detachment from Admiral Nagumo's *Kido Butai*. This comprised Carrier Division 2 (*Hiryū* and *Sōryū*) with a total of ninety-four operational aircraft.

On both the 21st and 22nd, *Sōryū* and *Hiryū* announced their presence with raids of forty-seven and thirty-nine aircraft, respectively. The last two operable Wildcats shot down three "Kates," but lost one Wildcat and pilot. The final Wildcat was damaged beyond repair. Wake's reports of the unmistakable presence of one or more Japanese carriers off Wake fundamentally changed the picture confronting Pye.

Indecipherable flashing lights to the north about 0200, 23 December (Wake time), forming cracks in what otherwise was the wall of stygian darkness around Wake, provided the first indication to the Americans that something was afoot. These were actually misdirected gunfire, but the flashes achieved what the shells did not: to shift American attention away from the south. One landing barge from *Kinryu Maru* with approximately 105 men fetched up on the Wilkes Island shore about 0320. There were a mere sixty-seven Marines on the island, joined in some cases by volunteers from the civilian contractors. The invaders sustained casualties getting ashore, and once there committed the literally fatal error of assuming the defenders had all retreated or fled to the east—not realizing they had left a sizable part of the island's garrison in their undefended rear. The defenders, fighting as makeshift infantry, proceeded to inflict severe losses on the Japanese trespassers on Wilkes by about 0700 at a cost of seven Marines dead. But prior to their demise, the invaders heavily decorated Wilkes's surface with Japanese flags. These were intended to prevent attacks by Japanese planes, but from the distance they led to a false belief that Wilkes had fallen, which exerted a powerful effect on the decisions of Devereux and Cunningham this day.

Kajioka's feints aimed to conceal his very audacious main effort. The admiral ordered *Patrol Boats 32* and *33* to sacrifice themselves by deliberate grounding on the south shore of Wake Island proper. *Patrol Boat 32* smashed its twenty-one-year-old hull plates over the reef and shuddered to a halt at 0230; its consort soon joined it. An American 3-inch antiaircraft gun completed the destruction of both. But the resolute armed landing parties, each man wearing a white sash on helmet or torso, swarmed ashore, soon joined by the Patrol Boat crews.

A series of confused encounters between the invaders and the defenders transpired throughout the remaining hours of darkness. At first light, the much-depleted Japanese assault force found itself recoiling under an improvised but effective counterattack from the west. But to the north and east, the Japanese overran the airfield and swung toward where Devereux and Cunningham maintained their command posts. Cunningham reported "Enemy on Island" and then added (borrowing a phrase from Anatole France's *Revolt of the Angels*): "Issue in Doubt." Pearl Harbor sent him the crushing news that not so much as an American submarine remained near Wake. Severed communications left Devereux with the false impression that not only was Wilkes in Japanese hands, but also that all the Americans on the southern arm of Wake were dead or captured. When Cunningham reluctantly proposed surrender to avoid needless loss of life, Devereux, exhausted by the strain of two weeks of sleepless command, concurred.

Proportionately to the value of the success, the Japanese sustained severe losses taking Wake: two destroyers, two patrol boats, a submarine, and seven aircraft, with at least 544 dead (39 air, 111 ashore, and 394 at sea). American losses totaled 124 dead, but of these just 49 were military personnel, the rest civilians. On the evening of 23 December, there were 1,593 Americans experiencing their first taste of Japanese captivity on Wake.

While the heroic defense of Wake served as a tonic to depressed American morale, the denouement of the navy's effort to relieve Wake proved a dreg more bitter than Pearl Harbor to many officers. When Pye and his staff received Cunningham's "Issue in Doubt" dispatch, they concluded Wake was lost and confronted the question of whether Task Force 14 should still seek battle. Though the navy and the nation pined sorely for a victory, Pye decided the risks far outweighed the potential gains and ordered Fletcher to withdraw. Within Task Force 14, Fletcher took off his hat and smashed it to the deck. Members of his staff urged him to ignore or claim "misunderstanding" of the order and press on to attack. Admiral Fitch, himself disgusted, recounted later that he retired to his cabin to escape the jabber of "mutinous" voices begging him to disregard Pye's command.

The notion that Kimmel's plan would have produced a victory lingered on but remains fanciful. The failure at Wake stemmed from an unsound plan, and command failure to instill the utmost urgency to get *Tangier* to Wake before 21 December. The plan left *Saratoga* alone to face a formidable combination of Japanese air and sea power some 2,000 miles from Pearl Harbor. Any damage to *Saratoga* would almost certainly have resulted in its loss long before distant *Lexington* or *Enterprise* could intervene. No one can look back with confidence on the potential outcome of a faceoff in December 1941 between *Saratoga* and *Hiryū* and *Sōryū* (whose air groups many Japanese regarded as the finest in the Imperial Navy). Pye's decision to abandon Wake without a fight marked the nadir of Pacific Fleet morale. But it was correct—as was Fletcher's obedience.

Echoes of the Battle of Wake Island lingered on for the whole war. Admiral Kajioka came ashore on December 23 to inspect his prize and foiled what appeared to the Marines to be a plan by one Japanese officer to execute the captured Americans. In January 1942 the Japanese evacuated all but 388 men. During passage to eventual prison camps, a Japanese officer selected four Marines and a sailor and beheaded them, apparently in revenge for losses at Wake. Another approximately two hundred contractors and the twenty sick servicemen were evacuated late in 1942. Of the remaining contractors on Wake, forty-five died as slave laborers and one was executed for stealing food.

In October 1943, Capt. Shigemitsu Sakaibara, the island commander, fearful that a raid by American carrier planes foretold a landing, ordered the remaining ninety-eight Americans killed. One American eluded the Japanese for a time, but when he was caught, Sakaibara dispatched him with his own sword—for which he was later executed as a war criminal.

All told, 244 Americans captured on Wake died in Japanese captivity. Of the captured Marines and sailors, only 27 died, or 5.7 percent—by far the lowest portion of any Allied contingent captured in these opening months of the war. The stature of Devereux in the eyes of his men soared even more when his tough discipline (along with a generous supply of good luck) proved instrumental in keeping their death rate suppressed. By contrast, Kajioka's subsequent assignments reflect dissatisfaction in Tokyo with his Wake performance. On 12 September 1944, he was killed in action when the US submarine *Growler* sank his flagship, the escort vessel *Hirado*.

Hong Kong

Hong Kong (Chinese for Fragrant Harbor) rests eighty miles southeast of Guangzhou (Canton). In 1842, the British seized it—and between 1860 and 1898, acquired the Kowloon Peninsula and a large expanse of "Leased Territories." Under British control, Hong Kong became a fabled and exotic international port, eclipsed only by Shanghai. The Sino-Japanese conflict propelled a tremendous refugee surge into the colony such that by December 1941, the population approximated three million. Most inhabitants, though ethnically Chinese, were Hong Kong–born British subjects.

Two prominent bank buildings seemingly provided graphs of enterprise in concrete, with the British structure just taller than its Chinese rival. In fact, Chinese merchants—exploiting the law and order widely deficient on the mainland—were surpassing their colonial masters on all economic fronts. But the British maintained a rigid racial social structure, with themselves on top, the Eurasians in an uneasy middle, and Asians at the bottom. Stella Benson, a feminist writer known for her cutting wit, acidly described the few thousand British expatriates who dominated Hong Kong as "tenth rate men married to eleventh rate women."

As the mini-Switzerland of the Orient, Hong Kong became a carousel of intrigue. The Japanese conducted secret diplomacy with Chiang and nourished his Chinese rivals through the city. No fewer than thirty-two different organs of Chiang's Nationalist government maintained offices in Hong Kong.

But Hong Kong's key role stood as the portal for supplies to the Nationalists. Early on some 60 to 70 percent of the war materials reaching the Nationalists passed through Hong Kong by rail to Guangzhou. Even after Guangzhou fell, the Japanese estimated that no less than 6,000 tons per month still reached Chiang by junks to transit points on the coast.

Hong Kong Island totals twenty-nine square miles dominated primarily by steep ridges. Victoria, the main port, spread across five miles of the western stretch of the north shore facing the mainland. Victoria replicated a European metropolis, with a university, a cathedral, and many fine buildings. Excellent paved roads girded the flat coastline of the island, with one north-south road bisecting the island. Only constricted narrow tracks not passable by vehicles gave rudimentary interior access. Kowloon, with its intricate fringe of wharfs and the "Leased Territories," totaled about four hundred square miles, with frontiers extending north up to seventeen miles inland. Rugged hills and ridges dominated this mainland region. Although the Tai Mo Shan massif, rising to 3,000 feet, formed a natural defense position, it is dominated by still more lofty ground beyond British territory.

From 1937, mindful of the rising German threat, the British Chiefs of Staff recognized that there was no realistic hope of defending the outpost of Hong Kong against a Japanese attack. By definition outposts are expendable. Thus, prior to 1941, four infantry battalions and twenty-nine coastal guns with only token air and sea contingents constituted the Hong Kong garrison. The British Chiefs of Staff rejected reinforcement proposals as "throwing good money after bad." Chiang recognized both Hong Kong's vital importance and its vulnerability. He offered 200,000 troops for defense, but the British rejected this offer in July 1941.

Then London's attitude abruptly reversed. For decades the official narrative was that the dispatch of two Canadian infantry battalions (the Royal Rifles of Canada and the Winnipeg Grenadiers) in late 1941 stemmed from the recommendation of an outgoing Hong Kong garrison commander, also a Canadian. But the real reason for this decision was ultimately to support the Soviet Union in conjunction with US and UK actions. Canadian prime minister William Mackenzie King explained: "a break in Chinese resistance will probably mean a break in Russian resistance." Hence, the reinforcements would bolster Chinese morale and head off combined catastrophes in Asia and Europe.

An ill-founded confidence afflicted the colony, which believed that, as in World War I, the conflict would not touch Hong Kong. The garrison commander, Maj. Gen. Christopher M. Maltby (who wore a face like "the mellowed red brick of an Elizabethan country house"), could not stir the civilian leadership to expensive and disruptive measures, such as comprehensive air raid preparations. While Englishmen and Eurasians were mustered into volunteer defense units, the British refused to arm Chinese. Security measures against espionage were risibly flabby.

War came at 0800, 8 December, when Japanese planes struck, destroying three of Hong Kong's five obsolete military planes. The alert defenders briskly settled the colony's perimeter along the 10.5 mile-long "Gindrinker's Line" (named for a bay on its west end). The Japanese attackers comprised about 15,000 men from the 38th Division ("an elite division with abundant battle experience") of Lt. Gen. Takashi Sakai's Twenty-Third (South China) Army. During 8 and 9 December, the Japanese drove in the screening force along the frontier. At darkness on 9 December, the three British battalions protecting the mainland hunkered in their designated positions.

The key to the whole west side of the "Gindrinker's Line" was the Shing Mun Redoubt. The redoubt lay in the zone of the Japanese 230th Infantry Regiment, but the troops that captured it came from the 228th Infantry. That unit's commander, Col. Teishichi Doi, recognized the supreme importance of the redoubt and decided to attack it without delay. About 2200, 9 December, two companies of Japanese soldiers in rubber-soled shoes stealthily snipped gaps in the wire entanglements and then sprang forward. By 0200, 10 December, the Japanese had overcome the forty-two defenders and held the entire redoubt. When Doi reported his triumph by radio to the division headquarters, he received not praise but a rebuke for crossing unit boundaries and was ordered to withdraw! Doi extracted grudging permission to remain, but the division's chief of staff apparently found time to conduct an inquisition into Doi's freelance exploits.[*] Further fighting along the "Gindrinker's Line" cost both sides heavily, and on the 11th, Maltby ordered withdrawal to Hong Kong Island.

At 0900, 13 December, a Japanese staff officer crossed the water under a white flag to deliver a surrender demand from Sakai's Twenty-Third Army. It warned that failure to comply would result in a severe aerial and artillery bombardment. Governor Sir Mark Young rejected the message (as he would a repetition on the 17th). Sakai's threat was not idle. Shells from the mainland, though carefully aimed at legitimate military targets, nonetheless also set

---

[*]   The chief of staff of the Twenty-Third Army, Maj. Gen. Tadamichi Kuribayashi, spoke up on Doi's behalf, only to be relieved of his duty by the army commander. Kuribayashi, now recognized as one of the great Japanese generals of the war, would die commanding the defense of Iwo Jima in March 1945.

many fierce fires in Victoria and broke water mains. Serial air raids added to the flames, which raged out of control. A dense pall of smoke roofed Hong Kong.

The Japanese also reaped handsome profits from their assiduous prehostility investment in espionage and subversion. Not only had the Japanese recruited disaffected Chinese and Indians, but they also had brought in spies from Taiwan and purchased the services of Triad underworld gangs. Guides steered Japanese assault parties around defensive positions pinpointed by spies. The Triad gangster underground and other agents caused civil commotion and spread propaganda that helped trigger the disappearance of many civilians tasked with providing much logistical support for the defenders. British authorities thwarted a reported Triad plot to murder all Europeans with the most effective means at hand: a handsome cash counteroffer to Triad bosses. British leaders, discarding all their prior reluctance at the potential political implications of such action, allied themselves with Chungking government secret services under the redoubtable one-legged Admiral Chak Chan. The admiral delicately named his vigilantes the Loyal and Righteous Charitable Association. Much of their "charity" consisted of an executioner's bullet, freely dispensed by the hundreds in a shared counterterror campaign with the elements of the Hong Kong police that remained loyal. This ruthless suppression curtailed but did not entirely halt "Fifth Column" activity.

News of the approach of a Nationalist relief force halted a slide in the defenders' morale, but later British accounts treated these stories as myths. They were not myths, but another instance of the intricate complexity of Chinese leadership. Gen. Hanmou Yu was commander in chief of the Guangdong War Zone with the Sixty-Third Army of three divisions. Yu generally exhibited skill at keeping a distance from Chiang and avoiding serious clashes with the Japanese. In this instance, however, his units drove close enough to Hong Kong that one regiment fought a battle at the last train station before the border. But the Japanese Twenty-Third Army stationed two divisions and a brigade to block Yu, and the powerful Japanese Eleventh Army began a battle toward Changsha, which pulled Chinese forces away from a relief of Hong Kong.

The Japanese scheme of attack during the night of 18–19 December was simple—and based on a Triad report that a British exercise in 1940 demonstrated an attack from the north would succeed. The 38th Division struck the northeast coast of Hong Kong Island. The assault crushed the single defending Indian Army battalion (5/7th Rajputs). Lt. Gen. Tadayoshi Sano, the division commander, stepped ashore about 0100 on the 19th. Fumbling attempts at counterattacks by other units failed in the darkness.

The one clear tactical error in the defense was that on the 19th, Brig. Cedric Wallis, commanding the East Brigade, withdrew his command south rather than west, opening a gap the Japanese exploited between his command and the West Brigade. From roughly this point onward, the story of Hong Kong's defenders is a long litany of company—or smaller size—elements, often intermixed with sailors and volunteers, being overwhelmed by tactically skilled Japanese forces enjoying advantages in numbers and usually firepower. Among the crippling Canadian officer losses was the West Brigade's Brig. J. K. Lawson, who died fighting it out at his command post.

Some isolated defenders continued to fight behind the Japanese line. Notable in this regard was the scratch force at the Power Station. It comprised a party of Middlesex regiment wounded and a detachment of the Hong Kong Volunteer Defense Command known as the "Hughesiliers," after the commander, Col. A. W. Hughes. These seventy men were all prominent businessmen past their fifty-fifth birthday—some with their last combat experience in the Boer War. They stymied Japanese regulars for eighteen hours, but were all captured or killed when they tried to break out.

By the 22nd, a shortage of water further sapped the rapidly thinning ranks of the defenders, while a crescendo of shells and bombs spread flames. One poetic police officer reported that oil tanks "blazed in anguish throughout the war, like three great wounds on the black body of the night." The continued dogged resistance enraged Japanese soldiers, who massacred at least 157 British and Canadian prisoners by bayonet, beheading, and in some cases burning alive (the flame-enshrouded victims "cried like a lot of pigs," noted one Japanese corporal). After slaughtering patients at a hospital, the Japanese threw mattresses upon a pile of corpses and proceeded to rape seven nurses. Three of these they then beheaded, piling their naked bodies outside. News of this episode soon spread far beyond Hong Kong's borders.

About 1515 on Christmas Day, Maltby informed Governor Young that his few remaining organized units had reached the end of effective resistance. Young formally surrendered that evening by candlelight to General Sasaki.

The fall of Hong Kong after only eighteen days shocked London. The Japanese exploited a detailed, though significantly flawed, intelligence portrait of Hong Kong's defenses and mustered a potent "Fifth Column" activity. The 38th Division was a combat-experienced well-honed team with aggressive and cunning officers and soldiers who displayed considerable initiative. The defenders, by contrast, were a confederation of disparate units wholly without combat experience. The Japanese offset approximate equality in infantry with an overwhelming superiority in artillery. Japanese command of the sea enforced tactical restraints on the defense by the always compelling concern for rear or flanking landings.

Casualties remain somewhat elusive. The official Commonwealth total was 4,420 casualties (including about 1,679 killed) of the 11,848 combatants present. These casualty numbers appear low. The Japanese reported total losses of 675 killed, 2,079 wounded, for a total of 2,754. Given the short duration of the battle and size of the opposing forces, these numbers testify to a savage conflict.

The Japanese failed to impose firm control for approximately twenty-four hours after the capitulation. The Chinese argue that the pause reflected a prior agreement with the Triads, who took the opportunity to conduct massive looting as well as general mayhem and rape. Then, notwithstanding Tokyo's orders for restraint, aimed at furthering Japan's professed commitment to Pan-Asian solidarity against colonialism, the Japanese conquerors unleashed days of plunder and violence, physical (the number of executions running into the hundreds, not thousands) and sexual (an estimated 10,000 rapes of Chinese women alone), directed primarily at the Chinese population—and ironically largely sparing the former British overlords. An intramural dispute between the Imperial Navy and Imperial Army prolonged the chaos until February. Ultimately, an army faction prevailed that advocated using Hong Kong as an access point for extracting the wealth of Southern China and as a platform for further attempts to undermine Chinese resistance by nourishing rivals to Chiang and the Nationalists.

Changsha—Disputed Victory

Gen. Korechika Anami, commander of the Eleventh Army, seethed over Chinese claims that they had defeated his September–October 1941 offensive aimed at Changsha. Now ostensibly Anami mounted a thrust with his army to support the Twenty-Third Army attack on Hong Kong. The effort originally aimed to drive south from below Hankou, east of the Hankou-Canton railway, roughly 18.6 miles and reach the Miluo River. Disregarding Imperial Headquarters directives, Anami drove on another approximately twenty-six miles for his real objective: Changsha. Anami's main forces amounted to twenty-seven battalions of infantry and ten artillery battalions plus one battery.

The Japanese attack commenced at dusk on 24 December (just a day before Hong Kong fell), led by the 6th and 40th Divisions. At first the Japanese bulldozed through Chinese defenders. By 29 December, the Japanese convinced themselves that Changsha was "inadequately defended," so Anami elected to capture Changsha to "add to the gains of the present operation." The 3rd Division and part of the 6th closed on Changsha, only to discover both numerous and resolute defenders. The 3rd Division at first penetrated into southeastern Changsha, but advanced no further. On 2 January, the 6th Division added pressure as Japanese soldiers beat upon the north, east, and south sides of the city. By dusk on 4 January, the Japanese occupied "all the important points of the city"—but found their units in danger of being surrounded by counterattacking Chinese forces.

Claiming success in supporting the Hong Kong Operation and occupying the major parts of Changsha, the Eleventh Army ordered a withdrawal along "predetermined routes" on the morning of the 4th. The Japanese admitted that "considerable hardship" attended the withdrawal as all units were desperately short of ammunition, especially artillery ordnance, and rations. The retreating columns fought off attacks by nine armies and over twenty divisions of Chinese, while burdened with protecting rear service units and large numbers of wounded. "In some cases" Japanese units were overwhelmed by the Chinese. Specifically, a detachment of two to three hundred men of the 9th Independent Mixed Brigade was wiped out on the night of 8–9 January, save for one man. When the operation ended on 15 January, the Japanese official account tabulated losses at 1,670 soldiers killed and 5,184 wounded as well as 1,120 horses killed and 646 injured. The Chinese version differed radically. Yue Xue, the Chinese commander, reported the Japanese did not just withdraw of their own accord but were repulsed with 33,941 killed and 23,003 severely wounded.

The irreconcilable differences between the Japanese and Chinese accounts of the battle are by no means unique. It is very unlikely that Japanese casualties matched Chinese claims, but the lack of surviving Imperial Army records and a general pattern of discrepancies between reported and actual losses meant Japanese losses may well have been higher than they stated. It is safe to assume that Chinese losses were several times greater than Japanese. The timing and conduct of the operation cast strong doubts over the actual Japanese intentions. The whole operation reflected haste and ill-planning, particularly as to Japanese logistics and ammunition supplies. Likewise, the Japanese severely underestimated both the number and the determination of the Chinese they might encounter. Given the fact that Changsha by now had great strategic and particularly symbolic value both as a blot on Anami's record that he took personally and as an exemplar of successful Chinese operations (just renewed the previous fall), it is more likely than not that, as earlier at Yichang, once the Japanese seized Changsha they intended to hold it, but the Chinese counterpunch was too much. If the battle was not the spectacular success claimed by the Chinese, it certainly demonstrated the ability of Chinese arms to inflict serious loss on Japanese forces and compel the enemy to withdraw, or at least deliver serious punishment to Japanese sallies. Moreover, the Chinese held the battlefield in the end. On these counts, the Chinese success was a great deal more than their Allies could claim in the six months after Pearl Harbor.

"Arcadia"

As new battles transpired, so too did a new alignment of allies and adversaries take shape. Chiang, after years of avoiding a formal declaration of war out of valid concerns that this would do more to harm than to aid China against Japan (US neutrality laws would have barred access to US supplies), acted swiftly to join the worldwide conflagration. On 9 December (Chongqing time) the Chinese government formally declared war on Japan, Germany, and Italy. The Americans, British, and Chinese all looked to Moscow to see whether the Soviet Union would declare war on Japan. As one US diplomat observed, however, Soviet foreign policy was "superlatively realistic." Stalin explained to Chiang that while he recognized China's contribution to the fight against their common enemies, Chiang should understand that his country could not join the war against Japan. In one of the more bizarre diplomatic footnotes to World War II, even now Japan did not and never would declare war on China.[*]

Meanwhile, Churchill wasted no time. Two days after Pearl Harbor he proposed a meeting with Roosevelt (code-named "Arcadia") to discuss strategy as well as munitions production "in light of reality and new facts." Roosevelt agreed. While extremely tempestuous seas contested Churchill's passage to the New World in the battleship *Duke of York* ("a submarine masquerading as a battleship," said one of the party), the exhilarated prime minister conjured dazzling visions in policy papers that explored all parts of the globe. In Europe he acknowledged that "Hitler's failure and losses in Russia are the prime fact in the war" and they must "weave the mighty Russian effort into

---

[*]   The main reason for this was the earlier disastrous declaration that Japan would not recognize Chiang as the head of the Chinese government. Thus, the Japanese faced the quandary of where to address their declaration of war, coupled to the fact that declaring war now on Chiang would serve to recognize his legitimacy.

the general texture of the war." He envisioned a joint British and American descent into Northwest Africa, Operation Gymnast. (This proposal particularly would consume a vast number of hours during the conference.) As for the Pacific, Churchill recognized sea power as the key, though he still thought first of restoring US and British battleship fleets while bending every effort to increase the number of carriers—but he firmly accorded the Pacific secondary rank.

As Churchill made his stormy transit, the naval fortunes for the US and Royal Navies plunged to a wartime nadir. Between 14 November and 21 December 1941, major losses included one fleet carrier (*Ark Royal*), one escort carrier, five Royal Navy battleships (*Barham*, *Prince of Wales*, and *Repulse* being outright sunk, while *Queen Elizabeth* and *Valiant* were disabled by Italian swimmers in Alexandria), five American battleships (*Arizona*, *Oklahoma*, *Nevada*, *California*, and *West Virginia*), and four British cruisers sunk as well as two American cruisers out of action. Although two British and three American battleships would be restored to action, the overall naval balance tilted sharply to the detriment of the Allied powers and would remain so for months.

Churchill reached Washington the evening of 22 December. "There was the President waiting in his car, I clasped his strong hand with comfort and pleasure," he recalled. At the Atlantic Conference in August 1941 the two leaders settled the overarching political issue of the basis on which the war would be fought and the central strategic issue of "Germany First." Now they would grapple with an array of political and strategic issues below those, but still of a momentous character. Their backgrounds were both alike and disparate in critical areas, so much so that it is important to recall that it was by no means certain their nascent close partnership was destined to endure in the tumult of full war.

Most conspicuously there yawned a vast chasm between their personal experiences on military matters. Churchill was trained as a soldier. He rode in the last British cavalry charge and personally shot men at close range. As a journalist, he observed and then cogently assessed several campaigns. He qualified as a pilot in the most perilous early days of flight, and survived two crashes before prudently abandoning personal piloting, though not his advocacy for military aviation. He had been first lord (the civilian head) of the British Navy and prepared it superbly for World War I. But as the principal exponent of the disastrous Gallipoli campaign, his reputation for sound judgment sustained a blow from which it never entirely recovered. He was dismissed as first lord and spent time commanding a battalion in the trenches before he returned to government to oversee war production. He maintained avid, lifelong interests in science (in 1924 he wrote an article envisioning nuclear bombs delivered by aerial means), secret intelligence, and the technology of warfare.

Against Churchill's depth on land, sea, and air warfare, Roosevelt's resume matched in only one respect: his extremely keen, lifelong interest in the US Navy and naval matters in general. He served as the assistant secretary of the navy in the Wilson administration during World War I, though this was overwhelmingly an administrative, not an operational remit. One notable facet of FDR's fascination with the US Navy was that he had, like that service, invested much time focused on a potential war with Japan.

As executives the Briton and the American were as different as night and day. Churchill's broad experience in cabinet positions, particularly during World War I, gave him a masterful sense of how to erect and manage the apparatus of wartime government that would effectively execute his intentions. A veritable human dynamo, Churchill reveled in detail and deluged his subordinates with ideas, perhaps one in ten of which had genuine merit. Though he was well schooled in war, he never once overruled the united opposition of his chiefs of staff.

It would be mid-1943 before Roosevelt finally completed an effective apparatus to execute his roles as commander in chief of the armed forces and chief executive of the government. He relished setting up officials with overlapping and often conflicting authorities. Perhaps the epitome of this was his early effort to mobilize the "Arsenal of Democracy." At one time he created sixteen different agencies to manage the different aspects of mobilization, all under the executive branch and all without a superior save for Roosevelt himself. This refusal to delegate power gained him a degree of control, but he lacked the time and interest in details to make such slapdash structures efficient.

Roosevelt relished mystery and surprise. He aptly described himself as a juggler who "never let my right hand know what my left hand is doing." As his close confederates learned in working with him, and as historians discovered often to their chagrin, Roosevelt kept a close lid on his real thoughts and often left lieutenants with conflicting understanding of his positions. The meticulously organized Stimson found sessions with Roosevelt exasperating because the president's mind "did not follow easily a consecutive chain of thought," and pursuing his views could be "very much like chasing a vagrant beam of sunshine around a vacant room." Churchill was the antithesis. He delighted in arguing out issues to a clear conclusion, did not shrink from verbal fisticuffs, and much respected those who went head-to-head with him.

One issue central to the Asia-Pacific War on which both men shared similar viewpoints was race. Both were children of the nineteenth century, when a mutilated form of Darwinism provided an all too casually accepted presumption that there was a hierarchy of races, with whites on top. Both generally believed that whites from their elevated status had a duty to "uplift" the "lesser races." Both had lacunas in this overall outlook. Churchill was severe or even shrill with respect to what his biographer, Andrew Roberts, termed "a rigid form of Islam" manifest in the Talib tribe (from whom the later Taliban take their name) and the peoples of India in general. Roosevelt regularly communicated with Professor Ales Hrdlicka of the Smithsonian Institution, a preeminent cultural anthropologist who clothed naked white supremacy in the robes of science. Roosevelt once lectured a British ambassador on Hrdlicka's explanation that Japanese delinquency derived from the fact that their skulls lagged whites' in development by two thousand years. Roosevelt also discoursed on ideas of racial crossbreeding to improve certain "lower races" and even the uses of sterilization to prevent what he regarded as excessive breeding by those races. These attitudes, however, did not extend to contemplation of the complete annihilation of other peoples, nor did it restrain Churchill and Roosevelt in their choice of military measures against Germans who shared a common racial classification.

The prime minister and a small party camped at the White House. That very night over dinner Roosevelt (soon seconded by his military chiefs) relieved the excruciating British anxiety by affirming that notwithstanding Pearl Harbor, the United States remained committed to "Germany First." Churchill soon cabled back that "We live here as one big family." The president's wife Eleanor would have amended that to add "but not one big happy family." She strained to conceal her distaste for this paragon of British imperialism. While the president worked hard and harmoniously with Churchill, he gave subtle and not so subtle indications of his distaste for Churchill's imperial ideology. The "British Lion" served as the very symbol of that nation's supremacy over the greatest empire in the world. At Roosevelt's direction, out of storage came a rug made from a dead lion skin that reposed symbolically on the floor of his office when he met the Briton. The elite accommodations, however, required the visitors to partake of daily culinary martyrdom with the president. The food-deprived Britons ravenously consumed the White House fare, blissfully ignorant that its overseer, Mrs. Henrietta Nesbitt, remains perhaps unchallenged as the worst White House manager in history.

Churchill displayed liberality in at least two dimensions. He consumed copious amounts of alcohol throughout the day and maintained bohemian working hours (a two-hour afternoon nap recharged Churchill to toil after dinner until about 0300) that taxed the White House staff and the president. He installed an elaborate "Map Room" containing intricately annotated maps and charts plotting daily progress on all fighting fronts. This inspired Roosevelt to create an even more elaborate version in the basement of the White House that served as his command post for the duration.

In public appearances Churchill burnished his reputation as an orator. When asked how long the war would take at a press conference on 24 December, Churchill quipped: "If we manage it well, it will only take half as long as if we manage it badly." Appearing before a joint session of Congress on 26 December, he commenced with a guileful sally that disarmed and amused, "I cannot help reflecting that if my father had been American and my mother British, instead of the other way round, I might have got here on my own." Deftly switching moods, he roused a growling roar when he asked about the Japanese: "What sort of people do they think we are?" That night, however, he sustained an attack of angina pectoris, with pain over his heart and down his left arm. His physician, Charles Wilson, later Lord Moran, sagely chose to tell him to avoid overexertion rather than try to prescribe six weeks of rest—which was quite out of the question.

The military staffs girded for a second meeting following the "Atlantic Charter" session. Each harbored doubts about the other. The Americans suspected British machinations to steer war strategy in ways that primarily served their imperial interests, and to poach American arms and troops while circumventing American participation in decisions about their use. The Americans bristled at British airs of superiority, especially since the British war record to date did not seem to merit such haughtiness. Exacerbating the foreboding of the American officers was the fact that Churchill billeted at the White House, where his informal access to the president might result in all kinds of mischief. The British viewed the North Americans as "unorganized, bureaucratic, ignorant of the realities of war and still reeling in shock from the Japanese attack." Field Marshal Sir John Dill, who genuinely admired the Americans, cabled that "the country has not—repeat not—the slightest conception of what the war means, and their armed forces are more unready for war than it is possible to imagine."

The first full meeting of the two executives and their military advisers on 23 December immediately humiliated Marshall: his staff had botched the elementary task of placing the gathering in a space adequate for the full company, requiring them to shuffle to a larger room. This augury fitted into the assessment of the assistant secretary of the war cabinet, Colonel Ian Jacob, that while "the President is a most impressive man and seems to be on the best of terms with all his advisers," he was yet a "child in Military affairs" compared to Churchill. Further "to our eyes the American machinery of government seems hopelessly disorganized. . . . [and the president] has no proper machinery through which to exercise command." The British immediately detected the unconcealed rivalry of the American Army and Navy, which presented an easily exploitable fractured front. The president's endorsement of General Arnold's proposal that they must open and maintain an aerial supply route to China (resulting in the "Over the Hump" from India to China air cargo project) constituted perhaps the most long-term consequence of this single session.

The worst fears of the president's military advisers materialized when he met with Churchill the evening of 24 December. The next morning a British memorandum on the substance of the conversations circulated in the War Department. It ignited an explosion. The memorandum indicated that Roosevelt had agreed that if reinforcements destined for the Philippines could not get through, they should be diverted to Singapore. "This astonishing paper made me extremely angry," recorded a furious and anxious Stimson. His anger stemmed from the insult that the president would make such a momentous decision without consulting Stimson or any of his senior military advisers. His trepidation arose from the potential political eruption over Washington's direction of the war if news burst out that the president contemplated writing off the Americans in the Philippines, and still worse that their intended reinforcements could be diverted to holding part of the British Empire. Stimson called Hopkins and notified him that he must resign if this decision stood. Roosevelt and Churchill innocently denied it was so to Hopkins. In fact, Churchill had cabled Australia after the session affirming Roosevelt had made just this pledge. Later that day, in conference with his advisers, Roosevelt offhandedly declared that a paper was going around which was "nonsense" about his conference with Churchill. Even without access to Churchill's cable to Australia, Stimson knew the paper had been accurate but discerned that Roosevelt had learned a lesson.

Harry Hopkins's outsize contribution in this episode and throughout the conference earned a salute from the British minister of supply, Lord Beaverbrook (Max Aiken), the energetic, outspoken, lightning-quick, Canadian-born entrepreneur and now Churchill protégé (they had been at odds in the 1930s). The controversial Beaverbrook wrote to Hopkins, "I bless and praise thy matchless might." If Hopkins had "might," it was in intellect and stamina, not physical presence. He was born in 1890 to a deeply religious family. After graduation from Grinnell College he pursued work in Christian reformism and the social gospel, eventually securing a job in relief work during the Great Depression for then–New York governor Franklin Roosevelt. Following Roosevelt to Washington, Hopkins moved from one position to another in a merry-go-round of Roosevelt's new agencies, becoming identified as a "big government free spender." He endured a dreadful year in 1937, when cancer first took his second wife and then Hopkins himself underwent stomach cancer surgery. He would remain emaciated and frail the rest of his life.

Officially titled special assistant to the president, Hopkins now literally lived in the White House. Although his prior career seemed embedded exclusively in domestic reform, effectively he functioned as a blend of two standard roles in later presidencies: chief of staff and national security adviser. He "shared or accepted most of the President's assumptions" and often acted as a surrogate for a president who could not travel easily. It was Hopkins who first personally met Churchill (describing his task as "a catalytic agent between two prima donnas") and then Stalin.* Energetic, a successful suitor of Churchill's respect, with a feline facility for reading the president's moods, his most valued trait was his complete loyalty to Roosevelt. Yet he also displayed a nimble mind capable of culling from a miasma of views the essential point (Churchill called him "Lord Root of the Matter"). In a paper surveying the worldwide situation just before the conference began, Hopkins raised the highly unsettling but prescient prospect that both the Philippines and Singapore might fall to the Japanese.

Although the conference featured clashes reflecting national, armed service, and personal conflicts, by any historical standard it ranks as a signal success, perhaps the most important of the war. It produced a roll of major achievements. On 1 January 1942 came the United Nations Declaration. The twenty-six signatory nations pledged themselves to the principles set forth in the Atlantic Charter and declared their determination to pursue cooperatively the complete defeat of the "savage and brutal forces seeking to subjugate the world."†

Articulating noble war aims was no small achievement, but the most important accomplishment at "Arcadia" was the establishment of the American and British command structure for the rest of the war. Though Churchill

---

* Roosevelt had met Churchill during World War I, but professed no memory of the encounter, much to Churchill's chagrin.

† Churchill pointed out to Roosevelt that the phrase "United Nations" had appeared in Lord Byron's poem *Childe Harold's Pilgrimage*, but Churchill's great biographer, Martin Gilbert, noted it had been used in June 1941 at a St. James Palace meeting in London. *The Road to Victory, 1941–1945* (Boston: Houghton Mifflin, 1986), 35.

and the British (particularly the Royal Navy) at first resisted, General Marshall pursued and won an agreement for the creation of "unity of command" in major theaters. A single supreme commander would control all land, air, and sea forces of any service or nationality in a single operational theater, thus at least permitting the unified application of Allied power. There were limited rights of appeal along national lines of the supreme commander's decisions, but in practice this was not permitted to erode seriously the authority of the theater commander. This was immediately followed by the appointment of British general Archibald P. Wavell as the supreme commander of the ABDA (American, British, Dutch, Australian) Theater to protect the Malay Barrier and the Netherlands East Indies.

The next step was the creation of the vital machinery between the theater commanders and Roosevelt and Churchill. When the chiefs of staff of the United States and Great Britain met, they would become the Combined Chiefs of Staff, the highest military body providing overall command and control immediately under the two chief executives. When the British Chiefs of Staff were not present, their representatives in Washington would work with the American Chiefs of Staff for day-to-day management. Roosevelt and Churchill agreed that the munitions and other resource production of their nations should become one common pool. They appointed a Munitions Assignment Board to decide under the Combined Chiefs of Staff how material would be distributed to the various theaters. Among the important supporting agencies for the Combined Chiefs and Munitions Assignment Board were joint intelligence and shipping bodies.

Lord Beaverbrook crusaded for drastically boosted American production goals for 1942 and 1943. Roosevelt, whose instincts channeled in a similar direction, issued an order to the War Department on 3 January 1942, steeply boosting aircraft production goals to 45,000 in 1942 and 100,000 in 1943. Tank production would be 45,000 and 75,000 respectively. On the same day, Roosevelt ordered merchant ship building goals for 1942 of eight million tons, rising to "a minimum" of 10 million in 1943.

There were and would continue to be major and even violent disagreements between Roosevelt and Churchill on policy and strategy. But the central pillar supporting the whole alliance was their mutual warmth and determination to cooperate. "The President made it perfectly clear," wrote Hopkins, "that he . . . was very pleased with the meeting. There is no question but that he grew genuinely to like Churchill and I am sure Churchill equally liked the President." If not the warmth, the determination to cooperate suffused the lower levels of the alliance and proved a profound product of Arcadia.

China: "Arcadia" and Realities

The attack on Pearl Harbor validated long-range Chinese strategy: the acquisition of allies capable of defeating Japan, unlike China alone. Chiang accepted Roosevelt's proposal to make the generalissimo the China Theater supreme commander. This seemed obvious since Allied forces in the region were overwhelmingly Chinese.

Two issues flared up immediately demonstrating the alliance would be rocky. When Wavell requested Chinese assistance in Burma, Chiang enthusiastically agreed to send a large Chinese force for defense of the British colony and the vital supply route to China. But the British fended off the offer, ostensibly because such large Chinese forces were not needed, but mainly because Wavell knew the Chinese had no supply system and stripped the land they marched over of food, placing the local population in peril. The Chinese presence in Burma also harbored important political issues. Wavell's request for a smaller force humiliated the generalissimo. Yet the American military mission leader, General Magruder, immediately identified an obvious contradiction between the British rejection of large bodies of Chinese troops as unneeded while the British simultaneously requested two of Chennault's three American Volunteer Group (AVG) fighter squadrons and seized Chinese Lend-Lease supplies in Rangoon. The seizure incensed Chiang: not over the material issue of China's desperate munitions needs, but the political issue of a stinging slap in the face to Chinese dignity that the British had not deigned to even ask permission. Chiang agreed to dispatch the AVG squadrons, and the Lend-Lease supply matter was smoothed over (but not forgotten in Chongqing).

The United States and Britain failed to disclose candidly to the Chinese (or other allies for that matter) that their fundamental strategic priority was "Europe First." In fact, Roosevelt disingenuously dispatched a personal message to Chiang that the Allies would treat equally the two phases of the global war. Chiang, however, suspected the European priority as early as 20 January 1942, but ascribed this primarily to British influence.

For Chiang and many other Chinese deeply infused with nationalist fervor, a towering issue was Allied treatment of China. On the one hand, the fact that China attained the status of one of the "Big Four" (with the United States, Britain, and the Soviet Union) on the United Nations declaration in January 1942 ostensibly lifted China to first rank among nations and marked a decisive break with China's lowly status since the 1840s. But a paper proclamation did not reflect British (or Soviet) opinion that this exalted status was not merited. Later, some Western accounts would dismiss this as merely an unearned favor benevolently dispensed by Roosevelt. Remarkably, Chiang privately believed China was too weak to warrant such recognition and would remain grateful to Roosevelt, despite other sharp disappointments. What seems stunning about the deprecation of China at this point is that it had been among the earliest and by now the longest suffering nation under Axis onslaught.

Chiang and other Chinese set great importance on whether China would participate as an equal at "Arcadia." Further, would it be an equal on the Combined Chiefs of Staff and the Munitions Assignment Board? In all instances, the answer would be no. Not only was there no high-level Chinese participation at the "Arcadia" Conference, but when Chiang actively pursued China's representation on the Combined Chiefs of Staff and the Munitions Assignment Board, he was rebuffed. Though Roosevelt seemed amenable to such an arrangement in conversation with Chinese foreign minister Soong, Marshall and the War Department adamantly rejected any such arrangement. The Soviets likewise did not sit at the Combined Chiefs of Staff, but they were not at war with Japan. The position of the United States and United Kingdom on the Munitions Assignment Board was that they alone were producing an excess of munitions and therefore they should decide on their distribution, hence the exclusion of both China and the Soviet Union.

Given Churchill's deprecating attitude toward China (widely shared at the top levels in the United Kingdom) as well as opposition within the US government, notably the War Department, little chance existed that China might have participated in top Allied war direction. But there was a reason for China's exclusion that did not rest on belittling of China's efforts or blatant or latent racism. The British had been reading top-level Chinese diplomatic code and cipher systems from prior to Pearl Harbor. The official records of the "Arcadia" Conference contain no clear reference to this—which is scarcely surprising, given the ultrahigh security status of code-breaking activities by Allied or Axis powers. But the minutes of a meeting of the US and British Chiefs of Staff on 10 January 1942 record that communication with the generalissimo was "difficult and subject to delay and *possible interception*" (italics added). From this it may be inferred that the British either informed their American counterparts about the vulnerability of Chinese secret communication systems or persuaded them that there was some other major compromise hazard. Therefore, permitting Chinese access to the highest levels of Western Allied counsels would be like granting Germany and Japan immediate and firsthand knowledge of Allied intentions and plans. This was no phantom fear: the Japanese had broken into Chinese diplomatic and military codes wholesale. Indeed, the insecurity of China's communications tainted its relations with its allies and degraded the performance of its armies in profound ways so far barely acknowledged or explored for the whole course of the Asia-Pacific War. In this regard, it is also instructive that the British remained well into 1942 quite reticent with the Americans about the extent of their success against German codes, because they deemed their US counterparts disorganized and insecure.

While the United States and Britain left China out of the top machinery of the alliance, keeping China in the war remained a major issue at "Arcadia" and beyond. A US paper warned of profound concern over the "progressive weakening, morally and materially, in China's war effort." For the immediate future, however, US planners offered only the maintenance of strength of the AVG, efforts to improve the supply route from Rangoon to Chungking (soon rendered moot), and the intent to equip some Chinese divisions for service under a US representative.

IN EARLY 1942, cables from Chongqing ignited an essay duel among American officials on China realities. The head of the military mission, Magruder, seeing a huge career opportunity, beseeched Chiang to recognize him as commander of US (as well as Allied) air forces in China. Chiang rebuffed Magruder on the grounds that all foreign forces based in China must be under the China Theater. Shortly afterward, Magruder wired Washington, describing Chiang as a "remarkable figure" who almost "alone" kept the Chinese together, but he insisted the United States must "oppose and temper [Chiang's] frequently exorbitant demands." Then, in February 1942, Magruder performed an abrupt about-face. He characterized the Chinese as "great believers in the world of make-believe" and condemned reports of "marvelous achievements and abilities of the Chinese Army" as "absolutely without foundation." Magruder maintained that the Chinese could not inaugurate any "large scale" offensive and failed even at "annoyance and attrition" of the Japanese. A message from the US naval attaché damned as "fatally defective" US news reports attaching high hopes to China's military value. He bluntly concluded that China's near total isolation now made it clear that "we will be well on our way toward defeating Japan by the time [supply] lines [to China] can be opened for delivery in real quantity."

State Department officials challenged these cables with a far broader view that contained truths that still resonate. Maxwell M. Hamilton, chief of the

Division of Far Eastern Affairs, underscored that "The Chinese have fought for four and one-half years. They have suffered tremendously in blood, in treasure, in forced removal from their accustomed homes. . . . The fact that they have kept going along in the face of what they have suffered is the most remarkable development of the last few years in the Far East." Career diplomat Stanley Hornbeck, the influential adviser to Cordell Hull, seconded this view and added that "most of the military experts of practically all the other powers (including Japan) thought and said at the outset and at intervals [that China's resistance] could not be continued beyond a few weeks or at the utmost a few months." He pointedly noted the dearth of supplies the Allies had provided China. Hornbeck admitted the Chinese victory at Changsha "was not as glorious as Chinese reports would indicate," but scored a stinging point that China had better grounds for presenting Changsha as a success than anything China's allies could recently claim. They might have pointed out one enormous contribution China made throughout the Asia Pacific: by joining the alliance with the United States and the British Commonwealth, China vitiated Japan's assertions that ultimately the war was about race between Asians and whites.

The end of 1941 fell just past the halfway mark in the War of Resistance—a moment to review China's situation, starting with its increasingly dismal domestic circumstances. In 1937 Chiang and the Nationalists claimed control of China, but Chiang's party only controlled seven provinces in the lower Yangtze region, albeit the most economically advanced, with roughly one-third of the nation's population. Absent the war, there is a high probability that the Nationalists would have gradually grasped real rather than nominal control through all or the majority of China. Where the writ of the Nationalists ran, they could select or dismiss local officials, collect taxes, and recruit "reasonably efficiently" for their armed forces.

The war radically diminished the power of Chiang and the Nationalists. By the end of 1941, the Nationalists had been ejected from their original urban power base and exerted much attenuated control over only about half of China's provinces, including most of the poorest and most backward. As historian Hsi-sheng Ch'i explained, Chiang's writ was further truncated by "at least 6 to 10 quasi-independent regional systems, each with its own entrenched power structures, leadership, and web of intricate interpersonal relations." Almost nowhere did the Nationalists command as much power as they had in their prewar base area, so that vital administrative functions like law and order, tax collection, and conscription remained almost everywhere under "a mass of local practices." Deprived of institutional control, Chiang and the Nationalists were reduced to veiled or open bargaining, threats of sanctions or outright retaliation, and major or minor accommodations with regional or local power brokers. Ironically, outsiders tended to accept at face value that Chiang and the Nationalists exercised effective control throughout China and thus to blame them for every abuse of power, mismanagement, and corruption.

Economically, Japan's blockade and seizure of coastal provinces nearly extinguished decades of advances in industrialization (reducing China to roughly its status in the 1870s) and clasped a near stranglehold over the import of munitions and supplies. In 1937 the combination of the Maritime Customs Service, the Salt Tax, and the Consolidated Tax generated 67 percent of the central government revenue. By 1939 those same sources produced only 6.3 percent of revenue. In accord with prewar planning, the Nationalists offset that loss by revenue generation aimed at the urban areas and the rich, while shielding rural areas. New taxes applied to consumption, excess war profits, and inheritance, and the income tax was adjusted. Consequently, up to 1941 the purchasing power of rural areas increased, while that of soldiers and civil servants sank to 22 percent and 16 percent, respectively, of their 1937 levels. The loss of most of the prewar income stream received by the central government not only administered a stunning blow to military efforts, it also deprived the government of vital resources to deal with the domestic catastrophes, such as the millions of refugees. The status of the *fabi* (the Nationalist money unit) eroded. Currency issued by regional or even local powers undermined the national-scale economy and provided bountiful opportunities for currency speculation, hoarding, smuggling, and the use of currency surrogates like opium.

Because highly populated and developed areas near the coast had become food deficit areas before the war, China depended on imports for 10–20 percent of its food. The tightening of the Japanese blockade ended this in 1941. Chiang and the Nationalists paid careful attention to food supplies. Government programs to encourage use of better seeds and pesticides, while expanding cultivated areas and encouraging other crops like wheat and potatoes, maintained an adequate food supply through 1940. This kept overall food production relatively stable until 1941, when a threatening decline first emerged.

Chiang's efforts on the military front suffered from increasingly crippling impediments. During the Northern Expedition, Chiang's small, loyal, but better-equipped and -trained army, backed by Guangdong and Guangxi regional units, all surging on nationalist fervor, directly or indirectly forced regional militarists to kowtow and offer at least outward allegiance. But Chiang found it prudent to leave most of them dominant in their local domains rather than engage in an endless succession of costly battles that might exhaust his forces before he secured complete ascendancy. Thus, Chiang's position hung heavily on the intimidation his army projected.

This army permitted Chiang to take on Japan, but only a select number of regional leaders gave full-hearted support to him. Most took a wait-and-see attitude to one degree or another. The devastating losses sustained by the Central Army in the first half-year of war undermined its intimidating aura. After the heavy loss of trained soldiers, new equipment, modern weapons, and most of all base areas, Chiang's loyal forces no longer clearly overmatched any individual, or even more, any groupings of regional powers. Some regions (Shanxi, Inner Mongolia, and the Muslim northwest provinces) professed to remain loyal to Chiang while working out accommodations with the Japanese and posing the threat of going over entirely to the Japanese or the puppet government if Chiang sought to bring them to heel.

And the army's deterioration extended ever deeper. Marked inequality and corruption plagued the conscription systems, now largely in the hands of regional and local power brokers outside Chiang's control. It was common for conscripts to be transported long distances in chains, without adequate nourishment or medical attention. Some died; others deserted. Nominally the army payroll provided for four or five million soldiers, but many were phantoms created so that their officers could scam their pay. Those dependent on government salaries, like soldiers and their officers, found their income too low to support families. The loss of German and then Soviet advisers degraded training standards as well as the quality of staff work. Moreover, the expenditure of the carefully built-up stockpiles of arms and supplies in the early months of the war far exceeded the paltry rate of resupply, which plummeted further in 1940–1941. Frequent condemnations by China's allies that its commanders were more concerned with hoarding their weapons and supplies than fighting, grate on the ear when it is considered that those same allies had failed to provide more than a tiny trickle of supplies compared to China's needs.

Other factors had also degraded Chiang's Central Army forces. Frequent and major defeats with heavy losses bored into morale. Moreover, now commanders also labored under administrative and territorial responsibility unlike during the pre-1937 years, when they were free from concerns about recruits, arms, or supplies. By 1941, in most areas the commanders effectively were living off the land and wrestling with local officials on taxes, food, and recruits. This took time away from training and created a reluctance to move once a routine was established. And once units became rooted in an area "they found it more difficult to resist the temptation of other forms of indulgence, embezzlement and corruption, cowardice, or pursuit of easy life styles. . . . The general tendency was that the longer a unit was stationed at a fixed location, the more it might become corrupt and less combat competent (e.g. Tang Enbo's troops in Henan province)."

As bad as this situation was, the loss of the supply channel via Hong Kong inflicted a major blow. Soon, worse was to come.

:

CHAPTER 13

"It Was Like Being Lost in Fog"

SINGAPORE SET UP

Far East Strategy

The end of the First World War found Britain and its global empire triumphant, but its economic position eroded. Its strategists ranked the security of the United Kingdom as its first priority. Japan's potential menace to Australia and New Zealand fixed the second priority. The Singapore naval base and the slogan "Main Fleet to Singapore" became the physical and political symbols of Britain's commitment to this second priority.

But in the words of historian Brian Farrell, Singapore was a "strategic delusion." Britain's economic weakness enforced budget stringencies that first mandated placing the base on the north shore, scarcely one mile across the Johore Straits from the Malayan Peninsula, to avoid expensive harbor defenses on the south shore. They further truncated the original massive complex for a dozen capital ships and a host of accompanying vessels to a three-capital-ship squadron capacity—while the Admiralty projected a minimum seven-ship battle squadron requirement to confront Japan.

By the late 1930s British policymakers sought to shore up the increasingly wobbly "Singapore Strategy" with two amendments. Like Greek playwrights, they wrote in a deus ex machina deliverance: fear of provoking a war with the United States would forestall a Japanese march south—though the United States refused to make such a commitment. The RAF advanced the second amendment: substitution of air power for scarce capital ships. While the new strategy provided the RAF with the opportunity to anoint one of its own as the commander in chief Far East, providing the quantity and quality of aircraft necessary to forge a defense proved another matter.

Sixty-two-year-old Air Chief Marshal Sir Robert Brooke-Popham was recalled from retirement to become the new Far East commander, notwithstanding his lack of any outstanding qualification for the post. Moreover, his writ provided an object lesson in how not to set up such a command. He held only general authority, not operational control, over air and land elements and not even general authority over the navy. He possessed no control over the civil administration—indeed civil and military chains of command in the Far East intersected only in London. Further, his bailiwick stretched from Burma through Singapore to Hong Kong, and he had to coordinate with the Dutch and the Australians—without so much as an adequate personal transport aircraft. "I fully realize that at the present time the requirements of Singapore must come a bad third to those of the British Isles and the Middle East," he wrote the day before leaving England.

In retrospect, the lethal blows to the already questionable "Singapore Strategy" occurred in June 1940 with the defeat of France and Italy's entry into the war. Britain now confronted naval challenges in the Atlantic and Mediterranean alone with no visible means of detaching a battle fleet to Singapore without abandonment of the Mediterranean. Abandoning the Eastern Mediterranean would rip a vast hole in the blockade, one of Britain's few remaining weapons against Germany. Further, if Britain lost access to the oil of Abadan and Bahrain that fueled the eastern reaches of its empire and their defense, there was no spare tanker capacity to replace it with oil from the United States. Abandoning its Mediterranean position would be devastating not just to the morale of the British public but also to American confidence in British stamina. As historian Raymond Callahan observed, "What [Churchill] did was to see clearly that Britain could fight one war—or lose two."

The logic of the British Mediterranean strategy remains defensible, but not Churchill's candor in his dealings with Australia and New Zealand. As first sea lord, Churchill pledged that the defense of Singapore remained the Empire's second priority. From the moment he became prime minister, however, Churchill rowed away from that promise with muffled oars, as he inveigled Australia and New Zealand to dispatch divisions for Mediterranean operations with assurances that, should Japan strike, Britain's second priority would revert to the Far East. But Australian leadership was by no means blameless. They issued protests but no emphatic objection as they watched Churchill cast off from the Singapore strategy. Then on 28 April

1941, Churchill issued a fiat that the government would grasp responsibility to provide the service departments with timely notice of the outbreak of war in the Far East. This bold pronouncement proved fatuous—no realistic plan followed for how, even assuming timely notice, reinforcements could be mustered in sufficient time.

But by the summer of 1941, British planners recognized that as much as 25 percent of the empire's war potential required holding the linked territories from Egypt, through the Middle East, the Indian Ocean (and India), and Australasia. This linkage dictated that holding both the Middle East and the Far East was mandatory, which, in turn, required maintaining maritime communications in the Indian Ocean. What it did not require was a strong forward defense of Singapore.

Malaya

In area, Malaya roughly equals England and Wales. It stretches four hundred miles on a north-south axis and its width ranges from sixty to two hundred miles. A mountain range in the peninsula's center forms a natural "spine." Fast flowing rivers serve as the "ribs" of this spine and create a set of hurdles to north-south movement. Very "dense jungle and graceful feathery clumps of bamboo" formed more than half of Malaya's area in 1941. An Australian officer described it as follows:

> As soon as we left the road and entered the trees it was like being lost in fog—nothing to indicate any direction whatever. There was no sun, only tall tree trunks festooned with every sort of creeper and the ground in between just covered with undergrowth.

In 1941 the population numbered about two million Malays, the original inhabitants, largely farmers. There were approximately two million Chinese who dominated the commercial structure, and around 9,000 Europeans who ruled from oversight positions in industry and government.

The typical rural dwelling featured a steep thatched roof of palm leaves, tightly woven and waterproof. The thatching of the walls left gaps through which breezes entered and fire smoke exited. Dogs or cats served as sentinels by the doors. Chinese or Indian structures employed dirt floors—seldom swept—whereas the Malays invariably built floors three to four feet off the ground. Inside were elaborately decorated walls with murals of newspaper and magazine clippings, with portraits of Hollywood stars accorded honored places. Each dwelling had "its own particular aroma, emanating chiefly from cesspits, pigstyes, and the Chinese methods of manuring, totally irrespective of the sources of the manure!" reported an Australian soldier.

Malaya's economic importance to Britain soared with the outbreak of the European war. Britain desperately needed dollars to purchase war materials from the United States. Enormous Malayan tin and rubber production filled tills in London with more precious dollars than any other imperial outpost except the dominions. London forcefully impressed upon the civil administration that maximizing output of these products constituted their overriding priority.

Malaya presented exceptional challenges to defense mobilization. The chaotic accretion of Britain's Far East Empire spawned no less than eleven administrative satrapies weakly bonded by the Malaya Civil Service of British professionals. At the apex of this jury-rigged structure was Sir Shenton Thomas, nearly sixty, who served simultaneously as the governor and commander in chief of the Straits Settlement (Singapore) and as the high commissioner of the Federated and Unfederated Malay States. An Australian observer condemned him as heavily disposed more to "producing reasons for not doing things than for doing them." His amiable, socially adept personality well fitted him for peacetime, but he was not rigged for war by background or self-identity.

Singapore Defenses: Ships, Planes, and Troops

Since June 1939, the overstretched Admiralty foresaw commitment of only a battle cruiser and an aircraft carrier to the Indian Ocean to counter Japanese cruiser raids, but not to confront a Japanese battle fleet. With increasing American assistance in the Atlantic, however, by mid-1941 the Admiralty projected a six-strong ship capital squadron for the Indian Ocean. But only two of the ships under consideration were more than obsolescent relics, and no balanced force mustering cruisers and destroyers could arrive before March 1942.

On 25 August, in response to a request from Australian prime minister Robert Menzies, Churchill proposed deployment of a "small but very powerful and fast force" to "eastern waters" to the first lord of the Admiralty, Fleet Admiral Sir Dudley Pound. This eventually became "Force Z" composed of the modern battleship *Prince of Wales* and aged battle cruiser *Repulse*. For decades, the disastrous fate of "Force Z" allegedly resulted from Churchill's forcing a resistant Admiralty to kneel to his fatuous proposal for offensive use of "Force Z." But historian Andrew Boyd retrieved the real story from neglected archival documents. Churchill envisioned "Force Z" to serve first as a strategic deterrent, along with American reinforcements to the Pacific. Should that fail, "Force Z" would revert to the mission of guarding Indian Ocean communications against Japanese cruiser raids. But in September and October 1941, the Admiralty itself conceived a new mission for "Force Z" and eventually a reinforced Eastern Fleet: project its power aggressively against Japanese communications into the South China Sea. If not the author, a major proponent for the new mission of "Force Z" was Admiral Tom Phillips, who became its commander. Phillips received a promotion to full admiral from his prior role as deputy chief of the Naval Staff. Churchill greatly admired the markedly diminutive Phillips (nicknamed "Tom Thumb") as a "fighting admiral," though in fact this officer's first combat in the war would prove his last. He was very intelligent, but inevitably his lack of experience left him basing decisions on theoretical knowledge.

Contrary to many later accounts, there is no evidence that the Admiralty ever earmarked the new carrier *Indomitable* as a definite consort for *Prince of Wales* and *Repulse*. *Indomitable* did sustain grounding damage during its "working up" training on 3 November, but even without that, absent abandonment of the work-up period it never could have reached Singapore by early December 1941. This makes speculation on its role with "Force Z" moot.

Megan Spooner, wife of Rear Admiral Ernest John "Jack" Spooner, flag officer Malaya, noted in her insightful diary that all of Singapore paused to watch the *Prince of Wales* and *Repulse* arrive on 2 December. They looked "very fine against the green hills of Johore" in their "exotic camouflage." Capturing the electric effect of their arrival, she added, "Never before surely can two ships of the Royal Navy have been more welcome nor given more confidence."

WITH REMARKABLE ACCURACY, British intelligence estimated the Japanese would attack Malaya with 600 aircraft; the actual total was 651 planes. In August 1940 the British Chiefs of Staff projected that Singapore security required 504 aircraft (336 aircraft as "initial establishment" plus half again as many aircraft as "immediate reserves"). At that time, Singapore's air arm numbered just eighty-eight aircraft, most of which vied for candidacy as museum exhibits or smelter feed. Despite the ominous tidings in the second half of 1941, the chief of the Air Staff confessed that the goal of 336 frontline planes could not be met by the end of 1941, nor even perhaps in 1942. The overwhelming reason for this empty cupboard was the Middle East. By mid-October 1941, the RAF in the Middle East counted 846 (92 percent modern) frontline aircraft.

The British shipped 200 fighters to the Soviet Union in July 1941, and the United States met Soviet demands by pledging about 1,800 aircraft previously earmarked for the United Kingdom. But given the fact that British shipments to the Middle East continued at high tempo, it is by no means clear that the aircraft shipped to the Soviet Union would otherwise have reached the Far East. This is particularly true as Soviet survival remained in doubt. A Soviet collapse would impose the need for yet another British army and air component to try to contain a German advance toward the Middle East from the north.

A combination of these priorities and shipping considerations induced the Air Ministry to deploy American aircraft reinforcements to Singapore. These included Brewster F2A Buffaloes to equip Singapore's four fighter squadrons, an aircraft deemed obsolescent for other theaters but an overmatch for expected Japanese opposition. One legend about the Malayan defeat is that the Imperial Navy's Mitsubishi A6M "Type Zero" fighters shot the Buffaloes out of the air. But Buffaloes very seldom encountered Imperial Navy fighters, including "Zeros." Rather, the Imperial Army provided by far the dominant winged element of Japan's offensive. That service deployed three fighter types. Of these, the Ki-44 "Tojos" appeared only as a handful of aircraft for operational testing and played no real role. The premier aircraft was the Nakajima Ki-43 "Oscar" that Allied fliers frequently misidentified as its much faster visual cousin, the "Zero." Moreover, the Japanese fielded just 59 Ki-43s, far fewer than the 123 Nakajima Ki-27 "Nates" with fixed undercarriages, a design generation behind the Buffalo.

By paper specifications, the Buffalo was on par with the "Oscar" in speed and faster than the "Nate," but by tests in operational service the Buffalo maximum speed was about 270 miles per hour (mph). Top speed for the Zero was 331.5 mph; the "Oscar" could reach 308 mph and even the "Nate" 292 mph. The conspicuously degraded speed of the Malaya (and Netherlands East Indies) Buffalo variants arose from their engine, which overheated in the tropics, splattered oil up on the canopy at high-power settings, and sometimes even forced the pilot to hand-operate a pump to supply enough fuel for top speed—which made accurate gunnery almost impossible. Further, the Buffalo's machine gun armament failed with disconcerting frequency. However, while every Japanese fighter outturned the Buffalo, they lacked the Buffalo's protective armor for the pilot and leakproof gas tanks.

Three other factors almost guaranteed Japanese combat superiority over

Malaya. First, the mere four Buffalo squadrons possessed just 60 aircraft, with 52 in reserve; they faced 228 Japanese peers. But Japanese dominance rested even more on better-trained and combat-seasoned pilots. Apart from a tiny leavening of battle-tested pilots from Europe and the Middle East, tyros filled the cockpits of Commonwealth fighters, mostly New Zealanders, fresh from basic levels of instruction. Finally, only a fraction of the planned radar sets was in place, and dated radio equipment limited effective ground control range of fighters to ten miles. These constituted much less noted but further severe technical detriments to RAF efforts in Malaya.

In theory, two torpedo bomber squadrons (twenty-nine aircraft and twelve reserves) formed the most potent element of Malaya's air command. The well-trained crews were grotesquely mismatched with their obsolete Vildebeest biplanes. The six squadrons equipped with Blenheim or Hudson bombers (the Hudson doubled as a reconnaissance plane) presented the opposite problem: dreadfully inexperienced crews manning reasonably modern aircraft (sixty-three aircraft and seventeen reserves). Thus, 92 front-line RAF strike aircraft faced 403 Japanese counterparts.

THE SEARCH FOR SOLDIERS for Singapore intersected with the overall plans for the Empire's armies. In September 1939, British leaders looked to create an army of fifty-five divisions to fight the war. Nearly one-third would be fielded by the Dominions and India: fourteen from the Dominions of Canada, Australia, New Zealand, and South Africa, and four from India. The catastrophe of 1940 left Britain's home army in a desperate state. Thereafter, Churchill's government only committed British soldiers overseas in large numbers to the Middle East. Accordingly, only the Dominions or India could supply a garrison for Malaya. The obvious importance of Singapore to Australia secured commitment of the 8th Australian Division (less one brigade) to its defense. That left only one other source for additional divisions: the Indian Army.

The Indian Army played a dominant role in the British Empire's Far Eastern campaigns from 1941 to 1945—from the early disasters to the final triumphs. The reasons for the initial failings and a benchmark for appreciating its later triumphs require examination. In 1939 the Indian Army comprised about 200,000 lightly equipped men. Notwithstanding the title "Indian Army," it was an entity commanded by British officers in British service fundamentally for internal control and security of India's northwest frontier. The army recruited enlisted men from a narrow sector of the spectacularly diverse population of India, the so-called "martial races," comprised of select ethnic groups of allegedly more warlike character. In British eyes, the "martial races" sprang overwhelmingly from northern regions of India. Not by coincidence, these inhabitants were taller, stronger on average, and lighter skinned. But even those with the correct ethnic credentials could be denied enlistment if they came from cities or towns, rather than rural stock, frequently from specific villages. By World War II, new recruits might well represent the fifth generation of their families to serve. This generated intense social pressure for every recruit to serve honorably to preserve the reputation of the village and hence opportunities for others.

Yet more complexities governed the Indian Army's composition. Atop ethnic criteria perched caste: a Jat Sikh could be an infantryman whereas Mazbhi and Ramdasia Sikhs were deemed fit only to be pioneers. Legacies from the 1857 Indian Mutiny added more convolutions. In many regiments each separate company derived recruits from different ethnic or caste origins on the premise that such divergent roots made it less likely that the enlisted men would unite in disobedience or mutiny. Further, British policy since the mutiny placed one battalion of British Army troops in each brigade of the Indian Army. Moreover, the British provided artillerymen (except mountain artillery) and most technical specialists.

Two sources produced officers for the Indian Army: British officers and "native" (later Viceroy) officers. The British officers trained at Sandhurst or its various Indian equivalents. The Viceroy Commissioned Officers (VCOs) were Indians selected by seniority rather than merit. But very sharp boundaries sundered these two categories. Only white British officers could command units of battalion size or larger. VCOs commanded platoons while British officers commanded companies or acted as company officers, but never under command of a VCO.

Sterling service in World War I resulted in Indian officers receiving "King's Commissions," meaning they were in theory on par with British officers. A quota of Indian officers attended Sandhurst and a separate Indian Military Academy at Dehra Dun, although the latter were not authorized to command British officers. This formed part of a broader tide of gradual devolution of more power into Indian hands in both civil and military spheres. Beginning in 1923, a very gradual and slender experiment in creating all-Indian units commenced.

The desperate crisis of 1940 induced a mammoth expansion of the Indian Army. Two divisions, partly trained and accoutered, deployed to the Middle East. The Indian Army instituted a program to stand up six additional infantry divisions by the summer of 1941, with six more divisions to follow (one armored) by the end of 1941. Such stupendous growth drastically diminished quality. A particularly acute issue was the Emergency Commissioned Officer program for British and Indian candidates. Instead of thirty months of training for British and forty-two months for Indian aspirants, both received just four to six months. Due to this abbreviated instruction, most British officers lacked mastery of Urdu, the universal language of the Indian Army, so they could not communicate effectively with their men. Compounding these severe deficiencies was a lack of modern equipment, and training oriented to open warfare in the Middle East rather than the jungles of Malaya or Burma.

The Indian troops sent to Malaya brought one open grievance with them and found another waiting. British authorities had plunged India into the war without any consultation with Indian political leadership. Arriving as saviors of the colony, Indian troops regardless of rank found the European ruling class scorned them and barred their admittance to clubs and swimming pools. The British civilian population and some officers also snubbed the Australians because, as one "digger" explained: "We were still thought of as colonials; we were a bit short on some forms of discipline and the niceties of cultured behavior; perhaps worst of all, we were too familiar with the native population." In Indian Army units another issue simmered beneath the surface: the effects of Indian independence agitation. Official records—created by the British—make this difficult to gauge. If this factor failed to compromise Indian unit effectiveness at the outset, it may have made them brittle in the face of the blows they would sustain.

Presiding over Malaya Command was Lt. Gen. Arthur E. Percival. Photographs reveal an elongated face terminating in "two protruding rabbit teeth" and a receding chin giving him the timid visage of perhaps an assistant headmaster at a second-tier school. His customary diffident, pleasant demeanor and his gangly, stoop-shouldered body reinforced this image. In this case, image mirrored reality for, as one officer said, Percival was "not the man for the whirlwind." His specific credential was service during 1936–1937 as chief of staff to the Malaya commander—when he drafted a prescient appreciation of the likely Japanese scheme of attack. Events proved that as a staff officer Percival had few peers; as a senior commander he had few inferiors.

Percival conspicuously lacked experience with the Indian Army troops who constituted the mainstay of Malaya Command. Exacerbating this situation was that Percival and the senior Indian Army officer, Lt. Gen. Sir Lewis Heath, represented two divergent types of officers in three dimensions. First, staff college and staff assignments dominated Percival's career path while Heath rigorously rejected staff positions to remain in troop assignments. Second, Percival radiated the typical class-based, condescending attitudes about Indian Army officers—like Heath—as distinctly second-team. Third, although Percival carried the ribbons testifying to his courageous performance in combat, it was only up to brigade level. Heath's background boasted military victory in Africa at division level (earning a knighthood). Finally, Heath could not forget that he had been the senior of the two until Percival's recent promotion.

The catalogue of command conflicts extended beyond Percival and Heath. The 8th Australian Division under Maj. Gen. Henry Gordon Bennett formed the other major Empire component of Malaya Command. Bennett was "prickly, obnoxious, demonstrative, suspicious" and boundlessly ambitious. Foremost among his overflowing reservoir of resentments was the fact that in 1916, at age twenty-nine, he had been the youngest brigadier in British Empire forces, and now he believed he had wrongly been denied the role of Australia's leading soldier for the new war. Bennett coupled a hair-trigger personality with special rights of appeal back to his government if his ire was provoked—and Bennett was easily provoked. The one bright spot at the senior level was that Percival and the senior air officer, Air Vice Marshal Pulford, formed a genuine friendship that sutured most of the rents in interservice relations.

Three disastrous dictates from their superiors shackled Percival and his subordinates. First, London declared that the fundamental mission of Malaya Command remained the defense of the Singapore naval base, despite the absence of a "main fleet" or prospect of its timely arrival. The British Chiefs of Staff imposed a second stricture that air power form the key element of Singapore's defenses. While the airmen assured Percival that they would destroy 40 percent of any invasion force, in December 1941 Empire air power existed mostly in aspiration. Worse yet, the RAF sited airfields in Malaya for their utility in projecting the reach of mostly nonexistent planes. The airmen expected any approaching invasion convoy to lack air cover, so they accorded no rigorous consideration to locating airfields where they could be best defended by ground forces. Finally, Far East Command directed Percival to orient his efforts to the defense of beaches, which further mandated a dispersal of Malaya Command.

If this trio of man-made handicaps was not enough, topography added two others. British Malaya commanders rightly concluded that, from a purely military standpoint, Malaya was best defended on terrain across the international border in the narrow Kra Isthmus of southern Thailand. Occupation of this ground would also deprive the Japanese of up to six airfield sites. Hence Malaya Command prepared Operation Matador to seize this area. The success of Matador, however, hinged on at least a twenty-four-hour early warning of a Japanese invasion and the political willingness to violate, if necessary, Thai neutrality. Even assuming the doubtful possibility of a timely early warning, London refused to delegate authority to execute Matador to local commanders because instigating unilateral hostilities with Japan or violating Thai neutrality might alienate American support, a far graver matter than local advantage, however great, in the Far East.

The second topographical issue stemmed from the characteristics of the Malaya peninsula. Prior to the 1930s, the prospect of an overland advance on Singapore from the north could be reasonably discounted. By 1941, the undeveloped east coast facing Japan and the jungle-covered mountains in the center of the peninsula still blocked a rapid advance. But the booming development in the western peninsula resulted in creation of a good north-south trunk road and a parallel rail line. There were, however, lateral roads running from the east coast at Kuantan and Mersing to the west coast. The road net from Mersing also connected to Singapore. To a soldier's eye, it was imperative to hold Kuantan and Mersing to prevent the Japanese from landing behind and cutting off the Empire formations in northern Malaya or even striking south to Singapore itself.

Malaya Command estimated it needed upwards of the equivalent of five divisions (fifteen brigades), not counting fortress troops. But in December 1941, it had just ten infantry brigades. They comprised three divisions each of two brigades (the 9th and 11th Indian, forming III Indian Corps, and the 8th Australian), as well as two brigades in the Singapore fortress, the 28th Indian Brigade as the III Indian Corps reserve, and the 12th Indian Brigade as the Malaya Command reserve. They were supported by second-line Indian battalions as airfield security and volunteer forces. There were thirty-two regular infantry battalions, plus artillery and engineers. (By contrast, at this time the British had stationed in the Middle East three armored and thirteen infantry divisions, as well as an array of separate brigades and battalions.) During the window from July to October 1941 when reinforcements might have reached the Far East in time, the Middle East received 770 tanks, 34,000 trucks, 600 field guns, 240 antiaircraft guns, 200 antitank guns, and 900 mortars.

Besides shortages of troops, Malaya Command faced a "nearly endless" list of deficiencies in weaponry and supplies. For example, the acute shortage of antiaircraft guns left virtually none for troops in the field. The War Office denied requests for armored vehicles from both Percival and his predecessor. There was an acute lack of Bren guns, the key firepower weapon of infantry sections, before November, which was the same month most artillery units received their new twenty-five-pounder field guns.

The matrix of obligations, terrain, and available forces induced Malaya Command's widely dispersed deployment. Heath's III Indian Corps headquarters reposed at Kuala Lumpur, some 200 miles north of Singapore and 250 miles from the Thai frontier. The 11th Indian Division (Maj. Gen. D. M. Murray-Lyon) faced the northwestern frontier, protecting airfields around Alor Star and on alert for Matador. The headquarters of the 9th Indian Division (Maj. Gen. A. E. Barstow) also sat in Kuala Lumpur, but its two brigades were deployed hundreds of miles distant to protect east coast airfields around Kota Bharu and Kuantan (the latter also being a critical lateral road entry point). Heath's reserve brigade, the 28th Indian Brigade, stood midway between Kuala Lumpur and the frontier. The 8th Australian Division guarded southern Malaya. Percival's reserve was the 12th Indian Brigade, by far the best trained and manned of the Indian brigades. It waited at Port Dickenson, about fifty miles south of Kuala Lumpur.

In the aftermath of the campaign, Percival and other officers heaped enormous blame on the civil government for failing to mobilize civilian labor for excavating defenses to free troops for training. The truth is that public officialdom and citizens did not lose Malaya, though Percival and his subordinates nonetheless identified valid faults—like the colonial administrative labyrinth. London created the root cause of military-civilian strife by instructing civilian authorities to maximize economic output while directing military authorities to prepare vigorously for defense.

Only three of Percival's ten brigades were prepared to fight the war that engulfed them. The mainspring of this preparation was Lt. Col. Ian M. Stewart of the 2nd Argyll and Sutherland Highlanders, 12th Indian Brigade. Stewart preached essentially an inversion of British Army doctrine which was mired in the art of 1918 with a few refinements. According to this doctrine, defense rested on static defense lines based upon the firepower of machine guns to hold up the enemy and then artillery to devastate it. Counterattacks were to restore a breach in the line. Formations had a distinct front and rear, with supplies flowing unimpeded from the latter to the former. The battle would be directed by colonels and above.

Stewart denounced such tactics as positively disastrous. The jungle restricted vision, denying automatic weapons the long-range dominance they possessed in other terrain, creating gaps between defensive positions and making them vulnerable to infiltration or being outflanked. No senior officer could exercise close control. Troops who sat meekly waiting in dense terrain for the enemy to strike them became psychologically vulnerable. Therefore, defense in the jungle must be active ("to lose the initiative in jungle is death"), with junior leaders constantly ranging out and about with patrols and small detachments to detect, confound, and foil the enemy with counterattacks. Roads were useful for distant movement and advancing supplies, but defenses must be stretched well out from roads and, above all, in great depth. The two Australian brigades also adopted this doctrine.

Intelligence on the Japanese flowing to and created by Malaya Command was not solely racist drivel. A 1939 *Handbook of the Japanese Army* from the Military Intelligence Directorate stated: "[The Japanese] are very well led, have excellent spirit, are well knit together, confident, and have exceptional powers of endurance." It graded the Imperial Army as "almost up to the highest standards." Likewise a manual issued by the Far East Command in 1941 accurately emphasized the Japanese proclivity for envelopment tactics at all levels, excellence at the small unit level, and capacity for night fighting. But the appraisal's final evaluation undercut this assessment by damning it as against merely presumptively inferior Chinese opposition. Notably, however, the Australians took the Japanese seriously and prepared accordingly. Far more defective was Commonwealth air intelligence, which in June 1941 grossly underestimated the range and bomb loads of Japanese aircraft.

Perhaps the largest element in the miscalculation derived from what is now called mirror imaging: gauging an opponent's capabilities in accordance with expectations about your own. The Japanese concentrated the forces for the Malaya campaign merely a few weeks before attacking—not the months the British assumed were required because they would need that long to mount so complex an operation. Wishful thinking likewise distorted British intelligence. Recognizing they were not ready, minds from London to Malaya arranged evidence to support the hopeful theorem that the Japanese would bide their time until the British were ready. The final component of the fatal intelligence failure was not simply underestimating the Japanese, but overestimating the readiness of Malaya Command.

Among several warnings from signals intelligence was an October intercept divulging a two-month-early termination of Combined Fleet sea exercises. A stream of intercepts emerged from the Japanese Consul-General's office in Singapore disclosing subversion and intelligence. In November, Tokyo ordered the Singapore consul to return to Japan (without relieving him) on the last Japanese vessel leaving Singapore on the 16th. Then the Imperial Navy changed call signs after only one month, instead of the usual six months. On the 18th, the dedicated Far East intelligence organization (the Royal Navy's Far East Combined Bureau [FECB]) warned that war was imminent. Yet as late as 27 November, Brooke-Popham in a message to London discounted the prospect of a Japanese attack.

Japanese Plans

Tokyo detailed the Twenty-Fifth Army under Gen. Tomoyuki Yamashita to conquer Singapore. Groomed by his country physician father as a soldier, Yamashita's impressive physical presence (he adopted a nom de plume at one point of *Daisen*, "Mighty Cedar") matched his rapid ascent in the Imperial Army. Yamashita's affinity to the "Imperial Way" faction led to what he rued as the great mistake of his career: he urged that an imperial witness be present for the suicides of the young officers convicted in the 26 February 1936 incident. This misstep angered the emperor and estranged Tôjô. While idling in a career wilderness, Yamashita accumulated an additional black mark by opposing the Tripartite Alliance. He owed his new appointment to his immediate superior, Field Marshal Count Hisaichi Terauchi of the Southern Army. Terauchi conspired with like-minded officers to mortify Tôjô by recruiting Yamashita.

Yamashita's army comprised what were regarded widely as the three best Imperial Army divisions. Lt. Gen. Takuro Matsui's 5th Division specialized in amphibious operations. Like the 5th Division, Lt. Gen. Renya Mutaguchi's 18th Division was battle-tested in China and specialized in light infantry operations in rough terrain. Yamashita forged an easy rapport with these subordinates. Lt. Gen. Takuro Nishimura's Imperial Guards Division presented a very different story. The well-connected Nishimura headed the army's most prestigious formation, but the division had last fought as a unit in 1905. Twenty-Fifth Army staff officers deemed the division's troops deficient in training and its officers arrogant and uncooperative. The Twenty-Fifth Army also included the 1st, 6th, and 14th Tank Regiments (battalion-sized formations) with a total of fifty-six medium and seventy-four light tanks. Confounding conventional thinking about fighting in jungle areas, these tanks played a huge role in the campaign. Lt. Col. Masanobu Tsuji, Yamashita's talented chief operations officer, "was widely seen as Tôjô's plant."

Contrary to later assertions, the Imperial Army devoted no rigorous attention to Malaya before August 1940. But during the next year, the Taiwan Army Research Section developed a very sound battle doctrine for the forthcoming campaign. This distilled wisdom was contained in a seventy-page pamphlet drafted by Tsuji and studied by all ranks, titled *Read This Alone—And the War Can Be Won.* Interspersed with savvy advice on jungle warfare were chatty sections, including a near travelogue on Malaya with helpful insight on native customs, and a "know your enemy" section highlighting as weaknesses the multiracial diversity of British forces—with singular contempt for Indian troops. Tsuji's pamphlet commanded the soldiers to "show compassion to those without guilt," but coupled this to the sinister qualification that the "Overseas Chinese" stood outside the "Asian Brotherhood." Yamashita saw the coming campaign as one of liberation. Hence he immediately enjoined his soldiers: "no looting, no rape, no arson."

Terauchi's naval counterpart was Vice Adm. Nobutake Kondo, who commanded the Southern Force. Yamashita's immediate naval partner was Vice Adm. Jisaburō Ozawa, commander of the Malaya Force that would lift the Twenty-Fifth Army to Thailand and Malaya. The Twenty-Fifth Army plan housed several notable points. First, Yamashita and Ozawa agreed on a simultaneous attack on Kota Bharu across the border in Malaya, with the landings in Thailand. This would protect the invasion force from air attack and promptly secure advanced air bases. Second, Yamashita decided to leave his reserve division, the 56th, behind to free shipping resources to maintain a flow of supplies to support a rapid advance.

But leaving the 56th Division behind (singularly few other generals in the war would have done this) meant that his army would amount to only two and three-quarters divisions (part of the 18th Division was tasked with attacking Borneo). Yamashita accepted inferiority in infantry because his vision of the campaign looked to substitute tactical and operational finesse for raw numbers. He called his scheme a "driving charge" (*Kirimomi Sakusen*), meaning he would seize the initiative from the outset and drive forward relentlessly, never permitting his numerically superior opponent to congeal into a formidable defensive stance or to receive reinforcements. If thin in infantry, the Twenty-Fifth Army was well endowed with artillery, armor, and engineer units, which would enable the army to administer powerful local blows and then sustain its advance. The final plan looked to destroy the defenders in Malaya and then capture Singapore. All of this would be made possible by Japanese dominance of both the sea and air. But ultimately Yamashita grounded his intentions on a fundamental premise: the Japanese were better fighters.

Japanese intelligence arrangements provide a story with high and low points. By late 1941, there were nearly three hundred Japanese agents in Malaya, sixty-two in Singapore alone. The Colonial Office's appeasement policy enhanced their work by blocking counterintelligence actions on the grounds they might be provocative. Japanese officers in mufti roamed Malaya and Singapore harvesting detailed information. They were coupled to blatant aerial reconnaissance overflights in late 1941—again the appeasement policy quashed proposals to intercept the planes grossly violating British airspace. Japanese signals intelligence proved much less capable than its Western counterparts. Hobbling all such efforts was the ferocious disharmony at the top between the Imperial Army and Navy.

The topic of intelligence brings us to the colorful and controversial *Automedon* affair. The German disguised merchant raider *Atlantis* intercepted a British ship, the *Automedon*, in the Indian Ocean on 11 November 1940. A boarding party returned for a second search of *Automedon* after the chivalrous German skipper, Bernard Rogge, acceded to the request of one passenger, Mrs. Violet Ferguson, for another effort to retrieve her luggage, which contained a tea set of sentimental value. On this serendipitous second excursion, the German sailors located a storeroom with Ferguson's luggage that also contained 123 mailbags, some packed with top secret papers intended for Brooke-Popham. The outstanding item was the minutes of a British cabinet meeting in August that reviewed a gloomy appreciation of the Far East situation by the British Chiefs of Staff. Besides full details of the state of Singapore's defenses and Royal Navy and Royal Air Force strengths there, it also specified British responses to further Japanese advances in the region, primarily one of avoiding war, given Britain's present weakness in the Far East.

The Germans handed over the documents to the Japanese, but could not resist substituting for the true story a claim that Berlin's espionage services had purloined the documents. The Japanese were extremely skeptical of this narrative and instead became suspicious that the documents were forgeries intended to goad Japan into attacking Singapore! Although some accounts attributed enormous significance to this episode, by 1941 much of the specific information and the August 1940 strategic appreciation was out of date. It does not appear to have played more than a subsidiary role in Japanese plans.

⦂

CHAPTER 14

"We Are Depending for Our Lives on Kindly but Slow-Witted Infants in Arms"

SINGAPORE FALLS

War Begins

On 5 November, London announced that Lt. Gen. Sir Henry Pownall would replace Brooke-Popham. This action reflected the very belated recognition that the army, not the air force, must mount the main defense of Malaya and Singapore. But arching across the Atlantic from Washington came another last-moment change. As noted, between 1 and 4 December President Roosevelt informed London that the United States would enter the war if Japan attacked the British or Dutch and further pledged to support Operation Matador. On 5 December, London authorized Brooke-Popham to order Matador on the threat of or the actual Japanese invasion of Thailand. Brooke-Popham's chief of staff thrust the message to him with the words: "They've now made you responsible for declaring war."*

On 6 December, British search planes located a large, heavily escorted

---

*   This episode does provide important evidence on conspiracy theories alleging the British had foreknowledge of Japanese plans from code breaking. If this was true, once Roosevelt pledged to support Matador, why would London hesitate to notify Brooke-Popham of Japanese intentions and direct him to execute Matador?

convoy with 22 transports over 185 miles due west of Kota Bharu. In dismal weather on 7 December, British search planes again sought the convoy. Japanese fighters destroyed a Catalina flying boat with eight men before it could report the assault convoy. These fliers became the first Allied casualties of the vastly expanded war.

The first confirmation of war came via a radar warning of seventeen Imperial Navy bombers approaching Singapore at 0320, 8 December. No one manned the civilian Air Raid Precaution Headquarters—it was assumed Singapore was beyond range of Japanese bombers—so no sirens startled the brilliantly lit city. The Japanese bombs inflicted scant damage but killed 61 civilians and wounded 133.

Just a quarter hour before the bombs fell on Singapore, the Japanese commenced landing at Singora and Patani in Thailand. A combination of two factors had kept the Thais admirably independent while almost all other Asians fell under colonial rule: (1) kind geography, tucking Thailand away from the main thoroughfares of the colonial conquest, and (2) clever leadership that played off potential overlords (mainly Britain and France) against each other. But in 1941, Thailand stood squarely in the path of Japan's southern advance. The premier, Songkhram Phibun, attempted to play Britain and the United States against Japan to maintain Thailand's independence, but overstretched Britain and unready America could provide no credible counter to the very real prospect of Japanese occupation. On 3 December, Phibun explained to his cabinet that if they resisted Japanese occupation, Thailand might survive the war, but their personal survival was unlikely. Thus his government acquiesced in accepting Japanese forces (and later would be compelled by Japan to declare war on the Allies). This decision, however, came so belatedly that some Thai units offered resistance until the premier ordered a halt. By morning, 13,500 men of the Japanese 5th Division and the Headquarters of the Twenty-Fifth Army stood ashore at Singora, and a regiment mustered at Patani. The Japanese 55th Infantry Division landed in Thailand and by 15 December seized the Victoria Point airfield at the extreme southern tip of Burma, thus severing the air reinforcement route for British aircraft attempting to reach Malaya from India.

At dawn, 8 December, Air Vice Marshal Pulford's Malaya air command comprised some 207 aircraft with just 87 on airfields in Malaya. No radar and few or no antiaircraft guns guarded the British airbases. British and Australian aircrew pressed home dawn attacks even after heavy loss against the Japanese landing areas. Lt. Gen. Michio Sugawara, commander, Third Air Brigade, orchestrated an "aerial extermination campaign" sending waves of Japanese fighters and bombers swarming over Malaya, thus liberating Imperial

Army aviators from the shackles of a close air support role into an independent air campaign. By day's end, the Japanese aviators and antiaircraft gunners destroyed or damaged at least forty-four British planes, most on the ground. They made operations from British airfields in Northern Malaya untenable. The confused, at points demoralized, evacuation of the airfields produced ugly scenes, including abandonment of undamaged airfields. But the Japanese lost some thirty-five aircraft: just six fighters in combat; eleven aircraft due to weather; and another eighteen on the ground, mostly to landing accidents.

Percival expected orders for Matador on 8 December, but Brooke-Popham delayed while awaiting a photo reconnaissance mission over Singora. When a heavily shot-up Beaufort staggered back to Kota Bharu with word of the landings, Brooke-Popham officially canceled Matador at about 0945. Subsequent events reveal it was extremely doubtful Matador could have been executed after hostilities broke out.

While the campaign generally unfolded as a triumphant Japanese parade, its opening hours off Kota Bharu were anything but when they encountered Brigadier B. W. Key's 8th Indian Brigade and Australian airmen. Key guarded three airfields near Kota Bharu, a town just south of the Thai border. Key shrewdly concentrated one company of the 3/17th Dogras on each of two three-mile-long beaches nearest the main Kota Bharu airfield.

Three Japanese transports bearing Maj. Gen. Hiroshi Takumi's command, about 5,300 men formed around the 56th Infantry Regiment, anchored off Kota Bharu before midnight, 7–8 December. The Indian troops detected the low silhouettes of armor-plated landing barges nudging toward shore. A few supporting field guns and the Dogras's machine guns sprang into action. The Japanese who landed on the intended beaches suffered severely, but some barges found a creek mouth that creased between the two beaches and deposited their occupants behind the defense lines. Despite being attacked from the front and rear, the Dogras fought ferociously—some posts to the last man.

The ruckus prompted eleven Hudsons of 1 R.A.A.F. Squadron at Kota Bharu field to mount fierce attacks in the darkness that seriously damaged all three Japanese transports, one fatally. One of two Hudsons shot down appeared to the Japanese deliberately to make a final suicide dive on a barge loaded with sixty soldiers, killing them all. The invasion shipping withdrew in daylight.

During the day the Japanese slowly gained the upper hand against the outnumbered defenders. Airmen abandoned the main Kota Bharu in panic-fevered disorder without destruction of the fuel supplies. This and subsequent episodes of terrorized Allied servicemen bolting stemmed in large measure from the stories of Japanese savagery—most based on truth—emanating from China and then Hong Kong. By 1800, Key received orders to withdraw his command before it was overwhelmed. When Key assembled his brigade on 11 December, his rolls were minus 68 dead, 37 missing, and 360 wounded. Japanese losses afloat and ashore in Takumi's command were much worse: 320 killed and 528 wounded.

For Malaya's aerial defenders, 9 December proved a day of decision. Repeating their successful tactics, the Japanese again devastated British airfields in Malaya. Individual heroism by British airmen proved of no avail. By the end of the day, remaining British air strength in northern Malaya numbered just ten planes. Rumors transformed an authorized evacuation of serviceable aircraft from Kuantan into a terror-stricken mass stampede. After observing a fellow officer seize the Post Office bus at pistol point as his personal transport to safety, another officer remarked, "for the first and last time I felt ashamed of being an Australian." On the 10th, Pulford ordered the remaining aircraft in northern Malaya back to Singapore.

Several factors contributed to the British aerial defeat. First, Pulford's airmen were heavily outnumbered. Second, the absence of early warning or base defense capability produced most losses on the ground, and the base abandonment turned damaged aircraft into outright losses. Third, while there were glimmers of effective efforts, the British air exertions were too dispersed and weak to deliver systematic concentrated blows. Fourth, such blows as were delivered were not massed where they should have been on Singora. Finally, failure to destroy forward bases made gifts to the Japanese.

The Death of *Prince of Wales* and *Repulse*

News of Japanese invasion forces presented Admiral Phillips with the choice of sailing to meet them, or moving Force Z to another more secure base. On 7 December, an Admiralty signal from London implied expectation of offensive action. But Phillips had endorsed the Admiralty plan for offensive projection of Force Z into the South China Sea in September and again intimated his intent to use Force Z aggressively when he met Admiral Hart in Manila on 4 December. Phillips believed he faced only the Japanese battleship *Kongo* (which *Prince of Wales* and *Repulse* clearly outmatched) and seven cruisers and twenty destroyers. In fact, *Kongo* sailed in company with its sister ship *Haruna* and ten cruisers, twenty-four destroyers, and twelve submarines. The four destroyers in Force Z (*Electra*, *Express*, *Vampire*, and *Tenedos*) were individually inferior to any prospective Japanese peer. Phillips had discarded his earlier cavalier attitude about the perils of air attack, but judged dive bombing the most dangerous threat. He discounted the possibility that Japanese torpedo planes could reach Force Z.

Force Z sortied from Singapore at 1730, 8 December. Capt. William Tennant of *Repulse* informed his crew: "We are off to look for trouble. I expect we shall find it." Before sailing, Phillips asked the RAF for reconnaissance ahead of his force on 9 December and off Singora in the morning of 10 December and fighter protection off Singora on 10 December. The RAF promised requested reconnaissance but not any fighter protection off Singora. The lack of fighter cover raised serious concern, but at this point Phillips could have reasoned that the season's cloudy weather and a little luck would shield him from Japanese detection or air attack. At 1700 9 December, Philipps became aware that a Japanese search plane had found him. Now stripped of both fighter cover and surprise, Phillips prudently elected to turn back.

Phillips's luck started a precipitous tumble at 2355 9 December, when a message from Singapore relayed a false report of a Japanese landing at Kuantan—much farther south than Singora on the Malayan coast. At 0052 10 December, Phillips turned Force Z southwest toward Kuantan, but did not notify Singapore of his intentions. Based on a sighting report of Force Z by a Japanese submarine, at daylight 10 December, the Imperial Navy's Twenty-Second Air Flotilla mounted a huge effort: eleven search planes followed by thirty-four bomb-equipped and fifty-one torpedo-equipped twin-engine G3M "Nells" and G4M "Bettys." Finding "complete peace" at Kuantan according to one destroyer skipper, Phillips resumed course for Singapore.

Force Z's luck ran out fully at 1015 10 December, when a Japanese search plane began reporting its position. The news electrified the exhausted crews of the attack planes, who had prowled almost to Singapore seeking Phillips. Eight "Nells" lunged at *Repulse* at 1115 in the first of a series of attacks. They bracketed the ship with leaping columns of water that doused British doubts about the capabilities of Japan's airmen. The sole hit on *Repulse*, however, inflicted no serious harm. Next came two squadrons of torpedo-equipped "Nells" of the Genzan Air Group. As they maneuvered around to assail *Prince of Wales* to port, an officer warned Phillips that they were intending a torpedo attack. Phillips replied, "No, they're not. There are no torpedo aircraft about."

A Hudson pilot on the scene vividly described the antiaircraft barrage:

> Grey smoke balls from exploding 5.25 inch shells festooned the air, while
> lighter puffs from thousands of rounds of smaller caliber shells laced

the bitterly contested airway around the Japanese. Steel fragments which fell into the sea, churned it into miniature geysers and white foam.

Captain Leach's confidence in the efficacy of *Prince of Wales*'s antiaircraft fire prompted him to hold a steady course too long before commencing an evasive swing to port.

At a cost of one of their number, the Japanese released their torpedoes in a fan-shaped pattern perhaps impossible to evade entirely. But *Prince of Wales*'s very wide turning radius for a capital ship of its generation made the situation worse. One torpedo hit to port aft at 1144. For some reason a second torpedo exploded just shy of the hull farther forward and flung a column of water as much as about two hundred feet high. Lt. D. B. H. Wildish described the sensation: "There was a terrific thump, and the ship whipped around like a spring-board for a few seconds." Divers learned years afterward that the actual hit weakened the strut securing the port outboard propeller shaft. This weapon—it may have missed had *Prince of Wales* commenced an earlier turn or possessed a smaller turning circle—caused the strut to fail, and this plus the shock transmitted by the explosion caused the shaft to disintegrate into its component segments. The emancipated, violently thrashing shaft segments vastly magnified the effect of the torpedo, slashing huge gouges in the ship's underbody all the way forward to the engine room. This single catastrophic initial hit alone doomed the ship. Torrents of water shortly stilled both port propellers, canted the ship over with a port list, and slowed it to only sixteen knots.

The Japanese officer leading the next of three squadrons of "Nells" to attack *Repulse* noted that its antiaircraft fire made his plane "reel and shake." Captain Tennant paced the bridge, calmly spinning his hand to indicate which way the rudder should be pivoted. His adroit handling caused fifteen torpedoes and six bombs to miss. To his amazement, Tennant learned that Phillips had failed to report the situation, so *Repulse*'s radio sounded the first word of Force Z's action at 1158. The message reached Singapore, and eleven Buffalo fighters scrambled at 1225.

Twenty-six "Bettys" of the Kanoya Air Group, desperately short of fuel, now appeared. Diving down, the Japanese airmen split up to attack both capital ships. Six aircraft put three torpedoes into *Prince of Wales*'s starboard side starting at 1233. Incredibly, one of these nearly replicated the effect of the hit on the port outer shaft on the starboard outer shaft but without disintegrating the shaft itself—a combination of events of almost unimaginable improbability. Eleven torpedo planes attacked *Repulse*. But Tennant steered

Repulse so adroitly that only one torpedo hit its port side, and it scurried on at twenty-five knots.

Captain Tennant reported coolly that as the last nine torpedo-carrying Kanoya Air Group planes approached *Repulse*, "I found the dodging of torpedoes quite interesting and entertaining until in the end they started to come in from all directions." At the cost of two of their number shot down and a third so damaged it crashed on landing, the squadron executed a devastating attack. The first torpedo plunged into the port side, jamming its rudder and depriving *Repulse* of its most effective defense, Tennant's elegant ship handling. In short order three more hits doomed the old ship. Tennant immediately ordered abandon ship, saving the lives of hundreds of men. Until just before the end, *Repulse* surged along at about sixteen knots, its propellers churning the stark blue seas into an ugly brown with the oil bleeding from its flanks.

As *Repulse* foundered at 1233, nine "Nells" missed it with their bombs, the only serious Japanese faux pas of the day. A Japanese squadron then managed one final bomb hit on *Prince of Wales*, which killed many men. In a scene that provided a historic photograph, destroyer *Express* pulled aside the now halted battleship. Displaying nerve and judgment in equal measures, its captain, Lt. Cdr. F. J. Cartwright, cast off at the last moment before *Prince of Wales* rolled over on its port side. Scores of men were wiggling down lines from the battleship to *Express*. When Cartwright roared "slip," sailors standing by each line immediately slashed the *Express* end and "all the ropes swung down, heavy with men, to crash sickeningly against the battleship's side." Belatedly scrambled Buffaloes arrived only in time to see *Prince of Wales* sink.

At a cost of six aircraft (including two search float planes) and twenty-one airmen, the Imperial Navy achieved a historic triumph: the first fully maneuverable capital ships sunk at sea by aircraft. Some 20 officers and 307 men perished with *Prince of Wales*, including Captain Leach and Admiral Phillips. With *Repulse*, 24 officers died and 486 ratings, making a total of 837 British seamen.

Churchill famously described how he received word of the disaster:

I was opening my boxes on the 10th when the telephone at my bedside rang. It was the First Sea Lord. He gave a sort of cough and gulp, and at first I could not hear quite clearly. "Prime Minister, I have to report to you that the *Prince of Wales* and *Repulse* have both been sunk by the Japanese—we think by aircraft. Tom Phillips is drowned." "Are you sure it's true?" "No doubt at all." So I put the telephone down. I was thankful to be alone. In all the war I never received a more direct shock.

In just three days, Japanese airmen knocked out both the American and British Pacific battle fleets. Yet it would be difficult to overstate the degree to which the symbolic value of the event eclipsed even the seismic military effects. The whole foundation of Britain's empire was prestige, particularly that of the Royal Navy. The destruction of Force Z—and its implicit demonstration of Japanese technical prowess—was read all over the region as a portent for the end of that empire and locally as a smashing blow to civilian and military morale.

Although Phillips's decision making has been subjected to minute scrutiny, his only material lapse of judgment was the failure to report promptly the sighting of Force Z about 1020 or at least the first attack about 1115, 10 December. An immediate report probably would have resulted in the Buffaloes arriving over Force Z in time to break up the attack by the Kanoya Air Group that sank *Repulse*.

Primary responsibility for the disaster rests with London and particularly the Admiralty, not Churchill. The internal Admiralty decision to reverse prior thinking and have Force Z project power into the South China Sea is the root cause of the disaster, not Churchill's vision of strategic deterrence followed by withdrawal to the Indian Ocean if that deterrence failed. As usual in war, fortune played no small role. The weather on 10 December proved clearer than normal, which permitted the Japanese to find and attack Force Z. The phenomenal luck of the key torpedo hit on *Prince of Wales* was another gift to the Japanese. But the Japanese were not just lucky: they were thoroughly prepared through careful planning and training to exploit the tilts of fortune.

Disaster at Jitra

With the Japanese ascendant over the Royal Air Force and Royal Navy, it befell the army to sustain the British position in Malaya and hold Singapore. The performance of Key's brigade at Kota Bharu evidenced credible performance by well-led Indian troops. But a second test of Indian troops around Jitra disclosed disturbing evidence about the state of the Indian Army, but even more about British leadership.

Maj. Gen. D. M. Murray-Lyon's 11th Indian Division crouched astride the trunk road and rail line threading down the west side of the Malaya peninsula to block a Japanese advance. But his orders also obligated him to protect advance air base sites. This compelled him to deploy his division far forward of three natural defensive positions on the much inferior ground near Jitra.

From Patani on Thailand's east coast near the border southwest to Kroh in Malaya ran a road that permitted rapid access to the deep right (east) rear of the Jitra position. Murray-Lyon planned to nullify this threat by dispatching a two-battalion task force up the road twenty-four miles into Thailand to "The Ledge." There demolitions of a six-mile stretch of road perched like a narrow top balcony in a large theater far above the Patani River could make the defile impassable for weeks.

Neither Brooke-Popham nor Percival impressed upon London that holding northern Malaya required the relatively modest violation of Thai neutrality to seize "The Ledge." Just one battalion, not two, under Lt. Col. H. D. Moorhead advanced to seize "The Ledge" at 1500, 8 December—eight hours after the Patani landing and four after the British learned of it. But the Indian soldiers placed second in a race where only first counted. A reinforced Japanese regiment not only reached "The Ledge" first, but also over three days smashed Moorhead's battalion with flanking movements and the first tanks most of the Indian soldiers had ever seen. Moorhead managed to extract only about 350 men.

"The Ledge" episode provided a telling reflection of the ponderous pace of British thinking and action in contrast to Japanese agility on both counts. Jitra proved much worse. Murray-Lyon pushed a detachment across the Thai border to act as an outpost for Jitra. On 9 December, about 2100, the glare of headlights provided the first indication to this contingent of a Japanese presence. The lights belonged to a Japanese column comprising merely five hundred men, primarily the 5th Division's reconnaissance battalion and part of the 1st Tank Regiment. It was a balanced force with ten medium and about twenty-five light tanks and armored cars as well as motorized infantry. For the loss of a few tanks, the Japanese flung back the Indian outpost. With an immediate perception of sagging enemy morale and a very informative captured map in hand, the Japanese charged right into the 14,000-man Indian division with its 50 field and 36 antitank guns.

The barreling column of tanks and motorized infantry next smashed through and captured most of the two advance battalions Murray-Lyon unwisely had deployed to delay the Japanese. Then the Japanese were temporarily checked, but this permitted part of a Japanese infantry brigade to join. With his front crumbling from infiltration and his right turned by the Japanese advancing from "The Ledge," Murray-Lyon ordered a withdrawal the evening of 12 December. It turned into a rout with the disintegration of the Fifteenth Indian Brigade and loss of most of the division's artillery and motor transport. Much worse, the division's morale sustained a blow from which there would be no recovery.

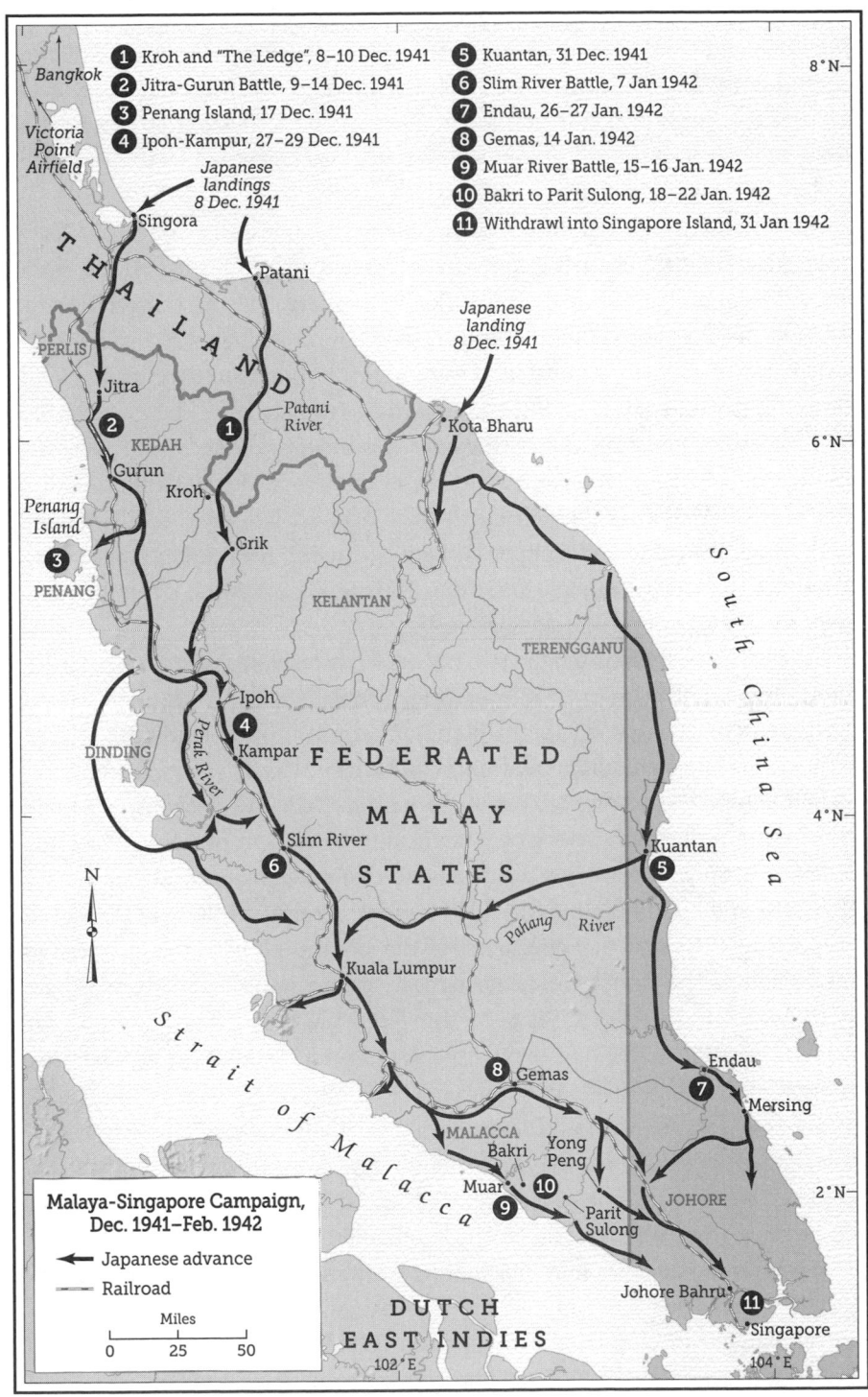

Bangkok

Victoria
Point
Airfield

1 Kroh and "The Ledge", 8–10 Dec. 1941
2 Jitra-Gurun Battle, 9–14 Dec. 1941
3 Penang Island, 17 Dec. 1941
4 Ipoh-Kampur, 27–29 Dec. 1941

5 Kuantan, 31 Dec. 1941
6 Slim River Battle, 7 Jan 1942
7 Endau, 26–27 Jan. 1942
8 Gemas, 14 Jan. 1942
9 Muar River Battle, 15–16 Jan. 1942
10 Bakri to Parit Sulong, 18–22 Jan. 1942
11 Withdrawl into Singapore Island, 31 Jan 1942

Japanese
landings
8 Dec. 1941

Singora

THAILAND

Patani

Japanese
landing
8 Dec. 1941

PERLIS

Jitra

2 KEDAH

Gurun

Kroh

Patani
River

Kota Bharu

6°N

Penang
Island

3

PENANG

1

Grik

KELANTAN

TERENGGANU

Ipoh

4

DINDING

Perak River

Kampar

FEDERATED

MALAY

Slim River

6

STATES

Kuantan

5

4°N

N

Kuala Lumpur

Pahang River

South China Sea

Strait of Malacca

8 Gemas

Endau

7

Mersing

MALACCA

Bakri

Yong
Peng

Muar

10

9

JOHORE

2°N

Parit
Sulong

Malaya-Singapore Campaign,
Dec. 1941–Feb. 1942

← Japanese advance

Railroad

Miles

0   25   50

DUTCH
EAST INDIES

102°E

Johore Bahru

11

Singapore

104°E

8°N

Historian Brian Farrell pronounced: "Jitra was without a doubt the most incompetently fought battle by a British Empire division in the Second World war, and the most decisive of the Malayan campaign." Fewer than 1,500 Japanese with a tank company and a few guns routed a division of 14,000. At least 75 percent of the minimum 3,000 casualties sustained by the Eleventh Indian Division were POWs.

Imperial Army officers instantly distilled critical lessons from Jitra. They recognized that the British Empire forces were capable foes if fighting from a fixed position backed by their formidable artillery. But the Imperial Army officers also diagnosed that the Empire forces were not adept at night battle, shied away from close combat, and were highly vulnerable to infiltration and flanking movements.

After two exhausting, dispiriting days of retreat, by 14 December, Murray-Lyon established a position at Guran further south astride the trunk road and the rail line. Whereas the debacle at Jitra involved two Japanese battalions with tanks, only one tank-supported battalion using infiltration tactics shattered the 6th Indian Brigade at Guran. Over the next several days, the Japanese took nearly 1,000 Indians prisoner.

As the Japanese trounced the 11th Indian Division at Jitra and Guran, Heath brought forward Brig. A. C. M. Paris's 12th Indian Brigade. Although Heath initially intended to send the 12th Indian Brigade to join the 28th Indian Brigade to restore the shattered front of the 11th Indian Division, he felt compelled to send the whole 12th Indian Brigade to Grik. Two reasons explained this emerging British pattern of piecemeal commitment of forces. First, the British not only credited the Japanese with double their actual strength (two divisions and a tank regiment), but also from Percival on down, they had to respect the flexibility that command of the sea and air gave the Japanese to strike behind the British in Malaya or even attempt a direct attack on Singapore Island. Further, Percival needed to keep the Japanese air bases as far away as possible for as long as possible to protect a series of convoys bearing reinforcements to Singapore.

By 23 December, the 11th Indian Division sat behind the Perak River, having fended off minor skirmishes for eight days. In contrast to their woeful, depleted opponents, Japanese soldiers advanced an average of 12.4 miles per day with soaring morale. The Japanese relentlessly pressed their attack with a well-balanced advance guard of infantry, armor, engineers, and light artillery. They traveled light and achieved remarkable mobility without logistical penalty by placing their unmotorized infantry on bicycles. Strapped to each bicycle was about eighty-eight pounds of cooking utensils, rice, and other rations. It was enough to keep a soldier going, but the average man lost twenty-two pounds during the campaign. At each contact they would either smash down the road with armor, or loop off the road around flanks. Envelopments involved two stages, a relatively short arc of encirclement to strike the flank coupled to a deeper arc designed to cut off the forces along the road.

The interlude of quiet at the Perak permitted the relief of the thoroughly discredited Murray-Lyon. Heath quite rightly recommended the Brigadier Key, whose performance so far had been the only shining light in a dark void of leadership. But Key, like Heath, was an Indian Army officer. Percival instead picked a British Army officer, Brig. Archibald Paris of the Twelfth Brigade. Replacing Paris in the Twelfth Indian Brigade was another British officer, Lt. Col. Ian M. Stewart of the Argyll and Sutherland Highlanders. Stewart was senior in grade, but he also had demonstrated prewar alertness to fighting in Malaya and a creditable performance so far.

Distant Decisions

The crowded agenda of Churchill's government as the New Year approached contained a brace of fundamental Far East strategic issues: defensive strategy in Malaya and the integration of Malaya into overall strategy. Churchill instinctively divined a sound theater strategy. Command of the sea empowered Japan to land anywhere along the Malay coast, thus any defensive stand north of Johore could only be a delaying action. He urged that defenses be concentrated in Johore and on Singapore Island. This strategy meant abandoning Singapore as a naval base because Japanese airpower would render it untenable.

But Percival believed his mission remained to fight his major battle along the Malaya peninsula to protect Singapore *as a naval base*. Percival also recognized he must keep Japanese air power at bay to permit the arrival of reinforcements. Despite his sound instincts, Churchill, distracted by other issues and thrown off balance by the speed of the Japanese advance, never forced his senior officers in London to acknowledge the end of Singapore's career as a naval base and thus permit the local commanders to adjust their plans accordingly.

The integration of Malaya into global strategy posed still more fraught issues. On Christmas Day, Gen. Alan Brooke persuaded the Chiefs of Staff to reverse immediate priorities with Singapore now to rank only behind defense of the United Kingdom itself. But the Japanese advance into Burma (addressed later) added another dimension to the crisis in the Far East. Burma ranked well above Malaya and Singapore in strategic importance. For the British, Burma's stature hinged on its status as the gateway to India, the proverbial "jewel in the crown." Churchill learned in Washington that the Americans likewise attached signal importance to Burma. The land link to Nationalist China comprised the Burmese port of Rangoon and a railway that connected to the western terminus of the Burma Road. In the first days after the outbreak of hostilities, London began to react to the situation by moving Burma from Brooke-Popham's overextended responsibilities and placing it where it more naturally belonged, under Wavell and the commander in chief in India. But standing up adequate defenses for Burma proved an issue that would stab into the very heart of Singapore's fate.

If his American allies pulled Churchill one way, his Australian allies made up for their relatively lesser pull with vigorous tugging in the other direction. Within days of the outbreak of war General Bennett in Malaya wired Canberra that the situation was critical. The Australian representative in Singapore, V. G. Bowden, telegraphed Canberra on Christmas Day that "the deteriorating situation in Malaya . . . is assuming land slide proportions." He prescribed massive air reinforcements from the Middle East and troop reinforcements. Australians from top to bottom now expected Britain to make good on oft-repeated promises that the defense of Singapore was second only to defense of the United Kingdom itself. On 27 December, Prime Minister Curtin embarrassed Churchill by publicly declaring, in effect, that Australia must henceforth look to its own defense and rely primarily not on "traditional links with the United Kingdom" but to the United States.

Gen. Sir Archibald Wavell became the commander in chief designate of the ABDA Command, but the position required more a Merlin than a mortal. Wavell's appointment extinguished the Far East Command, and its brief incumbent chief, Sir Henry Pownall, became Wavell's chief of staff. Pownall noted in his diary that of all the "raw deals" handed to Wavell, ABDA was the "worst." One of the most intriguing senior figures of World War II, Wavell's primary quality was his powerful intellect. His headmaster at Winchester School had written his father (a major general) that "There is no need for your son to go into the army; he is really quite intelligent." Although he saw enough combat to lose an eye to a shell splinter in 1915, his reputation rested on his superlative staff work. Wavell loved books and poetry and once admitted to Pownall, "My trouble is I am not really interested in war." But Wavell grossly and persistently underestimated the Japanese.

On 30 December, Percival articulated his "most determined attempt to pull together a coherent campaign strategy." He thought he faced three enemy divisions, with three more in reserve. The Japanese threatened the western trunk road and enjoyed the ability to make further assaults from sea. If the Japanese secured airfields in central Malaya, they could strangle Singapore's resupply and reinforcement access. Percival declared: "To achieve our objective of protecting the Naval Base it was necessary to fight the main battle on the mainland and it was hoped to be able to deploy all the reinforcements due to arrive in January for that purpose." The longer the Japanese were held in central Malaya "the better."

Vanishing Legitimacy at Penang; Fiasco on the Slim River

The legitimacy of 150 years of British rule rested on the principle that their rule was founded upon disinterested guardianship of all the peoples within their ambit. Sir Shenton Thomas in Singapore insisted that "If we are going to win this war, we must win it decently," i.e., without racial discrimination. But the Penang local commander, Brig. C. A. Lyon, ignored Thomas's injunction and spirited away all the Europeans, save three volunteers, leaving the Asians to Japanese mercy. A British woman denounced the abandonment as "a thing which I am sure will never be forgotten or forgiven." Historian Raymond Callahan declared, "The moral collapse of British rule in Southeast Asia came not at Singapore, but at Penang." When Yamashita learned of "indiscipline" among Japanese soldiers who occupied Penang, he had some tried and executed, while their commanders were placed under close arrest for thirty days.

To the surprised relief of the Japanese, Heath decided the front astride the formidable Perak River was far too wide for defense by the 11th Indian Division. He instead deployed the 12th and 28th Indian Brigades south around Ipoh and sent the 15th Indian Brigade (having absorbed survivors of the 6th Indian Brigade) twenty miles farther south to Kampar. While the Japanese 4th Imperial Guards Regiment administered jolts to Stewart's 12th Indian Brigade on 27 and 29 December, at Kampar Paris on the twelfth managed to hold and inflict loss on the Japanese. But Paris let slip through his fingers an opportunity to crush one Japanese regiment and abandoned Kampar when threatened by another Japanese amphibious hook down the west coast. By casting away a moment when the 11th Division grasped the upper hand, Paris stanched the incipient revival of morale among his Indian soldiers.

While the struggle in western Malaya provided by far the most drama by the New Year, a lesser variant with much the same themes played out in eastern Malaya. The Japanese 56th Infantry Regiment advanced along the seashore in the roadless reaches south of Kota Bharu toward Kuantan. It thrashed Brig. Gordon Painter's 22nd Indian Brigade near the Kuantan Airfield. For loss of about one-third of the brigade, Painter inflicted no commensurate loss on the Japanese.

At a senior officers' conference on 5 January, Percival unfolded a plan to evacuate Kuala Lumpur and pitch the next defense line along the northern border of Johore state. But Percival directed Heath to deny the Japanese use of the airfields at Kuala Lumpur and Port Sweetman until at least 14 January to cover a reinforcement convoy arrival. Accordingly, the 11th Indian Division deployed the 12th and 28th Indian Brigades around the vicinity of Trolak and the Slim River along generally excellent defensive terrain, with other elements some ten miles south in yet another potential delay position. Heath managed to anticipate and defeat two Japanese attempts to hook around his position along the west coast.

As formal Japanese plans foundered, an improvised scheme wildly prospered. In densely vegetated territory around Trolak, Stewart's 12th Indian Brigade covered the only two ready avenues: the rail line and the trunk road. But Stewart (supported by Paris) placed only one artillery battery to cover his position and, worse yet, he failed to provide adequate antitank defense. As evening came on 6 January, an Asian warned Stewart that the Japanese "iron land ships"—tanks—were gathering, but he ignored the warning.

A hell-for-leather armor officer, Major Shimada, convinced his superiors to release him for a full-throated attack with thirty tanks and supporting units straight down the trunk road. About 0330, 7 January, Shimada's tank unit with infantry and engineers in close support came roaring out of the darkness close behind a mortar and artillery barrage. The blow crumbled Stewart's Brigade. The supporting artillery battery simply fled. The British engineers failed to blow the bridge over the Trolak stream.

This proved merely an overture to vast disaster. The bold Japanese tankers kept motoring south. About 0730, they scattered and decimated a road-bound Indian infantry battalion, killing the commander. Knocking out antitank guns and racing past another infantry battalion, the Japanese armor next encountered the 2/1th Gurkhas. Maj. W. J. Winkfield reported an inexplicable approaching noise rippled the marching ranks with unease "the next thing I knew was a gun and machine gun blazing in my ear, a bullet grazed my leg, and I dived into the ditch the tank bore down on me." The scattered battalion's commander was mortally wounded.

The tanks then fell upon a British "regiment' (battalion) of artillery parked in a rubber tree plantation. The gunners panicked, spiked their guns, and scattered. The commander was killed. At 0840 the Japanese tankers seized the Slim River Bridge. About a dozen tanks surged on and encountered another British artillery "regiment." They killed their fourth British commander, but his gunners finally swerved field pieces into position to engage the raiders over open sights and knocked out the leading tank. Finally, after a nineteen-mile ride, the Japanese tankers were checked. Even on their withdrawal, they turned two more relatively intact Empire infantry battalions into disorganized mobs.

The defeat at the Slim River was a catastrophe for both the 11th Indian Division and the defense of Malaya. The Japanese count seems reasonable: 500 British-Indian dead (including some executed prisoners) and a total of about 3,200 prisoners. The Japanese seized immense quantities of desperately needed supplies and a fleet of motor transport. The 11th Indian Division lost about fifty lesser armored vehicles like armored cars and Bren carriers, sixteen twenty-five-pounder artillery pieces, and seven antitank guns. Just 14 officers and 409 enlisted men answered a 12th Indian Brigade roll call on 8 January. The 28th Indian Brigade mustered 750 officers and men.

In an assessment of responsibility for this debacle, Paris and Stewart earn rebuke for their failure to take reasonable precautions against tank attack. But there were also serious failings by the division's engineers, who failed to blow bridges, and inexplicable derelictions ranking as among the worst of the war by normally steadfast British gunners. Underlying all these command failures from division to battery probably rested the extremely potent factor of exhaustion within the 11th Indian Division. Thus, ultimate blame falls on Percival, who failed to replace the spent 11th Division after its month of battering on the battlefield and dispiriting and exhausting retreat.

The new ABDA commander in chief, Wavell, arrived at Singapore in the wake of the Slim River disaster. Wavell's chief of staff, General Pownall, confided in his diary Wavell's doubts about Percival ("an uninspiring leader, and rather gloomy") and Heath. Wavell's failure to oust Percival remains one of the great "what ifs" of the campaign. Wavell reported to London that he looked for but found no adequate replacement. But it appears likely that imperial politics also deterred Wavell: relieving Percival would confess that Britain had entrusted Australian defenses to incompetent hands. Yet in his private actions, Wavell communicated his lack of confidence in their chief to Percival's subordinates. Nor did Wavell stamp out the continuous strife between Heath and Percival. Wavell did contrive to place Australian general

Gordon Bennett in a vital post—only to have Bennett promptly demonstrate his limits.

On 8 January, Wavell flew to Kuala Lumpur. Wavell overruled Percival's plan to place eastern Johore under Bennett and western Johore under Heath. Instead, Wavell charged Bennett with command of the northwest front in Malaya while Heath and his battered III Indian Corps covered the eastern and southwestern coast.

Meanwhile, between sundown on 8 January and the morning of 10 January, the Japanese successively savaged the 15th and 28th Indian Brigades. Only now did Brigadier Key belatedly replace Paris in command of the 11th Indian Division. It was as if Key were handed the mere hilt of a sword with a broken blade.

Johore

During a relative pause, the Twenty-Fifth Army rested all but one regiment of the 5th Division after its punishing pursuit of the 11th Indian Division. Yamashita's soldiers reveled in "Churchill supplies": a cornucopia of captured British equipment and stores for both its ground and air forces around Kuala Lumpur, which lifted much strain from Japanese logistics. Meanwhile, two more Japanese regiments, the 21st Infantry (5th Division) and 5th Guards (Imperial Guards Division), marched from Thailand to join the modest four that had won repeated victories on the west. One regiment of the 18th Division continued down the east coast from Kota Bharu while a second regiment assembled at Kuantan in contemplation of a landing down the coast at Mersing toward the end of January. Altogether, Yamashita fielded eight infantry regiments at hand and one more en route to attack Johore.

Yamashita aimed to destroy Malaya Command in Johore by seizing the vital causeway linking the peninsula to Singapore Island at Johore Bahru. He launched four efforts: along the west coast, down the main trunk road, down the rail line, and along the east coast. But for once Twenty-Fifth Army's "driving charge" came up short. Yamashita lost one-third of his air support to meet Sumatra attack schedules. His depleted and reorganizing tank formations lacked a heavy punch. But most of all, Japanese logistics finally snapped. Yamashita sought to solve part of his supply problems as well as leapfrog forward his air units by sending a small convoy to land on the east coast at Endau with its two airfield sites on 26 January.

To meet the Endau landing, the RAF Far East Command mounted an aerial counterpart to "The Charge of the Light Brigade" spearheaded by two squadrons of wretchedly obsolete biplane Vildebeests and some nearly as obsolete biplane Albacores. Some twenty-two defending Japanese fighter planes (nearly all Ki-27s) met the seventy-four-plane British attack. At a cost of only one plane, the Japanese destroyed twelve Vildebeests, two Albacores, two Hudsons, and a Hurricane. The attack inflicted only modest damage on one transport.

In the early morning hours of 27 January, the World War I–era destroyers HMS *Thanet* and HMAS *Vampire* attempted to attack the shipping off Endau. Five vastly superior Japanese destroyers and a minesweeper sank *Thanet*. The thirty-one *Thanet* survivors rescued by destroyer *Shirayuki* were never heard from again. *Vampire* barely escaped. In Europe, the gallantry of airmen and sailors in these attacks would have been legendary; here it garnered virtually no notice.

As early as 9 January, Wavell informed London he would fight the "decisive battle" for Singapore in northwest Johore. He designated a line that secured two airfields and protected the last lateral road in Johore that would permit the shuffling of forces. A breach in this lateral road would render the whole position untenable. Wavell intended that the Australians with their aggressive jungle fighting tactics should be stationed to block the heretofore main Japanese axis along the trunk road. Wavell sought to buy time for the landing of reinforcements totaling five brigades (equal to half the original garrison), after which Malaya Command would counterattack. Just as important were expected air reinforcements: fifty-eight Blenheims, fifty-two Hudsons, and ninety-nine Hurricanes.

Percival, like Heath, wanted to fight a more conventional battle and effectively sabotaged Wavell's vision. He placed Bennett (now openly contemptuous of Heath) in command of "Westforce" to defend the trunk road and a line to the west coast. But Percival only gave Bennett the 22nd Australian Brigade and kept the 27th Australian Brigade with Heath's "Eastforce." Bennett placed his Australians along the trunk road and to their left (west) extended the line to the coast with first the 9th Indian Division (now only about 3,000 infantry) and then the newly arrived 45th Indian Brigade.

The Australians got off to a sound start on 14 January when the 2/30th Battalion ambushed two Japanese companies of bicyclists near Gemas.[*] Although the Australians claimed they inflicted massive casualties, the Japa-

---

[*]   As in World War I, Australia formed ground forces primarily by battalions numbered in sequence by arm of service. Under this system, the numbered battalions raised for World War II were the second raising of these battalions, hence the designation of 2/30th for the second constitution of the 30th Battalion.

nese sustained about seventy dead and fifty-seven wounded. The following day, stalwartly manned Australian antitank guns destroyed at least four Japanese tanks and repulsed a thrust down the trunk road.

Checked on the trunk road, the Japanese redirected their main effort at Brig. Hector Duncan's 45th Indian Brigade. Bennett not only assigned the green brigade just one battery of artillery, but also ordered a tactically disastrous deployment straddling the unbridged Muar River. On 15–16 January the Imperial Guards Division pounced. In close range fighting in which two battalion commanders were killed, the brigade crumpled rapidly. Other Japanese tramped to cut off the trunk road and the bulk of Bennett's forces at Yong Peng.

Bennett initially sent most of the 2/29th Battalion (Australian 27th Brigade), to stanch the danger Duncan reported as just two hundred Japanese—the real number was two regiments. On 18 January Japanese tanks unsupported by infantry clanked confidently down the road from the town of Muar toward Bakri into the sights of a pair of Australian antitank guns. In short order, the gunners knocked out five tanks at a distance close enough for a single photograph to clearly capture the combatants. The Australian gunners then destroyed three more, nearly wiping out the Japanese tank company. Then the Australian 2/19th Battalion occupied positions at Bakri where it crushed a Japanese battalion-strong infiltration effort. The Australians counted 140 dead Japanese, but the victors also learned that Japanese soldiers would not surrender.

Offsetting these successes, in the morning of 19 January a Japanese bomb hit the headquarters of the 45th Indian Brigade and severely wounded Duncan. Only about two hundred of Duncan's men assembled at Bakri. When they and the 2/29th Battalion withdrew in the evening, they ran into roadblocks established by the Japanese, and the Australian battalion commander was killed. The battalion split up. The Australians, too wounded to move, asked to be shot rather than being left to be bayoneted by the Japanese, as they knew by now the Japanese were not taking prisoners. This was done with pistol shots to the heart.

Lt. Col. Charles G. W. Anderson, a World War I veteran and interwar African game hunting guide, took charge of the survivors of the 45th Indian Brigade and the two Australian battalions in a breakout attempt from Bakri. With wounded loaded in vehicles, Anderson resolutely and skillfully directed the effort on 20–21 January. For fifty nearly continuous hours, the road-bound column smashed through successive roadblocks (Duncan heroically died leading an attack on one block). The "fighting mad" Australians performed feats of desperate valor—calling in mortar rounds within a few yards of their positions by voice, chopping down roadblocks with axes under heavy fire. Breakthrough assaults were repeatedly organized and often personally led by Anderson himself. Private Mac Reid, 2/19th Battalion, recalled how Anderson's "calm, clear voice," exhorting them to "Go for them," sent his small band charging onward at a roadblock. "I remember hearing the swish of bullets as they passed me, of seeing the fire-fly brilliance of tracers as they floated through the air. I was conscious that death was very near."

The Japanese also rose to heights of courage, holding positions to the death and charging at close quarters. But the sorely depleted column finally was checked at a bridge in the village of Parit Sulong. On the morning of 22 January, Anderson ordered the survivors to attempt to break out in small groups. About 110 Australian and 40 Indians too wounded to move fell into Japanese hands. Over the next day, the Japanese proceeded to massacre them by gunshot, bayonet, beheading, and burning prisoners alive. Survivors reaching British lines numbered about 400 Indians and 500 Australians out of an original force of 4,500. Anderson received a Victoria Cross for his valiant leadership. General Yamashita admitted later that the battles from Muar to Yong Peng were the "most savage" of the campaign. With losses numbering about a company of tanks and a battalion's worth of infantry, the Japanese for once paid a serious price for their victory.

But no amount of courage or skill at the British Commonwealth battalion level could offset the completely befuddled direction at higher levels induced by the tempo of Japanese units on the battlefield. Individual battalions of the Imperial Guards Division not only destroyed the 45th Indian Brigade and cut off the two Australian rescue battalions, but also thrashed the newly arrived British 53rd Brigade, 18th Division that Percival had sent to buttress his western front. A worse fate befell Brigadier Painter's 22nd Indian Brigade, 9th Indian Division. The Japanese cut off the brigade and the division commander, Maj. Gen. Arthur E. Barstow, was killed during a failed relief effort.

By this later phase of what Wavell envisioned as the "main battle" in Johore, the pervasive lack of mutual confidence among the commanders leached away any chance of Percival conducting a protracted defense in Johore. Moreover, it was obvious he intended the army to retreat to Singapore. Bennett held all Indian and British units in contempt. He sabotaged coordination to avoid any circumstance where his Australians would have to place vital reliance on other Commonwealth formations. Heath doubted Bennett's competence to direct a large battle and feared he would sustain disaster on the trunk road that would destroy the whole army. Each separate command and unit now nervously feared it would somehow be abandoned by a neighbor. One result of this was that the 15th Brigade (now all British) under Brig. B. S. Challen on the west coast became the next victim. The Japanese infiltrated behind the brigade and cut it off. Challen ordered his subordinates to break out. He was captured, but Rear Admiral Spooner in Singapore organized a naval evacuation operation on 30–31 January that brought out 1,500 men. Ultimately about 2,700 of Challen's men managed to reach British lines.

At 0700, 31 January, 250 men of the 2nd Argyll and Sutherland Highlands, two pipers in the lead, became the last organized units of Percival's army to cross the causeway from Johore to Singapore. An hour later, engineers destroyed the causeway. But behind was the 22nd Indian Brigade. Cut off like Challen's men, the brigade slowly disintegrated in the jungles; fewer than eighty made their way back to Singapore. According to the best figures available, casualties in Malaya Command up to the battle on Singapore Island numbered 19,123 killed, wounded, and mostly missing. Beyond the human toll, enormous quantities of equipment and supplies were lost or abandoned. Japanese losses were 1,793 dead and 2,772 wounded.

The collapse on Johore coincided with a dialogue on strategic priorities between Wavell, London, and Canberra. Wavell interjected grim clarity on 19 January by apprising Churchill that Singapore lacked landward defenses and thus was not a "fortress." Moreover, he advised London that Percival's demoralized command would mount no prolonged resistance once Johore was lost. Churchill was stunned. "The possibility of Singapore having no landward defenses no more entered my mind that that of a battleship being launched without a bottom," he later wrote.

The British Chiefs of Staff responded to Wavell that Singapore must be held for as long as possible. Churchill emended this directive with a rhetorical flourish that there must be "no question of surrender to be entertained until after protracted fighting among the ruins of Singapore City." But both London and Canberra now fully grasped the likely fall of Singapore; this recognition begat both a search for a new strategic approach and unseemly effort at blame shifting.

On 21 January Churchill and his chiefs of staff confronted the wretched question: Should they write off Singapore and concentrate reinforcements to save Burma to keep open the vital Burma Road? This issue was entwined with two fraught political considerations. First, in stark contrast to the unending retreat in Malaya, the Filipino-American Army appeared to be conducting a stout defense in the Philippines. Thus, "scuttling" Singapore would cause a severe loss of face to their American ally. Second, Churchill learned at

"Arcadia" just how vital the Americans viewed the Burma Road, but to abandon Singapore to hold Burma would betray two decades of pledges to Australia. Churchill and his military chiefs concluded that the best move would be to send the two Australian divisions en route from the Middle East, the rest of the British 18th Division and an armored brigade to Rangoon to hold Burma, and write off Singapore. The Australian special envoy in London heard erroneously that the British were contemplating evacuation of Singapore. This brought a 22 January cable from Prime Minister John Curtin to London that after the assurance that Singapore would be held, an evacuation would be treated in Australia as "an inexcusable betrayal." Although Churchill later denied it, his government sent the remainder of the British 18th Division to Singapore to try to appease the Australians and gain leverage for sending the Australian divisions to Burma.

The End in Singapore

In Singapore, the Chinese merchants signaled collapsing civilian morale as early as 12 January: they stopped accepting credit purchases from Europeans and demanded cash. This date brings us back to the air campaign. While Percival's army retreated in Malaya, after a lull following the initial raid on 8 December, the Imperial Army and Navy airmen embarked upon an aerial onslaught from 12 January. Up to three times per day, formations of Japanese bombers, sometimes fifty-four strong, winged across Singapore skies. The small number of antiaircraft guns provided no deterrent, and inadequate warning time prevented an effective fighter interception.

Despite their sea and air superiority, the Japanese conspicuously failed to halt the flow of reinforcements to Singapore. Convoys brought in the main body of British 18th Division, 44th Indian Brigade, the 2/4th Australian Machine Gun battalion, and 7,000 Indian and 1,900 Australian individual replacements. Escorts sank one Japanese submarine and weather frustrated Japanese airmen, though they did sink the large troop transport *Empress of Asia*. When the reinforcement convoys departed, they carried away approximately 9,000 British military personnel and mainly airmen, as well as European civilians. Many more civilians could have been evacuated, but while the colony's government quietly paid the fees of European civilians, it failed to assist or even notify the Asian population of the opportunity.

The wife of Rear Admiral Spooner, the commander of the naval base, wrote in her diary on 4 February after listening to stories of fighting in

Malaya: "I came away depressed as it seemed as though we were depending for our lives on kindly but slow witted infants in arms." Counting recent reinforcements, those "infants in arms" now numbered about 100,000 men, but most were Indians of severely compromised combat effectiveness. Twenty of twenty-one Indian infantry battalions still reeled from drubbings in Malaya; all but four comprised ad hoc amalgamations of original units. The 7,000 just debarked replacements had been jerked from training depots. The three British battalions originally in the III Indian Corps now formed one "British Battalion," while the 2nd Argyll and Sutherland Highlanders merged with the Royal Marine detachments from *Prince of Wales* and *Repulse* to a strength of about four hundred. The only bright spot was the largely intact III Indian Corps artillery.

The recently arrived British 18th Division (Maj. Gen. M. B. Beckwith-Smith) had trained for over two years for open warfare and debarked physically out of condition after the protracted ocean passage. Five of the seven infantry battalions of the 8th Australian Division remained in fit shape. According to one officer, the 1,900 Australian replacements were "not only almost useless but actually a positive menace" for want of discipline, physical fitness, and training (some had not even fired a rifle). Each Australian infantry battalion absorbed some replacements, but the 2/19th and 2/29th received six hundred and five hundred respectively after their severe losses in Johore. A small army of specialist and support units of negligible utility for infantry warfare filled the remaining ranks of the garrison. While most of the "volunteer" units of indigenous peoples had been disbanded, there remained a few, and four British officered Malay battalions. The morale of the garrison sagged still further from a series of blows: lack of prepared defenses on the island, destruction of the naval base whose protection was supposed to be the object of their efforts, and blatant Japanese air superiority culminating in the evacuation of the last Commonwealth air units.

Singapore's civilian population numbered roughly one million. With rationing, food sufficed for several months. Water from Johore was cut off, but three reservoirs in the center of the island could sustain all of its inhabitants with prudent use restrictions. Japanese bombing progressively killed numerous civilians and demoralized many more. The civil administration muddled along, still avoiding draconian measures for fear of causing "alarm and despondency."

Percival flunked his final examination question as a senior commander: Where would the Japanese attack? Singapore Island's 220 square miles of relatively flat land included about 70 miles of coast. Except for the six-mile stretch of waterfront on the south coast, elsewhere beaches generally mixed with jungle and mangrove swamp, especially along the Johore Strait. Wavell advised Percival to place the fresh 18th Division at the likely Japanese landing point: the island's northwest corner facing the narrowest span of the Johore Strait. But Percival (told by his intelligence officers Yamashita had 150,000 men and 300 tanks, more than double actual Japanese strength) instead decided the Japanese would attack in the east. There he placed the 18th Division, the best remaining Indian units and the strongest artillery concentration under Heath's III Indian Corps. Percival assigned the northwest coast to Bennett's Australians and the 44th Indian Brigade. Rather than massing a strong central reserve, Percival dissipated his remaining strength into beach defenses all around the rest of the island.

Inverting the British error, the Japanese underestimated enemy strength. Yamashita's plans rested on the notion that the Twenty-Fifth Army faced only about 30,000 effective defenders. An actual count of equivalent infantry formations discloses Yamashita with nine regiments while Percival commanded about thirteen brigades. Yamashita fielded 168 artillery pieces to Percival's 226. Contrary to the hoary myth that Singapore's heavy coast defense guns could only fire seaward, in fact most could fire on Johore. But armor-piercing shells in their magazines vastly outnumbered the high explosive projectiles needed for effective employment against troops. Yamashita faced severe logistical limitations, especially artillery ammunition. Nonetheless he planned to mount the attack on Singapore swiftly and to force surrender by 11 February, *Kigensetu*, the anniversary of the ascendancy of the semilegendary Emperor Jimmu.

In the Imperial Guards Division, Sgt. First Class Tominosuke Tsuchikane prepared for the final battle by honoring a pledge made at the outset of the campaign that everyone would enter Singapore. His unit had severed the left hand from each comrade killed, and now Tsuchikane and two other soldiers took the severed hands and burned away the flesh. One by one, the bones for each hand were picked out, carefully wrapped in cloth bags and given to a surviving soldier to carry into Singapore.

Although the Twenty-Fifth Army artillery deceptively fired into northeast Singapore from 4 February, Yamashita intended to land on the northwest coast manned by the Australians. There the Sungei Kranji (river) cleaved the Australian line into two unequal parts. Maxwell's 27th Brigade occupied a 4,000-yard front extending west from the Johore causeway to the Kranji. The three battalions of Taylor's 22nd Brigade held about eight miles of coast—six times that number of battalions held a comparable stretch of coast on the northeast.

About 2230, 8 February, Australians near the water's edge began to make out approaching dark shapes. This was the first of three assault waves totaling sixteen battalions from the 5th and 18th Divisions. The story of each Australia battalion merged into a common melancholy end, differing only in details. The Japanese encountered a hail of "enemy shells . . . flying amid crackling rifle fire raking down the mangrove leaves and ricocheting off the branches." They died in clusters where they debouched directly before defensive works. But lack of muzzle flashes identified gaps in the wide frontage through which the Japanese began infiltrating into the rear of the defenders. By organized units, comrades, or individuals, Australians—soot-smeared by smoke from oil fires, mud-stained, clothes torn, weapons sometimes lost or abandoned—sensed the inevitable trajectory of the fight, and to avoid inevitable piecemeal annihilation began backpedaling. Young males of both sides played a children's game of hide-and-seek in the dark, resulting in countless abruptly fatal collisions. By dawn, the fragmented 22nd Brigade leaked stragglers drifting all over the Australian sector. An Australian officer described these refugees as "quite out of control and leaderless [stating] they had had enough." Given the fact that the Australians to this point represented the one effective part of Singapore's defenders, the sight of "Diggers" in disarray exerted a crushing effect on the morale of civilians and other soldiers.

In the morning of 9 February, Percival vastly overestimated the number of Japanese on Singapore Island at about 23,000 rather than the real figure of perhaps 12,000. It says much that even the senior naval officer, Spooner, recognized the opportunity to turn the tables on the Japanese with massed counterattack to pounce on a fragment of Yamashita's army. According to his wife's diary, Spooner "tried to ginger up Percival to send reinforcements from anywhere [and] risk a 2nd attack as the chances were the Japs wouldn't know the troops had been moved for some time. But no—[Percival] had no fight left."

These same hours, the dysfunction in the Australian 8th Division leadership reached its nadir. Bennett failed to come forward to see the actual situation of Taylor's shattered 22nd Brigade. Instead, Bennett senselessly ordered Taylor to counterattack. Bennett also refused Maxwell's reasonable request to pull back his exposed left flank. Maxwell acted on his own to order his brigade

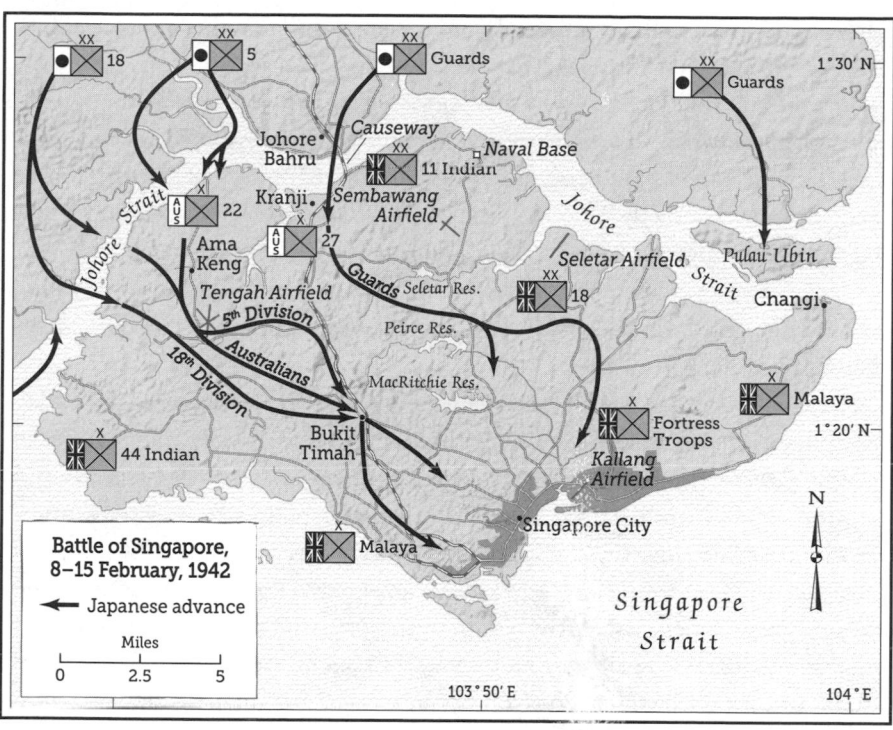

Battle of Singapore,
8–15 February, 1942

← Japanese advance

Miles
0   2.5   5

to pull back that night. About 2100, a demoralized Maxwell appeared at Bennett's headquarters. Bennett was absent, but Maxwell announced to a staff officer that he was going back to Percival "to urge him to surrender" to end the "senseless slaughter."

While Maxwell abdicated his responsibilities, the Imperial Guards Division attacked. Yamashita originally intended for the Guards to follow behind the 5th and 18th Divisions, but he unwisely yielded to pleas of the jealous Lieutenant General Nishimura for a separate role for his prestigious command. Yamashita authorized the Imperial Guards Division to cross the Johore Strait at the causeway on the night of 9–10 February. The Japanese who landed in front of the 2/30th Battalion near the causeway met a horrifying fate. Here an Australian engineer lieutenant cleverly managed to drain gasoline tanks into a mangrove swamp. When he ignited the gasoline, an inferno incinerated at least one Guard's company. But Maxwell's orders to retreat turned potential local victory into defeat. Meanwhile, a lurid tale reached Yamashita and Nishimura that flaming oil had immolated the Guard's entire vanguard. Nishimura urged a halt to the attack, but Yamashita prudently awaited further reports. When these demonstrated the situation was not so catastrophic, Yamashita ordered the attack pressed.

Wavell arrived in Singapore the morning of 10 February. Although he sensed bleak prospects for extended resistance, Wavell issued an Order of the Day that echoed an extraordinary cable from Churchill. The prime minister insisted (correctly) that Percival outnumbered the Japanese and should be able to destroy them. Churchill then declared: "There must be no thought of sparing the troops or the population. . . . Commanders and Senior Officers should die with their troops. The honour of the British Empire and of the British Army is at stake."

Once all three Japanese divisions were on the island supported by tanks, they defeated Percival's feeble efforts to halt them. The key moment came when Yamashita sent the 5th and 18th Divisions to seize the high ground around Bukit Timah (Silver Mountain), which contained the island's water reservoirs. This they secured about midnight 10–11 February. Yet the Japanese situation at sunrise on 12 February appeared to them serious, if not desperate. The Twenty-Fifth Army was outnumbered, outgunned, scattered, and nearly out of artillery ammunition. A lesser general would have turned cautious, but not Yamashita. Percival, however, was morally defeated and incapable of directing or inspiring effective resistance.

Singapore's last hours of British rule were marked by "gouts of black smoke . . . erupting from more than twenty fierce conflagrations, darken[ing] the high afternoon with the gloom of a heavy storm," recorded one British officer. Some heroic defenders assured that the Japanese did not have it all their way. The 11th Company, 114th Regiment, was cut down so swiftly that they lay in death in a clearly recognizable attack formation. Their dead commander was in the center, surrounded by several lifeless soldiers who had dragged him back from where he was initially hit. The attackers were shocked and infuriated by the nonstop barrages from the British guns they had thought had been suppressed. Lieutenant Colonel Tsuji went to the command post of the 18th Division of Lieutenant General Mutaguchi, where he reported, "The roar of the explosions [was] deafening and we could not hear one another even if we yelled at the top of our voices."

On this chaotic stage played out many ugly scenes. When British fire fell upon one Japanese unit, three Chinese girls about twenty years old were immediately—and almost certainly wrongly—suspected of signaling the enemy. They were lashed to poles and left out in terror as an artillery barrage sent their captors to earth. Then they were bayoneted to death. But the defenders likewise engaged in baseless executions of Asians falsely suspected of aiding the Japanese. Retreating troops fired from the grounds of Alexandria Hospital. The Japanese captured the building and proceeded to kill about fifty of the patients and staff. Another almost two hundred were systematically bayoneted to death over the next days by Japanese soldiers near the end of their tether with exhaustion and in fury over British artillery fire.

On 13 February, the senior British commanders met. General Heath stated that further resistance was futile. Bennett agreed. Percival responded that he was not authorized by Wavell to surrender and added, "I have my honour to consider and there is also the question of what posterity will think of us if we surrender this large Army and valuable fortress." By Percival's account, Heath then retorted, "You need not bother about your honour. You lost that a long time ago up in the North."

For several days, but particularly the night of 13–14 February, scenes unfolded evoking parallel moments in thousands of years of history of cities facing conquest. Rear Admiral Spooner ordered that all remaining vessels in Keppel Harbor sail the night of 13 February. There were about 3,000 spaces for passengers in about forty-four ships. Two of those spaces went to Spooner and Air Vice Marshal Pulford. Those with authorization or those who simply estimated their lives depended upon flight ransacked the waterfront of Singapore and filled every imaginable craft beyond the original forty-four with the faintest prospects of seaworthiness. Their last apocalyptic view of Singapore reported by one such escapee was of "the flare of the many fires tinged with the huge clouds of smoke . . . [that] hung over the city and . . . stretched for nearly a hundred miles out to sea."

But Japanese ships and planes wreaked slaughter on this exodus toward Sumatra and Java, leaving a four-hundred-square-mile area speckled with debris, bodies, oil, and desperate survivors of all races, ages, and backgrounds. Japanese destroyer skippers acted with compassion in seizing rather than sinking two ships mostly packed with civilians. But from another ship twenty-one captured Australian nurse survivors were machine-gunned by Japanese soldiers; only Vivian Bullwinkel lived. She survived to testify at a war crimes trial postwar and become an Australian heroine. A Japanese vessel forced the launch with Admiral Spooner and Air Marshal Pulford ashore on an uninhabited malarial island where most, including Spooner and Pulford, died.

The Li Wo, a former Yangtze paddle steamer commanded by Royal Navy Lt. Thomas Wilkinson, encountered two Japanese convoys. Although hopelessly outgunned, Wilkinson announced to his crew that he would engage and inflict what damage he could. He deliberately rammed a Japanese transport before he was killed as his ship was shot from under him. He received a posthumous Victoria Cross.

Nurse Margot Turner was sunk not once but twice. The second time she and another British Army nursing sister gathered fourteen other survivors, including six children, on two small rafts. But one by one, all the others died. Turner remembered it was particularly hard to tell if the small children were dead, but she "examined each of them with great care before committing their small bodies to the deep." On the fourth day, she was rescued by a Japanese warship, whose English-speaking doctor carefully kept her alive. After she was put ashore with other prisoners, the doctor visited her every day and on one visit brought her dress, cleaned and pressed, on a hanger.

The small Dutch steamer *Rooseboom* with over five hundred souls aboard provided the most horrific story. On 1 March, the Japanese submarine *I-59* torpedoed it, leaving about 130 survivors adrift with one lifeboat and scant supplies of food and water. Their numbers rapidly thinned. Eventually the haggard band in the rear of the lifeboat realized that a contingent of five soldiers in the bow had been systematically killing and eating other survivors. Sgt. Walter Gibson of the Argylls led a desperate struggle that heaved the cannibals overboard. Remorseless nature continued to take a toll until Gibson realized he and another man were the only Caucasians alive. His companion was killed by four Javanese survivors also reduced to cannibalism. At this point, after a month of drifting, the boat scraped ashore and Gibson and a young Chinese woman, Doris Lim, were taken prisoner by the Japanese.

A potential catastrophe of stupendous dimensions sat in a box in Singapore harbor. In response to a request from the FECB, the Government Code and Cipher School had shipped one of the precious "Purple" Machine analogues to Singapore. The machine arrived in late December, but the FECB fled Singapore for Ceylon on 5 January 1942 without the device. The fate of the machine remains unknown. Presumably it was either destroyed in the chaotic final days of the fortress or passed undiscovered or perhaps unrecognized by the Japanese.

The potential fallout from Japanese capture of this machine is breathtaking. Discovery that the Allies had not merely penetrated secret communications, but had re-created Japan's most sophisticated cipher machine, presumably would have sent shock waves through all Axis communications security organizations. It would have revealed a capability that demanded a vast upgrade of Axis communications security. Much of Allied success against the German Enigma and other secure communications methods hinged on careless errors in security practices founded on a blasé confidence in the impenetrability of those systems. A captured "Purple" Machine would have abruptly shattered this illusion.

The implications of this disaster are not confined to the Asian-Pacific area. The single most important insight into Hitler's strategic thinking was delivered to the Allies by the dispatches of the Japanese ambassador in Berlin who dutifully recounted Hitler's remarkably candid periodic interviews. An overall upgrade of Axis communications security methods might well have defeated or at least severely curbed the Allied success in this arena that the British authority on this subject, F. H. Hinsley, claimed shortened the war by three years. Another unpleasant residual of such a disaster would have been to deliver a body blow to the willingness of American code breakers to collaborate with their British counterparts. This alone would have retarded Allied efforts against Axis communications with incalculable results.

Percival gathered his commanders for a conference at 0930 on 15 February. Staff officers reported just one day's supply of water, gasoline, and artillery ammunition remained. Heath said that continued resistance would result in the wholesale death of Asians, a blot on the British record worse than surrender. All agreed a counterattack was not possible. Percival announced his decision to surrender.

Yamashita received Percival at a Ford Motor Company factory to the west of the city about 1715, 15 February. Looking "pale and thin and ill" according to a Japanese witness, Percival responded to Yamashita's demand for surrender by advancing a request for one thousand armed men to maintain order in the city. Suspecting wrongly that Percival was merely playing for time, Yamashita pounded a fist into the table, threatening to renew his attack that night, and demanded, "Is the British Army going to surrender or not. Answer (using the English words) YES or NO?" Even now, Percival displayed what a staff officer called "a painful inability to [make] a decision" and returned to his request for a body of armed men. In the legend, Yamashita was relentless; the more interesting reality is that he permitted Percival to follow a circuitous path to admitting capitulation. The agreement was signed about 1810. The two generals rose and shook hands as they had at the beginning.

As word spread of the surrender, there was a final surge to the waterfront for those seeking escape. Without notifying Percival or asking his government for permission (which Bennett correctly understood would not be forthcoming), Bennett and two staff officers slipped away by boat. He reached Australia on 2 March and gave as the spurious reason for his action that he carried valuable information and firsthand experience on how to defeat the Japanese.*

Aftermath

Notwithstanding the Churchillian pronouncement that Singapore was "the worst disaster and largest capitulation in British history," it never produced any official inquiry. This omission partly reflected the exceedingly explosive issues involving Australia: both the shortfalls between London promises and performance and the ugly stories of the behavior of some Australian troops. Another factor was that not only was defeat a common occurrence overall in Britain's war effort from 1940–1942, but also the event in distant Asia seemed less momentous to the British public than the new reversal in the Middle East and the epic death match on the Eastern Front. Moreover, the extremely daring German exploit of sailing two capital ships and a cruiser up the English Channel on 12 February, literally under British noses, constituted an extremely vivid and immediate distracting humiliation.

In Japan, the fall of Singapore marked perhaps the pinnacle of achievement of the Imperial Army. Yamashita became celebrated as "The Tiger of Malaya," although he cautioned his staff that this was but the opening phase of the war and there was far more war to come. When Yamashita publicly described Malays as "citizens" of the new Japanese empire, however, his rival Tôjô seized the purported miscue to transfer Yamashita back to Manchuria— even denying Yamashita's request for a visit to Japan en route.†

The vast haul of prisoners hugely surpassed Imperial Army estimates of Allied forces, and instilled prodigious Japanese contempt. On 17 February, the mass of European prisoners was marched off to Changi barracks in the northeast of the island. But the Japanese segregated approximately 55,000 Indian

---

* Appallingly, Bennett favorably impressed Army Minister Francis Forde, who was just then in the middle of appointing a commander in chief for the whole Australian Army. Fortunately, other Australian senior officers recognized Bennett's actual merits. Although he was promoted to lieutenant general and given an important command in Western Australia during the real threat of Japanese invasion, he secured no further combat role. Frustrated, Bennett resigned to return to civilian life in 1944.

† Kyoichi Tachikawa points out that the Japanese phrase tora ni naru, whose literal meaning is "to become a tiger," also carries a Japanese metaphor meaning "to be drunk." On that basis, Yamashita detested the nickname.

prisoners taken in Malaya and on Singapore from their erstwhile European comrades. Officers of Indian ethnicity and Viceroy Commissioned Officers (VCO) remained with the enlisted men. Maj. Iwaichi Fujiwara, a Japanese intelligence officer, launched a campaign to enroll these captives, whom he carefully called "brothers," into the Indian National Army (INA). This INA said Fujiwara and his Indian cohort, Capt. Mohan Singh, would work for Indian nationalism and independence—in cooperation with the Japanese.

The motivations of those joining the INA defy the simple categorizations of "traitors" or "nationalists." Initially, many Indians believed Japanese blandishments that their cause was to liberate fellow Asians. Knowledge of the widespread internal unrest sweeping over India in the summer of 1942, and the appearance that Japan might indeed invade India, afforded substance to the arguments of Fujiwara and Singh. Indian officers and VCOs carried deep psychic lacerations from discrimination in promotions and pay compared to those of their British peers. Yet afterward, relatively few Indian officers maintained that nationalist aspirations constituted the sole reason they joined the INA. Rather, some articulated the position that they saw that by joining the INA they would create an armed force that could free India from Britain *or* the Japanese. The Japanese induced VCOs to join the INA with promises that they would become junior officers. These considerations resulted in what a postwar estimate fixed as 50 percent of the Indian officers and 25 percent of VCOs joining the INA in 1942.

The expansive enrollment in the INA of Indian officers and VCOs influenced the rank and file. The circumstances in which most Indian soldiers had been rushed to Malaya without proper training or equipment, and then suffered the consequences of leadership failures—or rank incompetence—undermined the faith of many in Britain and the Allied cause. Then there was the grim dictate of self-preservation through captivity of uncertain duration. The Japanese deployed a full array of inducements from the subtle to the crude to herd Indian soldiers into the INA. Of the approximately 55,000 Indian prisoners of war, roughly 20,000 immediately joined the INA and another 20,000 between June and August. The 15,000 who refused represented those whose loyalty to Britain (as much due to community ties as individual faith) remained intact. Still, there were also those who doubted Japanese promises from the start.

Percival's surrender did not end the suffering of Singapore civilians. One postwar analysis concluded that from late January into early February, about 150 to 200 civilians died per day, mainly in the bombings. Some 6,000 to 7,000 were believed to have perished in the week before the capitulation. The

Japanese army moved rapidly to assert control. On-the-spot executions dealt summarily with looters. The Japanese embellished this universal practice for quelling breakdowns of authority with the added touch of public beheadings and displays of severed heads.

But the Japanese also instituted the *Sook Ching*, "purification by elimination." Yamashita believed the Chinese were implacable enemies of Japan, a view reinforced by desperate fighting by Chinese irregulars in Singapore. Therefore, Yamashita ordered a systematic combing of Singapore for hostile Chinese and then *Ganja Shogun* ("severe [or harsh] disposal"). Yamashita undoubtedly ordered some measures against the Chinese, but controversy remains about the precise character of his command and his knowledge about its implementation. Yamashita professed not to recall how his order was executed at a war crimes trial in Manila—a trial which resulted in his death by hanging. Whether Lt. Col. Tsuji played a key hand in the *Sook Ching* likewise is disputed. The military governor of Singapore, Maj. Gen. Saburo Kawamura, maintained that he questioned the order but was instructed that it carried Yamashita's emphatic sanction. Kawamura in turn directed the *kempeitai* (military police) commander of the city, Lt. Col. Masayuki Oishi, to discharge the order to "the letter and spirit of military law."

From 18 February the Japanese systematically rounded up Chinese males and screened them under standards ranging from the near whimsical to the sinister. Some Japanese interrogators merely asked a group of Chinese to raise hands in response to general questions. In others, the Chinese paraded one by one past hooded informers. Clear patterns emerged. Those detained had worked for the China Relief Fund, were schoolteachers or civil servants, and anyone with the bear tattoo of the Triads, communists, and those who spoke with a Hainanese dialect, whom the Japanese believed automatically marked communists. Those "cleared" walked away, some with ink stamps on skin or a piece of paper marked "Examined." Then the *kempeitai* as well as detachments from all three Japanese army divisions systematically exterminated the remaining detainees.

The details remain obscure because there were so few survivors, all of whom had been left for dead. A parallel process occurred on the Malayan peninsula. The exact death toll remains in dispute. Postwar senior Japanese officers admitted to a figure of 6,000. Historians have put the numbers steeply higher in the tens of thousands (50,000 in Singapore and perhaps 20,000 elsewhere). A senior Japanese intelligence officer, Col. Ichiji Sugita, reputedly admitted a figure of 25,000 to a Japanese reporter.

The threat of a second round of screening and potentially mass extinction terrorized the remaining Chinese and Malays into raising a huge indemnity of $50 million to purchase their lives. At the indemnity presentation ceremony, Yamashita explained that the Japanese were descended from gods, while Darwin had demonstrated that European ancestors were monkeys. In this war between gods and monkeys, the gods must prevail.

An official figure used for years provided Malaya Command casualties as totaling 138,708 (British 38,496, Australian 18,490, Indian 67,340, Malayan Volunteers, 14,382). This total is most likely somewhat too high, primarily because of overcounts of Indians and Malay Volunteers. One careful accounting placed actual battlefield losses as about 7,500 killed and 10,000 wounded with prisoners of war around 120,000 (a number depressed in part by the Japanese release of Malay volunteers). The low ratio of wounded to killed (in Europe the ratio ran more like three or four to one) reflects the savagery of combat against the Japanese and the dim prospects for survival of wounded in a hurried retreat. The Twenty-Fifth Army's losses on Malaya and Singapore numbered 3,507 killed and 6,150 wounded, for a total of 9,657. The campaign illustrated two grim features of the Asian-Pacific War. The number of Allied soldiers killed in battle would be less than one-third of those who perished as Japanese prisoners of war. And while total military fatalities on both sides during the campaign numbered about 11,000, civilian fatalities ran anywhere along a range from approximately 20,000 to perhaps as many as 83,000.

Air losses during the campaign were impressive. The Commonwealth air component started the campaign with 243 aircraft of all types. Virtually all were lost, as well as the approximately 200 reinforcements. The Japanese Third Air Division reported 331 aircraft lost from all causes during the campaign, but only about 92 in combat. The Twenty-Second Air Flotilla lost at least eleven aircraft, making total Japanese losses about 342.

Assessment

In the immediate aftermath of the defeat, excoriation cascaded down upon individual leaders or groups. The obvious lead goat was Percival. The first thing to be acknowledged is that no British Army commander in the war was so comprehensively let down by both the Royal Navy and the Royal Air Force. Further, his superiors chained him to the mission of defense of Singapore as a naval base and failed to provide adequate air power, yet dictated the dispersal of his forces to protect air bases. Others, not Percival, bore responsibility for the low effectiveness of Indian Army units assigned to Malaya. Percival's intelligence officers particularly ill served him. Further, thanks to thoughtlessness in London, the campaign began with a lame duck commander in chief.

But Percival authored much of the ignominious character of the defeat. He was thoroughly trounced by a foe he outnumbered in men and equipment— and he enjoyed generally better logistics. Even counting solely British and Australian units, he still wielded enough combat power to have sustained a much more vigorous defense. His signature blunder stands as the serial failure to concentrate combat power at decisive points. Perhaps in the broad view of history, the one thing to be said for Percival was that the surrender spared (most of) the civilian population of Singapore the sort of fate dealt to cities like Nanking and Manila by the Japanese.

Leaders below Percival also donated generously to disaster. Among the divisional and brigade commanders, Murray-Lyon, Paris, Duncan, and Barstow of the Indian units and Bennett and Maxwell of the Australians conspicuously failed. Even in the British Army's repetitive defeats in North Africa, it is hard to discern so much unrelieved deficient leadership from brigade level upwards. As for groups, the notion that the civil administration somehow contributed a vital measure to the disaster is without serious merit. Likewise, attempts to heap decisive responsibility on Indian or alternatively Australian soldiers invert cause and effect.[*]

But as is often the case in the recording of history, the more distant from the event, the more institutional issues loom large. The underlying causes for the Singapore disaster rest in post–World War I deficiencies in British mus-

---

[*]   Beyond the scope of this work is the ugly story of how some British leaders attempted to assign grossly disproportionate blame to the Australians. Under the massive blows Yamashita delivered, and in no small part due to Percival's and Bennett's failures, the 8th Australian Division did fracture on Singapore Island—as would any other Malaya Command unit. At least half the Japanese who died on Singapore were killed by the Australians. The papers of Maj. Gen. J. N. Kennedy, a member of the Imperial General Staff in London, contain a revealing document on the issue of overall sacrifice in the war a few months beyond this event. "Statistics of Casualties to 30 Sep. 42" tabulates army casualties of Commonwealth countries to date and calculates them as a percentage of each nation's population. The figures were: New Zealand (17,363) 1.1%; Australia (40,768) 0.58%; United Kingdom (195,200) 0.40%; Canada (7,043) 0.07% (not counting Dieppe); South Africa (21,520) 0.22%; and India (101,000) 0.03%. In other words, New Zealand's losses were almost three times and Australian losses almost 50 percent greater than those of the United Kingdom as a percentage of the population. Of course, if Royal Navy and Royal Air Force losses were factored in, the UK percentage would have been much greater, even allowing for losses in naval and air components of other Commonwealth nations. Papers of Major General J. N. Kennedy, Folder: Papers extracted from World War II diary—1942, 4/6, Liddell Hart Centre.

cle and brain power. One British admiral skewered Britain's Far East policy prior to 1941 as resting upon "the illusion that a Two-Hemisphere Empire can be defended by a One Hemisphere Navy." Then in the 1930s the men entrusted with Britain's fate misread Hitler and cast away opportunities to halt him before it was too late. Once France and the Netherlands were overrun, Churchill's government lacked any realistic prospect of checking a Japanese assault on Britain's Asian empire. Churchill's policy blended a steely ruthlessness with pious hopes. The ruthlessness involved prioritizing the defense of Britain, defense of the Middle East and, to a lesser extent, support for the Soviet Union. That left little sea or air power for the Far East—though the rich air assets conferred on the Middle East compared to the abject poverty of resources for the Far East remains questionable. Churchill's strategy also left the Far East with less than one-fifth of the ground forces deployed to the Middle East, and these numbers fail to reflect an even more lopsided ratio of actual capabilities. It remains shocking that up until 19 January, Churchill thought of Singapore as a "fortress" and his staff had never corrected this view, which apparently some shared.

Churchill's hopes rested on the deterrent effect of American arms in the Pacific coupled to the belief that if the United States, Britain, and the Dutch presented a united and firm diplomatic front, the Japanese might be dissuaded from adventurism. But American politics and institutions precluded such a firm front. While the London-generated causes of the disaster largely predated the advent of Churchill's government, what is not above censure is Churchill's lack of candor to the Australians and New Zealanders—although dominion leaders must share the blame for their failure to look clear-eyed at the peril facing them.

But in Malaya, victory was attained, not merely defeat gifted. In contemporary mythology, the Japanese Twenty-Fifth Army constituted superb jungle fighters. But the Japanese troops enjoyed no extended jungle training, nor for that matter was the Malaya campaign fought predominantly in true jungle. A real priceless Japanese advantage was that two divisions were combat-experienced. All Japanese combat units had trained hard for the campaign, and they were physically tougher than their opponents. The quality of Japanese leadership from top to bottom was also markedly superior. But above all, these Japanese strengths were merged with operational and tactical doctrines that matched the terrain. Except for the 12th Indian Brigade and the 8th Australian Division, Malaya Command was defeated because it was road-bound. With far fewer motor vehicles, the Japanese skipped about Malaya on foot and with bicycles and pack animals, continuously trapping the road-bound Commonwealth forces. Yamashita's soldiers triumphed from such mundane factors, not some magical elixir of "fanaticism." But it must be admitted that the reputation Japanese soldiers carried for ferocity, amply earned in displays before westerners in China, did leach away at steadfast-ness once the collapse began.

The fall of Singapore has been often cited as the death knell of Britain's Asian empire. This overstates the case, for India was on the path to indepen-dence before the war and the actual British withdrawal from the rest of its Asian possessions was far more gradual and generally successful than often assumed. But the loss of Malaya and Singapore inflicted an immediate and vast disaster on one country: China. The defense of the Burma Road, China's last land link to its Western allies, rested upon the premise that Japan would be halted in Malaya and Singapore before it could threaten Burma. The con-sequences of the loss of the Burma Road for the Nationalist government and ultimately the Chinese people would far exceed the cost of the end of Britain's Asian empire.

:

CHAPTER 15

"Men Would Follow Them, Suffer, and Be Glad About It"

LOSS OF THE NETHERLANDS EAST INDIES

Setting the Stage

Beginning in 1595 the Dutch colonized a vast territory in the Pacific between Malaya and Australia stretching about 2,275 miles east and west and 1,135 miles north to south. These boundaries encompassed thousands of islands straddling the equator, but the major ones were Java, Sumatra, Dutch Borneo, Celebes, Ambon, and Timor. In 1940 the estimated population approached 70.5 million—about the same as Japan's. Of these, Europeans numbered some 250,000 (less than 0.5 percent), Chinese totaled about one million, and over 98 percent of the rest comprised the indigenous peoples—whose armed resistance to Dutch rule persisted into the early twentieth century. The spark of an independence movement existed, especially among university students, but prewar it remained far from potent, much less an armed threat to Dutch control. After Germany overran Holland in 1940, the Dutch administration in the capital of Batavia (now Jakarta) exercised great autonomy, although legally subordinate to the Dutch government in exile in London. Armored by a sense of racial superiority (one Dutch girl recalled a rumor that "Japanese planes were made out of meat tins") and beguiled by government propaganda inculcating a false sense of security, the Dutch population lazed in a shroud of unreality.

The defense of the Netherlands East Indies hinged fundamentally upon the British Commonwealth and American forces holding Singapore and the Philippines, respectively. Consequently, initially the Dutch ungrudgingly forwarded air and naval assets to defend Malaya. But in short order the Dutch recalled their detachments to confront Japanese forces carving into their colony seeking, above all, its oil.

Japanese naval and amphibious operations from the Philippines, down through Malaya to the Netherlands East Indies, fell under overall command of Vice Adm. Nobutake Kondo, commander in chief, Second Fleet. The operational forces under Kondo ultimately targeting the main island of Java moved along three distinct avenues: (1) via northern Borneo, Banka, and Sumatra Islands (Western Force); (2) via Tarakan and eastern and southern Borneo (Central Force); and (3) via the Celebes, Ambon, and Timor (Eastern Force). Vice Adm. Jisaburō Ozawa, commander in chief, Southern Expeditionary Fleet, directed the Western Force. Vice Adm. Ibo Takahashi, commander in chief, Third Fleet directed the Eastern Force incorporating the Philippines, Makassar Strait, Java Sea, and waters eastward. Subordinate to Takahashi was a Central Force under Rear Adm. Sueto Hirose.

Nagumo's *Kido Butai* lent support at times, but remained under Combined Fleet control, as did the First Fleet (battleships), which remained in the Japanese homeland apart from two units with Nagumo and two with Kondo. Kondo deployed the bulk of the rest of the Combined Fleet as the Southern Task Force. Under his immediate command was a distant covering force built around battleships *Kongo* and *Haruna* and Cruiser Division 5 (heavy cruisers *Takao* [Kondo's flagship], *Atago*, and *Maya*). Ozawa's (Western Force) flag flew from heavy cruiser *Chokai*; it was joined by Cruiser Division 7 (heavy cruisers *Mogami*, *Mikuma*, *Suzuya*, and *Kumano*). Admiral Takahashi (Eastern Force) flew his flag on the heavy cruiser *Ashigara*. Rear Adm. Takeo Takagi commanded a covering element under Takahashi composed of Cruiser Division 4 (heavy cruisers *Nachi*, *Haguro*, and *Myoko*). This armada included three destroyer squadrons, seaplane carriers, and assorted lesser combatant ships (like minesweepers, patrol boats, and submarine chasers).

Ground forces committed to the advance on the Netherlands East Indies fell under command of Lt. Gen. Hitoshi Imamura's Sixteenth Army. The Sixteenth Army's order of battle listed the 2nd, 38th, and (from February 1942) 48th Divisions; the 56th Brigade (Sakaguchi Detachment after Maj. Gen. Shizuo Sakaguchi); and six units of Imperial Navy Special Naval Landing Forces

(SNLF) of roughly battalion or regimental strength (including airborne units) that nearly equaled the front-line combat power of another division.[*] The full authorized strength of the Sixteenth Army numbered 97,800 men, with another 10,000 personnel in army air units. Aviation units committed to the campaign included the Imperial Army's Third *Hiko Shidan* (Air Force), with air units authorized 321 aircraft, and the Imperial Navy's Twenty-First and Twenty-Third Air Flotillas, with roughly 150 aircraft, including flying boats.

Kondo's massive fleet vastly outnumbered and outgunned the Allied naval forces. The Dutch naval component formed the core with three cruisers, seven destroyers, fifteen submarines, and an assortment of small combatant and auxiliary ships. The British contributed one heavy cruiser, two elderly light cruisers, six destroyers (three very old), and two submarines. Australia provided two modern light cruisers, one sloop, and six corvettes. The Americans deployed the Asiatic Fleet consisting of one heavy cruiser, and one modern and one old light cruiser, thirteen elderly destroyers, fifteen modern and six old submarines, plus auxiliaries and smaller combatants.[†]

Allied air strength comprised a plethora of units and aircraft types, from the antique to the most up-to-date. At one extreme were a few British biplane Vildebeest torpedo bombers, while at the other were the latest models of the B-17F Flying Fortress and the Curtis P-40E fighter. Both the British and the Americans supplied new and replacement aircraft during the campaign, producing a rolling inventory. The Dutch air services started the war with

---

[*] Specifically, these special naval landing forces were: Sasebo Combined Special Landing Force (SNLF) (comprised of the Sasebo 1st SNLF and Sasebo 2nd SNLF, each about 800 strong); Kure 1st SNLF (about 820 men); Kure 2nd SNLF (about 1,000 men); Yokosuka 1st SNLF (airborne infantry capable of deploying 519 parachutists plus support units); Yokosuka 2nd SNLF (about 1,178 men); and Yokosuka 3rd SNLF (airborne unit of about 1,000).

[†] Of the Allied forces facing Japan in the opening months of the war, the fifteen Dutch submarines in the Far East stand out. They sank a Japanese destroyer and eight merchant or auxiliary ships—proportionately a much better record than their American counterparts with nearly double strength. But the Dutch submariners paid a heavy price. A secret Japanese mine field laid prior to hostilities began off Kota Bharu claimed Dutch submarines *O-16* on 15 December and *KXVII* about 21 December. *O-20*, depth-charged by Japanese destroyers off Kota Bharu on 19 December, was scuttled with the loss of seven men. Thirty-two men were captured. *KXVI* fell victim to a Japanese submarine on 25 December. A Japanese bomb destroyed *KVII* at Surabaya on 18 February. The Dutch scuttled *KX*, *KXIII*, and *KXVIII* at Surabaya on 2 March to prevent capture. Three Dutch submarines withdrew to Fremantle, Australia and four to Colombo. Data on Dutch Submarines: www.dutchsubmarines.com (accessed 16 November 2012).

about 254 aircraft of all types, plus 36 Catalina PBYs on hand or en route for replacement of the Dornier flying boats used by the Dutch naval air service. This overall figure included about 83 Model 139 WH-3/3As (export version of the obsolete Martin B-10, henceforth Martin bombers) and about 101 fighters (the majority Brewster Buffaloes). While the Japanese enjoyed a vast superiority at sea, the Allied air units were not vanquished simply by sheer numbers.

Allied forces facing the Japanese invasion of Java included about 5,100 RAF personnel and about 3,500 British soldiers in five antiaircraft "regiments" (battalions in other armies), supported by about 2,500 Indian drivers and other support personnel. Brigadier Arthur S. Blackburn commanded a hodgepodge of Australian units formed as a brigade equivalent (named "Black Force.") There was also a lone American artillery battalion some 558-men strong. Of these forces, the Australian brigade and American battalion proved to be by far the most formidable opponents the Japanese faced.

The predominant ground forces defending the Netherlands East Indies mustered as the Koninklijk Nederlands-Indisch Leger (KNIL or Royal Netherlands East Indies Army). Lt. Gen. Hein ter Poorten commanded the KNIL, as well as all other ground units in the Netherlands East Indies. Dutch law established the KNIL as entirely separate from the metropolitan Dutch Army, and no conscript from the Netherlands could be sent overseas to serve in the KNIL. As in other colonial armies, the vast bulk of the KNIL consisted of males from the various local populations. The Dutch believed the only reliable Indonesian units were those drawn from Ambonese and Mendoese, who historically had provided the most loyal Dutch subjects. They served under the command of Dutch officers. Enlistees of European extraction, a tiny fraction of the KNIL, essentially formed a Dutch version of the French Foreign Legion. Overall, the army comprised about forty Indonesians for every European. The KNIL order of battle divided its 25,000 regulars into four infantry regiments, with cavalry, artillery, support, and garrison units. KNIL infantry units employed only rifles (of four different calibers) and light machine guns and mortars. KNIL artillery was of the light mountain type, and the mechanized units boasted only light tanks or armored cars, plus an assortment of light trucks, a few of them armored. The vast majority of the Dutch males residing in the NEI up to age fifty-five served in reserve units. These reserve units, numbering about 40,000 men, although relatively well armed, lacked training and provided little combat power.

The Itinerary of Conquest: December Borneo

The "unparalleled magnitude" of the Japanese campaign to capture Java remains stellar in its stupendous span, intricate planning, deft coordination, and hypervelocity. Indeed, it arguably shines as the apex of military prowess by Imperial Japan's armed forces. The brilliance of Japanese operations emerges most evidently in a chronological framework.

In December 1941, the estimated fewer than three million inhabitants of Borneo lived largely in "primeval jungle" covering about 90 percent of the oil-rich island shaped like a portly *Tyrannosaurus Rex* with its head gazing east. British authority stretched along the northern seacoast, including the states of British North Borneo, the British Protectorate of Brunei, and Sarawak—the last a singular throwback to the nineteenth-century heyday of colonialism, for it was a "country" conquered and thereafter ruled by the Brooke family as a jungle Raj sheltered under the British ensign. The Dutch ruled the remaining approximately two-thirds of the island.

The British defenses of Borneo lacked resources but not color. Just one reinforced battalion, the 2/15th Punjab (about 1,050 men, largely British-officered Indian Army troops) served as the regular garrison, with the mission of covering planned demolitions of the oil fields to deny them to the Japanese. A contingent of locals, mostly Iban and Dyak (Dayak) tribesmen, brought the total force to 2,565. Japanese occupation would return the famously ferocious Dyaks back to their proclivity for headhunting. The Dutch garrison numbered about 750 men, mostly locals.

The Japanese targeted Borneo for its oil and to guard the flanks of their operations in Malaya and later toward Sumatra and Java. A heavily escorted convoy of ten transports bearing a reinforced regiment under Maj. Gen. Kiyotake Kawaguchi sighted Borneo just before midnight, December 15. Between that date and 9 March 1942, the contest on Borneo provided one of the most variegated miniature campaigns of the war. The Japanese seized key locations in both British and Dutch Borneo, often in small detachments maneuvering via barges or small native craft. In an epic jungle march eventually totaling some eight hundred miles, the 1/15th Punjab Battalion suffered and inflicted significant casualties but remained intact. Finally, with no hope of withdrawal or possibility of further resistance, the battalion's survivors surrendered on 9 March 1942. The Dutch garrison fought on till October 1942.

Borneo did not come cheap for Japanese sailors. Bombs from a Dutch

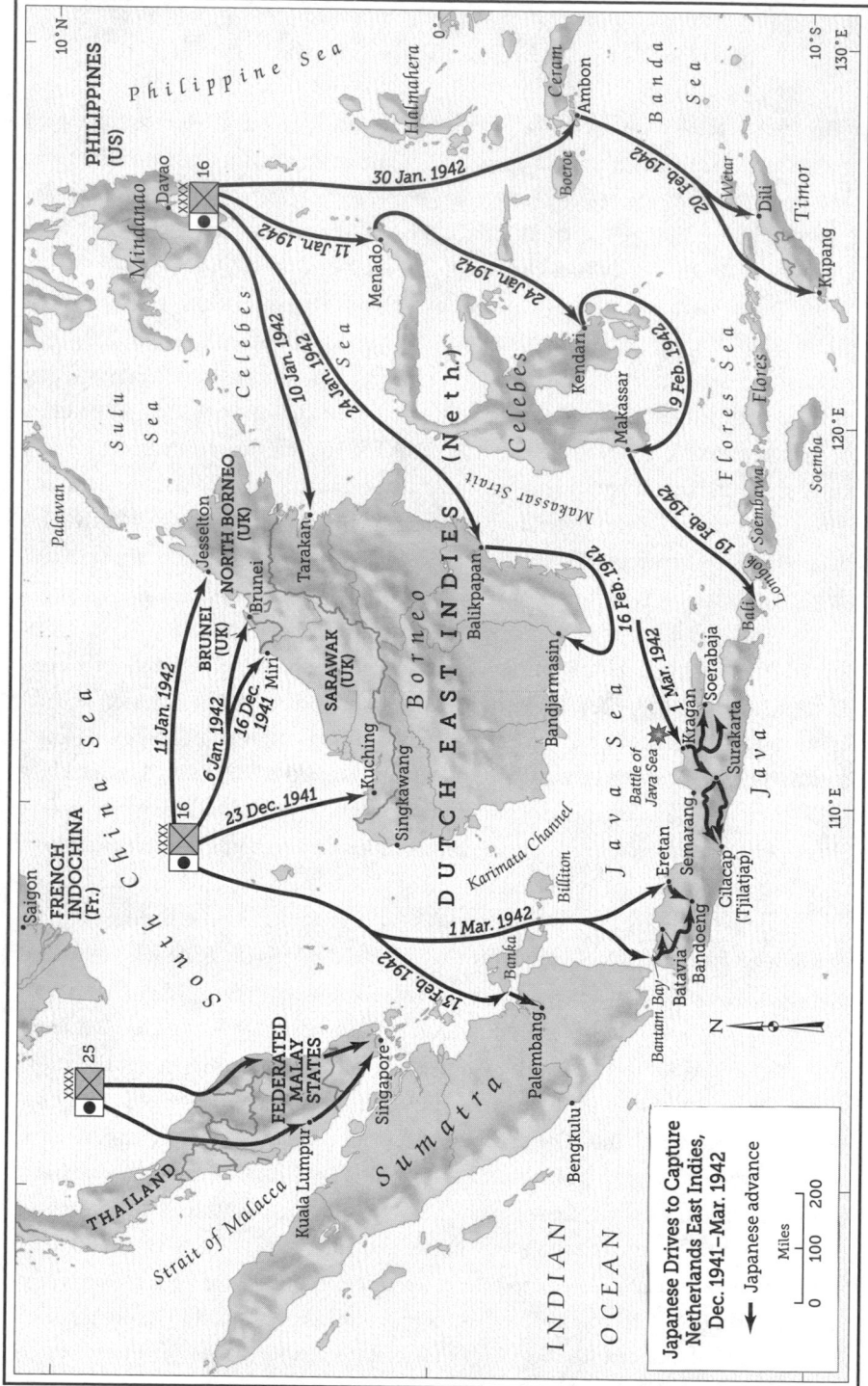

N

Japanese Drives to Capture
Netherlands East Indies,
Dec. 1941–Mar. 1942

→ Japanese advance

Miles

0   100   200

Do-24 seaplane blew up the destroyer *Shinonome* with its whole crew of 228 hands. The Dutch Submarine *KXVI* sank destroyer *Sagiri*, killing another 121 Japanese sailors. Mines and a Dutch submarine sank a total of four of the ten Japanese transports. Proportionally, Borneo ranks as the costliest Japanese naval expedition of the opening offensives.

January–February 1942: Menado and Tarakan, Balikpapan and Kendari, Ambon, Makassar

While Vice Admiral Ozawa's Western Force conducted operations at Borneo, the Japanese Eastern Force under Admiral Takahashi initiated a series of operations designed to move from Mindanao in the Philippines southward, ultimately alighting upon eastern Java. This effort commenced with a coordinated attack by amphibious and airborne units on Celebes at Menado. Perhaps the very strangest-looking island in the Pacific, Celebes resembles the misaligned merger of four peninsulas: one meandering northeast, a second stub peninsula roughly east, and two arranged like nutcrackers along the southeast and southern axes. Menado (now Manado) is at the tip of the northeast peninsula.

Protected by a strong naval escort, eight transports sent ashore Capt. Kunizo Mori's Sasebo 1st Combined SNLF (about 2,500 men) on both sides of the Menado Peninsula beginning at 0300, 11 January. About 1000, 28 G3Ms ("Nells") converted to troop transports began disgorging 334 paratroopers of the Yokosuka No. 1 SNLF over the Menado airfield. The defenders totaled about 1,500, though merely one-quarter were regular troops. By the evening of 12 January, the Japanese were masters of the area. Twenty parachutists died in the attack, but another twelve perished when a Japanese plane mistakenly downed their transport aircraft. The garrison withdrew and finally surrendered on 7 March. The Japanese promptly massacred most of the Dutch and the Christian Indonesians. Loss of the airfield on Menado cut off the Philippines from further Allied air reinforcements, except by heavy bombers.

The very same day (11 January) that Takahashi's Eastern Force attacked Menado, the Central Force assaulted Tarakan, an island brimming with oil fields off the east coast of Borneo. The overwhelming invasion force comprised the Sakaguchi Brigade (about 6,600 men total) loaded aboard 16 transports. During the approach, the Japanese escort dispatched a Dutch minelayer *Prins van Oranje*, with 102 Dutch sailors. The commander of the 1,300 Dutch defenders (few regulars) proposed to surrender. He warned the Japanese naval commander, Admiral Hirose, not to approach the Tarakan pier before the local coast defense battery received notice of the capitulation. Nonetheless, Hirose permitted six minesweepers to enter the bay where the Dutch gunners, unaware of the surrender, sank *W-13* and *W-14*, with 156 crewmen (by contrast only 55 Japanese died fighting ashore). The incensed Japanese leveled cruel vengeance by beheading some of the 219 men from the batteries and tying the others together in threes to drown or be eaten by crocodiles.

After only a slight pause, the Japanese Central force reloaded the Sakaguchi Brigade at Tarakan on 20 January and headed south to capture Balikpapan, a key oil production and refining center roughly halfway down the Makassar Strait on southeastern Borneo. With prompt news of the convoy, Admiral Hart coordinated a joint US-Dutch air, submarine, and surface-vessel effort to thwart the enemy design. A Dutch plane sank a transport on 23 January, but the Japanese landed before midnight 23–24 January. Refusing a Japanese surrender demand, the Dutch instituted a demolition program in the oil fields.

Hart's surface Striking Force under Rear Admiral Glassford at first labored under an unlucky star. Escort duties, an uncharted rock that slashed cruiser *Boise*'s hull requiring its withdrawal for repairs, and an engineering casualty on elderly *Marblehead* left Hart to launch the first US Navy surface action since the Spanish-American War with just four World War I–vintage "1,200 ton" destroyers, the "four pipers" (so called because of their four funnels) *John D. Ford*, *Pope*, *Parrot*, and *Paul Jones*.

Heavy weather slowed Cdr. Paul Talbot's quartet on their approach but also masked them from Japanese eyes before they reached Balikpapan at 0245, 24 January. There were anchored thirteen transports guarded by light cruiser *Naka* (a near match for Talbot's entire command) and ten modern destroyers completely outclassing Talbot's force. Also present were four minesweepers and three Japanese destroyers of the same vintage as Talbot's vessels, which the Japanese had demoted to "patrol boats."

The blazing oil facilities wafted oil fumes the Americans scented from 20 miles away. Up close, the fires backlighted low clouds, and smoke billowed over the water alternately outlining and shrouding the Japanese vessels, rendering the scene in the words of one American officer "a misplaced corner of Hell." Over the course of seventy-five minutes, Talbot's destroyers looped wildly at twenty-five knots between the anchored transports and their maneuvering screening vessels. The Americans emptied their torpedo tubes and in the last stages of the melee doled out gunfire. Early on, a *Parrot* torpedo touched off the ammunition cargo of *Sumanoura Maru*, which disappeared in a mighty blast, leaving only nine survivors. Two American torpedoes rendered *Patrol Boat 37* a constructive loss, removed permanently from service. Other such weapons sank transports *Tatukami Maru* and *Kuretake Maru*, and finished off *Tsuruga Maru* (damaged earlier that day by Dutch submarine *K-XVIII*). Casualties among Japanese seamen were serious, and at least 226 soldiers died in the melee.

Talbot's boldness earned a reward. Rear Admiral Nishimura, despite the alarms and fireworks at Balikpapan, kept his flagship *Naka* and the modern Japanese destroyers patrolling at a distance to the east, convinced no American force could pass them and reach the transports. Talbot's force sprinted away from the scene, having sustained just one hit on *John D. Ford*, which wounded four men.

Oddly enough, starting with Hart, American postmortems damned with faint praise Talbot's action. The reality is that Talbot's grossly outclassed force had displayed both daring and skill, sank one-quarter of the Japanese invasion force, and permanently removed a warship of about equal heft from Japanese service, with trivial damage in return. A latter Japanese history was more just: Talbot's band had "appeared out of nowhere like phantom killers, wreaked havoc in the dark, and disappeared like the wind." No US surface force would do as well until nineteen months later at the Battle of Vella Gulf. Notwithstanding Talbot's intervention, by nightfall that same day, 24 January, the Japanese expelled a weak Dutch battalion and held the town of Balikpapan. The Japanese punctuated their assertion of control by making the local inhabitants witness the execution of seventy-eight Dutch prisoners, including doctors, patients from a hospital, and priests. The Japanese Twenty-Third Air Flotilla opened operations from nearby airfields by 28 January, thus placing Java within range of their bombers.

Just as the Japanese coordinated a double move to Menado and Tarakan, so they coordinated a double move to Balikpapan and Kendari. Early on 24 January, the light cruiser *Nagara* and eight destroyers shepherding six transports bearing the Sasebo No. 1 SNLF closed on Kendari. The Dutch garrison of about four hundred men folded, and the Japanese promptly seized the excellent airfield at Kendari at a cost of only two wounded. The Twenty-First Air Flotilla soon advanced to Kendari.

After Kendari fell, Admiral Hart expected the Japanese to strike next 350 miles east at the modest island of Ambon. Ambon had once been coveted successively by the Portuguese, British, and Dutch for fabulously aromatic spices, but in early 1942 two airfields provided Ambon's main attraction.

Dutch Lt. Col. J. R. L. Kapitz commanded the island's defenses. These comprised about 2,600 Dutch defenders, mostly Indonesian troops under Dutch officers. The Australians provided the 2/21st Battalion (named "Gull Force") under Lt. Col. W. J. R. Scott numbering 1,100 men with attachments, but, like the Dutch, it lacked a full complement of weapons. Preliminary Japanese air raids had destroyed or driven away a smattering of Dutch, Australian, and American planes. Wavell overruled Hart's recommendation to withdraw the feeble Ambon garrison.

On 31 January, the main Japanese invasion force of a reinforced regiment (the 228th), totaling 5,300 men, landed to the south. Bolstering them was Rear Adm. Kouichiro Hatakeyama's Kure No. I and Sasebo Combined SNLF, which splashed ashore in the north. An overpowering naval covering force included softening-up strikes from carriers *Hiryū* and *Sōryū*. The substantial size of the island and the weakness of the scattered Dutch and Australian units rendered defensive prospects poor, but the Japanese reduced them to nil by cleverly landing away from the obvious localities and advancing at great speed from unexpected directions. All the Dutch and Australian defenders, save a few who escaped, were captured by 3 February. The Japanese claim to have killed 340 defenders and said their losses were 55 killed and 135 wounded.

Among all the many appalling examples of Japanese conduct with prisoners of war, Ambon earns a special niche. During the fighting, the main part of "Gull Force" suffered 15 known dead. But one major part of the battalion captured separately from the rest lost 309 dead, an unknown number in combat, the vast majority due to Japanese executions between 6 and 20 February, reportedly on orders of Admiral Hatakeyama as reprisal for the destruction of Japanese minesweeper *W-9* by a Dutch mine. The Japanese also executed surrendered Dutch troops and Royal Australian Air Force personnel. Of the 791 Australians taken prisoner and not executed shortly thereafter, no fewer than 405 died of the 528 held on Ambon. This provided a stark example of how, even among the awful death rates of prisoners held by the Japanese, those who found themselves in smaller batches often fared the worst.

As noted, the southern half of Celebes features two peninsulas roughly aligned like a nutcracker. Kendari is near the tip of the southeastern peninsula. At the tip of the southern peninsula is Makassar, to which an all–Imperial Navy invasion force in six transports steamed on 8 February. The transports carried the Sasebo Combined SNLF and two airfield construction units. The Japanese secured the area, but US submarine *S-37* sank Japanese destroyer *Natsushio*; eight crewmen perished.

Sumatra

The Japanese Western force gathered again to invade Sumatra, an island stretching about 1,000 miles long, bisected by the equator and six times larger than the Netherlands itself. With a mountainous spine to the west and vast level expanses of swamps and jungle, Sumatra featured poor interior communication. Economic development centered in the south, notably around Palembang, the capital. That town rested some fifty miles inland, but the Moesti (Moesi) River afforded access by oceangoing vessels. Oilfields, regarded as the best in Southeast Asia and accounting for about 40 percent of all oil production in the colony, stretched north about one hundred miles from Palembang. These fed major refineries about five miles east of Palembang at Pladjoe and Soengi (Sungei Gerong). A Japanese history remarked that "it is no exaggeration to say that the Greater East Asian War was launched for the oil in Palembang."

Two airfields flanked Palembang. One known to the British (and history) as P1 was the original concrete-paved civilian airfield about eight miles north of Palembang. Forty miles southwest of Palembang nestled P2, a huge grass field with a ten-mile, vegetation-framed perimeter affording instant cover for aircraft. The Japanese were oblivious to P2's existence until they physically occupied it. The Allied air units at Singapore largely withdrew to Sumatra in the latter part of January 1942. Allied fighters employed P1, while from P2 Allied bombers mounted small and ineffectual attacks on Malaya, usually at night. The Emperor's flyers struck back with much success at P1 due to erratic warnings from ground observers (there was no radar) and weak antiaircraft defenses.

On the morning of 14 February 1942, Allied air strength around Palembang comprised about thirty-five to thirty-nine Hudsons and about forty Blenheims at P2. At P1 waited approximately fifteen serviceable Hurricanes. Ground defenses of southern Sumatra totaled about 2,000 men, including a battalion of KNIL regulars, a reservist battalion, and eight fixed 75 mm guns at Palembang. The immediate P1 defenders numbered about 150 British soldiers manning antiaircraft guns, about 110 Indonesian soldiers, and an ad hoc 75-man contingent of RAF personnel.

The largely successful Allied sabotage of the refineries on Borneo and the Celebes created urgent Japanese needs for undamaged local refining capacity. The lengthy river pathway to the refineries gave the Dutch ample time to fire these facilities, so the Japanese selected a paratroop coup de main to seize them before they could be destroyed. Tactically, however, the parachute assault emphasized seizure of P1 as the indispensable base to sustain the airborne operations.

A Japanese invasion convoy of eight transports bearing part of the 229th Infantry Regiment of the 38th Division, fresh from conquest of Hong Kong, seized Banka Island early on the 14th. Attacks by Hudsons and Blenheims set one transport afire, but at a cost of nine Hudsons to Zeros of the Twenty-Second Air Flotilla. Behind this first echelon came another fourteen transports bearing the rest of the 229th Infantry Regiment and a battalion of the 230th Infantry Regiment. They prepared to hurry a relief force up the Moesti River to Palembang.

In early February, ABDA formed a combined Striking Force of Dutch, British, Australian, and American vessels and placed it under the command of Rear Adm. Karel Doorman. During its initial foray on 4 February, Japanese bombers attacked and scored a hit on American heavy cruiser *Houston*, knocking out its after main battery turret. The aging American light cruiser *Marblehead* barely survived two bomb hits by dint of the skill and resolution of its captain and crew. Now Doorman sailed again to intercept the Japanese invasion fleet bound for southern Sumatra. The Japanese again unleashed ferocious air attacks from land-based planes and light carrier *Ryujo*. Cruiser *Hobart*'s captain reported that "the bombs fell close enough for me to see the ugly red flash of their burst and to feel the heat of their explosions across my face." In the face of these attacks Doorman retired with damage to two American destroyers, but the Japanese postponed the seaward thrust to Palembang by a day.

In late morning of 14 February a massive flight of 150 Japanese aircraft (including 34 transports loaded with 240 paratroopers and 27 bombers carrying supply containers) droned at low altitude up the Moesti River. Paratroopers of the Imperial Army's 2nd Raiding Regiment jumped around P1, while one transport plane made a deliberate crash landing near P1 to deliver the commander of the Japanese parachute unit (Col. Seiichi Kume) and an antitank gun.*

The Japanese air assault on P1 ignited chaos that was memorable even by

---

* The Imperial Army had created its first parachute units expressly for the purpose of seizing the Palembang oil facilities. During passage from Japan, the ship bearing the 1st Raiding Regiment tasked for the Palembang drop experienced a disastrous accidental fire set off by incendiary bombs. Although escorts rescued the entire army contingent, the ship, with all the weapons and equipment of the regiment, was a total loss. At first canceling the air drop was deemed prudent; the 1st Raiding Regiment could not be reequipped in time and the 2nd Raiding Regiment was not nearly so well trained. Ultimately, the operation went ahead with the 2nd Raiding Regiment. Remmelink, *The Invasion of the Dutch East Indies*, 257–59, 272–74.

war standards. Clusters of Hurricanes, Blenheims, and Hudsons appeared almost simultaneously returning from attacks on the invasion convoy. Some Blenheims flew through clumps of Japanese paratroops swaying below white parachutes. Another flight of Hurricanes arrived on a ferry hop from Java desperately short of fuel. They became embroiled in low-level dogfights with Ki-43s. Two Hurricanes were shot down and three crash-landed, to no Japanese loss. On the airfield one newly landed Hudson crew snatched nearby ground personnel and one other Hudson crew and took off amid the attack. Some Hurricane pilots landed then and took wing again for P2.

The Japanese jumped carrying only pistols and hand grenades. All their other weapons reposed in containers, but most containers became lost or inaccessible in the vegetation. The heavy growth also impeded the linkup of the Japanese so that they only banded in small groups. A battalion commander, Maj. Takeo Komura, for example, never assembled more than thirty-four men until the end of the day.

In a particularly surreal incident, British Wing Cdr. H. C. Maguire, senior officer at P1, walked out to greet what he surmised was a Dutch relief force. Instead he bumped into over sixty Japanese. Maguire put down his Thompson submachine gun and, unarmed, "marched briskly" up to the closest Japanese and demanded that the soldier produce an officer. Obligingly, an English-speaking Japanese officer materialized. "I immediately demanded [their] surrender," recalled Maguire, "saying that I had a large force behind me. He replied that he had a large force and that he would give us safe conduct if we marched out." His bluff trumped by the Japanese bluff, Maguire announced he would have to go back and discuss the matter with his (nonexistent) senior officer. The Japanese officer released him unmolested. Meanwhile, the 99-man assault on the refineries seized Pladjoe intact, but demolitions destroyed about 80 percent of Soengi. Japanese paratrooper casualties were 39 killed (including two whose parachutes failed to open) and 37 wounded. As Sumatra fell, about 5,090 Allied military personnel and 1,000 civilians exited to Java. In early March 1942, the Japanese seized the northern stretches of Sumatra.

THE JAPANESE INVASION of southern Sumatra overlapped with a transnational clash over employment of the I Australian Corps (mainly the 6th and 7th Australian Divisions). Wavell discounted the ability of Allied defenders to withstand a Japanese onslaught against Java, expected around the end of February. He did not believe Australian units could reach Java in time ready to fight. Wavell thus advised: "Burma and Australia are absolutely vital for war against Japan. Loss of Java, though a severe blow from every point of view, would not be fatal." Therefore, on 16 February, Wavell recommended diversion to Burma of at least one division and preferably all of the I Australian Corps.

On 20 February, the British Chiefs of Staff cabled Wavell, stressing the vital importance of every day gained by a resolute defense of Java. They pointedly granted him freedom to augment the naval and air forces for Java's defense, but they said nothing about additional ground forces. The next day, the Chiefs of Staff informed Wavell that they were transferring Burma from his command to the India Command. This same day the Combined Chiefs of Staff in Washington directed him to withdraw his headquarters from Java to such a location as he deemed best. Wavell bluntly responded to these messages that the Dutch should take charge of the defense of Java, the only remaining area under his command. Therefore, rather his headquarters should be not withdrawn but abolished. With the approval of the Combined Chiefs in hand, Wavell formally closed the ABDA command on 25 February. Meanwhile, the Dutch and British insisted on the relief of American Admiral Hart, whom they viewed as "tired, over age and un-aggressive." Hart, who earlier almost endorsed this judgment to Wavell, was ignominiously relieved. Command of the final defense of Java fell entirely into Dutch hands, with Vice Adm. Conrad Helfrich overseeing naval forces, Maj. Gen. L. H. van Oyen air forces, and Lt. Gen. Hein ter Poorten ground forces.

The demise of the ABDA command still left open the issue of the employment of the I Australian Corps. But that matter coincided with the loss of Singapore and Churchill's serious domestic political troubles. Three days before the fall of Singapore, as mentioned earlier, two German battle cruisers and a heavy cruiser managed to stream up the English Channel in daylight. This "Channel Dash," as it became known, was a modest event in the global struggle, but it inflicted on the British public a stinging humiliation, seemingly a manifestation of gross incompetence in the direction of the war. "The country is more upset about the escape of the German battleships than about Singapore," wrote one diarist. Then on 18 February, Wavell cabled Churchill about the "lack of real fighting spirit" among British, Australians, and Indians not only in Malaya, but also "so far" in Burma. Brooke wrote in his diary that day, "If the Army cannot fight better than it is doing at the present we shall deserve to lose our Empire." The successive Far Eastern defeats and the "Channel Dash" compelled Churchill to shake up his government. Only to King George VI did Churchill admit his darkest fears, as recorded in the King's diary entry after their weekly luncheon on 22 February: "Burma, Ceylon, Calcutta and Madras in India and part of Australia may fall into enemy hands."

Churchill's intentions for the employment of the I Australian Corps thus must be placed in the context of this extremely somber backdrop of domestic and global strategic woes. The prime minister insisted that the Australians could stop the unraveling of the Far Eastern theater by debarking in Burma. President Roosevelt strongly supported him. From 17 to 23 February, a blizzard of sometimes barbed cable traffic swirled among London, Washington, and Canberra. Prime Minister Curtin and his government were livid to learn that Churchill had ordered leading ships bearing part of the I Australian Corps to turn for Burma on 20 February on the presumption that Australia would kowtow to London's vision. But the Australian government, braced by the recommendations of its senior army leadership, stood adamant that the I Australian Corps return to Australia—and so it did, to Churchill's enduring bitterness. After the war, Brooke claimed Burma could have been held with the Australian troops. But the Australians were right. With Japanese air and sea supremacy, adding Australians to the Allied ground forces soon to have their communications cut in Burma would only have magnified the ensuing debacle.*

This wrangle produced an important and enduring consequence. American support for Churchill's plea to debark Australian troops in Burma resulted in the dispatch of the US Army's 41st Infantry Division to Australia. Then in March, Churchill requested that US ground units deploy to Australia and New Zealand to permit retention of the 9th Australian and the 2nd New Zealand Divisions in the Middle East, where the situation was worsening. This prompted the transfer of the US 32nd Infantry Division to Australia and the US 1st Marine Division to New Zealand. The chain of events thus resulted in the fateful commitment of major American ground troops to the South Pacific.

Darwin Bombed

The Japanese administered a pointed reminder of Australia's vulnerability amidst the heated exchange over the disposition of Australian troops returning from the Middle East. The dazzling sunlight of a clear Pacific morning on 19 February hustled night shadows westward across the Timor Sea to reveal Admiral Nagumo's Striking Force of carriers *Akagi, Kaga, Sōryū,* and

---

* The Australian government relented to the extent of permitting the 16th and 17th Brigades (from the 6th Australian Division) to be diverted to defend Ceylon in March. They remained for about four months. Wigmore, *The Japanese Thrust,* 460.

Hiryū, escorted by two battleships, three cruisers, and seven destroyers. To support landings on Bali and Timor, the carriers slung aloft a massive strike of 188 planes—five more than the first wave to attack Pearl Harbor.

Darwin formed an obvious target as a key port and rear air base for Allied operations in the Netherlands East Indies. Anticipating a Japanese strike, all but 2,000 of the original 5,800 inhabitants evacuated the isolated frontier town. The harbor held this dawn some forty-seven naval and merchant vessels ranging from an 11,000-ton transport to a 12-ton patrol vessel. No fighters and few antiaircraft guns guarded Darwin.*

The aerial thunderbolt struck just before 1000. By chance, Zeros caught ten transient P-40s destined for Java on the ground or at low altitude and destroyed nine, killing four pilots. One American pilot courageously attacked the Japanese armada and damaged one dive bomber that ditched. The raiders lashed the town and nearby oil tanks hard, but struck their most devastating blows at the shipping. They sank the US destroyer *Peary*, killing ninety-one of its crew, many in the fuel oil inferno that topped the vessel's watery grave. The Japanese also sank two small naval craft and destroyed seven merchant vessels, including the heavily loaded transport *General M.C. Meigs*. Fuchida's flyers withdrew after ninety minutes, but at noon a second raid comprising fifty-four Imperial Navy "Nell" and "Betty" bombers from Kendari wheeled over Darwin to pummel the airfield. Counting the US fighters, the raids destroyed seventeen Allied combat aircraft. The Japanese lost four or five carrier planes; one pilot became the first Japanese prisoner of war taken in Australia.

This heavy dual raid struck a major blow at Allied efforts to hold Java and inflicted a serious loss on shipping. But its memory lingered long after in Australia as a font of national shame. The raids occurred just four days after the shocking fall of Singapore that marked Australia's greatest military disaster to date. They represented the first air attacks on Australian soil. The two closely timed aerial blows appeared as overtures to an actual invasion and snapped the resolve of the civilian and some of the uniformed leadership. They sparked

---

* En route to their target, nine Zeros peeled off to shoot down a Catalina PBY piloted by Lieutenant Thomas Moorer, who managed to get the flaming plane down onto the water. There the eight-man crew was picked up by the US Army chartered freighter *Florence D* on a blockade run to the Philippines. The returning Japanese carrier planes then sank *Florence D*. Thus, Moorer gained the dubious distinction of being shot down and then sunk within a few hours on the same day. Moorer rose to become US chief of Naval Operations (1967–1970) and then chairman of the Joint Chiefs of Staff (1970–1974). Peter Grose, *An Awkward Truth: The Bombing of Darwin 1942* (Crows Nest, UK: Allen & Unwin, 2011), 83, 134–35.

a panicked mass flight by civilians and military personnel that became deri-sively known as the "Adelaide Stakes" (a play on the idea that those fleeing Darwin were engaged in something akin to a horse race from Darwin to Ade-laide some 1,626 miles across the breadth of the continent). One especially energetic refugee turned up in Melbourne some 13 days and almost 2,000 miles later. Meanwhile scenes of confusion, fear, and looting unfolded in Dar-win for days. Deaths totaled at least 297 (including about 61 civilians).

Government censors could not suppress highly fevered accounts of the panic and flight. This delivered a jolt to the Australian psyche, which char-acteristically demands resolution, resourcefulness, and cheerfulness in the face of adversity. But lurid versions of the hours after the raids parted from the complex reality. In fact, great steadfastness, courage, and effectiveness marked the actions of servicemen and civilians alike to the first raid. Particu-larly commendable was Ivan Sinclair. Released from imprisonment on a fire-arms violation during the attack, instead of absconding he performed heroic rescue work, treating no fewer than 113 victims. It was the lack of effective resistance to the second mass bombing attack that shook loose the weak grip of the ineffectual civilian administration. It also triggered confusion, lead-ing to misinterpretation of orders on the military side, which precipitated a disordered evacuation of the airfields. Many Australians found it painful to admit that at least some of them reacted the way many other people did to heavy bombing.

Bali and Timor

One of the intended beneficiaries of Nagumo's Darwin raid was a Japanese force bound for Bali in two transports lugging a battalion from the 48th Divi-sion escorted by four destroyers. Light cruiser *Nagara* and three destroyers covered this modest contingent. At 0200, 19 February the troops commenced landing at Bali, meeting little resistance ashore, but attacks by Allied aircraft damaged both transports, delaying unloading.

News of the Bali landing found Doorman's Striking Force much depleted by escort duties and damage repairs. These circumstances prompted Door-man to sacrifice coordination for speed. He hurried away his available vessels in three separate waves—each attended by a fiasco. The first wave comprised Dutch cruisers *DeRuyter* and *Java*, with one Dutch and two American destroy-ers. The second wave numbered four American destroyers followed by Dutch light cruiser *Tromp*. Eight Dutch torpedo boats formed the third wave. The four defending Japanese destroyers, at a cost of heavy damage to *Michishio* and the loss of sixty-four killed, managed to sink Dutch destroyer *Piet Hein* (with an equal fatality list) and damage *Tromp* and an American destroyer. It was a decided victory for the outmatched Japanese.

The island of Timor sits east of Java, like a planned stepping stone for short-range aircraft of 1942 vintage winging from Australia to Java. An Australian officer described the interior, particularly to the northeast, as a "lunatic, contorted, tangled mass of mountains." Dutch colonial authorities administered the southwestern part, including the key port of Koepang (now Kupang), with its nearby air base and seaplane anchorages. About 400,000 Timorese and roughly 4,000 to 5,000 others of Dutch, Chinese, and Arabic descent populated Dutch Timor. The Portuguese claimed the northeast half of the island. Their capital at Dili featured a nearby airfield. About 500,000 Timorese plus roughly 300 Portuguese, 2,000 Chinese, and a handful of Japanese and Arabs inhabited Portuguese Timor.

The Dutch and Portuguese each deployed about six hundred men in Timor, mostly locals. The importance of Timor for the defense of Java prompted the Australians to deploy "Sparrow Force" to Dutch Timor. The heart of this 1,400-man unit was the 2/40th Infantry Battalion, the 2/2nd Independent (Commando) Company, and a coastal battery. The Australians faced the conundrum that Timor's security required the defense of its Portuguese half, but the presence of Australian defenders in Portuguese territory might incite a Japanese attack. Indeed, Japanese plans called for avoiding Portuguese Timor unless Allied forces entered it first. Over Portuguese protest, most of the 2/2nd Independent Company and about two hundred Dutch troops occupied Dili and vicinity. This preemptive violation of Portuguese neutrality provided the Japanese with a warrant to invade. On 16 February, Japanese aircraft turned back a convoy bearing an additional Australian battalion and an American artillery battalion. Tôjô pressed to have the Japanese withdraw from Portuguese Timor once Allied forces were expelled. The Imperial Navy insisted this territory was too valuable for operations against Australia to be surrendered. The upshot was a decision to propose withdrawing from Portuguese Timor once Allied forces were expelled, provided that the Portuguese could continue to maintain neutrality, which was not deemed likely.

During the night of 19–20 February, fourteen Japanese transports and three elderly destroyers, which were converted to high-speed small transports under the customary heavy naval escort, approached Timor bearing about 4,600 men. The Japanese put ashore landing parties in both Dutch Timor (on the far coast south of Koepang) and Portuguese Timor (at Dili). With daylight on the 20th, the Japanese dropped 308 paratroopers of the 3rd Yokosuka SNLF to block the potential retreat of the 2/40th Battalion into the interior of Dutch Timor. That Australian battalion fought hard to withdraw into the interior, clashing heavily with the paratroopers and being closely pursued by superior Japanese forces from the rear, accompanied by tanks. On 23 February, the largest portion of the 2/40th Battalion, exhausted, depleted, and now short of supplies and ammunition after four days of battle, surrendered. Imperial Army losses were seventy-four killed and fifty-six wounded on Timor.

In Portuguese Timor, a remarkable story began rather than ended. The 2/2nd Independent Company withdrew from around Dili to the southwest corner of the Portuguese territory. There they were eventually joined by about 200 Australian survivors from Dutch Timor (including Brig. W. C. D. Veale, the senior officer who had been cut off from the 2/40th Battalion) and about 150 Dutch troops. The last word from outside Timor that the Australians received was that Darwin was bombed on 19 February. Despite their seemingly forlorn situation, the Australians speedily established themselves. They mastered the food situation and mustered the help of the locals. An ingenious and diligent effort assembled a radio set that announced the existence of the guerrilla force to the startled Australian Army command on 20 April. The saga of this guerilla campaign on Timor, extending to February 1943, will be told later.

Java

Though Wavell, London, and Washington considered the Netherlands East Indies as good as lost, the local Dutch command refused to give up. The sheer size of Java (about 650 miles long and 130 miles wide) far overstretched the ground defense forces. Therefore, the Dutch kindled their hopes around the ability of air and sea forces to fend off the expected invasion.

The Dutch air commander, Maj. Gen. L. H. van Oyen, aimed to delay the Japanese invasion by striking at the key Japanese vulnerability: very thin logistical margins. The Imperial Army air contingents, poised to strike from the west, assembled at P1 on Sumatra. Van Oyen's bombers would retard the Japanese quest for air superiority by attacking the P1 aviation fuel stocks at hand and those en route by ship. The simultaneous bombing of Japanese aircraft on the ground at P1, as well as the attrition inflicted by Allied fighters against Japanese preinvasion air strikes on western Java, would secure a respite of a week or so. That would permit arrival of a stream of 113 expected fighter reinforcements that might permanently deny the Japanese air superiority over Java, without which the Japanese would cancel the invasion.

Van Oyen massed Dutch and British Commonwealth air assets in West Java, which the Dutch command regarded as the primary Japanese objective. Van Oyen left the air defense of eastern Java in American hands with about twenty heavy bombers and a fighter squadron. While Allied airmen in western Java faced mostly the Imperial Army aviators, the Americans in the east confronted almost entirely the more capable aircraft and excellent crews of the Imperial Navy.

Van Oyen's ends were sound, but his means were decidedly meager. On 19 February van Oyen launched his air campaign with just forty-three fighters, about one-third of the total he projected as necessary. He had a mere twenty-five operational bombers. The Imperial Army air units at P1 eventually mustered 167 aircraft while the Imperial Navy contributed fifteen Zeros and three reconnaissance planes. Although the Japanese countered van Oyen's forty-three fighters with just fifty-seven of their own, the lack of adequate radar warning resulted in the Japanese typically outnumbering Allied fighters two- or three-to-one in clashes over Western Java. Van Oyen's bombers obtained real but limited success against Japanese aviation fuel supplies and aircraft on the ground at P1. The few antiaircraft guns with very few shells left Dutch air bases highly vulnerable. In this air campaign from 19 to 27 February, the Japanese lost about thirty-five aircraft in the air or on the ground while Allied losses numbered about forty-five. The Allied airmen secured just a two-day delay in an invasion of Java to 28 February, not the postponement van Oyen hoped for.

Battle of the Java Sea

Allied air reconnaissance reported Japanese troop convoys approaching both eastern and western Java on 26 February. Even more than the modest attrition achieved by Allied airmen, the inability of thirty-seven Allied submarines near Java to inflict any damage on the Japanese convoys constituted a shocking failure. Meanwhile, a motley Allied surface-ship force of one modern light cruiser (the Australian *Hobart*), two elderly British light cruisers, and two aged British destroyers searched unsuccessfully for the reported western Japanese convoy. Thereafter, they managed to escape from the rolling disaster of the defense of Java.

The daylight hours of 27 February also found the American seaplane tender *Langley* about seventy-five miles from Tjilatjap, on Java's south coast, with its cargo of thirty-two desperately needed assembled P-40s on deck.[*] Sixteen Japanese bombers, with fifteen Zeros in escort, found *Langley*. Despite Cdr. Robert P. McConnell's skillful handling of plodding *Langley*, sixteen Japanese bombers ripped *Langley* with five bombs, halting it with raging fires—one of the most amazing examples of successful high-level bombing of a ship at sea in the war. Its escorting destroyers *Whipple* and *Edsall* picked up survivors and scuttled it.

With exhausted crews, Doorman's Combined Striking Force approached Surabaya this same morning to refuel after a night sweep when he received a report on the Japanese convoy. Doorman wheeled about with two heavy and three light cruisers and nine destroyers to meet the convoy. Simultaneously, the Japanese covering force of two heavy and two light cruisers and fourteen destroyers moved to block Doorman. The following table itemizes the armament of Doorman's command and his Japanese adversaries:

Allied and Japanese Ships at the Battle of the Java Sea: Armament Comparison

	GUNS						TORPEDO TUBES	
	8-INCH	6/5.9-INCH	5.5-INCH	5-INCH	4.7-INCH	4-INCH	21-INCH	24-INCH
	(203mm)	(155/149mm)	(140mm)	(127 mm)	(120mm)	(100mm)	(533mm)	(610 mm)
ALLIED								
Cruisers	12	25	0	8	0	16	14	0
Destroyers	0	0	0	0	21	19	72	0
Total	12	25	0	8	21	25	86	0

(The four US destroyers carried one short barrel 3-inch antiaircraft gun each. The two Dutch destroyers carried three 3-inch antiaircraft guns between them. These weapons were of no utility in this action for surface engagement.)

	8-INCH	6/5.9-INCH	5.5-INCH	5-INCH	4.7-INCH	4-INCH	21-INCH	24-INCH
JAPANESE								
Cruisers	20	0	14	16	0	0	0	48
Destroyers	0	0	0	78	0	0	0	114
Total	20	0	14	86	0	0	0	162

[*] In 1922, *Langley*, originally a collier, was converted into the US Navy's first aircraft carrier. In 1936, it reverted to the status of a seaplane tender. The forward 40 percent of its flight deck was dismantled so that it could not function as a carrier, but the after part of the former flight deck provided a ready parking area for assembled aircraft.

Japanese material superiority was still greater than this table conveys. The duo of Japanese heavy cruisers featured a combined total of twenty 8-inch guns of modern design aimed by sophisticated fire control systems. The British *Exeter* and American *Houston* mounted weapons and fire controls of comparable individual quality, but between them carried only twelve operational 8-inch guns (a bomb had destroyed Houston's aft triple turret). Australian *Perth* brought eight 6-inch and Dutch *DeRuyter* seven 5.9-inch guns to the affray with modern fire control, but they lacked the reach and punch of the 8-inch weapons. The Dutchman *Java* and its two Japanese counterparts *Jintsu* and *Naka*, represented the World War I lineage of light cruiser flotilla leaders designed basically to overwhelm destroyers at moderate to short range, not engage in long-range duels with peers.

The Allied situation in destroyers was much worse. The four antique American vessels could fire only three 4-inch guns on a broad side. Though the other five Allied destroyers were modern, only *Jupiter* matched any one of their fourteen Japanese counterparts. The Japanese destroyers also enjoyed large torpedo superiority, and the Type 93 Japanese 61 cm (24-inch) "Long Lance" torpedoes (which also fitted the Japanese cruisers) were the best in the world with markedly greater range, speed, and hitting power. The Japanese cruisers and destroyers mounted 162 torpedo tubes (to 86 Allied), but the Japanese ships also featured arrangements for reloading the tubes so that the actual number of available torpedoes favored the Japanese by 296 to 86.[*] Due to prior grounding damage, Dutch destroyer *Kortenaer* could only make 25 knots, thereby limiting the top speed of the Allied task force. But perhaps even more detrimental to Allied capabilities was the absence of common doctrine and even reasonably effective communications.

Curiously, in this first major surface battle of the Pacific War, the fifty-four-year-old Rear Adm. Takeo Takagi's primary career ladder was submarines while the fifty-two-year-old Rear Adm. Karel Willem Frederik Marie Doorman was in aviation. Both his superiors and his American (but not his Dutch) subordinates had questioned Doorman's tactical sagacity and determination in his weeks of command. Shortly before the battle, a pale and stooped Door-

---

[*] The Japanese outfitted the two heavy cruisers *Nachi* and *Haguro* with eight quick reload torpedoes, both light cruisers also carried eight quick-reload torpedoes, and all Imperial Navy destroyers carried one quick reload torpedo for each tube except *Sazanami* and *Ushio*, which carried only three spare torpedoes each. Thus while the Japanese had 162 torpedo tubes, they actually carried 296 torpedoes they could use in the battle.

man told his superior, Adm. Conrad Helfrich, that his task force had little chance and urged the ships to continue the fight elsewhere with the Allies. "The chance of success is slim," replied Helfrich, "but it is there." Doorman commented to another colleague on parting just before the battle that they would next meet in the afterlife. In contrast to Doorman's gloom, there were no desertions among Allied crewmen before they set out on an obviously perilous enterprise, including among the numerous Indonesians forming part of the complement of the Dutch ships.

At 1610, the *Jintsu*'s lookouts sighted Doorman's command, and two minutes later lookouts on British *Electra* spied *Jintsu*. At this moment, Doorman steamed northwest with his cruisers in column in order: *DeRuyter, Houston, Exeter, Perth,* and *Java*. The three British destroyers led on the starboard bow of the cruisers with the two Dutch and four American destroyers steamed on the port quarter of the cruiser column. The Japanese clotted the horizon to the north. From due north, *Jintsu* and four destroyers closed. To the west of *Jintsu* was a column of four destroyers, then the *Nachi* and *Haguro* in column, and finally a column of *Naka* and six destroyers.

Jintsu fired the first shots of the action at 1616; a minute later *Nachi* discharged its first salvo and *Houston* and *Exeter* replied shortly. Among the thousands of sailors present on both sides, one of just a handful who obtained a panoramic view of the battle was Tsuneji Tanaka, a gunnery officer on fleet flagship *Nachi*. "The sky was deep blue beyond the end of the ocean as far as we could see. Nothing obstructed our sight," he later wrote.

> I could see the white wavy lines created by each ship on the glassy surface of the ocean. . . . We were sailing at 32 knots. At that speed, we were like facing a typhoon in the fall. . . . I heard strong hissing noises from the mast. The battle scene was now mixed with bright flashes from our fire, shocks [and] thundering sounds.

Tanaka continued: "Huge water columns shot up everywhere. Those columns were colored red, white, and blue. It was a beautiful scene." Each Allied cruiser used a distinctive dye loaded into its projectiles so it could identify where its shells were landing by the color of the splashes. *Houston* employed a red dye, *Exeter* white, and *DeRuyter* blue. *Houston*'s particularly accurate shooting kept straddling *Nachi*. Tanaka observed that the face of Takagi's chief of staff was red from the dye in the spray tossed aboard by *Houston*'s near misses, while ordinary sailors "looked like red and blue devils running around."

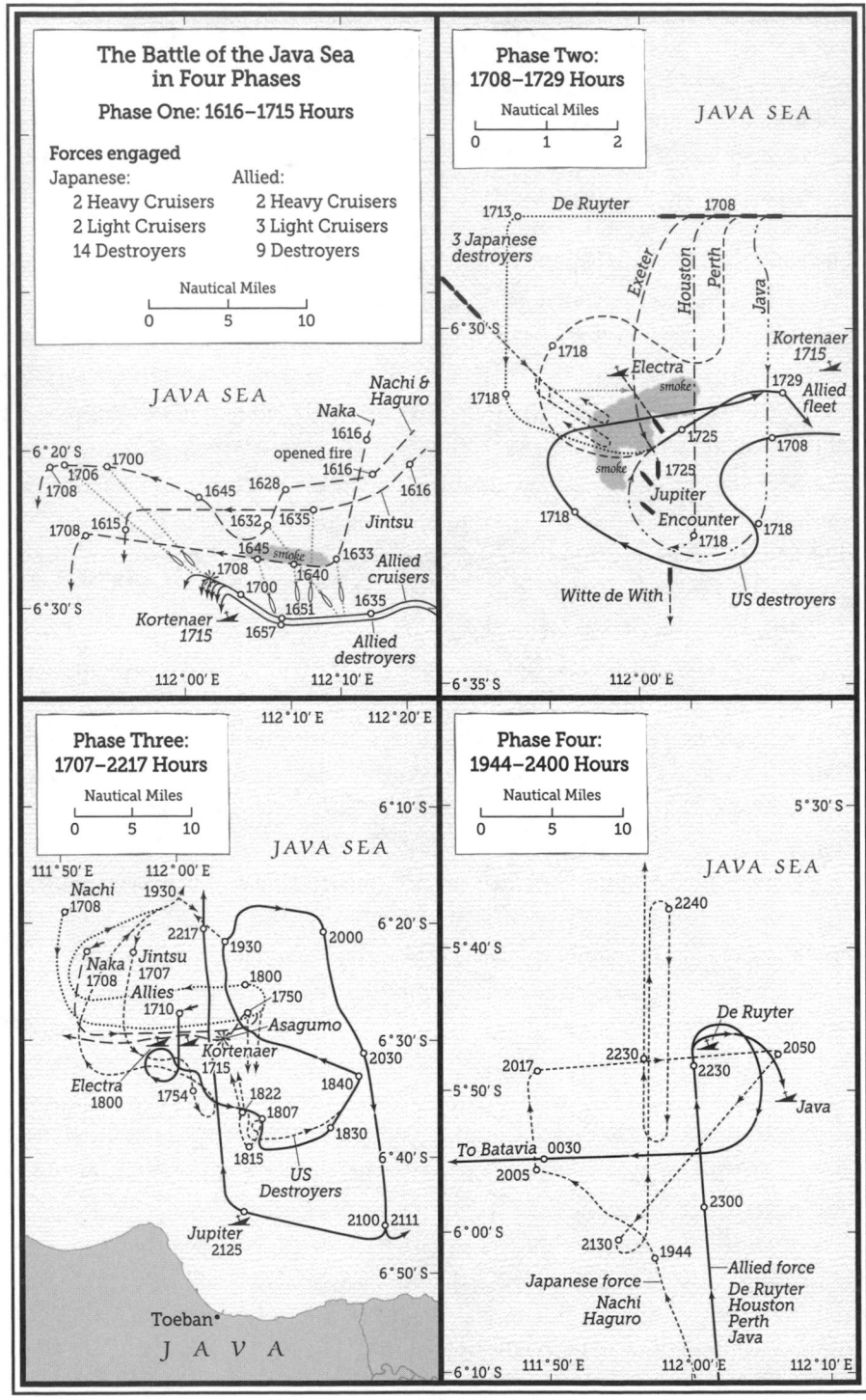

The Battle of the Java Sea in Four Phases

Phase One: 1616–1715 Hours

Forces engaged

Japanese:
- 2 Heavy Cruisers
- 2 Light Cruisers
- 14 Destroyers

Allied:
- 2 Heavy Cruisers
- 3 Light Cruisers
- 9 Destroyers

Nautical Miles
0   5   10

JAVA SEA

Nachi & Haguro

Naka
1616

opened fire
1616
1616
1616

Jintsu

6°20'S
1700
1706
1708
1645
1628
1632 1635
1708 1615
1645 smoke 1633
1708 1640 Allied cruisers
1700
1651 1635
6°30'S
Kortenaer 1715 1657
Allied destroyers

112°00'E   112°10'E

Phase Two: 1708–1729 Hours

Nautical Miles
0   1   2

JAVA SEA

De Ruyter
1713 1708

3 Japanese destroyers

Exeter Houston Perth Java

6°30'S
1718
1718
Electra
smoke
Kortenaer 1715
1729
Allied fleet
1725 1708
smoke
1725
Jupiter
1718 Encounter
1718
1718

Witte de With

US destroyers

6°35'S   112°00'E

Phase Three: 1707–2217 Hours

Nautical Miles
0   5   10

112°10'E   112°20'E

6°10'S
JAVA SEA

111°50'E   112°00'E
Nachi
1708
1930
6°20'S
2217
1930 2000
Naka Jintsu
1708 1707
Allies 1800
1710 1750
Asagumo
Kortenaer
1715
5°40'S
Electra
1800 1754 1822
1807
1840
1830
1815
US Destroyers
2100 2111
Jupiter
2125
Toeban•
JAVA

6°30'S
6°40'S
6°50'S

Phase Four: 1944–2400 Hours

Nautical Miles
0   5   10

5°30'S
JAVA SEA

2240
De Ruyter
2050
2017 2230 2230
Java
To Batavia 0030
2005
2300
2130 1944
Japanese force
Nachi
Haguro
Allied force
De Ruyter
Houston
Perth
Java

5°40'S
5°50'S
6°00'S
6°10'S
111°50'E   112°00'E   112°10'E

For almost an hour the heavy cruisers slugged away at each other on a northwesterly course at very long range and hence to scant effect, while at intervals Japanese cruisers and destroyers essayed torpedo attacks. At 1708, *Haguro* landed a blow that decided the course of the battle. One of its shells plunged into *Exeter* and knocked out six of eight boilers. *Exeter* staggered out of the Allied line to port rapidly losing headway. At 1713, one Type 93 torpedo erupted against *Kortenaer*. By the timepiece of the captain of *John D. Edwards*, the Dutch destroyer disappeared beneath the sea in just 110 seconds. This marked the end of the first phase of the battle. The Japanese fired 1,271 8-inch and 141 5.5-inch shells and 39 torpedoes. Just five shells struck, but only the shell that hit *Exeter* functioned properly. Just one torpedo from *Haguro* hit and sank *Kortenaer*. Allied ships fired a similar amount of shells, but obtained no hits.

Exeter began to withdraw to the southeast at about five knots, screened by *Perth* and one Dutch and three British destroyers. Doorman managed to reform his cruiser column, accompanied by the American destroyers, and likewise headed generally southeast. But Doorman was far from through. He turned his main body back northwest, and at about 1745 burst through smoke screens to reengage the Japanese. The Japanese heavy cruisers again fenced without effect against the Allied cruisers at long range.

Both Japanese destroyer squadrons mounted a second mass torpedo attack, but all ninety-eight Japanese Type 93s missed. British destroyers *Electra* and *Encounter* swung out to parry the Japanese onslaught with battle flags streaming from fore and mainmasts in Royal Navy tradition. Although *Electra*'s gunfire brought *Asagumo* to a halt, the Japanese destroyer returned the favor and its consort *Minegumo* sank *Electra*. Fifty-four members of its crew were rescued by the US submarine *S-38* the next morning.

Doorman marched his cruisers around in a circle ending up on a southeast heading paralleling the crippled *Exeter*. At this moment, the four American destroyers resolved their bafflement about Doorman's intentions by charging the Japanese and firing twenty-four torpedoes at the Japanese heavy cruisers. Takagi evaded the American torpedoes with ease, but he became anxious that he was approaching too close to the minefields protecting Surabaya. He broke off to the north while Doorman steamed east. During this second hour of engagement the Japanese fired 867 shells and 98 torpedoes.

Perhaps 99 percent of the admirals of all nationalities who served in World War II would have terminated the action at this point—but not Karl Doorman. At 1831 *DeRuyter* hoisted the "Follow Me" signal and the Dutchman led four cruisers and five destroyers (*Jupiter* and the American quartet) back to the northwest. This threatened the convoy, so Takagi ordered it to reverse course. Then Doorman took his reduced force looping around to the east and then west near the coast to try to slip past Takagi to get at the convoy. At this juncture, the leader of the American destroyers, Cdr. Thomas Binford, concluded that without torpedoes and low on fuel, his contingent must retire from the battle. During this excursion, at 2125 *Jupiter* collided with a Dutch mine that inflicted such damage that the British destroyer sank four hours later.

Now Karl Doorman steamed to his destiny. In darkness, only intermittent reports from his aircraft left Takagi groping for Doorman as the Dutchman sought to locate the convoy. At 2302 lookouts informed Takagi of Doorman's location. The Allied force opened fire at 2310; Takagi's cruisers only answered at 2321. Both sides were very low on ammunition and their crews drooped with exhaustion. At 2322 *Nachi* fired eight and *Haguro* four torpedoes. Unlike the earlier attempts, range was now only 14,000 yards—impossibly long for the Allies but reasonable for the Japanese. A torpedo from *Nachi* wrecked *Java*'s stern, and it sank rapidly with 512 men. *Haguro* hit *DeRuyter* with one torpedo that ignited a magazine. Despite the heroic struggle of the flagship's crew, *DeRuyter* sank with 344 men, including Doorman. *Houston* and *Perth* made off to the southeast.

The Battle of the Java Sea lasted over seven hours, by far the longest surface ship engagement of World War II. During the battle, the Japanese heavy cruisers fired a total of 1,619 rounds, the light cruisers 221 5.5-inch rounds, and the destroyers 516 5-inch shells. Apart from multiple hits on *Electra*, all this firing secured only five other hits, four of them duds. The Japanese fired 153 torpedoes that scored only three hits—but each torpedo hit sank an Allied ship. Human losses were overwhelmingly one-sided. Allied deaths were between 1,160 and 1,167 in the action to no more than perhaps 10 on the Japanese side. The battle broke Allied naval power and the last effective barrier before Java.

Java Sea Aftermath

Perth and *Houston*, with inexpressibly weary crews and desperately short of ammunition, returned to Batavia's port about noon. Admiral Helfrich ordered them to again give battle, but Capt. Hector ("Hec") M. L. Waller of *Perth*, the senior officer, recognized the suicidal futility of that directive. He led them both westward at 1900, 1 March, intending to depart Java via the Sunda Strait.

Bearing down to debark in western Java was a massive Japanese invasion convoy of fifty-six ships embarking the Sixteenth Army headquarters under Lt. Gen. Hitoshi Imamura, the 2nd Division, and other units. The convoy close escort under Rear Adm. Kenzaburō Hara comprised heavy cruisers *Mikuma* and *Mogami*, light cruisers *Natori*, *Yura*, and *Sendai*, and thirteen destroyers.

The main convoy closed into Java's northwest tip, particularly Bantam Bay. All was clear and quiet. Despite a Japanese plane's report of Allied warships at Batavia, Hara detailed only destroyer *Fubuki* to watch the bay's eastern approaches. *Fubuki* reported Waller's pair at 2314 approaching from the east but missed them with torpedoes. One minute later Waller realized he had stumbled into the dream of Allied sailors—a Japanese invasion convoy under his guns. Waller personally clutched *Perth's* wheel and plunged it into a duel with the Japanese, with *Houston* just astern brandishing its weapons like a loyal second.

The next seventy-eight minutes produced one of the wildest nights of the Pacific War. Waller spun *Perth* through a series of circles gradually edging westward with *Houston* faithfully following. General Imamura's aide, having just "heaved a sigh of disappointment to think that this landing operation was to be made without firing a single rifle or gun or without bloodshed," jolted to "the tremendous sound of guns." *Perth* sailors reported they heard bugle calls and the pop of gunfire from Japanese soldiers aboard transports.

Japanese warships, first destroyers and *Natori*, later joined by *Mikuma* and *Mogami*, encircled the Allied interlopers and stabbed at them from all points of the compass. One Japanese report noted: "The enemy ships fired red tracers and machine guns. Those bullets drew red lines in the smoke screen which was lit by flares." The smoke screen was an attempt by a Japanese destroyer to mask the transports in the clear night. The screen was pierced at intervals by the lingering light of flares, yellow gun flashes, and the "cold blue brilliance" of searchlight beams.

For a surprisingly long interval *Perth* and *Houston* enjoyed miraculous immunity from serious harm as they dodged forty-nine torpedoes and hundreds of shells. But Japanese torpedoes (presumably those from *Mogami* or *Fubuki*) did strike hulls—the hulls of Japanese transports *Sakura*, *Horai*, *Tatsuno*, and *Shinshu Maru*. They all sank in shallow water, spilling hundreds of soldiers, including General Imamura, into the waters. Lost with Imamura's headquarters ship (*Shinshu Maru*, also known as *Ryujo Maru*) were radios and code books, causing many problems in the first days on Java, as well as a "war chest" of six million yen. Imamura survived, drifting in oil-coated waters in his life jacket, but minesweeper *W-2* did not, eviscerated by a Japanese torpedo.*

As the clock swept up to midnight, the gunfire of the Allied cruisers slackened as *Perth* was reduced to firing practice shells, while on *Houston* crewmen labored to pass 8-inch projectiles from the after magazine to the operative forward guns. Recognizing they could no longer fight, Waller spun them for a last desperate lunge for Sunda Strait. A torpedo gouged *Perth* in the forward engine room. Its speed bled off, and then another torpedo erupted under its bridge. "Christ! That's torn it. . . . Abandon ship," Waller commanded. After two more Japanese torpedoes rent its hull, at 0012 *Perth* dipped its bow under, rolling to port, and sank. One of *Perth*'s sailors compared Waller to the legendary British Adm. Sir Andrew Cunningham as men "cast in the same mould; men would follow them, suffer, and be glad about it." Last seen with his arms holding the bridge and looking forward at its silent guns, Waller, an epic Australian hero, went down with *Perth* and 351 shipmates. There were 320 survivors, but 103 would expire in captivity.

Seeing escape blocked, Capt. Albert H. Rooks steered *Houston* back toward the anchored transports in Bantam Bay to sell his ship dearly. But Japanese shells and then three torpedoes now found their mark. Rooks ordered abandon ship just before a Japanese projectile cut him down. His Chinese steward Ah Fong, universally known as "Buda," was last seen cradling Rook's body repeating over and over "Captain die, *Houston* die, Buda die too." At 0033, *Houston*'s stern kicked up toward the night sky as it took a final plunge. Japanese searchlight beams revealed its colors still flying and at least one defiant machine gun loosing off ribbons of red racers as the waters closed over it. With *Houston* perished 693 men; there were only 368 survivors, of whom 284 survived Japanese captivity. Dutch destroyer *Evertsen*, lagging behind *Perth* and *Houston*, fell victim to Japanese destroyers. It was beached to prevent sinking, but some crewmen were slain by hostile locals and the balance captured, many dying as prisoners of war.

---

* *Shinshu Maru* was the world's first purpose-built landing ship, with a well deck for landing craft and a hangar for up to 26 small float planes. *Shinshu Maru*, IJA Landing Craft Depot Ships, www.combinedfleet.com (accessed 30 August 2016); Hansgeorg Jentschura, Dieter Jung, and Peter Mickel, *Warships of the Imperial Japanese Navy, 1869–1945* (Annapolis, MD: Naval Institute Press, 1977), 231. According to the official Imperial Army history volume, the navy, partly in jest, had cautioned Imamura that he would be wise to choose a much more modest ship for his headquarters as *Shinshu Maru* was likely to be a main target for the Allies. The fact their commander took a dip from a sunken ship into oil-smeared waters reportedly raised the morale of his soldiers. Remmelink, *The Invasion of the Dutch East Indies*, 244.

Other Allied vessels found varied fates. The same night *Perth* and *Houston* met their fatal rendezvous, Commander Binford took four American destroyers east on a successful night dash through Bali Strait and on safely to Australia. Shortly after Binford departed Surabaya, British *Exeter* (its speed limited) likewise sailed with *Encounter* and American *Pope*. The Japanese cornered them the next morning with recent adversaries *Nachi* and *Haguro* and two destroyers on the one hand, and heavy cruisers *Ashigara* and *Myoko* and a pair of destroyers on the other hand. The sole hit of 2,650 Japanese 8-inch shells fired brought *Exeter* to a halt. *Exeter*'s captain ordered the destroyers to take flight, but a Japanese shell halted *Encounter*. Its skipper ordered it scuttled. *Exeter* capsized at 1200. Seven *Encounter* and forty-one *Exeter* crew members died. The Japanese picked up 149 of *Encounter*'s complement and 651 from *Exeter*.

Cdr. Welford Blinn protracted *Pope*'s fate with a masterful repertoire of maneuvers to outwit Japanese gunners. Despite a bomb hit from a Japanese float plane, Blinn still evaded some thirty assorted bombs from *Ryujo* "Kates." Finally, with *Pope* clearly settling from cumulative damage, he ordered it scuttled. Two days later, a Japanese destroyer picked up 151 *Pope* sailors; only one man was killed in the action. One American lieutenant had been a language officer in Tokyo before the war and knew the skipper of the Japanese destroyer. The Japanese initially treated *Pope* survivors well, but twenty-seven would die in captivity. *Pope* was the last Allied warship at large north of Java.

As the sun rose on 1 March, the Imperial Navy positioned two major task forces to sweep up Allied shipping south of Java. First in precedence stood Nagumo's Striking Force of carriers, *Akagi*, *Kaga*, *Hiryū*, and *Sōryū*, escorted by two battleships, one light and two heavy cruisers, and seven destroyers. The second comprised Admiral Kondo's three heavy cruisers and two destroyers. Between them they reveled in four days of slaughter.

Nagumo's planes first spotted the American oiler *Pecos*. After hours of attacks by relays of "Vals," it finally succumbed. At least 456 sailors perished, including many previously rescued from *Langley*; there were just 233 survivors. Only minutes later, another plane of Nagumo's reported the presence of a "*Marblehead*-type" cruiser astern. Nagumo detached battleships *Hiei* and *Kirishima* and heavy cruisers *Chikuma* and *Tone* to deal with the "cruiser," which proved to be destroyer *Edsall*. Its skipper, Lt. Joshua J. Nix, handled his ship with consummate skill, using smoke and radical maneuvers (even charging *Chikuma* at one point) to evade a typhoon of over 1,100 major caliber Japanese shells equal to a major engagement. An attack by twenty-six "Vals" finally hit and slowed *Edsall* so that it could be overwhelmed by gunfire. The

Japanese rescued between seven and perhaps forty survivors; none survived the war and five were beheaded at Kendari. Nix had been a junior naval aide to Roosevelt and *Houston* had been a favorite ship of the president's; their losses personalized the distant war for him.

The following day, 2 March, Kondo's heavy cruiser *Maya* and two destroyers intercepted and sank the British destroyer *Stronghold* with eighty-three of its crew. A Dutch ship captured by the Japanese fished fifty survivors out and placed them aboard *Maya*, where they were well treated. But only a few hours after the end of *Stronghold*, Kondo's flagship cruiser *Atago* and its sister *Takao* caught American destroyer *Pillsbury* and sank it—with no survivors—in just seven minutes. *Pillsbury* left behind only a memorable Japanese picture taken of its end.

On 3 March Kondo's destroyers *Arashi* and *Nowaki* blasted the elderly American gunboat *Asheville* to the bottom. The Japanese plucked one lone survivor from the sea, who died in captivity after he recounted the vessel's demise to other prisoners. The following day, 4 March, Kondo's force fell upon a small convoy. Australian sloop *Yarra* (Lt. Cdr. Robert Rankin) put up a valiant fight against overwhelming odds before being sunk with 138 of its 151-man crew. Japanese weapons likewise put down the British auxiliary ship *Anking* (with the loss of 261 crew members), a tanker, and two small motor minesweepers. Nagumo's flyers struck Tjilatjap on 5 March. They sank one ship, but the Dutch subsequently scuttled sixteen, including two destroyers and three submarines. During their forays south of Java, Nagumo and Kondo sank twenty ships and captured three merchantmen. Meanwhile, over the span of the entire campaign, Japanese submarines accounted for forty-two Allied merchant ships.

Historian Vincent O'Hara provided an epitaph for the US Navy's fight from the Philippines to Java: "[The navy] demonstrated it would fight regardless of the odds, regardless of the hope for victory, [and] regardless of whether its battles would ever be known." The same applies to the sailors of the Dutch, Royal Navy, and Royal Australian Navy who fought side by side with the Americans.

Battles Ashore on Java

The final Japanese conquest of Java stemmed from guile and daring, not just brute force. It directed its main forces at east and west Java as the Dutch expected. The eastern effort involved the 48th Division (Maj. Gen. Yūitsu Tsuchihashi) and the Sakaguchi Brigade. Despite damage to two transports from relays of Allied air attacks, the assault convoy commenced landing operations at 0015, 1 March, at Kragan, ensconced along northern Java's east central coast. The heavy concentration of Dutch forces in west Java left only the KNIL 6th Infantry Regiment and a Dutch Marine battalion to defend the primary Japanese objective: the Surabaya (Soerabaja) naval base in central Java. East Java was virtually denuded of defenders.

Dutch and American aircraft continued attacks off Kragan in daylight, 1 March, but sustained major losses. The last twenty-one remaining American heavy bombers left for Australia, and American crews handed over the remaining fighters to the Dutch before attempting escape. By 6 March the 48th Division captured Surabaya while the Sakaguchi Brigade thrust west and south in a spectacular drive, capturing Tjilatjap.

The Dutch deployed by far the largest concentration of defenders in Western Java. The principal command was West Group under Maj. Gen. W. Schilling. It comprised the KNIL 1st Infantry Regiment, reinforced with artillery and cavalry and Blackforce. This latter unit, under Australian brigadier Arthur S. Blackburn, was a heterogeneous mixed motorized brigade over 3,000 strong comprised primarily of Australians, a British light tank company, and two American artillery batteries.[*] The KNIL 2nd Infantry Regiment, with the 1st Mountain Artillery Battalion, formed the West Java strategic reserve. Altogether, West Group fielded about 21,200 men.

The "Bandoeng Group" under Maj. Gen. J. J. Pesman protected the eastern reaches of west Java, particularly the vital military facilities and the military and civilian leadership center at Bandoeng. Presman directed the KNIL 4th Infantry Regiment with the 2nd Mountain Artillery Battalion and the KNIL Mobile Unit of twenty-four machine gun–armed light tanks, and an infantry company in light armored vehicles and trucks. The "Bandoeng Group" fielded about 5,900 troops.

After landing at Bantam Bay, the Imperial Army 2nd Division sent a regimental group to cover its southern flank while the other two regiments began thrusting east to attack Batavia from the southwest. They met cheers and

---

[*] The core of "Blackforce" consisted of Australian units that had the great misfortune to be landed on Java from the transport *Orcades* when other Australian units were diverted. These Australians numbered about 2,920 and included the 2/3rd Machine Gun Battalion, the 2/2nd Pioneer Battalion, and an assortment of support units and stragglers. Only the first two units could claim any role as infantry. Given these circumstances, their performance was highly commendable. Lionel Wigmore, *Australia in the War of 1939–1945*, Series One, Army, Vol. 4, *The Japanese Thrust* (Canberra: The Australian War Memorial, 1957), 454, 457.

received help from the local inhabitants. Light Dutch detachments fell back quickly, but Dutch demolitions slowed the Japanese advance to a crawl. Blackforce and a KNIL regiment prepared plans for a counterattack, but on 2 March for reasons we will see, the KNIL regiment was diverted back toward Bandoeng. Blackforce conducted a stalwart and successful defense (supported by very accurate US artillery fire) at a blown bridge over a river at Leuviliang between 2 and 4 March. Blackforce then executed a successful delaying action through 5 March. They then held open the withdrawal route for Dutch forces from Batavia trying to move to Bandoeng.

Eretan Wetan

A tremendous Japanese dare assured that, apart from Blackforce, the largest concentration of Java defenders in West Force never seriously engaged the invasion. While the main landings transpired at the western extremity of Java, Col. Toshishige Shoji's reinforced 230th Infantry Regiment, about 4,000 strong, landed from seven transports about 124 miles to the east at Eretan Wetan on the north coast of Java. The Imperial Navy initially opposed the effort since the detachment would be highly vulnerable to Allied air and sea attacks en route to the landing site. Further, once ashore, Shoji was beyond effective air support from Sumatra and distant from Japanese soldiers swarming ashore at Bantam Bay. There thus existed a serious peril that Shoji's command could be annihilated before any linkup.

The Sixteenth Army commander, Imamura, specially selected Shoji for this perilous mission. When Shoji was a probationary officer, Imamura personally trained him. They formed a very close bond, reinforced by later service together. Accordingly, Imamura handpicked Shoji on the basis that he might well be out of touch in a very difficult situation, but Imamura could be confident that Shoji would act exactly as Imamura would wish.

Despite damaging attacks in darkness by Allied bombers that inflicted about one hundred casualties, Shoji's command commenced landing at 0330, 1 March. One column of about 1,200 men (Maj. Minoru Wakamatsu) headed southwest for Kalidjati airfield, roughly forty-seven miles on a straight line from the beach. The second column of about 1,000 men (Maj. Masaru Egashira) marched west for the large bridge spanning the Tjitaroem River by Krawang. Another 1,000 men splashed ashore with Shoji, including aviation support elements to operate the airfield at Kalidjati and a mere fifty-combat-troop covering force for the beachhead.

Shoji's potent ally was surprise. The Dutch left Eretan Wetan undefended as they deemed that the "wet season" rough seas there precluded a landing. Moreover, the Japanese landed a company of ten light tanks and trucks to propel their vanguard to Kalidjati airfield by about 1230, 1 March, scarcely more than nine hours after the original landing. Other Japanese would pedal in on bicycles later. En route to and at Kalidjati, the Japanese executed many prisoners and some European civilians. In one swoop, they captured the airfield that permitted them to fly in their own aircraft the next day, and they destroyed or captured about eighty Allied planes. But British fighters strafed the second (Egashira) Japanese column headed for the Tjitaroem bridge, and handled it severely.

"The Japanese capture of Kalidjati," explained historian P. C. Boer, "was an enormous setback and completely unsettled the entire defense of western Java." Allied operational plans henceforth concentrated on defeating Shoji, recapturing the Kalidjati airfield, and then wheeling to deal with the main landing at the far western end of Java. The Allies had reasonably accurate intelligence on Shoji's strength, which appeared to demonstrate his command could be crushed. During the morning of 2 March the Dutch Mobile Unit (machine gun–armed light tanks and lightly armored truck-mounted infantry) attacked Japanese-held Soebang. The very hard-pressed Japanese defenders held on. Shoji fought personally as his headquarters was overrun.

On 3 March, Java's strategic reserve, the KNIL 2nd Infantry Regiment (Col. G. C. Toorop), reinforced with artillery, cavalry, antitank, and antiaircraft elements, and totaling about 3,500 men, all motorized, mounted an attack to retake Kalidjati. Only Wakamatsu's battalion faced them. Toorop's plodding approach the night before produced fatal delay. A Japanese ground assault on the last Allied airfield at Andir coincided purely by chance with raids by about fifty Imperial Navy aircraft to knock out Allied air cover. Although raids on Japanese air facilities at Kalidjati inflicted damage that same morning, the Japanese still readied twenty-seven freshly arrived fighters, assault planes, and light bombers to mount a series of strikes on Toorop's regiment—only a five-minute flight away. A bare dozen strong first wave of planes halted the Dutch columns by knocking out the lead and rear vehicles on open roads framed by impassable rice fields. Then, for almost five straight hours, Japanese planes assailed Toorop's men with ceaseless strafing and bombing attacks that by a Japanese count destroyed 176 vehicles. With those trucks went most of the regiment's ammunition, artillery, and equipment, as well as Toorop's key radio communications. A Japanese soldier described the carnage: "Some of the tanks were completely destroyed while armored vehicles and trucks [were] upside down, [had] nose dived into the fields or [had] hit trees." In perhaps their best ground support performance of the war, Japanese airmen killed few but wounded many and scattered the KNIL troops into the countryside.

When fading sunlight finally halted the aerial onslaught, a rout commenced. After dark, Toorop could muster only eighty men among his three battalions. The badly mauled Dutch had lost so much equipment and transport that the Japanese victory was an irretrievable disaster for the ground defense of Java. To round out a dismal day for the Dutch defenders, a supporting attack by a reinforced battalion on Soebang misfired, while small arms fire, vastly magnified by devastating bombardments by Japanese destroyers, halted another battalion-size attack on Eretan Wetan.

The aerial destruction of Toorop's command administered a tremendous physical and psychological blow to the Dutch command. It left scant combateffective forces to block an advance on Bandoeng. The desperate Dutch on 4 March ordered the West Group to abandon far Western Java and withdraw to the Bandoeng Plateau. In theory, this would permit a concentration of the defenders to strike against the Japanese. But Shoji blocked the direct route, forcing the West Group to march or move by train along a long southerly route that removed them from combat. Thus, Japanese airmen not only succeeded in destroying the most potent Dutch formation near Bandoeng on 3 March, they also tossed the largest Dutch ground force reeling into limbo for a week.

Besides scenting victory at arms, the steps of Shoji's men quickened with a swelling sense that they marched as liberators. "As we passed villages along the road" wrote one soldier, "the locals were waving Japanese flags with joy." Elsewhere he noted "hand-made Japanese flags were hoisted at every corner of the city as the locals started showing up outside showing 'thumbs-up' with a smile. They had been oppressed for three hundred years. . . . The Dutch made 60 million Indonesians to be their enemy."

Ironically, due to lack of radio communications thanks to loss of *Shinshu Maru*, the Sixteenth Army headquarters suffered tremendous anxiety that the Shoji Detachment faced near certain annihilation by vastly superior Allied forces. The angst was much increased by the inability of the 2nd Division to break through and link up, and by the Southern Army's dismissal of pleas for an airlift of reinforcements to Shoji. Further, one early Shoji report that did get through indicated Shoji projected the defeat or annihilation of his command. On 4 March, Shoji attacked toward Bandoeng—with an eye toward securing high ground for a final stand. The aggressive move nonetheless won emphatic approval from Major General Endo, commander of the Third Air

Division whose flyers were supporting Shoji. Endo unfavorably compared the performance of the Sixteenth Army so far with that of the Twenty-Fifth Army in Malaya and pledged all-out support to Shoji.

The Dutch still had about 9,000 men and looked to block Shoji's advance at the Tjiater and Tjisomang Passes athwart the northern roads to Bandoeng. But Shoji's warriors exuded sublime confidence in their superiority. An indicator of the contrasting morale between attacker and defender came on 4 March, when an Ambonese KNIL company panicked when they mistook the bursts of antiaircraft shells for Japanese paratroops. Another Japanese trump remained in play: just twenty-nine available Allied planes faced sixty-nine Japanese.

The final key battle for Java transpired at Tjiater Pass, which Shoji assaulted on 5 and 6 March. During tough fighting the overall Dutch commander of the defenses, Col. W. J. de Veer, died while personally leading a counterattack. A Japanese soldier provided his own idiosyncratic view of the postbattle scene: "I saw dead bodies of the Dutch soldiers all over. Their bodies were like cold, white wax dolls. They were kind of beautiful."

The defenders retreated to Lembang in the early hours of 7 March, but the Dutch command regarded this as just a temporary front to gain time before offering the Japanese a partial capitulation on the Bandoeng Plateau. As early as 1800, 5 March, however, General ter Poorten assembled his allied commanders and announced his intention to capitulate. He would not permit the fighting to envelop refugee-crowded Bandoeng. He also ruled out resorting to guerrilla fighting, admitting that "the great hostility of the Indonesians towards the Dutch" made this impossible. Parleys started on the 8th and ended with a formal surrender of the Dutch, as well as their British, Australian, and American allies, on 12 March. Not recognized then, this moment marked the effective end of nearly three and a half centuries of Dutch rule.[*]

The Sixteenth Army never deployed more than about 55,000 troops on Java. It reported capturing 82,618 prisoners of war (Dutch East Indies Armed

---

[*] On 8 May 1942, US submarine *Grenadier* (SS-210) sank the 14,503-ton transport *Taiyo Maru*. The ship carried 263 crewmen, 53 gunners, and 1,044 passengers, many of the last technicians and economic development personnel to exploit the newly captured territories in the Southern Area, especially its oil resources. Lost in the sinking were 656 passengers, 156 crewmen, and four gunners. The single submarine attack set back exploitation of the resources Japan desperately needed to fuel its war machine and heralded the devastating impact of American submarines on Japan's war economy. Tabular Record of Movement Rikugun Yuosen-IJA [Imperial Army] Transports, *Taiyo Maru*, combinedfleet.com (accessed 17 October 2016).

forces 66,219, Australian 4,890, British 10,626, and US 883). The Japanese captured 177 Allied aircraft and over a thousand vehicles of all types. The Sixteenth Army losses were 255 killed and 702 wounded on Java, plus 56 killed and 130 wounded in operations prior to January 31. Although the Japanese campaign to seize the Netherlands East Indies overall was stellar, operations on Java itself were not as impressive as those in Malaya or Burma.

Much like other campaigns from December 1941, the whole Netherlands East Indies drive formed a mosaic of murder and mercy by Imperial Japan's armed forces. Its final note occurred on Java. In April 1942, the Kempetai managed to round up most of an estimated two hundred Allied soldiers who attempted to maintain resistance. They were placed in three-foot-long bamboo pig baskets and transported to Surabaya. From there, they were taken out to sea and, still in the baskets, tossed into the shark-infested waters. An Australia military court convicted Imamura of responsibility for this crime and sentenced him to ten years' imprisonment.

::

"Only War Proves What Is Correct and What Is Wrong"*

THE PHILIPPINES

The Philippine Riddle

The Philippine Islands lie some 7,000 miles from the United States and comprise about 7,000 islands. The eleven largest islands constitute about 94 percent of the total area of 115,000 square miles. Luzon (40,420 square miles) and Mindanao (36,527 square miles) dominate by size and population. Just five hundred miles off the Asian coast, the Philippines straddle the key sea routes between Japan, China, Indochina, and the Netherlands East Indies. The population in 1939 was 16 million.

The United States seized sovereignty over the Philippines in 1898 from Spain during the Spanish-American War and then subdued a protracted insurgency by Filipinos seeking independence. American opinion sharply divided over the blatantly colonial character of the Philippine acquisition. The savagery of the pacification on southwest Luzon and Samar outraged anti-imperialists, who included such prominent figures as politician William Jennings Bryan, industrialist Andrew Carnegie, and author Mark Twain. If the United States had not annexed the Philippines, however, the islands' most

---

* "Only war proves what is correct . . .": Admiral Thomas C. Hart, Narrative of Events, Asiatic Fleet, Leading up to War, and from December 8, 1941 to February 15, 1942, 46, Fold3. com/WWII War Diaries/A/Admiral Thomas C. Hart (CINCAF), accessed 26 June 2016.

likely fate would have been German conquest followed by a Japanese "trustee-ship" under the League of Nations after World War I.

Over the next four decades, the Philippines posed a riddle for Ameri-can civilian and military leaders. Washington placed balm over conflicted American consciences by justifying occupation as simply a period of tute-lage in democracy and modernization as a prelude to independence. The 1934 Tydings-McDuffie Act mapped a timeline leading to Philippine independence in 1944. Free elections the next year installed Manuel Quezon as president of an interim commonwealth governing internal affairs, with the United States retaining control over foreign affairs and defense.

Two generations of US Army and Navy officers clashed over the defense of the Philippines. Some officers regarded the Philippines as a "sturdy out-post of American influence": a springboard for American trade in the Far East, a model of enlightened political institutions for Asians to follow, a shin-ing exemplar of intercultural relations between westerners and Asians and, if need be, a forward base for a war with Japan. These officers maintained that Manila Bay could be defended until a navy relief expedition arrived. A sec-ond faction believed the western perimeter of US defenses ran from Alaska through Hawaii to Panama. Some flatly rejected the whole colonial enterprise on both pragmatic (net drain on the US treasury and strategic vulnerability) and moral grounds. Further, seizing the distant Philippines compromised the moral right to enforce the Monroe Doctrine against foreign powers encroach-ing in the Americas. This group favored a minimal garrison only for internal order until Philippine independence. Since the islands lacked genuine strate-gic value to the United States and inevitably would be lost in a war with Japan, limited commitment would minimize useless loss. At least one general went so far as to condemn as immoral any futile effort to defend the islands against Japan that would result in the large loss of Filipino life.

From the outset, American Army and Navy officers identified Japan as the obvious threat to the Philippines and Hawaii. As one Army War College stu-dent stated, the Japanese soldier "probably has no superior." Far from dismiss-ing the skill of Japan's soldiers and sailors on racial grounds, in fact, repeated studies right up to 1941 emphasized the technical proficiency and warrior ethos of Japanese servicemen.

Efforts to supplement US forces with Filipinos during the insurgency resulted in creation of the Philippine Scouts (PS), an effective colonial army. The enlisted men were Filipinos while the US Army supplied almost all the officers. The scouts soon earned a reputation as first-class soldiers, at least for internal peacekeeping. It seemed imprudent to American officials, however, to expand the Filipino forces unless the initiative originated from the Philippine government. Although known as the "Paladin of Philippine Freedom," Quezon acutely recognized that independence might prove ephemeral in the international environment of the 1930s. He devised a hidden agenda to trade Philippine base rights for shelter beneath an American defense umbrella. A large Philippine army that could protect the bases would much enhance the value of Quezon's bargain. Accordingly, Quezon secured the services of Maj. Gen. Douglas MacArthur, the outgoing US Army chief of staff who shared Quezon's hidden agenda to create and command a new national army. MacArthur's ambitious vision of a huge if modestly equipped Philippine army that would deter invasion proved a fantasy. It foundered from a combination of MacArthur's unrealistic plans, an inability to develop adequate training and leadership cadres, Quezon's irresolute support, limited Philippine financial resources, limited time, and US parsimony with weapons, equipment, and supplies.

Maj. Gen. George Grunert arrived as the new Philippine Department commander in June 1940 just as Germany toppled the world strategic balance. In a bleak October 1940, the US Army War Plans Division recommended the complete withdrawal of army forces from the Philippines, maintaining that they lacked the strength to execute their mission of defending Manila Bay until relieved. The next month, Washington rebuffed Grunert's proposal to mobilize the Philippine Army—a major mistake, as the extra year of preparation might have made some difference. But with a brighter outlook at the New Year, Washington authorized some strengthening of forces, particularly the Scouts.

In July 1941, Washington abruptly and radically altered its Philippine strategy. The normally sober Secretary of War Henry Stimson, Chief of Staff Marshall, and President Roosevelt all championed the ill-founded concept that a force of 272 heavy bombers and a squadron of submarines based in the Philippines by April 1942 would either deter Japan, or at least provide a powerful counter to any attempted invasion. Their faith in B-17 and B-24 heavy bombers teetered on a quartet of erroneous beliefs: (1) that British naval losses off Crete stemmed from high-level bombing rather than low-level dive bombing, (2) that B-24s possessed the range to bomb Tokyo from the Philippine bases, (3) that Japanese aircraft could not climb to the altitude of American bombers, and (4) that the Japanese aviators were inferior. Marshall went so far as to argue that the US Navy would not play much of a role in a war with Japan. MacArthur reinforced this outlook with optimistic cables on the status of his forces, but the fundamental impetus for the shift to primarily a heavy bomber–based defense originated in Washington.

In 1941 Douglas MacArthur was 61 years old, with a distinguished, if controversial career behind him. He was the son of Arthur MacArthur, a Civil War officer awarded the Medal of Honor as a boy colonel in 1864. Arthur remained in the army and rose to major general. Douglas MacArthur graduated first in his class at West Point in 1901. Well decorated for his brilliant battlefield performance in World War I, postwar Douglas served as a very innovative superintendent of the West Point military academy. Arthur MacArthur commanded American forces during the Philippine Insurrection, and Douglas continued the family's strong ties to the Philippines with multiple tours of duty there. At a time when American elites were overwhelmingly Eurocentric, Arthur MacArthur proved an outspoken advocate for the idea that America's destiny rested in Asia, not Europe, and Douglas carried on his father's strategic outlook.

Douglas MacArthur secured the prize that had eluded his father, becoming chief of staff of the army in 1930. His tour was plagued by the fiscal stringencies of the Great Depression and then forever darkened by a crisis in 1932 when the army crushed a demonstration by veterans seeking early payment of a "bonus" for World War I service promised by Congress. MacArthur quite wrongly sensed the event as the overture to a left-wing insurrection. Violating instructions from President Herbert Hoover, MacArthur ordered troops to break up "Bonus Marcher" encampments, filled with wives and children. He thereafter became suspect as a political praetorian to many Americans, including Roosevelt. This view widely misjudged MacArthur, for his gargantuan ego disposed him to believe that the US public would one day recognize him as the most competent man in the United States and award him the presidency by acclamation, without a distasteful political campaign, much less a military coup.

Douglas MacArthur belonged to a generation of senior officers who mostly had died or retired by 1941. But Marshall and Roosevelt, despite reservations, recognized him as the American best fitted to the new Philippine command. His reputation as a general then stood high, but perhaps just as importantly Quezon and other Filipinos witnessed MacArthur's genuine affection for them, manifested by his "marked preference for the social company of prominent Filipinos rather than American expatriates." In an era of casually racist condescension, Filipinos found MacArthur an American around whom they gladly would rally. In July 1941, he was a trim 5 feet, 10¾ inches tall and weighed just 152 pounds, "leaner in fiber and tougher in spirit than most army men ten years his junior," noted one journalist. That journalist went on to identify one other attribute that armed MacArthur in councils throughout the war: he was "positively pyrotechnic" in conversation, "changing at will from mellifluous melodramatic whisper to a fiery snort, from brutal fact to flight of sheer rodomontade." He understood as few other US generals have the importance of public image, but his methods toward that end remained highly suspect.

Between July and December 1941, MacArthur received a steady infusion of weapons, supplies, and men. The most important reinforcements belonged to his Far Eastern Air Force (FEAF), particularly B-17 "Flying Fortress" bombers. To further the deterrent effect of the B-17s, the administration leaked to the *New York Times* newspaper not only word of the Philippine bomber buildup, but also the concept of what would later be called "shuttle bombing." The United States would obtain Moscow's authorization for US bombers to strike Japan, land in Soviet territory, refuel and rearm, and bomb Japan again on the way back to Philippine bases.

JAPANESE NAVAL OFFICERS had long contemplated seizing the Philippines as the opening step in a war with the United States. In theory, nonbelligerent American forces in a neutral Philippines posed no threat to Japanese designs for the resource-rich British and Dutch colonies in Southeast Asia. But should the United States enter hostilities against Japan, American Philippine-based sea and air forces could interdict the vital sea routes to the southern resource areas Japan must control to sustain the Home Islands. Thus, Tokyo concluded it could not ignore either immediate or delayed American belligerency.

Opposing Forces

The Imperial Army assigned Lt. Gen. Masaharu Homma's Fourteenth Army the mission of conquering the Philippines. The major components of the approximately 62,000-strong army were the excellent 48th Division, the 16th Division (which, according to Homma, "did not have a very good reputation for its fighting qualities" in China), and the novice 65th Brigade, plus major artillery attachments and two battalion-size tank units with fifty-two light and thirty-six medium tanks. Vice Adm. Ibo Takahashi's Third Fleet provided sea lift and protection. Japanese air units included the Imperial Army's Fifth Air Division, with 189 aircraft (72 Ki-27, 83 assorted bombers, 34 reconnaissance aircraft), and the Twenty-First and Twenty-Third Air Flotillas of Adm.

Nishizo Tsukahara's Eleventh Air Fleet with a combined 247 aircraft (114 fighters [90 A6M, 24 A5M], 97 bombers, 24 seaplanes, and 12 reconnaissance planes). The Japanese achieved a spectacular technical breakthrough in establishing that the Mitsubishi A6M2 Zero fighter with drop tanks could fly on a combat mission to a radius of 550 miles—i.e., from Japanese bases on Formosa to the central Philippines. No other fighter aircraft in the world matched this feat, and it contributed enormously to the surprise of the initial Japanese attacks. Other Imperial Navy aviation assets for the Philippine invasion included light aircraft carrier *Ryujo* (twelve fighters and fourteen bombers) and seaplane carriers *Mizuho, Chitose,* and *Sanuki Maru,* with a capacity for fifty-six assorted float planes.

The mobilized Philippine Army theoretically mustered about 120,000 men.[*] On paper, it fielded ten small (7,643 man) light infantry divisions. Seven divisions were concentrated on Luzon. The planned strength of each of the three infantry regiments per division numbered 92 officers and 1,620 enlisted men. Most of these divisions attained only 50 to 75 percent of authorized strength upon outbreak of the war. Many carried cast-off Lee-Enfield rifles, with stocks too long for the average diminutive Filipino. Defective extractors (the device that removed the spent cartridge casing from the chamber after firing) also plagued these weapons. Some Filipinos took to carrying a piece of bamboo they used like a ramrod to knock out each expended casing. This exercise rendered the weapons the near equivalent of muzzle-loaded muskets. Actual complements of automatic rifles and light machine guns fell well short of authorized levels, but even the ideal outfit left a Philippine Army regiment with just one-third the firepower of a similar Japanese unit. Due to lack of prewar training, many Filipino soldiers fired their first rounds in actual combat. Tables of organization and equipment provided 24 howitzers for each division's artillery regiment, but only two divisions were fully equipped. Each division was authorized engineer, signal, and medical units, but lacked any antitank or antiaircraft guns.

The lack of a common language formed the most serious challenge facing the Philippine Army. The Filipino elite spoke English and Spanish; the com-

---

[*] As Richard Meixsel explains, official US and Philippine documents contain a bewildering variety of figures from as few as 63,000 to as many as 1.25 million for the planned strength of the Philippine Army at various points. "Manuel L. Quezon, Douglas MacArthur, and the Significance of the Military Mission to the Philippine Commonwealth," *Pacific Historical Review* 70, no. 2, 271n33.

mon citizens spoke literally hundreds of dialects. Of the dialects, only Tagalog on Luzon and Visayan in the middle islands were widely spoken. One American officer reported his company spoke five different dialects. The problem was not just the inability of American advisers attached to Philippine units to speak in the language of the men in the unit. Quite commonly, Filipino officers, noncommissioned officers, and enlisted men could not communicate with each other.

On 30 November 1941, the US Army forces in the Philippines reportedly numbered 31,095 men, a figure that included 11,988 Philippine Scouts. This number is deceptive because a very large portion of US personnel served in aviation (5,609), coast defense (5,225), or service roles (4,268), not as frontline combatants. By far MacArthur's most potent ground element was the 10,233-man US Philippine Division with three infantry regiments. Just 1,400 men formed the only all-American rifle regiment, the 31st Infantry. The regiment's readiness was seriously diminished by the lack of many officers and sergeants, detached for service with other units, and the fact that draftees, usually with less than four months' service, filled nearly two-thirds of its ranks. The 45th and 57th Infantry Regiments (PS) had almost completely American officers commanding Filipino enlisted men. The latter ranged in service from six months (due to the doubling of scout strength in 1941) to over 20 years, with an average of about 7.5 years. The detachment of about 2,300 Scouts for duties with the Philippine Army left the 45th and 57th Infantry regiments at only about 1,750 men, but overall much better prepared than the 31st Infantry. On the plus side, all three Philippine Division infantry regiments boasted the excellent semiautomatic M-1 rifle and a full complement of automatic weapons, giving them much superior firepower.

The 26th Cavalry provided an elite Philippine Scout unit, but its field strength numbered just 682 men, and its mobility primarily depended on horses. The campaign demonstrated a comprehensive lack of understanding on the part of senior officers of how to employ the two light tank battalions (998 men) with 108 light M-3 ("Stuart") tanks just arrived in the Philippines. Two hastily formed battalions of World War I–vintage 75mm guns mounted upon M-3 half-tracks formed a late but very valuable addition. The Philippine Scouts also manned the most capable field artillery on the islands, the 86th and 88th Field Artillery Regiments (just 933 men total). The 4th Marine Regiment, withdrawn from Shanghai just before hostilities commenced, formed another component of MacArthur's command. This unit boasted highly professional officers and men, but mustered only about 1,440 personnel of all ranks. In summary, MacArthur's trained and equipped frontline fighters (infantry, cavalry, and tank and field artillery) numbered about 9,500.

MacArthur's Far East Air Force (FEAF) on 8 December 1941 notably included 35 B-17 Flying Fortresses, 67 P-40Es, 24 P-40Bs, and 26 P-35As among a total of 181 aircraft, compared to the Japanese total of 518. The FEAF strength included obsolete B-18 bombers and 0–52 and 0–46A observation planes with no real air combat utility. The Asiatic Fleet's air contingent included 28 PBYs, useful for patrol missions, but soon to be shown to be nearly suicidal as bombers against any defended target. The fledgling Philippine Air Force possessed just 12 P-26As and three B-10Bs, both types long out of date. The Asiatic Fleet, really a squadron rather than a fleet, counted one heavy and two light cruisers, thirteen vintage destroyers, twenty-nine submarines, and various auxiliaries. It was hopelessly outgunned by the Imperial Navy in the Western Pacific.

The Asiatic Fleet commander was sixty-four-year-old Adm. Thomas C. Hart. Though Hart's mind was sharp, and his temper and tongue feared by subordinates, physically he looked every bit his age, even frail. He had been a close friend of MacArthur's brother Arthur (a naval officer with a promising career cut short by illness). Hence, he had known Douglas for forty years. What he was seeing in the last half of 1941 disturbed him, as he noted: "Douglas knows a lot of things which are not so; he is an able and convincing talker—a combination that spells disaster."

The relationship between Filipinos and Americans was complex. Most Americans of that era harbored racist biases from mild to virulent. Antonio Aquino, a Philippine Army officer and son of the Speaker of the House of the Philippine Legislature, reported to President Quezon that "an undercurrent of antagonism" or annoyance rather than hatred ran between Americans and Filipinos. As Brig. Gen. Edward King explained to a group of American officers, the Filipinos were "a proud and sensitive race" who properly resented racial affronts. King lectured that "there was no such thing as racial superiority" and that "throughout history the Filipino soldier had demonstrated personal bravery and individual fighting ability, even against superior arms." One towering fact distinguished the Philippines from other Far Eastern colonial possessions: the US pledge of Philippine independence. Thus, a large majority of Filipinos saw themselves as fighting for their nascent nation, not in service of an oppressive occupier. Moreover, much of the Sino-Filipino elite were anti-Japanese. Accordingly, the central handicaps for the Philippine

Army were not motivation or aptitude for battle, but lack of acquired knowledge and first-class equipment.

8 December 1941, A Date That Will Live in Controversy

Unofficial word of the Pearl Harbor attack reached Manila about 0300, 8 December, roughly two hours after the attack, but across the international dateline. Approximately two hours later an official dispatch confirmed the attack and directed MacArthur to execute War Plan Rainbow 5. This sanctioned bombing Japanese targets within range. MacArthur's chief of staff, Brig. Gen. Richard K. Sutherland, relayed word of Pearl Harbor about 0400 to Maj. Gen. Lewis H. Brereton, the FEAF commander. A Naval Academy graduate much decorated in World War I, the newly arrived Brereton had no recent experience with heavy bombers or fighters. Indeed, the performance of his immediately prior command during maneuvers in the United States had been poor. Brereton replied to Sutherland that his B-17s "would be ready to attack Formosa at daylight." The group then manned nineteen B-17s at Clark Field on central Luzon; the other sixteen sat far to the south at Del Monte on Mindanao.

Initialing a series of much contested events, about 0500 Brereton arrived at MacArthur's headquarters and gained Sutherland's authorization to prepare an attack on Formosa—targeting shipping, not airfields—first with Clark-based B-17s and then a second wave of Del Monte B-17s. Brereton protested Sutherland's instructions (which Sutherland stated reflected MacArthur's order) to defer any offensive action pending MacArthur's express sanction. Brereton returned to his headquarters at 0715 and organized preparations for a reconnaissance of airfields on Formosa. Whether existing intelligence was adequate remains disputed, but prior to hostilities Washington had barred any such missions.

Meanwhile, reports reached Clark about 0800 of Japanese bombers approaching north Luzon. These were two flights of Imperial Army light and medium bombers that hit north Luzon and Baguio farther inland—but neither type possessed the range to reach mid-Luzon. Of the eighteen B-17s at Clark (one was on reconnaissance), fifteen took off to avoid being caught on the ground. Sutherland called Brereton at 0850 reaffirming the order to defer "bombing Formosa for present." Reports then reached Clark of a Japanese air attack at Davao on Mindanao. This was a strike by twenty-two planes from the carrier *Ryujo*. Brereton again phoned Sutherland to plead for authority to attack Formosa. Sutherland insisted that the FEAF stand on the defensive. Finally, 1014, over five hours since Brereton's opening proposal to attack Formosa, MacArthur called him personally to authorize the operation. Brereton replied that he planned to hold his bombers until he received reconnaissance reports.

Those B-17s airborne since about 0800 returned to Clark. By 1130, ground crews prepared three for a reconnaissance mission and the remainder (less one damaged in a prewar accident) for a planned dusk attack. Likewise, the fighter aircraft that had scrambled earlier recovered to their bases for refueling. At 1140, radar detected a large inbound raid. Imperial Navy airmen originally intended a massive dawn strike, but by a singular twist of fortune, fog blanketed Imperial Navy bases, but not Imperial Army bases on Formosa. Thus, while the Imperial Army flyers mounted their missions, for hours anxious Imperial Navy aviators feared the Americans might hit them first. The fog broke at 0750. By 0815 an aerial armada totaling 190 Imperial Navy aircraft (105 bombers, 85 fighters) adorned with red disc national insignia headed for Luzon.

The FEAF deployed five fighter squadrons of the 24th Pursuit Group. Although radar issued ample warning of the incoming Japanese raid, the controllers deployed one squadron each over Iba airfield, Manila, and Manila Bay. The only squadron detailed to protect Clark (with P-35As, the least capable fighters) never received orders and remained on the ground—nor was a fifth squadron scrambled. And no one warned the 19th Bomb Group, which was servicing its B-17s at Clark.

The startled Japanese never expected to find American planes on the ground at Clark but swiftly exploited American follies. Two neat formations of bombers in wide "Vs" approached Clark with motors roaring "like the deep growl of many powerful beasts—snarling as one." After the bombers released their loads with "diabolical accuracy," the escorting Zero fighters pounced in strafing runs. Altogether, explosives or bullets destroyed twelve B-17s. Three were damaged but repaired and one that had been damaged prewar never returned to service. Only two B-17s on reconnaissance missions and one on the ground escaped damage. The Japanese also destroyed thirty-four of the ninety-one available P-40s, including twenty of twenty-three at Clark. In one stroke the Japanese eliminated two of the five fighter squadrons as units; one of the three remaining flew obsolete P-35s. At day's end, merely fifty-eight of the original fighters were serviceable. American personnel losses (never exactly confirmed) included at least nine fighter pilots and ten bomber air-crew killed among total deaths of at least 77, with about 168 wounded. The triumphant Japanese aviators returned with the inflated reports of aerial vic-tories and accurate accounts of American aircraft lined up for destruction on airfields "almost as if the enemy did not know the war had started." Losses came to seven Zeros (all pilots killed) and two bombers with eight dead crew members.

The ineffectual American air defenses this day downed just seven Japanese planes, despite vital advantages the US airmen had over their counterparts in Hawaii. They knew a state of war existed, they had ample radar warning of nearing enemy aircraft, and they flew mostly more capable fighter aircraft (P-40Es rather than P-40Bs). The surprised Hawaiian defenders shot down at least eight, maybe as many as eleven Japanese planes. Both Hawaii and the Philippines sustained huge losses of aircraft on the ground, but the Philip-pines squandered a golden opportunity to avoid most if not all these losses.

As the overall commander, MacArthur bears ultimate local responsibil-ity for this fiasco. Simple math disproves the assertion in numerous later accounts that "all" or "most" of his planes were destroyed on the ground. But the exact distribution of blame remains a complex matter. Distance and the Japanese foreclosed an immediate inquiry, nor was there any subsequent investigation. The loss of records and passage of time rendered it difficult, if not impossible, to reconcile the sharply conflicting later accounts from Brere-ton, Sutherland, and MacArthur. Some mitigation of responsibility assign-able to MacArthur and his airmen is appropriate. The ability of the A6Ms to reach Central Luzon from Formosa, for example, represented an astonishing technological surprise.

A balanced assessment of the debacle of American airpower in the Philip-pines requires extending scrutiny to the end of December 1941. After weather imposed a one-day hiatus, from 10 December, the Imperial Navy, later joined by Imperial Army aircraft, mounted repeated blows against FEAF bases—though not without significant cost. On 10 December Japanese bombers devastated the Asiatic Fleet's main base at the Cavite Navy Yard adjacent to Manila, forcing its evacuation. The small squadron of Philippine Air Force in obsolete P-26As, led by Capt. Jesus A. Villamoor, also suffered serious loss but may have shot down two Japanese planes, a remarkable achievement. By 15 December, Japanese aircraft losses totaled fifty-four aircraft from all causes. On 19 December, the FEAF effectively declared defeat in the Philip-pines when the surviving B-17s flew out to Northern Australia. After that American fighters only found employment in reconnaissance and guerrilla-style hit-and-run raids. Driblets of B-17s from Australia mounted ineffectual pinpricks against the Japanese juggernaut.

On 31 December, MacArthur's airmen reported the operable aircraft in the Philippines numbered just four P-40s, five P-35s, one observation plane, and three assorted liaison aircraft. This represented just 7 percent of the combat strength available on 8 December, not counting B-17s. The approximately twelve Australian-based B-17s represented about 34 percent of the B-17 strength on 8 December. The figures for 31 December, not those for 8 December, reveal that a decisive cause of the extinction of American airpower in the Philippines was the loss of fighter aircraft (and effective air warning and interception control). With loss of local air control, the B-17s had to flee, thus stripping away even their feeble air offensive capability.

This in turn points to heavy responsibility in Washington. War experience demonstrated that high altitude bombers, like the B-17, very rarely hit maneuvering ships. Coupled to this misplaced faith that heavy bombers could protect the seas around the Philippines was the miscalculation that the relatively small numbers of Philippine-based heavy bombers could deter Japan in the last months of 1941. The execution of the heavy bomber deployment was arguably worse than these errors. Army air force planners had warned that building up Philippine airpower mandated the creation first of proper air base facilities. The second and third steps required creation of an initial followed by total base defense facilities. The fourth step involved the maintenance of forces in the United States able to sustain an air offensive against Japan. Instead, Washington attempted all four simultaneously—and did none adequately. To his credit, Brereton had warned Marshall and Arnold of the dangers to his B-17s unshielded by adequate defense, but they insisted this was a risk that had to be run. The Japanese did not find B-17s "wing tip to wing tip" at Clark, but tardy base development resulted in a lack of solid ground to allow adequate dispersal, which is why sixteen B-17s had been displaced to Del Monte.

As the overall commander, MacArthur's command responsibility cannot be waived, but his actual errors remain contested. The first of these is the failure to base all his B-17s only at Del Monte. He had been told that only there were they relatively secure from an attack. There is good evidence he had issued such orders, but FEAF failed to carry them out and MacArthur failed to ensure the orders were obeyed in timely fashion. The second is that Brereton never should have needed to beg for an audience on 8 December; MacArthur should have summoned him immediately. The third is the failure to grant Brereton's early requests to strike Formosa promptly on 8 December.

Brereton's plan presumably would have avoided the B-17 destruction on the ground. Even assuming all these errors can be laid to MacArthur, given the wartime record of small formations of B-17s, it seems highly speculative to assert that the available B-17s would have located the Imperial Navy airfields *and* delivered a devastating blow before the Japanese launched their own strike on 8 December. Without absolving Washington or MacArthur of their failures, however, the most underemphasized aspect of this debacle was the incredibly inept performance of the FEAF in the interception of the 8 December raid.

Unrestricted Submarine Warfare

The disaster to American airpower in the Philippines in December 1941 served to obscure an event of much greater significance: the policy of unrestricted warfare against Japan's shipping. The United States signed post–World War I treaties that codified the important, long-held American principle of "Freedom of the Seas" with respect to submarine warfare. The treaties extended the historic standard of "Cruiser Rules" to submarines. Under these rules, a warship could capture or sink a merchant vessel only after a "stop and search" to determine whether the vessel was carrying war-related material ("contraband"). Even if "contraband" were present, the intercepting warship must see to the safety of the merchant vessel crew.

As professional naval officers recognized, submarines could not wage World War I–style warfare against merchant trade under "Cruiser Rules." A submarine would have to surface at close range to the target and arrange confirmation of the nature of the target's cargo and, if necessary, see to the safety of the target's crew. The treaty further made "Cruiser Rules" applicable to both unarmed and armed merchant vessels. This made scant difference to heavily armed surface warships, but it placed submarines at impossible risk, as a single damaging hit from an armed merchantman could make it impossible for the submarine to submerge and thus condemn it to ultimate destruction.

Commencing about November 1940, Admiral Stark and his War Plans officer, Rear Adm. Richmond Kelly Turner, set a course for scuttling "Cruiser Rules" and authorizing "Unrestricted Submarine Warfare" within a week of outbreak of war with Japan. The Pearl Harbor attack before a declaration of war effectively mooted any legal quibble over the justification for the measure. With Stark's immediate authorization, Hart signaled the Asiatic Fleet to conduct "Unrestricted Air and Submarine Warfare." Obscured by the sad immediate failures in the Philippines, this order proved of cardinal importance in the ultimate defeat of Japan.

Ineffective performance initially masked the critical policy change. On 8 December 1941, the most potentially powerful component of the American defense of the Philippines resided in the Asiatic Fleet submarines (not B-17s). This comprised twenty-nine units: twenty-three large, modern "fleet boats" and six smaller, elderly S-Boats. They were commanded from 10 December by Cdr. John S. Wilkes.

Between 8 December 1941 and 1 April 1942, Asiatic fleet submarines claimed the destruction of forty-three Japanese vessels and damage to twelve others. Their actual achievement was two destroyers and twelve merchant ships sunk. They failed to inflict any serious impediment to the Japanese and lost four of their number. This ranks as one of the greatest but least heralded US Navy failures in the entire war.

Of the many reasons for this disappointing outcome, command issues stand foremost. Peacetime exercises greatly exaggerated the ability of surface ships to both detect and destroy submarines. They also instilled a morbid fear of aircraft. This background created a group of commanding officers inculcated with great caution, understandably enhanced by the unknown perils of the very first encounters with the enemy. The US Navy discovered that successful wartime submarine command demanded strengths of character no peacetime system could reliably predict. Unlike virtually any other type of naval command, that of a submarine skipper operated solo. Therefore, he alone determined how aggressive—or passive—he would be.

Many Asiatic Fleet submarine captains either were too cautious or were unskilled in their attacks. The most spectacular failure occurred only five days into the war, when Lt. Cdr. Morton C. Mumma Jr. of *Sailfish* cracked up during a depth charge attack. He told his executive officer to lock him in his stateroom and take command. Before the end of the campaign, Wilkes would relieve eight of his twenty-nine commanders, basically for lack of productive results.

Understandably, the skipper problem provoked much informal discussion as to what background produced the best commanders. Indeed, the record of American submarine commanders in World War II provides a unique case study in one of the most elusive issues in military history: exactly what foreshadows successful combat command? One school asserted that only the exceptionally cerebral captain could properly calculate the factors in any situation and produce results. Another faction argued that dullards provided the best prospects—men who would plunge ahead oblivious of the lethal hazards confronting them. But even the tiny sampling of early experience hinted at a disconcerting answer: no certain indicator existed to foretell combat success. One commander seemed to provide exhibit "A" in favor of the dullards. But his example was countered by *Salmon's* Lt. Cdr. Eugene B. McKinney. Not only was the soft-spoken McKinney thought to be overage (a presumptively negative indicator), he also had secured a law degree to boot (an achievement viewed as likely to promote caution)—factors taken by many of his crew as ineluctable predictors that they had drawn a dud for a skipper. But McKinney not only charged into the well-defended shallow waters of Lingayen Gulf to attack Japanese shipping when others did not, he also kept *Salmon* on the surface at night and stayed on the surface after being detected by destroyers.

But command failures also extended upward. For decades, army and navy officers predicted the Japanese would land at Lingayen Gulf. Yet with war obviously imminent, only one Asiatic Fleet submarine stood guard there. Worse, all but one of the other twenty-eight boats waited at Manila rather than along approaches to the Philippines or off Japanese bases. Once the war began, commanders diverted many submarines away from combat patrols to evacuation and supply tasks. (*Permit* at one point had 111 people aboard, double its complement.)

Material issues and Japanese actions also figured importantly in the outcome. Mechanical defects, most related to simple age, plagued the half-dozen elderly S-boats. Once expelled from the Philippines, they lacked the endurance for the long-distance patrols the Pacific demanded, so they were withdrawn. The destruction of the Cavite Navy Yard resulted in the loss of many spare parts and 233 reserve torpedoes, an event that would affect submarine operations for months.

One hope for future success was that the modern fleet boats proved superbly fitted to the Pacific War. Their survivability was assured by the remedial adjustments triggered by prewar live testing of depth charges against selected hulls. Their sophisticated torpedo data computers permitted accurate torpedo firing, and their air-conditioning proved essential to maintaining crew and equipment effectiveness in the tropics.

Nearly negating all this excellent material was the great torpedo fiasco. All of McKinney's daring in Lingayen Gulf came to naught when his torpedoes failed to connect. By the turn of the year, the evidence from early patrols convinced Wilkes that American torpedoes were "not functioning properly," and specifically they were running deep. By 2 January, the Bureau of Ordnance admitted that their torpedoes were running four feet deeper than set. But Wilkes suspected correctly that they were running still deeper.

In fact, at least two other major problems plagued American torpedoes well into 1943. The Navy's Bureau of Ordnance had developed prewar a supersecret magnetic exploder. It was expressly designed to work with a torpedo that ran *underneath* the target. Then a sensor in the exploder would detonate the torpedo. The explosion under the hull of the target would be much more destructive than a hit on the side of the hull. If the torpedo scored a hit on the side of a ship, the contact exploder proved too fragile and would often malfunction, resulting in no detonation of the torpedo warhead. The remedies for all these defects only came months later.

The Imperial Navy contributed in no small part to the failure of the Asiatic Fleet submarines. The Japanese severely inhibited submarine access by guiding invasion forces along and anchoring them in shallow waters. To American surprise, the Japanese not only possessed excellent sound detectors, they also employed active ranging devices. But thanks to the conceit that their adversaries' submarines were only as capable as theirs, the Japanese believed maximum American diving depths did not exceed nearly 150 feet—about half the real total. Consequently, American submariners swiftly learned that if they sought depths below 150 feet, they were immune to Japanese depth charges.

This overall record made the Americans frustrated and the Japanese complacent. In the long run, complacency would prove the more damaging.

Japanese Landings

From 1916 Washington dictated a broad mission for American forces in the Philippines, but left the specifics to local commanders. Some Philippine-originated plans prescribed a modest delaying action against a Japanese landing expected in Lingayen Gulf, which accessed a level plain, four miles wide and stretching one hundred miles south to Manila and containing two good roads. The delaying action would be followed by withdrawal to the Bataan peninsula or Corregidor Island. Some army officers (notably including MacArthur) from 1928 contested this view as tactically and psychologically unsound. In 1941 Grunert authored an aggressive plan premised on defeating any Japanese landing at Lingayen Gulf, primarily with American forces (including the Philippine Scouts), while the newly created Philippine Army mobilized.

MacArthur adopted Grunert's basic concept of beach defense at Lingayen Gulf, but inserted critical deviations. Reversing Grunert's scheme, MacArthur deployed to Lingayen Gulf almost solely ill-trained and ill-equipped Phil-

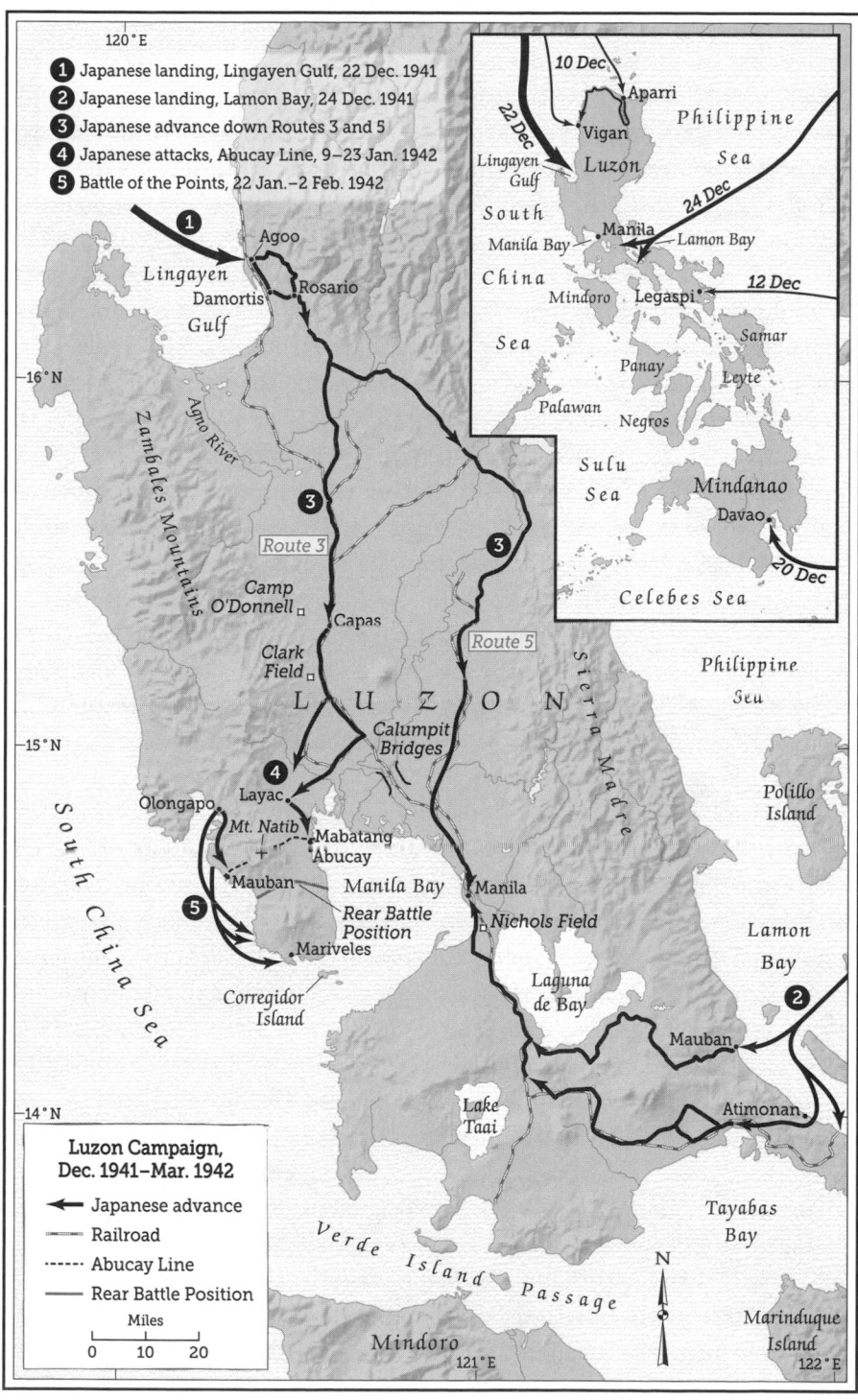

1 Japanese landing, Lingayen Gulf, 22 Dec. 1941
2 Japanese landing, Lamon Bay, 24 Dec. 1941
3 Japanese advance down Routes 3 and 5
4 Japanese attacks, Abucay Line, 9–23 Jan. 1942
5 Battle of the Points, 22 Jan.–2 Feb. 1942

Luzon Campaign,
Dec. 1941–Mar. 1942

→ Japanese advance
Railroad
Abucay Line
Rear Battle Position

Miles
0   10   20

ippine Army units. This was not necessarily a fatal defect, for even green and poorly armed troops might mount a serious landing beach defense. (The fresh example of this was Gallipoli in World War I.) But this scheme still mandated a capable reserve to exploit opportunities or to deal with failures. The sole first-class unit backing the Lingayen beach defenses was the 26th Cavalry (PS), numerically a medium-sized battalion of mostly horse-mounted light infantry. MacArthur retained the other US units in central Luzon. This may have reflected his overoptimistic evaluation of the combat effectiveness of Philippine Army units, but another and perhaps dominant explanation is that potential Japanese landings to the south, threatening Manila and Bataan, compelled him to abandon the thought of stationing any significant elements of the Philippine Division near Lingayen Gulf.

At 0200, 10 December six Japanese transports commenced landing 2,000 infantry from the 48th Division at Vigan on the western side of far northern Luzon. Serial attacks by FEAF B-17s, P-40s, and P-35s compelled the beaching of two damaged transports and sank minesweeper *W-10*. One B-17 piloted by Lt. Colin Kelly Jr. was shot down and he was killed. In the much trumpeted and exaggerated American version of these events, Kelly sank the battleship *Haruna*. His bombs damaged minesweeper *W-19*, which became a total loss. Kelly emerged as the first American air hero of the war and was even the subject of a national broadcast by President Roosevelt. These attacks represented the only vigorous opposition by FEAF to the landing. At the same time the similar Tanaka Detachment from the 48th Division landed near Aparri along the extreme north coast of Luzon. As MacArthur correctly reported to Washington, the Japanese intended these landings to secure air bases for shorter-range aircraft advancing from Formosa. On 12 December, a Japanese invasion force commenced landings at Legaspi on southern Luzon. The Japanese employed seven transports bearing 3,075 soldiers and naval infantry.

Approximately 20,000 of the 30,000 Japanese nationals living in the Philippines resided on Mindanao, with Davao the center of this community. The emperor expressed concern for their safety, so the Japanese accorded special attention in their planning to protection of their fellow countrymen. Principal forces detailed to secure Davao included the regimental-sized Sakaguchi Detachment under Maj. Gen. Shizou Sakaguchi and the Kure No. 2 Special Naval Landing Force. Fourteen transports carried these units under a heavy naval escort. Landings commenced before dawn on 20 December. The invaders sized the airfield and basked in the joy of the Japanese residents liberated from detention. The Japanese landing units then sailed to capture Jolo on 24–25 December.

On the morning of 22 December, eighty-five Japanese transports bearing the main body of the Fourteenth Army approached Lingayen Gulf's eastern reaches. The principal units comprised the 48th Division (less one regiment landed already), the 9th Infantry Regiment (from the 16th Division), and the 4th and 7th Tank "Regiments" (battalions) with a total of eighty-eight tanks and powerful artillery elements. The invasion convoy escort numbered two light cruisers and sixteen destroyers as well as lesser combatant vessels. Based on reasonably accurate reports of 70 to 80 transports at Lingayen Gulf, MacArthur signaled Washington that he faced "an enormous tactical discrepancy" since the Japanese numbered 80,000 to 100,000.

Between 0517 and about 0730, the Japanese landed three regiments along the Lingayen shores. The combination of darkness, dampness, and surf both knocked out radios and prevented landing of heavy equipment. The chief of staff of the Fourteenth Army, Lt. Gen. Maeda Masami, recalled that he could clearly see through his binoculars waves broaching and even overturning landing craft.

MacArthur's North Luzon Force (Maj. Gen. Jonathan Wainwright) deployed the 21st and 11th Divisions of the Philippine Army (PA) along the 120-mile beach front at Lingayen Gulf. A tall, very gaunt, cavalryman, the modest Wainwright inspired admiration and confidence up and down the chain of command. He was courageous to a fault. His forte was tactics, but his hard drinking did not bode well for higher command. Only in one location did the Filipino defenders seriously contest the far better trained and equipped Japanese. But a cautious Homma ordered the Japanese forces ashore not to launch a rapid advance but to secure the gulf's south shore, toward which he directed the shipping.

With news of the landing MacArthur sent north a dozen self-propelled 75 mm guns and the 192nd (Light) Tank Battalion. MacArthur placed neither of those under Wainwright's direct command, initiating confusion that spiraled through the day. Directly cantering to contact was the 26th Cavalry (PS) under Lt. Col. Clinton A. Pierce. At Damortis the Scouts dismounted and clashed with the Japanese 48th Reconnaissance Battalion. The Japanese ejected Pierce's exhausted cavalrymen from Damortis, and then Japanese tanks bludgeoned into the cavalry. A violent melee ensued in the darkness between Japanese tanks, weary cavalrymen seeking to withdraw, and terrified, rider-less horses. By a narrow margin, the 26th Cavalry extracted itself from a trap at Rosario. On 23–24 December, Philippine Army units continued their pattern of ineffectualness. On the other hand, the 26th Cavalry (PS) distinguished itself in checking the Japanese advance, although at heavy cost.

On 24 December, twenty-four Japanese transports put ashore about 7,000 men of the 16th Division under Maj. Gen. Susumu Morioka as well as naval ground units at Lamon Bay on southeastern Luzon. MacArthur's South Luzon Force had focused its deployments on southern Luzon's western beaches, which allowed ready access to an easy road to Manila from the south. Few defenders, with no artillery, guarded the eastern beaches chosen by the Japanese. But the trade-off was that from Lamon Bay, the Japanese had to vault the Tayabas Mountains to reach Manila. The Japanese at Lamon cut off part of the 51st Division (PA), and many of these troops dispersed and never returned to duty. Elsewhere, Philippine Army units either sharply contested or fell back quickly before Japanese thrusts. Spearheaded by armored cars, Morioka's command secured the roads across the Tayabas Mountains with unexpected dispatch, to the great surprise of Homma, and stood ready for a rapid advance on Manila.

Withdrawal to Bataan

Wainwright's request in the evening of 23 December for permission to withdraw confirmed the collapse of the Lingayen defenses. The same evening, MacArthur issued the fateful order for withdrawal to Bataan. The next day, MacArthur declared Manila an "Open City." This meant his forces would cease all military activities and defense of the city, and in exchange, the Japanese would not bomb or conduct fighting within the city. The reality was that military activity, at least of a logistical nature, continued in the city and some bombing resumed. President Quezon, US High Commissioner Francis Sayre, and their families and staffs moved to Corregidor on 24 December. That night, MacArthur's headquarters also moved to Corregidor.

The withdrawal plan (WPO-3) called for Wainwright's North Luzon Force to execute a withdrawal through five phase lines (designated D-1 to D-5) on the plain north of Manila, trading miles for hours. The last phase line was at the vital crossroads of San Fernando-Pampanga, where a key road turned into Bataan. Wainwright had to hold that locale as the South Luzon Force passed before him into Bataan. There were no similar preselected phase lines for the South Luzon Force, but the obvious critical locales were the road and rail Calumpit bridges over the Pampanga River, linking the withdrawal route to San Fernando and hence to Bataan. Brig. Gen. Albert M. Jones assumed command of the South Luzon Force.

Wainwright's actions over the rest of December teetered perilously between an organized withdrawal and a rout. The pullback of ill-trained Philippine Army troops in the face of the much better trained and equipped Japanese verged repeatedly near disaster. With a few exceptions, Philippine infantry started for the rear at first contact with the Japanese, and two Philippine divisions (71st and 91st) withdrew to reorganize due to heavy losses. The ranks of the North Luzon Force tumbled from 28,000 to 16,000, with few of the missing 12,000 killed or wounded. The 26th Cavalry (PS), and the pair of light tank battalions buttressed by the 75 mm guns on half-tracks, performed most of the actual fighting. Lacking infantry support, they could scarcely check the Japanese before being outflanked. Much credit for the sluggish Fourteenth Army pursuit is due to Wainwright's senior engineer Col. Harry A. Skerry, who oversaw the destruction of 184 bridges.

Fearing the D-5 line allowed too small a margin for defending the vital Calumpit bridges, Wainwright ordered the D-4 line near Layac to be held "at all costs until ordered withdrawn." The all-US 31st Infantry fought its first battle here, but did not distinguish itself. Two companies panicked and bolted from their positions, and a third was virtually destroyed in a disorganized withdrawal. The episode provides context for the performance of Philippine Army units in their own baptism of fire.

Down the clogged roads to Bataan tramped a highly variegated Filipino-American Army. By far the dominant component was wobbling columns of Philippine Army units: dull-eyed men or boys in "shoddy, dust white, denim blue" uniforms and canvas shoes, dangling bolo knives and clutching bolt-action rifles without slings, a size too large for their lithe frames. Military vehicles from Jeeps to 14-ton light tanks rumbled by, kicking up dusty gusts that tinted the vehicles' olive drab paint with light earthy tones in patches and streaks that daubed the roadside figures as well, providing a uniform hue their clothes lacked. Interspersed in the motor columns were civilian vehicles—often in garish orange or yellow—minuscule taxis, assorted trucks, and buses (some incongruously bearing advertising for various products). Saddest of all were the frightened, exhausted civilians who walked beside or swayed atop plodding carts cluttered with kettles, mattresses, wide-eyed children, cooped chickens, and strapped-down pigs.

Japanese miscalculation, not MacArthur's plan or Wainwright's management, contributed the most to the escape of the Filipino-American army into Bataan. Homma's orders identified Manila, not the enemy army, as his main objective. This reflects ill on Japanese intelligence, since American plans for

decades rested on a final stand on Bataan and Corregidor. The one deliberate Japanese thrust, apparently aimed to intercept the withdrawal by the 9th
Infantry Regiment, was halted and the Japanese commander killed.

To the amazement of Filipinos and Americans of all ranks, Japanese aircraft did not pummel the retreating, densely packed columns. The reasons
were a combination of lack of targeting orders and lack of accuracy in the consequent scattered attacks. But by no means were the roads safe thoroughfares.
Just north of the key road junction leading to Bataan sat two yellow Pampanga
Bus Company vehicles that on first glance appeared to hold sleeping Filipino
soldiers. On closer inspection, the buses bore signs of riddling by aircraft—
their dead occupants a feast now for a cloud of flies.

The men who trudged into Bataan soon found there "the cardinal blunder
of the entire campaign," a scandalous lack of stockpiled supplies, especially
food. Brig. Gen. Charles C. Drake, MacArthur's energetic quartermaster,
maintained afterward that he could have fully stocked Bataan and Corregidor, per prewar plans, within two weeks of 8 December. But Drake's declaration masked a critical command error. MacArthur inherited WPO-3's
logistical arrangements from Grunert. The August 1941 version of WPO-3
(after MacArthur took charge) provided for food stocks for 40,000 men on
Bataan and for 10,000 men on Corregidor, each for 180 days. The US garrison in the Philippines swelled in 1941 from about 22,500 to 31,000 (counting the Philippine Scouts). Around 10,000 men would occupy Corregidor,
and small detachments would be elsewhere in the Philippines. These calculations inferred that Philippine Army personnel participating in the defense of
Bataan would decline from roughly 27,000 to 20,000. In fact, WPO-3 stated
that "when and if troops designed to defend Bataan retire thereto, the remainder of the Philippine Army troops then in service on the Island of Luzon to be
organized into detachments for the conduct of such warfare as available supplies and munitions will permit."

Drake on his own initiative prepared a contingency plan for stocking
Bataan, but could not obtain an estimate of the troop strength earmarked for
Bataan's defense. Therefore, he simply presumed a figure of 43,000—slightly
above the original plan. But a head count of Bataan's garrison tallied about
104,000 persons. Filipino refugees numbered about 20,000 while another
6,000 Filipinos served as civilian USAFFE (US Army Forces in the Far
East) employees. The 6,000 civilian employees contributed materially to the
defense, but permitting 20,000 civilian refugees to enter Bataan was a tragic
mistake. Of the remaining 78,000 personnel, over 60,000 were members
of the Philippine Army. This number not only vastly exceeded prewar plans,

but also reveals a gross failure at MacArthur's headquarters to anticipate the correct numbers. It follows that Drake's claim that he could have adequately stocked Bataan in two weeks was not correct as to the actual Bataan garrison. And ultimately it underscores that despite the faltering combat performance of most Philippine Army units to that time and the significant numbers of stragglers or deserters, most of the green and ill-trained Philippine Army units reached Bataan as recognizable units.

If the prewar supply plan was manifestly deficient, two MacArthur decisions made the situation irretrievable. His quartermasters worked after 8 December to distribute supplies to four forward depots to support the beach defense scheme instead of provisioning Bataan. MacArthur's order to revert to the Bataan withdrawal plan on 24 December allowed his quarter-masters just a week to prepare. Little of the beach defense stockpiles could now be salvaged for Bataan. In accordance with the concerns of Philippine officials not to place the civilian population in jeopardy, MacArthur com-manded Drake not to remove rice from the huge ten-million-pound commer-cial store at Cabanatuan—rice that could have fed the garrison for a year. MacArthur even forbade the stripping of food from Japanese civilian enter-prises on Luzon.

As Drake's men desperately foraged to find supplies for Bataan not off limits by MacArthur's edicts, transportation loomed as another hurdle. The USAFFE quartermaster contingent numbered just about 1,300, roughly 4 per-cent of the US garrison, and they lacked trucks. The Luzon rail system and the functioning of the Manila docks collapsed as train crews and dockwork-ers fled to escape air attacks. All these factors considered, Drake's men did a remarkable job to get as many supplies to Bataan as they did, using comman-deered trucks and especially barges loaded in Manila and towed to Bataan. But as soon as the last units reached Bataan, the critical shortage of food became clear. The garrison went on half rations from 5 January. There is no attenuating MacArthur's responsibility for both grossly defective planning for and execution of the stockpiling of supplies on Bataan.

Deceptions

Washington's obligations to the US forces in the Philippines and to the loyal Filipinos were to attempt to provide relief, and if this proved futile, to acknowledge that fact candidly. Washington compiled a mixed record on the former responsibility. Its record on the latter responsibility was shameful.

As early as the evening of 8 December, Stimson recorded in his diary that due to naval losses, "we should be unable to reinforce [MacArthur] probably in time to save the islands." On 13 December, MacArthur relayed Hart's opinion that the islands were "doomed" due to Japan's unbreakable blockade. Yet not only did Marshall cable an implied rejection of Hart's verdict, during December a whole series of messages from the Army Department, as well as an address by the president, itemized reinforcements dispatched to the Pacific with clear implications they would reach the Philippines. Given these messages, it was reasonable for MacArthur initially to believe that the United States would maintain his lines of communication and thus sustain his command.

But the early message exchanges also disclosed a pattern of emphatic (and sometimes hysterical) communications that MacArthur would exhibit throughout the war. He immediately unveiled his enduring twin themes— that his command must enjoy priority over all other Allied global efforts, and that accordingly Washington must meet his demand for resources. One of the War Department staff reading MacArthur's barrage of messages was Brig. Gen. Dwight D. Eisenhower. Marshall had recalled him to Washington after Pearl Harbor expressly because of Eisenhower's long association with the Philippines and with MacArthur as a staff officer. Although initially quite impressed with MacArthur, Eisenhower became disgusted with MacArthur's supreme egotism and his concomitant propensity to see and state things as he wished them to be, not as they were. On 3 January 1942, Eisenhower reported that "it will be a long time before major reinforcements can go to the Philippines, longer than the garrison can hold out." Examining this "very gloomy" assessment, Stimson wrote in his diary, "everybody knows the chances are against our getting relief to [MacArthur], but there is no use in saying so before hand." Honor required that Washington directly acknowledge that relief could not come—but no such message was sent.

On 13 January, a dispatch from Marshall described heavy bomber reinforcements and convoys, with some 21,000 troops, destined for the Far East. Marshall added that the record of recent bombing attacks "indicate(s) probability" of "eventual reestablishment of naval equilibrium and superiority." This cable immediately preceded MacArthur's message to his entire command on 15 January, which declared: "Help is on the way from the United States. Thousands of troops and hundreds of planes are being dispatched." MacArthur's men would eventually—and quite properly—revile him over this failed promise, but at least equal blame rested in Washington. By about this point MacArthur should have understood that relief would not come.

The sense of betrayal and abandonment ran rampant through the garrison in the end, and was of importance in weakening the moral strength of the men as they entered brutal Japanese captivity, where every ounce of fortitude was essential.

Defense of the Abucay Line

Once on Bataan, MacArthur divided his command into Wainwright's 22,500-man I Philippine Corps (the former North Luzon Force) and Maj. Gen. George M. Parker's 25,000-strong II Philippine Corps (the former South Luzon Force). They formed along the Abucay Line at the northern end of the peninsula. The line measured about twenty miles from Mabatang (just north of Abucay) on the east coast to Mauban on the west coast. The defenders occupied only the easternmost and westernmost five-mile sectors of the line. American commanders smugly regarded the middle ten miles of the front, dominated by 4,222-foot-high Mt. Natib, as impassable to a military unit, but as historian John Whitman noted, impassable terrain "is often more a state of mind than a state of nature."

The eastern end of the Abucay Line stretched from the waters of Manila Bay across bare low areas, and then gradually rose into forested foothills before it reached the slopes of Mt. Natib. Threading this area was the north-south, well-graveled East Road, making this area the obvious attack point. Parker's II Corps deployed here with the 57th Infantry (PS) from the coast to across the road. The well-equipped and tautly trained Scouts prepared formidable positions. On the left of the Scouts stood the untested 41st Division (PA) under the very capable, West Point–trained Brig. Gen. Vicente Lim, and then the remnants of Brig. Gen. Jones's 51st Division (PA), which had sustained defeat and loss on southern Luzon. Two Philippine Army divisions formed the reserve. Along the far more difficult, steep, and forested terrain on the west, Wainwright held his I Corps main line with a collection of Philippine Army units.

Homma's men triumphantly entered Manila on 2 January. That same day, his superiors ordered him to release by far his best unit, the 48th Division, and most of the Fifth Air Division. Homma understood by the mores of the Imperial Army that, notwithstanding this major loss of strength, he must complete the campaign aggressively. A very erroneous grasp of the situation reinforced Homma's instincts: he believed loss of Manila had demoralized MacArthur's army, which now numbered only about 20–25,000 men. Tokyo goaded him further by advising him that the emperor only awaited the final Philippine conquest before issuing a coveted Imperial rescript commemorating the war dead to date.

Homma assigned the mission of clearing Bataan to Maj. Gen. Akira Nara's 65th Brigade. Formed in April 1941 to serve solely as an occupation force, the brigade comprised mostly conscripts with very minimal training. Its three rifle regiments (122nd, 141st, and 142nd) each fielded just two battalions. The brigade also lacked normal artillery and signal capabilities. Nara was deemed particularly fitted for occupational command in the Philippines. He had first-hand knowledge of Americans gleaned during his attendance at Amherst College with President Calvin Coolidge's son and the US Army Infantry School. Homma attached to Nara the 9th Infantry Regiment from the 16th Division and artillery and tank elements.

Nara planned a direct attack down or just west of the East Road with the 141st Infantry Regiment. But he also ordered the 9th Infantry Regiment to conduct an encircling march over Mt. Natib to roll up the left (west) flank of the II Corps. The 122nd Infantry Regiment, with one battalion from the belatedly attached 20th Infantry Regiment, 16th Division, would pry the Americans out of their position on the west coast. The 142nd Infantry Regiment formed Nara's reserve.

Nara's attack commenced at 0300, 9 January, with, by Japanese standards, a heavy artillery barrage. In two hard days, a costly Japanese penetration of the Scouts' line was contained and largely thrown back. The 21st Infantry (PA) sent up to reinforce the Scouts showed solid ability. But this was excelled by the remarkable performance of the 41st Division (PA), exemplified by the story of Sgt. Silvestre L. Tagarao, a college student with scant training who was made instant squad leader. In his first action, terror so paralyzed him that he could neither rise in his foxhole nor pick up his rifle. Another soldier shouted curses at him to do his part. Tagarao timidly stood up and discharged a shot without aiming, causing a "spurt of acrid smoke, burnt powder." Then, he recalled,

> it went into my nostrils, I smelled it. It was unpleasant, somewhat dizzying. . . . Another burst of fire and the effect became more pronounced. Another burst and bolder now, I aimed. I fired rapidly. Bullets came whizzing close to my head. I saw bodies topple over after I had aimed and pressed the trigger. . . . the smell of powder [is like strong wine]. It gets into your blood, warms it. The warmed blood then gets into your system and reaches your head [and heats it].

Showing, like Tagaro, a fortitude and resilience beyond any reasonable expectation, the repeatedly hammered 41st Division (PA) bent but did not break.

Nara's command gained the dubious distinction of becoming one of the few Japanese units (the Twenty-Fifth Army on Singapore Island was another) subjected to serious artillery bombardment in this phase of the war. Nara admitted that American artillery created "continuous havoc" with its "very accurate" fire of prodigious amounts of ammunition. On the first day of attack, one precisely aimed American shell wiped out the greater part of the Japanese artillery command.

Meanwhile, the encircling Japanese 9th Infantry Regiment endured a nightmare trek across Mt. Natib. The roads and even trails meandered aimlessly and then ended abruptly. The massively overgrown terrain was strewn with precipices and crosscut with numerous valleys and ravines, some of which could be traversed only with climbing ropes. In its initial foray, the disoriented 9th Regiment marched east instead of south and emerged behind the 141st Infantry. The last rations reached them on the 17th. Thereafter, to stave off starvation, the marchers hunted water buffalo and even scavenged for grass roots to eat.

Nara gradually shifted the focus of his efforts to his right and finally began to cave in the position of the shaken 51st Division (PA). Amazingly, a regiment of the 51st Division managed a counterattack, but exposed its left flank. By complete happenstance, the heretofore lost Japanese 9th Infantry Regiment at this moment crashed into this opening. With this, the 51st Division collapsed, never to be reconstituted, and the Japanese finally punched a hole in the Abucay Line.

Meanwhile, on the west coast, from 16 January the Japanese effort was under Maj. Gen. Natoki Kimura, commander of the 16th Division. As on the II Corps front, it proved impossible for Wainwright, despite a direct order from MacArthur, to establish a line defending the slopes of Mt. Natib and linking to II Corps. One Japanese battalion hacked its way across this ground and set up a roadblock on Wainwright's line of communications along the critical west coast road. Several small counterattacks failed, one by the 26th Cavalry (PS), marking the last horse-mounted charge in US military history, and another led by Wainwright personally. The necessity to retreat became manifest, but it led to a massive loss of vehicles and especially artillery.

MacArthur dispatched Sutherland to get a firsthand impression of the situation on 22 January. On Sutherland's recommendation, MacArthur ordered a withdrawal to the reserve battle position along the Pilar-Bagac Road. With good reason, American commanders harbored the greatest concern about II

Corps. The movement of this corps on the night of 25–26 January descended into mass confusion. Japanese artillery fire could have turned this into catastrophe, but none came.

MacArthur reported to Washington: "Under cover of darkness I broke contact with the enemy and without the loss of a man or ounce of material [and] am now firmly established on my main battle position. The execution of the movement would have done credit to the best troops in the world." The fantasy of this dispatch typified MacArthur's inveterate misrepresentation of events.

Battles of the Points and Pockets

Citing the success of such tactics in Malaya, Homma issued an order on 15 January for an amphibious hook on Bataan's west coast. Lt. Col. Nariyoshi Tsunehiro's 2nd Battalion, 20th Regiment (2/20th), drew the mission. The fresh battalion would land at Caibobo Point and block the west coast road, trapping and destroying Wainwright's I Corps. The target area lay within the sector of the Bataan Service Command, overwhelmingly an administrative and support organization. The only "combat" elements were three "regiments" just cobbled together from the paramilitary Philippine Constabulary, and an assortment of aviators and sailors crudely armed and formed as infantry.

Tsunehiro's battalion headed south on 22 January. In darkness and roiling seas, they stumbled onto patrolling *PT-34*, which scattered the barge convoy, sinking two barges and capturing the operations plan. The Japanese could not navigate accurately in darkness facing the indistinct steep coastline. Consequently, just 301 men of the 2/20th came ashore about ten miles south of their intended destination at Longoskawayan Point. The immediately available counter was Cdr. Francis J. Bridget's "naval battalion," formed from sailors and a few Marines assembled from various components of the Asiatic Fleet. The sailors wore mustard-colored uniforms, the result of a failed attempt to transform their regular white uniforms into something more adapted to fighting ashore. They were joined by equally novice army aviation personnel. The completely clueless Americans wandered about, yelling loudly at each other (prompting one Japanese diarist to marvel at the "completely without fear" Americans). The Japanese customary infiltration tactics failed against opponents blissfully ignorant of military maxims pronouncing it fatal to have your flanks turned and your rear occupied by the enemy contingents. The 2nd Battalion, 57th Infantry (PS) arrived to finish off the Japanese and awe the sailors and airmen with their proficiency and courage. A few Japanese were captured; most perished by 1 February. American and Scout losses came to twenty-four killed and missing and sixty-six wounded.

The bulk of the 2/20th groped ashore at Quinauan Point the night of 22–23 January. The defenders there initially were the heavily outnumbered 34th Pursuit Squadron, now serving as infantry. "All we lacked was training and equipment," explained one enlisted airman, "[but] fear we possessed." The Japanese failed to press forward and cut the west coast road, which might have caused the Americans major discomfort. Ultimately, the 3rd Battalion, 45th Infantry (PS) arrived. Even with tank support, rooting out the Japanese proved slow and costly. Nearly five hundred Americans and Filipinos were killed or wounded, but all six hundred–some Japanese died.

A second attempt at an amphibious hook transpired between 27 January and 16 February. This time Maj. Mituo Kimura's 1st Battalion, 20th Regiment (1/20th) landed in two echelons, the first at Silaiim Point/Anysan Bay and the second on Quinauan. Again, it was three battalions of Philippine Scouts (2nd Battalion, 45th Infantry and 1st and 3rd Battalions, 57th Infantry) (PS) that decided the matter. When it was over, the Japanese 1/20th was eradicated.

Even while fighting continued at the "Points," fresh actions flared along both the I and the II Corps fronts from 27 January to 17 February. Nara's 65th Brigade mounted another effort against the east section of II Corps. Fighting at Abucay reduced companies in the 141st and 142nd Regiments to half strength or less, with very few company officers. The 9th Regiment was better off, but disease had ravaged the whole brigade. "Those from the front line force who did not get diarrhea were just miraculously lucky," observed Nara's report. By dint of the energetic leadership of Brig. Gen. Clifford Bluemel and some luck, defenders fell into line just in the nick of time. The Japanese accomplished very little against mostly Philippine Army units and at a dreadful cost. The 41st Regiment (PA) particularly distinguished itself. By the time the fighting flickered out, Nara's 65th Brigade had lost nearly half its initial strength before the Abucay action.

The last battalion of the 20th Regiment, the 3rd, meanwhile advanced into Wainwright's front lines in extremely dense jungle. They cuffed aside a Filipino unit and penetrated south. No one on the Filipino-American side comprehended what had happened. The Japanese battalion split up and soon formed two pockets within the Filipino-American lines (hence the "Battle of the Pockets"). Gradually awakening to the situation, the 1st Battalion, 45th Infantry (PS), converged on the sector. Later, more and more Philippine Army units swarmed into the battle. Even with tank support, the fighting remained slow and costly, but the Philippine Army units now displayed a capacity for offensive action, something far beyond their repertoire at the start of hostilities. Eventually the 20th Regiment commander, Col. Yorimasa Yoshioka, and 377 men escaped. The rest of the regiment, except for three wounded men who were captured, was dead. It was an unmitigated disaster.

Homma's Fourteenth Army had shot its bolt. His chief of staff calculated that the effective combat strength of the army now amounted to a mere three battalions. Homma feared that a counterattack by the Filipino-American Army might recapture Manila—though the defenders were equally exhausted, if less depleted. Homma pulled the Fourteenth Army back several miles to assume the defensive and asked for reinforcements. This marked the Imperial Army's greatest setback against the United States and Britain in the first six months of operations after Pearl Harbor.

Quezon and MacArthur

Disillusioned by what he justifiably perceived as the abandonment of his country, on 8 February President Quezon challenged Roosevelt to grant immediate Philippine independence so the country could be neutralized. Thereafter, all foreign forces, Japanese and American, would be withdrawn and the Philippine Army disbanded. The senior American civilian official in the Philippines, High Commissioner Francis Sayre, fully supported Quezon, but Secretary of War Stimson was appalled that MacArthur's accompanying message seemed to go "more than half way" to support Quezon. Roosevelt emphatically rejected Quezon's demand and ordered MacArthur to "keep our flag flying in the Philippines so long as there remains any possibility of resistance."

Following this exchange, at Roosevelt's direction Quezon and Sayre and their families were evacuated by submarine to Australia to run a government in exile. Washington then confronted the prospect of the Japanese gaining a first-class propaganda coup by capturing MacArthur, the former chief of staff of the US Army. General Marshall brought up the subject of MacArthur's evacuation early in February, but MacArthur remained mute on the subject. Roosevelt's messages also discussed the evacuation of MacArthur and his family. MacArthur replied with "deep appreciation" for consideration of his family, but "I have decided that they will share the fate of the garrison." The prospect of MacArthur's family coming to harm was probably more than

Washington officials could contemplate. On 22 February, Roosevelt issued a direct order for MacArthur to proceed from Corregidor to Australia. MacArthur had no choice but to comply, though a sailor he was about to leave behind said later: "It was the only time [MacArthur] ever did what he was told to." But MacArthur insisted that he be permitted to choose the best "psychological time" for his departure.

Rear Adm. Francis Rockwell, the naval district commander who accompanied MacArthur and was involved in the planning, recorded that evidence of enhanced Japanese patrols prompted abandonment of the original plan for a submarine evacuation in favor of an earlier departure by Lt. John Bulkley's now much-heralded PT Boats. After dark on 11 March, MacArthur, his wife Jean, child Arthur, Arthur's Cantonese amah, and seventeen others boarded four PT Boats on Corregidor. Fortune cloaked the small flotilla as clouds blanked out the moon and prevented detection in the passage through Manila Bay. (But in the open ocean, pitching waters tormented the party, "a trip in a cement mixer," in MacArthur's words.) One of the boats had to be abandoned, but the other three, with all the passengers, reached Mindanao on 13 March. When MacArthur eyed the worn B-17s and fresh-faced crews sent to transport him to Australia he blew up, demanding better planes. During this wait he finalized his concept of Philippine command, dividing forces four ways, all under his continued control. Wainwright would lead only the forces on Bataan and Corregidor, likely because of doubts about his well-known alcoholism. Once a better set of planes arrived, MacArthur flew out on 17 March.

Alighting in Australia near Darwin, MacArthur and his family took a C-47 to lonely Alice Springs, in the desert center of the continent. There Roosevelt's representative Patrick Hurley met MacArthur and revealed to the weary general that he now orbited in American public renown at the level of such prior ultraheroes as Gen. John J. Pershing and aviator Charles Lindbergh. MacArthur boarded a special train, and at a stop before Adelaide, he announced to reporters that President Roosevelt had ordered him to Australia "for the purpose as I understand it, of organizing the American offensive against Japan, a primary object of which is the relief of the Philippines." And he famously added: "I came through and I shall return." He reached Melbourne on 21 March, finishing a nearly 3,000-mile journey.

MacArthur's learning curve in this first venture in high command was steep, costly, and controversial. One later critic described MacArthur's performance as a "supernova, a blaze of light without substance." MacArthur carried ultimate responsibility for the debacle of the comprehensively inept performance of the FEAF, but both Washington and Brereton contributed heavily toward this disaster. MacArthur's operational handling of his forces likewise reflected significant mistakes, notably the ill-judged arrangement of forces to defend Lingayen Gulf, the premature abandonment of Manila, and the indefensible failure to adequately stockpile supplies on Bataan. He bore substantial, though not total, responsibility for the deficiencies in the Philippine Army. However, he also inspired cooperation and performance from Filipinos, both military and civilian, as no other American could. Arithmetic disproved his claim of being heavily outnumbered, but in terms of capable, well-equipped frontline fighters, the Philippine defenders were at a great handicap. MacArthur benefited enormously from the long-term development of the Philippine Scouts, who proved the only indigenous force in the colonial possessions of the Western powers who could stand toe-to-toe with the Imperial Army. After the early and largely abysmal performances of the Philippine Army units, some elements displayed qualities vastly beyond any reasonable expectation. All of this, however, transpired in the context of how the world looked in 1942. At that point the Axis had reeled off a seemingly endless stream of triumphs since the mid-1930s, punctuated with very few setbacks. In these opening months of the expanded war in Asia and the Pacific, the Philippines seemed to gleam as the only clear case of sustained and successful resistance to the Japanese, and it inspired the later effective guerilla effort. This was of no little aid to the Allied cause.

A major part of that gleaming stemmed from MacArthur's 142 official communiqués, of which 109 featured only one name: MacArthur's. Vainglory and embellishment tilting toward fantasy, not fact, vied as the most reprehensible qualities of these dispatches. But another hugely tainted aspect of MacArthur's performance later emerged. On 13 February, Quezon signed an order authorizing the payment from Philippine funds of $500,000 for MacArthur and $135,000 for three other officers, including Sutherland. These sums arguably represented fulfillment of US-sanctioned payments under MacArthur's contract with the Philippine government as well as a contract-authorized performance bonus. Both Roosevelt and Stimson knew of and acquiesced in the payment, which may well represent their sense of guilt over their failure to succor the Philippines. The payments to the three staff officers, however, carried the strong odor of "hush money." Further, MacArthur remained on Corregidor while managing the Bataan campaign, making just one visit to Bataan. Some of his soldiers started the derisive and unfair sobriquet "Dugout Doug" that would tail him for years thereafter. On Corregidor, through bombing and shelling, however, he behaved with the casual courage, sometimes approaching recklessness, that he had exhibited in World War I. The eight army officers who accompanied him from Corregidor became known as "The Bataan Gang." Except for his intelligence officer, Charles Willoughby, this group did not fill all principal general staff functions as sometimes asserted, but did form a hyperloyal palace guard.

Unlike many other Allied officers found wanting in the early years of World War II, MacArthur would get a second chance. He would raise his level of performance, but debates about his real military competence would continue.

CHAPTER 17

"Abandoned My 100,000 Soldiers in Foreign Jungles"

BURMA FALLS

The Burma Battleground

Strategically and historically, the Japanese conquest of Burma ranks not far behind the thunderclap of Singapore's fall. For the British, Burma served as the gateway to India. Americans stressed Burma as the vital last land link to embattled China from the port of Rangoon up a railway that hooked into the western terminus of the Burma Road at Lashio. For the Chinese, loss of supplies via Burma carried dire ramifications both practically and for morale.

Burma rivals the combined size of France and Belgium. The topography resembles a "blind alley" or cul-de-sac open only to the south facing the Indian Ocean. The towering Himalayas form the "back wall" to the "blind alley," while hanging down from this "back wall" are two major subsidiary mountain ranges forming the "side walls." Four great rivers dominate the "blind alley." On the east, the Salween surges from China into Burma, etching part of the Thailand border. On the west, the Chindwin notches the Indian border, then turns southeast to merge with the great 1,300-mile-long Irrawaddy. The Irrawaddy is up to three miles wide and navigable some eight hundred miles inland. The much lesser Sittang, east of the Irrawaddy, still erects a major movement obstacle due to currents.

Two monsoon seasons affect Burma. From the middle of October to the middle of May, the relatively dry northeast monsoon dispenses cool, pleasant temperatures. In mid-May the southwest monsoon descends with massive rainfall; over two hundred inches deluge areas along the coast and the Assam border with India. Historian Louis Allen summed up Burma as "a country of immense topographical contrasts: high jungles, swampy coastal plains, alluvial deltas, a central plain with a dry triangle . . . in the middle."

Communication arteries in Burma overwhelmingly aligned north-south. Their utility fell in the order of river, rail, and road, with the Irrawaddy/Chindwin affording the most important internal network. All-weather roads existed in the Irrawaddy and Sittang valleys, but the former lacked bridges over many declivities, rendering it impassable in heavy rain. Practically no east-west roads existed.

Some 17 million people populated Burma in 1941: ten million Burmese, four million Karens, two million Shans, and a million hill tribesmen, including the Kachins and the Chins. Indians and Chinese constituted numerous minorities. The capital of Rangoon (population about 500,000) sat astride the Irrawaddy's alluvial delta, about twenty-five miles from the sea. Most inhabitants farmed rice, exported in vast quantities to India. Burma ranked as the world's premier supplier of "Brown Gold" (teak lumber), produced the highest quality jade (highly prized by the Chinese), and extracted much petroleum from the Yenangyaung oil fields.

Britain acquired Burma in phases between 1824 and 1891—with Winston Churchill's father, Randolph, annexing Upper Burma in 1886, the largest grab. Plenty of Englishmen came to do good in Burma; more came to do well. The idealistic minority imported solid education and law and order. The materialistic majority strived to export profits. The Burmese majority "wants to be rid of us" admitted Brooke-Popham, then the commander in chief Far East, in a message to London, citing three reasons: a presumption of racial superiority, lack of sympathetic understanding of Burmese aspirations, and blind obsession with extracting wealth without concern for the economic benefit of the population. Following the example of the Government of India Act of 1919, Britain granted the Burmese limited self-government in 1923, retaining British control over law and order, finance, and defense. Many Burmese, particularly university students, agitated for genuine independence.

The British governor entered Burma into the war without even token consultation with the Burmese legislature. When U Saw became prime minister in September 1940, he openly flaunted his desire for Burma's independence while secretly continuing Japanese contacts. In London he sought to trade Dominion status for cooperation in the war. En route back, U Saw talked with a Japanese ambassador, who cabled to Tokyo U Saw's promise to rebel against

Britain if Japan invaded. The decrypted message provided Churchill the warrant to arrest U Saw and intern him for the duration of the war.

The Japanese eagerly exploited Burmese disaffection with British rule. In May 1940 Col. Keiji Suzuki and two assistants arrived under cover in Rangoon. Suzuki's stolid façade masked a romantic sense of historic destiny wrapped in a personality of vigor and daring. He manifested an authentic devotion to Burmese independence; his superiors' devotion proved counterfeit.

Suzuki linked up with a group of young nationalists, the Thakins, and cemented his emotional bond with them in a "blood drinking ceremony." From this movement, Suzuki recruited "The Thirty Comrades." The Japanese slipped this cadre of young men out of Burma and put them through rigorous military training to prepare them for their roles as the leadership of the "Burma Independence Army" (BIA). The "army" initially numbered about three hundred men, but a liberal distribution of lofty ranks to "The Thirty Comrades" provided the hierarchy for a true army. The BIA played a vital role in the opening campaign—though not the one Suzuki had envisioned.

Burma's Defenses

Britain's Burma garrison braced only for internal revolt, not external attack: it mustered just six infantry battalions, only two British. The British deceptively titled the other four "The Burma Rifles" but filled their ranks not with Burmese but with Chins, Kachins, and Karens to assure fealty to London. Britain raised four additional "Burma Rifle" battalions by mid-1941 that enrolled far more Burmese—whose loyalty proved fragile. Moreover, the British stripped many men from the two British rifle battalions for cadre, leaving the pair at half strength. In July 1941, the British amalgamated all these battalions into the 1st and 2nd Burma Brigades. Combining them with the newly arrived 13th Indian Brigade, the British christened them the 1st Burma Division. The "division" title belied the fact that it lacked full artillery, engineers, and service elements, not to mention adequate equipment and training.

As for air defense, just sixteen Buffaloes equipped No. 67 Squadron, the sole Royal Air Force unit in Burma. New Zealanders lacking even modest combat training, much less combat experience, overwhelmingly manned these planes. Only two airstrips around Rangoon enjoyed the support of an observer system to permit timely warning of the approach of hostile aircraft. There was no external or internal intelligence organization whatever.

Having left Burma dreadfully vulnerable, London multiplied the odds against its defenders with terribly misguided command arrangements. Five days after the outbreak of hostilities, London severed Burma from Brooke-Popham's overextended responsibilities and placed it under Wavell, the commander in chief in India. Just a few days later, when Wavell took command of ABDA, he carried with him military control of Burma, but in a dreadful error, India retained administrative control. Worse yet, Wavell located his headquarters in Java, about 2,000 miles from Burma. Erratic radio links consigned Wavell to making decisions with out-of-date information. Wavell originally expected to bolster Burma's defenses with the 18th (British) Division and 17th Indian Division, only to have them diverted to Malaya, save for one brigade and the headquarters of the 17th Indian Division.

Wavell replaced the incumbent Burma commander with his own chief of staff, Lt. Gen. T. J. Hutton. A stop in Rangoon impressed upon Wavell the immense strategic importance of Burma to India and China, and the fact that highly vulnerable Rangoon was the key to holding Burma. Chiang required no such nudge: he had urged Allied actions to secure Burma from at least 1940. He offered the last of his best German-trained divisions, as well as his only motorized formations, to serve under British command in Burma. He also pledged to protect Burma with Claire Chennault's P-40 equipped American Volunteer Group (AVG), his only effective air unit. Wavell sidestepped the troop offer. He legitimately feared that a mass of Chinese troops, lacking any real logistical system, would live off the land at great cost to the Burmese population. In the background lurked the political implications of a Chinese presence in Burma, particularly a region recognized as falling under Chinese suzerainty. Further, Wavell did not conceal his low opinion of the Japanese. This roused Chiang presciently to emphasize to Wavell that he now faced not a mere colonial rebellion but a great power.

Opening Moves

The next British misstep involved tactical dispositions. The 1st Burma Division guarded the inland Shan States, wrongly deemed the most likely avenue of Japanese attack. Maj. Gen. John G. Smyth's 17th Indian Division held the front near the coast. It comprised the 2nd Burma Brigade and the newly arrived 16th and 46th Indian Brigades. Smyth intended to deploy his troops on the west side of the wide Sittang River, where the open country suited the limited training and low capability of his division, which was grossly deficient in artillery, engineers, and signalers. But Hutton, constrained by

Wavell's direct order not to cede ground and sharing Wavell's dismissive views of Japanese capabilities, compelled Smyth to disperse his command along the Thai border.

The Japanese detailed Lt. Gen. Shojiro Iida's Fifteenth Army to conquer Burma. It comprised the 33rd Division (less one regiment) and 55th Division, initially supported by the Tenth Air Brigade (thirty-seven fighters and twenty-eight light bombers). Once the Twenty-Fifth Army made satisfactory progress in Malaya, the Fifteenth Army would advance into southern Burma along the coastal region, capture Rangoon, and await orders to thrust into central or northern Burma. The 33rd Division's men, battle hardened in China, hailed from an area northwest of Tokyo. The 55th Division came from Shikoku, the smallest home island, and grew from a cadre in the summer of 1940. It lacked any combat experience.*

The Japanese 55th Division began its march to the Thai-Burmese border on 2 January 1942. One officer scribbled in his diary: "we were soon swallowed up in a deep jungle sea. We moved ahead single file, watching for rocks and tree roots: if you missed your footing, you'd be engulfed in the bottomless jungle floor." The calendar read 17 January when the division reached the frontier.

Meanwhile, the first Japanese encounter with the AVG on 20 December over Kunming previewed the initial major action in Burma. When ten unescorted Ki-48 ("Lilly") light bombers approached, some twenty-five P-40s pounced. The novice, adrenalin-pounding Americans perpetrated a number of miscues (recalled one, "I've never been a hero type, and I wasn't figuring on starting then"). But they applied Chennault's astute tactics that maximized the P-40's virtues and minimized its limitations. The Chennault catechism stressed fighting in basic pairs grouped in fours or sixes, not individually. The heavier, better-armed, and protected P-40s would fight in the vertical plane, climbing above the enemy and making diving passes, exploit-

---

* The large difference in strength of units of the same nominal title creates considerable confusion in the Burma campaign. A Japanese rifle company numbered about 180 officers and men, just about 50 percent larger than the strength of a comparable "rifle company" unit of Empire forces. Similar disparities existed at higher levels, so a rough rule of thumb is that Japanese units at the same level (i.e., company, battalion, regiment) were around one-third to one-half again as large as comparable Empire units. A Japanese division also possessed a full complement of artillery, engineer, signal, medical, and supply elements, whereas the Empire divisions were deficient in all these categories. Grant and Tamayama, *Burma 1942*, 374–77.

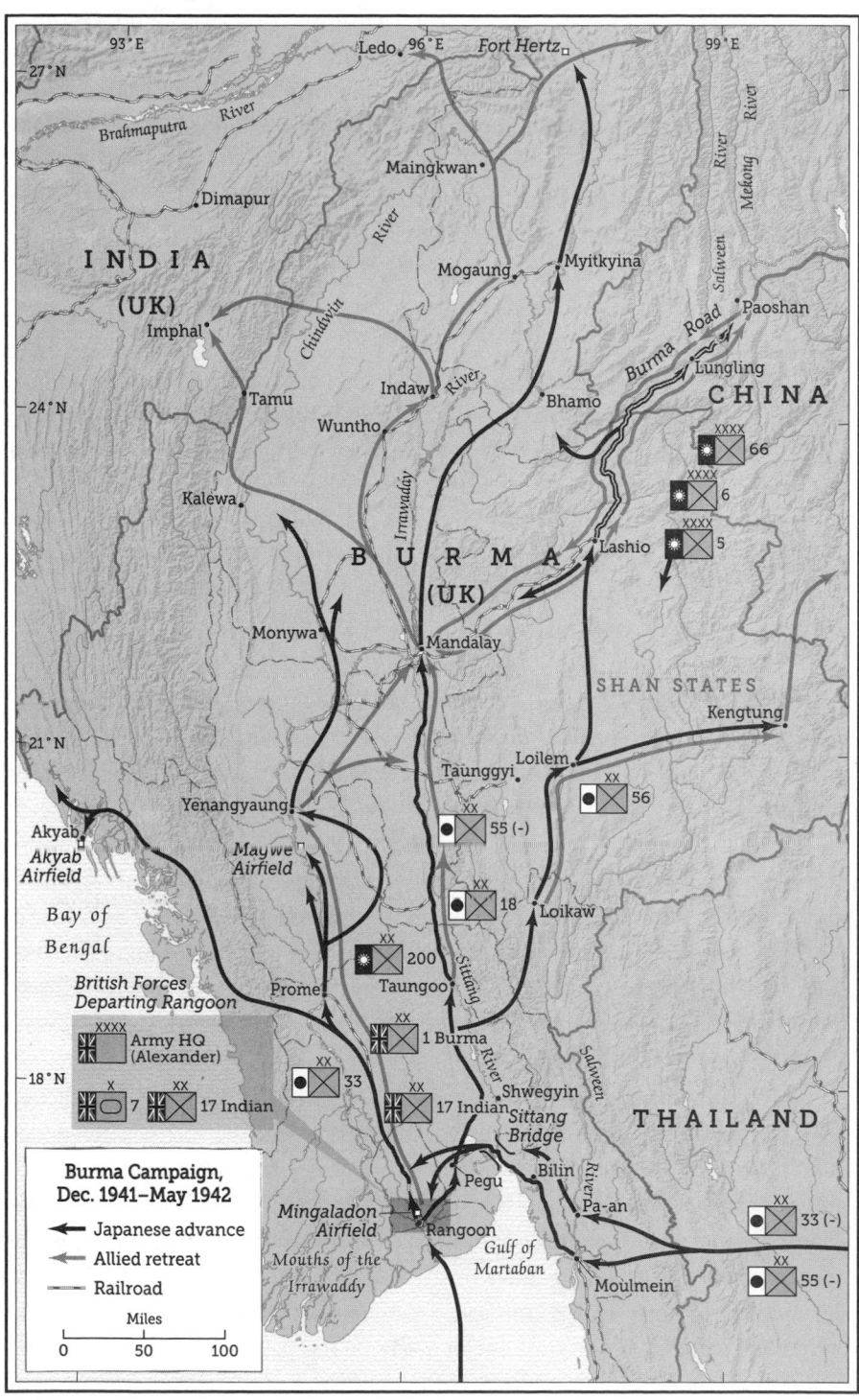

Burma Campaign, Dec. 1941–May 1942

→ Japanese advance
→ Allied retreat
— Railroad

Miles
0   50   100

ing their heavy firepower and then converting the dive energy into another climb. They would absolutely avoid being lured into fighting in the horizontal plane ("dog fighting"), where they became prey for the lethal turning superiority of Japanese fighters. The AVG pilots probably accounted for four bombers and saved Kunming from bombs. Ecstatic Chinese civilians marched to the airfield behind a band to hang purple silk award ribbons around the pilots' necks. The Japanese would not return to Kunming for a long time—but did not warn other units about the AVG, the sole Allied unit almost uniformly successful against the Japanese in the whole series of opening campaigns.

A long gash of a mouth below a prominent nose and dark, weary eyes dominated Chennault's face. His profession was military aviation, but his path always remained that of an outsider. Lacking the pedigree of a West Point military academy education, he further distanced himself as a rebel believer in fighter aircraft in a US Army Air Corps obsessed with bombers. His dissenting views as well as a hearing loss from flying in open cockpit planes led to his retirement from the Army Air Corps in April 1937, still only a captain after twenty years of service.

His dazzling exhibits of acrobatic flying during his service had already landed him another job as an aviation adviser to the fledgling Chinese Air Force. The employment was far more lucrative than his service pay, but much more importantly the role beckoned as a way to vindicate his personal worth and his theories about fighter aviation. On their first meeting, Chennault was smitten by Madame Chiang (who played a large role in the life of the Chinese Air Force) and thereafter always referred to her as "Princess." As a commander, Chennault was courageous, sternly demanding but manifestly compassionate about the fate of his men. He was rough-hewn and plainspoken, but innately courteous. The AVG proved he was master of tactical air combat and a superb trainer, but his competence at the larger issues of warmaking remained to be tested.

On 23 December, the Japanese sent 111 aircraft to attack Rangoon's docks and the nearby Mingaladon airfield. The defenders lofted fifteen Buffaloes and fifteen AVG P-40s. The AVG lost four aircraft and two pilots, while two Buffaloes were destroyed on the ground. Japanese losses numbered seven bombers. Accurate Japanese bombing knocked out the air defense control operations center at Mingaladon.

As one Burmese woman remarked, the population up to this point largely regarded themselves as "only incidentally in the path of the war monster's appetite." The raid's novelty attracted large street crowds to gaze overhead—

some cheering for the Japanese. Then exploding bombs dispersed spectators in "fear laden" sprints, said one shopkeeper. The bombs killed an estimated 1,000 and inflicted an equal number of injuries. The aerial pummeling spurred a massive flight by the mostly Indian dockworkers, creating an even greater impediment to Allied fortunes.

A still larger raid reached Rangoon on Christmas Day in two waves totaling 155 Japanese aircraft. Thirteen AVG P-40s and fourteen Buffaloes got airborne. Allied losses numbered two P-40s (one pilot wounded), four Buffaloes in the air (all pilots killed), and eight Buffaloes on the ground. Japanese loss reports recorded four bombers (one force-landed) and five fighters. Appalling civilian casualties in Rangoon may have reached 5,000 killed. These deaths sparked a panicky exodus. During the last of December to late January, the Burma air campaign simmered at a low level of intensity.

By 22 January, the arrival of the 4th Air Battalion from the Philippines gave the Japanese 150 fighters and bombers to support the Fifteenth Army. This same day the first three Hurricanes reached Rangoon's Mingaladon airfield. The British rated the Hurricane superior to the Buffalo, but while that was perhaps true of a "clean" Hurricane, these models featured drag-inducing bulky air filters and fixed under-wing fuel tanks. The Japanese attempted to gain air superiority from 23 to 29 January. Seventeen aircraft were shot down and ten badly damaged; the defenders lost two AVG and ten RAF aircraft. The Japanese then reverted to sporadic night attacks and missions against the defending army. At the end of January, three fully equipped Hurricane squadrons arrived, as did two Lysander army cooperation squadrons. A Blenheim squadron joined in early February.

To Wavell's consternation and condemnation, two regiments of the Japanese 55th Division ejected battalions of the Burma Rifles from the southern finger-like extrusion of Burma into the Kra peninsula. Then at the end of January, an inferior force of Japanese skillfully used infiltration and misdirection to confound, unnerve, and ultimately crush the defenders of Moulmein. The reverses created a bogeyman image of Imperial Army units appearing unheralded in overwhelming numbers. It also shattered confidence in the ultimate outcome, with potentially dire consequences for the families of the average Burmese soldier. The BIA quickly exploited this perception shift, causing many Burmese soldiers in British service to simply go home. By the end of the campaign, only eight hundred Burmese riflemen from the eight battalions would still be with Empire forces. Moreover, the raw 16th Indian Brigade likewise abandoned positions in panic and lost most of its equipment—as well as its morale. By contrast, the spirits of the novice Japanese 55th Division soared.[*]

The loss of Moulmein and consequent withdrawal prompted a critical decision by Hutton. He ordered the displacement of two-thirds of the 14,000 tons of stores in Rangoon to inland depots. These supplies—and some desperate fighting—would barely save the Empire defenders of Burma from annihilation.

Repeated disasters finally collapsed British objection to the movement of Chinese troops into Burma. The Sixth Chinese Army (Lt. Gen. Li-chu Kan), with the 49th, 55th, and 93rd Divisions, would cover the whole northern frontier with Thailand, freeing 1st Burma Division to redeploy to south of Toungoo. The Fifth Chinese Army (Lt. Gen. Yu-ming Tu), with the 22nd, 96th, and 200th Divisions would move to the Toungoo area to defend the Burma Road. Chinese designations did not match Commonwealth (or Japanese) nomenclature. Roughly, a Chinese regiment equaled a battalion, a division a regiment, and an army a division.

Wavell's inspection on 5–6 February produced decidedly mixed results. On the one hand he gleaned the false impression that the situation was in hand. On the other, he eyed the open ground west of the Sittang and decided that the 7th Armored Brigade must go to Rangoon. Since the brigade could not reach the front before 24 February, Hutton ordered Smyth to continue to hold forward near Bilin to buy time.

Disaster at the Sittang

With Moulmein in hand, General Iida ordered the 55th Division to cross the Salween on the Fifteenth Army's left (southern) front and advance along the road and rail line to Bilin. Led by the outstanding Lt. Gen. Seizo Sakurai, the 33rd Division would advance on the army's right (northern or inland) front. Sakurai issued stern commands to secure popular support, forbidding his soldiers from engaging in rape, pillage, and arson and demanding that anything taken from the Burmese must be paid for. The orders acknowledged that they represented a change from norms in China.

---

[*]   During the battles around Moulmein, two officers with the 4th Battalion, 12th Frontier Force Regiment were Capt. "Turk" Rahman and Capt. "Sam" Manekshaw. Two decades later these two friends were respectively the commanders in chief of the Pakistan and Indian armies during one of their wars. Grant and Tamayama, *Burma 1942*, 74–75.

Battles between the 46th Indian Brigade and the 55th Division between 9 and 19 February produced lopsided Indian casualties and convinced the Indians that the Japanese systematically killed all the wounded. Wavell's stinging rebuke for unauthorized withdrawal at the Salween River caused Smyth to fight forward even though he knew the Japanese were turning his left (northern) flank until 19 February, when he received express sanction to abandon Bilin. After his signalers intercepted a plain-language British withdrawal order, General Sakurai launched his 215th Regiment, with BIA guides, to streak cross-country to the north of the road and rail routes and seize the obvious bottleneck of the great bridge over the wide Sittang River estuary.

British misfortunes now came not as single spies, but in battalions. Both the RAF and the AVG mistakenly ravaged the retreating columns, inflicting heavy casualties, causing delay, and destroying many radios in the 17th Indian Division on 21 February, precluding the coordinated action desperately needed the following days. The commander of the belatedly arriving battalion charged with erecting a firm defense on the east side of the Sittang Bridge decided to wait till the next day to deploy his men. During the night, a massive jam developed on the east side—and then at dawn machine-gun fire burst to the northwest.

The machine guns heralding the dagger thrust for the bridge belonged to the Japanese 1st Battalion, 215th Regiment. From a hill commanding the eastern approaches to the bridge, the Japanese now threatened to cut off the Indian Division's motor transport and most fighting formations east of the river. Meanwhile, during the 22nd the Japanese 214th Regiment dispersed and divided the trailing 48th Indian Brigade.

As dawn approached on 23 February, Brig. Noel Hugh-Jones, exercising command of all troops west of the bridge, shouldered crushing responsibility. Strict orders admonished him not to permit the Sittang Bridge to fall into Japanese hands, but he had no reliable information on the status of 16th and 48th Indian Brigades. The commanders of the units manning the eastern bridgehead doubted they could repel an expected Japanese dawn attack. The engineer officer could not warrant that he could destroy the bridge in daylight if the Japanese held the east side. The detonator for the explosives sat in the open only three hundred yards from the east bank—with Japanese machine-gun fire already lancing down the bridge.

About 0415, Hugh-Jones determined he could not guarantee holding the bridge and sought Smyth's permission to destroy it. Given the information provided by telephone, Smyth authorized the action, and so the charges detonated.

After the deafening explosion, a momentary hush fell over the battlefield. The eruption transformed Japanese perceptions from the sense that they were failing to the conviction that they had won. Conversely, the explosion delivered a shattering blow to the morale of the Empire troops. The blast stranded on the east side of the destroyed bridge almost all the infantry and half the artillery of the 17th Indian Division.

Brig. "Jonah" Jones of the 16th Indian Brigade deployed troops to defend the east bank bridgehead during the day, and then attempt to cross the river that night. A cliff along the east bank of the river provided cover to Jones's and Ekin's men (46th Brigade) as they prepared to cross. In Brigadier Ekin's words:

> Here there was chaos and confusion; hundreds of men throwing down their arms, equipment and clothing and taking to the water . . . some bringing their arms with them on improvised rafts. . . . As we crossed, the river was a mass of bobbing heads. We were attacked from the air and sniped at continuously from the east bank.

From mid-afternoon and all through the night, men of the 17th Indian Division sought to cross the 1,100-yard-wide river, dotted with bobbing heads and odd-shaped rafts. The waters claimed many victims, demoralizing the nonswimmers waiting their turn. The next dawn, officers on the west bank watched helplessly as the thousands of stranded men fell prisoner to the Japanese. A muster showed that of the original approximately 8,000 men in the three brigades, only 3,484 were present.

The effective destruction of the original 17th Indian Division at the Sittang Bridge towers as the greatest catastrophe for British Commonwealth arms in the first Burma campaign. In assessing responsibility, perhaps last on the list should be Brigadier Hugh-Jones, who never should have been thrust into that situation. Smyth always insisted manfully that no blame should fall on anyone below him in the division. But Smyth also believed that the real cause of the disaster stemmed from the insistence by Wavell and Hutton that he fight east of the Sittang instead of behind it, given the limited capabilities of his troops. This is a valid point, but it is not the end of the matter.

Smyth possessed impeccable credentials for command of the 17th Indian Division: recipient of the Victoria Cross in World War I, well schooled professionally, an attractive extroverted personality, impressive range of talent (he wrote a novel), and effective performance as a brigade commander in the Dunkirk evacuation. But by the end of February 1942, Smyth was sick and exhausted from the campaign. He should have turned himself in as unfit to continue in command in favor of his very able deputy, Brig. David T. Cowan. Instead, Smyth successively failed to impose a sense of urgency about the withdrawal from the Bilin River, rejected Ekin's sound advice to get a solid force back to the bridge on the 21st, and positioned his headquarters on the west side of the Sittang, away from where the critical decision had to be made on the 23rd.

Rangoon Lost

Utterly unable to exploit the situation, Iida's triumphant command staggered at its far physical limits and tugged hopelessly on the end of its logistical leash. Moreover, Iida anticipated the intervention of British tanks in his front and Chinese armies on his northern flank. This gift of time found London for once sharply focused on its Far Eastern challenges. Over the week after the fall of Singapore, the British Chiefs of Staff decided to write off Java and concentrate all available resources on Ceylon, Burma, and Australia.

Contemptuous of the Japanese, Wavell reasoned the Japanese were not winning but the British were losing. Churchill, while shouldering full responsibility for the Far Eastern disasters, stood eager to appear to do something. Wavell fell in with Churchill's suggestion that one of the prime minister's favorite generals, Harold Alexander, replace Hutton. Alexander wore with modesty and great charm a renown as one of the bravest men in the twentieth-century British Army. Alas, as one of Alexander's able subordinates later in the war, Lt. Gen. Francis Tuker, bluntly pronounced, "I think he is quite the least intelligent commander I have ever met in a high position." Alexander simply adopted Wavell's plan. At the same time, David "Punch" Cowan replaced the wretchedly ill Smyth.

During 25–26 February the Japanese bid for air mastery over Rangoon. These clashes produced stunning overclaiming by both sides, with claims versus actual "kills" at Allied 46/7 and Japanese 23/3. But the dwindling inventory of Allied planes, coupled to the loss of bases and the air warning system, had enfeebled the Allied air effort. Heretofore, even single Japanese soldiers habitually cast anxious glances skyward, but henceforth, few Allied sorties managed to inhibit actions of the Imperial Army.

In the respite after the Sittang Bridge disaster, Empire forces in Burma acquired the entirely raw and very partially trained 63rd Indian Brigade. The brigade joined the reorganized 17th Indian Division, which distributed the survivors of the 46th Indian Brigade to the 16th and 48th Indian Brigades.

The arrival on 21 February of the well-trained and battle-experienced 7th Armored Brigade afforded the most important and brightest change in Allied fortunes. For the first time, the British in Burma possessed a first-class major unit with high morale, great firepower, and at least road-bound mobility.

Relieved from his ABDA command, Wavell devoted full attention to Burma. On meeting Chiang on 2 March, Wavell promised to try to hold Rangoon. Chiang responded with a pledge to advance the Fifth Chinese Army south to Toungoo as rapidly as feasible to permit the British to concentrate forces around Rangoon. Wavell instructed Alexander to hold Rangoon, but not permit the destruction of his army. If necessary, Alexander should hold northern Burma to permit construction of a road from India.

A week of recovery prepared the Japanese physically and logistically to advance on Rangoon. General Iida's plan called for the 33rd Division to swing wide around the north and northwest approaches to capture Rangoon by marching rather than fighting. The 55th Division would occupy British attention by striking through Pegu to Rangoon. Alexander, reaching Rangoon unaware of Japanese designs and accoutered with Wavell's orders, vetoed Hutton's plan to abandon the city. Alexander directed the 48th Indian Brigade, supported by the 7th Armored Brigade and the 63rd Indian Brigade, to hold at Pegu. An ill omen immediately beset Alexander's plan. On 5 March, a BIA ambush killed the brigade commander and the three battalion commanders of the newly arrived 63rd Brigade. At a stroke the newly arrived brigade lost its senior leadership before its first contact.

The next day, 6 March, Alexander awakened to the fact that the Japanese had outflanked Pegu. He now faced two crises. Only fierce fighting by Gurkha infantry, supported by the 7th Armored Brigade, avoided encirclement of much of Alexander's command at Pegu. Belatedly Alexander grasped that he must abandon Rangoon, but he failed to perceive that Japanese soldiers already blocked his withdrawal route.

Alexander left Rangoon the morning of 7 March. About twenty-one miles north of the capital the road forked. The right or east fork went to Pegu. The left or west fork went to Prome. Alexander discovered the Japanese had blocked the left fork road, trapping the 17th Indian Division, 7th Armored Brigade, and army headquarters. But the Japanese neither planned nor fathomed this situation. In the van of the 33rd Division's great wheeling movement around Rangoon marched Major Takanobe's 3rd Battalion, 214th Regiment, which had installed a block across the Prome road on 6 March. The Commonwealth forces surging up the road far outnumbered the Japanese defending the block on 7 March. But the resolute and skillful Japanese managed to repulse attacks that dribbled forward only by platoons or companies. At dark, Alexander faced a supreme crisis. He ordered the ill-trained 63rd Brigade, buttressed by the 7th Armored Brigade, to launch a desperation attack early on 8 March. But his absence of full confidence emerged in supplementary instructions to his command that if the attack failed, the army would break up into groups of twelve men and attempt to infiltrate north—a certain recipe for disaster.

During the night the wounded Major Takanobe—who, like his superiors, did not comprehend the priceless opportunity before him—elected to pull back his exhausted and depleted battalion. When the 63rd Brigade stumbled forward early on 8 March, they mercifully discovered the block abandoned. As Hutton later remarked, "Alex never had a greater stroke of luck in his life." While Alexander's army escaped, the Japanese 33rd Division tramped on to Rangoon. At the governor's house just before 1000, a soldier hoisted a small, tattered Japanese flag with many names on it. With a chorus of "Banzais" ringing from men clustered in the forecourt, he lofted high his rifle in one hand and in the other a container with ashes of dead comrades. General Sakurai's soldiers swelled with pride, for they had cut the Burma Road, thus aiding their comrades in the "Holy War" in China.

By the third week in February, about half the population of Rangoon had fled and only skeleton government staffs remained, the main body having retired to upper Burma. Criminals and the insane spurted from institutions; arson and looting erupted. Despite the demolition efforts of British so-called "last ditchers," Rangoon's infrastructure remained able to handle supplies for any feasible Japanese army. In a manic scene before departure, at the governor's mansion British officials capped a final banquet with a barrage of billiard balls flung at the gilt-framed paintings of past Imperial glories.

The loss of Rangoon levied immediate consequences. The Commonwealth forces now fought facing their former base. They could consume only those supplies Hutton managed to stockpile against this event. For the paltry Allied air forces, it was worse. Without any early warning system, their scant aircraft inventory faced extermination on the ground. On the other side of the coin, the Japanese Fifteenth Army now for the first time enjoyed secure logistical support and Japanese airmen gained advance bases. Alexander conceded that henceforth the very depressing influence on the morale of his soldiers was quite disproportionate to the actual damage Japanese airmen inflicted.

The melancholy story of the defense of Burma represents one of the low points of British direction in the entire war. But it had another aspect customarily neglected in Western accounts. The British not only lost Rangoon but also failed to provide timely notice of this fact to the Chinese. This experience fundamentally colored Chinese attitudes for the rest of the war. Profoundly distrustful, they viewed all British proposals as merely a means to sacrifice Chinese soldiers for British purposes.

Enter the Chinese—and Joseph Stilwell

As Rangoon fell, US leaders scrambled to provide an American officer to orchestrate efforts in the region. Attention first fell upon Lt. Gen. Hugh A. Drum, the army's senior line officer. Despite his lack of Asian experience, Drum submitted penetrating queries on China's place in US global strategy. These prescient observations clashed with Marshall's obdurate opposition to any substantial army commitment to China. Drum's mammoth ego propelled him to sketch a large US investment program he would command and to proclaim that anything less than a stellar role for him in China would squander his talents. That finished him with Marshall and Stimson.

With Drum out, eyes turned to Lt. Gen. Joseph Warren Stilwell. A West Point–educated infantryman, Stilwell enjoyed the added status of a China expert. Although credited with Chinese fluency, Stilwell lacked fully sophisticated proficiency; he habitually conducted sessions with Chiang with a translator present. Further, Stilwell knew few Chinese leaders and did not fathom the extraordinary complexity of Chinese military politics. Stilwell, however, stood tall in Marshall's estimation from prior troop assignments.

Stilwell arrived in Washington in December 1941 cast as the American commander-designate for Operation Gymnast, a proposed invasion of North Africa. Shelved in early 1942, Gymnast was resuscitated in the summer as Operation Torch, with Dwight Eisenhower as the American commander. Presented the China mission by Stimson, Stilwell replied simply, "I told him I'd go where I was sent." This stamped Stilwell as much more than an admirable contrast to Drum. Stimson and Marshall understood the Gymnast appointment had promised potentially great fame. But they also recognized that the China assignment probably meant a rugged road to obscurity. The deep reservoir of loyalty Stimson and Marshall retained for Stilwell throughout his travails in China likely stemmed from their gratitude for Stilwell's selflessness.

At fifty-eight, Stilwell exhibited the physical and mental vigor of a much younger man. He remained trim, if not gaunt. His neck comprised a stack of folds on which swiveled a fine head marred only by widely protruding ears. Behind wire-rimmed round glasses lurked a set of eyes with a natural wide-angled, quizzical view. A broad mouth and jutting chin conveyed command. The bristling gray hair at the sides merged incongruously with a very dark black bush on top that camouflaged his age. He radiated seething distaste for pomposity and pretentiousness that instantly won over reporters—who also marveled at his ability to smoke and chew gum at the same time. He always carried weapons in the field, as though he sought direct personal combat.

Stilwell's mien of gruff, modest simplicity, plus the extolling of his actions in China by journalists and historians, made him an attractive figure presented as enduring a tragic fate at the hands of venal and shortsighted men, both Chinese and American. But Stilwell's personality encompassed darker dimensions that make it impossible to see him following Eisenhower's rocket ascent. "Marshall knew that Stilwell was not a diplomat," observed the official US Army historians with studied understatement. For reasons unexplainable, Stilwell's slender frame housed a cauldron of prejudices. His diary demeans the Brits as "limeys," the French as "frogs," and Blacks as "niggers." He exhibited a vicious flare for degrading nicknames, such as "rubber legs" for polio-crippled FDR. Most famously or infamously, Stilwell referred to Chiang as "peanut," not simply in the privacy of his diary, but freely before his staff, so that predictably it soon got back to the Chinese leader and Marshall in Washington. Very ominously, even before reaching his new appointment, Stilwell demeaningly described Chiang as basically "a peasant [who] has the petty instincts of his class." Though Stilwell professed to love ordinary Chinese, American educated banker K. P. Chen translated this as actually meaning only Chinese "who obey and please." Stilwell also displayed a vicious temper and let loyalty trump competence or fitness, as exemplified by his appointment of Frank Merrill to command the later famous "Merrill's Marauders," though Merrill proved physically incapable of the job.

In contrast to Drum's searching critique of American objectives in China, Stilwell's evaluation to Marshall and Stimson emphasized that the Chinese soldiers would make first-rate soldiers, but only if they were placed under his command. In sum, Stilwell offered the prospect of potentially vast rewards for minimal investment, a view congruent with Marshall's and one attractive to Stimson. That combat-experienced Chinese officers might not simply kneel before a foreigner who had never led a unit in combat at any level above a platoon did not appear to occur to Stilwell's superiors.

After much discussion in Washington and exchanges with Chungking, Stilwell received his directives. As the senior American in the region, he simultaneously wore four hats: (1) chief of staff to the generalissimo (the commander in chief China Theater), (2) commanding general US Army forces in the China-Burma-India Theater, (3) US representative on any Allied war council, and (4) very importantly, supervisor of Lend-Lease programs for China.

Besides a potential overload of responsibilities, Stilwell's orders contained poisonous seeds of discord with the Chinese. Chiang originally requested an American chief of staff, a role identical to the ones held previously by German and Soviet officers. On that model, Chiang expected the American to remain largely in Chongqing. But the US warrant for Stilwell demanded a roving routine. Finally, Chiang had requested an American for *his* chief of staff, but Stilwell was dispatched as *Washington's* representative.

In a brief meeting with Stilwell on 9 February, President Roosevelt launched into what Stilwell damned as a "frothy" monologue that included the wildly optimistic assertion that the war would end in 1943 and the stunningly farsighted prediction that "one year from now" the great turn would come. Roosevelt instructed Stilwell to convey to Chiang Kai-shek that all Axis enemies were equal, whereas Stilwell knew that "Germany First" was the bedrock Anglo-American strategy. This sort of palaver reinforced Stilwell's perceptions that the president was "a rank amateur in military matters" and a "stooge" the British had "completely hypnotized."

American fighting participation in the new theater would be by air, not on the ground. To Stilwell's great relief, Chennault, now a world-renowned media hero for the work of his AVG, agreed to serve under his command. Through Chiang's intercession, Chennault duly returned to American service as the senior US airman in China—but to his chagrin, not the senior American airman in the theater. Chennault's AVG became the 23rd Fighter Group, with fifty-one new P-40Es en route as replacements—but only five of the original AVG pilots remained. An additional ninety-one assorted aircraft were earmarked for the theater, but to fall under command of the new Tenth Air Force in India. Maj. Gen. Lewis H. Brereton, with the remnants of his initial Philippine command (a mere eight B-17s and ten P-40s), headed the Tenth. In a forceful reminder of where China stood in American priorities, Brereton's heavy bombers all were diverted to support the British Eighth Army in the Middle East.

Stilwell met Chiang formally on 28 February. Their brief honeymoon relationship saw an abrupt deterioration during their conferences between 6 and 11 March. They agreed that the ultimate objective must be Rangoon, but they divided sharply over the means. Stilwell insisted that the Chinese and British Commonwealth Armies, or the Chinese alone if need be, should mount an all-out offensive to retake Burma's key port—and after that target Hanoi or Hankou! If this failed, Stilwell concurred with Chiang's plan to hold northern Burma in order to protect a land route to India. That stand would exploit the high ground around Mandalay. If the Allies could sustain a defense for a few weeks, the descent of horrendous monsoon conditions commencing about 15 May would stymie the Japanese for months. Stilwell's thinking rested upon a folio of military science abstractions: that the essence of war was battlefield triumph; that all resources must be committed to that end; and that only offensive action with all resources could secure victory. Defensive action bore the stigmas of passivity and defeatism, tainted further by a connotation of feminine rather than masculine traits.

Stilwell's élan initially impressed Chiang, but this lurched into alarm at Stilwell's recklessness. Chiang stressed that the Fifth and Sixth Armies were his last units that were German-trained and well-equipped; they must not be lost. He gave Stilwell a tutorial on their limitations in manpower, firepower, and logistics. Therefore, in the face of Japanese air and sea superiority, retaking Rangoon compelled a subtle approach. Chiang advised installing the main Chinese forces around Mandalay, luring the Japanese in deep, where their supply lines were overextended, and then counterattacking—the Chinese battle-tested successful counterpunch operational approach. Chiang further believed that Stilwell seriously underestimated the number of Japanese in or soon to be in Burma. This initial clash of visions raises profound questions about Stilwell's basic understanding of Chinese capabilities, which had just been demonstrated to be respectable at Changsha. It further suggests that Chiang should have immediately overruled Stilwell—and perhaps should have asked for his relief on the basis that Stilwell lacked a fundamental understanding of how China's armies could fight and win.

Based on a history extending back a century, Chiang—like a majority of Chinese—regarded the British as only somewhat less arrogant and rapacious than the Japanese. That general attitude gained potent reinforcement by the British refusal of Chiang's initial offers of forces to defend Burma, a policy only grudgingly reversed. Chiang vented in his diary: "The U.K. is engaged in a conspiracy to sacrifice others for its own benefits." Chiang warned Stilwell pointedly that the British were unreliable and might withdraw without notice, exposing the Fifth and Sixth Armies to destruction. Many of Chiang's actions in the ensuing campaign, particularly the reluctance to permit Chinese units to go deep into Burma, sprang from this conviction.

The shocking sights Chiang encountered during firsthand visits to Burma roused his distrust and contempt of the British even higher. On 7 April, Chiang, his wife, and Stilwell reached Mandalay, a city made famous by a Rudyard Kipling poem (he never actually visited it) and its enterprises in opium, rubies, and brothels. The American journalist Claire Boothe accompanied them. They witnessed scenes of disorganization, demoralization, incompetence, and panic among both military and civil institutions as well as ominously overt evidence of Burmese anti-British and pro-Japanese sentiment. A full two days after the last major Japanese air raid, relief and repair efforts appeared nonexistent, compared to much-bombed Chongqing. "As far as the eye could see," recounted Boothe, "it was met with a mass of smoldering grey and white charred timbers, twisted tin roofs." And her pen recorded that in "the long green moat that surrounded [Mandalay Palace, the central administrative hub] where lazy lotus pads drifted on the hot green scum, there floated many strange and hideous blossoms culled by the hand of death. The green little bottoms of babies, bobbing about like unripe apples. The gray, naked breasts of women, like lily buds and the white bellies of men—all with their limbs trailing like green stems beneath the stagnant water." Alexander admitted this was no fluke; "After a heavy raid on a town, life in that community came practically to a standstill." The abandonment of their jobs by railway and river barge operators severely disrupted internal communications.

Shortly after Stilwell's arrival, Lt. Gen. William Slim appeared to take command of Burma Corps. Unlike Stilwell's Brahmin ancestors, Slim's lower-middle-class family lacked the resources to provide him with a college education. When World War I erupted, Slim attained his ambition of becoming a soldier by finagling his way into an officer's training course. Arduous frontline service brought him wounds and decorations. But his lack of means drove him into the Indian Army after the war, where he could live on his pay, supplemented by income from writing magazine articles under a pseudonym. At the beginning of World War II, he led an Indian Army Brigade in Eritrea, where he sustained yet another wound. Although he harshly graded his own performance as a brigade commander, as major general he commanded with daring and great success the 10th Indian Division in the Middle East in 1941. This, and the stellar impression he made on British Army officers between the wars, brought him promotion and an assignment to Burma.

Historian Max Hastings provided a penetrating insight about Slim: "In contrast to almost every other outstanding commander of the war, Slim was a disarmingly normal human being, possessed of notable self-knowledge." Slim also harbored very rare acquired knowledge for a British officer. Before World War I he taught school in an economically very depressed district that accorded him direct experience with the "lower orders" of Britain's class-bound society. Between the wars his service, primarily with Gurhka units, instilled in him an understanding and respect for non-Europeans. One of his soldiers described him as "grim faced with that hard mouth and bulldog chin." Slim not only wielded a very sharp intellect but also an acute sensitivity to the inner motivations of his officers and men.

Besides the combat leadership experience from low to high level, Slim set himself apart from Stilwell in a telling manner. Reasoning that an actual victory over the Japanese could provide the best insight into how to fight them, Slim sought out a Changsha veteran Chinese general and listened attentively as this officer explained that the great Japanese weakness rested in their very thin logistical margins. If a Japanese advance could be contained for nine days, and they were denied the opportunity to seize Allied supplies, they were then highly vulnerable to counterattack. Here in a nutshell was the counterpunch tactic that Slim applied brilliantly in later campaigns. It also duplicated Chiang's counsel, which Stilwell dismissed as "a lot of crap tactics."

Command of Allied forces in Burma posed an incredibly thorny challenge. The British found it unthinkable that a foreigner would command Burma's defenses. On the other hand, the Chinese advanced a fair claim to command not only on the grounds of their investment in maintaining their last land link with their Western allies via Burma, but also their pledge of the greatest numbers of troops to halt the Japanese. American aspirations that Stilwell might prove a compromise commander proved wistful. In the end, Alexander described his status as the "nominal" overall commander, with Stilwell acting as his subordinate.

Double Disasters

In the three weeks after Rangoon fell, the Allies sustained devastating defeats in the air and on the ground. As the Japanese closed on Rangoon, the RAF command redeployed to Calcutta leaving two wings in Burma: one—with the AVG contingent—at Magwe, and the other at Akyab. In the morning of 21 March, a British strike from Magwe successfully hit Japanese aircraft clustered at Mingaladon. But Japanese airmen retaliated against Magwe with massive hammer blows (121 aircraft in one raid alone) on 21 and 22 March. The few surviving Allied planes left Burma. The Japanese then pummeled Akyab from 23 to 27 March and forced its abandonment. This left Allied commanders nearly blinded for lack of air reconnaissance.

The day before Rangoon fell, the Southern Army issued ambitious new orders to Iida's Fifteenth Army: crush British and Chinese forces in upper Burma and fling their remnants over Burma's borders. With secure communications through Rangoon, Iida welcomed the remaining regiment of the

33rd Division and then the 56th Division by 25 March and the 18th Division on 7 April. Iida also gained two tank regiments and artillery and engineer reinforcements. With aircraft transferred from Malaya and Java, the Fifth Air Division supported Iida with some 420 planes.

The Japanese launched the 33rd Division north up the Irrawaddy Valley via Prome to take Yenangyaung. The 55th Division marched north up the Sittang Valley from Pegu toward Mandalay. Meanwhile the new 56th Division executed a wide envelopment arc to the east, through Taunggyi and the Shan States to cut roads to China. The 18th Division constituted the reserve in the wake of the 55th Division.

Geography dictated to the Allies blocking deployments in the Irrawaddy and Sittang River valleys. But the approximately eighty miles of heavily vegetated elevations separating the two fronts afforded ideal opportunities for Japanese outflanking and deep penetration tactics. Despite the grim situation Slim faced, he sought to concentrate his corps for offensive operations. This meant that the Chinese Fifth Army must relieve the 1st Burma Division at Toungoo in the Sittang Valley so that the division could shift west to the Irrawaddy Valley. Chiang and Stilwell agreed to push the Chinese Fifth Army down to about Mandalay. Then Stilwell secured Chiang's approval for thrusting the 200th Division farther south to relieve the 1st Burma Division at Toungoo and for the 22nd Division to move to support the 200th Division. Deeply skeptical of the British commitment to hold Burma, Chiang initially refused to permit the 96th Division to venture so far south. While aware of Chiang's profound distrust of the British, Stilwell did not permit that to interfere with his own grand offensive designs. The abandonment of Rangoon, without proper notice to the Chinese, left Chiang ambivalent about further campaigning in Burma. He could well have decided to pull all his forces out of Burma, but instead he determined that his armies remain to stamp China's credentials as a solid ally.

The 200th Division represented by far the most potent Chinese formation in Burma, with about 8,500 men fully mechanized, including light armored vehicles.[*] Its two companion divisions in the Fifth Army each counted about

---

[*]   While Chinese organizational tables called for Soviet T-26 tanks in tank companies, the 200th Division had no such vehicles in Burma. Its available armored vehicles were only Italian CV-35 tankettes and French UEs (both armed only with machine guns). Also available were a few French Renault AMR-ZBs armed with either 37 mm guns or 13.2 mm machine guns. None of these vehicles was a match for Japanese light or medium tanks. Leeland Ness with Bin Shih, *Kangzhan: Guide to Chinese Ground Forces 1937–1945* (Solihull, UK: Helion, 2016), 110–15, 430.

6,000 soldiers, while the divisions in the Sixth Army mustered only about 5,700 each. These raw manpower totals deceive, as unarmed laborers numbered roughly one-third of each division's strength and provided the only immediate replacements. The Chinese forces also faced a dreadful mismatch in artillery. Chinese gunners lacked skill at basic firing, and they possessed effectively about twelve pieces with merely 5,000 rounds of artillery ammunition for the entire campaign.

The 200th Division's "experienced and resolute" General An-lan Tai erected a perimeter around Toungoo. Two Japanese regiments pitched back a covering force Tai positioned about twenty miles south of Toungoo between 21 and 24 March, although with high casualties in one regiment. On the 24th, one Japanese regiment looped west to capture airfield sites north of Toungoo. Then the 55th Division brought its full strength against Toungoo on the west bank of the Sittang and pounded away with heavy artillery.

When the motorized reconnaissance battalion of the Japanese 56th Division reached the area, it parked its vehicles and forded the Sittang. Then it closed in on the bridge spanning the Sittang, threatening the complete encirclement of Tai's division. All the Japanese accounts pay fulsome tribute to the skill and fighting spirit of Tai's command that resisted courageously and stubbornly house-to-house through Toungoo, mounting vigorous counterattacks. They only finally gave way on the 30th. The Chinese unit sustained severe casualties and lost all its heavy equipment. Much worse, it failed to destroy the Sittang Bridge—a disaster parallel to the British debacle on the Sittang in February. The seizure of Toungoo and the bridge gave the highly motorized 56th Division ready access to the northeastern road network toward China.

During the battle at Toungoo, Stilwell ordered the Chinese 55th Division to march to support the 200th and tried to hurry forward the 22nd and 96th Chinese Divisions, hoping to inflict a defeat on the Japanese. Stilwell's persistent underestimation of Japanese strength makes it difficult to avoid the conclusion that his orders would have magnified the disaster. The two, soon to be three, Japanese divisions in the Sittang Valley might have crushed all the Chinese units around Toungoo. But here as throughout the Burma campaign, Stilwell raged to Marshall and Stimson about the "incompetence, lethargy and disregard for orders amounting to disobedience on the part of [his subordinate] Division and Army commanders." He pungently added,"unfortunately, my powers stop well short of shooting." It is not that Stilwell lacked cause for his outbursts. His headquarters' records document a plethora of examples of noncompliance or flat disobedience to his orders, interference by Chiang, General Cho-ying Lo (sent as Stilwell's deputy by Chiang), and the army com-

manders in executing Stilwell's instructions, and incompetence and malfeasance by some Chinese commanders. Further, a tenet of Chinese military
practice formed a centerpiece of Stilwell's frustration. As the official US Army
historians explained: "Orders through a staff officer meant nothing. Orders
had to come from the commander personally, and, if written, bear his seal or
chop." Chiang never equipped Stilwell with the vital commander's seal. Not
only did Chinese officers deem Stilwell as merely their titular commander,
Chiang's well-entrenched practice of long-distance micromanagement meant
Chinese generals often tarried awaiting Chiang's oft-delayed approval. While
these factors formed the central charges in the later indictment of the Chinese by Stilwell's advocates, even Stilwell in a candid moment in his diary
confessed: "In justice to all of them, however, it is expecting a great deal to
have them turn over a couple of armies in a vital area to a goddam foreigner
that they don't know and in who they can't have much confidence."

But Stilwell's own subordinate Lt. Col. Haydon L. Boatner identified the
fundamental reason that the 22nd and 96th Divisions never advanced to support the 200th Division as Stilwell ordered. Rather than Chinese insubordination or Chiang's interference, Boatner wrote that the Chinese, in fact, pleaded
with the British officer in charge for necessary transportation to advance, as
well as authority for more than one Chinese division to move south of Mandalay. But the British officers summarily denied the transportation means or
the necessary authorization.

Stilwell wrongly told Chiang of Japanese reinforcements shifting from the
Irrawaddy Valley to Toungoo, so Chiang asked Alexander for an attack by
Burma Corps to draw off the forces facing Toungoo. Slim duly dispatched a
motorized column of a battalion of light tanks, the equivalent of a little over
one infantry battalion. The Japanese nearly trapped the column, which barely
escaped disaster. Though overlooked in both British and Japanese accounts,
this episode loomed large in Burmese history as the first (and last) major
action by the BIA. Of some 1,300 men, nearly half the Burmese became casualties or stragglers.

Middle Burma

At a meeting with Wavell and Alexander on 1 April, Slim received instructions to withdraw from Prome and occupy a new line to protect the Yenangyaung oil fields and upper Burma. Using their customary flanking and
infiltration tactics, the Japanese preempted Slim by forcing the 17th Indian

Division out of Prome by 3 April. This compelled Slim to anchor his new line south of Magwe, in the dry belt of Burma. "Trees smouldered at the roadside creating a tunnel of heat," reported one historian as the weary columns faced north. Moreover, the contestants entered the near desert-like central Burma. A journalist watching the 1st Burma Division withdraw in 110 degree Fahrenheit heat recorded: "Bearded, dust covered men, with the sweat salt dried white across their shirts, their water-bottles clacking dry against their hips, fell into position as the sun sank behind the smoke from the burning city of Yenangyaung."

From 10 to 14 April, the Japanese deftly applied their infiltration tactics by land to the east and by water to the west to dissolve the Burma Corps front. On 14 April Slim authorized another withdrawal, this time against the backdrop of flaming oil rigs around Yenangyaung turning day into virtual night. But the Japanese trapped the 1st Burma Division on 18 April with yet another roadblock. Maj. Gen. Bruce Scott, the division commander, radioed Slim a plea that his men were utterly exhausted and near collapse for lack of water. He asked for permission to destroy their guns and transport and break out that night. Over two decades of service together, merged with a close personal relationship between their two families, endowed Slim with the conviction that Scott had not exaggerated his dire situation. Setting aside fears he might be ordering his close friend to his death, Slim told Scott to hang on through the night.

In part, Slim based his hopes on saving Scott's unit on the appearance of the Chinese 38th Division (roughly the equivalent of a brigade) of the Chinese Sixty-Sixth Army on the 18th. The redoubtable Gen. Li-jen Sun, a graduate of the Virginia Military Institute, commanded the division.[*] The tall, handsome, very youthful-looking Sun spoke excellent English. Slim immediately sensed a kindred spirit, for as one acute witness observed, Sun treated "the enlisted men much more courteously than their sergeants or lieutenants would have done." Slim directed that Scott's 1st Burma Division would venture a breakout from the south on 19 April against the Japanese block while Sun's division delivered a blow from the north. Much to the chagrin of the commander of the 7th Armored Brigade, Slim assigned some of that brigade's tanks and artillery to Sun.

---

[*] The 38th Division, formed in 1938, was organized from the elite Tax Police Division. This division originally contained six regiments, "highly motivated and trained," of more than 25,000 soldiers with "a backbone of tough and experienced officers who had previously served under northern warlord Zhang Zueliang." Harmsen, *Shanghai, 1937*, 163.

On the 19th, Scott's attack was unable to pierce the roadblock, and for hours the promised Chinese attack failed to materialize. With his command nearly beyond control and men dying of heatstroke and thirst, Scott led a desperate breakout sortie, abandoning guns and vehicles and most of his badly wounded men—whom the Japanese then slaughtered. Sun belatedly attacked that afternoon and did not break through, but his unit, with 7th Armored Brigade, covered the withdrawal of Scott's terribly mauled command. Scott escaped with roughly 3,200 soldiers still in the ranks, having lost about 800 men killed, wounded, and prisoners. The Japanese inflicted this disaster at a cost of just thirty-nine fatalities.

Meanwhile, in the Sittang Valley, the Japanese pushed north from Toungoo toward Mandalay. Although the two Chinese divisions (22nd and 96th), equivalent to about two regiments, put up stiff fights at points, two Japanese divisions (the 18th and 55th), reinforced with tanks, hurled them back. Farther east the Japanese 56th Division, adroitly led by Gen. Masao Watanabe, outfitted with 250 trucks and bolstered by a tank regiment, exploited the roads toward the Shan States, which had been flung open when the Japanese captured the bridge at Toungoo. With just two battalions, the 56th Division crushed the Chinese 55th Division and seized the vital bridge at Loikaw on 20 April. Maneuvering astutely, Watanabe dispersed the Chinese Sixth Army and on 29 April (the emperor's birthday) seized Lashio with its huge dump of 44,000 tons of supplies.

On 25 April, with the situation obviously deteriorating precipitously, Alexander met with Slim and Stilwell. They agreed it was time to withdraw. To Slim's great relief, rather than heading for China, the Burma Corps and the Chinese 38th Division would head to Assam, India. Stilwell looked to take his other Chinese units back to China. The British withdrew past Mandalay, thus evading Iida's next effort to trap and destroy Burma Corps against the Irrawaddy. Iida recast his plan with the 33rd Division forming the left claw of a pincer with elements along the Chindwin River to bar a British escape to India. Now reinforced with a motorized third regiment, the 56th Division exploited its extra strength not only to send elements toward the Chinese border (reached on 5 May but halted by demolition of the bridge over the Salween), but also to launch an advance from Lashio that captured Bhamo on 3 May and Myitkina on 8 May. This effectively now made it the right claw of a huge pincer movement endeavoring to encircle Burma Corps.

After a brief rest pause, the relentless General Sakurai (33rd Division) yet again attempted to trap and destroy part of Slim's command. Sakurai rushed one regiment up the west bank of the Chindwin. Catching the British completely unawares, the regiment crossed back over the river at Monywa, immediately blocking the path of 1st Burma Division and raising fears the Japanese might ascend the Chindwin first to Kalewa—the planned Burma Corps crossing point on the gateway to India. The 1st Burma Division managed an escape portal to the east, but again, after significant losses, including code books and strategic plans.

Burma Corps struggled mainly to Kalewa (1st Burma Division) and Shwegyin (17th Indian Division, 7th Armored Brigade), on the Chindwin. River steamers had to lift units at Shwegyin up to Kalewa, where the track for India started again. The Japanese closed up on Shwegyin on 10 May, and a series of desperate fights broke out to control the high ground around the basin containing the main British forces and the river steamer embarkation point. River steamer crews refused to continue the lift from Shwegyin in the face of Japanese air attack and direct fire from land. This compelled the units in the basin to abandon their guns and vehicles and trudge afoot with a few mules to Kalewa. This was the last real battle of the British retreat.

Slim's command finished a nine-hundred-mile march, the longest retreat in British history, reaching Imphal in India in late May. Rather than admiration and honor for this remarkable feat, their British hosts delivered a final insult: Slim's command should be content to be left scattered about in the open under the monsoon.

Immeasurable credit is due to Cowan and Scott but above all to Slim for maintaining cohesion under these almost unimaginably trying circumstances. Slim's own words cannot be surpassed in describing this moment:

> I stood on a bank besides the road and watched the rearguard march into India. All of them, British, Indian, and Gurkha, were gaunt and ragged as scarecrows. Yet, as they trudged behind their surviving officers in groups pitifully small, they still carried their arms and kept their ranks, they were still recognizable as fighting units. They might look like scarecrow, but they looked like soldiers too.

When Slim toured his units to bid farewell he reported: "To be cheered by troops whom you have led to victory is grand and exhilarating. To be cheered by the gaunt remnants of those whom you have led only in defeat, withdrawal, and disaster, is infinitely moving—and humbling."

Stilwell's "Walkout"

A 30 April meeting with Alexander sketched a last defense line in Burma roughly from Kalewa through Bhamo. If this failed, Stilwell planned to withdraw the 22nd, 96th, and 38th Divisions and Fifth Army troops to India. But from 6 May, Stilwell led a much celebrated "walkout" from Burma covering approximately 140 miles and auguring through corrugated jungle. His party eventually numbered over one hundred, notably including twenty-four Americans, Dr. Gordon Seagraves's medical unit of two doctors and nineteen Burmese nurses, several Britons, Indians, and Malayans—and just sixteen Chinese. In the torrid premonsoon heat, many wilted and not a few wavered, but Stilwell in his trademark Montana peaked hat welded the group together as they hiked toward India. On the 14th, just as a deluge from the sky threatened dissolution of the party, they providentially contacted a British civil officer. More weary steps brought them to Imphal on 20 May, admirably without the loss of a single person. Stilwell declared to the press: "We got a hell of a beating. It was humiliating as hell. We ought to find out why it happened and go back!" The "walkout" made Stilwell a legend among Americans.

But the episode invites another interpretation: Stilwell led two Chinese "armies" into Burma; he "walked out" with the equivalent of two Chinese squads. In Chiang's eyes, Stilwell "abandoned my 100,000 soldiers in foreign jungles." Stilwell justified the scant Chinese in his party to battlefield exigencies and the discipline breakdown among his Chinese forces. More pointedly Stilwell charged that his key Chinese subordinates, Generals Lo and Tu, severed contact with him and even alleged that Lo deserted. Although there were many stragglers (as was the case with British Commonwealth forces), there still existed ample organized bodies of Chinese soldiers when Stilwell decamped. Both Lo and Tu remained in Burma with their soldiers and maintained contact with Chiang until they eventually made their way out with organized Chinese units long after Stilwell reached India. If these circumstances had involved an American force of such size, Stilwell's failure to link up with any substantial unit would have been pointedly questioned.

Stilwell's claim that his Chinese subordinates had failed to maintain proper contact with their superior infuriated Chiang, for Stilwell had effectively broken contact with Chiang after 1 April. When Stilwell decided to leave Burma, he maintained that Lo confirmed that Chiang "desired" that Chinese units on the Irrawaddy front (a clear minority of Chinese forces) head to India. But Chiang insisted that he had instructed Stilwell explicitly that any withdrawal of Chinese forces from Burma must be to China. Even if Lo had so informed Stilwell about Chinese units on the Irrawaddy front (for which there is no support in Chinese sources), Stilwell plainly understood this was not authorization for *his* "walk out" from Burma. In fact, Stilwell queried Washington, not Chiang, whether he should head to India rather than China. Stanley Hornbeck of the US State Department was one of the few American officials, if not the only one, who was aghast that Stilwell did not first refer his personal destination to Chiang, not Washington, for authorization. By far the most likely interpretation of these events is that Stilwell's frustration over his lack of genuine authority over Chinese units in Burma, a situation almost certainly to continue if he went back to China, drove him to gather a Chinese Army in India that he could command effectively.

Flight from Burma

Burma not only represented one of the lowest points of British direction in the whole war, but also it produced two more characteristic features of the Asia-Pacific War: mass noncombatant fatalities and mass refugee flight. Over 5,000 noncombatants died in Japanese air raids in Burma, but the vast noncombatant death toll stemmed primarily from Burmese-Indian rifts. About one million Indians clustered mostly in the Irrawaddy delta and cities in the central and southern regions. Rangoon (53 percent Indian by population) prompted one inhabitant to comment drolly that "Rangoon isn't Burma really. It's much more an Indian City, with a bit of China thrown in, run by Scots and Irishmen."

Burmese nationalism incorporated a generalized antiforeigner cast, with particular animus at Indians. Many Indians viewed Burma as "a kind of Wild East," with the equally alluring scents of easy fortunes and allegedly sexually compliant Burmese women. Indian immigrants poured from the entrepreneurial class all the way down to untouchables. Indians acted as moneychangers and bought up land from hard-pressed Burmese, an explosive cause of ire. But low-caste Indians also formed the very basement of the labor force: the sweepers who removed human waste from dwellings in the cities. When they fled in 1942, Burma's urban areas became stinking vats of misery and disease.

The December 1941 air raids cued approximately 70,000 Indians to rush to the ports of Rangoon or Akyab (where an outbreak of cholera claimed many) for easy and safe passage to Chittagong, India. Officials, mostly Europeans themselves, favored other Europeans and Indo-European evacuees over those with darker skins. Nearly all the Europeans (about 25,000) abandoned Rangoon, though some headed north in the hope that it would be held. American pilots flying China National Aviation Company transports and braving all weathers extracted as many as 14,000 passengers, including no fewer than 5,000 Indians and 2,600 wounded.

With increasing portents of Japanese victory, Indians grasped all too well that without the protecting arm of the British colonial administration, some Burmese were apt to exact vengeance for real or imagined infringements. Indian flight first produced spectacularly overcrowded trains, but the local railway staff typically fled into the jungle during the day to evade bombing, magnifying the burgeoning chaos. Stations became nightmare scenes of confusion, then filthy percolators of smallpox and cholera. Hundreds of thousands of Indians, interspersed with some Europeans and Indo-Europeans, formed endless winding foot columns staggering north. Some set out with tremendous collections of goods and valuables, as though exchanging homes rather than fleeing for their lives. Even those anticipating a hike seldom equipped themselves with adequate sustenance, clothing, or footwear.

Three main escape routes emerged. One was via Akyab and hence by sea to Chittagong. The second and best route for those afoot meandered from Mandalay northwest, across the Chindwin River, and then into India at the frontier town of Tamu, and onward to Imphal and Dimapur. The third ran from Myitkyina west-northwesterly through the Hukawng Valley, then on to Ledo.

Despite the endeavors of some heroic officials, the tidal wave of frightened refugees trampled under the generally feeble performance of the Burma government. Way station camps often featured better sections reserved for Europeans and Anglo-Indians and might be divided between Muslim and Hindu sections. The alleged "better discipline" of the Europeans and Indo-Europeans, claimed one medical official, justified the apartheid camp system and preferential access to cholera vaccine. The camps normally lacked adequate food and water. The inevitable breakdown of hygiene not only accentuated the squalor, but also posed deadly peril.

Tens of thousands of the starved, diseased, and exhausted perished along the way. Bodies lay thicker on up slopes, and dozens lay clustered around every waterhole. Others chose to "[wander] away into the thick forest to find a peaceful and solitary ending." When the monsoon rains began in May, the situation descended into a new level of Hell. Under incessant downfalls, the trails became yard-deep bogs. In the soggy patches waited the leeches, who exhibited affection particularly for mucus membranes accessed particularly via the rectum and urethra. Their removal brought infections and tropical ulcers. More fatal still were the scourges of cholera, typhoid, typhus, black water fever, and above all, malaria. Torrential streams striated the pathways littered with human excrement and fresh, moldering, or skeletal corpses. Weakened men but particularly women and children collapsed into the mud and could not get up. In a macabre touch, the clouds of gorgeous butterflies, said to be the most beautiful ever in Assam, swarmed down on the dying and dead.

Amid this mass tragedy, a handful of heroes emerged. While Burmese hostility to Indians proved epidemic and sometimes lethal, many ordinary Burmese treated refugees with humanity. As the streams of refugees left the plains, they entered the territory of the Kachin and Naga hill peoples. Since the Raj respected their independent identities, true to their cultural traditions, they often welcomed the bedraggled crowds. But the interlopers unloosed a new, virulent dysentery that killed thousands of Nagas. The one component of the Burmese government that earned esteem was the Burma Forest Department. Forest officers guided columns along trails known only to them and helped them find food.

In Assam, the Indian authorities proved ineffective. Filling the desperate breach was the Assam Tea Planters Association, towering heroes of the whole tragedy. An elite group of thoroughly practical men, mostly of Scottish origins, dominated this organization. They were accustomed not to polo and gin drinking on the veranda, but to hard practical organizational work demanding an early rise and a full day's effort. They mobilized and deployed 60,000 workers on critical roads to support the military effort until they encountered the humanitarian disaster. They proceeded to round up the ragged, starved trekkers and assemble them in transient and reception camps the government failed to establish. Alastair Tainsh, a planter, noted: "We had to be absolutely ruthless in order to maintain control of a hunger maddened crowd." He did not hesitate to use "his cane liberally on men, women and children alike" to prevent "a survival of the fittest and the best armed" anarchy from overwhelming the fair distribution of precious food. Without their efforts thousands more would have died.

One British brigadier described the survivors who completed the trek:

> Complete exhaustion, physical and mental, with disease superimposed, is the usual picture. All social sense is lost . . . they suffer from bad nightmares and their delirium is a babble of rivers and crossings, of mud and corpses. . . . Emaciation and loss of weight is universal.

A British woman, Mrs. Wilby, embarked on an escape trek with her 2½-year-old baby, a 12-year-old son, two daughters, two nieces, and two adult male companions. After days of draining march, one exhausted adult male sat down and died. The other male became deranged and plunged into the forest to perish. When her baby starved to death, she abandoned it beside the road. Then the boy died a few days later and was abandoned. The grieving survivors trudged on until Mrs. Wilby toppled down and expired from starvation and exhaustion. Other marchers came upon the four girls dying by the corpse of Mrs. Wilby. The girls rejected pleas to continue and died next to Mrs. Wilby. The end of countless other lives remains unrecorded.

The monsoon stranded thousands along the saturated trails. The RAF attempted to air drop some supplies, but refugees continued to be brought in as late as November 1942. A part of this agonizing sequel was the use of elephants from the trek industry to rescue survivors, as only they could traverse the terrain. Survivors of the Chinese Fifth Army, one group about 2,500 strong, likewise suffered severely as they trudged to India.

It is uncertain how many Indians fled and how many became "green ghosts," the Burmese term for those meeting unexpected or violent death. The Indian Overseas Department of the Government of India determined that 500,000 refugees from Burma reached India, but this enumeration is confined to those seeking government help. Historians since have projected that by autumn of 1942, some 600,000 refugees reached India. Estimates of the dead range between one official figure of 4,268 to a toll ranging from 50,000 to 80,000 that is probably closer to the mark. While on an absolute basis this is far lower than deaths among Chinese refugees, it represents a far higher proportion of the original number of Indian residents in Burma. The British scorched-earth policy devastated the oil and mining industries and destroyed enormous numbers of boats and vehicles, with the upshot that many Burmese were impoverished for two generations.

As for the approximately 100,000 Chinese soldiers fighting in Burma, some 10,400 reached India, including 5,378 of Sun's exemplary 38th Division. About 54,000 gradually trekked out to China through the summer in all too many desperate scenes resembling those just described for Indian refugees.

Burma 1941–1942: Summing Up

By the official accounting, British Commonwealth forces sustained casualties of 1,499 killed, 2,595 wounded, and 9,369 missing and prisoners for a total of

13,463. The best estimate is that deaths among the "missing" likely reached another 2,000, for a final figure of about 3,500 dead. At a minimum, 30,000 of China's best soldiers died. There apparently are no reliable figures for Burmese combatant deaths fighting on either side. Japanese losses totaled 2,431 killed, a ratio of one death for about every fourteen Allied deaths. There are no figures on Japanese wounded or missing, although the latter were likely to be very few. The Japanese reported taking 4,918 prisoners of war, but did not break the figure down. Two captured British officers estimated this total included about 350 British, a mere 50 Chinese, and the balance Indians.

The Japanese campaign in Burma ranks only somewhat below the Malaya/ Singapore campaign as the outstanding performance by Japanese arms from 1941 onward. Iida's Fifteenth Army turned in a stellar performance, combining stunning, rapid maneuvers both by foot and motor across an enormous battlefield and consistent tactical finesse. Accolades fall not only upon Iida, but also upon General Sakurai of the 33rd and General Watanabe of the 56th Divisions and many of their subordinates. Sakurai, the extremely able but modest and humane commander of the 33rd Division, astounded his staff by ordering the creation of not only a victory memorial to honor Japanese dead, but also alongside this a small memorial for their dead British and Indian opponents. The BIA contributed significantly to Japanese success both in battlefield intelligence and in causing mass defections of Burmese soldiers concerned about their families.

The only wholly commendable performances on the Allied side came early in the air and at Toungoo (with qualification over the failure to destroy the Sittang Bridge). In general, for the Allies the first Burma campaign collapsed into inglorious defeat. This seemed the consequence of lack of preparations and forces as well as defective command arrangements. The rebuff of Chiang's offer of preemptive reinforcement appeared a notable error, and serious operational and tactical errors by Allied commanders contributed heavily to the comprehensiveness of the defeat. In the end, Japanese command of air and sea as well as by March both the means and the fierce resolve to take Burma to complete the isolation of China probably would have overcome any conceivable Allied effort to hold Burma.

Though they abandoned vehicles, weapons, and sometimes even wounded soldiers as they were booted from Burma, many Allied officers still carried their prejudices. The British foisted the major blame on the Chinese. Stilwell mounted an all-around defense of his performance. He excoriated the British for lacking commitment to the defense of Burma because they regarded it as not essential to holding India and because they did not want China to grow strong on Allied supplies. He attributed the failure of his Chinese armies to Chinese ineptitude, lack of offensive spirit, and above all to Chiang, who, Stilwell alleged, "double crossed me at every turn." Stilwell could not acknowledge that a major part of his struggles stemmed from Chinese loss of confidence in him over his lack of grasp of the strategic situation and of effective Chinese operational and tactical capabilities. It is telling that the Japanese, who conducted the most unbiased examination of Allied units, gave the Chinese the highest marks. In stark contrast to others, Slim stands out not only in his performance under severe trials, but also in his readiness to take blame and give credit to the Japanese. The 1942 Burma campaign provided the first head-to-head measurement of Stilwell and Slim. It did not favor Stilwell.

Though just as bitterly disappointed, Chiang placed first blame upon himself. He had permitted his desire to validate China's stance as a solid ally to overcome his better judgment that his correct course of action was to withdraw his troops from Burma after Rangoon fell before they came to great harm. He, too, was quick to give credit to the Japanese. Because for weeks Chiang lacked full comprehension of the disastrous withdrawal of his troops, his initial messages of support for Stilwell back to Washington gave a false impression of his final conclusions about the Burma campaign. The defeat fundamentally poisoned his relations thereafter with Stilwell and ratcheted up still more his profound distrust of the British.

It is difficult to overstate the importance of the loss of Burma to the path of Chinese history. The severing of the last major supply link from the United Kingdom and the United States to China crippled China's armed forces for the rest of the war. Moreover, the psychological impact of that isolation and consequent lack of support inevitably wilted Chinese morale. By May 1942, Chiang's overarching strategic vision of holding out until China gained the active alliance of Britain and the United States looked misjudged, if not bankrupt. In the six months after Pearl Harbor, China's strategic position had gone from bad to worse.

CHAPTER 18

"We Are Not Barbarians"

THE JAPANESE EMPIRE AT ZENITH

US Code-Breaking Reorganization

While Japan rampaged across Asia and the Pacific, the United States confronted a critical covert policy change and a very public issue that would haunt its history. After the Pearl Harbor attack, Stimson's rigorous mind recognized that the United States had ventured merely a "haphazard beginning in the field of signals intelligence." The smoothly churning "Magic" production system intercepted and decrypted some 7,000 diplomatic messages in the six months prior to Pearl Harbor, but exploitation of this treasure proved "elementary." The War and Navy Departments each assigned a single intelligence officer to cull out the messages to be forwarded to the tiny list of authorized recipients. Other heavy duties barred these officers from systematic study of the intercepts. The select recipients received the raw messages themselves only for a single day. They could retain no notes or files. Each recipient thus functioned as his personal intelligence officer, with a grasp sharply constrained by the bounds of his memory. Describing this situation, leading cryptanalyst William F. Friedman later wrote that "each message represented only a single frame, so to speak, in a long motion picture film—a film which . . . should have been intently studied as a continuous series of pictures, because they were telling a story."

Part of the problem started at the top. In early 1941 Stimson found the president shockingly indifferent to the value of "Magic." (The president manifested much more attention to "Magic" thereafter.) In January 1942, Stimson concluded that securing true mastery over the cryptographic output was of first importance. To formulate a plan, Stimson brought in Alfred McCormack, a lawyer with experience in litigating complex cases.

McCormack devised a very effective system. A cell of individuals who possessed "imagination coupled with analytical, judicial and unbiased minds" would have access to all the intercepts as well as all other sources of intelligence. They would then identify which intercepts should be forwarded to policymakers in the guise of a daily news summary titled the "'Magic' Diplomatic Summary." Each intercept would be placed in the context of the whole body of intercepts and any other relevant intelligence material. McCormack emphasized that the summary must be "quickly intelligible" to very busy officials and free from "bias." A similar format would be applied later to military intelligence for the Asia-Pacific and European-African theaters. This remains the basic concept behind the President's Daily Brief to this day. Without the shock of Pearl Harbor, it is impossible to say how long the United States would have continued to squander so much of the value of its radio intelligence.

The Internment of Japanese Americans

Substantial numbers of Chinese reached America for the first time during the California Gold Rush of 1849. Initially they met a benign greeting, but by the time the Japanese began arriving in Hawaii after 1885, things had shifted into an anti-Asian "Yellow Peril" attitude rooted in racism, xenophobia, and fears of economic competition. By the 1940 census, some 126,947 persons of Japanese descent resided in the continental United States (less than 0.01 percent of the total population), but no fewer than 90 percent of these individuals lived on the West Coast. The Territory of Hawaii housed far more, some 157,905 Japanese, aliens and citizens, making up 37 percent of the population.

Marked generational divisions separated persons of Japanese descent in the continental United States. About 47,305 (37.2 percent) were Issei, persons born in Japan but denied US citizenship by American law. The other 79,642 (62.7 percent) were Nisei (second generation), with a small number of Sansei (third generation). US law bestowed citizenship on the Nisei and Sansei based on their birth on American soil. In Hawaii, the numbers were approximately one-quarter *Issei* and about three-quarters Nisei and Sansei.

Other complexities marked the US population of Japanese ancestry. A large majority (73,281 of 119,361) of the Nisei and Sansei in Hawaii carried dual American-Japanese citizenship. About 85 percent of Nisei attended after-hours Japanese language schools. Exact numbers of those having dual citizenship and after-hours Japanese language instruction for the continental United States are lacking, but were presumably similar in proportion. Japanese US immigrants largely came from the rural poor, but their energy and ambition resulted in spectacular economic advance. For example, with 1 percent of California farmland, the Japanese earned 10 percent of farm income. Perversely this ascent increased rather than quieted hostility. In Hawaii, the Japanese formed the key plantation labor force, the foundation of the territory's economy.

On 19 February 1942, President Franklin D. Roosevelt signed Executive Order 9066. Under this authority, the army uprooted from their homes on the West Coast 119,803 men, women, and children of Japanese descent, aliens and citizens alike, and transported them to hastily built camps in the interior. Besides bewilderment and shame, most internees experienced severe economic losses involving homes, businesses, or jobs. This episode remains a huge blot on America's record in World War II.

Multiple but not equal forces spawned this tragedy. In the background rested racism and economic anxiety. Fear was generated by the increasingly stunning Japanese military successes overseas as well as very largely false reports of hostile Japanese acts, or subversion, close to home. Japan did deploy nine submarines to patrol along the West Coast in December 1941, resulting in the sinking of two tankers. In February 1942, submarine *I-17* fired seventeen shells ineffectually at a Santa Barbara oil facility. False reports included "sightings" of Japanese aircraft and tales of Japanese agents radioing to Japanese submarines. The most dramatic "sighting" was the "Battle of Los Angeles" on the night of 24–25 February. Some 1,400 antiaircraft shells were discharged on spurious reports of Japanese aircraft overhead. Two further specific factors also contributed. American "Magic" intercepts of Japanese coded diplomatic cables disclosed grand Japanese ambitions to instigate espionage and subversion in the United States and gave evidence of some success in espionage. In mid-1941, two undercover Japanese naval officers were apprehended with evidence that they secured military information from both Japanese citizens and aliens. Based on this prehostilities intelligence, American security services rounded up after the Pearl Harbor attack a total of about 3,849 persons, almost exclusively aliens. About half of these were Japanese.

Concrete evidence of acts of disloyalty, however isolated, resonated profoundly within the Roosevelt administration. Key figures, starting with the president but also including Secretaries Stimson, Knox, and Morgenthau, believed that subversive elements (so-called "Fifth Columnists") had played a key role in Axis triumphs, particularly in Europe. As noted, this conviction spurred measures by the FBI and Treasury Department to find supporting evidence, notably against those noninterventionists who opposed administration policy. Thus, potent fear of subversion existed quite independently of racial prejudice.

But the critical triggers for the mass internment order emanated fundamentally not from broad forces but from the acts of specific men. This list starts with Maj. Gen. Allen W. Gullion, the provost marshal general of the army, who cultivated a special interest in dealing with enemy aliens. Maj. Karl R. Bendetsen, Gullion's principal subordinate, proved a willing and adept accomplice. Together they displayed consummate skill at maneuvering to advance their role and their policy far beyond the inherent sway of their bureaucratic niche. They faced a pair of formidable obstacles to secure their goal of mass internment. First, military officers under US law only exercised control over civilians in the immediate area of a battlefield. Second, jurisdiction over aliens otherwise rested with the Department of Justice. This was important because Attorney General Francis Biddle was a committed civil libertarian determined not to abuse citizens or aliens, as had been the case with the anti-German hysteria during World War I and the Red Scare afterwards.

For weeks after Pearl Harbor, American national and local officials debated various schemes for dealing with the danger of espionage or subversion by Americans whose families came from one of the Axis nations. By 25 January 1942, these debates culminated in a proposal forwarded by Attorney General Biddle to Secretary of War Stimson that would have absolutely banned entry of enemy *aliens* (*not* US citizens) from 86 "Category A" sites (military installations and defense plants) and placed them under a tight "pass and permit" system in 80 "Category B" areas (a looser list of sensitive areas). This proposal would have affected fewer than 3,000 Japanese out of a total of 7,000 persons.

The date of this proposal is extremely significant. A postwar scholarly study reviewed 112 California newspapers from 8 December 1941 to 8 March 1942. It categorized opinion articles, readers' comments, and news articles as favorable or unfavorable to persons of Japanese descent. Tellingly the count of editorials was 105.5 favorable to 163.5 unfavorable overall, but prior to the week of 26 January 1942 the tide ran five to one favorable to unfavorable. After that date the tide dramatically reversed to about 6.5 to 1 against. These hard data on the government proposal and editorial opinion confirm a dramatic event of grave consequence that happened at the end of January 1942: publication of the Roberts Commission Report.

On 18 December 1941 President Roosevelt charged Associate Supreme Court Justice Owen J. Roberts and two flag officers each from the army and navy with determining whether Adm. Husband Kimmel and Lt. Gen. Walter Short were culpably negligent in the Pearl Harbor attack. Documentary evidence gathered after the attack revealed detailed Japanese intelligence on US installations. This raised the question of whether that intelligence came from persons of Japanese ancestry. The commission on its own initiative took testimony on that issue that followed three broad lines. Impressive witnesses attested that local authorities could deal with any disloyal elements among a predominantly loyal population of Japanese descent. Certain witnesses countered this testimony by asserting no broad loyalty could be expected, particularly in the real threat of invasion. Some witnesses tendered a third view: while they expected broad loyalty, no one could be sure short of an actual test.[*]

The Roberts Commission Report was released on 24 January 1942. It contained the following passage:

> There were, prior to December 7, 1941, *Japanese spies* on the island of Oahu. Some were Japanese consular agents *and others were persons having no open relations with the Japanese foreign service. The spies* collected and, through various channels transmitted, information to the Japanese Empire respecting the military and naval establishments and dispositions on the island. (italics added)

The greatest significance of this passage lay in what it did not say: it failed to affirm the basic loyalty of persons of Japanese descent. This omission prompted the public to assume the report confirmed widespread disloyalty. The effect of the report proved dramatic—and decisive. When Gen. John J. DeWitt, the army's West Coast commander, met with California governor Culbert L. Olson, a liberal Democrat, on 27 January, Olson declared a

---

[*] In the context of these conflicting opinions about loyalty, the commission heard evidence on the Niihau Incident. A Japanese pilot landed his crippled fighter plane on Niihau Island west of Oahu after the Pearl Harbor attack. On the island were one Issei and a Nisei couple. Although the Issei attempted to avoid any association with the pilot, the two Nisei assisted him in escaping custody. The Nisei husband helped the pilot obtain firearms and threaten the local Hawaiian population. Eventually, a Hawaiian couple taken hostage managed to kill the pilot, whereupon the Nisei husband killed himself. Although this episode by itself probably cannot be viewed as the pivotal cause of later events, it appeared to serve as a test case for the commission on the ambiguous responses witnesses provided about what the local Japanese population might do in the event of a Japanese invasion. The local army commander, however, properly viewed the episode as an aberration, compared to the complete absence of any other evidence of disloyalty.

tremendous public demand now raged to remove all Japanese, aliens and citizens. Olson explained that, "Since the publication of the Roberts Commission Report [the people of California] feel that they are living in the midst of a lot of enemies. They don't trust the Japanese, none of them." Two days later, California attorney general Earl Warren, a Republican, endorsed mass evacuation. The capitulation of these key bipartisan civilian authorities, who previously resisted mass evacuation, clearly influenced the indecisive DeWitt.

Roberts struck further blows against West Coast Japanese. He met with DeWitt and subsequently with Stimson for four hours on 20 January. To Stimson, Roberts stressed the danger the Japanese posed in Hawaii. Roberts also met with Roosevelt on 18 and 24 January. His comments are unrecorded but presumably followed his remarks to Stimson.

Biddle tried valiantly to stem the powerful wave of opinion surging toward mass evacuation. Stimson confided in his diary that he feared the Nisei more than the Issei, but that taking measures against the Nisei solely based on their "racial characteristics" would "make a tremendous hole in our constitutional system." DeWitt's views on internment changed multiple times. Assistant Secretary of War John J. McCloy also proved reluctant, but Gullion and Bendetsen finally convinced McCloy that nothing short of mass internment would deal with the threat.

On 11 February, Secretary Stimson telephoned President Roosevelt to discuss what he now understood was DeWitt's proposal to "relocate" 120,000 persons of Japanese descent, "including citizens." Stimson explained the plan to the president "and fortunately found that he was very vigorous about it and told me to go ahead on the line that I myself thought best." Although Roosevelt did not sign Executive Order 9066 until 19 February, this phone conversation with Stimson effectively locked the government onto the course to mass evacuation.*

A combination of circumstances and men explain the otherwise mystifying fact that there would be no mass evacuation or internment on Hawaii despite the (correct) fears it would become the target of a full-scale Japanese invasion. Following the Pearl Harbor attack, the army placed Hawaii under martial law with suspension of the writ of habeas corpus. Military authori-

---

* Public demand for internment of persons of Japanese descent developed earlier in Canada than in the United States. Ultimately the Canadian government would evacuate some 21,000 persons of Japanese descent from its Pacific Coast.

ties thus wielded tremendous powers over all aliens and citizens never duplicated on the West Coast. Territory and army authorities shut down Japanese
schools, cultural centers, and newspapers. Other factors also played important roles. First, a mass evacuation of Japanese aliens and citizens would
impose shipping demands that Marshall informed DeWitt might reduce the
program of Hawaiian reinforcements in men and matériel below necessary
minimums. Then there was the relatively tolerant racial climate in multieth-
nic Hawaii; the fact that most pressure for relocation emanated from outside
the army (i.e., no Hawaiian counterpart to Gullion and Bendetsen); and the
key role Japanese played in the local economy. While the proportion of persons of Japanese descent was incomparably higher in Hawaii than on the
West Coast, with the reinforcements rushed to the islands the ratio of troops
to civilians was much greater. By June 1942, the army garrison alone numbered 122,000 men (i.e., not counting sailors or Marines), about one soldier
for every four civilians.

The size of the Hawaii population of Japanese descent numerically and
proportionately created diverse tugs on wartime policies. Extensive prewar
investigations convinced the army and the FBI that they had identified those
of suspect loyalty. Further, prior to Pearl Harbor General Short announced
that so long as they remained loyal, the Japanese population would be treated
fairly. Short's replacement, Lt. Gen. Delos C. Emmons, reaffirmed this policy
on 21 December 1941, after a careful investigation confirmed there had been
no act of sabotage and only one act of disloyalty on Niihau Island (see footnote
on page 491) by any Japanese alien or citizen.

By far the most potent impetus for treating the Hawaiian Japanese like
their West Coast counterparts originated in Washington and particularly
with Navy Secretary Knox and the president. Schemes were examined
seriously that either the Japanese would be uprooted from Oahu and relocated to another island, or alternatively, shipped to camps on the mainland. On 13 March 1942, the president approved a recommendation from
his senior military officers to evacuate the bulk of the Japanese population
from Hawaii to the mainland. An inspection of Hawaii thereafter by Assistant Secretary of War McCloy convinced him that displacing the Japanese
to another island or the mainland was impractical, a view he reported local
army and navy authorities shared. Those opposed included Emmons, who,
in retrospect, appears to have staged a deliberate delaying action, raising one
obstacle after another to any mass evacuation scheme. Victory at the Battle
of Midway in June 1942 greatly eased concerns, and by July Emmons pro-

claimed the conduct of the mass of Japanese was "highly satisfactory." In the end, after scaling down the target figures drastically, Emmons transferred only 1,875 Hawaiian residents of Japanese ancestry to the mainland. And most of these fell not into a category of "suspect loyalty" but of what might best be termed "useless mouths."

US Pacific Fleet: Command and Strategy

In the grim days after the attack on Pearl Harbor, as spilled oil fires flickered out and bodies bobbed until recovered, widespread doubt spread about restoring sunken vessels to service—or even that Pearl Harbor could function as a fleet base. Then in January 1942 Capt. Homer N. Wallin appeared, a salvage mastermind. By mid-1942, sunken battleships *California* and *Nevada* were refloated. Damaged ships repaired included battleships *Maryland*, *Pennsylvania*, and *Tennessee*, cruisers *Honolulu*, *Helena*, and *Raleigh*, destroyer *Shaw*, repair ship *Vestal*, and seaplane tender *Curtiss*. Wrecked destroyers *Cassin* and *Downes* provided parts transported to the West Coast, which were mated with two new hulls under the old names, but which were effectively new vessels. Wallin's crews raised ancient minelayer *Oglala* (beyond worthwhile repair) to clear an important berth.

Battleship *West Virginia* presented a greater challenge. Seven torpedoes ripped huge gashes in its port side, and then a fierce oil fire torched many interior compartments. In June 1942 within its refloated hull, workers discovered three bodies (among sixty-six recovered) resting in a storeroom. A calendar near them revealed a poignant "X" mark through every day from 7 to 23 December 1941, when their air pocket finally ran out of oxygen. Battleships *California* and *West Virginia* underwent massive rebuilding, making them near equals to the most modern battleships, save for speed, but neither would be ready for operations before 1944.

This left the hardest cases. Battleship *Oklahoma* rested upside down with its heavy tripod masts embedded in the harbor bottom. Ingenious engineering righted and raised it, but it was too outmoded for worthwhile repair. Beyond restoration also was target ship *Utah*; its hulk did not impede use of an important mooring. It is one of two victims of the Sunday morning attack still at Pearl Harbor. The other is *Arizona*. The completely shattered forward half of the vessel barred rebuilding. Of the 3,000 dives during all recovery operations, those on *Arizona* proved the most macabre. Hard-hatted explorers found its interior a massive crypt. Bodies constantly bumped or nudged the divers. Over the weeks, bodies progressively lost heads and flesh to decomposition and crab scavenging. Diver Edward Raymer described his horrifying first encounter with a corpse. In the pitch-black interior, he did not realize he had found a body until he inadvertently pushed his hand through the rotting chest of the dead man. Later he became accustomed to the sound "like wind chimes" of fleshless fingers scraping across his helmet. Eventually, the hull was abandoned. It was dedicated as a memorial in June 1962 and draws thousands of visitors each year.

The Pearl Harbor debacle produced major American command changes. To lead the navy in war, President Roosevelt summoned to Washington the commander of the Atlantic Fleet, Ernest J. King. The president appointed King as commander in chief, US Fleet. But the acronym CINCUS was pronounced like "sink us," which would hardly do after Pearl Harbor. Roosevelt granted King's request that the new acronym become COMINCH, and the title and the new acronym became the ones for which King was ever after best known. Harold Stark remained the chief of Naval Operations. Though both King and Stark tried their best to make the awkward arrangement effective, the overlap of responsibilities proved unworkable. In March 1942, Roosevelt transferred Stark to command navy forces in Europe and gave the CNO title and job to King.

From duty as chief of the navy's personnel bureau, Chester W. Nimitz received Roosevelt's nod to take the helm of the Pacific Fleet. It proved one of Roosevelt's most inspired personnel choices in the war. Working for the exacting taskmaster King still guaranteed trials under the best of circumstances. Working for him when one fundamentally disagreed with King's ardently held strategic view came close to terminating Nimitz's tenure as Pacific Fleet commander. On 30 December 1941 King directed Nimitz to cover and hold the line Hawaii-Midway and maintain communications with the West Coast. But secondly and "only in small degree less important," he must protect the sea lanes from the United States to Australia, primarily by covering the line Hawaii-Samoa with an extension to the Fiji Islands at the earliest practical date. Nimitz, however, deemed holding Hawaii his essential task rather than dissipating his much-diminished command south of the equator.

If disagreement on the critical mission of the Pacific Fleet was not enough, King's underlying prejudices boded ill for Nimitz. All acknowledged King's professional competence and powerful intellect. He brought unusually broad experience with work in submarines, salvage, and a conversion to naval aviation at an advanced stage of his career. Although crushed when he was passed over in 1939 for the top job in the navy, King managed to claw his way back into the mainstream by impressing the secretary of the navy with his work on fleet antiaircraft defenses, and then pleasing Roosevelt with his performance as Atlantic Fleet commander in the undeclared war with Germany. Stark told him in the fall of 1941 that when war came, he would retain command of the Atlantic Fleet, but Royal Ingersoll, a deputy King deemed excellent, would take the Pacific Fleet, while Chester Nimitz would take charge of the small Asiatic Fleet.

To King's stern eye, Nimitz owed his position not to demonstrated performance in the fleet, but to his ability to please Washington power brokers during two tours in the navy's personnel department. King referred to such flag officers as "fixers" inherently unfit for wartime command because their talents rested in managing and soothing egos and avoiding the unpleasantness of relieving the unfit. Unintentionally, Roosevelt gave King a near perfect opportunity to replace Nimitz. The inability of his beloved navy to score any striking success against the Axis in the first three months following Pearl Harbor ignited Roosevelt's ire. He turned to Secretary of the Navy Knox and demanded a list of the 40 "best" of the 120 officers then of flag rank. Knox convened a secret selection board to assemble the list and delivered the board's selections to Roosevelt in March. Nimitz's name did not appear among the list of the "best." The implicit message was that not only King, but also a distinguished panel of navy elders deemed Nimitz unfit for the most prized theater command in the navy. Roosevelt fortunately took no action. There is a strong hint in Nimitz's correspondence with his wife that he had learned of his nonselection by the secret board.

Rabaul

Although geographically well separated from Japan's other operations from December 1941, the Japanese targeted Rabaul because it formed a vital node in the defensive perimeter enfolding the newly expanded empire. With a superb harbor and nearby sites for airfields, Rabaul perches on the northeast tip of New Britain. From Rabaul the Solomon Islands formed footsteps tracking southeast. To the south, aircraft from Rabaul could command the Papua Peninsula on New Guinea, the glacis plate for Australia. Seizing Rabaul would also keep allied bombers out of range of Japan's key central Pacific base

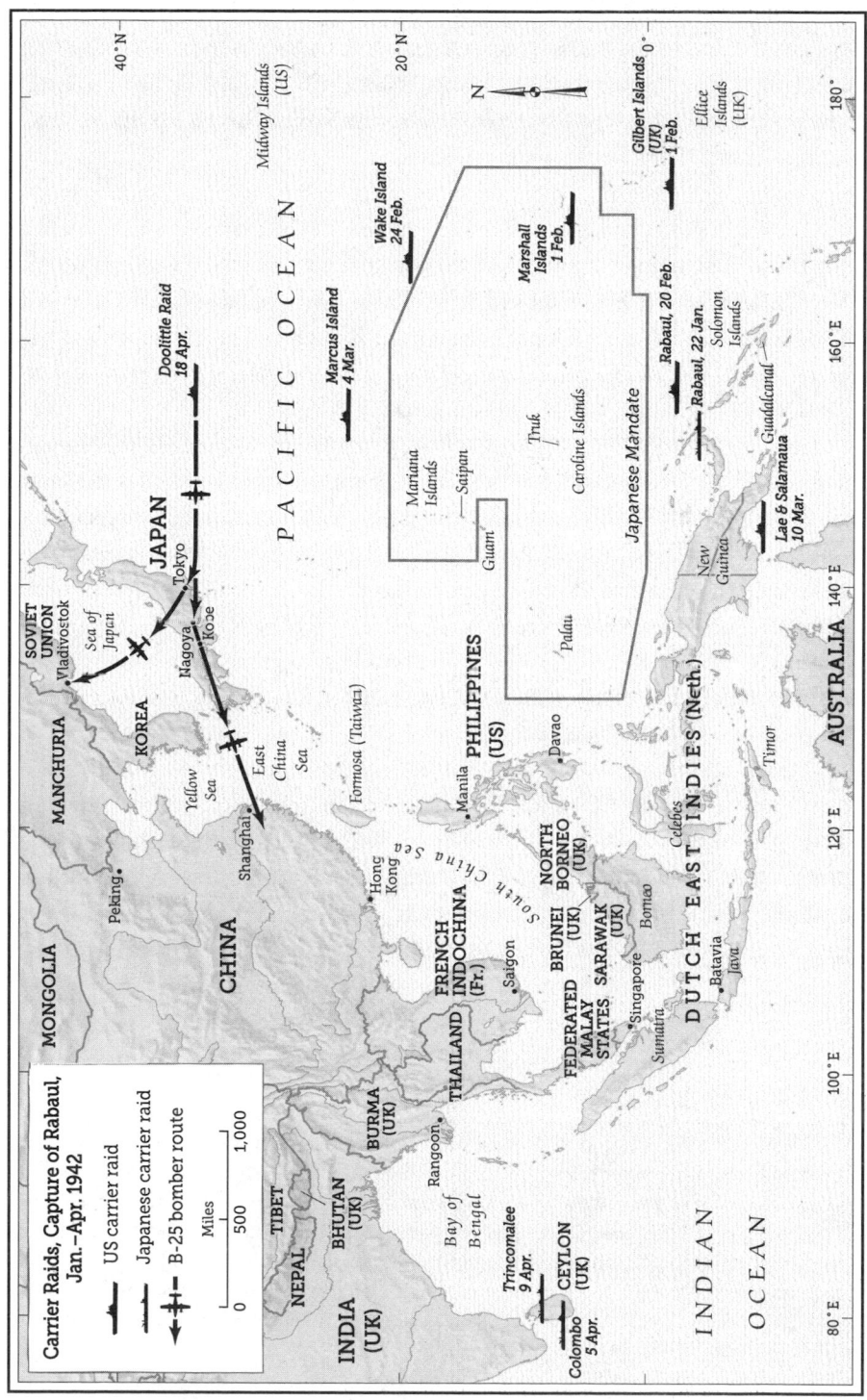

Carrier Raids, Capture of Rabaul,
Jan.–Apr. 1942

⌇ US carrier raid

⌇ Japanese carrier raid

✈ B-25 bomber route

Miles

0   500   1,000

at Truk. Australians readily recognized the strategic value of Rabaul but could spare only modest defenses. These comprised a battle group ("Lark Force") of 1,396 men (and six nurses). The air garrison consisted merely of four Hudsons and eight Wirraways.* Stern orders accompanied the senior officer, Col. John Scanlan: there would be no withdrawal.

The Japanese mounted a series of air raids on Rabaul on 4 January 1942, but the main effort commenced on 20 January. "Like a hunter sent to stalk a mouse with an elephant gun," said the strike leader, first line carriers *Akagi*, *Kaga*, *Shokaku*, and *Zuikaku* pummeled Rabaul with 101 aircraft. At a cost of one "Kate," they sank a merchant ship in the harbor and nearly wiped out the heroic attempted interception by eight hopelessly outclassed Wirraways (killing six and wounding 5 of 16 aircrew).

During the night of 22–23 January 1942, the Japanese landed three battalions of the 144th Regiment, South Seas Force commanded by Maj. Gen. Tomitaro Horii. Deciding that sustained resistance was futile, Scanlan declared it was "every man for himself." Part of the garrison trudged in great hardship to the northern coast and the other part to the southern coast. Those who went north eventually escaped by sea to Australia. The Japanese captured about 170 of those who went south at the Tol Plantation and executed some 160 by bayonet and bullet. Others escaped by sea and by air rescue. About 400 Australian servicemen reached Australia.

A cruel fate remorselessly pursued the Australians captured at Rabaul. In June the *Montevideo Maru* loaded Australian prisoners of war and civilian internees for passage to Japan. In the early hours of 1 July, the US submarine *Sturgeon* sank *Montevideo Maru*. The submarine crew of course had no inkling of their target's human cargo. All the 1,157 POWs and internees perished—the largest maritime disaster in Australian history—along with twenty crew and guards. The Japanese turned Rabaul into a bastion that became their key base in the South Pacific for two years.

---

* The two-seat Wirraway (an aboriginal word for "Challenge") was based on the US North American advanced trainer known variously as the AT-6 or SNJ. Australia adopted the Wirraway primarily as a stepping stone for development of its own aircraft industry based on its simple engine and airframe. Grotesquely outmatched by the Mitsubishi A6M "Zero," it was deemed a "temporary expedient" as a fighter bomber with a top speed straining for 220 mph and armament of three .30 caliber machine guns. Douglas Gillison, *Australia in the War of 1939–1945, Series Three, Air*, vol. 1, *The Royal Australian Air Force 1939–1942* (Canberra: Australian War Memorial, 1962), 46, 49, 137–38.

Initial US Carrier Raids

In the first weeks after Pearl Harbor, American carriers turned from the aborted relief of Wake Island to the shoring up of Hawaii's defenses. Reinforcing the small Marine garrison on Samoa with the 2nd Marine Brigade loomed as the largest January 1942 project. Carrier *Yorktown*, transferred from the Atlantic, escorted the Marines. Its arrival merely offset the temporary loss of *Saratoga*. After the Japanese submarine *I-6* put one torpedo into *Saratoga* on 11 January, the carrier sailed back for major repairs and alterations that would keep it out of action until June. As early as New Year's Day, Nimitz planned that Halsey's *Enterprise* task force would rendezvous with the *Yorktown* contingent, and the carrier duo would raid Japanese positions in the Gilbert and Marshall Islands.

Then the Japanese occupied Rabaul, an obvious springboard down into the South Pacific. Either in January or shortly thereafter, King's vision had leaped beyond a strategic defensive in the South Pacific. In one of the telling indicators of King's grasp as a strategist, he sidelined the US Navy's over-three-decades-old, sacrosanct War Plan Orange that called for a Central Pacific offensive mounted from Hawaii. But King balked at idleness in the Pacific. He plotted to create a necklace of bases across the South Pacific that not only secured Australia and New Zealand, but also afforded the foundation for an offensive that would pierce the Japanese defensive perimeter at the equator, not the international date line. Yet more impressive than even this farsighted plan stands King's basic conviction that the United States would produce enough resources for simultaneous offensives against Japan as well as Germany.

Very powerful crosscurrents from interservice clashes in Washington and global alliance politics ultimately advanced King's plan. The army air forces begrudged every plane and man diverted away from Northern Europe, where the army flyers intended to win the war by bombing Germany. A key February 1942 paper by then Brig. Gen. Dwight D. Eisenhower, now Marshall's chief planner, codified the army's strategic appraisal. Presuming the security of the United States and Hawaii, Eisenhower then set forth three prerequisites for winning the war: (1) maintain the United Kingdom, (2) keep the Soviet Union in the war, and (3) prevent Germany and Japan from linking up by protecting the Middle East and India. "We've got to go to Europe and fight," summarized Eisenhower, "we've got to quit wasting resources all over the world—and still worse—wasting time."

Eisenhower identified King—correctly—as the adamant American opponent of the army's plan. The acrimonious exchanges King generated prompted Eisenhower to scrawl in his diary: "One thing that might help win this war is to get someone to shoot King." But then the Japanese furthered King's vision by imperiling Australia and New Zealand. In his typically blunt way, King cut to the racial as well as strategic status of the two nations as "white men's countries," adding their loss would provoke adverse consequences "among the non-white races of the world." Though Churchill and Roosevelt were prepared to run risks in the Pacific to maintain their "Europe First" strategic vision, they would not abide the loss of these two British Commonwealth nations. The inescapable corollary to holding the two Commonwealth nations was that their communication lines also must be shielded. King labored assiduously to secure army cooperation in setting up a chain of bases that included Canton Island, Christmas Island, Fiji, Samoa, Bora Bora, and New Caledonia. Thus, King's island base network became an integral part of Allied global strategy.

During the exchanges between King and Nimitz, the Japanese occupied Rabaul, and radio intelligence pointed to a Japanese shift of forces out of the Marshalls toward the south. This combination prompted strident, even sarcastic, cables from King to Nimitz demanding action. On 24 January, *Enterprise* and *Yorktown* finally set course for the first American carrier raids of the war. An officer on *Enterprise* put the dominant attitude to verse: "An eye for an eye, a tooth for a tooth, this Sunday it's our turn to shoot." But Halsey's sailors understandably felt uncertain about what they would encounter. The actual defenders in the Marshalls and Gilberts belied Japan's formidable façade in the Pacific. Part of the Twenty-Fourth Air Flotilla (*kōkū sentai*) provided aerial defense with just forty-nine planes. The thirty-three fighters and nine land attack planes were both second line Mitsubishi products: the A5M ("Claude") and the G3M ("Nell"). Of the seven Kawanishi H6K ("Mavis") flying boats, the three at Makin constituted the sole aerial garrison of the Gilberts.

This would be the first battle of Halsey's career, but far from the last. He projected a powerful presence with his more than medium height, wide shoulders, and barrel chest. One journalist described how his "wide mouth held tight and turned down at the corners and exceedingly bushy eyebrows gave his face, in a grizzled sea dog way, an appearance of good humor." There was tremendous candle power when that broad mouth broke into a grin signaling Halsey's overall zest for life—and combat. No one mistook him for an intellectual, but he was aptly described as "brilliant in common sense," particularly about the importance of morale and above all aggression. Before the seasons would cycle, Halsey would emerge as Nimitz's most valued subordinate.

The dawn of 1 February found Halsey's Task Force 8 off the Marshalls shrouded in clouds and facing a dilemma about whether similar conditions cloaked their targets. An ingenious ploy overcame this quandary: the ship board radio intelligence detachment intercepted and decoded the local Japanese weather report predicting clear weather over the islands! *Enterprise* sliced off sixty-one planes to attack Kwajalein, Wotje, and Taroa. Halsey sent all his heavy cruisers and four destroyers to bombard Wotje and Taroa. This left *Enterprise* with a scant six F4Fs and three destroyers for self-defense. The scheme reflected Halsey's signature: overwhelming commitment to attack rather than prudent defense.

From dawn to early afternoon American planes swarmed over their targets while the cruisers and destroyers joined in the bombardment. At 1330, a formation of five "Nells" burst out of clouds to pounce on *Enterprise*, where Halsey stood conspicuously attired in a white sun helmet. The *Enterprise* adroitly sidestepped the Japanese bombs, but the lead plane with both engines ablaze veered around for a suicide attempt. The "Nell" scraped a wingtip along *Enterprise*'s flight deck before exploding in the water. The day's action cost Halsey one fighter in a takeoff accident and five SBDs, three to Japanese fighters. The Japanese lost four planes in the air and about ten on the ground. Halsey's flyers and gunners sank a transport and three small Japanese auxiliary vessels. They damaged the light cruiser *Katori*, a submarine, a submarine depot ship, and four transports. The attack wounded Vice Adm. Mitsumi Shimizu, Sixth (Submarine) Fleet commander, and killed Rear Adm. Yasuhiro Yukichi, the Marshall Islands commander. Yukichi was the first Japanese admiral killed in the war.

Much less luck attended Fletcher's *Yorktown* group off the Gilberts, where a feeble dawn revealed dense overcast and squalls. The Jaliut strike mission proved especially ill-starred. Weather claimed no fewer than four TBDs and two SBDs. Another SBD and a cruiser SOC were lost on local patrols over the task force. Of all these airmen, only one SBD crew was recovered. *Yorktown* fighters shot down one Japanese flying boat. That plane and two peers destroyed at their moorings represented the very small profit to offset the heavy losses.

Meanwhile Task Force 11 (Vice Adm. Wilson Brown), built around carrier *Lexington*, sortied from Pearl Harbor and headed south on 31 January. A major US Army garrison was detailed to land on New Caledonia, important for its location and its nickel deposits. At the same time, the ANZAC (Australia-New Zealand) Command had been set up under Vice Adm. Herbert F. Leary. Its original composition included Australian, New Zealand, and American cruisers and American destroyers. *Lexington* would cover the movement to New Caledonia and then join in the defense of the ANZAC area.

Reaching the Fijis by 14 February, Wilson Brown secured permission for a strike at Rabaul. On 20 February *Lexington*, by now with four heavy cruisers and ten destroyers, closed on Rabaul from the northeast. A Japanese "Mavis" flying boat from Rabaul detected Brown at 1030. The Twenty-Fourth Air Flotilla commander dispatched seventeen bomb-laden Mitsubishi G4M "Bettys" of the spanking new 4th Air Group, only formed at Truk on 10 February. No fighters accompanied the strike group. The leader, Lt. Cdr. Takuzō Itō, split his formation to multiply the chances of finding the Americans in the clouds. The second contingent of nine approached *Lexington* first. Wildcats accounted for five, including the leader. *Lexington* avoided bombs from the remaining four. One crippled bomber fell just short in a suicide attack. The last four "Bettys" fell to fighters and a dive bomber on withdrawal. The Japanese shot down two Wildcats, but one pilot survived.

Although all sixty-three Japanese airmen perished in this first wave, their sighting report brought the other eight "Bettys" boring in toward *Lexington*. The bad news for the Americans was that all but two of the available American fighters had been drawn away after the first contingent, and the guns of one of this last pair failed. The bad news for the Japanese was that Lt. Edward "Butch" O'Hare grasped the controls of the sole remaining effective defender. With deadly skill and determination, O'Hare executed repeated passes, shooting down three of the bombers outright. Another ditched due to the damage he inflicted. Then O'Hare's incredibly accurate fire literally blew one engine off the aircraft bearing Lt. Cdr. Itō. The Japanese bombs missed *Lexington*, but Itō's Betty bore in on a suicide dive. Antiaircraft machine guns on *Lexington* completed the job that O'Hare started. The valiant Japanese flyers died as their aircraft crashed astern of their target.

The aerial melee transpired in full view of the sailors of the task force. Admiral Brown admonished his exuberantly cheering staff that this was not "a football game." Of the second Japanese formation, one aircraft ditched at sea and three staggered back to Rabaul, where one ditched in the harbor. Thus, only two of the seventeen Bettys survived. Four Japanese search planes were also shot down or disappeared this day. Brown, with surprise lost and ignorant of his devastation of Rabaul's air garrison, called off the raid. For his performance, one of the greatest individual feats of the war, O'Hare was awarded the Medal of Honor.

February 24 found Halsey's *Enterprise* task force steaming toward Wake

Island into pitch blackness comprised of dense overcast punctuated by berserk winds and horizontal rains. In high humidity the propellers wiped the vivid blue tinted exhaust flames into blinding halos. One SBD of a strike group of fifty-one planes crashed on takeoff due to the pilot becoming disoriented from the halos. He survived but his gunner did not. It was a vivid example of the thousands of planes on both sides claimed by weather during the war.

At a cost of one SBD to antiaircraft fire and a Wildcat to an accident, the task force inflicted modest air and sea losses on the Japanese. Nimitz then authorized Halsey to raid Marcus Island, only 1,000 miles from Tokyo. Leaving his destroyers behind, Halsey took *Enterprise* and two heavy cruisers on a high-speed dash to launch a surprise strike scheduled to hit before dawn, 4 March. At a cost of one SBD, the *Enterprise* flyers beat up on Marcus.

While Halsey struck in the Central Pacific, Fletcher, in *Yorktown* with two heavy cruisers, six destroyers, and the ever-present oiler, sortied from Pearl Harbor on 16 February and pointed bows south. On 27 February, Nimitz ordered Fletcher to join Brown's *Lexington* task force and attack Rabaul. But the Japanese changed this plan when a twenty-two-ship task group commenced landing troops at Lae and Salamaua on the northern coast of New Guinea's Papuan Peninsula.

News of the Japanese landing reached American commanders on 8 March. Brown, the senior officer afloat, developed a plan to attack the Japanese ships unloading off Lae and Salamaua, but from the south, over the Owen Stanley Mountains from the Gulf of Papua. He intended this approach to keep the carriers out of sight of Japanese search planes from Rabaul. Hastily assembled information identified a pass through the mountains at 7,500 feet, normally cloud-free until about 1100. This became the approach path for a massive strike by fifty-two aircraft from each carrier. The first thirteen torpedo-armed TBDs failed to gain altitude as fast as the terrain rose, and it appeared they would have to turn back. But the squadron commander, Lt. Cdr. James Brett—an experienced glider pilot—recognized signs of an updraft and guided his squadron over the pass via this unorthodox climb technique. Although the American flyers seriously overstated the damage they inflicted, they managed to sink a transport and an auxiliary minelayer, and damage a light cruiser, three destroyers, the seaplane tender, two minelayers, and two minesweepers. This was by far the most telling blow struck by American carriers to date.

Later achievements vastly overshadowed these early American carrier raids, but they were extremely important. They rebuilt morale damaged by Pearl Harbor, but of even more significance, they validated prewar theoretical, operational, and basic tactical concepts and battle-tested the carrier air groups. Without this preparation, American carriers would have been at a severe disadvantage in the great carrier battles of 1942. Halsey became a public hero, a status he retained for the rest of the war.

Indian Ocean Raid

After just four months of spectacular triumphs, Japan had attained its core strategic objectives: to secure war-sustaining resources behind a defensive perimeter that would exhaust and drive to a negotiated peace its materially more powerful opponents. Imperial Navy strategists, heady with success, deemed it folly to yield the initiative to Japan's adversaries. They inspected three basic options: strike east against the Hawaiian-based US main fleet; strike south against Australia before it became a secure platform for counterattack; or strike west toward the Indian Ocean. They first chose option three, which also beckoned with the prospect of strategic convergence with Japan's German ally.

A sortie by major Japanese naval units into the Indian Ocean would ensure passage of Rangoon-bound convoys, thus accelerating the conquest of Burma, and solidify a western defensive perimeter coincident with seizure of the Andaman Islands on 23 March. For these purposes, the Imperial Navy dispatched two forces into the Indian Ocean. Nagumo's First Air Fleet would target British naval forces at Ceylon (now Sri Lanka). Simultaneously, Vice Adm. Jisaburō Ozawa's Second Expeditionary Fleet would maul Allied shipping and lash at land targets in India, in conjunction with long-range bombers.

When Nagumo surged into the Indian Ocean on 26 March, he commanded the most powerful single assemblage of naval might in the world, including five fleet carriers (*Akagi, Sōryū, Hiryū, Shokaku,* and *Zuikaku,* embarking some 275 aircraft), four fast battleships (*Hiei, Kirishima, Kongo,* and *Haruna*), two heavy cruisers, one light cruiser, and ten destroyers. On 1 April, Ozawa's formidable command sortied with light carrier *Ryujo,* four heavy cruisers, a light cruiser, four destroyers, and three oilers.

British code breakers correctly identified Colombo on Ceylon as a Japanese target, and Britain scrambled to bolster defenses of Ceylon and India. Vice Adm. James Somerville now commanded the Eastern Fleet, a leader who had done much with little in the Mediterranean. Somerville partly masked his high intelligence by standing out even among sailors with a "peculiar sense of bawdy humor" and profusely obscene conversation. But he led far more by inspiration than fear, particularly among ordinary sailors for whom he had displayed unusual paternal interest by Royal Navy standards.

Somerville divided his markedly heterogeneous command. Force A, the fast contingent, featured the new fleet carriers *Indomitable* and *Formidable*, the modernized battleship *Warspite*, two old but fast 6-inch gun cruisers, and six destroyers. Between them the carriers counted just ninety-four aircraft. These included thirty-seven fighters (sixteen Grumman F4F Wildcats, known in British service as Martlet IIs, nine Sea Hurricanes, and a dozen Fulmars) and a fifty-seven-carrier attack aircraft (the plodding, dreadfully vulnerable Swordfish and Albacore biplanes). "I drove my car faster than I landed a Swordfish," lamented one British pilot. The Royal Navy possessed a reliable air-launched torpedo, and Albacores fitted with radar. This gave the Royal Navy an unmatched capability that Somerville seized as his only conceivable option: somehow, with slower ships, to get close enough to Nagumo to launch a surprise, radar-guided night torpedo plane attack. Force B, Somerville's slow division, consisted of the elderly small carrier *Hermes*, embarking a mere dozen Swordfish. Somerville intended to group it with four aged and sluggish "*Royal Sovereign*" class battleships, three cruisers (one Dutch), and eight destroyers. There were also seven submarines available. The British braced for what Churchill called "breath-taking events."

Based on erroneous intelligence that Nagumo had only two carriers and that he would strike on 1 April, Somerville stationed his Force A to the south of Ceylon. On 2 April he withdrew to refuel. This inadvertently avoided disaster as Nagumo's forces approached three days later and much farther westerly than Somerville expected. Had Somerville still been in his original waiting position, he would have been trapped with the Japanese between Force A and his base, with likely disastrous consequences for Britain's and the Allied cause in the Indian Ocean.

At 1100, 5 April—Easter Sunday, a date the Japanese hoped would find the British doubly unwary—127 Japanese carrier aircraft pierced through the stormy skies over Colombo, the naval base on the southwest coast of Ceylon. The A6Ms soundly thrashed the forty-two defending British fighters. The attackers proceeded to sink destroyer *Tenedos* and an armed merchant cruiser and to pummel the dock facilities. They destroyed in the air or on the ground thirty-three British planes. The Japanese paid for these achievements with just one A6M and six Vals.

Meanwhile a search plane sighted the British heavy cruisers *Dorsetshire* and *Cornwall* at sea, without air cover, about three hundred miles southwest of Ceylon and racing to rendezvous with Force A. Commencing at 1638, fifty-three "Vals" with "shiny black noses," noted a British officer, delivered one of the most impressive dive-bombing exhibitions of the war. About ten bomb hits sank *Dorsetshire* in just seven minutes; *Cornwall* lasted barely twelve minutes after nine direct hits and six near misses. Some 424 British sailors perished, but 1,122 were rescued. Worse still, had the Japanese surmised the presence of or detected Somerville's Force A merely seventy miles distant from the two cruisers, they might have inflicted a disaster greater than the loss of *Prince of Wales* and *Repulse*. Later that day, Somerville and Nagumo maneuvered much closer toward each other than either recognized, granting Somerville an opportunity to strike a deadly blow at Nagumo and Nagumo a chance to do the same to Somerville.

By 7 April, the Admiralty wisely authorized Somerville to retreat to the African coast to protect the vital shipping lanes to the Middle East. But Somerville pursued his now foolhardy stalking of far more powerful Nagumo as the latter wheeled away from Ceylon and then closed again to a launch position at dawn on 9 April, this time to strike the British base at Trincomalee on the northeastern coast of Ceylon. Some 132 Japanese planes sank one merchant ship in the nearly empty harbor, damaged the monitor *Erebus*, and blasted ship and nearby air facilities, shooting down nine British aircraft and destroying at least fourteen aircraft on the ground. A second strike of eighty-five "Vals" and nine Zeros harvested ships near Trincomalee. They savaged *Hermes* with many hits. The small carrier, as well as its escort, the destroyer *Vampire*, sank in fifteen minutes. The captains of both vessels perished, as did 313 other crew members. Other "Vals" also put down corvette *Hollyhock* (fifty-three dead), two fleet oilers, and a merchant ship, but spared a clearly marked hospital ship. Belatedly arriving Fulmars sent to save *Hermes* shot down four "Vals" in exchange for two of their number. Meanwhile, nine Blenheim bombers reached Nagumo's formation undetected, but their bombs missed flagship *Akagi* and battleship *Kongo*. Zeros then exchanged two of their number for five Blenheims. This was Nagumo's first taste of an enemy air attack.

While Nagumo administered his blows, Ozawa's fleet wreaked great execution against shipping in the Bay of Bengal. On 6 April, they sank nineteen ships, totaling about 88,165 tons, the worst single day loss of the war for Allied shipping. By the end of the cruise, Ozawa's command accounted for about twenty ships of approximately 93,247 tons. Meanwhile, six Japanese submarines operating on the west side of India sank another 32,000 tons. During this interval, *Ryujo* planes, as well as long-range aircraft from Burma, attacked several cities in Eastern India. Material damage was slight, but the attacks that seemed to herald an invasion caused a huge panic. Wavell, now the commander in chief, India, declared that this was "India's Most Dangerous Hour."

Churchill was now seriously wounded politically by the parade of catastrophes in the Far East and yet a new reversal in the Middle East, as Rommel counterattacked and regained much lost ground. The Imperial Navy Indian Ocean raid marked one of his lowest points in the war. In a 15 April cable to Roosevelt, Churchill warned that the Japanese pivot not only could herald the loss of Ceylon, but also the prospect of an invasion of Eastern India "with incalculable internal consequences to our whole war plan and including . . . all contact with the Chinese through Burma." But these represented only two selections on a menu of disasters. Interdiction of the sea lanes in the Western Indian Ocean threatened to collapse Britain's Middle Eastern position by cutting off the reinforcement route around Africa. It would extinguish Britain's ability to maintain air or land forces in the Indian Ocean area by denying the flow of oil from Abadan. It would also block any further shipping of supplies to the Soviet Union via the Persian Gulf. (It will be recalled that blocking an Axis linkup in the India Ocean ranked on Eisenhower's list as one of the three essential strategic prerequisites to Allied victory.) To deal with these "immense perils," Churchill pleaded for US naval resources. In his postwar memoirs, Churchill omitted this despairing message as apparently too painful to mention.

Roosevelt responded promptly but guardedly. He lamented "the present lack of naval butter to cover the bread," especially in the Indian Ocean. He promised more land-based planes, but declined to send US ships as requested. The US carrier *Ranger* brought some aircraft that could forestall a Japanese invasion of India while Britain built up strength in that region.

Even before Nagumo's raid, in early March Churchill declared to Roosevelt that the "greatest danger" would arise if the Japanese seized Madagascar from the Vichy French (who had yielded Indochina without a fight) and interdicted the critical shipping lanes around the Cape of Good Hope. Accordingly, the British mounted Operation Ironclad, a preemptive strike to deny Madagascar to the Japanese. Naval covering forces included two fleet carriers, *Illustrious* from the Mediterranean and *Indomitable* from Somerville's Eastern Fleet, a battleship, cruisers, destroyers, lesser warships, and vessels bearing the landing force composed of the 29th Independent Brigade and No. 5 Commando. Backing them were two brigades of the British 5th Division.

The surprise assault commenced before dawn on 5 May. By the 7th, British numbers and naval superiority won the day and the garrison surrendered.

Over a hundred British troops died and about three hundred were wounded. French casualties, mostly colonial troops, totaled 150 killed and some 500 wounded. British planes sank one French submarine. The Japanese responded with a midget submarine attack on 30 May. It seriously damaged battleship *Ramilles* and sank a British tanker. This operation was notable as the first British amphibious assault since the Dardanelles in World War I. The French still held central and southern Madagascar. After stalemated negotiations, and at the urging of Prime Minister Jan Smuts of South Africa, the British with African and South African troops mounted further operations that ultimately ended in the 6 November 1942 surrender of French forces.

India Crisis: The Cripps Mission

The Japanese raid into the Indian Ocean coincided with a political crisis in India. The slightest hint of the end of British rule of India turned Churchill incandescent with rage. Churchill's sojourn as a subaltern in India in the nineteenth century, untainted by any depth of knowledge of its peoples, formed his views. He retained a romantic vision of Britain as an enlightened steward over a mosaic of fractious peoples incapable of unity or self-government—a stance reformist India Secretary Leo Amery called "early Kipling." While most members of his cabinet did not partake Churchill's rigid stance, the British viceroy in India, Lord Linlithgow,[*] surpassed even Churchill's imperialist fervor. In February 1940, Churchill pronounced the "Hindu/Muslim feud" as "the bulwark of British rule in India." But therein lay one tragically true strand of Churchill's general belief system: by this point Indian independence meant partition of the country accompanied by an enormous eruption of internecine bloodletting.

Four events led the way to the 1942 crisis. Parliament passed Government of India Acts in 1919 and 1935, the latter over Churchill's vociferous objection. While they nudged forward the prospect of Indian democratic governance and dominion status within the British Commonwealth, this shimmered below a very indistinct future horizon. Then in September 1939, the viceroy declared India at war with Germany without any consultation with Indian

---

[*]   Victor Alexander John Hope, Second Marquess of Linlithgow. He served in the trenches in World War I and was active in politics. He was governor general and viceroy in India from 1936 to 1943, the longest tenure of any viceroy during the Raj. He is not fondly recalled in India.

leaders. In August 1940, Britain announced its objective of dominion status for India, and establishment of a representative body that would be set up after the war to devise a constitution. Churchill entered 1942 thinking this status quo would hold, but the stunning Japanese victories in Malaya and Burma raised not only a military threat to India, but also what many Indians embraced as the moment to secure their independence.

The complexity at this moment of the political firmament in India bars extended dissection. Hindu politicians reflecting the population's majority dominated the Congress Party (technically the Indian National Congress), the largest player. The party's goal: Indian independence as a unitary state within its existing borders. Though most leaders abhorred Hitler, Congress voted for neutrality at the beginning of the European war, arguing that independence formed the prerequisite for supporting Britain. Even as the Japanese advanced toward India's borders, Congress maintained that the Japanese would not attack an independent India.

The next-largest participant was the Muslim League, headed by Mohamed Ali Jinnah. By this time, Jinnah and his supporters believed a unified, independent India meant a Hindu-dominated state that would subject Muslims to religious, social, and political discrimination. Consequently, the Muslims advocated continued British rule, or separate independent Hindu and Muslim majority states. Quite apart from other considerations, the disproportionate Muslim share of the Indian Army (about one-third), then critically involved in Britain's war effort, left the British obliged to appease Jinnah and his party. The "princely states" formed the other major political player. These relics comprised a patchwork of widely disparate territories with perhaps 80 million inhabitants ruled by "princes" under British suzerainty. Their rulers knew an independent Indian government would waste little time in extinguishing their power, hence they preferred the continuation of British rule.

The spiritual, though not the official leader of the Congress Party, was the already internationally renowned figure of Mohandas K. Gandhi. He championed an independent unified India in which Hindus and Muslims would live in peace and harmony. His famous advocacy of nonviolence separated him from some Hindu leaders, who by no means rejected force.

Gandhi made Churchill apoplectic. There were reasons. Gandhi's aspirations for peaceful coexistence of Hindus and Muslims prompted him to tailor his statements regarding the Jews to maintain favor with Muslims. In November 1938, he counseled German Jews to adhere to a nonviolent path, even if that meant accepting "massacre" at German hands. Later he observed that it might take the "immolation of hundreds, if not thousands [of Jews], to appease the hunger of the dictators." At the time of Hitler's triumphs in 1940, Gandhi stated that he wished Britain neither defeated nor victorious, and he urged the British to fight the Germans without weapons and only with "non-violent arms" while inviting Hitler and Mussolini to "take what they want of the countries you call your possessions." Not only should the British offer all their material possessions to the dictators but also "you will allow yourself, every man, woman and child, to be slaughtered."

Because of the obvious critical importance of India to China's ability to sustain the war, Chiang and his wife traveled to India in February 1942. Chiang shared the goal of Indian independence, but he sought to mediate an interim agreement that would enlist the Indians to cooperate with the British and support China against Japan in return for immediate autonomy. He met with a vast spectrum of Indian and British leaders, including Gandhi, but the British refused to grant immediate autonomy and the Indians stood fast that without at least that, they would offer China no more than moral sympathy.

Although Churchill contemplated traveling to India himself, the press of events in early 1942 scotched that plan. Instead, Churchill sent Sir Stafford Cripps—a choice adding another layer of complexity, as Cripps at that time loomed with Anthony Eden as the most plausible candidates to replace the politically damaged Churchill as prime minister. Cripps carried a proposal embossed with the unanimous approval of the coalition War Cabinet promising postwar self-government, albeit with provisos that would have allowed for partition of India to accommodate Muslims and others, but insisting that India must conform to British rule during the war. Congress found the prospect of partition a bitter pill, but might have swallowed it had their counter-proposals been met. The British acceded to a demand for an Indian defense minister, but insisted the commander in chief could not surrender his major duties to a civilian head during the war. London also rejected the demand that the viceroy treat the new Indian council as a cabinet and follow its decisions. Fundamentally, Congress pursued effective Indian independence while the British stood adamant that they must continue to control India in wartime, and particularly its armed forces. The gap could not be bridged.

Pleased with this outcome Churchill recalled Cripps, but Roosevelt now intervened. Many Americans saw the situation in India as a rerun of the story of their own path to independence from Britain. Likewise, Gandhi enjoyed much admiration in the United States. On 11 April, Roosevelt cabled Churchill that most Americans were assigning blame overwhelmingly to Britain for not having recognized an Indian right of self-government, "notwithstanding the willingness of the Indians to entrust technical, military and naval defense control to competent British authorities"—a characterization that glided over the Indian demand for ultimate say over whether there should be any "defense" at all.

Hopkins was present when the message arrived and later told Secretary Stimson that it ignited from Churchill a "string of cuss words last[ing] two hours in the middle of the night." Churchill's eruption reflected his view that Roosevelt had intruded on a purely British matter and further, as historian Max Hastings has observed, Churchill deemed it "rank cant for a nation which had itself colonized North American continent, dispossessing and largely exterminating its indigenous population, and which still practiced racial segregation, to harangue others about the treatment of native peoples." Roosevelt's intrusion failed to alter the outcome of the Cripps Mission, but it served notice that the Americans would be unbounded in their willingness to meddle in the postwar order. The great crisis of 1942 in India was yet to come.

The Doolittle Raid

To Churchill's requests for US naval support against the Japanese intrusion into the Indian Ocean, Roosevelt replied that "measures now in hand by Pacific Fleet have not been conveyed to you in detail because of secrecy requirements but we hope you will find them effective when they can be made known to you shortly." This was a reference to the event that would be known as the Doolittle Raid. As early as 21 December 1941, Roosevelt demanded that the United States strike back by bombing Japan. The conventional story is that Capt. Francis Low (oddly, a submarine specialist) on Admiral King's staff proposed the innovative scheme of the carrier *Hornet* transporting army air force, twin-engine, B-25 medium bombers to a position from which they would take off and bomb Tokyo. But there was an intriguing prologue. In discussing plans for a landing in Northwest Africa during the "Arcadia" Conference, King brought up a proposal for using three carriers: one to haul fighters, a second to haul bombers, and a third to haul army bombers earmarked to carry supplies like bombs and gasoline ashore. This third carrier project required that army bombers take off from a navy carrier.

Volunteer B-25 crews practiced extremely short takeoff runs and then loaded onto *Hornet*. Carrier *Enterprise* accompanied it, as the B-25s blocked

Hornet's own flight operations. The task force, under Vice Adm. William F. Halsey Jr., included four cruisers, eight destroyers, and two oilers. The ultimate plan called for launching Doolittle's men about five hundred miles from Tokyo for a night attack, after which the planes would head for airfields readied for them in China. For security reasons (with the insecurity of Chinese codes no doubt in mind), the Chinese were not informed of the plan until a few days before the raid. Chiang immediately objected that he needed time to move his forces to protect the airfields, which the Japanese would strive to capture after the attack. Washington told him it was too late for delay, but that the sixteen planes would become part of his air force. On the morning of 18 April, Japanese patrol boats sighted the task force. Halsey and Doolittle agreed to an immediate takeoff, though this meant a daylight attack and the planes' having barely enough fuel to reach the Chinese bases.

Still and motion pictures of the dramatic launch remain classics of the war. *Hornet's* prow pointed into a wind registering over forty knots. The heavy swells tossed its bow in violent pitches, sometimes spewing green water across the flight deck. With a bare 467 feet of soaked flight deck before him, Doolittle piloted the first plane off in an agonizing climb at the edge of a fatal stall. The remaining fifteen wallowed off behind their leader. The raiders achieved complete surprise; although their bombs generally inflicted little material injury, they did damage the Japanese carrier *Ryuho*. One plane landed in the Soviet Union, where its crew was interned. The other fifteen, fuel exhausted, crashed in China, with three crewmen killed. The Japanese captured eight flyers and executed three as "war criminals."

The "Doolittle Raid" would long be celebrated in the United States, where word of the brave feat sent American morale soaring. Doolittle received the nation's highest decoration, and all his men were rightly honored as heroes. Understandably, the episode would not be fondly recalled in Japan, where it came as a tremendous psychological shock. Nor would the raid arouse pleasant memories in China, for the Japanese struck with pitiless reprisals against civilians in the areas where Doolittle's men landed. A justly irate Chiang cabled Marshall that not only had the Japanese overrun the eastern airfields as predicted, but also that they unleashed their rage by "slaughtering every man, woman and child in these areas—let me repeat every man, woman and child." Estimates of Chinese military and civilian deaths ran as high as 250,000—if this figure is correct, it would likely exceed fatalities from the atomic bombs. Moreover, Chiang committed troops to confront the Japanese in Zhejiang and Jiangxi provinces, and suffered some 30,000 casualties.

Bataan Falls

The fate of besieged Bataan was determined not by Japanese arms but by malaria and malnutrition. Malaria is endemic to the Philippines. Supplies of quinine, the only control method available to USAFFE, ran out by 15 February. Thereafter, malaria raged within the Bataan garrison, but it was neither the only disease nor the only factor gradually reducing the defenders to a paralyzing debility.

The garrison went on half rations on 5 January. Initially these provided a maximum of 2,000 calories per day, but were grossly deficient in protein, fat, and vitamins. The official daily ration sank to 1,000 calories by early March and sank near the vanishing point by 1 April. One Philippine Scout officer explained, "because of filching along the way," a "half ration" became more like a quarter ration" when it reached his men. The ration fell short of daily dietary needs on Bataan by about one-half and later three-quarters, so each man's body ransacked stored fat and then muscle mass to meet metabolic needs—typically reducing a soldier's weight by one-third. Obviously, this had a devastating effect on stamina and susceptibility to other maladies. It triggered diseases—beriberi, pellagra, scurvy, and rickets among them. This constellation assaulted the peripheral and central nervous system and motor functions, producing symptoms of pain, weakness, lethargy, night blindness, hand and foot drop, and mental impairment.

Clipped clinical descriptions offer a very pale reflection of Bataan's reality. Because of contaminated water and poor nutrition, a host of digestive diseases, dysentery foremost among them, made diarrhea epidemic. Men would not or could not take basic sanitary measures, and the front lines and encampments could be located by the stench of feces alone. Up to early March, the hospitals coped with the patient load, but from around 7 March, a surge of hundreds of cases a day overwhelmed the hospital system. By the end of that month, malaria admissions alone touched a thousand cases per day. The hospital admission figures understate the problem, for as many as 7,000 or more sick men remained with their units. "Men with malaria and temperatures of 102 and 103 degrees [Fahrenheit] lay beside their foxholes because they could not be moved to the rear." Even more pitiful were the civilian encampments. A combination of the lack of available food and abysmal sanitary conditions produced an appalling death rate.

This somber recitation depicts a portrait of human torment that extends

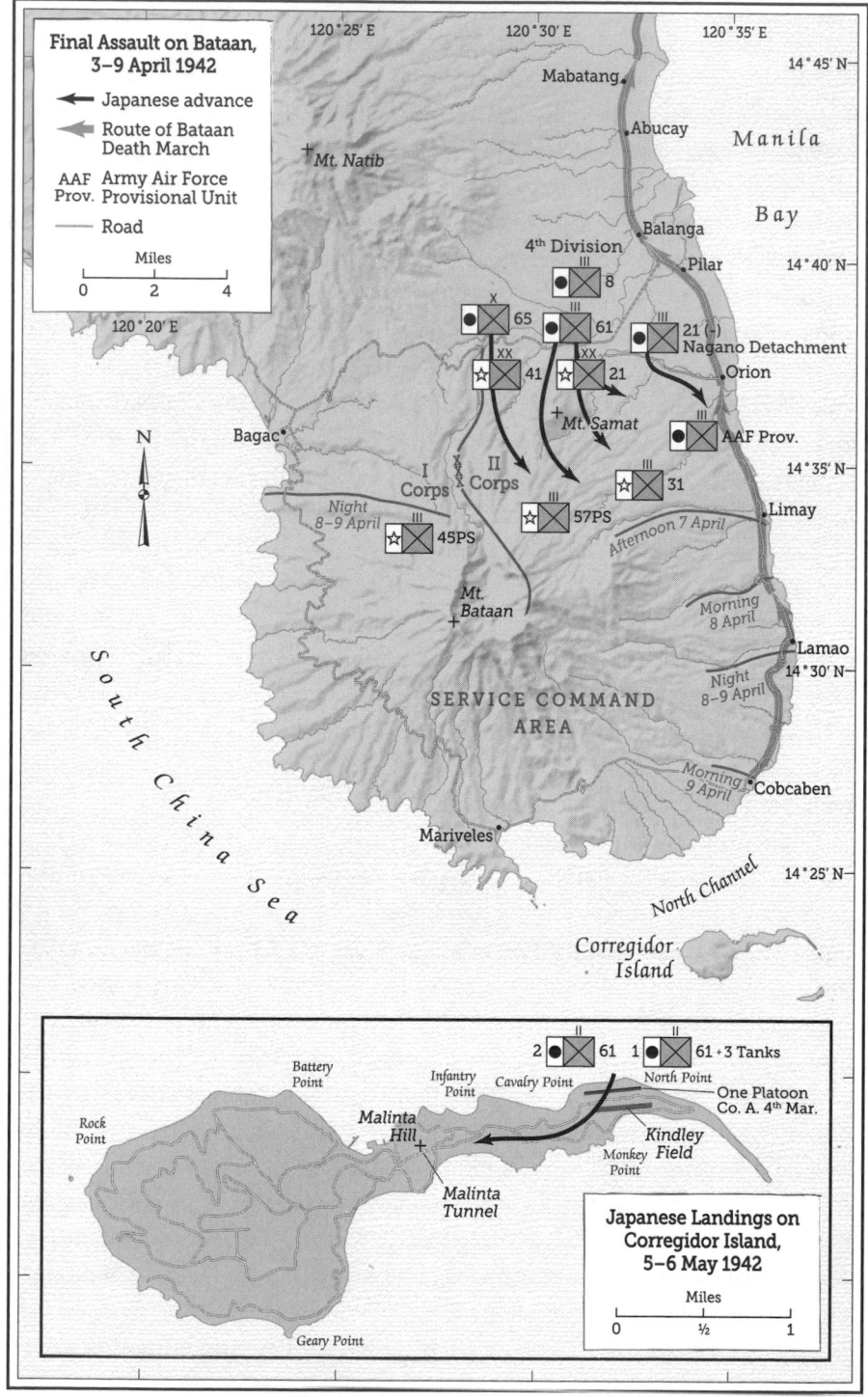

Final Assault on Bataan,
3–9 April 1942

→ Japanese advance

← Route of Bataan
Death March

AAF   Army Air Force
Prov.   Provisional Unit

━━ Road

Miles
0   2   4

N

Mt. Natib

Mabatang

Abucay

Manila

Balanga

Pilar

Bay

4th Division   8

65   61   21 (-)
                          Nagano Detachment

41   21   Orion

Mt. Samat   AAF Prov.

Bagac

I
Corps

II
Corps

31

Night
8–9 April   57PS   Limay

45PS   Afternoon 7 April

Mt.
Bataan

SERVICE COMMAND
AREA

Morning
8 April

Lamao

Night
8–9 April

Morning
9 April   Cobcaben

South China Sea

Mariveles

North Channel

Corregidor
Island

2   61   1   61 + 3 Tanks

Battery
Point

Rock
Point

Infantry
Point   Cavalry Point   North Point

One Platoon
Co. A. 4th Mar.

Malinta
Hill

Kindley
Field

Monkey
Point

Malinta
Tunnel

Japanese Landings on
Corregidor Island,
5–6 May 1942

Miles
0   ½   1

Geary Point

far beyond Bataan. The majority of the deaths in the Asia-Pacific War, numbering in the tens of millions, stemmed from starvation and disease. In most
cases, particularly among Asians, we lack specific clinical details of the type
recorded here with respect to the Filipino-American garrison on Bataan. Still
later, more Imperial Army soldiers would die from starvation and disease
than would perish in battle.

HOMMA'S COMMAND HAD been built up to 67,000 men on Bataan, bolstered
by the 7th Tank Regiment, and no fewer than 196 artillery pieces of 75 mm or
above. Reinforcements lifted the strength of the Fifth Air Division to at least
147 aircraft (also counting 18 G4Ms of the Imperial Navy). Although aware
that the defenders were debilitated, Homma remained quite wary, expecting
stiff resistance.

Homma massed six of his ten infantry regiments for his main effort to
break through the western end of the II Philippine Corps and capture the
dominating Mt. Samat. On the morning of 3 April, the Japanese commenced
a massive artillery barrage that to one American officer was "like the beating
of huge drums with the answering clash of cymbals." Joining this eruption
of blast and steel were dense mortar barrages and serial air attacks ("The sky
was black with planes," recorded one American) dumping sixty tons of high
explosive. The barrage focused on the front of the 41st Division (PA). It cast up
massive smoke and dust billows, set vegetation afire, and ripped apart labo-
riously constructed wire entanglements and defensive positions, until that
front resembled a World War I "No Man's Land."

The realities of the final Japanese offensive appear in microcosm in the
attack of the 65th Brigade, supported by light tanks, on the 42nd Infantry
Regiment (PA) in the 41st Division's (PA) center. The status of one of its battalions illustrates the state of this and other units: although officially counting
399 men, 125 men lay sick in aid stations, 150 were sick but with the unit, and
just 17 men were deemed fit for duty. Following the deluge of Japanese shells
and bombs, the grossly debilitated 42nd and the adjacent 43rd Infantry Regiments (PA) disintegrated. The Japanese cuffed aside the 41st Infantry on the
left flank, but the 41st Artillery Regiment (PA) stood to their guns with tremendous bravery and skill, extracting at least some penalty on the Japanese.
On 4 April, the Japanese with a similar application of artillery (kicking up so
much dust that men could not be seen ten yards away) and tank-supported
infantry similarly totally overpowered the next unit to the east, the 21st Division (PA), which also disintegrated.

Slowly recognizing the extreme peril poised by the Japanese thrust, the senior American officers mustered virtually all available reserve units to try to restore the line. The 33rd Infantry Regiment (PA) was sent into the maelstrom and disappeared. The all-white 31st Infantry, its men at desperate low ebb and down to fewer than fifty per rifle company, lurched into a floundering counterattack. There were several self-inflicted wounds by men trying to avoid what looked like a suicidal mission; other desperately sick men rose from their beds to fall into ranks. When the regiment attacked, there were many heroes in the ranks where there should have been few or none.

On 5 April, Japanese officers exhorted their men forward to capture dominant Mt. Samat, correctly believing its loss would be a mortal blow to the defense of Bataan. The Japanese attack seized the summit. The last of the stalwart gunners of the 41st Artillery (PA) were overrun and in some cases heaved their guns over cliffs to prevent them from falling to the Japanese. The loss of observation posts on Mt. Samat and the urgent necessity to displace guns to the rear nearly neutralized defensive artillery fire. The attempted counterattacks this day all misfired or failed. These events, particularly the disruption of any defensive artillery fire, effectively ended any chance of stopping the Japanese.

The events over the next two days juxtaposed fantasy and reality. Roosevelt's stern order prohibiting surrender remained in effect. Then on 4 April, MacArthur, with Marshall's blessing, issued a delusional directive to Wainwright that the Bataan garrison should mount a final desperate offensive to break out of Bataan to carry on the fight in Central Luzon before any consideration of capitulation. It made no difference that the Japanese left the I Philippine Corps largely unmolested because the II Philippine Corps was rapidly dissolving.

As units disintegrated, bodies of sick, emaciated, exhausted, and demoralized men—Philippine Army, Philippine Scouts, and Americans, enlisted men, and even field-grade officers—stumbled rearward in growing numbers. Sometimes they expended precious strength to try to carry their wounded and sometimes they abandoned the wounded. Often staggering in a mental twilight from lack of sleep, severe malnutrition, and debilitating disease, pathetically vulnerable to contagious panic, abandoning weapons and equipment, they clogged trails and then the East Road, where vehicles snarled three abreast. Japanese air attacks exacerbated the chaos. Standing like a rocky albeit small pinnacle in this flood was Brig. Gen. Clifford Bluemel. Virtually without sleep and partaking little food over nearly five days, Bluemel desperately attempted to cajole, exhort, intimidate, or physically throw men into new defense lines. Yet still some men in units like the ragged, pitiful remnants of the proud 26th Cavalry (PS) or the 4th Constabulary Regiment (PA) somehow found reserves of morale and physical strength to attempt organized resistance. On the 6th, Maj. Gen. Edward P. King, the Luzon Force commander, defined a still effective soldier as one who could walk one hundred yards carrying his weapon without a rest halt. His staff estimated this fitted about 15 percent of the men in the command.

A well-respected veteran artilleryman, with a quiet, innately courteous manner, King displayed at this most tragic moment of his life towering moral courage. He recognized the end had come and took personal responsibility for technically disobeying orders from Wainwright to counterattack and from Roosevelt forbidding surrender. It was the 77th Anniversary of the surrender of Gen. Robert E. Lee to Gen. Ulysses S. Grant at Appomattox during the American Civil War, and King believed if he survived the war he would be court-martialed for the largest surrender in American history. He met with Col. Motoo Nakayama, senior operations officer of the Fourteenth Army, who insisted that King must surrender all American forces in the Philippines. King explained he only commanded forces on Bataan and repeatedly requested that he be permitted to move his starved and exhausted men to any point the Japanese directed via the vehicles he had reserved for that purpose. Although Nakayama believed the meeting failed to settle matters, effectively the surrender of Bataan took hold. When King asked if his men would be treated as prisoners of war under international law, Nakayama replied: "We are not barbarians."

Most of the Filipino-American army was gathered around Mariveles at the time of surrender, but not all. The Japanese separated out about three hundred to four hundred officers and senior noncommissioned officers of the 91st Division (PA) in the mistaken belief that they had continued fighting that morning and inflicted serious losses on the 65th Brigade. They were bound with wire and aligned in rows. Japanese officers commenced decapitating men at one end while Japanese soldiers commenced bayoneting from the other end. Five men, including two officers, miraculously survived multiple bayonet wounds and lived to tell the tale. Approximately 70,000 Filipinos and Americans commenced a trek a distance of about ninety miles toward Camp O'Donnell, near Capas, Tarlac, to the north. It was, said one survivor, "a feast of hate." It became infamous as "The Bataan Death March."

Arranged in columns usually of four, the starved and exhausted men plodded north. They soon left the shaded area at the southern end of Bataan and walked beneath a brutal sun with temperatures of 95 to 104 degrees Fahrenheit during the rest of the route. Treatment by the guards varied widely.

The first Japanese that Private Leon Beck encountered after surrender were nonabusive combat troops who seemed to show the mutual respect of combat troops for their peers. A Japanese tank officer reached Hospital Number 1, packed with 3,000 helpless patients and staff. There he found that the Japanese prisoners-of-war patients had been treated well. He directed that the staff be treated with consideration. Although the prisoners were soon mostly relieved of personal valuables, some guards permitted halts in the shade and opportunities for food and water.

Most prisoners found these generous conquerors the minority. The majority of guards seemed to revel in opportunities to torment, to pummel, or to kill. Due to infrequent halts, the multitude with dysentery just let the filth run down their legs. When the march stopped for the night, the prisoners were herded into locations occupied the night before by another group, who left the ground coated with waste. Water was seldom allowed and guards particularly took pains to take away canteens. Japanese passing by in trucks took sport in swinging rifle butts, bayonets, rods of bamboo, and even looted golf clubs at walking prisoners.

Exhaustion from the siege and the toll of the march soon sent men collapsing to the ground. Some guards would permit other prisoners to help the fallen, but all too often if a prisoner remained recumbent, a guard would put a bayonet through his temple, and if the body still wiggled, fire a round into his head. An American surgeon, Alvin Poweleit, saw a dead American every couple yards and even more Filipinos. Another officer began counting just beheaded bodies; he counted twenty-seven in an equal number of miles before he stopped, as the task was causing him too much stress. At the tail of many columns, a Japanese "buzzard squad" killed those who fell out or fell behind. Some prisoners were selected as burial details and sometimes obliged to throw men not yet dead into graves and beat them down if they struggled. One American sailor recalled how these sights inspired him to follow two rules of perseverance: "Rule one is you take one more step. Rule two, when you don't think you can take one more step, refer back to rule one."

The exact death toll in the final Bataan battles and the Death March could never be ascertained; the numbers range from fewer than 500 to 2,350 Americans and from 5,000 to possibly more than 10,000 Filipinos. It was not clear how many men died in the final Japanese offensive—perhaps several thousand, mostly Filipinos. Then there are those who escaped to Corregidor, those who never surrendered, those who escaped during the march (with figures as high as 12,000 Filipinos and a few Americans), and those who remained in hospitals or were assigned to work details by the Japanese and never made the march. Reasonable estimates of American dead on the march fall around 500 to perhaps 600. Filipino deaths were much higher, perhaps as many as ten times or more above the American toll.

After several days or three weeks on the march, the prisoners reached Camp O'Donnell. Conditions were even worse there. An American general spoke of the camp as a place where he would awake with "a fog of death laying on the ground and the taste of death in my mouth." Exhausted by the siege, wracked by disease, depleted further by the march and abuse, and in some cases simply abandoning the will to live, by one accounting 29,589 men perished during 1942 in the camp. About one in six of the Americans who survived the march expired in Camp O'Donnell; the Filipino death rate was vastly worse.

Fall of Corregidor

Homma ordered the 4th Division, reinforced with elements of the 7th Tank Regiment, to assault the island fortress of Corregidor, while elements of the 16th Division attacked the other three US-held islands in Manila Bay. The Fourteenth Army also gained the 1st Artillery Command, with 116 pieces, under Maj. Gen. Kineo Kitajima, an expert gunner. Kitajima's most potent weapons were ten 24 cm howitzers and ten 15 cm guns. Homma estimated that Corregidor held some 5,000 to 10,000 men. Corregidor actually held about 13,000 men, and the other three islands forming American defenses of Manila Bay held about another 1,550.

In the days leading up to the Japanese landing on Corregidor, artillery and air bombardment surged to a crescendo. There was no location topside beyond the reach of the 24 cm howitzers. Scores of Japanese guns knocked out large-caliber coast defense batteries as well as the smaller artillery, machine gun, and searchlight positions to ward off a direct landing. Life in Malinta Tunnel, the largest underground installation, became a nightmare of "dust, dirt, black flies and vermin" amid the bombing and shelling. One nurse reported "under the deepening shadow of death life on Corregidor took on a faster, more intense tempo . . . there was a heightened feeling that life was to be lived from day to day, without illusions of ultimate victory."

In the last hours of 5 May, the Japanese barrage reached peak ferocity. A naval officer offshore reported "the island appeared to be one vast sheet of flame. . . . Dust clouds arose which reached the proportions of heavy fog and island defense searchlights were rendered useless, appearing only as yellow spots in the dust fog." On the targeted eastern end of the island, the barrage inflicted two deadly blows to any hopes of effective defense: it knocked out a great many defensive positions, sharply suppressing defensive firepower, and it shattered all forms of communication except by human voice or written • note delivered by runner under intense fire, nearly extinguishing defensive coordination.

The Japanese landing plan seriously miscarried. In the darkness, the 1st and 2nd Battalions, 61st Regiment boat crews failed to recognize their assigned Infantry Point landing beaches, and tides pushed the 1st Battalion east toward North Point at the tail of Corregidor and the 2nd even farther eastward. The much-thinned American firepower still administered serious punishment to both Japanese battalions, with shells and bullets finding boats and bodies.

While the garrison totaled some 13,000, about 1,000 were already wounded and most severely debilitated. Only about one in eight was an infantryman, and they were spread all over the island. Just one Marine company manned the entire 10,000-yard northeast stretch of beaches; just one platoon confronted the Japanese landing force, numbering roughly 2,000. The attackers rapidly seized high ground commanding the eastern end of the island. American counterattacks, mostly of navy and army personnel, including some Philippine Scouts, were checked with heavy casualties. The fateful blow came around 0930 when the Japanese landed three tanks. One of them was a captured American M-3. It played a critical role by pulling the two Japanese tanks up slopes they could not themselves surmount. All three then advanced against the defenders. Wainwright learned of this at 1000. He later explained that "it was the terror that is vested in a tank that was the decisive factor" as above all he feared they would nose into Malinta Tunnel and massacre the wounded.

Under a white flag of surrender, Wainwright strode out to meet the Japanese. He could see on all sides of his route vast numbers of dead and dying, attesting to the ferocity of the struggle. Exactly how many perished in this fight is unclear. The Japanese reported 903 total casualties from 17 April to 7 May. This total included 435 killed and missing in the final assault on Corregidor. Exact losses among the defenders are unknown, but it appears likely that approximately 170 Americans and Filipinos died from 3 to 6 May, the majority in the last twenty-four hours of resistance.

Wainwright's surrender effort proved contorted. In likely anticipation of exactly these circumstances MacArthur, before he departed, ordered the division of command in the Philippines into four parts, each answering to him. At General Marshall's recommendation, however, the president over-ruled MacArthur and placed all Philippine forces under Wainwright. Shortly before the final act on Corregidor, Wainwright sought to divest himself of all other commands in the Philippines save for Manila Bay installations. Cor-rectly pointing out the public announcement of Wainwright's overall com-mand, Homma rejected out of hand Wainwright's belated and transparent ploy to claim only limited command and demanded Wainwright surrender all forces in the Philippines. What eventually swayed Wainwright was what he perceived as the implied threat of retaliation, including possibly massacre, of the nearly 13,000 personnel on Corregidor. Communications difficulties and the reluctance of subordinate commanders to surrender protracted the effec-tive final surrender of all forces in the Philippines until about 9 June.

In the last few hours on Corregidor, a radio operator in Hawaii recorded the official and personal messages of a radio operator in the Malinta Tunnel:

> "They've been shelling us faster than you can count . . . we may not be able to stand it . . ." "They bring in the wounded every minute and it's a horrible sight . . . I'm vomiting." "General Wainwright is a right guy and we [are] willing to go on for him. . ."
>
> "[Everyone] is bawling like a baby."
>
> "My name is Irving Strobing. Get this to my mother, Mrs. Minnie Strobing, 605 Barbey Street, Brooklyn, New York. . ."

When a transcript of the messages reached the desk of Secretary of War Stim-son, it created a very rare moment in this war: a top policymaker confronting his personal responsibilities via the direct, emotional, personal experiences of a specific soldier.

As the sun set on 6 May 1942, approximately 12,800 men and some nurses of the Corregidor garrison entered effective, if not yet official, captivity. This arguably marked the moment when the Imperial Japanese Empire reached its zenith. It now stretched across seven time zones and housed approximately 516 million people—far more than the approximately 360 million captive peo-ples controlled at the peak by Nazi Germany. In its campaigns since 7 Decem-ber 1941, Japan had killed approximately 65,000 Allied soldiers, airmen, and sailors while losing about 15,000 servicemen. Over 300,000 Allied person-nel had become prisoners of war. The Imperial Navy had lost no warship larger than a destroyer while savaging Allied naval forces. Although Japanese aircraft losses were lower, their aircrew losses, due to operational casualties, were not so disparate from Allied losses as on land and at sea.

But at this same moment in Hawaii and Washington, US sailors were logging in and processing intercepted messages in the Imperial Navy's JN-25B main code. After translation of the typically partial decrypts, officers probed for useful intelligence. Since early in 1942, a trickle of recoveries had turned into a stream as the Japanese advance precluded the distribution of new additive tables, thus leaving a cipher for JN-25B in use long past a prudent termination date. Armed with those intercepts, Admiral Nimitz had gathered carrier-centered task forces built around *Lexington* and *Yorktown* to meet an anticipated Japanese attempt to seize Port Moresby on New Guinea, supported by possibly three or four carriers. Tomorrow in the Coral Sea there would be the first carrier engagement in history.

The outcome of this battle marked the first step in the decline of the Imperial Japanese Empire.

ACKNOWLEDGMENTS

My first thanks must go to my original editor at Random House, Robert Loomis, a legendary figure in American letters. He guided me along through most of my career as a writer and particularly steered me toward this project of creating a trilogy on the Asia-Pacific War. My debts to Bob are beyond measure.

I must next thank Don Fehr at Trident Media. When the publication home of this work fell into doubt, Don picked up the gauntlet and steered me very shrewdly over the hurdles to a landing at W. W. Norton & Company. There it has been my great good fortune to work very happily and with enormous benefit with my editor John Glusman and his able assistant Helen Thomaides.

One quite unexpected relationship that fell my way thanks to Dr. Donald Miller was association with the US National World War 2 Museum in New Orleans. It became my privilege to serve there as a member of the Presidential Counselors, a body of outstanding scholars and leaders in public memory who have contributed importantly to telling the story of that epic struggle. I also became the principal historian for the museum's "Road to Tokyo" exhibit. It is difficult to exaggerate the ways that mingling with my fellow counselors and the scholars the museum brings to its international conferences, as well as working on that exhibit, enhanced my awareness of not only the interrelations of events across the Asia-Pacific region, but also the relationships between that region and the European theater of the war. The staff at the museum now includes many good friends who freely share their knowledge. I cannot say enough about the leadership of the museum in Nick Mueller, the rightly revered first President and Chief Executive Officer, now emeritus, and the current President and Chief Executive Officer, Stephen Watson, Nick's very able successor.

Any effort of this scope is sustained by the vital assistance of the staffs at an array of facilities. Although the specific work on this volume began in 2007, material gathered at multiple facilities much earlier figures in the text. It has been my good fortune to team with able, professional, and highly cooperative individuals at all the archives and libraries I have visited. Generally, at the very largest archives, unless one visits with great frequency, the researcher works with a rotating roster of staff members. At the smaller facilities, the contacts with staff are concentrated and much more personal.

The former Naval History Center, now the Navy History and Heritage Command, is my original home where I first cut my teeth as a researcher. The lessons instilled there serve me to this day. The individuals who provided this foundation in my life as a historian included Dr. Dean Allard, Dr. Ronald Spector, Dr. Jeffery Barlow, Michael Walker, and Robert Cressman. Still others during what is now four decades have also contributed in great and small ways, and my thanks go to you all.

The National Archives in College Park, Maryland contains the largest repository of American World War II records. Over many years I have been assisted by dozens of staff members. Indeed, I have generally worked through two generations of staff, so I must ask forgiveness in not naming each one. As anyone who has worked with World War II records learns, the most astute and expert of the archivists is Timothy Nenninger. He is, by acclaim, a national treasure and has aided me and very many others in too many ways to enumerate. In addition to Tim, I have particularly been aided in the reading room by Gibson "Sandy" Smith, Barry Zerby, Wil Mahoney, Nathanial Patch, Jacob Haywood, and Paul Cogan. In the still and motion picture branch, Sharon Culley and Holly Reed rendered expert assistance. I will never forget my educational contacts with the late John Tayler, an institution by himself at the National Archives.

The Nimitz Museum in Fredericksburg, Texas hosts a world class museum as well as research sections. It further boosts a wonderful community I have had the pleasure of visiting at least once a year for over a quarter century. The museum sponsors symposia each year that have permitted me to meet a vast number of veterans whose individual stories inspired and continue to inspire my efforts. I particularly thank Helen MacDonald and her husband Richard for their kind hospitality. Helen has retired but her enormous work in organizing the symposia for years has left its own monument of World War II sources. I also have had the privilege of working in the archives there and benefited from the helpful and expert assistance of the staff, particularly Reagan Grau and Chris McDougal. Of course, I am indebted more than I can say to the two executive directors I have had the honor of knowing and working closely with at the Nimitz, the late Rear Admiral Charles ("Chuck") Grojean, USN (Ret.), and the wonderfully warm and supporting current incumbent, General Michael Hagee, USMC (Ret.), a former commandant of the US Marine Corps.

At the George C. Marshall Library on the campus of Virginia Military

Institute I became accustomed to the extremely receptive and helpful work of the staff, particularly Paul Barron. This facility has a well-earned reputation as a gem.

At the Hoover library and archives at beautiful Stanford University, my thanks to Dr. Richard Sousa, the director, and to the staff members who assisted me during my visit: David Jacobs, David Sun, and Samira Bozorgi. A special thanks is due Carol Leadenham, who tendered assistance well beyond the normal boundaries on one vexing question.

The Joyner Library of East Carolina University contains a font of memoirs, oral histories, and personal papers of World War II veterans. I particularly wish to commend Arthur Carlson and Dr. Jonathan Dembo for the special assistance they provided to me. Both went far beyond the call to guide me through the collections, and Dr. Dembo shared his special insights into the Robert Ghormley papers.

One of the great pleasures of this project was to visit Canberra multiple times and work at the Australian War Memorial (AWM). There I found a wonderful group of fellow historians led by Ashley Ekins, Head of the Military History Section. I enjoyed the particularly invaluable support of Dr. Steve Bullard and Karl James. At the enormously helpful information service, headed by Ms. Jennie Norberry, I encountered the uniformly cheerful and efficient staff including Suzy Nunes, Jesse Webb, Shelly Blakeley, Eric Carpenter, and Sue Decker.

Any visit to Australia for historical research about World War II brings contact with a whole team of skilled, enthusiastic, and richly personable historians. In addition to historians at the AWM, including Dr. Lachlan Grant, I have profited from the deep and careful work of Peter Williams and Garth Pratten. Peter Dean, formerly at the Australian National University and now at the University of Western Australia in Perth, cheerfully guided me and even more cheerfully allowed me to copy some of his wonderful research files. Of course, in his own special category in Australia is my fellow Vietnam veteran, Dr. David Horner, the dean of all Australian World War II historians. His body of work touches all aspects of the Australian role in the war, which was mighty for the size of its population.

At the Liddell Hart Centre for Military Archives at Kings College, I was assisted by Kate O'Brien, Francis Pattman, and Linne Smith. They proved most knowledgeable, courteous, and efficient. Likewise, at what is now known as The National Archives in London, formerly universally known as Kew, I was efficiently assisted and expertly guided by the staff.

My gratitude goes to Allen Packwood, Director of the Churchill Archive

Centre, Churchill College, Cambridge, United Kingdom. The user-friendly finding aids resulted in an exceptionally efficient research visit. This experience was enhanced and made highly agreeable by the work of staff members Amada Hawkes, Sarah Lewery, Julie Sanderson, Katherine Thomson, Louise Watling, and Ann Woodman. They proved uniformly pleasant and efficient.

Over the course of many years, I have gained enormously from not only the written output of a host of talented colleagues, but also the opportunity to discuss sources and issues with them. They served to guide, sharpen, and temper this work in more ways than space permits me to enumerate. A few of those listed here provided these contributions in their writings, but most also contributed by personal contact. These colleagues include Sadao Asada, Rick Atkinson, William Bartsch, Sir Antony Beevor, Eric Bergerud, Tami Biddle, Raymond Callahan, Conrad Crane, Thomas Doherty, Edward Drea, Brian P. Ferrell, Thomas French, Norman Friedman, Stuart Goldman, Alonzo "Lon" Hamby, Robert Hanyok, Sir Max Hastings, Joel Holwitt, James Hornfischer, Eri Hotta, James C. Hsiung, Warren Kimball, Diana Lary, Brian Linn, David Lu, Peter Mauch, Donald Miller, Edward S. Miller, Arthur Nicholson, William D. O'Neil, Paul Stillwell, Mark Stoler, Jay Taylor, Haruo Tohmatsu, H. P. Willmott, and Alan Zimm. An individual salute is due Eri Hotta, who uncovered the story that yielded a quotation now serving as the title of this work. The late and much missed Dr. Mark Peattie significantly extended my vision of where this trilogy should travel. Although I never met him, the late Robert J. C. Butow gave us enduring, foundational work on Japan.

In his own distinct category is the great dean of World War II historians, Gerhard Weinberg. His monumental *A World at Arms* remains in my view the best single volume history of the conflict. The breadth and depth of the research in this work remains unsurpassed. On more than one occasion, I thought I had discovered some new fact or insight only to find that Gerhard got there first.

Allan Millett also deserves a special salute. His work over the decades in supervising the creation of more doctorates in military history than any other American has stamped two generations of scholars with his rigorous intellectual DNA. He has proved a wise and thoughtful colleague always pressing and probing.

One of the chief aspirations guiding this work and the succeeding volumes is to restore China to a far more significant place in the history of the Second World War that has been woven over some eight decades. In broad terms, for decades after Japan surrendered in August 1945, reliable archival information from both sides of the Taiwan Strait proved sparse to nonexistent. Historians perforce often relied extensively on foreign records reflecting only second-hand interpretations of internal Chinese events and Chinese figures. Over the past approximately two decades this situation materially changed. While complete access to all remaining records is not available, a vast trove of important records is now accessible. These records have provided the foundation for pioneering publications by a small body of scholars whose work has shaped this narrative.

It is in the context of the story of China that I must pay special tribute to two scholars, Dr. Rana Mitter of Oxford University and Dr. Hans van de Ven. Their own work forms a critical mass in the new scholarship and they have afforded me unfailing assistance, encouragement, and friendship.

I am proud to count myself among a special informal group of World War II Pacific historians who have not only lent encouragement, but have also acted as invaluable scouts for facts and sources. These individuals include Barrett Tillman, Charles "Chuck" Haberlein, John Lundstrom, Jon Parshall, James Sawruk, Barrett Tillman, Anthony Tully, and J. Michael Wenger. To my great pleasure, Jon and I have also collaborated in numerous teaching venues. There is a much longer list of scholars who have contributed in some way toward this work, but their names are found primarily in the sources cited.

A special salute and thanks must go to a group of personal friends: Dennis Fontana, Greg Embree, and Robert Sullivan. They are nonprofessional writers or historians but with deep interest and knowledge in the area. Their most valuable service to me has been to read and critique drafts, especially from the standpoint of flow and focus. I never fail to recommend to other historians that they find such readers.

Of course, whatever the contributions of this list of individuals to this work, the responsibility for any error of fact or interpretation remains mine alone.

Finally, the patience, support, and love of my wife Janet has sustained me now for almost four decades. Some debts are beyond measure.

NOTES

Prologue: The Marco Polo Bridge

1 **Lugouqiao Bridge:** This description was derived from numerous internet sites with descriptions of the bridge's background, with special attention to the extensive photographic coverage that reveals details of the structure's construction and ornamentation. Particularly helpful was http://www.beijinglandscapes.com/beijing_attractions/Lugouqiao-Bridge.html, accessed 14 September 2014.

1 **Fall of Qing; adequacy of term *warlord*; Chiang's early life and Sun Yat-sen:** Jay Taylor, *The Generalissimo: Chiang Kai-shek and the Struggle for Modern China* (Cambridge, MA: The Belknap Press of Harvard University Press, 2009), 12, 16–17, 19 [hereafter Taylor, *The Generalissimo*]; Jonathan D. Spence, *The Search for Modern China*, 3rd edition (New York: W. W. Norton, 2012), 262, 301 [hereafter Spence, *The Search for Modern China*]; Rana Mitter, *Forgotten Ally: China's World War II 1937–1945* (Boston: Houghton Mifflin Harcourt, 2013), 32–33 [hereafter Mitter, *Forgotten Ally*]. S. C. M. Paine, *The Wars for Asia 1911–1949* (New York: Cambridge University Press, 2012), xvi [hereafter Paine, *The Wars for Asia*], reflects a recent comment on the inadequacy of the term *warlord*.

2 **Sun's relations with Chiang, bestows name:** Taylor, *The Generalissimo*, 11, 40–41.

2 **Sun's death and alliance with Soviets:** Taylor, *The Generalissimo*, 42–44; Hans van de Ven, *War and Nationalism in China 1925–1945* (London: RoutledgeCurzon, 2003), 80–81 [hereafter van de Ven, *War and Nationalism in China*].

2 **Chiang's status among Nationalists and ordinary members; Chiang triumphs in power struggle:** Taylor, *The Generalissimo*, 48–57; Hans van de Ven, *China at War: Triumph and Tragedy in the Emergence of the New China* (Cambridge, MA: Harvard University Press, 2018), 27–31 [hereafter van de Ven, *China at War*].

2 **"was an aggregation of relatively autonomous cliques and powerful personalities . . ." and diverse components of Nationalists:** Gregor Benton, *New Fourth Army: Communist Resistance along the Yangtze and the Huai, 1938–1941* (Berkeley: University of California Press, 1999), 101–59 (quote at 101) [hereafter Benton, *New Fourth Army*].

2 **Chiang's leadership techniques:** Benton, *New Fourth Army*, 101.

3 **Northern Expedition:** Taylor, *The Generalissimo*, 50, 55–59, 61; Spence, *The Search for Modern China*, 312–26; van de Ven, *War and Nationalism in China*, 105, 129–30; Mark R. Peattie, "The Dragon's Seed: Origins of the War," in Mark Peattie, Edward Drea, and Hans van de Ven, eds., *The Battle for China: Essays on the Military History of the Sino-Japanese War 1937–47* (Stanford, CA: Stanford University Press, 2010), 63 [hereafter Peattie, "The Dragon's Seed" and Peattie, Drea, and van de Ven, *The Battle for China*].

3   **Chiang's campaigns against Communists; status of Communist position in 1937:**
    Alexander V. Pantsov and Stephen I. Levine, *Mao: The Real Story* (New York:
    Simon & Schuster, 2012), 274–88 [hereafter Pantsov and Levine, *Mao: The Real
    Story*]; Taylor, *The Generalissimo*, 98–99, 110–12, 114; Mitter, *Forgotten Ally*, 69–
    70, 191. The numbers in the text are generally from Pantsov and Levine, 288,
    for Communist military strength, and Mitter, 191, for total population of Com-
    munist area (and assuming national population then 450 million). Taylor offers
    figures of 25,000 "fighters" at the beginning of the "Long March" and 7,000 to
    9,000 at the end.

3   **"Boxer" Rebellion and aftermath:** Paul A. Cohen, *History in Three Keys: The Box-
    ers as Event, Experience and Myth* (New York: Columbia University Press, 1997);
    Spence, *The Search for Modern China*, 222–24.

3   **Background of the Marco Polo Bridge:** David Lu, "Introduction to the Marco Polo
    Bridge Incident," in James Morley, ed., *Japan's Road to the Pacific War: The China
    Quagmire: Japanese Expansion on the Asian Continent, 1933–1941* (New York: Colum-
    bia University Press, 1983), 233 [hereafter Lu, "Introduction to the Marco Polo
    Bridge Incident" and Morley, *The China Quagmire*]; Spence, *The Search for Modern
    China*, 397–400; Diana Lary, *China's Republic* (New York: Cambridge University
    Press, 2007), 113 [hereafter referred to as Lary, *China's Republic*].

5   **Incident of 7 July 1937:** Edward Drea, "The Japanese Army on the Eve of the War,"
    105–6; Satoshi Hattori and Edward J. Drea, "Japanese Operations, from July to
    December 1937," in Peattie, Drea, and van de Ven, *The Battle for China*, 161 [hereaf-
    ter Hattori and Drea, "Japanese Operations, from July to December 1937"]; Taylor,
    The Generalissimo, 145; Ikuhiko Hata, "The Marco Polo Bridge Incident," in Mor-
    ley, *The China Quagmire*, 248 [hereafter Hata, "The Marco Polo Bridge Incident"];
    Sekiguchi Takashi, *Who Destroyed the Ikki Unit; Battle of Guadalcanal*. Tokyo: Fuyo
    Shobo, 2018, 18–21. Although the exact responsibility for the first shots has never
    been resolved definitively, Taylor flatly attributes the firing to Chinese soldiers, and
    this seems the most likely source. Professor Takashi discovered through contacts
    with Ikki's family that the correct rendering of the family name was Ikki, not Ichiki
    as it appeared for decades in the literature.

5   **"In Chinese philosophy, the number seven . . .":** Paine, *The Wars for Asia*, 128.

6   **8 July skirmish and Prince Kan'in directive:** Hata, "The Marco Polo Bridge Inci-
    dent," 247–48.

6   **Shimura killed in Burma; fate of Mutaguchi and Ikki:** Lu, "Introduction to the
    Marco Polo Bridge Incident," 233; Louis Allen, *Burma: The Longest War, 1941–1945*
    (London: Phoenix Press, 2000), 153, 193; Richard B. Frank, *Guadalcanal: The Defini-
    tive Account of the Landmark Battle* (New York: Random House, 1990), 156 [hereafter
    Frank, *Guadalcanal*].

1: "China Cannot Be Lost"

9   **"Something troubling has occurred," "Something wonderful has happened":** Edward
    J. Drea, "The Japanese Army on the Eve of War," in Peattie, Drea, and van de Ven,
    The Battle for China, 135.

9   **Sino-Japanese War of 1894–1895 effect on Japanese opinion:** Edward J. Drea, *Japan's
    Imperial Army: Its Rise and Fall, 1853–1954* (Manhattan: Kansas University Press,

2009), 87 [hereafter Drea, *Japan's Imperial Army*]; Marius B. Jansen, *The Making of Modern Japan* (Cambridge, MA: The Belknap Press of Harvard University Press, 2000), 433 [hereafter Jansen, *The Making of Modern Japan*]; Spence, *The Search for Modern China*, 349 ("[China] is . . . dead, only its corpse is wriggling").

10 **Japan's economic troubles of the 1920s and early 1930s:** Takafusa Nakamura, "The Japanese Economy in the Interwar Period: A Brief Summary," in Ronald Dore and Radha Sinha, *Japan and World Depression: Then and Now* (New York: St. Martin's Press, 1987), 52–82; Jansen, *The Making of Modern Japan*, 528–36, 567–68; 582–83; Drea, *Japan's Imperial Army*, 159–61.

10 **Viewpoints of Japanese officers; economic depression and Soviet military and ideological threat; liberalism versus ultranationalist/militarist currents; Japanese actions provoke steep rise in Chinese nationalism:** Drea, "The Japanese Army on the Eve of War," 106–11; Mark R. Peattie, *Ishiwara Kanji and Japan's Confrontation with the West* (Princeton, NJ: Princeton University Press, 1975), 286 [hereafter Peattie, *Ishiwara Kanji*]; Jansen, *The Making of Modern Japan*, 526–77; Odd Arne Westad, *Restless Empire: China and the World Since 1750* (New York: Basic Books, 2012), 248 [hereafter Westad, *Restless Empire*]; Paine, *The Wars of Asia*, 21–25.

11 **"the immediate ideological genesis":** Eri Hotta, *Pan-Asianism and Japan's War, 1931–35* (New York: Palgrave Macmillan, 2007), 89 [hereafter Hotta, *Pan-Asianism and Japan's War*].

11 **Ishiwara's background and the "Final War":** Peattie, *Ishiwara Kanji*, ch. 3, 319–20; Hata, "The Marco Polo Bridge Incident," 251.

11 **Manchurian Incident and reaction of Wakatsuki:** Hiroharu Seki, "The Manchurian Incident, 1931," and Toshihiko Shimada, "The Extension of Hostilities, 1931–1932," in James William Morley, ed., *Japan's Road to the Pacific War, Japan Erupts: The London Naval Conference and the Manchurian Incident, 1928–32* (New York: Columbia University Press, 1984) [hereafter Shimada, "The Extension of Hostilities, 1931–1932"]; Hotta, *Pan-Asianism and Japan's War*, 87.

11 **Fall of Wakatsuki, assassination of Inukai and consequences, creation of Manchukuo, plot to assassinate Charlie Chaplin:** Shimada, "The Extension of Hostilities, 1931–1932"; Jensen, *The Making of Modern Japan*, 504–11, 584, 591–92; Hotta, *Pan-Asianism and Japan's War*, 87; Paine, *The Wars of Asia*, 30; Shibly Nabhan, "No Laughing Matter," *Japan Times*, 15 May 2005, www.japantimes.co.jp/life/2005/05/15/to-be-sorted/no-laughing-matter, accessed 11 August 2017. After Inukai's assassination, there would be thirteen cabinets through August 1945. Fumimaro Kone headed three of them and Koki Hirota and Kiichiro Hiranuma one each. The other eight were all headed by generals or admirals. Thomas French pointed out to the author that the moves toward democracy in the early twentieth century were more halting steps than large strides, as the period also produced significant censorship and repression as described, for example, by Jansen.

12 **Japanese investment in Manchuria:** Morley, *The China Quagmire*, 6. By far the most comprehensive and insightful treatment of "Manchukuo" is Louise Young's *Japan's Total Empire: Manchuria and the Culture of Wartime Imperialism* (Berkeley: University of California Press, 1999). Among her most significant observations is that whatever the origins of "Manchukuo" in the machinations of the Imperial Army, the enterprise subsequently enlisted support across almost the whole spectrum of

Japanese society. Paine, *The Wars of Asia,* 27–34, provides a condensed and revealing set of statistics about Manchuria under Japanese rule.

12 **Distant roots of Manchurian Incident and terror:** Jansen, *The Making of Modern Japan,* 577–86; Hotta, *Pan-Asianism and Japan's War,* 87.

13 **Historical interpretations of Japan's path from 1931 to 1945:** Jun'ichiro Shoji, "Historical Perception in Postwar Japan Concerning the Pacific War," *National Institute of Defense Studies,* no. 4 (March 2003): 109–33. This essay is written from the viewpoint of historical debate in Japan, but the debates there are paralleled by outside historical frameworks.

13 **Variants of Pan-Asianism:** Hotta, *Pan-Asianism and Japan's War,* 30, 44–48.

13 **Ishiwara's stance on Marco Polo Bridge Incident:** Drea, *Japan's Imperial Army,* 190; Hata, "The Marco Polo Bridge Incident," 251; Peattie, *Ishiwara Kanji,* 296–97; Peattie, "The Dragon's Seed," 75–77; Michael Barnhart, *Japan Prepares for Total War: The Search for Economic Security, 1919–1941* (Ithaca, NY: Cornell University Press, 2015), 89 ("endless bog").

14 **Ishiwara's allies:** Hata, "The Marco Polo Bridge Incident," 249.

14 **"The mood in the army today . . .":** Herbert P. Bix, *Hirohito and the Making of Modern Japan* (New York: HarperCollins, 2000), 322 [hereafter Bix, *Hirohito and the Making of Modern Japan*].

14 **Divisions within the Imperial Army following the Marco Polo Bridge Incident, manipulation of news accounts:** Hata, "The Marco Polo Bridge Incident," 249, 252–56; Drea, "The Japanese Army on the Eve of War," 110–11; Peattie, *Ishiwara Kanji,* 292–93; Yoshitake Oka, *Konoe Fumimaro: A Political Biography* (Tokyo: University of Tokyo Press, 1983), 55 [hereafter Oka, *Konoe*]. The counsel of the chief of staff and war minister to the emperor is described in Bix, *Hirohito and the Making of Modern Japan,* 320.

14 **Tokyo vacillates, July 9–27; Konoe's peace negotiators arrested:** Hata, "The Marco Polo Bridge Incident," 248–61; Taylor, *The Generalissimo,* 145; Peattie, *Ishiwara Kanji,* 297–303; Ken Kotani, *Japanese Intelligence in World War II* (Oxford, UK: Osprey Publishing Ltd., 2006), 19–20 [hereafter Kotani, *Japanese Intelligence in World War II*].

15 **Japanese and Chinese strength at start of conflict:** van de Ven, *War and Nationalism in China,* 193–94; Hattori and Drea, "Japanese Operations from July to December 1937," 161.

15 **Japanese reinforcements and quick capture of Beijing and Tianjin:** Drea, *Japan's Imperial Army,* 191; Hattori and Drea, "Japanese Operations from July to December 1937," 161.

15 **Tongzhou incident:** Yang Daqing, "Atrocities in Nanjing: Searching for Explanations," in Diana Lary and Stephen MacKinnon, eds., *Scars of War: The Impact of Warfare on Modern China* (Vancouver: University of British Columbia Press, 2001), 77, 93n3; Philip Jowett, *Rays of the Rising Sun,* vol. 1: *Japan's Asian Allies 1931–45, China and Manchukuo* (Warwick, UK: Helion, 2005), 43; Takashi Yoshida, "Wartime Accounts of the Nanjing Atrocity," in Bob Tadashi Wakabayashi, ed., *The Nanking Atrocity 1937–38: Complicating the Picture* (New York: Berghahn Books, 2007), 260 [hereafter Wakabayashi, *The Nanking Atrocity 1937–38*]; Kazuo Yagami, *Konoe Fumimaro and the Failure of Peace in Japan 1937–1941* (Jefferson, NC: McFarland Publishers, 2006), 48 [hereafter Yagami, *Konoe Fumimaro*].

16 **Formation of North China Area Army:** Hattori and Drea, "Japanese Operations from July to December 1937," 161–62. The North China Area Army was organized as follows: the First Army included the 6th, 14th, and 20th Divisions; the Second Army comprised the 10th, 16th, and 106th Divisions. Directly under the North China Area Army were the 5th and 109th Divisions.

16 **North China Area Army maneuver scheme and logistical constraints:** Hattori and Drea, "Japanese Operations from July to December 1937," 161–62; Marvin Williamsen, "The Military Dimension, 1937–41," in James C. Hsiung and Steven I. Levine, eds., *China's Bitter Victory: The War with Japan 1937–1945* (Armonk, NY: M. E. Sharpe, 1992), 136–37 [hereafter Williamsen, "The Military Dimension, 1937–41" and Hsiung and Levine, *China's Bitter Victory*]; Drea, *Japan's Imperial Army*, 194–95.

16 **"ragamuffin hordes" that "broke like a wall of dust":** Theodore White and Annalee Jacoby, *Thunder Out of China* (New York: William Sloane Associates, 1961), 49 [hereafter White and Jacoby, *Thunder Out of China*].

16 **"most forces simply have never offered resistance":** van de Ven, *War and Nationalism in China*, 193–96.

16 **Terauchi's operations, attitudes, and casualties:** Hattori and Drea, "Japanese Operations from July to December 1937," 162–63, 168.

16 **Kwantung Army seizes Chahar, Suiyuan, and northern Shanxi provinces; disbands mechanized unit:** Hattori and Drea, "Japanese Operations from July to December 1937," 163–64, 167–68.

17 **Pingxingguan Pass and mythology:** Hattori and Drea, "Japanese Operations from July to December 1937," 164–67; http://www.yangkuisong.net/2tlw/sjyj/0000223 .htm, accessed October 2010; Axis History Forum, "The Battle of Pingxingguan 1937," with translation of analysis by Professor Yang Kui Song. Hattori and Drea report Chinese claims that Japanese losses in all the fighting around the pass were about 3,000 while Chinese losses were ten times that number. One of the earliest of the numerous examples of the mythology of a major Communist victory at Pingxingguan Pass (also rendered as P'inghsingkuan) is found in White and Jacoby, *Thunder Out of China*, 50–51 (which says the action "cut an entire division almost to pieces from the rear") and Williamsen, "The Military Dimension, 1937–41," 136 (which depicts Japanese losses as a brigade). Diana Lary, *The Chinese People at War: Human Suffering and Social Transformation, 1937–1945* (Cambridge: Cambridge University Press, 2010), 16, points out the absence of any major conventional fight by the Red Army in this first phase of the war.

17 **"a failure, a piece of Chinese flotsam . . ." and "Now it is not so easy to be sure":** Jonathan Spence, "The Enigma of Chiang Kai-shek," *New York Review of Books*, October 22, 2009, vol. 56, no. 16, p. 32 [hereafter Spence, "The Enigma of Chiang Kai-shek"].

17 **Resurrection of Chiang's reputation in People's Republic of China:** Mitter, *Forgotten Ally*, 9, provides an excellent benchmark pointing out that Chiang's restored villa in Huangshan today provides a detailed and positive description of his life, with little comment about his clash with the Communists and nothing "painting him as a bourgeois reactionary lackey." This would have been unimaginable a generation ago.

18 **Chiang's early life and Sun Yat-sen:** Taylor, *The Generalissimo*, 12, 16–17, 19; Spence, *The Search for Modern China*, 248–49, 262, 301–2; Mitter, *Forgotten Ally*, 32–33.

18 **"fiery temper, and your hatred of mediocrity":** Taylor, *The Generalissimo*, 36.

18 **Chiang described, "magnificent flashing eyes":** Hallett Abend, *My Life In China 1926–1941* (New York: Harcourt, Brace, 1943), 20–21; "large, very dark and bright, extremely intelligent, completely unrevealing . . .,": Freda Utley, *China at War* (London: Faber and Faber, 1938), 244 [hereafter Utley, *China at War*]. The famous American novelist Pearl S. Buck communicated her core reading of Chiang when she compared his face to that of a tiger with "the high forehead sloping, the ears flaring backward, the wide mouth seeming always ready to smile yet cruel." Hilary Sperling, *Pearl Buck in China: Journey to The Good Earth* (New York: Simon & Schuster, 2010), 180.

18 **Chiang's left-leaning economic views and rejection of Marxism:** Taylor, *The Generalissimo*, 39.

18 **". . . [an] emphasis on character development, self-discipline . . ." and "based on the political order and had a political objective . . .":** Taylor, *The Generalissimo*, 14.

18 **Diversity of Chiang's military background:** This observation expands slightly on the original insight of Jonathan Spence in "The Enigma of Chiang Kai-shek," 32. On Chiang's relationship with Zhou Enlai, see Taylor, *The Generalissimo*, 45. Mitter, *Forgotten Ally*, 33, notes Chiang first traveled outside the country to the Soviet Union and later to Japan.

19 **Northern Expedition:** Taylor, *The Generalissimo*, 50, 55–59, 61; Spence, *The Search for Modern China*, 312–26; van de Ven, *War and Nationalism in China*, 105, 129–30; Peattie, "The Dragon's Seed," 63.

19 **Chiang launches terror against Communists; "When the [Nationalist] Right is of no more use . . .":** Taylor, *The Generalissimo*, 66–68; van de Ven, *War and Nationalism in China*, 107–20.

19 **Chiang marries Soong Mayling; Madame Chiang described:** Taylor, *The Generalissimo*, 27–28; Department of State, Division of Far Eastern Affairs, 22 December 1936, The China Situation, p. 3, President's Secretary File, Box 26, Diplomatic, Chile Jul-Dec 1941 thru China 1938, Folder Diplomatic Correspondence China 1933-36, Franklin D. Roosevelt Library [hereafter FDRL]; President's Secretary File, Box 27, China: 1938—Military Dispatches thru China 1945, Folder Diplomatic Correspondence China: Lauchlin Currie Report 3/15/41 ("she is intelligent, liberally minded, self-assertive . . ."), FDRL; "Man and Wife of the Year," *Time* magazine, 3 January 1938 ("No woman in the West holds so great a position . . .").

19 **Soong family:** Taylor, *The Generalissimo*, 27–28; Paine, *The Wars of Asia*, 55–56.

19 **Chiang seizes Nanjing:** Lary, *China's Republic*, 83.

19 **Costs of Northern Expedition:** Peattie, "The Dragon's Seed," 64.

19 **"Nanjing Decade" begins in chaos and strife:** Spence, *The Search for Modern China*, 327–55.

19 **Shift of historical perspective:** Perhaps the best recognized representative of the older generation of historians who condemned "The Nanjing Decade" was Lloyd Eastman in *The Abortive Revolution: China Under Nationalist Rule, 1927–1937* (Cambridge, MA: Harvard University Press, 1974). In the same camp fell Hung-mao Tien, *Government and Politics in Kuomintang China, 1927–1937* (Stanford, CA: Stanford University Press, 1972). Benchmarks in the shift to a more positive view of "The Nanjing Decade" include Arthur Young, *China's National Building Effort: The Financial and Economic Record, 1927–37* (Stanford, CA: Hoover Institution Press,

1971); Robert E. Bedeski, *State Building in Modern China: The Kuomintang in the Prewar Period* (Berkeley, CA: The Center for Chinese Studies, 1981); William Kirby, *German and Republican China* (Stanford, CA: Stanford University Press, 1984); Paine, *The Wars for Asia*, 57–64. Of course, Taylor, *The Generalissimo*, takes the positive note. Of recent historians, the respected Diana Lary remains close to the older view, *China's Republic*, ch. 3, 81–111,

20 **"aesthetic of vigorous nationalist modernity" and Chiang's vision for the armed forces and nation:** van de Ven, *War and Nationalism in China*, 13, 131–32; Chiang's German-trained and -equipped forces and General von Falkenhausen's views: Taylor, *The Generalissimo*, 143. Von Falkenhausen also urged Chiang to defend coastal areas and the Yangtze valley, Taylor, *The Generalissimo*, 121.

20 **Suppression of critics and corruption issues:** Taylor, *The Generalissimo*, 1, 50–51, 100, 221–22; Mitter, *Forgotten Ally*, 57. The actual preferred tactic of Nationalist police with captured Communists was to provide them with a choice between death and public renunciation. The "loss of face" renunciation involved not only release, but even assignment to important positions on the premise that such individuals would now serve the Nationalists with special zeal. Pantsov and Levine, *Mao: The Real Story*, 227.

20 **"a far-seeing leader . . ." and "The people's confidence . . .":** quoted in Taylor, *The Generalissimo*, 122.

20 **Balanced view of Chiang's reforms:** This is a generalization based primarily on my interpretation of Spence, *The Search for Modern China*, 331–41, who provides only grudging and limited support for Chiang's reforms, and van de Ven, *War and Nationalism in China*, 169; Taylor, *The Generalissimo*, 121. For a divergent view of the "Nanking Decade" portraying the period as one of high hopes disintegrating into deep failure, see Lary, *China's Republic*, ch. 3, 81–111. Although by no means alone, Barbara Tuchman is probably the most widely known historian who finds few if any redeeming qualities in Chiang. Her *Stillwell and the American Experience in China* (New York: Macmillan, 1971) fitted into a trend growing since the latter part of the Second World War. This tide was accelerated from the divisive "Who Lost China" debate of the late 1940s in the United States and the decades-long bitterness it spawned. The acquisition of a great deal more archival material concerning Chiang, the Nationalists, and the Communists now makes it impossible in my view to depict Chiang, without overlooking his manifold flaws and mistakes, as a leader without a trace of honor or without a case, particularly in comparison with Mao.

21 **Chiang's image for the decade prior to 1937:** Taylor, *The Generalissimo*, 95; Lary, *China's Republic*, 195; van de Ven, *China at War*, 32.

21 **Xi'an Incident as forcing Chiang to fight the Japanese:** Spence, *The Search for Modern China*, 387 characterizes the outcome as Chiang having "implicitly given his word to change the direction of his policies." For another recent account explaining events as coercion at Xi'an promoting Chiang's decision for war, see Lary, *China's Republic*, 109–10. Taylor, *The Generalissimo*, 126–32, and van de Ven, *War and Nationalism in China*, 171–72, 177–78, 186–88, provide counterarguments on the significance of Xi'an. Even if one attaches great significance to Xi'an, it did not mark an abrupt reversal of Chiang's overall strategic vision.

21 **Background to Xi'an Incident:** Spence, *The Search for Modern China*, 385–87; Taylor, *The Generalissimo*, 125; van de Ven, *China at War*, 61–64, 88.

21 **Zhang's opium addiction and mistresses:** Stephen Kotkin, *Stalin: Waiting for Hitler,*
    1929–1941 (New York: Penguin Press, 2017), 360 [hereafter Kotkin, *Stalin: Waiting*
    for Hitler].

22 **"higher than that of any leader in modern Chinese history":** Edgar Snow, *Red Star*
    Over China (London: Victor Gollancz, Ltd., 1937; New York: Random House, 1938),
    471. More recently, Taylor summarized that despite international economic woes,
    civil war, and depredations by Japan, "the power and authority of the Chinese cen-
    tral government was greater than at any time since the Taiping Uprising." *The Gen-*
    eralissimo, 121.

22 **Denouement of Xi'an Incident and "Chiang had left for Xi'an a popular leader . . .":**
    Taylor, *The Generalissimo,* 128–29, 131–35; van de Ven, *China at War,* 61–64; "extraor-
    dinarily widespread," President's Secretary File, Box 26, Diplomatic, Chile Jul–Dec
    1941 thru China 1938, Folder Diplomatic Correspondence China 1933–36, page 5,
    FDRL. Spence, *The Search for Modern China,* 386, puts the "rapturous" crowd in
    Nanjing at 400,000. Lary, *China's Republic,* 109, however, describes the scene as
    "less than a hero's welcome." Taylor, *The Generalissimo,* 136–37, notes the irony that
    Chiang had probably ordered Zhou released in 1927 as Zhou faced death; now the
    roles were reversed.

22 **Possible consequences of Chiang's death:** Kotkin, *Stalin: Waiting for Hitler,* 365–67.

22 **Excessive optimism of Chiang and von Falkenhausen, they converse in Japanese:**
    Taylor, *The Generalissimo,* 143–44; Peter Harmsen, *Shanghai 1937: Stalingrad on the*
    Yangtze (Philadelphia and Oxford: Casemate Publishers, 2013), 76 [hereafter Harm-
    sen, *Shanghai 1937*].

22 **Strength and characteristics of Chinese armies in 1937:** This discussion merges
    information from Taylor, *The Generalissimo,* 143 (giving the 2,029,000 total and
    50,000 strength of Red Army forces) and Steven MacKinnon, "The Defense of the
    Central Yangtze," Peattie, Drea, and van de Ven, *The Battle for China,* 184–88, for
    the differing origins and loyalties of the Chinese armies. MacKinnon gives the total
    Chinese strength as 1.7 to 2.2 million. He believes the first two categories numbered
    about 900,000, the other regional armies about a million, and the combination of
    Red Army and Northeastern and Manchuria forces about 300,000, with Red Army
    strength at 100,000. MacKinnon gave slightly different total strength figures of 1.7
    to 2.4 million in *Wuhan, 1938: War, Refugees, and the Making of Modern China* (Berke-
    ley: University of California Press, 2008), 22–23 [hereafter MacKinnon, *Wuhan*].

23 **Chiang's March 1934 predictions:** Taylor, *The Generalissimo,* 100. Taylor makes the
    interesting observation that in terms of forces and popular opinion, this was the
    best time for Chiang to strike against the CCP, but he did not. Taylor reported that
    keeping his promise on unity, Chiang began to send 200,000 to 300,000 yuan a
    month to the Communists. *The Generalissimo,* 142. Subsequently, Taylor agreed the
    actual arrangement was $300,000 per year. My thanks to Professor Rana Mitter for
    pointing this out.

23 **Chiang's preparations for war from 1932:** van de Ven, *War and Nationalism,* 151–56,
    161–63; Chang Jui-te, "The Nationalist Army on the Eve of War," in Peattie, Drea,
    and van de Ven, *The Battle for China,* 85–88, 92–94 [hereafter Chang Jui-te, "The
    Nationalist Army on the Eve of War"]; Paine, *The Wars for Asia,* 143–44.

23 **"If we allow one more inch of our territory to be lost . . .":** Spence, *The Search for*
    Modern China, 400.

23 **Conflict between Chiang's views as a soldier and as a statesman:** John W. Garver, "China's Wartime Diplomacy," in Hsiung and Levine, *China's Bitter Victory*, 6–7 [hereafter Garver, "China's Wartime Diplomacy"]. Garver argues that the decision not to fight would endanger Chiang's regime. His analysis is shrewd and bears review, but appeared earlier than some of the documentation exploited by later historians.

24 **"the turning point for existence or obliteration":** Mitter, *Forgotten Ally*, 81.

24 **Debates on Chinese strategy, von Falkenhausen's warning:** van de Ven, *China at War*, 34; van de Ven, *War and Nationalism in China*, 157–60.

24 **Huge risks faced by Chiang:** Garver, "China's Wartime Diplomacy," 6.

24 **Other Chinese leaders urge avoidance of war:** Tianshi Yang, "Chiang Kai-shek and the Battles of Shanghai and Nanjing," in Peattie, Drea, and van de Ven, *The Battle for China*, 143–44 [hereafter Yang, "Chiang Kai-shek and the Battles of Shanghai and Nanjing"]; "at best both sides lose": Paine, *The Wars for Asia*, 129.

24 **"Is this an isolated episode . . .":** van de Ven, *War and Revolution in China*, 188; Yang, "Chiang Kai-shek and the Battles of Shanghai and Nanjing," 143–44.

24 **"one iota of sovereignty," orders to military and civilian authorities, dispatch of divisions to North China, and "I am now determined to declare war on Japan":** Taylor, *The Generalissimo*, 145.

24 **"War is inevitable. We must fight . . .":** Yang, "Chiang Kai-shek and the Battles of Shanghai and Nanjing," 145.

24 **Chiang summons meeting of National Defense Council and results:** Yang, "Chiang Kai-shek and the Battles of Shanghai and Nanjing," 145 46; Chang Jui-te, "The Nationalist Army on the Eve of War," 83–85; Taylor, *The Generalissimo*, 146–48; Mitter, *Forgotten Ally*, 94–95 ("Do we fight, or shall we be destroyed?").

25 **Prediction by W. H. Donald:** van de Ven, *War and Nationalism in China*, 175.

25 **Chiang's reasons for fighting at Shanghai:** van de Ven, *War and Revolution in China*, 175–78, 196–203; Taylor, *The Generalissimo*, 147–48; Edward Drea and Hans van de Ven, "An Overview of Major Military Campaigns during the Sino-Japanese War, 1937–1945," in Peattie, Drea, and van de Ven, *The Battle for China*, 28 [hereafter Drea and van de Ven, "An Overview of Major Military Campaigns during the Sino-Japanese War, 1937–1945"]. In van de Ven's judgment, Chiang did fight in Shanghai with public relations in mind. But van de Ven explains: "Although we do not know for certain, it is possible that [Chiang] did hope that Western diplomatic intervention, combined with a determined show of strength in Shanghai, where this was possible unlike in the north, could cause the Japanese to pull back from the brink. But domestic opinion was at least as important." Much early postwar literature asserted Chiang's overwhelming if not sole motivation for fighting at Shanghai was to induce Western intervention. Taylor highlights Barbara Tuchman's acid remarks as an example: "from first to last, Chiang Kai-shek had one purpose: to destroy the Communists and wait for foreign help to defeat the Japanese." *Sand Against the Wind: Stilwell and the American Experience in China* (London: Macmillan, 1971), 168. Van de Ven cites similar analysis from Frank Dorn, *The History of the Sino-Japanese War: From Marco Polo Bridge to Pearl Harbor* (New York: Macmillan, 1974), 67, 78 [hereafter Dorn, *The History of the Sino-Japanese War*], and Lloyd Eastman, "Nationalist China During the Sino-Japanese War," in John Fairbank and Denis Twitchett, eds., *The Cambridge History of China*, vol. 13 (Cambridge, UK: Cambridge

University Press, 1986), 551. This charge ignores the depth of Chiang's commitment of his best units that he would have needed to deal with the Communists if all he was seeking was Western intervention to drive out the Japanese. Peter Harmsen offered the astute observation that Chiang may have been influenced by the course of the battle in 1932 in Shanghai. *Nanjing: Battle for a Doomed City* (Philadelphia: Casemate, 2015), 84.

26 **Chiang sends two divisions to Shanghai and restricts local commander:** Yang, "Chiang Kai-shek and the Battles of Shanghai and Nanjing," 146.

26 **"The Chinese [troops] wear olive drab uniforms . . .":** *New York Times*, 14 August 1937, 3; 50,000 refugees to International Settlement: "Some Phases of the Sino-Japanese Conflict (July to December 1937), Compiled from the records of the Command in Chief Asiatic Fleet . . . Shanghai, China December 1938," 14, Charles J. Whiting Papers, Box 5, Hoover Institution, Standford University [hereafter Hoover Institution].

27 **"[look] as though a full–scale war could be averted" and rejection of concept Imperial Navy caused expansion of war:** Hata, "The Marco Polo Bridge Incident," 261–62.

27 **Japanese see Shanghai as new theater and first clash:** Yang, "Chiang Kai-shek and the Battles of Shanghai and Nanjing," 148–49.

27 **13 August 1937, Chinese air strike at Shanghai:** Yang, "Chiang Kai-shek and the Battles of Shanghai and Nanjing," 146–47. *New York Times*, 16 August 1937, 1, gives figure of 1,142 dead.

27 **Opening clashes in Shanghai; Japanese air raids:** Hattori and Drea, "Japanese Operations from July to December 1937," 168–69; Mitsura Hagiwara, "The Japanese Air Campaigns in China, 1937–1945," in Peattie, Drea, and van de Ven, *The Battle for China*, 242–44 [hereafter Hagiwara, "The Japanese Air Campaigns in China, 1937–1945"]; *New York Times*, 16 August 1937, 1.

27 **Imperial Navy advocates campaigns from Shanghai to Nanjing; Japanese defenders initially outnumbered ten to one:** Bix, *Hirohito and the Making of Modern Japan*, 323; Spence, *The Search for Modern China*, 400.

27 **Matsui described:** Hallett Abend, "Matsui is grieved by World's View," *New York Times*, 12 October 1937, 2.

27 **Shanghai Expeditionary Army created; chiefs of staff offer strategy to emperor:** Hattori and Drea, "Japanese Operations from July to December 1937," 169.

28 **Initial Chinese assault against Japanese enclave in Shanghai:** Harmsen, *Shanghai 1937*, 51, 70–72, 82–83, 88–89.

28 **"Every building was bullet-marked . . .":** Jeff E. Long, "The Japanese Literati and the 'China Incident': Hayashi Fusao Reporting the Battle of Shanghai," *Journal of Sino-Chinese Studies* 15 (April 2003): 36.

28 **Chinese Shanghai offensive stalls, August 20 "General War Directive," and "point of no return":** van de Ven, *War and Nationalism in China*, 198–99.

28 **Arrival of 3rd and 11th Divisions, importance of Luodian:** Hattori and Drea, "Japanese Operations from July to December 1937," 169; Harmsen, *Shanghai 1937*, 99.

28 **Table and discussion of comparative combat capabilities of Japanese and Chinese ground units:** Chang, "The Nationalist Army on the Eve of War," 124–28, including Table 1 from Xu Yong, *The Conqueror's Dream: Japan's Strategy of Invading China* (Guilin: Guangxi Normal University Press, 1993), 28; Ryoichi Tobe, "The Japanese Eleventh Army in Central China, 1938–1941," in Peattie, Drea, and van de Ven, *The Battle for China*, 210–11 [hereafter Tobe, "The Japanese Eleventh Army in Central China"].

29 **Imperial Army opinion on quality of Chinese forces:** Chang, "The Nationalist Army on the Eve of the War," 103.

30 **Japanese estimates of comparative capabilities of Imperial Army and Chinese units:** Tobe, "The Japanese Eleventh Army in Central China," 211.

30 **Evaluation of Dorn:** Dorn, *The History of the Sino-Japanese War,* 6–10.

30 **Obstacles in front of 11th Division:** Hattori and Drea, "Japanese Operations from July to December 1937," 169–70.

30 **"large and small conical grave mounds . . .":** *New York Times,* 8 September 1937, 1.

30 **". . .a maze of tiny streets . . .":** "The Story of the Jacquinot Zone, Shanghai China," Father Jacquinot de Besange , S.J., p. 9, Vertical File, China, History, 1937, FDRL.

31 **Obstacles in front of 3rd Division:** Hattori and Drea, "Japanese Operations from July to December 1937," 170.

31 **"The anti-Japanese feeling of the Chinese people is now at such a pitch. . .":** *New York Times,* 2 September 1937, 3. Two days later, this paper reported that thousands of Chinese soldiers in plain clothes left behind in areas overrun by the Japanese "made much trouble" for the Japanese, *New York Times,* 4 September 1937, 1.

31 **Imperial Headquarters mobilizes reserve battalions and factors raising Japanese casualties:** Hattori and Drea, "Japanese Operations from July to December 1937," 170–71.

31 **Dismissal of Ishiwara:** Peattie, *Ishiwara Kanji,* 303–6.

32 **Chiang's commitment to Shanghai and tie to political goals:** Taylor, *The Generalissimo,* 147; Yang, "Chiang Kai-shek and the Battles of Shanghai and Nanjing," 150–51.

32 **"international sympathy, though the source of great encouragement . . .":** *New York Times,* 10 October 1937, 39.

32 **Shanghai's International Settlement:** "Shanghai Lifeless City Weary of War," *New York Times,* 25 October 1937, 1.

33 **Reinforcements and Matsui's new orders:** Hattori and Drea, "Japanese Operations from July to December 1937," 171–74. By 23 September, Japanese Shanghai casualties numbered over 2,500 killed and 9,800 wounded.

33 **Fierce Chinese resistance, concentrated artillery fire, close range tactics, failure to take prisoners:** Hattori and Drea, "Japanese Operations from July to December 1937," 173–74; Harmsen, *Shanghai 1937,* 165; "Both Sides Shoot Soldiers Who Could be Taken Captive—League Survey Starts," *New York Times,* 26 September 1937, 35; Harmsen, *Shanghai 1937,* 181. On 21 October, more than nine weeks after fighting began, a *New York Times* reporter asked about prisoners of war taken by the Imperial Navy in Shanghai. He was taken to a temple and shown just twenty-seven Chinese and told these were the only prisoners taken since the start of the fighting. The reporter noted neither side routinely took prisoners. *New York Times,* 21 October 1937, 15.

33 **"viewed [China] as a dog, [it] now emerges as a wolf":** Tsuneo Watanabe and James E. Auer, eds., *Who Was Responsible?: From Marco Polo Bridge to Pearl Harbor* (Tokyo: The Yomuri Shimbun, 2006), 70 [hereafter Watanabe and Auer, *Who Was Responsible?*].

34 **Chinese failure to create defense in depth:** van de Ven, *War and Nationalism in China,* 216.

34 **The 101st Division and fighting along Suzhou Creek and beyond:** Hattori and Drea, "Japanese Operations from July to December 1937," 173–74.

34 **"In explanation of the slowness of their progress . . .":** *New York Times,* 29 September 1937, 1. The same paper published an article on 1 October 1937, 11, "Military Experts See Weak Japan," with a subhead: "Assert Shanghai Fight Shows No Major Power Need Fear Japan."

34 **Celebration in Tokyo of collapse of Chinese resistance in Shanghai:** *New York Times,* 27 October 1937, 2.

35 **Japanese losses in Shanghai, reaction of Japanese public:** Hattori and Drea, "Japanese Operations from July to December 1937, 174–75"; Drea, *Japan's Imperial Army,* 196; *New York Times,* 27 October 1937, 2.

DIVISION	PREWAR STRENGTH	KILLED	WOUNDED	TOTAL CASUALTIES
3rd	14,624	3,013	8,578	11,591 (79%)
9th	13,182	3,883	527	12,410 (94%)
11th	12,795	2,293	6,084	8,377 (65%)
13th	13,614	1,010	4,140	5,150 (38%)
101st		873	3,801	4,674
Total		11,072	31,130	42,202

35 **Official Chinese losses and later estimate:** Yang, "Chiang Kai-shek and the Battles of Shanghai and Nanjing," 154; Spence, *The Search for Modern China,* 401.

35 **Chinese losses in Shanghai, loss of academy-trained officers:** Taylor, *The Generalissimo,* 150; MacKinnon, *Wuhan,* 23.

35 **"We were totally defeated. It was my fault":** Yang, "Chiang Kai-shek and the Battles of Shanghai and Nanjing," 153.

35 **Genuine coalition of China's armed forces emerges:** van de Ven, *China at War,* 88–89.

35 **Unprecedented patriotic fervor kindled in China, "The Lost Battalion":** Lary, *The Chinese People at War,* 17, 38; Harmsen, *Shanghai 1937,* 190, 195–96, 198, 204–6; van de Ven, *China at War,* 91.

36 **Chinese slogans and mass singing:** Lary, *The Chinese People at War,* 4, 41, 54.

36 **"The March of the Volunteers":** Lary, *The Chinese People at War,* 13.

2: "The Bombs and the Bullets and the Bayonets of the Japanese Are Ruthless"

37 **Creation of Tenth Army:** Hattori and Drea, "Japanese Operations from July to December 1937," 176. The Tenth Army comprised the 18th and 114th Divisions from Japan and the 6th and 16th Divisions from North China.

37 **"our biggest strategic mistake":** Yang, "Chiang Kai-shek and the Battles of Shanghai and Nanjing," 153–54.

37 **Defeat became rout:** Yang, "Chiang Kai-shek and the Battles of Shanghai and Nanjing," 154–56; Hattori and Drea, "Japanese Operations from July to December 1937," 176.

37 **Chinese retreat from Shanghai described:** Williamsen, "The Military Dimension, 1937–41," 143.

38 **Divided opinion in Imperial Army over advance to Nanjing and distance:** Yang, "Chiang Kai-shek and the Battles of Shanghai and Nanjing," 154; Drea and van de Ven, "An Overview of Major Military Campaigns during the Sino-Japanese War, 1937–45," 31.

38 **Creation of Central China Field Army and split advance of Shanghai Expeditionary Army and Tenth Army:** Hattori and Drea, "Japanese Operations from July to December 1937," 176; Yang, "Chiang Kai-shek and the Battles of Shanghai and Nanjing," 154–55.

38 **Yanagawa urges thrust to Nanjing, Yanagawa proposes use of gas, Prince Kan'in rejects use of gas, concurrence of Yanagawa and Mitsui on opportunity to end war:** Hattori and Drea, "Japanese Operations from July to December 1937," 176–77; Spence, *The Search for Modern China*, 401; Bob Tadashi Wakabayashi, "Leftover Problems," in Wakabayashi, *The Nanking Atrocity 1937–38*, 386 [hereafter Wakabayashi, "Leftover Problems"].

38 **Chiang moves government to Chungking and his headquarters to Wuhan:** Taylor, *The Generalissimo*, 150.

38 **"Should we defend Nanjing or abandon it?" and split among Chinese leaders and von Falkenhausen:** Yang, "Chiang Kai-shek and the Battles of Shanghai and Nanjing," 155; Taylor, *The Generalissimo*, 150.

38 **"a sacrifice which is unnecessary, meaningless and without strategic benefit":** Yang, "Chiang Kai-shek and the Battles of Shanghai and Nanjing," 155.

38 **Chiang faces internal advocates for appeasement, "men of letters," and "lost their guts":** Yang, "Chiang Kai-shek and the Battles of Shanghai and Nanjing," 155–56.

39 **Soviet treaty, supplies, and communications and their impact on Chiang:** Yang, "Chiang Kai-shek and the Battles of Shanghai and Nanjing," 157; Drea and van de Ven, "An Overview of Major Military Campaigns during the Sino-Japanese War, 1937–45," 31. Yang makes a direct connection between defense of Nanjing and hope for Soviet intervention. Drea and van de Ven are more generalized that defense of the capital was important for international as well as domestic reasons.

40 **"was the only instance in which the high commands of both countries agreed . . .":** Hata, "The Marco Polo Bridge Incident, 1937," 279.

40 **Trautmann Mediation Effort:** Hata, "The Marco Polo Bridge Incident, 1937," 279–86; Yang, "Chiang Kai-shek and the Battles of Shanghai and Nanjing," 15–57; Zhang Baijia, "China's Quest for Foreign Military Aid," in Peattie, Drea, and van de Ven, *The Battle for China*, 297.

40 **"Tang's distinguishing feature . . .":** Spence, *The Search for Modern China*, 401.

40 **"It is hard to defend Nanjing . . .":** Yang, "Chiang Kai-shek and the Battles of Shanghai and Nanjing," 155.

40 **Geography of Nanjing:** Map 6, The Nanjing Campaign, November–December 1937, in Peattie, Drea, and van de Ven, *The Battle for China*, after p. 26; F. Tillman Durdin, "Japanese Atrocities Marked Fall of Nanking," *New York Times*, 9 January 1937, 38 [hereafter Durdin, "Japanese Atrocities Marked Fall of Nanking"].

41 **"in a final heroic gesture so dear to the Chinese heart":** Durdin, "Japanese Atrocities Marked Fall of Nanking."

41 **Establishment of Imperial General Headquarters and the Liaison Conference:** Hata, "The Marco Polo Bridge Incident, 1937," 268–72.

41 **November 25 Imperial Conference, creation of Imperial General Headquarters:** Hattori and Drea, "Japanese Operations from July to December 1937," 176–77.

41 **Tokyo authorizes seizure of Nanjing, creation of Central China Area Army, crumbling Chinese defenses:** Hattori and Drea, "Japanese Operations from July to December 1937," 177; Yang, "Chiang Kai-shek and the Battles of Shanghai and Nanjing," 156.

41 **Stalin's message of 5 December 1937 and Chiang's message to his commanders, December 6:** Taylor, *The Generalissimo*, 151; Yang, "Chiang Kai-shek and the Battles of Shanghai and Nanjing," 157–58.

42 **Japanese advance on Nanjing:** Hattori and Drea, "Japanese Operations from July to December 1937," 177–78.

42 **History of Nanjing and remodeling:** Mitter, *Forgotten Ally*, 50; Lary, *China's Republic*, 83; John E. Woods, *The Good Man of Nanking, The Diaries of John Rabe* (New York: Alfred A. Knopf, 1998), xv–xvi [hereafter Woods, *The Good Man of Nanking*]; Hattori and Drea, "Japanese Operations from July to December 1937," 178.

43 **Size of Nanjing Safety Zone:** Hua-ling Hu and Zhang Lian-hong, eds., *The Undaunted Women of Nanking: The Wartime Diaries of Minnie Vautrin and Tsen Shui-Fang* (Carbondale: Southern Illinois University Press, 2010), 2 [hereafter Hu and Lian-Hong, *The Undaunted Women of Nanking*]. "Tsen Shui-Fang" was the Romanization used contemporaneous to 1937 events. This account uses the more conventional subsequent rendering of "Cheng Ruifang" in the text and in the notes, except when the book title is used.

43 **International Committee, Nanjing Safety Zone and background on Rabe:** Rabe diary, November 19, 22, 23, and 1–2 December 1937, as quoted in Woods, *The Good Man of Nanking*, 25, 27–28, 46–47. The original members who comprised the Safety Committee and those who remained were: Americans 7 (6); British 4 (1); Germans 4 (3); and Danes 1 (0). Woods, *The Good Man of Nanking*, 43. By 21 December 1937, the list of foreign nationals in Nanjing totaled 22: Germans 5, White Russians 2, Austrians 1, Americans 14. Woods, *The Good Man of Nanking*, 272. For a detailed exploration of the Western and American presence in Nanjing in December 1937, see David Askew, "The International Community for the Nanjing Safety Zone: An Introduction," *Journal of Sino-Japanese Studies* 14 (April 2002): 3–22. Askew concluded that as many as 29 to 31 foreigners were in Nanjing as the Japanese Army approached. Of this total, five were journalists and twenty-two signed a petition as members of the International Committee. There were possibly as many as four other foreigners.

43 **"something very like an acting mayor":** Rabe diary, 8 December 1937, as quoted in Woods, *The Good Man of Nanking*, 54.

43 **"Every inch of soil that the Japanese conquer should be fertilized with our blood . . .":** Rabe diary, 6 December 1937, as quoted in Woods, *The Good Man of Nanking*, 41.

43 **International Committee gathers food, etc., attempts to keep Chinese soldiers out of Safety Zone:** Rabe diary, 9 December 1937, in Woods, *The Good Man of Nanking*, 55–57.

43 **"We assured them that if they gave up their equipment their lives would be spared . . .":** "Occupation of Nanking, Two Accounts by Eye-witnesses," Randall Gould Papers, Box 4, Folder "The Occupation of Nanking," p. 4, Hoover Institution.

44 **Order of battle of Chinese defenders of Nanjing:** David Askew, "Defending Nanjing:

An Examination of the Capital Garrison Forces," *Journal of Sino-Japanese Studies* 15 (April 2003): 148–73, esp. 151, 153 [hereafter Askew, "Defending Nanjing: An Examination of the Capital Garrison Forces"].

44 **Sichuan troops bolt away from Nanjing:** Yang, "Chiang Kai-shek and the Battle of Shanghai and Nanjing," 156.

44 **Best estimate of defenders:** Askew, "Defending Nanjing: An Examination of the Capital Garrison Forces," 152.

45 **Horst Baerensprung observations:** From his diary excerpt quoted in Woods, *The Good Man of Nanking*, 23–24.

45 **"entire columns . . . without any footwear . . .":** Rabe diary, 17–18 November 1937, as quoted in Woods, *The Good Man of Nanking*, 22–23. Like Askew, Yang also emphasizes the high proportion of raw recruits in Chinese ranks. "Chiang Kai-shek and the Battles of Shanghai and Nanjing," 157.

45 **Effective figures for "fighting troops":** Askew, "Defending Nanjing: An Examination of the Capital Garrison Forces," 151–53, 163. Askew points out that all the defenders except for the two divisions of the "Second Army" had fought at Shanghai.

45 **Chinese defense lines for Nanjing and Japanese attacks on 10 December 1937:** Hattori and Drea, "Japanese Operations from July to December 1937," 178.

45 **Chinese "scorched earth" tactics:** Durdin, "Japanese Atrocities Marked Fall of Nanking"; diary of Minnie Vautrin, 12 December 1937 [hereafter Vautrin diary], in Hu and Lian-hong, *The Undaunted Women of Nanking*, 31.

45 **Fighting on 10–12 December 1937:** Hattori and Drea, "Japanese Operations from July to December 1937," 178; Yang, "Chiang Kai-shek and the Battles of Shanghai and Nanjing," 157.

46 **"When Purple Mountain burns, Nanking is lost" and refugees in his compound:** Rabe diary, 12, 24 December 1937, as quoted in Woods, *The Good Man of Nanking*, 63, 92. On 26 December Rabe managed to save all of them from potentially being "selected" by Japanese for labor or execution. Rabe diary, 26 December 1937, as quoted in Woods, 97.

46 **Belated decision by Chiang and Tang to abandon Nanjing:** Hattori and Drea, "Japanese Operations from July to December 1937," 178–79.

46 **Scenes at Yijiang and Xiaguan Gates:** Yang Daqing, "Atrocities in Nanjing: Searching for Explanations," 91–92; Durdin, "Japanese Atrocities Marked Fall of Nanking"; A. T. Steele, "Japanese Troops Kill Thousands," *Chicago Daily News*, 15 December 1937, 1; "Occupation of Nanking, Two Accounts by Eye-witnesses," Randall Gould Papers, Box 4, Folder "The Occupation of Nanking," 4, 6, Hoover Institution; Rabe diary, 7 January 1938 (streets full of corpses being eaten by dogs), in Woods, *The Good Man of Nanking*, 115.

46 **Matsui orders, Tenth Army enters city in force; "meaning everyone from prisoners of war to suspicious-looking civilians":** Hattori and Drea, "Japanese Operations from July to December 1937," 179.

47 **"At first sight of the Japanese, a sense of relief . . .":** Rabe diary, 15 December 1937 (quoting a Reuters correspondent), as quoted in Woods, *The Good Man of Nanking*, 72–73.

47 **Display of Japanese flags:** Vautrin diary, 14 December 1937, in Hu and Lian-hong, *The Undaunted Women of Nanking*, 36.

47 **"certain Japanese officers tempered power with generosity and compassion":** Durdin, "Japanese Atrocities Marked Fall of Nanking."

47   "We have had some very pleasant Japanese who have treated us with courtesy and
     respect . . .": "The Occupation of Nanking, A Second Account by an Eye Witness," 2.

47   "The Japanese might have gained a wide measure of support and confidence . . .":
     Durdin, "Japanese Atrocities Marked Fall of Nanking."

47   Japanese soldiers first seek food and shelter: Vautrin and Cheng diaries, 13–14
     December 1937, in Hu and Lian-hong, *The Undaunted Women of Nanking*, 33–36;
     New York Times, 18 December 1937, "Butchery Marked Capture of Nanking," 1; Dur-
     din, "Japanese Atrocities Marked Fall of Nanking."

47   "The Japanese march through the city in groups of ten to twenty soldiers . . .": Rabe
     diary, 13 December 1937, as quoted in Woods, *The Good Man of Nanking*, 67.

48   "Open Door Policy": Cheng diary, 14–15 December 1937, in Hu and Lian-hong, *The
     Undaunted Women of Nanking*, 37–38.

48   "Every foreign house is a sight to behold . . .": "The Occupation of Nanking, A Sec-
     ond Account by an Eye Witness," 1.

48   Massive looting of stores and homes followed by arson: Vautrin diary 14,
     26, 31 December 1937, 2 February 1938 ("cover up evidence of very thorough loot-
     ing"), in Hu and Lian-hong, *The Undaunted Women of Nanking*, 36, 68, 76, 131.

48   Last fires seen 17 January 1938: Minnie Vautrin, "At a Refugee Camp: 14 January
     1938–31 March 1938," in Hu and Lian-hong, *The Undaunted Women of Nanking*, 190.

48   "Rape! Rape! Rape! . . .": "The Occupation of Nanking, A Second Account by an Eye
     Witness," 1.

48   Japanese soldiers seek "hwa guniang" (young girls), women from twelve to sixty, and
     teenage boys: Vautrin diary, 24 December 1937 and 7 and 13 February 1938, in Hu
     and Lian-hong, *The Undaunted Women of Nanking*, 64, 137, 146. Also in the same
     source, 183, Minnie Vautrin, "A Review of the First Month: 13 December 1937–13
     January 1938."

48   Ginling College as refugee camp for women and children: Hu and Lian-hong, *The
     Undaunted Women of Nanking*, 2, 25.

48   A sampler of the Vautrin diary entries referring to rapes, attempted rapes, and her
     efforts to break up rapes includes the following (pp. in parentheses): 16 December
     1937 (40); 17 December (43); 19 December (actual rape in progress) (51); 22 Decem-
     ber (56); 25 December (67–68); 1 January 1938 ("we believe that the raping of
     women has decreased although a few days ago twenty-seven women were raped
     on B.T.T.S. [Bible Teachers Training School])" (77–78); 21 January (foils rape in
     progress) (113); 24 January (foils rape in progress) (118); 1 February (129); 2 Feb-
     ruary (131); 4 February (133); 7 February (137); 8 February (foils rape in progress)
     (138); 9 February (142). From the same source, some references in the Cheng
     diary include: 18 December (50); 22 December (58); 27 December (70). The
     Rabe diary also addresses rapes. The American contemporary accounts are in
     the Randall Gould Papers, Box 4, Folder "The Occupation of Nanking," Hoover
     Institution.

49   "one poor woman was raped thirty-seven times . . .": "The Occupation of Nanking, A
     Second Account by an Eye Witness," 1.

49   "If husbands or brothers intervene, they are shot": Rabe diary, 17 December 1937, in
     Woods, *The Good Man of Nanking*, 77.

49   "a woman six months pregnant, who resisted . . .": "The Occupation of Nanking, A
     Second Account by an Eye Witness," 1.

49 **"Many young women are faced with a terrible dilemma . . .":** Vautrin diary, 24 December 1937, in Hu and Lian-hong, *The Undaunted Women of Nanking,* 64.

49 **"Japanese Troops Gently Sooth the Refugees . . .":** Vautrin diary, 21 January 1938, in Hu and Lian-hong, *The Undaunted Women of Nanking,* 123.

49 **Women from disbanded camps seek refuge at Ginling:** Vautrin diary, 5 February 1938, in Hu and Lian-hong, *The Undaunted Women of Nanking,* 135.

49 **Figures for rapes in Nanjing and between Nanjing and Shanghai:** Bob Tadashi Wakabayashi, "The Messiness of Historical Reality," in Wakabayashi, *The Nanking Atrocity,* 8 [hereafter Wakabayashi, "The Messiness of Historical Reality"]; Kasahara Tokushi, "Massacres Outside Nanking City," in Wakabayashi, *The Nanking Atrocity 1937–38,* 58; Masahiro Yamamoto, "A Tale of Two Atrocities: Critical Appraisal of American Historiography," in Wakabayashi, *The Nanking Atrocity 1937–38,* 298 [hereafter Yamamoto, "A Tale of Two Atrocities: Critical Appraisal of American Historiography"]; van de Ven, *China at War,* 98. In a pathbreaking work, reporter Honda Katsuichi collected a massive number of Chinese recollections of murder and rape by Imperial Army soldiers on the march from Shanghai to Nanjing. This has been published in English as *The Nanjing Massacre: A Japanese Journalist Confronts Japan's National Shame* (Armonk, NY: M. E. Sharpe, 1999). Honda's reliance on remote Chinese recollections was attacked by some Japanese historians. As Daqing Yang recounts, in an effort to counter the charges of Honda and others, as well as disprove the existence of a massive amount of looting, rape, and murder in Nanjing itself, Kaikosha, a fraternal organization of former Japanese military academy graduates, solicited reports from its members. Far from disproving the work of Honda and others, the eventual text published by the association focuses mainly on military operations but contains numerous side references to murders of prisoners. With this support for the reports of Honda et al. of murder, it is impossible to discount their parallel evidence on rape. "Convergence or Divergence? Recent Historical Writings on the Rape of Nanjing," *The American Historical Review* 104, no. 3 (June 1999): 845–46, 849 [hereafter Daqing Yang, "Convergence or Divergence?"].

49 **"came out to identify three men she did not know at all . . .":** Cheng diary, 29 December 1937, in Hu and Lian-hong, *The Undaunted Women of Nanking,* 73–74.

49 **"The only thing that had saved the Chinese people from utter destruction . . .":** Vautrin diary, 18 December 1937, in Hu and Lian-hong, *The Undaunted Women of Nanking,* 49.

50 **"The Goddess of Mercy":** Cheng diary, 26 December 1937, 20 February 1938, in Hu and Lian-hong, *The Undaunted Women of Nanking,* 69, 156; both refer to Vautrin title as "Goddess of Mercy."

50 **"very capable and courageous" and "all knelt and began to weep and implore":** Cheng diary, 17 February 1938; Vautrin diary, 17 February 1938, in Hu and Lian-hong, *The Undaunted Women of Nanking,* 151–52.

50 **Scenes as Chinese units disintegrate and soldiers flee via Xiaguan Gate:** *New York Times,* 16 December 1937, 1, 5; "Butchery Marked Capture of Nanking," 18 December 1937, 10; Durdin, "Japanese Atrocities Marked Fall of Nanking"; "Occupation of Nanking, Two Accounts by Eye-witnesses," 4, Randall Gould Papers, Box 4, Folder "The Occupation of Nanking," Hoover Institution.

50 **Legal status of "plain clothes soldiers":** Wakabayashi, "Leftover Problems," 372. Wakabayashi notes cases reported in Japanese records and diaries of Chinese feign-

ing surrender to kill with concealed weapons or waving Japanese flags to ambush Japanese troops.

50 **Evidence to establish "plain clothes soldiers":** Durdin, "Japanese Atrocities Marked Fall of Nanking"; "The Occupation of Nanking, A Second Account by an Eye Witness," 3.

51 **Durdin's eyewitness reports:** F. Tillman Durdin, "Butchery Marked Capture of Nanking," *New York Times*, 18 December 1937, 1, 10.

51 **Report of Reuters correspondent:** Rabe diary, 15 December 1937, as quoted in Woods, *The Good Man of Nanking*, 72–73.

51 **Burned survivors of mass executions:** "The Occupation of Nanking, A Second Account by an Eye Witness," 2.

51 **"scores of black charred bodies and among them two empty kerosene or gasoline":** Vautrin diary, 26 January 1938, in Hu and Lian-hong, *The Undaunted Women of Nanking*, 122. In a subsequent letter, Vautrin reported that two ponds alone contained a total of 143 bodies, Minnie Vautrin, "At a Refugee Camp: 14 January 1938– 31 March 1938," in Hu and Lian-hong, *The Undaunted Women of Nanking*, 192.

51 **Reports of executions from Ninth and Sixteenth Divisions:** Hattori and Drea, "Japanese Operations from July to December 1937," 179.

51 **Battle Report, 1st Battalion, 66th Regiment:** Wakabayashi, *The Nanking Atrocity 1937–38*, 42–43.

52 **Mufushan slaughters:** Kenji Ono, "Massacres Near Mufushan," in Wakabayashi, *Nanjing Atrocity 1937–38*, 70–85 [hereafter Ono, "Massacres Near Mufushan"].

52 **"the prisoner's agonized cries of death were indescribably horrific" and "Having witnessed a scene never to be forgotten in our lives . . .":** Ono, "Massacres Near Mufushan," 77.

52 **"I figured that I'd never get another chance like this . . .":** Ono, "Massacres Near Mufushan."

52 **"a totally inconceivable, unimaginable sight":** Ono, "Massacres Near Mufushan," 81.

52 **Estimates of "clearly," "estimated illegal," and "arguably illegal" killings:** Wakabayashi, "Leftover Problems," 369–72.

53 **Disputed temporal and geographic span of massacre:** Wakabayashi, "Leftover Problems," 361–62.

53 **Contested Nanjing victim numbers:** This account draws on the discussion of the historical evolution of the numbers issue in Wakabayashi, "The Messiness of Historical Reality," 3–5; Yamamoto, "A Tale of Two Atrocities: Critical Appraisal of American Historiography," 398; Wakabayashi, "Leftover Problems," 377. Wakabayashi reports that by 1983, the PRC claimed the number of deaths was 340,000, not including any combatants. Also useful is David Askew, "Part of the Numbers Issue: Demography and Civilian Victims," in Wakabayashi, *The Nanking Atrocity*, 86–87 [hereafter Askew, "Part of the Numbers Issue"]. An authoritative source for the postwar Tokyo trials is R. John Pritchard and Sonia Magbanua Zaide, comps., *International Military Tribunal for the Far East: The Tokyo War Crimes Trials*, 22 vols. (New York, 1981–1987), 49604–8. Wakabayashi notes that on this issue, history in the PRC proved quite plastic. Early on, partial culpability was assigned to Chiang and Tang. Later this charge disappeared as a part of the standard history. In the early decades of the PRC, westerners were depicted as vile accomplices of Japanese slaughter, but by the 1980s they became luminous humanitarians.

53 **Evacuation of Nanking by civilians; "For days and days . . .":** Minnie Vautrin, "A Review of the First Month: 13 December 1937–13 January 1938," in Hu and Lian-hong, *The Undaunted Women of Nanking*, 176. Background on Vautrin role may be found in Hu and Lian-hong, *The Undaunted Women of Nanking*, 2.

54 **"only the very poor are still here":** Rabe diary, 7 December 1937, as quoted in Woods, *The Good Man of Nanking*, 52.

54 **Western estimates of Nanjing population at time city fell:** Askew, "Part of the Num-bers Issue," 87–90. Askew notes the one outlier figure by Rabe in a 14 January 1938 letter to Japanese authorities of "250,000 to 300,000." This was based on what Askew deems an inaccurate report, and he notes Rabe the same day used the figure of 200,000 as the population of the International Safety Zone in letters to Seimens and to the German embassy. Two contemporary sources that use the 200,000 figure are Vautrin diary, 22 December 1937, in Hu and Lian-hong, *The Undaunted Women of Nanking*, 56, and "Occupation of Nanking, Two Accounts by Eye-witnesses," Randall Gould Papers, Box 4, Folder "The Occupation of Nanking," 1, Hoover Institution.

54 **Japanese registration figures and adjustment:** David Askew, "Part of the Numbers Issue: Demography and Civilian Victims," in Wakabayashi, *The Nanking Atrocity 1937–38*, 94–95. Another cross-check is afforded by the report of an American State Department official on 22 January 1938. He cabled that Rabe stated that the num-ber of Chinese in the Safety Zone at that time was "approximately 250,000." *FRUS, 1938*, vol. 3, 49–50.

54 **Higher numbers for Nanjing population:** Iris Chang, *The Rape of Nanking: The Forgotten Holocaust of World War II* (New York: Basic Books, 1997), 100 [hereafter Chang, *The Rape of Nanking*].

55 **Wakabayashi definition of perimeters of "Rape of Nanking" and death tolls with scholarly support:** Wakabayashi, "Leftover Problems," 362.

55 **Estimate of over 100,000 but less than 200,000:** Once again, it is impossible to definitively support any set of numbers. These numbers accord with a swath of scholarship including Wakabayashi, "Leftover Problems," 384, and the estimate by Honda Katsuichi of more than 100,000 but less than 200,000 reported in Frank Gibney, "Editor's Introduction" to Honda Katsuichi, *The Nanjing Massacre: A Japa-nese Journalist Confronts Japan's National Shame* (Armonk, NY: M. E. Sharpe, 1999), xiii–xiv. Lary cites Rabe's estimate of 50,000 civilian deaths, a figure not including military deaths. Lary, *The Chinese People at War*, 21. Spence, *The Search for Modern China*, 401–2, cites "estimates" of 30,000 soldiers and 12,000 civilians killed with "other contemporary estimates made by Chinese observers [that] were as much as ten times higher." Spence appears to be referring to only the first seven days of Japa-nese occupation.

56 **Analysis of causes of events in Nanjing:** This analysis combines the work of Yang Daqing cited in Hattori and Drea, "Japanese Operations from July to December 1937," 179; Spence, *In Search of Modern China*, 402; and Fujiwara, "The Nanking Atrocity: An Interpretive Overview," in Wakabayashi, *The Nanking Atrocity 1937–38*, 36.

56 **Imperial rescripts invoking international law and 5 August 1937 Army Ministry directive:** Fujiwara, "The Nanjing Atrocity: An Interpretative Overview," in Waka-bayashi, *The Nanking Atrocity 1937–38*, 33–36, 41.

56 **"[to] those who bear arms against Japan":** *New York Times,* 9 October 1937, 2.

56 **Legal significance of "war" versus "incident" and fundamental Japanese views of China and the Chinese:** Fujiwara, "The Nanjing Atrocity: An Interpretative Overview," 35–36.

57 **Executions, lack of food:** Fujiwara, "The Nanjing Atrocity: An Interpretative Overview," 48, 72, and Wakabayashi, "Leftover Problems," 373.

57 **Socialization in the Imperial Army:** Drea, *Japan's Imperial Army,* 68, 133–35; Meirion and Susie Harries, *Soldiers of the Sun: The Rise and Fall of the Imperial Japanese Army* (New York: Random House, 1991), 482.

57 **Losses in Ninth Division:** Hattori and Drea, "Japanese Operations from July to December 1937," 175, 179.

57 **Chinese resistance to Japan's cause particularly infuriating:** Mitter, *Forgotten Ally,* 143.

58 **"To be perfectly frank, the ways you (Matsumoto) and I look at the Chinese are fundamentally different . . .":** Hotta, *Pan-Asianism and Japan's War, 1931–45,* 152.

58 **Postwar conviction of Matsui on charges of crimes of omission:** Timothy Brook, "Ralhabinod Pal on the Rape of Nanking," in Wakabayashi, *The Nanking Atrocity 1937–38,* 156, and Yamamoto, "A Tale of Two Atrocities: Critical Appraisal of American Historiography," 293–94.

58 **Short-term effects of Nanjing events:** Hattori and Drea, "Japanese Operations from July to December 1937," 179. Dr. Rana Mitter pointed out that the Nanjing massacre was not well publicized during the war, hence its immediate effects were limited.

3: "Water as a Substitute for Soldiers"

59 **Konoe Government "rethink"; 11 January 1938, Imperial conference; 16 January announcement:** Hata, "Marco Polo Bridge Incident," in Morley, *The China Quagmire,* 279–86; Drea, *Japan's Imperial Army,* 199; Taylor, *The Generalissimo,* 153; Bix, *Hirohito and the Making of Modern Japan,* 343–46; Oka, *Konoe,* 67–70; Yagami, *Konoe Fumimaro,* 51–55.

60 **"no large amount of intelligence is necessary . . .":** Paine, *The Wars of Asia,* 162. Konoe and Kido's views, Yagami, *Konoe Fumimaro,* 52–55.

60 **Mistaken reports of the end of Chinese resistance:** Lary, *The Chinese People at War,* 19, 44; Mitter, *Forgotten Ally,* 116–17.

60 **"Defeatist Tone of Official Chinese Statements . . .":** *New York Times,* 1 January 1938, 1.

60 **Japan seen as modernizing force for China:** Stephen MacKinnon, "The Defense of the Central Yangtze," in Peattie, Drea, and van de Ven, *The Battle for China,* 184 [hereafter MacKinnon, "The Defense of the Central Yangtze"]; MacKinnon, *Wuhan,* 98–99.

60 **"One phase of this war which I had not expected . . .":** President's Secretary File, Box 26, Diplomatic, Chile Jul-Dec 1941 thru China 1938, Folder Diplomatic Correspondence China 1938, FDRL.

61 **"No government in China could today . . .":** Memorandum, 19 February 1938, from Admiral William D. Leahy, forwarding letter from Captain Riley F. McConnell, Chief of Staff, Asiatic Fleet, to Rear Admiral J. O. Richardson, President's Secretary

File, Box 26, Diplomatic, Chile Jul-Dec 1941 thru China 1938, Folder Diplomatic Correspondence China 1938, FDRL.

61 **Chiang argues China has achieved a strategic success at January 1938 meeting:** van de Ven, *War and Nationalism in China*, 218–19.

61 **Execution of General Han Fuju:** MacKinnon, *Wuhan*, 18–19; van de Ven, *War and Nationalism in China*, 195.

61 **"presiding coordinator of a loose federation of forces":** Jonathan D. Spence, *The Search for Modern China* (New York: W. W. Norton, 1990 edition), 460 [hereafter Spence, *The Search for Modern China* (1990 edition)].

62 **"The aim was to nurture a new type of officer . . .":** van de Ven, *War and Nationalism in China*, 83.

62 **Whampoa Academy prewar classes and selectivity:** Chang, "The Nationalist Army on the Eve of War," in Peattie, Drea, and van de Ven, *The Battle for China*, 96, 100–101.

62 **Dominance of Baoding Academy graduates in top positions in Chinese Army:** Chang, "The Nationalist Army on the Eve of War," in Peattie, Drea, and van de Ven, *The Battle for China*, 99–102.

62 **Differences between Baoding and Whampoa Military Academies:** MacKinnon, "The Defense of the Central Yangtze," 188–89, 205 (quote).

62 **Bonding of top Chinese commanders:** MacKinnon, "The Defense of the Central Yangtze," 205.

62 **"This decision was perhaps the most important [Chinese decision] of the war":** MacKinnon, *Wuhan*, 23.

62 **Regional armies provide main strength for Wuhan campaign:** MacKinnon, *Wuhan*, 23; Lary, *China's Republic*, 60 ("China's Sparta").

63 **"aggressive, ambitious, intelligent, nationalistic, puritanical, efficient, honest, daring, and innovative":** Benton, *New Fourth Army*, 102, quoting Eugen Levich, the historian of the Guangxi clique.

63 **Organization of Fifth and Ninth War Zones, widened gap between Chinese and Japanese units:** MacKinnon, *Wuhan*, 23–24; Taylor, *The Generalissimo*, 154; MacKinnon, "The Defense of the Central Yangtze," 191.

63 **March–April 1938 Nationalist Party Congress:** van de Ven, *War and Nationalism*, 219–20.

65 *Hanjian:* van de Ven, *War and Nationalism in China*, 220. Very important in this connection is Frederick Wakeman, "'Hanjian' (Traitor)!: Collaboration and Retribution in Wartime Shanghai," in Yeh Wen-hsin, ed., *Becoming Chinese: Passages to Modernity and Beyond* (Berkeley: University of California Press, 2000), 298–341 (esp. 298–309, 323–25).

65 **Imperial Headquarters orders halt to offensive operations:** Drea, *Japan's Imperial Army*, 197–98; Drea and van de Ven, "An Overview of Major Military Campaigns during the Sino-Japanese War, 1937–1945," 33; Tobe, "The Japanese Eleventh Army in Central China, 1938–1941," 207–8.

65 **Distribution of Japanese regulars and reservists:** Drea, *Japan's Imperial Army*, 198.

65 **Japanese predilection for widely dispersed columns in flanking movements:** Drea, *Japan's Imperial Army*, 200.

65 **Battles at Teng and Linyi:** MacKinnon, "The Defense of the Central Yangtze," 192–93; MacKinnon, *Wuhan*, 33–34; Chang, "The Nationalist Army on the Eve of War," 90.

66 **Battle of Taierzhuang:** MacKinnon, "The Defense of the Central Yangtze," 193–94; Tobe, "The Japanese Eleventh Army in Central China, 1938–1941," 208–9; van de Ven, *War and Nationalism in China*, 221–22, 224, 228; Drea, *Japan's Imperial Army*, 200–201; MacKinnon, *Wuhan*, 34; Drea and van de Ven, "Overview of Major Military Campaigns," 33.

66 **"Failure" to follow up victory at Taierzhuang:** MacKinnon also notes the criticism by the likes of von Falkenhausen, the Russian Kalyagin, and American attaches Carlson, Stilwell, and Dorn for the lack of Chinese pursuit of the Japanese after success at Linyi and Taierzhuang. But as MacKinnon correctly notes: "In retrospect, the charge seems unrealistic, given the inadequacy of equipment, absence of airpower, and the badly battered state of Chinese troops at the time. The Japanese were stopped but not beaten. The high morale of the Chinese troops alone could not have driven the Japanese into the sea." "The Defense of the Central Yangtze Valley," 196.

66 **Chinese soldiers fight for the nation of China:** Paine, *The Wars of Asia*, 139.

67 **Strategic position and importance of Xuzhou:** MacKinnon, "The Defense of the Central Yangtze," 186–87; van de Ven, *War and Nationalism in China*, 217.

67 **Virtues of Xuzhou and Chinese anticipate battle at Xuzhou prewar:** van de Ven, *War and Nationalism in China*, 217.

67 **Flaws in Chinese dispositions:** MacKinnon, "The Defense of the Central Yangtze," 186–87; van de Ven, *War and Nationalism*, 217.

68 **Fall of Xuzhou and Japanese boasts of historic annihilation battle at Xuzhou:** van de Ven, *War and Nationalism in China*, 225; MacKinnon, "The Defense of the Central Yangtze," 194; Tobe, "The Japanese Eleventh Army in Central China," 209.

68 **Campaign around Xuzhou and Chinese withdrawal:** MacKinnon, *Wuhan*, 35; MacKinnon, "The Defense of the Central Yangtze", 194–95; Drea, *Japan's Imperial Army*, 201; Tobe, "The Japanese Eleventh Army in Central China," 209.

68 **Devastation of Xuzhou:** Diana Lary, "A Ravaged Place: The Devastation of the Xuzhou Region, 1938," in Lary and MacKinnon, *Scars of War*, 101 [hereafter Lary, "A Ravaged Place"].

68 **Li as poet:** Lary, "A Ravaged Place," in Lary and Mackinnon, *Scars of War*, 115n21.

68 **Li's breakdown:** MacKinnon, *Wuhan*, 37.

68 **Effects of Taierzhuang and Xuzhou on Chinese morale and Japanese plans:** MacKinnon, "The Defense of the Central Yangtze," 195–97; van de Ven, *War and Nationalism*, 225.

69 **Imperial General Headquarters and Japanese cabinet plan, May 1938:** Drea, *Japan's Imperial Army*, 201; van de Ven, *War and Nationalism in China*, 226.

69 **Yellow River background and "lead to an obsession with control, and an authoritarian system of government which endured that control":** Diana Lary, "Drowned Earth: The Strategic Breaching of the Yellow River Dyke, 1938," *War in History* 8, no. 2 (2001): 191–92 [hereafter Lary, "Drowned Earth"].

69 **Need of China to buy time and the origins of decision to order breach of the dykes:** Lary, "Drowned Earth," 197; Lary, *The Chinese People at War*, 61. Mitter, *Forgotten Ally*, 157, states that at this moment, senior Chinese leadership believed "there was a serious chance that the entire Chinese war effort might collapse." Taylor states that General von Faulkenhausen, seconded by Chen Guofu, proposed breaching the dykes to halt the Japanese. Chen Guofu was head of the Central Political Training Institute that instructed Nationalist cadre. *The Generalissimo*, 154–55.

70 Breach and then flow of flood: Lary, "Drowned Earth," 199–201.

70 Calamity of flood: Lary, "A Ravaged Place," 112; Taylor, *The Generalissimo*, 155.

70 Casualty figures from Yellow River flood, June 1938: Lary, "A Ravaged Place," 112, from Li Wenhai et al., *Zhongguo jindaishi da zaihuang* (Disasters in China's modern history) (Shanghai: Renmin chubanshe, 1994), 254–55.

71 Still higher numbers for death toll: Taylor, *The Generalissimo*, 155.

71 Casualty figures: Lary, "Drowned Earth," 205–6.

71 Propaganda and blame for the disaster: Lary, "Drowned Earth," 199, 204–5.

71 Confusion and panic drive decision; scholarship showing Japanese had halted their advance: Lary, *The Chinese People at War*, 61-62; van de Ven, *China at War*, 107.

71 Chiang's silence on the Yellow River dyke breaching: Taylor, *The Generalissimo*, 155. Taylor points out few leaders in these circumstances would have done differently.

71 Disputed strategic effects of breach of Yellow River dykes: Lary, "Drowned Earth," 210, acknowledges the halt of the advance on Zhengzhou, but argues the overall effects were minimal. Van de Ven, *War and Nationalism*, maintains the effect was to gain the Chinese a five-month delay. Had the advance to Zhengzhou not been blocked at this time, it appears very likely the Japanese would have reached Wuhan months earlier without the significant losses sustained on the Yangtze route. Given how the delayed capture of Wuhan affected the Imperial Army strategists, it appears the horrific costs of the breaching of the dykes did purchase an important advantage. But it may also have inflicted a terrible blow to the long-term legitimacy of the Nationalist government.

71 Virtually no media coverage of flood in 1938: Lary, *The Chinese People at War*, 62.

71 "We are left to make an almost impossible leap in imagination . . .": Lary, "Drowned Earth," 206.

72 Clash at Zhangguofeng: Drea, *Japan's Imperial Army*, 201–2.

73 "Wuhan Summer" and preview of political and artistic freedom: MacKinnon, *Wuhan*, ch. 4–6; Lary, *The Chinese People at War*, 44.

73 "coppery brown, turbid with the red soil of the west . . .": Han Suyin, *Destination Chungking* (Hertfordshire, UK: Panther Books Limited, 1973), 54 (reprint of 1942 edition) [hereafter Han, *Destination Chungking*].

73 Description of Wuhan tri-cities: MacKinnon, *Wuhan*, 52–53.

73 Intellectual elite to Wuhan: MacKinnon, *Wuhan*, 62.

73 "Uniting to make a last stand became a moral necessity . . .": MacKinnon, *Wuhan*, 114.

73 Free press among regions of divided China and Western enclaves: MacKinnon, *Wuhan*, 63–64.

74 "more diversity of public opinion in Wuhan than in any Chinese capital before or since": MacKinnon, *Wuhan*, 65. Lary, *The Chinese People at War*, 44, supports this assessment.

74 Explosion of print outlets: MacKinnon, *Wuhan*, 63. MacKinnon noted that one Chinese journalist calculated that of the twenty-six fellow journalists he knew prior to 1938, sixteen died very early, mostly from violence. *Wuhan*, 64.

74 Range of political opinion and role of CCP: MacKinnon, *Wuhan*, 64, 113.

74 Cultural earthquake in Wuhan: MacKinnon, *Wuhan*, 62, 71–75.

74 College and secondary institutions, student populations, movement to Wuhan, social background: MacKinnon, *Wuhan*, 83–84.

74 **Role of Chinese students:** MacKinnon, *Wuhan*, 83–85.

75 **Steps toward political pluralism:** MacKinnon, *Wuhan*, 66–67.

75 **New precedents for national social services:** MacKinnon, *Wuhan*, 54–60. MacKinnon disagrees with Eastman's criticism that efforts in Wuhan were inadequate to the circumstances by maintaining they were at least equal to those in foreign concessions in Shanghai.

75 **"off stage a war, thuds like the slamming of a distant door":** W. H. Auden, "Hong Kong," from W. H. Auden, *Collected Poems* (London, 1976), 144, cited in Philip Snow, *The Fall of Hong Kong: Britain, China, and the Japanese Occupation* (New Haven, CT: Yale University Press, 2003), 32 [hereafter Snow, *Hong Kong*].

76 **Old guard of diplomats, journalists, and soldiers:** MacKinnon, *Wuhan*, 99–101.

76 **"being invaded and brutalized":** Stephen R. MacKinnon and Oris Friesen, *China Reporting: An Oral History of American Journalism in the 1930s and 1940s* (Berkeley: University of California Press, 1987), 39–41; MacKinnon, *Wuhan*, 100, 104. On Smedley, a detailed and highly sympathetic portrait is provided in Ruth Price, *The Lives of Agnes Smedley* (New York: Oxford University Press, 2005).

76 **Belden warns of path of Chinese Communist Party in power:** Jack Belden, *China Shakes the World* (New York: Harper's, 1949), esp. pp. 472–73. His "Brooklyn taxi driver" speech was noted in Henrietta Thompson, "Walk a Little Faster, Escape from Burma with General Stilwell in 1942," 4, Box 2, John L. Christian Papers, Hoover Institution.

76 **Walther Stennes:** Taylor, *The Generalissimo*, 156.

77 **Germany principal arms supplied for the first sixteen months of war:** Paine, *The Wars of Asia*, 144.

77 **German advisers depart, Soviet arms, advisers, and pilots arrive:** MacKinnon, *Wuhan*, 101–2; Paine, *The Wars of Asia*, 144.

77 **Role of American attachés:** MacKinnon, *Wuhan*, 103–4.

78 **Tong's handling of Western correspondents, favorable coverage for China:** MacKinnon, *Wuhan*, 104–6, 109.

78 **Chinese News Service:** MacKinnon, *Wuhan*, 105.

78 **Tong's policy of open contact and work of pro-Communist journalists:** MacKinnon, *Wuhan*, 106.

78 **Edgar Snow:** *Red Star Over China*; MacKinnon, *Wuhan*, 106. For a favorable take on Snow, see John Hamilton Maxwell, *Edgar Snow: A Biography* (Bloomington: Indiana University Press, 1988).

78 **Generalissimo and Madame Chiang as Man and Wife of the Year:** *Time*, vol. 31, no. 1, 3 January 1938.

78 **Japanese strategic plan and creation of Eleventh Army:** van de Ven, *War and Nationalism in China*, 226; MacKinnon, *Wuhan*, 106; Tobe, "The Japanese Eleventh Army in Central China, 1938–41," 207–8, 210.

78 **Japanese plan for capture of Wuhan:** MacKinnon, "The Defense of the Central Yangtze," 196; Drea and van de Ven, "Overview of Major Military Operations," 34. MacKinnon gives forces involved as "at least 800,000" Chinese and 400,000 Japanese, whereas Drea and van de Ven give numbers of "eventually 300,000 Japanese and 1 million Chinese troops."

79 **Overall Chinese defense scheme:** MacKinnon, "Defense of the Central Yangtze," 196–97; MacKinnon, *Wuhan*, 37–38.

79 **Geographical advantages and disadvantages, weather and disease:** Tobe, "The Japanese Eleventh Army in Central China," 210–11; MacKinnon, *Wuhan*, 37–38; van de Ven, *War and Nationalism*, 226.

79 **Japanese air superiority and use of poison gas:** van de Ven, *War and Nationalism*, 226; Drea, *Japan's Imperial Army*, 203; Drea and van de Ven, "Overview of Major Military Campaigns," 34; Jack Belden, "Japan's Drive on Hankow," 3, Jack Belden Papers, Folder, "In the Air" & "Japan's Drive on Hankow," Hoover Institution. Belden's description of the symptoms of gassed Chinese soldiers points to mustard gas or, less likely, lewisite.

79 **Fall of Anqing and Madang:** MacKinnon, *Wuhan*, 38–39; MacKinnon, "The Defense of the Central Yangtze," 197–98; Tobe, "The Japanese Eleventh Army in Central China," 211–12; van de Ven, *War and Nationalism in China*, 226–27.

79 **Hukou, Jiujiang, and Ruichang:** MacKinnon, "The Defense of the Central Yangtze," 198; Tobe, "The Japanese Eleventh Army in Central China," 212; MacKinnon, *Wuhan*, 39–40.

80 **Fierce resistance in Fifth War Zone:** MacKinnon, "The Defense of the Central Yangtze," 198–99; Tobe, "The Japanese Eleventh Army in Central China," 212–13; MacKinnon, *Wuhan*, 40.

80 **Tianjiazhen:** MacKinnon, *Wuhan*, 40; MacKinnon, "The Defense of the Central Yangtze," 199; Tobe, "The Japanese Eleventh Army in Central China," 213; van de Ven, *War and Nationalism in China*, 227.

80 **Second Army maneuvers, Xinyang:** van de Ven, *War and Nationalism in China*, 227; MacKinnon, "The Defense of the Central Yangtze," 198; MacKinnon, *Wuhan*, 40–41.

80 **Fall of Wuhan:** MacKinnon, *Wuhan*, 41; MacKinnon, "The Defense of the Central Yangtze," 199–200; Tobe, "The Japanese Eleventh Army in Central China," 213–14; Taylor, *The Generalissimo*, 157.

81 **Chinese losses in Wuhan Campaign:** MacKinnon, *Wuhan*, 42–43.

81 **Eleventh Army casualty numbers:** Tobe, "The Japanese Eleventh Army in Central China," 214 25.

81 **Loss of Guangzhou (Canton):** MacKinnon, *Wuhan*, 41; MacKinnon, "The Defense of the Central Yangtze," 200; Tobe, "The Eleventh Army in Central China," 213; Drea, *Japan's Imperial Army*, 203.

81 **Background on Changsha:** Lary, *The Chinese People at War*, 62.

81 **Destruction of Changsha:** Lary, *The Chinese People at War*, 63–64; MacKinnon, *Wuhan*, 42; van de Ven, *China at War*, 108; MacKinnon, "The Defense of the Central Yangtze," 200.

81 **Scorched earth policy:** van de Ven, *China at War*, 105–9, 119; Lary, *The Chinese People at War*, 60–61.

82 **"New Order in East Asia":** Paine, *Wars of Asia*, 160.

82 **Japanese seek rival Chinese leader:** van de Ven, *War and Nationalism*, 230.

82 **Wang's background and "In this poet I discover a fervent reformer . . .":** Lary, *The Chinese People at War*, 47–48; Paine, *Wars of Asia*, 165–67; Mitter, *Forgotten Ally*, 38–39 ("like a crazed lion" quote and recklessness).

83 **Wang's negotiation with Japan:** van de Ven, *War and Nationalism*, 230; Lary, *The Chinese People at War*, 48–49. Morley, *The China Quagmire*, 379–96 provides the convoluted details of the negotiations conducted by Wang with the Japanese, updated by van de Ven, *China at War*, 117–21.

83 **"traitor for a thousand generations":** as quoted in Mitter, *Forgotten Ally*, 7.

83 **Wang followed by few political and no important military leaders:** MacKinnon, "The Defense of the Central Yangtze," 205–6; van de Ven, *China at War*, 119–20.

83 **Chinese situation end of 1938:** MacKinnon, "The Defense of the Central Yangtze Valley," 200–201; Drea and van de Ven, "Overview of Major Military Campaigns," 35.

84 **November 1938 Chinese military conference:** van de Ven, *War and Nationalism*, 230–32. By contrast, MacKinnon sees Chiang as acting with "less bravado" than at the January 1938 conference and as more modest in his achievements. *Wuhan*, 111–12.

84 **Chiang's subordinates recognize his symbolic importance and his physical courage:** MacKinnon, "The Defense of the Central Yangtze Valley," 206.

84 **Changes in Japanese strategic perceptions, extent of Japanese control:** Drea, *Japan's Imperial Army*, 203; Drea and van de Ven, "Overview of Major Military Operations," 35; Tobe, "The Japanese Eleventh Army in Central China," 215; MacKinnon, *Wuhan*, 42–43; van de Ven, *War and Nationalism*, 227; Lary, *The Chinese People at War*, 46; Yagami, *Konoe Fumimaro*, 68.

85 **Paradox of Wuhan:** MacKinnon, *Wuhan*, 110.

4: "The Greatest Migration of People in All History"

86 **"conduct was excellent":** quoted in Liu, "A Whole Nation Walking," 29.

86 **"Is war so dreadful? Not at all . . .":** Liu, "A Whole Nation Walking," 33.

86 **"By the twentieth century, urban populations in particular . . .":** Stephen MacKinnon, "Refugee Flight at the Outset of the Anti-Japanese War," in Diana Lary and Stephen MacKinnon, eds., *Scars of War: The Impact of Warfare on Modern China* (Vancouver: UBC Press, 2001), 118, 121 [hereafter MacKinnon, "Refugee Flight at the Outset of the Anti-Japanese War" and Lary and MacKinnon, *Scars of War*].

87 **Fear of warlord soldiers in Chinese populace, "Burn, Kill, Rape . . .":** Edward A. McCord, "Burn, Kill, Rape, and Rob: Military Atrocities, Warlordism, and Anti-Warlordism in Republican China," in Lary and MacKinnon, *Scars of War*, 22–29.

87 **Japanese rampage worse than internal or Western imperialist incursions:** Lary, *The Chinese People at War*, 1, 12.

87 **Japanese air raids August to mid-October 1937:** MacKinnon, "Refugee Flight at the Outset of the Anti-Japanese War," 120–21; Lary, *The Chinese People at War*, 22–23.

87 **"ghosts and spirits":** Mitter, *Forgotten Ally*, 118.

87 **Reasons for flight of refugees besides air raids:** Lary, *The Chinese People at War*, 21, 25–26.

87 **"After the Nanjing Massacre . . .":** Lary, "A Ravaged Place," 101.

88 **"devils" and "tone was quite different . . .":** Lary, *The Chinese People at War*, 20–21.

88 **"the first war of the entire nation in Chinese history . . .":** quoted in Liu, "A Whole Nation Walking," 39.

88 **"survivor flight":** MacKinnon, "Refugee Flight at the Outset of the Anti-Japanese War," 118. Liu points out that there were two other mass migrations during the war. The Nationalists mobilized their own troops and those of regional origins and dispatched them all over the country. Second, the war period was also marked by the emigration of Chinese overseas and the immigration of foreign peoples such as Koreans and Jews into China. Liu, "A Whole Nation Walking," 3–4.

88 **"On the road to the southwest, a long ribbon of ox carts stretches without interruption . . .":** Lary, "A Ravaged Place," 105.

88 **"one of the greatest mass migrations in human history":** White and Jacoby, *Thunder Out of China*, 55.

88 **No Chinese Tolstoy:** MacKinnon, "Refugee Flight at the Outset of the Anti-Japanese War," 119.

88 **Political suppression of Chinese history of the war:** Lary, *The Chinese People at War*, 5, 8–10, 12–13.

88 **All or parts of twenty-one provinces under Japanese rule:** MacKinnon, "Refugee Flight at the Outset of the Anti-Japanese War," 121.

88 **Spectrum of refugee totals:** MacKinnon, "Refugee Flight at the Outset of the Anti-Japanese War," 121; Lary, *The Chinese People at War*, 28; Hsi-sheng Ch'i, "The Military Dimension, 1942–45," in Hsiung and Levine, *China's Bitter Victory*, 180; Mitter, *Forgotten Ally*, 123.

89 **45 million refugees:** The issue of the refugee totals provides an example of the chronic challenge of statistics about the War of Resistance. As Dr. Lu Liu noted with admirable understatement, "Official statistics on the human dimensions of the civilian movement are scattered and contradictory." The "three million" number was an early estimate that, in view of other figures just involving selected Chinese cities, can be safely discarded as a vast underestimate. The formal agency to minister to refugees (the DRC) did not exist until April 1938. By no means did all refugees register with this entity, while undoubtedly its methods resulted in double counting of some individuals. Further, enormous numbers of government functionaries and industrial workers evacuated under separate programs were not counted by the DRC. During the war, the Nationalist government at one point numbered the refugees as 26.7 million from April 1938 to December 1941 and 49 million by the end of 1944, after a massive Japanese offensive produced a further burst of refugee flight. Postwar the Nationalist government issued a figure of 95 million refugees, but this certainly included double counting (or worse) of some refugees, particularly if they moved more than once. (The official archival source is *Nanmin ji liuli renmin zongshu biao*, 1946.) An academic working for the Nationalist government calculated the refugee total at 30 million. Two "statisticians" produced a notably wide estimate of 30 to 60 million refugees in 1938. The China Yearbook for 1946 advanced a figure of 40 million people. A notable Chinese newspaper *Dagong bao* (*L'Impartial*) touted a figure of over 80 million in 1944. Further complicating the issue is that some refugees, particularly farmers, generally only left their homes for relatively short periods and then returned. Other refugees trekked far away from the Japanese, but then later trickled back to their homes. Both these categories escaped accurate enumerations. Recently Dr. Rana Mitter in his excellent work offered that the number of refugees "may have reached more than 80 million." *Forgotten Ally*, 5. Later he reports the number as "80 million to 100 million." *Forgotten Ally*, 378. This writer follows Liu who, based on her dedicated grappling with this morass of complications, arrives at an estimate that the number of refugees equaled around 45 million, about 10 percent of China's population. This may well be low, but this work will generally favor the lower end of plausible numbers in such areas where the data are so unsatisfactory. Liu, "A Whole Nation Walking," 4, 11–13; MacKinnon, "Refugee Flight," 121; Lary,

The Chinese People at War, 28; Ch'i, "The Military Dimension, 1942–45," in Hsiung and Levine, *China's Bitter Victory*, 180.

89 **Prewar Chinese population; Chinese within Japanese-controlled areas:** Spence, *The Search for Modern China* (1990 edition), 424 (population figure). A 1946 report of the United Nations Relief and Rehabilitation Administration (UNRRA), kindly provided by Dr. Hans van de Ven, stated that 266 million Chinese were in areas controlled by Japan. This was presumably for the entire war. The great majority of these fell under Japanese control in the first two years or so of the war before the fronts substantially stabilized. Then, in 1944, a renewed Japanese offensive added extensive territories at least nominally within Japanese control. Given these considerations, a reasonable estimate would be that prior to 1944, about 200 million Chinese, though perhaps more, were in areas under Japanese control. Taylor estimated that three-quarters of China's population remained in areas under Nationalist control after the fall of the Wuhan cities. *The Generalissimo*, 160. That would suggest that 120 million were in areas under Japanese control, but this seems low if the 1946 figure is at least approximately correct. A further confounding problem is how many refugees eventually settled back into areas under Japanese control. It appears impossible to certify any exact figure for Chinese in areas under Japanese control. The numbers offered here represent at best reasonable approximations based on the evidence now available.

89 **Refugee totals in France and the Soviet Union:** I. C. B. Dear and M. R. D. Foot, *The Oxford Companion to World War II* (Oxford: Oxford University Press, 1995), 391–92, 1212 [hereafter Dear and Foot, *The Oxford Companion to World War II*].

89 **Three waves of migration:** MacKinnon, "Refugee Flight at the Outset of the Anti-Japanese War," 123–24. Lary estimated that there were 300,000 refugees in Shanghai. *The Chinese People at War*, 27.

90 **"cultural and educational workers accounted for 55% . . .":** quoted in Liu, "A Whole Nation Walking," 14.

90 **Composition of refugees:** MacKinnon, "Refugee Flight at the Outset of the Anti-Japanese War," 124–26; Lary, *The Chinese People at War*, 5–6.

90 **Life in Chinese countryside:** Lary, *China's Republic*, 89, 96; Lary, *The Chinese People at War*, 3. Rural population percentages: Spence, *The Search for Modern China* (1990 edition) notes on page 296 that "at least" 75 percent of the population was rural in the opening decades of the twentieth century and on page 688 cites a table showing the urban population in 1949 was only 10.6 percent with 89.4 percent in rural areas. An 85 percent figure for the proportion of Chinese living in the countryside is provided by Dear and Foot, *The Oxford Companion to World War II*, 211.

91 **Entry of modernity:** Spence, *The Search for Modern China*, 198–99, 215–16, 343–46; Lary, *The Chinese People at War*, 15.

91 **Western-oriented Chinese elites and their attitudes:** Lary, *The Chinese People at War*, 14–15, 20.

91 **Free expression in 1930s China:** Lary, *China's Republic*, 88–90.

91 **City dwellers head for ancestral homes:** Liu, "A Whole Nation Walking," 186.

91 **"endless and incessant bitterness":** quoted in Liu, "A Whole Nation Walking," 251.

92 **"fate (*yuanfen*), the mysterious force . . .":** Lary, *The Chinese People at War*, 32.

92 **"spawned desperate romance":** MacKinnon, *Wuhan*, 54.

92 **"fellowship of war and misfortune and hope":** Lary, *The Chinese People at War*, 32.

92 "at times of crisis, the family was the core default unit": R. Keith Schoppa, *In a Sea of Bitterness: Refugees During the Sino-Japanese War* (Cambridge, MA: Harvard University Press, 2011), 305 [hereafter Schoppa, *In a Sea of Bitterness*].

92 "Many [families] had been on the march for weeks . . .": Utley, *China at War*, 46.

93 "China's population was being forcefully redistributed and remixed . . .": MacKinnon, "Refugee Flight at the Outset of the Anti-Japanese War," 124.

93 "it did not become a chaotic rout but rather unrolled with a great deal of dignity . . .": Lary, *The Chinese People at War*, 28.

93 Early refugee relief efforts in Shanghai; creation of Emergency Refugee Relief Commission: Liu, "A Whole Nation Walking," 189–90. Liu reports the international committee in Shanghai only supported 2,000 people.

93 Deaths in Shanghai: MacKinnon, "Refugee Flight at the Outset of the Anti-Japanese War," 123–24.

94 "The government is duty bound to do all the work related to [the refugees] alleviation and relief . . .": Liu, "A Whole Nation Walking," 248.

94 Creation of DRC: Liu, "A Whole Nation Walking," 198–203.

94 DRC network and accomplishments through 1941: Liu, "A Whole Nation Walking," 209–11, 216, 240n11.

94 "Who did a better job in the battle, Chinese or Japanese?": Liu, "A Whole Nation Walking," 225–26.

94 DRC instills larger narrative of refugees as warriors: Liu, "A Whole Nation Walking," 225–26.

94 "people of righteousness" and increased demands of refugees: Liu, "A Whole Nation Walking," 5, 28.

95 "In a time of national resistance against the Japanese, to sacrifice all that we have is our duty . . .": Quoted in Liu, "A Whole Nation Walking," 263.

95 Effects of massive refugee flight on the state, society, and individual: Liu, "A Whole Nation Walking," 229, 248; Lary, "A Ravaged Place," 114; Lary, *The Chinese People at War*, 20; MacKinnon, *Wuhan*, 118; Mitter, *Forgotten Ally*, 122. Schoppa, *In a Sea of Bitterness*, particularly in the concluding chapter, finds little or no positive aspects of the refugee crisis. This work, however, is based only on the experiences in Zhejiang province.

95 "You are building your conception of an Asia which would be raised on a tower of skulls": Hotta, *Pan-Asianism and Japan's War*, 32, 154–55.

95 Seizure of Manchuria changes US policy: Norman A. Graebner, "Hoover, Roosevelt and the Japanese," in Dorothy Borg and Shumpei Okamoto, eds., *Pearl Harbor as History: Japanese American Relations 1931–1941* (New York: Columbia University Press, 1973), 25–26 [hereafter Graebner, "Hoover, Roosevelt and the Japanese" and Borg and Okamoto, *Pearl Harbor as History*].

96 Hoover's "nonrecognition" policy; lack of Chinese resistance: Graebner, "Hoover, Roosevelt and the Japanese," 25–28; Youli Sun, "Chinese Military Resistance and Changing American Perceptions, 1937–1938," in Robert David Johnson, ed., *On Cultural Ground: Essays in International History* (Chicago: Imprint Publications, 1994), 82–83 [hereafter Sun, "Chinese Military Resistance and Changing American Perspectives"].

96 US investment figures in China: Spence, *In Search of Modern China*, 344.

96 US trade with China and Japan: Justus D. Doenecke, *Storm on the Horizon: The*

Challenge to American Intervention, 1939–1941 (Lanham, MD: Rowman & Little-field), 293–94 [hereafter Doenecke, *Storm on the Horizon*].

96 **Advocates of abandonment of US interests in the Far East and the Philippines; Tyd-ings-McDuffie Act:** Doenecke, *Storm on the Horizon*, 293–94, 298–302; Wayne S. Cole, "The Role of the United States Congress and Political Parties," in Borg and Okamoto, *Pearl Harbor as History*, 316–17.

97 **Gallup polls reflecting American opinion tilt to China:** Hadley Cantril, ed., *Public Opinion 1935–1946* (Princeton, NJ: Princeton University Press, 1951), 1081–82 [here-after Cantril, *Public Opinion*].

97 **1940 US Census:** teaching resources.atltas.illinois.edu/Chinese_exp/resources/, accessed 12 August 2016; digitalhistory.uh.edu/active_learning/explorations/japa, accessed 12 August 2016.

97 **American discrimination against Asians versus American romance with China:** *Chae Chan Ping v. United States* (130 U.S. 581) (9 S.Ct. 623, 32 L.Ed. 1068) (Uphold-ing the Chinese Exclusion Act of 1882); Paine, *Wars for Asia*, 172.

97 **Newsreels shaping American opinion in favor of China:** Professor Thomas Doherty of Brandeis University brought this to the author's attention. Doherty is an expert in not only feature films, but also newsreels, and he noted that the imagery of Japa-nese actions in China in these typically biweekly films is far more graphic than anything Americans saw of German atrocities prior to Pearl Harbor. His *Projec-tions of War: Hollywood, American Culture, and World War II* (New York: Columbia University Press, 1993) (esp. pp. 229–50 on newsreel programs) and *Hollywood and Hitler 1933–1939* (New York: Columbia University Press, 2013), particularly 264–65, are highly recommended.

97 **Religion shaping American public opinion:** Mitter, *Forgotten Ally*, 31–32, 51–52, 239–41; Michael Snape, *God and Uncle Sam: Religion and America's Armed Forces in World War II* (Woodbridge, UK: Boydell Press, 2015), 470–71. Taylor, *The Generalis-simo*, 2, 9, 108–9, dispels any illusion that Chiang's Christianity was insincere.

97 **Communications from missionaries:** Gerhard Weinberg first brought this to the author's attention. The author located anecdotal references to this factor demonstrat-ing it existed. Documenting its exact scope and content, however, proved impossi-ble despite multiple efforts. I am indebted to Jay Fagel, who embarked on his own research to locate contemporary documentation from various religious groups in the United States that supported missionary work in China. Unfortunately, neither Mr. Fagel nor I was able to locate contemporary evidence that would permit more than a general acknowledgment of this factor. This is a subject deserving of further research.

97 **"as that of Genghis Khan" and *Chicago Tribune* comment:** as quoted in Doenecke, *Storm on the Horizon*, 285.

98 **FDR idea of a naval blockade and sanctions in 1937:** Sun, "Chinese Military Resis-tance and Changing American Perspectives," 84; Robert Dallek, *Franklin D. Roos-evelt and American Foreign Policy 1932–1945* (Oxford: Oxford University Press, 1981), 147–49 [hereafter Dallek, *Franklin D. Roosevelt and American Foreign Policy*].

98 **"many mansions of anti-interventionism":** Doenecke, *Storm on the Horizon*, 1.

98 **Diversity of viewpoints among "anti-interventionists":** Doenecke, *Storm on the Hori-zon*, 1–8. For evidence suggestive that support for Roosevelt's policies encountered stronger support from middle- and lower-income groups than high-income groups,

but still relatively close levels of majority support across all income groups, see the polling results in Cantril, *Public Opinion*, 1158–59.

99 **"Isolationism" as the traditional American foreign policy and its two main prongs:** Wayne S. Cole, *Roosevelt & The Isolationists 1932–45* (Lincoln: University of Nebraska Press, 1983), ix [hereafter Cole, *Roosevelt & The Isolationists*]. Cole's excellent scholarly work provides an astute and sympathetic account of the movement, illustrating how grossly distorted many characterizations of this viewpoint have been in texts and popular culture.

99 **Outlook on foreign and domestic affairs by "isolationists," "progressive" leaders:** Cole, *Roosevelt & The Isolationists 1932–45*, 37–50, 128–29, 136–37.

99 **America First Committee:** Doenecke, *Storm on the Horizon*, 165.

100 **Foreign policy preferences and the shared features of domestic and foreign policy of "anti-interventionists":** Cole, *Roosevelt & The Isolationists 1932–45*, 37–38.

100 **Minority of "anti-interventionists" exempt Asia and Latin America:** Cole, *Roosevelt & The Isolationists 1932–45*, 78, 239–41.

100 **"probably the most effective medium for channeling American public opinion into isolationism during this period":** Cole, *Roosevelt & The Isolationists 1932–45*, 161. Cole provides a fascinating description of the Nye hearings. Usually overlooked in such accounts is that the final written report of Nye's committee admitted their examination did not establish "that wars have been started solely because of the activities of munitions makers and their agents." Cole, *Roosevelt & The Isolationists 1932–45*, 141–61.

100 **Neutrality Laws:** Cole, *Roosevelt & The Isolationists 1932–45*, 163 86, 233–34.

101 **Roosevelt's depletion of his political capital in 1937.** David M. Kennedy, *Freedom from Fear: The American People in Depression and War, 1929–1945* (New York: Oxford University Press, 1999), 323–50 [hereafter Kennedy, *Freedom from Fear*]; Dallek, *Franklin D. Roosevelt and American Foreign Policy*, 136–37, 140, 153.

101 **Roosevelt's approach to Brussels conference:** Graebner, "Hoover, Roosevelt and the Japanese," 38–41.

101 **Loss of *Panay*:** Commanding Officer, U.S.S. Panay, Subject: U.S.S. Panay, loss of by sinking as a result of bombing by Japanese planes, 12 December 1937, 21 December 1937 and Commander in Chief, Asiatic Fleet, to Secretary of the Navy 23 Dec 1937, President's Secretary File, Box 26, Diplomatic, Chile Jul-Dec 1941 thru China 1938, Folder Diplomatic Correspondence China 1937, FDRL; Okumiya Masatake with Roger Pineau, "How the Panay Was Sunk," *U.S. Naval Institute Proceedings*, June 1953, 587, 590.

102 **Japanese reaction to sinking of *Panay*:** John Prados, *Combined Fleet Decoded: The Secret History of American Intelligence and the Japanese Navy in World War II* (New York: Random House, 1995), 48–51 [hereafter Prados, *Combined Fleet Decoded*].

102 **Newsreel footage of *Panay* attack edited:** Kenneth S. Davis, *FDR: Into the Storm 1937–1940 A History* (New York: Random House, 1993), 157–58 [hereafter Davis, *FDR: Into the Storm*].

102 **Ludlow Amendment:** Cole, *Roosevelt & The Isolationists, 1932–1945*, 253–62.

103 **Shifting attitudes of American diplomats and attaches in China; key role of Carlson:** Sun, "Chinese Military Resistance and Changing American Perspectives," 85–87; MacKinnon, *Wuhan*, 103–4; John Gunther, *Roosevelt in Retrospect, A Profile in History* (New York: Harper and Brothers, 1950), 73.

103 **"serious blow to Chinese morale and American hopes"**: Sun, "Chinese Military Resistance and Changing American Perspectives," 86.

103 **"China is helpless and China as an independent nation is finished"**: The Second Secretary of the Embassy in China (Atcheson) to the Secretary of State, December 6, 1937, *FRUS, 1937*, vol. 3, *The Far East*, 766.

103 **Gloom followed by renewed confidence among US observers of China's resistance:** Sun, "Chinese Military Resistance and Changing American Perspectives," 86–88; The Ambassador to China (Johnson) to the Secretary of State, March 4, 1938, *FRUS, 1938*, vol. 3, *The Far East*, 115–16 ("it is possible for China to win").

104 **American loan to China in the fall of 1938:** Dallek, *Franklin D. Roosevelt and American Foreign Policy*, 193; Sun, "Chinese Military Resistance and Changing American Perspectives," 88–91.

5: "A Despicable Urge to Live!"

105 **War becomes stalemate:** Lary, *The Chinese People at War*, 78; Marci, *Clash of Empires in South China*, 125.

105 **Attrition characterizes new phase of war:** van de Ven, *War and Nationalism*, 232–33; MacKinnon, "Defense of the Central Yangtze Valley," 201, 204–5.

105 **Konoe resignation; Hiranuma cabinet:** Yagami, *Konoe Fumimaro*, 51, 66, 71–75.

105 **Chiang and Mao recognize China needs allies to win:** Taylor, *The Generalissimo*, 155–56.

105 **Nationalist strategy in 1939:** Drea and van de Ven, "An Overview of Major Military Campaigns during the Sino-Japanese War," 35; van de Ven, *War and Nationalism in China*, 234–35; Paine, *The Wars of Asia*, 150.

106 **Sources of income for national government:** van de Ven, *War and Nationalism*, 75–76; Spence, *The Search for Modern China*, 69–70, 244–45, 269–70.

106 **T. V. Soong reforms and 1937 budget:** Spence, *The Search for Modern China*, 333.

106 **Nationalist income at end of 30 June 1937 fiscal year:** Arthur N. Young, *China's Nation Building Effort 1927–1937: The Financial and Economic Record* (Stanford, CA: Hoover Institution Press, 1971), appendix 1, Receipts and Expenditures from July 1, 1928 to June 30, 1937 [hereafter Young, *China's Nation Building Effort 1927–1937*].

107 **Nationalist budget deficit:** Paine, *The Wars of Asia*, 136.

107 **War inflicts "economic catastrophe" on Nationalist government finances; conflicting figures:** Lary, *The Chinese People at War*, 36; Arthur N. Young, *China's Wartime Finance and Inflation, 1937–1945* (Cambridge, MA: Harvard University Press, 1965), 11–21 [hereafter Young, *China's Wartime Finance and Inflation*]. Wartime figures on Nationalist finances are problematic, not least because of inflation. Lary, *The Chinese People at War*, 33–34.

107 **Loss of value of Nationalist currency 1937–1941; loss of purchasing power of government workers and soldiers:** Paine, *The Wars of Asia*, 136.

107 **China's internal economy ravaged:** Lary, *The Chinese People at War*, 37.

107 **"Between November 21st and December . . .":** Lary, *The Chinese People at War*, 34.

108 **"records, books, letters and mementoes":** Lary, *The Chinese People at War*, 34.

108 **Chinese industrial development prewar:** Liu, "A Whole Nation Walking," 134–35.

108 **National Resources Committee:** Liu, "A Whole Nation Walking," 133, 136.

108 **Weng Wenhao:** Liu, "A Whole Nation Walking," 139.

108 **"a tiny man, a scholarly doodler . . ." never accused of corruption:** White and Jacoby, *Thunder Out of China,* 55.

108 **Weng's background and planning by NDRC/NRC:** Liu, "A Whole Nation Walking," 138–41.

109 **Shanghai factory total and importance:** Liu, "A Whole Nation Walking," 143, 146.

109 **"seeing their colleagues die, they simply move the corpse aside . . .":** quoted in Liu, "A Whole Nation Walking," 145.

109 **Evacuation of factories from Shanghai and north, east, and south China:** Liu, "A Whole Nation Walking," 146, 152.

109 **"zealous for the common weal and steadfastly pursuing righteousness . . .":** quoted in Liu, "A Whole Nation Walking," 149.

109 **"The large majority of industrialists . . . preferred the amenities of Hong Kong . . .":** quoted in Liu, "A Whole Nation Walking," 148.

109 **Reasons why factories not evacuated, failure to destroy facilities:** Liu, "A Whole Nation Walking," 146–48, 150–51, 162–64.

110 **"China's Dunkirk Retreat":** Liu, "A Whole Nation Walking," 152–56.

110 **Lu Zuofu's role in evacuation:** Liu, "A Whole Nation Walking," 159. Liu reports that Lu lost 16 steamers and 177 employees. Of the 200,000 total tons moved, the junks hauled only 25,000 tons.

110 **"walking on rocks hundreds of feet above the river line" and "We were embracing chilly winds . . .":** quoted in Liu, "A Whole Nation Walking," 160.

110 **Industrialists, technical experts, and workers and geographically defined patriotism:** Liu, "A Whole Nation Walking," 164–65.

110 **Japanese seize Hainan Island:** Marci, *Clash of Armies in South China,* 110–13; "Assault on Hainan Island 1939," *Rising Storm*—the Imperial Japanese Navy and China 1931–1945, combinedfleet.com, accessed 9 April 2013.

110 **Struggle for Nanchang:** Drea and van de Ven, "Overview of Major Military Campaigns," 35–36; MacKinnon, "The Defense of the Central Yangtze," 201–2; Tobe, "The Japanese Eleventh Army in Central China," 216–18; van de Ven, *War and Nationalism,* 236; Paine, *The Wars of Asia,* 146.

111 **Importance of Changsha in 1939:** Marci, *Clash of Empires in South China,* 6–7, 45, 47, 165, 169–70.

111 **Chiang's instructions for defense of Changsha and detailed planning by Xue Yue:** van de Ven, *War and Nationalism in China,* 239.

112 **Changsha battle 1939:** Drea and van de Ven, "Overview of Major Military Campaigns," 36; van de Ven, *War and Nationalism in China,* 238–39; MacKinnon, "The Defense of the Central Yangtze," 202; Tobe, "The Japanese Eleventh Army in Central China," 217–18.

112 **Foreign observers' estimates of losses at Changsha:** Marci, *Clash of Empires in South China,* 165.

112 **Battles for Shiqi June to October 1939:** Marci, *Clash of Empires in South China,* 137–44.

113 **Manchurian border and clashes:** Hata Ikuhiko, "The Japanese Soviet Confrontation, 1935–39," in James W. Morley, ed., *Japan's Road to the Pacific War: Deterrent Diplomacy, Japan, Germany, and the USSR 1935–1939* (New York: Columbia University Press, 1976), 133 [hereafter Hata, "The Japanese Soviet Confrontation, 1935–39"];

Alvin D. Coox, *Nomonhan: Japan Against Russia, 1939* (Stanford, CA: Stanford University Press, 1990) (two vols. combined), 92, 94, 99 [hereafter Coox, *Nomonhan*]. Coox's work is a magnificent monument to scholarship.

113 **Amur River encounter, June–July 1937:** Hata, "The Japanese Soviet Confrontation, 1935–1939," 137–40; Coox, *Nomonhan*, 115–17.

113 **Changkuofeng clash:** Hata, "The Japanese Soviet Confrontation, 1935–1939," 140–49; Edward J. Drea, *Nomonhan: Japanese-Soviet Tactical Combat, 1939*, Leavenworth Papers no. 2, Combat Studies Institute, Fort Leavenworth, Kansas, January 1981, 13–14 [hereafter Drea, *Nomonhan: Japanese-Soviet Tactical Combat*]; Coox, *Nomonhan*, 134.

113 **Imperial Army's "lessons" from Changkuofeng:** Drea, *Nomonhan: Japanese-Soviet Tactical Combat*, 20–21.

113 **Blyukher tortured to death:** Jonathan Haslam, *The Soviet Union and the Threat from the East, 1933–41* (Pittsburgh, PA: University of Pittsburgh Press, 1992), 119–20 [hereafter Haslam, *The Soviet Union and the Threat from the East*].

113 **Emperor dresses down chief of staff; army deceives emperor:** Coox, *Nomonhan*, 130, 134.

114 **Imperial Japan's strategic plans, Imperial Army priority for Russia:** Hata, "The Japanese Soviet Confrontation, 1935–1939," 131.

114 **"supreme command exhausted its wits in thinking out countermeasures":** Coox, *Nomonhan*, 85–87.

114 **"As long as the essence of the Russian people does not change" and "in a state of confusion, and corrupt in morale . . .":** Coox, *Nomonhan*, 86–87.

114 **Imperial Army integrated strategic, operational, and tactical doctrine:** Drea, *Nomonhan: Japanese-Soviet Tactical Combat*, 18–20, 86–90.

114 **Japanese soldiers inculcated with absolute conviction in ultimate victory; "that night attacks exploited the unique Japanese characteristics . . .":** Drea, *Nomonhan: Japanese-Soviet Tactical Combat*, 18–20; Coox, *Nomonhan*, 86–87, 1,083.

115 **"but it required high-quality, well-trained junior officers . . .":** Drea, *Nomonhan: Japanese-Soviet Tactical Combat*, 19.

115 **How to Fight the Soviets and "a despicable urge to live":** Drea, *Nomonhan: Japanese-Soviet Tactical Combat*, 21, 30–31; Coox, *Nomonhan*, 1,089.

115 **May 1939 border skirmishes:** Coox, *Nomonhan*, 183–212; Drea, *Nomonhan: Japanese-Soviet Tactical Combat*, 28.

115 **Terrain around Nomonhan/Khalkhin Gol:** Drea, *Nomonhan: Japanese-Soviet Tactical Combat*, 21; Coox, *Nomonhan*, 291, 502.

115 **Kwantung Army orders 23rd Division to attack; status of 23rd Division and Yasuoka Detachment:** Coox, *Nomonhan*, 174–79, 181, 260–62, 545.

116 **"amoral and devious attitude":** Hata, "The Japanese Soviet Confrontation, 1935–1939," 165–70; Stuart Goldman, *Nomonhan 1939: The Red Army's Victory that Shaped World War II* (Annapolis, MD: Naval Institute Press, 2012), 108–9 [hereafter Goldman, *Nomonhan 1939*].

116 **Tsuji and Hattori; Japanese plan of attack:** Drea, *Nomonhan: Japanese-Soviet Tactical Combat*, 32.

116 **23rd Division launches attack; "human bullets" and fate of Yasuoka tank units:** Coox, *Nomonhan*, 301, 425; Goldman, *Nomonhan 1939*, 115–19.

116 **Imperial Army commits heavy artillery:** Hata, "The Japanese Soviet Confrontation, 1935–1939," 165–70; Coox, *Nomonhan*, 179, 373–74, 486, 491, 544–45; Goldman, *Nomonhan 1939*, 127–29.

118 **Japanese detect signs of Soviet offensive; Imperial Army miscalculation of Soviet capabilities:** Drea, *Nomonhan: Japanese-Soviet Tactical Combat*, 24, 71; Coox, *Nomonhan*, 491.

118 **Soviets gather forces and logistical support:** Drea, *Nomonhan: Japanese-Soviet Tactical Combat*, 71 (including 9,200 figure); Coox, *Nomonhan*, 580. Coox offers figures of 3,500 supply and 1,400 tanker trucks.

118 **Zhukov strength and plan of attack:** Coox, *Nomonhan*, 587–89; Tomoyuki Hanada, "The Nomonhan Incident and the Japanese-Soviet Neutrality Pact," Kiyotada Tsutsui, ed., *Fifteen Lectures on Showa Japan: Road to Pacific War in Recent Historiography* (Tokyo: Japan Publishing Industry for Culture, 2016), 184–85 [hereafter Tsutsui, *Fifteen Lectures on Showa Japan*]; Drea, *Nomonhan: Japanese-Soviet Tactical Combat*, 71.

118 **Soviets launch attack, artillery, and aerial bombardment:** Coox, *Nomonhan*, 570, 664, 668 ("like the gongs of hell"), 823.

118 **Soviet infantry and armored attacks:** Coox, *Nomonhan*, 667–79, 677 ("spitting like the tongues of snakes,"), 750, 757, 759.

119 **Last minutes of 71st Infantry Regiment:** Coox, *Nomonhan*, 825–28 ("I am Lieutenant Colonel Higashi, 49 years old!").

119 **Japanese counterattack smashed, Komatsubara ordered out:** Coox, *Nomonhan*, 712, 835, 842.

119 **German-Soviet Nonaggression Pact; Stalin's remarks:** Coox, *Nomonhan*, 496–98, 892–95, 902.

120 **Japanese losses:** Coox, *Nomonhan*, 914–18, Appendices J, K.

120 **Soviet losses:** for old figures, see Drea, *Nomonhan: Japanese-Soviet Tactical Combat*, 11; Coox, *Nomonhan*, 918; for new figures, see Goldman, *Nomonhan 1939*, 149.

120 **Air strengths and losses over Nomonhan:** Nicholas Millman, *Osprey Aircraft of the Aces, 103, Ki-27 "Nate" Aces* (Oxford: Osprey Publishing, 2013), 21, 48.

120 **Japanese retrieve dead:** "bordering on the supernatural . . .": Coox, *Nomonhan*, 922, 924.

120 **Fate of Japanese captured by Soviets; stories of Corporal Negishi and Lt. Col. Ioki:** Coox, *Nomonhan*, 930–40, 949–51, 959–60; Goldman, *Nomonhan 1939*, 143–45.

121 **Concepts of surrender from Tokugawa Era to Russo-Japanese War:** Drea, *Japan's Imperial Army*, 17–18, 45, 119–20.

121 **Kugo and the three "human bombs" in Shanghai:** Drea, *Japan's Imperial Army*, 172–73.

122 **Public announcement of loss and "purge":** Hata, "The Japanese Soviet Confrontation, 1935–1939," 171–72; Coox, *Nomonhan*, 874–76, 914, 956–57.

122 **Faltering justice of post-Nomonhan "purge":** Coox, *Nomonhan*, 876–78; Hata, "The Japanese Soviet Confrontation, 1935–1939," 176.

122 **Zhukov fame; Shtern fate:** Coox, *Nomonhan*, 991–92.

122 **Damage to image of Kwantung Army at Nomonhan:** Hata, "The Japanese Soviet Confrontation, 1935–1939," 176.

123 **"To alter drastically [Imperial Army] tactical doctrine . . .":** Drea, *Nomonhan: Japanese-Soviet Tactical Combat*, 90.

123 **Administration stance in mid-1939 and public opinion:** Langer and Gleason, *The Challenge to Isolationism,* 148–52.

123 **"Moral embargo," Pittman proposal for trade embargo:** Langer and Gleason, *The Challenge to Isolationism,* 149–59.

123 **Chinese welcome to "moral embargo":** Usui, "The Politics of War, 1937–1941," 365.

123 **Mixed fruits of Nomonhan:** van de Ven, *War and Nationalism,* 236–37; Paine, *The Wars of Asia,* 5.

124 **News of the August 1939 Nazi-Soviet Pact reaches Japan and its effect:** Bix, *Hirohito and the Making of Modern Japan,* 354–55; Hosoya Chihiro, "The Japanese Soviet Neutrality Pact," in Morley, *The Fateful Choice,* 17.

124 **Nazi-Soviet Pact prompts settlement in Nomonhan:** Hosoya Chihiro, "The Japanese Soviet Neutrality Pact," in Morley, *The Fateful Choice,* 18.

124 **Fall of Abe government:** Bix, *Hirohito and the Making of Modern Japan,* 355.

124 **Challenges facing Chiang in fall of 1939:** van de Ven, *War and Nationalism in China,* 240–41.

125 **Nationalists Winter Offensive, 1939:** van de Ven, *War and Nationalism in China,* 239–40.

125 **Chiang at the Second Nanyue Military Conference:** van de Ven, *War and Nationalism in China,* 242–43.

125 **Japanese land in Guangxi Province and capture Nanning:** Marci, *Clash of Empires in South China,* 177–80; Paine, *Wars of Asia,* 148.

126 **Chiang's assessment of Winter Offensive:** van de Ven, *War and Nationalism in China,* 243.

126 **Nanning and Kunlan Pass:** Marci, *Clash of Empires in South China,* 181–86; Paine, *Wars of Asia,* 148.

126 **Japanese assessment in China of Winter Offensive; losses in Eleventh Army:** Tobe, "The Japanese Eleventh Army in Central China," 219–20; van de Ven, *China at War,* 128.

126 **View from Tokyo and proposals to withdraw troops from China:** Tobe, "The Japanese Eleventh Army in Central China," 220–21.

6: "Japan's Prince of Self-Destruction"

128 **Japanese penetration of Chinese codes; Japanese launch Zaoyang-Yichang offensive:** Kotani, *Japanese Intelligence in World War II,* 19; "cannot sustain an offensive for longer than a week . . .": van de Ven, *War and Nationalism in China,* 245; MacKinnon, "The Defense of the Central Yangtze," 202–3; Tobe, "The Japanese Eleventh Army in Central China," 221–23.

128 **Japanese capture of Yichang:** Tobe, "The Japanese Eleventh Army in Central China," 222–23; MacKinnon, "The Defense of the Central Yangtze," 203 ("devastating blow"); Tobe, "The Japanese Eleventh Army in Central China," 223–24; van de Ven, *War and Nationalism,* 237–38, 245. Paine, *Wars of Asia,* 148–49, lists Chinese losses at 51,000 killed.

129 **Nakajima advocated bombing civilians:** H. P. Ned Willmott, *The Second World War in the East* (London: Cassell, 1999), 38 [hereafter Willmott, *The Second World War in the East*].

129 **World War I airship and bomber raids on Britain:** John Terraine, *A Time for Courage:*

The Royal Air Force in the European War, 1939–1945 (New York: Macmillan, 1985), 10; Jim McGuigan, "British Identity and the 'People's Princess,'" *The Sociological Review* (2000): 7; Ian Castle, *London 1917–18: The Bomber Blitz* (New York: Osprey Publishing Ltd., 2010), 33.

130 **Colonial "policing" by bombing:** Sven Lindqvist, *A History of Bombing* (New York: New Press, 2001), 2, 5, 37, 42, 45, 50–51, 61, 68–69 [hereafter Lindqvist, *A History of Bombing*].

130 **Bombing prophets and popular fears of city attacks:** Lindqvist, *A History of Bombing*, 42–76.

130 **"the most destructive aerial attack on an urban center . . .":** Mark R. Peattie, *Sunburst: The Rise of Japanese Naval Air Power, 1909–1941* (Annapolis, MD: Naval Institute Press, 2001), 50–51 [hereafter Peattie, *Sunburst*]; Donald Jordan, *China's Trial by Fire: The Shanghai War of 1932* (Ann Arbor: University of Michigan Press, 2001), 192–93.

130 **Guernica in fact and image:** Williamson Murray, *Luftwaffe* (Baltimore, MD: Nautical and Aviation Publishing Co. of America, 1985), ch. 1; James S. Corum, *The Luftwaffe: Creating the Operational Air War, 1918–1940* (Lawrence: University Press of Kansas, 1997), 199–200.

130 **"the first country to be subjected to systematic bombing of civilian targets":** Lary, *The Chinese People at War*, 22–23.

130 **Strength of Imperial Army and Navy air arms:** Hagiwara Mitsuru, "The Japanese Air Campaigns in China, 1937–1941," 239–40 in Peattie, Drea, and van de Ven, *The Battle for China* [hereafter Hagiwara Mitsuru, "The Japanese Air Campaigns in China, 1937–1941"]; Peattie, *Sunburst*, 102–4; Hattori, "Japanese Operations from July to December 1937," 160.

131 **Japanese divide air responsibilities, first Chinese bombing attack:** Hagiwara, "The Japanese Air Campaigns in China, 1937–1945," 241–43; Yang, "Chiang Kai-shek and the Battles of Shanghai and Nanjing," 146–47.

131 **Japanese aircraft losses in early operations:** Peattie, *Sunburst*, 106–10; Hagiwara, "The Japanese Air Campaigns in China, 1937–1945," 243–44.

132 **Chinese Air Force situation from August to November 1937:** Hakan Gustavsson, *Sino-Japanese Air War 1937–1945: The Longest Struggle* (Croydon, UK: Fonthill, 2016), 13–31 [hereafter Gustavsson, *Sino-Japanese Air War 1937–45*]; "Sino Japanese Air War 1937–1942," http://surfcity.kund.dalnet.se/sino-japanese_sources.htm (accessed 31 December 2013). The numbers in the text are from Gustavsson.

132 **Soviet Union provides China with aircraft and volunteer airmen; status of Chinese Air Force to end of 1938:** Gustavsson, *Sino-Japanese Air War 1937–1945*, 31–38; "Sino Japanese Air War 1937–1942," http://surfcity.kund.dalnet.se/sino-japanese_sources.htm (accessed 31 December 2013).

132 **December 1938 Imperial Headquarters directives:** Tow, "The Great Bombing of Chongqing and the Anti-Japanese War, 1937–1945," 259.

132 **Attacks on transportation targets:** Hagiwara, "Japanese Air Campaigns in China," 246–48.

132 **Chongqing as most bombed city and status in 1939:** Lary, *The Chinese People at War*, 85, 89; Tow, "The Great Bombing of Chongqing," 268–69; White and Jacoby, *Thunder Out of China*, 4–5, 9–10.

132 **"All the dialects of China mixed together in Chungking . . ." and "A foreigner who asked directions . . .":** White and Jacoby, *Thunder Out of China*, 8.

133 **Chongqing described:** Tow, "The Great Bombing of Chongqing," 261; White and Jacoby, *Thunder Out of China*, 6, 8; Lindqvist, *A History of Bombing*, 75.

133 **Climate of Chongqing:** White and Jacoby, *Thunder out of China*, 9–10; Lary, *The Chinese People at War*, 87; Hagiwara, "The Japanese Air Campaigns in China," 249.

133 **Raid of 3–4 May 1939:** Tow, "The Great Bombing of Chongqing," 260–61; Lary, *The Chinese People at War*, 87.

133 **"Hundreds tried to escape . . .":** as quoted in Lindqvist, *The History of Bombing*, 75.

133 **Reaction of population to May 1939 raid:** White and Jacoby, *Thunder Out of China*, 12–13.

133 **Air raid warning system:** White and Jacoby, *Thunder Out of China*, 14; Tow, "The Great Bombing of Chongqing," 271–72.

134 **"people were rushing in every direction . . .":** Lary, *The Chinese People at War*, 88.

134 **"there is haste but no confusion . . .":** Han Suyin, *Destination Chungking* (Hertfordshire, UK: Panther Books, 1973), 224 [hereafter Han, *Destination Chungking*].

134 **"elaborate privately run shelters charging admission fees and offering such amenities as chairs and tables . . .":** Tow, "The Great Bombing of Chongqing," 268–70.

134 **Creation of air raid shelters, evacuation fire break programs:** Tow, "The Great Bombing of Chongqing," 268–72; White and Jacoby, *Thunder Out of China*, 14–15; Han, *Destination Chungking*, 224.

135 **"We sit in the stifling damp, drenched with sweat . . .":** Han, *Destination Chungking*, 224.

135 **Chongqing scenes under bombing; Chiang extols city:** White and Jacoby, *Thunder Out of China*, 14–15; Tow, "The Great Bombing of Chongqing," 268, 272–74; Han, *Destination Chungking*, 218–19, 225–26; Mitter, *Forgotten Ally*, 177–78.

135 **"Operation 101":** Peattie, *Sunburst*, 118–19; van de Ven, *War and Nationalism in China*, 245–46; Willmott, *The Second World War in the East*, 38–39.

136 **"honey-combed ruins [of Chongqing] looked like the excavated remains . . ."** and **"bursting and throwing up myriads of freakish cloud formations . . .":** Lary, *The Chinese People at War*, 88–89.

136 **Chongqing defenses; debut of Mitsubishi A6M:** Peattie, *Sunburst*, 91–92, 119–20; "Sino Japanese Air War 1937–1942," for dates September 13, 1940 and March 14, 1941, http://surfcity.kund.dalnet.se/sino-japanese_sources.htm, accessed 31 December 2013. The summary conclusion about the reduction of Chinese Air Force activities is based on the monthly and daily summaries in this source during 1940–1941.

136 **Summary of Japanese bombing in 1940:** Peattie, *Sunburst*, 120–21.

137 **Grew and the "sword of Damocles":** quoted in Anderson, Irvine H. Jr., *The Standard-Vacuum Oil Company and United States East Asian Policy, 1933–1941* (Princeton, NJ: Princeton University Press, 1975), 124 [hereafter Anderson, *The Standard-Vacuum Oil Company and United States East Asian Policy*].

137 **German conquest of Denmark and Norway:** Dear and Foot, *The Oxford Companion to World War II*, 293–95 (Denmark), 819–23 (Norway).

137 **Strength of Allied and German forces in the Western European campaigns of 1940:** Karl-Heinz Frieser, *The Blitzkrieg Legend: The 1940 Campaign in the West* (Annapolis, MD: Naval Institute Press, 2005), 34–54, contains the best numerical comparisons, allowing sensibly for a host of complexities.

137 **Fall of Luxemburg, Belgium, and France:** Dear and Foot, *The Oxford Companion to World War II*, 118–22, 293–95, 347, 414, 701, 785.

138 **Peacetime draft and upsurge of defense appropriations in 1940:** For establishment of peacetime draft and restrictions on where draftees could serve, see Dear and Foot, *The Oxford Companion to World War II*, 996. For appropriations surge, see Davis, *FDR: Into the Storm*, 603–5.

138 **American 1940 naval expansion acts:** Joel R. Davidson, *The Unsinkable Fleet: The Politics of U.S. Navy Expansion in World War II* (Annapolis, MD: Naval Institute Press, 1996), 18–22.

138 **American Two Ocean Navy building program and its effect on naval strength ratios between United States and Japan:** Sadao Asada, *From Mahan to Pearl Harbor: The Imperial Japanese Navy and the United States* (Annapolis, MD: Naval Institute Press, 2006), 240–41 [hereafter Asada, *From Mahan to Pearl Harbor*]; Morley, *The Final Confrontation*, 270, 272; Lisle Rose, *Power at Sea*, vol. 2, *The Breaking Storm 1919–1945* (Columbia: University of Missouri Press, 2007), 134–35.

138 **"about one in three":** quoted in Dallek, *Franklin D. Roosevelt and American Foreign Policy*, 243.

138 **Roosevelt grapples with conflicting concerns in the Atlantic and Pacific, creation of Export Control Administration:** Anderson, *The Standard-Vacuum Oil Company and United States East Asian Policy*, 129–30; Edward S. Miller, *Bankrupting the Enemy: The U.S. Financial Siege of Japan Before Pearl Harbor* (Annapolis, MD: Naval Institute Press, 2007), 85–87 [hereafter Miller, *Bankrupting the Enemy*].

139 **Morgenthau four-point program:** Dallek, *Franklin D. Roosevelt and American Foreign Policy*, 239.

139 **Roosevelt authorizes restrictions on aviation grade petroleum products:** Anderson, *The Standard-Vacuum Oil Company and United States East Asian Policy*, 131–37, 143–44.

140 **Mers-el-Kébir:** Gerhard L. Weinberg, *A World at Arms: A Global History of World War II*, 2nd ed. (Cambridge: Cambridge University Press, 2005), 147–48.

140 **Impact of Mers-el-Kébir on Roosevelt:** Martin Gilbert, *Winston S. Churchill*, vol. 6, *Their Finest Hour* (Boston: Houghton Mifflin, 1983), 628–44 [hereafter Gilbert, *Finest Hour*].

140 **"brought the United States definitely near to us and to the war":** Winston C. Churchill, *The Second World War, Their Finest Hour* (Boston: Houghton Mifflin, 1949), 347 [hereafter Churchill, *Their Finest Hour*]; Cole, *Roosevelt & the Isolationists*, 370–74.

140 **"golden opportunity that comes once in a thousand years":** Chihiro Hosoya, "The Japanese Soviet Neutrality Pact," in Morley, *The Fateful Choice*, 40 [hereafter Hosoya, "The Japanese Soviet Neutrality Pact"].

140 **Sentiment among Imperial Army officers:** Bix, *Hirohito and the Making of Modern Japan*, 368.

140 **Attitude of emperor and Imperial Navy leaders to German alliance:** Bix, *Hirohito and the Making of Modern Japan*, 386–89.

141 **Fall of Yonai; appointment of Konoe; background:** David Lu, *The Agony of Choice: Matsuoka Yosuke and the Rise and Fall of the Japanese Empire, 1880–1945* (Lanham, MD: Lexington Books, 2002), 144 [hereafter Lu, *The Agony of Choice*]; Bix, *Hirohito and the Making of Modern Japan*, 367–68, 370–71, 373.

141 **"Modern Japanese history has not known . . .":** Jensen, *The Making of Modern Japan*, 618.

141 **Konoe's birth and family background:** Jensen, *The Making of Modern Japan*, 618; Oka, *Konoe Fumimaro*, 3–4; Yagami, *Konoe Fumimaro*, 134.

141 **Konoe's tragic childhood:** Oka, *Konoe Fumimaro*, 3–6.

141 **Konoe's education and presence at Versailles Conference:** Jensen, *The Making of Modern Japan*, 519; Oka, *Konoe Fumimaro*, 5–13; Yagami, *Konoe Fumimaro*, 16–20. Oka and Yagami both stress that Konoe's article after the Versailles Conference represented his lifelong attitudes to foreign policy.

141 **Konoe's rise in politics, personal characteristics, and public expectations:** Oka, *Konoe Fumimaro*, 3–6, 19–43, 46–47.

142 **Konoe was prone to indecision:** Lu, *Agony of Choice*, 145.

142 **Matsuoka background:** Lu, *The Agony of Choice*, 1–16, 98, 144. An example of works attributing Matsuoka's attitude to bitter experiences in his youth in the United States is the otherwise quite exemplary Iguchi Takeo, *Demystifying Pearl Harbor: A New Perspective from Japan* (Tokyo: International House of Japan, 2010), 48.

142 **"The era of democracy is finished . . .":** quoted in Bix, *Hirohito and the Making of Modern Japan*, 374.

142 **Relationship of Matsuoka and Konoe:** Lu, *The Agony of Choice*, 144; Yagami, *Konoe Fumimaro*, 87.

143 **Background of Hidenori Tôjô and Hideki Tôjô's early life and personality:** Robert J. C. Butow, *Tojo and the Coming of the War* (Stanford, CA: Stanford University Press, 1961), 3–6, 9, 12–13 ("If only you apply yourself" quote), 41–42 [hereafter Butow, *Tojo and the Coming of War*].

143 **Tôjô's War College experience, stint in Europe; Imperial Army gap in understanding of Anglo-Americans:** Butow, *Tojo and the Coming of War*, 14–16; Watanabe and Auer, *Who Was Responsible?*, 92.

143 **February 1936 mutiny, Tôjô's outlook:** Butow, *Tojo and the Coming of War*, 72–74.

143 **The "Four Pillars Conference":** Lu, *The Agony of Choice*, 145–48; Chihiro Hosoya, "The Tripartite Pact, 1939–1940," in James W. Morley, ed., *Japan's Road to the Pacific War, Deterrent Diplomacy: Japan, Germany, and the USSR 1935–1940* (New York: Columbia University Press, 1976), 217–19 [hereafter Hosoya, "The Tripartite Pact, 1939–1940"].

144 **Matsuoka's image and the "Cyclone":** Lu, *The Agony of Choice*, 148–50.

144 **Matsuoka seeks German alliance; Japan mesmerized by German triumphs:** Lu, *The Agony of Choice*, 154; Hosoya, "The Japanese Soviet Neutrality Pact," 205–6.

144 **Matsuoka's lack of anti-Semitism and views:** Lu, *The Agony of Choice*, 135–36, 155–59. Lu describes Matsuoka's support for covert aid to Jews fleeing Nazi Germany.

145 **Hitler sends Stahmer to Tokyo; Imperial Navy opposition to Tripartite Pact; Yoshida replaced by Oikawa:** Lu, *The Agony of Choice*, 135–36, 155–59; Hosoya, "The Tripartite Pact, 1939–1940," 220–24, 226–30.

145 **Provisions of Tripartite Pact signed on 27 September:** Hosoya, "The Tripartite Pact," appendix 7, 298–99; Lu, *The Agony of Choice*, 159–64. The 19 September Imperial Conference sanctioning the treaty proved far more than the usual perfunctory session ratifying positions long since worked out. When Prince Fushimi, the chief of naval operations, raised the issue of how Japan could expect to obtain oil to carry on

a protracted war with the United States, Matsuoka could only offer the completely unsatisfactory answer that somehow Germany would compel oil to be shipped from the Dutch East Indies. Fushimi countered that the only practical way for Japan to secure essential oil supplies was to occupy the Netherlands East Indies. Lu, *The Agony of Choice*, 165–67.

145 **Matsuoka exchanges letters with Ott and Stahmer; letters not forwarded to Berlin and Rome:** Hosoya, "The Tripartite Pact," 250–55.

146 **Tripartite Pact produces both allies and enemies:** Akira Iriye, *Power and Culture: The Japanese American War 1941–1945* (Cambridge, MA: Harvard University Press, 1982), 10–12.

146 **"From the British and American point of view . . .":** Paine, *The Wars of Asia*, 177. Yagami maintains that Konoe correctly believed the pact did not directly lead to a more stringent US posture against Japan. *Konoe Fumimaro*, 100–101. Even if this is true, the pact certainly cemented in the minds of the public a direct link between Germany and Japan that heretofore was only implied.

146 **"Japan's prince of self-destruction":** Sherman Xiaogang Lai, "A War within a War: The Road to the New Fourth Army Incident in January 1941," *Journal of Chinese Military History* 2, no. 1 (2013): 19.

146 **Matsuoka's benefits and perils from the Tripartite Pact:** Lu, *The Agony of Choice*, 168–69.

146 **Japanese occupation of Northern Indochina:** the best and most detailed account in English remains Ikuhiko Hata, "The Army's Move into Northern Indochina," in Morley, *The Fateful Choice*, 155–208. Also important is Lu, *The Agony of Choice*, 184–87.

148 **Matsuoka's terrible error on Southern Indochina advance:** Lu, *The Agony of Choice*, 187–88.

148 **Breaking "Purple":** The fundamental source for the story of breaking "Purple" is William F. Friedman, "Preliminary Historical Report on the Solution of the 'B' Machine," October 14, 1940, SRH-111, RG 457, Entry 9002, National Archives and Records Administration [hereafter NARA]. Friedman's handwritten note on the file copy states that after October 23, 1940, for security purposes the machine was designated as "Purple." The technical Japanese name for the machine was 97-shiki obun inji-ki ("System 97 Printing Machine for European Characters") or Angoki Taipu-B ("Type B Cipher Machine").

151 **First breakthrough of "Purple" and team reaction:** Frank B. Rowlett, *The Story of Magic: Memoirs of An American Cryptologic Pioneer* (Laguna Hills, CA: Aegean Park Press, 1998), 151–53.

152 **Comparison of "Purple" and Enigma machines:** Stephen J. Kelly, *Big Machines: Study of the Cryptographic Security of the German ENIGMA, Japanese PURPLE and U.S. SIGABA/ECM Cipher Machines* (Walnut Park, CA: Aegean Park Press, 2001), 178, 181–82, 187–96. Kelly provides an in-depth, mathematically robust analysis of the theoretical and practical security of the three premier cipher machines of World War II. He concludes that PURPLE was theoretically more secure than the three-rotor ENIGMA and nearly as secure as the four-rotor ENIGMA. The US SIGABA/ECM II was theoretically vastly more secure than either Axis system. Kelly concludes that the creation of the PURPLE analog was "perhaps the most

remarkable achievement of cryptanalysis against an electro mechanical system in history" (187).

152 **The 1940 presidential election:** Davis, *FDR: Into the Storm*, 593–624, and Jean Edward Smith, *FDR* (New York: Random House, 2007), 450–63, 472–80 [hereafter Smith, *FDR*], provide the bases for the facts concerning this campaign.

153 **"the most dictatorial and arbitrary act of any President in the history of the United States," and "I have said this before, and but shall say it again and again and again . . .":** quoted in Davis, *FDR: Into the Storm*, 611, 621.

153 **"appeaser fifth-columnists":** Franklin D. Roosevelt address, July 19, 1940, Democratic National Convention, http://millercenter.org/president/speeches/detail/3318, accessed 10 January 2014.

153 **"who consciously or unconsciously are playing the traitor's part":** "Ickes Denounces 'Traitor' Activity," *New York Times*, 17 November 1941, 2.

153 **Belief in "fifth column" or traitorous activity:** Cole, *Roosevelt & the Isolationists*, 484–87. Stimson's diary provides evidence of Roosevelt and Stimson's belief that their domestic opponents had crossed over into treasonous activity. See entries of Stimson's diary for July 24 and December 4–5, 1941.

154 **"In 1937 . . . the [Chinese Communist Party, or CCP] was still . . .":** Lary, *The Chinese People at War*, 15.

154 **No inevitability to Communist triumph in China:** Lary, *The Chinese People at War*, 3–4.

154 **Mao and Japanese prime minister:** van de Ven, *China at War*, 134.

154 **Creation of Chinese Communist Party, first party congress attended by Mao:** Spence, *The Search for Modern China*, 258, 295–99; Pantsov and Levine, *Mao: The Real Story*, 98–106.

154 **Mao's birth and family background:** Pantsov and Levine, *Mao: The Real Story*, 5–6, 12, 14–17, 25–28, 66–67, 210; Philip Short, *Mao: A Life* (New York: Henry Holt, 1999), 19–20, 27–30 [hereafter Short, *Mao: A Life*].

155 **Mao's reading, school experiences, and sense of superior station:** Pantsov and Levine, *Mao: The Real Story*, 17–18, 28–29, 35–36, 43, 66, 455–56; Short, *Mao: A Life*, 23–27, 82.

155 **"[Mao] wrote quickly . . .":** Pantsov and Levine, *Mao: The Real Story*, 38.

155 **Mao's appearance, first wife, income compared to rickshaw puller's:** Pantsov and Levine, *Mao: The Real Story*, 39, 56–57, 64, 73, 76, 96–97, 204; Short, *Mao: A Life*, 2, 83–87; Benton, *New Fourth Army*, 364.

156 **Formation of Chinese Communist Party, "the romance of universal equality . . .":** Pantsov and Levine, *Mao; The Real Story*, 92–94, 101–3; Spence, *The Search for Modern China*, 296–97.

156 **CCP financially controlled from Moscow:** Pantsov and Levine, *Mao: The Real Story*, 115, 135; Short, *Mao: A Life*, 122.

156 **Mao's first two critical contributions to rise of CCP, "political power is obtained from the barrel of the gun" and "the enemy advances, we retreat . . .":** Pantsov and Levine, *Mao: The Real Story*, 92, 222.

156 **Mao's emphasis on the rural masses, not the proletariat, and his reputation as expert on peasantry:** Pantsov and Levine, *Mao: The Real Story*, 124–25, 141–42, 151–52, 157, 164, 171–72; Spence, *The Search for Modern China*, 322–25, 365–68.

157 **"One characteristic feature of village life in China . . ." and chasm between landless and landholders:** Pantsov and Levine, *Mao: The Real Story*, 167–68.

157 **Rural clan divisions, the *Hakka*:** Pantsov and Levine, *Mao: The Real Story* 168–69; Spence, *The Search for Modern China*, 13–15, 360–65.

157 **Background to and course of 12 April Shanghai "White Terror":** van de Ven, *War and Nationalism in China*, 115–20; Taylor, *The Generalissimo*, 64–68 ("When the [Nationalist] Right is of no more use . . ." at 66); Pantsov and Levine, *Mao: The Real Story*, 170–79, 185. Pantsov and Levine note that the "barbaric" acts unleashed in the countryside by the CCP were indiscriminate, killing the innocent and the guilty alike. Their targets were frequently related to both the left- and right-wing members of the Revolutionary Army officer corps, thus making retribution inevitable.

158 **The Futian Incident:** Pantsov and Levine, *Mao: The Real Story*, 239–45; Short, *Mao: A Life*, 268–80. Short concluded that the "best informed Chinese historians say merely that 'tens of thousands' died" (279).

158 **Chiang's "Anti-Bandit" Campaigns:** Taylor, *The Generalissimo*, 98–99.

158 **The "Long March":** *Pantsov and Levine*, 274–88; Taylor, *The Generalissimo*, 99, 110–12, 114; Mitter, *Forgotten Ally*, 69–70 ("glorious foundation myth"). The numbers in the text are from Pantsov and Levine, 274, 288.

158 **Mao urges guerilla strategy; denial of Japanese control in countryside:** Yang Kuisong, "The Evolution of the Relationship Between the Chinese Communist Party and the Comintern during the Sino-Japanese War," in Hans van de Ven, Diana Lary, and Stephan R. MacKinnon, *Negotiating China's Destiny in World War II* (Stanford, CA: Stanford University Press, 2015), 70–90 [hereafter Yang, "The Evolution of the Relationship Between the Chinese Communist Party and the Comintern"]; Mitter, *Forgotten Ally*, 167–69, 189, 191; Pantsov and Levine, *Mao: The Real Story*, 313–14. Mitter provides the population estimate for the Special Zone, and a figure of roughly 450 million is the number used for the total population.

159 **Mao's orders on division of forces; Zhou's report read by Stalin, January 1940:** Pantsov and Levine, *Mao: The Real Story*, 313–14; Yang, "The Evolution of the Relationship Between the Chinese Communist Party and the Comintern," 72; Taylor, *The Generalissimo*, 169. While Pantsov and Levine state Mao committed only 25 percent of Red Army forces against the Japanese, the text follows Yang, who gives the figure as 33 percent. Taylor found the report in the Comintern archives in Moscow. It apparently covered the period from July 1937 to August 1939.

159 **Mao era narrative of CCP rise:** Benton, *New Fourth Army*, 6, 49, 168–69.

159 **Origins and profile of New Fourth Army, emphasis on unity over class struggle, and appeal to widely varied classes, groups, and associations:** Benton, *New Fourth Army*, 14, 19–24, 66–71, 84, 98, 100, 175, 226–27, 230–33, 242–45, 249 ("Machiavelli, not Marx").

160 **Contrasting geographic and political situations in northwestern and east Central China:** Benton, *New Fourth Army*, 30–32.

160 **"not to be bound by the Kuomintang's restrictions":** Taylor, *The Generalissimo*, 172.

160 **Strength of New Fourth and Eighth Route Armies:** Benton, *New Fourth Army*, 84.

160 **Chiang-Zhou agreement on territorial divisions; rejection by Mao:** Taylor, *The Generalissimo*, 172–73.

161 **The "Hundred Regiments" campaign:** Yang, "Nationalist and Communist Guerilla Warfare," 320–24; Paine, *The Wars for Asia 1911–1949*, 155; Spence, *The Search for Modern China*, 413–14; Taylor, *The Generalissimo*, 173–74; Lary, *The Chinese People at War*, 81–82.

161 **New Fourth Army crushes Nationalist Eighty-Ninth Army; ordered to move north of Yangtze and Yellow Rivers:** Taylor, *The Generalissimo*, 175–76.

161 **Basic facts about New Fourth Army (or Wannan) Incident of January 1941:** Taylor, *The Generalissimo*, 176–77; Benton, *New Fourth Army*, 511, 545, 572–77; van de Ven, *War and Nationalism in China*, 246.

162 **Varied explanations for Xiang's actions leading to incident:** Benton, *New Fourth Army*, ch. 14–15 provide an extended discussion of these theories. He favors a major role for Mao. Mitter, *Forgotten Ally*, 225–26, calls Mao's messages to Xiang Ying "ambiguous" on the route to follow and adds that Mao "may not have been sure what he wanted to achieve, half hoping and half fearing to provoke an incident."

162 **Yang's assessment of the New Fourth Army incident:** van de Ven, *China at War*, 148–49.

162 **Effects of New Fourth Army Incident:** Benton, *New Fourth Army Incident*, 590–97, 601, 726–28; "nothing out of the New Fourth Army Incident to offset his enormous loss in the propaganda war": Taylor, *The Generalissimo*, 177. Diana Lary called the New Fourth Army Incident "the last straw" in a "souring" relationship resulting in a clear breakdown of the "United Front" by early 1941. *The Chinese People at War*, 81–82. Other historians, like van de Ven, do not see the episode as such a stark departure point.

162 **"The Nationalists were on their knees":** van de Ven, *War and Nationalism in China*, 246.

7: "One Hundred Evils and Not a Single Good"

163 **"Matsuoka troupe" and Matsuoka as diplomatic "star":** Hosoya Chihiro, "The Japanese-Soviet Neutrality Pact," in Morley, *The Fateful Choice*, 64 [hereafter Hosoya, "The Japanese-Soviet Neutrality Pact"]; Lu, *The Agony of Choice*, 197–98.

163 **Matsuoka's ruminations on the train to Moscow:** Lu, *The Agony of Choice*, 199.

163 **Matsuoka's stop in Berlin, Hitler's pledge, Oshima's counsel:** Hosoya, "The Japanese-Soviet Neutrality Pact," 71; Lu, *The Agony of Choice*, 200–203.

164 **Italian attack on Greece; German conquest of Yugoslavia, Greece, and Crete:** Weinberg, *A World at Arms*, 215–22, 227–31; Max Hastings, *Inferno: The World at War 1939–1945* (New York: Alfred A. Knopf, 2011), 113–21 ("The infallibility of the Germans is an idea that is rapidly gaining ground" at 121); Hosoya, "The Japanese-Soviet Neutrality Pact," 74–75.

165 **"I can now have my treaty":** Lu, *The Agony of Choice*, 204.

165 **Japanese leader's outlook on Russia/Soviet Union:** Hosoya, "The Japanese-Soviet Neutrality Pact," 30–35, 40–41.

165 **Japanese-Soviet neutrality treaty:** Lu, *The Agony of Choice*, 204–7; Hosoya, "The Japanese-Soviet Neutrality Pact," 44–45, 78–79.

165 **Stalin sees off Matsuoka at the train station:** Lu, *The Agony of Choice*, 206.

165 **Chiang and US response to Japanese-Soviet Neutrality Pact:** Hosoya, "The Japanese Soviet-Neutrality Pact," 84–85.

166 **Lend-Lease program:** Gilbert, *Their Finest Hour*, 936–38; Smith, *FDR: The War President*, 81–89, 99–100, 135–36; Heinrichs, *The Threshold of War*, 11.

166 **Battle of Southern Henan:** van de Ven, *War and Revolution in China*, 246.

166 **Battle of Shanggao, loss of Zhongtiao Mountains:** van de Ven, *War and Revolution in China*, 246–47.

167 **Currie Mission:** Folder Diplomatic Correspondence China: Lauchlin Currie Report 3/15/41, President's Secretary File, Box 27, China: 1938—Military Dispatches thru China 1945, FDRL [hereafter Currie Report]. An edited version of Currie's report appears in *FRUS, 1941*, vol. 4, *The Far East*, 81–95. Currie's status as a Soviet agent (code named "Page") is noted in, among other places, Allen Weinstein and Alexander Vassiliev, *The Haunted Wood: Soviet Espionage in America—The Stalin Era* (New York: Random House, 1999), 48, 106, 161–63, and Macri, *Clash of Empires*, 254. At this point, however, Moscow's interest was in bolstering Chiang's government and its resistance to Japan, not undercutting those efforts.

167 **James Roosevelt trip to China:** Macri, *Clash of Empires*, 254–55.

167 **Chongqing financial situation in 1941:** Currie Report, especially 8–13; "Memorandum by Arthur M. Young, American Adviser to the Chinese Ministry of Finance, May 13, 1941," *FRUS, 1941*, vol. 5, *The Far East*, 647–48; "The Ambassador in China (Gauss) to the Secretary of State, December 21, 1941," *FRUS, 1941*, vol. 5, *The Far East*, 766–77.

168 **"the outlook for German-Soviet relations . . .":** Hosoya, "The Japanese-Soviet Neutrality Pact," 82.

168 **Nomura's appointment and background:** Mauch, *Sailor Diplomat*, ch. 1–4, particularly 14, 45, 57, 63, 66 67; Lu, *The Agony of Choice*, 219; Heinrichs, *Threshold of War*, 49. In a 24 July 1941 letter, Admiral Harold Stark wrote that Nomura "has many friends in our Navy," Hearings before the Joint Committee on the Investigation of the Pearl Harbor Attack, Congress of the United States, Seventy-ninth Congress (Washington, DC), July 1946, PHA, Part 5, 2114 [hereafter PHA].

168 **Nomura's grasp of the situation and hope to have senior naval leadership head off war:** Mauch, *Sailor Diplomat*, 115, 134.

169 **Oikawa and Toyoda urge Nomura to take the ambassador position and set up direct communications channel:** Mauch, *Sailor Diplomat*, 135–37. Nomura's messages were to go to Oikawa; Toyoda, chief of the Naval General Staff; Prince Fushimi; Vice Chief of Staff Nobutake Kondo; director of the Navy Ministry's powerful Naval Affairs Bureau Takazumi Oka; and chief of the Naval General Staff Operations Division Matsome Ugaki.

169 **Assurances about Tripartite Pact from Konoe, Oikawa, and Fushimi, warnings from Yamamoto and Yonai:** Lu, *The Agony of Choice*, 219; Mauch, *Sailor Diplomat*, 131; Morley, *The Final Confrontation*, 17–19.

169 **Matsuoka's attitudes to Nomura and comments December 1941:** Lu, *The Agony of Choice*, 219–20.

169 **Yokoyama's stance and "one hundred evils and not a single good":** Mauch, *Sailor Diplomat*, 144.

169 **ABC-1 Agreement and "The question as to our entry into the war . . .":** Patrick Abbazia, *Mr. Roosevelt's Navy: The Private War of the Atlantic Fleet 1939–1942* (Annapolis, MD: Naval Institute Press, 1976), 39–42; Heinrichs, *Threshold of War*, 38–39; Barnhart, *Japan Prepares for Total War*, 220.

170 **Meeting on 14 February 1941 of Nomura and Roosevelt:** Mauch, *Sailor Diplomat*, 141–43; Memorandum by the Secretary of State, February 14, 1941, *FRUS, Japan, 1931–1941*, vol. 2, 387–89 (includes "marked spirit of cordiality and personal friendliness" quote).

170 **Background of Drought and Walsh and their private diplomatic effort:** Morley, *The Final Confrontation*, 20–22, 33–34, 36–37, 59; Ike, *Japan's Decision for War*, xx.

170 **Iwakuro background:** Morley, *The Final Confrontation*, 20–22.

170 **Meetings with Matsuoka and Roosevelt:** Lu, *The Agony of Choice*, 221–22; January 23, 1941, Franklin D. Roosevelt Day by Day, January 23, 1941, FDR Presidential Library.

171 **Drought and Walsh's Tokyo and Washington memoranda:** Mauch, *Sailor Diplomat*, 145; Morley, *The Final Confrontation*, 21–22; Ike, *Japan's Decision for War*, xx–xxi.

171 **Drought's manipulations; Nomura's doubts:** Mauch, *Sailor Diplomat*, 145–47.

171 **March Nomura cable to naval leadership and cable from Tokyo:** Mauch, *Sailor Diplomat*, 147.

171 **Confusion over whether "Draft Understanding" represented a Japanese or American proposal:** Lu, *The Agony of Choice*, 226–27.

172 **Nomura fails to forward Hull's "four principles" to Tokyo; Hull's intent inverted:** Mauch, *Sailor Diplomat*, 160–61; Morley, *The Final Confrontation*, 53–57; Barnhart, *Japan Prepares for Total War*, 223–24 ("disposed to yield on some important issues as a result").

172 **Matsuoka gains first knowledge of "Draft Understanding" and reacts:** Lu, *The Agony of Choice*, 228; Morley, *The Final Confrontation*, 56–58, 76.

173 **Matsuoka unhinged by "Draft Understanding":** Lu, *The Agony of Choice*, 228–29; Mauch, *Sailor Diplomat*, 169.

173 **Response of naval leadership to Nomura May 8:** Mauch, *Sailor Diplomat*, 173–74.

173 **Matsuoka's revision of the "Draft Understanding":** *FRUS, Japan 1931–1941*, vol. 2, 420–25; Mauch, *Sailor Diplomat*, 174–75; Lu, *The Agony of Choice*, 231. In an "oral" explanatory section appended to the formal proposal, the Japanese note required that the United States enter into a "separate and secret" written understanding that if Chiang's government refused to follow a US recommendation that it enter into negotiations with Japan, the United States would "discontinue" its assistance to Chiang's government. If the United States would not execute such a written declaration, then "a definite pledge by some highest authority will suffice." In a conversation with Maxwell Hamilton of the State Department on May 30, 1941, Colonel Iwakuro set out Japanese concepts for stationing troops in China for "defense against communistic activities" per Matsuoka's revision of the "Draft Understanding." Basically, Iwakuro portrayed deployments that American officials deemed as equaling domination of the five northern provinces of China (Hopei, Shantung, Shansi, Chahar, and Suiyan) encompassing an area of over 400,000 square miles and a population of more than 80 million people. *FRUS, Japan 1931–1941*, vol. 2, 334, 444–45.

173 **Trans-Pacific defeat of Matsuoka's request to meet Roosevelt:** Lu, *The Agony of Choice*, 230–35.

174 **May 31 American response to Matsuoka's May 11 "revised Draft Understanding" and reaction in Tokyo:** "American Draft Proposal Handed to the Japanese Ambassador

(Nomura) on 31 May 1941," *FRUS, Japan, 1931–1941*, vol. 2, 446–54; Mauch, *Sailor Diplomat*, 177–78.

174 Trio of evils inflicted by "John Doe Associates": Lu, *The Agony of Choice*, 232.

174 Matsuoka's lost opportunity to settle the China Incident; Tôjô's support and opposition to settlement within Imperial Army: Lu, *The Agony of Choice*, 174–83, 193–94.

8: "Leaping off the Veranda"

175 Background of Joseph Grew: David Mayers, *FDR's Ambassadors and the Diplomacy of Crisis* (Cambridge: Cambridge University Press, 2013), 15–29 [hereafter Mayers, *FDR's Ambassadors*].

175 "I believe that the fundamental proposition . . .": Joseph C. Grew, *Turbulent Era: A Diplomatic Record of Forty Years 1904–1945*, vol. 2 (Boston: Houghton Mifflin, 1952), 1255–61.

176 Hitler's decision to attack the Soviet Union: Weinberg, *A World at Arms*, 179–81, 187–89.

176 Soviet warnings to Stalin of German Attack: David M. Glantz and Jonathan House, *When Titans Clashed: How the Red Army Stopped Hitler* (Lawrence, KS: University Press of Kansas, 1995), 41–44. I am indebted to Gerhard Weinberg, who pointed out to me that Soviet intelligence had acquired a copy of Hitler's December 1940 directive.

176 Warnings from the United States and from Churchill to Stalin and Eden to Maisky of German plans to attack the Soviet Union; Stalin's reaction: William I. Langer and S. Everett Gleason, *The Undeclared War, 1940–1941* (New York: Harper & Brothers, 1953), 336–37 [hereafter Langer and Gleason, *The Undeclared War*]; Hosoya Chihiro, "The Japanese-Soviet Neutrality Pact," in Morley, *The Fateful Choice*, 86–87; Gilbert, *Finest Hour*, 1050–51; David M. Glantz, "The Impact of Intelligence Provided to the Soviet Union by Richard Zorge on Soviet Force Deployments from the Far East to the West in 1941 and 1942," paper kindly provided by the author. Glantz's deeply researched paper demonstrates that though Stalin did not change deployments or the alert status of units along the western border immediately facing the Germans (which understandably led to the conclusion that the intelligence reports had no effect on his actions), his customary deeply suspicious or even "paranoid" outlook prompted him to order the mobilization of large numbers of units then positioned as deep reserves. These reserves played a key role in stalling the German attack. As will be noted further below, the stalling of the German thrusts in the last part of July would have a significant effect on American decision making. Glantz notes Sorge's contribution to the array of intelligence reaching Stalin before 22 June, but points out his messages were only part of a large body of evidence and hence cannot be assigned critical value.

176 German and Allied forces deployed at opening of Barbarossa: Glantz and House, *When Titans Clashed*, 31–33.

176 Opening phases of Operation Barbarossa: Glantz and House, *When Titans Clashed*, 49–55; Richard Lourie, *Sakharov: A Biography* (Hanover, MA: Brandeis University Press, 2002), 46 ("I prefer fear to convictions, because convictions change"). As to what the outside world could discern, an excellent indicator is the *New York*

Times, 22 June 22–19 July 1941. Nearly every day contained a reprint of official German and Soviet communiqués, normally on p. 2, often with maps.

177 **"thoroughly occupied with beating Russia for a minimum of one month and a possible maximum . . .":** Stimson diary, June 23, 1941.

177 **"Grave" Soviet military situation; "concert pitch" counterinvasion preparations:** Gilbert, *Finest Hour*, 1125–26, 1128.

177 **Stimson background:** Godfrey Hodgson, *The Colonel: The Life and Wars of Henry Stimson 1867–1950* (New York: Alfred A. Knopf, 1990), 17, 372; Elting E. Morison, *Turmoil and Tradition: A Study of the Life and Times of Henry L. Stimson* (Boston: Houghton Mifflin, 1960), 202; Jonathan W. Jordan, *American Warlords: How Roosevelt's High Command Led America to Victory in World War II* (New York: NAL Caliber, 2015), 158.

177 **Reality versus appearance of Barbarossa:** of the recent works on Barbarossa, this account follows the explicit analysis in David Stahel, *Operation Barbarossa and Germany's Defeat in the East* (Cambridge: Cambridge University Press, 2009). Particularly important are pp. 127–38 on the completely deficient German logistics, and the details in following chapters on the fierce fighting and high losses of German units. Much the same analysis appears in the numerous works by David Glantz that contain vast detail, particularly from Soviet archives.

177 **Chinese Communist reaction to German invasion of Soviet Union:** Yang, "The Evolution of the Relationship between the Chinese Communist Party and the Comintern during the Sino-Japanese War," 85–86.

178 **Comparative statistics on death tolls in September 1939 and June 1941:** Figures of Hitler and Stalin by September 1939 from Timothy Snyder, *Bloodlands: Europe Between Hitler and Stalin* (New York: Basic Books, 2010), vii, x [hereafter Snyder, *Bloodlands*]. Of course, there are numerous estimates that find or clearly imply that Stalin's death toll by September 1939 must have climbed steeply above eight million. For example, Steven Rosefielde, *Red Holocaust* (Routledge, 2009), 17, maintains that it is "beyond reasonable doubt" Stalin killed "more than 13 million" between 1929 and 1953 "and that this figure could rise above 20 million." Sebag Montefiore, *Stalin: The Court of the Red Tsar* (New York: Knopf, 2004), 649, speaks of "perhaps 20 million" killed by Stalin (but this number extends to 1953). Alexander N. Yakovlev, *A Century of Violence in Soviet Russia* (New Haven, CT: Yale University Press, 2002), 234, one of Mikhail Gorbachev's lieutenants, puts the total fatalities during the period of Soviet power (thus including Lenin) for political repression at 20 to 25 million and he adds about 10.5 million killed in famines for which Soviet leadership bore responsibility. Although there is little doubt that the number of deaths in Chinese internal conflict from 1928 to 1937 was large, an exact figure is impossible to state with confidence. After looking at a variety of estimates, the figure here is derived from R. J. Rummel, *China's Bloody Century: Genocide and Mass Murder Since 1900* (New Brunswick, NJ: Transaction Publishers, 2008 reprint), 77–101. Figures for Japanese killing in China are based on a linear projection starting from an overall estimate that 15 million Chinese perished due to Japan's aggression between July 1937 and August 1945. The "in excess of 600,000" figure for Hitler by June 1941 includes the larger portion of the 200,000 Poles who died in the 1939 campaign or the severe repression during German and Soviet occupation. Snyder, *Bloodlands*, vii. Primary source for other figures between Sep-

tember 1939 and June 22, 1941 is Michael Clodfelter, *Warfare and Armed Conflicts: A Statistical Reference to Casualty and Other Figures, 1500-2000*, 3rd edition (Jefferson, NC: McFarland Publishers, 2008), 465–67, 469–71, 477–78 [hereafter Clodfelter]. Although caution is in order over death statistics in World War II, generally those for Western Europe are more reliable and Clodfelter's numbers appear reasonable in most cases when compared to other sources. Alternative sources are used when in the author's judgment they appear more reliable, and ranges are used where sources differ materially. These numbers combine to total between 553,714 and 617,714. The specific sources for these figures are from the following. Poland 1939–1941: Polish and Soviet Losses, Clodfelter, 465–66; Tadeusz Piotrowski, *Poland's Holocaust: Ethnic Strife, Collaboration with Occupying Forces and Genocide in the Second Republic, 1918–1947* (Jefferson, NC: McFarland Publishers, 1998), 301. Finland: Finnish, German, and Soviet losses, Clodfelter, 465–66. 1940 Western European campaigns: German, British, and French losses, Karl-Heinz Frieser, *The Blitzkrieg Legend: The 1940 Campaign in the West* (Annapolis, MD: Naval Institute Press, 2005), 318. Belgian losses, Jean Paul Pallud, *Blitzkrieg in the West Then and Now* (London: After the Battle, 1991), 609 (combatants) [hereafter Pallud], Clodfelter, 469 (noncombatants). Danish Losses: Clodfelter, 466. Netherlands losses: Pallud 609 (combatants), Clodfelter, 469 (noncombatants). Other German losses in 1940–1941: Battle of Britain (for period 1 August 1940 to 31 March 1941), Clodfelter, 471; Greece and Crete, Clodfelter, 478; Yugoslavia, Clodfelter, 478. German Euthanasia program: Christopher R. Browning with contributions by Jürgen Matthäus, *The Origins of the Final Solution: The Evolution of Nazi Jewish Policy, September 1939–March 1942* (Lincoln: University of Nebraska Press, 2004), 184–93 (70,000 "by August 1941" at 191). All losses in Norwegian campaign from http://www.feldgrau.com/norwegian .html, accessed 11 November 2013. British losses: Battle of Britain, Clodfelter, 470–71; Greece and Crete, Clodfelter, 478. Greek losses: Clodfelter, 478. Yugoslav losses: No figures for combatants could be located. The noncombatant figures are from Clodfelter, 477.

178 **Upward leap of German terror from June 1941:** Snyder, *Bloodlands*, ch. 5–7, and Browning, *The Origins of the Final Solution*, ch. 7–9; Antony Beevor, *The Second World War* (New York: Little, Brown, 2012) 210–18.

178 **"Hunger plan":** Snyder, *Bloodlands*, xiv, 162–63, 168–72; Adam Tooze, *The Wages of Destruction: The Making and Breaking of the Nazi Economy* (New York: Viking, 2006), 476–85, 538–44. Figures for deaths of Soviet prisoners of war are from Browning, *The Origins of the Final Solution*, 244.

179 **Churchill's emotional basis for depicting the Soviet alliance; Roosevelt's decision to depict the Soviets as sharing values with the United States and UK; "regardless of Soviet realities":** Roberts, *Walking With Destiny*, 661; Dallek, *Franklin D. Roosevelt and American Foreign Policy*, 298.

179 **Orwell's protest of misrepresentation of the Soviet Union:** Richard Overy, *Why the Allies Won* (New York: W.W. Norton, 1995), 296–97.

179 **Roosevelt on Soviet "religious freedom" and "To welcome Russia as an associate in the defense of democracy . . .":** Dallek, *Franklin D. Roosevelt and American Foreign Policy*, 297–98.

179 **Matsuoka receives news of German attack on the Soviet Union, meets with emperor:** Lu, *The Agony of Choice*, 235; Nobutaka Ike, *Japan's Decision for War: Records of the*

1941 Policy Conferences (Stanford, CA: Stanford University Press, 1967), 46–47 [hereafter Ike, *Japan's Decision for War*]; Tsunoda, *The Final Confrontation*, 122–26.

180 **Meiji constitution and "right of autonomous command":** Jansen, *The Making of Modern Japan*, 390–95, 414–19, 496 ("a curious sort of pluralism . . ."); Drea, *Japan's Imperial Army*, 65.

180 ***Genro* and *Jushin*:** Jansen, *The Making of Modern Japan*, 420–23; Keiichiro Komatsu, *The Origins of the Pacific War and the Importance of 'Magic'* (London: Routledge, 1999), 4–5 [hereafter Komatsu, *The Origins of the Pacific War and the Importance of 'Magic'*].

180 **Structural defects in Japanese government:** Komatsu, *The Origins of the Pacific War and the Importance of 'Magic,'* 2–3, 280–82. When Tôjô Hideki became prime minister in October 1941, he also retained the position of army minister. This was not a sinister lunge for unbridled power, but a bid to gain access to military decision making that had been legally denied to Konoe. It would also position Tôjô to exercise some influence over the army.

181 **Power of the elite bureaucracy:** Komatsu, *The Origins of the Pacific War and the Importance of 'Magic,'* 4. One of the major criticisms of postwar reform is that the bureaucracy escaped accountability and if anything achieved greater power during the war, which it sustained into the postwar period.

181 **Role of Imperial Household Ministry, Kido:** Bix, *Hirohito and the Making of Modern Japan*, 76, 177–78, 370–72; Robert Butow, *Japan's Decision to Surrender* (Stanford, CA: Stanford University Press, 1954), 12–15.

181 **Division within Imperial Army; "Imperial Way" and "Control" factions in the Imperial Army:** Drea, *Japan's Imperial Army*, 22, 50, 174–81.

182 **Konoe's perception of effects of ascendancy of "Control" over "Imperial Way" officers in 1941:** Yagami, *Konoe Fumimaro*, 35–36.

182 **Factionalism in the Imperial Navy:** Asada, *From Mahan to Pearl Harbor*, 244–46, 272 ("ratio neurosis"); Morley, *The Final Confrontation*, 167–68.

183 **Role of *bakuryo*:** Eri Hotta, *Japan 1941: Countdown to Infamy* (New York: Alfred A. Knopf, 2013), 124–25, 185–87, 196 [hereafter Hotta, *Japan 1941*]. She explains the origins of the term *bakuryo* as follows: "In the olden days, the word *baku* (curtains) had double meaning in explaining concentration of power. One was political, synonymous with the government, as in *bakufu* (shogunate), meaning 'a regime behind the curtains.' The other was strategic, alluding to the makeshift curtain used in encampments during field combat to identify the headquarters, where strategies were secretly debated among the select few. In prewar Japan, *bakuryo* had come to assume both the political task of negotiating and liaising with different sources of power and the more practical task of planning strategies. Because of the pivotal role *bakuryo* would come to assume in directing Japan's policy after July, the term evokes the image of war planners furtively creating bellicose policies in the name of assisting and advising their superiors." *Japan 1941*, 125.

183 **Culture of insubordination and rebellion:** Danny Orbach, *Curse Upon This Country: The Rebellious Army of Imperial Japan* (Ithaca and London: Cornell University Press, 2017), 4–5, 190, 256, 260, 261–65 [hereafter Orbach, *Curse Upon This Country*].

184 **Imperial Navy reaction to outbreak of Soviet-German war:** Mauch, *Sailor Diplomat*, 178–79, 183.

184 **Policy conferences among Japanese leaders in June:** Ike, *Japan's Decision for War,* 56–75 (Matsuoka quote at 72, navy minister quote at 59, Tôjô quote at 74); Tsunoda, *The Final Confrontation,* 124–26; Lu, *The Agony of Choice,* 236. Historian Herbert Bix frames the role of China at this juncture in a different light. To fight in China from 1937, the Imperial Army expanded from 17 to 51 divisions and from 250,000 to 2.1 million men, and he attributes an expansion of the Imperial Navy to the same cause. This is an interesting argument, but it can be challenged on several fronts. First, the primary rationale for the naval expansion programs preexisted that conflict. Second, to the degree the army buildup sustained a huge commitment to China, it did not prepare the army to fight the Soviets. Third, without the war in China, or an early settlement thereof, a modest expansion program that German triumphs may well have triggered might also have positioned Japan to contemplate war in late 1941 with the Soviets as well as the United States and Great Britain. Bix, *Hirohito and the Making of Modern Japan,* 396.

185 **"Outline of National Policies in View of the Changing Situation":** Ike, *Japan's Decision for War,* 78–79. This version can be compared to that in Tsunoda, *The Final Confrontation,* 128–29.

185 **"Outline" first document to contemplate war with Britain and the United States; discussions at July 2 Imperial Conference:** Bix, *Hirohito and the Making of Modern Japan,* 397–98; Ike, *Japan's Decision for War,* 80–82; Asada, *From Mahan to Pearl Harbor,* 251.

186 **Japanese fail to anticipate American reaction to advance into southern Indochina:** Mauch, *Sailor Diplomat,* 183–84. Asada notes that "again the navy's concern for budget and material was the real but hidden motive for its belligerent stance." Without an objective assessment of the international situation and the chances for victory, the navy became absorbed in domestic dispute with the army. The Liaison Conference meeting failed to discuss whether advance into southern Indochina would trigger a total American embargo. Asada, *From Mahan to Pearl Harbor,* 252.

186 **Matsuoka predicts "disaster":** Hotta, *Japan 1941,* 128–30, 133, 136, 141–42.

186 **"Outline" does not authorize or lead inexorably to attacks on Malaya or the Netherlands East Indies:** Tsunoda, *The Final Confrontation,* 129–30. David A. Titus in his "Introductions" (pp. xxv–xxvi) to *The Final Confrontation* finds much to praise in Tsunoda's work, but Titus observes that it is astonishing that Tsunoda presents the key imperial conferences' decisions to sanction the southern advance on 2 July and 6 September as mere "semantics" or "rhetoric."

186 **The limited authorization for actual action and dangerous momentum in the "Outline of National Policies in View of the Changing Situation":** Komatsu, *The Origins of the Pacific War and the Importance of 'Magic,'* 126–43; Morley, *The Final Confrontation,* 129–30. Tsunoda calls the July 2 policy "inherently ambiguous" and not a commitment to war.

187 **Southern Indochina plays no role in China Incident:** Miller, *Bankrupting the Enemy,* 173, makes the point that there were no transportation links between Southern Indochina and China.

187 **Hull's note and oral statement of June 21:** Lu, *The Agony of Choice,* 237–38.

187 **Matsuoka thrown from cabinet:** Ike, *Japan's Decision for War,* 93–104; Lu, *The Agony of Choice,* 238; Mauch, *Sailor Diplomat,* 188; Hotta, *Japan 1941,* 136–40. Lu points

out that among his traits, Matsuoka could neither forgive insults nor pass up opportunities to get even. The most spectacular single example of this trait transpired during a March 1941 meeting with the emperor present. Years earlier when Matsuoka had been president of the South Manchurian Railway, General Sugiyama had twice insulted him. Now in a session over policy about French Indochina, Matsuoka shattered the customary rigid decorum of such assemblies by lashing back at Sugiyama—now army chief of staff—"You fool, look, you are the one who spent three and a half years in China and still cannot solve it." Sugiyama and Tôjô were speechless. *The Agony of Choice*, 190–92, 194. Yagami reports that Konoe saw Matsuoka as an obstacle to reaching a settlement with the United States, but Yagami does not depict Konoe as believing that Matsuoka was the singular obstacle to a settlement. Yagami further notes that between the disruptive behavior of Matsuoka and reports that Germany was about to attack the Soviet Union, Konoe talked about resigning. Kido dissuaded him. *Konoe Fumimaro*, 113.

187 **"engaged in a real drag down and knockout fight . . .":** as quoted in Langer and Gleason, *The Undeclared War*, 646.

187 **"Magic" version of Tokyo's report of July 2, Imperial Conference:** Department of Defense, *The "Magic" Background of Pearl Harbor*, 8 vols. (Washington, DC: Government Printing Office, 1977), vol. 2, p. 36, appendix 2, A56–57, Tokyo to Berlin, no. 1390 (Parts 1 and 2), 2 July 1941 [hereafter *The "Magic" Background of Pearl Harbor*]. The key passage was translated as: "The Imperial Government shall continue its endeavor to dispose of the China incident, *and shall take measures with a view to advancing southward* in order to establish firmly a basis for her self-existence and self-protection." (Italics added.) Of further note is that this message was only translated on August 8. This is interesting because Stimson's diary for that date notes: "I had brought with me the last magics [the 2 July message was in two parts] that I had received which gave a very recent example of Japan's duplicity and I found that Hull had not read both of them, so I showed them to him." Stimson diary, August 8, 1941.

188 **Japanese ultimatum to French authorities:** *The "Magic" Background to Pearl Harbor*, vol. 2, pp. 63–64, appendix, vol. 2, A419–22, no. 171, Tokyo to Vichy, no. 273, Parts 1 & 2, 12 July 1941 (translated 14 July); no. 173, Tokyo (Matsuoka) to Vichy, no. 274, Parts 1 & 2, 12 July 1941 (translated 14 July). French yield, vol. 2, 157–58, appendix, vol. 2, A446–47, Vichy to Tokyo, no. 395 (Part 1 only), 21 July 1941 (translated 23 July).

188 **Welles warning and Roosevelt neutralization proposal:** "Memorandum by the Acting Secretary of State (Welles)," 21 July 1941, *FRUS, Japan, 1931–1941*, vol. 2, 520–23; "Memorandum by the Acting Secretary of State (Welles)," 24 July 1941, *FRUS, Japan, 1931–1941*, vol. 2, 527–30; "Memorandum by the Acting Secretary of State (Welles)," 21 July 1941, *FRUS, Japan, 1931–1941*, vol. 2, 520–23; "Memorandum by the Acting Secretary of State (Welles)," 24 July 1941, *FRUS, Japan, 1931–1941*, vol. 2, 527–30.

188 **Japan occupies southern Indochina and responds to Roosevelt's neutralization proposal:** Hotta, *Japan 1941*, 155; "Proposal by the Japanese Government Handed by the Japanese Ambassador (Nomura) to the Secretary of State on August 6, 1941," *FRUS, Japan, 1941*, vol. 2, 549–50. The Japanese note also offered a Japanese pledge to recognize Philippine neutrality and asked for recognition of Japan's "special status" in Indochina after its troop withdrawal.

189 **Magruder mission to China:** Charles F. Romanus and Riley Sunderland, *The United States Army in World War II, China-Burma-India Theater, Stilwell's Mission to China* (Washington, DC: Office of the Chief of Military History, 1953), 27–32 [hereafter Romanus and Sunderland, *Stilwell's Mission to China*]. The title of Magruder's team was American Military Mission to China (AMMISCA).

189 **"willing to give Chiang Kai-shek just enough . . ." and negative reports from China reaching Washington:** Heinrichs, *Threshold of War*, 131–32.

189 **July 1941 tonnage authorizations:** Jonathan G. Utley, *Going to War with Japan, 1937–1941* (Knoxville: University of Tennessee Press, 1985), 135–36.

189 **Japan's naval blockade of China:** Ken-ichi Arakawa, "Japanese Naval Blockade of China in the Second Sino-Japanese War, 1937–41," in Bruce A. Elleman and S. C. M. Paine, *Naval Blockades and Seapower, Strategies and Counter-Strategies* (London and New York: Routledge, 2006), 105–16. This source gives an accounting of the origins and progression of the blockade.

189 **Hong Kong Supply route:** Macri, *Clash of Empires in South China*, 17, 35–38 ("the primary source of war material from aboard"), 45–46, 84, 109–10.

189 **Soviet supply route to China:** Macri, *Clash of Empires in South China*, 46–47, 146.

189 **Burma Road:** Macri, *Clash of Empires in South China*, 7, 46, 83, 106–7; Romanus and Sunderland, *Stilwell's Mission to China*, 45–46 ("for private profit"); Karl C. Dod, *The United States Army in World War II, The Technical Services, The Corps of Engineers in the War Against Japan* (Washington, DC: Office of the Chief of Military History, 1966), 413 [hereafter Dod, *The Corps of Engineers in the War Against Japan*]. Roosevelt had dispatched Lauchlin Currie from his staff to China. Currie submitted a March 1941 report urging major support for China, including improvements in the Burma Road. Folder Diplomatic Correspondence China: Lauchlin Currie Report 3/15/41, President's Secretary File, Box 27, China: 1938–Military Dispatches thru China 1945, FDRL.

190 **Formation of American Volunteer Group:** Daniel Ford, *Flying Tigers: Claire Chennault and the American Volunteer Group* (Washington: Smithsonian Institution Press, 1991), 36–37, 41–48, 54, 59–60, 65–66 [hereafter Ford, *Flying Tigers*].

190 **Creation of United States Army Forces in the Far East; recall of MacArthur:** Louis Morton, *United States Army in World War II, the War in the Pacific, the Fall of the Philippines* (Washington, DC: Office of the Chief of Military History, 1953), 14–19 [hereafter Morton, *The Fall of the Philippines*].

191 **"the terrible German Moloch . . .":** Stimson diary, 2 July 1941.

191 **German advance halted in Soviet Union; a turning point reached in August; implications as to China:** For what American officials could discern for themselves, see the official German and Soviet daily communiqués, usually on p. 2, *New York Times*, 19–31 July 1941. For what actually transpired on the ground, David Glantz awards primary credit to Soviet fighting in his two volumes: *Barbarossa Derailed: The Battle of Smolensk 10 July–10 September 1941*, vol. 1, *The German Advance, the Encirclement Battle, and the First and Second Soviet Counteroffensives, 10 July–24 August 1941* (Solihull, UK: Helion & Company Ltd., 2010) and *Barbarossa Derailed: The Battle of Smolensk 10 July–10 September 1941*, vol. 2, *The German Offensives on the Flanks and the Third Soviet Counteroffensive, 25 August–10 September 1941* (Solihull, UK: Helion & Company Ltd., 2011). Gerhard Weinberg's magisterial account gives much credit to Soviet fighting, but also assigns major weight to German logistical short-

comings, inherent in the planning phase, now becoming handcuffs on German options. *A World at Arms*, 187–98, 268–70. David Stahel's *Operation Barbarossa* advances these points and rests on the basic thesis that the German failure to crush Soviet armies near the borders was clear by August 1941, and this was decisive for the whole German-Soviet conflict as this was the only path to German victory. He restates this point in *Operation Typhoon: Hitler's March on Moscow, October 1941* (Cambridge: Cambridge University Press, 2013), 305.

191 **Roosevelt's three-tiered policy:** Heinrichs, *Threshold of War*, 135–36. On 6 August, Nomura delivered a Japanese proposal to Hull. This was described as a reply "in a way" to Roosevelt's 24 July proposal (to neutralize Indochina). The key terms set forth in the proposal were that (1) Japan had no intention of advancing farther south beyond Indochina, but the United States must recognize Japan's "special right" to this area even after the end of war in China, (2) Japan guaranteed the neutrality of the Philippines, (3) the United States would cease military buildup in the South-west Pacific, (4) the United States would restore trade with Japan and assist it to secure resources from the NEI, and (5) that the United States would urge Chiang's government to enter into direct negotiations with Japan. Although this omitted the onerous terms for a settlement between Japan and China, it effectively demanded that the United States recognize Japan's occupation of Indochina and restore trade. *FRUS, Japan 1931–1941*, vol. 2, 548–50.

192 **"quite a lecture" and "was still unwilling to draw the noose tight . . .":** as quoted in Dallek, *Franklin D. Roosevelt and American Foreign Policy*, 274.

192 **Accounts attributing oil embargo to bureaucratic usurpation of policy:** Jonathan G. Utley, *Going to War with Japan, 1937–1941* (New York: McGraw-Hill, 1985), 153–56; Robert L. Beisner, *Dean Acheson: A Life in the Cold War* (Oxford: Oxford University Press, 2006), 1, 15, 663n17 [Beisner, *Acheson*]; Asada, *From Mahan to Pearl Harbor*, 258–59; Dallek, *Franklin D. Roosevelt and American Foreign Policy*, 274–75. This writer's view is that the theory that Acheson surreptitiously veered policy to a confrontation with Japan is not frivolous and is one way to look at the evidence. Certainly, Roosevelt's comments prior to the last days of July 1941 indicate his original intent was for a flexible system to apply pressure, not to inflict a total embargo. But for reasons elaborated below in the text, I believe that evidence suggesting the survival of the Soviet Union, which only became available in the last ten days of July and early August, prompted Roosevelt to shift his stance.

192 **Welles's order to take no action on Japanese applications to unfreeze funds:** Heinrichs, *Threshold of War*, 135, 246n68.

192 **Meeting at Placentia Bay and arrival of *Prince of Wales*:** *FRUS, 1941*, vol. 1, *General, Soviet Union*, 341–69; Kenneth S. Davis, *FDR: The War President 1940–1943* (New York: Random House, 2000), 256 ("high mountains, deep water, & fjord like arms of the sea," FDR quote) [hereafter Davis, *FDR: The War President*].

192 **10 August services on *Prince of Wales*:** Churchill, *Their Finest Hour*, 1159; Max Hastings, *Winston's War: Churchill 1940–1945* (Alfred A. Knopf, 2010), 168 ("You would have had to be pretty hard boiled . . ."); Davis, *FDR: The War President*, 259–60; David Hein, "Vulnerable: HMS *Prince of Wales* in 1941," *Journal of Military History* 77, no. 3 (July 2013): 971 (clarifies that "Eternal Father" was Roosevelt's selection).

193 **"in the highest degree important":** *FRUS, 1941 General, Soviet Union*, 355.

193 **"Atlantic Charter":** "Joint Statement by President Roosevelt and Prime Minister

Churchill, August 14, 1941" [containing "Atlantic Charter"], *FRUS, 1941 General, Soviet Union*, 367–69. A memo by Sumner Welles reflects that on 10 August in a conversation with Roosevelt, Churchill suggested incorporating in the charter an endorsement of a postwar international organization. Roosevelt declined on the basis that this would stir up too much current political opposition, but he said that after the war was over and before an international body established, the world would enter a period where the peace would be enforced by an "international police force" consisting of the United States and United Kingdom. *FRUS, 1941, General, Soviet Union*, 358.

193 **"the political basis for waging and winning the war":** Heinrichs, *Threshold of War*, 151.

193 **Hopkins mission to the Soviet Union and interviews with Stalin and Molotov:** Davis, *FDR, The War President 1940–1943*, 235–49 ("Give us anti-aircraft guns, and the aluminum . . ." at 241 and "would come to the assistance of the Soviet Union" at 243).

194 **Roosevelt dares not reverse the oil embargo due to its popularity:** Miller, *Bankrupting the Enemy*, 203–4; Langer and Gleason, *The Undeclared War*, 646 (on public opinion), 655; Barnhart, *Japan Prepares for War*, 231–32.

194 **Roosevelt allows the oil embargo to continue; "might encourage or permit":** Heinrichs, *Threshold of War*, 141–42. It is in this writer's view hard to overstate the importance of Heinrichs's recognition of the link between the oil embargo and deterrence of a Japanese attack on the Soviet Union. One other piece of information reaching Roosevelt on this issue was from Chiang Kai-shek via a letter from Owen Lattimore to Lauchlin Currie, 22 July 1941. Lattimore reported that the "Generalissimo [is] now confident Japan will attack Soviets within a few weeks." The reasons cited were that (1) the Kwantung Army would take the initiative, and (2) fear of revolution in Japan absent decisive action. President's Secretary File, Box 27, China: 1938–Military Dispatches thru China 1945, Folder Diplomatic Correspondence China 1941, FDRL. The effect of Chiang's message on Roosevelt is unknown, but the prospect of unilateral action by the Kwantung Army was by no means a fanciful matter. As noted, the Japanese War Ministry likewise had fears of unilateral action by the Kwantung Army.

194 **Japanese dependence on oil imports from United States:** Miller, *Bankrupting the Enemy*, 162.

195 **Discouragement in Britain; Churchill's claim to close personal relationship with Roosevelt; Roosevelt's strategy to confine the US role to support of Allies to defeat Axis:** Dallek, *Franklin D. Roosevelt and American Foreign Policy*, 286–87; Gilbert, *Their Finest Hour*, 1161, 1165, 1167–68 ("he would wage war, but not declare it" and "I am sure I have established . . ."), 1230; Weinberg, *A World at Arms*, 84–85, 154–60.

195 **Konoe stunned by freeze:** Oka, *Konoe*, 135–36.

195 **Nomura meets with Hull and Roosevelt:** "Memorandum of a Conversation, 8 August 1941," *FRUS, Japan, 1931–1941*, vol. 2, 550–51; *The "Magic" Background of Pearl Harbor*, vol. 3, 4–7, appendix 3, 19–20.

195 **Folly of rejecting neutralization proposal before seeking summit meeting:** Hotta, *Japan 1941*, 156.

196 **Arguments by Konoe and foreign ministry officials for leaders meeting:** "Memorandum by the Ambassador in Japan (Grew), 18 August 1941," *FRUS, Japan 1931–1941*,

vol. 2, 560–64 (Toyoda and Grew); "Memorandum by the Counselor of the Embassy in Japan (Dooman), 27 August 1941," *FRUS, Japan 1931–1941,* vol. 2, 568–69 (Terasaki and Dooman); "Memorandum by the Ambassador to Japan (Grew), August 29, 1941," *FRUS, Japan 1931–1941,* vol. 2, 579–80 (Terasaki and Grew); "Memorandum by the Ambassador to Japan (Grew), 6 September 1941," *FRUS, Japan 1931–1941,* vol. 2, 603–4 (Terasaki and Grew); "Memorandum of the Ambassador to Japan (Grew), 6 September 1941," *FRUS, Japan 1931–1941,* vol. 2, 604–6 (Konoe and Grew); "Memorandum by the Ambassador to Japan (Grew), 17 September 1941," *FRUS, Japan 1931–1941,* vol. 2, 624–25 (Shigemitsu and Grew); "Memorandum by the Counselor of the Embassy in Japan (Dooman), 7 October 1941," *FRUS, Japan 1931–1941,* vol. 2, 662–63 (Ushiba and Dooman); and "Memorandum by the Under Secretary of State (Welles), 13 October 1941," *FRUS, Japan 1931–1941,* vol. 2, 680–86 (Kaname Wakasugi and Welles).

196 **"with all the force at [his] command . . . [and] very prayerful consideration":** "The Ambassador in Japan (Grew) to the Secretary of State, 18 August 1941," *FRUS, Japan, 1931–1941,* vol. 2, 565.

196 **"appalling consequences":** "Memorandum by the Ambassador to Japan (Grew), 13 September 1941," *FRUS, Japan, 1931–1941,* vol. 2, 621–22.

196 **Roosevelt meets with Nomura; United States pursues Japanese statement of "attitude and plans":** "Memorandum by the Secretary of State, 17 August 1941," *FRUS, Japan 1931–1941,* vol. 2, 554–59 ("clearer statement" and "attitude and plans" at 559); "ratification of essential points": "Memorandum of a Conversation, 28 August 1941," *FRUS, Japan 1931–1941,* vol. 2, 576–79.

196 **Imperial Army General Staff "Strike North" calculations and weather:** Drea, *Japan's Imperial Army,* 216–17; Komatsu, *The Origins of the Pacific War and the Importance of 'Magic',* 293–94 (December Manchuria troop number).

197 **"extremely difficult" and "securing enough oil suppressed . . .":** Oka, *Konoe,* 136.

197 **Draft extension passed:** Dallek, *Franklin D. Roosevelt and American Foreign Policy,* 277; Davis, *Into the Storm,* 273. With the vote at 203–202, several members approached the well below the speaker's rostrum apparently intent on changing their vote. House Speaker Sam Rayburn seized the moment to declare the measure passed and banged down his gavel, closing the vote. Absent Rayburn's quick thinking, the bill might have been defeated. Stimson recorded in his diary that he was told the closeness of the vote was due to "deep hostility to Roosevelt and second, cowardice about the coming election next year and their fear of the [draftees]' vote if they made such an extension." Henrichs attributes the near failure of the extension to a subtle set of circumstances. He notes that many representatives felt honor-bound by their original pledge to the conscripts that they only faced one year of service. These individuals were joined by "hard core isolationists, most Republicans and all Roosevelt haters" as well as "the complacent" to produce the close vote. *Threshold of War,* 160. This analysis is probably correct as to the factors motivating the representatives, but to the world it had to look like a strong statement of opposition to plunging into hostilities.

197 **Imperial Conference of 6 September and "The Essentials for Carrying Out the Empire's Policies":** Ike, *Japan's Decision for War,* 135–36. One other lesser term in "The Essentials" was that the United States and Great Britain must also agree not to pursue base rights in the Far East or to increase their forces beyond the current

level. Eri Hotta argues that while the paper appeared to be a "strong push for war," a more sophisticated reading would be that it was a cloak of face-saving bravado for the militarists who fully expected to make concessions involving troop withdrawal. Hotta's reading is as usual quite plausible, but later powerful factions within the military insisted upon such conditions controlling the troop "withdrawal" as to make the promise almost meaningless (i.e., that withdrawal from China would stretch over twenty-five years). *Japan 1941*, 171.

198 **"displayed the incisiveness he was capable of when utterly compelled . . .":** Hotta, *Japan 1941*, 174.

198 **Konoe, Sugiyama, and Nagano meet with Kido and emperor on 5 September:** Kawamura, *Emperor Hirohito and the Pacific War*, 92–95; Hotta, *Japan 1941*, 174–75; Morley, *The Final Confrontation*, 174; Oka, *Konoe Fumimaro*, 145–46; Ike, *Japan's Decision for War*, 133–34. In Bix, *Hirohito and the Making of Modern Japan*, 409–13, the emperor is portrayed at this meeting as failing to take a clear stance against the march to war. The text follows the persuasive arguments of Kawamura based on more sources than Bix that the emperor's comments were more extensive than Bix recounted and that they do show an attempt by the emperor to steer Japan to peace.

198 **Nagano analogy to surgical operation:** Bix, *Hirohito and the Making of Modern Japan*, 412.

198 **Konoe's and Nagano's remarks at beginning of Imperial Conference:** Ike, *Japan's Decision for War*, 138–39.

199 **Document accompanying "The Essentials for Carrying Out the Empire's Policies":** Ike, *Japan's Decision for War*, 152–63.

199 **Exchange of Hara and Oikawa:** Morley, *The Final Confrontation*, 175–76.

199 **Emperor reads poem; "I always read this composition with humility . . ."; "His Majesty's wish is for peace, I tell you!"; "War is absolutely out of the question . . .":** Morley, *The Final Confrontation*, 176–77; Bix, *Hirohito and the Making of Modern Japan*, 413–14. Hotta notes that Tôjô took the poem as "imperial encouragement for the military in the face of long odds." Tôjô further harbored the view that the Anglo-Americans would turn to attack Japan after they finished with Germany in pursuit of establishing their hegemonic power throughout Asia. *Japan 1941*, 178–79.

199 **Psychological barriers to settlement terms:** Hotta, *Japan 1941*, 177.

200 **"trying to nail jelly to a wall":** Morley, *The Final Confrontation*, 180.

200 **Konoe and foreign ministry fail to convey to United States the complete proposals adopted at the Imperial Conference on 6 September and later drafts:** Ike, *Japan's Decision for War*, 172–73, 176–78.

200 **Key events on Japanese-American exchanges on proposal terms September/October 1941:** "Memorandum of a Conversation, September 6, 1941," *FRUS, Japan 1931–1941*, vol. 2, 606–7; "Draft Proposal Handed by the Japanese Ambassador (Nomura) to the Secretary of State, September 6, 1941, *FRUS, Japan 1931–1941*, vol. 2, 608–9 [a copy of the same document had been delivered to Ambassador Grew on 4 September]; "Memorandum of the Ambassador to Japan (Grew), September 6, 1941," *FRUS, Japan 1931–1941*, vol. 2, 604–6; "Memorandum by the Ambassador to Japan (Grew) September 10, 1941," and the "Statement Handed by the Ambassador to Japan (Grew) to the Japanese Foreign Minister (Toyoda) on September 10, 1941," *FRUS, Japan 1931–1941*, vol. 2, 610–13; "Memorandum of a Conversation, September 10, 1941," *FRUS, Japan 1931–1941*, vol. 2, 614–19 (Japanese diplomatic officials

in Washington confirmed clearly that the 6 September Japanese draft agreement required the United States to stop all aid to China); "Proposed Instructions to the Japanese Ambassador (Nomura), Handed by the Japanese Foreign Minister (Toyoda) to the American Ambassador to Japan (Grew) on September 13, 1941," *FRUS, Japan 1931–1941,* vol. 2, 623–24; "The Japanese Minister of Foreign Affairs (Toyoda) to the American Ambassador to Japan (Grew), Text of Basic Japanese Terms of Peace with China, September 22, 1941," *FRUS, Japan 1931–1941,* vol. 2, 633 (this provided Japan's proposed terms for settlement with China, including "cooperative defense" to prevent "communist or other subversive activities," and required the stationing of Japanese troops in China for a "necessary time"); "Japanese Proposals Submitted to the American Ambassador in Japan (Grew) on September 25, 1941," *FRUS, Japan 1931–1941,* vol. 2, 637–41 (this and the 10 September exchange made clear that Japan sought American good offices to bring China to negotiations with Japan, followed by the US abandonment of all support for China); "Oral Statement Handed by the Secretary of State to the Japanese Ambassador (Nomura) on October 2, 1941, *FRUS, Japan 1931–1941,* vol. 2, 656–61; "Memorandum by the Ambassador in Japan (Grew), October 10, 1941," *FRUS, Japan 1931–1941,* vol. 2, 677–79 (Foreign Minister Toyoda tells Grew that "under present conditions the full extent of the undertaking that the Japanese government was willing to assume could not be set forth prior to the meeting"); "Memorandum of a Conversation, October 9, 1941," *FRUS, Japan 1931–1941,* vol. 2, 672–77; "Memorandum by the Under Secretary of State (Welles), October 13, 1941," *FRUS, Japan 1931–1941,* vol. 2, 680–86.

A telling example about the consistently mixed signals the Japanese sent comprised the meetings of Minister Kaname Wakasugi with Welles on October 13 and with Hull on October 17. On the former occasion Wakasugi stated the Japanese government was prepared to withdraw all its troops from China. But on the 17th, Wakasugi talked earnestly about how the United States should recognize the Japanese need to maintain troops in China. "Memorandum by the Under Secretary of State (Welles), October 13, 1941," *FRUS, Japan 1931–1941,* vol. 2, 680–86; "Memorandum by the Secretary of State, October 17, 1941," *FRUS, Japan 1931–1941,* vol. 2, 687. Likewise, Konoe himself told Grew on 6 September that he accepted Hull's "Four Principles" as the basis for a settlement, and affirmed that he accepted responsibility for the current strained state of affairs between the two nations. Konoe went on to stress that he was the only Japanese prime minister who could now bring matters to a satisfactory conclusion. He further assured Grew that while there were elements in the armed forces that might oppose a settlement, he had the support of the top officers of the army and navy and could thus assure that the settlement would be carried out. "Memorandum by the Ambassador in Japan (Grew), September 6, 1941," *FRUS, Japan 1931–1941,* vol. 2, 604–6.

200 **"was obsessed with holding the summit . . .":** Morley, *The Final Confrontation,* 184.

200 **"offer assurances which, because of their far reaching character . . .";** **"Japanese psychology . . . cannot be measured . . .":** "The Ambassador in Japan (Grew) to the Secretary of State, September 29, 1941," *FRUS, Japan 1931–1941,* vol. 2, 645–50.

200 **Proposed October 15 diplomatic deadline and Konoe's panic:** Hotta, *Japan 1941,* 187–88.

200 **Fukudome's projection; Tōjō's doubts about outcome of war; Oikawa abdication of responsibility:** Morley, *The Final Confrontation,* 214–28; Hotta, *Japan 1941,* 198–99.

201 **Konoe's draft negotiating position for summit:** Hotta, *Japan 1941*, 162–63, 172; Bix, *Hirohito and the Making of Modern Japan*, 404. Bix speculates that "perhaps Konoe was calculating on deceiving Roosevelt—the master dissimulator—by leaving issues vague." This proposition finds support in Konoe's resignation letter. There Konoe expressed the view that even the troop stationing issue could be finessed if Japan "takes the attitude of yielding to them as formality, in effect keeping in substance what we abandon in name." Morley, *The Final Confrontation*, 226.

201 **Tôjô says the only United States answer to Japanese terms "yes" or "no":** Ike, *Japan's Decision for War*, 180. This was at the October 4, 1941, Liaison Conference. Bix, *Hirohito and the Making of Modern Japan*, 419, describes Tôjô as "the army's strongest advocate for war and the main opponent of troop withdrawal from China." I concur.

202 **Tôjô reacts to report of the Total War Research Institute:** Hotta, *Japan 1941*, 164–67 ("grew noticeably pale. . ." at 167).

202 **Various Imperial Army officers favor or predict that a settlement is better than war with the United States:** Hotta, *Japan 1941*, 170–71, 191.

202 **"A war with so little chance of success should not be fought":** Hotta, *Japan 1941*, 191–92.

202 **Oikawa's "swallow all the U.S. demands" comment and Nagano's reported agreement:** Hotta, *Japan 1941*, 197–98.

202 **"It is no longer time for discussion . . .":** Hotta, *Japan 1941*, 197–98.

202 **Oikawa meets Tôjô October 5 and "That, I am afraid, I do not have . . .":** Hotta, *Japan, 1941*, 198–99. In another exchange in October, Mutô Akira, chief of the Military Affairs Bureau of the army, spoke to Kenji Tomita, the chief secretary to the cabinet. Muto stated that if the navy would make clear its lack of confidence in a war with the United States, this would assist Konoe in controlling the army and top army officers in maintaining order among their bellicose subordinates. Yagami, *Konoe Fumimaro*, 129. This again underscores the critical importance of an official navy pronouncement on the prospects for a war with the United States.

202 **Konoe meets with Tôjô, October 6:** Hotta, *Japan 1941*, 200–201.

203 **"present to the Japanese people some reward for . . .":** "Memorandum of a Conversation, October 9, 1941," *FRUS, Japan 1931–1941*, vol. 2, 672–77 (quote at 676).

203 **"more jingoistic than Japan's top leaders from 1931 to 1941":** David A. Titus, "Introduction," in Morley, *The Final Confrontation*, xxiii–xxiv.

203 **Konoe resignation:** Hotta, *Japan 1941*, 208–14.

203 **Background of Sorge and Ozaki; their espionage and arrest:** Hotta, *Japan 1941*, 119–21, 159–60, 183, 211–12, 217; Jonathan Haslam, *Near and Distant Neighbors: A New History of Soviet Intelligence* (New York: Farrar, Straus and Giroux, 2015), 28, 59, 61–63, 118, 126–28.

204 **Prince Higashikuni considered and rejected for prime minister:** Morley, *The Final Confrontation*, 232–35, 242; Bix, *Hirohito and the Making of Modern Japan*, 418–19; Butow, *Tôjô*, 286–87, 293–94.

204 **Tôjô selected as prime minister and cabinet:** Ike, *Japan's Decision for War*, 184–85; Bix, *Hirohito and the Making of Modern Japan*, 418–20 ("absolutely . . . dumbfounded" at 419); Morley, *The Final Confrontation*, 237–40, 252 ("a simpleton"); Butow, *Tôjô*, 293–94.

205 **Tôgô's background and appearance:** Hagihara Nobutoshi, *Tōgō Shigenori: Denki to*

Kaisetsu (*Tōgō Shigenori: A Biography and Commentary*) (Tokyo: Hara Shobō, 1985), 14, 27–29, 32–33, 112, 114, 126 (translation kindly provided by Dr. Brian Walsh); Hotta, *Japan 1941*, 216.

205   **Kido's "wipe the slate clean" message:** Morley, *The Final Confrontation*, 243–44.

206   **Tôjô as outstanding clerk, fails to secure "wipe the slate clean review" by fresh personnel:** Morley, *The Final Confrontation*, 245–46, 251; Watanabe and Auer, *Who Was Responsible*, 247.

206   **Liaison conference meetings October 23–30:** Hotta, *Japan 1941*, 219–21, 223, 225–29.

206   **Review of merchant shipping situation:** Ike, *Japan's Decision for War*, 187–91; Watanabe and Auer, *Who Was Responsible*, 115–16; Hotta, *Japan 1941*, 222–23. A June 1941 appraisal by a Navy Ministry officer, Ishikawa Shingo, had cheerfully concluded Japan might lose 600,000 tons of shipping per year but could build 800,000 tons. But the chief of the Naval General Staff Operations Bureau countered with an estimate that Japan would lose a disastrous 1.4 million tons per year. *Who Was Responsible*, 115–16. The actual figures for losses for the first three years of war are from Morley, *The Final Confrontation*, 278–79.

206   **"It is first and foremost necessary. . .":** Hotta, *Japan 1941*, 225; Ike, *Japan's Decision for War*, 130. This quote is from the journal of the War Guidance office of the Imperial Army General Staff.

206   **Army officers argue Imperial Navy responsible for comparing US-Japan capabilities:** Ike, *Japan's Decision for War*, 130.

206   **"would it not be pointless to occupy the East Indies?":** quoted in Asada, *From Mahan to Pearl Harbor*, 236.

206   **"great tension and angry exchanges between participants":** Ike, *Japan's Decision for War*, 199.

206   **Shimada becomes war proponent and demands more steel for the navy:** Tsunoda, "The Decision for War," 253–58; Ike, *Japan's Decision for War*, 200–201. Hotta, *Japan 1941*, 217, 225, points out Shimada's initial opposition to war and explains that his views were altered after a 27 October conference with prowar Imperial Prince Fushimi Hiroyasu, the former chief of staff of Naval General Staff.

207   **Trio of options:** Ike, *Japan's Decision for War*, 198–200; Tsunoda, "The Decision for War," 255, 258–59.

207   **Suzuki's stance:** Hotta, *Japan 1941*, 224. She notes that Konoe wanted Suzuki to stay on as a voice against war. Years later, Suzuki confessed his dereliction.

207   **Japan's prospects in a Pacific War, skeptics denied facts:** Ike, *Japan's Decision for War*, 201–2; Morley, *The Final Confrontation*, 270–71.

207   **"At the time of the Russo-Japanese War . . .":** as quoted in Bix, *Hirohito and the Making of Modern Japan*, 420.

207   **Setting a deadline for diplomacy:** Ike, *Japan's Decision for War*, 203–4, 206; Morley, *The Final Confrontation*, 259–62.

208   **"a way of saying close to eternity":** Morley, *The Final Decision*, 252.

208   **Proposals A and B:** Tsunoda, *The Decision for War*, 261–65, appendix 9; Ike, *Japan's Decision for War*, 209–11.

208   **True meaning of Item 4 of Proposal B:** The "Draft Proposal Handed by the Japanese Ambassador (Nomura) to the Secretary of State on September 6, 1941," *FRUS, Japan 1931–1941*, vol. 2, 608–9, provided that: "the United States will refrain from any measures or actions which will be prejudicial to the endeavor by Japan concern-

ing the settlement of the China Affair." At a subsequent meeting, Japanese officials made clear to the State Department that these seemingly mild words actually meant the United States would withdraw all support for China. "Memorandum of a Conversation, September 10, 1941," *FRUS, Japan 1931–1941,* vol. 2, 614–19 (at 618). In a November 10, 1941, message from Tokyo to Washington, Foreign Minister Tōgō made it clear that if China were brought into negotiations with Japan, the United States must promise "cessation of activities for aiding CHIANG." No. 65 Tokyo to Washington, no. 755, November 10, 1941, *The "Magic" Background to Pearl Harbor,* appendix 4, A-30-1. When formally presented with Proposal B on November 20, Hull rejected the whole thrust of Japanese diplomatic proposals, which as he knew from code breaking included Proposal B, on the basis that they aimed to have the United States cease all support for China. "Memorandum of a Conversation, November 20, 1941," *FRUS, Japan 1931–1941,* vol. 2, 753–55 (at 754); "Draft Proposal Handed by the Japanese Ambassador (Nomura) to the Secretary of State, November 20, 1941," *FRUS, Japan 1931–1941,* vol. 2, 755–56. When Tōgō conferred with Ambassador Grew on November 24, Tōgō made it clear that if as Roosevelt had earlier suggested Chiang issued a statement indicating a desire to restore peace, Japan immediately would respond in kind and enter negotiations. But he further clarified that the Japanese expected the United States then to halt "action which is calculated to aid Chinese military forces." "The Ambassador to Japan (Grew) to the Secretary of State, November 24, 1941," *FRUS, Japan 1931–1941,* vol. 2, 762–64 (at 763).

208 **Statements of Tōgō, Suzuki (President of Cabinet Planning Board), Kaya, Nagano, Sugiyama at Imperial Conference:** Ike, *Japan's Decision For War,* 208–39 ("there is no prospect of the negotiations . . ." at 213; "for a while we will have to pursue . . ." at 224).

9: "Our Anxiety Is About China"

210 **November 5 memorandum to Roosevelt from Marshall and Stark:** PHA, Part 14, 1061–62.

210 **Marshall's November 10 memorandum to Roosevelt:** Heinrichs, *Threshold of War,* 204.

211 **War with Japan "almost certain":** quoted in Marci, *Clash of Empires,* 278.

211 **Roosevelt warns Balfour of "blowup" of Japanese relations:** Tsunoda, "The Decision for War," 302–3.

211 **Tokyo sends Washington embassy Proposals A and B, Tōgō's "exhortations," deadline of November 25:** no. 20, Tokyo to Washington, November 2, 1941; no. 22–30, all Tokyo to Washington, November 4, 1941; no. 44, Tokyo to Washington, November 5, 1941, *The "Magic" Background to Pearl Harbor,* appendix 4, A-12-16, 89.

211 **Situation on Eastern Front August to November 1941:** Glantz and House, *When Titans Clashed,* 74–87.

211 **Soviet fortunes reflected in Stimson diary:** diary September 10, 11; October 10, 20, 1941.

211 **Reports of US Soviet embassy; Soviet and German communiqués:** Heinrichs, *Threshold of War,* 201, 202.

211 **Reports of situation on Soviet front:** *New York Times,* 28 October–16 November 1941, p. 1 or 2 daily. The German November 10 communiqué appears on p. 2 of the 11 November edition.

211 "Winter and Russians Rob Hitler of Victory": *New York Times*, 16 November 1941, section 4, p. 4.

212 Strain on Chinese morale; Japanese plans for Second Battle of Changsha: Drea, *Japan's Imperial Army*, 215, 218–19; Macri, *Clash of Empires*, 286–87, 290, 301; van de Ven, *War and Nationalism in China*, 247.

212 Terrain on Changsha approaches; order of battle of opposing forces: Macri, *Clash of Empires*, 292–93; van de Ven, *War and Nationalism in China*, 247.

212 Japanese capture Changsha; Chinese counterpunch: Macri, *Clash of Empires*, 294.

212 Soviet advisers and the attempt to retake Yichang: Macri, *Clash of Empires*, 295–96.

213 Battle of the Atlantic, *Kearny* and *Reuben James*: Clay Blair, *Hitler's U-Boat War, The Hunters 1939–1942* (New York: Random House, 1996), 370, 375, appendix 18; Samuel Elliot Morison, *History of United States Naval Operations in World War II*, vol. 1, *The Battle of the Atlantic 1939–1943* (Boston: Little, Brown, 1966), 92–94; Heinrichs, *Threshold of War*, 205–6.

213 5 November, public opinion poll: Cantril, *Public Opinion* 1, 172.

213 Marshall orders November 8; Churchill statement November 10; Roosevelt orders November 14: Heinrichs, *Threshold of War*, 205; *New York Times*, 11 November 1941, 1.

213 Germans renew drive on Moscow over frozen ground: Glantz and House, *When Titans Clashed*, 83–87; *New York Times*, 21–22, 24–26 November 1941, pp. 1 and 2, International Situation reports and communiqués.

214 Grew main themes: "Memorandum by the Ambassador in Japan (Grew), October 25, 1941," *FRUS, Japan, 1931–1941*, vol. 2, 697–98 (one and two); "Memorandum by the Ambassador in Japan (Grew), October 30, 1941," *FRUS, Japan, 1931–1941*, vol. 2, 699 (two); November 3, 1941, "Memorandum by the Ambassador in Japan (Grew), November 3, 1941," *FRUS, Japan, 1931–1941*, vol. 2, 700–701 (one); "The Ambassador to Japan (Grew) to the Secretary of State, November 3, 1941," *FRUS, Japan, 1931–1941*, vol. 2, 701–4 (four); "Memorandum by the Ambassador in Japan (Grew), November 7, 1941," *FRUS, Japan, 1931–1941*, vol. 2, 705–6 (three and four); "Memorandum by the Ambassador in Japan (Grew), November 12, 1941," *FRUS, Japan, 1931–1941*, vol. 2, 719–22 (three and four); "Memorandum of Comment by the Ambassador in Japan (Grew), November 12, 1941," *FRUS, Japan, 1931–1941*, vol. 2, 722 (three).

214 "Japanese sanity cannot be measured by . . ." and "rush headlong into a suicidal struggle . . .": "The Ambassador to Japan (Grew) to the Secretary of State, November 3, 1941," *FRUS, Japan, 1931–1941*, vol. 2, 701–4.

214 Grew warns Washington not to expect forewarning of attack: "The Ambassador in Japan (Grew) to the Secretary of State, November 17, 1941," *FRUS, Japan, 1931–1941*, vol. 2, 743–44.

214 Tōgō cables proposals to Nomura, appoints Kurusu as special envoy: Mauch, *Sailor Diplomat*, 207; Hotta, *Japan 1941*, 245–46.

214 Kurusu described: Hotta, *Japan 1941*, 242; Prange, *At Dawn We Slept*, 175–76.

214 Nomura presents Proposal A: "Memorandum of a Conversation, November 7, 1941," *FRUS, Japan 1931–1941*, vol. 2, 706–9; "Document handed by the Japanese Ambassador (Nomura) to the Secretary of State on November 7, 1941," *FRUS, Japan 1931–1941*, vol. 2, 709–10.

215 Tōgō meets with Grew: Memorandum by the Ambassador in Japan (Grew), November 10, 1941, *FRUS, Japan 1931–1941*, vol. 2, 710–14.

215 **November 6, Roosevelt proposes six-month "truce":** Stimson diary, November 6–7, 1941.

215 **Nomura presents paper, Roosevelt raises modus vivendi:** "Memorandum of Conversation, November 10, 1941," *FRUS, Japan 1931–1941,* vol. 2, 715–19; Tsunoda, "The Decision for War," 302.

216 **Nomura's report to Tokyo on modus vivendi:** Tsunoda, "The Decision for War," 302; no. 79, Washington (Nomura) to Tokyo, no. 1070, November 10, 1941, translated November 13, 1941, *The "Magic" Background to Pearl Harbor,* vol. 4, appendix, A-38-39.

216 **Roosevelt's view of Hull and the State Department:** Mayers, *FDR's Ambassadors,* 2.

216 **"every economic weapon they possess" and "for the sake of peace in the Pacific . . .":** no. 110, Washington (Nomura) to Tokyo, no. 1090, November 14, 1941, *The "Magic" Background to Pearl Harbor,* appendix 4, A-56-57.

216 **17 November 1941, Kurusu and Nomura meet FDR in White House:** "Memorandum by the Secretary of State, November 17, 1941," *FRUS, Japan 1931–1941,* vol. 2, 740–43; no. 135-37, Washington (Nomura) to Tokyo, November 17, 1941, *The "Magic" Background to Pearl Harbor,* appendix 4, A-71-74. Nomura's messages provide a more detailed and balanced account of the session. The "Bad Cop"/"Good Cop" analogy is from Mauch, *Sailor Diplomat,* 208.

217 **Roosevelt proposal to Hull:** President Roosevelt to the Secretary of State, n.d.; *FRUS, 1941, The Far East,* vol. 4, 626. As Heinrichs, *Threshold of War,* 208n95, argues, the undated memorandum seems very likely to have been sent on November 17. In this he concurs with the original insight by Langer and Gleason, *The Undeclared War,* 872. The judgment that it was sent after the meeting with Nomura and Kurusu is based on the presumption that if Roosevelt had this whole set of terms in mind before or during meeting Nomura and Kurusu, he presumably would have sketched them out in a recognizable form.

217 **The situation in Japan "very pressing" and Nomura-Kurusu proposal:** Memorandum of a Conversation, November 18, 1941, *FRUS, Japan 1931–1941,* vol. 2, 744–51; Mauch, *Sailor Diplomat,* 208–10; no. 171, Washington to Tokyo, no. 1180, November 26, 1941, *The "Magic" Background to Pearl Harbor,* appendix 4, A-93 ("would have to wait until the end of the world").

217 **Tōgō rejects Nomura-Kurusu offer of November 18:** Mauch, *Sailor Diplomat,* 209–10. As in other instances, Mauch here relies on the Japanese Foreign Ministry version of cables.

217 **"Please bear in mind that . . .":** Tokyo to Washington 19 Nov 41 Translated 11/20/41, SRDJ 16,735, Box 19, RG 457, NARA.

217 **Nomura submits original version of Proposal B; reports Hull finds abandonment of China an impossible term:** "Memorandum of a Conversation, November 20, 1941," *FRUS, Japan 1931–1941,* vol. 2, 753–56; no. 1159, Washington to Tokyo, November 23, 1941, *The "Magic" Background to Pearl Harbor,* appendix 4, A-87-9. On November 24, in Washington to Tokyo, no. 1147, *The "Magic" Background to Pearl Harbor,* appendix 4, A84, Nomura and Kurusu reiterated that Hull stated that it was as impossible for the United States to cease aiding China as to cease aiding England.

218 **Hull assembles drafts of modus and comprehensive agreement with Japan:** "Draft of a Proposed 'Modus Vivendi" with Japan, November 22, 1941," and "Outline of a Proposed Basis for an Agreement Between the United States and Japan, November

22, 1941," *FRUS, 1941, The Far East*, vol. 4, 635–40, 642–46; Heinrichs, *Threshold of War*, 208–9.

219 **Hull meets ambassadors November 22:** "Memorandum of a Conversation, November 22, 1941," *FRUS, 1941, The Far East*, vol. 4, 640.

219 **British intercepts of Chongqing and German Eastern Front messages:** During the fall of 1941, and usually several times per day, new intercepts were forwarded personally to Churchill. They are now assembled in the approximately HW 1/38 (1 September 1941) to HW 1/330 (21 December 1941) range, The National Archives, UK [hereafter TNA]. These intercepts also included Turkish and Mexican diplomatic messages, and the originals disclose Churchill's marginal annotations in distinctive red ink. What is not present in the intercepts or Churchill's marginalia is any indication of foreknowledge of the Pearl Harbor attack.

219 **Churchill to Eden, November 23:** cited in David Klein and Hilary Conroy, "Churchill, Roosevelt and the China Question in Pre-Pearl Harbor Diplomacy," Hilary Conroy and Harry Wray, in *Pearl Harbor Reexamined: Prologue to the Pacific War* (Honolulu: University of Hawaii Press, 1990), 134.

220 **Formal British Foreign Office comments:** "The British Embassy to the Department of State" (received November 25, 1941), *FRUS, 1941, The Far East*, vol. 4, 655–57. This message contained the position the British War Cabinet had adopted the day before. During that session, Eden conveyed his opinion that the Japanese had put out a bargaining position containing maximum demands and minimum concessions, and that the reply by the United States and United Kingdom should follow the same stance. Confidential Annex Agenda: (3) The Far East Negotiations Between the United States and Japan, CAB 65/24/7, 24 November 1941, TNA. The interesting question is whether knowing of the fast-approaching deadline and the Japanese note emphasizing the unacceptable demand that the United States abandon China, Eden basically reached the same conclusion as Hull would (and later much condemned): that the negotiations were hopeless and that for the sake of history, Britain should endorse a ringing rejection of Japanese terms.

220 **Chiang reaction via Lattimore, Shi Hu, and T. V. Soong:** "Telegram for the Chinese Minister for Foreign Affairs (Quo Tai-chi) to the Chinese Ambassador (Hu Shih), November 24, 1941," *FRUS, 1941, The Far East*, vol. 4, 654; "Mr. Owen Lattimore to Mr. Lauchlin Currie, Administrative Assistant to President Roosevelt, November 25, 1941," *FRUS, 1941, The Far East*, vol. 4, 652. Lattimore's message is also found in President's Secretary File, Box 28, China: Currie, Lauchlin 1941–42 Outgoing thru Finland: 1939–40 Folder Diplomatic Correspondence Lattimore, Owen: 1941–42, FDRL.

220 **Chiang's comments, "leaving Japan entrenched in China"; "completely sacrificed," etc.:** "Dr. T. V. Soong, of China Defense Supplies, Inc., to the Secretary of War (Stimson), November 25, 1941 (enclosing message from Generalissimo Chiang Kaishek)," *FRUS, 1941, The Far East*, vol. 4, 660–61.

220 **Roosevelt forwards copy of draft modus to Churchill:** "The Secretary of State to the Ambassador in the United Kingdom (Winant), November 24, 1941," *FRUS, 1941, The Far East*, vol. 4, 648–49. The draft of the message was prepared by Hull, but *FRUS* notes that the comments quoted were added personally by the president.

220 **Churchill's message received in Washington, 0055, 26 November 1941:** "The Ambassador to the United Kingdom (Winant) to the Secretary of State (Hull)," *FRUS, 1941, The Far East*, vol. 4, 665.

220 **Magic disclosures November 22–24:** Tokyo to Washington, November 22, 1941, SDRJ 16849, 16850, 16852 (translated November 24), Box 20, SDRJ series, RG 457, NARA; Tokyo to Washington, no. 823, November 24, 1941, *The "Magic" Background to Pearl Harbor*, appendix 4, A89. In SDRJ 16850, Tōgō made it clear that "our demand for a cessation of aid to CHIANG (the acquisition of Netherlands East Indies goods and at the same time the supply of American petroleum to Japan as well) is the most essential condition." Sidney Pash quotes a report from Grew after a conference with Tōgō on November 24 in which Grew characterizes as merely "face saving" Tōgō's clearly emphasized point on the importance of the discontinuance of US aid to Chiang. *The Currents of War: A New History of American-Japanese Relations, 1899–1941* (Lexington: University of Kentucky Press, 2014), 242 [hereafter Pash, *The Currents of War*]. (Grew's memo is in *FRUS, Japan 1931–1941*, vol. 2, 762–64.) Although Pash's research is admirable in many ways, his analysis here seems unsupported to say the least. The overwhelming evidence is that US abandonment of Chiang was a critical term, and as Tōgō stated, if the United States would not meet it, there could be no agreement. If Grew really believed this point was merely "face saving," it only serves to illustrate how badly Grew misread Japanese intentions on this point.

221 **"we were likely to be attacked perhaps next Monday . . .":** Stimson diary, November 25, 1941.

221 **"first shot" quote and concerns about Japanese attacks solely on British and Dutch colonial possessions:** Pash, *The Currents of War*, 242. Pash cites the analysis of Richard N. Current, "How Stimson Meant to 'Maneuver' the Japanese," *Mississippi Valley Historical Review* 40, no. 1 (June 1953).

221 **Movements of Japanese warships and transports assembling for opening offensives:** the combinedfleet.com website (accessed 2 February 2014) provides documentation of these movements in the Tabular Records of Movement, combinedfleet.com [hereafter TROM] for both warships and auxiliaries. A selection of entries demonstrating the numbers, types, movement dates, and destinations includes the following examples: carrier *Ryujo*; battleship *Kongo*; heavy cruisers *Chokai* and *Mogami*; light cruisers *Kinu, Yura, Sendai, Naka,* and *Natori*; virtually all destroyers of the *Mutsuki, Fubuki, Akatsuki, Hatsuhara, Shiratsuyu, Asashio,* and *Kagero* classes; submarines *I-53, I-56, I-62, I-65, I-121,* and *I-123*; Imperial Army auxiliary transports *Miike Maru, Macassar Maru, Havre Maru, Sidney Maru, Brisbane Maru,* and *Aden Maru*; and Imperial Navy auxiliary transport *Nojima Maru*. Each of these entries contains the identification of numerous other vessels participating in this activity. The TROMs generally show warships heading to assembly points from November 20. The dates that auxiliary vessels headed south are usually not supplied, but the arrival dates sometimes are. Given the much slower speeds of the auxiliary vessels, their movement had to have started days earlier than November 20.

221 **Stimson sees report of convoy and notifies Hull and the White House:** Stimson diary, November 25, 1941. Iguchi, *Demystifying Pearl Harbor*, 116–17, points out that Rear Adm. Edwin T. Layton, Roger Pineau, and John Costello, *"And I Was There"* (New York: William Morrow, 1985), 200–202, purportedly representing the memoirs of Edwin Layton, the Pacific Fleet Intelligence officer, and John Costello, *Days of Infamy* (New York: Pocket Books, 1994), chap. 6, both cast doubts about the accuracy of the report reaching Stimson. They cite what they take as the original message, which only referred to fewer and anchored transports in Shanghai with the

interpretation by army G-2 that this was part of a routine troop shift. *"And I Was There"* was completed after Layton's death, and as historian John Lundstrom points out, conflicts on material points with Layton's views in his writings and discussions with other historians. *"And I Was There"* seeks to deprecate Stimson's diary entry as the real reason for a change in American attitude toward the modus vivendi to set up an argument that the actual reason involved a decryption of a purported "sailing message" of the Japanese Pearl Harbor attack force on November 25. But this feat Costello and company attributed to the Dutch or British, as they found no evidence that the United States intercepted and broke such a message. As discussed in the next chapter, neither the British nor the Dutch achieved such a breakthrough against the main Japanese naval code prior to Pearl Harbor.

There is a controversy over this part of Stimson's 25 November diary entry. Historians have argued that the apparent G-2 report in question gave figures of ten to thirty ships, not thirty to fifty, interpreted this as a "more or less normal movement," and placed the ships not at sea but still in Shanghai. The G-2 report was accompanied by a British intelligence appreciation that envisioned one more Japanese effort at settlement. If it failed, the appreciation predicted the Japanese would then invade Thailand. Does this evidence contradict Stimson's diary entry or even indicate that Stimson entered deliberate misstatements in his diary? There are multiple reasons to doubt these interpretations. First, Stimson dictated his diary entries at the end of the day, usually relying on memory and when possible selected documents. His secretary transcribed the dictation, which Stimson did not check. Thus, it is by no means clear that Stimson misrepresented the contents of the document. Robert J. C. Butow, "How Roosevelt Attacked Japan at Pearl Harbor Myth Masquerading as History," *Prologue* 28, no. 3 (Fall 1996): 3n9, www.archives.gov/publications/prologue/1996/fall/butow.html, accessed 20 August 2016. Further evidence that Stimson's diary entry misstated rather than deliberately misrepresented the facts emerges in Stimson's official memorandum to the president on 25 November, which accurately reflects the content of the G-2 report. This further clarified that the phrase "more or less normal movement" reflects earlier "Magic" intercepts showing the Japanese were deploying another 50,000 troops to Indochina, in addition to the 40,000 already there. This smacked of offensive, not innocuous, intentions. Memorandum for the President, November 25, 1941, RG 107, Entry 99 "Safe File," Box 11, Folder Philippines, NARA. Second, Army G-2 compiled a dismal record for accuracy in its 1941 projections, headed by its prediction of certain Soviet collapse. Further, as will be noted in the next chapter, just two days before the Pearl Harbor attack and Japan's multiple offensives across the Asian-Pacific region, G-2 held that Germany was the only Axis power capable of "large scale strategic offensives." Third, the handling of the "Magic" summaries—raw messages without interpretation—effectively made Stimson accustomed to acting in the role of his own intelligence officer. Given these circumstances, Stimson's ominous interpretation demonstrates that he, not G-2, was far more alert to Japan's capabilities and intentions. Fourth, we cannot be entirely sure that Stimson in fact saw more than the G-2 report he specifically mentioned. When he prepared the diary entry, his error was not that he falsely reported what he saw, but that, in this extremely busy and tumultuous period, he did not get the details of what he saw correctly as to Japanese movements. Indeed, the very next day an appreciation by the Sixteenth Naval District (the Philippines) reached Stimson. It noted that for the past month the Japanese had organized a very large "naval task force" (including "all large carrier forces" numbering ten carriers) projected to be heading for operations in Southeast Asia, with components operating from Palau and the Marshall Islands. Memorandum for the Chief of Staff, November 26, 1941, Subject: Japanese Naval Task Force, RG 107, Entry 99, "Safe File," Box 11, Folder: Philippines, NARA. Finally, we know for a fact that by 25–26 November there was in progress a massive movement of Japanese warships and shipping to assembly points for the start of hostilities. Therefore, Japan was preparing for hostilities exactly as Stimson reported, an action that would have made their diplomacy appear in bad faith to American officials.

222 **Stimson phone calls with Hull and Roosevelt early 26 November:** Stimson diary, November 26, 1941.

222 **On 26 November, Hull meets Nomura and Kurusu and "Hull Note":** Memorandum of a Conversation, November 26, 1941, FRUS, *Japan 1931–1941*, vol. 2, 764–68; "Document Handed by the Secretary of State to the Japanese Ambassador (Nomura) on November 26, 1941," *FRUS, Japan 1931–1941*, vol. 2, 768–70.

223 **"was struck by despair . . ." and "the note rejected willfully . . .":** Hotta, *Japan 1941*, 269.

223 **"Hull Note" not legally an ultimatum:** Iguchi, *Demystifying Pearl Harbor*, 137–38, 168, 265.

223 **"nothing short of a miracle":** Hotta, *Japan 1941*, 269.

223 **"washed my hands of [the negotiations] . . .":** Stimson diary, November 27, 1941.

223 **Roosevelt and Hull meet Nomura and Kurusu, 27 November:** "Memorandum by the Secretary of State, November 27, 1941," FRUS, *Japan 1931–1941*, vol. 2, 770–72.

224 **Stimson presents G-2 report, 28 November:** Stimson diary, November 28, 1941.

224 **"superhuman efforts" and "the negotiations will be de facto ruptured . . .":** Tokyo to Washington, no. 844, November 28, 1941, *The "Magic" Background to Pearl Harbor*, appendix 4, A118.

224 **"Magic" translations challenged:** the most comprehensive work to address this issue is Komatsu, *Origins of the Pacific War and the Importance of 'Magic.'* There is no disputing the difficulty of rendering precise translations of the intercepted Japanese cables. John Hurt, the longest serving and best army translator in 1941, would later write: "The shades of meaning in Japanese text cannot be rendered in their exact tone in English. English is not one-third as highly integrating to a tongue as Japanese; so, in translating, we had to break the sentences up into shorter ones, moreover we had to use many circumlocutions and resort to a number of other devices to convey the real intended sense and weight of the original. . . . Learned Japanese diplomats are prone to vie with one another in the use of their classical language. They are not hampered to the same extent as most government officials are in most other countries by a set manner of writing." SRH-252, p. 39, RG 457, NARA. Komatsu shows numerous instances in which he argues that specific words or phrases were mistranslated. He argues that the vector of these errors was almost wholly toward making the Japanese stance seem more rigid and to cast doubts on Japan's sincerity in pursuing a settlement. But Komatsu treats the overall American approach to Japanese diplomacy as though messages in the summer and fall of 1941 should have been read without regard to events from 1931 to 1941. Further, he does not come to grips with the central problem, which was not mood or nuance but an unbridgeable gap between rival substantive terms for an agreement.

10: "This Dispatch Is to Be Considered a War Warning"

228 **Influence of Mahan and historical and indigenous roots of Japanese strategy:** Asada, *From Mahan to Pearl Harbor*, 26–44; Toshi Yoshihara and James R. Holmes, "Japanese Maritime Thought: If Not Mahan, Who?" *Naval War College Review* 59, no. 3 (Summer 2006): 27–31.

229 **Washington agreements of 1922; London Treaty of 1930:** Richard W. Fanning, *Peace and Disarmament: Naval Rivalry & Arms Control 1922–1933* (Lexington: University Press of Kentucky, 1995), 1–16, 106–32, 140; David C. Evans and Mark Peattie, *Kaigun: Strategy, Tactics and Technology in the Imperial Japanese Navy, 1887–1941* (Annapolis, MD: Naval Institute Press, 1997), 187, 199–212 [hereafter Evans and Peattie, *Kaigun*].

229 **Assassination of prime ministers over naval treaties:** Jansen, *The Making of Modern Japan*, 503–4.

229 *Yogeki sakusen:* Evans and Peattie, *Kaigun*, 273–86.

229 **Prewar American recognition of Japanese strategic planning:** Douglas Ford, *The Elusive Enemy: U.S. Naval Intelligence and the Imperial Japanese Fleet* (Annapolis, MD: Naval Institute Press, 2011), ch. 1 [hereafter Ford, *The Elusive Enemy*].

230 **"possesses more brains than any other Japanese in High Command":** Prange, *At Dawn We Slept*, 291.

230 **"his pronounced individuality [which] was so rare among Japanese navy men . . .":** Asada, *From Mahan to Pearl Harbor*, 275.

230 **Japanese *Kantai Kessen* war games and prewar exercises:** James Morley, ed., *Japan's Road to the Pacific War, The Final Confrontation* (New York: Columbia University Press, 1994), 271–72 [hereafter Morley, *The Final Confrontation*]; Evans and Peattie, *Kaigun*, 429–30.

230 **Yamamoto's background, interests in aviation and gambling:** Hiroyuki Agawa, *The Reluctant Admiral Yamamoto and the Imperial Navy* (Annapolis, MD: Naval Institute Press, 1979), 1–2, 6, 8, 17–18, 85–86, 89–90, 158–64 [hereafter Agawa, *The Reluctant Admiral*].

230 **Yamamoto first thinks of Pearl Harbor attack; Taranto attack; and "If I am told to fight regardless of the consequences" . . .:** Prange, *At Dawn We Slept*, 10; Asada, *From Mahan to Pearl Harbor*, 279–80; Willmott, *Pearl Harbor*, 49–50; Thomas P. Lowry and John W. G. Wellham, *The Attack on Taranto: Blueprint for Pearl Harbor* (Mechanicsburg, PA: Stackpole Books, 2000 edition), 87–94.

230 **Yamamoto's January 1941 letter to Oikawa:** Prange, *At Dawn We Slept*, 16.

230 **Summary of historical evaluations of Yamamoto:** Zimm, *Attack on Pearl Harbor*, 365–70.

231 **Yamamoto's variable views on the vulnerability of American morale:** Agawa, *The Reluctant Admiral*, 243–44.

231 **"There are those who say that if we give a terrible blow to the enemy . . .":** Agawa, *The Reluctant Admiral*, 280.

231 **Goal of sinking or disabling four battleships:** Zimm, *Attack on Pearl Harbor*, 26–29. Zimm notes it is not clear how the Japanese arrived at the number four, but it appears related to the calculations done in conjunction with interwar planning whereby the Japanese believed the United States would not embark on a campaign unless they had a 10:6 or better ratio of battleships. This guideline would predict no American advance if the United States had fourteen or fewer battleships available

at any point prior to May 1942. In December 1941, the United States had seventeen battleships in commission and could expect to place one more in service by April 1942. Destruction or disabling of four through May 1942 would presumably secure Japan's advance from interference by the US Pacific Fleet.

232 **Vulnerability of carriers:** This point weaves together discussion in Norman Friedman, *U.S. Aircraft Carriers: An Illustrated Design History* (Annapolis, MD: Naval Institute Press, 1983), 8–16, 43–44, 83–90, and Hans Lengerer, "Akagi & Kaga," in John Roberts, ed., *Warship VI* (London: Conway Maritime Press, 1982), 127–39; and Lengerer, "The Aircraft Carriers of the Shōkaku Class," in John Jordan, *Warship 2015* (London: Conway Maritime Press, 2015), 90–109.

232 **Carrier defensive vulnerability prompts dispersion:** Thomas C. Hone, Norman Friedman, and Mark D. Mandeles, Naval War College Papers 37: Innovation in Carrier Aviation, 2011, 17; Norman Friedman, *Naval Anti-Aircraft Guns & Gunnery* (Annapolis, MD: Naval Institute Press, 2013), 288–89. The Naval War College paper notes that up to the spring of 1941 "no navy knew how to protect a carrier from an effective strike staged by opposing carrier-based bombers."

232 **Evolution of carrier doctrine to creation of First Air Fleet:** Peattie, *Sunburst*, 75, 147–55. The concept of massing carriers originated among Ozawa's staff, but he supported it. Yamamoto initially rejected the proposal and Ozawa took it to the navy minister before Yamamoto agreed.

233 **Unprecedented operation of six fleet carriers in one formation:** I am indebted to H. P. Willmott for pointing out that the Pearl Harbor attack was the sole occasion in history when six fleet carriers operated in one tactical formation. *Pearl Harbor*, 76. Later in the war, the US Navy would group up to three fleet and two (or once three) light carriers in one formation and operate up to six much smaller escort carriers in one formation.

233 **US development of carrier defensive capabilities from 1943:** David L. Boslaugh, Capt. Ret. USN, "Radar and the Fighter Directors," ch. 4–13, www.ethw.org/Radar -and-the-Fighter-Directors, accessed 8 October 2016. This article nicely explains the systematic developments in electronics and command and control that permitted effective defense of carrier task groups from 1943.

233 **Nagumo described:** Prange, *At Dawn We Slept*, 106–7, 574.

233 **Kusaka and Genda and his contributions:** Prange, *At Dawn We Slept*, 20–24, 107–8; Willmott, *Pearl Harbor*, 83; Zimm, *Attack on Pearl Harbor*, 23.

234 **Fuchida and his contributions:** Prange, *At Dawn We Slept*, 195–201, 258–60, 265–73; Jonathan Parshall and J. Michael Wenger, "Pearl Harbor's Overlooked Answer," *Naval History* 25, no. 6 (December 2011): 19. Ford, *The Elusive Enemy*, ch. 1, again covers the prewar efforts of US naval intelligence to develop an accurate portrait of the Imperial Japanese Navy.

234 **First Air Fleet aircraft complement, air crew quality issues, solution to shallow water launch of aerial torpedoes; location of factory making modified torpedoes:** Prange, *At Dawn We Slept*, 320–24; Zimm, *Attack on Pearl Harbor*, 86, 289–95; Willmott, *Pearl Harbor*, 60–61; Richard B. Frank, *Downfall: The End of the Imperial Japanese Empire* (New York: Random House, 1999), 284. I am indebted to Mike Wenger, who shared his research indicating that individual flight experience was comparable on average across all the air groups, but Carrier Division 5 had not had time to develop the level of teamwork in the other two carrier divisions.

234 **Converting 16.1-inch naval shells to armor-piercing bombs and bombing technique:** Prange, *At Dawn We Slept*, 268–69; Zimm, *Attack on Pearl Harbor*, 62–64, 131–32.

235 **"Val" bomb load and capability:** Zimm, *Attack on Pearl Harbor*, 84–85. Zimm provides a lengthy critique of planning defects in the employment of the three types of Japanese aircraft. It is a very shrewd analysis, as is characteristic of the overall outstanding work, but it serves unfortunately to underplay the full extent of the Japanese operational successes. *Attack on Pearl Harbor*, 87, 105–11, 116–17, 121–22, 123, 131, 135–36, 145–48, 193–94, 374, 376–77.

236 **Japanese submarines deployed to support Pearl Harbor attack:** Willmott, *Pearl Harbor*, 65, 69.

236 **Yamamoto authorizes harbor penetration by midget submarines:** Willmott, *Pearl Harbor*, 69–71; Prange, *At Dawn We Slept*, 340–41.

236 **Consideration of landing in Hawaii in conjunction with carrier raid:** John J. Stephan, *Hawaii Under the Rising Sun: Japan's Plans for Conquest after Pearl Harbor* (Honolulu: University of Hawaii Press, 1984), 81–82 [hereafter Stephen, *Hawaii Under the Rising Sun*]; Willmott, *Pearl Harbor*, 58–59.

236 **Final approval of Pearl Harbor attack:** Asada, *From Mahan to Pearl Harbor*, 278–82. Asada notes that Yamamoto's prestige within the whole navy is what made the threat work.

236 **Striking Force sails:** Prange, *At Dawn We Slept*, 390–91; Willmott, *Pearl Harbor*, 78–79, 81, 192–95.

237 **Yamamoto's judgment:** Zimm, *Attack on Pearl Harbor*, 264, 365, 367–69.

237 **FDR Moves Pacific Fleet to Pearl Harbor:** Skipper Steely, *Pearl Harbor Countdown: Admiral James O. Richardson* (Gretna, LA: Pelican Publishing, 2008), 165, 170–72, 174, 179, 188.

237 **"Complaining, allegedly the sole right accorded servicemen . . .":** Raymond G. O'Connor, "The American Navy, 1939–1941: The Enlisted Perspective," *Military Affairs* 50, no. 4 (October 1986): 176.

237 **Richardson does not protest Pearl Harbor vulnerability to attack; fired by FDR:** Steely, *Pearl Harbor Countdown*, 181, 227–31. At the postwar hearings, Richardson expressly testified that in his September 1940 letter, he listed seven reasons it was disadvantageous to base the fleet at Pearl Harbor, but he stated, "I did not consider it was likely that the fleet would be attacked by a carrier raid." PHA, Part 1, 285. Richardson's charge that Hornbeck was orchestrating deployment of the fleet was based on what he was told by the new US ambassador to Australia, Clarence E. Gauss, who stopped at Pearl Harbor en route from Washington to his post. Steely, *Pearl Harbor Countdown*, 181–82.

238 **FDR appoints Kimmel:** Prange, *At Dawn We Slept*, 50–51.

238 **"Energetic, Highly able. Bold in contrast to most. . .":** Vice Admiral William Ward Smith, USN (Ret.) papers, held by Col. William Ward Smith Jr., US Army (Ret.) via John Lundstrom, with much thanks.

238 **Caliber of officers commanding the Hawaiian Department between the wars:** Brian Linn, *Guardians of Empire: The U.S. Army in the Pacific, 1902–1941* (Chapel Hill: University of North Carolina Press, 1999).

238 **Short's appointment and orders:** PHA 15: 1601–2; Prange, *At Dawn We Slept*, 53–54.

238 **Size of Hawaii garrison, Short's promotion:** Prange, *At Dawn We Slept*, 52–53; Stet-

son Conn, Rose E. Engelman, and Byron Fairchild, *United States Army in World War II, Guarding the United States and Its Outposts* (Washington, DC: Center of Military History, 1989), 163, 171 [hereafter Conn, Engelman, and Fairchild, *Guarding the United States and Its Outposts*]. I am indebted to Dr. Brian Linn, the acknowledged expert on Hawaii's interwar defenders, for his insight into the exceptional talents of the Hawaiian Department commanders and for his views on Marshall's rationale for appointing Short. For an extremely clear and succinct appraisal of Short, see William D. O'Neil, *Undefending Pearl Harbor*, sections "Lieut. Gen. Walter Short" and "Short in the Air" (Amazon Kindle, 2016) [hereafter O'Neil, *Undefending Pearl Harbor*]. O'Neil emphasizes that Short was obsessively detail-oriented. In Hawaii Short found himself in a huge command that was beyond even his considerable ability to micromanage without vigorous support from a staff. Short, however, failed to adjust his leadership style to permit his staff to keep track of the huge number of details involved in so large a command.

239 **Lack of unity of command; Bloch responsible for base defense:** Prange, *At Dawn We Slept*, 53–54, 93.

239 **"Admiral Bloch . . . looked down his nose at Admiral Kimmel":** as cited in Gregory J. W. Urwin, *Facing Fearful Odds: The Siege of Wake Island* (Lincoln: University of Nebraska Press, 2002), 11 [hereafter Urwin, *Facing Fearful Odds*]. Worse still, Bloch was a battleship admiral, "dismissive of innovative ideas" like the potential of carrier aviation: Albert A. Nofi, *To Train the Fleet for War: The U.S. Navy Fleet Problems, 1923–1940* (Newport, RI: Naval War College Press, 2010), 224–25, 227–28, 232–33, 240, 309.

239 **Effects of legal restrictions on congressionally appropriated funds dictating the schedule of fleet operations:** I am indebted to William O'Neil, who clarified this important point. The original draft blamed Bloch for dictating the predictable operating schedule based on the testimony he provided to the Roberts Commission that he followed this practice to economize. PHA, Part 22, 490–91. O'Neil explained that Bloch's testimony excerpt did not fully explain what was transpiring. Bloch, like all other officers, was legally obligated to follow the regular schedule to keep base operation and development within the limited appropriations.

239 **Lack of oil tankers constricts fleet operations:** Husband E. Kimmel, *Admiral Kimmel's Story* (Chicago: Henry Regnery, 1955), 28–29.

239 **Taranto attack and correspondence on antitorpedo measures for Pearl Harbor:** PHA, Part 14, 973–75, 991; Part 1, 285; Part 5, 2266; Part 23, 1137; Part 33, 1283; Michael Gannon, *Pearl Harbor Betrayed: The True Story of a Man and a Nation Under Attack* (New York: Henry Holt, 2001), 174–80 [hereafter Gannon, *Pearl Harbor Betrayed*]; Zimm, *Attack on Pearl Harbor*, 124, 357. Antony Summers and Robbyn Swan, *A Matter of Honor: Pearl Harbor: Betrayal, Blame and a Family's Quest for Justice* (New York: Harper, 2016), 84–87, cites a US naval attaché report that contained a chart of Taranto Harbor allegedly showing the launch of torpedoes during the attack in water only twenty-four feet deep. This chart reportedly was not forwarded to Kimmel. This evidence is far from clear. The chart is undated, and its actual depth notations are not clarified as to whether they are in fathoms or meters (it appears to be an Italian chart). Harbors like Taranto are notorious for rapid and shifting silting, so even if the original notation of depth was accurate, there is no guarantee the depths

were the same at the time of the attack. Finally, the accompanying British report shows the torpedoes were set to run at thirty-three feet, which raises a question as to what would happen if they were dropped in only twenty-four feet.

239 **Martin-Bellinger Report, March 1941:** PHA, Part 22, 349–53. In August 1941, Martin sent to Washington a report describing the worst danger his command faced as "6 enemy carriers against Oahu simultaneously each approaching on a different course." Interestingly, this reflects the expectation that even if the Japanese deployed six carriers against Hawaii, they would be dispersed. Headquarters Hawaiian Air Force, 20 August 1941, Enclosure 1: "Plan for the Employment of Bombardment Aviation in the defense of Oahu," PHA, Part 14, 1030.

240 **Status of available PBYs, morning 7 December 1941:** Commander Task Force Nine (Commander Patrol Wing Two), 20 December 1941, Subject: Operations December 7, 1941, which lists sixty-nine PBYs on Oahu and twelve at Midway. Mike Wenger, who has done very detailed research, provided a figure of sixty-six on Oahu, with the difference of three fewer PBYs at Ford Island. The text follows Wenger.

240 **Search plane issues:** I am indebted to William O'Neil, who shared his professional experience with designing search plane programs and his analysis of the situation at the time of the Pearl Harbor attack. He particularly was persuasive that Kimmel, even if he had significantly more search planes, would have preserved them for his own offensive plans rather than committed them to intensified searches in December 1941. All of this analysis appears in O'Neil, *Undefending Pearl Harbor*, section "Impossibility of Proof," paragraphs 1–10.

The evidence and literature on the search plane issue is extensive. This writer, after plowing through this evidence, eventually concluded that Kimmel never would have used much greater resources for an enhanced search program even after "War Warnings" he received later. Those who wish to examine the dense detail on this issue can consult: PHA, Part 6, 2533; John W. Lambert and Norman Polmar, *Defenseless: Command Failure at Pearl Harbor* (St. Paul, MN: Motor Books International, 2003), 105–10 [hereafter Lambert and Polmar, *Defenseless*]; Zimm, *Attack on Pearl Harbor*, 357; Conn, Engelman, and Fairchild, *Guarding the United States and Its Outposts*, 205. See also the exchange noted in the text about when Kimmel's War Plans Officer, Capt. Charles E. McMorris, completely dismisses the prospect of a Japanese air attack on Hawaii.

240 **Failure to ready air warning system:** PHA, Part 26, 375–85; Lambert and Polmar, *Defenseless*, 44–51; Zimm, *Attack on Pearl Harbor*, 268, 354–57. The official army historians argue essentially that Short could not have created an effective air warning system because a shortage of spare parts and unreliable power supply limited radar operations to about three to four hours per day, and the information center had achieved only an embryonic state by 7 December. Taylor's detailed testimony, however, is very compelling that these obstacles could have been surmounted with command emphasis. Moreover, the actual events on 7 December bear out Taylor. Conn, Engelman, and Fairchild, *Guarding the United States and Its Outposts*, 167–68.

241 **Lack of navy liaison officers for air warning service:** Lambert and Polmar, *Defenseless*, 49–51, 118–25, contains a good summary and appraisal of the testimony on this point.

241 **Antiaircraft gun in Hawaii:** Conn, Engelman and Fairchild, *Guarding the United States and Its Outposts*, 168–69; PHA, Part 26, 375–82.

241 **Army Air Force air garrison in Hawaii 7 December:** the totals presented here are an amalgamation of information from three sources, two enumerations in the congressional investigation that do not match (PHA, Part 12, 234 and Part 24, 1833), and the Army Air Forces Historical Study no. 41, Operational History of the Seventh Air Force, 7 December 1941 to 6 November 1943, p. 2, MilSpecManuals.com. The miscellaneous types included four AT-6 modern trainers, two C-33 cargo aircraft, five BT-2s, and thirteen tactical observations planes (one OA-8, three OA-9s, seven O-47Bs, and two O-49s). All three sources agree that 64 P-40s and 20 P-36s were operational but not armed the morning of 7 December. PHA, Part 24, 1833 is more comprehensive on other types, noting for example the presence of the single B-24 type and BT-2s. Therefore, totals in the text reflect primarily this second itemization in the PHA, slightly modified with the Army Air Forces Historical Study.

241 **Aircraft sent to Philippines and the Soviet Union:** William H. Bartsch, *December 8, 1941: MacArthur's Pearl Harbor* (College Station: Texas A & M Press, 2003), appendix C; PHA, Part 24, 1842–44.

241 **Sea services aircraft garrison in Hawaii 7 December:** Commander in Chief, United States Pacific Fleet, Serial 0479, February 15, 1942, Enclosure D. Other sources give smaller numbers, in large part because of the omission of aircraft in storage. This total is supplemented by details in Lambert and Polmar, *Defenseless*, appendices D and E.

242 **Effective American operational combat aircraft on December 7:** this number includes eighty-four army fighters (sixty-four P-40s and twenty P-36s), twenty-five army bombers (twelve B-17s, one B-24 derivative, and twelve A-20s), ten navy fighters, and forty-one navy scout bombers. As detailed in the next chapter, the Japanese launched 350 aircraft in two waves.

242 **Reallocation of part of Pacific Fleet to Atlantic:** Prange, *At Dawn We Slept*, 127–34.

242 **Naval Force Strength and Dispositions, 7 December 1941:** table adapted from Willmott, *Pearl Harbor*, 199, and Harruo Tohmatsu and H. P. Willmott, *A Gathering Darkness: The Coming of War to the Far East and the Pacific, 1921–1942* (Lanham, Boulder, New York, Toronto, Oxford: SR Books, 2004), 119. As of this day, the British Commonwealth deployed in the Pacific and Indian Oceans three capital ships, one light carrier, two heavy cruisers, eight light cruisers, and seven frontline destroyers. The Royal Netherlands Navy added three light cruisers, six destroyers, and twelve submarines to the total of Allied forces.

243 **"take such steps on such days to see that proper watches and precautions are in effect":** PHA, Part 14, 1395.

243 **General Andrews institutes high alert in Panama Canal Zone in response to "War Warning":** Conn, Engelman, and Fairchild, *Guarding the United States and Its Outposts*, 349.

243 **Short orders full alert July 1941:** PHA, Part 27, 138–40.

243 **Stark message 16 October on Japanese cabinet changes:** PHA, Part 14, 1402.

243 **"Personally I do not believe the Japs are going to sail into us . . .":** PHA, Part 16, 2214.

243 **"tension between United States and remains stained . . .":** Conn, Engelman, and Fairchild, *Guarding the United States and Its Outposts*, 175.

244 "Chances of favorable outcome of negotiations with Japan very doubtful . . .": PHA, Part 14, 1405.

244 Turner's background and personality, assessments of Japanese intentions, misinformation about location of "Purple" machine in Hawaii: Prange, *At Dawn We Slept*, 40, 45; PHA, Part 4, 1731, 1939–40, 1975–77, 1983, Part 10, 4714–17, Part 11, 5363–64. Turner did draft a memo in January 1941 warning that hostilities with Japan would likely commence with an attack on Pearl Harbor, and the first two types of likely attack were by air bombing or torpedo attack.

244 Performance of army intelligence, appreciations of 28 November and 5 December; Stimson and Roosevelt aim to relieve Miles: Conn, Engelman, and Fairchild, *Guarding the United States and Its Outposts*, 176; Heinrichs, *Threshold of War*, 20–21.

244 "Negotiations with Japan appear to be terminated to all practical purposes . . .": PHA, Part 11, 5424; Part 14, 1328.

245 Army sabotage warnings: PHA, Part 7, 2935; Part 14, 1330; Conn, Engelman, and Fairchild, *Guarding the United States and Its Outposts*, 178–79.

245 Navy Department warning against sabotage November 28: PHA, Part 14, 1406.

245 "alerted to prevent sabotage": PHA, Part 14, 1330.

245 Short's response to November 27 alert: PHA, Part 7, 2941; Part 15, 1440–44; Part 27, 156–58; Zimm, *Attack on Pearl Harbor*, 355; Conn, Engelman, and Fairchild, *Guarding the United States and Its Outposts*, 179–80. "Alert no. 1" as defined in the order of 5 November 1941 at Headquarters Hawaiian Department, Standing Operating Procedure, 5 November 1941, PHA, Part 24, 2107–20 (Alert no. 1 at 2010).

245 Short on 27 June 1940 message Marshall to Herron: PHA, Part 7, 2930.

245 The "do's" and "don'ts" of the 27 November 1941 message: PHA, Part 7, 2985.

245 Short on the stricture that "no international incident must take place in Hawaii that would provoke the Japanese . . .": PHA, Part 7, 3032. Stimson's diary entry notes that there were numerous interruptions during the day as he and others worked up the draft of this "War Warning." This may explain how the problems in the draft went unnoted in Washington. Stimson diary, 27 November 1941.

246 Short's replies reviewed by Bundy, Gerow, and Marshall: Gannon, *Pearl Harbor Betrayed*, 137–38.

246 "That was my opportunity to intervene . . .": PHA, Part 3, 1421–22.

246 Gerow testimony and death of Bundy: Prange, *At Dawn We Slept*, 589, 686–87.

246 "This dispatch is to be considered a war warning . . .": PHA, Part 14, 1406.

246 Unprecedented status of term *war warning*: PHA, Part 33, 814. This matter is stated in the detailed and highly persuasive testimony of Admiral Royal Ingersoll about the circumstances of the drafting of the message.

246 Kimmel orders alert and depth charging of submarines: PHA, Part 32, 232–33; Part 17, 496.

246 Heavy bomber concentration in Philippines: W. F. Craven and J. L. Cate, eds., *The Army Air Forces in World War II*, vol. 1, *Plans and Early Operations January 1939 to August 1942* (Washington, DC: Office of Air Force History, 1983 [reprint]), 174–75, 185 [hereafter Craven and Cate, *Plans and Early Operations January 1939 to August 1942*]. The official history appears to overstate the case by reporting a like emphasis in the distribution of fighters. On 7–8 December, however, Hawaii had ninety-nine P-40s to ninety-four in the Philippines, with the most modern models in the Philippines.

247 **Washington orders to send P-40s and army troops to Wake and Midway and the response by Kimmel and Short, McMorris comment:** PHA, Part 5, 2153–54; Part 6, 2519–20; Part 26, 321–22; Part 27, 412; Part 28, 1497. The army aviator repeated this story to Prange in April 1961. *At Dawn We Slept*, 400–401. The message to Kimmel noted that the transfer of army planes could be accomplished by carrier if "feasible and desirable." In other words, Washington was not ordering the carriers out of Pearl Harbor but leaving their use up to Kimmel. Also since Washington specified no date for the transfer, these orders could not have been part of a conspiracy to "save" the carriers from an anticipated Japanese attack.

247 **Altered plans to send Marine aircraft via carriers to Wake and Midway:** PHA, Part 17, 2480–84, Part 6, 2519–20; John B. Lundstrom, *The First Team: Pacific Naval Air Combat from Pearl Harbor to Midway* (Annapolis, MD: Naval Institute Press, 1984), 3–15 [hereafter Lundstrom, *The First Team*].

247 **"My Peruvian Colleague told a member of my staff. . . .":** PHA, Part 14, 1042.

248 **Assessment and reaction to Grew's warning of Pearl Harbor attack:** Prange, *At Dawn We Slept*, 31–33.

248 **Yoshikawa's memoir accounts:** Dr. Brian Walsh reviewed Yoshikawa's postwar memoirs, *I Was the Pearl Harbor Spy*, for the author and prepared a report, submitted 4 September 2016 via email. These memoirs appeared in 1963 and 1985 with a third posthumous edition in 2015. Walsh reviewed the 1985 and 2015 editions and states that the 1985 version appears most accurate overall. Yoshikawa takes pains to insist that no Hawaiian residents of Japanese descent aided him and he took care to avoid them as he did not trust them (1985, 86–87, 309–10; 2015, 78–79). That said, Mr. Mikami, a cab driver whom Yoshikawa regularly employed on his information-gathering trips, plainly indicated by his actions to aid Yoshikawa that he understood Yoshikawa's real purpose (1985, 149–51, 208; 2015, 76–77, 141–42, 144, 207). The mistress of the Shunchōrō Restaurant Yoshikawa frequented (and where he maintained a telescope to observe Pearl Harbor) also had to be aware of what he was engaged in doing (1985, 96–97, 315, 2015, 88–89). The consul general, Mr. Kita, had himself served as a spy for the Imperial Navy before Yoshikawa arrived, and he knew Yoshikawa's mission. Since the consulate code clerk handled some of Yoshikawa's messages, it would be impossible for him to have missed Yoshikawa's spy activities (1985, 75–76; 2015, 70–71). Yoshikawa claimed to have no specific knowledge that the attack would come on 7 December (1985, 156; 2015, 149). This seems consistent with the fact that he had not succeeded in destroying all the code material before American authorities arrived (1985, 95, 100, 102, 126–28; 2015, 152). Yet he settled all of his bills on 6 December and reports that Kita also deduced an attack was coming (1985, 143, 150–52; 2015, 135, 152). One major reason Yoshikawa discerned that an actual attack was coming was the content of the questionnaire delivered to him by Japanese agents arriving in October posing as Japanese sailors. This included a specific question about which day of the week the most warships were in harbor (1985, 104, 116–21; 2015, 97, 109–13).

248 **American counterintelligence efforts on Oahu:** PHA, Part 23, 333, 335, 857–58, 875–78, 914; Part 10, 5089–90; Part 35, 84, 569; Part 36, 331.

248 **"Tricycle":** the story was first disclosed in J. C. Masterman, *The Double-Cross System in the War of 1939 to 1945* (New Haven, CT: Yale University Press, 1972), 79–81, appendix 2: Tricycle's American Questionnaire, 196–98. The best examination of

the issue is in Gordon W. Prange with Donald M. Goldstein and Katherine Dillon, *Pearl Harbor: The Verdict of History* (New York: McGraw-Hill, 1986).

249 **September 1941 "Bomb Plot Message":** PHA, Part 12, 261.

249 **"Bomb Plot Message":** PHA, Part 12, 261; Prange, *At Dawn We Slept*, 248–56.

249 **Congressional investigation of espionage in Hawaii aborted:** Prange, *At Dawn We Slept*, 256–57.

249 **Disposition of "Purple" Machines:** Prange, *At Dawn We Slept*, 80–82.

249 **Kimmel's dependency on Stark for intelligence information:** PHA, Part 6, 2539–43, 2550.

249 **Direction finding (DF):** R. Keen, *Wireless Direction Finding* (London: Wireless World and Iliffe & Sons, 1938), esp. 377–83, for the issues involved in DF of the high-frequency (HF) radio transmissions that navies largely depended on at that time. I am indebted to William O'Neil for bringing to my attention this and the following authorities on direction finding.

250 **Direction finding equipment:** P. G. Redgment, "High-Frequency Direction Finding in the Royal Navy: Development of Anti-U-Boat Equipment, 1941–5," in *The applications of radar and other electronic systems in the Royal Navy in World War 2*, ed. F. A. Kingsley (Basingstoke: Macmillan, 1995).

250 **Background on JN-25:** The following discussion of JN-25 and the efforts to break it is drawn particularly from the following sources, all of which are filed in RG 38, CNSG Library, NARA: Box 115, File 5750/197, History of GYP-1, pp. 1–4, 7–9, 12–13; Box 115, File 5750/198 Op-20 GY [Monthly Reports] February 1940 to January 1942, especially March 1940, January to March and August to December 1941, and January 1942; Box 116, File 5750/199 (2 of 3), Op-20-GYP History World War II, pp. 1–4, 7, 12–13; Box 116, File 5750/202 CNSG-History of OP-20-GYP-1 WWII (1 of 2), pp. 1–52, especially pp. 1–7, 11–14, 17–22, 25–26, 29. Unless otherwise indicated, the next section draws from these sources. The original American designation for the Japanese system was AN; it was changed to the now famous JN-25 in March 1942.

252 **Complacency of Imperial Navy code clerks, "no system's security [is] greater than the care of those who [use] it":** RG 38, CNSG Library, Box 116, 5750/202 CNSG-History of OP-20-GYP-1 WWII (1 of 2), 10, 13 (quote); RG 38, CNSG Library Box 116, File 5750/199 (2 of 3), Op-20-GYP History World War II, 7–8.

253 **Japanese Morse:** Michael Smith, *The Emperor's Codes* (London: Transworld Publishers, 2000), 64 [hereafter Smith, *The Emperor's Codes*]

253 **Recovery of code group values by 1 December 1941; reading of "movement reports":** the 3,800 figure is from Box 115, File 5750/198 Op-20-GY Monthly Report for January 1, 1942. This indicates that 2,380 code values were recovered in December 1941, bringing the total to "approximately 6,180 values recovered" by the end of the month (or 6,180 − 2,380 = 3,800 values at the beginning of the month. The claim that the unit in the Philippines even read a "movement report" is in RG 38, CNSG Library, File 5750/202, History of OP-20-GYP-1 WWII (1 of 2), 25–26. But a report (undated but by content around 10 March 1942) on the activities of the Philippine radio intelligence unit makes no mention of reading even "movement reports." RG 38, CNSG Library, Box 119, File 5750/221, "Summary of C.I. Activity." Another Washington report dated 8 January 1942 indicates "[JN-25B] Code Values recovered from all sources were counted. Total is 5,366, of which, roughly 3,000 are verified

values." RG 38, CNSG Library Box 116 File 5750/201 CNSG-OP-20-GY-P History (2 of 2) "File # 62, War diary File on History and Function of OP-20-G Officers from Dec 41–Oct 45. The tabulations of recovered code group values in Washington as of 8 January 1942, and by the Philippine unit (displaced to Australia) as of 10 March 1942, underscore how limited the valid recovered code group values were before Pearl Harbor. It is also to be noted that any conspiracy to the contrary would have to involve the alteration of these reports as well as those predating the Pearl Harbor attack.

254 **No JN-25B messages "read" prior to Pearl Harbor Attack:** RG 38, CNSG Library, Box 115, File 5750/197, "The Activities and Accomplishments of GY-1 During 1941, 1942 and 1943." This top secret wartime report provides data on additive and code group recoveries for all three years. From the three ciphers used in 1941, each of 50,000 additives, the additives recovered from each were: cipher (Book) 5, 22,900; cipher 6, 47,000; cipher 7, 36,600. The report goes on to list the total of actual messages read, but shows none read in all of 1941.

254 **Army communications personnel numbers Pearl Harbor to VJ Day:** SRH-134, William F. Friedman, Expansion of the Signal Intelligence Service from 1930–7 December 1941, 4 December 1945, 4, Box 40, Entry 9002, RG 457, NARA.

254 **Figures for Navy Department:** SRH-149, A Brief History of Communications Intelligence in the United States, by Laurance F. Stafford, Captain United States Navy, Retired (prepared 21–27 March 1952), 4, 6 (the 738 include eight men captured on Guam); SRH-197, "U.S. Navy Communication Intelligence Organization, Liaison and Collaboration 1941–45," both RG 457, NARA.

254 **Enhancement of capability from machinery:** One report shows that as of January 1942, the machinery at the Washington station totaled sixteen with a staff of nine men. By December 1943, there were 172 machines, staffed by eight officers, 169 enlisted men, and 229 enlisted WAVES. RG 38, CNSG Library, Box 110, 5750/150, Historical Review of Op-20G, 11.

255 **Staffing of US Navy Washington code breaking unit:** RG 38, CNSG Library, Box 115, File 5750/197, History of GYP-1, 4.

255 **Division of duties on "Purple" by army and navy:** SRH-134, William F. Friedman, Expansion of the Signal Intelligence Service from 1930–7 December 1941, 4 December 1945, 6–7, 16–22, RG 457, Entry 9002, Box 40, NARA.

255 **Translation bottleneck:** RG 457, SRH-149, A Brief History of Communications Intelligence in the United States, by Laurance F. Stafford, Captain United States Navy, Retired, 19; RG 457, SRH-252, A Version of the Japanese Problem In the Signal Intelligence Service (Later the Signal Security Agency) 1930–1945 by John B. Hurt, 28.

256 **Dutch and British code breaking work; FECB and Philippine exchanges:** The summary of Dutch and British efforts is drawn from Robert J. Hanyok and David P. Mowry, *United States Cryptologic History Series IV: World War II*, vol. 10: *West Wind Clear: Cryptology and the Winds Messages Controversy—A Documentary History* (Center for Cryptologic History, National Security Agency, 2008), 10. That resource particularly relies on H. L. Shaw, *History of HMS Anderson*, 24 May 1946, section 3, 2–4, and Smith, *The Emperor's Codes*, 78–90. The FECB and Philippine exchange is drawn from Robert L. Benson, *A History of U.S. Communications Intelligence during*

World War II: Policy and Administration (Fort Meade, MD: National Security Agency, 1997), 21–22. Although contact was first initiated in December 1940, actual information exchange did not commence until February 1941. The American version of the exchange is that the two centers had achieved "almost equal progress" in their recoveries. RG 38, CNSG Library, Box 116, 5750/202 CNSG-History of OP-20-GYP-1 WWII (1 of 2), 21.

256   **Cryptographic success and intelligence failure against JN-25 prior to Pearl Harbor:** A wartime report, RG 38, CNSG Library, Box 115, File 5750/197, "The Activities and Accomplishments of GY-1 During 1941, 1942 and 1943," 8–9, tabulates additive and code group recoveries for all three years. Although the report lists cipher (Additive Book) 8 as "1942," it was effective from 4 December 1941. It also had 50,000 additives, of which 47,700 were recovered. But the report is clear that during all of 1941, no actual messages were read.

257   **"Japanese May Strike Over Weekend":** Lambert and Polmar, *Defenseless*, 76–82. The samples of headlines and articles in the *Honolulu Advertiser* and the *Honolulu Star Bulletin* emphatically convey crisis for more than a week before the attack.

257   **Japanese merchant ships heading home:** OPNAV to CINCAF, CINCPAC, etc., 14 August 1941 (Japanese "rapidly completing" withdrawal of merchant ships homeward from world shipping lanes); OPNAV 4 to CINCPAC, etc., Nov 1941 (all but one Japanese merchant ship withdrawn or preparing to withdraw from Western Hemisphere; no vessels sailing toward Western Hemisphere), PHA, Part 14, 1401, 1403.

257   **Intelligence reaching Kimmel and Short in Hawaii:** The actual daily summaries seen by Kimmel between 1 November and 6 December 1941 appear in PHA, Part 17, 2601–42 and SRH-147 Communications Intelligence Summaries 1 November–6 December 1941, Commandant, Fourteenth Naval District, United States Navy, RG 457, NARA. A very detailed discussion of all sources of information reaching Kimmel appears in the testimony of Capt. Edwin Layton before the Hewitt Investigation, PHA, Part 36, 111–30. Unless otherwise indicated, the actual daily summaries and Layton's testimony provide the basis for the discussion of intelligence reaching Kimmel that follows.

258   **Conflicting conclusions about presence of Japanese carrier division in the Marshalls:** No. 197, COM 14 260110 of November 1941 (Station Hypo) to OPNAV, info: CINCPAC, CINCAF, COM 16. This shows lineup of forces headed south, but placed Cardiv Three (*RYUJO* and one Maru) in Marshalls. No. 198, COM 16 261331, Nov 1941 (Station Cast) to CINCPAC, COM 14, OPNAV, CINCAF, *The "Magic" Background to Pearl Harbor*, appendix 4, page A107. This assessment largely agrees on the lineup of units forming forces headed south, but Station Cast does not agree with Station Hypo on carriers and submarines in Marshalls. *The "Magic" Background to Pearl Harbor*, vol. 4, page A107. The 27 November estimate that ten carriers were part of the naval task force assembled for operations in Southeast Asia is in Memorandum for the Chief of Staff, November 26, 1941, Subject: Japanese Naval Task Force, RG 107, Entry 99, "Safe File," Box 11, Folder: Philippines, NARA. Testimony by Capt. Arthur M. McCollum, Officer in Charge, Far Eastern Division, Office of Naval Intelligence in 1941, at the Hewitt investigation in 1945 disclosed the opinion that Station Cast was deemed more accurate because it was closer to Japanese signals and the traffic analysis section was stronger and had more continuity. PHA, Part 36, 14–15.

258 **2 December exchange between Kimmel and Layton:** PHA, Part 36, 128.

258 **Loss of track of Japanese carriers for fifteen to twenty-five days:** PHA, Part 10, 4837–38.

259 **US Fleet vital to defense of United States and British Asian Empire:** this point was nicely made by no less a figure than William Friedman. RG 457, Entry 9002, NARA, SRH-125 "Certain Aspects of 'Magic' in the Cryptological Background of the Various Official Investigations into the Attack on Pearl Harbor," by William F. Friedman, n.d. (circa 1957, sometime after 4 Jan 57), 37–38.

260 **Japanese radio deception plans:** Robert J. Hanyok, "'Catching the Fox Unaware': Japanese Radio Denial and Deception and the Attack on Pearl Harbor," *Naval War College Review* 2008, vol. 61, no. 4, 103–12, provides the best single discussion of the Japanese efforts at radio deception. Hanyok points out that a successful British direction finding achievement in July 1941 against a Japanese carrier rendered the Imperial Navy extremely wary of the capability of Allied radio intelligence efforts and prompted the comprehensive deception and denial plan for the Pearl Harbor attack. Further, while the Striking Force itself maintained radio silence, intelligence, weather, and other information was sent to it by broadcasts from Japan using multiple messages over multiple frequencies. The battleships *Hiei* and *Kirishima*, with the best and most sensitive antennas, made sure the messages were disseminated by visual signals within the task force.

260 **Short's decrease in defensive preparations and delink of air raid warning capability and the ability to intercept raid:** The 1945–46 congressional investigation properly emphasized this aspect of Short's culpability. Particularly telling proved a comparison of Short's reaction to the "War Warning" message and the response of commanders in the Philippines, the West Coast, and Panama. PHA, Part "4.0," Congressional Committee Report and Conclusions, 126, 129–30.

260 **Kimmel's failure to verify defenses to protect fleet:** PHA, Part 6, 2579–89.

260 **Failure to invoke plans for unity of command and joint operations:** Conn, Engelman, and Fairchild, *Guarding the United States and Its Outposts*, 182.

261 **1 December Imperial Conference:** Ike, *Japan's Decision for War*, 262–83.

261 **Japanese leaders miss opportunity to see German defeat in the Soviet Union:** this very intriguing fact was pointed out to the author by Gerhard Weinberg. Email to Author, 1 November 2016.

261 **Code machine and code destruction orders:** Tokyo messages, December 1–2, *The "Magic" Background to Pearl Harbor*, appendix 4, A122–23.

261 **"should Japan become engaged in a war against the United States . . .":** Berlin to Tokyo, no. 1393, November 29, 1941, *The "Magic" Background to Pearl Harbor*, appendix 4, A382–84.

261 **"may come quicker than anyone realizes":** Tokyo to Berlin, no. 985, November 30, 1941, *The "Magic" Background to Pearl Harbor*, appendix 4, A384–85.

261 **FDR's pledges on 1 and 4 December:** Heinrichs, *Threshold of War*, 216–17; Callahan, *The Worst Disaster*, 168–69; Franklin D. Roosevelt, Day by Day, December 1, 1941, FDRL.

262 **"Defensive Information Patrol":** OPNAV to CINCAF 012356 Dec 41, *The "Magic" Background to Pearl Harbor*, appendix 4, A124–25.

262 ***Chicago Tribune* story on "Victory Program":** *Chicago Tribune*, 4 December 1941, 1;

Stimson diary, December 4–5, 1941; Murray Klein, *A Call to Arms: Mobilizing America for World War II* (New York: Bloomsbury Press, 2013), 207, 271–72, 363–64, 378–79 [hereafter Klein, *A Call to Arms*]; Lynne Olson, *Those Angry Days: Roosevelt, Lindbergh, and America's Fight over World War II, 1939–1941* (New York: Random House, 2013), 411–23, 430. A thread running through Klein's magisterial account of mobilization is Roosevelt's refusal to delegate authority or set firm priorities, which resulted in a far less than optimal effectiveness from 1939 to 1943. Olson constructs a case that the actual source of the *Chicago Tribune* leak was none other than General Henry ("Hap") Arnold, the chief of the Army Air Forces, who faulted the plan as failing to provide adequately for his service.

The Hearst paper disclosures of December 1941 were not the first public intimations of the "Victory Program." A 20 October 1941 *Barron's* article had disclosed the existence of a "victory program" for a stupendous increase in military production "needed to crush Hitler." Stimson's "Safe File" contains copy apparently indicating he was aware of the leak. RG 107, Entry 180, Box 4, Folder Victory Program, NARA.

263 **British Desert Offensive:** In the *New York Times*, 28 November–6 December 1941, each day articles on pp. 1-2 provided British and German communiqués and news coverage. A good account of the battle, called "Operation Crusader" by the British, placed in context in the overall African campaigns, is Barrie Pitt, *The Crucible of War: Western Desert 1941* (New York: Paragon House, 1989), ch. 11–12.

263 **Eastern Front Situation:** *New York Times*, 24 November–6 December 1941. As with the British offensive in the Western Desert, pp. 1–2, each day provided Soviet and German communiqués and news coverage. On 28 November, Hanson Baldwin wrote a shrewd article assessing the situation. "Struggle For Moscow Crucial Point of War," *New York Times*, 28 November 1941, section E, p. 2.

263 **"The Germans are making a supreme effort . . .":** Ickes diary, Sunday, December 7, 1941, pp. 6105–6.

263 **Approach of Japanese Striking Force:** Willmott, *Pearl Harbor*, 78–79.

264 **Roosevelt's telegram to the emperor:** "President Roosevelt to Emperor Hirohito of Japan, December 6, 1941," *FRUS, Japan 1931–1941*, vol. 2, 784–86. This was transmitted 2100 hours (local), 6 Dec 1941 from Washington. Iguchi makes a strong case that Roosevelt's telegram was a sincere effort to avoid war, not just an attempt to create a favorable paper record. Iguchi additionally shows that the long delay between when Roosevelt's telegram reached Tokyo and when it reached the emperor was due to deliberate delay by the Imperial Army. Further, the delay of this telegram played a role in the delayed dispatch of the final Japanese diplomatic message. *Demystifying Pearl Harbor*, 222–25, 237–40.

264 **Roosevelt seeks draft statement to justify entering war with Japan if Japan only attacks British or Dutch possessions or Thailand:** Davis, *FDR: The War President*, 337.

265 **Schultz delivers "Magic" of 13-part message to Roosevelt and Hopkins:** PHA, Part 10, 4,661–72; 13-part message: "Memorandum Handed by the Japanese Ambassador (Nomura) to the Secretary of State, December 7, 1941," *FRUS, Japan 1931–1941*, vol. 2, 787–92. The note was in English, so there is no question about the translation on 6 December. Schultz's testimony is one of the real gems uncovered by the postwar congressional investigation. Schultz's appearance was riveting and utterly convincing.

265 Thirteen-part message delivered to other officials; none take further action: Prange, *At Dawn We Slept*, 474–76.

11: "Air Raid, Pearl Harbor, This Is No Drill"

266 Launch of midget submarines: Willmott, *Pearl Harbor*, 95; Dorr Carpenter and Norman Polmar, *Submarines of the Imperial Japanese Navy* (Annapolis, MD: Naval Institute Press, 1986), 130–31.

266 *Condor-Ward* initial encounter with midget submarine: Commander in Chief, United States Pacific Fleet, Serial 0479, February 15, 1942, Part II, 21 [hereafter CinCPac Serial 0479]; Norman Friedman, *U.S. Destroyers: A Design History* (Annapolis, MD: Naval Institute Press, 1982), 432; Narrative by William W. Outerbridge, USN, 18 February 1944, Office of the Chief of Naval Operations, Office of Naval Records and Library, World War II Oral Histories and Interviews, RG 38, Box 22, NARA [hereafter Outerbridge oral history].

267 Part 14 of diplomatic message received and interpreted: PHA, Part 12, 245; Part 11, 5273–74; Part 8, 3905–7, 3392–93.

267 Bratton and "one o'clock" message: PHA, Part 12, 248; Part 9, 4517, 4523–24, 4527, 4534, 4548, 4571.

267 Bratton notifies superiors, summons Marshall to War Department: PHA, Part 9, 4524–25, 4549, 4595; Part 3, 1114.

268 Meeting of Stimson, Knox, and Hull, "very certain that the Japs are planning some deviltry. . .": Stimson diary, December 7, 1941.

268 Kramer sees "one o'clock message": PHA, Part 8, 393–94, 447–48.

268 Kramer delivers "one o'clock message" to Stark and Knox: PHA, Part 8, 3909, 3430; Part 36, 26; Part 9, 4043, 4052–53; Part 5, 2095; Part 33, 859–60.

268 Development and delivery time of Japan's final note: Morley, *The Final Confrontation*, 327–29; Mauch, *Sailor Diplomat*, 212–13.

268 Notice to Washington embassy staff to prepare fourteen-part message for delivery; actions of staff; Nomura's attitude: Morley, *The Final Confrontation*, 330–38; Mauch, *Sailor Diplomat*, 213. The piquant detail that the embassy staff went to a Chinese restaurant is from Seishiro Sugihara, *Between Incompetence and Culpability: Assessing the Diplomacy of Japan's Foreign Ministry from Pearl Harbor to Potsdam* (Lanham, MD: University Press of America, 1997), 89 [hereafter Sugihara, *Between Incompetence and Culpability*].

269 Controversy over role of Washington embassy staff in "sneak attack": Morley, *The Final Confrontation*, 335–39; Sugihara, *Between Incompetence and Culpability*, ch. 3 and 5.

270 Striking Force preparation to launch aircraft carriers, aircraft, and crew members described: Prange, *At Dawn We Slept*, 490–91; Willmott, *Pearl Harbor*, 78–79; Jonathan Parshall and Andrew Tully, *Shattered Sword: The Untold Story of the Battle of Midway* (Washington, DC: Potomac Books, 2005), 6–10, 462–75. Motion pictures of the Striking Force this morning underscore the rough seas at the time of the launch.

270 Launch of first attack wave: Willmott, *Pearl Harbor*, 100, 191.

272 Miles reacts to fourteen-part and "one o'clock" messages: PHA, Part 2, 933.

272 Marshall reaches office and reads messages: PHA, Part 2, 929; Part 9, 4514, 4517–18; Part 29, 2309.

272 **Discussions between Marshall and Stark:** PHA, Part 9, 4518; Part 5, 2132–33; Part 15, 1633.

272 **Marshall hands message to Bratton; Marshall and Stark do not call Hawaii:** PHA, Part 9, 4518–19; Part 2, 931; Part 33, 882; Part 29, 2313.

273 **"Japanese are presenting at one p.m. Eastern Standard Time today what amounts to an ultimatum . . .":** PHA, Part 15, 1640.

273 **Bratton glances at watch:** PHA, Part 9, 4519.

273 **Fuchida leads first wave toward Pearl Harbor:** Prange, *At Dawn We Slept*, 490–91.

273 **Marshall's message transmission, ultimately by cable:** PHA, Part 9, 4555, Part 14, 1410–11; Part 27, 109–11, 114; Part 23, 1103; Part 34, 33.

273 *Antares* **and** *Ward* **encounter second midget submarine:** *Antares* AKS-3, December 10, 1941, Action Report; *Ward* (DD-139), December 13, 1941, Action Report; CinCPac Serial 0479, 21–22; Commander Task Force Nine (Commander Patrol Wing Two), 20 December 1941, Subject: Operations December 7, 1941, 2; Outerbridge oral history; Curtis Lim, "1941 Japanese mini sub found off Pearl Harbor," *Honolulu Advertiser*, 29 August 2002. Note that all "Action Reports" cited in this chapter are found in RG 38, NARA, where they are filed by ship or unit name and date.

273 *Ward* **sinks midget submarine, subsequently hulk located:** See note above on *Antares* and *Ward* encounter.

274 **Second strike launched:** Times the carriers turned into wind and immediately began launching aircraft based on study of Carrier Division 5 action report by Mike Wenger.

274 **Detection of reconnaissance float planes and Opana radar contacts and reports:** PHA, Part 27, 528–32, 569; Part 10, 5028–29, 5033, 5040–41, 5046, 5058 (and record of readings opposite this page); Part 18, 3015; Part 29, 2121; Part 32, 342; Conn, Engelman, and Fairchild, *Guarding the United States and Its Outposts*, 186–87.

275 **Tactical warnings:** Zimm, *Attack on Pearl Harbor*, 136, and ch. 9 give estimate of time required for battleships to get to general quarters and secure watertight enclosures given the circumstances in Pearl Harbor that morning. His ch. 9 explores at length the hypothetical situation of the American reaction with tactical warning. Zimm believes the two-float-plane reconnaissance mission unduly threatened to provide the Americans a tactical warning. *Attack on Pearl Harbor*, 173–74.

275 **Number of ships in Pearl Harbor at time of attack; situation of** *Enterprise*: CinCPac Serial 0479, 10, 13-4; navsource.org/Naval/pearl.htm (accessed 1 March 2010); Robert J. Cressman and J. Michael Wenger, *Steady Nerves and Stout Hearts: The Enterprise (CV-6) Air Group and Pearl Harbor, 7 December 1941* (Missoula, MT: Pictorial Histories Publishing, 1990), 9, 49–59 [hereafter Cressman and Wenger, *Steady Nerves and Stout Hearts*]. Enumerating the number of "ships" at Pearl Harbor at the time of the attack involves some judgment issues. The total given here of ninety-six follows the web source but excludes from the count as not "ships" four very small coastal minesweepers of less than 250 tons' displacement, eleven PT (Patrol Torpedo) Boats, and thirty-one assorted tiny yard and district craft. Also not counted are three cutters and two boats of the US Coast Guard in or off Honolulu Harbor. Willmott counts twenty-eight major warships (one carrier, one battleship, two light cruisers, nine destroyers, and fifteen submarines) on the US West Coast. This count does not include auxiliary vessels. *Pearl Harbor*, 199.

275   **Weather, status of ships in harbor readying for morning colors, aircraft heard and seen:** CinCPac Serial 0479, 10, 13–14; *Henley* (DD-371), December 15, 1941.

276   **Japanese aircraft radio deficiencies, effects on command and control:** Zimm, *Attack on Pearl Harbor*, 87–90, 375.

276   **Fuchida fumble with flare signal, "Tora Tora Tora" message:** Zimm, *Attack on Pearl Harbor*, 135–36, 155; Willmott, *Pearl Harbor*, 101.

276   **"with the same level of organization as the Kentucky Derby . . .":** Zimm, *Attack on Pearl Harbor*, 175.

277   **Attack on Kaneohe:** Commander, Patrol Wing One, 1 January 1942, Subject: Report of Japanese Air Attack on Kaneohe Bay, December 7, 1941; Commander VP-11, December 13, 1941, Subject: December 7, 1941, Air Raid, Report of. For a superb and meticulous recounting of the events at Kaneohe Bay, see J. Michael Wenger, Robert J. Cressman, John F. DiVirgilio, *No One Avoided Danger: NAS Kaneohe Bay and the Japanese Attack of 7 December 1941 (Pearl Harbor Tactical Series)* (Annapolis, MD: Naval Institute Press, 2015).

277   **Attack on Wheeler and Hickam Air Bases:** Craven and Cate, *Plans and Early Operations January 1939 to August 1942*, 195–98; Prange, *At Dawn We Slept*, 520–24, 530, 532–35, 538–39; Willmott, *Pearl Harbor*, 190; Zimm, *Attack on Pearl Harbor*, 156–57.

277   **Attack on Ewa:** Frank O. Hough, Verle E. Ludwig, and Henry I Shaw, *History of Marine Corps Operations in World War II:* vol. 1, *Pearl Harbor to Guadalcanal* (Historical Branch, Headquarters, US Marine Corps, Battery Press Reprint, 1993), 71–73.

277   **Defensive fighter sorties, losses, and successes:** Craven and Cate, *Plans and Early Operations January 1939 to August 1942*, 198–99; Prange, *At Dawn We Slept*, 524, 529, 532–34; Zimm, *Attack on Pearl Harbor*, 168–69. Zimm reports the US fighters destroyed eight and maybe as many as eleven Japanese planes.

277   ***Enterprise* participation and aircraft losses:** Cressman and Michael Wenger, *Steady Nerves and Stout Hearts*, 49–59; Lundstrom, *The First Team*, 15–22.

278   **B-17 flight arrives during attack:** Craven and Cate, *Plans and Early Operations January 1939 to August 1942*, 199–200. Mike Wenger provided updated information on the two Fortresses that never flew again.

278   **Torpedo plane attack targets and formations:** Zimm, *Attack on Pearl Harbor*, 158; Willmott, *Pearl Harbor*, 100–103. Information from Mike Wenger provided an updated account of the formations of these torpedo planes.

278   **Torpedo plane attack profile and challenges; level bomber formation approach:** Zimm, *Attack on Pearl Harbor*, 117, 165–66, 436n43; Willmott, *Pearl Harbor*, 101.

278   **Attack on Ford Island, "Air Raid, Pearl Harbor, This Is No Drill":** Commander Task Force Nine (Commander Patrol Wing Two), 20 December 1941, Subject: Operations December 7, 1941, 3.

280   **Damage to Ford Island and response:** Commander Task Force Nine (Commander Patrol Wing Two), 20 December 1941, Subject: Operations December 7, 1941; Commander VP-22, Commander VP-23, Commander VP-24; Commander VP-11, December 13, 1941, Subject: December 7, 1941, Air Raid, Report of; Commander VP-12, Commander VP-14.

280   ***Hiryū* and *Sōryū* torpedo planes attack north side of Ford Island:** David Aiken, "Torpedoing Pearl Harbor," *Military History*, vol. 18, no. 5 (December 2001): 48–50 [hereafter Aiken, "Torpedoing Pearl Harbor"]; Zimm, *Attack on Pearl Harbor*, 158–59, 180–81.

280 *Utah* sunk: Aiken, "Torpedoing Pearl Harbor," 49–50; Zimm, *Attack on Pearl Harbor*, 159; *Utah* (AG-16), December 15, 1941; *Raleigh* (CL-7), June 10, 1942; Norman Friedman, *U.S. Battleships: An Illustrated Design History* (Annapolis, MD: Naval Institute Press, 1985), 419. The times given are readjusted from those in *Utah*'s report, which has events about five minutes later than the actual time.

280 **Torpedo and bomb hits on Raleigh:** *Raleigh* (CL-7), December 13, 1941; June 10, 1942.

280 *Detroit* and *Tangier* participation: *Detroit* (CL-8) Serial 1471, December 10, 1941 (a very succinct report comprising only part of one page); *Tangier* (AV-8), January 2, 1942.

280 **Torpedo plane attack on *Helena* and *Oglala*, *Oglala* capsizes:** Aiken, "Torpedoing Pearl Harbor," 49–50; Zimm, *Attack on Pearl Harbor*, 159–60, 181–82; *Oglala* (CM-4), December 11, 1941.

281 *Helena* torpedo damage, engineers trapped: *Helena* (CL-50), December 14, 1941, Action Report, p. 9.

281 *Sōryū* and *Hiryū* torpedo planes join attack on "Battleship Row": Aiken, "Torpedoing Pearl Harbor," 51–53; Zimm, *Attack on Pearl Harbor*, 164–65.

282 **Japanese torpedo plane attack on "Battleship Row":** claimed and actual torpedo hits on battleships: Aiken, "Torpedoing Pearl Harbor," 50–53; Willmott, *Pearl Harbor*, 101, 106; Zimm, *Attack on Pearl Harbor*, 161–62. Aiken provides a very detailed account for each attacking "Kate" torpedo plane from which the following draws heavily. Mike Wenger clarified the number of *Sōryū* and *Hiryū* planes attacking "Battleship Row" and found that the *Hiryū* planes initially were assigned to attack the long pier (1010 pier) rather than "Battleship Row" proper.

282 *California* participation: Attack on *California* (BB-44), December 13 and December 22, 1941, Action Reports, NARA, RG 38; "U.S.S. California Torpedo and Bomb Damage," War Damage Report no. 21, 28 November 1942, RG 181, NARA.

282 *Neosho* participation: *Neosho* (AO-23), December 12, 1941; *Neosho* Deck Log, 6–7 December 1941, RG 38, NARA.

282 **Sinking of *Oklahoma*:** *Oklahoma* (BB-37), December 18, 1941, RG 38, NARA; Steven Bowder Young, *Trapped At Pearl Harbor: Escaping from Battleship Oklahoma* (Annapolis, MD: Naval Institute Press, 1991), 43–48 [hereafter Young, *Trapped at Pearl Harbor*]; Zimm, *Attack on Pearl Harbor*, 230. The destroyer *Mugford*'s report says *Oklahoma* capsized at 0808. *U.S.S. Mugford* (DD-389), December 9, 1941, Action Report, RG 38, NARA. Zimm, *Attack on Pearl Harbor*, 162, calculates first torpedo hit on a battleship was as early as 0757 and as late as 0759.

283 **Rescue of trapped *Oklahoma* sailors:** *Oklahoma* (BB-37), December 18, 1941, including particularly the report of Lt. Cdr. W. M. Hobby, Rescue and Salvage Work Report, December 12, 1941; Young, *Trapped at Pearl Harbor*, 135–45.

283 *Maryland* participation: *Maryland* (BB-46), December 11, 1941; *Maryland*, War diary, 7 December 1941, RG 38, Box 1183, NARA; *Maryland* (BB46), Serial 021, February 9, 1942; Maryland Deck Log, 7 December 1941, RG 38, NARA; United States Pacific Fleet, Battleships, Battle Force, Subject: Attack of Pearl Harbor by Japanese planes on December 7, 1941 (casualty totals, including flag personnel); Willmott, *Pearl Harbor*, 190–91.

283 *Tennessee* participation: *Tennessee* (BB-43), December 11, 1941.

284 *West Virginia* participation: *West Virginia* (BB-48), December 11, 1941.

284 *Arizona* attacked, "wish with a gust of hot air and sparks flew". . .: Willmott, *Pearl Harbor*, 190; Zimm, *Attack on Pearl Harbor*, 167–68, 185–86; *Arizona* (BB-39), December 13, 1941, Statement of Ens. G. S. Flanagan.

285 Initial bomb hit on *Arizona*: *Arizona* (BB-39), December 13, 1941, Statement of Ens. H. D. Davidson.

285 Destruction of *Arizona*: T. C. Hone, drawing by Joseph R. Beckenbach Jr., "The Destruction of the Battle Line at Pearl Harbor," *Naval Institute Proceedings*, vol. 103, no. 12, December 1977, 49–59; John F. Virgilio, "Seven Seconds to Infamy," *Naval Institute Proceedings*, vol. 123, no. 12, December 1997, pp. 62–65; CDR John Rogaard, USNR, Peter K. Hsu, Carroll L. Lucas, and CAPT Andrew Bache Jr., USNR (Ret.), "Death of the Arizona," *Naval Institute Proceedings*, vol. 15, no. 6, December 2001, 22–28; Commander, Navy Yard, Pearl Harbor, Subject: *U.S.S. Arizona* (BB-39) War Damage Report, C-L11-1/BB/NY10, 7 October 1943, NARA, RG 38. *Mugford's* report says *Arizona* blew up at 0808 (*U.S.S. Mugford* (DD-389), December 9, 1941, Action Report). *Tangier* (AV-8), January 2, 1941 says it blew up at 0806, and places time attack started at 0755. Zimm, *Attack on Pearl Harbor*, 235–36, 375, dismisses theory two as an attempt by designers to deny that *Arizona's* horizontal armor could have been defeated and shift blame to operators.

286 Casualties on *Arizona*: Paul Stillwell, *Battleship Arizona* (Annapolis, MD: Naval Institute Press, 1991), 254, 265–66, 273–78; *Arizona* (BB-39), December 13, 1941, Statement of Ens. Jim D. Miller.

286 *Vestal* participation: *Vestal* (AR-4), December 11, 1941.

286 Second wave attacks, difficulties for "Vals": Zimm, *Attack on Pearl Harbor*, 132–33, 169–71, 199, 254.

286 "Vals" attack *Nevada*: *Nevada* (BB-36), December 15, 1941; CINCPAC Serial 0479, 44–45; Zimm, *Attack on Pearl Harbor*, 204–5. Although some accounts credit the Japanese Vals with at least six hits on *Nevada*, Zimm argues five. Mike Wenger clarified that just the 23 *Kaga* "Vals" attacked *Nevada*.

286 Reasons for beaching of *Nevada*: Zimm, *Attack on Pearl Harbor*, 204–6, 375.

287 *Downes* and *Cassin* bombing: *Downes* (DD-375), December 17, 1941; *Cassin* (DD-372), December 13, 1941.

287 *Pennsylvania* participation: *Pennsylvania* (BB-38), December 16, 1941.

287 *Shaw* participation: *U.S.S. Shaw* (DD-373), Bomb Damage Pearl Harbor, 7 December 1941, RG 38, NARA; Willmott, *Pearl Harbor*, 116–17; Zimm, *Attack on Pearl Harbor*, 201; Prange, *At Dawn We Slept*, 537.

287 Vessels in Navy Yard, effectiveness against torpedo planes: *Bagley* (DD-386), Serial 0131, December 11, 1941; *Castor* (AKS-1), December 11, 1941; *Cummings* (DD-365), December 18, 1941; *Dolphin* (SS-169), Serial 055, December 10, 1941; *Hulbert* (AVD-6), December 8, 1941; *Jarvis* (DD-393), December 12, 1941; *Mugford* (DD-389), December 9, 1941; *Narwhal* (SS-167), December 12, 1941; *New Orleans* (CA-32), December 13, 1941; *Pelias* (AS-14), December 11, 1941; *Ramapo* (AO-12), December 11, 1941; *Sacramento* (PG-19), December 9, 1941; *San Francisco* (CA-38), December 10, 1941; *Sicard* (DM-21), December 9, 1941; *Sumner* (AG-32), December 11, 1941; *Swan* (AVP-7), December 11, 1941; *Tautog* (SS-199), December 12, 1941; *Thorton* (AVD-11), December 17, 1941; Aiken, "Torpedoing Pearl Harbor," 51–54; Zimm, *Attack on Pearl Harbor*, 162–63. Howell M. Forgy, *And Pass the Ammunition* (New York: D. Appleton-Century, 1944), 1–11.

287 *Monaghan* **destroys midget submarine:** U.S.S. *Monaghan* (DD-354), December 30, 1941; *Curtiss* (AV-4), December 16, 1941; *Tangier* (AV-8), January 2, 1942; *Medusa* (AR-1), December 16, 1941.

287 *Curtiss* **damaged:** *Curtiss* (AV-4), December 16, 1941. Times are from the report of *Tangier* (AV-8), January 2, 1942.

288 **Destroyer nests and tenders:** *Aylwin* (DD-355), December 12, 1941, and January 2, 1942; *Blue* (DD 387), December 11, 1941; *Dobbin* (AD-3), December 11, 1941; *Hull* (DD-350), December 9, 1941.

288 **US aircraft losses:** Willmott, *Pearl Harbor*, 134, 203.

288 **American service and civilian casualties:** Samuel Eliot Morison, *History of United States Naval Operations in World War II*, vol. 3, *The Rising Sun in the Pacific 1931–April 1942* (Boston: Little, Brown, 1963), 126 [hereafter Morison, *The Rising Sun in the Pacific*]. These figures are from the Navy Bureau of Medicine, Marine Corps Headquarters, the adjutant general of the army and (for civilians) the University of Hawaii War Depository as well as the local press for wounded civilians.

289 **Survival of sunken ships' crews:** Weinberg, *A World at Arms*, 261.

289 **US fleet antiaircraft fire and dead little girl:** CinCPac, Serial 0479, pp. 56–57; *Dale* (DD-353), December 28, 1941; Elizabeth P. McIntosh, "Honolulu after Pearl Harbor: A Report Published for the first time 71 years later," *Washington Post*, 6 December 2012. McIntosh submitted her article a week after the attack to the *Honolulu Star Bulletin*, but the editors declined to print it then due to its graphic content.

289 **Japanese losses, effect of tactical warning to defenders:** Willmott, *Pearl Harbor*, 131, 203; Zimm, *Attack on Pearl Harbor*, 202, ch. 9. Zimm provides a particularly thorough and sobering exploration of the scenario if the defenders enjoyed a tactical warning. Mike Wenger shared his findings on the number of aircraft jettisoned and the two ditched on return of the Japanese planes.

289 **Cult status of midget submarine crews:** Willmott, *Pearl Harbor*, 84.

290 **Assessment of effectiveness of attack and Japanese ordnance:** Zimm, *Attack on Pearl Harbor*, 211–12, 215–16, 375; Willmott, *Pearl Harbor*, 106, 128, 131.

290 **Japanese submarine force achievements and failures:** TROM *I-172*, www .combinedfleet.com/I-70.htm, accessed 22 June 2010; Jurgen Rohwer, *Axis Submarine Successes 1939–1945* (Annapolis, MD: Naval Institute Press, 1983), 278; Zimm, *Attack on Pearl Harbor*, 22. *I-26* sank freighter *Cynthia Olson* at 0808, December 7, simultaneously with the air raid on Pearl Harbor. None of its thirty-five crew and passengers survived.

290 **"Third Strike" thesis:** Willmott, *Pearl Harbor*, ch. 5; Zimm, *Attack on Pearl Harbor*, 289–321; Morison, *The Rising Sun in the Pacific*, 125. Willmott's brilliant analysis first thrashed the myth of the feasibility of a "Third Strike" and sets the record straight on Fuchida's role in propagating the hoax. Further details from Japanese records by Osamu Tagaya indicate that the operational "Val" total was only fifty-one, with no figure available for *Hiryū*. That carrier, like *Sōryū*, launched eighteen "Vals" in the second wave. All the "Val" units from the second wave for which data is available show very low operational totals after recovery (*Akagi* 2 operational of eighteen launched, *Kaga* 6/27, and *Sōryū* 7/18). This suggests only around sixty "Vals" would have been serviceable for a third strike (or 44 percent of those operational at start of day), of which some would have been held back to deal with American carriers.

Osprey Combat Aircraft, 63, Aichi 99 Kanbaku 'Val' Units 1937–42 (Oxford: Osprey Publishing, 2011), 38.

291 **"admitted that they did not expect [the air attack] . . .":** Report by Secretary of the Navy Knox to the President, 10–11, President's Secretary File, Departmental Navy, Box 59, Folder July–Dec 1941, FDRL.

291 **Roberts Commission Report:** PHA, Part 39, 1–21.

292 **Three army and navy investigations after Roberts Commission:** PHA, Part 39.

292 **Dorn Report:** Edwin Dorn, Assistant Secretary of Defense, December 15, 1995, Memorandum for the Secretary of Defense, Subject: Advancement of Rear Admiral Kimmel and Major General Short, www.ibiblio.org/pha/dorn/dornmemo.html, accessed 24 June 2010.

292 **"Navy is Superior . . .":** *New York Times,* 7 December 1941, 1.

292 **"a great majority of people still instinctively refuse to believe":** *New York Times,* 7 December 1941, 3.

293 **"The American people may feel fully confident . . .":** "Roosevelt Appeals Direct to Emperor . . ." and "At the moment this is written . . .": *Washington Post,* 7 December 1941, 1, 20, section B, 7.

293 **Gallup poll results:** Dr. George Gallup, "Polls Showed Majority Favored War," *Washington Post,* 9 December 1941.

293 **"unusually bare" and "the usual lines in front of the big motion picture houses . . .":** *New York Times,* 8 December 1941, "Winter and War Fall on Capital" by Frederick B. Barkley, 16; *Washington Post,* 8 December 1941, 1, 27.

293 **News of attack reaches White House:** Robert E. Sherwood, *Roosevelt and Hopkins: An Intimate History* (New York: Harper & Brothers, 1948), 430–31 [hereafter Sherwood, *Roosevelt and Hopkins*]. This account is based on Hopkins's memorandum about the day's events that night.

294 **"In all my 50 years of public service . . .":** Memorandum of a Conversation, December 7, 1941 (J. W. Ballantine), *FRUS, Japan, 1931–1941,* vol. 2, 786–87; Japanese note: Memorandum Handed by the Japanese Ambassador (Nomura) to the Secretary of State at 2:20 p.m. on December 7, 1941, *FRUS, Japan 1931–1941,* vol. 2, 787–92.

294 **"pale, formal paraphrase of the Secretary's words" and "abusive idiom":** Alistair Cooke, *The American Home Front 1941–1942* (New York: Atlantic Monthly Press, 2006), 9 [hereafter Cooke, *The American Home Front*].

294 **Hull waves out Nomura:** Prange, *At Dawn We Slept,* 554. The "scoundrels and pissants" remark is quoted in Mauch, *Sailor Diplomat,* 214. It should not be assumed this was the only earthy language Hull employed.

294 **Officials assemble in Roosevelt's office after 1500:** Prange, *At Dawn We Slept,* 555–56.

294 **Sun descending, 1420. White House announcement:** *New York Times,* 8 December 1941, 16; *Washington Post,* 8 December 1942, 15. Alistair Cooke confessed he was among many who were not sure exactly where Pearl Harbor was. *The American Home Front,* 6.

294 **"A crowd arose as though from the streets . . .":** "The crowd included men, women and children . . ."; and "a lot of quiet evenly spoken, emphatic and bitter cussing": *Washington Post,* 8 December 1941, 3.

294 **Redskins-Eagles football game, "Japan Kicks Off":** *Washington Post,* 8 December 1941, 24.

295   **Scene at Japanese embassy:** *New York Times*, 8 December 1941, 5, 16.

295   **America First Committee meeting in Pittsburgh:** Cole, *Roosevelt and the Isolationists*, 501–2.

295   **"The White House press room . . .":** Cooke, *The American Home Front*, 7.

295   **Armed guards appear around White House and government buildings:** *Washington Post*, 8 December 1941, 3.

295   **Senators O'Daniels and Connolly:** "Cheering Crowds Line Pennsylvania Avenue," *New York Times*, 8 December 1941, 4.

296   **"opened by telling us that this was the most serious meeting of the Cabinet . . .":** Stimson diary, December 7, 1941; meeting in Red Room: "The U.S. At War: National Ordeal," *Time*, 15 December 1941.

296   **"the president was his usual calm self . . .":** Francis Biddle Papers, 1912–1967, Aliens and Immigration—Correspondence, Container 1, Folder Cabinet Meetings, 1941, FDRL.

296   **"had lost his air of bravado":** Claude R. Wickard Papers, Dept. of Agriculture Files A–D, 1933–45, Container 13, Folder Cabinet Meetings 1941–42, FDRL [hereafter Wickard Account December 7, 1941 cabinet meeting].

296   **"the most important war in 500 years . . ." and "inspired and planned this whole affair":** Wickard Account December 7, 1941 cabinet meeting; Stimson diary, December 7, 1941.

296   **Roosevelt meets with congressional leaders:** Franklin D. Roosevelt, Speech Files, 1391–1401, November 4, 1941 to December 9, 1941, Folder December 7, 1941, Remarks to Cabinet Members and Legislative Leaders, FDRL (also found at PHA, Part 19, 35002-7); Wickard Account December 7, 1941 cabinet meeting.

296   **"Yesterday, December 7, 1941, a date which will live in world history . . .":** Draft no. 1, December 7, 1941, Message to Congress, Franklin D. Roosevelt, Speech Files, 1391–1401, November 4, 1941 to December 9, 1941, Folder December 7, 1941, First Draft of December 8 speech, FDRL.

297   **"Our planes were destroyed on the ground, by God, on the ground":** Alexander Kendrick, *Prime Time: The Life of Edward R. Murrow* (Boston: Little, Brown, 1969), 240; Davis, *FDR: The War President*, 342.

297   **Officers wear uniforms to work:** "Winter and War Fall on Capital" by Frederick B. Barkley, *New York Times*, 8 December 1941, 16.

297   **Front page headlines and photograph:** *Washington Post*, 8 December 1941, 1.

297   **Summary of newspaper headlines and Baldwin analysis:** *New York Times*, 8 December 1941, 5.

297   **"sublime insanity . . .":** "War With Japan," *New York Times*, 8 December 1941, 16.

297   **News reports:** *New York Times*, 8 December 1941, 4, 6, 13; *Washington Post*, 8 December 1941, 1, 6.

298   **"For the Japanese Plan of Attack . . .":** *New York Times*, 8 December 1941, 6.

298   **Presidential motorcade to the capitol; security at capitol:** Cooke, *The American Home Front*, 10–11; "Capital Swings Into War Stride" by James B. Reston, *New York Times*, 9 December 1941, 5 [hereafter Reston, "Capital Swings Into War Stride"]; "The U.S. At War: National Ordeal," *Time*, 15 December 1941.

298   **"looked as serious as I have ever seen him . . .":** Claude R. Wickard Papers, Dept. of Agriculture Files A–D, 1933–45, Container 13, Folder Cabinet Meetings 1941–42, FDRL.

298 **Scene on the House floor, entry of the Senate, Supreme Court, and cabinet:** Cooke, *The American Home Front,* 11–12.

299 **"Mr. Roosevelt gripped the reading clerk's stand . . .":** "The U.S. At War: National Ordeal," *Time,* 15 December 1941.

299 **Roosevelt acknowledges crowd:** Reston, "Capital Swings Into War Stride."

299 **Congressional votes; Rankin votes "no"; president signs declaration of war:** *New York Times,* 9 December 1941, 3; *Washington Post,* 9 December 1941, 6, 9; "The U.S. At War: National Ordeal," *Time,* 15 December 1941.

300 **"Today all of us . . .":** *United States Department of State, Foreign Relations of the United States, 1941, The Far East,* 735.

300 **"But the war came as a great relief . . .":** "The U.S. At War: National Ordeal," *Time,* 15 December 1941.

300 **"You and I know this continuous putting pins in rattlesnakes finally got the country bitten . . .":** Small collections, Elinor & James Hendrick, etc., Herbert Hoover to Hoyt, Morgan H., Folder Hoover, Herbert Pearl Harbor Materials, FDRL.

12: "Issue in Doubt"

301 **Japanese reaction to news of war:** Haruko Taya Cook and Theodore F. Cook, *Japan at War: An Oral History* (New York: New Press, 1992), 71–72; Donald Keene, ed., *So Lovely a Country Will Never Perish* (New York: Columbia University Press, 2010), 11–27.

301 **Hitler's declarations of war:** Weinberg, *A World at Arms,* 261–63; William Remmelink, ed., *War History Series,* vol. 3, *The Invasion of the Dutch East Indies* (Leiden University Press, 2015), 105, 168–69 [hereafter Remmelink, *The Invasion of the Dutch East Indies*]. This volume is a translation under the auspices of the Netherlands Institute of Military History of the relevant volume of the massive Senshi Sosho (*War History Series*) compiled by the War History Office of the National Defense College of Japan. That effort totaled 102 volumes published between 1966 and 1980.

302 **Japanese Southern Operations strategic plan:** Remmelink, *The Invasion of the Dutch East Indies,* 269. By Japanese figures, the NEI produced about eight million tons of oil. Japan needed at the outset of the war five million tons, but domestic Japanese production fell short of even 10 percent of this figure (pp. 11–12).

302 **Japanese forces deployed for Southern Operations:** Remmelink, *The Invasion of the Dutch East Indies,* 4, 6–7, 28, 36, 41–49.

302 **Guam background and defenses:** Morison, *The Rising Sun in the Pacific,* 32–34, 184; Hough, Ludwig, and Shaw, *Pearl Harbor to Guadalcanal,* 7, 75–76.

302 **Battle and surrender of Guam:** Morison, *The Rising Sun in the Pacific,* 184–86; Hough, Ludwig, and Shaw, *Pearl Harbor to Guadalcanal,* 76–78; TROMs Imperial Army Auxiliary Transports *Clyde* and *Cheribon Marus,* cruiser *Aoba,* combinedfleet.com, accessed 30 May 2016.

303 **"[a] horseshoe of bright turquoise, framed in flashing white . . .":** Robert Cressman, *The Magnificent Fight: The Battle for Wake Island* (Annapolis, MD: Naval Institute Press, 1995), 1 [hereafter Cressman, *The Magnificent Fight*].

303 **Wake atoll described:** Gregory J. W. Urwin, *Facing Fearful Odds: The Siege of Wake Island* (Lincoln: University of Nebraska Press, 1997), 7–8 [hereafter Urwin, *Facing Fearful Odds*]; Cressman, *The Magnificent Fight,* 7–8; Lt. Col. Walter L. J. Bayler, *Last Man off Wake Island* (Indianapolis: Bobbs-Merrill, 1943), 62.

303   **Strategic importance of Wake as base; Kimmel's war plans:** Urwin, *Facing Fearful Odds*, 17, 31, 49–50, 64, 123; Cressman, *The Magnificent Fight*, 8, 10–11; John Lundstrom, MS chapter, "The Pacific Fleet's 1941 War Plans and the Attack on Pearl Harbor," 2–9. Lundstrom's work explains Kimmel's plans for Wake and was kindly shared with the author.

303   **Base building on Wake:** Urwin, *Facing Fearful Odds*, 69–72, 80, 89, 94–95, 106, 109.

303   **Defenses of Wake:** Hough, Ludwig, and Shaw, *Pearl Harbor to Guadalcanal*, 96–99, 103; Urwin, *Facing Fearful Odds*, 69–72, 96–99, 103.

303   **Civilian and military personnel on Wake:** Hough, Ludwig, and Shaw, *Pearl Harbor to Guadalcanal*, 104; Urwin, *Facing Fearful Odds*, 160–65, 183, 213, 388, 571–72.

303   **Last minute bolstering of Wake defenses:** Hough, Ludwig, and Shaw, *Pearl Harbor to Guadalcanal*, 102, 104; Urwin, *Facing Fearful Odds*, 173–75, 183.

305   **Wake alert and bugle calls:** Urwin, *Facing Fearful Odds*, 226–29.

305   **Japanese air raid 8 December:** Hough, Ludwig, and Shaw, *Pearl Harbor to Guadalcanal*, 107–9; Cressman, *The Magnificent Fight*, 86–87, 90, appendix 3, 270–74; Urwin, *Facing Fearful Odds*, 242–59, 262.

305   **Japanese raids 9–10 December; contractor volunteers:** Cressman, *The Magnificent Fight*, 107; Urwin, *Facing Fearful Odds*, 279–82, 288, 298–300.

305   **Wake Island Attack Force:** combinedfleet.com/kaigun.htm, TROMs *Yubari*, *Tatsuta*, *Tenryu*, *Hayate*, *Kisaragi*, *Kinryu Maru*, *Kongo Maru*, *RO-62*, and *RO-66*, accessed 8 January 2018; Cressman, *The Magnificent Fight*, 112–14.

305   **Kajioka's intelligence information and plan:** Cressman, *The Magnificent Fight*, 112–14; Urwin, *Facing Fearful Odds*, 312–14.

305   **Kajioka begins attack:** Cressman, *The Magnificent Fight*, 117; Urwin, *Facing Fearful Odds*, 321–22.

305   **Devereux described and his reasoning:** Urwin, *Facing Fearful Odds*, 127–28, 316–17; Cressman, *The Magnificent Fight*, 41.

306   **Marine batteries open fire, *Yubari* escapes damage:** Cressman, *The Magnificent Fight*, 118–19; Urwin, *Facing Fearful Odds*, 322–23; combinedfleet.com/kaigun.htm, *Yubari* TROM, accessed 8 January 2018.

306   **Destruction of *Hayate*:** combinedfleet.com/kaigun.htm, *Hayate* and *Yubari* TROMs, accessed 8 January 2018; Cressman, *The Magnificent Fight*, 121.

306   **Air attacks on retreating Japanese:** combinedfleet.com/kaigun.htm, *Kisaragi* and *Kongo Maru* TROMs, accessed 8 January 2018; Cressman, *The Magnificent Fight*, 123–25; Urwin, *Facing Fearful Odds*, 331–33.

306   **"Kimmel's plan for relieving Wake was sound . . .":** Morison, *The Rising Sun in the Pacific*, 235–36; Lundstrom, *Black Shoe Carrier Admiral*, 45–47.

306   **Kimmel's basic plan for Wake; Fletcher's fuel and speed issues:** Lundstrom, *Black Shoe Carrier Admiral*, 19–27, 30–32; Cressman, *The Magnificent Fight*, 151. Cressman emphasizes that it was Kimmel's high regard for Fletcher, not seniority, that motivated Fletcher's appointment. Lundstrom thoroughly refutes the blame (and scorn) heaped on Fletcher in the influential postwar account by Morison, followed by others. Cressman provides a cogent defense of Kimmel's oiler distribution.

307   **Pye relieves Kimmel; Pye's background:** Lundstrom, *Black Shoe Carrier Admiral*, 28, 32–33; Cressman, *The Magnificent Fight*, 166–69.

307   **Fletcher's orders and progress 22–23 December:** Lundstrom, *Black Shoe Carrier Admiral*, 23–26, 34–35. For a critique of Morison on the controversial refueling

issue, compare Morison, *The Rising Sun in the Pacific*, 243–44, 251–52, with Lundstrom, *Black Shoe Carrier Admiral*, 34–36.

307 **Loss of *RO-66*:** combinedfleet.com/kaigun.htm, *RO-66* TROM, accessed 8 January 2018.

307 **Kajioka's composition and plans for second invasion attempt:** Cressman, *The Magnificent Fight*, 176–77.

307 **Attachments to Kajioka's second invasion force:** Lundstrom, *Black Shoe Carrier Admiral*, 30, 33, 43; Cressman, *The Magnificent Fight*, 157–59.

307 **Strikes by *Sōryū* and *Hiryū*, Pye's reaction:** Cressman, *Magnificent Fight*, 177–79, 183, 184–89.

307 **Action on Wilkes December 23:** Cressman, *The Magnificent Fight*, 195–97, 217–19; Urwin, *Facing Fearful Odds*, 452–75.

308 **Grounding and destruction of *Patrol Boats 32* and *33*; Landings on Wake Island:** Cressman, *The Magnificent Fight*, 193–99, 205; Hough, Ludwig, and Shaw, *Pearl Harbor to Guadalcanal*, 134–37; Urwin, *Facing Fearful Odds*, 454.

308 **Fighting on Wake Island and surrender:** Cressman, *The Magnificent Fight*, 199–207, 210–17, 219–21, 225–37; Urwin, *Facing Fearful Odds*, 477–529

309 **Japanese fatalities for Wake:** figures from Cressman, *The Magnificent Fight*, 90, 107, 121, 125, 128–29, 135, 168–69, 205, 239–40, and combinedfleet.com/kaigun.htm website for relevant ships.

309 **American fatalities:** Urwin, *Facing Fearful Odds*, 540. American dead included just thirteen members of 1st Marine Defense Battalion, and three sailors but five officers and twenty-eight enlisted men of VMF-211. Civilian dead numbered sixty-five contractors and ten Guamains employed by Pan Am.

309 **Pye's order to retire; "dismay and indignation"; reaction in Task Force 14:** Morison, *The Rising Sun in the Pacific*, 252; Lundstrom, *Black Shoe Carrier Admiral*, 37–41; Cressman, *The Magnificent Fight*, 207–10, 221–24. For a thorough evisceration of Morison's factually challenged and often vicious false charges against Fletcher, see Lundstrom, 534n47.

309 **Pye's decision and Fletcher's obedience were correct:** Lundstrom, *Black Shoe Carrier Admiral*, 42–47.

309 **Kajioka foils massacre:** Urwin, *Facing Fearful Odds*, 534–55.

309 **Evacuation of prisoners, fate of contractors left on Wake:** Urwin, *Facing Fearful Odds*, 542–53; Cressman, *The Magnificent Fight*, 247–48, 254. For an account both gripping in detail and nuanced in its analysis of the POW experience of the Wake defenders, see Gregory J. W. Urwin, *Victory in Defeat: Wake Island Defenders in Captivity, 1941–1945* (Annapolis, MD: Naval Institute Press, 2010).

310 **Death of Kajioka:** combinedfleet.com/kaigun.htm, TROMs, *Hirado*, accessed 8 January 2018.

310 **Hong Kong background:** Maj. Gen. S. Woodburn Kirby, *History of the Second World War, United Kingdom Military Series, The War Against Japan*: vol. 1, *The Loss of Singapore* (Uckfield, UK: Naval & Military Press, Ltd., reprint 2004), 107–8 [hereafter, Kirby, *The Loss of Singapore*].

310 **Hong Kong economics and social structure:** Snow, *Hong Kong*, 1–4, 18–21, 70.

310 **Hong Kong's role in intrigue and supplies for the Nationalists:** Snow, *Hong Kong*, 27, 34–35; Kwong Chi Man and Tsoi Yiu Lun, *Eastern Fortress: A Military History of Hong Kong, 1840–1970* (Hong Kong: Hong Kong University Press, 2014), 146–54

[hereafter Man and Lun, *Eastern Fortress*]. *Eastern Fortress* is a particularly admirable study of Hong Kong military history, set very intelligently in broader political, economic, and social context.

311 **Hong Kong geography in 1941:** Kirby, *The Loss of Singapore*, 107–8.

311 **Hong Kong defenses and British appreciation:** Maj. Gen. C. M. Maltby, M.C., Operations in Hong Kong, 8th to 25th December 1941, Supplement to the *London Gazette*, 27 January 1948, appendix A War Narrative, Part I, Own forces—before outbreak of war with Japan, para. 1 [hereafter Maltby Dispatch]; Man and Lun, *Eastern Fortress*, ch. 5, 6, and 7; Kirby, *The Loss of Singapore*, 17–18, 109–10.

311 **Canadian reinforcements:** Christopher M. Bell, "Our Most Exposed Outpost: Hong Kong and British Far Eastern Strategy, 1921–1941," *Journal of Military History* 60, no. 1 (January 1996): 61–88; Kirby, *The Loss of Singapore*, 81–82; Snow, *Hong Kong*, 40–41; MacKenzie King diary 6 Nov 41 ("a break in Chinese resistance will probably mean . . ."), www.bac-lac.gc.ca/eng/discover/politics-government/primeministers/william-lyon-mackenzie-king, accessed 31 July 2016; Marci, *Clash of Armies*, 217, 270, 338.

311 **Cloud of misplaced confidence, limited mobilization, refusal to arm Chinese, and lax security measures:** Snow, *Hong Kong*, 41, 47–48; Kirby, *The Loss of Singapore*, 110–12. Man and Lun, *Eastern Fortress*, 154–59, argues that Hong Kong was "perhaps" better prepared than other British and Allied possessions.

312 **Outbreak of war:** Maltby Dispatch, appendix A, Part I, para. 1, Part III, para. 14–16; Kirby, *The Loss of Singapore*, 117–18.

312 **Japanese forces and "Gindrinker's Line":** Man and Lun, *Eastern Fortress*, 174–75; Kirby, *The Loss of Singapore*, 119–20; Snow, *Hong Kong*, 53; Remmelink, *The Invasion of the Dutch East Indies*, 23.

312 **Fall of Shing Mun Redoubt:** Man and Lun, *Eastern Fortress*, 175–78; Kirby, *The Loss of Singapore*, 121–22; Maltby Dispatch, appendix A, Part III, para. 20; John Cartwright, "The Defense of Hong Kong, Shing Mun Redoubt and the Gin Drinker's Line," http://hksw.org/Shing%20Mun.htm, accessed 16 September 2013.

312 **Withdrawal from mainland:** Maltby Dispatch, appendix A, Part III, para. 29–36; Man and Lun, *Eastern Fortress*, 178–82; Kirby, *The Loss of Singapore*, 124–25.

312 **Surrender demands, bombardment and Japanese espionage and subversion campaign; Adm. Chak:** Man and Lun, *Eastern Fortress*, 182–84, 188–90, 220–21; Kirby, *The Loss of Singapore*, 127, 129; Maltby Dispatch, appendix A, Part III, para. 37, 40–41, 44, 50–51, 54, 57, 60, 62; Snow, *Hong Kong*, 36–39; Kotani, *Japanese Intelligence in World War II*, 48–50. The Japanese leveraged their lavish investment in subversion by counterfeiting and drug sales.

313 **Maltby's situation, Chinese relief efforts, and Japanese deployments:** Kirby, *The Loss of Singapore*, 120, 127–29; Snow, *Hong Kong*, 74–75; Romanus and Sunderland, *Stilwell's Mission to China*, 53. Man and Lun, *Eastern Fortress*, 213, notes that Admiral Chak did give faked reports on the Chinese relief effort on 22 December as he had not heard from Yu since 20 December. Major blame for the failed Chinese relief effort lies with the British, who turned down Chiang's initial offer of help and then issued affirmations that Hong Kong would hold out into January, which proved entirely too optimistic. I am indebted to Dr. Hans van de Ven for explaining the situation of General Yu (email to author, 2016).

313 **Japanese landing:** Man and Lun, *Eastern Fortress*, 191–97; Kirby, *The Loss of Singapore*, 131; Snow, *Hong Kong*, 39; Maltby Dispatch, appendix A, Part III, para. 63, appendix B. The 5/7th Rajputs sustained 100 percent casualties among its seventeen officers during the battle, with only seven wounded surviving. Overall, 212 of 538 officers (39.5 percent) in the garrison became casualties. For those seeking more description of the military actions on Hong Kong Island, Man and Lun provide meticulous tactical detail on all the battles.

314 **Defense of rest of Hong Kong Island:** Man and Lun, *Eastern Fortress*, 197–218; Kirby, *The Loss of Singapore*, 132–35, 140–41; Maltby Dispatch, appendix A, Part III, para. 63–150, particularly 63(y).

314 **Defensive posts overrun at landing area, "Hugesiliers":** Man and Lun, *Eastern Fortress*, 196–97; Kirby, *The Loss of Singapore*, 133; Maltby Dispatch, appendix A, Part III, para. 63(i); Snow, *Hong Kong*, 67.

314 **Lack of water, fires set by shells and bombs, massacre of prisoners, and slaughter and rape at auxiliary hospital:** Man and Lun, *Eastern Fortress*, 192, 214, 218; Snow, *Hong Kong*, 65, 79–80; "A Nursing Sisters Story, in Memory of Lieutenant Kay Christie," www.hkvca.ca/historical/accounts/christie.htm, accessed 5 October 2009.

314 **Surrender of Hong Kong:** Kirby, *The Loss of Singapore*, 141–45; Maltby Dispatch, appendix A, Part III, para. 116, 150; Snow, *Hong Kong*, 72.

314 **London shocked, overall assessment:** Kirby, *The Loss of Singapore*, 145–49; Japanese "Fifth Column" activity: a prehostilities estimate by the army and navy sections of Imperial General Headquarters was that taking Hong Kong would require four weeks. Remmelink, *The Invasion of the Dutch East Indies*, 35. The thoughtful assessment in Man and Lun, *Eastern Fortress*, 222–24, notes that Japanese intelligence prior to the battle was actually deficient compared to the length of time the Japanese had to prepare. This especially showed up in the careful plan for assaulting the mainland compared to the crude scheme for attacking Hong Kong Island. They further note the novice Canadians inflicted significantly more casualties on the Japanese than might have been expected on several occasions.

315 **Casualties and assessment of battle:** Kirby, *The Loss of Singapore*, 149–51; Man and Lun, *Eastern Fortress*, 222–24.

315 **Rampages by Triads and Japanese, Japanese intramural struggles finally settled for occupation regime:** Snow, *Hong Kong*, 80–90.

315 **Changsha:** This account is based upon *Japanese Monograph no. 71, Army Operations in China, December 1941 to December 1943*, particularly 56–58, 63–71, 76, Maps 6 and 7 ibiblio.org/hyperwar/Japan/Monos/pdfs/JM-71/JM-71.pdf, accessed 1 June 2016, much supplemented with communications with Jon Parshall and Lu Yu, who offered information from important online and published sources as well as valuable overall insight. Finally, key insight was provided by Dr. Edward Drea, whose command of the Imperial Army's operations is exemplary. The final interpretation, however, is the author's.

317 **China declares war on Japan, Germany, and Italy; Soviets do not join war against Japan; Japan does not declare war on China:** "Declaration of War on Japan," and "Declaration of War on Germany and Italy," *FRUS, 1941, The Far East*, vol. 5, 550–51; The Chargé in the Soviet Union (Thurston) to the Secretary of State December 17, 1941, *FRUS, 1941, The Far East*, 755–56 ("superlatively realistic"); Yuzhen Li, "Chi-

ang Kai-shek and Joseph Stalin during World War II," 152–55, and Akio Tsuchida, "Declaring War as an Issue in Chinese Wartime Diplomacy," 124–26, both in Hans van de Ven, Diana Lary, and Stephan R. MacKinnon, *Negotiating China's Destiny in World War II* (Stanford, CA: Stanford University Press, 2015), 153–54. On December 24, Churchill commented during a meeting in Washington that Stalin reported that the Soviet Union might join the war against Japan in the spring. This, of course, did not happen. Meeting of United States and British Chiefs of Staff, December 24, 1941, United States Department of State, *Foreign Relations of the United States, the Conferences at Washington, 1941–1942, and Casablanca, 1943 (1941–1943)*, 82–90 [hereafter *FRUS, Conferences at Washington and Casablanca (1941–1943)*].

317 **"in light of reality and new facts"**: Prime Minister to President Roosevelt, December 9, 1941, *FRUS, Conferences at Washington and Casablanca (1941–1943)*, 5.

317 **"a submarine masquerading as a battleship"**: Max Beaverbrook quoted in Max Hastings, *Winston's War: Churchill 1940–1945* (New York: Alfred A. Knopf, 2010), 184.

317 **Churchill's strategic overview paper:** Memorandum by the Prime Minister, December 16–20, 1941, *FRUS, Conferences at Washington and Casablanca (1941–1943)*, 21–37. This same source shows entries during the conference, too numerous to itemize, on the subject of Gymnast (later confined to a British attack alone) and later Super Gymnast (a joint US-British assault).

318 **Losses of British and American warships:** David Brown, *Warship Losses of World War II* (New York: Arms and Armour, 1990), 52–55.

318 **Churchill's background in military matters:** Roberts, *Walking With Destiny*, 28–35, 47–48, 52–53, 57–58, 111, 116, 128, 160, 170–72, 187, 196–204, 238–41, 273–74, 306, 323, 400–401, 449–50, 357, 413–14, 418, 442, 444, 518, 538–39.

318, 320 **Churchill's arrival in Washington; relations with Eleanor Roosevelt; encampment at the White House**: Winston S. Churchill, *The Second World War*, vol. 3, *The Grand Alliance* (Boston: Houghton Mifflin, 1950), 558 ("There was the President. . ."); Martin Gilbert, *The Road to Victory, 1941–1945* (Boston: Houghton Mifflin, 1986), 23–24, 27, 36 [hereafter Gilbert, *The Road to Victory*]; David Bercuson and Holger Herwig, *One Christmas in Washington: Roosevelt and Churchill Forge the Grand Alliance* (Woodstock and New York: Overlook Press, 2006), 125–27, 129–30 [hereafter Bercuson and Herwig, *One Christmas in Washington*].

319 **Roosevelt's personal experience in military affairs:** Eric Larrabee, *Commander in Chief: Franklin Delano Roosevelt, His Lieutenants & Their War* (New York: Harper & Row, 1987), 40–95, 210–11, 218–23, 642 [hereafter Larrabee, *Commander in Chief*]; Smith, *FDR*, 23, 29–35, 96–138, 339, 546. Larrabee's account remains a classic. Roosevelt displayed a strong advocacy for aircraft production, but he did not know the technical details of aviation the way he knew nautical technology. He was also still finding his way on the army at this point.

319 **Churchill as executive:** Roberts, *Walking With Destiny*, 229, 263–64, 512, 514–25, 608, 662, 664, 689–90.

319 **Roosevelt as executive:** Klein, *A Call to Arms*, 555–56.

319 **Roosevelt's love of mystery and surprise; as "juggler"; Stimson quote; Churchill's opposite qualities:** Samuel I. Rosenman, *Working with Roosevelt* (New York: Harper and Brothers, 1952), 440–42; Warren Kimball, *The Juggler: Franklin Roosevelt as Wartime Statesman* (Princeton, NJ: Princeton University Press, 1991), 7 [hereafter Kimball, *The Juggler*]: Gunther, *Roosevelt in Retrospect*, 50–53; Stimson diary, Octo-

ber 25, 1940; Roberts, *Walking With Destiny*, 229, 523–25. Just about every Roosevelt scholar learns all too quickly that clear-cut, reliable information on Roosevelt's thinking at any juncture can be very hard to find.

319 **Churchill and Roosevelt racial views:** Roberts, *Walking With Destiny*, 39, 43, 52–53, 143, 351, 415, 976; Christopher Thorne, *Allies of a Kind: The United States, Britain, and the War Against Japan, 1941–1945* (Oxford: Oxford University Press, 1978), 5–7, 8–9, 158–59, 167–68n68, 355–57 [hereafter Thorne, *Allies of a Kind*].

320 **Churchill's liberality and the "Map Room":** Bercuson and Herwig, *One Christmas in Washington*, 129–32; Davis, *FDR: The War President*, 366.

321 **Churchill's rhetorical flourishes and attack of angina pectoris:** Gilbert, *The Road to Victory*, 29, 31–32.

321 **Doubts with American and British military staffs:** Mark Stoler, *Allies and Adversaries: The Joint Chiefs of Staff, the Grand Alliance, and U.S. Strategy in World War II* (Chapel Hill and London: University of North Carolina Press, 2000), 37–38, 45–46, 67–70 [hereafter Stoler, *Allies and Adversaries*]; Bercuson and Herwig, *One Christmas in Washington*, 137.

321 **First session of Roosevelt and Churchill and their military advisers:** Bercuson and Herwig, *One Christmas in Washington*, 142; Memorandum of Lieutenant General Arnold, December 23, 1941, White House Conference, *FRUS, Conferences at Washington and Casablanca (1941–1943)*, 74–80.

322 **Eruption over Roosevelt's conversation with Churchill evening of December 24:** Secretary of the British Chiefs of Staff (Hollis) to the Secretary, War Department General Staff (Smith), December 24, 1941, *FRUS, Conferences at Washington and Casablanca (1941–1943)*, 267; Memorandum of Conversations, by Mr. Stewart of the Division of European Affairs, January 12, 1942, *FRUS, Conferences at Washington and Casablanca (1941–1943)*, 321–25; Stimson diary, December 25, 1941.

322 **Hopkins role and background:** The British Minister of Supply (Beaverbrook) to the President's Special Assistant (Hopkins), January 11, 1942, *FRUS, Conferences at Washington and Casablanca (1941–1943)*, 135; Kimball, *The Juggler*, 9, 92–93; Warren F. Kimball, *Forged in War: Roosevelt, Churchill, and the Second World War* (New York: William Morrow, 1997), 77; Bercuson and Herwig, *One Christmas in Washington*, 134–36; Memorandum, Harry Hopkins to the President, 17 Dec 1941, President's Secretary File, Germany: May 1941–1944 thru Marshall, George C: 1941–4/14/42, Box 3, Folder Safe File Hopkins, Harry, FDRL. Roosevelt had met Churchill during World War I, but to Churchill's dismay had completely forgotten the occasion.

323 **Success and importance of Arcadia:** Mark A. Stoler, *Allies in War: Britain and America Against the Axis Powers* (New York: Hodder Education, 2005), 37 [hereafter Stoler, *Allies in War*]; United Nations Declaration, Signed January 1, 1942, *FRUS, 1942, General: The British Commonwealth; the Far East*, 25–26. One conspicuous omission from the signatory governments was France.

323 **Unity of command, Combined Chiefs of Staff, Munitions Assignment Board and other joint bodies established:** Meeting of the United States and British Chiefs of Staff, January 14, 1942, *FRUS, Conferences at Washington and Casablanca (1941–1943)*; Meeting of President Roosevelt, Mr. Hopkins and General Marshall, January 14, 1942, *FRUS, Conferences at Washington and Casablanca (1941–1943)*, 202–3; Stoler, *Allies in War*, 37–39, 41–45; Gilbert, *Road to Victory*, 31–33; Robert Sherwood,

Roosevelt and Hopkins: An Intimate History (New York: Harper & Brothers, 1948), 455–57, 471–72 [hereafter Sherwood, *Roosevelt and Hopkins*].

324   **Beaverbrook advocates steep rises in production goals; FDR orders major production goal increases:** The British Minister of Supply (Beaverbrook) to President Roosevelt, December 27, 1941, *FRUS, Conferences at Washington and Casablanca (1941–1943)*, 328–30; The President to the Secretary of War (Stimson), January 3, 1942, *FRUS, Conferences at Washington and Casablanca (1941–1943)*, 342–43; The President to the Chairman of the United States Maritime Commission (Land), January 3, 1942, *FRUS, Conferences at Washington and Casablanca (1941–1943)*, 343–44. Actual 1942 aircraft production would be 47,826 and in 1943 85,898. Likewise figures for tanks were 24,997 and 29,497. Klein, *A Call to Arms*, 515. The reduction in tank production stemmed from a presidential decision in August 1942 to cut back sharply on munitions for the army in favor of air and sea power. Phillips Payson O'Brien, *How the War Was Won: Air-Sea Power and Allied Victory in World War II* (Cambridge: Cambridge University Press, 2015), 243–44.

324   **"The President made it perfectly clear . . .":** Memorandum by the President's Special Assistant (Hopkins), January 15, 1942, *FRUS, Conferences at Washington and Casablanca (1941–1943)*, 209.

325   **Chiang supreme commander China Theater:** President Roosevelt to the President of the Chinese Executive Yuan (Chiang), December 29, 1941, *FRUS, 1941, The Far East*, 763; Generalissimo Chiang Kai-shek to President Roosevelt [received January 2, 1942], *FRUS, 1942, China*, 1–2 [hereafter *FRUS, 1942, China*].

325   **Chiang offers troops for defense of Burma:** Hsi-sheng Ch'i, *The Much Troubled Alliance: US-China Military Cooperation During the Pacific War, 1941–1945* (Hackensack, NJ: World Scientific, 2016), 30–31; Secretary of War to President, Magruder message, 26 December 1941, President's Secretary File, Box 2, Australia through Germany, September 1939–1941, FDRL.

325   **Chiang's reaction to seizure of Lend Lease supplies:** Ch'i, *The Much Troubled Alliance*, 25–30; The Coordinator of Information (Donovan) to President Roosevelt, January 9, 1942, with attached message of January 7, 1942, from Chiang, *FRUS, 1942, China*, 2–3.

325   **Chiang's thoughts on American entry and strategic priority:** Ch'i, *The Much Troubled Alliance*, 12–13.

325   **China's status in United Nations Proclamation; Chiang's view of China's status:** Ch'i, *The Much Troubled Alliance*, 13–19.

326   **Chiang seeks a seat for China at Combined Chiefs of Staff and on Munitions Assignment Board:** Generalissimo Chiang Kai-shek to the Chinese Minister of Foreign Affairs (Soong), April 19, 1942, *FRUS, 1942, China*, 33–34.

326   **Chiang pursues Chinese representation on Combined Chiefs of Staff and Munitions Assignment Board and rejection:** Generalissimo Chiang to President Roosevelt, December 24, 1941, *FRUS, Conferences at Washington and Casablanca (1941–1943)*, 268–69; Ch'i, *The Much Troubled Alliance*, 11, 17–19. On December 29, Hopkins related to Marshall that Roosevelt "desired Chiang's participation with the senior members of the Allied Nations in conversations relating to all theaters." Meeting of Secretary Stimson with Mr. Hopkins and General Marshall, December 29, 1941, *FRUS, Conferences at Washington and Casablanca (1941–1943)*, 134.

326 **Churchill's and high level British policymakers' attitudes toward China:** Throne, *Allies of a Kind*, 6, 184–97. Although it is a bleak trek to review British racist attitudes toward the Chinese people, as Throne points out the British were not wholly indifferent to China's suffering and contributions.

326 **China's insecure codes:** see the HW 1/38 (1 September 1941) to HW 1/330 (21 December 1941) range, TNA; Meeting of the United States and British Chiefs of Staff, January 10, 1942, *FRUS, Conferences at Washington and Casablanca (1941–1943)*, 171–74.

327 **Japanese success against Chinese diplomatic and military codes:** Kotani, *Japanese Intelligence in World War II*, 19–21.

327 **British reticence to United States about breaking German codes:** Bradley F. Smith, *The Ultra-Magic Deals and the Most Secret Special Relationship 1940–1946* (Novato, CA: Presidio, 1994), 72, 90, 120–22. Smith goes on later to note that by 1944 the United States and United Kingdom were both reading Chinese cipher systems, and they obtained from Japanese intercepts a solid basis to doubt the security of Chinese secret communications from Axis penetration. A parallel problem arose regarding the security of Free French secret communications against Axis penetration (188–92).

327 **Concern over China and plans to assist:** Meeting of the United States and British Chiefs of Staff, January 10, 1942, *FRUS, Conferences at Washington and Casablanca (1941–1943)*, 171–74; "Immediate Assistance to China, January 10, 1942," *FRUS, Conferences at Washington and Casablanca (1941–1943)*, 319–21.

327 **Chiang rejects Magruder appointment; Magruder cables:** Ch'i, *The Much Troubled Alliance*, 38 41; The Military Mission in China to the War Department, January 5, 1942, *FRUS, 1942, China*, 769–71; The Military Mission in China to the War Department, February 10, 1942, *FRUS, 1942, China*, 13–16.

327 **"fatally defective" and "we will be well on our way . . .":** The Office of the Chief of Naval Operations to the Department of State, April 16, 1942, *FRUS 1942, China*, 31.

328 **"The Chinese have fought for four and one-half years . . .":** Memorandum by the Chief of the Division of Far Eastern Affairs (Hamilton), February 16, 1942, *FRUS, 1942, China*, 18–19.

328 **"most of the military experts . . .":** Memorandum by the Adviser on Political Relations (Hornbeck) to the Under Secretary of State (Welles), February 16, 1942, *FRUS, 1942, China*, 20–21. Similar notes were sounded by Gauss, the ambassador in China. The Ambassador in China (Gauss) to the Secretary of State, February 21, 1942, *FRUS, 1942, China*, 24–25.

328 **Summary of situation for Chiang and Nationalists in 1937:** Ch'i, *The Much Troubled Alliance*, xii–xiii. Ch'i provides a concise survey of China's situation circa December 1941–January 1942.

328 **Effects of ejection of Nationalists from power base:** Ch'i, *The Much Troubled Alliance*, xiii–xv.

329 **Wartime tax loss and Nationalist adjustments to increase revenue:** van de Ven, *War and Nationalism in China*, 258–60.

329 **China's economic woes:** Ch'i, *The Much Troubled Alliance*, xv–xvi.

329 **Inflation in China:** The Ambassador in China (Gauss) to the Secretary of State, March 6, 1942, *FRUS, 1942, China*, 25–26, describes currency inflation as then "a major concern."

329   **Chiang and Nationalists deal with agricultural production through 1941:** van de Ven, *War and Nationalism in China*, 258–62.

329   **Deterioration of Chinese armies, particularly Central Army units:** Ch'i, *The Much Troubled Alliance*, xvi–xxi.

13: "It Was Like Being Lost in Fog"

332   **Britain's post–World War I position and strategic priorities:** Raymond Callahan, *The Worst Disaster: The Fall of Singapore* (Cranbury, NJ: Associated University Presses, 1977), 22–23 [hereafter Callahan, *The Worst Disaster*]; Brian P. Farrell, *The Defense and Fall of Singapore 1940–1942* (Stroud, UK: Tempus, 2006), 13, 24–25 [hereafter Farrell, *The Defense and Fall of Singapore*]; Christopher Bayly and Tim Harper, *Forgotten Armies: The Fall of British Asia, 1941–1945* (Cambridge, MA.: Belknap Press of Harvard University Press, 2004), 106 [hereafter: Bayly and Harper, *Forgotten Armies*].

332   **Singapore as "strategic delusion":** Farrell, *The Defense and Fall of Singapore*, 24–26. Callahan gives the number of necessary capital ships to take on Japan as nine. *The Worst Disaster*, 34.

332   **United States as the *deus ex machina* for the Singapore strategy:** Farrell, *The Defense and Fall of Singapore*, 34–35.

332   **Air power substitute for capital ships; disastrous complication:** Callahan, *The Worst Disaster*, 35–36, 50–51.

333   **Brooke-Popham:** Callahan, *The Worst Disaster*, 66–69, 112.

333   **Mediterranean strategy rationale:** Callahan, *The Worst Disaster*, 43–44, 58–59, 271; Farrell, *The Defense and Fall of Singapore*, 51–52, 72. Farrell (62) flatly says: "The fall of France, more than any other single event, compromised Singapore." For a deeply researched and revisionist account of Royal Navy planning as to Far East contingencies, see Andrew Boyd, *The Royal Navy in Eastern Waters: Linchpin of Victory 1935–1942* (Barnsley, UK: Seaforth Publishing, 2017) [hereafter Boyd, *The Royal Navy in Far Eastern Waters*].

333   **Churchill's candor with Australia and New Zealand:** Callahan, *The Worst Disaster*, 24–25, 32–33, 53, 59–60, 78, 83–85, 102–6, 165–66; Alan Warren, *Britain's Greatest Defeat: Singapore 1942* (London: Hambledon and London, 2002), 289–90 [hereafter Warren, *Britain's Greatest Defeat*]. Farrell argues that the Australians engaged in self-deception. *The Defense and Fall of Singapore*, 49. Along the same lines is Augustine Meaher IV, *The Road to Singapore: The Myth of British Betrayal* (Melbourne: Australian Scholarly Publishing, 2010). David Horner illustrated how some Australian officials, notably Frederick Shedden, the senior civil servant in the defense structure, although initially inclined to follow British advice, in 1941 would warn repeatedly of the vulnerability of Singapore and urge remedies. *Defense Supremo: Sir Frederick Shedden and the Making of Australian Defense Policy* (St. Leonards, Australia: Allen & Unwin, 2000), 70–71, 84–89, 96–99, 104–6.

333   **Churchill's 28 April 1941 fiat:** Callahan, *The Worst Disaster*, 86–92; Farrell, *The Defense and Fall of Singapore*, 89–91.

334   **British planners recognize huge importance of Far Eastern reaches of Empire:** Boyd, *The Royal Navy in Far Eastern Waters*, 312–16, 165–67, 400.

334   **"As soon as we left the road and entered the trees it was like being lost in fog . . .":**

"Singapore Story" by R. F. Oakes, p. 10, MSS 0776 Oakes, Roland Frank Lieutenant Colonel, Australian War Memorial [hereafter Oakes, "Singapore Story"].

334 **Malaya land area and 1941 population:** Kirby, *The Loss of Singapore*, 153–56; "dense jungle and graceful feathery clumps of bamboo": Oakes, "Singapore Story," 10.

334 **Malayan dwellings and villages:** "Boong House" by WC Bayliss, MSS 0921 Australian War Memorial.

335 **Malaya's contributions to Imperial Defense and economic importance:** Callahan, *The Worst Disaster*, 29–30, 116; Kirby, *The Loss of Singapore*, appendix 1. London ordered Malaya to double the 1939 output of tin and rubber in 1941.

335 **Sir Shenton Thomas:** Callahan, *The Worst Disaster*, 63; Bayly and Harper, *Forgotten Armies*, 107.

335 **London views on capital ship deployments to Far East 1939 to mid-1941:** Callahan, *The Worst Disaster*, 26, 144–45; Boyd, *The Royal Navy in Far Eastern Waters*, 67, 82–115, 271–84. For the change of strategy to operations forward of Singapore, Boyd, *The Royal Navy in Far Eastern Waters*, 284–87.

335 **"small but very powerful and fast force":** Callahan, *The Worst Disaster*, 144–45.

335 **Formation of "Force Z":** Boyd, *The Royal Navy in Far Eastern Waters*, 277, 279–80, 284–87, 289–93, 295–97. Churchill was made the culprit for the loss of "Force Z" from the official Royal Navy history, Captain S. W. Roskill, *The War at Sea*, vol. 1: *The Defensive* I (London: Her Majesty's Stationery Office, 1954), 555–56. For an overall excellent account of "Force Z," though it places heavy responsibility on Churchill, see Arthur Nicholson, *Hostages to Fortune: Winston Churchill and the Loss of the Prince of Wales and Repulse* (Stroud, UK: Sutton Publishing, 2005) [hereafter Nicholson, *Hostages to Fortune*].

336 **Phillips described:** Stephen Martin, *Fighting Admirals: British Admirals of the Second World War* (Annapolis, MD: Naval Institute Press, 1991), 115 [hereafter Martin, *Fighting Admirals*]; Roberts, *Walking With Destiny*, 600, 695; Nicolson, *Hostages to Fortune*, 24–27.

336 **Carrier support for "Force Z":** Boyd, *The Royal Navy in Far Eastern Waters*, 301–2, 331; Nicholson, *Hostages to Fortune*, 41–44.

336 **Arrival of Force Z:** diary of Megan Spooner, December 2, 1941, Liddell Hart Centre [hereafter Spooner diary]; Farrell, *The Defense and Fall of Singapore*, 105.

336 **Japanese air strength:** figures adopted from Christopher Shores and Brian Cull with Yasuho Izawa, *Bloody Shambles*, vol. 1, *The Drift to War to the Fall of Singapore* (London: Grub Street, 1992), 52–54 [hereafter Shores, Cull, and Izawa, *Bloody Shambles*, vol. 1]. The Imperial Army's Third Air Wing deployed 191 fighters (123 Ki-27 "Nates," 59 Ki-43 "Oscars," 9 Ki-44 "Tojos"), 239 heavy and light bombers (124 Ki-21 "Sallys," 91 Ki-48 "Lillys," and 24 Ki-30 "Anns"), and 89 army cooperation and reconnaissance planes (Ki-15 "Babs," Ki-46 "Dinahs," Ki-51 "Ednas"). The Imperial Navy's Twenty-Second Air Flotilla in Indochina fielded another 142 aircraft, including 37 fighters (25 A6M "Zeros," 12 A5M "Claudes") and 99 bombers (72 G3M "Nells" and 27 G4M "Bettys"), plus 6 reconnaissance planes (C5M "Babs"). Japanese planners intended that the Imperial Army's Fifth Air Division, with yet another 189 aircraft, would join this armada after operations in the Philippines.

336 **August 1940 aircraft strength projection by Chiefs of Staff and Brooke-Popham estimates:** Callahan, *The Worst Disaster*, 49–50, 69–70, citing Kirby, *Singapore the Chain of Disaster*, 50, 58–60.

336 **1941 British Chiefs of Staff review of reinforcements for Singapore:** Callahan, *The Worst Disaster*, 143–49; Farrell, *The Defense and Fall of Singapore*, 91.

337 **British strength in Middle East in 1941:** Callahan, *The Worst Disaster*, 150–52. Between January and October 1941, Britain shipped 1,996 aircraft to the Middle East, including 857 Hurricanes.

337 **Aircraft to Soviet Union:** Callahan, *The Worst Disaster*, 95, 153–54.

337 **Comparative speed performance of opposing fighters over Malaya:** Rene J. Francillon, *Japanese Aircraft of the Pacific War* (Annapolis, MD: Naval Institute Press, 1979), 196–203, 206–14, 362–77; Christopher Shores, *Aircraft in Profile*, vol. 10 (Windsor, UK, 1971), 134–56. Although Shores gives the top speed of the Buffalo as 323 mph, Dan Ford, who cites actual testing of the models used in Malaya, placed their best speed at 313 mph. See Ford, *The Sorry Saga of the Brewster Buffalo: A 'Flying Coffin' to the Marines, but a 'Sky Pearl' to the Finns* (Warbird Books, 2010) [hereafter Ford, *The Sorry Saga of the Brewster Buffalo*], and "Annals of the Brewster Buffalo," warbirdforum.com/buff, accessed 15 December 2012. Peter Preston-Hough, *Commanding Far Eastern Skies: A Critical Analysis of the Royal Air Force air superiority campaign in India, Burma and Malaya 1941–1945* (Helion, 2015), 142–44 [hereafter Preston-Hough, *Commanding Far Eastern Skies*], cites a July 1941 test report placing Buffalo's top speed at only 270 mph. He also quotes pilot reports complaining of the Buffalo's lack of speed even when pursuing bombers. Although the Buffalo figures prominently in many discussions of "Worst Aircraft of World War II," its phenomenal record with Finland must be recognized. Finnish Buffalo pilots from June 1941 to May 1944 reportedly shot down 459 Soviet aircraft while losing only 15 Buffaloes in air combat, four in accidents and two in air raids. Twelve Finnish pilots were killed in Buffaloes. Frigid Finnish temperatures prevented many engine defects. Kari Stenman and Andrew Thomas, *Osprey Aircraft of the Aces 91: Brewster F2A Buffalo Aces of World War II* (Oxford: Osprey Publishing, 2010), 41.

337 **Comparison of Buffalo to Japanese fighters and technical defects of Buffalo:** Ford, *The Sorry Saga of the Brewster Buffalo* and "Annals of the Brewster Buffalo"; Shores, Cull, and Izawa, *Bloody Shambles*, vol. 1, 85, 89.

337 **Buffalo technical and manufacturing defects; Japanese and RAF pilot experience levels:** Dan Ford, "Annals of the Brewster Buffalo"; Shores, Cull, and Izawa, *Bloody Shambles*, vol. 1, 64–65; Farrell, *The Defense and Fall of Singapore*, 134–35. Callahan points out the RAF dispatched a mere eight experienced fighter pilots to Malaya in January 1941. *The Worst Disaster*, 120–21.

338 **Radar and radio shortcomings:** Preston-Hough, *Commanding Far Eastern Skies*, 31–49; Callahan, *The Worst Disaster*, 123.

338 **RAF attack strength:** Shores, Cull, and Izawa, *Bloody Shambles*, vol. 1, 57; Farrell, *The Defense and Fall of Singapore*, 134–35.

338 **Army mobilization plans for British Empire:** Callahan, *The Worst Disaster*, 30.

338 **Expansion of Indian Army; enlisted and officer recruits; British presence in Indian Army ranks:** Marston, *Phoenix from the Ashes*, 13, 25, 33n43; Srinath Raghavan, *India's War: World War II and the Making of Modern South Asia* (New York: Basic Books, 2016), 33–38, 66–67, 70 [hereafter Raghavan, *India's War*]; Callahan, *The Worst Disaster*, 57. Raghavan notes strength of Indian Army in October 1939 was 194,373 and the army would grow by a factor of ten during the war (64) and a factor of 4.5 by December 1941 alone (68).

339 **Officers for Indian Army:** Marston, *Phoenix from the Ashes*, 15–16.

339 **Post–World War I reforms of Indian Army:** Marston, *Phoenix from the Ashes*, 15–20, 23.

339 **Indian Army expansion, 1940–41:** Marston, *Phoenix from the Ashes*, 42–43; Raghavan, *India's War*, 63–70; Callahan, *The Worst Disaster*, 56. Farrell points out, for example, the "milking" of 5/11 Sikhs noted in the unit diary prior to sailing, where it discloses that the battalion acquired 450 recruits and six British officers who did not speak Urdu. Farrell, *The Defense and Fall of Singapore*, 127–28.

340 **Color line faced by Indians; Australian relations with locals:** Farrell, *The Defense and Fall of Singapore*, 128. "We were still thought of as colonials . . .": PR83/68 Memoirs of Cpl J. G. Morris, Australian War Memorial. Lachlan Grant cautions that, while there was certainly evidence of friendly relations between the typically egalitarian-minded Australians and the diverse nonwhite local population, these relations are "open for interpretation." He suggests the Australian soldiers produced comments that accorded with official views on relations, and that beneath this surface were a casual acceptance of a racial hierarchy with whites on top. *Australian Soldiers in Asia-Pacific in World War II* (Sydney: NewSouth Publishing, 2014), ch 3 (quote at 66).

340 **Effects of Indian independence agitation:** Marston, *Phoenix from the Ashes*, 23–24, 26, acknowledges awareness of this issue among Indian soldiers of all ranks. He reports the convention was not openly to discuss it and on the whole tends to play it down as a factor in Malaya. Farrell presents inferential evidence that political dissatisfaction had in fact crept into the Indian units in Malaya. Farrell, *The Defense and Fall of Singapore*, 127–28. Bond concludes this factor made the morale of Indian units brittle. Brian Bond, "Introduction," in Brian Bond and Kyoichi Tachikawa, *British and Japanese Military Leadership in the Far Eastern War 1941–1945* (Oxon, UK: Frank Cass, 2004), 2 [hereafter Bond and Tachikawa, *British and Japanese Military Leadership in the Far Eastern War*].

340 **Percival:** Callahan, *The Worst Disaster*, 111; Farrell, *The Defense and Fall of Singapore*, 71, 107, 109; Carl Bridge, "Crisis of Command: Major-General Gordon Bennett and British Military Effectiveness in the Malaya Campaign," in Bond and Tachikawa, *British and Japanese Military Leadership in the Far Eastern War*, 66 [hereafter Bridge, "Crisis of Command"] .

341 **Percival and Heath:** Farrell, *The Defense and Fall of Singapore*, 108, 110; Callahan, *The Worst Disaster*, 111.

341 **Henry G. Bennett; Pulford:** Bridge, "Crisis of Command," 65; Farrell, *The Defense and Fall of Singapore*, 107–8. The all too pervasive toxic or ineffectual command relations in the 8th Division, including much troubled relations within battalions up to and including mutiny, are presented and analyzed by Garth Pratten in his excellent *Australian Battalion Commanders in the Second World War* (Cambridge and New York: Cambridge University Press, 2009), 130–64. A major theme is that the 8th was the last division formed in the Australian Imperial Force, and accordingly, suffered from dilution of the pool of talent for command slots from battalion on up.

341 **Dictates governing Percival and his subordinates:** Farrell, *The Defense and Fall of Singapore*, 56–57, 71, 198–99, 111–12.

341 **Kra Isthmus and Operation Matador:** Callahan, *The Worst Disaster*, 127–29. On 9 August 1941, during the Atlantic Conference, Under Secretary of State Sumner Welles informed the British permanent under secretary of state for foreign affairs,

Sir Alexander Cadogan, that the president directed him to inform Britain that, even if Japan occupied Thailand, the United States did not wish for Britain to treat this as casus belli. "Memorandum by the Under Secretary of State (Welles) of Conversation with the British Permanent Under Secretary of State for Foreign Affairs (Cadogan)," August 9, 1941, *FRUS, 1941, General, Soviet Union*, 345–54 (reference at 347). This confirmed, if not settled, British policy to avoid executing Matador preemptively.

342 **Ease of advance on west coast of Malaya Peninsula and road net from east coast:** Farrell, *The Defense and Fall of Singapore*, 54.

342 **Malaya Command's order of battle December 1941:** Callahan, *The Worst Disaster*, 35–36, 50–51; Farrell, *The Defense and Fall of Singapore*, 95.

342 **British strength in Middle East in 1941:** Callahan, *The Worst Disaster*, 150–52.

342 **Deficiencies of Malaya Command equipment:** Callahan, *The Worst Disaster*, 175–77.

342 **Deficiencies in weapons and equipment:** Farrell, *The Defense and Fall of Singapore*, 129.

343 **Percival's deployment of ground forces:** Callahan, *The Worst Disaster*, 203–4; Farrell, *The Defense and Fall of Singapore*, 114.

343 **Military-civilian relations at the time and the later controversy:** Farrell, *The Defense and Fall of Singapore*, 122–26.

343 **Stewart's jungle fighting doctrine:** Farrell, *The Defense and Fall of Singapore*, 130–32, 134.

344 **Malaya Command intelligence portraits of Japanese ground and air forces:** Farrell, *The Defense and Fall of Singapore*, 140–41.

344 **Mirror imaging:** Farrell, *The Defense and Fall of Singapore*, 145.

344 **Far East radio intelligence from August to November 1941:** Farrell, *The Defense and Fall of Singapore*, 144.

344 **Yamashita background:** Kyoichi Tachikawa, "Yamashita and His Style of Leadership," in Bond and Tachikawa, *British and Japanese Military Leadership in the Far Eastern War*, 75–76 [hereafter Tachikawa, "Yamashita and His Style of Leadership"]; Bayly and Harper, *Forgotten Armies*, 113–14, citing Yoki Akashi, "General Yamashita Tomoyuki: Commander of the Twenty-fifth Army," in Brian Ferrell and Sandy Hunter, eds., *Sixty Years On: The Fall of Singapore Revisited* (Singapore: Times Academic Press, 2003), 85–207; Farrell, *The Defense and Fall of Singapore*, 109–10.

345 **Twenty-Fifth Army divisions, Tsuji:** Farrell, *The Defense and Fall of Singapore*, 110, 136–37; Tachikawa, "Yamashita and His Style of Leadership," 80–81. Tank strength and organization: "The History of Battles of Imperial Japanese Tanks," Imperial Japanese Army Page, www3.plala.org.jp/takihome, accessed 26 December 2012. This is also known as "Taki's Home Page" and is based on original Imperial Army documents.

345 **Japanese begin planning Malaya campaign August 1940;** *Read This Alone—And the War Can Be Won:* Tachikawa, "Yamashita and His Style of Leadership," 76; Bayly and Harper, *Forgotten Armies*, 114–15; Farrell, *The Defense and Fall of Singapore*, 118, 136–37. The very low opinion of Indian troops (and not much better opinion of Australians) in the pamphlet reflected the conclusions of Imperial Army intelligence officers. Kotani, *Japanese Intelligence in World War II*, 115–16.

346 **Distinct features of Twenty-Fifth Army plans:** Farrell, *The Defense and Fall of Singapore*, 118–20.

346 **Japanese intelligence gathering in Malaya:** Kotani, *Japanese Intelligence in World War II*, 48, 53, 55, 115–16, 141–42; Farrell, *The Defense and Fall of Singapore*, 146–49.

347 **The *Automedon* episode:** Eiji Seki, *Mrs. Ferguson's Tea-Set, Japan and the Second World War: The Global Consequences following Germany's Sinking of the SS Automedon in 1940* (London: Global Oriental, 2007), 68–72, 85–88, 149. It does appear that after Japan's own intelligence estimates verified the authenticity of the *Automedon* data, the documents were accepted as authentic. Miraculously Violet Ferguson was reunited with her tea set postwar.

14: "We Are Depending for Our Lives on Kindly but Slow-Witted Infants in Arms"

348 **Pownall designated to replace Brooke-Popham:** Callahan, *The Worst Disaster*, 161–62.

348 **FDR's pledges on 1 and 4 December:** Callahan, *The Worst Disaster*, 168–69; "They've now made you responsible for declaring war": Bayly and Harper, *Forgotten Armies*, 109.

348 **6–7 December air searches:** Shores, Cull, and Izawa, *Bloody Shambles*, vol. 1, 74–78, 80.

349 **First air raid on Singapore:** Shores, Cull, and Izawa, *Bloody Shambles*, vol. 1, 85–87; Callahan, *The Worst Disaster*, 193–94.

349 **Thailand's failed attempts to maintain neutrality; declaration of war on the Allies:** E. Bruce Reynolds, *Thailand and Japan's Southern Advance 1940–1945* (London: Macmillan, 1994), ch. 1–4.

349 **Initial Japanese landings:** Shores, Cull, and Izawa, *Bloody Shambles*, vol. 1, 85; Farrell, *The Defense and Fall of Singapore*, 179.

349 **British aircraft status; "aerial extermination campaign" and effects of Japanese air attacks December 8:** Shores, Cull, and Izawa, *Bloody Shambles*, vol. 1, 58, 80–99; Hisayuki Yokoyama, "Air Operational Leadership in the Southern Front," in Bond and Tachikawa, *British and Japanese Military Leadership*, 134–49; Callahan, *The Worst Disaster*, 196–97. The text follows Shores et al. on aircraft totals and dispositions. Yokoyama provides a very insightful explanation of how revolutionary Sugawara's operational concept was in the history of the Imperial Army's air service.

350 **Final cancellation of Matador; unlikeliness of successful execution:** Callahan, *The Worst Disaster*, 194; Farrell, *The Defense and Fall of Singapore*, 155.

350 **Deployment of Key's brigade:** Alan Warren, *Britain's Greatest Defeat*, 59–60; Raghavan, *India's War*, 190–92.

350 **Defense of Kota Bharu:** Alan Warren, *Britain's Greatest Defeat*, 60–62; Raghavan, *India's War*, 190–92; Shores, Cull, and Izawa, *Bloody Shambles*, vol. 1, 85.

350 **Air action off Kota Bharu, early 8 December:** Shores, Cull, and Izawa, *Bloody Shambles*, vol. 1, 80–83.

351 **End of battle at Kota Bharu, casualties:** Warren, *Britain's Greatest Defeat*, 62–64; Shores, Cull, and Izawa, *Bloody Shambles*, vol. 1, 85. On the effect of stories of Japanese ferocity in China, see Callahan, *The Worst Disaster*, 197, and Bayly and Harper, *Forgotten Armies*, 121–22 (which adds Hong Kong).

351 **Air actions 9 December:** Shores, Cull, and Izawa, *Bloody Shambles*, vol. 1, 101–6; Farrell, *The Defense and Fall of Singapore*, 158.

351 "for the first and last time I felt ashamed . . ."; aircraft status; Pulford orders aircraft back to Singapore: Shores, Cull, and Izawa, *Bloody Shambles*, vol. 1, 101–2; Callahan, *The Worst Disaster*, 197–98.

351 Factors contributing to the British defeat in the air: Farrell, *The Defense and Fall of Singapore*, 158–60.

351 Phillips's decision to attack with Force Z, attitude about air threat: Boyd, *The Royal Navy in Far Eastern Waters*, 277, 279–80, 284–87, 289–93, 295–97, 335–37, 347–51; Nicholson, *Hostages to Fortune*, 25–28, 68–88, 95–96, 101–2, 147.

352 "We are off to look for trouble": Nicholson, *Hostages to Fortune*, 104.

352 Phillips's request for air support and decision to proceed: Nicholson, *Hostages to Fortune*, 104–5.

352 Force Z detected and decision to turn back: Nicholson, *Hostages to Fortune*, 106–9; Shores, Cull, and Izawa, *Bloody Shambles*, vol. 1, 111.

352 Diversion to Kuantan: Nicholson, *Hostages to Fortune*, 114–15.

352 Force Z sighted and initial attacks: Nicholson, *Hostages to Fortune*, 118–19, 123–24; Shores, Cull, and Izawa, *Bloody Shambles*, vol. 1, 113–16.

352 "Grey smoke balls from exploding 5.25 inch shells . . .": Shores, Cull, and Izawa, *Bloody Shambles*, vol. 1, 118.

353 Leach holds course; ineffective British antiaircraft fire: Norman Friedman, *British Battleships 1906–1946* (Annapolis, MD: Naval Institute Press, 2015), 355–56.

353 Initial torpedo hits on *Prince of Wales*: William H. Garkze Jr., Robert O. Dulin Jr., and Kenvin V. Denlay, "Death of a Battleship: The Loss of HMS Prince of Wales December 10, 1941, A Marine Forensics Analysis of the Sinking (2012 Revision)," 13–33, 55–62, at rina.org.uk, accessed 1 February 2013 [hereafter Garkze, Dulin, and Denlay, "Death of a Battleship"]; Nicholson, *Hostages to Fortune*, 124–26, 169; Garkze, Dulin, and Webb, *Allied Battleships*, 196–204. Nicholson (169) cites an Admiralty study pronouncing that at 14.5 knots and 35 degrees of rudder, a *King George V* class battleship needed 930 yards to turn, whereas the American *Washington* needed only 575 yards in identical conditions.

353 "There was a terrific thump . . .": William H. Garzke Jr., Robert O. Dulin Jr., and Thomas G. Webb, *Battleships: Allied Battleships of World War II* (Annapolis, MD: Naval Institute Press, 1980), 196 [hereafter Garzke, Dulin, and Webb, *Allied Battleships*].

353 Catastrophic damage to *Prince of Wales*: Garzke, Dulin, and Denlay, "Death of a Battleship," 13–33; Garzke, Dulin, and Webb, *Allied Battleships*, 202–3.

353 Attacks on *Repulse*: Nicholson, *Hostages to Fortune*, 126–27.

353 Tennant's report: Nicholson, *Hostages to Fortune*, 127.

353 Final torpedo hits on *Prince of Wales*, initial hit on *Repulse*: Nicholson, *Hostages to Fortune*, 127–28; Garzke, Dulin, and Denlay, "Death of a Battleship," 28–32; Garzke, Dulin, and Webb, *Allied Battleships*, 196, 204–7.

354 "I found the dodging of torpedoes quite interesting and entertaining . . .": Tennant's report of loss of *Repulse*, quoted in R. A. Burt, *British Battleships 1919–1939*, revised edition (Annapolis, MD: Naval Institute Press, 2012), 240 [hereafter Burt, *British Battleships*].

354 Fatal attack on *Repulse*: Nicholson, *Hostages to Fortune*, 131–32; Shores, Cull, and Izawa, *Bloody Shambles*, vol. 1, 120–21.

354 Last attacks, *Prince of Wales* sinks: Nicholson, *Hostages to Fortune*, 133–36, 163, 170–

74; Garkze, Dulin, and Denlay, "Death of a Battleship," 32–35, 41–50; Shores, Cull, and Izawa, *Bloody Shambles*, vol. 1, 123; "all the ropes swung down, heavy with men, to crash sickeningly against the battleship's side": A. B. H. Nelson, manuscript copy of H.M.S. *Prince of Wales: Ship of Destiny*, ch. 8, p. 29, A. B. H. Nelson papers, Churchill Archives. The loss of the new *Prince of Wales* administered a severe jolt to the Royal Navy. Lacking a grasp of the fluke effects of the torpedo hits on the port and starboard outer propeller shafts, the investigators imputed a major cause of the loss to a lack of discipline or panic by the crew, thus blackening the reputation of the ship and its survivors. This was most unjust.

354 **Casualties, significance:** Nicholson, *Hostages to Fortune*, 137; Shores, Cull, and Izawa, *Bloody Shambles*, vol. 1, has the most accurate Japanese loss data. Despite some Allied concerns, the Japanese were not able to retrieve anything of intelligence value from the wrecks. TROM kaibokun *Shimushu*, combinedfleet.com, accessed 7 January 2013.

354 **"I was opening my boxes on the 10th when . . .":** Winston S. Churchill, *The Second World War*, vol. 3, *The Grand Alliance* (Boston: Houghton Mifflin, 1950), 620.

355 **Significance of event:** Callahan, *The Worst Disaster*, 202–3; Bayly and Harper, *Forgotten Armies*, 118.

355 **Phillips's failure to break radio silence:** Nicholson, *Hostages to Fortune*, 140–52; Shores, Cull, and Izawa, *Bloody Shambles*, vol. 1, 118, 125.

355 **Apportioning responsibility:** Nicholson, *Hostages to Fortune*, 179–89.

355 **Murray-Lyon's compromised mission:** Farrell, *The Defense and Fall of Singapore*, 97.

356 **"The Ledge" battle:** Farrell, *The Defense and Fall of Singapore*, 114–15, 168–69; Warren, *Britain's Greatest Defeat*, 79–80; Callahan, *The Worst Disaster*, 206–7; Kirby, *The Loss of Singapore*, 184–86.

356 **Disastrous defeat at Jitra:** Warren, *Britain's Greatest Defeat*, 81–94; Raghavan, *India's War*, 192–93; Farrell, *The Defense and Fall of Singapore*, 170–71.

358 **"Jitra was without a doubt . . ." and casualties:** Farrell, *The Defense and Fall of Singapore*, 170, 176. Raghavan, *India's War*, 192–93, likewise grades it as the most decisive battle in Malaya.

358 **Imperial Army assessment of Jitra:** Farrell, *The Defense and Fall of Singapore*, 178.

358 **Defeat of 11th Indian Division at Guran:** Warren, *Britain's Greatest Defeat*, 102–9.

358 **Heath brings forward 12th Brigade; rationale for piecemeal commitment of British forces:** Warren, *Britain's Greatest Defeat*, 105–6, 111–13.

358 **Japanese tactics and logistics:** Farrell, *The Defense and Fall of Singapore*, 178–79; Warren, *Britain's Greatest Defeat*, 114; Henry Frei, *Guns of February: Ordinary Japanese Soldiers' Views of the Malaya Campaign & the Fall of Singapore* (Singapore: Singapore University Press, 2004), 46, 76 [hereafter Frei, *Guns of February*].

359 **British command changes:** Warren, *Britain's Greatest Defeat*, 115.

359 **Strategic decisions in London in December 1941 regarding the Far East:** Warren, *Britain's Greatest Defeat*, 116–18; Callahan, *The Worst Disaster*, 211–13, 222–25; "not much liked, but he knew his onions": Nicolson, *Hostages to Fortune*, 27.

359 **Churchill and Percival's differing views on Singapore and Churchill's failure to confront the issue:** Farrell, *The Defense and Fall of Singapore*, 187, 191.

359 **Brooke's strategic Christmas Day appreciation:** Farrell, *The Defense and Fall of Singapore*, 185.

360 **Strategic significance of Burma:** Callahan, *The Worst Disaster*, 257–58. Callahan

notes that on 20 January, Churchill sent a minute stating that keeping the Burma Road open was more important than holding Singapore.

360 **Curtin's statement and Australian demands for return of troops:** Farrell, *The Defense and Fall of Singapore*, 188–89; Callahan, *The Worst Disaster*, 228–34.

360 **"There is no need for your son to go into the army . . ." and Wavell's background:** Warren, *Britain's Greatest Defeat*, 118–19; "raw deals" and "My trouble is I am not really interested in war": Pownall Diaries, volume June 1940 to December 1941, end of volume, "On Wavell," Liddell Hart Centre: "a more completely lotus eating land . . .": Papers of Hutton, Lt. Gen. Sir Thomas Folder 3/1-6, Letter, Wavell to Hutton, 18 January 1942, Liddell Hart Centre.

360 **Percival's December 30 vision:** Farrell, *The Defense and Fall of Singapore*, 200.

361 **Thomas's attempt to assure equal treatment of Asians and "the moral collapse of British rule in Southeast Asia . . .":** Callahan, *The Worst Disaster*, 242–45; "a thing which I am sure will never be forgotten or forgiven": Bayly and Harper, *Forgotten Armies*, 119–21.

361 **Yamashita deals with "indiscipline" at Penang:** Bayly and Harper, *Forgotten Armies*, 121.

361 **Delay and retreat at Kampar:** Warren, *Britain's Greatest Defeat*, 119–24; Farrell, *The Defense and Fall of Singapore*, 204–10.

361 **Painter at Kuantan:** Farrell, *The Defense and Fall of Singapore*, 201–4; Warren, *Britain's Greatest Defeat*, 124–27.

362 **Slim River positions and protection of coastal flank:** Warren, *Britain's Greatest Defeat*, 129–30.

362 **Stewart's dispositions and ignores warning:** Warren, *Britain's Greatest Defeat*, 130–34.

362 **Shimada recasts plan:** Warren, *Britain's Greatest Defeat*, 129–30, 134.

362 **Destruction of 12th Brigade; unfolding sequence of disasters as Japanese tanks advance; Japanese tank attack past 12th Brigade:** Warren, *Britain's Greatest Defeat*, 134–37, 139.

363 **Japanese tank attack checked:** Warren, *Britain's Greatest Defeat*, 141–43.

363 **Casualties at Slim River disaster:** Warren, *Britain's Greatest Defeat*, 144–45.

363 **Exhaustion of commanders as key factor:** Raghavan, *India's War*, 195, notes Wavell interviewed the commanders afterward and his aide noted in his diary, "I have never seen men look so tired."

363 **"he is an uninspiring leader . . .":** Warren, *Britain's Greatest Defeat*, 144.

363 **Wavell and Percival:** Farrell, *The Defense and Fall of Singapore*, 254–55.

363 **Wavell's arrival and new plans:** Farrell, *The Defense and Fall of Singapore*, 223–25; Warren, *Britain's Greatest Defeat*, 147–48.

364 **Paris replaced by Key:** Warren, *Britain's Greatest Defeat*, 149–50, 154.

364 **Twenty-Fifth Army situation by 8 January:** Warren, *Britain's Greatest Defeat*, 152, 154; Farrell, *The Defense and Fall of Singapore*, 228.

364 **Yamashita plan for Johore battle:** Farrell, *The Defense and Fall of Singapore*, 228, 267–70, 318–19; Warren, *Britain's Greatest Defeat*, 151–53.

364 **Endau convoys and air attacks:** Farrell, *The Defense and Fall of Singapore*, 319–20; Christopher Shores and Brian Cull with Yasuho Izawa, *Bloody Shambles*, vol. 2: *The Defense of Sumatra to the Fall of Burma* (London: Grub Street, 1993), 17–42 [hereafter Shores, Cull, and Izawa, *Bloody Shambles*, vol. 2]; Peter Cannon, "Night

Action, Malaya 1942," in John Jordan, ed., *Warship 2015* (Annapolis, MD: Naval Institute Press, 2015), 62–80; TROM *Sendai* in *Junyokan*, combinedfleet.com, accessed 19 July 2016.

365 **Wavell's plan undermined by Percival, reinforcements and Bennett's dispositions:** Farrell, *The Defense and Fall of Singapore*, 186, 223–24, 250–55, 258–59, 263, 267–70.

365 **Australian success at Gemas:** Warren, *Britain's Greatest Defeat*, 154–59; Farrell, *The Defense and Fall of Singapore*, 257–58. The Australians inflicted these setbacks on the Japanese 9th Brigade, 5th Division.

366 **Imperial Guards Division attacks 45th Indian Brigade:** Farrell, *The Defense and Fall of Singapore*, 226–27, 254–55, 270–71; Warren, *Britain's Greatest Defeat*, 153, 159–62.

366 **Bennett reacts and Australian antitank success:** Warren, *Britain's Greatest Defeat*, 165–67.

366 **2/19th Battalion at Bakri:** Warren, *Britain's Greatest Defeat*, 168.

366 **Retreat of 45th Brigade and 2/29th Battalion survivors from Bakri:** Warren, *Britain's Greatest Defeat*, 169–71.

367 **"calm, clear voice . . .":** Pte. Mac Reid 2/19th Bn, "Road Block," MSS 1629, Australian War Memorial.

367 **Anderson's retreat:** Farrell, *The Defense and Fall of Singapore*, 276–80; Warren, *Britain's Greatest Defeat*, 172–79.

367 **22nd Brigade cut off, Barstow killed:** Farrell, *The Defense and Fall of Singapore*, 328–34; Warren, *Britain's Greatest Defeat*, 193–97.

367 **Pervasive lack of trust among Commonwealth commanders; destruction of 15th Brigade:** Warren, *Britain's Greatest Defeat*, 183–87; Farrell, *The Defense and Fall of Singapore*, 292–98, 323–25.

368 **2nd Argylls cross causeway; end of the 22nd Indian Brigade:** Warren, *Britain's Greatest Defeat*, 200–201; Farrell, *The Defense and Fall of Singapore*, 334–35.

368 **Casualties prior to battle on Singapore Island:** Warren, *Britain's Greatest Defeat*, 205.

368 **Wavell's report Singapore not a fortress and "The possibility of Singapore . . .":** Winston S. Churchill, *The Second World War*. Vol. 4. *The Hinge of Fate* (Boston: Houghton Mifflin, 1950), 49 [hereafter Churchill, *The Hinge of Fate*]; Callahan, *The Worst Disaster*, 60–61; Farrell, *The Defense and Fall of Singapore*, 310.

368 **January 20 message and "no question of surrender to be entertained . . .":** Callahan, *The Worst Disaster*, 257.

368 **New strategic approach and blame shifting between London and Canberra:** Farrell, *The Defense and Fall of Singapore*, 306–16; Callaghan, *The Worst Disaster*, 256–60; Warren, *Britain's Greatest Defeat*, 179–81.

369 **Chinese merchants, air raids from 12 January:** Farrell, *The Defense and Fall of Singapore*, 340; Warren, *Britain's Greatest Defeat*, 203–5; Shores, Cull, and Izawa, *Bloody Shambles*, vol. 1, ch. 8 and 9 provide details of air battles.

369 **Reinforcements arrive in Singapore, evacuation of military personnel and European civilians:** Warren, *Britain's Greatest Defeat*, 208. On 17 January British destroyer *Jupiter* sank Japanese submarine *I-60*. TROM *I-60*, combinedfleet.com, accessed 20 July 2016.

370 **"I came away depressed as it seemed as though . . .":** Spooner diary, February 4, 1942.

370 **Status of Percival's forces on Singapore Island:** Warren, *Britain's Greatest Defeat*, 208–10; Farrell, *The Defense and Fall of Singapore*, 363.

370   **Blows to morale of garrison:** Farrell, *The Defense and Fall of Singapore,* 355–57.

370   **Situation of Singapore civilians:** Warren, *Britain's Greatest Defeat,* 211–12; Farrell, *The Defense and Fall of Singapore,* 340–47. "alarm and despondency" phrase from Ashby, Hugh King, Wallet One, "Notes by Hugh King Ashby on his experiences as a Prisoner of War, POW, under the Japanese 1942–1945," PR 03218, Australian War Memorial.

370   **Percival prepares for attack in east:** Warren, *Britain's Greatest Defeat,* 213–14; 354–55, 357.

371   **Japanese underestimate strength of Malaya Command; actual infantry and artillery strengths:** Farrell, *The Defense and Fall of Singapore,* 112, 348–49, 358–59; Warren, *Britain's Greatest Defeat,* 215; Bayly and Harper, *Forgotten Armies,* 107. There were fifty high-explosive rounds for each of the eighteen 6-inch guns and just twenty-five for the 9.2-inch. There was none for the 15-inch guns.

371   **Yamashita's shortage of artillery ammunition, plan to force surrender by 11 February:** Farrell, *The Defense and Fall of Singapore,* 347–48, 350. Yamashita's staff figured the ammunition supply on hand consisted of 10.5 standard loads. The plan called for 1.5 in the preliminary bombardment, 4 for the assault, and 2.5 for the advance to the commanding high ground around Bukit Timah. This left only 2.5 loads for contingencies.

371   **Bones of fallen soldiers carried into Singapore in Imperial Guards Division:** Frei, *Guns of February,* 135–36.

371   **Yamashita's intentions and Australian dispositions:** Farrell, *The Defense and Fall of Singapore,* 348, 362; Warren, *Britain's Greatest Defeat,* 221–23; Tachikawa, "Yamashita and His Style of Leadership," 77, 83.

372   **"enemy shells . . . flying amid crackling rifle fire raking . . .":** Frei, *Guns of February,* 88.

372   **Initial Japanese assault on 22nd Brigade:** Warren, *Britain's Greatest Defeat,* 226–30; Farrell, *The Defense and Fall of Singapore,* 348, 369–70.

372   **Percival's opportunity to defeat initial landing and "tried to ginger up Percival to send reinforcements from anywhere . . .":** Spooner diary, February 9, 1942; Farrell, *The Defense and Fall of Singapore,* 370–73; Warren, *Britain's Greatest Defeat,* 230–31.

372   **Dysfunction of 8th Australian Division leadership:** Farrell, *The Defense and Fall of Singapore,* 370–73; Warren, *Britain's Greatest Defeat,* 230–32. Bridge, "Command Crisis," 72, assigns large blame to Bennett for Maxwell's retreat on the basis that Bennett issued confusing orders.

373   **Assault of the Imperial Guards Division, night of 9–10 February:** Farrell, *The Defense and Fall of Singapore,* 350, 376; Warren, *Britain's Greatest Defeat,* 233–35; Tachikawa, "Yamashita and His Style of Leadership," 84.

374   **Wavell's arrival, orders from Churchill and Wavell:** Warren, *Britain's Greatest Defeat,* 242–43.

374   **Japanese thrust to Bukit Timah:** Warren, *Britain's Greatest Defeat,* 243–45; Farrell, *The Defense and Fall of Singapore,* 379–81.

374   **Situation on 12 February:** Warren, *Britain's Greatest Defeat,* 253–55.

374   **"gouts of black smoke . . . erupting from more than twenty fierce conflagrations":** diary of Lieutenant Colonel Andre from 9–15 February 1942, Liddell Hart Centre.

374   **11th Company, 114th Regiment dies in formation:** Frei, *Guns of February,* 129–30.

374   **"The roar of the explosions were deafening . . .":** MSS 769, *Japan Times and Adver-*

tiser, 8 April 1942, p. 26, Australian War Memorial. Frei, *Guns of February*, 112, addresses the anger of Japanese soldiers at the intense artillery fire.

374 **Death of Chinese girls:** Frei, *Guns of February*, 106–8; execution of Asians by defenders: see Sergeant Lennon, John L., diary entry, February 13, 1942, PR 00875, Australian War Memorial for just one example.

375 **Alexandria Hospital massacre:** Warren, *Britain's Greatest Defeat*, 261; Farrell, *The Defense and Fall of Singapore*, 404.

375 **Percival's command meeting 13 February:** Warren, *Britain's Greatest Defeat*, 257–58; Farrell, *The Defense and Fall of Singapore*, 404–5.

375 **Armada fleeing Singapore:** Geoffrey Brooke, *Singapore's Dunkirk: The Aftermath of the Fall* (London: Leo Cooper, 1989), 23, 157–61, 177–81 [hereafter, Brooke, *Singapore's Dunkirk*]; Warren, *Britain's Greatest Defeat*, 259.

375 **"The flare of the many fires tinged with the huge clouds of smoke . . .":** James, Lieutenant Colonel Noel, Commanding Officer, Ordnance Ammunition dumps, Singapore 1942, Liddell Hart Centre.

375 **Massacre of Australian nurses; Bullwinkel:** PR01216 Papers of Bullwinkel, Vivien, Series 1, Folder 3 of 3, Testimony at the International Tribunal for the Far East, transcript, pp. 13, 454–76, Australian War Memorial.

375 **Death of Pulford and Spooner:** Shores, Cull, and Izawa, *Bloody Shambles*, vol. 2, 80–81.

376 **Margot Turner:** Brooke, *Singapore's Dunkirk*, 37, 46–49. Later she became Dame Margot Turner for her heroic nursing career that ended in her appointment as Britain's chief military nurse.

376 ***Rooseboom* story:** Brooke, *Singapore's Dunkirk*, 216–20; TROM *I-159*, combined fleet. com, accessed 20 July 2016. *I-59* was renumbered *I-159* on 20 May 1942.

376 **Loss of "Purple" Machine:** Ralph Erskine, "When a Purple Machine Went Missing: How Japan Nearly Discovered America's Greatest Secret," *Intelligence and National Security* 12, no. 3 (1997): 185–89. In gross violation of orders, the machine had been transferred from a warship to the merchant vessel *Sussex* in Durban. The master of the *Sussex* reported that he had delivered the crate bearing the machine to Singapore in late December 1941. Also with regard to security matters, an Irish-Burmese intelligence officer, Capt. Patrick Heenan, had been recruited by the Japanese during a long leave in Japan in 1939. He was caught red-handed in the act of espionage early on. Contrary to some accounts, his information only refined details of the essential picture the Japanese gathered themselves and did not serve importantly in the fall of Singapore. Heenan apparently was executed just before the surrender. Bayly and Harper, *Forgotten Armies*, 127; Warren, *Britain's Greatest Defeat*, 65.

377 **Percival meeting, morning 15 February:** Warren, *Britain's Greatest Defeat*, 233–35, 263; Farrell, *The Defense and Fall of Singapore*, 406–7.

377 **Meeting of Yamashita and Percival 15 February:** Warren, *Britain's Greatest Defeat*, 265–66.

377 **Bennett's flight and subsequent fate:** Warren, *Britain's Greatest Defeat*, 267–68; David Horner, *Blamey: The Commander in Chief* (Canberra: Allen & Unwin, 1998), 273–74, 447–48. When Percival was finally liberated, he reported Bennett had no authority to leave Singapore. Although the enmity between Percival and Bennett was apparent, the Australian Army and later the government appointed inquiries.

Both concluded Bennett acted improperly. He did retain the loyalty of many members of his division.

378 **"the worst disaster and largest capitulation in British history"; no official inquiry:** Churchill, *The Hinge of Fate*, 92; Warren, *Britain's Greatest Defeat*, 269–70.

378 **Japan celebrates fall of Singapore, Yamashita's fame and fall:** Warren, *Britain's Greatest Defeat*, 272; Farrell, *The Defense and Fall of Singapore*, 417.

378 **Japanese handling of prisoners:** Bayly and Harper, *Forgotten Armies*, 147; Farrell, *The Defense and Fall of Singapore*, 415. Bayly and Harper point out that before Fujiwara spoke, a British Colonel Hunt addressed the Indian captives. Later, some Indians alleged their actions were legitimized by Hunt's claimed statement that "now you belong to the Japanese army." Raghavan notes that Singh was captured during the debacle at Jitra. *India's War*, 192. This event would undoubtedly have severely shaken his faith in British leadership.

379 **Indian officers and VCOs' response to Japanese appeals:** Warren, *Britain's Greatest Defeat*, 274–75.

379 **Enlistment in and resistance to the INA:** Warren, *Britain's Greatest Defeat*, 275–76.

379 **Singapore civilian casualties; Japanese assert control:** Warren, *Britain's Greatest Defeat*, 271–72, 278.

380 **The *Sook Ching*:** Warren, *Britain's Greatest Defeat*, 278–79; Bayly and Harper, *Forgotten Armies*, 208–14; Farrell, *The Defense and Fall of Singapore*, 416–17. Hayashi Hirofumi summarized his extensive findings in a 2014 article "The Battle of Singapore: The Massacre of Chinese and Understanding of the Issue in Postwar Japan," http://japanfocus.org/-Hayashi-Hirofumi/3187, accessed 19 February 2014. After his extensive research in records from Singapore, Japan, and Great Britain, he concluded that there is lack of support for figures as high as 50,000 deaths. Hayashi stated that at least 5,000 Chinese were killed, but he could not venture a guess as to a maximum. He reported a diary entry by Kawamura showing a death toll of 5,000 and a document in the intelligence record of the Twenty-Fifth Army reporting a total of 11,110 deaths through 28 May 1942. This latter number, however, included those who died in bombing raids as well as the purge. Hayashi says only the Imperial Guards Division participated in the purge on Singapore Island, but the 5th and 18th Divisions carried out such activities on the Malay peninsula. The single substantial Chinese formation fighting the Japanese was the "Dalforce," named after its commander, John Dalley. One Chinese leader predicted all too accurately that the Japanese would seize upon the existence of the unit (and its stiff fighting at Singapore) to justify savage reprisals against the Chinese community. Bayly and Harper, *Forgotten Armies*, 135–36.

380 **Yamashita at indemnity presentation ceremony:** Bayly and Harper, *Forgotten Armies*, 214–17.

381 **Malaya Command and civilian casualties:** Warren, *Britain's Greatest Defeat*, 301–2; Callahan, *The Worst Disaster*, 270; Twenty-fifth Army losses: Farrell, *The Defense and Fall of Singapore*, 451. Of the Japanese losses, 5,092 (1,714 killed and 3,378 wounded) occurred on Singapore Island. By divisions, Japanese casualties were Imperial Guards, 1,579; 5th Division, 3,694; and 18th Division, 3,646.

381 **Aircraft losses:** Shores, Cull, and Izawa, *Bloody Shambles*, vol. 1, 338–39, 384–85.

381 **Percival as lead "goat":** Callahan, *The Worst Disaster*, 247–48.

382 **Malaya Command leadership failures:** Warren, *Britain's Greatest Defeat*, 290–92; Callahan, *The Worst Disaster*, 244–45.

383 **"the illusion that a Two-Hemisphere Empire can be defended . . .":** Warren, *Britain's Greatest Defeat*, 272, 289–90; Callahan, *The Worst Disaster*, 150–51.

383 **Underlying causes of Japanese victory:** Callahan, *The Worst Disaster*, 246–47.

15: "Men Would Follow Them, Suffer, and Be Glad About It"

385 **History of Dutch East Indies:** Forgotten Campaign: The Dutch East Indies Campaign 1941–1942 website, dutcheastindies.webs.com, accessed 20 November 2012; Peter Post, William H. Frederick, Iris Heidebrink, and Shigeru Sato, *The Encyclopedia of Indonesia in the Pacific War* (Leiden and Boston: Brill, 2010), 6, 29, 45–46, 498–500, 510–11, 594–96; Remmelink, *The Invasion of the Dutch East Indies*, 10.

385 **Dutch population delusions:** Tom Womack, *The Allied Defense of the Malay Barrier 1941–1942* (Jefferson, NC: McFarland Publishers, 2016), 30 [hereafter Womack, *The Allied Defense of the Malay Barrier*]; Elizabeth van Kampen, "Memories of My Youth and the Years of Japanese Occupation in the former Dutch East Indies During World War Two," ch. 21, Walking With My Father ("Japanese planes were . . ."), http://www.dutch-east-indies.com/chapter_21T.html, accessed 30 March 2016.

386 **Japanese naval commands:** Remmelink, *The Invasion of the Dutch East Indies*, 4–8; Kirby, *The Loss of Singapore*, 291–92.

386 **Japanese naval forces committed to Netherlands East Indies Campaign:** Remmelink, *The Invasion of the Dutch East Indies*, 4–8; TROMs *Kongo, Nachi, Ashigara, Takao, Mogami, Yura, Jintsu, Naka*, combinedfleet.com, accessed 19 November 2012.

386 **Strength of Sixteenth Army and Japanese air units committed against the Netherlands East Indies:** Remmelink, *The Invasion of the Dutch East Indies*, 95, 98, 262; Shores, Cull, and Izawa, *Bloody Shambles*, vol. 1, 52–53.

387 **Strength of Allied naval forces:** F. C. van Oosten, *The Battle of the Java Sea* (Annapolis, MD: Naval Institute Press, 1976), appendix 11 [hereafter van Oosten, *The Battle of the Java Sea*]; Morison, *The Rising Sun in the Pacific*, 271–73.

387 **Dutch air strength:** Shores, Cull, and Izawa, *Bloody Shambles*, vol. 1, 60; "Dutch Air Force Order of Battle," The Netherlands East Indies 1941–1942, 1–7, dutcheastindies .webs.com, accessed 19 November 2012.

388 **Allied ground forces on Java:** "The Conquest of Java Island, March 1942," The Netherlands East Indies 1941–1942, 1–7, dutcheastindies.webs.com, accessed 20 November 2012.

388 **Organization of Dutch ground forces:** "The Conquest of Java Island, March 1942," The Netherlands East Indies 1941–1942, 1–7, dutcheastindies.webs.com, accessed 20 November 2012; Lionel Wigmore, *Australia in the War of 1939–1945*, Series One, Army, vol. 4, *The Japanese Thrust* (Canberra: The Australian War Memorial, 1957), 442 [hereafter Wigmore, *The Japanese Thrust*].

389 **"unparalleled magnitude":** Wigmore, *The Japanese Thrust*, 508.

389 **Borneo and its British defenses:** Kirby, *The Loss of Singapore*, 223–24; L. Klemen, "The Invasion of Borneo," ©1999–2000, The Netherlands East Indies 1941–1942, 1–7, dutcheastindies.webs.com/sarawak.html, accessed 24 October 2012 [hereafter Klemen, "The Invasion of Borneo"].

389   **Japanese seizure of Borneo; fighting of defenders:** Klemen, "The Invasion of Borneo," 7–13; Kirby, *The Loss of Singapore*, 223–27; Dear and Foot, *The Oxford Companion to World War II*, 787.

389   **Japanese ship losses off Borneo; loss of Dutch *KXVI*:** Klemen, "The Invasion
of Borneo," 7–9, 13–14; TROMs *Yura, Sagiri, Shinonome*, combinedfleet.com,
accessed 30 March 2016.

391   **Capture of Menado:** Remmelink, *The Invasion of the Dutch East Indies*, 182–84; Kirby,
The Loss of Singapore, 292–93; TROM *Jintsu*, combinedfleet.com, accessed 23 Octo-
ber 2012; Womack, *The Allied Defense of the Malay Barrier*, 139; G. Rottman & A.
Takizawa, *Japanese Paratroop Forces of World War II* (Oxford: Osprey Publishing,
2005), 20–24 [hereafter Rottman & Takizawa, *Japanese Paratroop Forces of World
War II*].

391   **Capture of Tarakan:** Willem Remmelink, ed., *War History Series*, vol. 26, *Operations
of the Navy in the Dutch East Indies and the Bay of Bengal* (Leiden: Leiden University
Press, 2018), 126–49 [hereafter Remmelink, *Operations of the Navy in the Dutch
East Indies and the Bay of Bengal: The Invasion of the Dutch East Indies*]. This volume
is a translation under the auspices of the Netherlands Institute of Military History
of the relevant volume of the massive *Senshi Sosho* (War History Series) compiled
by the War History Office of the National Defense College of Japan. Also see Remmelink, *The Invasion of the Dutch East Indies*, 75, 176–81, 208; Womack, *The Allied
Defense of the Malay Barrier*, 60, 111–14; "The Capture of Tarakan Island," The Netherlands East Indies 1941–1942, 1–7, dutcheastindies.webs.com, accessed 21 November 2012; TROM *W-14*, combinedfleet.com, accessed 25 October 2012; van Oosten,
The Battle of the Java Sea, appendix 8.

392   **Balikpapan, Japanese and Allied reaction:** TROM *Naka*, combinedfleet.com,
accessed 26 October 2012; Kirby, *The Loss of Singapore*, 296–97. For coverage of the
landing and subsequent events, including the naval battle, see Remmelink, *Operations of the Navy in the Dutch East Indies and the Bay of Bengal: The Invasion of the
Dutch East Indies*, 178–98.

392   **Night action off Balikpapan:** Commander in Chief, United States Asiatic Fleet,
serial CF-0020, January 29, 1942, Subject: Naval Engagement off Balikpapan, Borneo, N.E.I. on January 24, 1942, with attached reports from Commander, Destroyer
Division Fifty-Nine, Serial CF-005, January 26, 1942; *John D. Ford* (DD-228), January 25, 1942; *Pope* (DD-225), January 25, 1942; *Parrott* (DD-218), January 26, 1942;
Paul Jones (DD-230), January 24, 1942, all in RG 38, Box 1, NARA. Japanese participation from Vincent P. O'Hara, *The U.S. Navy Against the Axis* (Annapolis, MD:
Naval Institute Press, 2007), 20–26; TROM, *Patrol Boat 37*, www.combinedfleet
.com, accessed 10 December 2016; Womack, *The Allied Defense of the Malay Barrier*,
119–21. The translated Japanese official history is Remmelink, *The Invasion of the
Dutch East Indies*, 358 ("appeared out of nowhere like phantom killers . . .").

393   **Capture of Balikpapan, advance of Twenty-Third Air Flotilla:** Remmelink, *The Invasion of the Dutch East Indies*, 348–61; "The Japanese Invasion of Balikpapan" and
"Massacres in the Dutch East Indies, 1941–1942," subhead "The Balikpapan Massacre, February 1942," The Netherlands East Indies 1941–1942, 1–7, dutcheastindies.
webs.com, accessed 21 November 2012; Kirby, *The Loss of Singapore*, 298; Shores,
Cull, and Izawa, *Bloody Shambles*, vol. 1, 229.

393   **Kendari invasion, advance of Twenty-First Air Flotilla:** "The Fall of Kendari,

1942," The Netherlands East Indies 1941–1942, 1–7, dutcheastindies.webs.com, accessed 21 November 2012; TROM *Nagara*, combinedfleet.com, accessed 26 October 2012; Morison, *The Rising Sun in the Pacific*, 293–94; Shores, Cull, and Izawa, *Bloody Shambles*, vol. 1, 226.

393 **Ambon described; Dutch and Australian defense forces:** Wigmore, *The Japanese Thrust*, 418–21, 423, 426–27; Douglas Gillison, *Australia in the War of 1939–1945*, Series 3, *The Air Force*, vol. 1, *The Royal Australian Air Force 1939–1942* (Canberra: Australian War Memorial, 1962), 374–75 [hereafter Gillison, *Royal Australian Air Force 1939–1942*].

394 **Wavell overrules Hart on withdrawal from Ambon:** Morison, *The Rising Sun in the Pacific*, 296.

394 **Japanese forces deployed to attack Ambon; Australian and Dutch defenders overwhelmed by 3 February:** Remmelink, *The Invasion of the Dutch East Indies*, 361–72; The Netherlands East Indies 1941–1942, 1–7, dutcheastindies.webs.com, accessed 21 November 2012; TROMs *Hiryū*, *Jintsu*, combinedfleet.com, accessed 26 October 2012; Wigmore, *The Japanese Thrust*, 427–40; "The Japanese Invasion of Ambon Island, January 1942".

394 **Executions of Australian and Dutch Prisoners 1942:** Wigmore, *The Japanese Thrust*, 436; Gillison, *Royal Australian Air Force 1939–1942*, 377n6; TROM *Jintsu*, combinedfleet.com, accessed 10 October 2019. By Japanese count, they captured 782 Australians, 334 Dutch troops, and 1,066 indigenous troops. Remmelink, *The Invasion of the Dutch East Indies*, 372.

394 **Deaths of Australian prisoners of war held on Ambon:** Wigmore, *The Japanese Thrust*, 606–11.

394 **Makassar seized:** TROMs *Nagara*, *Natsushio*, combinedfleet.com; Remmelink, *The Invasion of the Dutch East Indies*, 394–97.

395 **Sumatra described:** Kirby, *The Loss of Singapore*, 354–55; Gillison, *Royal Australian Air Force 1939–1942*, 382; Dear and Foot, *The Oxford Companion to World War II*, 786 (oil production figures).

395 **"it is no exaggeration to say that the Greater East Asian War . . .":** Remmelink, *The Invasion of the Dutch East Indies*, 269. For a description of Japanese naval operations at Sumatra, see Remmelink, *Operations of the Navy in the Dutch East Indies and the Bay of Bengal: The Invasion of the Dutch East Indies*, 258–304.

395 **Allied air units on Sumatra; first Japanese raids:** Shores, Cull, and Izawa, *Bloody Shambles*, vol. 2, 27, 34, 43, 45, 50, 56–58, 62–69, 70, 75–79; Gillison, *Royal Australian Air Force 1939–1942*, 382, 384, 388.

395 **Allied deployments around Palembang 14 February 1942:** *The Battle for Palembang, Forgotten Campaign: The Dutch East Indies Campaign 1941–1942*, accessed 12 November 2012; Shores, Cull, and Izawa, *Bloody Shambles*, vol. 2, 89; Gillison, *Royal Australian Air Force 1939–1942*, 394, 391–92.

396 **Japanese invasion fleets for southern Sumatra:** *The Japanese Invasion of Sumatra Island, Forgotten Campaign: The Dutch East Indies Campaign 1941–1942*, accessed 12 November 2012; TROMs *Yura*, *Sendai*, combinedfleet.com, accessed 12 November 2012.

396 **Formation of ABDA Striking force; bombing on 4 February; "the bombs fell close enough for me to see the ugly red flash . . .":** Gill, *Royal Australian Navy, 1939–1942*, 574; O'Hara, *The U.S. Navy Versus the Axis*, 26. During Doorman's maneuvers, the Dutch destroyer *Van Ghent* ran aground and became a total loss.

396 **Japanese parachute assault on P1 and oil refineries and subsequent fighting:** Remmelink, *The Invasion of the Dutch East Indies*, 286, 316–42; Shores, Cull, and Izawa, *Bloody Shambles*, vol. 2, 93–107; Rottman & Takizawa, *Japanese Paratroop Forces of World War II*, 30–32, 41–43.

397 **"I immediately demanded surrender . . .":** Shores, Cull, and Izawa, *Bloody Shambles*, vol. 2, 105–6; Remmelink, *The Invasion of the Dutch East Indies*, 325–32.

397 **Capture of refineries on Sumatra:** Remmelink, *The Invasion of the Dutch East Indies*, 324, 329–32, 344–45.

397 **Fall of Sumatra:** Remmelink, *The Invasion of the Dutch East Indies*, 333–44; The Japanese Invasion of Sumatra, The Battle for Palembang, The Japanese Invasion of Northern Sumatra, *Forgotten Campaign: The Dutch East Indies Campaign 1941–1942*, accessed 12 November 2012; Rottman & Takizawa, *Japanese Paratroop Forces of World War II*, 43.

397 **Wavell's 16 February assessment; "Burma and Australia are absolutely vital for war against Japan . . .":** Wigmore, *The Japanese Thrust*, 442–46.

398 **Wavell's ABDA command ends:** Kirby, *The Loss of Singapore*, 424, 429; Gill, *Royal Australian Navy, 1939–1942*, 596–97.

398 **Hart relieved; Dutch command of final defense of Java:** Womack, *The Allied Defense of the Malay Barrier*, 152–53, 156.

398 **"The country is more upset about the escape of the German battleships . . .":** Gilbert, *The Road to Victory*, 56. "lack of real fighting spirit" and "If the Army cannot fight better . . .":** Gilbert, *Road to Victory*, 62–63.

398 **Churchill's government shake-up and "Burma, Ceylon, Calcutta and Madras . . .":** Gilbert, *The Road to Victory*, 63–67.

398 **I Australian Corps returned to Australia, not diverted to Burma:** Horner, *Defense Supremo*, 134–39; Wigmore, *The Japanese Thrust*, ch. 20; Gilbert, *The Road to Victory*, 63–67.

399 **US ground units deployed to South Pacific:** Louis Morton, *United States Army in World War II, The War in the Pacific, Strategy and Command: The First Two Years* (Washington, DC: Office of the Chief of Military History, 1962), 202–3, 220–21; Grace Person Hayes, *The History of the Joint Chiefs of Staff in World War II: The War Against Japan* (Annapolis, MD: Naval Institute Press, 1982), 111–12 [hereafter Hayes, *The History of the Joint Chiefs of Staff in World War II*]; Frank, *Guadalcanal*, 46–47.

399 **Nagumo's Striking Force launches Darwin raid 19 February:** Peter Grose, *An Awkward Truth: The Bombing of Darwin 1942* (Crows Nest: Allen & Unwin, 2011), 81 [hereafter Grose, *An Awkward Truth*]; TROM Chikuma, combinedfleet.com, accessed 23 October 2012; G. Hermon Gill, *Australia in the War of 1939–1945, Series Two, Navy*, vol. 1, *Royal Australian Navy, 1939–1942* (Canberra: Australian War Memorial, 1957), 590 [hereafter Gill, *Royal Australian Navy, 1939–1942*]. Japanese naval operations regarding Darwin are covered in Remmelink, *Operations of the Navy in the Dutch East Indies and the Bay of Bengal: The Invasion of the Dutch East Indies*, 330–42.

400 **Darwin background and weakness of defenses:** Grose, *An Awkward Truth*, 2, 23–24, 26; Gillison, *Royal Australian Air Force 1939–1942*, 426–32.

400 **Ship losses:** Gill, *Royal Australian Navy, 1939–1942*, 594–95; Grose, *An Awkward Truth*, 105–8; Gillison, *Royal Australian Air Force 1939–1942*, 431.

400 **Air events:** Grose, *An Awkward Truth*, 84, 88–89, 91–93, 115–16, 137; Gillison, *Royal*

Australian Air Force 1939–1942, 425, 429; TROM *Chikuma*, combinedfleet.com, accessed 26 October 2012.

400 **Breakdown in civilian and military leadership and death totals:** Grose, *An Awkward Truth*, 56–60, 67–71, ch. 11 to 13, 191–93.

401 **Grose on the complex reality of the reaction of Darwin civilians and military personnel:** Grose, *An Awkward Truth*, 130–31, 136, 151, 178–87, 200–201.

401 **Seizure of Bali:** Remmelink, *The Invasion of the Dutch East Indies*, 397–403.

401 **Action in Badung Strait:** O'Hara, *The U.S. Navy Against the Axis*, 26–33; TROMs *Asashio*, *Oshio*, and *Michishio*, combinedfleet.com, accessed 26 October 2012. Destroyer *Stewart* was damaged in this sortie. Despite efforts to scuttle it in dry dock, the Japanese captured it and returned it to service as *Patrol Boat 102*. *Stewart* returned to US control at the end of the war. TROM *Patrol Boat 102 (ex-Stewart)*, combinedfleet.com, accessed 26 October 2012.

402 **Timor described and "Sparrow Force":** Wigmore, *The Japanese Thrust*, 466–69.

402 **Conundrum facing Australians over Portuguese Timor:** H. P. Willmott, *The Barrier and the Javelin* (Annapolis, MD: Naval Institute Press, 1983), 142–43 [hereafter Willmott, *The Barrier and the Javelin*].

402 **Occupation of Portuguese Timor by Australians and Dutch; reinforcement convoy turned back; Japanese debates on occupation of Portuguese Timor:** Wigmore, *The Japanese Thrust*, 469–70, 474; James Hornfischer, *Ship of Ghosts: The Story of the USS Houston, FDR's Legendary Lost Cruiser and the Epic Saga of Her Survivors* (New York: Bantam Books, 2006), 52–54 [hereafter Hornfischer, *Ship of Ghosts*]; Remmelink, *The Invasion of the Dutch East Indies*, 381–85.

402 **Japanese attack on Timor:** Remmelink, *The Invasion of the Dutch East Indies*, 403–15; Wigmore, *The Japanese Thrust*, 482–90; Rottman & Takizawa, *Japanese Paratroop Forces of World War II*, 25–27; TROM *Jintsu*, combinedfleet.com, accessed 25 October 2012.

403 **Australian and Dutch forces in Portuguese Timor commence guerilla warfare:** Wigmore, *The Japanese Thrust*, 472–82, 491–94; Dudley McCarthy, *Australia in the War of 1939–1945, Series 1-Army*, vol. 5, *Southwest Pacific Area—First Year: Kokoda to Wau* (Canberra: Australian War Memorial, 1959), appendix 2: Timor.

403 **Oyen's plan:** P. C. Boer, *The Loss of Java, The Final Battles for the Possession of Java Fought by Allied Air, Naval and Land Forces in the Period of 18 February–7 March 1942* (Singapore: NUS Press, 2011), xxiv–xxv, 5–7 [hereafter Boer, *The Loss of Java*]; Womack, *The Allied Defense of the Malay Barrier*, 189–90.

404 **Allied air efforts to postpone Java invasion:** Boer, *Loss of Java*, 4–6, 11, 16, 18–28, 59–60, 66, 79–80, 102–3, 115, 162, 182; Remmelink, *The Invasion of the Dutch East Indies*, 417–19; Cull and Izawa, *Bloody Shambles*, vol. 2, 191–255.

404 **Battle of Java Sea:** Remmelink, *Operations of the Navy in the Dutch East Indies and the Bay of Bengal: The Invasion of the Dutch East Indies*, 431–65, provides the official Japanese account. Although it is valuable and detailed, there are a number of errors in this account such that subsequent specific citations about this battle are from other sources.

404 **Air detection of invasion convoys; failures of Allied submarines; western surface Striking Force:** Womack, *The Allied Defense of the Malay Barrier*, 179–91; Remmelink, *The Invasion of the Dutch East Indies*, 442.

405 **Loss of *Langley*:** Dwight R. Messimer, *Pawns of War: The Loss of the USS Langley and*

the USS Pecos (Annapolis, MD: Naval Institute Press, 1983), ch. 4–6 [hereafter Messimer, *Pawns of War*].

405 **Armament comparisons:** Eric LaCroix and Linton Wells II, *Japanese Cruisers of the Pacific War* (Annapolis, MD: Naval Institute Press, 1997), 38, 208–9, 246–52, 262–71; van Oosten, *The Battle of the Java Sea*, Appendix Twelve; M. J. Whitley, *Destroyers of World War Two: An International Encyclopedia* (Annapolis, MD: Naval Institute Press, 1988), 198–22; O'Hara, *The U.S. Navy Against the Axis*, 36–38. On 17 January, British destroyer *Jupiter* sank Japanese submarine *I-60*, but lost one of its forward twin 4.7-inch gun mounts in the battle. It was replaced in Surabaya with a single 4.7-inch mount; thus *Jupiter* carried five, not six 4.7-inch guns. Christopher Langtree, *The Kelly's: British J, K & N Class Destroyers in World War II* (Annapolis, MD: Naval Institute Press, 2002), 144.

406 **Superiority of Japanese Type 93 torpedoes:** John Campbell, *Naval Weapons of World War Two* (Annapolis, MD: Naval Institute Press, 1985), 84–85, 158, 204–8, 396.

406 ***Kortenaer* limited speed; lack of common doctrine and effective communications:** Womack, *The Allied Defense of the Malay Barrier*, 196, 204, 232.

406 **Backgrounds of Doorman and Takagi:** van Oosten, *The Battle of the Java Sea*, 44–45.

407 **Doorman's ill health and gloom:** Womack, *The Allied Defense of the Malay Barrier*, 137–38, 153, 194 ("The chance of success is slim . . ."), 232.

407 **No desertions among Allied crewmen:** Womack, *The Allied Defense of the Malay Barrier*, 197.

407 **"The sky was deep blue beyond the end of the ocean . . ." and "I heard strong hissing noises from the mast . . .":** "The Battle at Java Sea" by Tanaka Tsuneji, 204, 209 [hereafter Tanaka, "The Battle at Java Sea"]. A copy of this article was generously supplied by Vincent O'Hara.

407 **"Huge water columns shot up everywhere. Those columns were colored red, white and blue," and "looked like red and blue devils running around":** Tanaka, "The Battle at Java Sea," 213, 217.

409 ***Exeter* hit:** Womack, *The Allied Defense of the Malay Barrier*, 205–13; O'Hara, *The U.S. Navy Against the Axis*, 38–41; van Oosten, *The Battle of the Java Sea*, 46–47.

409 ***Perth* protects *Exeter*, *Kortenaer* sunk; first phase ends:** Womack, *The Allied Defense of the Malay Barrier*, 213–15; O'Hara, *The U.S. Navy Against the Axis*, 38–41; van Oosten, *The Battle of the Java Sea*, 47; LaCroix and Wells, *Japanese Cruisers of the Pacific War*, 298.

409 **Second phase of engagement, sinking of *Electra*:** Womack, *The Allied Defense of the Malay Barrier*, 215–21; O'Hara, *The U.S. Navy Against the Axis*, 41–43; van Oosten, *The Battle of the Java Sea*, 51–52; D. D. Nowlin, U.S.S. *John D. Ford*, "My diary (December 8, 1941 to June 12, 1942)" (British destroyers streaming battle flags), kindly provided by Barrett Tillman via CV-6 Association.

409 **Final phase of battle; loss of *Java* and *DeRuyter*; Allied personnel losses:** Womack, *The Allied Defense of the Malay Barrier*, 222–32; O'Hara, *The U.S. Navy Against the Axis*, 43–44; van Oosten, *The Battle of the Java Sea*, 52–55; LaCroix and Wells, *Japanese Cruisers of the Pacific War*, 298. By count, Allied losses were: *DeRuyter*, 375; *Java*, 512; *Kortenaer*, 56–59; *Electra*, 109; *Jupiter*, 95; and *Exeter*, 13. In addition, the Japanese captured 113 *DeRuyter* and 57 *Java* survivors (of these, 14 died in captivity). US submarines rescued two *DeRuyter* and 54 *Electra* survivors. Losses on *DeRuyter*, *Java*, and *Kortenaer* taken from "Cruiser De Ruyter (I) history" at netherlandsnavy.

nl/ruyter; "History of the cruiser Java" at netherlandsnavy.nl/java; and "Admirlen-class destroyers" at netherlandsnavy.nl/Admirlen.htm. These were all accessed via Uboat.net/allies/warship/war_losses, accessed 30 October 2012. Losses on *Korten-aer* were listed as 56 to 59; *Java* apparently had 512 killed in the battle. Another 14 apparently died as POWs and 43 eventually were repatriated. Losses on *Exeter*, *Elec-tra*, and *Jupiter* taken from "Casualty Lists for the Royal Navy and Dominion Navies, World War 2, February 1942" at naval-history.net, accessed 30 October 2012. This site also lists three RN personnel who died on *DeRuyter* and one on *Java*. It is not clear whether their deaths were counted in the figures for those ships on Dutch sites.

410 **Japanese losses:** *Jintsu*, one killed, four wounded; *Asagumo*, four killed, nineteen wounded; *Minegumo*, four wounded; *Ushio*, "a few" casualties; and *Sazanami*, "a few" casualties. Losses from: *Jintsu*, LaCroix, and Wells, *Japanese Cruisers of the Pacific War*, 432; *Asagumo* and *Minegumo* from TROMs *Asagumo* and *Minegumo*, combinedfleet.net, accessed 30 October 2012; *Ushio* and *Sazanami*, van Oosten, *The Battle of the Java Sea*, appendix 17.

410 **Waller sorties with *Perth* and *Houston*, Japanese invasion convoy approaches, Waller lulled:** Womack, *The Allied Defense of the Malay Barrier*, 241–43; O'Hara, *The U.S. Navy Against the Axis*, 46–48. The Japanese side of the action with *Perth* and *Houston* is in Remmelink, *Operations of the Navy in the Dutch East Indies and the Bay of Bengal: The Invasion of the Dutch East Indies*, 465–74.

411 **Waller encounters invasion fleet, opens fire:** O'Hara, *The U.S. Navy Against the Axis*, 48–50; Gill, *The Australian Navy, 1939–1942*, 620.

411 **"heaved a sigh of disappointment to think . . .":** Gill, *The Australian Navy, 1939–1942*, 620.

411 ***Perth* sailors hear bugles and gunfire:** Kenneth Sydney Wallace, *Last Day of Summer* (Sydney: Drawquick Publishing, 2007), 23.

411 **"The enemy ships fired red tracers and machine guns . . .":** quoted in O'Hara, *The U.S. Navy Against the Axis*, 53.

411 **Effects of flares, gunfire, and the "cold blue brilliance" searchlights:** Gill, *The Australian Navy, 1939–1942*, 621.

411 **Immunity of *Perth* and *Houston* from damage; loss of transports and *W-2*:** O'Hara, *The U.S. Navy Against the Axis*, 53–54; TROMs *Mogami*, *W-2*, combinedfleet.com, accessed 2 November 2012; Remmelink, *The Invasion of the Dutch East Indies*, 470–74, 486–88.

412 **"Christ! That's torn it. . . . Abandon ship . . .":** Gill, *The Australian Navy, 1939–1942*, 621–22; "men would follow them, suffer, and be glad about it": Ray Parkin, *Out of the Smoke* (New York: William Morrow, 1960), 223; O'Hara, *The U.S. Navy Against the Axis*, 53–54.

412 **Loss of *Houston*; "Captain die, *Houston* die, Buda die too":** W. G. Winslow, *The Ghost That Died at Sunda Strait* (Annapolis, MD: Naval Institute Press, 1984), 141.

412 **Japanese searchlights show *Houston*'s colors and last machine gun fire:** Hornfischer, *Ship of Ghosts*, 145. This work provides a superb and wrenching account of the struggles of *Houston*'s survivors.

412 ***Houston*'s final moments and survivor count:** Hornfischer, *Ship of Ghosts*, ch. 16–20; O'Hara, *The U.S. Navy Against the Axis*, 54–55.

412 **Fate of *Evertsen*:** Womack, *The Allied Defense of the Malay Barrier*, 246–47.

413 **Binford's quartet escapes:** O'Hara, *The U.S. Navy Against the Axis*, 55–57.

413 **End of *Exeter* and *Encounter*:** Womack, *The Allied Defense of the Malay Barrier*, 248–51; O'Hara, *The U.S. Navy Against the Axis*, 57–60; TROMs *Nachi, Ashigara, Myoko*, combinedfleet.com, accessed 23 November 2012; losses on *Encounter* and *Exeter* from "Casualty Lists for the Royal Navy and Dominion Navies, World War 2, February 1942" at naval-history.net, accessed 30 October 2012. Of prisoners captured from the British vessels, 152 *Exeter* and 38 *Encounter* survivors died in captivity.

413 **End of *Pope*:** O'Hara, *The U.S. Navy Against Japan*, 60–61; TROMs *Nachi, Ashigara, Myoko*, combinedfleet.com, accessed 23 November 2012.

413 **Loss of *Pecos*:** Messimer, *Pawns of War*, ch. 8–10.

413 **Loss of *Edsall*:** O'Hara, *The U.S. Navy Against the Axis*, 63; TROMs *Kirishima, Chikuma, Tone*, combinedfleet.com, accessed 5 April 2016; Hornfischer, *Ship of Ghosts* (covers numerous cruises of FDR in *Houston*); Donald M. Kehn Jr.'s *A Blue Sea of Blood: Deciphering the Mysterious Fate of the USS Edsall* (Minneapolis, MN: Zenith Press, 2009). The exact number of *Edsall* survivors remains unclear, ranging from seven to over forty. The remains of five beheaded *Edsall* sailors were found at Kendari after the war.

414 **Loss of *Stronghold* and *Pillsbury*:** O'Hara, *The U.S. Navy Against the Axis*, 64–65; TROMs *Maya, Atago, Takao*, combinedfleet.com, accessed 23 November 2012; crew loss on *Stronghold* from "Casualty Lists for the Royal Navy and Dominion Navies, World War 2, February 1942" at naval-history.net, accessed 30 October 2012.

414 **Loss of *Ashville*; destruction of *Yarra* convoy:** Gill, *Royal Australian Navy, 1939–1942*, 626–27, 630–32; TROMs *Maya, Atago*, combinedfleet.com, accessed 23 November 2012; crew loss on *Anking* from "Casualty Lists for the Royal Navy and Dominion Navies, World War 2, February 1942" at naval-history.net, accessed 30 October 2012.

414 **Nagumo attacks Tjilatjap; Dutch scuttle vessels:** TROMs *Kaga, Sōryū*, combinedfleet.com, accessed 23 November 2012; Australian Naval History, 632; Womack, *The Allied Defense of the Malay Barrier*, 309–11; van Oosten, *The Battle of the Java Sea*, appendix 8. The major warships scuttled included two destroyers (*Witte de With, Banekert*), three submarines (*K X, K XIII, K XIV*), four minelayers, and three minesweepers.

414 **Allied shipping lost to Nagumo and Kondo, March 1–5; losses to Japanese submarines:** Gill, *Royal Australian Navy, 1939–1942*, 632; Womack, *The Allied Defense of the Malay Barrier*, 108–9.

414 **"[The navy] demonstrated it would fight regardless of the odds . . .":** O'Hara, *The U.S. Navy Against the Axis*, 66.

415 **Disposition of ground defense units on eastern Java:** Boer, *The Loss of Java*, xxvi–xxvii; "The Conquest of Java Islands, March 1942," The Netherlands East Indies 1941–1942, 1–7, dutcheastindies.webs.com, accessed 17 November 2012.

415 **Air attacks on eastern invasion convoy, American aircraft withdrawal:** Bartsch, *Every Day a Nightmare*, 307–12, 316–34; Shores, Cull, and Izawa, *Bloody Shambles*, vol. 2, 303–6; Boer, *The Loss of Java*, 232; Remmelink, *The Invasion of the Dutch East Indies*, 552, 559, 569.

415 **Japanese advances in East Java, capture of Surabaya:** Remmelink, *The Invasion of the Dutch East Indies*, 460–61, 537–47, 549; "The Conquest of Java Islands, March

1942," "The East Java Campaign, March 1942," The Netherlands East Indies 1941–1942, 1–7, dutcheastindies.webs.com, accessed 17 November 2012.

415 **West Group:** Boer, *The Loss of Java*, xxvi–xxvii, 19–21; "Java Campaign," "The Conquest of Java Islands, March 1942," The Netherlands East Indies 1941–1942, 1–7, dutcheastindies.webs.com, accessed 17 November 2012; Wigmore, *The Japanese Thrust*, 495–96.

415 **Bandoeng Group:** Boer, *The Loss of Java*, 221.

415 **Japanese advance from landing at Bantam Bay; maneuvers of Blackforce; withdrawal of KNIL troops:** "The Conquest of Java Island, March 1942," The Netherlands East Indies 1941–1942, 1–7, dutcheastindies.webs.com, accessed 24 November 2012; Remmelink, *The Invasion of the Dutch East Indies*, 475; Wigmore, *The Japanese Thrust*, 499–506.

416 **The daring of Shoji's landing at Eretan Wetan:** Remmelink, *The Invasion of the Dutch East Indies*, 244, 462–63, 505–7; Boer, *The Loss of Java*, 236–37.

416 **Imamura's selection of Shoji:** Remmelink, *The Invasion of the Dutch East Indies*, 251.

416 **Shoji's landing and deployments:** Remmelink, *The Invasion of the Dutch East Indies*, 505–9; TROM *Choko Maru*, combinedfleet.com, accessed 9 April 2016; Boer, *The Loss of Java*, 239, 261, 289, 297.

417 **Shoji seizes Kalidjati airfield, Allied air situation:** Remmelink, *The Invasion of the Dutch East Indies*, 505–9; Boer, *The Loss of Java*, 276; "The Conquest of Java Island, March 1942," The Netherlands East Indies 1941–1942, 1–7, dutchcastindies.webs.com, accessed 24 November 2012.

417 **"The Japanese capture of Kalidjati. . ." and reordered defensive plans:** Boer, *The Loss of Java*, 285, 287–88.

417 **Accurate intelligence Allied estimates and counterattacks on March 2:** Remmelink, *The Invasion of the Dutch East Indies*, 509–10; Boer, *The Loss of Java*, 288–89, 302–3.

417 **Japanese aircraft rout Toorop's regiment:** Remmelink, *The Invasion of the Dutch East Indies*, 510–14, 521; Boer, *The Loss of Java*, 334–43, 348–49, 351, 366; "Some of the tanks were completely destroyed . . .": Noriki Deguchi, ed., *Maru Bessatsu—Sensho no Hibi* (Tokyo: Ushio Shobo, 1988), 358 [hereafter Deguchi, *Maru Bessatsu—Sensho no Hibi*].

418 **Allied counterattacks on Soebang and Eretan Wetan fail:** Remmelink, *The Invasion of the Dutch East Indies*, 514–23; Boer, *The Loss of Java*, 343–46, 347–48, 349, 366.

418 **Dutch withdraw West Group toward Bandoeng:** Boer, *The Loss of Java*, 392–93.

418 **"As we passed villages along the road . . .":** Deguchi, *Maru Bessatsu—Sensho no Hibi*, 358. Remmelink, *The Invasion of the Dutch East Indies*, 585, says that everywhere Japanese were welcomed with cheers by the indigenous peoples, and they had no fear of local resistance.

418 **Sixteenth Army fears for Shoji Detachment:** Remmelink, *The Invasion of the Dutch East Indies*, 480, 488–89, 502–3, 498–501. The captured skipper of a British destroyer, presumably Lt. Cdr. N. V. J. T. Thew of *Jupiter*, told his captors that two Australian divisions had been landed on Java. This presumably was misinformation, and it had the desired effect of causing tremendous anxiety among some staff officers of the Sixteenth Army, particularly as regards Shoji. The army's chief of staff, Maj. Gen. Seizaburō Okazaki, however, correctly assessed the information as false. Remmelink, *The Invasion of the Dutch East Indies*, 481–82.

419   **Shoji attacks toward Bandung; Endo's support:** Remmelink, *The Invasion of the Dutch East Indies*, 517–18, 521–22.

419   **Shoji plans to advance on Bandoeng; Dutch defenders and air situation:** Boer, *The Loss of Java*, 367–68, 382–84.

419   **Fighting in Tjiater Pass 5–6 March:** Boer, *The Loss of Java*, 398, 404–5, 493–95; Remmelink, *The Invasion of the Dutch East Indies*, 523–26.

419   **Withdrawal to Lembang; Dutch Command stance; "the great hostility of the Indonesians towards the Dutch":** Boer, *The Loss of Java*, 495; Wigmore, *The Japanese Thrust*, 502–3.

419   **Sixteenth Army accounts of achievements:** Remmelink, *The Invasion of the Dutch East Indies*, 364, 568–69. This source quotes Dutch accounts as reporting that the Japanese captured a total of 93,000 Dutch servicemen in the NEI.

420   **Fate of Allied soldiers who attempt guerilla warfare on Java:** "The Conquest of Java Island, March 1942," The Netherlands East Indies 1941–1942, dutcheastindies. webs.com, accessed 24 November 2012.

16: "Only War Proves What Is Correct and What Is Wrong"

421   **Philippines Islands described:** Morton, *The Fall of the Philippines*, 4–5; Department of Commerce, Washington, Basic Data on the Philippines, December 11, 1941, Folder Wars: WWII Operations—Philippines (1 of 2), United States Marine Corps History Center, Quantico, Virginia.

421   **US seizure of the Philippines and the insurgency:** for an excellent overall history, see Brian McAllister Linn, *The Philippine War, 1899–1902* (Lawrence: University Press of Kansas, reprint edition 2000). The seizure fits into the background of Linn's further advance of the story in his also superlative *Guardians of Empire* (Chapel Hill and London: University of North Carolina Press, 1997), 14–15, 17–18 [hereafter Linn, *Guardians of Empire*]. For a decidedly contrary view of the Philippine insurgency, see Stuart C. Miller, *Benevolent Assimilation: The American Conquest of the Philippines, 1899–1903* (New Haven, CT: Yale University Press, reprint 1984).

422   **American policy toward the Philippines, Tydings-McDuffie Act (Public Law 73-127, 48 Stat. 456, March 24, 1934):** Morton, *The Fall of the Philippines*, 4, 13, 61.

422   **Factions among American officers on the Philippines:** Frazier Hunt, *The Untold Story of Douglas MacArthur* (New York: Devin-Adair, 1954), 35 ("sturdy outpost of American influence"); Linn, *Guardians of Empire*, 21, 82–83, 86–87, 100, 178–79, 181.

422   **Views of Japan and high quality of Japanese armed forces:** Linn, *Guardians of Empire*, 88 ("probably has no superior"), 220. Linn quotes studies demonstrating a consistency of respectful views of Japanese armed forces that, if anything, increased between the 1920s and 1930s. The WPO-3 G-2 Annex as of April 1941 gave a very respectful treatment to the Japanese armed forces, especially the Imperial Navy. Philippine Department Plan Orange (1940 Revision), G-2 Annex (as of 4/1/41), Contributions from the Public, Folder no. 4, Papers of John Gordon, Box 49, MacArthur Memorial and Library [hereafter MML]. Norman Friedman has carefully reviewed the extensive naval war plans files and notes, which also show very respectful, nonracist appreciations of the Japanese armed forces.

422   **Creation of Philippine Scouts; Quezon's vision, hiring of MacArthur; failure of plan**

to develop a Philippine Army: Richard B. Meixsel, "Manuel L. Quezon, Douglas MacArthur, and the Significance of the Military Mission to the Philippine Commonwealth," *Pacific Historical Review* 70, no. 2, 255–92 (esp. 266–72); D. Clayton James, *The Years of MacArthur*, vol. 1, *1880–1941* (Boston: Houghton Mifflin, 1970), 470–76, 485, 503–4 [hereafter James, *The Years of MacArthur*, vol. 1]; Linn, *Guardians of Empire*, 59, 100–101, 103, 148–49; Ricardo Trota Jose, *The Philippine Army 1935–1942* (Manila: Atneo do Manila University Press, 1992), 216; Morton, *Fall of the Philippines*, 9–11; Richard B. Meixsel, "Major General George Grunert, WPO-3, and the Philippine Army, 1940–1941," *Journal of Military History* 59, no. 2 (April 1995) [hereafter Meixsel, "Major General George Grunert, WPO-3, and the Philippine Army, 1940–1941"]; Louis Morton, "The Philippine Army 1935–39: Eisenhower's Memorandum to Quezon," *Military Affairs* 12, no. 2 (Summer 1948): 103–7 [this actually is then-Maj. Gen. Dwight Eisenhower's June 1942 memorandum to President Manuel Quezon on the development of the Philippine Army]; William D. O'Neil, "Transformation and the Officer Corps: Analysis in the Historical Context of the U.S. and Japan Between the World Wars," Center for Naval Analysis, CME D0012589.A2, September 2005, 111 [hereafter O'Neil, "Transformation and the Officer Corps"]. Although the title reflects the basic focus of the article, an account by Kerry Irish provides an insightful summary of the problems with creating a Philippine Army: "Dwight Eisenhower and Douglas MacArthur in the Philippines: There Must Be a Day of Reckoning," *Journal of Military History* 74 (April 2010): 439–73 [hereafter Irish, "Dwight Eisenhower and Douglas MacArthur in the Philippines"]. I am also much indebted to Dr. Richard M. Meixsel of James Madison University for his very insightful comments on these issues. I follow his interpretation of Quezon's and MacArthur's shared hidden agendas. Why the development of the Philippine Army fell well short of MacArthur's vision is a complex and controversial topic beyond the scope of this work.

423 **Grunert arrives; October 1940 War Plans division recommendation; failure to mobilize Philippine Army in 1940:** Meixsel, "Major General George Grunert, WPO-3, and the Philippine Army, 1940–1941," 312; Mark S. Watson, *U.S. Army in World War II, The War Department, Chief of Staff Prewar Plans and Preparations* (Washington, DC Historical Division, Department of the Army, 1950), 418–19; Heinrichs, *Threshold of War*, 130–31; Willmott, *Empires in Balance*, 119–20.

423 **July 1941 radical alteration of Philippine policy:** Morton, *Fall of the Philippines*, 31; Heinrichs, *Threshold of War*, 130–31; Jeffery S. Underwood, *The Wings of Democracy: The Influence of Air Power on the Roosevelt Administration, 1933–1941* (College Park: Texas A&M University Press, 1991), 166–83 [hereafter Underwood, *The Wings of Democracy*]; Willmott, *Empires in Balance*, 125–26; Henry L. Stimson and McGeorge Bundy, *On Active Service in Peace and War* (New York: Harper & Brothers, 1948), 193. Stimson's diary contains multiple entries reflecting his extremely overconfident belief in the ability of heavy bombers parked in the Philippines to deter Japan and defend the islands. See Stimson diary, August 4, October 28, and November 10, 1941. The diary shows that Stimson's faith in the efficacy of high level bombing of ships by B-17s endured at least through the Battle of Midway (see sample diary entries for March 17, April 16, and June 6, 1942). The figures for heavy bombers are from Wesley Frank Craven and James Lea Cate, *The Army Air Forces in World War II*, vol. 1, *Plans and Early Operations January 1939 to August 1942* (Washington, DC:

Office of Air Force History, 1983 reprint), 178. This text is somewhat unclear as it describes a force of four groups "to consist of 272 with 68 in reserve." This appears to indicate four groups, each of 51 heavy bombers, with 68 such aircraft in reserve.

424 **MacArthur background:** these high points of his career prior to World War II are drawn from the indispensable source, D. Clayton James's magisterial and measured three-volume biography *The Years of MacArthur*. The background sketch of MacArthur's career up to 1941 is from vol. 1, *1888–1941* (Boston: Houghton Mifflin, 1970). Given MacArthur's divisive position in American history, he has also inspired biographies tilted from adulatory, notably William Manchester's *American Caesar: Douglas MacArthur 1888–1964* (Boston: Little, Brown, 1978), to the sharply critical like Michael Schaller's *Douglas MacArthur: The Far Eastern General* (New York: Oxford University Press, 1989). For MacArthur's height and weight in 1941 and promotion to full general, see Application for Identity Card and War Department to CG USAFFE, no. 859, December 22, 1941, Folder no. 2, AG 201, MacArthur, Douglas, Personal File, July 1941–March 1942, RG 2 USAFFE, Box 3, MacArthur Archive. Also useful is Duncan Anderson, "Douglas MacArthur and the Philippines," in Brian Bond, ed., *Fallen Stars*, 166 ("marked preference for the social company of prominent Filipinos rather than American expatriates") [hereafter Anderson, "Douglas MacArthur and the Philippines," and Bond, "Douglas MacArthur and the Philippines"]. The reporter was Clare Boothe, "MacArthur of the Far East," *Life* magazine, vol. 11, no. 23, 8 December 1941, 123–39 ("leaner in fiber and tougher in spirit . . ." at 139 and "positively pyrotechnic" at 135). Ironically, MacArthur appeared as the cover photo in the *Life* magazine issue the day after the Pearl Harbor attack.

425 **Reinforcements to MacArthur:** Morton, *Fall of the Philippines*, ch. 3, The Reinforcement of the Philippines; James, *The Years of MacArthur*, vol. 1, 611–12.

425 **Strength of FEAF:** William C. Bartsch, *December 8, 1941: MacArthur's Pearl Harbor* (College Station: Texas A&M University, 2003), appendix C [hereafter Bartsch, *December 8, 1941: MacArthur's Pearl Harbor*].

425 *New York Times* **story of Philippine bomber buildup:** "Philippines as a Fortress," *New York Times*, 19 November 1941, 1.

425 **Composition of Fourteenth Army and "did not have a very good reputation for its fighting qualities":** Morton, *Fall of the Philippines*, 56, 139. Although records appear incomplete, the figure for the strength of the Fourteenth Army is based upon the following reported totals in landing in the Philippines detailed in the text: 2,000 men each in landings at Vigan and Aparri, 2,500 at Legaspi, 7,000 at Lamon Bay, approximately 1,000 at Davao (the regimental size Sakaguchi Detachment actually was only briefly attached to the Fourteenth Army and then reverted to the Sixteenth Army control), 43,110 at Lingayen Gulf during 22–28 December, and at least 5,238 in the 65th Brigade.

426 **Japanese air units committed to Philippines:** Shores, Cull, and Izawa, *Bloody Shambles*, vol. 1, 53–54; Jiro Horikoshi, *Eagles of Mitsubishi: The Story of the Zero Fighter* (University of Washington Press, 1981), 125; Zimm, *Attack on Pearl Harbor*, 24, 56, 430–31n11; TROMs *Ryujo*, *Mizuho*, *Chitose*, and *Sanuki Maru*, combinedfleet.com, accessed 14 June 2014.

426 **Organization and strength of Philippine Army and its divisions:** Morton, *The Fall of the Philippines*, 26–27 (gives estimate of 120,000 men total in mobilized Philippine Army); "Philippine Department Plan Orange (1940 Revision), G-1 Annex,

Exhibit D, Data on the Philippine Army (revised as of 4/1/41), "Contributions from the Public," Box 4, Folder no. 4, Papers of John Gordon, MacArthur Archive; 98-USFI-0.3, "Report of Operations of USAFFE and USFIP in the Philippine Islands, 1941–1942," 10–13 (Wainwright Report on First Philippine Campaign), RG 407, Entry 427, Box 1156, NARA [hereafter "Report of Operations of USAFFE and USFIP in the Philippine Islands, 1941–1942"]; John W. Whitman, *Bataan: Our Last Ditch* (New York: Hippocrene Books, 1990), 60–61 (bamboo ramrods) [hereafter Whitman, *Bataan: Our Last Ditch*].

426 **Philippine Army lack of common language:** Whitman, *Bataan: Our Last Ditch*, 28.

427 **Strength of MacArthur's American forces:** Morton, *The Fall of the Philippines*, 33, 49 (Table 4); Whitman, *Bataan: Our Last Ditch*, 22–28; Hough, Ludwig, and Shaw, *Pearl Harbor to Guadalcanal*, 190–91. The 9,500 number comprises three infantry regiments (4,800); one cavalry battalion (682); two tank battalions (998); two artillery regiments (933); two self-propelled 75 mm gun battalions (estimated as about 600 men total); and 1,440 Marines. It must be noted that Table 4, page 49 in Morton's official history shows a return for strength of US forces in the Philippines as of 30 November 1941. The total strength given is 31,095; however, the subtotals on the table for headquarters units, the Philippine Division, Harbor Defenses, Aviation units, and Service Detachment, as well as 19 unassigned officers, is only 26,025, thus seemingly leaving 5,070 men not accounted for. The two commanders of the self-propelled 75 mm gun battalion died as prisoners of war, and no unit reports are available. This is especially regrettable as these two battalions and the tank battalions played crucial roles during the withdrawal to Bataan. On their fate, see The Harold K. Johnson Collection, Box 201, Folder 1, Oral Histories, Interview with D. Clayton James, 7–8, the United States Army Heritage and Education Center, Carlisle Barracks, Pennsylvania [hereafter USAHEC]. A 1901 law capped the size of the Philippine Scouts at 12,000. This law was not altered. Further, the additional manpower for the scouts came from Philippine Army soldiers who had completed their basic training, thus depriving the Philippine Army of freshly trained men. Meixsel, "Major General George Grunert, WPO-3, and the Philippine Army, 1940–1941," 314–15. The US Marine Corps history provides slightly different figures on pp. 190 and 191 and may not include some men already lost on Bataan.

428 **MacArthur's aviation units:** Bartsch, *December 8, 1941*, appendix C; Shores, Cull, and Izawa, *Bloody Shambles*, vol. 1, 56. There are slight differences between Bartsch and Shores. For example, Shores shows just 72 P-40s and 18 P-35As. The US Navy also had a handful of float aircraft. The text follows Bartsch for FEAF strength.

428 **Asiatic Fleet Strength:** Morison, *The Rising Sun in the Pacific*, 158–60.

428 **Hart described:** James Leutze, *A Different Kind of Victory: A Biography of Admiral Thomas C. Hart* (Annapolis, MD: Naval Institute Press, 1981), 163–64, 279–81, 284.

428 **"an undercurrent of antagonism":** Toland Papers, Series 1, The Rising Sun, Box 1, Folder, Aquino, Antonio, FDRL.

428 **"a proud and sensitive race . . . there was no such thing . . . throughout history":** Col. Richard C. Mallonee, *Battle for Bataan, An Eyewitness Account* (Novato, CA: Presidio Press, 1997), 5. My thanks to Dr. Allan Millett, who pointed out that the Sino-Filipino elite were anti-Japanese.

429 **News of Pearl Harbor attack reaches MacArthur; War Department order; Brereton notified:** Report of Operations, USAFFE and USFIP, 17, 25, RG 407, Entry 427, Box

1157 (which states unofficial word came via a correspondent calling one of MacArthur's aides at 0300; this is earlier than in other accounts, placing the time MacArthur was notified at 0330; Morton, *The Fall of the Philippines*, 90; D. Clayton James, *The Years of MacArthur*, vol. 2, *1941–1945* (Boston: Houghton Mifflin, 1975), 2, 7–15 [hereafter *James*, vol. 2]; Roger G. Miller, "A 'Pretty Damn Able Commander': Lewis Hyde Brereton: Part II," *Air Power History* 48, no. 1 (Winter 2001): 25–26, 32 [hereafter Miller, "A 'Pretty Damn Able Commander' "]; Bartsch, *December 8, 1941*, 276, appendix C (disposition of B-17s).

429 **Brereton meets Sutherland 0500 and 0715; preparations to attack shipping:** Bartsch, *December 8, 1941*, 276–77, 281–83, 416; Miller, "A 'Pretty Damn Able Commander,' " 25–26, 32. Bartsch reports that staff officers of the 19th Bomb Group first identified shipping as the target; Brereton, who previously called Takao harbor the "juiciest" target in range, confirmed this. This is an important point, for if the B-17s left early enough to catch Imperial Navy aircraft pinned to the ground by fog, the American objective would have been shipping, specifically Takao harbor. This makes it dubious that the bombers would have diverted to strike the airfields. Miller maintains that Brereton intended to attack both Takao harbor and the nearby naval airfield. Assuming this is true, this dispersion of an already small formation makes the prospect very dim of inflicting serious damage on the Imperial Navy's aircraft on the ground.

429 **Imperial Army raids, *Ryujo* raid on Davao; Brereton finally obtains authority to strike Formosa and plan:** Bartsch, *December 8, 1941*, 271–75, 279–82, 287, 292–94, 296; TROM *Ryujo*, combinedfleet.com, accessed 19 June 2014; Miller, "A 'Pretty Damn Able Commander,' " 32–33.

430 **FEAF aircraft recover; delayed Imperial Navy strikes take off:** Bartsch, *December 8, 1941*, 267–71, 286, 288–90; Shores, Cull, and Izawa, *Bloody Shambles*, vol. 1, 165–66.

430 **Mismanagement of interception of raid:** Bartsch, *December 8, 1941*, 299–310. Daniel Ford, "Informed Airmen? The US Army Air Forces Intelligence on Japanese Fighter Tactics in the Pacific Theater, 1941–5," *International History Review* 34, no. 4 (2012), explains that the Army Air Forces' neglect of intelligence on Japanese fighter tactics formed an important part of the reason for the poor showing of AAF fighters early in the war.

430 **Imperial Navy strike hits Clark and other bases; American interception:** Bartsch, *December 8, 1941*, 311–61, 409, appendices C, H, I; Shores, Cull, and Izawa, *Bloody Shambles* vol. 1, 163–75; Col. E. B. Miller, *Bataan Uncensored* (Minnesota Military Museum, Military Historical Society of Minnesota, 1991; reprint of 1949 volume), 66–67 ("like the deep growl of many powerful beasts—snarling as one" and "diabolical accuracy") [hereafter Miller, *Bataan Uncensored*]. There are slight differences in figures between Bartsch and Shores et al. Although Shores et al. are excellent, the text follows Bartsch as the newer work.

431 **Japanese aviators return; Japanese losses:** Barstch, *December 8, 1941*, 288, 399–403 ("almost as if the enemy did not know the war had started" at 402).

431 **Accounts of Sutherland, MacArthur, and Brereton cannot be reconciled:** not only were their postwar statements in conflict, examination of what is purported to be the contemporary record of Brereton's headquarters appears extremely suspicious as to its authenticity, at least for 8 December. The document in question is titled

"Headquarters, Far East Air Force, Office of the Commanding General." A copy reposes in Folder no. 3, Far East Air Force Operations 8 December 1941–24 February 1942, RG 2 USAFFE, Box 3, MML. The entries for December 8, 1941, and several other dates in December 1941 are typed as "1942." Mistakenly recording dates into the New Year with the past year's date is perhaps understandable, but not so repeatedly recording "1942" for contemporary 1941 dates. The first entry for December 8 is timed at 0730, thus omitting any reference to Brereton's asserted earlier meetings with Sutherland. Astonishingly, the contents fail to reflect *any* reports or inquiries as to damage, losses, and claims by the FEAF fighter command for 8 December. The only entry with respect to B-17 losses is clearly incomplete. Finally, the report fails to mention Brereton's meeting with MacArthur that took place at 1550 according to MacArthur's office diary. The overpowering inference is that this document was prepared later and carefully edited to obscure evidence of the disasters of 8 December. The skepticism many writers have directed at MacArthur's and Sunderland's accounts is easily understood and concurred in by this writer. But the supposed "official" records of Brereton's headquarters demonstrates that his accounts should be treated with vast skepticism.

431 **Air situation over the Philippines from December 10 to 31; bombing of Cavite Navy Yard:** Shores, Cull, and Izawa, *Bloody Shambles,* vol. 1, 176–97 (FEAF strength December 10, 183, Japanese loss figures 186, 191); Morison, *The Rising Sun in the Pacific,* 171–72. Japanese losses by 15 December included eighteen Ki-27s, one Ki-48, and one Ki-51 of the Imperial Army and Imperial Navy; losses to all causes totaled four G4M, six G3M, twenty-three A6Ms, and one transport aircraft. The combined total was fifty-four aircraft.

432 **Operable American aircraft in Philippines on 31 December 1941:** Headquarters, Fifth Interceptor Command, December 31, 1941, RG 2, Personal Files, Correspondence of General MacArthur, Box 2, November 25, 1941 to April 17, 1942, Folder 3, December 25, 1941 to January 22, 1942. B-17 strength as of 22 December was fourteen, and two were damaged beyond repair for further operations on the 25th. Thus, about twelve B-17s were still on hand on 31 December. Shores, Cull, and Izawa, *Bloody Shambles,* vol. 1, 191–97.

432 **Inadequacy of Clark as air base; warning from Army Air Force planners:** Bartsch, *December 8, 1941,* 119–20, 164–65, 218; Underwood, *The Wings of Democracy,* 148, 173; Miller, "A 'Pretty Damn Able Commander,'" 29. It bears noting that MacArthur and his aviators kept requesting more aircraft than the available bases would properly support, but Washington carried the first responsibility to assure that bases and defenses were adequate for the FEAF.

432 **MacArthur and orders to send all B-17s to Del Monte:** Walter D. Edmonds, *They Fought With What They Had* (Boston: Center for Air Force History, Little, Brown, 1951), 63 [hereafter Edmonds, *They Fought With What They Had*] states flatly that MacArthur's headquarters ordered all B-17s to Mindanao to keep them out of Japanese reach prior to 8 December, although noting Brereton later claimed the order was his. This writer finds Edmonds's work highly credible as it was based on review of contemporary records and extensive interviews of many principals during or shortly after the war. (The one conspicuous exception among interviewees is Brereton, who declined an interview.) Further support, albeit much after the fact, was provided by Hugh Casey, the distinguished engineer officer who served under MacArthur from

the Philippines onward. In a 1979 interview, Casey insisted he was present when Sutherland, upon learning that the B-17s had not all been moved to Del Monte as MacArthur ordered, called Brereton's chief of staff and ordered them moved immediately, but this was not done. Engineer Memoirs, Major General Hugh J. Casey, Pamphlet no. 870-1-18, pp. 149–50, www.publications.usace.army.mil/Portals/76/Publications/EngineerPamphlets/EP_870-1-18.pdf, accessed 20 September 2016. Though, as noted, this writer is not disposed to accept casually after-the-fact statements from MacArthur or Sutherland, he finds Brereton grossly lacking in credibility. Besides the obvious problem with Brereton's headquarters report dated "December 8, 1942," as noted above, another telling indicator is Geoffrey Perret, *Old Soldiers Never Die: The Life of Douglas MacArthur* (New York: Random House, 1996), 253–54. Perret is scathing about Brereton, noting that review of more than a thousand interviews for his prior work on the Army Air Forces revealed no one who found Brereton competent. In a 29 November 1941 letter to Marshall, MacArthur stated that "the location of potential enemy bombardment airdromes and the types of aircraft available to him indicate that heavy bombers should be located south of the island of Luzon, where they are reasonably safe from attack, but from where, through partial utilization of auxiliary fields, they can deliver their own blows." MacArthur pointed out that Del Monte still presented problems as "the defensive location of the Bomber Command base in Mindanao is not acceptable because that Island is strategically a salient and its defense a difficult problem with the force now in contemplation." Letter MacArthur to Marshall, November 29, 1941, RG 2, Personal Files, Correspondence of General MacArthur, Box 2, November 25, 1941 to April 17, 1942, Folder no. 1, November 25, 1941 to December 15, 1941, MML. Another intriguing communication from MacArthur to Marshall, on 1 December 1941, indicates MacArthur's aviators advised him that the location of Japanese bases and capabilities of their aircraft placed "definite limitation" on their ability to project strikes by escorted bombers, unless the Japanese coordinated bombers with carrier-based fighters, or until the Japanese could establish forward air bases on Luzon. This indicates that MacArthur had been advised to be wary that Japanese carriers could be operating off the Philippines. This in turn meant that Formosa by no means represented the only vector from which a Japanese air strike could originate. There is no direct evidence MacArthur was thinking this way on 8 December, but it is notable that this Japanese capability seems to be completely disregarded in the literature on the Japanese strike. Letter MacArthur to Marshall, December 1, 1941, i RG 2, Personal Files, Correspondence of General MacArthur, Box 2, November 25, 1941 to April 17, 1942, Folder no. 1, November 25, 1941 to December 15, 1941, MML.

433   **Effects of theoretical B-17 strike on Formosa in morning hours of 8 December:** Bartsch, a very insightful historian of these events, argued that such a raid could have devastated Imperial Navy aircraft waiting at their bases. Bartsch, *December 8, 1941*, 412. This writer respectfully disagrees. It is conceivable that had the raid been launched, as Brereton urged, the B-17s might have arrived over Formosa as the weather broke. Even assuming this was so, there remained major hurdles raised by the "fog of war": would the American strike have located the correct airfield or airfields from which the Japanese mounted the strikes, and would the American bombing have caused more than modest damage? The likely outcome would be that the B-17s would miss the opportunity by failing to choose the right targets or to hit

them effectively. At a minimum, the Japanese used multiple bases which would have left some free of harm or split the bombing effort into small and probably ineffective parcels. Further, as noted above, Miller's account maintains the small B-17 strike would have been divided between shipping and airfield targets, making devastation of grounded Japanese aircraft even less likely.

433 **Unrestricted air and submarine warfare policy change:** Joel Holwitt, *Execute Against Japan: The U.S. Decision to Conduct Unrestricted Submarine Warfare* (College Station: Texas A&M University Press, 2009). Hoelwitt, a currently serving US submarine officer, performed the fascinating detective work on this hugely important but overlooked issue. He found no documentary evidence that Stark presented the issue to Secretary of the Navy Knox or President Roosevelt. This raises an important issue about the American principle of subordination of the military to the political authorities. Given Roosevelt's intense scrutiny of the activities of his navy, and his penchant for refusing to have written records made of his conversations or decisions, this writer's view is that Stark very likely did discuss this momentous matter with Roosevelt and obtained the president's approval.

434 **US submarine force, Asiatic Fleet, December 8, 1941:** Commander Submarines, U.S. Asiatic Fleet, Serial S518, April 1, 1942, RG 38, NARA, 1–2, 5 [hereafter Commander Submarines, US Asiatic Fleet]. Supporting the submarines were three tenders (*Canopus, Holland*, and *Otus*) and one rescue vessel (*Pigeon*).

434 **Claimed successes versus reality:** Commander Submarines, U.S. Asiatic Fleet, 1 (note this was an amendment of the original tabular data, which showed thirty-six sunk and eleven damaged at page 71); John D. Alden and Craig R. McDonald, *United States and Allied Submarine Successes in the Pacific and Far East During World War II*, 4th edition (Jefferson, NC: McFarland Publishers, 2009), 27–34. Of the twelve ships sunk, one was later salvaged and one was Norwegian, but almost certainly would have been seized and used by Japan. The Asiatic fleet lost *Sealion* on 10 December to Japanese bombs at Cavite with four killed. *S-36* became a total loss when it ran aground on 19 January. Fortunately, the whole crew of forty-seven was saved. On 11 February, the Japanese destroyer *Yamakaze* caught *Shark* on the surface and sank it with gunfire. All fifty-eight men were lost. A series of depth charge attacks during 1–3 March inflicted progressive damage that forced the crew of *Perch* to scuttle their boat. All sixty-four survived to be captured. Vernon J. Miller, "US Submarine Losses," *Warship XII*, 45, 51, 54.

434 **Claimed versus actual sinkings, problems with submarine commanders:** Commander Submarines, U.S. Asiatic Fleet, 1, 53–55; Clay Blair, *Silent Victory: The U.S. Submarine War Against Japan* (Philadelphia and New York: J. B. Lippincott, 1975), 45–46, 118–21, 125–26, 129, 132–33, 176–78 [hereafter Blair, *Silent Victory*]. Blair's book remains the monumental narrative of the US submarine war, comprehensive, balanced, and highly readable. Later work by Alden and McDonald, however, has raised some of the confirmed sinking credits above that available when Blair worked.

434 **Submarine commander problems; McKinney:** Blair, *Silent Victory*, 125–26, 176–78.

435 **Failure of defense of Lingayen Gulf; diversions of submarines:** Commander Submarines, U.S. Asiatic Fleet, 43; Blair, *Silent Victory*, 149–52.

435 **Material issues; loss of torpedoes and spare parts:** Commander Submarines, U.S. Asiatic Fleet, 56; Blair, *Silent Victory*, 133–34, 136. An excellent description of all

the material deficiencies that rendered the S-Boats of low value is provided in Lt. Cdr. C. N. G. Hendrix, Fold3.com/WWII War Diaries/P/Personnel Interviews/333, accessed 26 June 2016.

435 **Fleet boats prove value:** Commander Submarines, U.S. Asiatic Fleet, 50, 56.

435 **Torpedo failure:** Commander Submarines, U.S. Asiatic Fleet, 44–47; Robert Gannon, *Hellions of the Deep: The Development of American Torpedoes in World War II* (University Park: Pennsylvania State University Press, 1996), ch. 6; Blair, *Silent Victory*, 118, 137.

436 **Imperial Navy effectiveness:** Commander Submarines, U.S. Asiatic Fleet, 9, 20, 48; Blair, *Silent Victory*, 175.

436 **Luzon plain and Evolution of Philippine defense plans, Grunert's 1941 plan:** Dod, *The Corps of Engineers in the War Against Japan*, 73–74; Meixsel, "Major General George Grunert, WPO-3, and the Philippine Army, 1940–1941," 316–17; 98 USFI-0.3 (Wainwright Report on First Philippine Campaign, Annex IV), Report of Operations of North Luzon Force and I Philippine Corps in the Defense of North Luzon and Bataan, 2–3, RG 407, Entry 427, Box 1156, NARA [hereafter Report of Operations of North Luzon Force and I Philippine Corps].

438 **Philippine Division role:** James Havens Birdseye, "Japanese and Philippine-American Logistics: The Philippine Dilemma, 1935–1942" (University Microfilms International, unpublished diss., 1995), 408–9.

438 **Vigan landings and FEAF attacks:** "The Philippine Campaign, Phase I" (n.d.), 18, 23 (translated report of operations, Fourteenth Army), D767.4.P44, USAHEC [hereafter Report of Operations, Fourteenth Army, Phase I]; TROMs *W-10, Brisbane Maru* (IJA auxiliary transport), combinedfleet.com, accessed 6 May 2014; Shores, Cull, and Izawa, *Bloody Shambles*, vol. 1, 176–77.

438 **Aparri landing:** Report of Operations, Fourteenth Army, Phase I, 18, 23, 25; Morton, *Fall of the Philippines*, 104–6.

438 **MacArthur assessment of purpose of Vigan and Aparri landings:** MacArthur to War Department, December 13, 1941, RG 2, Personal Files, Correspondence of General MacArthur, Box 2, November 25, 1941 to April 17, 1942, Folder no. 1, November 25, 1941 to December 15, 1941, MML.

438 **Legaspi landing Force:** Report of Operations, Fourteenth Army, Phase I, 19, 26; TROMs *Nagara, Shinryu Maru* (Zatsuyosen [Imperial Army transports]), *Ikushima Maru* (Zatsuyosen [Imperial Navy transports]), combinedfleet.com, accessed 14 July 2014.

438 **Japanese landing at Davao and Jolo:** Remmelink, *The Invasion of the Dutch East Indies*, 88, 103–14; Report of Operations, Fourteenth Army, Phase I, 7, 28; TROM *Jintsu*, combinedfleet.com, accessed 20 August 2014; ATIS, no. 355, "Luzon Campaign of 16 Division, 24 Dec 41–3 Jan 42," RG 3, Box 139, SWPA, ATIS: Enemy Publications no. 312–356, MacArthur Archive [hereafter "Luzon Campaign of 16 Division, 24 Dec 41–3 Jan 42"].

439 **Strength of Japanese forces landing at Lingayen Gulf:** Report of Operations, Fourteenth Army, Phase I, Table 1, 30–31. For the equipment of the two tank regiments, see "The History of Battles of Imperial Japanese Tanks, Part I," ww3.plala.or.jp/takihome/history.htm, accessed 13 May 2014. One set of figures indicates the Fourteenth Army, counting shipping and aviation units, landed a total of 43,110 men at Lingayen Gulf from 22 to 28 December. Morton, *The Fall of the Philippines*, 125n5.

Thus, the eighty-five Japanese transports carried on average five hundred men each. By World War II standards, and particularly those of the Japanese later in the war, this was remarkably low. Part of the seeming light loading of troops may be due to the large numbers of horses needed for Japanese transportation, particularly artillery. Much literature looks askance at MacArthur's claims that he was heavily outnumbered. To be fair, however, MacArthur's original report of massive Japanese strength reasonably matched the size of the invasion fleet. If fault is to be found, it should be assigned to the subsequent campaign, where contact with Japanese units should have yielded a more accurate picture.

439 **MacArthur's report to the War Department:** MacArthur to War Department radio of December 22, 1941, RG 2, Personal Files, Correspondence of General MacArthur, Box 2, November 25, 1941 to April 17, 1942, Folder 2, December 16, 1941 to December 24, 1941, MML.

439 **Lingayen landings, December 22:** Report of Operations, Fourteenth Army, Phase I, 30–31; Maeda, Lieutenant General Masami, Fourteenth Army Chief of Staff, Interrogations of Former Japanese Officers, Philippines-Japanese Invasion, USAHEC.

439 **Ineffective defense of Lingayen Gulf landing sites; Wainwright described:** Report of Operations of North Luzon Force & I Philippine Corps, 2–8; Morton, *Fall of the Philippines*, 131; Report of Operations, Fourteenth Army, Phase I, 30–31; John Jacob Beck, *MacArthur and Wainwright: Sacrifice in the Philippines* (Albuquerque: University of New Mexico Press, 1974), 240.

439 **MacArthur sends forward reinforcements, battles at Damortis and Rosario, performance of 26th Cavalry (PS):** Report of Operations of North Luzon Force & I Philippine Corps, 8–10; Morton, *Fall of the Philippines*, 133–36; Report of Operations, Fourteenth Army, Phase I, 34–35.

440 **Lamon Bay landing:** Report of Operations, Fourteenth Army, Phase I, 33; TROMs *Bengal Maru*, *Ikushima Maru* IJA transport (Yusosen), combinedfleet.com, accessed 14 July 2014; "Luzon Campaign of 16 Division, 24 Dec 41–3 Jan 42."

440 **Lamon Bay defenders and Japanese advances:** Morton, *The Fall of the Philippines*, 139–44; The Philippine Campaign I, 15, 33, 38–40; "Luzon Campaign of 16 Division, 24 Dec 41–3 Jan 42."

440 **Wainwright calls, permission granted, Manila declared "Open City":** Report of Operations, USAFFE and USFIP, 33–34; James, *The Years of MacArthur*, vol. 2, 22, 30–31.

440 **WPO-3 withdrawal plan:** Report of Operations, USAFFE and USFIP, 33–34; Report of Operations of North Luzon Force & I Philippine Corps, 11.

441 **Wainwright's withdrawal down corridor from Lingayen Gulf to Manila:** Report of Operations of North Luzon Force & I Philippine Corps, 11–13, 15; Whitman, *Bataan: Our Last Ditch*, 101, 106–7.

441 **Defense of Layac:** Whitman, *Bataan: Our Last Ditch*, 69–87 (esp. 81, 83, 85); Morton, *Fall of the Philippines*, 180.

441 **Columns retreating into Bataan:** Donald Young, *The Battle of Bataan: A Complete History* (2nd edition) (Jefferson, NC: MacFarland Publishers, 2009), 9 ("shoddy, dust white, denim blues" [plural in original], from Henry G. Lee's poem, "Abucay Withdrawal"); Whitman, *Bataan: Our Last Ditch*, 1–2.

441 **Japanese miscalculation on Bataan withdrawal:** Report of Operations, Fourteenth Army, Phase I, 4, 10–11, 44–45, 46, 50–53, 60–62. Extensive postwar commentary

on the failure of the Fourteenth Army to foresee or cut off the retreat to Bataan is found in Interrogations of Former Japanese Officers, Philippines-Japanese Invasion, USAHEC: Akiyama, Col. Monjiro Third Department, IGHQ (Army air section), 3–4; Inagaki, Major Shojo, Fourteenth Army Staff, Line of Communications, 3; Kawagoe, Col. Morigi, Chief of Staff 48th Division, 5; Maeda, Lieutenant General Masami, Fourteenth Army Chief of Staff, 2–3; Morioka, Lieutenant General Susumu, 16th Division Commander, 4–5; Nakayama, Colonel Motoo, Fourteenth Army, Senior Operations Officer, 3–5; Nakayama, Col. Motoo, Replies to Inquiries, 21 Mar 50, 1–2; Maeda, Masami, 2 Mar 50 "Answers," 2–3; and Kawagoe Miriji, former Chief of Staff, 48th Division, Reply, 9 Mar 50, 1–2.

442   **Buses with dead Filipino soldiers:** Whitman, *Bataan: Our Last Ditch*, 2.

442   **"the cardinal blunder of the entire campaign":** James, *The Years of MacArthur*, vol. 1, 30.

442   **Drake states he could have stocked Bataan in two weeks in accordance with pre-war plan:** Report of Operations Quartermaster Corps U.S. Army, in the Philippine Campaign 1941–42, 21–22, by Maj. Gen. Charles C. Drake, Chief Quartermaster USAFFE and USFIP 98 USFI-0.3 (Wainwright Report Annex XIII), RG 407, Entry 427, Box 1159, NARA [hereafter Drake, Report of Operations of Quartermaster Corps]. Drake was a colonel until December 18, 1941, when he was promoted to brigadier general.

442   **Expectations as to Philippine Army personnel participating in defense of Bataan:** "Philippine Department Plan Orange (1940 Revision) (with August 13, 1941 amendment, Subject: Changes to G-4 Annex to HPD WPO-3)," section 2, Mission and General Plan ("when and if troops designed to defend Bataan retire thereto, the remainder of the Philippine Army troops . . ."); Strength of US forces in Philippine Department from Morton, *The Fall of the Philippines*, 24, 49. Morton (254) states that as of 23 December, the quartermasters understood they needed to stock Bataan for 80,000 troops. Assuming this is so, it still indicates that plans on 8 December based on the current WPO-3 would have grossly underestimated the amount of required supplies.

442   **Drake presumes 43,000-man garrison on Bataan:** Drake, Report of Operations Quartermaster Corps, 21–22.

442   **Number of persons on Bataan:** Drake, Report of Operations Quartermaster Corps, 31–34; Morton, *The Fall of the Philippines*, 254; Whitman, *Bataan: Our Last Ditch*, 49, 125. These sources agree on the number of Filipino civilians, including civilian employees of USAFFE, but disagree somewhat on the number of combatants. The figures in the text should be deemed approximations rather than an exact count. Whitman figures the numbers of American service personnel on Bataan at 15,000, with the rest Filipinos. The text allows for more Americans in view of the presence of naval personnel. Whichever way the existing numbers are calculated, however, it is clear that the number of Philippine Army personnel reaching Bataan far exceeded prewar plans.

443   **MacArthur's two decisions create insurmountable obstacles to stocking adequate supplies on Bataan; garrison goes on half rations:** Drake, Report of Operations Quartermaster Corps, 5, 21–22, 28–30; Report of Operations, USAFFE and USFIP in Philippines, 42; Alvin P. Stauffer, *United States Army in World War II, The Technical Services, The Quartermaster Corps: Operations in the War Against Japan* (Washington, DC: Office of the Chief of Military History, 1956), 9–13; James, *The Years of*

MacArthur, vol. 1, 29–34; Whitman, *Bataan: Our Last Ditch*, 46; Morton, *Fall of the Philippines*, 164–65, 179–80.

443 **Resupply efforts:** Stanley Falk, "Ships that Never Came In," *Military History Quarterly* 7, no. 2 (Winter 1994): 43–45. This account shows that all resupply efforts in total moved to MacArthur about 4,900 tons of rations, plus eight submarine deliveries, each with about half a day's supply, plus antiaircraft ammunition.

444 **"we should be unable to reinforce [MacArthur]...":** Stimson diary, December 8, 1941.

444 **Hart advises that the islands are "doomed":** Radio MacArthur to Marshall, December 13, 1941, Personal Files, Correspondence of General MacArthur, Box 2, November 25, 1941 to April 17, 1942, Folder no. 1, November 25, 1941 to December 15, 1941, RG 2, MML.

444 **December messages and president's address:** a sampling of these messages includes Marshall to MacArthur, December 11, 1941 ("We are making every effort to reach you..."), Personal Files, Correspondence of General MacArthur, Box 2, November 25, 1941 to April 17, 1942, Folder no. 1, November 25, 1941 to December 15, 1941, RG 2, MML; Headquarters USAFFE to Commanding General, Far East Air Force, December 22, 1941 (Washington promises over 260 aircraft for the Philippines and specifics), Personal Files, Correspondence of General MacArthur, Box 2, November 25, 1941 to April 17, 1942, Folder 2, December 16, 1941 to December 24, 1941, RG 2, MML ("the President [has] again personally directed the Navy to make every effort to support you"); Radio, Washington to USA Forces Far East Manila (apparently December 25, 1941) and signed "Marshall," RG 2, Personal Files, Correspondence of General MacArthur, Box 2, November 25, 1941 to April 17, 1942, Folder 3, December 25, 1941 to January 22, 1942, RG 2, MML; James, *The Years of MacArthur*, vol. 2, 49, citing a Roosevelt address implying major relief is on the way to the Philippines and a Navy Department announcement of December 28, 1941, appearing to confirm this. On 18 December, MacArthur ordered his engineers to begin preparing landing strips on Bataan, but also outside Bataan, first for fighters and later for bombers expected to arrive. Dod, *The Corps of Engineers in the War Against Japan*, 79. This order, obviously based upon promises of aircraft reinforcements, raises the issue of whether MacArthur made decisions through December based on the need to retain territory on Luzon for the promised aircraft.

444 **MacArthur advocates priority for the Philippines, urges his demands for reinforcements be met:** for example, MacArthur to Marshall, February 4, 1942 (Allies making "a fatal blunder" in not making flank attack to support Philippines), and MacArthur to Marshall, January 1, 1942 (advocating "an immediate combined effort of all the resources of the United States and her allies by land, sea and air" to relieve the Philippines), and demands his requirements be met as an Allied priority (messages too numerous to itemize from December 1941 through February 1942), all in Folder no. 1, Chief of Staff Dealing with Plans and Policies November 1941 to February 1942, RG 2 USAFFE, Box 3, MML. An example of what fairly can be called a hysterical communication is MacArthur's message to Marshall in June 1942 claiming that in the 1930s when he was chief of staff, he discovered a navy "master plan" to take over national defense and reduce the army to a much inferior role. Frank, *Guadalcanal*, 33–34.

444   **Eisenhower recalled to Washington, relationship with MacArthur:** Irish, "Dwight Eisenhower and Douglas MacArthur in the Philippines," 439–73.

444   **"it will be a long time before major reinforcements . . ." and "Everybody knows the chances are against . . .":** Stimson diary, January 5, 1942. Eisenhower had prepared a similar assessment for Marshall as early as December 14, 1941. James, *Years of MacArthur,* vol. 2, 51.

444   **Marshall dispatch, 13 January:** Marshall to MacArthur, 13 January 1942, Personal Files, Correspondence of General MacArthur, Box 2, November 25, 1941 to April 17, 1942, Folder 3, December 25, 1941 to January 22, 1942, RG 2, MML.

444   **"Help is on the way from the United States . . .":** Headquarters USAFFE, January 15, 1943, Subject: Message from General MacArthur, Personal Files, Correspondence of General MacArthur, Box 2, November 25, 1941 to April 17, 1942, Folder 3, December 25, 1941 to January 22, 1942, RG 2, MML.

445   **Sense of betrayal weakens Americans and Filipinos in captivity:** Matthew S. Klimow, "Lying to the Troops: American Leaders and the Defense of Bataan," *Parameters* 20, no. 4 (December 1990): 57–58. Klimow provides a thorough and thoughtful assessment of this issue.

445   **MacArthur organizes I and II Philippine Corps; establishes Abucay Line:** Headquarters, USAFFE, General Orders no. 56, 6 January 1942, RG 2, Personal Files (Correspondence of General MacArthur), Box 2, November 25, 1941 to April 17, 1942, Folder 3, December 25, 1941 to January 22, 1942; Report of Operations USAFFE & USFIP in Philippines, 43–45; Report of Operations of North Luzon Force and I Philippine Corps, 16–20; Morton, *Fall of the Philippines,* 266; Whitman, *Bataan: Our Last Ditch,* 89–91 ("is often more a state of mind . . ." at 91).

445   **Dispositions of II Philippine Corps:** Whitman, *Bataan: Our Last Ditch,* 96–99, 116; Wainwright Report on First Philippine Campaign, Annex V Report of Operations of South Luzon Force and II Philippine Corps, RG 407, Entry 427, Box 1156, NARA.

445   **Dispositions of I Philippine Corps on Abucay Line:** Report of Operations of North Luzon Force & I Philippine Corps, 16–18; Whitman, *Bataan: Our Last Ditch,* 112–13.

445   **Homma loses units; misinformation about Bataan defenders, impetus to attack:** Report of Operations, Fourteenth Army, Phase I, 60–65; Interview, Lieutenant General Masami, Fourteenth Army Chief of Staff, 6; Whitman, *Bataan: Our Last Ditch,* 124–26.

446   **Background 65th Brigade, Nara and attachment 9th Infantry Regiment:** ATIS: 151, "Combat in the Mt. Natib Area Bataan," 2–3, MacArthur Archive, RG 3, Box 130, SWPA, ATIS: Enemy Publications no. 146-166 [hereafter "Combat in the Mt. Natib Area Bataan"]; Whitman, *Bataan: Our Last Ditch,* 123–24, 127. "Combat in the Mt. Natib Area Bataan" was the translated detailed report of the 65th Brigade of battles in January 1942. The report was captured in 1944.

446   **Japanese attacks 9–10 January 1942:** "Combat in the Mt. Natib Area Bataan," 15–17; Whitman, *Bataan: Our Last Ditch,* 128–31.

446   **"spurt of acrid smoke, burnt powder" and "It went into my nostrils . . .":** Silvestre L. Tagarao, *This Was Bataan* (Quezon City: New Day Publishers, 1991), 38.

447   **65th Brigade suffers under American artillery fire:** "Combat in the Mt. Natib Area Bataan," 10, 12–13, 15, 27.

447   **Travails of 9th Infantry Regiment:** "Combat in the Mt. Natib Area Bataan," 4, 22, 31; Whitman, *Bataan: Our Last Ditch,* 162.

447 **The 9th Regiment on Mt. Natib:** hole driven in Abucay line: "Combat in the Mount Natib Area Bataan," 30–32; Operations of the Philippine Division, 12–14; Whitman, *Bataan: Our Last Ditch*, 168–72.

447 **Japanese cut west coast road, force retreat of I Corps:** Whitman, *Bataan: Our Last Ditch*, 209–26.

447 **MacArthur orders retreat from Abucay Line:** USFI-0.3 Report of Operations USAFFE & USFIP in Philippines, vol. 1, 48–49; James, *The Years of MacArthur*, vol. 2, 57–58.

447 **Retreat of II Corps:** Whitman, *Bataan: Our Last Ditch*, 227–46.

448 **MacArthur message to Washington; MacArthur's communiqués:** Whitman, *Bataan: Our Last Ditch*, 246 (quotes MacArthur report of withdrawal).

448 **Battle at "Points" with 2/20th:** Young, *The Battle of Bataan*, 75–105; Whitman, *Bataan: Our Last Ditch*, 249–93 ("completely without fear" at 260 and "All we lacked was training and equipment . . ." at 276).

449 **Destruction of 1/20th:** Whitman, *Bataan: Our Last Ditch*, 295–322; Young, *The Battle of Bataan*, 2nd edition, 106–29.

449 **Attacks of 65th Brigade in eastern sector of II Corps from 27 January:** 65th Brigade Combat Report on Philippine Operation, 26 Jan to 24 Feb 1942, 2, 6–15, 21, ATIS no. 289, Box 136, RG 3, MML; Whitman, *Bataan: Our Last Ditch*, 325–45.

449 **Battle of the Pockets:** Whitman, *Bataan: Our Last Ditch*, 347–72; Young, *The Battle of Bataan*, 2nd edition, 130–50.

450 **Homma assumes defensive:** Whitman, *Bataan: Our Last Ditch*, 373–80; Young, *The Battle of Bataan*, 2nd edition, 148–50.

450 **Quezon proposes neutralization of the Philippines; supported by Sayre and MacArthur:** the original messages are in *FRUS, 1942, General; the British Commonwealth; the Far East*, 894–99; Stimson diary, February 8, 1941 ("more than half way").

450 **Roosevelt rejects Quezon proposal; orders to MacArthur:** *FRUS, 1942, General; the British Commonwealth; the Far East*, 899–900; James, *The Years of MacArthur*, vol. 2, 96–97.

450 **Evacuation of Quezon, Sayre, and Roosevelt's order to MacArthur:** Blair, *Silent Victory*, 151–52; James, *The Years of MacArthur*, vol. 2, 97–99; Dick Harrelson oral history, transcribed March 22, 2006, National Museum of the Pacific War, 5 ("It was the only time . . .").

451 **Evacuation by PT Boat instead of submarine:** Rear Adm. F. W. Rockwell to The Commander in Chief, U.S. Fleet, August 1, 1942, Subject: Narrative of Naval Activities in Luzon Area, December 1, 1941 to March 19, 1942, 20 (fold3.com/image 267942048), accessed 24 September 2016.

451 **MacArthur's journey from Corregidor to Melbourne; "I shall return" statement:** James, *The Years of MacArthur*, vol. 2, 99–110; Bulkley, *At Close Quarters*, 16–18. My thanks to Australia's distinguished historian David Horner, who pointed out that the accounts that indicate MacArthur's famous "I shall return" statement was made in Adelaide are mistaken. He made the comment in Terowie, about 132 miles north of Adelaide.

451 **"supernova, a blaze of light without substance":** Anderson, "Douglas MacArthur and the Philippines," 166.

452 **MacArthur's performance in the First Philippine Campaign:** James, *The Years of MacArthur*, 151–54; Frank, *MacArthur*, 52–54.

452 **MacArthur's communiqués:** James, *The Years of MacArthur*, vol. 2, 89–90. A very astute scholar, Eric Bergerud, correctly observes that the manipulation of the press is hardly a sin that can be solely attributed to MacArthur. Allied communiqués during the half decade before 1942, and much of the next two years, are full of exaggerations and distortions, some of rather spectacular character (to pick but one example, the US Eighth Air Force wildly exaggerated claims that bomber gunners were shooting down vast numbers of German fighters). Bergerud further argues that MacArthur's use of the press secured for him his subsequent theater command and the resources to conduct a successful campaign against Japan.

452 **Quezon offers payments to MacArthur and three other officers:** copies of original documents, including confirmation that Roosevelt and Stimson were aware of the payments, are in Folder no. 7, President of the Philippines Executive Order no. 1, 22 February 1942, RG 2 USAFFE, Box 3, MML. Quezon's Executive Order describes the sums to be given as follows: "In recognition of outstanding service to the Commonwealth of the Philippines and pursuant to the authority granted me by Commonwealth Act number one and especially by the Emergency Powers Law, the officers named below are hereby granted recompense and reward, however inadequate, for distinguished service rendered between November 15, 1935 and December 30, 1941. . . ." Payments included $75,000 to Sutherland, $45,000 to Richard J. Marshall, and $20,000 to Sidney J. Huff. Carol Petillo uncovered this story in *Douglas MacArthur: The Philippine Years* (Bloomington: Indiana University Press, 1981), 204–11, 230. Geoffrey Perret mounted a robust challenge to the usual interpretation that it was a "corrupt transaction," at least as to MacArthur; *Old Soldiers Never Die* (New York: Random House, 1996), 271–73. Basically, the adjutant general ruled that when MacArthur took up his appointment in the Philippines, he was specifically exempted from the law against serving officers receiving sums from foreign governments and thus could receive any amount of money the Philippine government chose to give him. In 1937 Roosevelt had a chance to revoke that authority but did not (nor apparently did the matter come up in 1941 when MacArthur was recalled to active service). This may explain why Roosevelt, Stimson, and Marshall mounted no objection to the transaction, and one cannot overlook what may have been their guilt over the failure of the efforts to at least provide some major support to the garrison, if not its relief. Then there is the further aspect that MacArthur may have never expected to live to have access to the money. Perret further notes that the sum involved as to MacArthur was vastly exceeded by offers for his memoirs (Viking alone proposed a million dollars for such a work while MacArthur was on Corregidor, but he ignored the offer), corporate directorships and "other profitable ventures" he passed up after 1935, and even a "sizable" figure offered to Jean about her life with MacArthur. Perret called the sums paid to the other officers "more than a little dubious." This writer remains convinced that whatever the specific legality of the payment to MacArthur may have been, the failure to recognize its tainted appearance alone warrants condemnation. At the same time, anyone with an appreciation for MacArthur's gigantic ego can see how he could have accepted the money as his due, and at least himself thought it would have no effect on his judgment on official matters.

452 **"Dugout Doug":** James, *The Years of MacArthur*, vol. 2, 74–75, 153.

17: "Abandoned My 100,000 Soldiers in Foreign Jungles"

454 **Burma's topography and climate:** Kirby, *India's Most Dangerous Hour*, 1–5; Louis Allen, *Burma: The Longest War 1941 to 1945* (London: Phoenix Press, 2000), 8 [hereafter Allen, *Burma: The Longest War*].

455 **"So Burma was a country of immense topographical contrasts . . .":** Allen, *Burma: The Longest War*, 8.

455 **Burma's communications:** Kirby, *India's Most Dangerous Hour*, 4.

455 **Burma's population and economy:** Kirby, *India's Most Dangerous Hour*, 5; Allen, *Burma: The Longest War*, 6–8; Felicity Goodall, *Exodus Burma: The British Escape Through the Jungle of Death 1942* (Spellmount, 2011), 23 ("Brown Gold") [hereafter Goodall, *Exodus Burma*]. Dr. Hans van de Ven kindly pointed out Burma's jade production and its attraction to the Chinese.

455 **British colonization of Burma; "wants to be rid of us"; Indian influx issue:** Allen, *Burma: The Longest War*, 9, 13–15; Roberts, *Walking with Destiny*, 17; Captain Nadir Salahuddin Tyabji, "Burma Story," 1941–1942, Amitvaghosh.com/blog/?cat=30&paged=2, accessed 23 January 2016.

455 **Burma politics:** Allen, *Burma: The Longest War*, 9.

455 **Burma prime minister and the war:** Allen, *Burma: The Longest War*, 15–16; Kirby, *India's Most Dangerous Hour*, 5–6.

456 **Suzuki, "The Thirty Comrades," and the Burmese Independence Army:** Allen, *Burma: The Longest War*, 12, 17–21; Grant and Tamayama, *Burma 1942*, 45–46.

456 **Burma's garrison:** Kirby, *India's Most Dangerous Hour*, 8–9, 12; Allen, *Burma: The Longest War*, 13; Grant and Tamayama, *Burma 1942*, 38–39. The colonial administration also created six Burma Frontier Force battalions (staffed by Indians and Gurkhas domiciled in Burma) for intelligence and outpost duty, not regular combat. Graham Dunlop, *Military Economics, Culture and Logistics in the Burma Campaign, 1942–1945* (London: Pickering & Chatto, 2009), 20.

456 **Burma's initial air defense arrangements:** Kirby, *India's Most Dangerous Hour*, 10; Shores, Cull, and Izawa, *Bloody Shambles*, vol. 1, 235–37.

456 **Lack of intelligence organization:** Report by Lt. Gen. T. J Hutton, C.B., M.C., on Operations in Burma from 27th December, 1941, to 5th March, 1942, www.Britain-at-war.org.uk/ww2/London_Gazette/Burma_Dec_1941_to_May_1942/html/part_ix.htm, accessed 6 January 2016.

456 **Burma command arrangements:** "Operations in Burma from 15th December 1941 to 20th May 1942," section I, Supplement to the London Gazette, 11 March 1948, www.Britain-at-war.org.uk/ww2/London_Gazette/Burma_Dec_1941_to_May_1942/, accessed 17 April 2015; Kirby, *India's Most Dangerous Hour*, 21; Grant and Tamayama, *Burma 1942*, 42–43.

457 **Reinforcements denied and promised to Wavell:** Kirby, *India's Most Dangerous Hour*, 21–22.

457 **Wavell appoints Hutton; initial visit and appraisal:** Kirby, *India's Most Dangerous Hour*, 14–16.

457 **Chiang urges actions to secure Burma from 1940:** Ch'i, *The Much Troubled Alliance*, 99–100.

457 **Chiang's pledges to defend Burma, Wavell's meeting with Chiang:** Taylor, *The Gen-*

eralissimo, 190–91; Westad, *Restless Empire*, 266; Romanus and Sunderland, *Stilwell's Mission to China*, 53–55; Kirby, *India's Most Dangerous Hour*, 7–19.

457 **British operational and tactical arrangements at start of campaign:** Allen, *Burma: The Longest War*, 24–28, 30; Kirby, *India's Most Dangerous Hour*, 26–30, 73–74. Grant Tamayama, *Burma 1942*, 343, points out that during the first phase of the Burma campaign, Empire forces were supported by the equivalent of one-half field "regiment" (a battalion in other armies) and two mountain regiments. During the second phase, there were never more than 1.5 field regiments and one mountain regiment. In 1944–1945 some seventy field regiments supported the British Fourteenth Army.

458 **Fifteenth Army plans, background of 33rd and 55th Divisions:** Kirby, *India's Most Dangerous Hour*, 23–24; Grant and Tamayama, *Burma 1942*, 46–48; Leland Ness, *Rikugun: Guide to Japanese Ground Forces 1937–1945*, vol. 1, *Tactical Organization of Imperial Army & Navy Ground Forces* (Solihull, UK: Helion, 2014), 18, 25, 64–65, 70.

458 **". . . we were soon swallowed up in a deep jungle sea . . .":** Allen, *Burma: The Longest War*, 23–24.

458 **20 December Kunming interception; Chennault's tactics:** Daniel Ford, *Flying Tigers: Claire Chennault and the American Volunteer Group* (Washington, DC: Smithsonian Institution Press, 1991), 77–78, 111–19 ("I've never been a hero type . . ." at 117) [hereafter Ford, *Flying Tigers*]. Ford's excellent account notes that exact Japanese losses are unknown, but four seems the reasonable toll. This victory of the AVG also stands as stinging condemnation of the competence of American air commanders in the Philippines, who failed to prepare their pilots for fighting Japanese aircraft, a point further reinforced by the fact that US Navy fighter pilots digested Chennault's reports and devised tactics that would enable them to meet successfully the fabled Japanese Zero. Lundstrom, *The First Team*, 478–81. Most famous of the navy fighter tactics was the "Thach Weave" (or technically the "Beam Defense Maneuver"). Lt. Cdr. John S. "Jimmy" Thach developed the tactic based on reports he received of the performance of the Japanese Zero that showed it was faster and more maneuverable and could climb faster than the navy's standard Grumman F4F Wildcat. Although it is not definitely established that the reports Thach saw came directly from Chennault, it seems obvious that what reached Thach had been informed from Chennault's observations and certainly originated in China.

460 **Chennault background and personality:** Martha Byrd, *Chennault: Giving Wings to the Tiger* (Tuscaloosa: University of Alabama Press, 1987), ix–xiii, 4–5, 20–21, 27, 33–34, 36–47, 60–61, 69.

460 **23 December air action:** Ford, *Flying Tigers*, 125–38 ("fear laden" at 135); Shores, Cull, and Izawa, *Bloody Shambles*, vol. 1, 241–46; Kirby, *India's Most Dangerous Hour*, 24–25; Allen, *Burma: The Longest War*, 35.

461 **25 December air action:** Shores, Cull, and Izawa, *Bloody Shambles*, vol. 1, 246–51.

461 **Simmering level of air combat, December into January:** Shores, Cull, and Izawa, *Bloody Shambles*, vol. 1, 251–58.

461 **Air action January 22–29:** Ford, *Flying Tigers*, 191–93; Shores, Cull, and Izawa, *Bloody Shambles*, vol. 1, 258, 260–61, 263–70; Grant and Tamayama, *Burma 1942*, 70.

461 **Initial defeats of Burma Rifles and 16th Indian Brigade:** Allen, *Burma: The Longest*

War, 29–30; Grant and Tamayama, *Burma 1942*, 52–53, 60–69, 344; Kirby, *Indian's Most Dangerous Hour*, 29.

462 **Hutton's critical decision after Moulmein:** Kirby, *India's Most Dangerous Hour*, 32–33.

462 **Chinese troops deployed to Burma:** Kirby, *India's Most Dangerous Hour*, 44, 52–53.

462 **Wavell's visit 5–6 February:** Grant and Tamayama, *Burma 1942*, 80–81; Kirby, *India's Most Dangerous Hour*, 75–77.

462 **Orders from Iida and 33rd Division:** Grant and Tamayama, *Burma 1942*, 85.

463 **55th Division battles 46th Indian Brigade; Smyth hesitates to withdraw from Bilin:** Grant and Tamayama, *Burma 1942*, 87–94, 97–105; Kirby, *India's Most Dangerous Hour*, 54–62.

463 **General Sakurai reacts to intercept of withdrawal order:** Grant and Tamayama, *Burma 1942*, 105–8.

463 **Delayed British withdrawal 21 February:** Grant and Tamayama, *Burma 1942*, 116–19, 121, 124.

463 **Dispositions and actions east of Sittang Bridge, 22 February:** Grant and Tamayama, *Burma 1942*, 122, 126–31, Map 12: The Battle for the Sittang Bridge.

463 **Destruction of Sittang Bridge 23 February:** Grant and Tamayama, *Burma 1942*, 131–33; Allen, *Burma: The Longest War*, 37–43; Kirby, *India's Most Dangerous Hour*, 64–72.

464 **Japanese and Empire perceptions of destruction of the bridge:** Grant and Tamayama, *Burma 1942*, 134–35.

464 **"Here there was chaos and confusion . . .":** Kirby, *India's Most Dangerous Hour*, 72.

464 **Attempts to cross Sittang and strength of 17th Indian Division after disaster:** Grant and Tamayama, *Burma 1942*, 134–40; totals for losses and average brigade strength extrapolated from www.Britain-at-war.org.uk/ww2/London_Gazette/Burma_Dec_1941_to_May_1942/html/part_xvi.htm, accessed 6 January 2016.

464 **Appraisal of responsibility for Sittang Bridge disaster:** Grant and Tamayama, *Burma 1942*, 140.

465 **Japanese pause after Sittang Bridge; London plans:** Grant and Tamayama, *Burma 1942*, 143–44; Kirby, *India's Most Dangerous Hour*, 56–58. To date, the Fifteenth Army had survived solely on the supplies it had carried into Burma.

465 **Relief of Hutton and Smyth, appointment of Alexander:** Allen, *Burma: The Longest War*, 48–52; Grant and Tamayama, *Burma 1942*, 145–48.

465 **Air clashes 25–26 February and effects:** Shores, Cull, and Izawa, *Bloody Shambles*, vol. 1, 279–84; Grant and Tamayama, *Burma 1942*, 148–49.

465 **Reorganization and reinforcement of Empire forces in Burma:** Grant and Tamayama, *Burma 1942*, 144, 155.

466 **Wavell's trip to Burma and orders to Alexander:** Grant and Tamayama, *Burma 1942*, 149–51; Kirby, *India's Most Dangerous Hour*, 86.

466 **Iida's plan to capture Rangoon:** Grant and Tamayama, *Burma 1942*, 154–55.

466 **Alexander reaches Rangoon:** Grant and Tamayama, *Burma 1942*, 158.

466 **Loss of leaders of 63rd Indian Brigade:** Grant and Tamayama, *Burma 1942*, 159–60; Kirby, *India's Most Dangerous Hour*, 85. It speaks much of the intelligence void facing Alexander that the first hint of the existence of the Burmese Independence Army only came on 27 February.

466 **British evade trap at Pegu:** Grant and Tamayama, *Burma 1942*, 160–65. The failure
     to trap the British at Pegu cost the commander of the Japanese 112th Regiment and
     one of his battalion commanders their jobs.

466 **Takanobe abandons road block; Alexander escapes; Japanese capture Rangoon:**
     Grant and Tamayama, *Burma 1942*, 175–86; Allen, *Burma: The Longest War*, 54–57
     ("Alex never had a greater stroke of luck in his life"); Kazuo Tamayama and John
     Nunneley, *Tales by Japanese Soldiers* (London: Cassell, 2000), 44.

467 **Flight of Rangoon's population; final scenes of disorder, destruction, and fire:** Kirby,
     India's Most Dangerous Hour, 93–95; Grant and Tamayama, *Burma 1942*, 169–75;
     Allen, *Burma: The Longest War*, 52–53.

467 **Consequences of loss of Rangoon:** Kirby, *India's Most Dangerous Hour*, 100; "Opera-
     tions in Burma from 15th December 1941 to 20th May 1942," section 3, Supplement
     to the *London Gazette*, 11 March 1948, www.Britain-at-war.org.uk/ww2/London_
     Gazette/Burma_Dec_1941_to_May_1942/html/part_xxvii, accessed 6 January 2016.

467 **Long-term effect of loss of Rangoon on Chinese attitudes:** Ch'i, *The Much Troubled
     Alliance*, 110.

468 **Drum offered China Mission:** Ch'i, *The Much Troubled Alliance*, 61–66, 86–87;
     Romanus and Sunderland, *Stilwell's Mission to China*, 63–70; Larry I. Bland, Joellen
     K. Bland, and Sharon Titenor Stevens, eds., *George C. Marshall Interviews and Remi-
     niscences for Forrest C. Pogue* (Lexington, VA.: George C. Marshall Research Founda-
     tion, 1991), 605; Tuchman, *Stilwell and the American Experience in China*, 240–43.
     In Drum's brief orbit through Washington, he and his hastily assembled staff wrote
     a paper that proved all too prescient as to future events in what became the China-
     Burma-India Theater.

468 **Stilwell's actual Chinese proficiency; lack of understanding of complexity of Chinese
     military politics:** Ch'i, *The Much Troubled Alliance*, 54n; Guangqiu Xu, "The Issue of
     US Air Support for China during the Second World War, 1942–45," *Journal of Con-
     temporary History* 36, no. 3 (July 2001): 459–60. Ch'i makes a convincing case that
     Stilwell's Mandarin was modest. Reading between the lines, Tuchman's descrip-
     tion of Stilwell's Chinese language instruction suggests the same (*Stilwell and the
     American Experience in China*, 66–67), but the fact that a translator was present
     for virtually every meeting of Stilwell and Chiang speaks for itself. Further, as the
     official US Army history explains, all orders drafted in Stilwell's headquarters were
     then sent to the Chinese General Staff Mission in Burma to be translated into Chi-
     nese. Romanus and Sunderland, *Stilwell's Mission to China*, 105.

468 **Marshall's high opinion of Stilwell:** Romanus and Sunderland, *Stilwell's Mission to
     China*, 70–71; Stilwell diary, January 1, 1942, Box 38, File 38-1 Black and White
     Books, no. 1, Dec 41 to January 1942, Hoover Institution [hereafter Stilwell diary];
     Shelford Bidwell, *The Chindit War: Stilwell, Wingate, and the Campaign in Burma:
     1944* (New York: Macmillan Publishing, 1979), 31 [hereafter Bidwell, *The Chindit
     War*]. Bidwell's work stands the test of time with honor.

468 **Stilwell offered North Africa command; creates reservoir of loyalty in Marshall and
     Stimson:** Stimson diary 14 January 1942; Stilwell diary, 14 January 1942 ("I told
     him I would go where I was sent"); Tuchman, *Stilwell and the American Experience
     in China*, 231–33, 240–44; Ch'i, *The Much Troubled Alliance*, 88–89. The origins of
     Stilwell's great store of loyalty from Marshall and Stimson were first pointed out to
     the author by Dr. Gerhard Weinberg.

468 **Stilwell's appearance, distaste for pomposity or pretentiousness, ability to smoke and chew gum simultaneously:** photographs from 1942, notably those in Tuchman, *Stilwell and the American Experience in China*, and Bidwell, *The Chindit War*; Claire Boothe, "Burma Mission," *Life*, vol. 12, no. 24, 15 June 1942, 95; World War II Diaries of Joseph W. Stilwell, 11, 14, 30 January 1942, Hoover Institution [hereafter Stilwell Diaries].

469 **Stilwell's personality:** Romanus and Sunderland, *Stilwell's Mission to China*, 70–71; Slim, *Defeat into Victory*, 51; Tuchman, *Stilwell and the American Experience in China*, 4, 126–27, 283; Bidwell, *The Chindit War*, 32, 36; Dorn, *Walkout with Stilwell in Burma*, 42–43 ("basically [is] a peasant" . . .); John Pomfret, *The Beautiful Country and the Middle Kingdom: America and China, 1776 to the Present* (New York: Henry Holt, 2016), 283–84. Merrill was appointed to command the "Marauders," but shortly after the unit entered combat, he suffered a heart attack and Col. Charles H. Hunter assumed command. Hunter earned the greatest credit for the success of the unit. Charlton Ogburn, *The Marauders* (New York: Harper & Brothers, 1956), 2.

469 **Stilwell's assertion that Chinese soldiers would be first rate, but only under his command:** Ch'i, *The Much Troubled Alliance*, 75–77.

469 **Stilwell's directives and tasks:** Romanus and Sunderland, *Stilwell's Mission to China*, 71–78; Tuchman, *Stilwell and the American Experience in China*, 246–47.

470 **Seeds of discord in Stilwell's assignment of responsibilities:** Ch'i, *The Much Troubled Alliance*, 69–75. Ch'i points out that both McCloy and Stimson in written communications in January 1942 affirmed that the senior American officer sent would spend most of his time in Chongqing.

470 **Meeting with Roosevelt:** Stilwell diary, December 29, 1941 ("rank amateur" and "completely hypnotized"), January 6 ("stooge"), January 24, and February 9, 1942 ("frothy"). The February entry is in Stilwell Papers, Box 38, File 38-2 Black and White Books, no. 2, 1942, February 8 to April 18, Hoover Institution. Also important is Tuchman, *Stilwell and the American Experience in China*, 249–50.

470 **American air role and command in China:** Romanus and Sunderland, *Stilwell's Mission to China*, 78–79, 93; Craven and Cate, *Plans & Early Operations, January 1939 to August 1942*, 492–95. The ninety-one additional aircraft assigned comprised thirty-three A-29 dive bombers for the Chinese Air Force under Lend Lease, twenty-three B-24 heavy bombers, and thirty-five DC-3/C-47s transports. Col. James Doolittle's sixteen B-25s that raided Japan in April also were earmarked for China, but all were lost. Brereton's B-17s did briefly perform air ferry duties from India to Burma.

470 **Initial meetings of Stilwell and Chiang; Stilwell's strategy:** Taylor, *The Generalissimo*, 196–200; Romanus and Sunderland, *Stilwell's Mission to China*, 97–98; Ch'i, *The Much Troubled Alliance*, 108, 114–15; van de Ven, *War and Nationalism in China*, 9–10; Dorn, *Sino-Japanese War*, 65, 113, 120, 128. Van de Ven provides a particularly acute and devastating assessment of the origins and ramifications of Stilwell's attitudes.

470 **Chiang's strategic views:** Ch'i, *The Much Troubled Alliance*, 108–13, 149–52; Taylor, *The Generalissimo*, 195, 197–98.

471 **Chiang's attitudes about the British:** Ch'i, *The Much Troubled Alliance*, 106, 108–9, 112, 118, 123 ("The U.K. is engaged . . ."); Taylor, *The Generalissimo*, 195.

471 **Scenes in Mandalay, 7 April 1942:** Claire Boothe, "Burma Mission," *Life*, vol. 12,
no. 24, 15 June 1942, 94–106 (quotes on 102); Ch'i, *The Much Troubled Alliance*,
120–23; Goodall, *Exodus Burma*, 97–98. Chiang and his wife conveyed their scathing reports on these scenes in messages by Chiang to Churchill, with a copy to
FDR, and by his wife to Currie. Generalissimo Chiang Kai Shek to Prime Minister, 17 April 1942, President's Secretary File, Box 2, Australia through Germany,
September 1939–1941, Folder China, FDRL; Cablegram from Madame Chiang Kai-
shek to Laughlin Currie, April 12, 1942, President's Secretary File, Box 2, Australia
through Germany, September 1939–1941, Folder China, FDRL.

472 **Effects of Japanese bombing on Burmese towns:** The Campaign in Burma (from
March 10th to June 1st, 1942), Stilwell Papers, Box 21, File 21-9, 47, Hoover Institution [hereafter The Campaign in Burma]; www.Britain-at-war.org.uk/ww2/
London_Gazette/Burma_Dec_1941_to_May_1942/html/part_ix/htm and part_xx,
accessed 6 January 2016 ("After a heavy raid on a town . . .").

472 **Slim's background:** Russell Miller, *Uncle Bill: The Authorized Biography of Field
Marshall Viscount Slim* (London: Weidenfeld & Nicholson, 2013), ch. 1–9 [hereafter
Miller, *Uncle Bill*]; Robert Lyman, *Slim, Master of War* (London: Constable, 2004),
appendix 1. Lyman explains that prior accounts attributing Slim's appointment
to a recommendation by Alexander are incorrect. The original recommendation
for Slim to command Burma Corps originated with Lt. Gen. T. W. Corbett, commander 4 India Corps in Iraq. Coincidentally, Lyman gives important weight to the
strong endorsement of Slim to General Alan Brooke, chief of the Imperial General
Staff, by Lieutenant General Archibald Nye, fortuitously then the vice chief of the
Imperial General Staff. Slim had deeply impressed Nye during their stint together
at a staff college.

472 **"In contrast to almost every other outstanding commander of the war . . .":** Max
Hastings, *Retribution: The Battle for Japan 1944–45* (New York: Alfred A. Knopf,
2008), 68–69.

473 **Slim seeks advice from Chinese general:** William Slim, *Defeat into Victory* (London:
Pan Books, 1999, reprint of 1956 edition), 17–18 [hereafter Slim, *Defeat into Victory*];
Ch'i, *The Much Troubled Alliance*, 109 ("a lot of crap tactics"), quoting from Stilwell's
diary.

473 **Allied command set up:** Despatch to the Secretary of State for War by General Sir
Archibald Wavell, July 14, 1942, on Operations in Burma from December 15, 1941
to May 20, 1942, covering reports by Lieutenant General T. J. Hutton on Operations
in Burma from December 27, 1941 to March 5, 1942, and by General the Honor-
able Sir Harold R. L. G. Alexander on Operations in Burma from March 5, 1942 to
May 20, 1942, supplement to the *London Gazette*, 11 March 1948, www.thegazette
.co.uk/London/Issue/38228/Page/1695 [hereafter Wavell Despatch, Operations in
Burma]; "Operations in Burma from 15th December 1941 to 20th May 1942," section 3, Supplement to the *London Gazette*, 11 March 1948, www.Britain-at-war.org
.uk/ww2/London_Gazette/Burma_Dec_1941_to_May_1942/html/part_xxvii.htm
accessed 6 January 2016 (quotes Alexander on "nominal" command); Allen, *Burma:
The Longest War*, 58–59; Romanus and Sunderland, *Stilwell's Mission to China*, 94–95.

473 **Japanese force abandonment of Magwe and Akyab:** Shores, Cull, and Izawa, *Bloody
Shambles*, vol. 2, 350–60; Slim, *Defeat into Victory*, 41–42; Grant and Tamayama,
Burma 1942, 198–99.

473 **New Japanese plans and reinforcements:** Kirby, *India's Most Dangerous Hour*, 145–46; Grant and Tamayama, *Burma 1942*, 188; TROM Minelayer *Hatsutaka*, combinedfleet.com (for details of convoy movements, accessed 2 August 2015).

474 **Plans of Fifteenth Army for thrusts into central and northern Burma:** Allen, *Burma: The Longest War*, 59; Kirby, *India's Most Dangerous Hour*, 146.

474 **Chiang and Stilwell agreements on disposition of Fifth Army:** Ch'i, *The Much Troubled Alliance*, 111–15: www.Britain-at-war.org.uk/ww2/London_Gazette/Burma_ Dec_1941_to_May_1942/html/part_xx.htm. Chiang and Stilwell initially agreed that the Chinese units should hold around Mandalay (to allay British fears of Chinese territorial designs on Burma), with the British defending areas to the south.

474 **Chiang and Stilwell redeploy divisions of Fifth Army:** Ch'i, *The Much Troubled Alliance*, 119.

474 **Strength of Chinese Fifth and Sixth Army formations:** Allen, *Burma: The Longest War*, 59–61.

475 **Chinese artillery in Burma:** Sources differ on exact figures for Chinese artillery pieces. This account follows Stilwell's report, The Campaign in Burma, 8, 46.

475 **General Tai and early battles over Toungoo:** The Campaign in Burma, 1–5; Grant and Tamayama, *Burma 1942*, 191; Allen, *Burma: The Longest War*, 61.

475 **Heroic defense of Toungoo; loss of Sittang bridge:** The Campaign in Burma, 5–8; Grant and Tamayama, *Burma 1942*, 191–92; Allen, *Burma: The Longest War*, 63.

475 **Stilwell's orders and rage over his Chinese subordinate commanders and underestimate of Japanese strength:** Kirby, *India's Most Dangerous Hour*, 156–57; Stilwell to Sec of War and Chief of Staff, April 1, 1942, President's Secretary File, Box 2, Australia through Germany, September 1939–1941, Folder China ("incompetence, lethargy and disregard for orders . . ."), FDRL. Stilwell's headquarters report, The Campaign in Burma, contains notations almost too numerous to count to illuminate his frustrations. Just some particular examples are at pp. 5–8, 27, 31, 34, 36, 44, 46, and 51. The background for this issue is found in Romanus and Sunderland, *Stilwell's Mission to China*, 36 ("Orders through a staff officer meant nothing . . ."); Ch'i, *The Much Troubled Alliance*, 110–12, 115–17; Kirby, *India's Most Dangerous Hour*, 36–37. Ch'i's revelations about Chiang's ambivalence on defending Burma after the loss of Rangoon and his loss of faith in the British provides vital context for these events. An example of how seriously Stilwell misjudged Japanese strength is manifest in the estimate of his intelligence officer as late as April 21 still placing the Japanese 18th Division in Thailand rather than in Burma. Romanus and Sunderland, *Stilwell's Mission to China*, 132. One piece of evidence on how Chinese generals regarded Stilwell is reported in Allen, *Burma, The Longest War*, 58. This work says that when Stilwell presented himself as the commander of Chinese forces in Burma, the commander of the Fifth (Chinese) Army, General Tu Lu Ming, had already presented himself to Alexander as that officer. When the governor of Burma, Dorman-Smith, pressed Tu about the actual hierarchy, Tu replied: "the American General only thinks he is commanding. In fact he is doing no such thing. You see, we Chinese think that the only way to keep Americans in the war is to give them a few commands on paper. They will not do much harm as long as we do the work."

476 **Real reason 22nd and 96th Divisions do not come to support of 200th Division:** Headquarters U.S. Force in China, Burma & India, 13 May 1942, Subject: Anglo-

Chinese Relations at Lashio, March 21–April 25, 1942, by H. L. Boatner, Lieutenant Colonel General Staff, Stilwell Papers, Box 22, File 22-19, Hoover Institution. Boatner was at Lashio and witnessed this whole disheartening episode. He reported that "for several days the Chinese expressed their great concern for the safety of the 200th Division and pleaded for transportation to move the two rear divisions of the 5th Army close to Taungoo and to shift the 55th Division to the Loikaw area."

476 **British thrust to draw off Japanese allegedly reinforcing front at Toungoo:** Grant and Tamayama, *Burma 1942*, 206–16; Allen, *Burma: The Longest War*, 62–63; Slim, *Defeat into Victory*, 44–46; Kirby, *India's Most Dangerous Hour*, 158–62.

476 **Loss of Prome; new Burma Corps line at Magwe:** Grant and Tamayama, *Burma 1942*, 249; Goodall, *Exodus Burma*, 79–80 ("Trees smouldered at the roadside . . ."); Miller, *Uncle Bill*, 173–75 ("Bearded, dust covered men . . ." at 175).

477 **1st Burma Division trapped:** Grant and Tamayama, *Burma 1942*, 230–41, 250–56; Miller, *Uncle Bill*, 179–82.

477 **38th Division and General Sun Li-jen:** Grant and Tamayama, *Burma 1942*, 252–53; Miller, *Uncle Bill*, 180; Allen, *Burma: The Longest War*, 65–69 ("the enlisted men much more courteously . . ." at 66).

478 **Break out of 1st Burma Division:** Grant and Tamayama, *Burma 1942*, 256–59; Miller, *Uncle Bill*, 183–84.

478 **Japanese drive out of Toungoo up Sittang Valley to Lashio:** Grant and Tamayama, *Burma 1942*, 262–65; The Campaign in Burma, April 22, pp. 23, 50; Romanus and Sunderland, *Stilwell's Mission to China*, 134–35.

478 **April 25 meeting, withdrawal orders:** Grant and Tamayama, *Burma 1942*, 267–68. Stilwell's general report of the campaign fails to mention this important meeting. The Campaign in Burma, 26–27.

478 **Iida's new scheme of maneuver:** Grant and Tamayama, *Burma 1942*, 283.

478 **Advances of reinforced 56th Division:** Grant and Tamayama, *Burma 1942*, 283–85.

478 **Japanese thrust to Monywa:** Grant and Tamayama, *Burma 1942*, 289–94; The Campaign in Burma, 34. Stilwell's report claims the 1st Burma Division lost "all of the British codes, including the entire plan of defense of the Mandalay and the eventual withdrawal of the British Army."

479 **Last battle of British retreat at Kalewa and Shwegyin:** Grant and Tamayama, *Burma 1942*, 297–313.

479 **Burma Corps arrived in Imphal:** Miller, *Uncle Bill*, 201; Grant and Tamayama, *Burma 1942*, 320. At that time the two main formations numbered 9,908 men in the 17th Indian Division and just two thousand in the 1st Burma Division, as the Burmese, who constituted originally about two-thirds of the division, had mostly left the ranks.

479 **"I stood on a bank besides the road . . .":** Slim, *Defeat into Victory*, 109–10.

479 **"To be cheered by troops whom you have led to victory . . .":** Slim, *Defeat into Victory*, 114; Miller, *Uncle Bill*, 204–5.

480 **April 30 meeting and Stilwell's "walkout":** The Burma Campaign, 32–33; Tuchman, *Stilwell and the American Experience in China*, 292–99; Romanus and Sunderland, *Stilwell's Mission to China*, 142–43. Both accounts present the "walk out" in a highly favorable light. The sole reporter with Stilwell, Jack Belden, wrote *Retreat With Stilwell* (New York: Knopf, 1943), which celebrated the "walkout" and burnished Stilwell's image still further.

480 **Stilwell's failure to march out with any significant body of Chinese troops:** Ch'i, *The*

Much Troubled Alliance, 135–48; Taylor, *The Generalissimo*, 204–7 ("abandoned my 100,000 soldiers in foreign jungles" at 205); The Campaign in Burma, 35–36. Stilwell's report describing his decision to head to India asserts that "Chinese troops were rapidly beginning to disintegrate into relatively small independent units" (36). Yet this same report, on pp. 35–36, shows for instance that on May 4 about 8,000 men of the 22nd and 96th Divisions were at Shwebo, the 38th Division was "intact" north of Shwebo. The official US Army history (Romanus and Sunderland, *Stilwell's Mission to China*, 138) states that Stilwell started May 5 at Indaw (about 130 miles north of Shwebo) with the intention to head to Myitkyina, but when he learned the Japanese were at Bhamo "within easy striking distance" of Myitkyina, Stilwell decided to "walk out" of Burma. At that point the history acknowledges Stilwell knew he was only "a few hours" ahead of the Fifth Army. It is hard to read these accounts and believe that Stilwell could not have linked up with substantial bodies of organized Chinese troops for his "walkout."

480 **Stilwell's explanations for his "walkout" and Chiang's reactions:** The Burma Campaign, 36; Ch'i, *The Much Troubled Alliance*, 114, 135–36, 147, 153. Ch'i could find no support in Chinese sources for the proposition that Chiang ever authorized the withdrawal of units to India, as Stilwell claimed Lo informed him.

481 **Noncombatant deaths in Burma:** Allen, *Burma: The Longest War*, 80; Bayly and Harper, *Forgotten Armies*, 87, 167–68 ("Rangoon isn't Burma really . . ."); Goodall, *Exodus Burma*, 18.

481 **Burmese and Indian immigrants:** Bayly and Harper, *Forgotten Armies*, 9 ("as unscrupulous opportunists . . ."), 86–87, 90–92.

481 **Initial flight after air raids by sea:** Allen, *Burma: The Longest War*, 80–81, 83–85; Bayly and Harper, *Forgotten Armies*, 167–69; Grant and Tamayama, *Burma 1942*, 170.

482 **Air evacuation:** Allen, *Burma: The Longest War*, 83–84; Goodall, *Exodus Burma*, 94–95; Bayly and Harper, *Forgotten Armies*, 185, 187. Kirby, *India's Most Dangerous Hour*, 213–14, gives figures for air evacuation of 8,600, including 2,600 wounded.

482 **Railway overcrowding and disorder:** Goodall, *Exodus Burma*, 102–3.

482 **Refugee foot columns:** Goodall, *Exodus Burma*, 126–27, 144–45.

482 **Main escape routes:** Grant and Tamayama, *Burma 1942*, 169–70.

482 **Burma government efforts, banditry and looting; Mandalay:** Bayly and Harper, *Forgotten Armies*, 175–76; Goodall, *Exodus Burma*, 102–3, 126; Allen, *Burma: The Longest War*, 83.

482 **Thousands die along the trek:** Bayly and Harper, *Forgotten Armies*, 182–83, 185; Goodall, *Exodus Burma*, 123 ("[wander] away into the thick forest . . ."), 173–74, 177, 180–81.

483 **Heroes of the refugee flight:** Bayly and Harper, *Forgotten Armies*, 182, 184, 203; Goodall, *Exodus Burma*, 211.

483 **Assam Tea Planters Association, Alastair Tainsh quotes:** A Report on the Evacuation of Refugees from Burma to India (Assam) (January–July 1942) by Major General E. Wood, Administrator General of Eastern Communications, Calcutta, 1 October 1942 (John L. Christian Papers, Box 2, Folder, British Papers Released 2010, Hoover Institution), 10, para. 10 [hereafter Wood Report on Evacuation of Refugees from Burma]; Allen, *Burma: The Longest War*, 90; Bayly and Harper, *Forgotten Armies*, 184–85; Goodall, *Exodus Burma*, 204–8.

483 **"Complete exhaustion, physical and mental . . .":** quoted in Allen, *Burma: The Longest War,* 89.

484 **Fate of Wilby family:** Goodall, *Exodus Burma,* 212.

484 **Refugees rescued to November 1942; role of elephants; rescue of Chinese soldiers:** Goodall, *Exodus Burma,* 225–30; Bayly and Harper, *Forgotten Armies,* 181. For a popular account of the role of elephants, see Andrew Martin, *Flight by Elephant: The Untold Story of World War II's Most Daring Jungle Rescue* (London: Fourth Estate, 2013).

484 **Numbers of refugees and deaths, economic cost of scorched earth policy:** Kirby, *India's Most Dangerous Hour,* 192–93; Allen, *Burma: The Longest War,* 90; Bayly and Harper, *Forgotten Armies,* 167 (gives 80,000 figure), 180; Goodall, *Exodus Burma,* 230–32; Hugh Tinker, "A Forgotten Long March: The Indian Exodus from Burma, 1942," *Journal of Southeast Asia Studies* 6. no. 1 (March 1975): 1–15 (50,000 figure for deaths). A very early official report on the evacuation of refugees gives a total of 218,455 evacuees, of whom 4,268 were known dead and an estimated 20 to 25 percent more may have died. Wood Report on Evacuation of Refugees from Burma, 21, para. 34. In light of the other and later evidence, the 4,268 number appears extremely low and unlikely.

484 **Chinese soldiers trek out of Burma:** Box 22, File 22-10, "Headquarters Combat Troops Ledo Sector, 11 June 1943, Subject: Random Notes on Evolution and Organization of the Chinese Army in India [Brig. Gen. H. (Haydon) L. Boatner]; Box 25, File 25-21 Memoranda on food dropped to Chinese troops in India by Frank Merrill, Memorandum, August 27, 1942, Stilwell Papers, Hoover Institution.

484 **Military Casualties in Burma:** British Commonwealth casualties from Maj. Gen. S. Woodburn Kirby, *The War Against Japan,* vol. 5, *The Surrender of Japan* (Uckfield, UK: The Naval & Military Press Ltd., 2004), appendix 31; Grant & Tamayama, *Burma 1942,* 378–79; Chinese fatalities from Ch'i, *The Much Troubled Alliance,* 143; Japanese losses, Grant & Tamayama, *Burma 1942,* 379–80.

485 **Sakurai orders memorials created:** Grant & Tamayama, *Burma 1942,* 333n10.

485 **Assessments by British officers and Stilwell:** Grant and Tamayama, *Burma 1942,* 329, 339–49; Stilwell Papers, Box 38, File 38-2 Black and White Books, no. 2, 1942, February 8 to April 18, undated, pp. 47, 49 ("double crossed me at every turn"), Hoover Institution; The Campaign in Burma (from March 10th to June 1st, 1942), 43–51, Stilwell Papers, Box 21, File 21-9, Hoover Institution; Slim, *Defeat into Victory,* 111–21; Miller, *Uncle Bill,* 208–9.

486 **Chiang's reflections on defeat:** Ch'i, *The Much Troubled Alliance,* 155–61.

18: "We Are Not Barbarians"

487 **Background on handling "Magic" pre–Pearl Harbor; Roosevelt's disinterest; Stimson's intervention:** SRH-116, "Origins, Functions and Problems of the Special Branch, M.I.S.," 4–6, RG 457, Entry 9002, NARA; SRH-125, "Certain Aspects of "Magic," 59 ("each message represented only a single frame . . ."), RG 457, Entry 9002, NARA; SRH-005, "Use of CX/MSS Ultra by the United States War Department (1943–1945)," 4 ("haphazard beginning" and "elementary") [hereafter SRH-005]; Stimson diary January 2, 1941 (where Stimson records that Roosevelt was not reading "Magic" intercepts). Joseph E. Persico's *Roosevelt's Secret War: FDR and*

World War II Espionage (New York: Random House, 2001) covers in detail Roosevelt's enthusiasm for espionage, a good deal of it amateurish. Roosevelt's comments to Churchill and others demonstrate he was reading "Magic" much more attentively later in 1941.

488 **"imagination coupled with analytical, judicial and unbiased minds" and "quickly intelligible" and free of "bias":** SRH-005, 13, 29.

488 **Background of Japanese immigrants:** Roger Daniels, *Concentration Camps, U.S.A: Japanese Americans in World War II* (New York: Holt, Rinehart and Winston, 1971), 2–5 [hereafter Daniels, *Concentration Camps, U.S.A.*].

488 **1940 Census totals for United States:** United States Census Bureau, 1940 Census, 6, 1209–10, www.census.gov/prod/www/decennial/html, accessed 3 April 2015; Conn, Engelman, and Fairchild, *Guarding the United States and Its Outposts*, 115–16; Daniels, *Concentration Camps, U.S.A.*, 1, table p. 21.

488 **Population of Hawaii:** United States Census Bureau, 1940 Census, 1209–10, www .census.gov/prod/www/decennial/html, accessed 3 April 2015; PHA, Part 18, 3136 (reproduction of 1940 census publication on Hawaii). This latter shows Hawaii had 423,330 inhabitants.

488 **Japanese generations, dual citizenship, and after-hours Japanese language schools:** Stephen, *Hawaii Under the Rising Sun*, 23–25; Daniels, *Concentration Camps, U.S.A.*, table p. 21.

488 **Japanese economic success:** Greg Robinson, *By Order of the President: FDR and the Internment of Japanese Americans* (Cambridge, MA: Harvard University Press, 2001), 54 [hereafter Robinson, *By Order of the President*].

489 **Executive Order 9066:** FDR: Day by Day, February 19, 1942, FDRL; Conn, Engelman, and Fairchild, *Guarding the United States and Its Outposts*, ch. 5 details events from the military context. The exact number of persons interned under this order is somewhat elusive as there are various categories such as "voluntary residents" or former residents of "institutions" that are subject to debate. The Report of the Commission on Wartime Relocation and Internment of Civilians, published as *Personal Justice Denied* (Washington, DC: The Civil Liberties Public Education Fund, 1997), 150 [hereafter *Personal Justice Denied*].

489 **False and actual Japanese military activities on the West Coast:** TROM I-17, combinedfleet.com, accessed 7 April 2015; Conn, Engelman, and Fairchild, *Guarding the United States and Its Outposts*, 86–88, 120.

489 **"Magic" messages on espionage; undercover Japanese naval officers:** *The "Magic"Background of Pearl Harbor*. Lowman cites specific messages in ch. 7–14, and maintains that there were over 5,000 "Magic" messages and that "more than half relate to espionage." *Magic: The Untold Story of U.S. Intelligence and the Evacuation of Japanese Residents from the West Coast During World War II* (Athena Press, 2000), 68 [hereafter Lowman, *Magic: The Untold Story*]. A cross-check of a large sample of messages in Lowman against the Department of Defense volumes verifies Lowman's accuracy. Peter Irons described the arrest of Lt. Cdr. Itaru Tachibana and noted that "There is no question that Tachibana headed an espionage ring on the West Coast that enlisted a number of Japanese Americans, both aliens and citizens, nor that the government knew about the identities of its members." *Justice at War* (Berkeley: University of California Press, 1983), 22–23 [hereafter Irons, *Justice at War*]. Much of this evidence came from a break-in at the Japanese consulate in

Los Angeles that retrieved Tachibana's papers. Tachibana was deported in July 1941. Lowman also identifies Lieutenant Commander Okada in the Seattle area. *Magic: The Untold Story*, 144, 154. The uncovering of the Tachibana spy ring gave the local Office of Naval Intelligence officer, Lt. Cdr. K. D. Ringle, confidence that US authorities had isolated the actual threat of espionage and thus that the loyalty of the overall Japanese community was vindicated.

Significant controversy lingers over the role played by "Magic" intercepts and other intelligence information in the mass internment. The Report of the Commission on Wartime Relocation and Internment of Civilians (*Personal Justice Denied*) properly found the mass internment a grave injustice. That said, the report's treatment of intelligence is grossly defective. It simply ignores "Magic" messages as well as the arrest in mid-1941 of Tachibana and Okada. It further conceals the Niihau Incident in an obscure footnote. Into this opening stepped Lowman, who pointed out the indisputable fact that the "Magic" intercepts contained numerous references to Japanese ambitions to instigate espionage and subversion and reports of actual though limited espionage activities. In *Magic: The Untold Story*, ch. 7 to 14, Lowman quotes verbatim scores of "Magic" messages on espionage and subversion. Lowman also quotes verbatim intelligence reports asserting security threats from persons of Japanese descent, including one maintaining the existence of espionage rings as late as February 1942. Ch. 15–17, particularly p. 239. Then Michelle Malkin offered the incendiary title *In Defense of Internment; The Case for "Racial Profiling" in World War II and the War on Terror* (Washington, DC: Regnery Publishers, 2004). This followed Lowman in many ways and triggered an acrimonious public exchange. This narrative takes the view that ignoring the "Magic" intercepts and, for example, the arrest of Tachikawa and Okada, is historical malpractice of a particularly egregious type. Even so, acknowledging the existence of these plain facts is not tantamount to finding the actions taken by the US government were justified.

490 **Post–Pearl Harbor roundup:** Daniels, *Concentration Camps, U.S.A.*, 34–35. Figures are from *Personal Justice Denied*, 284. As Daniels observes, this roundup involved about 1 percent of all persons of Japanese descent. The action was even applauded by some Japanese Americans.

490 **Role of Gullion, Bendetsen, and Biddle:** for a factual recital of the key role of Gullion and Bendetsen and Biddle's steadfast opposition, see Conn, Engelman, and Fairchild, *Guarding the United States and Its Outposts*, ch. 5. For characterization of the roles of Gullion, Bendetsen, and Biddle, see, for example, Irons, *Justice at War*, 29–31, 34–36, 38–46, 49–55, 59–63, 363.

490 **25 January 1942, "Category A and B" proposal:** Daniels, *Concentration Camps, U.S.A.*, 50.

490 **Findings on California newspapers:** Morton Grodzins, *Americans Betrayed: The Politics of the Japanese Evacuation* (Chicago: University of Chicago Press, 1949), appendix 1, 377. This study showed that demands for evacuation remained minuscule prior to the week ending 25 January and then soared to tremendous heights from the date of publication of the Roberts Commission Report. This remains an extremely important piece of evidence on the causes of the internment.

490 **Roberts Commission:** PHA, Part 22, 79, 195–96, 327, 396–97, 545.

491 **Testimony before Roberts Commission:** PHA, Part 23, especially 820–27, 857–74, 884–85, 890–91, 916–24, 948–1009, 1022–25; Part 24, 1312–13, 1447–50.

491 **Roberts Commission Report:** PHA, Part 39, 2, 12–13.

491 **Importance of Roberts Commission Report:** Conn, Engelman, and Fairchild, *Guarding the United States and Its Outposts*, 121–22. These official historians note: "The publication of the report of the Roberts Commission, which had investigated the Pearl Harbor attack, on 25 January had a large and immediate effect both on public opinion and on government action." Another historian emphasizing the importance of the report is Robinson, *By Order of the President*, 95–97. Finally, the distinguished historian David M. Kennedy in his Pulitzer Prize–winning work described the report as "the decisive blow" leading to the mass internment. *Freedom from Fear*, 750–51. Ignoring the Roberts Commission Report or placing it on the periphery of events is another instance of egregious historical malpractice on this issue.

491 **Olson, Warren, and DeWitt exchanges and change of opinion:** Robinson, *By Order of the President*, 95–97; Conn, Engleman, and Fairchild, *Guarding the United States and Its Outposts*, 117–23.

492 **Roberts meets with DeWitt, Stimson, and Roosevelt:** Stimson diary, January 20, 1942; Daniels, *Concentration Camps, U.S.A.*, 49–50, Irons, *Justice at War*, 40–41; Davis, *FDR: The War President*, 421; Conn, Engelman, and Fairchild, *Guarding the United States and Its Outposts*, 195–96.

492 **"racial characteristics" would "make a tremendous hole . . .":** Stimson diary, February 10, 1942.

492 **Bendetsen and Gullion sway McCloy between 6 and 10 February:** Daniels, *Concentration Camps, U.S.A.*, 63–65.

492 **11 February decision:** Stimson diary, February 11, 1942; Daniels, *Concentration Camps, U.S.A.*, 65. At the time this matter appeared before Roosevelt, Singapore appeared about to fall, which carried dire implications for the ability of China to stay in the war, an issue involving the fate of over 450 million people. Likewise, President Quezon had submitted his request for the United States to grant the Philippines immediate independence so Quezon could secure neutralization of the nation, an event concerning the fate of 16 million people. This background serves to place in context Roosevelt's willingness to dispose of a matter involving 120,000 persons by telephone.

492 **General factors foreclosing evacuation from Hawaii:** Conn, Engelman, and Fairchild, *Guarding the United States and Its Outposts*, 206–7, 214–16. I am indebted to Edward Drea for bringing to my attention Marshall's statements to DeWitt on the shipping situation.

493 **Hawaii Japanese population features, prewar investigations; official policies toward Japanese population:** Conn, Engelman, and Fairchild, *Guarding the United States and Its Outposts*, 207.

493 **JCS recommends and president approves mass evacuation from Hawaii:** Conn, Engelman, and Fairchild, *Guarding the United States and Its Outposts*, 216.

493 **McCloy inspection and Emmons's maneuvers to avoid mass evacuation:** Memorandum [from McCloy] for General Eisenhower, March 28, 1942, Subject: Evacuation of Japanese from Hawaii, RG 107, Entry 180, Box 6, Folder Hawaii, NARA; Conn, Engelman, and Fairchild, *Guarding the United States and Its Outposts*, 210–14; Robinson, *By Order of the President*, 146–48; Irons, *Justice at War*, 269. Admittedly, Emmons did not directly declare he was deliberating staving off a mass evacuation,

but I concur with Robinson and Irons that when you place his actions in context, it seems manifest that while Emmons professed seeming agreement with various mass evacuation schemes, he was in fact calculating how best to defeat them on pragmatic grounds.

493 **Emmons's delaying actions and ultimate evacuation:** Conn, Engelman, and Fairchild, *Guarding the United States and Its Outposts*, 212–14. In May, Emmons did implement one evacuation. The 298th and 299th Infantry Regiments of Hawaii included many enlisted men and officers of Japanese ancestry. By May 1942, Emmons received enough replacements to remove all the Japanese from these two units and to ship a contingent of 29 officers and 1,277 enlisted men to the mainland. These men became the nucleus of the Japanese-American 100th Infantry Battalion that served in Europe.

493 **Doubts about Pearl Harbor as fleet base after attack:** PHA, Part 22, 520–21, 544. In testimony before the Roberts Commission, Captain Walter S. Delany, assistant chief of staff and operations officer, Pacific Fleet, expressed the view that Pearl Harbor was not suitable as a fleet base given current resources. Admiral William Pye testified that Pearl Harbor must be held and used as a base, but emphasized that this would require reinforcement of defenses.

494 **Wallin and Pearl Harbor salvage efforts:** Salvage Officer, Navy Yard, Pearl Harbor, Serial 01873, October 17, 1942, RG 38, NARA.

494 **Salvage efforts on *Arizona*:** Commander Edward C. Raymer, *Descent into Darkness: Pearl Harbor, 1941, A Navy Diver's Memoir* (Navato, CA: Presidio Press, 1996), 4–5, 45–46. *Arizona*'s two after main battery turrets, each mounting three 14-inch guns, remained intact. In a priceless example of the unbounded bureaucratic mind, a salvage officer authorized "*loan* of turrets no. 3 and no. 4 to the Army." (Emphasis added.) In the fevered atmosphere of 1942, the army promptly began building two huge coast defense sites, each employing one of the *Arizona* turrets. Work throttled back as the threat of further Japanese attack or invasion dissipated. In August 1945, the one complete battery conducted its sole test firing, more in celebration of the victory than for practical purposes. Salvage Officer, Navy Yard, Pearl Harbor, Serial 01873, October 17, 1942, p. 14; Stillwell, *Battleship Arizona*, 279–81.

495 **King appointed COMINCH; Stark transferred:** Thomas B. Buell, *Master of Sea Power: A Biography of Fleet Admiral Ernest J. King* (Annapolis, MD: Naval Institute Press, 1980), 151–54, 178–79 [hereafter Buell, *Master of Sea Power*].

495 **December 30 directive to Nimitz:** COMINCH to CINCPAC 301740 Dec 41, in the War diary of the Pacific Fleet, p. 121, identified as the CINCPAC Gray Book or as "Captain Steele's Running Estimate and Summary, 7 December 1941 to 31 August 1942" [hereafter Gray Book], www.ibiblio.org/anrs/graybook.html, accessed 28 December 2016; John Lundstrom, *The First South Pacific Campaign Pacific Fleet Strategy December 1941 to June 1942* (Annapolis, MD: Naval Institute Press, 1976), 19 [hereafter Lundstrom, *The First South Pacific Campaign*]. Lundstrom's book remains on the short list of indispensable works on Pacific 1942 naval air and naval strategy subjects.

496 **King's background; Stark's plan for fleet commanders in the fall 1941:** Buell, *Master of Seapower*, ch. 2–10; Lundstrom, *Black Shoe Carrier Admiral*, 48. This superb work not only powerfully restores the reputation of Frank Jack Fletcher, it also comprises the best description of Pacific Fleet command in the first year of the war.

496 **King's doubts about Nimitz as a "fixer":** Lundstrom, *Black Shoe Carrier Admiral*, 48–49.

496 **FDR's secret flag selection board:** Richard B. Frank, "Picking Winners?" *Naval History* 25, no. 3 (June 2011): 24–30. Dr. Jeffrey Barlow, a distinguished historian formerly at the Naval Heritage and History Command, found Knox's memo at the FDRL. He very graciously shared it with the author and encouraged the preparation of the article on this very striking episode.

496 **Rabaul and its garrison:** Wigmore, *The Japanese Thrust*, 397, 673; Gillison, *Royal Australian Air Force 1939–1942*, 234, 369; Bruce Gamble, *Book One of the Rabaul Trilogy: Invasion Rabaul: The Epic Story of Lark Force, the Forgotten Garrison, January–July 1942* (Minneapolis, MN: Zenith Press, 2014), 45–47, 52–53 [hereafter Gamble, *Invasion Rabaul*]. Gamble's three volumes on the role of Rabaul in the war are highly recommended.

498 **Air battle of 20 January:** Gillison, *The Royal Australian Air Force 1939–1942*, 398–99; Gamble, *Invasion Rabaul*, 74–77 (like a hunter . . ." at 75); TROMs *Akagi*, and *Shokaku*, combinedfleet.com, accessed 20 July 2016.

498 **Japanese landing 22–23 January; South Seas Force:** Wigmore, *The Japanese Thrust*, 412; Gamble, *Invasion Rabaul*, 65, 115, 122, 93–125; TROM minelayer *Tsugaru*, combinedfleet.com, accessed 21 July 2016. Horii's South Sea Force totaled about 5,300 men at this stage. Besides the 144th Regiment, it included a battalion of antiaircraft guns and company-size or smaller detachments of horse-mounted cavalry, engineers, signalers, and transportation, veterinarian, and medical units, as well as the Maizuru 2nd Special Naval Landing Force. During fighting on the 23rd, Japanese reported losses were sixteen killed and forty-seven wounded. The best reconstructed Australian figures are fifty-seven dead on 23 January.

498 **Scanlan orders; northern and southern contingents of "Lark Force"; Tol Plantation massacre:** Gamble, *Invasion Rabaul*, 115, 122, ch. 8–12. Gamble provides a graphic description from both sides of the weeks after the capture of Rabaul and the rescue of part of "Lark Force." He identifies the unit responsible for the Tol massacre as the 8th Company, 144th Regiment. Survivors reported the Japanese unit exchanged radio messages with a headquarters at Rabaul just before the massacre began, plainly implying the executions were by order of the regimental commander or Horii. The balance, which particularly included an RAAF contingent, were evacuated mostly by daring rescue flights by PBYs that took out 244. Altogether about four hundred men of Scanlan's command escaped to Australia. Wigmore, *The Japanese Thrust*, appendix 4: Ordeal on New Britain, 653–74.

498 **Tragedy of *Montevideo Maru*:** Gamble, *Invasion Rabaul*, 240–42, 247–48; TROM *Montevideo Maru*, IJN auxiliary transport, combinedfleet.com, accessed 20 July 2016. There are small discrepancies as to the total of POWs and internees on *Montevideo Maru*. One report puts the total at 1,061 whereas another postwar Japanese report puts the number at 1,054.

499 **Marine reinforcements to Samoa; plans for carrier strikes; damage to *Saratoga* and sinking of *Neches*:** Lundstrom, *The First Team*, 52–53, 58–61. Lundstrom, *Black Shoe Carrier Admiral*, 56–62; Damage to *Saratoga*: TROM *I-6*, combinedfleet.com, accessed 4 February 2013.

499 **King's strategic vision for South Pacific offensive:** Buell, *Master of Sea Power*, 188–89; Larrabee, *Commander in Chief*, 173–74; Lundstrom, *The First South Pacific Cam-*

paign; Lundstrom, *Black Shoe Carrier Admiral*, 61. Buell calls King's drive to follow an offensive cast to Pacific operations at the same time, not after, operations proceeded against Hitler "the most important contribution he would make to victory in the Second World War."

499 **Conflicts between American services on Pacific strategy:** Hayes, *History of the Joint Chiefs of Staff*, 38, 57, 118; Lundstrom, *The First South Pacific Campaign*, 50–51, 55, 129; Craven and Crate, *Plans and Early Operations January 1939 to August 1942*, 47–50; Louis Morton, *United States Army in World War II, The War in the Pacific, Strategy and Command: The First Two Years* (Washington, DC: Office of the Chief of Military History, Department of the Army, 1962), 217–19 [hereafter Morton, *Strategy and Command*]; Robert H. Ferrell, ed., *The Eisenhower Diaries* (New York: W. W. Norton, 1981), 44 ("we've got to go to Europe and Fight . . .") [hereafter Ferrell, *The Eisenhower Diaries*].

500 **"white men's countries":** King to Roosevelt, 5 Mar 42, cited in Thorne, *Allies of a Kind*, 7, 259.

500 **King as opponent of army plans; effects of Australian and New Zealand demands for return of ANZAC forces; string of army bases:** Morton, *Strategy and Command*, 198–224; Hough, Ludwig, and Shaw, *Pearl Harbor to Guadalcanal*, 84–92; Lundstrom, *The First South Pacific Campaign*, 48–49; Ferrell, *The Eisenhower Diaries*, 50 ("one thing that might help win this war . . .").

500 **Plan for carrier raids of Gilberts and Marshalls and defenses there:** Lundstrom, *Black Shoe Carrier Admiral*, 60–62. Originally the Gilberts/Marshalls raid would have been the second American carrier raid of the war. But when Japanese submarine *I-72* sank the American oiler *Neches* on 23 January, it forced cancelation of a raid on Wake Island by the *Lexington* task force. TROM *I-172*, combinedfleet.com, accessed 4 February 2013. In May 1942, the Japanese renumbered many submarines. One of them was the *I-72* renumbered to *I-172*.

500 **Halsey described:** Robert Trumball, "All Out with Halsey," *New York Times Magazine*, 6 December 1942; James Hornfischer, *Neptune's Inferno: The U.S. Navy at Guadalcanal* (New York: Bantam Books, 2011), 210.

501 **Use of intercepted weather reports:** Memorandum for Cdr. P. P. Leigh, USNR, Subject: Task Force Sixteen (U.S.S. Enterprise) 10 February 1942 to 10 March 1942, 10 September 1945, 1, SRH-313, Pacific Ocean Mobile Radio Intelligence Unit Reports 1942, RG 457, NARA.

501 **Halsey's aggressive attack in Marshalls, attack on *Enterprise*; losses on both sides:** The Commanding Officer, U.S.S. Enterprise (CV-6), 7 February 1942, Serial 026, Report of Action on February 1, 1942, RG 38, NARA; Lundstrom, *The First Team*, 60–77; TROM *Katori*, combinedfleet.com, accessed 2 February 2013; Richard Fuller, *Shōkan: Hirohito's Samurai, Leaders of Japanese Armed Forces, 1926–1945* (London: Arms and Armour Press, 1992), 307. This raid by Halsey at first prompted Combined Fleet on 5 February to cancel intended employment of *Kido Butai* to support southern operations and assign it to the Fourth Fleet on the Pacific front. Then on 8 February, the Combined Fleet decided to send *Kido Butai* to Southern Operations, but retain Carrier Division 5 (two fleet carriers) on the mainland. Remmelink, *The Invasion of the Dutch East Indies*, 377.

501 **Yorktown *strike at Gilberts:*** Lundstrom, *Black Shoe Carrier Admiral*, 65–71.

501 **Lexington*'s aborted attack on Rabaul:*** Commanding Officer, Task Force Eleven, Feb-

ruary 23, 1942, Serial 004, Report of Air Attack on Lexington February 20, 1942, RG 38, NARA; Lundstrom, *The First Team*, 83–110.

502 **Halsey's raids on Wake and Marcus Islands:** Commanding Officer, U.S.S. Enterprise (CV-6), 8 March 1942, Report of Action on February 24, 1942; Commanding Officer, U.S.S. Enterprise (CV-6), 9 March 1942, Serial 055, Report of Action on March 4, 1942, RG 38, NARA; Lundstrom, *The First Team*, 111–21.

503 **Strikes at Lae and Salamaua:** Commanding officer, U.S.S. Yorktown, March 12, 1942, Serial 022, Attack Made by Yorktown Air group Against Enemy Forces on Salamaua and Lae, New Guinea, RG 38, NARA; Lundstrom, *The First Team*, 122–32; TROMs cruiser *Yubari*, destroyer *Asanagi*, auxiliary seaplane tender *Kiyokawa Maru*, and auxiliary cruiser *Kongo Maru*, combinedfleet.com, accessed 25 June 2016.

504 **Japanese strategic options:** H. P. Willmott, *Empires in the Balance: Japanese and Allied Pacific Strategies to April 1942* (Annapolis, MD: Naval Institute Press, 1982), 435–42.

504 **Composition of Nagumo's and Ozawa's forces:** the First Air Fleet composition follows TROM *Akagi*, combinedfleet com, accessed 22 September 2014. Figures on air complement from Boyd, *The Royal Navy in Far Eastern Waters*, 488–89n84. The composition of Ozawa's raiding force follows TROM *Ryujo*, combinedfleet.com, accessed 22 September 2014.

504 **British detect Colombo as target, preparations to defend Ceylon and India:** Michael Smith, *The Emperor's Codes* (New York: Arcade Publishing, 2007), 128; Shores, Cull, and Izawa, *Bloody Shambles*, vol. 2, 383–94.

504 **Somerville.** Captain's Confidential Reports, http://www.admirals.org.uk/admirals/fleet/somervillejf.php, accessed 24 September 2014; Stephen Roskill, *Churchill and the Admirals* (New York: William Morrow, 1978), 270–71 ("peculiar brand . . ." at 270); Stephen Martin, *Fighting Admirals: British Admirals of the Second World War* (Annapolis, MD: Naval Institute Press, 1991), 83–84, 209. Roskill's account is particularly validated by his close work with many of the subjects, including Somerville.

505 **"I drove my car faster than I landed a Swordfish":** Max Arthur, *Lost Voices of the Royal Navy: Vivid Eyewitness Accounts of Life in the Royal Navy for 1914 to 1945* (London: Hodder & Stoughton Ltd., 2005), 289.

505 **Composition and capabilities of Eastern Fleet:** Willmott, *Empires in Balance*, 440; Shores, Cull, and Izawa, *Bloody Shambles*, vol. 2, 386.

505 **"breath-taking events":** Churchill, *The Hinge of Fate*, 154.

505 **Faulty British intelligence and Somerville's near disaster:** Boyd, *The Royal Navy in Eastern Waters*, 366–69.

505 **Attack on Colombo, sinking of *Dorsetshire* and *Cornwall*:** ADM 199/1389; ADM 358/3178, 358/3229, TNA; Shores, Cull, and Izawa, *Bloody Shambles*, vol. 2, 395–408; *Dorsetshire* and *Cornwall*, Allied Warships, Warship losses, 5 April 1942, uboat.net, accessed 24 September 2014.

506 **Somerville and Nagumo missed opportunities on 5 April:** Boyd, *The Royal Navy in Far Eastern Waters*, 368–85.

506 **Nagumo's attack on Trincomalee:** Shores, Cull, and Izawa, *Bloody Shambles*, vol. 2, 412–30; TROMs *Akagi* and *Kongo*, combinedfleet.com, accessed 24 September 2014; *Hermes*, *Vampire* and *Hollyhock*, Allied Warships, Warship losses, 9 April 1942, uboat.net, accessed 24 September 2014.

506 **Ozawa's depredations in the Bay of Bengal, attack on Indian cities:** TROMs *Ryujo, Chokai, Suzuya, Kumano, Mogami, Mikuma, I-2, I-3, I-4, I-5, I-6, I-7,* combinedfleet. com, accessed 29 September 2014; Shores, Cull, and Izawa, *Bloody Shambles,* vol. 2, 408–11, 429–31; Kirby, *India's Most Dangerous Hour,* 119–20, 125–26.

507 **"India's Most Dangerous Hour":** Kirby, *India's Most Dangerous Hour,* 131.

507 **Churchill's 15 April cable:** Warren F. Kimball, ed., *Churchill & Roosevelt: The Complete Correspondence,* vol. 1, *Alliance Emerging, October 1933–November 1942* (Princeton, NJ: Princeton University Press, 1984), 452–54 [hereafter Kimball, *Churchill & Roosevelt: The Complete Correspondence,* vol. 1]. Specifically, Churchill asked that the modern US fast battleship *North Carolina* and fleet carrier *Ranger* move to the Indian Ocean. Alternatively, *North Carolina* could relieve the British battleship *Duke of York* in British waters for duty in the Indian Ocean with *Ranger.* These exchanges can also be found online in the Franklin D. Roosevelt Papers as President: Map Room Papers, 1941–1945, Franklin D. Roosevelt Presidential Library & Museum, fdrlibrary.marist.edu/_resources/images, accessed 30 September 2014. The omission of Churchill's April 15 message can be observed in *Hinge of Fate,* 159–60, where Churchill records Roosevelt's response but omits his own message.

507 **Roosevelt's reply to Churchill's April 15 message:** Roosevelt to Churchill, no. 134, April 16, 1942, in Kimball, *Churchill & Roosevelt: The Complete Correspondence,* vol. 1, 455–56.

507 **Background to Operation Ironclad:** Churchill to Roosevelt, no. 44, March 14, 1942, in Kimball, *Churchill & Roosevelt: The Complete Correspondence,* vol. 1, 404–5; Kirby, *India's Most Dangerous Hour,* 133–35.

507 **Order of battle for Operation Ironclad:** Kirby, *India's Most Dangerous Hour,* 133–35, appendix 9. The establishment of this naval force triggered a complex rearrangement of US and British warships, with a major US detachment going to the Home Fleet to free British ships to replace Force H at Gibraltar while ships from Force H went to Madagascar. See Roosevelt to Churchill, Nos. 119 and 120, March 16, 1942, and no. 123, March 18, 1942, in Kimball, *Churchill & Roosevelt: The Complete Correspondence,* vol. 1, 406–7, 419–22.

507 **Landing on Madagascar; subsequent naval, military, and political events:** Kirby, *India's Most Dangerous Hour,* 135–44; Kimball, *Churchill & Roosevelt: The Complete Correspondence,* vol. 1, 483. The submarine lost was the *Bévéziers. Ramilles* was severely damaged and out of the war for twelve months. Burt, *British Battleships,* 188–91. During the follow-on campaign in 1942, the 29th Independent and 23rd East African Brigades suffered relatively few battle casualties but did experience a high rate of malarial sickness, which left Wavell without their services when he needed them in the fall of 1942.

508 **Churchill's attitude toward India:** Thorne, *Allies of a Kind,* 61–62; Hastings, *Winston's War,* 214–15.

508 **Background events in India by early 1942:** Thorne, *Allies of a Kind,* 60–61; Roberts, *Walking With Destiny,* 341–43, Roberts makes the point that it was Churchill's opposition to granting of Dominion status to India, not his warnings about Nazi Germany, that propelled Churchill into what was called his "Wilderness Years" in the 1930s within the Conservative Party.

509 **Political complexion of India; Gandhi:** Raghavan, *India's War,* 7, 10–19; Yasmin Kahn, *India at War: The Subcontinent and the Second World War* (Oxford: Oxford

University Press, 2015), 7–11, 15–17 [hereafter Kahn, *India at War*]; Yogesh Chadha, *Gandhi: A Life* (New York: John Wiley & Sons, 1997), 362–74 [hereafter Chadha, *Gandhi: A Life*]. All these works are of great value.

509 **"nonviolent arms"; "immolation of hundreds, if not thousands . . ."; "take what they want of the countries . . ."; "you will allow yourself . . ."**: Chadha, *Gandhi: A Life*, 362–64, 369. In addition to these quotes, in May 1940 Gandhi wrote, "I do not consider Hitler to be as bad as he is depicted. He is showing an ability that is amazing and he seems to be gaining his victories without much bloodshed." Chadha, *Gandhi: A Life*, 363. Then in May 1942, he told the press that the United States should have stayed out of the war. Raghavan, *India's War*, 241.

510 **Chiang visits India**: Yang Tianshi, "Chiang Kai-shek and Jawaharlal Nehru," in van de Ven, Lary, and MacKinnon, *Negotiating China's Destiny in World War II*, 131–37.

510 **Failure of Cripps mission**: Raghavan, *India's War*, 233–39, 241; Kahn, *India at War*, 132–35; Gilbert, *The Road to Victory*, 63, 78, 87–88; Hastings, *Winston's War*, 200, 205–6, 214. The failure of the Cripps mission remains a very much alive and controversial topic in India.

510 **Roosevelt attempts to intervene in Cripps Mission**: Roosevelt to Churchill, no. 132, April 11, 1942, Kimball, *Churchill & Roosevelt: The Complete Correspondence*, vol. 1, 446–47; Hastings, *Winston's War*, 214.

511 **"string of cuss words last[ing] two hours . . ."**: Stimson diary, April 22, 1942.

511 **"rank cant for a nation . . ."**: Hastings, *Winston's War*, 215.

511 **"Measures now in hand . . ."**: Roosevelt to Churchill, no. 134, April 16, 1942, Kimball, *Churchill & Roosevelt: The Complete Correspondence*, vol. 1, 454 55.

511 **Roosevelt's demand; King's proposal for army bombers to fly from a carrier**: Glines, *The Doolittle Raid: America's Daring First Strike Against Japan* (New York: Orion Books, 1988), 9–10, 12–15 [hereafter Glines, *The Doolittle Raid*]; "Meeting of President Roosevelt and Prime Minister Churchill with their Military Advisers," January 4, 1942, *FRUS, Conferences at Washington and Casablanca (1941–1943)*, 161–70.

511 **Doolittle plan; the task force**: James H. Doolittle to The Commanding General of the Army Air Forces, Subject: Report on the Aerial Bombing of Japan, June 5, 1942, http://doolittleraider.com/interviews.htm# at doolittleraider.com, accessed 28 December 2014; Commander Task Force 16, War diary, 4/1–30, 1942, serial 0025 (enclosures include reports of *Hornet* and *Enterprise*) [hereafter Commander Task Force 16, War diary, 4/1–30, 1942], RG 38, NARA.

512 **Original plan for Doolittle launch, decision to launch early, lack of notice to Chinese, and American, Japanese, and Chinese reactions**: http://doolittleraider.com/interviews.htm# at doolittleraider.com, accessed 28 December 2014; Commander Task Force 16, War diary, 4/1–30, 1942; Glines, *The Doolittle Raid*, 92, 103, ch. 10, esp. 150–51, 180–82, 217; The Chief of Staff (Marshall) to Generalissimo Chiang Kai-shek, April 17, 1942, *FRUS, 1942, China*, 32. The 250,000 figure is from Claire Lee Chennault, *Way of a Fighter: The Memoirs of Claire Lee Chennault, Major General, U.S. Army (Ret.)* (New York: G. P. Putnam's Sons, 1949), 168. It is possible that the 250,000 figure for Chinese deaths in Japanese reprisals is high, but the retribution was savage and widespread. For an excellent recent account of the raid and horrific descriptions of Japanese reprisals, see James M. Scott, *Target Tokyo: Jimmy Doolittle and the Raid that Avenged Pearl Harbor* (New York: W. W. Norton, 2015), 105–6, 380–85, 389–90. One of the Doolittle raiders captured by the Japanese was

Cpl. Jacob D. DeShazer. After his release, he kept a vow he made to become a Christian missionary in Japan. During this phase of his life, one of his converts was Mitsuo Fuchida, who was the air leader of the Japanese attack on Pearl Harbor.

513 **Malaria and quinine:** Paul F. Russell, M.D., M.P.H., Sc.D., Introduction, *Medical Department, United States Army, Preventative Medicine in World War II*, vol. 6, *Communicable Diseases: Malaria* (Washington, DC: Office of the Surgeon General, Department of the Army, 1963), 4–6, http://history.amedd.army.mil/booksdocs/ wwii/Malaria/chapterI.htm, accessed 21 August 2014), and Maj. Gen. James O. Gillespie, MC, USA (Ret.), "Malaria and the Defense of Bataan," ch. 9, Communicable Diseases, *Medical Department, United States Army, Preventative Medicine in World War II*, vol. 6, *Communicable Diseases: Malaria* (Washington, DC: Office of the Surgeon General, Department of the Army, 1963), 4–6, 503–4, http://history.amedd .army.mil/booksdocs/wwii/Malaria/chapterIX.htm, accessed 21 August 2014 [hereafter Gillespie, "Malaria and the Defense of Bataan"].

513 **Rations on Bataan:** Gillespie, "Malaria and the Defense of Bataan," 504–5.

513 **Pilferage of rations:** "because of filching along the way": The Harold K. Johnson Collection, Box 201, Folder 1 Oral Histories, Interview with D. Clayton James, 14, USAHEC. At least one historian charges that the failure of MacArthur to take (presumably) draconian action to stamp out pilferage of rations constitutes one of his greatest command failures in the Philippines. Bond, "Douglas MacArthur and the Philippines," 182. On January 17, 1942, USAFFE issued a memorandum titled "Noncompliance with Orders" condemning both the overstating of ration strengths of units to secure more rations and the pilferage of rations. This seems wholly inadequate to address the issue. Headquarters, USAFFE, 17 January 1942, Subject: Noncompliance with Orders, RG 2, Personal Files, Correspondence of General MacArthur, Box 2 November 25, 1941 to April 17, 1942, Folder 3, December 25, 1941 to January 22, 1942, MML.

513 **Effects of starvation and resulting diseases:** William D. O'Neil, "Transformation and the Officer Corps: Analysis in the Historical Context of the U.S. and Japan between the World Wars," Center for Naval Analysis, CME D0012589.A2, September 2005, 118–19; Whitman, *Bataan: Our Last Ditch*, 449; Gillespie, "Malaria and the Defense of Bataan," 504–5.

513 **Frontline conditions:** Whitman, *Bataan: Our Last Ditch*, 394.

513 **Hospital admissions, sick men in front lines:** Gillespie, "Malaria and the Defense of Bataan," 505–7; Whitman, *Bataan: Our Last Ditch*, 450.

513 **Civilian encampments:** Whitman, *Bataan: Our Last Ditch*, 412.

515 **Homma's built-up command:** Whitman, *Bataan: Our Last Ditch*, 475, 477, 528; Shores, Cull, and Izwa, *Bloody Shambles*, vol. 2, 136–38. There was a brief appearance of "Vals" of the 31st Air Group. Among the well-traveled Imperial Army Ki-21 "Sally" crews, Corregidor gained the reputation of having the most troublesome antiaircraft fire. Email of Osamu "Sam" Tagaya, 23 December 2014. He is an expert on Japanese World War II aviation, and much else.

515 **Homma's plan and opening barrage:** Whitman, *Bataan: Our Last Ditch*, 475–80; Young, *The Battle of Bataan*, 2nd edition, 189–91 ("the sky was black with planes" at 191).

515 **Collapse of 41st and 21st Divisions (PA):** Whitman, *Bataan: Our Last Ditch*, 478, 489.

515   **Counterattacks by 33rd Infantry Regiment (PA) and 31st Infantry Regiment:** Morton, *The Fall of the Philippines*, 434–37; Whitman, *Bataan: Our Last Ditch*, 491–92, 508, 552.

516   **Japanese seize Mt. Samat:** Whitman, *Bataan: Our Last Ditch*, 494–96.

516   **Fantasy versus reality:** Whitman, *Bataan: Our Last Ditch*, 487–88; James, *The Years of MacArthur*, vol. 2, 144–46.

516   **Disintegration of Luzon Force:** Whitman, *Bataan: Our Last Ditch*, 510–11, 513, 534–37, 544–46, 550–53, 559–61, 563–66; Shores, Cull, and Izawa, *Bloody Shambles*, vol. 2, 137–39; Richard C. Mallonee II, ed., *The Naked Flag Pole* (San Rafael, CA: Presidio Press, 1980), 128.

517   **King described and his decision to surrender:** Stanley Falk, *Bataan: The March of Death* (New York: W. W. Norton, 1962), 29 [hereafter Falk, *Bataan: The March of Death*]; Whitman, *Bataan: Our Last Ditch*, 583–89. At a conference on 18 March, the Luzon force quartermaster, Drake, informed Wainwright of the dwindling food situation that he projected would only permit carrying on until on or about the middle of April. Wainwright said his planning date was 15 April. Even without the Japanese offensive, it appears Bataan might have surrendered no later than about 15 April. Report of Operations Quartermaster Corps, p. 43, Wainwright Report, RG 407, NARA.

517   **Massacre of 91st Division (PA) officers and noncommissioned officers:** Falk, *The March of Death*, 107–12; Young, *The Battle of Bataan*, 2nd edition, 254–55. The area of the massacre was controlled by the 65th Brigade. There was evidence that General Nara had appeared before the massacre and issued some order. The massacre followed, suggesting he ordered it. There was no solid evidence that the officer was Nara and the matter was never pursued in postwar trials.

517   **Number of prisoners set to marching out from Bataan, characterization of the march:** Falk, *Bataan: The March of Death*, 194–95; Whitman, *Bataan: Our Last Ditch*, 589; Capt. Paul L. Ashton, *Bataan diary* (privately published, 1984), 159 ("a feast of hate") [hereafter Ashton, *Bataan diary*]. Whitman estimates garrison of Bataan at 74,000 at time of surrender, and Falk puts the garrison total at time of surrender at about 78,100. Falk estimates that about 2,000 men escaped to Corregidor, about 4,000 or so were hospital patients, and others retained by the Japanese on work details did not make the march.

518   **Heat, generous treatment by some guards:** Donald Knox, *Death March: The Survivors of Bataan* (New York: Harcourt Brace Jovanovich, 1981), 117 [hereafter Knox, *Death March*], 117; Gavin Daws, *Prisoners of the Japanese: POWs of World War II in the Pacific* (New York: William Morrow, 1994), 77 [hereafter Daws, *Prisoners of the Japanese*], 77; Falk, *Bataan: The March of Death*, 93.

518   **Abusive guards:** Falk, *Bataan: The March of Death*, 87; Knox, *Death March*, 117; Daws, *Prisoners of the Japanese*, 77; Ashton, *Bataan diary*, 161.

518   **Killing of marchers who fell down or out:** Daws, *Prisoners of the Japanese*, 75–76; Ashton, *Bataan diary*, 9–10; Oral History Robert A. Brown, May 15, 2002, National Museum Pacific War ("Rule one is you take one more step . . .").

518   **Death March fatality figures:** among the major published sources, Falk, *Bataan: The March of Death*, 194–99, attempted as rigorous an assessment as possible of the many unknowns that compromise any attempt to develop precise figures on march deaths. He ventures that about 600 to 650 Americans and between 5,000 and 10,000 Filipinos perished. Daws, *Prisoners of the Japanese*, 80, estimates between

500 and 1,000 Americans and "possibly as many as ten thousand" Filipinos died. Knox, *Death March*, 154–55, puts American deaths between 600 and 700 and Filipino deaths "probably between 5,000 and 10,000." John Toland, *The Rising Sun* (New York: Random House, 1970), 375, reports as many as 2,330 Americans died on the march, a figure that seems improbably high, and may have stemmed from including in the "dead" approximately 1,500 hospital patients on Bataan who simply did not make the march. Dr. Richard Meixsel of James Madison University was kind enough to share his deep research on these topics from US and Philippine sources. Essentially, the numbers had to be reassembled after the war and thus were subject to great uncertainty, which Meixsel lays out in detail. Some of the sources would place the number of American deaths on the march as probably several hundred, but fewer than five hundred. There seems no doubt that the number of Filipino deaths, even allowing for large-scale escapes on the march, was several multiples of US deaths.

519   **Camp O'Donnell:** Falk, *Bataan: The March of Death*, 200 ("a fog of death laying on the ground . . ." at 200); Daws, *Prisoners of the Japanese*, 87; Gillespie, "Malaria and the Defense of Bataan," 510. Again Dr. Meixsel details the great range of figures for deaths at Camp O'Donnell. But there is no question the number much exceeded deaths on the march from Bataan.

519   **Fourteenth Army preparations to take Corregidor:** Fourteenth Army Operations, part 10, 129–32, USAHEC; Morton, *The Fall of the Philippines*, 521–27, 552–53. Figures for the American garrison are from Morton, 529, based on numbers for 15 April 1942.

519   **Japanese shelling of Corregidor; crescendo on 5 May:** John Gordon, *Fighting For MacArthur: The Navy and Marine Corps' Desperate Defense of the Philippines* (Annapolis, MD: Naval Institute Press, 2011), 255–61 [hereafter Gordon, *Fighting For MacArthur*]; Morton, *The Fall of the Philippines*, 536–51 ("dust, dirt, black flies and vermin" and "under the deepening shadow of death . . ." at 542); Hough, Ludwig, and Shaw, *Pearl Harbor to Guadalcanal*, 185–87, 189–92; Surrender of Corregidor, Scuttling of U.S.S. Quail. (No Serial), June 16, 1942, 2–3, "the island appeared to be one vast sheet of flame . . ."), Fold3/WWII War Diaries/U/USS Quail, accessed 23 June 2016.

520   **Japanese final assault on Corregidor:** Gordon, *Fighting For MacArthur*, 271–309; Morton, *The Fall of the Philippines*, 552–61; Hough, Ludwig, and Shaw, *Pearl Harbor to Guadalcanal*, 191–201; Wainwright, *General Wainwright's Story*, 119 ("it was the terror that is vested in a tank . . ."). In this writer's view, the painstaking re-creation of the last fighting on Corregidor by army and Marine Corps historians is one of their finest achievements in their histories of World War II. As the Marine Corps historians pointed out, relatively few men who fought against the Japanese landing on Corregidor survived the fighting and the war. The 4th Marine Regiment tragically sustained massive losses of its officers held as prisoners of war when American submarines sank ships transporting them out of the Philippines. Notwithstnading all these issues, Gordon's account is also outstanding.

520   **Wainwright's surrender, casualties:** Morton, *The Fall of the Philippines*, 560–61; Hough, Ludwig, and Shaw, *Pearl Harbor to Guadalcanal*, 199–200; Gordon, *Fighting For MacArthur*, 304–6. Figures for American and Filipino casualties remain unclear. The 4th Marines, who formed the backbone if not a majority of the defend-

ers, alone lost 330 killed and missing and 357 wounded in the whole Philippine campaign. It appears that the great majority of this total fell in this last action. Gordon, however, presents good evidence from various US and Japanese figures and the recollections of those on burial details after the battle that make the 170 number persuasive.

521 **Roosevelt overrules MacArthur original command structure; Wainwright's appointment; Japanese reject Wainwright's attempt to surrender only Manila Bay installations:** Morton, *The Fall of the Philippines*, 360–66, 570–72; James, *The Years of MacArthur*, vol. 2, 141–43; Wainwright, *General Wainwright's Story*, 133. MacArthur described the rationale for the divided command as "special problems" and "the intangible of the situation in the Philippines." This seems to imply his foresight that protracted resistance and encouragement of guerilla operations warranted the divided command. Marshall's understandable arguments were that MacArthur could not exercise effective command at a distance of 4,000 miles and that MacArthur as a supreme Allied commander could not simultaneously exercise direct control of a single national force.

521 **Protracted surrender of forces in the Philippines:** Morton, *The Fall of the Philippines*, 572–82.

521 **Strobing messages:** "Copy, Fort Mills (WVDM) radio operator to Fort Shafter (WTJ) radio operator," RG 107, Entry 99 "Safe File," Box 11, Folder Philippines, NARA.

521 **Population of Imperial Japanese Empire at zenith:** The calculation of this figure is derived from totals provided in Dear and Foot, *The Oxford Companion to World War II*, unless otherwise indicated: Burma (Myanmar): 17 million; China: 266 million in areas controlled by Japan (per a figure in a 1946 report of the United Nations Relief and Rehabilitation Administration [UNRRA], kindly provided by Dr. Hans van de Ven); Formosa: 5 million; French Indochina: 25 million; Hong Kong: 1.4 million; Japan: 70 million; Korea: 23.5 million; Netherlands East Indies: 70.5 million; Malaya/Singapore: 5.5 million; Philippines: 17 million; Thailand: 15.9 million; and total: 516.8 million. These numbers were cross-checked against www.populstat .info, accessed 25 June 2016, and although differences were present (usually somewhat higher in the latter source), they were found to be reasonably consistent. The figures do not include Pacific islands, apart from the Philippines and the Netherlands East Indies, occupied by Japan; however, those numbers are at most in the thousands. No representation is made that these numbers are precise; however, they give a reasonable approximation.

Approximate population in German Empire (for this purpose including Italy) in 1942: Albania: 1 million; Austria: 6.7 million; Belgium: 8.2 million; Czechoslovakia (aggregated after breakup): circa 14 million; Denmark: 3.85 million; Finland: 3.6 million (1936); France: 41.1 million (1936); Germany: 79.5 million; Greece: 7.345 million; Hungary: 8 million; Italy: 42 million (1936); Luxembourg: 293,000; Netherlands: 9 million; Norway: 3 million; Poland: 35 million; Romania 16.7 million (website); Soviet Empire: 65 million; and Yugoslavia: 16 million. The total is 360.288 million. The sources for these numbers are the same as for the Imperial Japanese Empire with the same qualifications. The figure of the population within the German occupied sphere of the Soviet Empire was kindly provided by Dr. Evan Maudsley. Obviously, given the wide gap between figures for the Imperial Japanese and German Empires, the basic point that the Imperial Japanese Empire included a much larger population appears beyond reasonable dispute, whatever the exact figures may be.

521 **Japanese versus Allied losses in campaigns from 7 December 1941:** the source of the figures used here is from a Microsoft Excel sheet prepared using the data presented in ch. 12–18. These data are admittedly incomplete, but they do give an approximation of the disparity between Allied and Japanese casualties. Figures on aircrew losses are particularly incomplete, but such figures as are available do show that Japanese losses in the air, when operational losses are factored in, were not so disparate as those in ground and sea combat.

522 **Scene of "decryption line":** 5750/202 CNSG-History of OP-20-GYP-1 WWII (1 of 2), 30, RG 38, CNSG Library, Box 116, NARA.

BIBLIOGRAPHY

A Note on Sources

Because of the immense scope and novel perspective of this trilogy, its primary character is synthesis. The synthesis is a result of a combination of sources and a network of colleagues who have provided invaluable guidance to sources and knowledgeable critiques of drafts. The author has also chosen certain areas to drill down to original source material. Some of these areas include American and British radio intelligence, the diplomatic exchanges between the United States and Japan in 1941, and the Pearl Harbor attack. Radio intelligence forms an often veiled key to decision making. The diplomatic and military developments leading to the American entry into World War II form, together with China's sustained hostilities against Japan for eight years, two of the most significant aspects of this narrative.

The following materials are the selected sources that have provided the sinews of this work. The multitude of other sources examined but not used are not listed.

Archives

US National Archives, College Park. Maryland
Library of Congress, Washington, DC
Hoover Institution, Stanford University, Stanford, California
Franklin D. Roosevelt Presidential Library, Hyde Park, New York
Harry S. Truman Presidential Library, Independence, Missouri
The National Archives, Kew, United Kingdom
Imperial War Museum, London, United Kingdom
Liddle Hart Centre, Kings College, London, United Kingdom
Churchill Library, Cambridge, United Kingdom
Australian War Memorial, Canberra, Australia
Australian National University, Canberra, Australia
George C. Marshall Library, Lexington, Virginia
Joseph Mark Lauinger Memorial Library, Georgetown University, Washington, DC
Naval History and Heritage Command, Washington Navy Yard, Washington, DC
United States Marine Corps History Center, Quantico, Virginia
United States Army Heritage and Education Center, Carlisle, Pennsylvania
MacArthur Memorial and Library, Norfolk, Virginia
Nimitz Museum, Fredericksburg, Texas
Pritzker Military Library and Museum, Chicago, Illinois
University of Wisconsin, Milwaukee
Nimitz Library, United States Naval Academy, Annapolis, Maryland

US National World War II Museum, New Orleans, Louisiana
Joyner Library, East Carolina University, Greenville, North Carolina
US Naval War College, Newport, Connecticut
Northern Virginia Community College, Annandale, VA
Arlington County Public Library, Arlington, VA

Books

Abbazia, Patrick. *Mr. Roosevelt's Navy: The Private War of the Atlantic Fleet 1939–1942.* Annapolis, MD: Naval Institute Press, 1976.

Abend, Hallett. *My Life in China 1926–1941.* New York: Harcourt, Brace, 1943.

Agawa, Hiroyuki. *The Reluctant Admiral Yamamoto and the Imperial Navy.* Annapolis, MD: Naval Institute Press, 1979.

Alden, John D., and Craig R. McDonald. *United States and Allied Submarine Successes in the Pacific and Far East During World War II.* 4th edition. Jefferson, NC: McFarland Publishers, 2009.

Allen, Louis. *Burma: The Longest War 1941 to 1945.* London: Phoenix Press, 2000.

Anderson, Irvine H., Jr. *The Standard-Vacuum Oil Company and United States East Asian Policy, 1933–1941.* Princeton, NJ: Princeton University Press, 1975.

Arthur, Max. *Lost Voices of the Royal Navy: Vivid Eyewitness Accounts of Life in the Royal Navy for 1914 to 1945.* London: Hodder & Stoughton Ltd., 2005.

Asada, Sadao. *From Mahan to Pearl Harbor: The Imperial Japanese Navy and the United States.* Annapolis, MD: Naval Institute Press, 2006.

Ashton, Captain Paul L. *Bataan Diary.* Privately published, 1984.

Barnhart, Michael. *Japan Prepares for Total War: The Search for Economic Security, 1919–1941.* Ithaca, NY: Cornell University Press, 2015.

Bartsch, William H. *December 8, 1941: MacArthur's Pearl Harbor.* College Station: Texas A&M Press, 2003.

———. *Every Day a Nightmare: American Pursuit Pilots in Defense of Java, 1941–1942.* College Station: Texas A&M University Press, 2010.

Bayler, Lieutenant Colonel Walter L. *Last Man off Wake Island.* Indianapolis: Bobbs-Merrill, 1943.

Bayly, Christopher, and Tim Harper. *Forgotten Armies: The Fall of British Asia, 1941–1945.* Cambridge, MA: Belknap Press of Harvard University Press, 2004.

Beck, John Jacob. *MacArthur and Wainwright: Sacrifice in the Philippines.* Albuquerque: University of New Mexico Press, 1974.

Bedeski, Robert E. *State Building in Modern China: The Kuomintang in the Prewar Period.* Berkeley, CA: Center for Chinese Studies, 1981.

Beevor, Antony. *The Second World War.* New York: Little, Brown, 2012.

Beisner, Robert L. *Dean Acheson: A Life in the Cold War.* Oxford: Oxford University Press, 2006.

Belden, Jack. *China Shakes the World.* New York: Harper's, 1949.

———. *Retreat with Stilwell.* New York: Knopf, 1943.

Benson, Robert L. *A History of U.S. Communications Intelligence during World War II: Policy and Administration.* Fort Meade, FL: National Security Agency, 1997.

Benton, Gregor. *New Fourth Army: Communist Resistance along the Yangtze and the Huai, 1938–1941.* Berkeley: University of California Press, 1999.

Bercuson, David, and Holger Herwig. *One Christmas in Washington: Roosevelt and Churchill Forge the Grand Alliance*. Woodstock and New York: Overlook Press, 2006.

Bidwell, Shelford. *The Chindit War: Stilwell, Wingate, and the Campaign in Burma: 1944*. New York: Macmillan Publishing, 1979.

Birdseye, James. "Japanese and Philippine-American Logistics: The Philippine Dilemma, 1935–1942." University Microfilms International, unpublished diss., 1995.

Bix, Herbert P. *Hirohito and the Making of Modern Japan*. New York: HarperCollins Publishers, 2000.

Blair, Clay. *Hitler's U-Boat War, The Hunters 1939–1942*. New York: Random House, 1996.

———. *Silent Victory: The U.S. Submarine War Against Japan*. Philadelphia and New York: J. B. Lippincott, 1975.

Bland, Larry I., Joellen K. Bland, and Sharon Ritenor Stevens, eds. *George C. Marshall Interviews and Reminiscences for Forrest C. Pogue*. Lexington: George C. Marshall Research Foundation, 1991.

Boer, P. C. *The Loss of Java, The Final Battles for the Possession of Java Fought by Allied Air, Naval and Land Forces in the Period of 18 February–7 March 1942*. Singapore: NUS Press, 2011.

Bond, Brian, ed. *Fallen Stars: Eleven Studies in Twentieth Century Military Disasters*. London: Brassey's Putnam Aeronautical, 1992.

Bond, Brian, and Kyoichi Tachikawa. *British and Japanese Military Leadership in the Far Eastern War 1941–1945*. Oxon, UK: Frank Cass, 2004.

Borg, Dorothy, and Shumpei Okamoto, eds. *Pearl Harbor as History: Japanese American Relations 1931–1941*. New York: Columbia University Press, 1973.

Boyd, Andrew. *The Royal Navy in Eastern Waters: Linchpin of Victory 1935–1942*. Barnsley, UK: Seaforth Publishing, 2017.

Brooke, Geoffrey. *Singapore's Dunkirk: The Aftermath of the Fall*. London: Leo Cooper, 1989.

Brown, David. *Warship Losses of World War II*. New York: Arms and Armour, 1990.

Browning, Christopher R., with contributions by Jürgen Matthäus. *The Origins of the Final Solution: The Evolution of Nazi Jewish Policy, September 1939–March 1942*. Lincoln: University of Nebraska Press, 2004.

Buell, Thomas B. *Master of Sea Power: A Biography of Fleet Admiral Ernest J. King*. Annapolis, MD: Naval Institute Press, 1980.

Bulkley, Robert J. *At Close Quarters: PT Boats in the United States Navy*. Washington. DC: Naval History Division, Navy Department, 1962.

Burt, R. A. *British Battleships 1919–1939*. Revised edition. Annapolis, MD: Naval Institute Press, 2012.

Butow, Robert J. C. *Japan's Decision to Surrender*. Stanford, CA: Stanford University Press, 1954.

———. *Tojo and the Coming of the War*. Stanford, CA: Stanford University Press, 1961.

Byrd, Martha. *Chennault: Giving Wings to the Tiger*. Tuscaloosa: University of Alabama Press, 1987.

Callahan, Raymond. *The Worst Disaster: The Fall of Singapore*. Cranbury: Associated University Presses, 1977.

Campbell, John. *Naval Weapons of World War Two*. Annapolis, MD: Naval Institute Press, 1985.

Cantril, Hadley, ed. *Public Opinion 1935–1946*. Princeton, NJ: Princeton University Press, 1951.

Carpenter, Dorr, and Norman Polmar. *Submarines of the Imperial Japanese Navy*. Annapolis, MD: Naval Institute Press, 1986.

Castle, Ian. *London 1917–18: The Bomber Blitz*. New York: Osprey Publishing Ltd., 2010.

Chadha, Yogesh. *Gandhi: A Life*. New York: John Wiley & Sons, 1997.

Chang, Iris. *The Rape of Nanking: The Forgotten Holocaust of World War II*. New York: Basic Books, 1997.

Chennault, Claire Lee. *Way of a Fighter: The Memoirs of Claire Lee Chennault, Major General, U.S. Army (Ret.)*. New York: G. P. Putnam's Sons, 1949.

Ch'i, Hsi-sheng. *The Much Troubled Alliance: US-China Military Cooperation During the Pacific War, 1941–1945*. Hackensack, NJ: World Scientific, 2016.

Churchill, Winston C. *The Second World War*. Vol. 2. *Their Finest Hour*. Boston: Houghton Mifflin, 1949.

———. *The Second World War*. Vol. 3. *The Grand Alliance*. Boston: Houghton Mifflin, 1950.

———. *The Second World War*. Vol. 4. *The Hinge of Fate*. Boston: Houghton Mifflin, 1950.

Clodfelter, Michael. *Warfare and Armed Conflicts: A Statistical Reference to Casualty and Other Figures, 1500–2000*. 3rd edition. Jefferson, NC: McFarland Publishers, 2008.

Cohen, Paul A. *History in Three Keys: The Boxers as Event, Experience and Myth*. New York: Columbia University Press, 1997.

Cole, Wayne S. *Roosevelt & The Isolationists 1932–45*. Lincoln: University of Nebraska Press, 1983.

Conn, Stetson, Rose E. Engelman, and Byron Fairchild. *United States Army in World War II, Guarding the United States and Its Outposts*. Washington, DC: Center of Military History, 1989.

Conroy, Hilary, and Harry Wray, eds. *Pearl Harbor Reexamined: Prologue to the Pacific War*. Honolulu: University of Hawaii Press, 1990.

Cook, Alistair. *The American Home Front 1941–1942*. New York: Atlantic Monthly Press, 2006.

Cook, Haruko Taya, and Theodore F. Cook. *Japan at War: An Oral History*. New York: New Press, 1992.

Coox, Alvin D. *Nomonhan: Japan Against Russia, 1939*. Stanford, CA: Stanford University Press, 1990. 2 vols.

Corum, James S. *The Luftwaffe: Creating the Operational Air War, 1918–1940*. Lawrence: University Press of Kansas, 1997.

Costello, John Costello. *Days of Infamy*. New York: Pocket Books, 1994.

Craven, W. F., and J. L. Cate, eds. *The Army Air Forces in World War II*. Vol. 1, *Plans and Early Operations January 1939 to August 1942*. Washington, DC: Office of Air Force History, 1983. Reprint.

Cressman, Robert J. *The Magnificent Fight: The Battle for Wake Island*. Annapolis, MD: Naval Institute Press, 1995.

Cressman, Robert J., and J. Michael Wenger. *Steady Nerves and Stout Hearts: The Enterprise (CV-6) Air Group and Pearl Harbor, 7 December 1941*. Missoula, MT: Pictorial Histories Publishing, 1990.

Dallek, Robert. *Franklin D. Roosevelt and American Foreign Policy 1932–1945*. Oxford: Oxford University Press, 1981.

Daniels, Roger. *Concentration Camps, U.S.A: Japanese Americans in World War II*. New York: Holt, Rinehart and Winston, 1971.

Davidson, Joel R. *The Unsinkable Fleet: The Politics of U.S. Navy Expansion in World War II.* Annapolis, MD: Naval Institute Press, 1996.

Davis, Kenneth S. *FDR: Into the Storm 1937–1940.* New York: Random House, 1993.

———. *FDR: The War President 1940–1943.* New York: Random House, 2000.

Daws, Gavin. *Prisoners of the Japanese: POWs of World War II in the Pacific.* New York: William Morrow, 1994.

Dear, I. C. B., and M. R. D. Foot. *The Oxford Companion to World War II.* Oxford: Oxford University Press, 1995.

Deguichi, Noriki, ed. *Maru Bessatsu—Sensho no Hibi.* Tokyo: Ushio Shobo, 1988.

Dod, Karl C. *The United States Army in World War II, The Technical Services, The Corps of Engineers in the War Against Japan.* Washington. DC: Office of the Chief of Military History, 1966.

Doenecke, Justus D. *Storm on the Horizon: The Challenge to American Intervention, 1939–1941.* Lanham, MD: Rowman & Littlefield Publishers, 2000.

Doherty, Thomas. *Hollywood and Hitler 1933–1939.* New York: Columbia University Press, 2013.

———. *Projections of War: Hollywood, American Culture, and World War II.* New York: Columbia University Press, 1993.

Dore, Ronald, and Radha Sinha. *Japan and World Depression: Then and Now.* New York: St. Martin's Press, 1987.

Dorn, Frank. *The History of the Sino-Japanese War: From Marco Polo Bridge to Pearl Harbor.* New York: Macmillan, 1974.

———. *Walkout with Stilwell in Burma.* New York: Crowell, 1971.

Drea, Edward J. *Nomonhan: Japanese-Soviet Tactical Combat, 1939.* Leavenworth Papers No. 2, Combat Studies Institute, Fort Leavenworth, Kansas, January 1981.

———. *Japan's Imperial Army: Its Rise and Fall, 1853–1954.* Manhattan: University Press of Kansas, 2009.

Dunlop, Graham. *Military Economics, Culture and Logistics in the Burma Campaign, 1942–1945.* London: Pickering & Chatto, 2009.

Eastman, Lloyd. *The Abortive Revolution: China Under Nationalist Rule, 1927–1937.* Cambridge, MA: Harvard University Press, 1974.

Edmonds, Walter D. *They Fought With What They Had.* Boston: Center for Air Force History, Little, Brown, 1951.

Elleman, Bruce A., and S. C. M. Paine. *Naval Blockades and Seapower, Strategies and Counter-Strategies.* London and New York: Routledge, 2006.

Evans, David C., and Mark Peattie. *Kaigun: Strategy, Tactics and Technology in the Imperial Japanese Navy, 1887–1941.* Annapolis, MD: Naval Institute Press, 1997.

Falk, Stanley. *Bataan: The March of Death.* New York: W. W. Norton, 1962.

Fanning, Richard W. *Peace and Disarmament: Naval Rivalry & Arms Control 1922–1933.* Lexington: University Press of Kentucky, 1995.

Farrell, Brian P. *The Defense and Fall of Singapore 1940–1942.* Stroud, UK: Tempus, 2006.

Farrell, Brian P., and Sandy Hunter, eds. *Sixty Years On: The Fall of Singapore Revisited.* Singapore: Times Academic Press, 2003.

Ferrell, Robert H., ed. *The Eisenhower Diaries.* New York: W. W. Norton, 1981.

Ford, Dan. *The Sorry Saga of the Brewster Buffalo: A 'Flying Coffin' to the Marines, but a 'Sky Pearl' to the Finns.* Durham: Warbird Books, 2010.

Ford, Daniel. *Flying Tigers: Claire Chennault and the American Volunteer Group.* Washington, DC: Smithsonian Institution Press, 1991.

Ford, Douglas. *The Elusive Enemy: U.S. Naval Intelligence and the Imperial Japanese Fleet.* Annapolis, MD: Naval Institute Press, 2011.

Francillon, Rene J. *Japanese Aircraft of the Pacific War.* Annapolis, MD: Naval Institute Press, 1979.

Frank, Richard B. *Downfall: The End of the Imperial Japanese Empire.* New York: Random House, 1999.

———. *Guadalcanal: The Definitive Account of the Landmark Battle.* New York: Random House, 1990.

———. *MacArthur.* New York: Palgrave McMillan, 2007.

Frederick, H., Iris Heidebrink, and Shigeru Sato. *The Encyclopedia of Indonesia in the Pacific War.* Leiden and Boston: Brill, 2010.

Frei, Henry. *Guns of February: Ordinary Japanese Soldiers' Views of the Malaya Campaign & the Fall of Singapore.* Singapore: Singapore University Press, 2004.

Friedman, Norman. *British Battleships 1906–1946.* Annapolis, MD: Naval Institute Press, 2015.

———. *Naval Anti-Aircraft Guns & Gunnery.* Annapolis, MD: Naval Institute Press, 2013.

———. *U.S. Aircraft Carriers: An Illustrated Design History.* Annapolis, MD: Naval Institute Press, 1983.

———. *U.S. Battleships: An Illustrated Design History.* Annapolis, MD: Naval Institute Press, 1985.

———. *U.S. Destroyers: An Illustrated Design History.* Annapolis, MD: Naval Institute Press, 1982.

Frieser, Karl-Heinz. *The Blitzkrieg Legend: The 1940 Campaign in the West.* Annapolis, MD: Naval Institute Press, 2005.

Fuller, Richard. *Shōkan: Hirohito's Samurai, Leaders of Japanese Armed Forces, 1926–1945.* London: Arms and Armour Press, 1992.

Gamble, Bruce. *Book One of the Rabaul Trilogy: Invasion Rabaul: The Epic Story of Lark Force, the Forgotten Garrison, January–July 1942.* Minneapolis, MN: Zenith Press, 2014.

Gannon, Michael. *Pearl Harbor Betrayed: The True Story of a Man and a Nation Under Attack.* New York: Henry Holt, 2001.

Gannon, Robert. *Hellions of the Deep: The Development of American Torpedoes in World War II.* University Park: Pennsylvania State University Press, 1996.

Garkze, William H., Jr., Robert O. Dulin, Jr., and Thomas G. Webb. *Battleships: Allied Battleships of World War II.* Annapolis, MD: Naval Institute Press, 1980.

Gilbert, Martin. *Winston S. Churchill.* Vol. 4, *Their Finest Hour, 1939–1941.* Boston: Houghton Mifflin Company, 1983.

———. *Winston S. Churchill.* Vol. 7. *The Road to Victory, 1941–1945.* Boston: Houghton Mifflin, 1986.

Gill, G. Hermon. *Australia in the War of 1939–1945, Series 2, Navy.* Vol. 1. *Royal Australian Navy, 1939–1942.* Canberra: Australian War Memorial, 1957.

Gillison, Douglas. *Australia in the War of 1939–1945, Series 3, The Air Force.* Vol. 1. *The Royal Australian Air Force 1939–1942.* Canberra: Australian War Memorial, 1962.

Glantz, David M., and Jonathan House. *When Titans Clashed: How the Red Army Stopped Hitler.* Manhattan: University Press of Kansas, 1995.

Glantz, David. *Barbarossa Derailed: The Battle of Smolensk 10 July–10 September 1941*. Vol. 1. *The German Advance, the Encirclement Battle, and the First and Second Soviet Counter-offensives, 10 July–24 August 1941*. Solihull, UK: Helion & Company Ltd., 2010.

———. *Barbarossa Derailed: The Battle of Smolensk 10 July–10 September 1941*. Vol. 2. *The German Offensives on the Flanks and the Third Soviet Counteroffensive, 25 August–10 September 1941*. Solihull, UK: Helion & Company Ltd., 2011.

Glines, Carroll V. *The Doolittle Raid: America's Daring First Strike Against Japan*. New York: Orion Books, 1988.

Goldman, Stuart. *Nomonhan 1939: The Red Army's Victory that Shaped World War II*. Annapolis, MD: Naval Institute Press, 2012.

Goodall, Felicity. *Exodus Burma: The British Escape Through the Jungle of Death 1942*. Stroud: Spellmount, 2011.

Gordon, John. *Fighting for MacArthur: The Navy and Marine Corps' Desperate Defense of the Philippines*. Annapolis, MD: Naval Institute Press, 2011.

Grant, Ian Lyall, and Kazuo Tamayama. *Burma 1942: The Japanese Invasion*. Chichester, UK: The Zampi Press, 1999.

Grant, Lachlan. *Australian Soldiers in Asia-Pacific in World War II*. Sydney: NewSouth Publishing, 2014.

Grew, Joseph C. *Turbulent Era: A Diplomatic Record of Forty Years 1904–1945*. Vol. 2. Boston: Houghton Mifflin, 1952.

Grodzins, Morton. *Americans Betrayed: The Politics of the Japanese Evacuation*. Chicago: University of Chicago Press, 1949.

Grose, Peter. *An Awkward Truth: The Bombing of Darwin 1942*. Crows Nest: Allen & Unwin, 2011.

Gunther, John. *Roosevelt in Retrospect, A Profile in History*. New York: Harper and Brothers, 1950.

Gustavsson, Hakan. *Sino-Japanese Air War 1937–1945: The Longest Struggle*. Croydon: Fonthill, 2016.

Hagihara, Nobutoshi. *Tōgō Shigenori: Denki to Kaisetsu (Tōgō Shigenori: A Biography and Commentary)*. Tokyo: Hara Shobō, 1985.

Han, Suyin. *Destination Chungking*. Hertfordshire: Panther Books Limited, 1973. Reprint of 1942 edition.

Hanyok, Robert J., and David P. Mowry. *United States Cryptologic History Series 4: World War II*. Vol. 10. *West Wind Clear: Cryptology and the Winds Messages Controversy—A Documentary History*. Center for Cryptologic History, National Security Agency, 2008.

Harmsen, Peter. *Nanjing: Battle for a Doomed City*. Philadelphia: Casemate Publishers, 2015.

———. *Shanghai 1937: Stalingrad on the Yangtze*. Philadelphia and Oxford: Casemate Publishers, 2013.

Harries, Meirion, and Susie Harries. *Soldiers of the Sun: The Rise and Fall of the Imperial Japanese Army*. New York: Random House, 1991.

Haslam, Jonathan. *The Soviet Union and the Threat from the East, 1933–41*. Pittsburgh: University of Pittsburgh Press, 1992.

Hastings, Max. *Inferno: The World at War, 1939–1945*. New York: Alfred A. Knopf, 2011.

———. *Retribution: The Battle for Japan 1944–45*. New York: Alfred A. Knopf, 2008.

———. *Winston's War: Churchill 1940–1945*. New York: Alfred A. Knopf, 2010.

Hayes, Grace Person. *The History of the Joint Chiefs of Staff in World War II: The War Against Japan*. Annapolis, MD: Naval Institute Press, 1982.

Heinrichs, Waldo. *The Threshold of War: Franklin D. Roosevelt & American Entry into World War II*. Oxford: Oxford University Press, 1988.

Hodgson, Godfrey. *The Colonel: The Life and Wars of Henry Stimson 1867–1950*. New York: Alfred A. Knopf, 1990.

Holwitt, Joel. *Execute Against Japan: The U.S. Decision to Conduct Unrestricted Submarine Warfare*. College Station: Texas A&M University Press, 2009.

Honda, Katsuichi. *The Nanjing Massacre: A Japanese Journalist Confronts Japan's National Shame*. Armonk, NY: M. E. Sharpe, 1999.

Horikoshi, Jiro. *Eagles of Mitsubishi: The Story of the Zero Fighter*. Seattle: University of Washington Press, 1981.

Horner, David. *Blamey: The Commander in Chief*. Canberra: Allen & Unwin, 1998.

———. *Defense Supremo: Sir Frederick Shedden and the Making of Australian Defense Policy*. St. Leonards: Allen & Unwin, 2000.

Hornfischer, James. *Neptune's Inferno: The U.S. Navy at Guadalcanal*. New York: Bantam Books, 2011.

———. *Ship of Ghosts: The Story of the USS Houston. FDR's Legendary Lost Cruiser and the Epic Saga of Her Survivors*. New York: Bantam Books, 2006.

Hotta, Eri. *Japan 1941: Countdown to Infamy*. New York: Alfred A. Knopf, 2013.

———. *Pan-Asianism and Japan's War, 1931–35*. New York: Palgrave Macmillan, 2007.

Hough, Frank O., Verle E. Ludwig, and Henry I. Shaw. *History of Marine Corps Operations in World War II*. Vol. 1. *Pearl Harbor to Guadalcanal*. Historical Branch, Headquarters US Marine Corps. Battery Press, 1993. Reprint.

Hsiung, James C., and Steven I. Levine, eds. *China's Bitter Victory: The War with Japan 1937–1945*. Armonk, NY: M. E. Sharpe, 1992.

Hu, Hua-ling, and Zhang Lian-hong, eds. *The Undaunted Women of Nanking: The Wartime Diaries of Minnie Vautrin and Tsen Shui-Fang*. Carbondale: Southern Illinois University Press, 2010.

Hunt, Frazier. *The Untold Story of Douglas MacArthur*. New York: Devin-Adair, 1954.

Iguchi, Takeo. *Demystifying Pearl Harbor: A New Perspective from Japan*. Tokyo: International House of Japan, 2010.

Ike, Nobutaka. *Japan's Decision for War: Records of the 1941 Policy Conferences*. Stanford, CA: Stanford University Press, 1967.

Iriye, Akira. *Power and Culture: The Japanese American War 1941–1945*. Cambridge, MA: Harvard University Press, 1982.

Irons, Peter. *Justice at War*. Berkeley: University of California Press, 1983.

James, D. Clayton. *The Years of MacArthur*. Vol. 1. *1880–1941*. Boston: Houghton Mifflin, 1970.

———. *The Years of MacArthur*. Vol. 2. *1941–1945*. Boston: Houghton Mifflin, 1975.

Jansen, Marius B. *The Making of Modern Japan*. Cambridge, MA: The Belknap Press of Harvard University Press, 2000.

Johnson, Robert David, ed. *On Cultural Ground: Essays in International History*. Chicago: Imprint Publications, 1994.

Jordan, Donald. *China's Trial by Fire: The Shanghai War of 1932*. Ann Arbor: University of Michigan Press, 2001.

Jordan, John, ed. *Warship 2015*. Annapolis, MD: Naval Institute Press, 2015.

Jordan, Jonathan W. *American Warlords: How Roosevelt's High Command Led America to Victory in World War II.* New York: NAL Caliber, 2015.

Jose, Ricardo Trota. *The Philippine Army 1935–1942.* Manila: Ateneo do Manila University Press, 1992.

Jowett, Philip. *Rays of the Rising Sun.* Vol. 1. *Japan's Asian Allies 1931–45, China and Manchukuo.* Warwick, UK: Helion and Company Ltd., 2005.

Kahn, Yasmin. *India at War: The Subcontinent and the Second World War.* Oxford: Oxford University Press, 2015.

Keen, R. *Wireless Direction Finding.* London: Wireless World and Iliffe & Sons Ltd., 1938.

Keene, Donald, ed. *So Lovely a Country Will Never Perish.* New York: Columbia University Press, 2010.

Kehn, Donald M., Jr. *A Blue Sea of Blood: Deciphering the Mysterious Fate of the USS Edsall.* Minneapolis, MN: Zenith Press, 2009.

Kelly, Stephen J. *Big Machines: Study of the Cryptographic Security of the German ENIGMA, Japanese PURPLE and U.S. SIGABA/ECM Cipher Machines.* Walnut Park, CA: Aegean Park Press, 2001.

Kendrick, Alexander. *Prime Time: The Life of Edward R. Murrow.* Boston: Little, Brown, 1969.

Kennedy, David M. *Freedom from Fear: The American People in Depression and War, 1929–1945.* Oxford: Oxford University Press, 1999.

Kimball, Warren. *Forged in War: Roosevelt, Churchill, and the Second World War.* New York: William Morrow, 1997.

———. *The Juggler: Franklin Roosevelt as a Wartime Statesman.* Princeton, NJ: Princeton University Press, 1991.

Kimball, Warren F., ed. *Churchill & Roosevelt: The Complete Correspondence.* Vol. 1. *Alliance Emerging, October 1933–November 1942.* Princeton, NJ: Princeton University Press, 1984.

Kimmel, Husband E. *Admiral Kimmel's Story.* Chicago: Henry Regnery, 1955.

Kingsley, F. A., ed. *The Applications of Radar and Other Electronic Systems in the Royal Navy in World War 2.* Basingstoke, UK: Macmillan, 1995.

Kirby, Major General S. Woodburn. *History of the Second World War, United Kingdom Military Series, The War Against Japan.* Vol. 1. *The Loss of Singapore.* Uckfield, UK: Naval & Military Press, Ltd., 2004. Reprint of 1957 edition.

———. *History of the Second World War, United Kingdom Military Series, The War Against Japan.* Vol. 2. *India's Most Dangerous Hour.* Uckfield, UK: Naval & Military Press, Ltd., 2004. Reprint of 1958 edition.

Kirby, William. *Germany and Republican China.* Stanford, CA: Stanford University Press, 1984.

Klein, Murray. *A Call to Arms: Mobilizing America for World War II.* New York: Bloomsbury Press, 2013.

Knox, Donald. *Death March: The Survivors of Bataan.* New York: Harcourt Brace Jovanovich, 1981.

Komatsu, Keiichiro. *The Origins of the Pacific War and the Importance of 'Magic'.* London: Routledge, 1999.

Kotani, Ken. *Japanese Intelligence in World War II.* Oxford: Osprey Publishing Ltd, 2006.

Kotkin, Stephen. *Stalin: Waiting for Hitler, 1929–1941.* New York: Penguin Press, 2017.

LaCroix, Eric, and Linton Wells II. *Japanese Cruisers of the Pacific War.* Annapolis, MD: Naval Institute Press, 1997.

Lambert, John W., and Norman Polmar. *Defenseless: Command Failure at Pearl Harbor.* St. Paul, MN: Motor Books International, 2003.

Langer, William L., and S. Everett Gleason. *The Challenge to Isolationism, 1937–1940.* New York: Harper & Brothers, 1952.

———. *The Undeclared War, 1940–1941.* New York: Harper & Brothers, 1953.

Langtree, Christopher. *The Kelly's: British J, K & N Class Destroyers in World War II.* Annapolis, MD: Naval Institute Press, 2002.

Larrabee, Eric. *Commander in Chief: Franklin Delano Roosevelt, His Lieutenants & Their War.* New York: Harper & Row, 1987.

Lary, Diana. *China's Republic.* Cambridge University Press, 2007.

———. *The Chinese People at War: Human Suffering and Social Transformation, 1937–1945.* Cambridge: Cambridge University Press, 2010.

———, and Stephen MacKinnon, eds. *Scars of War: The Impact of Warfare on Modern China.* Vancouver: University of British Columbia Press, 2001.

Layton, Rear Admiral Edwin T., Roger Pineau, and John Costello. *"And I Was There."* New York: William Morrow, 1985.

Leutze, James. *A Different Kind of Victory: A Biography of Admiral Thomas C. Hart.* Annapolis, MD: Naval Institute Press, 1981.

Lindqvist, Sven. *A History of Bombing.* New York: New Press, 2001.

Linn, Brian. *Guardians of Empire: The U.S. Army in the Pacific, 1902–1941.* Chapel Hill: University of North Carolina Press, 1999.

———. *The Philippine War, 1899–1902.* Lawrence: University Press of Kansas. Reprint edition, 2000.

Lourie, Richard. *Sakharov: A Biography.* Hanover, MA: Brandeis University Press, 2002.

Lowman, David D. *Magic: The Untold Story of U.S. Intelligence and the Evacuation of Japanese Residents from the West Coast During World War II.* Athena Press, 2000.

Lowry, Thomas P., and John W. G. Wellham. *The Attack on Taranto: Blueprint for Pearl Harbor.* Mechanicsburg, PA: Stackpole Books, 2000.

Lu, David. *The Agony of Choice: Matsuoka Yosuke and the Rise and Fall of the Japanese Empire, 1880–1945.* Lanhan, MD: Lexington Books, 2002.

Lu, Liu. "A Whole Nation Walking: The 'Great Retreat' in the War of Resistance, 1937–45." PhD diss., University of California, San Diego, 2002. Proquest Information and Learning.

Lundstrom, John B. *Black Shoe Carrier Admiral.* Annapolis, MD: Naval Institute Press, 2006.

———. *The First South Pacific Campaign: Pacific Fleet Strategy December 1941 to June 1942.* Annapolis, MD: Naval Institute Press, 1976.

———. *The First Team: Pacific Naval Air Combat from Pearl Harbor to Midway.* Annapolis, MD: Naval Institute Press, 1984.

Lyman, Robert. *Slim. Master of War.* London: Constable, 2004.

MacKinnon, Stephen R. *Wuhan, 1938: War, Refugees, and the Making of Modern China.* Berkeley: University of California Press, 2008.

———, and Oris Friesen. *China Reporting: An Oral History of American Journalism in the 1930s and 1940s.* Berkeley: University of California Press, 1987.

Malkin, Michelle. *In Defense of Internment; The Case for "Racial Profiling" in World War II and the War on Terror.* Washington, DC: Regnery Publishers, 2004.

Mallonee, Col. Richard C. II, ed. *Battle for Bataan, An Eyewitness Account.* Novato, CA: Presidio Press, 1997.

———. *The Naked Flag Pole*. San Rafael, CA: Presidio Press, 1980.

Man, Kwong Chi, and Tsoi Yiu Lun. *Eastern Fortress: A Military History of Hong Kong, 1840–1970*. Hong Kong: Hong Kong University Press, 2014.

Manchester, William. *American Caesar: Douglas MacArthur, 1888–1964*. Boston: Little, Brown, 1978.

Marci, Franco David. *Clash of Empires in South China: The Allied Nation's Proxy War with Japan, 1935–1941*. Lawrence: University Press of Kansas, 2012.

Marston, Daniel P. *Phoenix from the Ashes: The Indian Army in the Burma Campaign*. Westport, CT: Praeger, 2003.

Martin, Andrew. *Flight by Elephant: The Untold Story of World War II's Most Daring Jungle Rescue*. London: Fourth Estate, 2013.

Martin, Stephen. *Fighting Admirals: British Admirals of the Second World War*. Annapolis, MD: Naval Institute Press, 1991.

Masterman, J. C. *The Double-Cross System in the War of 1939 to 1945*. New Haven, CT: Yale University Press, 1972.

Mauch, Peter. *Sailor Diplomat: Nomura Kichisaburō and the Japanese American War*. Cambridge, MA: Harvard University Press, 2011.

Maxwell, John Hamilton. *Edgar Snow: A Biography*. Bloomington: Indiana University Press, 1988.

Mayers, David. *FDR's Ambassadors and the Diplomacy of Crisis*. Cambridge: Cambridge University Press, 2013.

McCarthy, Dudley McCarthy. *Australia in the War of 1939–1945, Series 1, Army*. Vol. 5. *Southwest Pacific Area—First Year: Kokoda to Wau*. Canberra: Australian War Memorial, 1959.

Meaher, Augustine IV. *The Road to Singapore: The Myth of British Betrayal*. Melbourne: Australian Scholarly Publishing, 2010.

Messimer, Dwight R. *Pawns of War: The Loss of the USS Langley and the USS Pecos*. Annapolis, MD: Naval Institute Press, 1983.

Miller, Col. E. B. *Bataan Uncensored*. Camp Riley: Minnesota Military Museum, Military Historical Society of Minnesota, 1991. Reprint of 1949 edition.

Miller, Edward S. *Bankrupting the Enemy: The U.S. Financial Siege of Japan Before Pearl Harbor*. Annapolis, MD: Naval Institute Press, 2007.

Miller, Russell. *Uncle Bill: The Authorized Biography of Field Marshall Viscount Slim*. London: Weidenfeld & Nicholson, 2013.

Miller, Stuart C. *Benevolent Assimilation: The American Conquest of the Philippines, 1899–1903*. New Haven, CT: Yale University Press. Reprint, 1984.

Millman, Nicholas. *Osprey Aircraft of the Aces, 103, Ki-27 'Nate' Aces*. Oxford: Osprey Publishing, 2013.

Mitter, Rana. *Forgotten Ally: China's World War II 1937–1945*. Boston: Houghton Mifflin Harcourt, 2013.

Montefiore, Sebag. *Stalin: The Court of the Red Tsar*. New York: Knopf, 2004.

Morison, Elting E. *Turmoil and Tradition: A Study of the Life and Times of Henry L. Stimson*. Boston: Houghton Mifflin, 1960.

Morison, Samuel Elliot. *History of United States Naval Operations in World War II*. Vol. 1. *The Battle of the Atlantic 1939–1943*. Boston: Little, Brown, 1966.

———. *History of United States Naval Operations in World War II*. Vol. 3. *The Rising Sun in the Pacific 1931–April 1942*. Boston: Little, Brown, 1963.

Morley, James W., ed. *Japan's Road to the Pacific War: The China Quagmire: Japanese Expansion on the Asian Continent, 1933–1941*. New York: Columbia University Press, 1983.

———. *Japan's Road to the Pacific War. Deterrent Diplomacy: Japan, Germany, and the USSR 1935–1940*. New York: Columbia University Press, 1976.

———. *Japan's Road to the Pacific War. The Fateful Choice: Japan's Advance into Southeast Asia, 1939–1941*. New York: Columbia University Press, 1980.

———. *Japan's Road to the Pacific War. The Final Confrontation, Japan's Negotiations with the United States, 1941*. New York: Columbia University Press, 1994.

———. *Japan's Road to the Pacific War. Japan Erupts: The London Naval Conference and the Manchurian Incident, 1928–32*. New York: Columbia University Press, 1984.

Morton, Louis. *United States Army in World War II, The War in the Pacific, Strategy and Command: The First Two Years*. Washington, DC: Office of the Chief of Military History, 1962.

———. *United States Army in World War II, The War in the Pacific, the Fall of the Philippines*. Washington, DC: Office of the Chief of Military History, 1953.

Murray, Williamson. *Luftwaffe*. Baltimore: Nautical and Aviation Publishing Company of America, 1985.

Ness, Leland. *Rikugun: Guide to Japanese Ground Forces 1937–1945*. Vol. 1. *Tactical Organization of Imperial Army & Navy Ground Forces*. Warwick, UK: Helion & Co., 2014.

Nicholson, Arthur. *Hostages to Fortune: Winston Churchill and the Loss of the Prince of Wales and Repulse*. Stroud, UK: Sutton Publishing Limited, 2005.

Nofi, Albert A. *To Train the Fleet for War: The U.S. Navy Fleet Problems, 1923–1940*. Newport: Naval War College Press, 2010.

O'Brien, Phillips Payson. *How the War Was Won: Air-Sea Power and Allied Victory in World War II*. Cambridge: Cambridge University Press, 2015.

Ogburn, Charlton. *The Marauders*. New York: Harper & Brothers, 1956.

O'Hara, Vincent P. *The U.S. Navy Against the Axis*. Annapolis, MD: Naval Institute Press, 2007.

Oka, Yoshitake. *Konoe Fumimaro: A Political Biography*. Translated by Shumpei and Patricia Murray. Tokyo: University of Tokyo Press, 1983.

Olson, Lynne. *Those Angry Days: Roosevelt, Lindbergh, and America's Fight over World War II, 1939–1941*. New York: Random House, 2013.

O'Neil, William D. *Transformation and the Officer Corps: Analysis in the Historical Context of the U.S. and Japan Between the World Wars*. Center for Naval Analysis, CME D0012589.A2. September 2005.

———. *Undefending Pearl Harbor*. Amazon Kindle, 2016.

Orbach, Danny. *Curse Upon This Country: The Rebellious Army of Imperial Japan*. Ithaca and London: Cornell University Press, 2017.

Overy, Richard. *Why the Allies Won*. New York: W. W. Norton, 1995.

Paine, S. C. M. *The Wars for Asia 1911–1949*. New York: Cambridge University Press, 2012.

Pallud, Jean Paul. *Blitzkrieg in the West Then and Now*. London: After the Battle, 1991.

Pantsov, Alexander V., and Stephen I. Levine. *Mao: The Real Story*. New York: Simon & Schuster, 2012.

Parkin, Ray. *Out of the Smoke*. New York: William Morrow, 1960.

Pash, Sydney. *The Currents of War: A New History of American-Japanese Relations, 1899–1941*. Lexington: University of Kentucky Press, 2014.

Peattie, Mark. *Ishiwara Kanji and Japan's Confrontation with the West.* Princeton, NJ: Princeton University Press, 1975.

———. *Sunburst: The Rise of Japanese Naval Air Power, 1909–1941.* Annapolis, MD: Naval Institute Press, 2001.

Peattie, Mark, Edward Drea, and Hans van de Ven, eds. *The Battle for China: Essays on the Military History of the Sino-Japanese War 1937–47.* Stanford, CA: Stanford University Press, 2010.

Perret, Geoffrey. *Old Soldiers Never Die: The Life of Douglas MacArthur.* New York: Random House, 1996.

Persico, Joseph E. *Roosevelt's Secret War: FDR and World War II Espionage.* New York: Random House, 2001.

Petillo, Carol. *Douglas MacArthur, the Philippine Years.* Bloomington: Indiana University Press, 1981.

Pitt, Barrie. *The Crucible of War: Western Desert 1941.* New York: Paragon House, 1989.

Pomfret, John. *The Beautiful Country and the Middle Kingdom: America and China, 1776 to the Present.* New York: Henry Holt, 2016.

Prados, John. *Combined Fleet Decoded: The Secret History of American Intelligence and the Japanese Navy in World War II.* New York: Random House, 1995.

Prange, Gordon W. *At Dawn We Slept: The Untold Story of Pearl Harbor.* New York: McGraw-Hill, 1981.

———, with Donald M. Goldstein and Katherine Dillon. *Pearl Harbor: The Verdict of History.* New York: McGraw-Hill, 1986.

Pratten, Garth. *Australian Battalion Commanders in the Second World War.* Cambridge: Cambridge University Press, 2009.

Preston-Hough, Peter. *Commanding Far Eastern Skies: A Critical Analysis of the Royal Air Force Air Superiority Campaign in India, Burma and Malaya 1941–1945.* Warwick, UK: Helion & Co. Limited, 2015.

Price, Ruth. *The Lives of Agnes Smedley.* New York: Oxford University Press, 2005.

Pritchard, R. John, and Sonia Magbanua Zaide, comps. *International Military Tribunal for the Far East: The Tokyo War Crimes Trials.* 22 vols. New York, 1981–1987.

Raghavan, Srinath. *India's War: World War II and the Making of Modern South Asia.* New York: Basic Books, 2016.

Raymer, Commander Edward C. *Descent into Darkness: Pearl Harbor, 1941, A Navy Diver's Memoir.* Navato, CA: Presidio Press, 1996.

Remmelink, William, ed. and trans. *War History Series.* Vol. 3. *The Invasion of the Dutch East Indies.* Leiden: Leiden University Press, 2015. [This volume and the following are complete translations under the auspices of the Netherlands Institute of Military History of the relevant volumes of the massive *Senshi Sosho* (War History Series) compiled by War History Office of the National Defense College of Japan.]

———. *War History Series.* Vol. 26. *Operations of the Navy in the Dutch East Indies and the Bay of Bengal.* Leiden: Leiden University Press, 2018.

Reynolds, E. Bruce. *Thailand and Japan's Southern Advance 1940–1945.* London: Macmillan, 1994.

Roberts, Andrew. *Churchill: Walking with Destiny.* New York: Viking, 2018.

Robinson, Greg. *By Order of the President: FDR and the Internment of Japanese Americans.* Cambridge, MA: Harvard University Press, 2001.

Rohwer, Jurgen. *Axis Submarine Successes 1939–1945*. Annapolis, MD: Naval Institute Press, 1983.

Romanus, Charles F., and Riley Sunderland. *The United States Army in World War II, China-Burma-India Theater, Stilwell's Mission to China*. Washington, DC: Office of the Chief of Military History, 1953.

Rose, Lisle. *Power at Sea*. Vol. 2. *The Breaking Storm 1919–1945*. Columbia: University of Missouri Press, 2007.

Rosefielde, Steven. *Red Holocaust*. London: Routledge, 2009.

Rosenman, Samuel I. *Working with Roosevelt*. New York: Harper and Brothers, 1952.

Roskill, Captain S. W. *Churchill and the Admirals*. New York: William Morrow, 1978.

———. *The War at Sea*. Vol. 1. *The Defensive*. London: Her Majesty's Stationery Office, 1954.

Rottman, G., and A. Takizawa. *Japanese Paratroop Forces of World War II*. Oxford: Osprey Publishing, 2005.

Rowlett, Frank B. *The Story of Magic: Memoirs of An American Cryptologic Pioneer*. Laguna Hills, CA: Aegean Park Press, 1998.

Rummel, R. J. *China's Bloody Century: Genocide and Mass Murder Since 1900*. New Brunswick, NJ: Transaction Publishers. Reprint, 2008.

Schaller, Michael. *Douglas MacArthur: The Far Eastern General*. Oxford: Oxford University Press, 1989.

Schoppa, R. Keith. *In a Sea of Bitterness: Refugees During the Sino-Japanese War*. Cambridge, MA: Harvard University Press, 2011.

Scott, James M. *Target Tokyo: Jimmy Doolittle and the Raid that Avenged Pearl Harbor*. New York: W. W. Norton, 2015.

Seki, Eiji. *Mrs. Ferguson's Tea-Set, Japan and the Second World War: The Global Consequences following Germany's Sinking of the SS Automedon in 1940*. London: Global Oriental, 2007.

Sherwood, Robert E. *Roosevelt and Hopkins: An Intimate History*. New York: Harper & Brothers, 1948.

Shores, Christopher. *Aircraft in Profile*, Vol. 10. Windsor, and Berkshire, UK: Profile Publications, Ltd., 1971.

Shores, Christopher, and Brian Cull, with Yasuho Izawa. *Bloody Shambles*. Vol. 1. *The Drift to War to the Fall of Singapore*. London: Grub Street, 1992.

———. *Bloody Shambles*. Vol. 2. *The Defense of Sumatra to the Fall of Burma*. London: Grub Street, 1993.

Short, Philip. *Mao: A Life*. New York: Henry Holt, 1999.

Simpson, B Mitchell III. *Admiral Harold R. Stark: Architect of Victory 1939–1945*. Columbia: University of South Carolina Press, 1989.

Slim, William. *Defeat Into Victory*. London: Pan Books, 1999. Reprint of 1956 first edition.

Smith, Bradley F. *The Ultra-Magic Deals and the Most Secret Special Relationship 1940–1946*. Novato, CA: Presidio, 1994.

Smith, Jean Edward. *FDR*. New York: Random House, 2007.

Smith, Michael. *The Emperor's Codes*. London: Transworld Publishers, 2000.

Snape, Michael. *God and Uncle Sam: Religion and America's Armed Forces in World War II*. Woodbridge: Boydell Press, 2015.

Snow, Edgar. *Red Star Over China*. London: Victor Gollancz, Ltd., 1937; New York: Random House, 1938.

Snow, Philip. *The Fall of Hong Kong: Britain, China, and the Japanese Occupation*. New Haven, CT: Yale University Press, 2003.

Snyder, Timothy. *Bloodlands: Europe Between Hitler and Stalin*. New York: Basic Books, 2010.

Spence, Jonathan D. *The Search for Modern China*. New York: W. W. Norton, 1990.

———. *The Search for Modern China*. 3rd edition. New York: W. W. Norton, 2012.

Sperling, Hilary. *Pearl Buck in China: Journey to The Good Earth*. New York: Simon & Schuster, 2010.

Stahel, David. *Operation Barbarossa and Germany's Defeat in the East*. Cambridge: Cambridge University Press, 2009.

———. *Operation Typhoon: Hitler's March on Moscow, October 1941*. Cambridge: Cambridge University Press, 2013.

Stauffer, Alvin P. *United States Army in World War II, The Technical Services, The Quartermaster Corps: Operations in the War Against Japan*. Washington, DC: Office of the Chief of Military History, 1956.

Steely, Skipper. *Pearl Harbor Countdown: Admiral James O. Richardson*. Gretna, LA: Pelican Publishing, 2008.

Stenman, Kari, and Andrew Thomas. *Osprey Aircraft of the Aces 91: Brewster F2A Buffalo Aces of World War II*. Oxford: Osprey Publishing, 2010.

Stephan, John J. *Hawaii Under the Rising Sun: Japan's Plans for Conquest after Pearl Harbor*. Honolulu: University of Hawaii Press, 1984.

Stillwell, Paul. *Battleship Arizona*. Annapolis, MD: Naval Institute Press, 1991.

Stimson, Henry L., and McGeorge Bundy. *On Active Service in Peace and War*. New York: Harper & Brothers, 1948.

Stoler, Mark. *Allies and Adversaries: The Joint Chiefs of Staff, the Grand Alliance, and U.S. Strategy in World War II*. Chapel Hill and London: University of North Carolina Press, 2000.

———. *Allies in War: Britain and America Against the Axis Powers*. New York: Hodder Education, 2005.

Sugihara, Seishiro. *Between Incompetence and Culpability: Assessing the Diplomacy of Japan's Foreign Ministry from Pearl Harbor to Potsdam*. Translated by Norman Hu. Lanham, MD: University Press of America, 1997.

Summers, Antony, and Robbyn Swan. *A Matter of Honor. Pearl Harbor: Betrayal, Blame and a Family's Quest for Justice*. New York: Harper, 2016.

Tagarao, Silvestre L. *All This Was Bataan*. Quezon City: New Day Publishers, 1991.

Tamayama, Kazuo, and John Nunneley. *Tales by Japanese Soldiers*. London: Cassell, 2000.

Taylor, Jay. *The Generalissimo: Chiang Kai-shek and the Struggle for Modern China*. Cambridge, MA: The Belknap Press of Harvard University Press, 2009.

Terraine, John. *A Time for Courage: The Royal Air Force in the European War, 1939–1945*. New York: Macmillan, 1985.

Throne, Christopher. *Allies of a Kind: The United States, Britain, and the War Against Japan*. Oxford: Oxford University Press, 1978.

Tien, Hung-mao. *Government and Politics in Kuomintang China, 1927–1937*. Stanford, CA: Stanford University Press, 1972.

Tohmatsu, Haruo, and H. P. Willmott. *A Gathering Darkness: The Coming of War to the Far East and the Pacific, 1921–1942*. Lanham, Boulder, New York, Toronto, and Oxford: SR Books, 2004.

Toland, John. *The Rising Sun.* New York: Random House, 1970.

Tooze, Adam. *The Wages of Destruction: The Making and Breaking of the Nazi Economy.* New York: Viking, 2006.

Tsutsui, Kiyotada. ed. *Fifteen Lectures on Showa Japan: Road to Pacific War in Recent Historiography.* Tokyo: Japan Publishing Industry for Culture, 2016.

Tuchman, Barbara. *Stillwell and the American Experience in China.* New York: Macmillan, 1971.

Underwood, Jeffery S. *The Wings of Democracy: The Influence of Air Power on the Roosevelt Administration, 1933–1941.* College Station: Texas A&M University Press, 1991.

United States Department of Defense. *The "Magic" Background of Pearl Harbor.* 8 vols. Washington, DC: Government Printing Office, 1977.

United States Department of State. *Foreign Relations of the United States, 1931–1942.* Washington, DC: Government Printing Office.

Urwin, Gregory J. W. *Facing Fearful Odds: The Siege of Wake Island.* Lincoln: University of Nebraska Press, 2002.

———. *Victory in Defeat: Wake Island Defenders in Captivity, 1941–1945.* Annapolis, MD: Naval Institute Press, 2010.

Utley, Freda. *China at War.* London: Faber and Faber, 1938.

Utley, Jonathan G. *Going to War with Japan, 1937–1941.* New York: McGraw-Hill, 1985.

van de Ven, Hans. *China at War: Triumph and Tragedy in the Emergence of the New China.* Cambridge, MA: Harvard University Press, 2018.

———. *War and Nationalism in China 1925–1945.* London: RoutledgeCurzon, 2003.

van de Ven, Hans, Diana Lary, and Stephan R. MacKinnon. *Negotiating China's Destiny in World War II.* Stanford, CA: Stanford University, 2015.

van Oosten, F. C. *The Battle of the Java Sea.* Annapolis, MD: Naval Institute Press, 1976.

Wainwright, General Jonathan M. *General Wainwright's Story: The Account of Four Years of Humiliating Defeat, Surrender and Captivity.* Garden City: Doubleday, 1946.

Wakabayashi, Bob Tadashi, ed. *The Nanking Atrocity 1937–38: Complicating the Picture.* New York: Berghahn Books, 2007.

Wallace, Kenneth Sydney. *Sunda Strait: The Last Day of Summer.* Sydney: Drawquick Publishing, 2007.

Warren, Alan. *Britain's Greatest Defeat: Singapore 1942.* London: Hambledon and London, 2002.

Watanabe, Tsuneo, and James E. Auer, eds. *Who Was Responsible?: From Marco Polo Bridge to Pearl Harbor.* Tokyo: The Yomiuri Shimbun, 2006.

Watson, Mark S. *U.S. Army in World War II, The War Department, Chief of Staff Prewar Plans and Preparations.* Washington, DC: Historical Division, Department of the Army, 1950.

Weinberg, Gerhard. *A World at Arms: A Global History of World War II,* 2nd ed. Cambridge: Cambridge University Press, 2005.

Weinstein, Allen, and Alexander Vassiliev. *The Haunted Wood: Soviet Espionage in America—The Stalin Era.* New York: Random House, 1999.

Wenger, J. Michael, Robert J. Cressman, and John F. Di Virgillo. *No One Avoided Danger: NAS Kaneohe Bay and the Japanese Attack of 7 December 1941 (Pearl Harbor Tactical Series).* Annapolis, MD: Naval Institute Press, 2015.

Westad, Odd Arne. *Restless Empire: China and the World Since 1750.* New York: Basic Books, 2012.

White, Theodore, and Annalee Jacoby. *Thunder Out of China*. New York: William Sloane Associates, 1961.

Whitley, M. J. *Destroyers of World War Two: An International Encyclopedia*. Annapolis, MD: Naval Institute Press, 1988.

Whitman, John W. *Bataan: Our Last Ditch*. New York: Hippocrene Books, 1990.

Wigmore, Lionel. *Australia in the War of 1939–1945, Series One, Army*. Vol. 4. *The Japanese Thrust*. Canberra: The Australian War Memorial, 1957.

Willmott, H. P. *The Barrier and the Javelin*. Annapolis, MD: Naval Institute Press, 1983.

———. *Empires in Balance: Japanese and Allied Pacific Strategies to April 1942*. Annapolis, MD: Naval Institute Press, 1982.

———. *The Second World War in the East*. London: Cassell, 1999.

Willmott, H. P., with Tohmatsu Haruo and W. Spencer Johnson. *Pearl Harbor*. London: Cassel, 2001.

Winslow, W. G. *The Ghost That Died at Sunda Strait*. Annapolis, MD: Naval Institute Press, 1984.

Womack, Tom. *The Allied Defense of the Malay Barrier 1941–1942*. Jefferson, NC: McFarland Publishers, 2016.

Woods, John E. *The Good Man of Nanking, The Diaries of John Rabe*. New York: Alfred A. Knopf, 1998.

Xu, Yong. *The Conqueror's Dream: Japan's Strategy of Invading China*. Guilin: Guangxi Normal University Press, 1993.

Yagami, Kazuo. *Konoe Fumimaro and the Failure of Peace in Japan 1937–1941*. Jefferson, NC: McFarland Publishers, 2006.

Yakovlev, Alexander N. *A Century of Violence in Soviet Russia*. New Haven, CT: Yale University Press, 2002.

Young, Arthur N. *China's National Building Effort: The Financial and Economic Record, 1927–37*. Stanford, CA: Hoover Institution Press, 1971.

———. *China's Wartime Finance and Inflation, 1937–1945*. Cambridge, MA: Harvard University Press, 1965.

Young, Donald. *The Battle of Bataan: A Complete History*. 2nd edition. Jefferson, NC: MacFarland, 2009.

Young, Louise. *Japan's Total Empire: Manchuria and the Culture of Wartime Imperialism*. Berkeley: University of California Press, 1999.

Young, Steven Bowder. *Trapped at Pearl Harbor: Escaping from Battleship Oklahoma*. Annapolis, MD: Naval Institute Press, 1991.

Zimm, Alan D. *Attack on Pearl Harbor: Strategy, Combat, Myths, Deceptions*. Philadelphia and Newbury: Casemate, 2011.

Articles

Aiken, David. "Torpedoing Pearl Harbor." *Military History* 18, no. 5 (December 2001): 46–53.

Akashi, Yoki. "General Yamashita Tomoyuki: Commander of the Twenty-fifth Army." In *Sixty Years On: The Fall of Singapore Revisited*. Edited by Brian Ferrell and Sandy Hunter. Singapore: Times Academic Press, 2003.

Anderson, Duncan. "Douglas MacArthur and the Philippines." In *Fallen Stars: Eleven Studies in Twentieth Century Military Disasters*. Edited by Brian Bond. London: Brassey's Putnam Aeronautical, 1992.

Arakawa, Ken-ichi. "Japanese Naval Blockade of China in the Second Sino-Japanese War, 1937–41." In *Naval Blockades and Seapower, Strategies and Counter-Strategies*. Edited by Bruce A. Elleman and S. C. M. Paine. London and New York: Routledge, 2006.

Askew, David. "Defending Nanjing: An Examination of the Capital Garrison Forces." *Journal of Sino-Japanese Studies* 15 (April 2003).

———. "The International Community for the Nanjing Safety Zone: An Introduction." *Journal of Sino-Japanese Studies* 14 (April 2002).

———. "Part of the Numbers Issue: Demography and Civilian Victims." In *The Nanking Atrocity 1937–38: Complicating the Picture*. Edited by Bob Tadashi Wakabayashi. New York: Berghahn Books, 2007.

Bell, Christopher M. " 'Our Most Exposed Outpost': Hong Kong and British Far Eastern Strategy, 1921–1941." *Journal of Military History* 60, no. 1 (January 1996).

Bond, Brian. "Introduction." In *British and Japanese Military Leadership in the Far Eastern War 1941–1945*. Edited by Brian Bond and Kyoichi Tachikawa. Oxon, UK: Frank Cass, 2004.

Boothe, Clare. "MacArthur of the Far East." *Life* 11, no. 23 (December 8, 1941).

———. "Burma Mission." *Life* 12, no. 24 (June 15, 1942).

Boslaugh, David L. Capt. Ret. USN. "Radar and the Fighter Directors." Chapters 4–13. www.ethw.org/Radar-and-the-Fighter-Directors.

Bridge, Carl. "Crisis of Command: Major-General Gordon Bennett and British Military Effectiveness in the Malaya Campaign." In *British and Japanese Military Leadership in the Far Eastern War 1941–1945*. Edited by Brian Bond and Kyoichi Tachikawa. Oxon, UK: Frank Cass, 2004.

Brook, Timothy. "Radhabinod Pal on the Rape of Nanking." In *The Nanking Atrocity 1937–38: Complicating the Picture*. Edited by Bob Tadashi Wakabayashi. New York: Berghahn Books, 2007.

Butow. Robert J. C. "How Roosevelt Attacked Japan at Pearl Harbor: Myth Masquerading as History." *Prologue* 28, no. 3 (Fall 1996). www.archives.gov/publications/prologue/1996/fall/butow.html.

Cannon, Peter. "Night Action, Malaya 1942." In *Warship 2015*. Edited by John Jordan. Annapolis, MD: Naval Institute Press, 2015.

Cartwright, John. "The Defense of Hong Kong, Shing Mun Redoubt and the Gin Drinker's Line." http://hksw.org/Shing%20Mun.htm.

Chang, Jui-te. "The Nationalist Army on the Eve of War." In *The Battle for China: Essays on the Military History of the Sino-Japanese War 1937–47*. Edited by Mark Peattie, Edward Drea, Hans van de Ven. Stanford, CA: Stanford University Press, 2010.

Cole, Wayne S. "The Role of the United States Congress and Political Parties." In *Pearl Harbor as History: Japanese American Relations 1931–1941*. Edited by Dorothy Borg and Shumpei Okamoto. New York: Columbia University Press, 1973.

Current, Richard N. "How Stimson Meant to 'Maneuver' the Japanese." *Mississippi Valley Historical Review* 40, no. 1 (June 1953).

Drea, Edward. "The Japanese Army on the Eve of the War." In *The Battle for China: Essays on the Military History of the Sino-Japanese War 1937–47*. Edited by Mark Peattie, Edward Drea, and Hans van de Ven. Stanford, CA: Stanford University Press, 2010.

———, and Hans van de Ven. "An Overview of Major Military Campaigns during the Sino-Japanese War, 1937–1945." In *The Battle for China: Essays on the Military His-*

tory of the Sino-Japanese War 1937–47. Edited by Mark Peattie, Edward Drea, and Hans van de Ven. Stanford, CA: Stanford University Press, 2010.

Durdin, F. Tillman. "Japanese Atrocities Marked Fall of Nanking." New York Times, 9 January 1937.

Eastman, Lloyd. "Nationalist China During the Sino-Japanese War." In The Cambridge History of China. Vol. 13. Republican China, 1912–1949. Vol. 2. Edited by John Fairbank and Albert Feuerwerker. Cambridge: Cambridge University Press, 1986.

Erskine, Ralph. "When a Purple Machine Went Missing: How Japan Nearly Discovered America's Greatest Secret." Intelligence and National Security 12, no. 3 (1997).

Falk, Stanley. "Ships that Never Came In." Military History Quarterly 7, no. 2 (Winter 1994).

Ford, Dan. "Annals of the Brewster Buffalo." warbirdforum.com/buff.

Ford, Daniel. "Informed Airmen? The US Army Air Force's Intelligence on Japanese Fighter Tactics in the Pacific Theater, 1941–5." The International History Review 34, no. 4 (2012).

Frank, Richard B. "Picking Winners?" Naval History 25, no. 3 (June 2011).

Fujiwara, Akira. "The Nanking Atrocity: An Interpretive Overview." In The Nanking Atrocity 1937–38: Complicating the Picture. Edited by Bob Tadashi Wakabayashi. New York: Berghahn Books, 2007.

Gallop, Dr. George. "Polls Showed Majority Favored War." Washington Post, 9 December 1941.

Garkze, William H., Jr., Robert O. Dulin, Jr., and Kevin V. Denlay. "Death of a Battleship: The Loss of HMS Prince of Wales December 10, 1941, A Marine Forensics Analysis of the Sinking." 2012 revision. https://rina.org.uk.

Garver, John W. "China's Wartime Diplomacy." In China's Bitter Victory: The War with Japan 1937–1945. Edited by James C. Hsiung and Steven I. Levine. Armonk, NY: M. E. Sharpe, 1992.

Graebner, Norman A. "Hoover, Roosevelt and the Japanese." In Pearl Harbor as History: Japanese American Relations 1931–1941. Edited by Dorothy Borg and Shumpei Okamoto. New York: Columbia University Press, 1973.

Hagiwara, Mitsuru. "The Japanese Air Campaigns in China, 1937–1945." In The Battle for China: Essays on the Military History of the Sino-Japanese War 1937–47. Edited by Mark Peattie, Edward Drea, and Hans van de Ven. Stanford, CA: Stanford University Press, 2010.

Hanada, Tomoyuki. "The Nomonhan Incident and the Japanese-Soviet Neutrality Pact." In Fifteen Lectures on Showa Japan: Road to Pacific War in Recent Historiography. Edited by Kiyotada Tsutsui. Tokyo: Japan Publishing Industry for Culture, 2016.

Hanyok, Robert J. " 'Catching the Fox Unaware': Japanese Radio Denial and Deception and the Attack on Pearl Harbor." Naval War College Review 61, no. 4 (2008).

Hata, Ikuhiko. "The Army's Move into Northern Indochina." In Japan's Road to the Pacific War. The Fateful Choice: Japan's Advance into Southeast Asia, 1939–1941. Edited by James W. Morley. New York: Columbia University Press, 1980.

———. "The Japanese Soviet Confrontation, 1935–39." In Japan's Road to the Pacific War: Deterrent Diplomacy. Japan, Germany, and the USSR 1935–1939. Edited by James W. Morley. New York: Columbia University Press, 1976.

———. "The Marco Polo Bridge Incident." In Japan's Road to the Pacific War: The China

Quagmire: Japanese Expansion on the Asian Continent, 1933–1941. Edited by James W. Morley. New York: Columbia University Press, 1983.

Hattori, Satoshi, and Edward Drea. "Japanese Operations from July to December 1937." In *The Battle for China: Essays on the Military History of the Sino-Japanese War 1937–47*. Edited by Mark Peattie, Edward Drea, and Hans van de Ven. Stanford, CA: Stanford University Press, 2010.

Hayashi, Hirofumi. "The Battle of Singapore: The Massacre of Chinese and Understanding of the Issue in Postwar Japan." http://japanfocus.org/-Hayashi-Hirofumi/3187.

Heim, David. "Vulnerable: HMS *Prince of Wales* in 1941." *Journal of Military History* 77, no. 3 (July 2013).

Hone, T. C., with drawing by Joseph R. Beckenbach, Jr. "The Destruction of the Battle Line at Pearl Harbor." *Naval Institute Proceedings* 103, no. 12 (December 1977).

Hone, Thomas C., Norman Friedman, and Mark D. Mandeles. *Naval War College Papers 37: Innovation in Carrier Aviation*. 2011.

Hosoya, Chihiro. "The Japanese Soviet Neutrality Pact." In *Japan's Road to the Pacific War. The Fateful Choice: Japan's Advance into Southeast Asia, 1939–1941*. Edited by James W. Morley. New York: Columbia University Press, 1980.

———. "The Tripartite Pact, 1939–1940." In *Japan's Road to the Pacific War: Deterrent Diplomacy. Japan, Germany, and the USSR 1935–1939*. Edited by James W. Morley. New York: Columbia University Press, 1976.

Irish, Kerry. "Dwight Eisenhower and Douglas MacArthur in the Philippines: There Must Be a Day of Reckoning." *The Journal of Military History* 74, no. 2 (April 2010).

Kasahara, Tokushi. "Massacres Outside Nanking City." In *The Nanking Atrocity 1937–38: Complicating the Picture*. Edited by Bob Tadashi Wakabayashi. New York: Berghahn Books, 2007.

Klein, David, and Hilary Conroy. "Churchill, Roosevelt and the China Question in Pre–Pearl Harbor Diplomacy." In *Pearl Harbor Reexamined: Prologue to the Pacific War*. Edited by Hilary Conroy and Harry Wray. Honolulu: University of Hawaii Press, 1990.

Klimow, Matthew S. "Lying to the Troops: American Leaders and the Defense of Bataan." *Parameters* 20, no. 4 (December 1990).

Lary, Diana. "Drowned Earth: The Strategic Breaching of the Yellow River Dyke, 1938." *War in History* 8, no. 2 (2001).

———. "A Ravaged Place: The Devastation of the Xuzhou Region, 1938." In *Scars of War: The Impact of Warfare on Modern China*. Edited by Diana Lary and Stephen MacKinnon. Vancouver: University of British Columbia Press, 2001.

Lengerer, Hans. "The Aircraft Carriers of the Shōkaku Class." In *Warship 2015*. Edited by John Jordan. London: Conway Maritime Press, Ltd., 2015.

———. "Akagi & Kaga." In *Warship VI*. Edited by John Roberts. London: Conway Maritime Press, Ltd., 1982.

Li, Yuzhen. "Chiang Kai-shek and Joseph Stalin during World War II." In *Negotiating China's Destiny in World War II*. Edited by Hans van de Ven, Diana Lary and Stephan R. MacKinnon. Stanford, CA: Stanford University Press, 2015.

Long, Jeff E. "The Japanese Literati and the "China Incident." In Hayashi Fusao, "Reporting the Battle of Shanghai." *Journal of Sino-Chinese Studies* 15 (April 2003).

Lu, David. "Introduction to the Marco Polo Bridge Incident." In *Japan's Road to the Pacific War: The China Quagmire: Japanese Expansion on the Asian Continent, 1933–1941*. Edited by James W. Morley. New York: Columbia University Press, 1983.

Lundstrom, John B. Manuscript Chapter. "The Pacific Fleet's 1941 War Plans and the Attack on Pearl Harbor." Manuscript chapter, n.d. [This was a deleted section of Lundstrom's *The First Team: Pacific Naval Air Combat from Pearl Harbor to Midway*. Annapolis, MD: Naval Institute Press, 1984.]

MacKinnon, Stephen. "Refugees Flight at the Outset of the Anti-Japanese War." In *Scars of War: The Impact of Warfare on Modern China*. Edited by Diana Lary and Stephen MacKinnon. Vancouver: University of British Columbia Press, 2001.

———. "The Defense of the Central Yangtze." In *The Battle for China: Essays on the Military History of the Sino-Japanese War 1937–47*. Edited by Mark Peattie, Edward Drea, and Hans van de Ven. Stanford, CA: Stanford University Press, 2010.

"Man and Wife of the Year." *Time* magazine 31, no 1, 3 January 1938.

McGuigan, Jim. "British Identity and the 'People's Princess.' " *The Sociological Review* 7 (2000).

McIntosh, Elizabeth P. "Honolulu after Pearl Harbor: A Report Published for the First Time 71 Years Later." *Washington Post*, 6 December 2012.

Meixsel, Richard B. "Major General George Grunert, WPO-3, and the Philippine Army, 1940–1941." *The Journal of Military History* 59, no. 2 (April 1995).

———. "Manuel L. Quezon, Douglas MacArthur, and the Significance of the Military Mission to the Philippine Commonwealth." *Pacific Historical Review* 70, no. 2 (Spring 2002).

Miller, Roger G. "A 'Pretty Damn Able Commander': Lewis Hyde Brereton." Part 2. *Air Power History* 48, no. 1 (Winter 2001).

Miller, Vernon J. "US Submarine Losses." In *Warship XII*. Edited by Ian Grant. Annapolis, MD: Naval Institute Press, 1988.

Morton, Louis. "The Philippine Army 1935–39 Eisenhower's Memorandum to Quezon." *Military Affairs* 12, no. 2 (Summer 1948).

Nakamura, Takafusa. "The Japanese Economy in the Interwar Period: A Brief Summary." In *Japan and World Depression: Then and Now*. Edited by Ronald Dore and Radha Sinha. New York: St. Martin's Press, 1987.

"A Nursing Sisters Story. In Memory of Lieutenant Kay Christie." www.hkvca.ca/historical/accounts/christie.htm.

O'Connor, Raymond G. "The American Navy, 1939–1941: The Enlisted Perspective." *Military Affairs* 50, no. 4 (October 1986).

Okumiya, Masatake, with Roger Pineau. "How the Panay Was Sunk." *U.S. Naval Institute Proceedings* 79, no. 10 (June 1953).

Parshall, Jonathan, and J. Michael Wenger. "Pearl Harbor's Overlooked Answer." *Naval History* 25, no. 6 (December 2011).

Peattie, Mark R. "The Dragon's Seed: Origins of the War." In *The Battle for China: Essays on the Military History of the Sino-Japanese War 1937–47*. Edited by Mark Peattie, Edward Drea, and Hans van de Ven. Stanford, CA: Stanford University Press, 2010.

Redgment, P. G. "High-Frequency Direction Finding in the Royal Navy: Development of Anti-U-Boat Equipment, 1941–5." In *The Applications of Radar and Other Electronic Systems in the Royal Navy in World War 2*. Edited by F. A. Kingsley. Basingstoke: Macmillan, 1995.

Rogaard, CDR John USNR, Peter K. Hsu, Carroll L. Lucas, and CAPT Andrew Bache Jr., USNR (Ret.). "Death of the Arizona." *Naval Institute Proceedings* 127, no. 6 (December 2001).

Seki, Hiroharu. "The Manchurian Incident, 1931." In *Japan's Road to the Pacific War. Japan Erupts: The London Naval Conference and the Manchurian Incident, 1928–32*. Edited by James W. Morley. New York: Columbia University Press, 1984.

Shimada, Toshihiko. "The Extension of Hostilities, 1931–1932." In *Japan's Road to the Pacific War. Japan Erupts: The London Naval Conference and the Manchurian Incident, 1928–32*. Edited by James W. Morley. New York: Columbia University Press, 1984.

Shoji, Jun'ichiro. "Historical Perception in Postwar Japan Concerning the Pacific War." National Institute of Defense Studies, no. 4 (March 2003).

Spence, Jonathan. "The Enigma of Chiang Kai-shek." *New York Review of Books* 56, no. 16 (October 22, 2009).

Sun, Youli. "Chinese Military Resistance and Changing American Perceptions, 1937–1938." In *On Cultural Ground: Essays in International History*. Edited by Robert David Johnson. Chicago: Imprint Publications, 1994.

Tachikawa, Kyoichi. "Yamashita and His Style of Leadership." In *British and Japanese Military Leadership in the Far Eastern War 1941–1945*. Edited by Brian Bond and Kyoichi Tachikawa. Oxon, UK: Frank Cass, 2004.

Takashi, Yoshida. "Wartime Accounts of the Nanjing Atrocity." In *The Nanking Atrocity 1937–38: Complicating the Picture*. Edited by Bob Tadashi Wakabayashi. New York: Berghahn Books, 2007.

Tanaka, Tsuneji. "The Battle at Java Sea." A copy of this article was generously supplied by Vincent O'Hara.

Tinker, Hugh. "A Forgotten Long March: The Indian Exodus from Burma, 1942." *Journal of Southeast Asia Studies* 6, no. 1 (March 1975).

Titus, David. "Introduction." In *Japan's Road to the Pacific War, The Final Confrontation, Japan's Negotiations with the United States, 1941*. Edited by James W. Morley. New York: Columbia University Press, 1994.

Tobe, Ryōichi. "The Japanese Eleventh Army in Central China, 1938–1941." In *The Battle for China: Essays on the Military History of the Sino-Japanese War 1937–47*. Edited by Mark Peattie, Edward Drea, and Hans van de Ven. Stanford, CA: Stanford University Press, 2010.

Tow, Edna. "The Great Bombing of Chongqing and the Anti-Japanese War, 1937–1945." In *The Battle for China: Essays on the Military History of the Sino-Japanese War 1937–47*. Edited by Mark Peattie, Edward Drea, and Hans van de Ven. Stanford, CA: Stanford University Press, 2010.

Trumball, Robert. "All Out with Halsey." *New York Times Magazine*, 6 December 1942.

Tsuchida, Akio. "Declaring War as an Issue in Chinese Wartime Diplomacy." In *Negotiating China's Destiny in World War II*. Edited by Hans van de Ven, Diana Lary, and Stephan R. MacKinnon. Stanford, CA: Stanford University, 2015.

Tyabji, Captain Nadir Salahuddin. "Burma Story, 1941–1942." https://Amitvaghosh.com/blog/?cat=30&paged=2

Usui, Katsumi. "The Politics of War, 1937–1941." In *Japan's Road to the Pacific War: The China Quagmire: Japanese Expansion on the Asian Continent, 1933–1941*. Edited by James W. Morley. New York: Columbia University Press, 1983.

Virgilio, F. "Seven Seconds to Infamy." *Naval Institute Proceedings* 123, no. 12 (December 1997).

Wakabayashi, Bob Tadashi. "Leftover Problems." In *The Nanking Atrocity 1937–38: Compli-*

cating the Picture. Edited by Bob Tadashi Wakabayashi. New York: Berghahn Books, 2007.

———. "The Messiness of Historical Reality." In *The Nanking Atrocity 1937–38: Complicating the Picture.* Edited by Bob Tadashi Wakabayashi. New York: Berghahn Books, 2007.

Wakeman, Frederick. "'Hanjian' (Traitor)!: Collaboration and Retribution in Wartime Shanghai." In *Becoming Chinese: Passages to Modernity and Beyond.* Edited by Yeh Wen-hsin. Berkeley: University of California Press, 2000.

Williamsen, Marvin. "The Military Dimension, 1937–41." In *China's Bitter Victory: The War with Japan 1937–1945.* Edited by James C. Hsiung and Steven I. Levine. Armonk, NY: M. E. Sharpe, 1992.

Xiaogang Lai, Sherman. "A War within a War: The Road to the New Fourth Army Incident in January 1941." *Journal of Chinese Military History* 2, no. 1 (2013).

Xu, Guangqiu. "The Issue of US Air Support for China during the Second World War, 1942–45." *Journal of Contemporary History* 36, no. 3 (July 2001).

Yamamoto, Masahiro. "A Tale of Two Atrocities: Critical Appraisal of American Historiography." In *The Nanking Atrocity 1937–38: Complicating the Picture.* Edited by Bob Tadashi Wakabayashi. New York: Berghahn Books, 2007.

Yang, Daqing. "Atrocities in Nanjing: Searching for Explanations." In *Scars of War: The Impact of Warfare on Modern China.* Edited by Diana Lary and Stephen MacKinnon. Vancouver: University of British Columbia Press, 2001.

———. "Convergence or Divergence? Recent Historical Writings on the Rape of Nanjing." *The American Historical Review* 104, no. 3 (June 1999).

Yang, Kuisong. "The Evolution of the Relationship Between the Chinese Communist Party and the Comintern during the Sino-Japanese War." In *Negotiating China's Destiny in World War II.* Edited by Hans van de Ven, Diana Lary, and Stephen R. MacKinnon. Stanford, CA: Stanford University Press, 2015.

———. "Nationalist and Communist Guerilla Warfare in North China." In *The Battle for China: Essays on the Military History of the Sino-Japanese War 1937–47.* Edited by Mark Peattie, Edward Drea, and Hans van de Ven. Stanford, CA: Stanford University Press, 2010.

Yang, Tianshi. "Chiang Kai-shek and the Battles of Shanghai and Nanjing." In *The Battle for China: Essays on the Military History of the Sino-Japanese War 1937–47.* Edited by Mark Peattie, Edward Drea, and Hans van de Ven. Stanford, CA: Stanford University Press, 2010.

Yokoyama, Hisayuki. "Air Operational Leadership in the Southern Front." In *British and Japanese Military Leadership in the Far Eastern War 1941–1945.* Edited by Brian Bond and Kyoichi Tachikawa. Oxon, UK: Frank Cass, 2004.

Yoshida, Takashi. "Wartime Accounts of the Nanjing Atrocity." In *The Nanking Atrocity 1937–38: Complicating the Picture.* Edited by Bob Tadashi Wakabayashi. New York: Berghahn Books, 2007.

Yoshihara, Toshi, and James R. Holmes. "Japanese Maritime Thought: If Not Mahan, Who?" *Naval War College Review* 59, no. 3 (Summer 2006).

Zhang, Baijia. "China's Quest for Foreign Military Aid." In *The Battle for China: Essays on the Military History of the Sino-Japanese War 1937–47.* Edited by Mark Peattie, Edward Drea, and Hans van de Ven. Stanford, CA: Stanford University Press, 2010.

Major Online Sites

These sites generally contain enormous collections of records rivaling or exceeding large archives. Others are more specialized but contain rich primary sources.

http://www.admirals.org.uk. A wonderful collection of records on officers attaining flag rank. Particularly useful are the "confidential reports" prepared by superiors, which are remarkably vivid as to personal qualities both positive and negative.

www.ibiblio.org/anrs/graybook.html. This site contains the multivolume document that effectively is a War Diary of Admiral Chester W. Nimitz, the commander in chief, Pacific Fleet and Pacific Ocean Areas. It was called "The Graybook" after its original cover. This document includes copies of numerous original messages, staff studies, and other papers covering all phases of the war in the Pacific from strategic level decision making to the most mundane details. It is by far the single most important record of the US role in the maritime war with Japan.

Fold3 (Fold3.com). This site contains a massive and ever-growing collection of records from all US armed services during World War II, as well as other periods of history. It is now established as one of the most valuable of all sources of US World War II records.

Franklin D. Roosevelt Presidential Library and Museum (fdrlibrary.marist.edu). This site contains voluminous records from the presidency of Franklin D. Roosevelt.

Hyperwar: A Hypertext History of the Second World War (ibiblio.org/hyperwar). This site contains both original records and online copies of many official histories.

Imperial Japanese Navy Page (www.combinedfleet.com). This site contains a massive assembly of data on Japan's maritime war from 1937 to 1945. Notwithstanding the title, the records assembled on this constantly growing site cover not only Japanese warships, but also auxiliary vessels (including impressed merchant vessels) and essays on topics related to the maritime war.

Naval-History.net (naval-history.net). Valuable records, notably including ship loss and casualty records in the British Royal and US Navies.

The Netherlands East Indies 1941–1942 (dutcheastindies.webs.com); www.dutch-east -indies.com. These two sites contain detailed records on the role of the Dutch armed forces in the Netherlands East Indies.

Royal Netherlands Navy Warships of World War II (netherlandsnavy.nl). This site contains records of the Dutch Navy, including during the World War II period.

Pearl Harbor History Associates (www.ibiblio.org/pha). This site contains all forty volumes recording the hearings and evidence gathered by the US congressional investigation of the Pearl Harbor Attack (PHA). The topics covered ranged well beyond the boundaries of events on 7 December 1941 and its antecedents.

Sino Japanese Air War 1937–1942 (http://surfcity.kund.dalnet.se/sino-japanese_sources .htm). This site assembles records from all participants on the air war over China (1937–1942).

Uboat.net (uboat.net). Notwithstanding the title implying a focus on German submarines, this site contains massive data on worldwide naval activities during World War II.

United States Census Bureau (www.census.gov). US census records of particular use with respect to not only the total US population but its breakdowns by race and location.

University of Wisconsin–Madison Digital Libraries (http://digital.library.wisc.edu/1711.dl/ FRUS). This site contains the records assembled by the US Department of State of US diplomatic papers in yearly sets of volumes titled *Foreign Relations of the United States*. The volumes used in this work were 1931–1942.

Periodicals

Barron's
The Chicago Daily News
Chicago Tribune
Honolulu Advertiser
Japan Times and Advertiser
Life
Los Angeles Times
New York Times
Time
Washington Post
Washington Times-Herald

MAP AND ILLUSTRATION CREDITS

Maps by Glen Pawelski and Mapping Specialists, Ltd.

Dueling Visions for China

Generalissimo Chiang Kai-Shek: Magnum Photos BOB1938014W00011/ICP329
Mao Zedong speaking in 1938: Magnum Photos DRF1976099W07285-36C

Critical Battles, 1937

USS *Augusta* in Shanghai: From the American Geographical Society Library, University of Wisconsin Libraries AGLS fr207213
Admiral Harry Yarnell: National Archives and Records Administration 208-PU-224UU
Chiang Kai-shek's German-equipped and trained troops: From the American Geographical Society Library, University of Wisconsin Libraries AGLS fr208105
Japanese troops triumph in Nanjing: National Archives and Records Administration 306-NT-1318-110

Chinese Retreat; Japanese Bombing; American Reaction

Wartime capital in Chongqing: From the American Geographical Society Library, University of Wisconsin Libraries AGLS fr205592
Shanghai bombed: From the American Geographical Society Library, University of Wisconsin Libraries AGLS fr 207026
Baby in Shanghai Rail Station: W. S. Wong/Hulton Archive via Getty Images
Aftermath of Japanese Air Raid on Chongqing: Corbis Historical via Getty Images

Agonies of the Chinese People

Chinese refugees: From the American Geographical Society Library, University of Wisconsin Libraries AGLS fr207083
The breaching of the Yellow River dykes: From the American Geographical Society Library, University of Wisconsin, Libraries AGLS fr209570

A Global War

President Franklin D. Roosevelt: National Archives and Records Administration 208-PU-172A
Hitler's attack on the Soviet Union: National Archives and Records Administration 242-GAP-251-C

The Atlantic Conference: National Archives and Records Administration 80G 268500

Japan's Desperate Plunge

Emperor Hirohito: National Archives and Records Administration 208-PU-93S-2
Gen. Hideki Tôjô: National Archives and Records Administration 208-PU-1990U-2

Ill-Fated Diplomacy

Ambassador Joseph Grew: © Philippe Halsman Archive/Magnum Photos
Ambassador Kichisaburō Nomura and Special Envoy Saburō Kurusu: National Archives
    and Records Administration 208-PU-146

"Air Raid, Pearl Harbor, This Is No Drill"

Opening minutes of Pearl Harbor attack: National Archives and Records Administration
    80G 30454
USS *Arizona*: National Archives and Records Administration 80G 32920
President Roosevelt delivers his "Day of Infamy" speech: National Archives and Records
    Administration 208-PU-168, Folder A043

Allied Disaster in the South China Sea

Battleship *Prince of Wales*: © Imperial War Museum (A 006786)
Battlecruiser *Repulse*: © Imperial War Museum (FL 012335)
The last minutes of *Prince of Wales*: © Imperial War Museum (HU 002675)

Key Aerial Adversaries

Mitsubishi G3M "Nell" Bomber: National Archives and Records Administration 80G 12745
Brewster Buffalo fighter aircraft: © Imperial War Museum (CF 000758)
Mitsubishi A6M "Zero" Fighter: National Archives and Records Administration 342-FH-
    3B 35161
Nakajima B5N2 "Kate" Bomber: National Archives and Records Administration 80G
    182245

Singapore: Greatest Japanese Military Triumph

Lt. Gen. Archibald E. Percival: © Imperial War Museum (K 001261 A)
Gen. Tomoyuki Yamashita: National Archives and Records Administration 208-PU-224RR-4
Australian antitank gun crew: Australian War Memorial 011302-2-seq 1
British surrender delegation at Singapore: © Imperial War Museum (HU 002781)

Defense of the Philippines

Gen. Douglas MacArthur: National Archives and Records Administration 319-AP Box 283,
    Folder 14443

USS *Swordfish*: National Archives and Records Administration 80G 456121

The "Flying Tigers"

Claire Chennault: National Archives and Records Administration 80G-331333
"Flying Tigers": National Archives and Records Administration 208-N-6688, Box 12037

Fate of the Netherlands East Indies

Palembang Oil Refineries on Sumatra: National Archives and Records Administration
    80-CF-79321-10
Capt. Hector "Hec" Waller: Australian War Memorial
USS *Houston*: National Archives and Records Administration 80G 466533

Burma

Lt. Gen. Joseph W. Stilwell's "Walkout": National Archives and Records Administration
    111-PP-29 SC 138413
Stilwell inset: National Archives and Records Administration 111-PP Box 29 SC 134625-a
Gen. William Slim: © Imperial War Museum (IND 3595)

Glimmers of Allied Hope

Gen. Douglas MacArthur confers with Prime Minister John Curtin: Australian War
    Memorial 042774-1
Adm. Chester W. Nimitz with Adm. William F. Halsey, Jr.: National Archives and Records
    Administration 2-8-PU 146
USS *Enterprise*: National Archives and Records Administration 80G 410094
Doolittle Raid: National Archives and Records Administration 80 G 411961

INDEX

Page numbers followed by *m* indicate maps. Page numbers followed by *n*
indicate footnotes. All page numbers after page 528 refer to notes.
Ships and aircraft are listed alphabetically.